Year	Federal Finances: Federal Budget Totals (Billions of Dollars): Fiscal Year Outlays	Fiscal Year Receipts	Surplus (+) or Deficit (−)	National Debt: Billions of Dollars	As a Percent of GDP	Size of Government as a Share of GDP: Federal, State, and Local Government: Expenditures (Percent of GDP)	Purchases of Goods & Services (% of GDP)
1959	92.1	79.2	−12.8	287.5	58.5	23.0	22.1
1960	92.2	92.5	0.3	290.5	56.1	23.1	21.5
1961	97.7	94.4	−3.3	292.6	55.1	24.0	22.2
1962	106.8	99.7	−7.1	302.9	53.4	24.1	22.5
1963	111.3	106.6	−4.8	310.3	51.9	24.1	22.3
1964	118.5	112.6	−5.9	316.1	49.4	23.7	21.8
1965	118.2	116.8	−1.4	322.3	46.9	23.4	21.3
1966	134.5	130.8	−3.7	328.5	43.6	24.2	22.0
1967	157.5	148.8	−8.6	340.4	41.9	26.1	23.3
1968	178.1	153.0	−25.2	368.7	42.5	26.8	23.3
1969	183.6	186.9	3.2	365.8	38.6	26.9	22.8
1970	195.6	192.8	−2.8	380.9	37.8	28.3	22.8
1971	210.2	187.1	−23.0	408.2	37.9	28.7	22.2
1972	230.7	207.3	−23.4	435.9	37.0	28.5	21.7
1973	245.7	230.8	−14.9	466.3	35.7	28.0	20.8
1974	269.4	263.2	−6.1	483.9	33.6	29.3	21.6
1975	332.3	279.1	−53.2	541.9	34.9	31.6	22.2
1976	371.8	298.1	−73.7	629.0	36.3	30.6	21.2
1977	409.2	355.6	−53.7	706.4	35.8	29.9	20.6
1978	458.7	399.6	−59.2	776.6	35.1	28.7	20.0
1979	504.0	463.3	−40.7	829.5	33.2	28.4	19.8
1980	590.9	517.1	−73.8	909.1	33.4	30.2	20.6
1981	678.2	599.3	−79.0	994.8	32.6	30.6	20.3
1982	745.8	617.8	−128.0	1,137.3	35.4	32.5	21.1
1983	808.4	600.6	−207.8	1,371.7	40.1	32.4	20.9
1984	851.9	666.5	−185.4	1,564.7	41.0	31.1	20.4
1985	946.4	734.1	−212.3	1,817.5	44.3	31.4	20.9
1986	990.5	769.2	−221.2	2,120.6	48.5	31.6	21.2
1987	1,004.1	854.4	−149.8	2,346.1	50.9	31.4	21.2
1988	1,064.5	909.3	−155.2	2,601.3	52.5	30.7	20.4
1989	1,143.7	991.2	−152.5	2,868.0	53.6	30.5	20.1
1990	1,253.2	1,032.0	−221.2	3,206.6	56.4	31.4	20.5
1991	1,324.4	1,055.0	−269.4	3,598.5	61.4	32.1	20.7
1992	1,381.7	1,091.3	−290.4	4,002.1	65.1	33.1	20.2
1993	1,409.4	1,154.4	−255.0	4,351.4	67.2	32.7	19.6
1994	1,461.7	1,258.6	−203.1	4,643.7	67.8	31.9	18.9
1995	1,515.7	1,351.8	−163.9	4,921.0	68.4	31.8	18.7
1996	1,560.5	1,453.1	−107.5	5,181.9	68.6	31.3	18.3
1997	1,601.2	1,579.3	−21.9	5,369.7	67.2	30.5	17.9
1998	1,652.6	1,721.8	69.2	5,478.7	65.2	29.8	17.5

Sources: *Economic Report of the President,* 1999, and *Survey of Current Business,* March 1999.

Ninth Edition

MICROECONOMICS

Private and Public Choice

Ninth Edition

James D. Gwartney
Florida State University

Richard L. Stroup
Montana State University

Russell S. Sobel
West Virginia University

THE DRYDEN PRESS
A DIVISION OF HARCOURT COLLEGE PUBLISHERS
Fort Worth Philadelphia San Diego New York Orlando Austin San Antonio
Toronto Montreal London Sydney Tokyo

Publisher MIKE ROCHE
Acquisitions Editor GARY NELSON
Market Strategist DEBBIE K. ANDERSON
Developmental Editor AMY RAY
Project Editor LAURA J. HANNA
Art Director BURL SLOAN
Production Manager LOIS WEST

Cover image: © The Stock Market

ISBN: 0-03-021292-8

Library of Congress Catalog Card Number: 99-64605

Address for Domestic Orders
The Dryden Press, 6277 Sea Harbor Drive, Orlando, FL 32887-6777
800-782-4479

Address for International Orders
International Customer Service
The Dryden Press, 6277 Sea Harbor Drive, Orlando, FL 32887-6777
407-345-3800
(fax) 407-345-4060
(e-mail) hbintl@harcourtbrace.com

Address for Editorial Correspondence
The Dryden Press, 301 Commerce Street, Suite 3700, Fort Worth, TX 76102

Web Site Address
http://www.hbcollege.com

Printed in the United States of America

9 0 1 2 3 4 5 6 7 8 048 9 8 7 6 5 4 3 2 1

The Dryden Press
Harcourt College Publishers

THE DRYDEN PRESS SERIES IN ECONOMICS

Baldani, Bradfield, and Turner
Mathematical Economics

Baumol and Blinder
Economics: Principles and Policy
Eighth Edition
(also available in Micro and Macro paperbacks)

Baumol, Panzar, and Willig
Contestable Markets and the Theory of Industry Structure
Revised Edition

Breit and Elzinga
The Antitrust Casebook: Milestones in Economic Regulation
Third Edition

Brue
The Evolution of Economic Thought
Sixth Edition

Callan and Thomas
Environmental Economics and Management: Theory, Policy, and Applications
Second Edition

Edgmand, Moomaw, and Olson
Economics and Contemporary Issues
Fourth Edition

Gardner
Comparative Economic Systems
Second Edition

Gwartney, Stroup, and Sobel
Economics: Private and Public Choice
Ninth Edition
(also available in Micro and Macro paperbacks)

Gwartney and Stroup
Introduction to Economics: The Wealth and Poverty of Nations

Hess and Ross
Economic Development: Theories, Evidence, and Policies

Hirschey and Pappas
Fundamentals of Managerial Economics
Sixth Edition

Hirschey
Managerial Economics
Revised Edition

Hyman
Public Finance: A Contemporary Application of Theory to Policy
Sixth Edition

Kahn
The Economic Approach to Environmental and Natural Resources
Second Edition

Kaserman and Mayo
Government and Business: The Economics of Antitrust and Regulation

Kaufman
The Economics of Labor Markets
Fifth Edition

Kennett and Lieberman
The Road to Capitalism: The Economic Transformation of Eastern Europe and the Former Soviet Union

Kreinin
International Economics: A Policy Approach
Eighth Edition

Mankiw
Principles of Economics
(also available in Micro and Macro paperbacks)

Nicholson
Intermediate Microeconomics and Its Application
Seventh Edition

Nicholson
Microeconomic Theory: Basic Principles and Extensions
Seventh Edition

Ramanathan
Introductory Econometrics with Applications
Fourth Edition

Rukstad
Corporate Decision Making in the World Economy: Company Case Studies

Rukstad
Macroeconomic Decision Making in the World Economy: Text and Cases
Third Edition

Samuelson and Marks
Managerial Economics
Third Edition

Santerre and Neun
Health Economics: Theories, Insights, and Industry Studies
Revised Edition

Scarth
Macroeconomics: An Introduction to Advanced Methods

Sexton
Exploring Economics: Pathways to Problem Solving
(also available in Micro and Macro paperbacks)

Stockman
Introduction to Economics
Second Edition
(also available in Micro and Macro paperbacks)

Walton and Rockoff
History of the American Economy
Eighth Edition

Welch and Welch
Economics: Theory and Practice
Sixth Edition

Yarbrough and Yarbrough
The World Economy: Trade and Finance
Fifth Edition

PREFACE

We are dogmatic about some things. *We believe that a course on economics principles should focus on the power and relevance of the economic way of thinking.* It is this belief and corresponding writing approach that have made *Economics: Private and Public Choice* one of Harcourt College Publishing's most solid and enduring texts—a cornerstone of its economics program for more than 25 years. With the eighth edition having sold more copies than any prior edition, our commitment to this approach is strengthened.

While models, formulas, and mechanical exercises can be helpful, they should be viewed as tools. In a principles course, they are secondary to the development of the economic way of thinking. Throughout this text, we integrate applications and real-world data in an effort to make the basic concepts of economics come alive for the reader. The book's exercises, testing questions, and even the PowerPoint package developed for this edition are designed to encourage and promote economic reasoning.

The study of economics does not have to be either difficult or "watered down." *Economics: Private and Public Choice* is a comprehensive text, rich in detail. But it is written with the student in mind. We have avoided abstractions and mechanical exercises that stress obscure details rather than basic concepts. The primary objective of our writing style is clarity. We have worked hard to make the material as clear as possible. Examples, illustrations, and visual aides are used to reinforce basic concepts. Simplicity, however, is not substituted for depth. Rather, our aim is to highlight the power, accessibility, and relevance of economic concepts.

This is an exciting time to study economics. More than ever before, the world is characterized by dynamic change, instant communication, and interaction between people in different nations. New products and technologies are constantly replacing the old ways of doing things. In fact, sometimes new products become obsolete just a few years after they are introduced. How will these developments affect your life? What will the U.S. economy be like ten or twenty years from now? Why has the U.S. economy experienced persistent growth during the last 16 years? Why do some countries prosper while others regress? As we proceed, we will use the tools of economics to address these and many other important issues that affect us so dramatically.

CHANGES IN THE NINTH EDITION

A noteworthy change with this edition is the inclusion of new coauthor Russell S. Sobel of West Virginia University. For the better part of a decade, Professor Sobel has contributed significantly to the development and improvement of both *Economics: Private and Public Choice* and its ancillary package. We are convinced that his contributions will continue for many years to come.

To the text itself, we have made a number of structural changes that make this edition more flexible and user-friendly. Additionally, the supplements for this edition—both print and electronic—have been markedly improved. (Please review the "Supplementary Materials" section later in this preface to learn about these exciting new enhancements.) Important changes to the textbook follow.

Division into "Core" Chapters and "Special Topic" Applications

The core chapters found in this edition cover all of the material taught in most principles courses and they are presented in the usual manner. Examples and data from the real world are used to reinforce the analysis. In addition, the final part of the text (Applications and Special Topics), contains a number of short features on high-profile topics. The applications are crisp and clearly focused—about one-third the length of a chapter. They are designed for coverage in a single class period. These features provide a solid foundation for discussing important topics such as the stock market, the future of social security, the impact of unions, welfare reform, natural resources, and environment protection. Instructors stressing applications may choose to build their course around Parts 1 and 2, plus the final part, "Applications and Special Topics." Others may want to use several of the applications to buttress various points as they progress through the core material, or they may want to combine the applications and chapters for the purpose of teaching a survey course. Still others—particularly those teaching honors classes—may want to use the applications as the focal point for special projects or classroom debates. The format of this edition provides each instructor with maximum flexibility. Directly following this preface, you will find some sample course outlines with suggestions for the integration of these applications.

A More Visual Textbook

Today's students read less, but they are better prepared to learn from the superior visual aides and technologies that we can now offer them. Accordingly, we have reduced the number of words in this edition by about 10 percent—taking care to not omit important material or oversimplify the analysis. Illustrative graphics, diagrams, pictures, cartoons, and other visual aides are frequently used to highlight the content and reinforce important points. An example of this is the feature on "Facts and Figures of Government" between Chapters 5 and 6. Rather than using 8 to 10 text pages to present this material as in the last edition, the ninth edition uses graphs and pictures with brief descriptions to illustrate the major points. You will notice that the part openers in the text have also been given special treatment. Each is a photo/graphical montage intended to pique the student's curiosity about the material that follows. You will notice that the end-of-chapter summary paragraphs have been rewritten into point-by-point "key topic" lists. The new format helps students immediately recognize the most important aspects of each chapter, making for easier student review.

More Supply and Demand

Following Chapter 3 on supply, demand, and the market process, we have added a new chapter on applications and extension of the supply and demand model. Instructors tell us that they are using supply and demand more and more to address topics of interest to students. This is precisely what Chapter 4 does. Fun topics integrated into this chapter include black markets, illegal drug trade, rent controls, the minimum wage, actual versus statutory tax incidence, and the Laffer curve.

The Role of Government and Collective Choice

While Chapters 3 and 4 focus on markets, Chapters 5 and 6 analyze the functions and operations of government. These two chapters focus on the protective role of government, why governments are often involved in the provision of public goods, and how the political process actually works. This material consolidates four chapters from the last edition. Regardless of the emphasis placed on the public choice approach, we believe that Chapters 5 and 6 add an important dimension to an economics course. This material will enliven a principles course, while enhancing student understanding of the real world and some of its imperfections. Taken together, the four chapters in Part 2 provide a solid foundation for the topics covered throughout the remainder of the text.

Core Micro

Our approach to microeconomics continues to highlight the importance of information supplied by markets, competition as a process, and the role of entrepreneurship. The micro section has been streamlined. The core micro contains only nine chapters, two fewer than in the last edition. Five of the chapters focus on product markets, three on resource markets, and one on income differences and poverty. Several of the applications in the final part of the text—for example, the ones on regulation, unionization, welfare reform, natural resources, and environment economics—provide supplementary material for the core micro.

ORGANIZATIONAL FEATURES

We have employed several organizational features designed to make the presentation both more interesting and more understandable.

1. **Myths of Economics.** In a series of boxed articles, commonly held fallacies of economic reasoning are dispelled. Each myth is followed by a concise explanation of why it is incorrect, and each one is presented within a chapter containing closely related material.
2. **Applications and Measures in Economics.** The application boxed features apply economic theory to real-world issues and controversies. The measures explain how important economic indicators such as the unemployment rate and the index of leading indicators are assembled.
3. **Chapter Focus Questions and Closing "Key Point" Summaries.** Each chapter begins with several questions that summarize the focus of the chapter. Following the end of each chapter is a Key Points section that provides the student with a concise statement of the material (chapter learning objectives). Reviewing the focus questions and these concise "key points" will help the student better understand the material and integrate it into the broader economic picture.
4. **Key Terms.** The terminology of economics is often confusing to introductory students. Key terms are introduced in the text in bold type; simultaneously, each term is defined in the margin opposite the first reference to the term. A glossary containing the key terms also appears at the end of the book.
5. **Critical Analysis Questions.** Each chapter concludes with a set of discussion questions and problems designed to test the student's ability to analyze economic issues and to apply economic theory to real-world events. Appendix B at the end of the text contains suggested answers for approximately half of the critical analysis questions. We think these answers, illustrating the power of economics, will interest students and will help them develop the economic way of thinking.

SUPPLEMENTARY MATERIALS

***Wall Street Journal* Edition.** Instructors can enhance the real-life applications in the text by ordering *The Wall Street Journal* Edition of the textbook instead of the regular textbook. This special edition of the textbook is the same as the standard edition but includes a discounted 20-week *Wall Street Journal* subscription for students. Professors get a free subscription when 10 or more of their students order the *Journal. The Wall Street Journal* provides a nice tie-in with the text, since new examples of economic principles can be found in each day's paper. Students can activate their subscriptions by simply completing and mailing the business reply card found in the back of the book. Instructors interested in finding out more about this program can contact their sales representative or simply call 800-782-4479. This option is available for both the hardcover version of the book and paperback splits.

Coursebooks

The Coursebooks for this edition were prepared by coauthor Professor Russell Sobel and are now available not in two, but three versions, covering all three courses: economics, microeconomics, and macroeconomics. The Coursebooks are more than study guides. Each includes numerous multiple-choice, true/false, and discussion questions permitting students to self-test their knowledge of each chapter. Answers and short explanations for most questions are provided in the back of the Coursebooks. Each chapter also contains problem and project exercises designed to improve the student's knowledge of the mechanics. A set of short readings chosen to supplement the classroom teaching of important topics is also included. Like the textbook, the Coursebooks are designed to help students develop the economic way of thinking.

EconActive Student-Learning CD ROM

Our new EconActive student-learning CD is html-based and very easy to use. Students will navigate through the software as effortlessly as they do a website. The CD ROM contains chapter-review sections, automatically graded practice quizzes, "cyberproblems" that launch to the worldwide web, and more. It also includes interactive graphs, and graphing problems where students are required to give the correct answers by graphing the solutions. They are then given feedback when they draw the wrong solution. Like the Coursebook, the EconActive CD ROM is designed to help students develop the economic way of thinking within a multimedia environment.

Test Banks

The Test Banks for the ninth edition were prepared by David MacPherson of Florida State University. The two Test Banks contain approximately 7,000 questions—multiple-choice and short answer—most of which have been class tested. Within each chapter, the questions correspond to the major subheadings of the text. The first ten questions of each chapter are suitable for use as a comprehensive quiz covering the material of the chapter.

Computerized Test Banks

The computerized Test Banks for this edition have been enhanced significantly. EXAMaster99 includes a more intuitive graphic interface, increased test sizes of up to 500 questions, the capacity to create up to 99 versions of any one test, on-line testing and grade-book keeping, and many more features. The new software is now available on CD ROM in Windows and Macintosh formats. A more detailed explanation of the enhancements of EXAMaster99 can be found at the front of the Instructor's Manual accompanying this text.

PowerPoint CD-ROM

Prepared by David MacPherson, Chuck Skipton, and James Gwartney, we believe our PowerPoint presentation is the best you will find in the principles market. The new package provides chapter-by-chapter lecture notes with fully animated slides of the textbook's exhibits. The dynamic slides and accompanying captions make it easy for instructors to present (and students to follow) sequential changes. The dynamic graphics are also used to highlight various relationships among economic variables. In order to facilitate discussion and interaction, questions designed to help students develop the economic way of thinking are strategically located throughout each chapter. We have used the material in our own classes and can assure you that students find this method of presentation both enjoyable and helpful. As the graphics are built step-by-step, the accompanying dialogue guides the student through the underlying economic analysis. Economic principles are developed rather than merely portrayed. This makes it so much easier to visualize relationships.

Instructions explaining how professors can easily add, delete, and modify slides in order to tailor-make the presentation to their liking are included with the PowerPoint CD-ROM. If instructors want to make the PowerPoint presentation available to students, they can place it on their web site (or the site for their course). It is also available on the web site for this text at **www.dryden.com/econ/gwartney** and on the EconActive Student-Learning CD ROM. The PowerPoint package also includes self-test quizzes covering the major concepts of each chapter. This is a powerful teaching tool that will both attract student interest and enrich the learning process.

PowerPoint Lecture Notes

For years, we have encouraged students to think rather than focus on note-taking in our classes. It was a hard sell—many feel uncomfortable if they are not developing a set of notes. This booklet contains the PowerPoint slides (both the notes and graphics), along with space for additional note-taking next to each slide. This supplement permits students to focus on the classroom activities while providing them with confidence that they have an excellent set of notes for future reference. Professors who choose to customize their PowerPoint presentations and would like to do the same with their accompanying customized printed lecture notes can do so via Harcourt's custom publishing program. Visit **www.harcourtcollege.com/custom** for more information. Once at the Website, you can locate your area's custom publishing representative by clicking the "Contact Us" icon.

Web-Based Course Management Software

Harcourt now offers instructors html-based software to help them build web-based learning sites for their students. This software can be utilized by nontechnical users to create entire web-based courses, or simply to post office hours or supplementary course materials for students. Instructors can design websites that provide a full array of educational tools, including communications with their students, web testing, student grade tracking with access control, database collaboration and searching, and more. It is free of charge to adopters. For more information, call Harcourt's customer service line at 800-237-2665, or visit our home page at **www.harcourtcollege.com.**

Web Site

Resources for instructors and students, including the PowerPoint slides and Instructor's Manual, can be found at **www.dryden.com/econ/gwartney**. Students will find there chapter-by-chapter links to economic Internet sites, automatically graded practice quizzes, PowerPoint slides for their review, sample chapters from the study guide and EconActive CD ROM, and other resources. Career listings for students, leading economic-indicator information, and an economic URL database can be found at **www.dryden.com.** Because the Internet has become so integral to learning and to our lives, you will notice bound into this book a quick Internet reference card listing important URLs. We hope you and your students find it useful and tear it out for your reference.

Instructor's Manual with Classroom Games

The Instructor's Manual was also prepared by David MacPherson. Instructions and information on how to use and modify the PowerPoint material is contained in the front of the manual. Also included at the front of the manual is information on the enhancements to the new EXAMaster99 testing software. The remainder of the manual is divided into three parts. The first part is a detailed outline of each chapter in lecture-note form. It is designed to help instructors organize and structure their current lecture notes according to the format of the ninth edition. Instructors can easily prepare a detailed, personalized set of notes by revising the computerized form of the notes. The second part of the Instructor's Manual contains teaching tips, sources of supplementary materials, and other helpful information. Part 3 provides instructors with in-class games designed to illustrate and enliven important economic concepts. Contributed in part by Professor Charles Stull of Kalamazoo College, the games are an enormously popular feature with instructors. We hope you will try them. We believe you will find them extremely useful for classroom learning.

Instructor's CD ROM

For the first time, the instructor's supplements accompanying this textbook are now conveniently available on one CD ROM. Included on the CD ROM are the PowerPoint slides, Instructor's Manual, and Test Banks. The CD ROM also displays a navigation bar, allowing professors to easily search among the microeconomics and macroeconomics versions of the supplements.

Color Transparencies

Color transparencies of the major exhibits of the ninth edition have been prepared for use with overhead projectors. They are available to adopters upon request in sets for microeconomics and macroeconomics.

Harcourt College Publishing will provide complimentary supplements or supplement packages to those adopters qualified under our adoption policy. Please contact your sales representative to learn how you may qualify. If as an adopter or potential user you receive supplements you do not need, please return them to your sales representative or send them to:

Attn: Returns Department
Troy Warehouse
465 South Lincoln Drive
Troy, MO 63379

ACKNOWLEDGMENTS

A project of this type is a team effort. Several people contributed substantially to the development of this edition.

We would like to express our appreciation to David MacPherson, who prepared both the Test Banks and Instructor's Manual for this edition. He also directed the development of the PowerPoint slides and assisted us in numerous other ways. We are also indebted to Chuck Skipton who put in numerous hours programming the animation for the PowerPoint slides. Together MacPherson and Skipton have developed what we believe to be the very best PowerPoint materials accompanying a principles text.

In the past, Woody Studenmund of Occidental College prepared the Coursebook and Gary Galles of Pepperdine University coauthored the Instructor's Manual. Both of these supplements still bear the imprint of their contribution. Through the years, numerous people have supplied us with quality questions for the Test Banks. We would like to acknowledge specifically the contributions of J. J. Bethune, University of Tennessee—Martin; Edward Bierhanzl, Florida A&M University; Tim Sass, Florida State University; and Woody Studenmund. Both Amy Gwartney and Kathy Makinen helped with the proofing and provided assistance in several other areas.

We have often revised material in light of suggestions made by reviewers, users, friends, and even a few competitors. In this regard, we would like to express our appreciation to the following people for their contributions to recent editions: Robert N. Baird, Case Western Reserve University; Fred Beebe, Long Beach Community College; John W. Dodge, Jr., University of Sioux Falls; Charles J. Ellard, University of Texas—Pan American; T. Windsor Fields, James Madison University; Joseph Fuhrig, Golden Gate University; Ralph C. Gamble, Jr., Fort Hays State University; Joseph D. Greene, Augusta College; Anthony L. Ostrosky, Illinois State University; Robert C. Rencher, Jr., Liberty University; Torsten Schmidt, University of New Hampshire; Paul M. Taube, University of Texas—Pan American; Donna Thompson, Brookdale Community College; Roger Trenary, Kansas State University.

Many people made important contributions to the ninth edition by providing us with insightful feedback and astute reviews. Their comments enabled us to write a superior ninth edition. We are indebted to them: Douglas Agbetsiafa, Indiana University, South Bend; James C.W. Ahiakpor, California State University, Hayward; Ali T. Akarca, University of Illinois at Chicago; Stephen A. Baker, Capital University; Alana Bhatia, University of Colorado at Boulder; Edward J. Bierhanzl, Florida A&M University; Charles A. Booth, University of Alabama at Birmingham; Ford J. Brown, University of Minnesota—Morris; Dennis Brennen, Harper College; James Bryan, Manhattanville College; Darcy R. Carr, Coastal Carolina University; Mike Cohick, Collin County Community College; David S. Collins, Virginia Highlands Community College; Jim F. Couch, University of North Alabama; Steven R. Cunningham, University of Connecticut; George W. Dollar, Clearwater Christian College; Jeff Edwards, Collin County Community College; Robert C. Eyler, Sonoma State University; James R. Fain, Oklahoma State University; Kathryn Finn, Western Washington University; Andrew W. Foshee, McNeese State University; Marsha Goldfarb, University of Maryland Baltimore County; David Harris, Northwood University; Ronald Helgens, Golden Gate University; Robert E. Herman, Nassau Community College/SUNY; William D. Hermann, Golden Gate University, San Francisco; Brad Hobbs, Florida Gulf Coast University; Woodrow W. Hughes, Jr., Converse College; Rob H. Kamery, Christian Brothers University; Frederic R. Kolb, University of Wisconsin, Eau Claire; Barbara Kouskoulas, Lawrence Technological University; David W.

Kreutzer, James Madison University; George Kuljurgis, Oakland University; Randy W. LaHote, Washtenaw Community College; Tsung-Hui Lai, Liberty University; Bob Lawson, Capital University; Don R. Leet, California State University, Fresno; George P. Lephardt, Milwaukee School of Engineering; Joe LeVesque, Northwood University; G. Dirk Mateer, Grove City College; John McArthur, Wofford College; Ed Mills, Kendell College; David M. Mitchell, Oklahoma State University; Hadley T. Mitchell, Taylor University; Glen A. Moots, Northwood University; John R. Neal, Lake-Sumter Community College; Lloyd Orr, Indiana University, Bloomington; Judd W. Patton, Bellevue College; Robert Reinke, University of South Dakota; Robert C. Rencher, Jr., Liberty University; Dan Rickman, Oklahoma State University; Karin L. Russell, Keiser College; Lewis F. Schlossinger, Community College of Aurora; Thomas W. Secrest, USC Coastal Carolina; Ben S. Shippen, Jr., Mercer University; Charles D. Skipton, Florida State University; Ken Somppi, Southern Union State Community College; William A. Steiden, Jefferson Community College; Richard D.C. Trainer, Warsaw School of Economics; Scott Ward, East Texas Baptist University; Tom Lee Waterston, Northwood University; Jim Wharton, Northwood University; Janice Yee, Wartburg College; and Anthony Zambelli, Cuyamaca College.

We are also indebted to the excellent team of professionals at Harcourt College Publishers: Gary Nelson, acquisitions editor, for his help and support of our efforts; Amy Ray, associate editor, who managed the project and performed countless other tasks for us; Laura Hanna, senior project editor, for orchestrating the copyediting, proofreading, and indexing; Burl Sloan, senior art director, who designed the book; Lois West, senior production manager, who kept it on schedule; Linda Blundell, art and literary rights editor, who helped us locate and obtain permissions for the many photos; and Debbie Anderson, product manager, who worked hard to market the book. Finally, we would like to acknowledge the assistance of Amy Gwartney, Jane Shaw Stroup, and Terri Sobel for their encouragement throughout the project. Without their contributions, we would have been unable to meet the demands and deadlines of this project.

A NOTE TO STUDENTS

This text contains several features that we think will help you maximize (a good economic term) the returns derived from your study effort. Our past experience indicates that awareness of the following points will help you to use the book more effectively.

- Each chapter begins with a series of focus questions that communicate the central issues of the chapter. Before you read the chapter, briefly think about the focus questions, why they are important, and how they relate to the material of prior chapters.

- The textbook is organized in the form of an outline. The headings within the text (highlighted with a color background) are the major points of the outline. Minor headings are subpoints under the major headings. In addition, important subpoints within sections are often set off and numbered. Bold italicized type is used to highlight material that is particularly important. Sometimes thumbnail sketches are included to help the reader better organize important points. Careful use of the headings, highlighted material, and the thumbnail sketches will help you master the material.

- A "Key Points" summary appears at the end of each chapter. Use the summary as a checklist to determine whether you understand the major points of the chapter.

- A review of the exhibits and illustrative pictures will also provide you with a summary of the key points of each chapter. The accompanying legend briefly describes the content and analysis of each feature.

- The key terms introduced in each chapter are defined in the margins. As you study the chapter, go over the marginal definition of each key term as it is introduced. Later, you may also find it useful to review the marginal definitions. If you have forgotten the meaning of a term introduced earlier, consult the glossary at the end of the book.

- The boxed features provide additional depth on various topics without disrupting the flow of the text. In general, the topics of the boxed features have been chosen because of their relevance as an application of the theory or because of past student interest in the topic. Reading the boxed features will supplement the text and enhance your understanding of important economic concepts.

- The critical analysis questions at the end of each chapter are intended to test your understanding of the economic way of thinking. Solving these questions and problems will greatly enhance your knowledge of the material. Answers to approximately half of these questions are provided in Appendix B.

If you need more practice, be sure to obtain a Coursebook and solve the questions and problems for each chapter. The Coursebook also contains the answers to the multiple-choice questions and a brief explanation of why an answer is correct (and other choices incorrect). In most cases, if you master the concepts of the test items in the Coursebook, you will do well on the quizzes and examinations of your instructor. For extra help utilizing multimedia tools, obtain a copy of the book's EconActive Student-Learning CD ROM or go to **www.dryden.com/econ/gwartney**, where you will find practice quizzes and PowerPoint reviews of each chapter. If your bookstore doesn't carry the Coursebook or the EconActive CD ROM, you can order them by calling 800-782-4479.

APPLICATION GUIDE

APPLICATION: A check (✓) indicates that the application would go well with or immediately following the chapter.

CHAPTER NUMBER	APPLICATION NUMBER 1	2	3	4	5	6	7	8
1								
2								
3								
4			✓	✓			✓	✓
5	✓	✓		✓	✓	✓	✓	✓
6	✓	✓		✓	✓	✓	✓	✓
7								
8								
9								
10								
11				✓				
12						✓		
13	✓							✓
14			✓					
15		✓			✓	✓	✓	✓
16								
17								

CONTENTS IN BRIEF

Relationship between MAIN EDITION AND MACRO/MICRO EDITIONS

TABLE OF CONTENTS

The economic way of thinking

Economics is about how people choose. The choices we make influence our lives and those of others. Your future will be influenced by the choices you make with regard to education, job opportunities, savings, and investment. We live in a dynamic world. Changes in technology, demographics, communications, and transportation are constantly altering the attractiveness of various options and the opportunities available to us.

Think for a moment about how the lives of Americans have changed and are changing in three areas: (1) population composition, (2) the workforce, and (3) interaction with people in other countries.

THE WALL STREET JOURNAL
MONEY & INVESTING
Concerned About Sagging Stocks
Life is a series of choices with regard to how we earn, spend, save and invest.

ABY BOOMERS AND DEMOGRAPHIC CHANGES

following the Second World War, there crease in the number of births. As a re- third of Americans were age 15 years 960 (see Exhibit I-A). The baby boomers prime working-age years of life. Com- he percentage of Americans 40 to 55 risen sharply, while the share of population under 15 years of age has declined substantially. During the next several decades, there will be still more change. By 2025, the proportion of the population age 65 and over will soar to 18.7 percent, more than twice the figure for 1960. Meanwhile, both the young and prime-age workers will decline as a share of the population.

EXHIBIT I-A

SOURCES: Statistical Abstract of the United States *(various years).*

WOMEN AND COLLEGE GRADUATES ARE AN INCREASING SHARE OF THE LABOR FORCE

Since 1950 the labor force has seen a huge influx of women, particularly married women. Today, women comprise 46.2 percent of the labor force, up from 29.6 percent in 1950 (see Exhibit I-B). The proportion of workers with a college degree has also increased substantially. As Exhibit I-B shows, college graduates now comprise 28.5 percent of the labor force, up from 6.2 in 1950 and 14.1 in 1970.

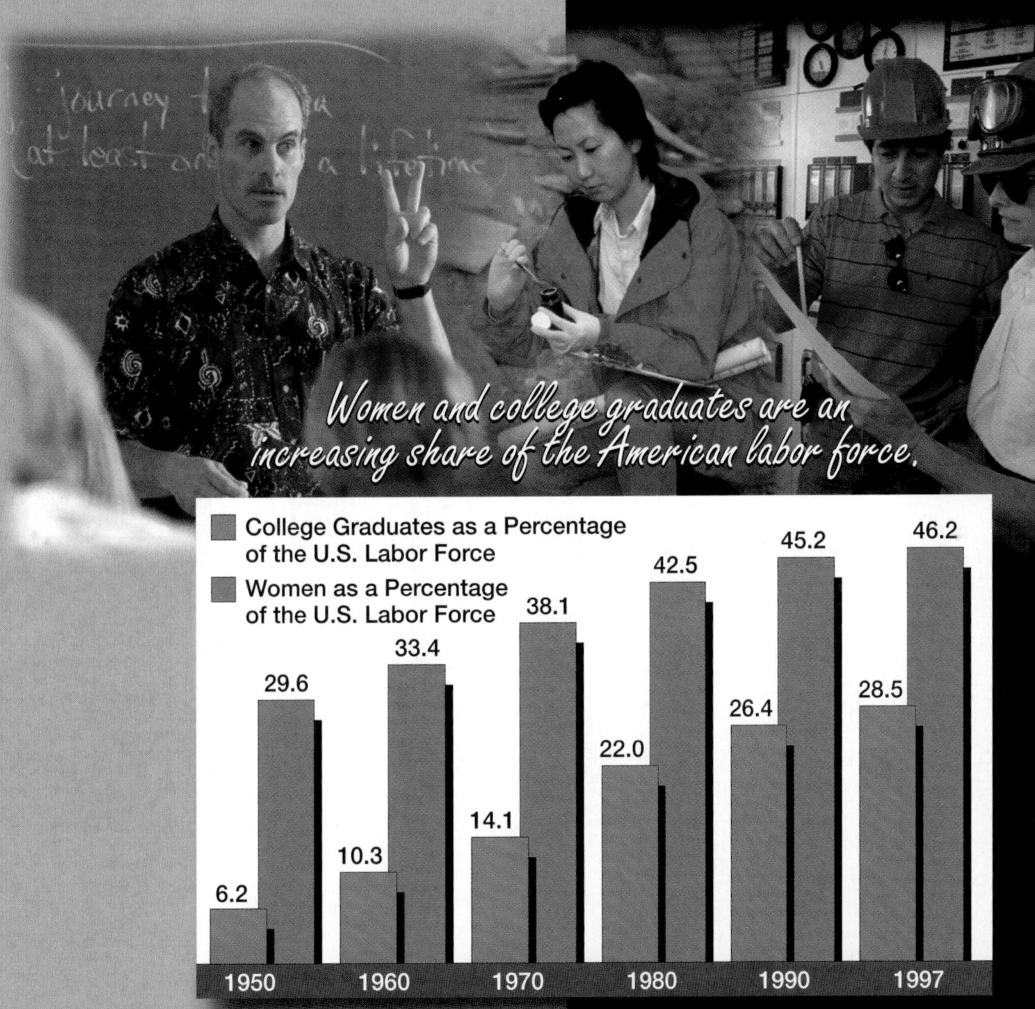

SOURCES: Statistical Abstract of the United States *(various years) and* Employment and Training Report of the President *(1979). Note the 1950 figure is for persons age 25 years and older.*

EXHIBIT I-B

INCREASINGLY, WE ARE INVOLVED IN A GLOBAL ECONOMY

The world is shrinking. In recent decades, transportation and communication costs have fallen dramatically. Increasingly, Americans are buying, investing, traveling, and even working abroad. At the same time, foreigners are more likely to do these same things in the United States. As a share of the economy, the size of the international trade sector (exports plus imports) has tripled since 1960 and doubled since 1980.

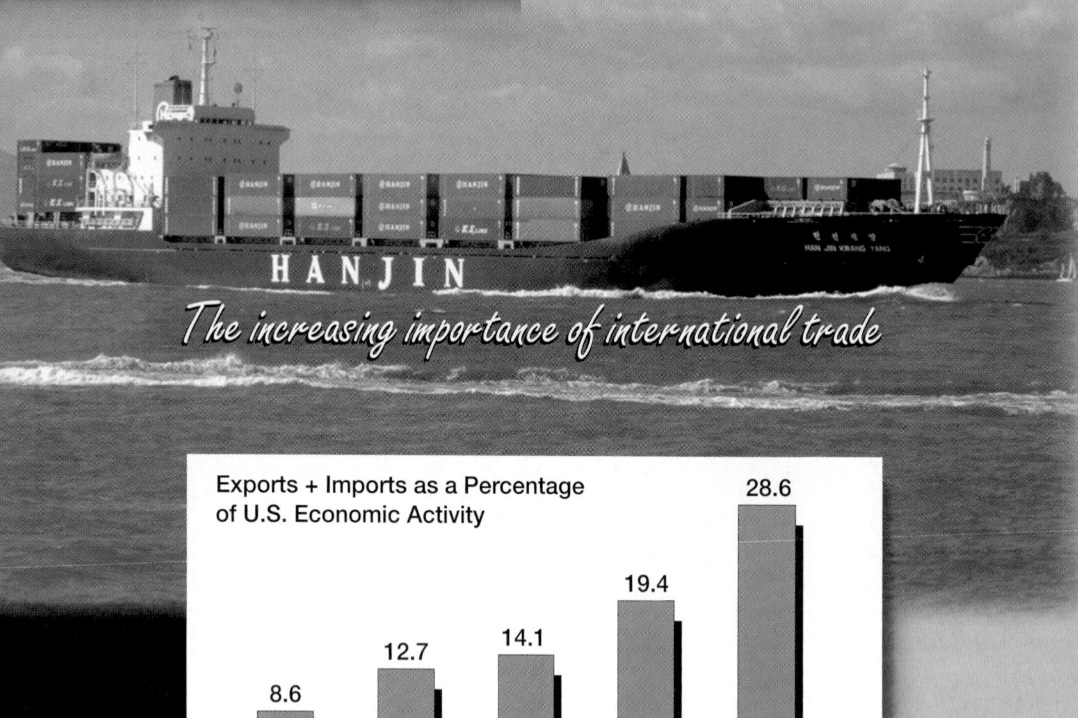

EXHIBIT 1-C

SOURCE: Economic Report of the President: 1998, *table B-2.*

SIGNIFICANCE OF OUR CHANGING ECONOMY

An increase in the number of elderly Americans, more women and college grads in the workforce, and the globalization of economic activity: How will these megatrends influence your job opportunities and quality of life? The tools of economics can enhance your understanding of these factors and numerous others that will affect your life. The economic way of thinking will help you make better choices in our dynamic world.

CHAPTER 1

[Economics] is not a body of concrete truth, but an engine for the discovery of concrete truth.

Alfred Marshall[1]

The Economic Approach

CHAPTER FOCUS

- Why is scarcity a key economic concept, even in an affluent economy?
- How does scarcity differ from poverty? Why does scarcity necessitate rationing and cause competition?
- What are the basic principles underlying the economic way of thinking? What is different about the way economists look at choices and human decision making?
- What is the difference between positive and normative economics?

[1]Alfred Marshall, *The Present Position of Economics* (1885), p. 25.

Now is an exciting time to study economics. Recent political campaigns in the United States have centered on such economic issues as budget deficits, the structure and level of taxes, and social security reform. The market economies of Western Europe are struggling to develop a single, integrated economy with a common currency and legal structure. Several countries of Eastern Europe and the former Soviet Union are continuing their struggle to move from socialist central planning toward market-directed economies. Several Asian nations are trying to recover from recent financial difficulties and regain the prosperity they achieved throughout most of the 1980s and 1990s. Latin American and African leaders are searching for economic prescriptions that will generate prosperity and upgrade living standards.

Simultaneously, economies around the world are becoming more and more interrelated. Many of the goods at your favorite shopping mall are produced, at least in part, by people who speak a different language and live in a country far from your own. Similarly, many Americans work for companies that market their products in Europe, Japan, Latin America, or Africa. The pension funds of American workers commonly own stocks from around the world. Ownership shares of American companies are traded not only in New York City but also on stock exchanges in London, Tokyo, and throughout the world.

How will our current economic policies and rapidly changing world affect the economic status of Americans? What impact will the globalization of our economy have on our living standards, lifestyles, and future opportunities? This book will help you better understand the world in which you live. This is not to imply that economics provides easy answers for problems. As Alfred Marshall stated more than a century ago, economics is a discovery process—a way of thinking—rather than a "body of concrete truth" (see chapter opening quote). Our goals are to present the tools of economics and illustrate how the economic way of thinking can enhance your understanding of our rapidly changing world.

WHAT IS ECONOMICS ABOUT?

[Economics is] the science which studies human behavior as a relationship between ends and scarce means which have alternative uses.

Lionel Robbins[2]

Economics is about people and the choices they make. The unit of analysis in economics is the individual. Of course, individuals group together to form collective organizations, such as corporations, labor unions, and governments. Individual choices, however, still underlie and direct these organizations. Thus, even when we study collective

[2]Lionel Robbins, *An Essay on the Nature and Significance of Economic Science* (1932).

organizations, we will focus on the ways in which their operation is affected by the choices of individuals.

Scarcity and Choice

Would you like some new clothes, a nicer car, and a larger apartment? How about better grades and more time to watch television, go skiing, and travel abroad? Most of us would like more of all these goods. The human desire for goods is virtually unlimited. We cannot, however, have more of everything. Both individually and collectively we face a constraint called **scarcity.** Goods are scarce because people's desire for things is far greater than what is freely available from nature. Because scarcity prevents us from having as much as we would like of **economic goods,** we are forced to choose from a restricted set of potential alternatives. **Choice,** the act of selecting among alternatives, is the logical consequence of scarcity. These two—*scarcity* and *choice*—are the basic ingredients of an economic topic.

Scarcity
Fundamental concept of economics that indicates that a good is less freely available than consumers would like.

Economic good
A good that is scarce. The desire for economic goods exceeds the amount that is freely available from nature.

Choice
The act of selecting among alternatives.

Resource
An input used to produce economic goods. Land, labor, skills, natural resources, and capital are examples. Our history is a record of our struggle to transform available, but limited, resources into things that we would like to have—economic goods.

Resources are inputs used to produce goods and services. In essence, they are tools that we can use to battle scarcity. There are three general categories of resources. First, there are human resources—the productive knowledge, skill, and strength of human beings. Second, there are physical resources—things like tools, machines, and buildings that enhance our ability to produce goods. Economists often use the term *capital* when referring to these human-made resources. Third, there are natural resources—things like land, mineral deposits, oceans, and rivers. The ingenuity of humans is often required in order to make these natural resources useful in production. For example, until recently the yew tree was considered a "trash tree," having no value. Then, scientists discovered that the tree produces taxol, a substance that could be used to fight cancer. Human knowledge and ingenuity made yew trees a valuable resource. Natural resources are important, but recognizing the best ways to produce goods, and which goods to produce under changing circumstances, is as important as the existence of the resources themselves.

Exhibit 1–1 provides a listing of the various categories of both desired goods and the limited resources that might be utilized to produce them. Put simply, the basic economic problem concerns how we can best use the limited resources to produce the desired goods. With the passage of time, investment activities—the development of better tools and improved knowledge, for example—can increase the availability of resources; but more investment requires the sacrifice of additional current consumption. If we use more of today's resources to produce education and skill enhancement, more tools and machines, or more factories, then fewer resources will be available to produce goods for consumption right now. Economics is about trade-offs.

During the past 250 years, we have loosened the grip of scarcity a little. Think for a moment what life was like in 1750. People all over the world struggled 50, 60, and 70 hours a week to obtain the basic necessities of life—food, clothing, and shelter. Manual labor was the major source of energy. Animals provided the means of transportation. Tools and machines were primitive by today's standards. As the English philosopher Thomas Hobbes stated in the 17th century, life was "solitary, poor, nasty, brutish, and short."[3]

Throughout much of South America, Africa, and Asia, economic conditions continue to make life difficult. In North America, Western Europe, Oceania, and some parts of Asia, however, substantial economic progress has been made. Of course, scarcity is still a fact of life in these areas, too; the desire for goods and services still far

[3]Thomas Hobbes, *Leviathan* (1651) Part I, Chapter 13.

History is a record of our struggle to transform available, but limited, resources into things that we would like to have—economic goods.

EXHIBIT 1-1

A GENERAL LISTING OF DESIRED ECONOMIC GOODS AND LIMITED RESOURCES

Economic Goods	Limited Resources
Food (bread, milk, meat, eggs, vegetables, coffee, etc.)	Land (various degrees of fertility)
Clothing (shirts, pants, blouses, shoes, socks, coats, sweaters, etc.)	Natural resources (rivers, trees, minerals, oceans, etc.)
Household goods (tables, chairs, rugs, beds, dressers, television sets, etc.)	Machines and other human-made physical resources
Education	Nonhuman animal resources
National defense	Technology (physical and scientific "recipes" of history)
Leisure time	Human resources (the knowledge, skill, and talent of individual human beings)
Entertainment	
Clean air	
Pleasant environment (trees, lakes, rivers, open spaces, etc.)	
Pleasant working conditions	

outstrips the ability of people to produce them. But from a material standpoint, life is more comfortable. As diet and health care have improved, so has life expectancy. Modern energy sources, means of transportation, appliances, and recreational opportunities have reduced physical hardship and the drudgery of life in North America and other wealthy parts of the world. In these areas, a typical family might worry about financing a summer vacation, obtaining a better home computer or an additional car, and providing for the children's college education. Subsistence levels of food, shelter, and clothing are taken for granted.

It is important to note that scarcity and poverty are not the same thing. Poverty implies some basic level of need, either in absolute or relative terms. Absence of poverty means that the basic level has been attained. In contrast, the absence of scarcity would imply that we have as much of all goods as we would like. Both individuals and countries may win the battle against poverty—people may achieve income levels that allow them to satisfy a basic level of need. But it is painfully obvious that we will not triumph over scarcity. Even in the wealthiest of countries, productive capabilities cannot keep pace with material desires. People always want more goods for themselves and others they care about; societies always want more and better medical care, schooling, and national defense than can be produced with available resources.

Rationing
An allocation of a limited supply of a good or resource to users who would like to have more of it. Various criteria, including charging a price, can be utilized to allocate the limited supply. When price performs the rationing function, the good or resource is allocated to those willing to give up the most "other things" in order to obtain ownership rights.

Scarcity Necessitates Rationing

When a good (or resource) is scarce, some criterion must be set up for deciding who will receive the good (or resource) and who will do without it. Scarcity makes **rationing** a necessity.

Several possible criteria could be used in rationing a limited amount of a good among citizens who would like to have more of it. The rationing criterion chosen will influence human behavior. If the criterion were first-come, first-served, goods would be allocated to those who were fastest at getting in line or to those who were most willing to wait in line. If beauty were used, goods would be allocated to those who were thought to be most beautiful. The political process might determine allocations, and goods would be distributed on the basis of political status and ability to manipulate the political process to personal advantage. In a market setting, price is used to ration things; goods and resources are allocated to those willing to pay the highest prices. One thing is certain: Scarcity means that methods must be established to decide who gets the limited amount of available goods and resources.

Competition Results from Scarcity

Competition is a natural outgrowth of scarcity and the desire of human beings to improve their conditions. Competition exists in every economy and every society. It exists both when goods are allocated by price in markets and when they are allocated by other means—political decision making, for example.

Moreover, the rationing criterion will influence which competitive techniques will be used. When the rationing criterion is price, individuals will engage in income-generating activities that enhance their ability to pay the price. The market system encourages individuals to provide goods and services to others in exchange for income. In turn, the income will permit them to procure more scarce goods.

A different rationing criterion will encourage other types of behavior. When the appearance of sincerity, broad knowledge, fairness, good judgment, and a positive television image are important, as they are in the rationing of elected political positions, people will use resources to project these qualities. They will hire makeup artists, public relations experts, and advertising agencies to help them compete. We can change the form of competition, but no society has been able to eliminate it, because no society has been able to eliminate scarcity and the resulting need for rationing. When people who want more scarce goods seek to meet the criteria established to ration those goods, competition occurs.

THE ECONOMIC WAY OF THINKING

It [economics] is a method rather than a doctrine, an apparatus of the mind, a technique of thinking which helps its possessor to draw correct conclusions.

John Maynard Keynes[4]

One does not have to spend much time around economists to recognize that there is an "economic way of thinking." Admittedly, economists, like others, differ widely in their ideological views. A news commentator once remarked that "any half-dozen economists will normally come up with about six different policy prescriptions." Yet, in spite of their philosophical differences, the approach of economists covers a common ground.

[4]John Maynard Keynes (1883–1946) was an English economist whose writings during the 1920s and 1930s exerted an enormous impact on both economic theory and policy. Keynes established the terminology and the economic framework that are still widely used when economists study problems of unemployment and inflation.

Reprinted by permission: Tribune Media Services.

Economic theory
A set of definitions, postulates, and principles assembled in a manner that makes clear the "cause-and-effect" relationships of economic data.

That common ground is **economic theory,** developed from basic postulates of human behavior. Economic theory, like a road map or a guidebook, establishes reference points indicating what to look for, and how economic issues are interrelated. To a large degree, the basic economic principles are merely common sense. When applied consistently, however, these commonsense concepts can provide interesting and powerful insights.

Eight Guideposts to Economic Thinking

The economic way of thinking requires the incorporation of certain guidelines—some would say the building blocks of basic economic theory—into one's thought process. Once these guidelines are incorporated, we believe that economics can be a relatively easy subject to master. Students who have difficulty with economics have almost always failed to assimilate these principles. We will outline and discuss eight principles that characterize the economic way of thinking and that are essential to understanding the economic approach.

1. The Use of Scarce Resources to Produce a Good Is Always Costly. Economists sometimes refer to this as "There Ain't No Such Thing As A Free Lunch," or the "TANSTAAFL" principle. The use of resources to produce one good diverts the resources from the production of other goods that are also desired. No option is free of cost. The highest valued alternative that must be sacrificed is the **opportunity cost** of the option. For example, if you use one hour of your scarce time to study economics, you will have one hour less time to watch television, read magazines, sleep, work at a job, or study other subjects. Time spent working at a job, or even time spent sleeping, might be viewed as your highest valued option forgone. The cost of an action is always the highest valued option given up in order to choose the action.

Opportunity cost
The highest valued alternative that must be sacrificed as a result of choosing among alternatives.

It is important to recognize that the "scarce resources have a cost" concept is true regardless of who pays for the good or service produced. In many countries, various kinds of schooling are provided free of charge *to students.* However, provision of the schooling is not free *to the community.* The scarce resources (for example, buildings, equipment, and skills of teachers) used to produce the schooling could have been used instead to produce more recreation, entertainment, housing, or other goods. The cost of the schooling is the highest valued option that must now be given up because the resources required for its production were instead used to produce the schooling.

By now the central point should be obvious. Economic thinking recognizes that the use of a scarce resource always involves a cost. The use of more resources to do one thing implies fewer resources with which to achieve other objectives. In the next chapter we will look more closely at this key concept and some of its implications.

2. Individuals Choose Purposefully; They Try to Get the Most From Their Limited Resources. Recognizing the restrictions imposed by the limited resources available to them (income, time, talent, and so on), individuals will try to select those options that best advance their personal objectives. They will not deliberately waste their valuable resources. In turn, the objectives or preferences of individuals are revealed by the choices they make. **Economizing behavior** results directly from purposeful (rational) decision making. Economizing individuals will seek to accomplish an objective at the least possible cost to themselves. When choosing among things that yield equal benefit, an economizer will select the cheapest option. For example, if a pizza, a lobster dinner, and a sirloin steak are expected to yield identical benefits (including the enjoyment of eating them!), economizing behavior implies that the cheapest of the three alternatives, probably the pizza, will be chosen. In the same way, when choosing among alternatives of equal cost, economizing decision makers will select the option that yields the greatest benefit. If the price of several dinner specials are equal, for example, economizers will choose the one they like the best—the one that provides them the most benefit.

Economizing behavior
Choosing with the objective of gaining a specific benefit at the least possible cost. A corollary of economizing behavior implies that, when choosing among items of equal cost, individuals will choose the option that yields the greatest benefit.

Purposeful choosing implies that decision makers have some basis for their evaluation of alternatives. Economists refer to this evaluation as **utility**—the benefit or satisfaction that an individual expects from the choice of a specific alternative. The utility of an alternative is highly subjective, often differing widely from person to person. The steak dinner that delights one person may be repulsive to another (a vegetarian, for example).

Utility
The benefit or satisfaction expected from a choice or course of action.

OUTSTANDING ECONOMIST

The Importance of Adam Smith, the Father of Economics

Economics is a relatively young science. The foundation of economics was laid in 1776, when Adam Smith (1723–1790) published *An Inquiry Into the Nature and Causes of the Wealth of Nations.* Smith presented what at that time was a revolutionary view. He argued that the wealth of a nation did not lie in gold and silver, but rather in the goods and services produced and consumed by people. According to Smith, coordination, order, and efficiency would result without the planning and direction of a central authority.

Adam Smith was a lecturer at the University of Glasgow, in his native Scotland. Morals and ethics actually were his concern before economics. His first book was *The Theory of Moral Sentiments.* For Smith, self-interest and sympathy for others were complementary. However, he did not believe that charity alone could provide the essentials for a good life. He stressed that free exchange and competitive markets would harness self-interest as a creative force. Directed by the "invisible hand" of market prices, individuals *pursuing their own interests* would be encouraged to produce the goods and supply the resources that others value most highly (relative to costs).

Ideas have consequences. Smith's ideas greatly influenced not only Europeans but also those who mapped out the structure of the U.S. government. Since then, the effectiveness of the "invisible hand" of the market has become accepted as critical to the prosperity of nations.[1]

[1]For an excellent biographical sketch of Adam Smith, used to prepare this feature, see David Henderson, ed., *The Fortune Encyclopedia of Economics* (New York: Warner Books, 1993), pp. 836–838.

THE FAMILY CIRCUS® By Bil Keane

"Everybody wants to be sick. I'm using M&M's for pills."

3. Incentives Matter—Choice Is Influenced in a Predictable Way by Changes in Economic Incentives. This guidepost to clear economic thinking might be called the basic postulate of all economics. ***As the personal benefits from choosing an option increase, other things constant, a person will be more likely to choose that option. In contrast, as the personal costs associated with the choice of an item increase, the individual will be less likely to choose that option.*** For a group, this basic economic postulate suggests that making an option more attractive will cause more people to choose it. In contrast, as the cost of a selection to the members of a group increases, fewer of them will make this selection.

This basic postulate of economics is a powerful tool because its application is so widespread. Incentives affect behavior in virtually all aspects of our lives, ranging from market decisions about what to buy to political choices concerning for whom to vote. If beef prices rise, making beef consumption more expensive relative to other goods, the basic postulate indicates that consumers will be less likely to choose it. As a result, less beef will be consumed at the higher price. Similarly, the "incentives matter" postulate indicates that a voter will be less likely to support candidates favoring higher taxes to provide goods the voter finds unattractive.

To show its broad scope, we can apply this basic postulate of economics to the examination process. If a classroom instructor makes it more costly to cheat, students will be less likely to do so. There will be little cheating on a closely monitored, individualized essay examination. Why? Because it is difficult (that is, costly) to cheat on such an exam. Suppose, however, that an instructor gives an objective "take-home" exam, basing students' course grades entirely on the results. Among the same group of students, more will be likely to cheat because the benefits of doing so will be great and the risk (cost) minimal. (The boxed feature "Incentives Matter" gives yet another application of this principle.)

Marginal
Term used to describe the effects of a change in the current situation. For example, the marginal cost is the cost of producing an additional unit of a product, given the producer's current facility and production rate.

4. Economic Thinking Is Marginal Thinking. Fundamental to economic reasoning and economizing behavior are the effects of decisions made to change the status quo. Economists describe such decisions as **marginal.** Marginal choices always involve the

APPLICATIONS IN ECONOMICS

Incentives Matter: Drinking and Driving in Norway

How generally can we apply the "incentives matter" principle? Do differences in incentives influence, for example, the incidence of drinking and driving? Consider the case of Norway, the country that has the toughest drunk-driving laws in the Western world.[1] Drinking a single can of beer before driving can put a first offender in jail for a minimum sentence of three weeks. These drivers generally lose their licenses for up to two years and often get stiff fines as well. Repeat offenders are treated even more harshly. These laws are far more draconian than those of the United States. Surveys indicate that:

1. One out of three Norwegians arrives at parties in a taxi, while nearly all Americans drive their own cars.
2. One out of ten Norwegian partygoers spends the night at the host's home; Americans seldom do.
3. In Norway, 78 percent of drivers totally avoid drinking at parties, compared to only 17 percent of American drivers.

Norwegians do like to drink, though they consume only half as much alcohol as Americans. The strong incentives built into Norwegian law, however, clearly make a difference. Once again, incentives do matter, and matter in a big way.

[1]The information in this feature is from L. Erik Calonius, "Just a Bottle of Beer Can Land a Motorist in Prison in Norway," *Wall Street Journal,* August 16, 1985, p. 1.

effects of net additions to or subtractions from the current conditions. In fact, the word *additional* is often used as a substitute for *marginal.* For example, we might ask, "What is the marginal (or additional) cost of producing one more unit?"

Marginal decisions may involve large or small changes. The "one more unit" could be a new factory or a new stapler. It is marginal because it involves additional costs and additional benefits. Given the current situation, what marginal benefits (additional sales revenues, for example) can be expected from the new factory, and what will be the marginal cost of constructing it? The answers to these questions will determine whether building the new factory is a good decision.

It is important to distinguish between *average* and *marginal.* A manufacturer's current average cost of producing a specific automobile (total cost divided by total number of the cars produced to date) may be $20,000, but the marginal cost of producing an additional automobile (or an additional 1,000 automobiles) might be much lower, say, $5,000 per car. Costs associated with research, testing, design, molds, heavy equipment, and similar factors of production must be incurred whether the manufacturer is going to produce 1,000 units, 10,000 units, or 100,000 units. Such costs will clearly contribute to the average cost of an automobile. However, since these activities have already been undertaken to produce the manufacturer's current output level, the cost of producing additional units (automobiles) will change them very little. Thus, the marginal cost of

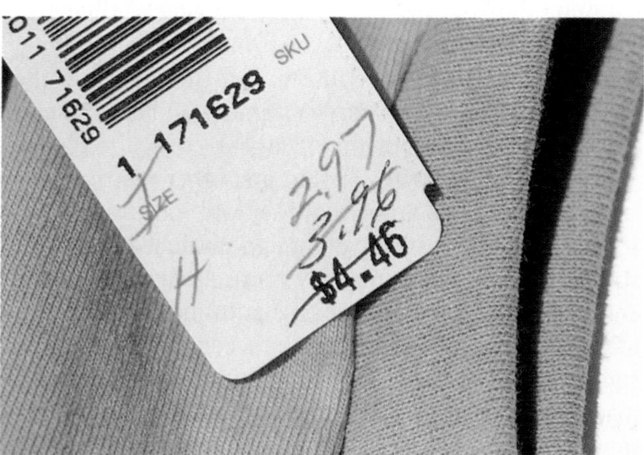

Why do store owners reduce their prices on various items? Do they believe that consumers respond to incentives?

additional units may be substantially less than the average cost. Should production be expanded or reduced? That choice should be based on marginal costs, which indicate the *change* in total cost due to the decision, rather than the current average cost.

We often confront decisions involving a possible change from the current situation. The *marginal benefits* and *marginal costs* associated with the choice will determine the wisdom of our decisions. What happens at the margin is therefore an important element of the economic way of thinking.

5. Although Information Can Help Us Make Better Choices, Its Acquisition Is Costly. Thus we will almost always make choices based on limited knowledge. Information that will help us make better choices is valuable. Like other resources, however, it is also scarce and therefore costly to acquire. As a result, individuals will economize on their search for information just as they economize on the use of other scarce resources. For example, when purchasing a pair of jeans, you may check price and evaluate quality at several different stores. At some point, though, you will decide that additional shopping—that is, acquisition of additional information—is simply not worth the trouble. You will make a choice based on the limited knowledge that you already possess.

The process is similar when individuals search for a restaurant, a new car, or a roommate. They will seek to acquire some information, but at some point, they will decide that the expected benefit derived from still more information is simply not worth the cost. When differences among the alternatives are important to the decision maker, more time and effort will be spent to make a better individual decision. Even then, limited knowledge and resulting uncertainty about the outcome characterize the decision-making process.

6. Economic Actions Often Generate Secondary Effects in Addition to Their Immediate Effects. Failure to consider these secondary effects is the most common source of economic error. Frederic Bastiat, a nineteenth-century French economist, stated that the difference between a good and a bad economist is that the bad economist considers only the immediate, visible effects, whereas the good economist is also aware of the **secondary effects,** effects that result from the initial policy, but that may be seen or felt only with the passage of time.

Secondary effects
Economic consequences of an economic change that are not immediately identifiable but are felt only with the passage of time.

Perhaps a simple example involving both immediate and secondary effects will help us grasp this point. The immediate effect of an aspirin is a bitter taste in one's mouth. The secondary effect, which is not immediately observable, is relief from a headache. The immediate effect of drinking six quarts of beer might be a warm, jolly feeling. The secondary effect is likely to be a sluggish feeling the next morning, and perhaps a pounding headache.

In economics, the immediate, short-term effects that are highly visible are often quite different from the long-term effects. Changes in economic policy often alter the structure of incentives, which indirectly affects how much people work, earn, invest, and conserve for the future. But the impact of the secondary effects is often observable only after the passage of time—and even then only to those who know what to look for in evaluating them.

Consider tariffs, quotas, and other restrictions that limit imports. Proponents of such restrictions argue that they will increase employment; indeed, at first they do. If, for example, the supply of foreign-produced automobiles to the U.S. market were restricted, Americans would buy more American-made automobiles, increasing output and employment in the domestic auto industry. These would be the immediate, easily identified effects. But consider the secondary effects. The restrictions would also reduce supply to the domestic market and increase the price of both foreign- and American-made automobiles. As a result of the higher prices, many auto consumers would pay more for automobiles and thus be forced to curtail their purchases of food, clothing,

Reprinted with special permission of King Features Syndicate.

recreation, and literally thousands of other items. These reductions in spending would mean less output and employment in those areas. There would also be a secondary effect on sales to foreigners. Since foreigners would be selling fewer automobiles to Americans, they would acquire fewer dollars with which to buy American-made goods. U.S. exports, therefore, would fall as a result of the restrictions on automobile imports.

Once the secondary effects are considered, the net impact on employment of the import restrictions is no longer obvious. Although restrictions may increase employment in the auto industry, they will reduce employment in other industries, particularly export industries. Primarily, they will reshuffle employment rather than increase it. As this example illustrates, consideration of secondary effects is an important ingredient of the economic way of thinking.

7. The Value of a Good or Service Is Subjective. Preferences differ, sometimes dramatically, between individuals. How much is a ticket to see tonight's performance of the Bolshoi Ballet worth? Some would be willing to pay a very high price, while others might prefer to stay home and avoid the ballet performance, even if tickets were free! Circumstances can change from day to day, even for a given individual. Alice, a ballet fan who usually would value the ticket at more than its price of $50, is invited to a party, and suddenly becomes uninterested in the ballet tonight. Now what is the ticket worth? If she knows a friend who would give her $20 for the ticket, it is worth at least that much. If she advertises on a bulletin board and gets $40 for it, a higher value is created. But if someone who doesn't know of the ticket would have paid even more, then a potential trade that would have created even more value is missed. If tonight's performance is sold out, perhaps someone in town would be willing to pay $70! One thing is certain: The value of the ticket depends on several things, including who uses it and under what circumstances.

Seldom will one individual know how others would value an item. Consider how difficult it often is to know what would make a good gift, even for a close friend or family member! So, arranging trades, or otherwise moving items to higher-valued users and uses, is not a simple task. The entrepreneurial individual, who knows how to locate the right buyers and arranges for the goods to flow to higher-valued uses, can create huge increases in value from existing resources. In fact, encouragement of individuals to (a) move goods toward those who value them most and (b) combine resources into goods that individuals value more highly than the resources required for their production is a vitally important source of economic progress. As we proceed, we will investigate this issue in detail.

Scientific thinking
Development of a theory from basic postulates and the testing of the implications of that theory as to their consistency with events in the real world. Good theories are consistent with and help explain real-world events. Theories that are inconsistent with the real world are invalid and must be rejected.

8. The Test of a Theory Is Its Ability to Predict. Economic thinking is **scientific thinking.** The proof of the pudding is in the eating. The usefulness of an economic theory is proved by its ability to predict the future consequences of economic action. Economists develop economic theory from scientific thinking, using basic postulates to analyze how incentives will affect decision makers, and comparing the analysis against events in the real world. If the events in the real world are consistent with a theory, we say that the theory has *predictive value* and is therefore valid.

If it is impossible to test the theoretical relationships of a discipline, the discipline does not qualify as a science. Because economics deals with human beings, who can think and respond in a variety of ways, can economic theories really be tested? The answer to this question is yes, if, on average, human beings respond in predictable and consistent ways to certain changes in economic conditions. The economist believes that this is the case even though not all individuals will respond in a specified manner. Economists usually do not try to predict the behavior of a specific individual; instead, they focus on the general behavior of a large number of individuals.

In the 1950s, economists began to do laboratory experiments to test economic theories. Individuals were brought into laboratories to see how they would act in buying and selling situations, under differing rules. For example, small but concrete cash rewards were given to individuals who, when an auction was conducted among them, were able to sell at high prices and to buy at low prices, thus approximating real-world market incentives. These experiments have verified many of the important propositions of economic theory.

Laboratory experiments, however, cannot duplicate all real economic interactions. How can we test economic theory when controlled experiments are not feasible? This is a problem, but economics is no different from astronomy in this respect. Astronomers can use theories tested in physics laboratories, but they must also deal with the world as it is. They cannot change the course of the stars or planets to see what impact the change would have on the gravitational pull of the earth. Similarly, economists cannot arbitrarily change the prices of cars or unskilled labor services in real markets, just to observe the effects on quantities purchased or levels of employment in the real world outside the laboratory. However, economic conditions (for example, prices, production costs, technology, and transportation costs), like the location of the planets, do change from time to time. As actual conditions change, an economic theory can be tested by comparing its predictions with real-world outcomes. Just as the universe is the main laboratory of the astronomer, the real economic world is often the laboratory of the economist.

POSITIVE AND NORMATIVE ECONOMICS

A positive science may be defined as a body of systematized knowledge concerning what is; a normative or regulative science is a body of systematized knowledge relating to criteria of what ought to be, and concerned therefore with the ideal as distinguished from the actual.

John Neville Keynes[5]

Positive economics
The scientific study of "what is" among economic relationships.

Economics as a social science is concerned with predicting or determining the impact of changes in economic variables on the actions of human beings. Scientific economics, commonly referred to as **positive economics,** attempts to determine "what is." Positive economic statements postulate a relationship that is potentially verifiable or refutable. For example: "If the price of gasoline were higher, people would buy less." Or, "As the money supply increases, the price level will go up." We can statistically investigate (and estimate) the relationship between gasoline prices and gallons sold,

[5]John Neville Keynes, *The Scope and Method of Political Economy,* 4th ed. (1917), pp. 34–35.

or between the supply of money and the general price level. We can analyze the facts to determine the correctness of a statement about positive economics.

Normative economics involves the advocacy of specific policy alternatives, because it uses ethical or value judgments as well as knowledge of positive economics. Normative economic statements concern "what ought to be," given the preferences and philosophical views of the advocate. Value judgments may be the source of disagreement about normative economic matters. Two persons may differ on a policy matter because one is a socialist and the other a libertarian, because one wants cheaper food while the other favors organic farming, or even because one values wilderness highly while the other wants more improved campsites that can be easily reached by roads. They may agree as to the expected outcome of altering an economic variable (that is, the positive economics of an issue), but disagree as to whether that outcome is desirable.

Normative economics
Judgments about "what ought to be" in economic matters. Normative economic views cannot be proved false, because they are based on value judgments.

In contrast with positive economic statements, normative economic statements can neither be confirmed nor proven false through scientific testing. "Business firms should not maximize profits." "The use of pesticides on food to be sold in stores should not be allowed." "More of our national forests should be set aside for wilderness." These normative statements cannot be scientifically tested because their validity rests on value judgments.

Normative economic views can sometimes influence our attitude toward positive economic analysis. When we agree with the objectives of a policy, it is easy to overlook warnings of potential problems implied by positive economics. Although positive economics does not tell us which policy is best, it can provide knowledge that will help reduce the likelihood of false expectations. Desired objectives are not the same as workable solutions. The actual effects of policy alternatives often differ dramatically from the objectives of their proponents. A new law forcing employers to pay all employees at least $12 per hour might be intended to help low-skill workers, but the resulting decline in the number of workers employed (and increase in the number unemployed) would be disastrous despite the good intentions. Proponents of such a law, of course, would not want to believe the economic analysis that predicted the unfortunate outcome.

The task of the professional economist is to expand our knowledge of how the real world operates, both in the private and the public sectors. If we do not fully understand the implications, including the secondary effects, of alternative actions, we will not be able to choose intelligently. Yet, it is not always easy to use economic thinking to isolate the impact of a change in an economic variable or a change in policy. Let us consider some of the potential pitfalls to avoid in economic thinking.

PITFALLS TO AVOID IN ECONOMIC THINKING

VIOLATION OF THE CETERIS PARIBUS CONDITION

Economists often preface their statements with the words **ceteris paribus,** a term from Latin meaning "other things constant." "Other things constant, an increase in the price of housing will cause buyers to reduce their purchases." Unfortunately for the economic researcher, we live in a dynamic world. Other things seldom remain constant. For example, as the price of housing rises, the income of consumers may also be increasing. Each of these factors—higher housing prices and an expansion in consumer income—will have an impact on housing purchases. In fact, we would generally expect them to have opposite effects: higher prices reducing housing purchases but the rise in consumer income increasing the demand for housing. The task of sorting out the specific effects of two or more variables when all are changing at the same time is difficult,

Ceteris paribus
A Latin term meaning "other things constant," used when the effect of one change is being described, recognizing that if other things changed, they also could affect the result. Economists often describe the effects of one change, knowing that in the real world, other things might change and have their effects, too.

though with a strong grip on economic theory, some ingenuity, and enough data, it can often be done. In fact, the major portion of the day-to-day work of many professional economists consists of statistical research.

Association Is Not Causation

In economics, causation is very important, and statistical association alone cannot establish causation. Perhaps an extreme example will illustrate the point. Suppose that each November a witch doctor performs a voodoo dance designed to arouse the cold-weather gods of winter, and that soon after the dance is performed, the weather in fact begins to turn cold. The witch doctor's dance is associated with the arrival of winter, but does it cause the arrival of winter? Most of us would answer in the negative, even though the two are linked statistically.

Unfortunately, cause-and-effect relationships in economics are not always self-evident. For example, it is sometimes difficult to know whether a rise in income has caused people to buy more or, conversely, whether an increase in people's willingness to buy more has created more business and caused incomes to rise. Similarly, economists sometimes argue whether rising money wages are a cause or an effect of inflation. Economic theory, if rooted to the basic postulates, can often help to determine the source of causation, even though competing theories may sometimes suggest differing directions of causation.

Fallacy of Composition

What is true for the individual (or subcomponent) may not be true for the group (or the whole). If you stand up for an exciting play during a football game, you will be better able to see. But what happens if everyone stands up at the same time? What benefits the individual does not necessarily benefit the group as a whole. When everyone stands up, the view for individual spectators fails to improve; it may even become worse.

Fallacy of composition
Erroneous view that what is true for the individual (or the part) will also be true for the group (or the whole).

People who argue that what is true for the part is also true for the whole may be mistaken because of the **fallacy of composition.** Consider an example from economics. If you have an extra $10,000 in your bank account, you will be better off. But, what if everyone suddenly has an additional $10,000? This increase in the money supply will result in higher prices, as people with more money bid against one another for the existing supply of goods. Without an increase in the availability (or production) of scarce economic goods, the additional money will not make anyone better off. What is true for the individual can be misleading and is often fallacious when applied to the entire economy.

Potential error associated with the fallacy of composition highlights the importance of considering both a micro view and a macro view in the study of economics. Because individual decision makers are the moving force behind all economic action, the foundations of economics are clearly rooted in a micro view. **Microeconomics** focuses on the decision making of consumers, producers, and resource suppliers operating in a narrowly defined market, such as that for a specific good or resource.

Microeconomics
The branch of economics that focuses on how human behavior affects the conduct of affairs within narrowly defined units, such as individual households or business firms.

Macroeconomics
The branch of economics that focuses on how human behavior affects outcomes in highly aggregated markets, such as the markets for labor or consumer products.

As we have seen, however, what is true for a small unit may not be true in the aggregate. **Macroeconomics** focuses on how the aggregation of individual micro-units affects our analysis. Like microeconomics, it is concerned with incentives, prices, and output. Macroeconomics, however, aggregates markets, lumping all 100 million households in this country together to study such topics as consumption spending, saving, and employment. Similarly, the nation's 20 million business firms are lumped together in "the business sector."

What factors determine the level of aggregate output, the rate of inflation, the amount of unemployment, and interest rates? These are macroeconomic questions. In

MYTHS OF ECONOMICS

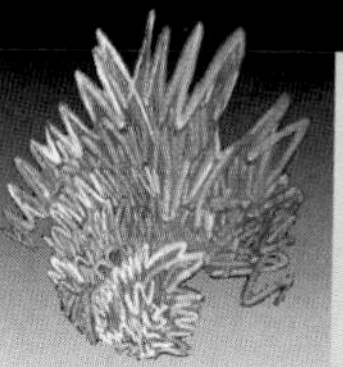

"Economic analysis assumes people act only out of selfish motives. It rejects the humanitarian side of humankind."

Probably because economics focuses on efforts of individuals to satisfy material desires, casual observers often argue that its relevance hinges on selfishness. This view is false. People are motivated by a variety of goals, some humanitarian and some selfish. The basic postulate of economics applies to both. As an action becomes more costly, both the altruist and the selfish egotist will be less likely to choose it. Similarly, when the cost of an option declines, both will be more likely to choose it. Changes in benefits and cost will influence the choices of both. For example, both the altruist and the egotist will be more likely to attempt the rescue of a small child in a three-foot swimming pool than in the rapid currents approaching Niagara Falls. Similarly, both are more likely to give a needy person their hand-me-downs rather than their best clothes.

Sometimes people confuse a focus on narrow goals with selfishness. The two are not the same thing. Many people, humanitarians as well as egotists, focus on a narrow set of objectives. For example, the late Mother Teresa focused on a narrow goal—the improvement in the material and spiritual well-being of the indigent and the sick of Calcutta. Her tireless work in this area was legendary. The late John Muir's love of wilderness and his focus on its eternal protection for all humankind was also legendary. The goals of both Mother Teresa and John Muir were noble and altruistic rather than narrowly selfish. The same could be said of passionate advocates for cancer research, education, historic preservation, the arts, aid to underprivileged children, and a thousand other worthy causes. Advocates in all these areas argue passionately for additional funding and support of their mission at the expense of the "missions" of others. Even without selfishness, the narrow focus of individuals with different primary goals will assure strong competition for scarce resources, economizing behavior, and predictable responses to changes in incentives.

short, macroeconomics examines the forest rather than the individual trees. As we move from the micro components to a macro view of the whole, it is important that we beware of the fallacy of composition.

ECONOMICS AS A CAREER

If you find yourself doing well in this course, and find economics an interesting field of study, you may want to think about majoring in economics. Graduating with a major in economics provides a variety of choices. Many students go on to graduate school in economics, business, public administration, or law. Graduate M.B.A. and law programs find economics majors particularly attractive because of their strong analytical skills.

A graduate degree (a master's or doctorate) in economics is typically required to pursue a career as a professional economist. About one-half of all professional economists are employed by colleges and universities as teachers and researchers. Professional economists also work for the government or private businesses. Most major corporations have a staff of economists to advise them in business decisions, while governments employ economists to analyze the impact of policy alternatives. The federal government has a Council of Economic Advisers whose purpose is to provide the president with analyses of how the activities of the government influence the economy. The chairmanship of the Council of Economic Advisers is a cabinet-level position.

Students who major in economics, but who do not pursue graduate school, have many job opportunities. Because economics is a way of thinking, knowledge of economics is a valuable decision-making tool on almost any job. Undergraduate majors in economics typically work in business, government service, banking, or insurance. There are even increasing opportunities for persons with only undergraduate economics majors to teach economics at the high school level.

The average salary offer for a beginning economics graduate is comparable to those with finance and accounting majors, and is generally higher than for management or marketing. Professional economists with graduate degrees in economics who work for private business average approximately $70,000 per year, and those who choose to work as teachers and researchers at colleges and universities earn approximately $60,000 annually. Although salaries vary substantially, the point is that a career in economics can be rewarding both personally and financially. If you are interested in learning more about a major in economics, and the job opportunities available for economics majors, you might visit your school's career center or speak with your school's undergraduate advisor in economics.

Even if you choose not to major in economics, you will find that your economics courses will broaden your horizons and increase your ability to understand and analyze what is going on around you in the world of politics, business, and human relations. Economics is a social science, often overlapping with the fields of political science, sociology, and psychology. Because the economic way of thinking is so useful in making sense of the abundance of available economic observations and data, and because there is ample opportunity for productive research using economic science in the real world, economics has sometimes been called the "queen of the social sciences." Reflecting the scientific nature of economics, the Swedish Academy of Science in 1969 instituted the Nobel Prize in economic science. The men and women of genius in economics take their place alongside those in physics, chemistry, physiology and medicine, peace, and literature.

LOOKING *Ahead*

The primary purpose of this book is to encourage you to develop the economic way of thinking so that you can separate sound reasoning from economic nonsense. Once you have developed the economic way of thinking, economics will be relatively easy. Using the economic way of thinking can also be fun. Moreover, it will help you become a better citizen. It will give you a different and fascinating perspective on what motivates people, why they act the way they do, and why their actions sometimes go against the best interest of the community or nation. It will also give you some valuable insight into how people's actions can be rechanneled for the benefit of the community at large.

KEY POINTS

➤ Scarcity and choice are the two essential ingredients of an economic topic. Goods are scarce because desire for them far outstrips their availability from nature. Scarcity forces us to choose among available alternatives.

➤ Every society will have to devise some method of rationing the scarce resources among competing uses. Competition is a natural outgrowth of the need to ration scarce goods.

➤ Scarcity and poverty are not the same thing. Absence of poverty implies that some basic level of need has been met. An absence of scarcity would imply that all our desires for goods were fully satisfied. We may someday eliminate poverty, but scarcity will always be with us.

➤ Economics is a way of thinking that emphasizes eight points:

1. Among economic goods, there are no free lunches. The use of scarce resources to produce a good is always costly.

2. Individuals make decisions purposefully, always seeking to choose the option they expect to be most consistent with their personal goals.

3. Incentives matter. The likelihood of people choosing an option increases as personal benefits rise and personal costs decline.

4. Economic reasoning focuses on the impact of marginal changes; decisions will be based on marginal costs and marginal benefits (utility).

5. Since information is scarce, uncertainty is a fact of life.

6. In addition to their initial impact, economic events often generate secondary effects that may be felt only with the passage of time.

7. The value of a good or service is subjective and varies with individual preferences and circumstances.

8. The test of an economic theory is its ability to predict and to explain events in the real world.

➤ Economic science is positive; it attempts to explain the actual consequences of economic actions. Normative economics goes further, applying value judgments to make suggestions about what "ought to be."

➤ Microeconomics focuses on narrowly defined units, while macroeconomics is concerned with highly aggregated units. When shifting focus from micro- to macrounits, one must beware of the fallacy of composition.

➤ The origin of economics as a systematic method of analysis dates to the publication of *The Wealth of Nations* by Adam Smith in 1776. Smith believed a market economy would bring individual self-interest and the public interest into harmony.

CRITICAL ANALYSIS QUESTIONS

1. Indicate how each of the following changes would influence the incentive of a decision maker to undertake the action described.

   a. A reduction in the temperature from 80° to 50° on one's decision to go swimming.

   b. A change in the meeting time of the introductory economics course from 11:00 A.M. to 7:30 A.M. on one's decision to attend the lectures.

   c. A reduction in the number of exam questions that relate directly to the text on the student's decision to read the text.

   d. An increase in the price of beef on one's decision to have steak.

   e. An increase in the rental price of apartments on one's decision to build additional housing units.

*2. "The government should provide such goods as health care, education, and highways because it can provide them free." Is this statement true or false? Explain your answer.

3. Is the following disagreement between Senator Dogooder and Senator Donothing positive or normative? Explain.

Senator Dogooder: I favor an increase in the minimum wage because it would help the unskilled worker.

Senator Donothing: I oppose an increase in the minimum wage because it would cause the unemployment rate among the young and unskilled to rise.

*4. Some groups in the United States have asked for an increase in the personal income tax exemption provided to parents for each dependent child. According to the basic postulate of economics, how would this change affect the birth rate?

*5. "The economic way of thinking stresses that good intentions lead to sound policy." Is this statement true or false? Explain your answer.

6. Economic theory postulates that self-interest is a powerful motivation for action. Does this imply that people are selfish and greedy? Do self-interest and selfishness mean the same thing?

*7. Congress and government agencies often make laws to help protect the safety of product consumers. New cars, for example, are required to have many safety features before they can be sold in the United States. These rules do indeed provide added safety for buyers, although they also add to the cost and price of the new vehicles. But can you think of secondary effects of the laws that tend to undercut or reduce the intended effect of increasing auto safety?

*8. "Individuals who economize are missing the point of life. Money is not so important that it should rule the way we live." Evaluate this statement.

*9. "Positive economics cannot tell us which agricultural policy is better, so it is useless to policymakers." Evaluate this statement.

*10. "I examined the statistics for our basketball team's wins last year and found that, when the third team played more, the winning margin increased. If the coach played the third team more, we would win by a bigger margin." Evaluate this statement.

---

*Asterisk denotes questions for which answers are given in Appendix B.

ADDENDUM

Understanding Graphs

Economists often use graphs to illustrate economic relations. Graphs are like pictures. They are visual aids that can communicate valuable information in a small amount of space. A picture may be worth a thousand words, but only to a person who understands the picture (and the graph).

This addendum illustrates the use of simple graphs as a way to communicate. Many students, particularly those with some mathematics background, are already familiar with this material, and can safely ignore it. This addendum is for those who need to be assured that they can understand graphic illustrations of economic concepts.

The Simple Bar Graph

A simple bar graph helps us to visualize comparative relationships and to understand them better. It is particularly useful for illustrating how an economic indicator varies among countries, among time periods, or under alternative economic conditions.

Exhibit 1A–1 is a bar graph illustrating economic data. The table in part a presents data on the income per person in 1997 for several countries. Part b uses a bar graph to illustrate the same data. The horizontal scale of the graph indicates the total income per person in 1997. A bar is made indicating the income level (see the dollar scale on the *x*-axis) of each country. The length of each bar is in proportion to the per person income of the country. Thus, the length of the bars provides a visual illustration of how per capita income varies across the countries. For example, the extremely short bar for Nigeria shows immediately that income per person there is only a small fraction of the comparable income figure for the United States, Switzerland, Japan, and several other countries.

Linear Graphic Presentation

Economists often want to illustrate variations in economic variables with the passage of time. A linear graph with time on the horizontal axis and an economic variable on the vertical axis is a useful tool to indicate variations over time. **Exhibit 1A–2** illustrates a simple linear graph of changes in consumer prices (the inflation rate) in the United States between 1960 and 1997. The table of the exhibit presents data on the percentage change in consumer prices for each year. Beginning with 1960, the horizontal axis indicates the time period (year). The inflation rate is plotted vertically above each year. Of course, the height of the plot (line) indicates the inflation rate during that year. For example, in 1975 the inflation rate was 6.9 percent. This point is plotted at the 6.9 percent vertical distance directly above the year 1975. In 1976 the inflation rate fell to 4.9 percent. Thus, the vertical plot of the 1976 inflation rate is lower than that for 1975. The inflation rate for each year (part a) is plotted at the corresponding height directly above the year. The linear graph is simply a line connecting the points plotted for each of the years 1960 through 1997.

The linear graph is a visual aid to understanding what happens to the inflation rate during the period. As the graph shows, the inflation rate rose sharply between 1967 and 1969, in 1973–1974, and again in 1977–1979. It was substantially higher during the 1970s than in the early 1960s or the mid-1980s. Although the linear graph does not communicate any information not in the table, it does make it easier to see the pattern of the data. Thus, economists often use simple graphics rather than tables to communicate information.

Direct and Inverse Relationships

Economic logic often suggests that two variables are linked in a specific way. Suppose an investigation reveals that, other things constant, farmers supply more wheat as the price of wheat increases. **Exhibit 1A–3** presents hypothetical data on the relationship between the price of wheat and the quantity supplied by farmers, first in tabular form (part a) and then as a simple two-dimensional graph (part b). Suppose we measure the quantity of wheat supplied by farmers on the *x*-axis (the horizontal axis) and the price of wheat on the *y*-axis (the vertical axis). Points indicating the value of *x* (quantity supplied) at alternative values of *y* (price of wheat) can then be plotted. The line (or curve) linking the points illustrates the relationship between the price of wheat and the amount supplied by farmers.

In the case of price and quantity supplied of wheat, the two variables are directly related. When the *y*-variable increases, so does the *x*-variable. When two variables are directly related, the graph illustrating the linkage between the two will slope upward to the right (as in the case of *SS* in part b).

Sometimes the *x*-variable and the *y*-variable are inversely related. A decline in the *y*-variable is associated with an increase in the *x*-variable. Therefore, a curve picturing the inverse relationship between *x* and *y* slopes downward to the right. **Exhibit 1A–4** illustrates this case. As the data of the table indicate, consumers purchase less as the price of wheat increases. Measuring the price of wheat on the *y*-axis (by convention, economists always place price on the *y*-axis) and the quantity of wheat purchased on the *x*-axis, the relationship between these two variables can also be illustrated graphically. If the price of

EXHIBIT 1A-1

INTERNATIONAL COMPARISON OF INCOME PER PERSON

COUNTRY	TOTAL INCOME PER PERSON, 1997
United States	$28,740
Switzerland	26,320
Japan	23,400
Canada	21,860
Germany	21,300
United Kingdom	20,520
Sweden	19,030
Mexico	8,120
China	3,570
India	1,650
Nigeria	880

(a)

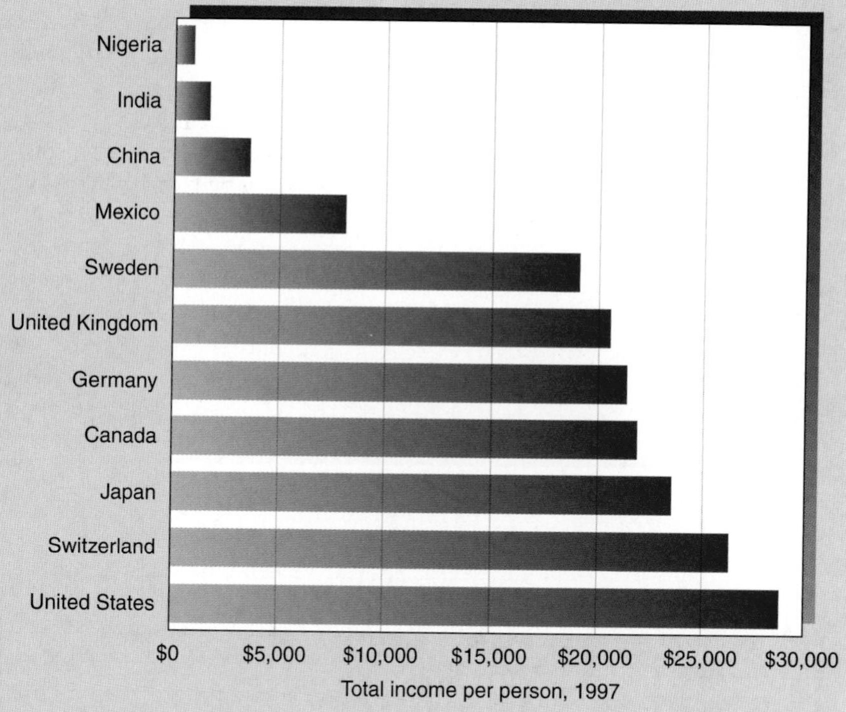

(b)

SOURCE: The World Bank, World Development Report, 1998/99, *Table 1. The income comparisons were derived by the purchasing power parity method.*

wheat were $5 per bushel, only 60 million bushels would be purchased by consumers. As the price declines to $4 per bushel, annual consumption increases to 75 million bushels. At still lower prices, the quantity purchased by consumers will expand to larger and larger amounts. As part b illustrates, the inverse relationship between price and quantity of wheat purchased generates a curve that slopes downward to the right.

EXHIBIT 1A-2

The tabular data (a) of the inflation rate are presented in graphic form in (b).

SOURCE: Economic Report of the President, 1991, *Table B-61; and* Economic Report of the President, 1998, *Table B-63.*

CHANGES IN LEVEL OF PRICES IN UNITED STATES, 1960–1997

Year	Percent Change in Consumer Prices	Year	Percent Change in Consumer Prices
1960	1.4	1979	13.3
1961	0.7	1980	12.5
1962	1.3	1981	8.9
1963	1.6	1982	3.8
1964	1.0	1983	3.8
1965	1.9	1984	3.9
1966	3.5	1985	3.8
1967	3.0	1986	1.1
1968	4.7	1987	4.4
1969	6.2	1988	4.4
1970	5.6	1989	4.6
1971	3.3	1990	6.1
1972	3.4	1991	3.1
1973	8.7	1992	2.9
1974	12.3	1993	2.7
1975	6.9	1994	2.7
1976	4.9	1995	2.5
1977	6.7	1996	3.3
1978	9.0	1997	1.7

(a)

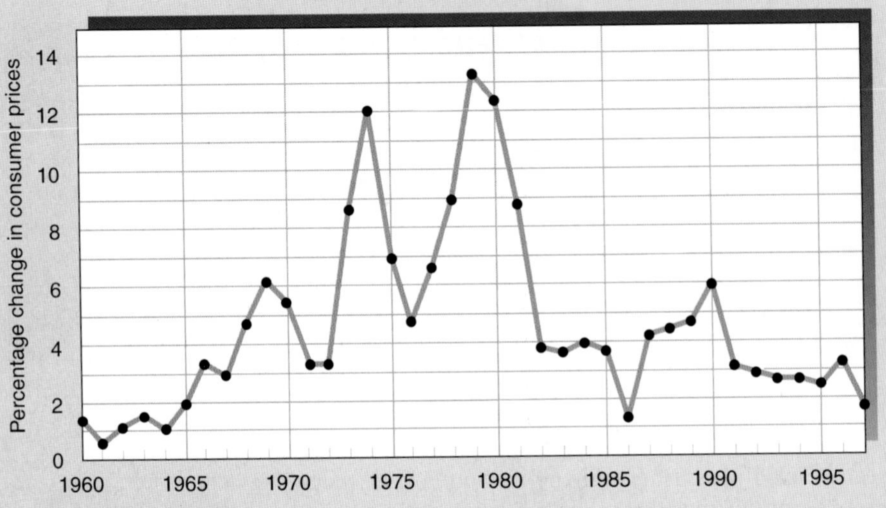

(b)

EXHIBIT 1A-3

DIRECT RELATIONSHIP BETWEEN VARIABLES (HYPOTHETICAL DATA)

PRICE	AMOUNT OF WHEAT SUPPLIED BY FARMERS PER YEAR (MILLIONS OF BUSHELS)
$1	45
2	75
3	100
4	120
5	140

(a)

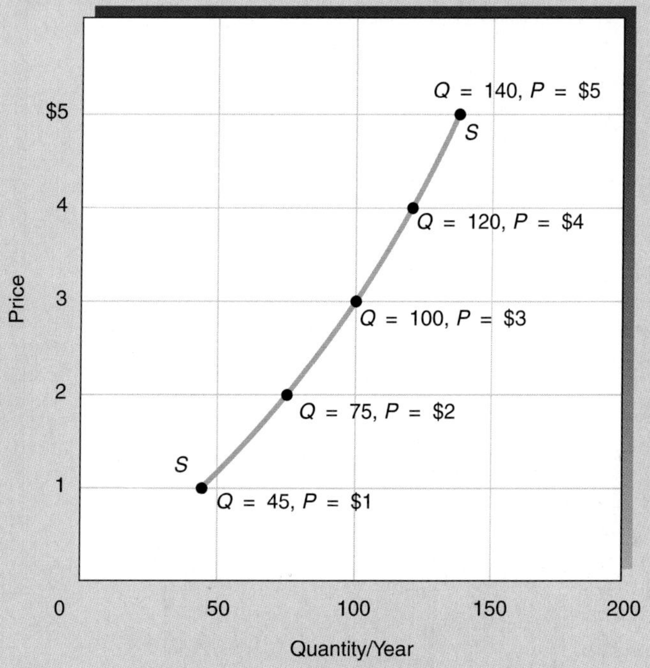

(b)

As the table (a) indicates, farmers are willing to supply more wheat at a higher price. Thus, there is a direct relation between the price of wheat and the quantity supplied. When the x- *and* y- *variables are directly related, a curve mapping the relationship between the two will slope upward to the right like* SS.

Complex Relationships

Sometimes the initial relationship between the x- and y-variables will change. **Exhibit 1A–5** illustrates more complex relations of this type. Part a shows the typical relationship between annual earnings and age. As a young person gets work experience and develops skills, earnings usually expand. Thus, initially, age and annual earnings are directly related; annual earnings increase with age. However, beyond a certain age (approximately age 55), annual earnings generally decline as workers approach retirement. As a result, the initial direct relationship between age and earnings changes to an inverse relation. When this is the case, annual income expands to a maximum (at age 55) and then begins to decline with years of age.

Part b illustrates an initial inverse relation that later changes to a direct relationship. Consider the impact of travel speed on gasoline consumption per mile. At low speeds, the automobile engine will not be used efficiently.

EXHIBIT 1A-4

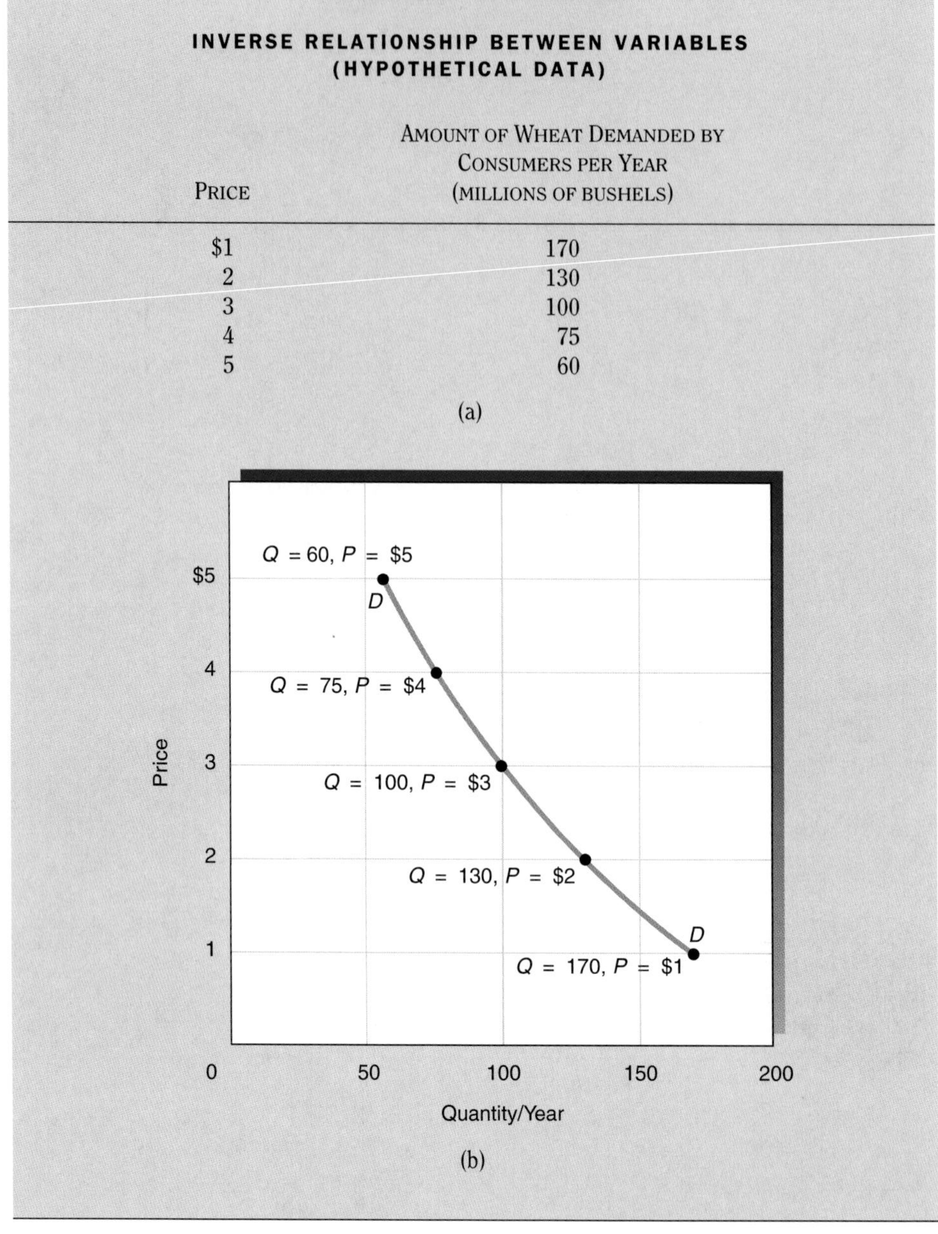

INVERSE RELATIONSHIP BETWEEN VARIABLES (HYPOTHETICAL DATA)

PRICE	AMOUNT OF WHEAT DEMANDED BY CONSUMERS PER YEAR (MILLIONS OF BUSHELS)
$1	170
2	130
3	100
4	75
5	60

(a)

(b)

As the table (a) shows, consumers will demand (purchase) more wheat as the price declines. Thus, there is an inverse relationship between the price of wheat and the quantity demanded. When the x- and y-variables are inversely related, a curve showing the relationship between the two will slope downward to the right like DD.

As speed increases from 5 mph to 10 mph and on to a speed of 40 mph, gasoline consumption per mile declines. In this range, there is an inverse relationship between speed of travel (x) and gasoline consumption per mile (y). However, as speed increases beyond 40 mph, air resistance increases and more gasoline per mile is required to maintain the additional speed. At very high speeds, gasoline consumption per mile increases substantially with speed of travel. Thus, gasoline consumption per mile reaches a minimum, and a direct relationship between the x- and y-variables describes the relationship beyond that point (40 mph).

Slope of a Straight Line

In economics, we are often interested in how much the y-variable changes in response to a change in the x-variable. The slope of the line or curve reveals this information. Mathematically, the slope of a line or curve is equal to the change in the y-variable divided by the change in the x-variable.

EXHIBIT 1A–5

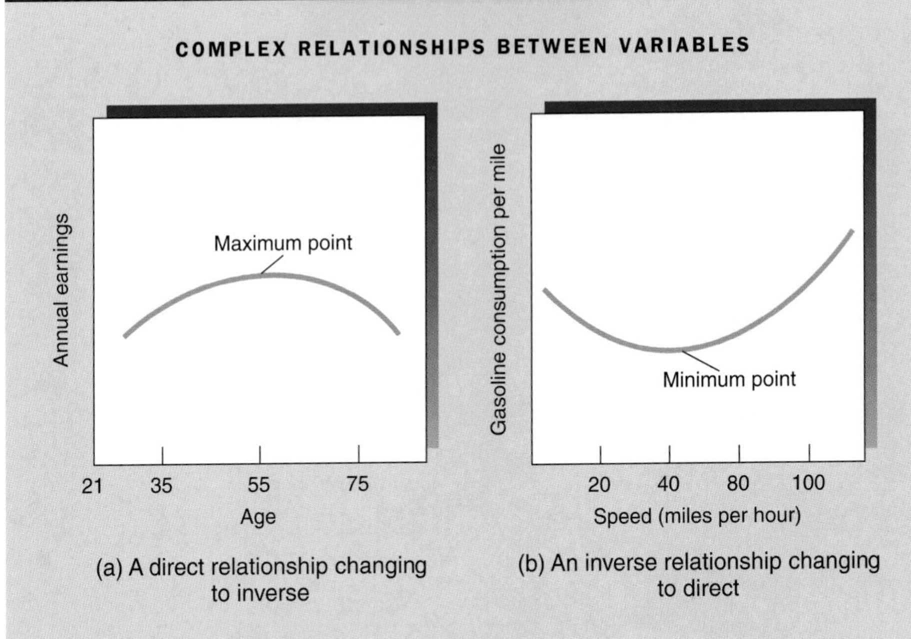

(a) A direct relationship changing to inverse

(b) An inverse relationship changing to direct

At first, an increase in age (and work experience) leads to a higher income, but later earnings decline as the worker approaches retirement (a). Thus, age and annual income are initially directly related but at approximately age 55 an inverse relationship emerges. Part (b) illustrates the relationship between travel speed and gasoline consumption per mile. Initially, gasoline consumption per mile declines as speed increases (an inverse relationship), but as speed increases above 40 mph, gasoline consumption per mile increases with the speed of travel (direct relationship).

Exhibit 1A–6 illustrates the calculation of the slope for a straight line. The exhibit shows how the daily earnings (y-variable) of a worker change with hours worked (the x-variable). The wage rate of the worker is $10 per hour, so when 1 hour is worked, earnings are equal to $10. For 2 hours of work, earnings jump to $20, and so on. A 1-hour change in hours worked leads to a $10 change in earnings. Thus, the slope of the line ($\Delta y/\Delta x$) is equal to 10. (The symbol Δ means "change in.") In the case of a straight line, the change in y, per unit change in x, is equal for all points on the line. Thus, the slope of a straight line is constant for all points along the line.

Exhibit 1A–6 illustrates a case in which a direct relation exists between the x- and y-variables. For an inverse relation, the y-variable decreases as the x-variable increases. So, when x and y are inversely related, the slope of the line will be negative.

Slope of a Curve

In contrast with a straight line, the slope of a curve is different at each point along the curve. The slope of a curve at a specific point is equal to the slope of a line tangent to the curve at the point, meaning a line that just touches the curve.

Exhibit 1A–7 illustrates how the slope of a curve at a specific point is determined. First, consider the slope of the curve at point A. A line tangent to the curve at point A indicates that y changes by one unit when x changes by two units at point A. Thus, the slope ($\Delta y/\Delta x$) of the curve at A is equal to 0.5.

Now consider the slope of the curve at point B. The line tangent to the curve at B indicates that y changes by two units for each one unit change in x at point B. Thus, at B the slope ($\Delta y/\Delta x$) is equal to 2. At point B, a change in the x-variable leads to a much larger change in y than was true at point A. The greater slope of the curve at B reflects this greater change in y per unit change in x at B relative to A.

Graphs Are Not a Substitute for Economic Thinking

By now you should have a fairly good understanding of how to read a graph. If you still feel uncomfortable with graphs, try drawing (graphing) the relationship between several things with which you are familiar. If you work, try graphing the relationship between your hours worked (x-axis) and your weekly earnings (y-axis). Exhibit 1A–6 could guide you with this exercise. Can you graph the relationship between the price of gasoline and your expenditures on gasoline? Graphing these simple relationships will give you greater confidence in your ability to grasp more complex economic relationships presented in graphs.

This text uses only simple graphs. Thus, there is no reason for you to be intimidated. Graphs look much more complex than they really are. In fact, they are nothing more than a simple device to communicate information

EXHIBIT 1A-6

The slope of a line is equal to the change in y divided by the change in x. The line opposite illustrates the case in which daily earnings increase by $10 per hour worked. Thus, the slope of the earnings function is 10 ($10 ÷ 1 hr). For a straight line, the slope is constant at each point on the line.

SLOPE OF A STRAIGHT LINE

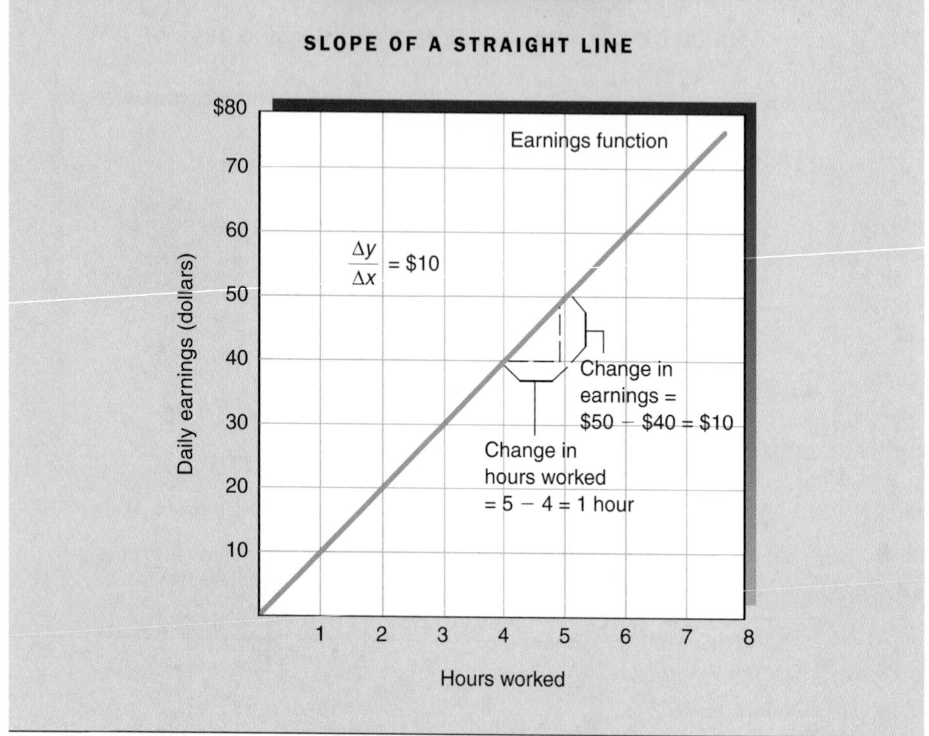

EXHIBIT 1A-7

The slope of a curve at any point is equal to the slope of the straight line tangent to the curve at the point. As the lines tangent to the curve at points A and B illustrate, the slope of a curve will change from point to point along the curve.

SLOPE OF A NONLINEAR CURVE

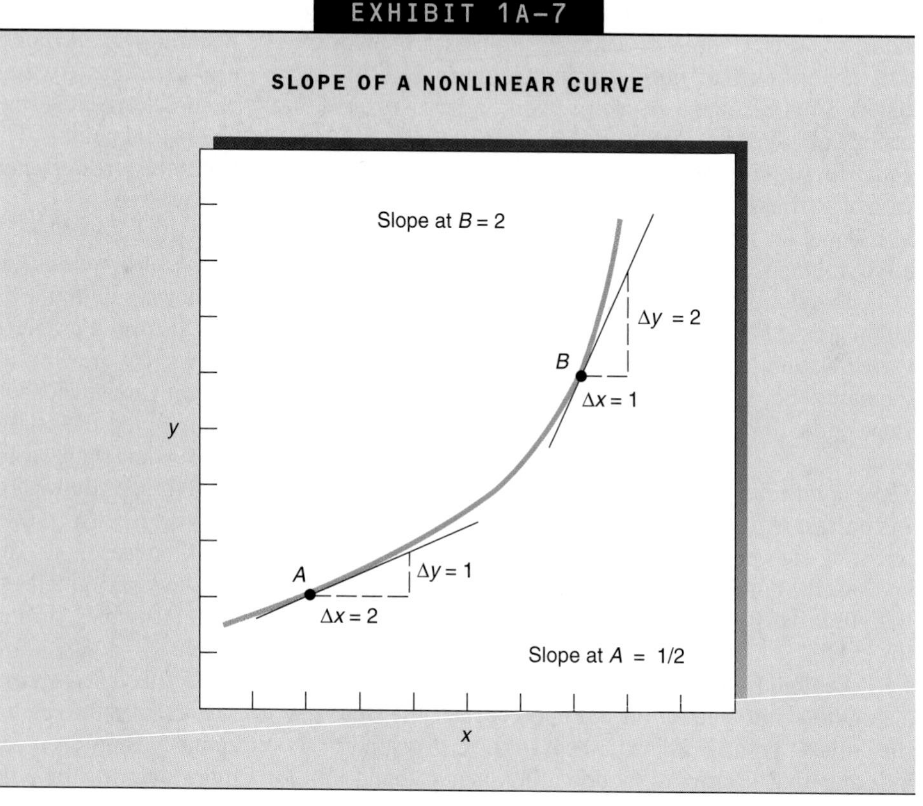

quickly and concisely. Nothing can be communicated with a graph that cannot be communicated verbally.

Most important, graphs are not a substitute for economic thinking. Although a graph may illustrate that two variables are related, it tells us nothing about the cause-and-effect relationship between the variables. To determine probable cause and effect, we must rely on economic theory. Thus, the economic way of thinking, not graphs, is the power station of economic analysis.

CHAPTER 2

The key insight of Adam Smith's Wealth of Nations is misleadingly simple: if an exchange between two parties is voluntary, it will not take place unless both believe they will benefit from it. Most economic fallacies derive from the neglect of this simple insight, from the tendency to assume that there is a fixed pie, that one party can gain only at the expense of another.

Milton and Rose Friedman[1]

Some Tools of the Economist

CHAPTER FOCUS

- What is opportunity cost? Why do economists place so much emphasis on it?
- Why do people engage in exchange?
- How does private ownership affect the use of resources? Will private owners pay any attention to the desires of others?
- What does a production-possibilities curve demonstrate?
- What are sources of gains from trade? How does trade influence our modern living standards?
- What are the two major methods of economic organization? How do they differ?

[1]Milton and Rose Friedman, *Free To Choose* (Harcourt Brace, 1990), p. 13.

In the preceding chapter, you were introduced to the economic way of thinking. We will now begin to apply that approach. This chapter focuses on four topics: opportunity cost, trade, property rights, and the potential output level of an economy. These seemingly diverse topics are in fact highly interrelated. The opportunity cost of goods determines which ones it makes sense for an individual or a nation to produce and which should be acquired through trade. In turn, the structure of both trade and property rights will influence the level of output. We will begin by taking a closer look at the concept of opportunity cost.

WHAT SHALL WE GIVE UP?

Scarcity calls the tune in economics. We cannot have as much of everything as we would like. Most of us would like to have more time for leisure, recreation, vacations, hobbies, education, and skill development. We would also like to have more wealth, a larger savings account, and more consumable goods. However, all these things are scarce, in the sense that they are limited. Our efforts to get more of one will conflict with our efforts to get more of the others.

OPPORTUNITY COST

An unpleasant fact of economics is that the choice to do one thing is, at the same time, a choice not to do something else. Your choice to spend time reading this book is a choice not to spend the time playing tennis, listening to a math lecture, or attending a party. These things must be given up because of your decision to read. As we indicated in Chapter 1, the highest valued alternative sacrificed in order to choose an option is the opportunity cost of that choice.[2]

Costs are subjective. (So are benefits. After all, a cost is a sacrificed benefit!) A cost exists in the mind of the decision maker. It is based on expectation—the expected value of the forgone alternative. Cost can never be directly measured by someone other than the decision maker because only the decision maker can place a value on what is given up.[3] Others, including experts and elected officials, who try to choose for the individual (or group of individuals), face an exceedingly difficult information problem. Individuals differ in the trade-offs they prefer to make, and those preferences change with time and circumstances. Only individuals are in a position to properly evaluate options for themselves, and to decide whether a specific trade-off is a good thing for them, in their specific circumstances of time and place.

---

[2]See also David Henderson, "Opportunity Cost," in *The Fortune Encyclopedia of Economics,* ed. David Henderson (New York: Warner Books, Inc., 1993), pp. 44–45.

[3]See James M. Buchanan, *Cost and Choice* (Chicago: Markham, 1969), for an analysis of the relationship between cost and choice.

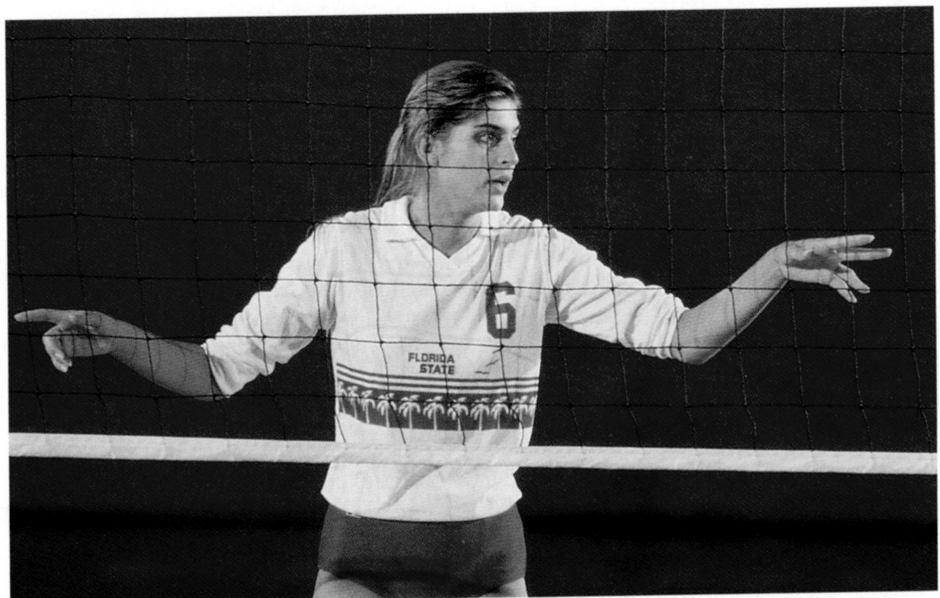

Gabrielle Reece understands opportunity cost. A star volleyball player at Florida State University, she forfeited her $4,500 scholarship (the NCAA prohibits outside employment by scholarship athletes) in order to embark on a six month modeling tour following her freshman year. After an appearance on the cover of Vogue, *her modeling opportunities soared. Even though she was both a good student and super volleyball player, she left school prior to graduation. Given her potential earnings as a model, the opportunity cost of school was simply too great.*

Cost, however, often has a monetary component that enables us to approximate its value. For example, the cost of attending a ballet (or a football game) is the highest valued opportunity lost as a result of (1) the time necessary to attend and (2) the purchasing power—the money—necessary to obtain a ticket. The monetary component is, of course, objective and can be measured. So long as individuals are paying the money price in voluntary exchange, it represents for them opportunity costs. When *nonmonetary* considerations are relatively unimportant, the monetary component will approximate the total cost of an option. We should notice, though, that to a buyer (or to one who refuses to sell), the item is probably worth more than the market price. However, to a seller (or one who does not buy), the item is worth less than the market price.

Opportunity Cost and the Real World

Is real-world decision making influenced by opportunity cost? Remember, the basic economic postulate states that an option is more likely to be chosen when its cost to the decision maker is less. So economic theory does tell us that differences (or changes) in opportunity cost will influence decisions. Recognizing opportunity costs can help us to understand decisions—those made by college students, for example.

Consider your own decision to attend college. Your opportunity cost of going to college is the value of the next best alternative, which could be measured as the salary you would earn if you had chosen to work rather than go to college. Every year you stay in college, you give up what you could have earned by working that year. Changes in the opportunity cost of going to college will affect the choices of potential students. Suppose, for example, that you received a job offer today for $250,000 per year as an athlete or an entertainer, but the job would require so much travel that school would be impossible. Would this change in the opportunity cost of going to college affect your continuation in school? For many students it would; such a large increase in the cost of remaining in school would cause many students to leave. (See feature on Gabrielle Reece above.) It is clear that one of the most important costs of attending college is the value of the next best alternative: the opportunity cost.

Even when their parents pay all the monetary expenses of their college education, some students are surprised to learn that they are actually incurring more of the total cost of going to college than their parents. For example, the average monetary cost (tuition, room and board, books, and so forth) for a resident student attending a public four-year college is about $10,000 per year. Even if the student's next best alternative was working at a job that paid only $15,000 per year, then over a four-year college career, he or she will incur $60,000 of the cost of college in the form of forgone earnings, while the parents will incur only about $40,000 of the cost.[4]

Now consider another decision made by college students—whether to attend a particular meeting of class. The monetary cost of attending a class (bus fare or parking and gasoline, and so on) remains fairly constant from day to day. Why then do students choose to attend class on some days and not on others? Even though the monetary cost is fairly constant, the opportunity cost—the highest valued alternative given up—can change dramatically from day to day. Some days the next best alternative to attending class may be sleeping in or watching TV. Other days, the opportunity cost may be substantially larger, perhaps the value of attending a big football game, getting an early start on a holiday break, or having additional study time for a crucial exam in another class. As options like this increase the cost of attending class, more students will decide not to attend.

Failure to consider opportunity cost often leads to unwise decision making. Suppose that your community builds a beautiful new civic center. The mayor, speaking at the dedication ceremony, tells the world that the center will improve the quality of life in your community. People who understand the concept of opportunity cost may question this view. If the center had not been built, the resources might have funded contruction of a new hospital, improvements to the educational system, or housing for low-income families. Will the civic center contribute more to the well-being of the people in your community than these other facilities? If so, it was a wise investment. If not, however, your community will be worse off than it might have been if decision makers had chosen a higher-valued project (that must now be forgone).

TRADE CREATES VALUE

We learned in the preceding chapter that preferences are subjective, they are known only to the individual, and they differ among individuals. That is why the value of an item can vary greatly from one person to another. In turn, this means that simply trading—rearranging goods and services among people to get them to higher-valued uses and users—can create value. In our Chapter 1 example, the value to Alice of a ticket to attend the Bolshoi Ballet performance was zero once she received the party invitation, but the value to other individuals had not declined. Suppose Jim, who bought it at the advertised price of $40, actually valued it at $55. An unforeseen change in Alice's schedule had destroyed the value of the performance that evening for her, but trading (selling) the ticket to Jim created $40 in value for her, and it netted $15 in value for Jim—the $55 value he placed on the performance minus the $40 he gave to Alice. The performance remained the same, and the seats available remained the same, but trade had created value just as surely as if an additional seat had been made available.

It is wrong to assume that a particular good or service has a fixed value just because it exists.[5] As the example of the ballet ticket illustrates, the value of goods and

---

[4]From the standpoint of the family's total economic cost of sending a child to college, some of the monetary costs, such as room and board, are not costs of choosing to go to college. The cost of living does have to be covered, but it would be incurred whether or not the student went to college.

[5]An illuminating discussion of this subject, termed the "physical fallacy," is found in Thomas Sowell, *Knowledge and Decisions* (New York: Basic Books, 1980), pp. 67–72.

OUTSTANDING ECONOMIST

Thomas Sowell (1930–)

Thomas Sowell, a senior fellow at the Hoover Institution, recognizes the critical importance of the institutions—the "rules of the game"—that shape human interactions. His book, *Knowledge and Decisions,* stresses the difficulty of obtaining knowledge and explores the way different institutional arrangements provide different kinds and amounts of scarce information.

services generally depends on who uses them, and on circumstances, such as when and where they are used, as well as on the physical characteristics. This explains why trades can make existing goods more valuable simply by getting them to the people who value them more.

Transaction Costs—A Barrier to Trade

Unfortunately, Alice did not know about Andrew, another ballet fan, who would have been willing to pay $60 for the ticket. Andrew lives off campus and failed to see the bulletin board ad, so the potential for another $5 increase in value failed to materialize. But if Jim and Andrew happen to meet before the show and the topic of the ballet comes up, the additional $5 in value for the ticket might be created by another transaction: Jim trading the ticket to Andrew. Such a transaction is unlikely, because getting together requires either good luck or costly measures, such as searching bulletin boards. Of course, new and cheaper marketing methods, such as electronic online bulletin boards, can reduce the cost and increase the frequency of value-creating trades. Still, not every trade that could potentially create value will be discovered and made.

Although exchange creates value, it is also costly. The costs of the time, effort, and other resources necessary to search out, negotiate, and conclude an exchange are called **transaction costs.** *Transaction costs reduce our ability to produce gains from potential trades.*

Transaction costs
The time, effort, and other resources needed to search out, negotiate, and consummate an exchange.

Because of transaction costs, we should not expect all potentially valuable trades to take place, any more than we expect all useful knowledge to be learned, all safety measures to be taken, or all potential "A" grades to be earned. Frequent fliers know that if they never miss a flight, they are probably spending too much time waiting in airports. Similarly, the seller of a car, a house, or a ballet ticket knows that to find that one person in the world who would be willing to pay the most money is not worth the enormous effort required to locate that buyer. Information is costly. That is one reason that perfection in exchange, as in most things we do, is seldom reached.

Middleman as Cost Reducer

Because gains from exchange are facilitated by information, some people, called **middlemen,** specialize in providing information at a lower cost, and in arranging trades. Middlemen are generally not very popular; many think that they just add to the buyer's expense without performing a useful function. Once we recognize that transaction costs deter gains from trade, the real contribution of middlemen is obvious: They provide services that reduce the cost of transactions and thereby promote the realization of additional gains from trade. The auto dealer, for example, can help both the

Middleman
A person who buys and sells, or who arranges trades. A middleman reduces transaction costs.

manufacturer and the buyer. By keeping an inventory of autos, and by hiring knowledgeable salespeople, the dealer lowers the cost for the car shopper to learn about the many cars offered, and how each car looks, performs, and "feels." (Since preferences are subjective and not objectively known to others, the reports of other users may not fully inform the potential buyer.) Car buyers also like to know that the local dealer will honor the warranty and provide parts and service for the car. The car maker, by using the dealer as a middleman, is able to concentrate on designing and making cars, leaving to middlemen—that is, dealers—the tasks of marketing and servicing.

Grocers also provide middleman services. Each of us could avoid the grocer by dealing with farmers and other food producers directly. If we did, though, transaction costs would be high and it would be more difficult to squeeze the tomatoes! Alternatively, we could form consumer cooperatives, banding together to eliminate the middleman, using our own warehouses and our own volunteer labor to order, receive, display, redistribute, and collect payment for the food. In fact, some cooperatives like this do exist, but most people prefer instead to pay the grocer to provide all these middleman services.

Stockbrokers, publishers of the Yellow Pages, and merchants of all sorts are middlemen—specialists in selling, guaranteeing, and servicing the items traded. For a fee, they reduce transaction costs both for the shopper and for the seller. By making exchange cheaper and more convenient, middlemen cause more efficient trades to happen. In so doing, they themselves create value.

THE IMPORTANCE OF PROPERTY RIGHTS

> *[A] private property regime makes people responsible for their own actions in the realm of material goods. Such a system therefore ensures that people experience the consequences of their own acts. Property sets up fences, but it also surrounds us with mirrors, reflecting back upon us the consequences of our own behavior.*
>
> *Tom Bethell*[6]

Property rights
The right to use, control, and obtain the benefits from a good or service.

Private property rights
Property rights that are exclusively held by an owner, or group of owners, and that can be transferred to others at the owner's discretion.

The buyer of an apple, a CD, a television set, or an automobile generally takes the item home. The buyer of a steamship or an office building, though, may never touch it. When exchange occurs, it is really the rights—the **property rights**—to the item that change hands.

Private property rights involve three things: (1) the right to exclusive use, (2) legal protection against invaders—those who would seek to use or abuse the property without the owner's permission, and (3) the right to transfer to (exchange with) another. Private owners cannot do anything they want with their property. Most significantly, they cannot use their property in a manner that invades or infringes on the property of another. For example, I cannot throw the hammer that I own through the television set that you own. If I did, I would be violating your property right to your television. The same is true if I operate a factory that harms you or your land by spewing air pollution.[7] Because an owner has the right to control the use of property, the owner also must accept responsibility for the outcomes of that control.

---

[6]Tom Bethell, *The Noblest Triumph* (New York: St. Martin's Press, 1998), p. 10.

[7]For a detailed explanation of how property rights protect the environment, with several real-world examples, see Roger E. Meiners and Bruce Yandle, *The Common Law: How It Protects the Environment* (Bozeman, Mont.: PERC, 1998), available online at <www.perc.org>.

As Tom Bethell (see quotation at left) points out, powerful incentive effects follow from private ownership of goods and resources. The following four factors are particularly important.

1. *Private owners can gain by employing their resources in ways that are beneficial to others.* And they bear the opportunity cost of ignoring the wishes of others. If someone values an asset more than its current owner, the current owner can gain by paying heed to the wishes of others. For example, suppose Ed owns a car that others would also like to have. What incentive is there for Ed to pay attention to the desires of the others? If Ed values the car at $4,000, he can gain by selling it at any price in excess of that amount. If transaction costs are low (search is relatively cheap), Ed may well gain by searching for people (potential buyers) who value the car more than he does. Suppose that a potential buyer makes Ed an offer of $4,500 for the car. Turning down this offer will cost Ed a potential net gain of $500. If Ed fails to consider the desires of others, he may penalize potential buyers, but he will also be hurting himself. Thus, when cars and other goods are privately owned and easily transferable, potential buyers and sellers have a strong incentive to search out mutually advantageous trades. After all, if they find such a trade, only the buyer and seller have to approve the deal in order to realize the mutual gain.

As a second example, suppose Ed owns a house and will be out of town all summer. Will the house stay vacant, or will Ed let someone else use it during those months? We don't know, but we do know that Ed can rent the house to someone else if he chooses, and that if he does not, he will incur the opportunity cost—the rental payments he could get, minus any damages, added upkeep, and transaction costs. Even if he is unwilling to rent the house, ownership of the private property rights again faces Ed with the opportunity costs of not renting it out, thereby providing him with a strong incentive to consider the wishes of others regarding the use of his property.

How about the owners of investment properties and businesses—do they have an incentive to heed the desires of others? Consider the owner of an apartment complex near your campus. The owner may not care much for swimming pools, workout facilities, study desks, or green areas, for example. Nonetheless, private ownership provides the owner with a strong incentive to provide these items if students and other potential customers value them enough to cover the cost of their provision. Why? The owner will be able to lease the apartment units for more if they include amenities that are highly valued by others. Investment property owners have a strong incentive to consider the desires of others.

2. *The private owner has a strong incentive to care for and properly manage what he or she owns.* Will Ed change the oil in his car? Will he take care to see that the seats do not get torn? Probably so, since being careless about these things would reduce the car's value, both to him and to any future owner. The car and its value—the sale price if he sells it—belong just to Ed, so he would bear the burden of a decline in the car's value if the oil ran low and ruined the engine, or if the seats were torn. Similarly, he would capture the value of an expenditure that improves the car, such as providing a new paint job. As the owner, Ed has both the authority and the incentive to protect the car against harm or neglect, and even to enhance its value. Private property rights concentrates the owner's interest and attention, providing a strong incentive for good stewardship.

"Their house looks so nice. They must be getting ready to sell it."

From the *Wall Street Journal*—permission, Cartoon Features Syndicate.

The incentive for good care and management by the individual extends also to private investments that yield income. The owner of a hotel does not want to neglect electrical or plumbing problems, if taking care of them now avoids large repair costs due to electrical fires or water leaks. The wealth of the owner, in the form of the value of hotel ownership, is a hostage to the owner's good management. Poor management will reduce the hotel's value, and thus the owner's personal wealth. Again, ownership concentrates the owner's interest and attention on good management of the asset owned.

3. *The private owner has an incentive to conserve for the future if the property's value is expected to rise.* Suppose our man Ed owns a case of very good red wine, which is only two years old. Age will improve it substantially if he puts it in his cellar for another five years. Will he do so? Well, if he does not, he will personally bear the consequences. He (and presumably his friends) will drink wine sooner, but they will sacrifice quality. Also, Ed will forgo the chance to sell the wine later for much more than its current worth. The opportunity cost of drinking the wine now is its unavailability later, for drinking or for sale. Ed bears that cost. Private property rights assure that Ed has the authority to preserve the wine, and that he gains the benefits if he does so. If the greater quality is expected to be worth the wait, then Ed can capture the benefits of not drinking the wine "before its time."

In a similar way, if Ed owns land, or a house, or a factory, he has a strong incentive to bear costs now, if necessary, to preserve the asset's value. His wealth is tied up in its value, which reflects nothing more than the net benefits that will be available to the owner in the future. So Ed's wealth depends on his willingness and ability to look ahead, maintain, and conserve those things that will be highly valued in the future.

4. *With private property rights, the property owner is accountable for damage to others through misuse of the property. Private ownership links responsibility with the right of control.* Ed, the car owner, has a right to drive his car, but he has no right to drive in a drunken or reckless way that injures Alice. A chemical company has control over its products, but, exactly for that reason, it is legally liable for damages if it mishandles the chemicals. Courts of law recognize and enforce the authority granted by ownership, but they also enforce the responsibility that goes with that authority. Once again, property rights hold accountable the person (owner) with authority over property, concentrating the owner's attention on avoiding the cost of liability for damage done.

Private Ownership and Markets

The incentives provided by the private ownership of property are very useful. As we will discuss in more detail later, private ownership and competitive markets provide the foundation for cooperative behavior among individuals. They provide each individual, however selfish or narrow-minded, with both the information and the incentive to engage in productive activities and cooperate with others. ***When private property rights are protected and enforced, permission of the owner is required for the use of a resource. Put another way, if you want to use a good or resource, you must either buy or lease it from the owner. This means that each of us faces the cost of using scarce resources.*** Furthermore, when their actions are directed by market price signals, private owners have a strong incentive to consider the desires of others and to use and develop their resources in ways that are valued highly by others. The resulting market exchanges generate what F. A. Hayek, the 1974 Nobel laureate in economics, called the "extended order." Hayek used this expression to describe the tendency of markets to direct individuals from throughout the world to cooperate with each other in mutually beneficial ways despite the fact that they do not know each other, and that they often have vastly different backgrounds, lifestyles, and cultural values.

When apartments and other investment properties are owned privately, the owner has a strong incentive to provide amenities that others value highly relative to their cost.

In contrast, in a community that does not recognize private ownership rights, whoever has the power or the political authority can simply take command of an item, ignoring the wishes of both the person in possession and other potential users. Without private property rights, other methods must be found to provide the incentives for good stewardship of property, and for proper concern for others by the users of property. For example, if the owners of a factory are not held responsible for damages their pollutants impose on the person and property of others, then other measures may be needed to control polluting behavior. We will return to this issue in Chapter 5 and in other sections of the book.

PRODUCTION POSSIBILITIES CURVE

The resources of every individual are limited. Purposeful decision making and economizing behavior imply that individuals seek to get the most from their limited resources. They do not deliberately waste resources.

The nature of the economizing problem can be made more clear with the use of a conceptual tool, the production possibilities diagram. A **production possibilities curve** from this diagram reveals the maximum amount of any two products that can be produced from a fixed set of resources, and the possible trade-offs in production between them.

Production possibilities curve
A curve that outlines all possible combinations of total output that could be produced, assuming (1) the utilization of a fixed amount of productive resources, (2) full and efficient use of those resources, and (3) a specific state of technical knowledge. The slope of the curve indicates the rate at which one product can be traded off to produce more of the other.

Exhibit 2–1 illustrates the production possibilities curve for Susan, an intelligent economics major. This curve indicates the combinations of English and economics grades that she thinks she can earn if she spends a total of 10 hours per week studying for the two subjects. Currently she is choosing the material to study in each course that she expects will help her grade the most, for the time spent, and she is allocating 5 hours of study time to each course. She expects that this amount of time, carefully spent on each course, will allow her to earn a B grade in both, indicated at point *T*. But if she took some time away from studying one of the two subjects and spent it studying the other, she could raise her grade in the course receiving more time. If she

EXHIBIT 2–1

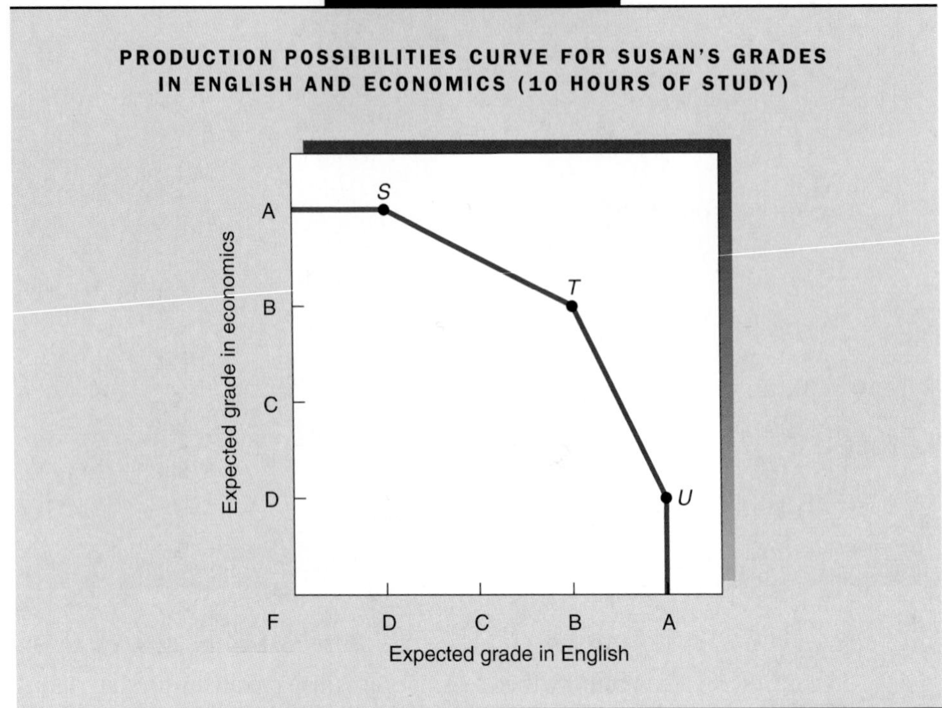

The production possibilities for Susan, in terms of grades, are illustrated for 10 hours of total study time. If Susan studied 10 hours per week in these two classes, she could attain (1) a D in English and an A in economics (point S), (2) a B in English and a B in economics (point T), or (3) a D in economics and an A in English. [Note: Spending even more of her 10 hours on economics than at point S, moving along the curve to the left, would decrease her English grade toward an F, but could not improve her A in economics. Similarly, spending more time on English than at point U, moving her downward on the curve from there, would decrease her economics grade toward an F, but could not increase her A in English, so we assume that Susan will not choose to spend time on these parts of her production possibilities curve.] Could Susan move the entire curve outward, making higher grades in both? Yes, if she were willing to apply more rescources, perhaps by giving up some leisure or her job.

spent more hours on economics and fewer on English, for example, her expected economics grade would rise as a result, while her English grade would fall.

Susan's production possibilities curve indicates that the additional study time required to raise her economics grade by one letter, to an A (point *S*), would require giving up two grades in her English class, not just one grade, reducing her English grade to a D. As she shifts more time away from English, she gives up some time that would have been spent studying the most important (grade-increasing) material. In contrast, as she reallocates more and more study time to economics, much of that time is spent studying additional material that is likely to be a little less helpful in producing grade points than the material chosen at point *T*. The curve is flatter to the left of point *T*, and steeper to the right, showing that, as Susan takes more and more of her resources (time, in this case) from one course and puts it into the other, she must give up greater and greater amounts of productivity in the course getting fewer resources.

Of course, Susan could study more economics *without* giving up her English study time, if she gave up some leisure, or study time for other courses, or her part-time job in the campus bookstore. If she gave up leisure or her job to add to the 10 hours of study time for economics and English, the entire *STU* portion of the curve in Exhibit 2–1 would shift outward. She could get better grades in both classes by devoting more of her scarce time to studying for both of them.

Can the production possibilities concept be applied to the entire economy? The answer is yes. We can grow more soybeans if we grow less corn, since both can be grown on the same land. Beefing up the military requires the use of resources that otherwise could be used to produce nonmilitary goods. When scarce resources are being used efficiently, more of one thing requires the sacrifice of others.

Exhibit 2–2 shows a production possibilities curve for an economy producing only two goods: food and clothing. The curve is convex, or bowed out from the origin,

EXHIBIT 2–2

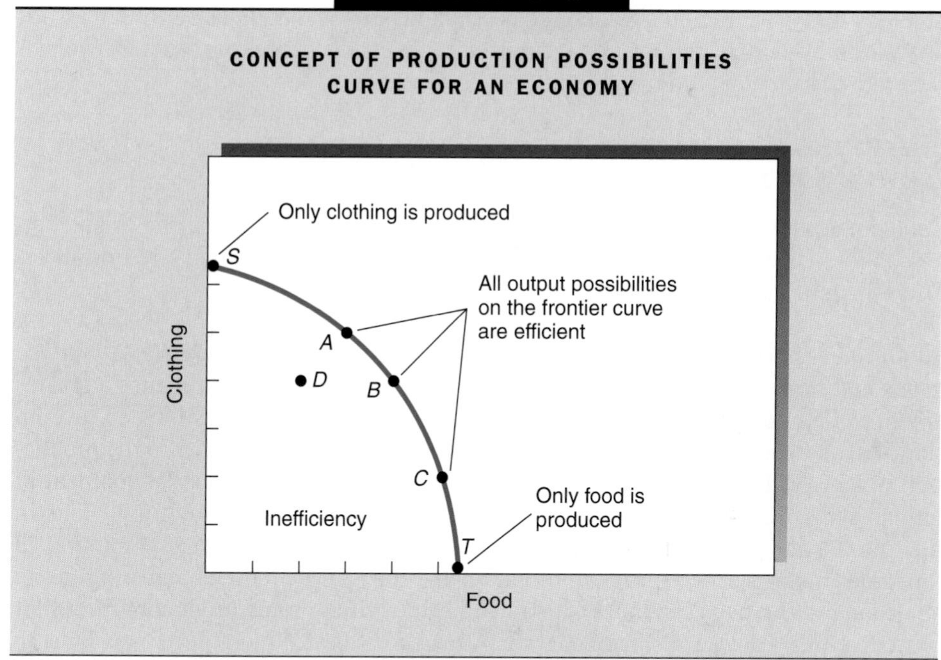

When an economy is using its limited resources efficiently, production of more clothing requires the economy to give up some other goods—food in this simple example. With time, a technological discovery, expansion of the economy's resource base, or improvement in its economic organization could make it possible to produce more of both, shifting the production possibilities curve outward.

Or the citizens of the economy might decide to give up some leisure for more of both goods. These factors aside, limited resources will constrain the production possibilities of an economy.

just as Susan's was in the previous exhibit. Why? Resources are not equally well suited to produce food and clothing. Consider an economy that is using all its resources to produce clothing. At that point (*S*), food production can be expanded by transferring those resources that are best suited for production of food (and least suitable for clothing production) from clothing to food production. Since the resources transferred are chosen to be those that are highly productive in food and not very productive in clothing, in this range the opportunity cost (clothing forgone) of producing additional food is low. However, as more and more resources are devoted to food production, and successively larger amounts of food are produced (moving from *S* to *A* to *B* and so on), the opportunity cost of food will rise. This results because as more and more food is produced, additional food output can be achieved only by using resources that are less and less suitable for the production of food relative to clothing. Thus, as food output is expanded, successively larger amounts of clothing must be forgone per unit of additional food.

What restricts the ability of an economy, once resources are fully utilized, from producing more of everything? The same constraint that kept Susan from making a higher grade in both English and economics—lack of resources. There will be various maximum combinations of goods that an economy will be able to produce when:

1. It uses some fixed quantity of resources.
2. The resources are used efficiently.
3. The level of technology is constant.

When these three conditions are met, the economy will be at the edge of its production possibilities frontier (points such as *A*, *B*, and *C* in Exhibit 2–2). Producing more of one good, such as clothing, will necessitate less production of other goods (for example, food).

When the resources of an economy are used inefficiently, the economy is operating at a point inside the production possibilities curve—point *D*, for example. Why might this happen? It happens if the economy is not properly solving the economizing problem. A major function of economic decision making is to help us get the most out of available resources, to move us out to the production possibilities frontier. We will return to this problem again and again.

Shifting the Production Possibilities Curve Outward

Could an economy ever have more of all goods? In other words, could the production possibilities curve be shifted outward? The answer is yes, under certain circumstances. There are four major possibilities.

Capital formation
The production of buildings, machinery, tools, and other equipment that will enhance the ability of future economic participants to produce. The term can also be applied to efforts to upgrade the knowledge and skill of workers and thereby increase their ability to produce in the future.

1. *An increase in the economy's resource base would expand our ability to produce goods and services.* If we had more and better resources, we could produce a greater amount of all goods. Many resources are human-made. If we were willing to give up some current consumption, we could invest more of today's resources into the production of long-lasting physical structures, machines, education, and the development of human skills. This **capital formation** would provide us with better tools and skills in the future and thereby increase our ability to produce goods and services. **Exhibit 2–3** illustrates the link between capital formation and the future production possibilities of an economy. The two economies illustrated begin with the same production possibilities curve (*RS*). However, since Economy A (part a) allocates more of its resources to investment than does Economy B, A's production possibilities curve shifts outward with the passage of time by a greater amount. The growth rate of A—the expansion rate of the economy's ability to produce goods—is enhanced because the economy allocates a larger share of its output to investment. Of course, more investment in machines and human skills requires a reduction in current consumption.

Here we illustrate two economies that initially confront identical production possibilities curves (RS). The economy illustrated on the left allocates a larger share of its output to investment (I_a, compared to I_b for the economy on the right). As a result, the production possibilities of the high-investment economy will tend to shift outward by a larger amount than will be true for the low-investment economy.

EXHIBIT 2–3

INVESTMENT AND PRODUCTION POSSIBILITIES IN FUTURE

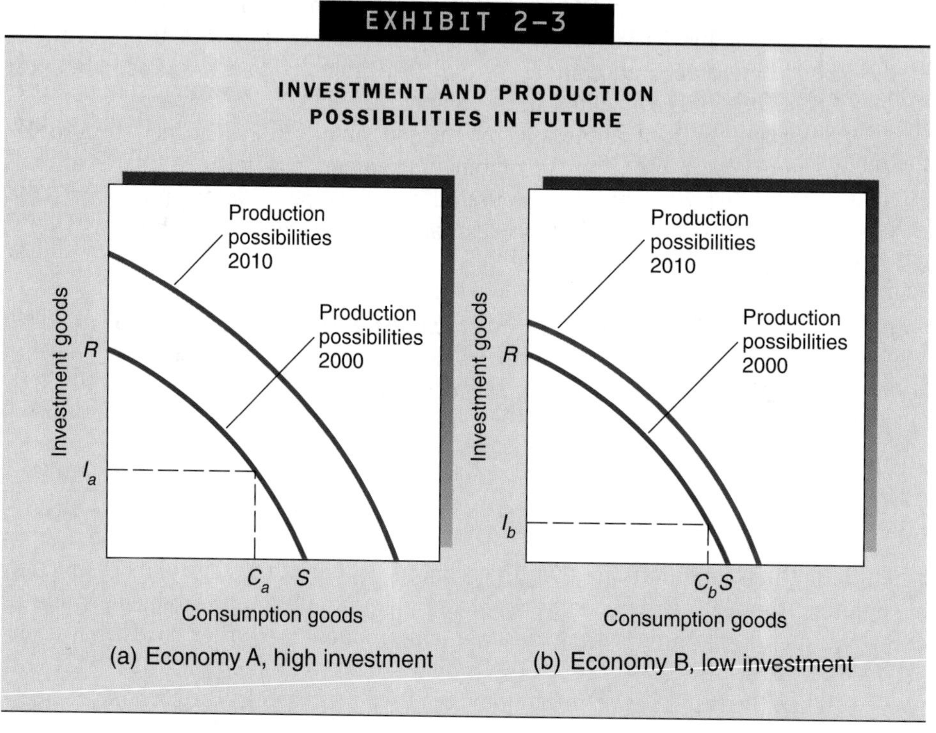

2. *Advancements in technology can expand the economy's production possibilities.* **Technology** determines the maximum physical output obtainable from any particular set of resource inputs. New technology can make it possible to get more from our given base of resources.[8] An important form of technological change is **invention**—the use of science and engineering to create new products or processes. In recent years, for example, inventions have allowed us to develop photographs faster and cheaper, get more oil from existing fields, and send information instantly and cheaply by satellite. Such technological advances increase our production possibilities, shifting the entire curve outward.

Technology
The technological knowledge available at any given time. The level of technology establishes the relationship between inputs and the maximum output they can generate.

Invention
The creation of a new product or process, often facilitated by the knowledge of engineering and scientific relationships.

An economy can also benefit from technology change through **innovation**—the practical and effective adoption of new techniques. Such innovation is commonly carried out by an **entrepreneur**—one who seeks profit by introducing new products or improved techniques to satisfy consumers at a lower cost.[9] To prosper, an entrepreneur must undertake projects that convert and rearrange resources in a manner that will increase their value, thus expanding our production possibilities. Perhaps a few examples will illustrate the importance of this point.

Innovation
The successful introduction and adoption of a new product or process; the economic application of inventions and marketing techniques.

Entrepreneur
A profit-seeking decision maker who decides which projects to undertake and how they should be undertaken. A successful entrepreneur's actions will increase the value of resources.

One entrepreneur, Henry Ford, changed car-making technology by pioneering the assembly line. With the same amount of labor and materials, Ford made more cars, more cheaply. Another entrepreneur, the late Ray Kroc, purchased a hamburger restaurant from Richard McDonald and went on to build the world's largest hamburger chain. In addition to a popular restaurant menu, Kroc provided information to potential customers. By carefully designing a limited menu that could be prepared according to strict formulas, setting up a training school (Hamburger University, outside Chicago) for managers, and providing a program for regular inspection of restaurants, he could guarantee uniformity (known products and quality level) to each customer. Once the McDonald's reputation spread, hungry people knew what to expect at the "golden arches" without even having to enter the restaurant.

Another type of entrepreneur takes inventions produced by others and applies them more effectively. Steven Jobs, cofounder of the Apple Computer Corporation, is an example. He and his firm used the new computer technology to create personal and small-business computers, and pioneered the "user-friendly" software needed by most of us to use such machines. Selling the combination helped make computers useful to millions of people, both at home and on the job, and brought the new technology within their financial reach. Other entrepreneurs subsequently developed hardware and software that has greatly enhanced the usefulness of the personal computer, time and again increasing our ability to find, process, and utilize information, thus further expanding our production possibilities.

3. *An improvement in the rules under which the economy functions can increase output.* The legal system of a country influences the ability of people to cooperate with one another and produce desired goods. Changes in legal institutions that

---

[8]Without modern technical knowledge, it would be impossible to produce the vast array of goods and services responsible for our standard of living. Thomas Sowell makes this point clear when he notes: "The cavemen had the same natural resources at their disposal as we have today, and the difference between their standard of living and ours is a difference between the knowledge they could bring to bear on those resources and the knowledge used today." See Thomas Sowell, *Knowledge and Decisions* (New York: Basic Books, 1980), p. 47.

[9]This French word literally means "one who undertakes." The entrepreneur is the person who is ultimately responsible. Of course, this responsibility may be shared with others (partners or stockholders, for example) or it may be partially delegated to technical experts. Nevertheless, the success or failure of the entrepreneur is dependent on the outcome of the choices he or she makes.

promote social cooperation and enhance the incentive of people to produce will shift the production possibilities curve outward.

Historically, legal innovations have been an important source of economic progress. During the eighteenth century, a system of patents provided inventors with a private property right to their ideas. At about the same time, the recognition of the corporation as a legal entity reduced the cost of forming large firms that were often required for the mass production of manufactured goods. Both of these legal changes improved economic organization and thereby accelerated the growth of output (that is, shifted the production possibilities curve outward more rapidly) in Europe and North America.

Sometimes governments, perhaps as the result of ignorance or prejudice, adopt legal institutions that reduce production possibilities. Laws that restrict or prohibit trade among various groups provide an illustration. For example, the laws of several southern states prohibited the employment of African Americans in certain occupations, and restricted other economic exchanges between blacks and whites for almost 100 years following the Civil War. This legislation was not only harmful to African Americans, it retarded progress and reduced the production possibilities of these states.

The recent experience of Russia illustrates the importance of economic institutions. Following the collapse of communism, Russia was unable to develop legal institutions capable of protecting property rights and enforcing contracts. The absence of these institutions not only retarded investment and gains from trade, but also led to inefficient use of resources and movement of capital to other places where property rights were more secure. Therefore, even though Russia has a well-educated labor force and abundant natural resources, its economic performance has been abysmal. The weak legal structure and insecurity of ownership rights are important elements underlying the economic struggles of Russia.

4. ***By working harder and giving up current leisure, we could increase our production of goods and services.*** Strictly speaking, this is not an expansion in the production frontier because leisure is also a good. We are giving up some of that good to have more of other things.

The work effort of individuals depends not only on their personal preferences but also on public policy. For example, high tax rates may induce individuals to reduce their work time. The basic economic postulate implies that, as high tax rates reduce the personal payoff from working (and earning taxable income), individuals will shift more of their time to other, untaxed activities, including the consumption of leisure, moving the production possibilities curve for market goods inward. (Recall, from Exhibit 2–1, how Susan's production possibilities for grades would shift *outward* if she changed from 10 hours of study per week to more than 10 hours. The reverse would occur if she were to reduce study time below 10 hours.) Any reduction in market work time due to higher taxes not only reduces output directly, but is likely also to reduce the gains from the division of labor, as more people do more work for themselves because doing so is untaxed. We turn now to look at why such a reduction is important.

DIVISION OF LABOR, SPECIALIZATION, AND PRODUCTION POSSIBILITIES

In a modern economy, individuals do not produce most of the items they consume. Instead, we sell our labor services (usually agreeing to do specified productive work) and use the income we get in exchange to buy what we want.

Gains from the Division of Labor and Adoption of Mass Production Processes

Specialization, exchange, and the **division of labor** often allow us to produce far more goods and services through cooperative effort than we could if each household produced its own food, clothing, shelter, transportation, and other desired goods. The most famous example in economics was given over 200 years ago by Adam Smith. Observing the operation of a pin manufacturer, Smith noted that specialization and division of labor permitted far more output. When each worker specialized in a productive function, ten workers were able to produce 48,000 pins per day, or 4,800 pins per worker. Without specialization and division of labor, Smith doubted an individual worker could produce even 20 pins per day.[10]

Division of labor
A method that breaks down the production of a commodity into a series of specific tasks, each performed by a different worker.

The division of labor separates production tasks into a series of related operations. Each worker performs one or a few out of perhaps hundreds of tasks necessary to produce a commodity. There are several reasons why the division of labor often leads to enormous gains in output per worker. First, specialization permits individuals to take advantage of their existing abilities and skills. (Put another way, specialization permits an economy to take advantage of the fact that individuals have different skills.) Different types of work can be assigned to those individuals who are able to accomplish them most efficiently. Second, a worker who specializes in just one narrow area becomes more experienced and more skilled in that task with the passage of time. Third, and perhaps most important, the division of labor lets us adopt complex, large-scale production techniques unthinkable for an individual household. As our knowledge of technology and the potential of machinery expands, capital-intensive production procedures and the division of labor permit us to attain living standards undreamed of just a few decades ago.

Gains from Specialization and Comparative Advantage

Economizing means getting the most out of our available resources. How can this be accomplished? How can we reach our production possibilities curve and achieve the maximum value from our productive activities? To answer these questions, we must understand a basic truth known as the **law of comparative advantage,** which lies at the heart of economizing behavior for any economy. ***Initially developed in the early 1800s by the great English economist David Ricardo, the law of comparative advantage states that the total output of a group of individuals, an entire economy, or a group of nations will be greatest when the output of each good is produced by the person (or firm) with the lowest opportunity cost.***

Law of comparative advantage
A principle that states that individuals, firms, regions, or nations can gain by specializing in the production of goods that they produce cheaply (that is, at a low opportunity cost) and exchanging those goods for other desired goods for which they are high-opportunity-cost producers.

Once one thinks about it, the law of comparative advantage is almost common sense. It simply means that if we want to get a job done (something produced) with the smallest sacrifice, each of us should specialize in that part of the job that we do best, comparatively speaking. If we are going to get the most out of our resources, products must be produced by the low-opportunity-cost producers. If someone else is willing to supply us with a good at a lower cost than we can produce it ourselves, we will be better off to trade for it and use our resources to produce more of the things for which we are a low-cost producer. Failure to have activities carried out by the low-opportunity-cost producers means that we are not economizing—we are getting less than the potential output from our resources.

[10]See Adam Smith, *An Inquiry into the Nature and Causes of the Wealth of Nations* (1776; Cannan's ed., Chicago: University of Chicago Press, 1976), pp. 7–16, for additional detail on the importance of the division of labor.

The principle of comparative advantage is universal. It is just as valid in socialist countries as it is in capitalist countries. It is just as applicable to trade among individuals as it is to trade among nations. Consider the situation of an attorney who can type 120 words per minute. The attorney is trying to decide whether to hire a secretary, who types only 60 words per minute, to complete some legal documents. If the lawyer does the typing job, it will take four hours; if a secretary is hired, the typing job will take eight hours. At first glance, we might think that the cost of the typing is less if the lawyer does it (4 hours) than if the secretary does it (8 hours). Certainly, the lawyer can do the job more quickly than the prospective employee. The *cost* of her time, though, is the $50 per hour she can earn when working as a lawyer, while the typist's time is worth just $7 per hour.

Although she is a fast typist, the attorney is still a high-opportunity-cost producer of typing service. If she types the documents, the job will cost $200, the opportunity cost of four hours of lost time as a lawyer. Alternatively, the cost of having the documents typed by the typist is only $56 (eight hours of typing service at $7 per hour). The lawyer's comparative advantage thus lies in practicing law. She will increase her own productivity, and gain income accordingly, by hiring the typist rather than personally performing the task.

Division of Labor, Specialization, and Exchange

It is difficult to exaggerate the gains derived from division of labor, specialization, and exchange in accordance with the law of comparative advantage. These factors are the primary source of our modern standard of living. Can you imagine the difficulty involved in producing your own housing, clothing, and food, to say nothing of radios,

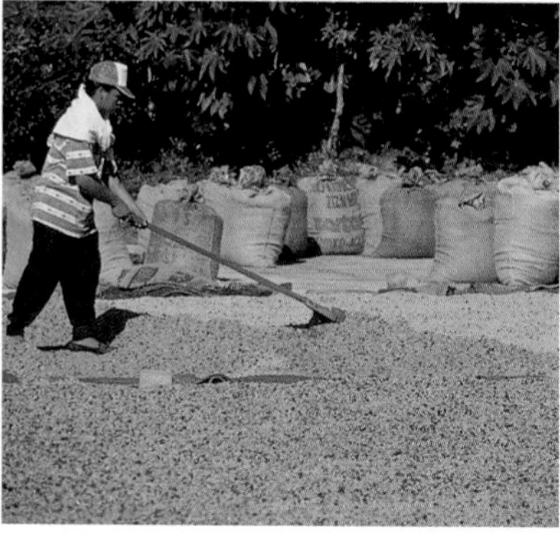

Trade channels goods to those who value them most and permits us to achieve a larger output as the result of specialization, division of labor, and use of mass production techniques. These factors underlie our modern living standards.

MYTHS OF ECONOMICS

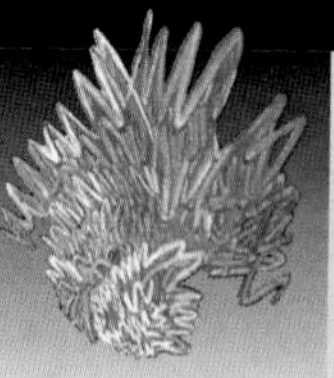

"In exchange, when someone gains, someone else must lose."

People tend to think of making, building, and creating things as productive activities. Agriculture and manufacturing are like this. They create something genuinely new, something that was not there before. On the other hand, trade—the mere exchanging of one thing for another—does not create new material items. Therefore, some conclude that it is a zero-sum game in which one person's gain is necessarily a loss to another. A closer look at the motivation for trade helps us see through this popular fallacy. Exchange is based on the mutual expectation of gain. If both parties did not expect the trade to improve their well-being, they would not agree to the trade. Because trade is mutually advantageous, it must be a positive-sum productive activity.

There are three major reasons why trade is a positive-sum activity. ***First, trade channels goods and services to those who value them most.*** It is easy to think of material things as wealth, but material things are not wealth until they are in the hands of someone who values them. The preferences, knowledge, and goals of people vary widely. A good that is virtually worthless to one may be a precious gem to another. For example, a highly technical book on electronics that is of no value to an art collector may be worth several hundred dollars to an engineer. Similarly, a painting that is unappreciated by an engineer may be of great value to an art collector. Therefore, a voluntary exchange that moves the electronics book to the engineer and the painting to the art collector will increase the value of both goods. Thus, transactions that channel goods and resources toward those who value them most create wealth for both the trading partners and the nation.

Second, exchange permits trading partners to gain from a larger total output as the result of specialization in those areas where they have a comparative advantage. A group of individuals, regions, or nations will be able to produce a larger joint output when each specializes in those productive activities that it does best. In turn, the larger total output allows both trading parties to gain when they produce those goods they can provide at a low cost and use the revenue generated from their sale to purchase desired products that they could produce only at a high cost. For example, exchange permits a skilled carpenter to concentrate on building house frames, while contracting for electrical and plumbing services from others who have comparative advantages in those areas. Similarly, trade permits a country such as Canada to specialize in the production of wheat, while Brazil specializes in coffee. Because the joint output of the two countries is enlarged as the result of this specialization, both can gain from the exchange of Canadian wheat for Brazilian coffee.

Third, voluntary exchange makes it possible for individuals to produce more goods through division of labor and adoption of mass production methods. In the absence of exchange, productive activity would be limited to the individual household. Self-provision and small-scale production would be the rule. Exchange permits business firms to sell their output over a broad market area, so they can plan for large outputs and adopt complex large-scale production processes. Using such mass production procedures often leads to a more efficient utilization of both labor and machinery and enormous increases in output per worker. Without exchanges, these gains could not be achieved.

television sets, dishwashers, automobiles, and telephone services? Yet, most families in North America, Western Europe, Japan, and Australia enjoy all these conveniences. They are able to do so largely because their economies are organized in such a way that individuals can cooperate, specialize, and trade, thereby reaping the benefits of the enormous increases in output—both in quantity and diversity—thus produced.

Gains from trade are a key to economic progress. Human-made obstacles that retard exchange also retard the realization of gains from specialization, comparative advantage, and division of labor. Countries that impose such trade barriers fail to realize their full potential. (See the "Myths of Economics" box concerning gains from trade.)

Personal Motivation, Specialization, and Exchange

Economic thinking implies that people will choose an alternative only if they expect that it will provide benefits (utility) in excess of opportunity costs. Purposeful decision makers will be motivated by the pursuit of personal gain. They will never knowingly choose an alternative when they expect the opportunity cost to exceed the benefits. To do so would be to sacrifice the preferred course of action. That simply would not make sense.

When an individual's interests, aptitudes, abilities, and skills make it possible to gain by exchanging low-opportunity-cost goods for those things that could be produced only at a high opportunity cost, pursuit of the potential gain will motivate the individual to trade precisely in this manner. If free exchange is allowed, people will not have to be ordered to perform the "right" job. In a market setting, the incomes of people will be higher if they produce and sell items for which they have a comparative advantage (items they can produce cheaply). Similarly, they will promote their own interests by buying goods that others can produce more cheaply.

ECONOMIC ORGANIZATION

Every economy must answer three basic questions: (1) What will be produced? (2) How will goods be produced? and (3) For whom will they be produced? These questions are highly interrelated. Throughout, we will consider how alternative forms of economic organization address these three questions.

As we have stressed in this chapter, the availability of most goods we enjoy—our food, clothing, housing, medical services, and so on—reflects cooperative efforts by numerous people, most of whom we have never met. This cooperation does not occur automatically. Economic organization and institutions influence both the type and degree of cooperation.

Two Methods of Economic Organization: Markets and Political Planning

There are two broad ways that an economy can be organized: markets and government (or political) planning. Let us briefly consider each.

Market organization
A method of organization that allows unregulated prices and the decentralized decisions of private property owners to resolve the basic economic problems of consumption, production, and distribution.

Capitalism
An economic system based on private ownership of productive resources and allocation of goods according to the signals provided by market prices.

Market Organization. Private ownership, voluntary contracts (often these contracts are verbal), and reliance upon market prices are the distinguishing features of market organization, or **capitalism,** as it is sometime called.[11] In market economies, people have private ownership rights to productive assets, as well as to consumption goods and their own labor services. Private parties are permitted to buy and sell ownership rights at mutually acceptable prices in unregulated markets. Government plays the limited role of a rule maker and neutral referee. The rule maker role involves the development of a legal structure that recognizes, defines, and protects private ownership rights, enforces contracts, and protects people from violence and fraud. But the government is not an active player in the economy; ideally, the political process avoids modifying market outcomes or favoring some participants at the expense of others. For example, the government does not prevent sellers from undertaking price reductions and quality improvements to compete with other sellers. Nor does it prevent buyers from offering higher prices to bid products or productive resources away from others. No legal restraints (for example, government licensing) limit potential buyers or sellers from producing, selling, or buying in the marketplace. Under market organization, there is no central planning authority. The three basic economic questions are answered through market coordination of the decentralized choices of buyers and sellers.

[11]*Capitalism* is a term coined by Karl Marx.

Political Planning. The major alternative to market organization is **collective decision making,** the use of political organization and government planning to allocate resources. An economic system in which the government owns the income-producing assets (machines, buildings, and land) and directly determines what goods they will produce is called **socialism.** Alternatively, the government may maintain private ownership in name, but use taxes, subsidies, and regulations to resolve the basic economic questions. In either instance, political rather than market forces direct the economy. In both cases, government officials and planning boards hand down decisions to expand or contract the output of education, medical services, automobiles, electricity, steel, consumer durables, and thousands of other commodities. This is not to say that the preferences of individuals have no importance. If the government officials and central planners are influenced by the democratic process, they have to consider how their actions will influence their election prospects. Otherwise, like the firm in a market economy that produces a product that consumers do not want, their tenure of service is likely to be a short one.

Collective decision making
The method of organization that relies on public-sector decision making (voting, political bargaining, lobbying, and so on) to resolve basic issues.

Socialism
A system of economic organization in which (1) the ownership and control of the basic means of production rest with the state, and (2) resource allocation is determined by centralized planning rather than by market forces.

Exit and Voice: Two Methods of Sending Messages

Individual choice provides the foundation for economic analysis. Individuals have two major methods of sending messages and thereby influencing market and political decision makers. First and most directly, they have a **voice**—they can communicate complaints, desires, and suggestions to decision makers. Second, individuals can **exit,** or withdraw from an economic relationship with another person or organization. The individual's voice will generally be more persuasive if exit is also available.

Voice
The ability to communicate complaints, desires and suggestions to decision makers who may be private buyers or sellers, or may be decision makers in government.

Exit
The ability to withdraw from an economic relationship with another person or organization.

The exit option is generally much easier to exercise in a market setting. If you are a dissatisfied customer—if you are unhappy with a retail store, an automobile manufacturer, or a local restaurant—what do you generally do? Some may write a letter of complaint (the voice option), but most of us simply take our business elsewhere (the exit option). The exit option provides us with a relatively easy way of dealing with poor service, shoddy products, and high prices. It is the primary way that customers communicate with business firms.

The exit option is also an effective method of sending a message to corporate managers and labor union leaders. For example, if a stockholder is unhappy with the corporate strategy of a firm, the voice strategy—writing company officers or voicing dissatisfaction at the annual stockholder meeting—is an option. But the exit option, the selling of one's stock, is likely to be both less costly and more effective. When a substantial number of fellow stockholders agree and also sell their stock, the price of the stock will fall and the likelihood of a management shake-up or change of direction will almost certainly increase.

The exit option is generally more difficult to use in a system of political planning than in a market system. This is particularly true at the national level, where an exit message can only be sent by moving to another country. While exit is a more feasible option at the local government level—for example, it may be possible to move from one school district to another at a low cost—even here it is generally more costly to choose the exit option than is true in a market setting. Voice is generally the primary means of sending messages to government officials. In a democratic setting, competitive political parties are present, discussion is encouraged, and the right to speak out is recognized and protected. The vote is another form of voice, but as we will see later, the incentive structure often reduces its potency.

In summary, the exit choice is the primary method of communication among participants in the marketplace. This option is generally limited in the political arena.

Thus, individuals have to rely mostly on voice when sending messages to political decision makers. How will this difference in the importance of the exit option as a method of communication influence the allocation of resources and operation of the two sectors? This question will be dealt with as we analyze the operation of the two sectors in subsequent chapters.

LOOKING *Ahead*

The next two chapters present an overview of the market sector, with real-world applications of the supply and demand model of market behavior. Chapters 5 and 6 focus on how the public sector—the democratic collective decision-making process—functions. The tools of economics can be used to analyze the operation of and allocation of resources in both the market and political sectors.

We think this approach is important, fruitful, and exciting. How does the market sector really work? What does economics say about which activities should be handled by government? What types of economic policies are politically attractive to democratically elected officials? Why is sound economic policy sometimes in conflict with good politics? All these questions will be tackled in the next four chapters.

KEY POINTS

➤ The highest valued activity sacrificed in making a choice is the opportunity cost of the choice; differences (or changes) in opportunity costs help explain human behavior.

➤ Mutual gain is the foundation of trade.

➤ Transaction costs—the time, effort, and other resources necessary to search out, negotiate, and conclude an exchange—are an obstacle to the realization of gains from trade.

➤ Private property rights provide strong incentives for owners to use their resources in ways that benefit others.

➤ The production possibilities curve reveals the maximum combination of any two products that can be produced with a fixed quantity of resources and constant level of technology.

➤ With the passage of time, the production possibilities curve of an economy can be shifted outward through (1) investment, (2) technological advances, (3) improved institutions, and (4) greater work effort (the forgoing of leisure).

➤ The joint output of individuals, regions, or nations will be maximized when goods are exchanged between parties in accordance with the law of comparative advantage.

➤ Voluntary exchange channels goods toward those who value them most and permits us to realize gains from specialization, division of labor, mass production, and cooperative effort among individuals. These elements underlie our modern living standards.

➤ The two basic methods of making economic decisions are the market mechanism and public-sector decision making; in each, the decisions of individuals using voice and exit strategies will influence the result.

➤ The tools of economics are general; they are applicable to choices that influence both market- and public-sector decisions.

CRITICAL ANALYSIS QUESTIONS

1. "If Jones trades $5,000 to Smith for a used car, the items exchanged must be of equal value." Is this statement true, false, or uncertain?

*2. Economists often argue that wage rates reflect productivity. Yet, the wages of house painters have increased nearly as rapidly as the national average, even though these workers use approximately the same methods that were applied 50 years ago. Can you explain why the wages of painters have risen substantially even though their productivity has changed so little?

3. It takes one hour to travel from New York City to Washington, D.C., by air, but it takes five hours by bus. If the air fare is $110 and the bus fare is $70, which would be cheaper for someone whose opportunity cost of travel time is $6 per hour? For someone whose opportunity cost is $10 per hour? $14 per hour?

*4. "People in business get ahead by exploiting the needs of their consumers. The gains of business are at the expense of suffering imposed on their customers." Evaluate this statement from the producer of a prime-time television program.

5. With regard to the use of resources, what is the objective of the entrepreneur? What is the major function of the middleman? Is the middleman an entrepreneur?

6. If you have a private ownership right to something, what does this mean? Does private ownership give you the right to do anything you want with the things that you own? Explain. How does private ownership influence the incentive of individuals to (a) take care of things, (b) conserve resources for the future, and (c) develop and modify things in ways that are objectionable to others? Explain.

7. What is the law of comparative advantage? According to the law of comparative advantage, what should be the distinguishing characteristics of the goods that a nation produces? What should be the distinguishing characteristics of the goods that the nation imports? How will international trade of this type influence the level of production and living standard of the populace? Explain.

*8. Does a 60-year-old tree farmer have an incentive to plant and care for Douglas fir trees that will not reach optimal cutting size for another 50 years?

*9. What forms of competition does a private-property, market-directed economy authorize? What forms does it prohibit?

10. What are the three major sources of gains from trade? Why is exchange important to the prosperity of a nation? How do physical obstacles (such as rivers, mountains, and bad roads) that increase transaction costs influence gains from trade and the prosperity of a nation? How do human-made obstacles (for example, tariffs, quotas, and legal restrictions limiting trade) that increase transaction costs influence gains from trade and prosperity?

*11. "Really good agricultural land should not be developed for housing. Food is far more important." Evaluate this statement.

*12. In many states, the resale of tickets to sporting events at prices above the original purchase price ("ticket scalping") is prohibited. Who is helped and who is hurt by such prohibitions? Can you think of ways ticket owners who want to sell might get around the prohibition? Do you think it would be a good idea to extend the resale prohibition to other things—automobiles, books, works of art, or stock shares, for example? Why or why not?

13. "When you're dealing with questions related to human life, economic costs are irrelevant." Evaluate this statement made by a congressman.

14. Consider the questions below:

a. Do you think that your work effort is influenced by whether there is a close link between personal output and personal compensation (reward)? Explain.

b. Suppose the grades in your class were going to be determined by a random draw at the end of the course. How would this influence your study habits?

c. How would your study habits be influenced if everyone in the class were going to be given an A grade? How about if grades were based entirely on examinations composed of the multiple-choice questions in the coursebook for this textbook?

d. Do you think the total output of goods in the United States is affected by the close link between productive contribution and individual reward? Why or why not?

---

*Asterisk denotes questions for which answers are given in Appendix B.

PART 2

Markets and governments

There are two primary methods of allocating scarce resources among alternative uses: markets and governments.

VISUALIZING MARKET ALLOCATION

Exhibit II-A provides a visual representation of how markets allocate resources toward the production of products (goods and services). Business firms purchase resources, such as materials, labor services, tools, and machines, from households in exchange for income (bottom of diagram). Firms incur costs as the resources are bid away from their alternative uses. Businesses transform the resources into products, such as shoes, automobiles, food products, and medical se vices, and supply them to households in exchange revenues (top of diagram). Whether a product is p duced depends on sales revenue relative to producti costs. *In a market economy, business firms will co tinue to supply a good or service only if the revenu from the sale of the product are sufficient to cover t cost of the resources required for its production.*

EXHIBIT II-A

VISUALIZING ALLOCATION THROUGH GOVERNMENT

As Exhibit II-B illustrates, allocation through government involves a more complex three-sided ex- ange. In a democratic political setting, a legislative dy levies taxes on voter-citizens and these revenues e subdivided into budgets, which are allocated to gov- nment bureaus and agencies. In turn, the bureaus and gencies use the funds from their budgets to supply oods, services, and income transfers to voter-citizens. ne legislative body is like a board of directors elected the citizens. The competitive pressure to be elected rovides legislators with a strong incentive to cater to the views of voters. In turn, a voter will be more likely to support a legislator if the value of the goods, services, and transfers received by the citizen (link between bureau and citizen) is large relative to the citizen's tax liability (link between voter and legislator). *Goods, services, and income transfers will tend to be supplied through government if, and only if, a majority of the legislators perceive that the provision will enhance their electoral prospects—in other words, the likelihood they will win the next election.*

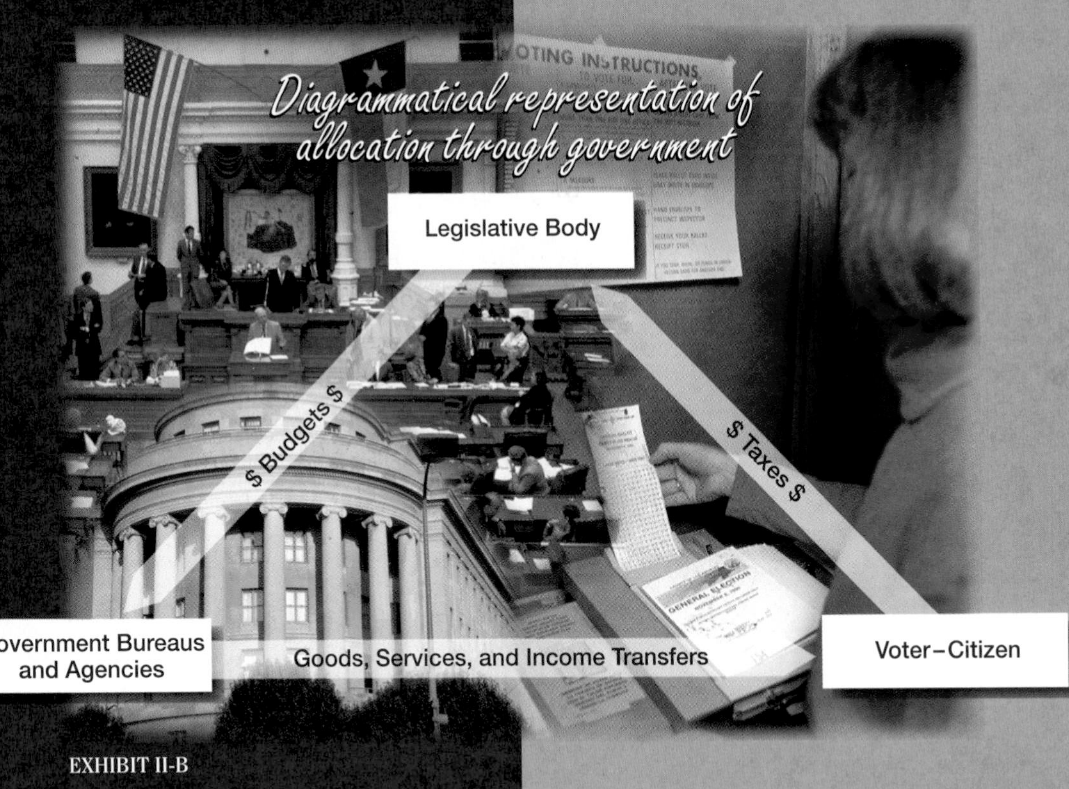

EXHIBIT II-B

SIGNIFICANCE OF ECONOMIC THEORY

Economics has a great deal to say about how both markets and governments allocate scarce resources. It provides insights concerning the conditions under which each will likely work well (and when each will likely work poorly). The next four chapters will focus on this topic.

CHAPTER 3

I am convinced that if it [the market system] were the result of deliberate human design, and if the people guided by the price changes understood that their decisions have significance far beyond their immediate aim, this mechanism would have been acclaimed as one of the greatest triumphs of the human mind.

Friedrich Hayek, Nobel Laureate[1]

From the point of view of physics, it is a miracle that [seven million New Yorkers are fed each day] without any control mechanism other than sheer capitalism.

John H. Holland, scientist, Santa Fe Institute

Supply, Demand, and the Market Process

CHAPTER FOCUS

- What are the laws of demand and supply?
- How do consumers decide whether to purchase a good? How do producers decide whether to supply it?
- How do buyers and sellers respond to changes in the price of a good?
- What are profits and losses? What must a firm do in order to make a profit?
- How is the market price of a good determined?
- How do markets adjust to changes in demand? How do they adjust to changes in supply?
- What is the "invisible hand" principle?

---

[1]Friedrich Hayek, "The Use of Knowledge in Society," *American Economic Review* 35 (September 1945), pp. 519–530.

To those who study art, the Mona Lisa is much more than a famous painting of a woman. Looking beyond the overall picture, they see and appreciate the brush strokes, colors, and techniques embodied in the painting. Similarly, studying economics can help you to gain an appreciation for the details behind many things from your everyday life. On your last visit to the grocery store, you probably noticed the fruit and vegetable section. Next time, take a moment to ponder how potatoes from Idaho, oranges from Florida, apples from Washington, bananas from Honduras, kiwi fruit from New Zealand, and other items from around the world got to your local grocery store. Literally thousands of different individuals, *working independently,* were involved in the process. Their actions were coordinated such that the quantity of each good was just about right for your local community. Furthermore, the goods, including those transported great distances, were both fresh and reasonably priced.

How does all this happen? The short answer is, "It is the result of market prices, and the incentives and coordination that flow from them." To the economist, the operation of markets—including the local grocery market—is analogous to the brush strokes and techniques underlying a beautiful painting. Reflecting on this point, Professor Hayek speculates that if the market system had been deliberately designed, it would be "acclaimed as one of the greatest triumphs of the human mind." Similarly, computer scientist John H. Holland argues that, from the viewpoint of physics, the feeding of millions of New Yorkers "day after day with very few shortages or surpluses" is a miraculous feat.

Amazingly, markets coordinate the actions of millions of individuals *without* central planning. There is no individual, political authority, or central planning committee in charge. Considering that there are over 260 million Americans with widely varying skills and desires, and roughly 7 million businesses producing a vast array of

The produce section of your local grocery store is a great place to see economics in action. Literally millions of individuals from around the world have been involved in the process of getting these goods to the shelves in just the right quantities. Market prices underlie this feat.

products ranging from diamond rings to toilet paper, the coordination derived from markets is an awesome achievement.

This chapter focuses on supply, demand, and the determination of market prices. For now, we will analyze the operation of competitive markets—that is, markets with rival sellers (and buyers) without restrictions limiting potential rivals from entering and competing in the market. We will also assume that the property rights to both resources and goods are well defined. Later, we will consider what happens when these conditions are absent.

When you sell a car through a classified newspaper ad, as the seller you have in mind a minimum price you will accept for your car. A potential buyer, on the other hand, has in mind a maximum price he or she will pay for the car. If the potential buyer's maximum price is greater than your minimum price, mutual gains from trade are possible. As this simple example shows, the desires and incentives of both buyers and sellers underlie the operation of markets and the determination of prices. We will begin with the demand (buyer's) side, then turn to the supply (seller's) side of the market.

CONSUMER CHOICE AND LAW OF DEMAND

Our desire for goods is far greater than our income. Even high-income consumers are unable to purchase everything they would like. We all must make choices as consumers. Seeking as much satisfaction (value) as possible from our limited income, we choose those alternatives that are expected to enhance our welfare the most, relative to their cost. Clearly, prices influence our decisions. As the price of a good increases, we are required to give up more of *other* goods if we buy at the more expensive price. Thus, we might say that as the price of a good rises, its opportunity cost increases (in terms of other goods forgone).

The basic postulate of economics says that incentives matter: An increase in the cost of an alternative reduces the likelihood that it will be chosen. A straightforward application suggests that consumers will purchase fewer units of a good in response to an increase in its price. ***The* law of demand *states that there is an inverse relationship between the price of a good and the quantity of it that consumers are willing to purchase. As the price of a good rises, consumers buy less of it, and, as the price falls, consumers buy more.***

The availability of **substitutes**—goods that perform similar functions—underlies the negative relationship between price and quantity purchased. No single good is absolutely essential (see Myths of Economics box); each good can be replaced by other goods. Margarine can be substituted for butter. Wood, aluminum, bricks, and glass can take the place of steel. Going to the movies, playing tennis, watching television, and going to a football game are substitute forms of entertainment. When the price of a good increases, people turn to substitute products and economize on their use of the more expensive good. Prices really do matter.

Law of demand
A principle that states there is an inverse relationship between the price of a good and the amount of it buyers are willing to purchase. As the price of a product increases, other things constant, consumers will purchase less of the product.

Substitutes
Products that serve similar purposes. They are related such that an increase in the price of one will cause an increase in demand for the other (for example, hamburgers and tacos, butter and margarine, Chevrolets and Fords).

MARKET DEMAND SCHEDULE

Exhibit 3–1 shows a hypothetical demand schedule for cellular telephones with differing prices and the quantities that consumers would demand at each price.[2] Here, price

[2]These data are actual prices (adjusted to 1994 dollars) and quantities annually for 1988 to 1994 taken from *Statistical Abstract of the United States: 1995* (Washington, D.C.: U.S. Bureau of the Census, 1995). *If we could assume that other demand determinants (income, prices of related goods, etc.) had remained constant,* then this hypothetical demand schedule would be accurate for that time period. Because it is possible that some of these other factors changed, we treat the numbers as hypothetical, depicting alternative prices and quantities *at a given time.* Since 1995, there have been additional price reductions.

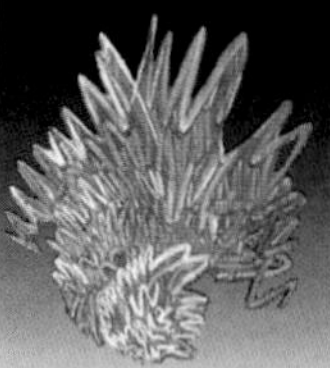

MYTHS OF ECONOMICS

"The Demand Curve for Some Goods Is Vertical, Because Fixed Amounts of Them Are Needed for Consumption."

Noneconomists often ignore the impact of price and make statements implying that, for some goods, there is a fixed amount that must be available for consumption. "During the next five years the United States will need 30 million barrels of oil." "Next year the United States will need 20,000 more physicians." Have you ever heard popular commentators make statements like these, implying that the demand for some commodity is vertical?

Two points should be recognized when evaluating such statements. ***First, we live in a world of substitutes.*** There are alternative ways of satisfying needs. For example, a fax, an e-mail, or a telephone call is a substitute for a letter. Sometimes the substitutes are seemingly unrelated. For example, reading, staying home and watching television, and picnicking in the backyard are substitutes for gasoline used for a Sunday drive. In varying degrees, there are substitutes for everything.

Second, since scarcity and limited income restrict our options, each of us will have to forgo many things that we "need"—or at least think we need. Given our limited income, purchasing them would mean that we would have to give up other things that we value more highly and therefore apparently need more urgently. The concept of need changes with differences in income, preferences, and cultural factors. In affluent countries, families are thought to need at least one bathroom with hot and cold running water, a sink, a toilet, and a bathtub or shower. Yet the typical family in many poorer countries would perceive such a bathroom to be a luxury.

There are substitutes for everything, and price influences the amount "needed" of each good. Thus, the vertical demand curve, like the unicorn, is a myth.

is measured as the average monthly cost, and quantity demanded is the number of subscribers to cellular phone service. In the table, when the price of cellular phone service is $123 per month, just over 2 million consumers subscribe. As the price falls to $107, the quantity rises to 3.5 million; when the price falls to $56 per month, the quantity of subscribers increases to 24.1 million.

Exhibit 3–1 also provides a graphic presentation of the law of demand called the *demand curve.* When representing the demand schedule graphically, economists measure price on the vertical, or *y*-axis, and the amount demanded on the horizontal, or *x*-axis. Because of the inverse relationship between price and amount purchased, the demand curve will slope downward to the right.

Read horizontally, the demand curve shows how much of a particular good consumers will buy at a given price. Read vertically, the demand curve also reveals important information about consumer preferences—their valuation of goods. ***The height of the demand curve at any quantity shows the maximum price that consumers are willing to pay for that additional unit.*** If consumers value an additional unit of a product highly, they will be willing to pay a large amount (a high price) for it. Conversely, if their valuation of an additional unit of the good is low, they will be willing to pay only a small amount for it.

Because the amount a consumer is willing to pay for a good is directly related to the good's value to the consumer, the demand curve indicates the marginal benefit consumers receive from additional units. When viewed in this manner, the demand curve reveals that as consumers have more and more of a product, they will value additional units less and less.

Consumer Surplus

Previously, we indicated that voluntary exchange makes both the buyer and seller better off. The demand curve can be used to illustrate the gains of the consumers. Suppose that you value a particular good at $50, but you are able to purchase it for only $30.

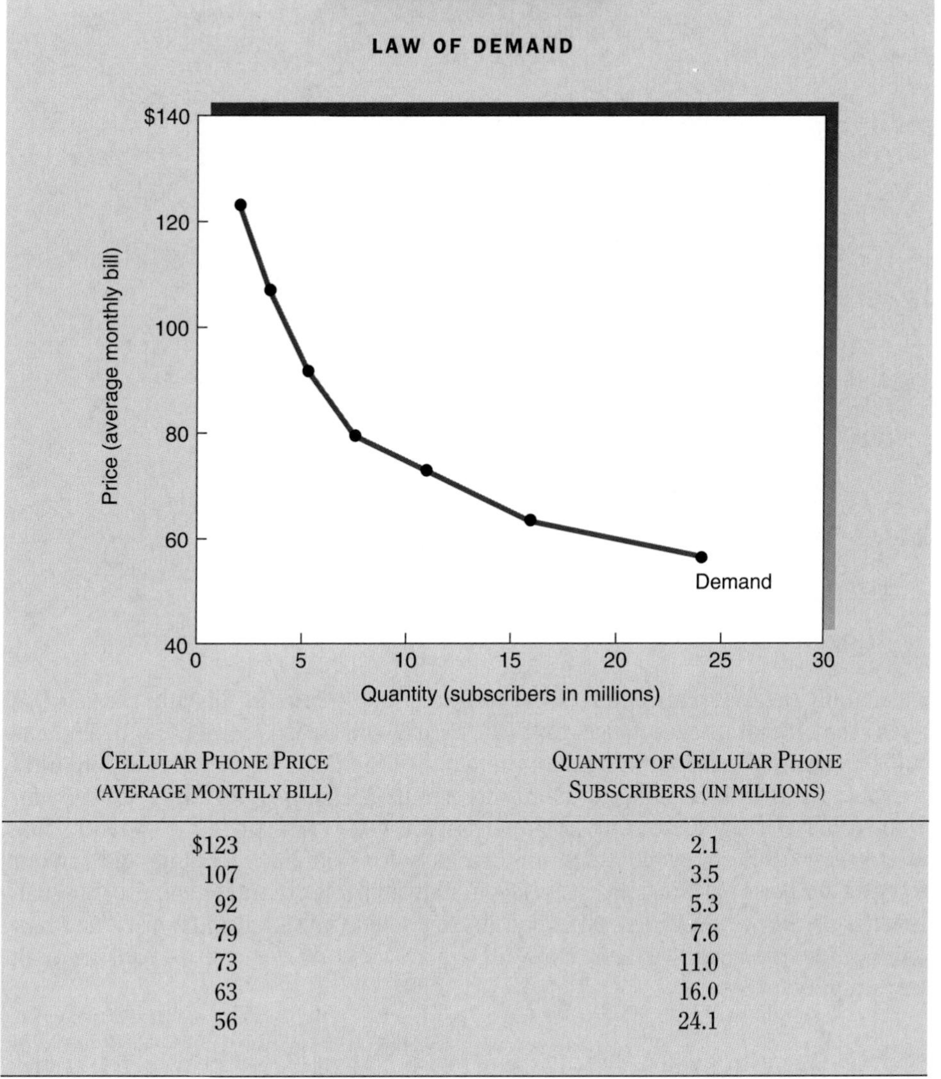

Cellular Phone Price (average monthly bill)	Quantity of Cellular Phone Subscribers (in millions)
$123	2.1
107	3.5
92	5.3
79	7.6
73	11.0
63	16.0
56	24.1

As the table indicates, the number of people subscribing to cellular phone service (just like the consumption of other products) is inversely related to price. The data from the table are plotted as a demand schedule in the graph. The inverse relation between price and amount demanded reflects the fact that consumers will substitute away from a good as it becomes more expensive.

Your net gain from buying the good is $20. Economists call this net gain of buyers **consumer surplus.** In effect, consumer surplus is the difference between the amount that consumers would be willing to pay and the amount they actually pay for each unit of a good. Exhibit 3–2 illustrates the measurement of consumer surplus. The height of the demand curve measures how much the various buyers value each unit of the good, while the price indicates the amount they actually pay. The difference between these two—the area under the demand curve but above the price paid—is a measure of consumer surplus. The size of the consumer surplus is affected by the market price. A reduction in the market price will lead to an expansion in quantity purchased and a larger consumer surplus. Conversely, a higher market price will reduce the amount purchased and shrink the surplus (net gain) of consumers.

Consumer surplus
The difference between the maximum price consumers are willing to pay and the price they actually pay. It is the net gain derived by the buyers of the good.

In aggregate, the total value (area under the demand curve) to consumers of the units purchased may be far greater than the amount they pay. When additional units are available at a low price, the marginal value of a good may be quite low, even though its total value to consumers is exceedingly high. For example, this

Consumer surplus is the area below the demand curve but above the actual price paid. This area represents the net gains to buyers from market exchange.

EXHIBIT 3-2

CONSUMER SURPLUS

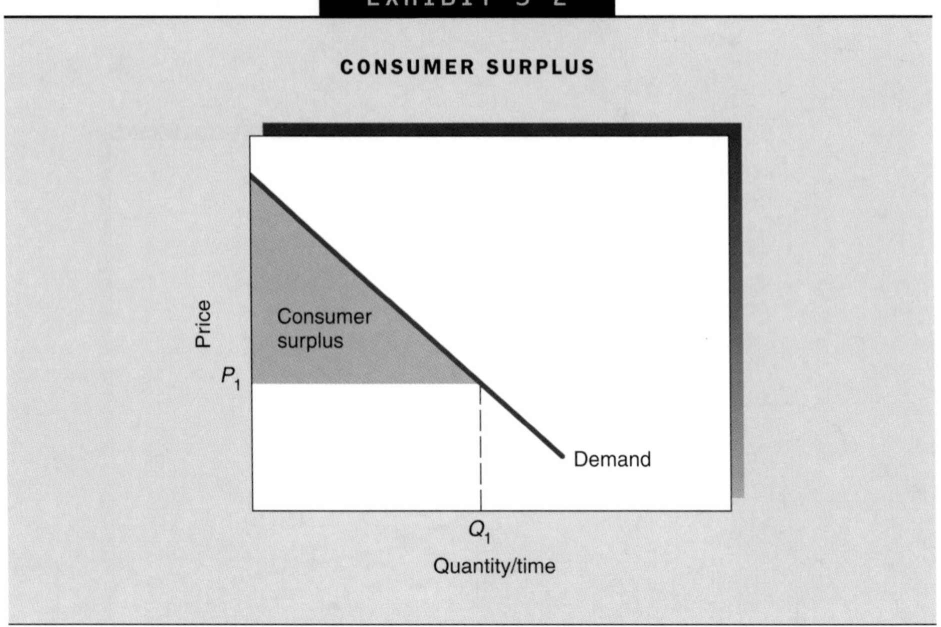

is generally the case with water. Of course, water is essential for life and the value derived from the first few units consumed per day will be exceedingly high. The consumer surplus derived from these units will also be large when water is plentifully available at a low price. As more and more units are consumed, however, the *marginal* value of even something as important as water will fall to a low level. Thus, when water is cheap, people will use it not only for drinking, cleaning, and cooking, but also for washing cars, watering lawns, flushing toilets, and keeping fish aquariums. Thus, while consumers will tend to expand consumption until price and *marginal value* are equal, price reveals little about the *total value* derived from the consumption of a good.

Responsiveness of Quantity Demanded to Price: Elastic and Inelastic Demand Curves

As we previously noted, the availability of substitutes is the main reason why the demand curve for a good slopes downward. Some goods, however, are much easier to substitute away from than others. As the price of tacos rises, most consumers find hamburgers a reasonable substitute. Because of the ease of substitutability, the quantity demanded of tacos is quite sensitive to a change in their price. Economists would say that the demand for tacos is relatively *elastic* because a small price change will cause a rather large change in the amount purchased. Alternatively, such goods as gasoline and electricity have fewer good substitutes. When their prices rise, it is harder for consumers to easily substitute away from these products. When good substitutes are unavailable, even a large price change may not cause much of a change in the quantity demanded. Economists would say that the demand for such goods is relatively *inelastic*.

Graphically, this different degree of responsiveness is reflected in the steepness of the demand curve, as is shown in **Exhibit 3–3**. The flatter demand curve (D_1, left frame) is for a product—tacos—for which the quantity demanded is highly responsive

EXHIBIT 3-3

ELASTIC AND INELASTIC DEMAND CURVES

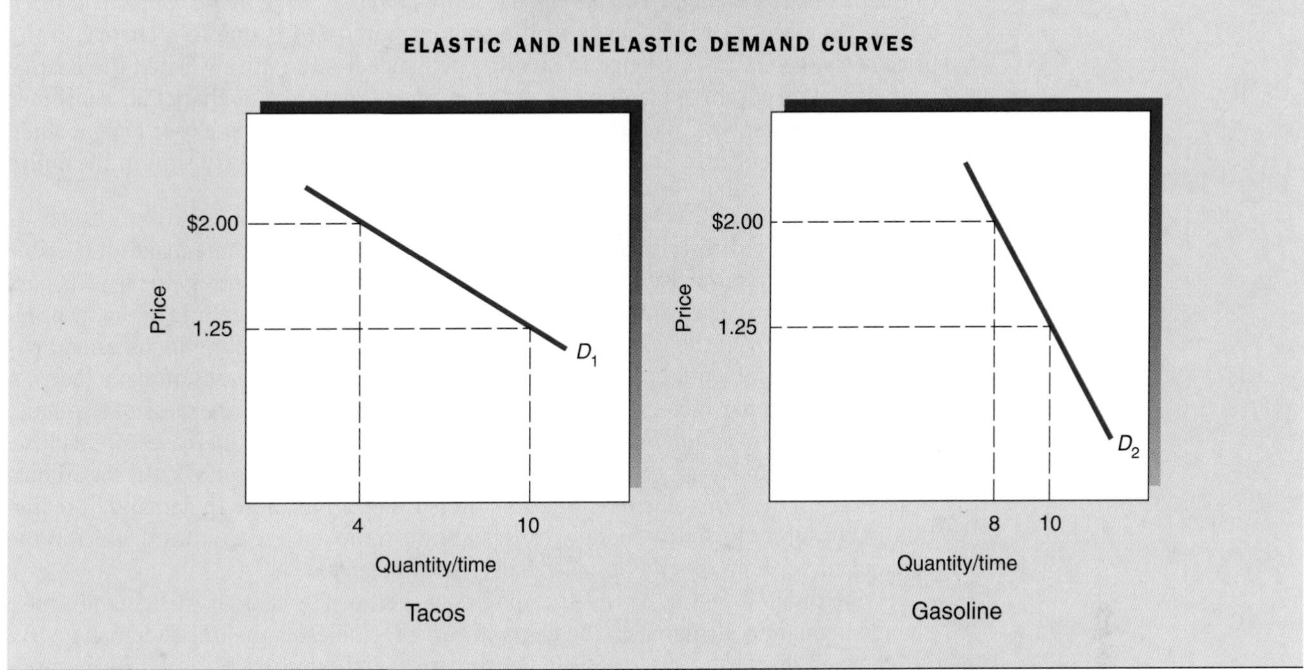

The responsiveness of consumer purchases to a change in price is reflected in the steepness of the demand curve. The flatter demand curve (D_1) *for tacos shows a higher degree of responsiveness and is called relatively elastic, while the steeper demand curve* (D_2) *for gasoline shows a lower degree of responsiveness and is called relatively inelastic.*

to a change in price. As the price increases from $1.25 to $2.00, the quantity demanded falls sharply from 10 to 4 units. The steeper demand curve (D_2, right frame) is for a product—gasoline—where the quantity purchased is much less responsive to a change in price. For gasoline, an increase in price from $1.25 to $2.00 results in only a small reduction in the quantity purchased (from 10 to 8). An economist would say that the flatter demand curve D_1 was relatively elastic, while the steeper demand curve D_2 was relatively inelastic. The availability of substitutes is the main determinant of whether the demand curve is relatively elastic or inelastic.

CHANGES IN DEMAND VERSUS CHANGES IN QUANTITY DEMANDED

The demand curve isolates the impact of price on the amount of a product purchased. Economists refer to a change in the quantity of a good purchased that occurs in response to a price change as a "change in *quantity demanded.*" A change in quantity demanded is a movement along a demand curve from one point to another. Changes in factors like income and the prices of closely related goods will also influence the decision of consumers. If one of these other factors changes, the entire demand curve will shift inwards or outwards. Economists refer to such shifts in the demand curve as a "change in *demand.*"

Failure to distinguish between a change in demand and a change in quantity demanded is one of the most common mistakes made by beginning economics

students.[3] ***A change in demand is a shift in the entire demand curve. A change in quantity demanded is a movement along the same demand curve in response to a price change.*** In essence, if the change in the amount purchased is due to a change in the price of the good, it is a change in quantity demanded. Alternatively, when the change in the amount purchased is due to *anything other than price* (a change in consumer income, for example), it is a change in demand. Let us now take a closer look at some of the factors that cause a change in demand—an inward or outward shift in the entire demand curve.

1. Changes in Consumer Income. An increase in consumer income makes it possible for consumers to purchase more goods. If you were to win the lottery, or if your boss were to give you a raise, you would respond by increasing your spending on many products. Alternatively, if the economy were to go into a recession, falling incomes and rising unemployment would cause consumers to reduce their purchases of many items. A change in consumer income will result in consumers buying more or less of a product *at all possible prices for the product.* When consumer income increases, individuals will generally purchase more of a good. This is shown by a shift to the right (or an outward shift) in the demand curve. Such a shift is called an increase in demand. A reduction in consumer income generally causes a shift to the left (or an inward shift) in the demand curve, which would be called a decrease in demand.

Exhibit 3–4 highlights the difference between a change in demand and a change in quantity demanded. The demand curve D_1 indicates the initial demand curve for compact discs. At a price of $30, consumers would purchase Q_1 units. If the price declined to $10, there would be an increase in *quantity demanded* from Q_1 to Q_3. Arrow A indicates the change in *quantity demanded*—a movement along the original

Arrow A *indicates a change in* quantity demanded, *a movement along the demand curve* D$_1$*, in response to a change in the price of compact discs. The* B *arrows illustrate a change in* demand, *a shift of the entire curve, in this case due to an increase in consumer income.*

EXHIBIT 3–4

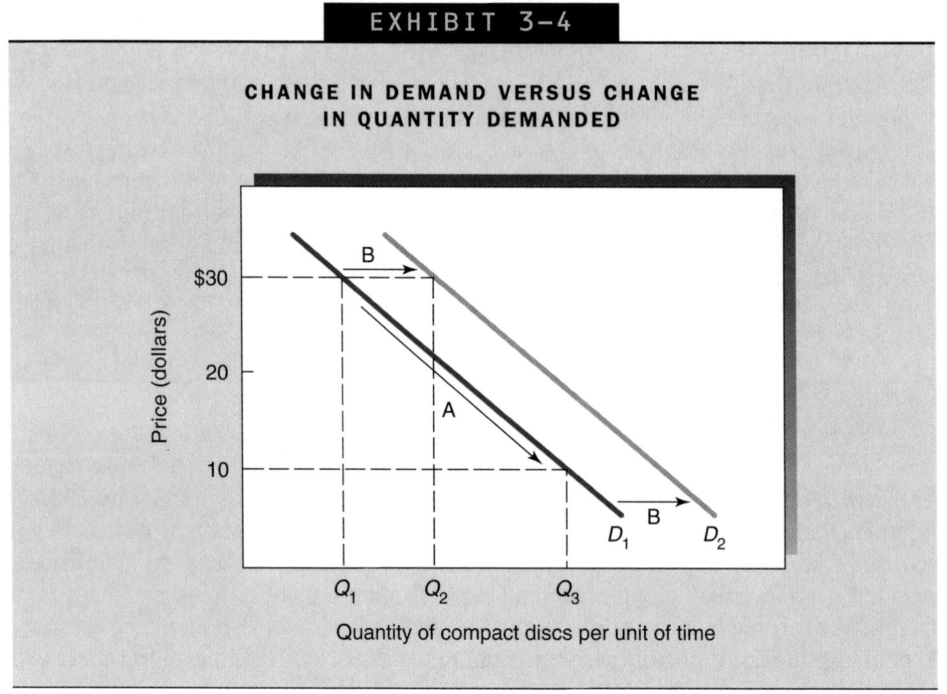

[3]Questions designed to test the ability of students to make this distinction are favorites of many economics instructors. A word to the wise should be sufficient.

EXHIBIT 3–5

A DECREASE IN DEMAND

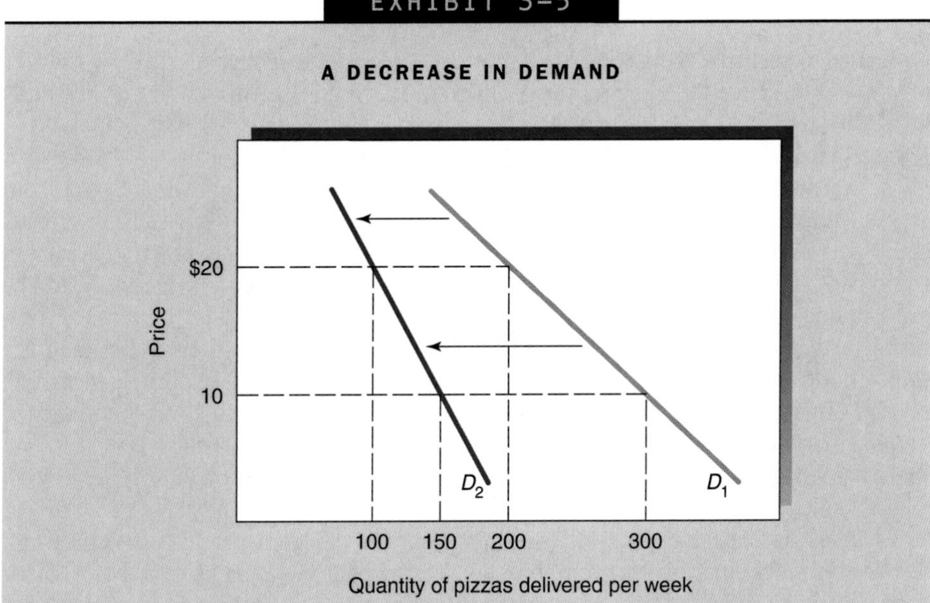

When students go home for the summer, the demand for pizza delivery in college towns decreases. A decrease in demand is a leftward shift in the entire demand curve. Fewer pizzas are demanded at every price.

demand curve D_1. Now, alternatively suppose that there is an increase in consumer income. The *demand* for compact discs would increase from D_1 to D_2. As indicated by the B arrows, the entire demand curve would shift. At the higher income level, consumers would be willing to purchase more compact disks than before. This is true at a price of $30, at $20, at $10, and at every other price. The increase in income leads to an increase in *demand*—a shift in the entire curve. Alternatively, a decrease in consumer income would have led to a decrease in demand—the demand curve would have shifted in the opposite direction (for example, from D_2 inward to D_1).

2. Changes in the Number of Consumers in the Market. Businesses that sell products in college towns are greatly saddened when summer arrives. As you might expect, the demand for many items—from pizza delivery to beer—falls during the summer. **Exhibit 3–5** shows how the falling number of consumers in the market caused by students going home for the summer affects the demand for pizza delivery. With fewer customers, the demand curve shifts inward from D_1 to D_2. There is a decrease in demand; pizza stores will sell fewer pizzas than before regardless of what price they were originally charging. Had their original price been $20, then demand would have fallen from 200 pizzas per week to only 100. Alternatively, had their original price been $10, then demand would have fallen from 300 pizzas to 150. When fall arrives and the students come back to town, there will be an increase in demand, restoring the curve to near its original position. As cities grow and shrink, and as international markets open for domestic firms, changes in the number of consumers have an effect on the demand curves for many products.

3. Changes in the Price of a Related Good. Changes in prices of closely related products also influence the choices of consumers. Related goods may be either substitutes or complements. When two products perform similar functions or fulfill similar needs, they are generally *substitutes.* Economists define goods as substitutes when there is a direct relationship between the price of one and the demand for the other (an increase in the price of one increases demand for the other). For example, margarine is a substitute for butter. If the price of butter rises, it will increase the demand for margarine. Consumers substitute margarine for the more expensive butter. Similarly, lower butter prices would reduce the demand for margarine, shifting the entire curve to the left. A substitute relationship exists between beef and chicken, pencils and pens, apples and oranges, coffee and tea, and so forth.

Other closely related products are consumed jointly, so the demands for them are linked together in a positive way. Examples of goods that "go together," so to speak, could be bread and peanut butter, CDs and CD players, or tents and other camping equipment. For these combinations of goods, called **complements,** a decrease in the price of one will not only increase its quantity demanded, it will also increase the demand for the other. With complements, there is an inverse relationship between the price of one and the demand for the other. For example, lower prices for videocassette players during the 1980s increased the demand for videocassette tapes. Similarly, if hamburger is on sale this week at the grocery store, the store can also expect to sell more hamburger buns, even if the price of buns is unchanged.

Complements
Products that are usually consumed jointly (for example, peanut butter and jelly). They are related such that a decrease in the price of one will cause an increase in demand for the other.

4. Changes in Expectations. Consumers' expectations about the future also can affect the current demand for a product. If consumers begin to expect that a major hurricane will strike their area, the current demand for such goods as batteries and canned food will rise. Expectations about the future direction of the economy can also affect current demand. If consumers become pessimistic about the economy, they might start spending less, causing the current demand for goods to fall. Of perhaps most importance is how a change in the expected future price of a good affects the current demand. When consumers expect the future price of a product to rise, their current demand for it will increase. "Buy now, before the price goes up." On the other hand, consumers will delay a purchase if they expect the item to decrease in price. No doubt you have heard someone say, "I'll wait until it goes on sale." When consumers expect the price to be lower in the near future, they will reduce their current demand for the product.

5. Demographic Changes. The demand for many products is strongly influenced by the demographic composition of the market. An increase in the size of the elderly population during the past decade increased the demand for medical care, retirement housing, and vacation travel, shifting the demand for these goods to the right. During the 1980s, population in the 15–24 age grouping fell by more than 5 million. Because young people are a major part of the U.S. market for jeans, the demand for jeans declined. Sales, which had topped 500 million pairs in 1980, fell to less than 400 million pairs in 1989.[4]

6. Changes in Consumer Tastes and Preferences. Why do preferences change? Preferences change because people learn and change. Consider how consumers responded in the 1980s to new medical information linking certain fats and oils to heart disease. They purchased less of such products as whole milk, butter, and beef, which were thought to be dangerous, and increased their demand for such goods as olive oil and canola oil, thought to be much more "heart-healthy." Sales of olive oil doubled between 1984 and 1989, while canola oil sales doubled between 1988 and 1990. Consumption of butterfat fell at the same time. By 1995, Americans ate 25 percent less beef than they

---

[4]These figures are from Suzanne Tregarthen, "Market for Jeans Shrinks," *The Margin* 6, no. 3 (January–February 1991), p. 28.

THUMBNAIL SKETCH

This factor increases (decreases) the quantity demanded of a good:

1. A decrease (increase) in the price of the good

These factors increase (decrease) the demand for a good:

1. A rise (fall) in consumer income
2. An increase (decline) in the number of consumers in the market

3a. A rise (fall) in the price of a substitute good
3b. A fall (rise) in the price of a complementary good
4. A rise (fall) in the expected future price of the good
5. Demographic changes: Population increases (decreases) in age groups with strong demand for a good
6. Preferences: Increased (reduced) consumer desires for the good

had in 1970. As consumers became more aware of the health implications of their diet, their preferences changed, shifting the demand for various foods. Trends in clothing, toys, collectables, and in the types of leisure activities that are popular cause continuous changes in the demand for products. Firms may even try to increase the demand for their own products through advertising and information brochures targeted at changing consumer tastes.

The **Thumbnail Sketch** above summarizes the major factors that cause a change in *demand*—a shift of the entire demand curve—and points out that *quantity demanded* (but not demand) will change in response to a change in the price of a good.

PRODUCER CHOICE AND LAW OF SUPPLY

We have now completed the examination of demand and will shift our focus to the supply side of the market. How does the market process determine the amount of each good that will be produced and supplied to the market? We cannot answer this question properly unless we understand the factors that influence the choices of those who supply goods, the producers of goods and services. Often using the business firm, producers:

1. organize productive inputs and resources, such as land, labor, capital, natural resources, and intermediate goods;
2. transform and combine these factors of production into goods and services; and
3. sell the final products to consumers for a price.

Production involves the conversion of resources into commodities and services. Producers will have to purchase the necessary resources at prices that are determined by market forces. Predictably, owners will only supply resources at prices that are at least equal to what they could earn elsewhere. Stated another way, each resource employed has to be bid away from all other uses; its owner will have to be paid its opportunity cost. ***The sum of the producer's cost of employing each resource required to produce the good will equal the product's* opportunity cost of production.**

Opportunity cost of production
The total economic cost of producing a good or service. The cost component includes the opportunity cost of all resources, including those owned by the firm. The opportunity cost is equal to the value of the production of other goods sacrificed as the result of producing the good.

There is an important difference between the opportunity cost of production and standard accounting measures of a firm's cost. Accountants generally do not count the cost of such assets as buildings, equipment, and financial resources *owned by the firm.* These assets have alternative uses and, therefore, costs are incurred when they are used to produce a good. Unless these costs are covered, the resources will eventually be employed in other ways. For now, it is sufficient to think of this cost of employing assets owned by the firm as a normal return (or "normal profit rate") that these assets could earn if employed in another way. For example, the millions of dollars worth of capital, buildings, and equipment held by a shirt manufacturer could also be used in other ways. For one thing, the firm's operating funds could be drawing interest at a bank. If the interest rate was 10%, a firm with $100,000 worth of operating capital could place these funds in a bank (or mutual fund) and earn $10,000 in interest income per year. This income forgone because the funds are tied up running the business is an opportunity cost.

Firms will not remain in business for long unless they are able to cover the cost of all resources employed, including the opportunity cost of resources owned by the firm. Typically, economists will use some measure of an average or normal rate of return as an indicator of the employment cost of assets owned by the firm.

Role of Profits and Losses

Profit
An excess of sales revenue relative to the opportunity cost of production. The cost component includes the opportunity cost of all resources, including those owned by the firm. Therefore, profit accrues only when the value of the good produced is greater than the value of other goods that could have been produced with those same resources.

Business decision makers have a strong incentive to undertake activities that generate **profit,** revenues greater than cost. If an activity is to be profitable, the revenue derived from the sale of the product must exceed the cost of employing the resources required for its production. The opportunity cost of producing a good indicates the value of other goods that might have been produced with the same resources. For example, if the opportunity cost of producing a pair of jeans is $30, this means that the resources used to produce the jeans could have been used to produce other items worth $30 to consumers (perhaps a denim backpack). If consumers are willing to pay more than $30 for the jeans, producing them increases the value of the resources. ***Firms that use resources to supply goods and services for which consumers are willing to pay more than the opportunity cost of the resources will make a profit. The willingness of consumers to pay a price greater than a good's opportunity cost indicates that they value the good more than other things that could have been produced with the same resources.*** Viewed from this perspective, profit is a residual "income reward" earned by entrepreneurs that increase the value of resources.

Loss
Deficit of sales revenue relative to the opportunity cost of production. Losses are a penalty imposed on those who misuse resources in lower-valued uses as judged by buyers in the market.

Sometimes decision makers use resources unwisely. When resources are employed to produce a good or service that has less value to consumers than other things that might have been produced, losses are incurred. **Loss** results because the sales revenue derived from the project is insufficient to cover the opportunity cost of the resources. Losses indicate that the firm has reduced the value of the resources. It would have been better if the resources had been used to produce other things. In a market economy, losses will eventually cause firms to go out of business and the resources will be directed toward other things that are valued more highly.

Profits and losses play a very important role in a market economy. They determine which firms and products will expand and survive, and which will contract and be driven from the market. In 1996, nearly 800,000 new businesses were incorporated in the United States. During the same year, more than 70,000 businesses failed. Although the business failure rate was only 90 out of every 10,000 firms, many more firms incurred losses. Some were taken over by new owners. Marketing studies indicate that only about 55 to 65 percent of the new products introduced are still on the market five years later.[5] Firms come and go at a rapid rate. Business failures are not necessarily bad. To the contrary—as our preceding discussion highlights, losses and business failures direct resources that are being used unwisely toward productive activities that are more highly valued.

Losses are capable of disciplining even the largest of firms. For example, in 1987, General Motors launched the Cadillac Allanté as a $54,700 coupe that would

[5]See "Flops," the *Business Week* cover story, August 16, 1993, pp. 76–82, for a history and explanation of new-product failures in the United States.

appeal to car buyers shifting their demands to European cars in that price range. But the car did not have the qualities consumers wanted at that price. It never sold even half of the 7,000 cars per year that General Motors planned. In 1993, the Allanté went out of production.

Supply and the Entrepreneur

Entrepreneurs undertake production organization, deciding what to produce and how to produce it. The business of the entrepreneur is to figure out which projects will be profitable, and then to convince a corporation, a banker, or individual investors to invest the resources needed to give the new idea a chance. Since the profitability of a project is affected by the price consumers are willing to pay for a product, the price of resources required to produce it, and the cost of alternative production processes, successful entrepreneurs must either be knowledgeable in each of these areas or be able to obtain the advice of others who have such knowledge. Being an entrepreneur means taking on the risk of failure.

To prosper, business entrepreneurs must convert and rearrange resources in a manner that will increase their value. An individual who purchases 100 acres of raw land, puts in a street and a sewage-disposal system, divides the plot into one-acre lots, and sells them for 50 percent more than the opportunity cost of all resources used is clearly an entrepreneur. This entrepreneur "profits" because the value of the resources has been increased. Sometimes entrepreneurial activity is less complex. For example, a 15-year-old who purchases a power mower and sells lawn service to the neighbors is also an entrepreneur seeking to profit by increasing the value of resources—his time and equipment. In a market economy, profit is the reward to the entrepreneur who discovers and acts upon an opportunity to produce a good or service that is valued more highly than the resources required for its production. Profit also creates an incentive for rival entrepreneurs to enter the market and further expand the production of the good for consumers.

Market Supply Schedule

How will producer-entrepreneurs respond to a change in product price? Other things constant, a higher price will increase the producer's incentive to supply the good. New entrepreneurs, seeking personal gain, will enter the market and begin supplying the product. Established producers will expand the scale of their operations, leading to an additional expansion in output. Higher prices will induce producers to supply a greater amount. ***The* law of supply *states that there is direct relationship between the price of a product and the amount of it that will be supplied. As the price of a product increases, producers will be willing to supply more. Correspondingly they will supply less, if the price declines.***

Law of supply
A principle that states there is a direct relationship between the price of a good and the amount of it offered for sale. As the price of a product increases, other things constant, producers will increase the amount of the product supplied to the market.

Like the law of demand, the law of supply reflects the basic economic postulate that incentives matter. Higher prices increase the reward entrepreneurs receive from selling their product. When it becomes more profitable, they will be willing to supply more. Conversely, as the price of the good falls, so does the profitability, and thus the incentive to supply the good. Just think about how many hours of tutoring services you would supply for different prices. Would you be willing to supply more hours of work at a wage of $50 per hour than at $5 per hour? The law of supply suggests that you would, and producers of other goods and services are no different.

Exhibit 3–6 provides a graphic presentation of the law of supply called the *supply curve.* Because of the direct relationship between price and the amount offered for sale by suppliers, the supply curve will slope upward to the right. Read horizontally, the supply curve shows how much of a particular good producers are willing to

As the price of a product increases, other things constant, *producers will increase the amount of the product supplied to the market.*

EXHIBIT 3–6

SUPPLY CURVE

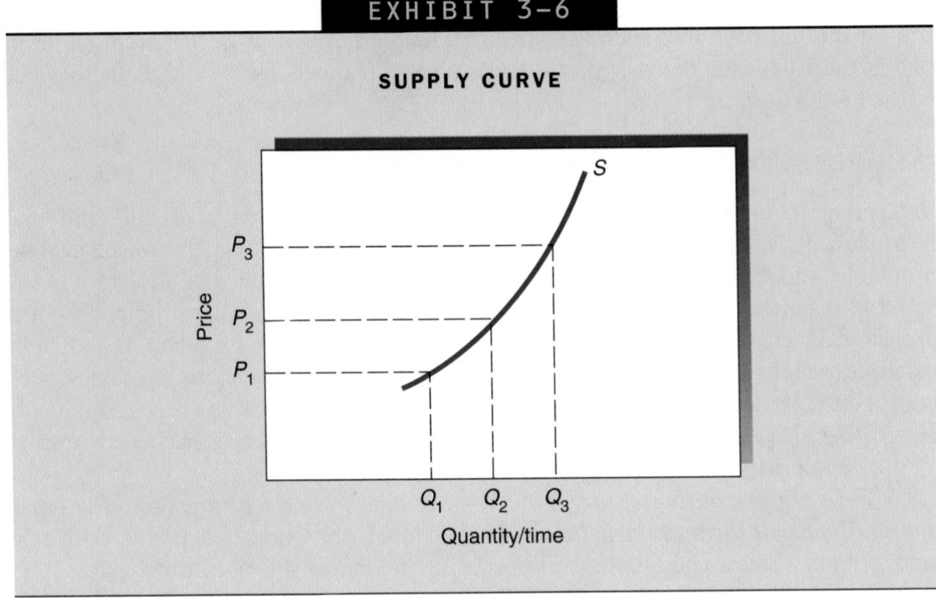

produce and sell at a given price. Read vertically, the supply curve reveals important information about the cost of production. ***The height of the supply curve indicates both (1) the minimum price necessary to induce producers to supply that additional unit and (2) the opportunity cost of producing the additional unit of the good.*** These are both measured by the height because the minimum price required to induce a supplier to sell a unit is precisely the marginal cost of producing it. Just as the demand curve can also be used as a marginal benefit curve, the supply curve can also be used as a marginal cost curve.

PRODUCER SURPLUS

We previously used the demand curve to illustrate consumer surplus, the net gains of buyers from market exchange. The supply curve can be used in a similar manner to derive the net gains of producers and resource suppliers. The height of the supply curve shows both the marginal cost of providing various quantities of a good and the minimum price required to induce suppliers to produce these quantities. As the shaded area of Exhibit 3–7 shows, the net gain of suppliers from the production and exchange of a good is the difference between the market price and the height of the supply curve. This net gain is called **producer surplus.** Suppose that you are a musician and that you would be willing to perform a two-hour concert for $50. If a promoter offers to pay you $200 to perform the concert, you will accept, and receive $150 more than your minimum price. This $150 represents your producer surplus.

Producer surplus
The difference between the minimum supply price and the actual sales price. It measures the net gains to producers and resource suppliers from market trade. It is not the same as profit.

It is important to note that producer surplus represents the gains that accrue to all parties that contribute resources used to produce the good. Producer surplus is fundamentally different from profit. Remember, profit is a return that accrues to the owners of the firm when sales revenues exceed the *total* cost of production. The supply curve reflects *marginal* costs (not total or average) of producing various quantities. As production of a good is expanded, the prices of the resources required to produce the good may rise. If so, the rising resource prices generate gains for resource suppliers and these gains are an integral part of producer surplus. In contrast, the higher

EXHIBIT 3–7

PRODUCER SURPLUS

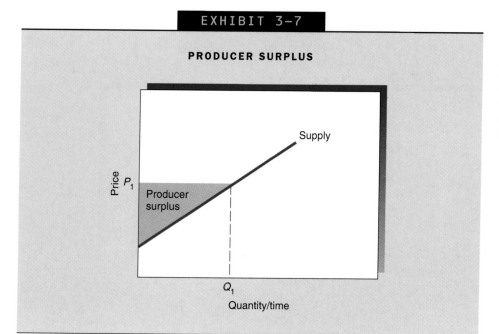

Producer surplus is the area above the supply curve but below the actual sales price. This area represents the net gains to producers and resource suppliers from production and exchange.

resource prices increase the costs of firms producing the good, and thereby reduce their profit. Profit accrues to the owners of the firm, while producer surplus encompasses the net gains derived by all resource owners that help to produce the good, including those employed by or selling resources to the firm.

RESPONSIVENESS OF QUANTITY SUPPLIED TO PRICE: ELASTIC AND INELASTIC SUPPLY CURVES

As in the case of demand, the responsiveness of quantity supplied to a change in price will differ among goods. For some goods, a change in price will lead to a relatively large change in quantity supplied. This will be true when producers can obtain additional resources with only a small increase in their price. When this is the case, the supply curve will be relatively flat. Economists would say that the supply curve is elastic. When quantity supplied is not very responsive to a change in price, supply is said to be inelastic. **Exhibit 3–8** shows both relatively elastic and inelastic supply curves. The flatter supply curve (S_1, on the left) is relatively elastic, while supply curve S_2 (right frame) is relatively inelastic. In the case of the relatively elastic supply curve S_1, an increase in

OUTSTANDING ECONOMIST

Alfred Marshall (1842–1924)

The most influential economist of his era, Marshall introduced many of the concepts and tools that form the core of modern microeconomics, including the short run, the long run, and equilibrium.

EXHIBIT 3-8

ELASTIC AND INELASTIC SUPPLY CURVES

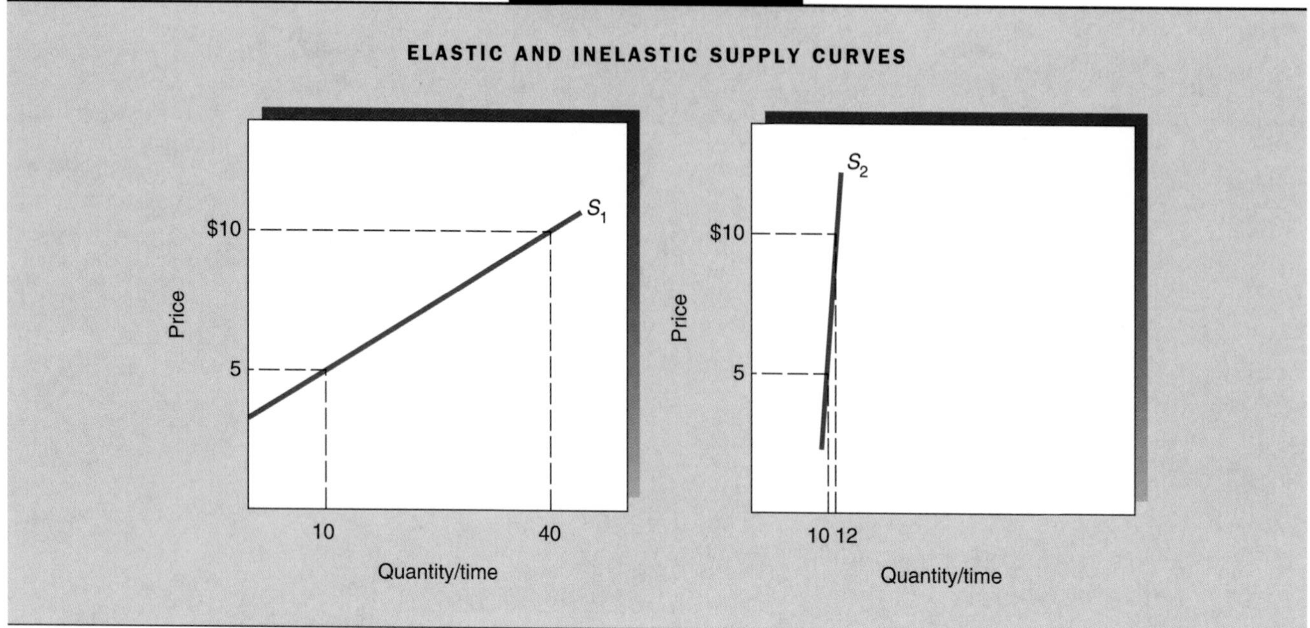

The responsiveness of producer supply to a change in price is reflected in the steepness of the supply curve. The flatter supply curve (S_1) shows a higher degree of responsiveness and is called relatively elastic, while the steeper supply curve (S_2) shows a lower degree of responsiveness and is called relatively inelastic.

price from $5 to $10 leads to an increase in the quantity supplied from 10 units to 40 units. For the inelastic supply curve S_2, the same increase in price leads to an increase in quantity supplied from 10 units to only 12 units. The more inelastic supply, the smaller the output response to a change in price.

The responsiveness of supply to a change in price is affected by time. The great English economist Alfred Marshall introduced the concepts of *short run* and *long run* in order to highlight this point. In the **short run,** firms do not have enough time to build a new plant or expand the size of their current one. Producers are stuck with their existing facility in the short run; they can increase output only by using that facility more intensely. As a result, the immediate supply response to a price change will be limited. Thus, the supply curve for many goods will be relatively inelastic (like the right frame of Exhibit 3–8) in the short run.

Short run
A time period of insufficient length to permit decision makers to adjust fully to a change in market conditions. For example, in the short run, producers will have time to increase output by using more labor and raw materials, but they will not have time to expand the size of their plants or to install additional heavy equipment.

Long run
A time period of sufficient length to enable decision makers to adjust fully to a market change.

The **long run** is a time period lengthy enough for existing firms to alter the size of their plant and for new firms to enter (or exit) the market. Predictably, the change in quantity supplied in response to a change in the price of a good will be greater in the long run than in the short run. Compared to the short run, the supply curve in the long run will be much more elastic (like the left frame of Exhibit 3–8).

CHANGES IN SUPPLY VERSUS CHANGES IN QUANTITY SUPPLIED

As with demand, it is important to distinguish between a change in *quantity supplied* and a change in *supply.* When sellers alter the number of units supplied in response to a change in price, this movement along the same supply curve is referred to as a "change in *quantity supplied.*"

As we previously discussed, profit-seeking entrepreneurs will produce a good only if the sales price of the good is expected to exceed its opportunity cost. Therefore, changes that affect the opportunity cost of supplying a good will also influence the amount of it that producers are willing to supply. These "other factors," such as the price of resources and level of technology, are held constant when drawing a supply curve. Changes in these other factors that influence the opportunity cost of providing the product will shift the entire supply curve for the good. This shift in the entire supply curve is referred to as a "change in *supply*." Factors that increase the opportunity cost of providing a good will discourage production and decrease supply (shift the entire curve inward to the left). Similarly, changes that decrease the opportunity cost of producers will increase supply (shift the entire curve outward to the right).

Let us now take a closer look at the primary factors that will cause a change in supply, a shift in the entire curve to either the right or the left.

1. Changes in Resource Prices. How will an increase in the price of a resource, such as the wages of workers or the materials used to produce a product, affect the supply of the good? There are two ways to view the effects of changing resource prices. First, higher resource prices will increase the cost of production, reducing the profitability of firms buying the resources to supply the good. The higher cost will induce firms to cut back their output. With time, some may even be driven out of business. As **Exhibit 3–9** illustrates, the higher resource prices and increased opportunity cost will reduce the supply of the good, causing a shift to the left in the supply curve from S_1 to S_2. A second way to view the effect of a change in resource prices is to remember that the height of the supply curve measures the marginal cost of production. Thus higher production costs can be thought of as shifting the supply curve upward, showing that the cost of producing each and every unit has now gone up. We would encourage you, however, to think of an increase in supply as a shift to the right and a decrease as a shift to the left. When remembered this way, decreases in both supply and demand are shown by a shift to the left, while increases in both are shifts to the right.

EXHIBIT 3–9

A DECREASE IN SUPPLY

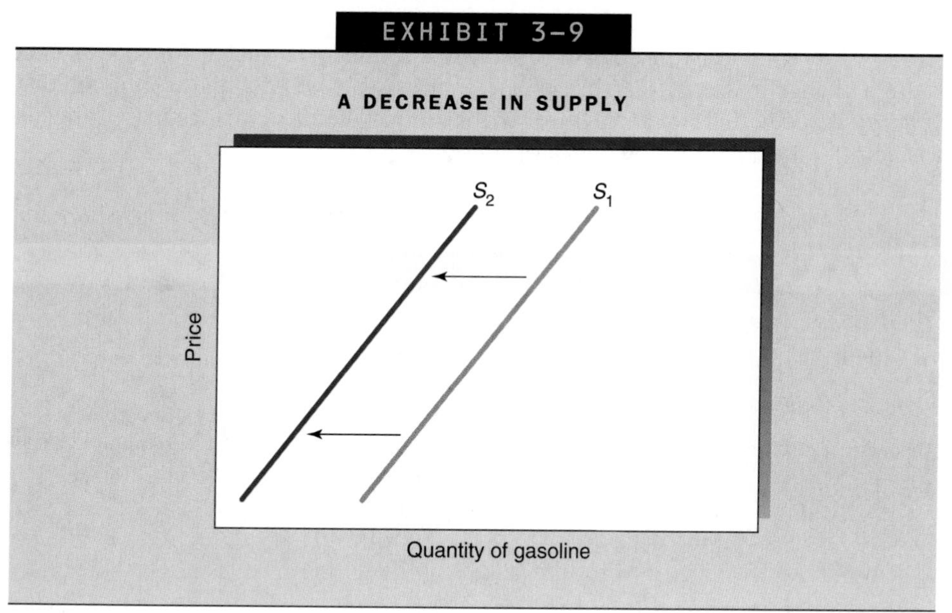

Crude oil is a resource used to produce gasoline. When the price of crude oil rises, it increases the cost of producing gasoline and results in a decrease in the supply of gasoline.

Suppose that the price of a resource used to produce a good falls. How will this affect the supply of the good? Lower resource prices will reduce the cost of producing the good. Suppliers will respond with a larger output, causing the supply curve to shift outward to the right.

2. Changes in Technology. Like lower resource prices, technological improvements—the discovery of new, lower-cost production techniques—reduce production costs, and thereby increase supply (shift the curve to the right). Technological advances have in fact affected the cost of almost everything. Before the invention of the printing press, books had to be handwritten. Just imagine the massive reduction in cost and increase in the supply of books caused by this single invention. Technologically improved farm machinery has reduced cost and vastly expanded the supply of agricultural products through the years. Recent technological improvements in the production of computer chips have drastically reduced the cost of producing such electronic products as calculators, VCRs, microwave ovens, and compact disc players. Robotics have reduced the cost of airplanes, automobiles, and several other types of machinery.

3. Elements of Nature and Political Disruptions. Natural disasters and changing political conditions may also alter supply, sometimes dramatically. During some years, highly favorable weather can lead to higher yields and "bumper crops," increasing the supply of various agricultural products. At other times, droughts may reduce yields, reducing supply. War and political unrest in Iran exerted a major impact on the supply of oil in the late 1970s, as did the invasion of Kuwait by Iraq in 1990. Such factors as these will reduce supply.

4. Changes in Taxes. If the government increases the taxes on the sellers of a product, the result will be the same as any other increase in the cost of doing business. The added tax to be paid by sellers will reduce their willingness to sell at any given price. At each price, only those units for which the price covers all opportunity costs, including the tax, will be offered for sale. For example, the Superfund law placed a special tax on petroleum producers based on petroleum output (not on the producer's past or present pollution level). That raised the cost of producing petroleum products, decreasing the supply of those products.

The accompanying **Thumbnail Sketch** summarizes the major factors that cause a change in *supply*—a shift of the entire supply curve—and points out that *quantity supplied* (but not supply) will change in response to a change in the price of a good.

THUMBNAIL SKETCH

Factors That Cause Changes in Supply and Quantity Supplied

This factor increases (decreases) the quantity supplied of a good:

1. An increase (decrease) in the price of the good

These factors increase (decrease) the supply of a good:

1. A fall (rise) in the price of a resource used in producing the good
2. A technological change allowing cheaper production of the good
3. Favorable weather (bad weather or a disruption in supply due to political factors or war)
4. A reduction (increase) in the taxes imposed on the producers of the good

HOW MARKET PRICES ARE DETERMINED: SUPPLY AND DEMAND INTERACT

Consumer-buyers and producer-sellers make decisions independent of each other, but markets coordinate their choices and influence their actions. To the economist, a **market** is not a physical location, but an abstract concept that encompasses the forces generated by the buying and selling decisions of economic participants. A market may be quite narrow (for example, the market for grade A jumbo eggs), or it may be quite broad when it is useful to aggregate diverse goods into a single market, such as the market for all "consumer goods." There is also a wide range of sophistication among markets. The New York Stock Exchange is a highly computerized market in which, each weekday, buyers and sellers, who seldom formally meet, exchange shares of corporate ownership worth billions of dollars. In contrast, the neighborhood market for lawn-mowing services, or tutoring in economics, may be highly informal, since it brings together buyers and sellers primarily by word of mouth.

Market
An abstract concept that encompasses the trading arrangements of buyers and sellers that underlie the forces of supply and demand.

Equilibrium *is a state in which conflicting forces are in balance. When a market is in equilibrium, the decisions of consumers and producers are brought into harmony with one another. In equilibrium, it will be possible for both buyers and sellers to realize their choices simultaneously.* What could bring these diverse interests into harmony? We will see the answer is market prices.

Equilibrium
A state of balance between conflicting forces, such as supply and demand.

MARKET EQUILIBRIUM

As Exhibit 3–1 illustrates, a higher price will reduce the amount of a good demanded by consumers. On the other hand, Exhibit 3–7 shows that a higher price will increase the amount of a good supplied by producers. The market price of a commodity will tend to change in a direction that will bring into balance the quantity of a good desired by consumers with the quantity supplied by producers. That is, price will tend to move toward equilibrium. If the price is too high, the quantity supplied will exceed the quantity demanded. Producers will be unable to sell as much as they would like unless they reduce their price. Alternatively, if the price is too low, the quantity demanded will exceed the quantity supplied. Some consumers will be unable to get as much as they would like, unless they are willing to pay a higher price. Thus, there will be a tendency for the price in a market to move toward the price that brings the quantity demanded by consumers into balance with the quantity supplied by producers.

Exhibit 3–10 illustrates supply and demand curves in the market for oversize playing cards. At a high price—$12, for example—card producers will plan to supply 600 decks of the cards per month, whereas consumers will choose to purchase only 450. An excess supply of 150 decks (distance *ab* in the graph) will result. Production exceeds sales, pushing the inventories of producers upward. To reduce undesired inventories, some producers of the oversized cards will cut their price in order to increase their sales. Other firms will have to lower their price also, or sell even fewer decks. The lower price will make production of the cards less attractive to producers. Some producers may go out of business, while others will reduce their output. How low will the price go? When it has declined to $10, the quantity supplied by producers and the quantity demanded by consumers will be in balance at 550 decks per month. At this price ($10), the choices of buyers and sellers are brought into harmony. The amount that producers are willing to supply just equals the amount that consumers want to purchase.

What will happen if the price per deck is lower—$8, for example? The amount demanded by consumers (650 units) will exceed the amount supplied by producers (500

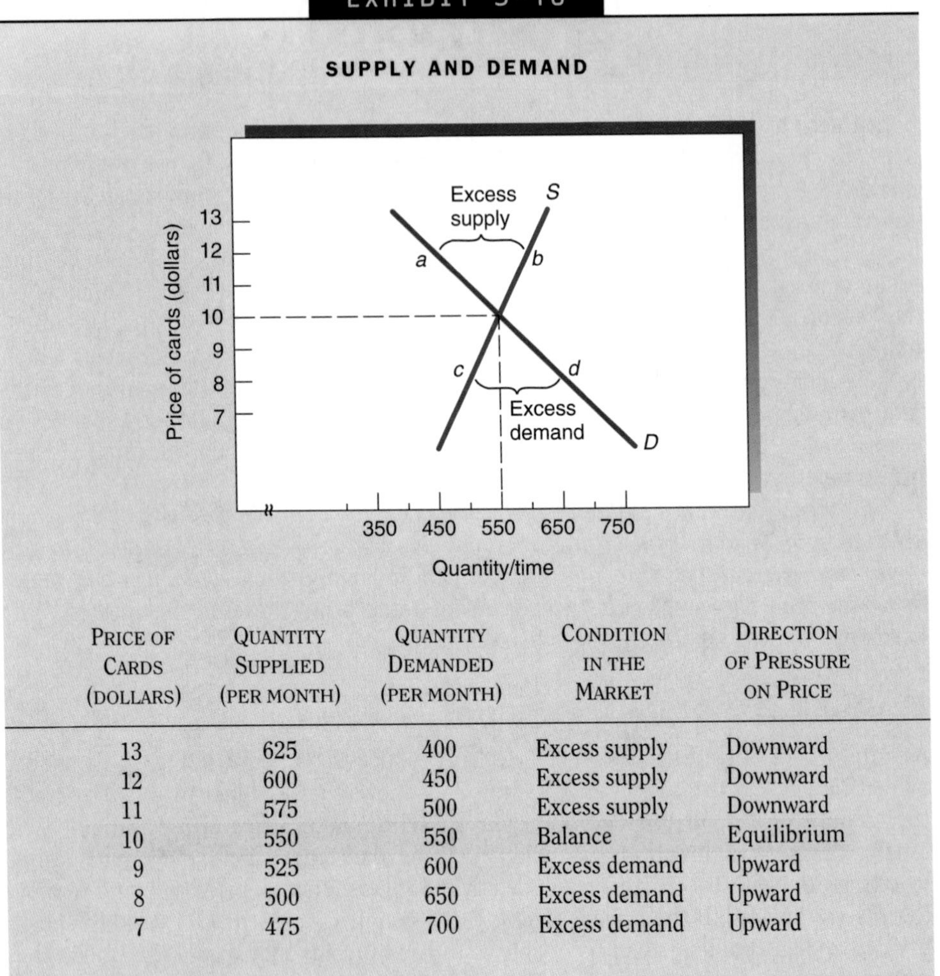

The table indicates the supply and demand conditions for oversized playing cards. These conditions are also illustrated by the graph. When the price exceeds $10, an excess supply is present, which places downward pressure on price. In contrast, when the price is less than $10, an excess demand results, which causes the price to rise. Thus, the market price will tend toward $10, at which point supply and demand will be in balance.

PRICE OF CARDS (DOLLARS)	QUANTITY SUPPLIED (PER MONTH)	QUANTITY DEMANDED (PER MONTH)	CONDITION IN THE MARKET	DIRECTION OF PRESSURE ON PRICE
13	625	400	Excess supply	Downward
12	600	450	Excess supply	Downward
11	575	500	Excess supply	Downward
10	550	550	Balance	Equilibrium
9	525	600	Excess demand	Upward
8	500	650	Excess demand	Upward
7	475	700	Excess demand	Upward

units). An excess demand of 150 units (*cd* in the graph) will be present. Some consumers who are unable to purchase the cards at $8 per unit because of the inadequate supply would be willing to pay a higher price. Recognizing this fact, producers will raise their price. As the price increases to $10, producers will expand their output and consumers will cut down on their consumption. At the $10 price, equilibrium will be restored.

People have a tendency to think of consumers wanting lower prices and producers wanting higher prices. Although true, price changes frequently work in exactly the opposite direction. When a local store has an excess supply of a particular item, how does it get rid of it? By having a sale or somehow otherwise lowering its price (a "blue-light special"). Firms often lower their prices in order to get rid of excess supply. On the other hand, excess demand is solved by consumers bidding up prices. Children's toys around Christmas provide a perfect example. When first introduced, both the Cabbage Patch Doll and the Tickle-Me-Elmo stuffed animal were immediate successes. The firms producing these products had not anticipated the overwhelming demand for their products. Soon every child wanted one of these dolls for Christmas. Lines of parents were forming outside stores before they even opened. Only the first few in line would be able to get the dolls before the store would quickly run out (a sure sign that the store had set the price below equilibrium). Out in the parking lots, and in the classified ads, parents were offering up to $100 or more for these items. If stores were not going to set the prices right, parents in these informal markets would. These examples show that rising prices are often the result of consumers bidding up prices when excess demand is present.

EFFICIENCY AND MARKET EQUILIBRIUM

When a market reaches equilibrium all the gains from trade have been fully realized; **economic efficiency** is present. This criterion is important because economists often use it as a standard with which to judge outcomes under alternative circumstances. The central idea of efficiency is a cost versus benefit comparison. Undertaking an economic action will be efficient only if it generates more benefits than costs. On the other hand, undertaking an action that generates more costs than benefits is inefficient. For a market to satisfy the criterion of economic efficiency, all trades that generate more benefits than costs need to be undertaken. In addition, economic efficiency requires that no trades creating more costs than benefits be undertaken.

Economic efficiency
A market meets the criterion of economic efficiency if all the gains from trade have been realized. An action is consistent with efficiency only if it creates more benefits than costs. With well-defined property rights and competition, market equilibrium is efficient.

A closer look at the way in which markets work can help us to understand the concept of efficiency. The supply curve reflects producers' opportunity costs. Each point along the supply curve indicates the minimum price for which the units of a good could be produced without a loss to the seller. On the other side of the market, each point along the demand curve indicates the consumer's valuation of an extra unit of the good—the maximum amount the consumer is willing to pay for the extra unit. Any time the consumer's valuation of a unit (the benefit side) exceeds the producer's minimum supply price (the cost side), producing and selling the unit is consistent with economic efficiency. The trade will result in mutual gain to both parties. When property rights are well defined, and only the buyers and sellers are affected by production and exchange, competitive market forces will automatically guide a market toward an equilibrium level of output that satisfies economic efficiency.

Exhibit 3–11 illustrates why this is true. Suppliers of a good, bicycles in this example, will produce additional units as long as the market price exceeds the production

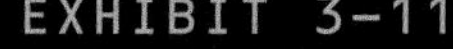
EXHIBIT 3–11

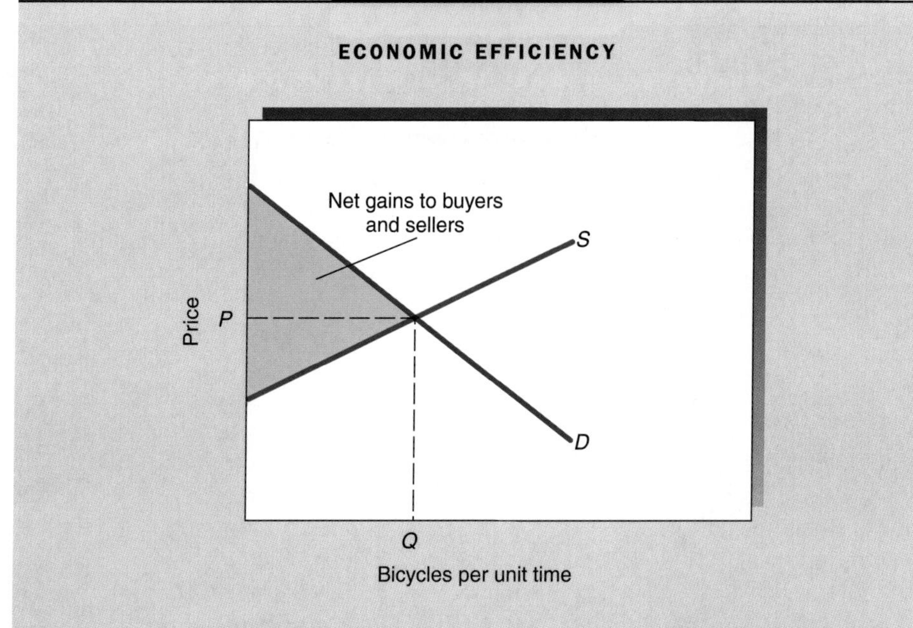

When markets are competitive and property rights are well defined, the equilibrium reached by a market satisfies economic efficiency. All units that create more benefit (the buyer's valuation shown by the height of the demand curve) than cost (opportunity cost of production shown by the height of the supply curve) are produced. This maximizes the total gains from trade, the combined area represented by consumer and producer surplus.

cost. Similarly, consumers will gain from the purchase of additional units as long as their benefits, revealed by the height of the demand curve, exceed the market price. Market forces will result in an equilibrium output level of Q: All units providing benefits to consumers that exceed the costs to suppliers will be produced. Economic efficiency is met because all potential gains from exchange (the shaded area) between consumers and producers are fully realized.

If less than Q bicycles were produced, economic efficiency would be violated and inefficiency would result. This is because the market did not provide all units for which benefits were greater than costs. If more than Q bicycles were produced, inefficiency would also result because units were produced that cost more than the benefits created. With competitive markets, consumers and producers alike will be guided by the pricing system to output level Q, just the right amount from the standpoint of economic efficiency.

HOW MARKETS RESPOND TO CHANGES IN DEMAND AND SUPPLY

How will a market adjust to a change in demand? **Exhibit 3–12** illustrates the market adjustment to an increase in demand. For most of the year, the demand for eggs is primarily for breakfast or the making of other food products. The demand D_1 and supply S indicate the typical conditions throughout most of the year. Typically, the equilibrium price of eggs is P_1. Around Easter time, however, many people purchase extra eggs to decorate or dye with coloring. During the two weeks before Easter, U.S. farmers sell about 600 million more eggs than the average throughout the rest of the year. Thus, at Easter time, there is a sharp increase in demand for eggs (shift from D_1 to D_2 in Exhibit 3–12). This increase in demand for eggs will push their price upward. During the holiday, egg prices are typically about 20 cents higher per dozen. Note that if the price of eggs did not rise, excess demand would be present. At the P_1 price present throughout

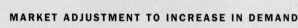

MARKET ADJUSTMENT TO INCREASE IN DEMAND

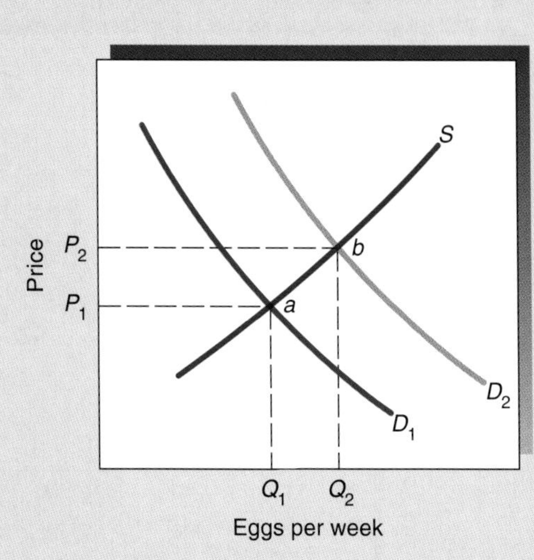

Here we illustrate how the market for eggs adjusts to an increase in demand such as generally occurs around Easter time. Initially (before the Easter season), the market for eggs reflects demand D_1 and supply S. The increase in demand (shift from D_1 to D_2) pushes price up and leads to a new equilibrium at a higher price (P_2 rather than P_1) and larger quantity traded (Q_2).

The tradition of coloring and hunting for eggs causes an increase in demand for eggs around Easter. As Exhibit 3-12 illustrates, this leads to higher egg prices and costly actions by producers to supply a larger quantity during this period.

most of the year, consumers at Easter time would want to purchase more than producers were willing to supply. At the higher P_2 price, consumers will moderate their additional purchases and producers will supply a larger quantity (Q_2 rather than Q_1). Because hens lay fewer eggs when they are molting, farmers take costly steps to avoid having the hens molt around Easter. This can be done by changing the quantity and types of feed used, and by changing the brightness of lighting in the birds' sheds. In addition, farmers attempt to build up larger than normal inventories of eggs before Easter. Eggs are typically about two days old when consumers buy them, but can be up to seven days old during Easter.

In a market economy, when the demand for a good increases, its price will rise, which will provide (1) consumers with more incentive to search for substitutes and to moderate their additional purchases and (2) producers with a stronger incentive to supply more of the product. These two forces will keep the quantity demanded and quantity supplied in balance.

When the demand for a product declines, the adjustment process will provide buyers and sellers with just the opposite signals. Take a piece of paper and see if you can show how a decrease in demand will affect a market. If you've done it correctly, a decline in demand (a shift to the left in the demand curve) will lead to a lower price and a lower quantity traded. What's going on in the diagram is that the lower price (caused by lower consumer demand) is reducing the incentive of producers to supply the good. Thus, when consumers no longer want as much of a good, market prices send the signal to producers to cut back on their production. The reduced production allows these resources to be freed up to go into the production of other goods.

How will markets respond to changes in supply? **Exhibit 3-13** uses the example of romaine lettuce to illustrate the market's adjustment to a reduction in supply. Severe rains and flooding in California during the spring and early summer of 1998 destroyed a large portion of the romaine lettuce crop. This reduction in supply (shift from S_1 to S_2)

EXHIBIT 3-13

MARKET ADJUSTMENT TO A DECREASE IN SUPPLY

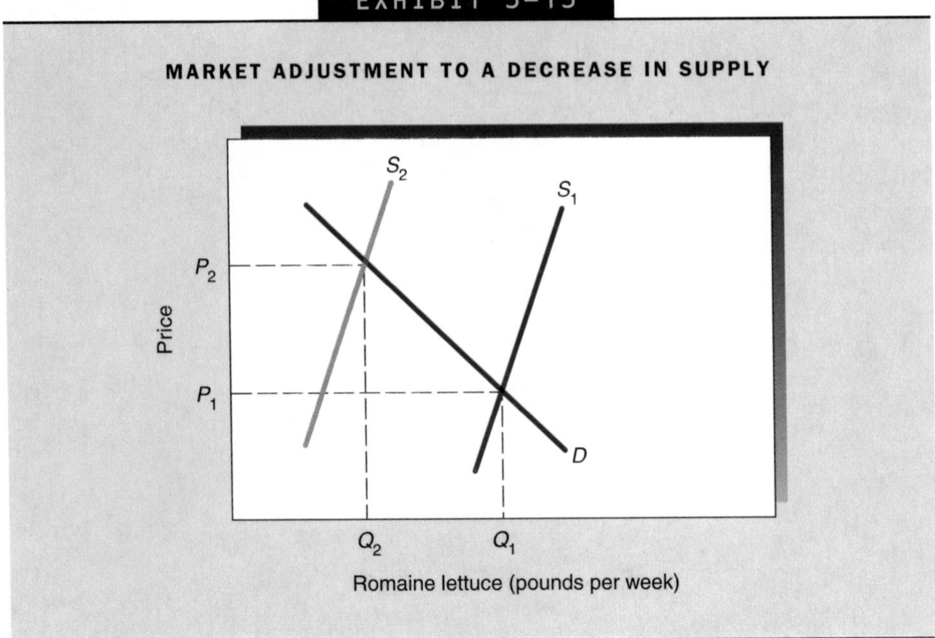

Here, using romaine lettuce as an example, we illustrate how a market adjusts to a decrease in supply. Adverse weather conditions substantially reduced the supply (shift from S_1 to S_2) of romaine during the spring and summer of 1998. The reduction in supply led to an increase in the equilibrium price (from P_1 to P_2) and a reduction in the equilibrium quantity traded (from Q_1 to Q_2).

caused the price of romaine to increase sharply (to P_2). Consumers cut back on their consumption of the now more expensive good. Some switched to substitutes—in this case, probably other varieties of lettuce and leafy vegetables. Producers took extraordinary steps to expand output and replenish the supply. Vegetable farmers shifted from other crops to romaine lettuce. Some greenhouses were even converted to produce romaine lettuce. The higher prices kept the quantity demanded and quantity supplied in balance and provided suppliers with an incentive to expand supply. Eventually, weather patterns returned to normal and the price fell from its temporary high level.

As the lettuce example illustrates, a decrease in supply will lead to higher prices and a reduction in the equilibrium quantity. How would the market adjust to an increase in supply, such as would result from a technological breakthrough or lower resource prices that reduce production cost of a good? Again, try to draw the appropriate supply and demand curves to illustrate this case. If you do it correctly, the graphic will illustrate that an increase in supply (a shift to the right in the supply curve) leads to a lower market price and a larger quantity.

The following **Thumbnail Sketch** summarizes the impact of changes—both increases and decreases—in demand and supply on the equilibrium price and quantity. Sometimes market conditions can be affected by a simultaneous shift in both demand and supply. For example, consumer income might increase at the same time that a technological advance was reducing the cost of producing a good. These two changes will cause demand and supply to increase at the same time. Both curves will shift to the right. The new equilibrium will definitely be at a larger quantity, but the direction of the change in price is indeterminate. Price may either increase or decrease, depending on whether the increase in demand or increase in supply is larger. When both supply and demand shift, either the resulting price (or quantity) will be indeterminate. Which would be indeterminate if an increase in supply and a reduction in demand occurred at the same time? The correct answer is: Price will definitely fall, but the new equilibrium quantity may either increase or decrease. Draw the supply and demand curves for this case and make sure that you understand why.

THUMBNAIL SKETCH

How Changes in Demand and Supply Affect Market Price and Quantity

Changes in Demand

1. An increase in demand (a shift to the right of the demand curve) will cause an increase in both the equilibrium price and quantity.
2. A decrease in demand (a shift to the left of the demand curve) will cause a decrease in both the equilibrium price and quantity.

Changes in Supply

1. An increase in supply (a shift to the right of the supply curve) will cause a decrease in the equilibrium price and an increase in the equilibrium quantity.
2. A decrease in supply (a shift to the left of the supply curve) will cause an increase in the equilibrium price and a decrease in the equilibrium quantity.

TIME AND THE ADJUSTMENT PROCESS

When market prices change, both consumers and producers adjust their behavior to the new structure of incentives. The adjustment process will not be instantaneous, though. Sometimes various signals are sent out by changing market prices and are acted upon only gradually, with the passage of time.

Using gasoline as an example, **Exhibit 3–14** illustrates the role of time as market participants adjust to a decline in supply. During the late 1970s, political turmoil in Iran—an important oil producer—caused a reduction in supply of gasoline, represented by the shift from S_1 to S_2. This led to sharply higher prices for gasoline. Adjusted for inflation, gasoline prices rose from $0.70 in 1978 to $1.20 in 1980. *Initially,* consumers responded to rising prices by cutting out some unnecessary trips and leisure driving, and by accelerating more slowly in order to get better gasoline mileage. Adjustments like these allowed consumers to reduce their consumption of gasoline,

EXHIBIT 3–14

TIME, AND ADJUSTMENT TO A REDUCTION IN SUPPLY

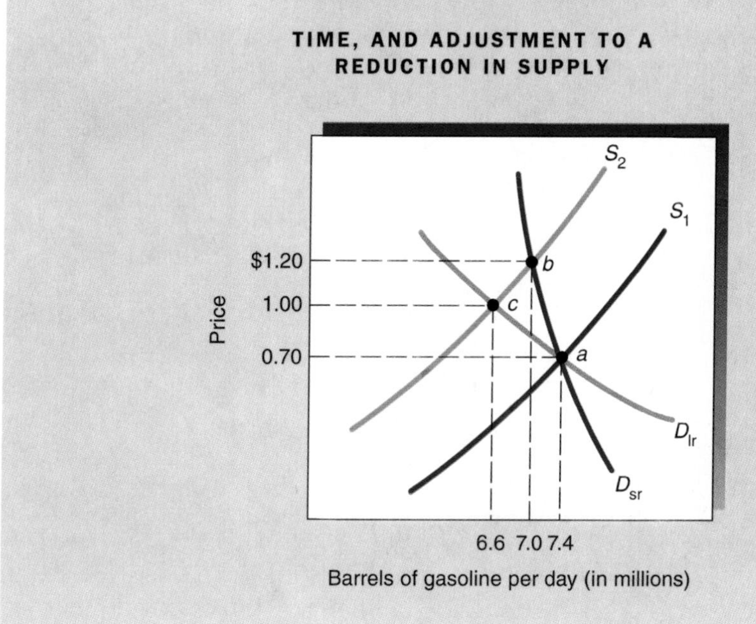

Here we illustrate the adjustment of a market to an unanticipated reduction in supply, such as occurred in the market for gasoline during 1978–1982. Initially, the price of gasoline was 70 cents (equilibrium a*). Supply declined (shifted from* S_1 *to* S_2*) as the result of military conflict and political unrest in the Middle East. In the short run, prices rose sharply to $1.20, and consumption declined by only a small amount (equilibrium moved from* a *to* b*). In the long run, however, the demand for gasoline was more responsive to the price change. As a result, in the long run the price increase was more moderate (equilibrium moved from* b *to* c*).*

but only by a small amount (from 7.4 million to 7.0 million barrels per day), moving them up D_{sr} from point *a* to point *b*. The demand for gasoline in the short run was relatively inelastic, being not very responsive to the change in price.

Given additional time, however, consumers were able to make other adjustments that influenced their consumption of gasoline. For example, as larger cars that used a lot of gasoline became old and worn out, new car purchases shifted toward smaller cars with better gas mileage. Adjustments like this caused a more price-responsive long-run demand for gasoline. By late 1981, consumption of gasoline had declined to 6.6 million barrels per day, and there was downward pressure on prices.

This adjustment process for gasoline is typical. The consumption response to a price change will usually be smaller in the short run than over a longer period of time. As a result, an unexpected reduction in the supply of a product will generally push the price up more in the short run than in the long run.

Similarly, the adjustments of producers to changing market conditions take time. Suppose that specialized new computer software is developed that causes an increase in demand for notebook computers. How will this change be reflected in the market? **Exhibit 3–15** provides an overview. The increase in demand is shown by the shift from D_1 to D_2. Initially, suppliers of notebook computers see a decline in their inventories as the computers move off their shelves more rapidly. Discounts will be more difficult to find, deliveries to buyers will be slower, and prices will begin to rise as sellers ration their limited supplies among the increased number of buyers. The market price rises from P_1 to P_2.

A few aggressive entrepreneurs in the computer-producing business may quickly expand their production of notebook computers. They increase the quantity supplied quickly, by rush orders of new materials, having employees work overtime, and so on. But since it is costly to expand output quickly, the higher market price (P_2) will lead to only a modest increase in output from Q_1 to Q_2 in the short run. The higher prices and improved profitability, however, will encourage other, more deliberate efforts

EXHIBIT 3-15

TIME, SUPPLY, AND ADJUSTMENT TO AN INCREASE IN DEMAND

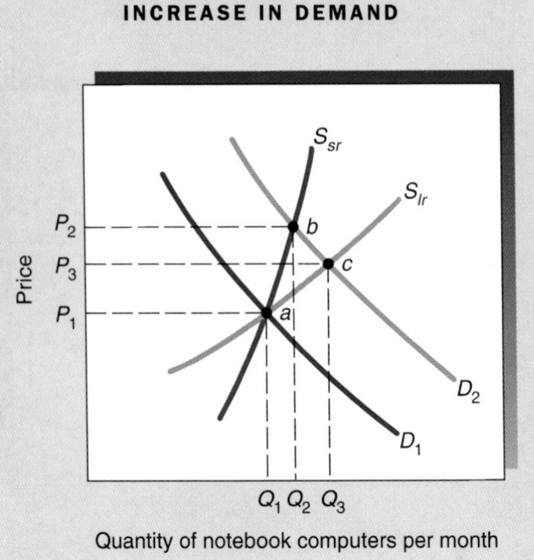

The quantity supplied is generally more responsive to a price change in the long run than in the short run. If the market for notebook computers was initially in equilibrium at P_1 and Q_1, an unexpected increase in demand would push the price of the notebooks up sharply to price P_2 (moved from a to b). Given more time, however, producers will expand output by a larger amount. Therefore, the long-run supply curve will be more responsive to a price change than the short-run curve (S_{lr} is flatter than S_{sr}). The more responsive supply will place downward pressure on price (moved from b to c) with the passage of time.

to supply more notebooks. *With the passage of time,* more resources will be brought into notebook computer production. Some resource prices will have to be bid higher in order to obtain larger quantities. This raises costs, but over time relatively low cost expansion will take place. In the long run the quantity supplied will be more responsive (S_{lr} rather than S_{sr}) and the price increase will be more moderate (P_3 rather than P_2). All these responses will take time, however, even though economists sometimes talk as if the process were instantaneous.

INVISIBLE HAND PRINCIPLE

More than 200 years ago, Adam Smith, the father of economics, stressed that personal self-interest *when directed by the market prices* is a powerful force promoting economic progress. In a famous passage in his *Wealth of Nations,* Smith put it this way:

> Every individual is continually exerting himself to find out the most advantageous employment for whatever capital [income] he can command. It is his own advantage, indeed, and not that of the society which he has in view. But the study of his own advantage naturally, or rather necessarily, leads him to prefer that employment which is most advantageous to society. . . . He intends only his own gain, and he is in this, as in many other cases, led by an invisible hand to promote an end which was not part of his intention. By pursuing his own interest he frequently promotes that of the society more effectually than when he really intends to promote it.[6]

Using the terminology employed by Smith, economists refer to the tendency of competitive markets to direct the actions of self-interested individuals and bring them into harmony with the general welfare (economic progress) as the **invisible hand principle.** Smith's major point was that market prices are able to harness self-interest and put it to work for the benefit of society. Is this really true? Next time you sit down to have a nice dinner, think about all the people who help make it possible. It is unlikely that any of them, from the farmer to the truck driver to the grocer, was motivated by a concern that you have an enjoyable meal. Market prices, however, bring their interest into harmony with yours. Farmers who raise the best beef or turkeys receive higher prices; truck drivers and grocers earn more money if their products are delivered fresh and in good condition; and so on. Let us now take a closer look at how the invisible hand of market prices brings the interests of individuals into harmony with economic progress.

Invisible hand principle
The tendency of market prices to direct individuals pursuing their own interests into productive activities that also promote the economic well-being of the society.

Communicating Information to Decision Makers

Communication of information is one of the most important functions of markets. Markets register information reflecting the choices of consumers, producers, and resource suppliers and tabulate it into a summary statistic called the *market price.* This statistic provides decision makers with valuable information that would be difficult to obtain by any other means. For example, suppose that a drought in Colombia severely reduced the supply of coffee. To ration this reduced supply necessitates that individuals reduce their consumption of coffee. One possibility is to have bulletins on radio and television telling people about the necessity to reduce consumption. However, the information role played by market prices accomplishes this automatically without individuals even knowing about the situation in Colombia. Consumers will see higher

[6]Adam Smith, *An Inquiry into the Nature and Causes of the Wealth of Nations* (New York: Modern Library, 1937), p. 423.

prices for coffee and, even if they have no idea why the prices have changed, they will respond by cutting back on their consumption of coffee.

On the production side, market prices communicate up-to-date information about consumers' valuation of additional units of each commodity. Higher prices signal to producers that the commodity is now more highly valued and encourage producers to expand production. Lower prices signal a reduced desire for the commodity and encourage resources to flow away from the production of such goods into the production of others that are valued more highly relative to their cost. A farmer deciding on the allocation of land between, say, planting corn or green beans would ideally make the decision based upon how intensively consumers want each of the products. Market prices direct the farmer to do just that. When there is a strong demand for corn and therefore its price is relatively high, farmers will plant more corn and fewer green beans. Conversely, if something happened that lowered the demand for and price of corn, farmers will devote less land to corn and more to green beans. Farmers do not need to know how or why consumers decide what to buy. Market prices convey all the information needed for farmers (and other sellers) to make wise decisions.

Market prices also communicate important information about the usage of inputs in the production process. The cost of production, driven by the opportunity cost of resources, tells the business decision maker the relative importance others place on factors of production (for example, skill categories of labor, natural resources, and machinery). A boom in the housing market might cause lumber prices to rise. In turn, furniture makers seeing these higher prices will turn to substitute raw materials such as metal and plastic. Because of market prices, furniture makers will conserve on their usage of lumber, just as if they had known that lumber was now more urgently needed for constructing new housing.

Coordinating Actions of Market Participants

Market prices also coordinate the choices of buyers and sellers, bringing their decisions into line with each other. Excess supply will lead to falling prices, discouraging production and encouraging consumption until the excess supply is eliminated. Alternatively, excess demand will lead to price increases, encouraging consumers to economize on their uses of the good and encouraging suppliers to produce more of it, eliminating the excess demand and bringing the choices of market participants into harmony.

Suppose that farmers produce too few potatoes relative to the desire of consumers. This would lead to higher potato prices. Temporarily, the higher potato prices would discourage consumers from using as many, helping to keep their consumption in balance with the level of production. On the supply side, the higher potato prices would make it more profitable to plant potatoes. In the future, more potatoes will be planted and harvested. Market prices induce responses on both sides of the market in the proper direction to help correct the situation.

The combination of product and resource prices will determine profit (and loss) rates for alternative projects and thereby direct entrepreneurs to undertake the production projects that consumers value most intensely (relative to their cost). If consumers really want more of a good—for example, luxury apartments—the intensity of their demand will lead to a market price that exceeds the opportunity cost of constructing the apartments. The profitable opportunity thus created will soon be discovered by entrepreneurs who will undertake the construction, expanding the availability of the apartments. In contrast, if consumers want less of a good—large cars, for example—the opportunity cost of supplying such cars will exceed the sales revenue from their production, penalizing those who undertake such unprofitable production.

An understanding of the importance of the entrepreneur also sheds light on the market-adjustment process. Since the future is not fully predictable, and information is imperfect, the move toward equilibrium will typically be a groping process. With time, however, successful entrepreneurial activity will be more clearly identified. Successful methods will be copied by other producers. Learning-by-doing and trial-and-error will help producers sort out attractive projects from "losers." The process, though, will never quite be complete. By the time entrepreneurs discover one intensely desired product (or a new, more efficient production technique), change will have occurred elsewhere, creating other unrealized profitable opportunities. The wheels of dynamic change never stop.

Motivating Economic Players

As many leaders of centrally planned economies discovered, people must be motivated to act before production plans can be realized. Market prices establish a reward-penalty (profit-loss) structure that induces participants to work, cooperate with others, use efficient production methods, supply goods that are intensely desired by others, and invest for the future.

No government agency needs to tell business decision makers to use resources wisely (minimize per-unit cost) or to produce those goods intensely desired by consumers. Self-interest and the pursuit of profit will do these jobs. Self-interested entrepreneurs will seek to produce those goods, and only those goods, that consumers value enough to pay a price that is sufficient to cover their costs. Self-interest will also encourage producers to use efficient production methods and adopt cost-saving technologies because lower costs will mean greater profits. Firms that fail to do so, as even giant firms have learned, will be unable to compete successfully in the marketplace.

Similarly, no one has to tell resource suppliers to invest and develop productive resources. Why are many young people willing to undertake the necessary work, stress, late hours of study, and financial cost to acquire a medical or law degree, or an advanced degree in economics, physics, or business administration? Why do others seek to master a skill requiring an apprentice program? Why do individuals save to buy businesses, machines, and other capital assets? The expectation of financial reward is not the only factor, but it is an important stimulus, providing motivation to work, create, develop skills, and supply capital assets to those productive activities most desired by others.

Remember, when you sell something in the market, whether it be a product, a home, or your labor services, the price you will receive is determined by how much other people value what you are selling. To get the most from the sale, you must figure out the best way to provide the most value to potential buyers. The same incentive that motivates sellers to fix up homes before selling them, motivates workers to invest in an education in a field valued by others.

Prices and Market Order

At the beginning of this chapter, we asked you to reflect on why the grocery stores in your local community have approximately the right amount of milk, bread, vegetables, and other goods—an amount sufficiently large that the goods are nearly always available but not so large that spoilage and waste are a problem. We might also reflect on other products. How is it that refrigerators, automobiles, and VCRs, produced at diverse places around the world, are supplied in the U.S. market in approximately the same amount that they are demanded by consumers? The answer is that the invisible hand of market prices directs self-interested individuals into cooperative action and brings their choices into harmony.

The invisible hand principle is difficult for many people to grasp because there is a natural tendency to associate order with central direction. Surely some central authority must be in charge. But this is not the case. ***The pricing system, reflecting the choices of literally millions of consumers, producers, and resource owners, is providing the direction.*** The market process works so automatically that most give little thought to it. They simply take it for granted that the goods most people value will be produced in approximately the quantities that consumers want to purchase.

Perhaps an illustration will enhance your understanding of both the operation and importance of the invisible hand principle. Visualize a busy limited-access highway with four lanes of traffic moving in each direction. No central planning agency assigns lanes and directs traffic. No one tells drivers when to shift to the right, middle, or left lane. Drivers are left to choose for themselves. Nonetheless, they do not all try to drive in the same lane. Why? Drivers are alert for adjustment opportunities that offer personal gain. When traffic in a lane slows due to congestion, some drivers will shift to other lanes and thereby smooth out the flow of traffic among the lanes. Even though central planning is absent, this process of mutual adjustments by the individual drivers results in order and social cooperation. In fact, the degree of social cooperation is generally well beyond what could be achieved if central coordination were attempted—if, for example, each vehicle were assigned a lane. Drivers acting in their own interests and switching to less congested lanes promote the most orderly and quickest flow of traffic for everyone.

Market participation is a lot like driving on the freeway. Success is dependent upon one's ability to act on opportunities. Like the amount of traffic in a lane, profits and losses provide market participants with information concerning the advantages and disadvantages of alternative economic activities. Losses indicate that an economic activity is congested, and, as a result, producers are unable to cover their costs. Successful market participants will shift their resources away from such activities toward other, more valuable uses. Conversely, profits are indicative of an open lane, the opportunity to experience gain if one shifts into an activity where price is currently high relative to per-unit cost. As producers and resource suppliers shift away from activities characterized by congestion and into those characterized by the opportunity for gain (profit), they smooth out economic activity and enhance its flow. Order is the result, even though central planning is absent. This coordination brought about by market prices is precisely what Adam Smith was referring to when he spoke of the "invisible hand" more than 200 years ago.

Qualifications

As we noted at the beginning, the focus of this chapter was the operation of markets where rival firms are free to enter and compete and where property rights are clearly defined and secure. ***The efficiency of market organization is dependent on (1) competitive markets and (2) well-defined private property rights.*** Competition, the great regulator, can protect both buyer and seller. The presence (or possible entry) of independent alternative suppliers protects the consumer against a seller who seeks to charge prices substantially above the cost of production. The existence of alternative resource suppliers protects the producer against a supplier who might otherwise be tempted to withhold a vital resource unless granted exorbitant compensation. The existence of alternative employment opportunities protects the employee from the power of any single employer. Competition can equalize the bargaining power between buyers and sellers.

Understanding the information, coordination, and motivation results of the market mechanism helps us see all the more clearly the importance of property rights, the things actually traded in markets. Property rights force resource users—including users who own the resources—to bear fully the opportunity cost of their actions, and prohibit persons from engaging in destructive forms of competition. When property rights are well defined, secure, and tradeable, suppliers of goods and services will be required to pay resource owners the opportunity cost of each resource employed. They will not be permitted to seize and use scarce resources without compensating the owners—that is, without bidding the resources away from alternative users. Neither will they be permitted to use violence (for example, to attack or invade the property of another) as a means to achieve an economic objective.

LOOKING *Ahead*

Although we incorporated numerous examples designed to enhance your understanding of the supply-and-demand model throughout this chapter, we have only touched the surface. In various modified forms, this model is the central tool of economics. The following chapter will explore several specific applications and extensions of this important model.

KEY POINTS

➤ The law of demand states that there will be an inverse relationship between the price of a good and the amount consumers will want to purchase. The height of the demand curve at any quantity shows the maximum price that consumers are willing to pay for that unit.

➤ The degree of responsiveness of consumer purchases to a change in price is shown by the steepness of the demand curve. The more (less) responsive buyers are to a change in price, the flatter (steeper) the demand curve.

➤ A movement along a demand curve is called a change in quantity demanded. A shift of the entire curve is called a change in demand. A change in *quantity demanded* is caused by a change in the price of the good. A change in *demand* can be caused by several factors, such as a change in consumer income or a change in the price of a closely related good.

➤ The opportunity cost of producing a good is equal to the cost of bidding the resources required for the production of the good away from their alternative uses. Profit indicates that the producer has increased the value of the resources used, while a loss indicates that the producer has reduced the value of the resources.

➤ The law of supply states that there is a direct relationship between the price of a product and the amount supplied. An increase in the price of a product will induce established firms to expand their output and new firms to enter the market.

➤ A change in the price of a good will cause a change in *quantity supplied,* a movement along a single supply curve. A change in *supply* is a shift in the curve caused by other factors, such as a change in the price of resources or a technological improvement.

➤ The responsiveness of supply to a change in price is shown by the steepness of the supply curve. The more willing producers are to alter the quantity supplied in response to a change in price, the more elastic (flatter) the supply curve. The supply curve for most products is more elastic in the long run than in the short run.

➤ Market prices will bring the conflicting forces of supply and demand into balance. There is an automatic tendency for prices to bring about an equilibrium where quantity demanded equals quantity supplied.

➤ Consumer surplus represents the net gain to buyers from market trade, while producer surplus represents the net gain to producers and resource suppliers. In equilibrium, competitive markets maximize these gains, a condition known as economic efficiency.

➤ Changes in the prices of goods are caused by changes in supply and demand. An increase (decrease) in demand will cause prices to rise (fall) and quantity supplied to increase (decline). An increase (decrease) in supply will cause prices to fall (rise) and quantity demanded to expand (decline).

➤ Market prices communicate information, coordinate the actions of buyers and sellers, and provide the incentive structure that motivates decision makers to act. As Adam Smith noted long ago, market prices are generally able to bring the personal self-interest of individuals into harmony with the general welfare (the invisible hand principle). The efficiency of the system is dependent on (1) competitive market conditions and (2) securely defined private property rights.

CRITICAL ANALYSIS QUESTIONS

*1. Which of the following do you think would lead to an increase in the current demand for beef?

a. higher pork prices
b. higher incomes
c. higher prices of feed grains used to feed cattle
d. good weather conditions leading to a bumper (very good) corn crop
e. .an increase in the price of beef

2. What is being held constant when a demand curve for a specific product (like shoes or apples, for example) is constructed? Explain why the demand curve for a product slopes downward to the right.

3. What is the law of supply? How many of the following "goods" do you think conform to the general law of supply? Explain your answer in each case.

a. gasoline
b. cheating on exams
c. political favors from legislators
d. the services of heart specialists
e. children
f. legal divorces
g. the services of a minister

*4. A drought during the summer of 1988 sharply reduced the 1988 output of wheat, corn, soybeans, and hay. Indicate the expected impact of the drought on the following:

a. Prices of feed grains and hay during the summer of 1988
b. Price of cattle during the summer and fall of 1988
c. Price of cattle during the summer and fall of 1989

5. What is being held constant when the supply curve is constructed? Explain why the supply curve slopes upward to the right.

6. Define consumer and producer surplus. What is meant by economic efficiency, and how does it relate to consumer and producer surplus?

7. Recent tax reforms make college tuition partially tax deductible for certain families. This should lead to more people wishing to attend college (a higher demand for a college education). How will this affect tuition prices? How will this affect the cost of college to families who do not qualify for the tax deduction?

*8. "The future of our industrial strength cannot be left to chance. Somebody has to develop notions about which industries are winners and which are losers." Is this statement by a newspaper columnist true? Who is the "somebody"?

9. What role does time play in the market adjustment process? Explain why the response of both consumers and producers to a change in price will be greater in the long run than in the short run.

*10. Production should be for people and not for profit." Answer the following questions concerning this statement:

a. If production is profitable, are people helped or hurt? Explain.
b. Are people helped more if production results in a loss than if it leads to profit? Is there a conflict between production for people and production for profit?

11. What is the opportunity cost of production? What does it tell us about the value of other goods that could have been made with the resources? Within this context, define profit and loss.

*12. Suppose a drought destroyed half the wheat crop in France. What is the expected impact on the market price of wheat in France?

13. **What's Wrong with This Way of Thinking?** "Economists claim that when the price of something goes up, producers bring more of it to the market. But the last year in which the price was really high for oranges, there were not nearly as many oranges as usual. The economists are wrong!"

14. What is the *invisible hand principle?* Does it indicate that "good intentions" are necessary if one's actions are going to be beneficial to others? What are the necessary conditions for the invisible hand to work well? Why are these conditions important?

*15. A popular California winery, and the restaurant on its grounds, can be reached only by a tram with gondola cars, similar to those used at ski resorts. Suppose the owners are charging $3 to winery visitors and restaurant diners alike, but are thinking about providing "free rides" to diners. Explain how this change would affect the following conditions:

a. The demand for dining at the restaurant

b. The price and quantity of meals served at the restaurant

16. **What's Wrong with This Way of Thinking?** "Economists argue that lower prices will necessarily result in less supply. However, there are exceptions to this rule. For example, in 1970, ten-digit electronic calculators sold for $100. By 1995 the price of the same type of calculator had declined to less than $15. Yet business firms produced and sold five times as many calculators in 1995 as in 1970. Lower prices did not result in less production or in a decline in the number of calculators supplied."

---

*Asterisk denotes questions for which answers are given in Appendix B.

CHAPTER 4

The division of labour, from which so many advantages are derived, is not originally the effect of any human wisdom, which foresees and intends that general opulence to which it gives occasion. It is the necessary, though very slow and gradual consequence of a certain propensity in human nature . . . ; the propensity to truck, barter, and exchange one thing for another.

Adam Smith[1]

Nations stumble upon establishments, which are indeed the result of human action, but not the execution of any human design.

Adam Ferguson[2]

Supply and Demand: Applications and Extensions

CHAPTER FOCUS

- Can wage rates, interest rates, and exchange rates be analyzed within the supply and demand framework?
- What happens when prices are set by law above or below the market equilibrium level?
- How do rent controls affect the maintenance and quality of rental housing? How do minimum wage rates influence the job opportunities of low-skilled workers?
- What are "black markets"? How does the lack of a well-structured legal environment affect their operation?
- How does the imposition of a tax affect a market? What determines the distribution of the tax burden between buyers and sellers?
- What is the Laffer curve? What does it indicate about the relationship between tax rates and tax revenues?

---

[1]Adam Smith, *An Inquiry into the Nature and Causes of the Wealth of Nations* (New York: Modern Library, 1937), p. 13.

[2]Adam Ferguson, *An Essay on the History of Civil Society* (London, 1767), p. 187.

Markets are everywhere. They exist in many different forms and degrees of sophistication. In elementary schools, children trade baseball cards; in households, individuals trade chores ("I'll clean the bathroom if you'll clean the kitchen"); on street corners, people buy and sell illegal drugs or tickets to concerts and sporting events; and in the stock market, individuals who have never met exchange shares of corporate stock and other financial assets worth billions of dollars each business day. Even in the nonmarket-based former Soviet Union, black markets were present where individuals bought and sold goods at market-determined prices.

Markets will exist regardless of whether they are legal or illegal, formal or informal. Why? Trading with other individuals is a natural part of human behavior that exists regardless of legal and societal conditions. As Adam Smith put it more than 200 years ago (see quotation, opening of chapter), human beings have a natural propensity "to truck, barter, and exchange one thing for another." We all want to improve our standard of living, and recognize that trading with other individuals is the primary way we can achieve this goal. Whenever and wherever people trade, there is a market. Markets are a result of human action, not of human design, as Adam Ferguson points out.[3]

In the previous chapter we saw how market prices, determined by supply and demand, work through the invisible hand to coordinate the actions of buyers and sellers. In this chapter we explore several important applications and extensions of supply and demand. We will begin by analyzing interest rates, wage rates, and foreign exchange rates within the context of supply and demand. We will then see how several types of government interventions alter the operation of markets.

WAGE RATES, INTEREST RATES, AND EXCHANGE RATES

As Juliet says to Romeo in William Shakespeare's *Romeo and Juliet,* "What's in a name? That which we call a rose by any other name would smell as sweet." In different markets, different names are sometimes used for price. The price of labor is generally referred to as a *wage rate.* The term *interest rate* is used when referring to the price paid by a borrower or received by a lender of loanable funds. The price of one currency in terms of another is called the *exchange rate.* Despite their different names, they are still prices. Therefore, when analyzing these markets, these special names will be measured along the vertical (or *price*) axis of a supply and demand diagram. In some instances, special names for the quantity traded in the market are used as well. In the labor market, the number of workers holding jobs, or the number of hours they work in aggregate, is called *employment* rather than *quantity.* Although the names have been changed, the forces of supply and demand and the workings of price within the market remain the same.

---

[3]This theme was a focus of much of the work of Nobel Prize–winning economist Friedrich Hayek.

Linkage between Labor and Product Markets

The production process generally involves (a) the purchase of resources—such things as raw materials, labor services, tools, and the services of machines; (b) transformation of these resources into products (goods and services); and (c) the sale of the goods and services in the product market. Business firms are generally utilized to undertake production. Typically, business firms demand resources—labor services and raw materials, for example—while households supply them. Firms demand resources *because* they contribute to the production of goods and services. In turn, households supply them in order to earn income.

Just as in product markets, the demand curve in a **resource market** is typically downward-sloping and the supply curve upward-sloping. An inverse relationship will exist between the amount of a resource demanded and its price because businesses will substitute away from a resource as its price rises. In contrast, there will be a direct relationship between the amount of a resource supplied and its price because a higher price will make it more attractive to provide the resource. As in the case of consumer goods, prices will coordinate the choices of buyers and sellers in resource markets, bringing the quantity demanded into balance with the quantity supplied.

Resource market
Market for inputs used to produce goods and services.

The labor market is a large and important component of the broader resource market. It is important to note that there is not just one market for labor, but rather many labor markets, one for each different skill-experience-occupational category.

The markets for resources and products are closely linked. Changes in one will also alter conditions in the other. Using the labor market for low-skill, inexperienced workers, Exhibit 4–1 illustrates this point. Reflecting demographic factors, in many areas the supply of youthful, inexperienced workers has declined in recent years. This reduction in supply has pushed the wages of youthful workers upward (increase from \$5.25 to \$6.50 in Exhibit 4–1a). The higher price of this resource increases the

EXHIBIT 4–1

RESOURCE PRICES, OPPORTUNITY COST, AND PRODUCT MARKETS

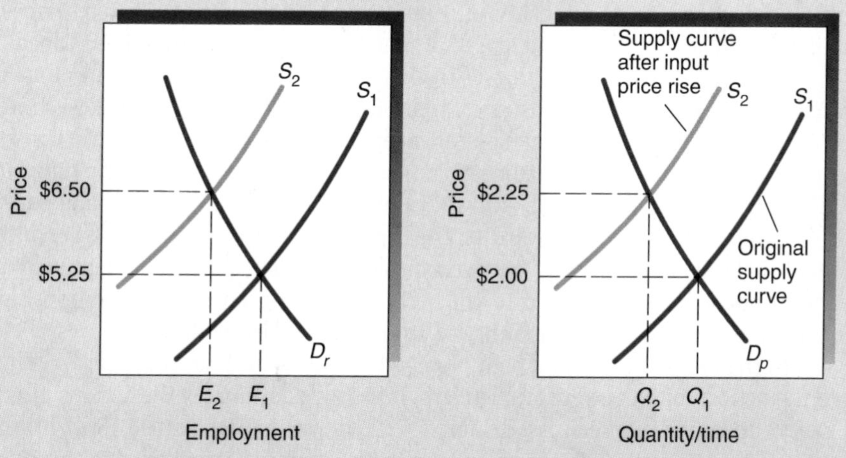

(a) Resource market (youthful, inexperienced labor)

(b) Product market (fast-food hamburgers)

Suppose a reduction in the supply of youthful, inexperienced labor pushes the wage rates of workers hired by fast-food restaurants upward (a). In the product market (b), the higher wage rates will increase the restaurant's opportunity cost, causing a reduction in supply (shift from S_1 *to* S_2*), leading to higher hamburger prices.*

opportunity cost of goods and services the youthful workers help to produce. In turn, the higher cost reduces the supply (shift from S_1 to S_2) of products like hamburgers at McDonald's and other fast-food restaurants, pushing their price upward (Exhibit 4–1b). When the price of a resource increases, it will lead to higher cost, a reduction in supply, and higher prices for the goods and services produced with the resource.

Of course, lower resource prices would exert the opposite effect. A reduction in resource prices will reduce costs and expand the supply (a shift to the right) of consumer goods using the lower-priced resources. The increase in supply will lead to a lower price in the product market.

There is also a close relation between the demand for products and the demand for the resources required for their production. An increase in demand for a consumer good, automobiles for example, will lead to higher auto prices, which will increase the profitability of automakers and provide them with an incentive to expand output. But the expansion in output of automobiles will also increase the demand for and prices of the resources (for example, steel, rubber, plastics, and the labor services of autoworkers) required for the production of automobiles. The higher prices of these resources will cause other industries to conserve on their usage, making it possible for automakers to utilize the additional resources required for the expansion in the output of automobiles.

Of course, the process will work in reverse in the case of a decrease in product demand. A reduction in demand for a product will not only reduce the price of the product but also reduce the demand for and prices of the resources required for its production. As we analyze changes in various markets, we will return to the linkage between product and resource markets again and again.

Loanable Funds Market and the Interest Rate

Loanable funds market
A general term used to describe the broad market that coordinates the borrowing and lending decisions of business firms and households. Commercial banks, savings and loan associations, the stock and bond markets, and insurance companies are important financial institutions in this market.

The **loanable funds market** is highly diverse. Banks, insurance companies, and brokerage firms often act as intermediaries (middlemen) between lenders and borrowers. Bank deposits, bonds, and mutual funds are important financial instruments in this market. In the loanable funds market, borrowers demand the current use of funds in exchange for later repayment, while lenders supply them. As we previously mentioned, the interest rate is the price of loanable funds. To keep things relatively simple, we will assume that there is only a single interest rate. In reality, of course, there is a multitude of interest rates, depending on such factors as risk and length of time the funds are borrowed (or loaned).

The demand and supply curves in this market look like they do in other markets. As part a of **Exhibit 4–2** illustrates, more funds will be borrowed at lower interest rates. A lower interest rate will make it cheaper for households to purchase consumption goods and for businesses to undertake investment projects *during the current period.* Thus, they will borrow more at lower rates, and, as a result, the demand curve for loanable funds will slope downward to the right. On the other hand, lower interest rates will make it less attractive to save (and loan funds). Thus, the supply curve for loanable funds will slope upward to the right, indicating an inverse relationship between the interest rate and the quantity of funds supplied by lenders.

In the loanable funds market, price—the interest rate in this case—will coordinate the actions of borrowers and lenders, just as it coordinates the actions of buyers and sellers in other markets. As Exhibit 4–2a shows, interest rate r_1 will bring the quantity of funds demanded into balance with the quantity supplied. At interest rates greater than r_1, lenders would want to save more than borrowers will demand. This excess supply of loanable funds will place downward pressure on interest rates, pushing them toward equilibrium. If the interest rate was less than r_1, the quantity of funds demanded by borrowers would exceed the quantity supplied by lenders, placing upward

EXHIBIT 4-2

INCREASE IN THE DEMAND FOR LOANABLE FUNDS

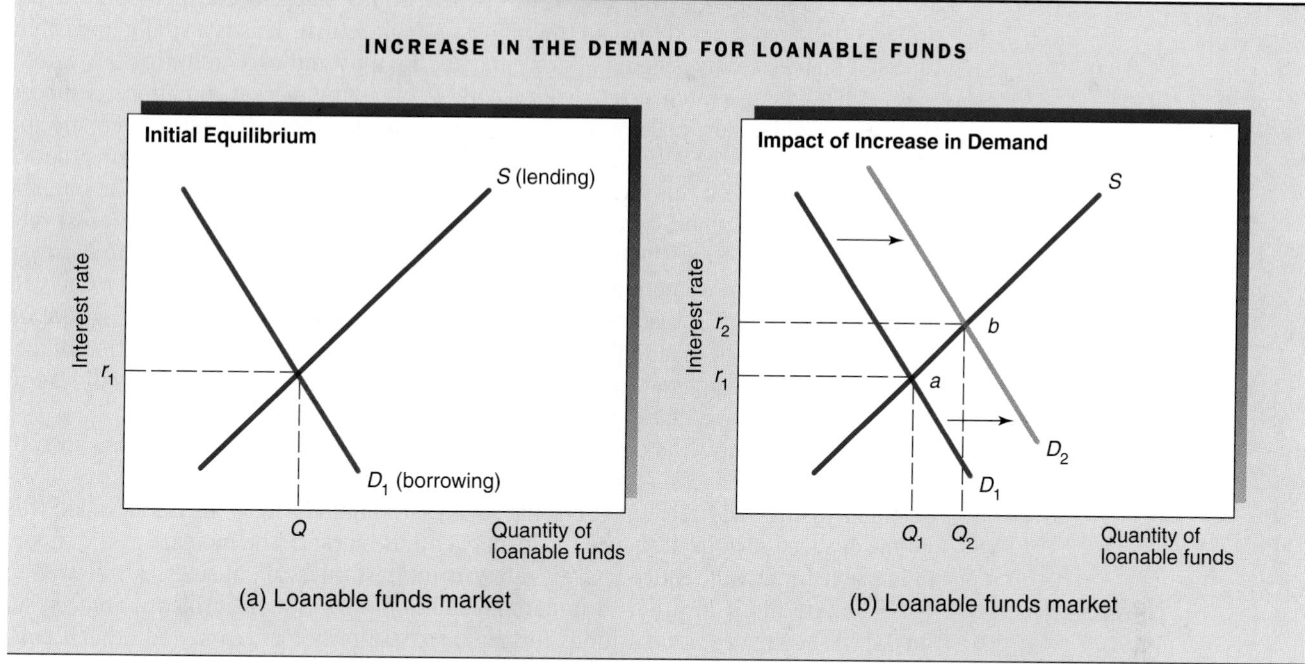

The interest rates will bring the quantity of loanable funds demanded by borrowers into balance with the quantity supplied by lenders (frame a). An increase in demand for loanable funds will push the interest rate up from r_1 to r_2 (frame b). The higher interest rate will encourage additional savings, making it possible to fund more borrowing.

pressure on the interest rates. Thus, market forces will direct the interest rate toward r_1, the rate that brings the choices of borrowers and lenders into harmony.[4]

The interest rate is vitally important because it connects the price of things today with their price in the future. In essence, it is the price that must be paid for earlier availability. This relative price—the cost of spending today relative to spending in the future—is central to the decision making of both households and businesses. Should you buy a car this year or wait until next year? Should you reduce your current consumption so you can save more? The interest rate helps you evaluate choices like these. An increase in the interest rate will make it more expensive for households to purchase a car, house, vacation, or any other good during the current period rather than waiting until next year or some other time in the future. The interest rate is a primary determinant of how households allocate their income between current consumption of goods and services and savings for future consumption.

The interest rate is also central to the investment choices of business decision makers. At any point in time, there are literally millions of potential investment projects that might be undertaken. However, profit-seeking business decision makers will only want to undertake projects that are expected to yield a rate of return greater than or equal to the interest rate. If a project's rate of return is less than the interest rate, the potential investor would be better off simply putting the funds into a savings account or using them to purchase a bond. The interest rate confronts business

[4]The expectation of inflation will influence the nominal interest rate. This topic will be discussed in a later chapter. For now, when we speak of a change in interest rates, we are referring to a change after adjustment for the effects of inflation.

decision makers with the opportunity cost of funds, providing them with a strong incentive to economize on the use of investment funds and allocate them toward the projects that are expected to yield the highest rate of return. This is a vitally important function if an economy is going to grow and get the most out of its resources.

The market interest rate will respond to changing market conditions. Suppose that business decision makers become more optimistic about the future demand for their product, and therefore seek additional funds to expand the scale of their productive capacity. How will this increase in demand for loanable funds influence the interest rate? As part b of Exhibit 4–2 shows, the stronger demand will push the interest rate up from r_1 to r_2. In turn, the higher interest rate will encourage households to increase their savings (the movement along the supply curve from a to b). The higher rate will also discourage some investors from undertaking marginal projects—ones that are no longer expected to be profitable at the higher rate of interest. This combination of factors—increased saving and reduction in borrowing for marginal projects—will lead to a new equilibrium at a higher interest rate.

Alternatively, let's consider how the market would respond to a change in supply. Suppose that a social security reform is enacted that increases the incentive of individuals to channel funds into personal savings accounts for retirement. How will this inflow of added savings influence the loanable funds market? The increase in the supply of loanable funds will reduce interest rates. As interest rates fall, businesses will wish to borrow more funds in order to undertake additional investment projects, and households will borrow additional funds for the purchase of homes, cars, and other items. The result: At the lower market interest rate, businesses and households will want to borrow the additional savings.

Market for Foreign Exchange

Foreign exchange market
The market in which the currencies of different countries are bought and sold.

The **foreign exchange market** is the market where the currency of one country is traded for the currency of another. Americans demand various foreign currencies so they can buy goods, services, and assets from sellers in these countries. If you were to go on vacation to Mexico, for example, you would want to conduct many transactions in the Mexican currency, the peso. One of your first transactions would be to trade some dollars for pesos in the foreign exchange market. However, even if you purchase a Mexican-made product in the United States, it will generally result in a conversion of dollars to pesos so that the Mexican firm can pay its domestic resource suppliers in pesos.

Although purchases from foreigners underlie the demand for a foreign currency, sales to foreigners give rise to the supply. For example, when an American firm sells lumber to a Japanese purchaser, the Japanese buyer will supply yen to the foreign exchange market in order to acquire the dollars used for the lumber purchase. Thus, the sale of goods, services, and assets to foreigners creates a supply of foreign exchange.

Exchange rate
The price of one unit of foreign currency in terms of the domestic currency. For example, if it takes $1.50 to purchase an English pound, the dollar-pound exchange rate is 1.50.

Using the currency of Guatemala—the quetzal—part a of **Exhibit 4–3** shows how "price," the **exchange rate** between the dollar and the quetzal, is determined in the foreign exchange market. (Note: In order to keep the example simple, we assume that the U.S. and Guatemala only trade with each other.) When the dollar price of the quetzal is low, Guatemalan goods will be cheap for Americans. Therefore, Americans will purchase more Guatemalan goods *and therefore more quetzals* at the lower dollar price of the foreign currency. As a result, the dollar demand for quetzals slopes downward to the right. On the other hand, when the dollar price of the quetzal is high, American-produced goods will be cheap for Guatemalans, which will induce them to buy more American goods. Thus, at the higher dollar price of quetzals, American sales to Guatemalans will be greater. As a result, the supply curve for the quetzal will slope upward to the right. The exchange rate will tend to move toward the equilibrium price

EXHIBIT 4–3

INCREASE IN DEMAND FOR FOREIGN EXCHANGE

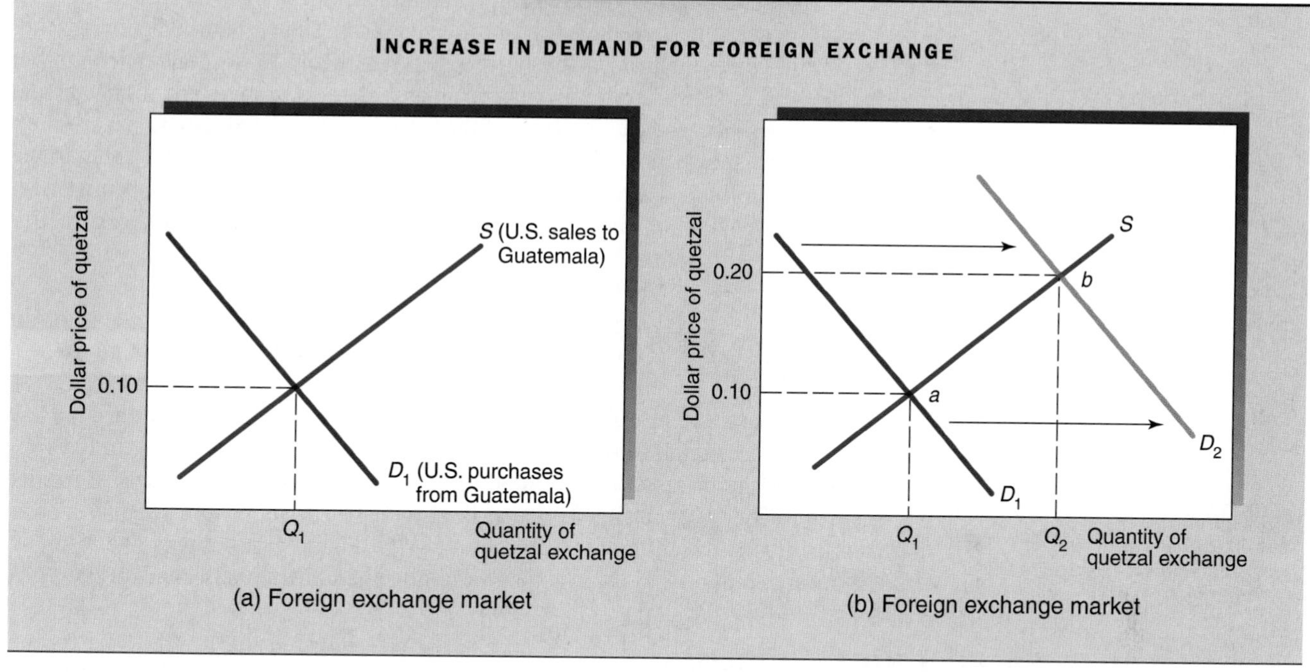

Initially, when the dollar price of the Guatemalan quetzal is $0.10 (10 US cents = 1 quetzal), equilibrium is present in this foreign exchange market (frame a). An increase in the demand of Americans for Guatemalan coffee will also increase the demand for the quetzal. As a result, the dollar price of the quetzal will rise (frame b).

of $0.10 (10 US cents = 1 quetzal), which will bring the quantity demanded of quetzals into equality with the quantity supplied.

Suppose that U.S. citizens suddenly increased their desire for Guatemalan coffee. How will this affect the dollar-quetzal exchange rate? Because every purchase of Guatemalan coffee generates a demand for quetzals, the increase in coffee purchases will increase the demand for quetzals. As part b of Exhibit 4–3 shows, this increase in demand will cause the dollar price of the quetzal to rise to $0.20 (20 cents). How will this affect the cost to a Guatemalan citizen of purchasing a product made in the United States? To answer this, we must first express the exchange rate from the perspective of a Guatemalan citizen. Prior to this change, one quetzal was equal to 10 U.S. cents. Thus, it took 10 quetzals to buy one U.S. dollar. After the dollar price of the quetzal increased to 20 U.S. cents, one U.S. dollar could be purchased for only 5 quetzals. Thus, a U.S.-made product that sells for a price of $100 used to cost the Guatemalan citizen 1,000 quetzals. At the new exchange rate, however, the price of the $100 product has fallen to 500 quetzals. The lower price means that Guatemalan citizens will purchase more American-made products. Thus, the higher U.S. demand for Guatemalan coffee, which results in more imports from Guatemala, will also encourage American exports to Guatemala.

Changes in the exchange rate are vitally important because they alter the prices of all goods, services, and assets that are traded in international markets. They also provide business decision makers with information that will help them compare purchase prices and production costs across countries. Should a business choose to produce output in Mexico, Thailand, the United States, or some other country? Wage rates for most types of labor are likely to be lower in Mexico and Thailand than in the

United States. However, there are several disadvantages of locating a plant in another country. If the good is going to be sold in the United States, transportation costs will probably be higher if it is produced in another country. The risks accompanying contract violations and insecurity of property rights are likely to be greater in another country. Exchange rates will help businesses analyze cost advantages and disadvantages like these. As we proceed, we will return to these topics and related issues.

We have shown how market prices, from wage rates to interest rates to exchange rates, coordinate the actions of buyers and sellers. What would happen if prices were fixed either below or above the market equilibrium? We will now turn to this question.

THE ECONOMICS OF PRICE CONTROLS

Buyers often believe that prices are too high, while sellers complain that they are too low. Unhappy with prices established by market forces, various groups may seek to have the government set the prices of certain products. Government-mandated prices are called **price controls.** They may be either price ceilings, which set a maximum price for a product, or price floors, which impose a minimum price. Fixing prices seems like a simple, straightforward solution. However, do not forget the phenomenon of secondary effects.

Price controls
Government-mandated prices; they may be either greater or less than the market equilibrium price.

PRICE CEILINGS

A **price ceiling** is a legal restriction that prohibits exchanges at prices greater than a designated price—the ceiling price. When imposed below the market equilibrium, the price ceiling will alter the operation of the market. **Exhibit 4–4** illustrates the impact of fixing a price of a product below its equilibrium level. Of course, the price ceiling does result in a lower price than market forces would produce, at least in the short run. At the lower price, however, the quantity that producers are willing to supply decreases,

Price ceiling
A legally established maximum price that sellers may charge for a good or resource.

EXHIBIT 4–4

THE IMPACT OF A PRICE CEILING

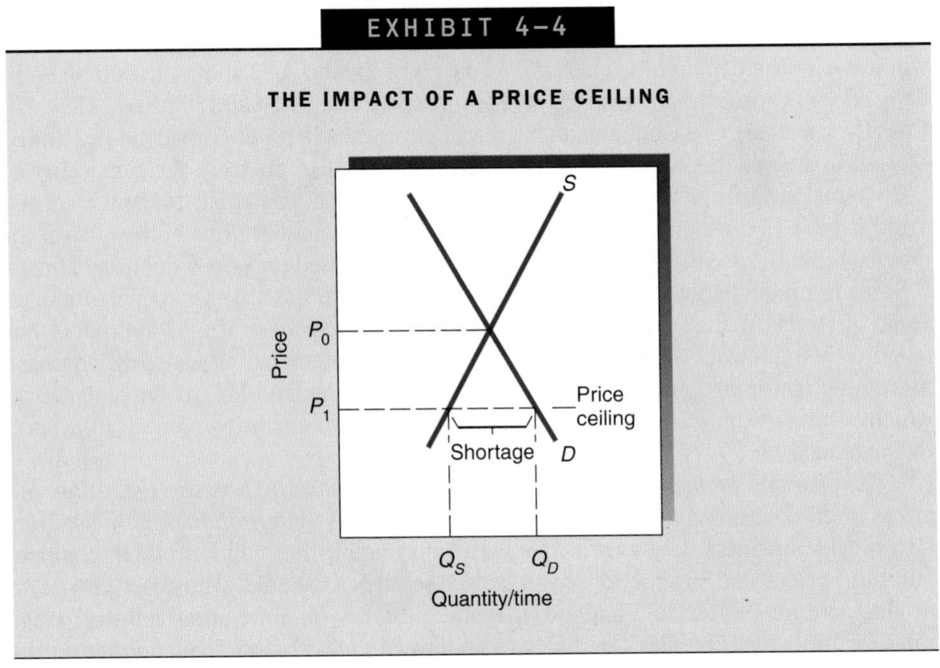

When a price ceiling like P_1 pushes the price of a product (rental housing, for example) below the market equilibrium, a shortage will develop. Because prices are not allowed to direct the market to equilibrium, nonprice elements will become more important. Given the shortage, the nonprice factors will change in ways favorable to sellers.

while the quantity that consumers would like to purchase increases. A **shortage** (Q_D—Q_S) of the good will result, a situation in which the quantity demanded by consumers exceeds the quantity supplied by producers *at the existing price.* After the imposition of the price ceiling, the quantity of the good exchanged declines and the gains from trade fall as well.

Shortage
A condition in which the amount of a good offered for sale by producers is less than the amount demanded by buyers at the existing price. An increase in price would eliminate the shortage.

Normally, the higher price would ration the good to the buyers most willing to pay for it. Because the price ceiling keeps this from happening, other means must be used to allocate the smaller quantity Q_s among consumers seeking to purchase Q_d. Predictably, nonprice factors will become more important in the rationing process. Producers must discriminate on some basis other than willingness to pay as they ration their sales to eager buyers. Sellers will be partial to friends, to buyers who do them favors, and even to buyers who are willing to make illegal "under-the-table" payments. (The accompanying Applications in Economics box, "The Imposition of Price Ceilings during Hurricane Hugo," highlights this point.) Time may also be used as the rationing device, with those willing to wait in line the longest being the ones able to purchase the good. In addition, the below-equilibrium price reduces the incentive of sellers to expand the future supply of the good. With the passage of time, the shortage conditions will worsen. At the lower price, suppliers will direct resources away from production of this commodity and into other, more profitable areas.

What other secondary effects can we expect? ***In the real world, there are two ways that sellers can raise prices. First, they can raise their money price, holding quality constant. Or, second, they can hold the money price constant while reducing the quality of the good.*** (The latter could include a reduction in the size of the product, such as a decline in the size of a candy bar or loaf of bread.) Confronting a price ceiling, sellers will rely on the latter method of raising prices. Rather than do without the good, some buyers will accept the lower-quality product. It is not easy to repeal the laws of supply and demand.

It is important to note that a shortage is not the same as scarcity. ***Scarcity is inescapable.*** Scarcity exists whenever people want more of a good than nature has provided. This means, of course, that almost everything of value is scarce. ***Shortages, on the other hand, are avoidable if prices are permitted to rise.*** A higher, unfixed price (P_0 rather than P_1 in Exhibit 4–4) would stimulate additional production, discourage consumption, and increase the incentive of entrepreneurs to search for and develop substitute goods. This combination of forces would eliminate the shortage.

Rent Control: A Closer Look at a Price Ceiling

Over 200 American cities maintain rent controls, intended to protect residents from high housing prices. Rent controls are a price ceiling. When they push the price of rental housing below the equilibrium level, the amount of rental housing demanded by consumers will exceed the amount landlords will make available. Initially, if the mandated price is only slightly below equilibrium, the impact of rent controls may be barely noticeable. With the passage of time, however, their effects will grow. Inevitably, rent controls will lead to the following results.

1. Shortages and black markets will develop. Since the quantity of housing demanded will exceed the quantity supplied, some persons who value rental housing highly will be unable to find it. Frustrated by the shortage, they will seek methods by which they may induce landlords to rent to them. Some will agree to prepay their rent, including a substantial damage deposit. Others might agree to rent or buy the landlords' furniture at exorbitant prices in order to obtain an apartment. Still others will make under-the-table (black market) payments to secure the cheap housing.

APPLICATIONS IN ECONOMICS

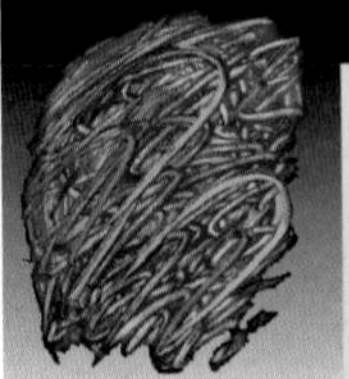

The Imposition of Price Ceilings during Hurricane Hugo

In the fall of 1989 Hurricane Hugo struck the coast of South Carolina, causing massive property damage and widespread power outages lasting for weeks. The lack of electric power meant that gasoline pumps, refrigerators, cash registers, ATM machines, and many other types of electrical equipment did not work. In the hardest hit coastal areas, such as Charleston, the demand for such items as lumber, gasoline, ice, batteries, chain saws, and electric generators increased dramatically. A bag of ice that sold for $1 before the hurricane went up in price to as much as $10, the price of plywood rose to about $200 per sheet, chain saws soared to the $600 range, and gasoline sold for as much as $10.95 per gallon. At these higher prices, individual citizens from other states were renting trucks, buying supplies in their home state, driving them to Charleston, and making enough money to pay for the rental truck and the purchase of the goods and to compensate them for taking time off from their regular jobs.

In response to consumer complaints of "price gouging," the mayor of Charleston signed emergency legislation making it a crime, punishable by up to 30 days in jail and a $200 fine, to sell goods at prices higher than their pre-hurricane levels in the city. The price ceilings kept prices down, but also stopped the flow of goods into the area almost immediately. Shippers of items such as ice would stop outside the harder-hit Charleston area, to avoid the price controls, and sell their goods. Shipments that did make it into the Charleston area were often greeted by long lines of consumers, many of whom would end up without goods after waiting in line for up to five hours. Some of the lucky people who got these items would then drive them back out of the city to sell them at the higher, noncontrolled prices. Shortages became so bad that military guards were required to protect shipments of the goods and maintain order when a shipment did arrive.

The price controls resulted in serious misallocations of resources. Grocery stores could not open because of the lack of electric power; inside the stores, food items were spoiling—thousands of dollars' worth, in some stores. Gasoline pumps require electricity to operate, so, although there was fuel in the underground tanks, there was a shortage of gasoline because of the inability to pump it. Consumers were faced with problems of obtaining money, as ATM machines and banks could not operate without electric power. Hardware stores that sold gasoline-powered electric generators before the hurricane typically had only a few in stock, but suddenly hundreds of businesses and residents wanted to buy them. In the absence of price controls, these generators would have risen to thousands of dollars in price. Individual homeowners would have been outbid by businesses who could have put the generators to use in opening stores and gasoline stations and operating ATM machines. It would have been these uses that could have generated enough revenue to cover the high price of the generators. Individuals who had generators at home would have even found it in their interest to sell them to businesses for the high sum of money involved.

However, the price ceilings prevented prices from allocating these generators to those most willing to pay. Instead, individuals kept their generators, and it was commonplace for hardware store owners who had a few generators on hand to take one home for their family, and then sell the others to their close friends, neighbors, and relatives. In the absence of price rationing, these nonprice factors played a larger role in the allocation process. While these families used the generators for household uses (such as running television sets, lighting, electric razors, and hair dryers), gasoline stations, grocery stores, and banks were closed because of their inability to purchase generators. Thousands of consumers could not get goods they urgently wanted because these businesses were closed. In addition, the flow of new generators into the city effectively ceased, and some were being taken from the city to the less-damaged outlying areas to be sold at higher (noncontrolled) prices. Without price controls, the price of generators would have been bid up to the point where they would be (1) purchased by those who had the most urgent uses for them, and (2) imported into the city fairly rapidly because of the high prices they commanded.

The secondary impacts of the price controls used during Hurricane Hugo in Charleston, South Carolina, highlight the importance of understanding economics and the role of prices in our economy. It is during emergency times such as this, when major reallocations of goods and resources are needed, that reliance on market-determined prices is of most importance. Despite pleas from economists in local newspapers and in the *Wall Street Journal,* the price controls remained in effect, increasing the suffering and retarding the recovery of the areas most severely damaged by the hurricane.[1]

[1]See David N. Leband, "In Hugo's Path, a Man-Made Disaster," *Wall Street Journal,* September 27, 1989, p. A22; and Tim Smith, "Economists Spurn Price Restrictions," *Greenville News,* September 28, 1989, p. C1.

2. The future supply of rental houses will decline. The below-equilibrium price will discourage entrepreneurs from constructing new rental housing units. Private investment will flow elsewhere, since the controls have depressed the rate of return in the rental housing market. In the city of Berkeley, rental units available to students of the University of California reportedly dropped 31 percent in the first five years after the city adopted rent controls in 1978.[5]

3. The quality of rental housing will deteriorate. Economic thinking suggests that there are two ways to raise prices. The nominal price can be increased, quality being held constant. Alternatively, quality can be reduced, while the nominal price is maintained. When landlords are prohibited from adopting the former, they will use the latter. Normal maintenance and repair service will deteriorate. Tenant parking lots will be eliminated (or rented). Eventually, the quality of the rental housing will reflect the controlled price. Cheap housing will be of cheap quality.

4. Nonprice methods of rationing will increase in importance. Because price is no longer allowed to play its normal role, other forms of competition will develop. Prohibited from price rationing, landlords will have to rely more heavily on nonmonetary discriminating devices. They will favor friends, persons of influence, and those with lifestyles similar to their own. In contrast, applicants with many children or unconventional lifestyles, and perhaps racial minorities will find fewer landlords who will rent to them. Since the cost to landlords of discriminating against those with characteristics they do not like has been reduced, such discrimination will become more prevalent in the rationing process.

5. Inefficient use of housing space will result. The tenant in a rent-controlled apartment will think twice before moving. Why? Even though the tenant might want a larger or smaller space or might want to move closer to work, he or she will be less likely to move because it is much more difficult to find a vacancy if rent control ordinances are in effect. Turnover will be lower, and many will find themselves in locations and in apartments not well-suited to their needs. In a college town, apartments will end up being rented too heavily to students whose parents live locally (at the cheaper rent they will be less likely to remain living at home and also their parents will have the best connections to local landlords), while students from farther away, to whom the apartments would be better allocated, will find it harder to find a place to rent.

6. Long-term renters will benefit at the expense of newcomers. People who stay for lengthy periods in the same apartment often pay rents substantially below market value (because the controls restrict rent increases), while newcomers are forced to pay exorbitant prices for units sublet from tenants or for the limited supply of unrestricted units—typically newly constructed and thus temporarily exempted. Distortions and inequities result. A book on housing and the homeless by William Tucker reports several examples, such as "actress Ann Turkel, who paid $2,350 per month for a seven-room, four-and-a-half bathroom duplex on the East Side (of New York City). . . . Identical apartments in the building were subletting for $6,500."[6] Turkel had been spending only two months each year in New York. "Former mayor Edward Koch . . . pays

[5]William Tucker, *The Excluded Americans* (Washington, D.C.: Regnery Gateway, 1990), p. 162. For a more detailed exposition on rent controls, see Walter Block, "Rent Controls," in *Fortune Encyclopedia of Economics,* ed. David Henderson (New York: Warner Books, 1993).

[6]Tucker, *The Excluded Americans,* p. 248.

Rent controls lead to shortages, poor maintenance, and deterioration in the quality of renting housing.

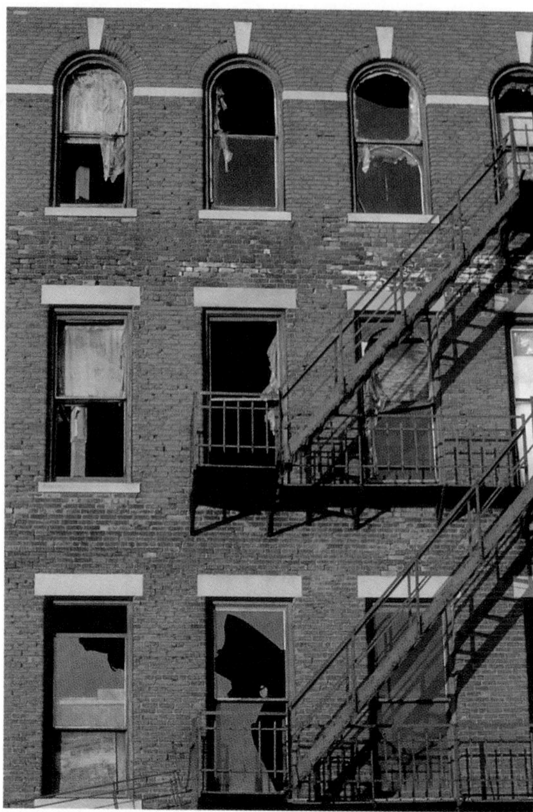

$441.49 a month for a large, one-bedroom apartment . . . that would probably be worth $1,200 in an unregulated market. Koch kept the apartment the entire twelve years he lived in Gracie Mansion (the official mayor's residence)." Tucker uses these and many other such cases to illustrate the distortions brought on by the control of rental prices.

Imposition of rent controls may look like a simple method of dealing with high housing prices. However, the analysis of price ceilings and the experiences where they have been imposed indicate that they cause other problems, including a decline in the supply of rental housing, poor maintenance, and shortages. In the words of Swedish economist Assar Lindbeck: "In many cases rent control appears to be the most efficient technique presently known to destroy a city—except for bombing."[7] Though this may overstate the case somewhat, Lindbeck's point is well taken.

Price floor
A legally established minimum price that buyers must pay for a good or resource.

Surplus
A condition in which the amount of a good offered for sale by producers is greater than the amount that buyers will purchase at the existing price. A decline in price would eliminate the surplus.

Price Floors

While price ceilings set a maximum price, **price floors** establish a minimum price that can legally be charged. **Exhibit 4–5** illustrates the case of a price floor, which fixes the price of a good or resource above the market equilibrium level. At the higher price, sellers will want to bring a larger amount to the market, while buyers will choose to buy less of the good. A **surplus** (Q_S—Q_D) will result. As in the case of the price ceiling, nonprice factors will play a larger role in the rationing process because the price control stifles the normal function of prices. But, because there is a surplus rather than a

[7]Assar Lindbeck, *The Political Economy of the New Left* (New York: Harper and Row, 1972), p. 39.

EXHIBIT 4-5

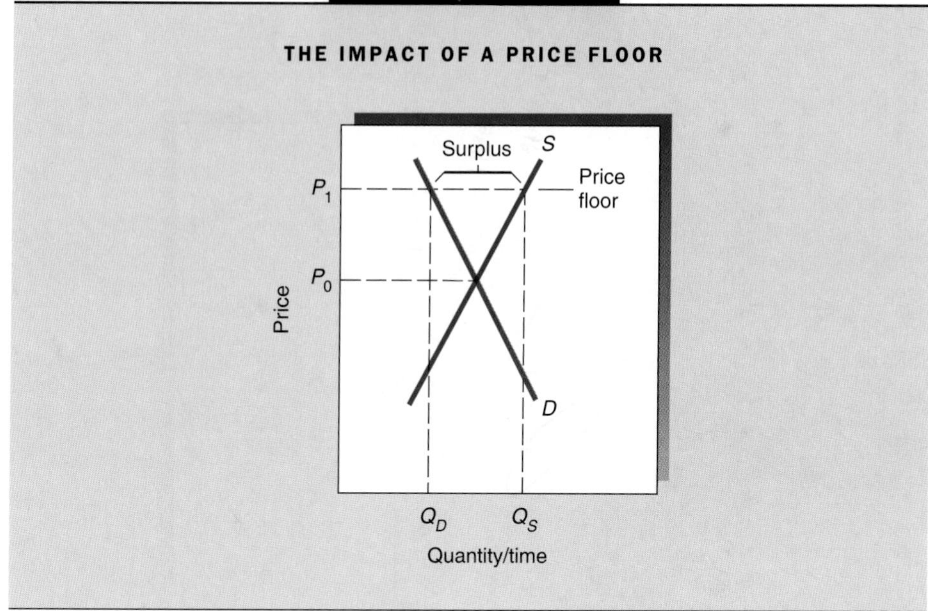

When a price floor like P_1 keeps the price of a good or service above the market equilibrium, a surplus will result. The surplus will cause the nonprice elements of exchange to change in ways favorable to buyers.

shortage, this time it is buyers who will be in a position to be more selective. Buyers can be expected to seek out sellers willing to offer them favors (better service, discounts on other products, or easier credit, for example). Some sellers may be unable to market their product or service. Unsold merchandise and underutilized resources will result.

Note that a surplus does not mean the good is no longer scarce. People still want more of the good than is freely available from nature, even though they desire less *at the current price* than sellers desire to bring to the market. A decline in price would eliminate the surplus but not the scarcity of the item.

Minimum Wage: A Closer Look at a Price Floor

In 1938 Congress passed the Fair Labor Standards Act, which provided for a national **minimum wage** of 25 cents per hour. During the past 50 years, the minimum wage has been increased several times. The current minimum wage is $5.15 per hour.

Minimum wage
Legislation requiring that workers be paid at least the stated minimum hourly rate of pay.

The minimum wage is a price floor. Because most employees in the United States earn wages in excess of the minimum, their employment opportunities are largely unaffected. However, the wages of low-skilled and inexperienced workers will be affected. **Exhibit 4–6** provides a graphic illustration of the direct effect of a $5.15-per-hour minimum wage on the employment opportunities of a group of low-skill workers. Without a minimum wage, the supply of and demand for these low-skill workers would be in balance at a wage rate of $4.00. Because the minimum wage makes low-skill labor service more expensive, employers will substitute machines and more highly skilled workers (whose wages have not been raised by the minimum) for the now more expensive low-skill employees. Fewer low-skill workers will be hired when the minimum wage pushes their wages up. As the wages of low-skill workers are pushed above equilibrium, there will be more unskilled workers looking for jobs than businesses are willing to employ at the minimum wage. Theory indicates that minimum-wage legislation increases the rate of unemployment among low-skill workers. The exceedingly high

If the market wage of a group of employees were \$4.00 per hour, a \$5.15-per-hour minimum wage would increase the earnings of persons who were able to maintain employment but would reduce the employment of others (E_0 to E_1), pushing them onto the unemployment rolls or into less-preferred jobs.

EXHIBIT 4-6

EMPLOYMENT AND THE MINIMUM WAGE

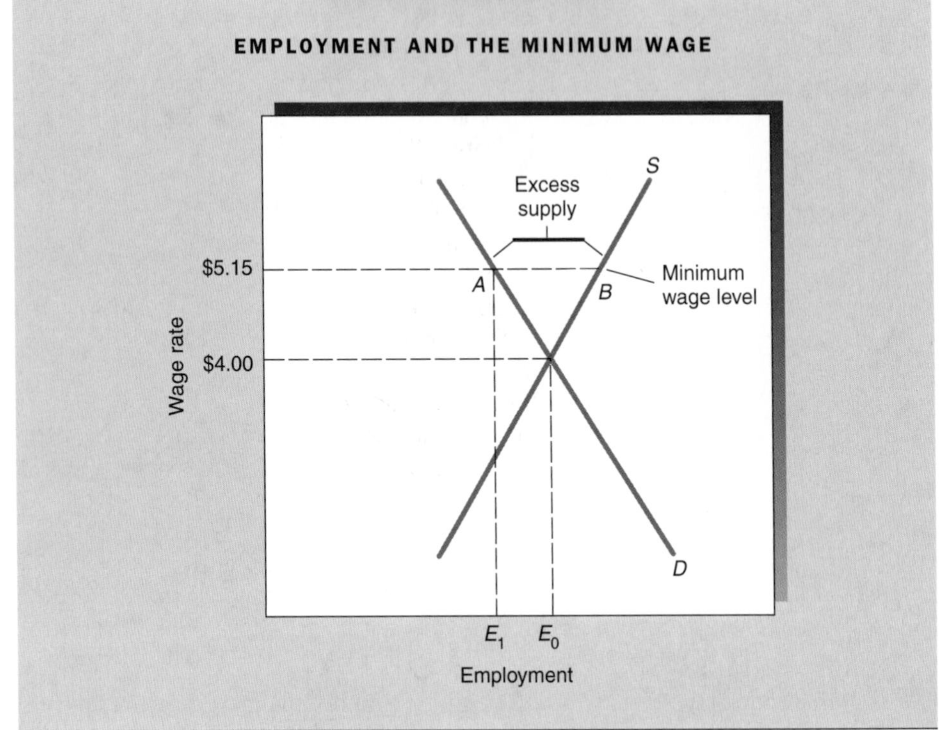

unemployment rate of teenagers (one of the most affected groups) is consistent with this view. In the United States, the unemployment rate for teenagers is more than three times the national average, and the rate for black youth has generally exceeded 30 percent in recent years.

When analyzing the effects of the minimum wage, we must not forget that money wages are only one dimension. As we noted in the previous section, a price ceiling will lead to a deterioration in product quality because sellers have little incentive to maintain quality in order to attract buyers. Correspondingly, when a price floor pushes price—remember wage rates are a price—above equilibrium, buyers will have little incentive to offer nonprice terms of trade attractive to sellers. At an above-equilibrium wage, employers will have no trouble hiring low-skill workers. Therefore, they will have little incentive to offer them convenient working hours, training opportunities, continuous employment, and other benefits and nonwage amenities. Predictably, a higher minimum wage will lead to a deterioration of the nonwage attributes of minimum-wage jobs.

The impact of the minimum wage on the opportunity of youthful workers to acquire experience and training is particularly important. Many young, inexperienced workers face a dilemma: They cannot find a job without experience (or skills), but they cannot obtain experience without a job. Low-paying, entry-level jobs can provide workers with experience that will help them move up the job ladder to higher-paying positions. Employment experience obtained at an early age, even on menial tasks, can help one acquire self-confidence, work habits, attitudes, skills, and a reputation for these attributes that will enhance one's value to employers in the future. The minimum wage makes this process more difficult. It also reduces the number of jobs providing low-skill workers with training. Because the minimum wage prohibits the payment of even a temporarily low wage, it is often too costly for employers to offer low-skill workers jobs with training.[8] Not surprisingly, most minimum-wage jobs are dead-end positions with little opportunity for future advancement.[9]

Of course, workers who are able to maintain employment—most likely the better qualified among those with low-skill levels—gain when the minimum wage is increased. Other low-skill workers, particularly those with the lowest prelegislation wage rates and skill levels, will find it more difficult to find employment. How large are the employment reductions of low-skill workers? Studies indicate that a 10 percent increase in the minimum wage reduces the employment of low-skill workers by 1 percent to 3 percent. This relatively small decline in employment is not surprising given the ability of employers to cut training programs and other forms of compensation. Minimum-wage supporters argue that the higher wages for low-skill workers are worth these relatively small reductions in employment and job training opportunities.

The proponents of a higher minimum wage nearly always argue that it will help the poor. The composition of minimum-wage workers should cause one to question its effectiveness as an antipoverty device. Perhaps surprising to some, in 1997 more than half of all the minimum-wage workers were members of a family with an income above the median. Only a small proportion of minimum-wage workers—12 percent in 1997—were sole earners responsible for the support of a family. A majority (53 percent) of the minimum-wage workers were voluntarily working part-time. Approximately one-third (31 percent) were teenagers. The typical minimum-wage worker is a spouse or a teenage member of a household with an income well above the poverty level. Therefore, even if the adverse impacts of a higher minimum wage on employment and nonwage forms of compensation were small, a higher minimum wage would exert little impact on the income of the poor.[10]

BLACK MARKETS AND THE IMPORTANCE OF THE LEGAL STRUCTURE

Not all markets operate within the framework of the law. Some drugs, such as marijuana and cocaine, are illegal. Prostitution is illegal in all states except Nevada. Many states have passed laws making it illegal to sell (and in some cases buy) tickets to concerts and sporting events at prices in excess of the original purchase price. Despite the legal restrictions, when demand is strong and gains from trade are present, markets will develop. Markets that operate outside the legal system, either by selling illegal items or items at illegal prices or terms, are called **black markets.** People may also turn to black markets in order to avoid high taxes and costly regulations. High taxes have created substantial black markets for cigarettes in such countries as England, Italy, Germany, and Canada. Employees in the United States and other countries are sometimes hired "off the books" and paid in unreported cash in order to avoid payroll and income taxes.

Black market
A market that operates outside the legal system, either by selling illegal goods or by selling goods at illegal prices or terms.

[8]In order the reduce this obstacle, the Netherlands permits the temporary employment of youthful workers at wage rates that are substantially below the minimum wage of that country.

[9]For evidence that the minimum wage limits training opportunities, see Masanori Hashimoto, "Minimum Wage Effects on Training on the Job," *American Economic Review* 72 (December 1982): 1070–1087; and Charles Brown, "Minimum Wage Laws: Are They Overrated?" *Journal of Economic Perspectives* (summer 1988): 133–145.

[10]See William E. Even and David A. MacPherson, "Consequences of Minimum Wage Indexing," *Contemporary Economic Policy,* 14 (October 1996), for evidence on this point.

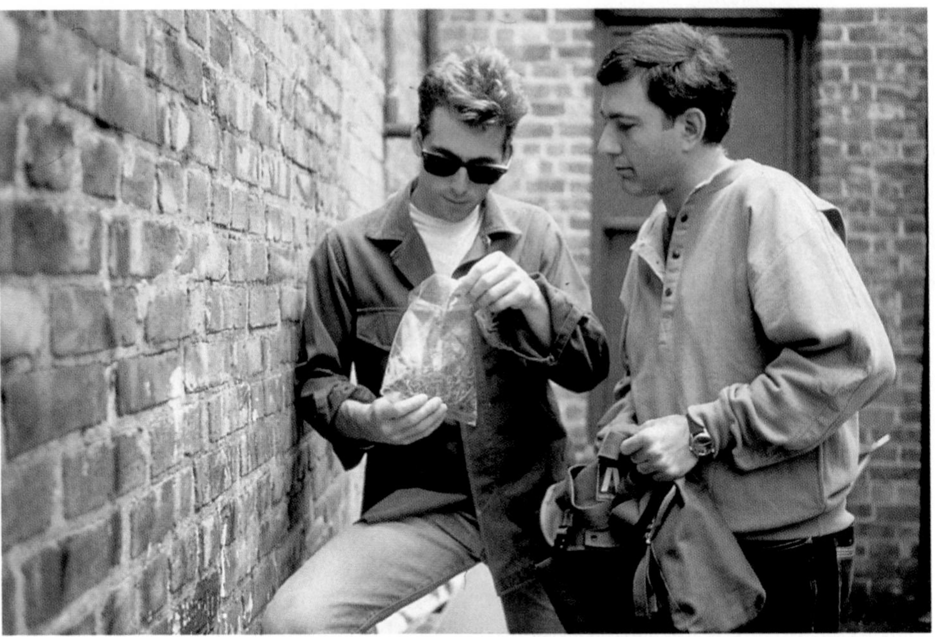

Black markets like those for illegal drugs are characterized by less dependable product quality and greater use of violence as a means of settling disputes between buyers and sellers.

How will black markets work? As in other markets, supply and demand will determine price in black markets. However, because they operate outside the official legal structure, enforcement of contracts and the dependability of quality will be less certain in these markets. Furthermore, participation in black markets involves greater risk, particularly for suppliers. Prices in these markets will have to be high enough to compensate suppliers for the cost of risks they are taking—the threat of arrest, possibility of a fine or jail sentence, and so on. Perhaps most important, there are no legal channels for the peaceful settlement of disputes in black markets. When a buyer or seller fails to deliver, it is the other party who must try to enforce it, usually through the threat of physical force.

Compared to normal markets, black markets are characterized by a higher incidence of defective products, higher profit rates (for those who do not get caught), and greater use of violence. The incidence of phony tickets purchased from street dealers and deaths caused by toxic drugs indicates that the presence of defective goods in these markets is high. Certainly the expensive clothes and automobiles of many drug dealers suggest that monetary profit is relatively high for those who manage to avoid major conflicts with the law. Evidence concerning the use of violence as a means of settling disputes arising from black market transactions is widespread. Illegal drug markets clearly illustrate this point. In New York City during a six-month period in 1988, there were 414 murders, of which 218 were classified as drug-related. Some were committed by persons under the influence of drugs who committed a crime they would not normally have committed. These drug-induced murders accounted for only 29 of the murders, and, of these, 21 were committed by individuals under the influence of alcohol. The remaining 189 murders were all associated with bad trades and competition among dealers in the illegal drug market.

The U.S. experience during the Prohibition era also illustrates the elevated role of violence in markets operating outside the rule of law. When the production and sale of alcohol was illegal during the 1920–1933 Prohibition period, gangsters dominated the alcohol trade, and the murder rate soared to record highs. There were also problems with product quality (such as tainted or highly toxic mixtures) similar to the ones present in modern-day illegal drug markets. When Prohibition was repealed and the market for alcoholic beverages once again began operating within the framework of law, these harmful secondary effects disappeared.

The operation of black markets highlights a point that is often taken for granted: A legal system that provides for secure private property rights, enforcement of contracts, and access to an unbiased court system for the settlement of disputes is vitally important for the smooth operation of markets. While markets will exist in any environment, they can be counted on to function efficiently only within the framework of a structured legal environment. Such an environment is largely absent in black markets; therefore, more fraud, deception, and violence are observed here. The analysis of black markets also provides insights into current conditions in Russia and much of the former Soviet Union. A well-structured legal system is currently absent in these areas. In fact, markets in Russia are quite similar to black markets in Western Europe and North America. So, too, is their operation. Fraud, deception, and the use of violence are widespread, and, from the viewpoint of economic efficiency, the performance of markets in these areas is relatively poor.

THE IMPACT OF A TAX

How do taxes affect market exchanges? When a tax is placed on the sale of a good, who bears the burden? Economists use the term **tax incidence** to indicate how the burden of a tax is *actually* shared between buyers (who pay more for what they purchase) and sellers (who receive less for what they sell). When a tax is imposed, the government can make either the buyer or the seller legally responsible for payment of the tax. The legal assignment is called the *statutory incidence* of the tax. However, the person who writes the check to the government—that is, the person statutorily responsible for the tax—is not always the one who bears the tax burden. The *actual incidence* of a tax may lie elsewhere. If, for example, a tax is placed statutorily on a seller, the seller may increase the price of the product to consumers, in which case the buyers ends up bearing some, or all, of the tax burden.

Tax incidence
The manner in which the burden of a tax is distributed among economic units (consumers, producers, employees, employers, and so on). The actual tax burden does not always fall on those who are statutorily assigned to pay the tax.

To illustrate, **Exhibit 4–7** shows how a $1,000 tax placed on the sale of used cars would affect the market. (In this hypothetical example, we simplify by assuming that all used cars are identical.) Here, the tax has statutorily been placed on the seller. When a tax is imposed on the seller, it shifts the supply curve upward by exactly the amount of the tax, $1,000 in this example. To understand why, remember that the height of the supply curve at a particular quantity shows the minimum price required to cause enough sellers to offer that quantity of cars for sale. Suppose that you were a potential seller, willing to sell your car for any price over $6,000, but unwilling unless you can pocket at least $6,000 from the sale. Because you will have to pay a tax of $1,000 when you sell your car, the minimum price you will accept *from the buyer* must now rise to $7,000 so that after paying the tax, you will retain $6,000. Other potential sellers will be in an identical position. The tax will push the minimum price at which each seller will be willing to supply the good upward by $1,000. Thus, the after-tax supply curve shifts vertically by this amount.

Before the imposition of the tax, used cars sold for a price of $7,000 (at the intersection of the original supply and demand curves shown by point A). After the imposition of this tax, the price of used cars will rise to $7,400 (the intersection of the new supply curve that includes the tax, and the demand curve, shown by point B). Thus, despite the tax being statutorily imposed on sellers, the higher price shifts some of the tax burden to buyers. A buyer will now pay $400 more for a used car after the imposition of the tax. A seller now receives $7,400 from the sale of a used car, but, after sending the tax of $1,000 to the government, the seller retains only $6,400. This is exactly $600 less

EXHIBIT 4-7

THE IMPACT OF A TAX IMPOSED ON SELLERS

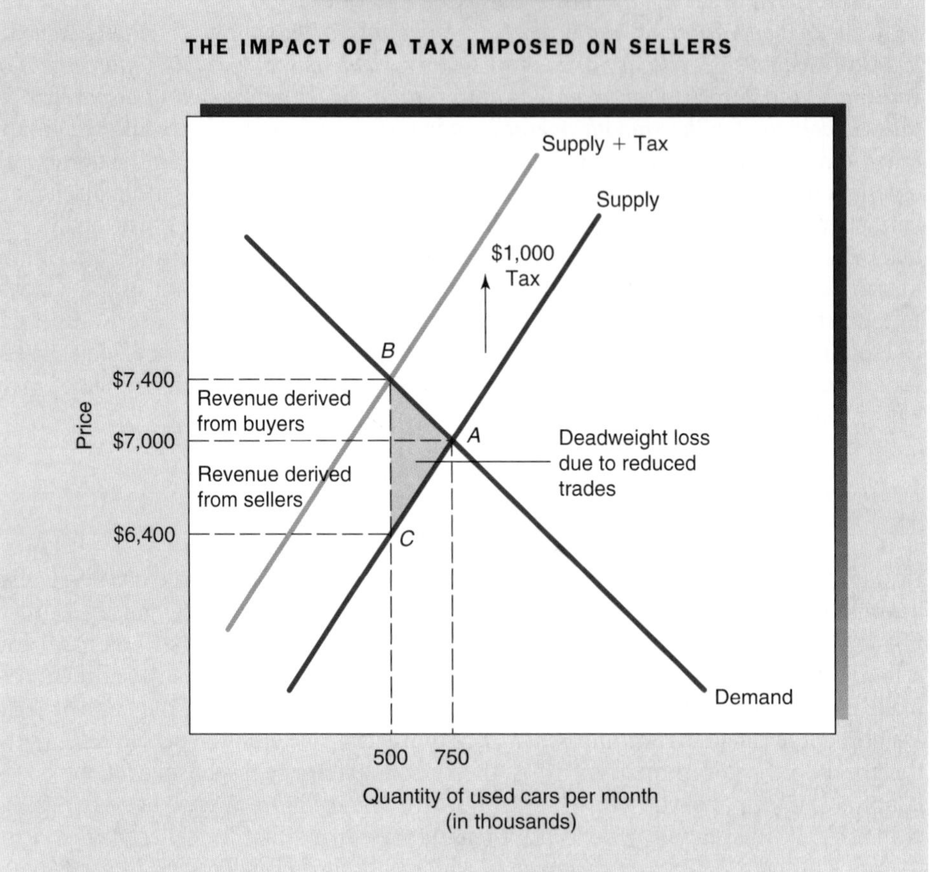

When a $1,000 tax is imposed statutorily on the sellers of used cars, the supply curve shifts vertically upward by the amount of the tax. The price of used cars to buyers rises from $7,000 to $7,400, resulting in buyers bearing $400 of the burden of this tax. The price received by a seller falls from $7,000 to $6,400 ($7,400 minus the $1,000 tax), resulting in sellers bearing $600 of the burden.

than the seller would have received had the tax not been imposed. Because the distance between the supply curves is exactly $1,000, this net price can be found in Exhibit 4-7 by following the vertical line down from the new equilibrium to the original supply curve (point *C*) and over to the price axis. In this case, each $1,000 of tax revenue transferred to the government imposes a burden of $400 on the buyer (in the form of higher used-car prices) and a $600 burden on sellers (in the form of lower net receipts from a car sale).

Tax base
The level or quantity of the economic activity that is taxed (e.g., gallons of gasoline sold per week). Because they make the activity less attractive, higher tax rates reduce the level of the tax base.

Tax rate
The per-unit amount of the tax or the percentage rate at which the economic activity is taxed.

The tax revenue derived from a tax is equal to the **tax base** (in this case, the number of used cars exchanged) multiplied by the **tax rate.** After the imposition of the tax, the quantity exchanged falls to 500,000 cars per month. In this case, the monthly tax revenue derived from the tax would be $500 million (500,000 cars multiplied by $1,000 tax per car).

The Deadweight Loss Accompanying Taxation

Sellers would like to pass the entire tax on to buyers, raising the price by the full amount of the tax, rather than paying any part of it themselves. However, as the price rises, customers respond by purchasing fewer units. Sales decline and sellers must then lower their price toward its pretax level, accepting part of the tax burden themselves in the form of a lower price net of tax. As Exhibit 4–7 shows, the imposition of the $1,000 tax on used cars causes the number of units exchanged to fall from 750,000 to 500,000.

Thus, the imposition of the tax reduces the quantity of units exchanged by 250,000 units. Remember, trade results in mutual gains for both buyers and sellers. The loss of the mutual benefits that would have been derived had the tax not eliminated 250,000 units of exchange also imposes a cost on buyers and sellers. Economists refer to this loss as the **deadweight loss** of taxation. In Exhibit 4–7, the triangle *ABC* measures the size of the deadweight loss. The deadweight loss generates neither revenue for the government nor gains for any other party. It is a burden imposed on buyers and sellers over and above the cost of the revenue transferred to the government. Thus, it is often referred to as the **excess burden of taxation.** It is composed of losses to both buyers (the lost consumer surplus that is the upper part of the triangle *ABC*), and sellers (the lost producer surplus that is the lower part of the triangle *ABC*).

Deadweight loss
A loss of gains from trade resulting from the imposition of a tax. It imposes a burden of taxation over and above the burden associated with the transfer of revenues to the government.

Excess burden of taxation
Another term for deadweight loss. It reflects losses that occur when beneficial activities are forgone because they are taxed.

When a tax is imposed on products currently being produced, the deadweight loss to sellers includes the indirect cost the tax imposes on suppliers of resources to the industry (such as workers). The 1990 luxury boat tax vividly illustrates the potential adverse impact on resource suppliers. Although supporters of the luxury boat tax wanted to shift more of the tax burden toward wealthy yacht purchasers, the actual effects were quite different. As the result of the tax, the sales of luxury boats fell sharply and thousands of workers lost their jobs in the yacht manufacturing industry. Clearly, the boat tax substantially reduced the gains from trade between boat producers and resource suppliers. Thus, the deadweight loss of the tax was quite large. Because of the sharp reduction in luxury boat sales, the tax generated only a meager amount of revenue. This combination—a large deadweight excess burden and meager revenues for the government—eventually led to its repeal.

Actual versus Statutory Incidence

Economic analysis indicates that the actual burden of a tax is independent of whether it is statutorily placed on the buyer or seller. To see this, we must first look at how the market responds to a tax statutorily placed on the buyer. Continuing with the above example, suppose that the government places the $1,000 tax on the buyer of the car, rather than the seller. After making a used-car purchase, the buyer must send a check to the government for $1,000. The imposition of a tax on buyers will shift the demand curve downward by the amount of the tax, as is shown in **Exhibit 4–8**. This is because the height of the demand curve represents the maximum price a buyer is willing to pay

The actual burden of a tax is independent of whether it is imposed on buyers or sellers.

By John Trever, Albuquerque Journal. *Reprinted by permission.*

EXHIBIT 4-8

THE IMPACT OF A TAX IMPOSED ON BUYERS

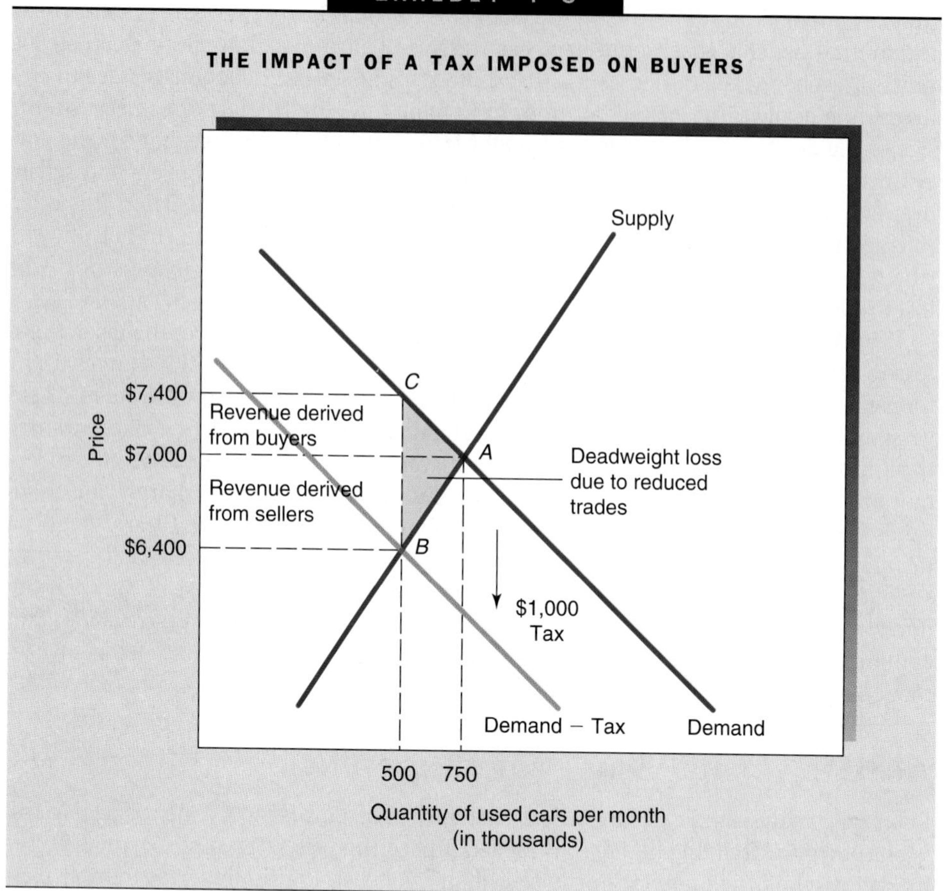

When a $1,000 tax is imposed statutorily on the buyers of used cars, the demand curve shifts vertically downward by the amount of the tax. The price of used cars falls from $7,000 to $6,400, resulting in sellers bearing $600 of the burden. The buyer's total cost of purchasing the car rises from $7,000 to $7,400 ($6,400 plus the $1,000 tax), resulting in buyers bearing $400 of the burden of this tax. The incidence of this tax on used cars is the same regardless of whether it is statutorily imposed on buyers or sellers.

for the car. If a particular buyer is willing and able to pay only $5,000 for a car, the imposition of the $1,000 tax would mean that the most the buyer would be willing to pay *to the seller* was now $4,000. This is because the total cost to the buyer is now the purchase price plus the tax.

As Exhibit 4–8 shows, the price of used cars falls from $7,000 (point *A*) to $6,400 (point *B*) when the tax is statutorily placed on the buyer. Even though the tax is placed on buyers, the resulting reduction in demand causes the price received by sellers to fall by $600. Thus, $600 of the tax is again borne by sellers, just as it was when the tax was placed statutorily on sellers. From the buyer's standpoint, a car now costs $7,400 ($6,400 paid to the seller plus $1,000 in tax to the government). Just as in the case when the tax was imposed on the seller, the buyer now pays $400 more for a used car.

A comparison of Exhibits 4-7 and 4-8 makes it clear that the actual burden of the $1,000 tax is independent of its statutory incidence. In both cases, buyers pay a total price of $7,400 for the car (a $400 increase from the pretax level), and sellers receive $6,400 from the sale (a $600 decrease from the pretax level). Correspondingly, the revenues derived by the government, the number of sales eliminated by the tax, and the size of the deadweight loss are identical regardless of whether the law requires payment of the tax by the sellers or by the buyers.

The equivalence of the actual burden of a tax regardless of its statutory assignment is true for any tax. The 15.3 percent social security payroll tax, for example, is statutorily levied as 7.65 percent on the employee and 7.65 percent on the employer.

The impact is to drive down the net pay received by employees and raise the employers' cost of hiring workers. Economic analysis tells us that the actual burden of this tax will probably differ from its legal assignment. The actual burden imposed on employees and employers, however, will be the same regardless of how the tax is statutorily assigned. Because market prices (here, workers' gross pay) will adjust, the incidence of the tax will be identical regardless of whether the 15.3 percent is levied on employees or on employers or is divided between the two parties.

Elasticity and the Incidence of a Tax

If the actual incidence of a tax is independent of its statutory assignment, what does determine the incidence? The answer: The incidence of a tax depends on the responsiveness of buyers and of sellers to a change in price. When buyers respond to even a small rise in price by leaving this market and buying other things, then they will not be willing to accept a price that is much higher. Similarly, if sellers respond to a small reduction in what they receive by shifting to other areas or going out of business, then they will not be willing to accept a much smaller payment, net of tax. The burden of a tax—its incidence—tends to fall more heavily on whichever side of the market has the least attractive options elsewhere, thus is less sensitive to price changes.

In the preceding chapter, we saw that the steepness of the supply and demand curves reflects the degree of responsiveness to a price change. Relatively inelastic demand or supply curves are steeper (more vertical), indicating less responsiveness to a change in price. Relatively elastic demand or supply curves are flatter (more horizontal), indicating a higher degree of responsiveness to a change in price.

Using gasoline as an example, part a of **Exhibit 4–9** illustrates the impact of a tax when demand is relatively inelastic and supply is relatively elastic. It will not be easy for gasoline consumers to shift—particularly in the short run—to other fuels in response to an increase in the price of gasoline. The inelastic demand reflects this point. When a 20-cent tax is imposed on gasoline, buyers end up paying 15 cents more per gallon ($1.15 instead of $1.00), while the net price of sellers is 5 cents less ($0.95 instead of $1.00). ***When, as in the case of gasoline, demand is relatively inelastic and supply elastic, the primary burden of a tax will fall on buyers.***

In contrast, more of the tax burden will fall on sellers and resource suppliers when demand is relatively elastic and supply inelastic. Using a tax on luxury boats as an example, part b of Exhibit 4–9 illustrates this point. As we mentioned earlier, Congress imposed a tax on the sale of luxury boats in 1990. Later, the tax was repealed because of its adverse impact on sales and employment in the industry. There are many things on which wealthy potential yacht owners can spend their money other than luxury boats *sold in the United States.* For one thing, they can buy a yacht someplace else, perhaps in Mexico, England, or the Bahamas. Or they can spend more time on the golf course, travel to exotic places, or purchase a nicer car or more expensive home. Because there are attractive substitutes, the demand for domestically produced luxury boats is relatively elastic compared to supply. Therefore, when a $25,000 tax is imposed on luxury boats, prices rise by only $5,000 (from $100,000 to $105,000) and output falls substantially (from 10,000 to 5,000). The net price received by sellers falls by $20,000. ***When, as in the case of luxury boats, demand is relatively elastic compared to supply, sellers (including resource suppliers) will bear the larger share of the tax burden.***

Elasticity and the Deadweight Loss

We have seen that elasticities of supply and demand determine how the burden of a tax is distributed between buyer and seller. These elasticities also influence the size of

EXHIBIT 4-9

HOW THE BURDEN OF A TAX DEPENDS ON THE ELASTICITIES OF DEMAND AND SUPPLY

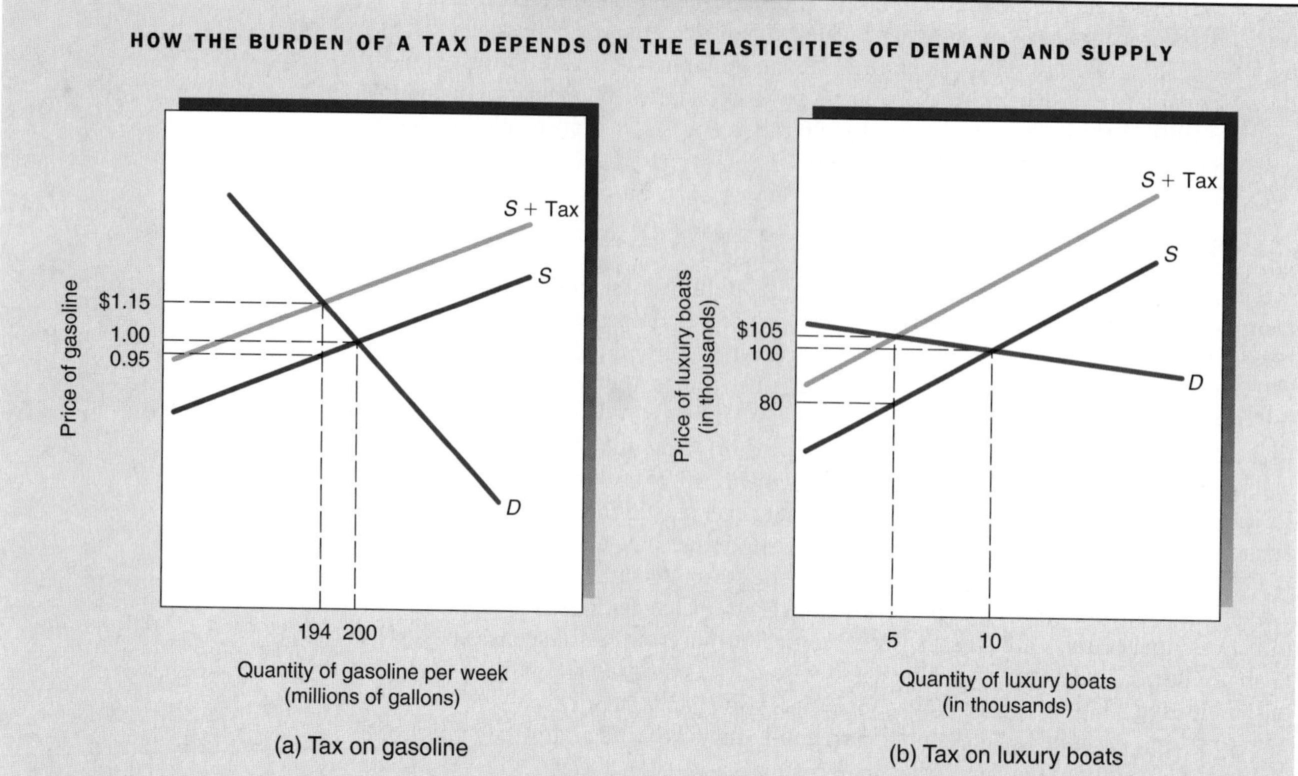

In part a when demand is relatively more inelastic than supply, buyers bear a larger share of the burden of the tax.

In part b when supply is relatively more inelastic than demand, sellers bear a larger share of the tax burden.

the deadweight loss caused by the tax because they determine the total reduction in the quantity of exchange. When either demand or supply is relatively inelastic, fewer trades will be eliminated by imposition of the tax, so the resulting deadweight loss is smaller. From a policy perspective, the excess burden of a tax system will therefore be lower if taxes are levied on goods and services for which either demand or supply is highly inelastic.

TAX RATES, TAX REVENUES, AND THE LAFFER CURVE

Average tax rate (ATR)
Tax liability divided by taxable income. It is the percentage of income paid in taxes.

When analyzing the impact of taxation, it is important to distinguish between the average and marginal rates of taxation. The **average tax rate (ATR)** can be expressed as follows:

$$\text{ATR} = \text{Tax liability/Taxable income}$$

Progressive tax
A tax in which the average tax rate rises with income. Persons with higher incomes will pay a higher percentage of their income in taxes.

For example, if a person's tax liability was $3,000 on an income of $20,000, her average tax rate would be 15 percent ($3,000 divided by $20,000). The average tax rate is simply the percentage of income that is paid in taxes. In the United States, the personal income tax provides the largest single source of government revenue. This tax is particularly important at the federal level. You may have heard reference to the federal income tax being "progressive." A **progressive tax** is defined as a tax in which the average tax rate rises with income. In other words, persons with higher income pay a larger *percentage of their income* in taxes. Alternatively, taxes can be proportional or regressive. A **proportional tax** is one for which the average tax rate is the same across income levels. Here, everyone would pay the same percentage of income in taxes. Finally, a **regressive tax** is one in which the average tax rate falls with income. If someone making $100,000 per year paid $30,000 in taxes (an ATR of 30 percent) while someone making $30,000 per year paid $15,000 in taxes (an ATR of 50 percent), the tax code would be regressive. Note that a regressive tax merely means that the *percentage* paid in taxes declines with income; the actual dollar amount of the tax bill might still be higher for those with larger incomes.

Proportional tax
A tax in which the average tax rate is the same at all income levels. Everyone pays the same percentage of income in taxes.

Regressive tax
A tax in which the average tax rate falls with income. Persons with higher incomes will pay a lower percentage of their income in taxes.

The economic way of thinking stresses that what happens at the margin is of crucial importance in personal decision making. The **marginal tax rate (MTR)** can be expressed as follows:

Marginal tax rate (MTR)
Additional tax liability divided by additional taxable income. It is the percentage of an extra dollar of income that must be paid in taxes. It is the marginal tax rate that is relevant in personal decision making.

$$\text{MTR} = \text{Change in tax liability/Change in income}$$

The MTR reveals both how much of one's *additional* income must be turned over to the tax collector and how much is retained by the individual. For example, when the MTR is 28 percent, $28 of every $100 of additional earnings must be paid in taxes. The individual is permitted to keep only $72 of his or her additional income. The marginal tax rate is vitally important because it affects the incentive to earn additional income. The higher the marginal tax rate, the less incentive individuals have to earn more income.

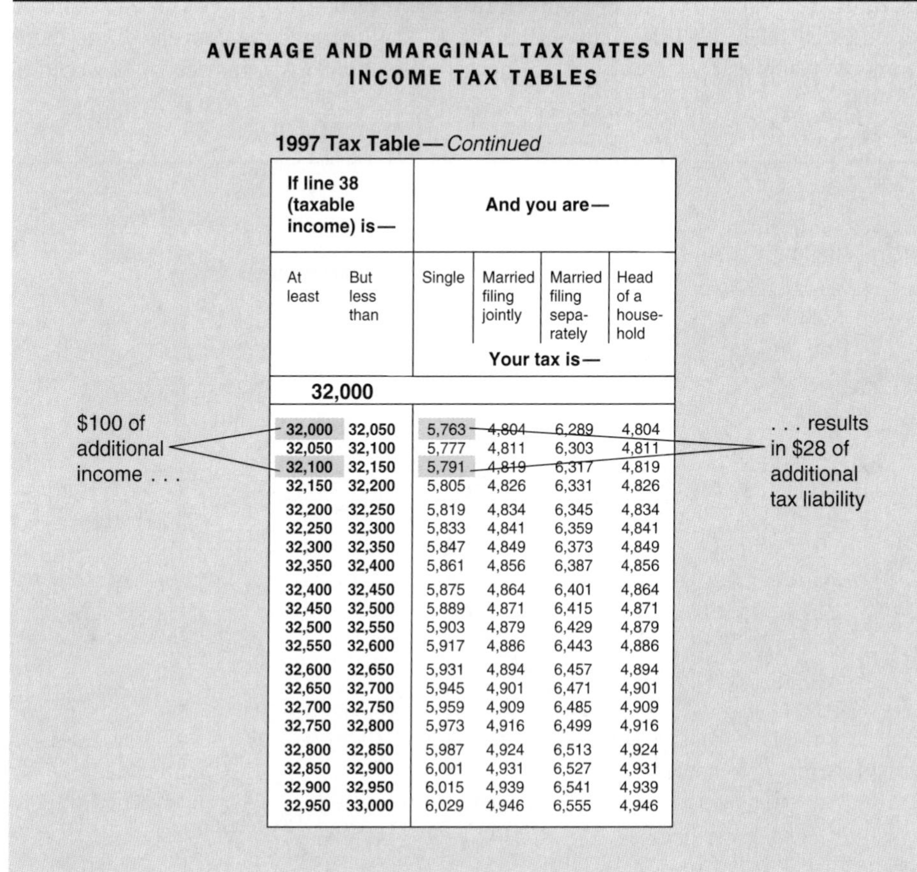

EXHIBIT 4-10

AVERAGE AND MARGINAL TAX RATES IN THE INCOME TAX TABLES

1997 Tax Table—*Continued*

If line 38 (taxable income) is— At least	But less than	And you are— Single	Married filing jointly	Married filing separately	Head of a household
		Your tax is—			
32,000					
32,000	32,050	5,763	4,804	6,289	4,804
32,050	32,100	5,777	4,811	6,303	4,811
32,100	32,150	5,791	4,819	6,317	4,819
32,150	32,200	5,805	4,826	6,331	4,826
32,200	32,250	5,819	4,834	6,345	4,834
32,250	32,300	5,833	4,841	6,359	4,841
32,300	32,350	5,847	4,849	6,373	4,849
32,350	32,400	5,861	4,856	6,387	4,856
32,400	32,450	5,875	4,864	6,401	4,864
32,450	32,500	5,889	4,871	6,415	4,871
32,500	32,550	5,903	4,879	6,429	4,879
32,550	32,600	5,917	4,886	6,443	4,886
32,600	32,650	5,931	4,894	6,457	4,894
32,650	32,700	5,945	4,901	6,471	4,901
32,700	32,750	5,959	4,909	6,485	4,909
32,750	32,800	5,973	4,916	6,499	4,916
32,800	32,850	5,987	4,924	6,513	4,924
32,850	32,900	6,001	4,931	6,527	4,931
32,900	32,950	6,015	4,939	6,541	4,939
32,950	33,000	6,029	4,946	6,555	4,946

$100 of additional income . . .
. . . results in $28 of additional tax liability

This excerpt from the 1997 federal income tax table shows that in the 28 percent federal marginal income tax bracket, each $100 of additional taxable income (from $32,000 to $32,100) results in tax liability increasing by $28 (from $5,763 to $5,791). Note that the average tax rate for a single taxpayer at $32,000 is about 18 percent ($5,763 ÷ $32,000).

At high marginal rates, spouses will choose to stay home instead of working, and others will choose not to take on second jobs or extra work. **Exhibit 4–10** illustrates the calculation of both the average and marginal tax rates within the framework of the 1997 income tax tables provided to taxpayers.

Generally, a person's income is subject to several taxes, and it is the combined marginal tax rate from all applicable taxes that matters to the individuals in their decision making. For example, in 1997, a married couple with $30,000 in taxable income living in Baltimore, Maryland, would face a 28 percent marginal federal income tax rate, a 7.65 percent marginal social security payroll tax rate, a 5 percent marginal state income tax rate, and a 2.5 percent marginal local income tax rate. If we ignore the relatively small deductions that one tax can generate in calculating certain others, the result is a combined marginal tax rate of 43.15 percent, meaning that an additional $100 of gross income would result in only a $56.85 increase in net take-home income.

Governments generally levy taxes in order to raise revenues. The revenue derived from a tax is equal to the tax base multiplied by the tax rate. As we previously noted, taxes will lower the level of the activity taxed. The basic postulate of economics indicates that when an activity is taxed more heavily, people will choose less of it. The higher the tax rate, the greater the shift away from the activity. If taxpayers can easily escape the tax by altering their behavior (perhaps by shifting to substitutes), the tax base will shrink significantly as rates are increased. This erosion in the tax base in response to higher rates means that an increase in tax rates will generally lead to a less than proportional increase in tax revenues.

Laffer curve
A curve illustrating the relationship between the tax rate and tax revenue. Tax revenue will be low for both very high and very low tax rates. Thus, when tax rates are quite high, a reduction in the tax rate can increase tax revenue.

Economist Arthur Laffer has popularized the idea that, beyond some point, higher tax rates will shrink the tax base so much that tax revenues will decline when tax rates are increased. The curve illustrating the relationship between tax rates and tax revenues is called the **Laffer curve.** Exhibit 4–11 illustrates the concept of the Laffer curve as it applies to income-generating activities. Obviously, tax revenues would be

Because taxation affects the amount of the activity being taxed, a change in tax rates will not lead to a proportional change in tax revenues. As the Laffer curve indicates, beyond some point (B), an increase in tax rates may actually cause tax revenues to fall. Because large tax rate increases will lead to only a small expansion in tax revenue as B is approached, there is no presumption that point B is an ideal rate of taxation.

EXHIBIT 4–11

LAFFER CURVE

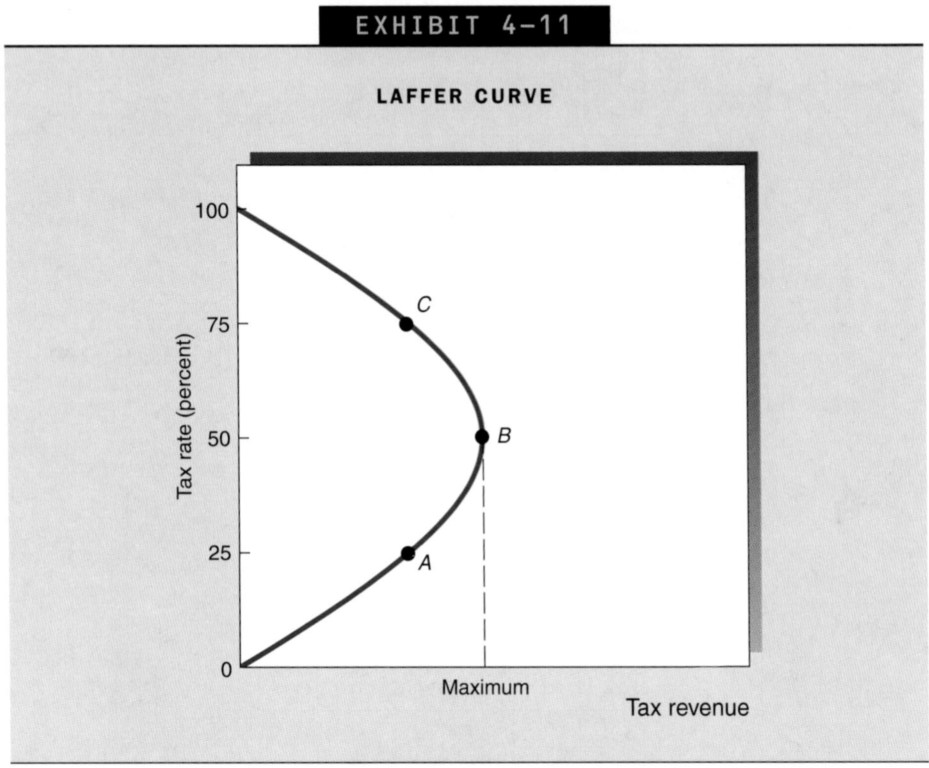

zero if the income tax rate were zero. What is not so obvious is that tax revenues would also be zero (or at least very close to zero) if the tax rate were 100 percent. Confronting a 100 percent tax rate, most individuals would go fishing—or find something else to do rather than engage in taxable productive activity, since the 100 percent tax rate would completely remove the material reward derived from earning taxable income.

As tax rates are reduced from 100 percent, the incentive to work and earn taxable income increases, income expands, and tax revenues rise. Similarly, as tax rates increase from zero, tax revenues expand. Clearly, at some rate greater than zero but less than 100 percent, tax revenues will be maximized (point *B* in Exhibit 4–11). This is not to imply that the tax rate that maximizes revenue is ideal. In fact, as rates are increased and the maximum revenue point (*B*) is approached, relatively large tax rate increases will be necessary to expand tax revenue by even a small amount. In this range, the excess burden of taxation in the form of reductions in gains from trade will be substantial. Thus, ideal tax rates will be lower than the rate that maximizes revenue.

The Laffer curve illustrates that it is important to distinguish between changes in *tax rates* and changes in *tax revenues.* Higher rates will not always lead to more revenue for the government. Similarly, lower rates will not always lead to less revenue. When higher tax rates lead to a substantial shrinkage in the tax base, the higher rates will raise little additional revenue. In extreme cases, revenue may even decline in response to higher tax rates. Correspondingly, tax rates can sometimes be lower without any significant loss of revenue.

It is interesting to view the 1980s within the framework of the Laffer curve. During the eighties there was a sharp reduction in marginal tax rates imposed on those with high incomes. The top marginal rate was reduced from 70 percent at the

APPLICATIONS IN ECONOMICS

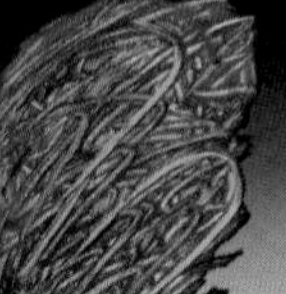

The Laffer Curve and Mountain Climbing Deaths

The Laffer curve is a tool that can be used to illustrate many relationships other than the one between tax rates and tax revenues. Economists J. R. Clark and Dwight Lee have used the Laffer curve framework to analyze the relationship between the safety of mountain climbing and the number of mountain climbing deaths on Mt. McKinley. As the probability of death from the climb fell due to increased government involvement in rescue attempts, the number of people seeking to "conquer the mountain" rose significantly. The increase in the number of climbers dominated the reduction in risk, leading to a Laffer curve–type relationship: An improvement in safety resulted in a *higher* number of total deaths.

Perhaps a numeric example can best illustrate why this might be the case. Assume that if the probability of death from an attempted climb was 90 percent, only 100 persons would attempt to climb the mountain each year, leading to an annual death rate of 90. Now suppose that increased rescue attempts lower this probability of death to 50 percent. Because incentives matter, the increased safety will result in an increase in the number of people attempting to climb the mountain. Suppose that the number of climbers increases from 100 to 200. With 200 climbers and a 50 percent probability of death, the annual number of fatalities would increase to 100, 10 more than before the improvement in safety. Viewing this within the Laffer curve framework, the total number of mountain climbing deaths is lowest both when there is a very high and a very low probability of death. The number of deaths is largest in the middle probability ranges. Thus, making a very risky mountain safer can result in more rather than fewer fatalities.

Besides mountain climbing, these same authors have explored a similar relationship between the average prison sentence length and total prison space occupied. Other authors have explored potential Laffer curve relations between the minimum-wage and the earnings of minimum wage workers and the regulatory costs of the Endangered Species Act on the acres of habitat for endangered species.[1]

[1]See J. R. Clark and Dwight R. Lee, "Too Safe to Be Safe: Some Implications of Short- and Long-Run Rescue Laffer Curves," *Eastern Economic Journal* 23 no. 2 (spring 1997): 127–137; Russell S. Sobel, "Theory and Evidence on the Political Economy of the Minimum Wage," *Journal of Political Economy,* forthcoming; and Richard L. Stroup, "The Endangered Species Act: The Laffer Curve Strikes Again," *The Journal of Private Enterprise,* vol. XIV (special issue 1998): 48–62.

EXHIBIT 4–12

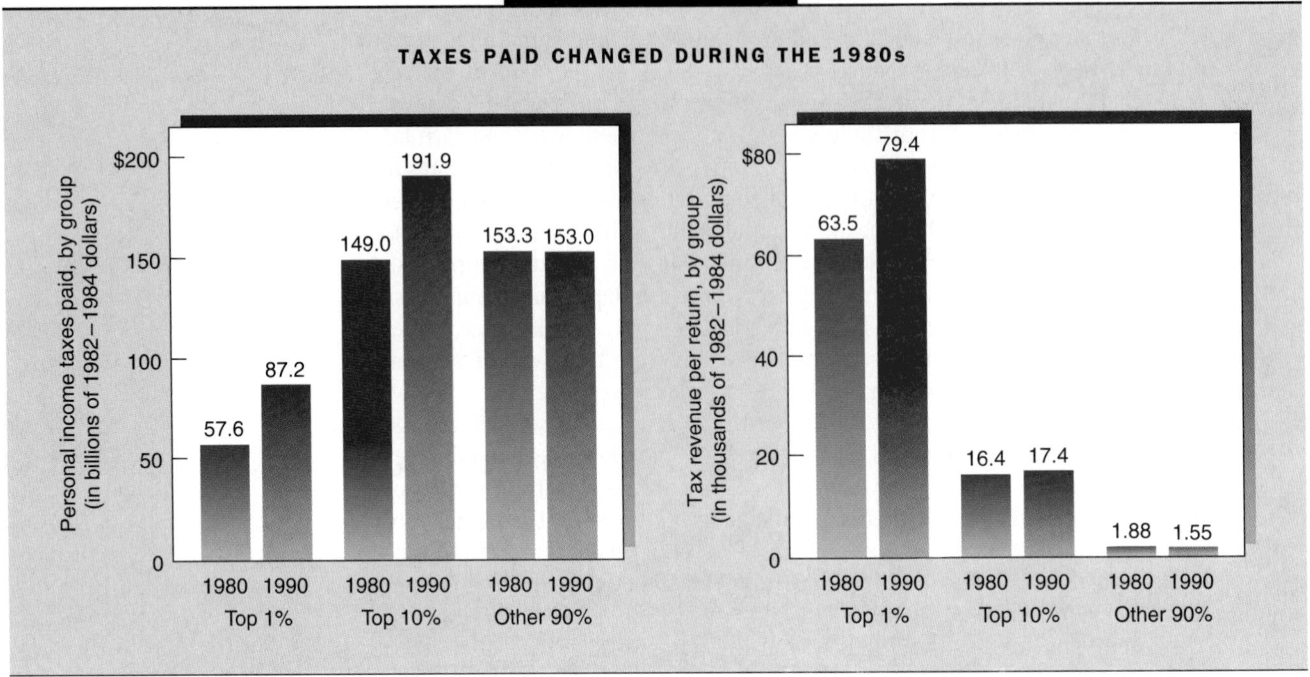

Measured in 1982–1984 dollars, the personal income taxes paid by the top 1 percent and the top 10 percent of income recipients increased between 1980 and 1990, even though their rates were reduced. In contrast, the tax revenue collected from other taxpayers was virtually unchanged during the decade (left frame). Per return, the revenue collected from the top 1 percent and the top 10 percent rose, while the revenue fell for other taxpayers (right frame).

beginning of the decade to 33 percent at the end of the decade. Focusing on this sharp reduction in the top marginal rate, critics charged that the 1980s' tax policies were a bonanza for the rich. When analyzing this view, once again it is important to distinguish between tax rates and tax revenue. Even though the top rates were reduced sharply, both the tax revenue (even after adjustment for inflation) and share of the personal income tax paid by high-income taxpayers rose during the 1980s. As **Exhibit 4–12** illustrates, the real tax revenue (measured in 1982–1984 dollars) collected from the top 1 percent of earners rose from $57.6 billion in 1980 to $87.2 billion in 1990, a whopping increase of 51.4 percent. For the top 10 percent as a whole, real revenue rose from $149.0 billion in 1980 to $191.9 billion in 1990. Meanwhile, the revenue collected from all other taxpayers was virtually unchanged.

Viewed as percentages of total income tax collections, in 1980 the top 1 percent of earners accounted for just over 19 percent of all income tax revenue collected. By 1990 at the lower tax rates, the top 1 percent accounted for more than 25 percent of income tax revenue. The top 10 percent of earners paid just over 49 percent of total income tax liability in 1980 and 55 percent in 1990. Interestingly, the top 10 percent of earners paid more than half of the total income tax liability.

The data from the 1980s are consistent with the Laffer curve. They indicate that in the case of most taxpayers (those in the range near point *A* of Exhibit 4–11), lower tax rates lead to a reduction in the revenue collected from the group. When tax rates are higher (in the range near *B* of Exhibit 4–11), tax rates can be reduced with little or no loss of revenue, and when rates get even higher (in the range near *C* of Exhibit 4–11), lowering tax rates will produce more tax revenue.

LOOKING Ahead

The last two chapters have focused on the operation of markets and the role of market prices. At various points, we have stressed the importance of legal structure and secure property rights for the smooth operation of markets. Governmental policies in these and other areas influence both economic efficiency and progress. The next two chapters will focus on the role and operation of government, a topic that is central to understanding the world in which we live.

KEY POINTS

➤ Wage rates, interest rates, and exchange rates are also market prices determined by the forces of supply and demand. In each, these prices play important roles in coordinating the actions of buyers and sellers. Changes in these markets lead to changes in other markets and alter the relative prices of many other goods.

➤ Legally imposed price ceilings result in shortages, while legally imposed price floors will cause surpluses. Both will also cause other harmful secondary effects. Rent controls, for example, will lead to shortages, less investment, poor maintenance, and a deterioration in the quality of rental housing.

➤ The minimum wage is a price floor for unskilled labor. It increases the earnings of some low-skill workers, but also reduces employment and leads to a reduction in training opportunities and a deterioration in the nonwage job benefits available to minimum-wage workers.

➤ Because black markets operate outside the legal system, they are often characterized by deception, fraud, and the use of violence as a means of enforcing contracts. A legal system that provides secure private property rights and unbiased enforcement of contracts enhances the operation of markets.

➤ The division of the actual tax burden between buyers and sellers is determined by the relative elasticities of demand and supply rather than on whom the tax is legally imposed.

➤ In addition to the cost of the tax revenues transferred to the government, taxes will eliminate trades in a market and thereby impose an excess burden or deadweight loss.

➤ Higher tax rates reduce the size of the tax base. The Laffer curve illustrates that when tax rates are quite high, a reduction in the tax rate can result in more tax revenue. The increase in tax revenue obtained from the wealthy as the result of income tax rate reductions during the 1980s is consistent with the Laffer curve.

CRITICAL ANALYSIS QUESTIONS

1. How will a substantial increase in demand for housing affect the wages and employment of carpenters, plumbers, and electricians?

2. Suppose there is a sharp reduction in lumber prices. How will this affect the market for newly constructed housing?

3. Why are nonprice factors, such as product quality, service, and the characteristics of potential trading partners, more important when price ceilings and price floors are imposed than when prices are freely determined?

*4. To be meaningful, a price ceiling must be below the market price. Conversely, a meaningful price floor must be above the market price. What impact will a meaningful price ceiling have on the quantity exchanged? What impact will a meaningful price floor have on the quantity exchanged? Explain.

5. Suppose that college students in your town convinced the town council to enact a law setting the maximum price for rental housing at $100 per month. Will this help or hurt college students who rent housing? In your answer address how this price ceiling will affect (a) the quality of rental housing, (b) the amount of rental housing available, (c) the incentive of landlords to

maintain their property, (d) the amount of racial, gender, and other types of discrimination in the local rental housing market, (e) the ease with which students will be able to find housing, and finally (f) whether a "black market" for housing would develop.

*6. Analyze the impact of an increase in the minimum wage from the current level to $8.00 per hour. How would the following be affected?

a. Employment in skill categories previously earning less than $8 per hour
b. The unemployment rate of teenagers
c. The availability of on-the-job training for low-skill workers
d. The demand for high-skill workers who provide good substitutes for the labor services offered by low-skill workers, who are paid higher wage rates due to the increase in the minimum wage

7. What is a black market? What are some of the main differences in how black markets operate relative to legal markets?

8. How do you think the markets for organ donation and child adoption would be affected if they were made fully legal with a well-functioning price mechanism? What would be the advantages and disadvantages relative to the current system?

9. What is meant by the incidence of a tax? Explain why the statutory and actual incidence of a tax can be different.

10. What conditions must be met for buyers to bear the full burden of a tax? What conditions would cause sellers to bear the full burden? Explain.

*11. What is the nature of the deadweight loss accompanying taxes? Why is it often referred to as an "excess burden" of the tax?

12. The demand and supply curves for unskilled labor in a market are given in the accompanying table.

a. Find the equilibrium wage and number of workers hired.
b. Suppose that a new law is passed requiring employers to pay an unemployment insurance tax of $1.50 per hour for every employee. What happens to the equilibrium wage rate and number of workers hired? How is this tax burden distributed between employers and workers?
c. Now suppose that, rather than being paid by the employers, the tax must be paid by workers. How does this affect the equilibrium wage rate and number of workers hired? How is this tax burden distributed between employers and workers?
d. Does it make a difference who is statutorily liable for the tax?

DEMAND		SUPPLY	
WAGE	QUANTITY DEMANDED	WAGE	QUANTITY SUPPLIED
$6.50	1,000	$6.50	1,900
$6.00	1,200	$6.00	1,800
$5.50	1,400	$5.50	1,700
$5.00	1,600	$5.00	1,600
$4.50	1,800	$4.50	1,500
$4.00	2,000	$4.00	1,400

13. Currently, the social security payroll tax is statutorily imposed at 7.65 percent on the employee and 7.65 percent on the employer. Show this graphically, being careful to distinguish between the total cost to the employer of hiring a worker, the employee's gross wage, and the employee's net wage. Show how the outcome would differ if all 15.3 percent were imposed on the employee or if all 15.3 percent were imposed on the employer.

*14. Suppose that, recognizing that one cannot support a large family at the current minimum wage, Congress passes legislation requiring that businesses employing workers with three or more children pay these employees at least $8.50 per hour. How would this legislation affect the employment level of low-skill workers with three or more children? Do you think some workers with large families might attempt to conceal the fact? Why?

15. "We should impose a 20 percent luxury tax on expensive automobiles (those with a sales price of $50,000 or more) in order to collect more tax revenue from the wealthy." Will the burden of the proposed tax fall primarily on the wealthy? Why or why not?

*Asterisk denotes questions for which answers are given in Appendix B.

CHAPTER 5

The principal justification for public policy intervention lies in the frequent and numerous shortcomings of market outcomes.

Charles Wolf[1]

The Economic Role of Government

CHAPTER FOCUS

- What is government?
- How does the nature of decision making in the political and market sectors differ?
- Do taxes measure the opportunity cost of a government?
- Which functions of government are most likely to promote economic well-being?
- Why might markets fail to achieve ideal economic efficiency?

---

[1]Charles Wolf, Jr., *Markets or Government* (Cambridge: MIT Press, 1988), p. 17.

About two-fifths of U.S. national income is channeled through various government departments and agencies. In addition, about two-fifths of the nation's land is owned by the government. Furthermore, the legal framework set by the government establishes many of the "rules of the game" for the market sector. Government regulation of prices and the use of land, water, and air, along with labor relations and business practices, exerts a major impact on the operation of the economy. Given the size, cost, and influence of government, it is important that we understand what government is, and the reasons that people sometimes turn to it, rather than to the private sector, to get what they want. In this chapter we will examine these issues, focusing in particular on situations in which markets cannot be expected to deliver ideal results.

WHAT IS GOVERNMENT?

At the most basic level, the distinguishing characteristic of government is its monopoly over the legitimate use of force to modify the actions of adults. Most societies allow parents to use force to influence the actions of their children. But with regard to adults, governments possess the exclusive right to use force. No individual or firm has a right to use violence—or the threat of violence—in order to take your wealth. If a business raises its price or performs unsatisfactorily, you always have the right to exit—to take your business elsewhere. But when a government decrees a tax or a new regulation, exit is possible only by moving out of the government's territory. And that is costly, especially when it comes to the national government. Its monopoly on the legitimate use of force to take from its citizens—to tax them and to control their behavior—makes government different from any other form of organization.

Given its unique powers, it is tempting to think of government, particularly democratically elected government, as a tool that can be used to solve all types of problems ranging from inadequate health care to the high cost of housing. Some even argue that government can use income transfers to achieve the "optimal distribution of income."

It is, of course, important to understand alternative actions that might *potentially* lead to outcomes that are more consistent with economic prosperity. But as we will see clearly in the next chapter, government is merely an alternative method of social organization—an institutional process through which individuals collectively make choices and carry out activities. No matter how lofty the rhetoric of political officials, the people (for example, voters, legislators, lobbyists, and bureau managers) who make the choices that determine political outcomes are ordinary mortals, persons with ethical standards, narrow interests, and personal motivations very much like those present in the market sector. Furthermore, government decision makers often confront a reward structure that encourages them to help narrow constituencies at the expense of economic efficiency and activities that are in the interest of all citizens.

Because the incentive structure in the political process generally differs from that of markets, collective outcomes will often differ from market outcomes. For some categories of economic activity, there are reasons to believe that democratic political procedures work quite well. In other instances, there are sound reasons to believe that government allocation will be counterproductive. This chapter and the next will help us understand when—and under what conditions—political decision making is likely to yield positive economic results.

DIFFERENCES AND SIMILARITIES BETWEEN MARKET AND COLLECTIVE ACTION

There is at least one important similarity between the market and the public sectors: The choices of individuals will influence outcomes in both. But there are basic structural differences in the way that individuals exercise their influence. Market transactions are characterized by voluntary exchange coordinated by prices. Only transactions that are voluntarily accepted by both buyer and seller will take place in markets. In contrast, when collective action occurs in a democratic setting, majority rule is the key, either directly or through legislative procedures. Let us take a look at both the differences and similarities between the two sectors.

1. **Competitive behavior is present in both the market and public sectors.** The market sector is sometimes called the "competitive sector," but competitive behavior is present in both sectors. Politicians compete for elective office. Bureau chiefs and agency heads compete for additional taxpayer dollars. Public-sector employees compete for promotions, higher incomes, and additional power, just as they do in the private sector. Lobbyists compete for program funding, for favorable bureaucratic rulings, and for legislation favorable to the interest groups they represent—including both private and government clients. (See Applications in Economics: Perspectives on the Cost of Political Competition.) The nature of the competition and the criteria for success differ between the two sectors, but people compete in both.
2. **Public-sector organization can break the individual consumption-payment link.** In the market, a consumer who wants a commodity must pay the price. In this respect, market and collective action differ in a fundamental way. The government usually does not establish a one-to-one relationship between the individual's payment and receipt of a good. Some individuals receive very large benefits from a government action without any significant impact on their personal tax bill. Others pay substantial taxes while receiving much smaller benefits. In contrast with the market, the amount one pays does not determine the amount one receives in the public sector.
3. **Scarcity imposes the aggregate consumption-payment link in both sectors.** Although the government can break the link between an individual's payment for a good and the right to consume the good, the reality of the ***aggregate consumption–aggregate payment*** link will remain. There are no free lunches. Someone must pay the cost of providing scarce goods, regardless of the sector used to produce (or distribute) them. Free goods provided in the public sector are "free" only to certain individuals. They are certainly not free from the viewpoint of society.
4. **Private-sector action is based on voluntary choice; public-sector action on majority rule.** In the private sector, when two parties engage in trade, they do so voluntarily. Corporations, like Exxon and General Motors, no matter how large or powerful, cannot levy a "tax" on your income or force you to buy their products. Although mutual gain is the foundation for market transactions, the political process generates losers

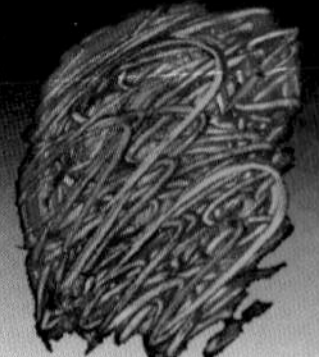

APPLICATIONS IN ECONOMICS

Perspectives on the Cost of Political Competition

We all have our own ideas about how government should be run. Because government is such an extremely important force in our economy and in our lives, individuals and groups try to influence election outcomes by voting, by contributing to political campaigns, and by ringing doorbells, among other activities. In addition, legislative and executive branch decisions can be influenced directly, by lobbying.

Competition for elective office is fierce and campaigns are expensive. In preparation for the 1998 elections, for example, candidates for U.S. House and Senate positions raised $207 million in 1997 alone. In the 1996 presidential race, candidates had spent $237 million through September 1996. Unlike bidders in a market auction, winners and losers alike pay the full costs of the election bid. It is common for lobbying groups to donate to opposing candidates in a close race.

During and after the election, lobbying groups compete for the attention—the ear—of elected officials. In fact, the greatest portion of campaign funds raised by incumbents is not raised at election time; rather, it accrues over their entire term in office. A large campaign contribution may not be able to "buy" a vote, but it certainly enhances the lobbyist's chance to sit down with the elected official to explain the power and the beauty of the contributor's position. In the competitive world of politics, the politician who does not at least listen to helpful "friends of the campaign" is less likely to survive.

Campaign contributions are only the tip of the lobbying iceberg. In Washington, D.C., alone, tens of thousands of individuals, many of them extremely talented, hard-working, and well paid, are dedicated to lobbying Congress and the executive branch of the federal government. Trade associations, for example, have more than 3,000 offices and 80,000 employees in Washington. Of these associations, at least 30 pay their highest officials between $400,000 and $900,000 per year.[1] Another indicator of the enormous amount of time and effort allocated to influencing government is that 65 percent of *Fortune* 200 chief executive officers travel to Washington at least every two weeks, on average. Billions of dollars in budgets, in taxes, and in expenditures required by regulation are at stake. When Congress and the agencies wield such power, competition to obtain the prizes and avoid the penalties naturally results in huge expenditures designed to influence government policy.

[1]The salary range is from Peter H. Stone, "Payday!" *National Journal* (December 17, 1994): 2948–2961. More details on campaign finance can be found in Michael Barone and Grant Ujifusa, *The Almanac of American Politics: 1996* (Washington, D.C.: National Journal, 1995).

as well as winners. If a legislative majority decides on a particular policy, the minority must accept the policy and help pay for it, even if that minority strongly disagrees. If $10 billion is allocated by the legislative branch for the development of a super weapon system (or for welfare programs, health care, or foreign aid), the dissenting minority is required to pay taxes that will help finance the project. Similarly, if government regulators mandate that private parties must provide a wildlife habitat, wetlands, housing at below-market prices, or other goods, both the providers of mandated goods and potential buyers who would like to purchase the same resources for their own use must comply with government orders. When issues are decided in the public sector, those who disagree must, at least temporarily, yield to the view of the current majority.

5. **When collective decisions are made legislatively, voters must choose among candidates who represent a bundle of positions on issues.** On election day, the voter cannot choose the views of Representative Frank Free Lunch on poverty and business welfare and simultaneously choose the views of challenger Amanda Austerity on national defense and tariffs. ***Inability to support a candidate's views on one issue while rejecting that candidate's views on another greatly reduces the voter's power to make preferences count on specific issues.*** Since the average representative is asked to vote on roughly 2,000 different issues during a two-year term, the enormity of the problem is obvious. The situation in a market is quite different. A buyer can purchase some groceries or items of clothing from one store, while choosing related items from different suppliers. There is seldom a bundle purchase problem in markets.

6. **Income and power are distributed differently in the two sectors.** Individuals who supply more highly valued resources in the marketplace have larger incomes. The number of dollar votes available to an individual will reflect his or her abilities, ambitions, skills, perceptiveness, past savings, inheritance, good fortune, and willingness to produce for others, among other things. An unequal distribution of consumer power is the result. In a democratic public sector, ballots call the tune. One citizen, one vote is the rule. But there are other, more powerful ways to deliver votes. An individual might donate money to help a campaign do its work better and capture more votes. Or an individual might provide more direct assistance to the campaign by visiting friends and neighbors, writing letters, or speaking publicly on behalf of the candidate (or party). The political process gives the greatest rewards to those who are best able and most willing to use their time, persuasive skills, organizational abilities, and financial contributions to help politicians get votes. Persons who have more money and skills of this sort—and are willing to spend them in the political arena—can expect to benefit more handsomely from the political process than can individuals who lack these personal resources. In the public sector as in the market, there is an unequal distribution of influence and "income," although the sources of success and influence differ between the two sectors.

THE OPPORTUNITY COST OF GOVERNMENT

Scarcity is inescapable in both the private and the public sectors. People often speak as if taxes are the cost of government. But the cost of any product is what we have to give up in order to produce it—the opportunity cost. Government is no exception. There are three types of cost incurred when an activity is undertaken by the government.

First, there is the opportunity cost of the resources used to produce goods supplied through the public sector. When governments purchase goods and services to provide missiles, education, highways, health care, and other goods, the resources needed must be bid away from private-sector activities. If they were not tied up producing goods provided by government, these resources would be available to produce private-sector goods. Note that this cost is incurred regardless of whether the provision of the public-sector goods is financed by current taxes, by an increase in government debt, or by money creation. This cost can be diminished only by reducing the size of government purchases. And a similar cost is incurred when government does not purchase goods, but orders the provision of goods without payment, or on terms decreed by regulators rather than terms voluntarily agreed upon by trading parties. The fact that government has not paid a market price does not reduce the cost. The Center for the Study of American Business estimated that the cost of complying with federal regulations, on the part of those regulated, was more than $340 billion (approximately $1,250 per person) in 1998. The first and often largest opportunity cost of an item supplied by government is the best alternative use that could have been made of the resources required to provide the good.

Second, there is the cost of resources expended in the collection of taxes and the enforcement of government mandates. Tax laws and regulatory orders must be enforced. Tax returns and formal notices of compliance with regulations must be prepared and monitored. Resources used to prepare, monitor, and enforce tax and regulatory legislation are unavailable for the production of either private- or public-sector goods. In the United States, studies indicate that it takes businesses and individuals approximately 5.5 billion worker-hours (the equivalent of 2.7 million full-time workers) each year just to complete the taxation paperwork. This means that every dollar of tax revenue raised by the government costs taxpayers approximately $1.15.

Finally, there is the excess burden (or deadweight loss) of taxation that we discussed in Chapter 4. Taxes distort incentives. When buyers pay more and sellers receive less due to the payment of a tax, trade and the production of output become less attractive. Trade and output will decline. Individuals will spend less time on productive (but taxed) market activities and more time on tax-avoidance and untaxed activities, such as leisure. Regulation also distorts incentives. When a government agency can mandate the supply of a resource—for example, a tract of land for use as an endangered species habitat—it will tend to allocate more of the "free" resource and less of other resources that it must purchase from its own budget. Regulatory powers, like taxes, distort prices and incentives, thus reducing economic efficiency.

In essence, the cost of government activities is the sum of (1) the opportunity cost of resources used to produce government-supplied goods and services, (2) the cost of tax and regulatory compliance, and (3) the excess-burden cost of taxation and regulation. Thus, government supply of goods and services generally costs the economy a good bit more than either the size of the tax bill or the level of budget expenditures implies.

Who pays the cost of government? Politicians often speak of imposing taxes on "business" as if part of the tax burden could be transferred from individuals to a nonperson (business). But business taxes, like all other taxes, are paid by individuals. A corporation or business firm may write the check to the government, but it does not pay the taxes. The business corporation merely collects the money from someone else—from its customers in the form of higher prices, from its suppliers (including employees) in the form of lower wages or prices paid, or from stockholders in the form of lower dividends paid—and transfers the money to the government. The same is true when a firm is forced by government mandate to provide goods. In order for government to provide goods and services, individuals must pay for them.

ECONOMIC EFFICIENCY AND THE ROLE OF GOVERNMENT

Government is a powerful force in the economy. It can produce much that is good. But using government is costly. Why do citizens turn to government? How large should the scope of governmental action be? From an economic viewpoint, what are the proper functions of government?

To address these questions, we need a criterion by which to judge alternative institutional arrangements—that is, market- and public-sector policies. Economists often use the standard of **economic efficiency.** The central idea is straightforward. It simply means that, for any given level of effort (cost), we want to obtain the largest possible benefit. A corollary is that we want to obtain any specific level of benefits with the least possible effort. Economic efficiency simply means getting the most value from the available resources—making the largest pie from the available set of ingredients, so to speak.

Economic efficiency
Economizing behavior. When applied to a community, it implies that (1) an activity should be undertaken if the sum of the benefits to the individuals exceeds the sum of their costs and (2) no activity should be undertaken if the costs borne by the individuals exceed the benefits.

Why efficiency? Economists acknowledge that individuals generally do not have the efficiency of the economy as a primary goal. Rather, each person wants the largest possible "piece of the pie." All might agree that a bigger pie is preferred, however, particularly if each is allowed a larger slice as a result. Thus, efficiency can be in everyone's interest because it makes a larger pie, and, therefore, a larger slice, possible.

What does efficiency mean when applied to the entire economy? Individuals are the final decision makers of an economy, and individuals will bear the costs and reap the benefits of economic activity. When applied to the entire economy, two conditions are necessary for ideal economic efficiency:

Rule 1. ***Undertaking an economic action will be efficient if it produces more benefits than costs for the individuals of the economy.*** Such actions make it possible to improve the well-being of at least some individuals without creating reductions in the welfare of others. Failure to undertake such activities means that potential gain has been forgone.

Rule 2. ***Undertaking an economic action will be inefficient if it produces more costs than benefits to the individuals.*** When an action results in greater total costs than benefits, somebody must be harmed. The benefits that accrue to those who gain are insufficient to compensate for the losses imposed on others. Therefore, when all persons are considered, the net impact of such an action is counterproductive.

Both failure to undertake an efficient action (Rule 1) and the undertaking of inefficient activities (Rule 2) will result in economic inefficiency. The concept of economic efficiency applies to each and every possible income distribution, although a change in income distribution may alter the precise combination of goods and services that is most efficient.[2] Positive economics does not tell us how income should be distributed. Of course, we all have ideas on the subject. Most of us would like to see more income distributed our way. Agreement on what is the best distribution of income is unlikely, but for any particular income distribution, there will be an ideal resource allocation that will be most efficient.

Economic efficiency provides us with a criterion for the evaluation of the scope of government. Of course, this does not completely resolve the issue. Philosophers, economists, and other scholars have debated this issue for centuries. While the debate continues, there is substantial agreement that at least two functions of government are legitimate: (1) protection against invasions by others and (2) provision of goods that cannot easily be provided through markets. These two functions correspond to what Nobel laureate James Buchanan conceptualizes as the protective and productive functions of government.

Protective Function of Government

The most fundamental function of government is the protection of individuals and their property against acts of aggression. As John Locke wrote more than three centuries ago, individuals are constantly threatened by "the invasions of others." Therefore, each individual "is willing to join in society with others, who are already united, or have a mind to unite, for the mutual preservation of their lives, liberties, and estates."[3]

---

[2]Note to students who may pursue advanced study in economics: Using the concept of efficiency to compare alternative policies typically requires that the analyst estimate costs and benefits that are difficult or impossible to measure. Costs and benefits are the values of opportunities forgone or accepted by individuals, *as evaluated by those individuals.* Then these costs and benefits must be added up across all individuals and compared. But does a dollar's gain for one individual really compensate for a dollar's sacrifice by another? Some economists simply reject the validity of making such comparisons. They say that neither the estimates by the economic analyst of subjectively determined costs and benefits nor the adding up of these costs and benefits across individuals is meaningful. Their case may be valid, but most economists today nevertheless use the concept of efficiency as we present it. No other way to use economic analysis to compare policy alternatives has been found.

[3]John Locke, *Treatise of Civil Government,* 1690 ed. Charles Sherman (New York: Appleton-Century-Crofts, 1937), p. 82.

APPLICATIONS IN ECONOMICS

The Importance of the Protective Function—The Case of Russia

Government does not always protect the rights of those who produce value. It sometimes joins with those seeking to restrict trade or plunder the goods of others. The recent experience of Russia vividly illustrates what happens when the protective function of government is poorly performed. Reporter Andrew Higgins, in a front-page article in *The Wall Street Journal* (October 16, 1998) described how regional officials, or "barons," sought to ban the movement of food out of their domains in order to keep food prices low for their regional constituents. "Eager to keep bread cheap, sausages plentiful and their own interests secure," various regional barons restricted the ability of farm producers to trade with buyers outside of their region. As a result, food prices in Moscow and other large northern cities were substantially higher than in the countryside where the food is produced. Sunflower oil, for example, was selling for 2,000 rubles a ton in one region, while the price was 5,000 rubles in another.

The article describes the plight of Mrs. Irina Radinsya, who stored over 250 tons of rye on her farm, along with barley and a sunflower crop. When she and other farmers tried to move their food 375 miles north to Moscow, where hungry people were willing to pay more, regional police stopped them. Some farmers were refused permission to proceed, and others were required to pay bribes of 150 rubles (about $11.50 at the time) per truck moved out of the region. Far from protecting the property of producers and traders, government officials were restricting trade and seizing property. Under these conditions, less food is produced. Furthermore, some of the harvest rots as farmers seek ways around the artificial trade barriers and the lawless demanding of bribes by government officials.

The protective function of government involves the maintenance of a framework of security and order— an infrastructure of rules within which people can interact peacefully with one another. It also entails the enforcement of rules against theft, fraud, physical harm to one's person and property, and the like. It also involves provision of national defense designed to protect domestic residents against invasion from a foreign power.

It is easy to see the economic importance of this function. When the protective function is performed well, the property of citizens is secure, freedom of exchange is present, and contracts are legally enforceable. With the freedom of exchange and assurance that if they sow (produce), they will be permitted to reap (enjoy the benefits of their output), individuals will move resources toward their highest valued uses. In

The English philosopher John Locke argued that people own themselves and, as a result of this self-ownership, they also own the fruits of their labor. Locke stressed that individuals are not subservient to government. To the contrary, the role of government is to protect the "natural rights" of individuals to their person and property. This view, also reflected in the "unalienable rights" of the American Declaration of Independence, undergirds the protective function of government.

contrast, when property rights are insecure and contracts unenforceable, productive behavior is undermined. Plunder, fraud, and economic chaos result. The recent experience of Russia illustrates this point. (See the accompanying Applications in Economics feature on Russia.)

Productive Function of Government

The nature of some goods makes them difficult to provide through markets. Sometimes it is difficult to establish a one-to-one link between payment for a good and receipt of the good. If this link cannot be established, the incentive of market producers to supply such goods is weak. In addition, high transaction costs—particularly, the cost of monitoring use and collecting fees—can sometimes make it difficult to supply a good through the market. When either of these conditions is present, it may be more efficient for the government to supply the good and use its taxing power to cover the cost.

Of all the productive functions that government can provide, a framework of a stable monetary and financial environment is perhaps the most important. That is so because markets work better within such a framework. Why? If markets are to function well, individuals need to know the value to others of what they are buying or selling. For market prices to convey this information, a stable monetary exchange system must be provided. This is especially true for the many market exchanges that involve a time dimension. Houses, cars, consumer durables, land, buildings, equipment, and many other items are often used and paid for over a period of months or even years. If the purchasing power of the monetary unit, the dollar in the United States, gyrated wildly, previously determined prices would not represent their intended values. Few would want to make transactions involving long-term commitments, due to uncertainty. The smooth functioning of the market would be retarded.

The government's spending and monetary policies exert a powerful influence on economic stability. If properly conducted, these policies contribute to economic stability, full and efficient utilization of resources, and stable prices. However, improper stabilization policies can cause massive unemployment, rapidly rising prices, or both.

Economists are not in complete agreement on the extent to which public policy can stabilize the economy and promote full employment. They often debate the impact of various policy tools. All agree, however, that a stable economic environment is vital to a market economy. (Those pursuing a course in macroeconomics will find both the potential and the limitations of government action as a stabilizing force discussed further in Part Three.)

Thus we can see that government may have a productive role along with its protective role; it may be able to engage in activities that will increase the size of the economic pie.

THE ROLE OF GOVERNMENT AND POTENTIAL SHORTCOMINGS OF THE MARKET

The protective and productive functions of government can be analyzed within the framework of the invisible hand principle. As we previously discussed, the invisible hand of market forces generally provides resource owners and business firms with a strong incentive to undertake projects that create value. Will this always be true? The answer to this question is no. There are four major factors that may undermine the invisible hand and reduce the efficiency of markets: (1) lack of competition, (2) externalities,

(3) public goods, and (4) poorly informed buyers or sellers. We will now consider each of these factors and explain why they may create the potential for productive action through government.

Lack of Competition

Competition is vital to the proper operation of the pricing mechanism. It is competition among sellers that drives the prices of consumer goods down to the level of their cost. Similarly, competition in markets for productive resources prevents (1) sellers from charging exorbitant prices to producers and (2) buyers from taking advantage of the owners of productive resources. The existence of competing buyers and sellers reduces the power of both to rig the market in their own favor.

Because competition is the enemy of prices higher than costs, sellers have a strong incentive to escape from its pressures. When there are only a few firms in a market, rather than competing, sellers may be able to collude effectively. Efforts in this direction should be expected. Competition is something that is good when the other guy faces it. Individually, each of us would prefer to be loosened from its grip. Students do not like stiff competitors at exam time, when seeking entry to graduate school, or in their social or romantic lives. Similarly, sellers prefer few real competitors.

Exhibit 5–1 illustrates how sellers can gain from collusive action. If a group of sellers could eliminate competition from new entrants to the market, they would be able to raise their prices. The total revenue of sellers is simply the market price multiplied by the quantity sold. The sellers' revenues may well be greater, and their total costs would surely be lower, if the smaller, restricted output Q_2 were sold rather than the competitive output Q_1. The artificially high price P_2 reflects not only resource scarcity, but also a premium due to the reduction in output resulting from collusion among sellers.

If a group of sellers can restrict the entry of competitors and collude to reduce their own output, they can sometimes obtain more total revenue by selling fewer units. Note that the total sales revenue P_2Q_2 for the restricted supply exceeds the sales revenue P_1Q_1 for the competitive supply, in this case. Such behavior reduces the gains from trade, making the market less efficient as a result.

EXHIBIT 5–1

RIGGING THE MARKET

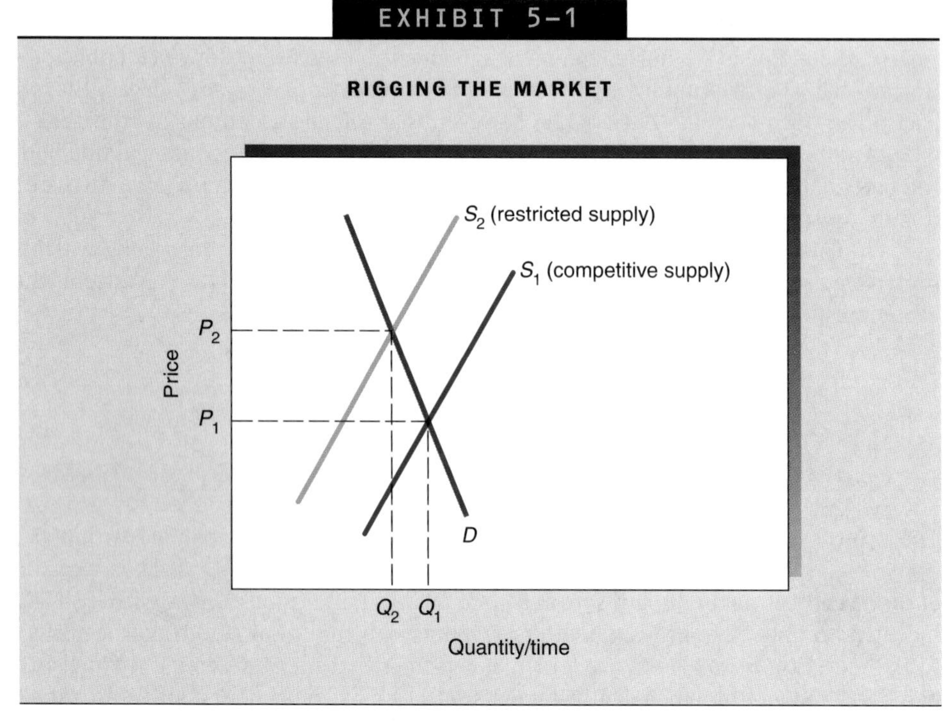

It is in the interest of consumers and the community that output be expanded to Q_1. At output Q_1, all units that are valued more than their cost are produced and sold. Thus, Q_1 is consistent with economic efficiency (Rule 1). It is in the interest of sellers, though, to make the good artificially scarce and raise its price. If sellers could restrict entry into the market and reduce output (to Q_2 for example), they could gain. If this happens, however, inefficiency would result because units valued more than their opportunity cost will not be supplied. There is a potential conflict between the interests of sellers and what is best for the entire community.

What can the government do to ensure that markets are competitive? The first guideline might be borrowed from the medical profession: Do no harm. A productive government will refrain from using its powers to impose licenses, discriminatory taxes, price controls, tariffs, quotas, and other entry and trade restraints that lessen the intensity of competition. Competition is ubiquitous. Without the help of government, sellers will generally find it very difficult to limit the entry of rival firms (including rival producers from other countries) into a market. When entry into a market is costly and there are only a few sellers, collusive behavior is more likely. In an effort to deal with such cases, the United States has enacted a series of antitrust laws, most notably the Sherman Antitrust Act (1890) and the Clayton Act (1914), making it illegal for firms to collude or attempt to monopolize a product market.

For the most part, economists favor the principle of government action to ensure and promote competitive markets. There is considerable debate, however, about the effectiveness of past public policy in this area. Many economists believe that, by and large, antitrust policy has been ineffective. Others stress that government regulatory policies have often been counterproductive by restricting entry, protecting existing producers from potential competitors, and limiting price competition. When government takes these actions, it actually reduces the competitiveness of markets. As we proceed, we will return to this topic and consider it in more detail.

Externalities—Failure to Register Fully Costs and Benefits

When property rights are not fully enforced, the actions of a producer or consumer might harm the property (or the person) of another, because the law fails to force the party doing the harm to bear the cost or to stop the harm. This failure results in spillover effects called **externalities,** actions of an individual or a group that influence the well-being of others without their consent. When spillover effects are present because, for example, the courts have failed to enforce rights against pollution, markets will fail to register the full costs of the resources used to produce a good or service. As a result, the information conveyed by prices is an inaccurate reflection of relative scarcity.

Externalities
The side effects, or spillover effects, of an action that influence the well-being of nonconsenting parties. The nonconsenting parties may be either helped (by external benefits) or harmed (by external costs).

Examples of externalities abound. The steel mill pouring pollution into the air imposes an external cost on surrounding residents. An apartment resident playing loud music may impose a cost on neighbors seeking to study, relax, or sleep. Driving your car during rush hour increases the level of congestion, thereby imposing a cost on other motorists. Similarly, litterbugs, drunk drivers, muggers, and robbers impose unwanted and *unauthorized* costs on others.

The existence of externalities implies the lack of property rights, or a lack of enforcement of those rights. The apartment dweller who is bothered by a neighbor's noise either does not have a right to quiet or is unable to enforce the right. In either case, the maker of the noise is not forced to take into account the resulting discomfort of neighbors. Similarly, each motorist adding his or her car to heavy traffic will not be forced to consider the effects on others, unless there is a highway access fee reflecting the costs of congestion. When enforceable property rights are absent, externalities are a natural occurrence.

Not all externalities result in the imposition of a cost. Sometimes human actions generate benefits for nonparticipating parties. The homeowner who keeps a house in good condition and maintains a neat lawn improves the beauty of the entire community, providing benefits for other community members. A flood-control dam project built by upstream residents for their benefit may also generate gains for those who live downstream. Scientific theories benefit their authors, but the knowledge gained also contributes to the welfare of others who do not help to pay for their development. Again, a lack of enforceable property rights to the created benefit prevents the producer of the good or service generating the positive-valued externalities from reaping the full benefit.

Why do externalities create problems for the market mechanism? **Exhibit 5–2** can help answer this question. With competitive markets in equilibrium, the cost of a good (including the opportunity cost borne by the producer) will be paid by consumers. Unless consumer benefits exceed the opportunity cost of production, the goods will not be produced. What happens, though, when externalities are present?

Suppose that a business firm discharges smoke into the air or sewage into a river. Valuable resources—clean air and pure water—are used essentially for garbage disposal. The polluter may benefit from the garbage removal, but if those downwind or downstream who are harmed cannot successfully sue for damages, neither the firm nor the consumers of its products will pay for these costs. As part a of Exhibit 5–2 shows, the supply curve will understate the opportunity cost of production when these external costs are present. Since the producer has to consider only the cost to the firm and can ignore the costs imposed on secondary parties, supply curve S_1 is present. If the producer had to pay all costs, a smaller supply (S_2) would result.

The actual supply curve S_1 does not register fully the opportunity cost of producing the good. For the producer, the opportunity cost paid is low enough to merit

When external costs are present (a), the output level of a product will exceed the desired amount. Some units (beyond Q_2) will be produced even though their costs exceed the benefits they generate, causing reduced efficiency. In contrast, market output of goods that generate external benefits (b) will be less than the ideal level. Production that could generate more benefits than costs is not undertaken, and a lack of efficiency results.

EXHIBIT 5–2

EXTERNALITIES AND PROBLEMS FOR THE MARKET

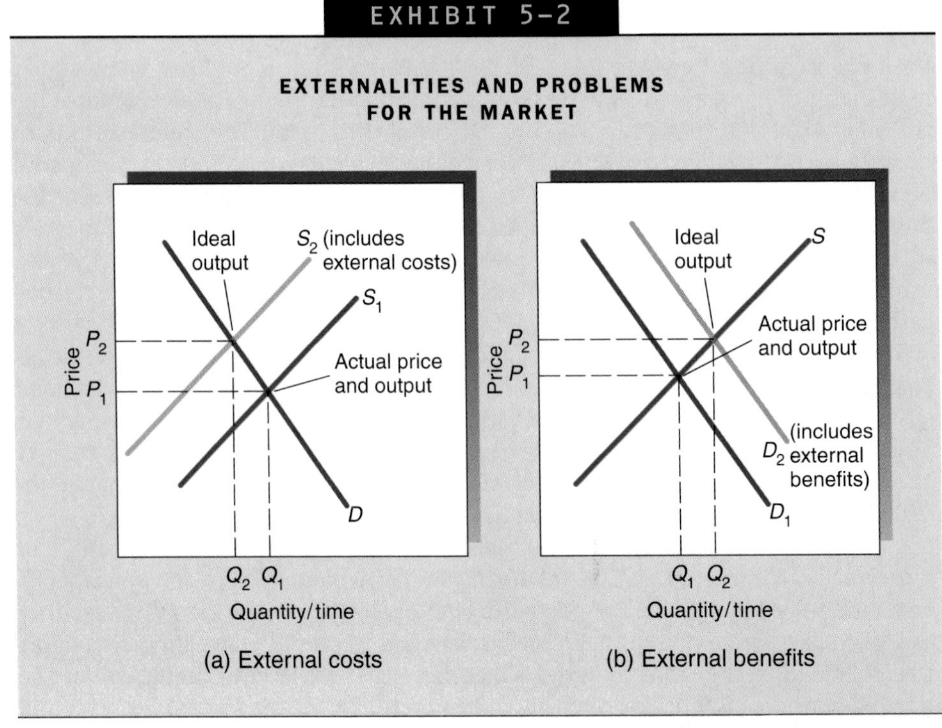

(a) External costs

(b) External benefits

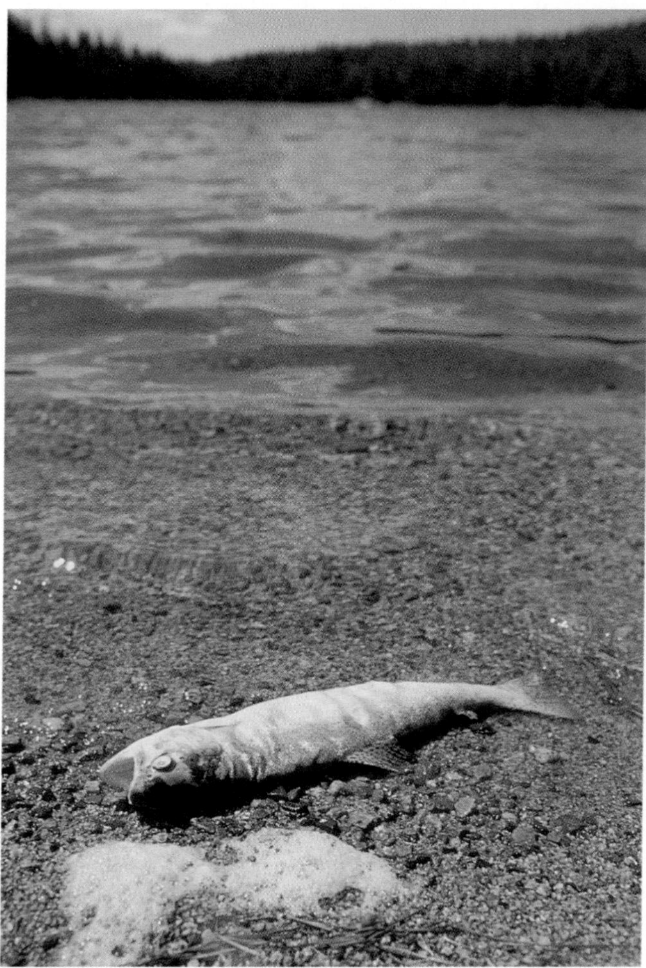

Externalities resulting from poorly defined and enforced property rights underlie the problems of excessive air and water pollution.

expansion in output beyond Q_2 (to Q_1), *even though the buyer's valuation of the additional units is less than their full opportunity cost.* The second efficiency condition, Rule 2, is violated. Inefficiency results because units are produced even though their value is less than their cost. Excessive air and water pollution are side effects. In the total picture, the harm caused by the added pollution outweighs the net benefits derived by buyers and sellers from the production of units beyond Q_2. The economy would have been better off if the units beyond Q_2 had not been produced. To repeat, this problem is caused by the inability or the failure of courts to protect the property rights of those downwind or downstream who are harmed.

As part b of Exhibit 5-2 shows, external benefits often result in opportunities forgone. A good, such as a flower garden in the front yard of a home, may be intended for private consumption. But others also benefit without having to shoulder any of the costs. Under these circumstances, the market demand curve D_1 will not register fully the total benefits, including those received by persons who do not help pay for their cost. Output Q_1 will result. Could the community gain from a greater output of the product? Yes. The demand curve D_2 reflects both the direct benefits to paying consumers and the benefits bestowed on secondary, nonpaying parties. Expansion of output beyond Q_1 to Q_2 would result in a net gain to the community. But because neither producers nor paying consumers can capture the secondary benefits, consumption level Q_1 will result. The potential net gain from the greater output level Q_2 will be lost. Rule 1 of our ideal efficiency criterion is violated. Once again, the failure of property rights enforcement causes the problem. In this case, producers are unable to collect payment from some of those who enjoy the goods or the services they produce.

Market participants can gain if they can figure out a way to capture the external benefits. Sometimes this can be done by expanding the functions of the firm. For example, developers of golf courses in recent years have typically purchased large tracts of land around the planned course *before it is built.* This places them in a position to resell the land at a higher price after the golf course has been completed, and thereby capture what would otherwise be external benefits.

The development of Walt Disney World in Florida provides an interesting case of entrepreneurial ingenuity designed to capture external benefits more fully. When Walt Disney developed Disneyland in California, the market value of the land in the immediate area soared as a result of the increase in demand for services (food, lodging, gasoline, and so on). Because the land in the area was owned by others, the developers of Disneyland were unable to capture these external benefits. However, when Walt Disney World was developed outside of Orlando, Florida, the owners purchased an enormous plot of land, far more than was needed for the amusement park. The value of this land soared, as the demand for hotels, restaurants, and other businesses increased with the development of Disney World. Through the years, the resale of land near the park has provided a major source of revenue for the Disney Corporation. While efforts of this type are helpful, they are unable to overcome fully the problems created by external benefits. Some unrealized potential gains remain, creating the potential for future improvement.

Summarizing, competitive markets will fail to give consumers and producers the correct signals and incentives when property rights are not fully defined and enforced, creating externalities. The market will tend to overallocate resources to the production of goods that impose external costs on nonconsenting parties and underallocate resources to the production of goods with external benefits. Government might be able to alter this situation. For example, it might be able to define and enforce property rights more clearly. Alternatively, it might levy a tax on goods that generate external costs and provide subsidies to activities that generate external benefits. While there is no assurance that government intervention will improve the situation, externalities do create the potential for productive action.

PUBLIC GOODS—A POTENTIAL PROBLEM FOR THE MARKET

Public goods
Jointly consumed goods that are not diminished when one person enjoys their consumption. When consumed by one person, they are also made available to others. National defense, flood control dams, and scientific theories are all public goods.

Public goods are difficult to provide commercially through the marketplace because there is no way to exclude nonpaying customers. For a good to be considered a public good, it must be (1) *joint-in-consumption* and (2) *nonexcludable.* A good is joint-in-consumption when many individuals can share in the consumption of the same unit of output. A radio broadcast signal, for example, can be shared by everyone within the listening range. When a good is joint-in-consumption, additional consumption by one person does not reduce the amount available to others. If an additional listener turns on her radio, this does not reduce the amount of the signal available for other listeners. Thus, the marginal cost of allowing an additional listener to share in the usage of the good is zero. Most goods do not have this shared consumption characteristic, but are instead rivals-in-consumption. Two individuals cannot simultaneously consume the same pair of jeans, for example. When one person purchases a pair of jeans, there is one less pair available for someone else.

The second characteristic of a public good is that it is nonexcludable. Nonexcludable means that it is impossible (or at least very costly) to exclude nonpaying customers from receipt of the good. Since those who do not pay cannot be excluded, no one has much incentive to help pay for such goods. This creates a problem with **free riders,** persons who receive the benefits of the good without helping to pay for its cost. When a large number of people become free riders, not very much of the public good is produced. This is precisely the problem with market provision in the case of public goods—they will be undersupplied by the market. This will be true even if the good is quite valuable. Suppose national defense were provided entirely through the market. Would you voluntarily help to pay for it? Your contribution would have little impact on the total supply of defense available to each of us, even if you made a large personal contribution. Many citizens, even though they might value defense highly, would become free riders, and few funds would be available for the finance of national defense.

Free rider
One who receives the benefit of a good without contributing to its costs. Public goods and commodities that generate external benefits offer people the opportunity to become free riders.

It is important to note that it is the characteristics of the good, not the sector in which it is produced, that distinguishes a public good. In reality, government produces both public and nonpublic goods, and so do private markets. Many goods provided in the public sector, ranging from medical services and education to mail delivery and trash collection, do not qualify as public goods. In fact, pure public goods are rare. National defense is probably the closest example. Keeping the air in a city clean also qualifies as a public good. Similarly, the actions of a central banking system and the judicial and legal systems could also be classified as public goods.

Just because a good is a public good does not necessarily mean that markets will fail to supply it. When the benefit of producing these goods is high, entrepreneurs will attempt to find innovative ways of overcoming the free rider problem. Radio broadcasts, which have both of the public good characteristics, are still produced well by the private sector. The free rider problem has been overcome through the use of advertising (which generates indirect revenue from listeners), rather than directly charging listeners. Private entrepreneurs have also used such devices as signal encoders for

The Dutch boy has his finger in the dike, to prevent the leak from becoming a torrent and breaking the dike. Will the man help out with a donation, or will he be a free rider?

television broadcasts like HBO, copy protection on videotapes, and tie-in purchases (for example, tying the purchase of a software instruction manual with the purchase of the software itself) to overcome the free rider problem. The marketing of computer software provides an interesting illustration. Since the same software program can be copied without reducing the amount available, and it is costly to prevent consumption by nonpayers, software clearly has public good characteristics. Nonetheless, Bill Gates became the richest man in the world by producing and marketing this public good!

Public goods often cause a breakdown in the harmony between self-interest and the public interest. In spite of the innovative efforts of entrepreneurs, the quantity of a public good supplied strictly through market allocation will often be smaller than the quantity consistent with economic efficiency. This will create the potential for productive public sector action.

Potential Information Problems

In the real world, market choices, like other decisions, are made with incomplete information. Consumers do not have perfect knowledge about the quality of a product, the price of alternative products, or side effects that may result from its use. They may make incorrect decisions, decisions they will later regret, because they do not possess good information.

The reality of imperfect knowledge is not the fault of the market. In fact, the market provides consumers with a strong incentive to acquire information. If they mistakenly purchase a "lemon" product, they will suffer the consequences. Furthermore, sellers have a strong incentive to inform consumers of the benefits of their products, especially in comparison to competing products. However, circumstances will influence the incentive structure confronted by both buyers and sellers.

The consumer's information problem is minimal if the item is purchased regularly. Consider the purchase of soap. There is little cost associated with trying alternative brands. Since soap is a regularly purchased product, trial and error is an economical means of determining which brand is most suitable to one's needs. Soap, like toothpaste, most food products, lawn service, and gasoline, is a **repeat-purchase item.** The consumer can use past experience to good advantage when buying such items.

Repeat-purchase item
An item purchased often by the same buyer.

When dependent on repeat-purchase customers, sellers have a strong incentive to supply consumers with accurate information. Failure to do so would adversely affect future sales. Because future demand is directly related to the satisfaction level of current customers, sellers of repeat-purchase items will want to help their customers make satisfying long-run choices. In this case, there is a harmony of interests between buyers and sellers.

This harmony, however, is not always present. Major problems of conflicting interests, inadequate information, and unhappy customers arise when goods are either (1) difficult to evaluate on inspection and seldom repeatedly purchased from the same producer or (2) potentially capable of serious and lasting harmful side effects that cannot be predicted by a layperson. Under these conditions, human nature being what it is, we would expect some unscrupulous producers to sell low-quality, defective, and even harmful goods.

When customers are unable to distinguish between high-quality and low-quality goods, business entrepreneurs have an incentive to cut costs by reducing quality. Consumers get less for their dollars. Since sellers in this situation are not dependent on repeat customers, those who cut costs by cutting quality may survive and even prosper in the marketplace. ***The probability of customer dissatisfaction is thus increased by the absence of adequate information. Accordingly, the case for an unhampered market mechanism is weakened.***

Consider the consumer's information problem when an automobile is purchased. Are most consumers capable of properly evaluating the safety equipment? Except for a handful of experts, most people are not. Some consumers might individually seek expert advice. And entrepreneurs have sometimes found ingenious ways to benefit from providing consumers with more reliable information. (See the feature on

APPLICATIONS IN ECONOMICS

Information Problems as Profit Opportunities

When consumers can benefit from additional information, entrepreneurs can profit if they find a way to be paid for providing the information. Entrepreneurs are always looking for ways to earn more by providing consumers things for which they are willing to pay. ***Consumers have the incentive to seek good information, even though it is costly. Entrepreneurial publishers and other providers of information help consumers find what they seek by providing expert evaluations of the special characteristics built into complex products.*** For car buyers and computer buyers, for example, publishers market dozens of specialized magazines containing expert analyses and opinions from almost any point of view. Laboratory test results and detailed product evaluations on a wide variety of goods are provided by *Consumer Reports, Consumer Research,* and other publications.

Franchises are another way that entrepreneurs have responded to the need of consumers for more and better information. The tourist traveling through an area for the first time—and very possibly the only time—may find that eating at a franchised food outlet and sleeping at a franchised motel are the cheapest ways to avoid annoying and costly mistakes. The franchiser sets the standards for all firms in the chain and establishes procedures, including continuous inspection, designed to maintain the standards. Franchisers have a strong incentive to maintain their reputation for quality, because if it declines, their ability to sell new franchises is hurt. Even though the tourist may visit a particular establishment only once, the franchise turns that visit into a "repeat purchase," since the reputation of the entire national franchise operation is at stake.

Similarly, the advertising of a brand name nationally develops a reputation that is at stake each time a purchase is made. How much would the Coca-Cola Company pay to avoid the sale of a dangerous bottle of Coke? Surely, it would be a large sum. The company's brand name is worth an estimated $24 billion, and that good name is a hostage to quality control. Because Coke is a household name, any serious quality-control problem would be broadcast worldwide and do enormous financial damage to the firm. Advertising investments play a part, too, helping to build a reputation that consumers know is at stake. The value of the reputation built with the help of advertising is threatened if the firm cheats customers.

Enterprising entrepreneurs have found ways to assure buyers that products meet high standards of quality, even when the producer is small and not so well known. Consider the case of Best Western Motels.[1] Best Western owns no motels; however, building on the franchise idea, it publishes rules and standards with which motel owners must comply if they are to use the Best Western brand name and the reservation service that the company also operates. In order to protect its brand name, Best Western sends out inspectors to see that each Best Western motel in fact meets the standards. Every disappointed customer harms the reputation and reduces the value of the Best Western name, and reduces the willingness of motel owners to pay for use of the name. The standards are designed to keep customers satisfied. Even though each motel owner has only a relatively small operation, renting the Best Western name provides the small operator with the kind of international reputation formerly available only to large firms. In effect, Best Western acts as a regulator of all motels bearing its name. As it does so, it provides both consumers and producers with a market solution to problems resulting from imperfect information.

Another kind of private regulator is Underwriters Laboratories, or UL. It establishes its own standards for safety in electrical equipment. Manufacturers voluntarily submit their equipment to UL and pay the firm to test their products. They do so because if UL certifies that the product meets UL standards, that fact can be advertised, and consumers, knowing the UL reputation, will be more willing to buy the product. Again, the certifying firm, UL in this case, has a strong incentive to certify only those electrical products that do indeed meet their safety standards, because the value of the UL name is at stake. That value depends entirely on the effectiveness of its claims that UL-certified products are safe to use.

As these examples indicate, entrepreneurial measures, such as assuring the quality of a firm or franchise, or otherwise protecting a brand name, can be both expensive and effective. But they cannot guarantee that customers will never be cheated or disappointed after a transaction. We live in a world of imperfect information.

[1]This section draws from Randall G. Holcombe and Lora P. Holcombe, "The Market for Regulation," *Journal of Institutional and Theoretical Economics* 142, no. 4 (1986): 684–696.

"Information Problems as Profit Opportunities.") In many cases, however, it may be more efficient to prevent market failure by having the government regulate automobile safety and require certain safety equipment.

As useful and important as are the published evaluations of experts, franchise operations, advertising, brand-name reputations, and private regulatory firms, they cannot solve a kind of information problem that has little to do with product design or manufacture. This is called the **asymmetric-information problem,** and it can make markets themselves, for some products, difficult to operate effectively. ***The problem of asymmetric information arises when either the potential buyer or potential seller has important information that the other side does not have.***

Asymmetric-information problem
A problem arising when either buyers or sellers have important information about the product that is not possessed by the other side in potential transactions.

Think for a moment about buyers trying to avoid "lemons" in the used car market. Sellers know which cars are above average quality and which are below average. Buyers, on the other hand, cannot tell which is which simply by looking at and test-driving them. Thus buyers will be willing to pay no more than what they believe is the average value of all cars on the market. But if better-than-average cars cannot bring better-than-average prices, then fewer of them will be sold in the market, and if below-average cars bring average prices, then more of the below-average cars will be offered. Buyers understand this, so they expect the average car in such a market to be below the average of all existing cars of that age and type. Owners of better cars are reluctant to sell at the low market price and it is hard to make a market for cars of above-average quality when buyers cannot be convinced that they actually are better than average.

Sellers of the better cars have an incentive to provide additional information in order to get a higher price for their superior goods. But how is this done? How can they support their claims about their product being better? The answers differ according to whether the seller is a private owner or a dealership. Car owners can present their records of oil changes and lubrications to show that these services, important to the long-run durability of a car, have been performed on schedule. Dealers, whose mechanics inspect the cars before they are offered for sale, may offer money-back guarantees, or warranties that promise free repairs if needed within a specified time, on the most reliable cars they sell. The other cars they sell will be sold "as is" with no warranty. Sellers of products can even give price guarantees, as some stores do when they advertise that, if the buyer finds a lower price for the same product within a specified period of time, the seller will refund the difference. By offering to bear quality and price risks for buyers, sellers provide credibility to their claims about better products and prices. In other words, they improve the quality of the information offered and reduce the problem of asymmetric information.

The problem of asymmetric information also arises when buyers know more than sellers. Consider the market for health insurance. Buyers know their own health problems better than insurance companies do. Those whose health history and lifestyle threaten greater potential health costs may pay the same as others but later collect more from the insurance company. In contrast, the same insurance at the same price is less attractive to the healthiest people, and fewer of them will buy it. When the company is unable to identify those with the greatest potential health costs and charge them more, it will have to charge its healthier customers a rate that exceeds their expected future insurance claims. But this would drive away even more of the healthier potential buyers, making the situation even worse. As in the case of used cars, asymmetric information reduces the effectiveness of the market. Just as the best used cars may be hard to sell at a price reflecting their full value, so, too, may the healthiest individuals find it hard to find reasonably priced insurance when asymmetric information is present.

What can be done about asymmetric information when buyers have information but sellers do not? Buyers, like sellers, are willing to provide information when it is to their advantage to do so. Insurance buyers with the best health record, who are therefore least likely to have future insurance claims, can often get lower insurance rates by opening their private medical records to the insurance company. Sellers who otherwise have no right to see that information may find it gladly offered by the healthiest buyers when buyers know they will be offered lower insurance prices as a result.

We have discussed many ways in which market participants can reduce the problems they face due to the scarcity and cost of information. These are not totally effective, however. As with imperfect competition, externalities and public goods, poor information remains a problem that keeps markets from reaching their hypothetical ideal.

LOOKING *Ahead*

This chapter focused on the role of government from the standpoint of economic efficiency. Our analysis indicates that government can contribute positively to the prosperity of people through the provision of a legal and monetary environment for the smooth operation of competitive markets. Government may also contribute by providing a limited set of public goods and following policies capable of minimizing problems arising from externalities and poor information.

The potential of government to promote economic efficiency does not necessarily mean that it will. The political process is merely an alternative method of organizing economic activity. There is no assurance that even a democratic government will always "do the right thing." Furthermore, people can be expected to turn to government for reasons other than economic efficiency—pursuit of personal gain through subsidies, income transfers, and regulation of rivals, for example. Political decision making is complex, but the tools of economics can enhance our understanding of how it works. The next chapter will focus on this topic—the operation of government, when it is likely to work well, and when there is reason to expect that it will not work so well.

KEY POINTS

➤ Government has the exclusive right to use coercive force. Individuals and groups compete to influence the use of government's powers to tax, spend, and regulate.

➤ Public-sector organization can take from some and give to others, but scarcity guarantees that someone always pays. Benefits and costs are distributed differently in the public sector, as opposed to the private sector.

➤ Voters face a bundle purchase problem and are unable to vote for some policies favored by one candidate and other policies favored by the candidate's opponent.

➤ To find the cost of government, add the opportunity cost of the resources used to produce goods provided through government, the cost of tax and regulatory compliance, and the excess-burden cost of taxation and regulation. Individuals bear the burden of taxes (and regulations), regardless of whether firms or individuals write the checks to government.

➤ The protective function of government provides a framework in which individuals gain by acting peacefully and constructively. The productive function of government can help people get goods that would not easily be supplied through market transactions.

➤ When markets fail to produce the ideal quantity and mix of outputs, the problems can generally be traced to one of four sources: absence of competition, externalities, public goods, and poor information. Externalities and public goods reflect a lack of fully defined, enforced, and tradeable property rights.

➤ Entrepreneurs in markets have an incentive to find solutions to each market problem, and new solutions are constantly being discovered. But problems remain, and each creates the potential for improvement through government action.

CRITICAL ANALYSIS QUESTIONS

*1. If producers are to be provided with an incentive to produce a good, why is it important for them to be able to prevent nonpaying customers from receiving the good?

2. Explain in your own words what is meant by external costs and external benefits. Why may market allocations be less than ideal when externalities are present?

3. Why are public goods troublesome for markets to allocate efficiently?

*4. Which of the following are public goods?
(a) an antimissile system surrounding Washington, D.C.
(b) a fire department
(c) tennis courts
(d) Yellowstone National Park
(e) elementary schools
Explain, using the definition of a public good.

5. Suppose that Abel builds a factory next to Baker's farm, and air pollution from the factory harms Baker's crops. Is Baker's property right to the land being violated? Is an externality present? What if the pollution invades Baker's home and harms her health? Are her property rights violated? Is an externality present? Explain.

6. English philosopher John Locke argued that the protection of each individual's person and property (acquired without the use of violence, theft, or fraud) was the primary function of government. Why is this protection important to the efficient operation of an economy?

7. "The protective function of government is a key to the success of the market sector in the economy." Is this true or false? Explain.

8. "The traveler, in a market economy, has no chance for a fair deal. Local people may be treated well, but the traveler has no way to know, for example, who offers a good night's lodging at a fair price, if the quality and price are not regulated by government." Is this true or false? Explain.

9. If sellers of toasters were able to organize among themselves, reduce their output, and raise their price, how would economic efficiency be affected? Explain in terms of the impact on the marginal costs to sellers of the last (marginal) units produced, and the marginal benefits to buyers of obtaining the last (marginal) units.

10. (a) Explain why economic inefficiency may result when a producer of copper imposes external costs on growers of alfalfa located downwind from the copper facility.
(b) In terms of property rights, what must be true if the costs on downwind farmers are external costs?

11. "Elementary education is obviously a public good. After all, it is provided by government." Evaluate this statement.

---

*Asterisk denotes questions for which answers are given in Appendix B.

Special Feature: The Size and Functions of Government—A Graphic and Pictorial Presentation

Chapter 5 has focused on how government might establish a framework for the smooth operation of markets and engage in certain activities—supply public goods and help deal with externalities, for example—that will make it possible to produce more value from the available resources. How do real-world governments fit this model? How have the size and functions of government changed through time? This brief special feature presents data on spending and taxation related to these questions.

GROWTH OF GOVERNMENT

As **Exhibit 5A–1** illustrates, the total government expenditures were only 10.1 percent of GDP in 1929, and most of that was at the state and local levels. (Note: GDP is a measure of the size of the economy. The term will be explained more fully in Chapter 7.) Federal expenditures accounted for only 3 percent of total output in 1929. During the 1930–1970 period, both the size and composition of government changed dramatically. By 1970 total government expenditures had risen to 32.5 percent of the economy, more

EXHIBIT 5A–1

THE GROWTH OF GOVERNMENT EXPENDITURES, 1929–1997

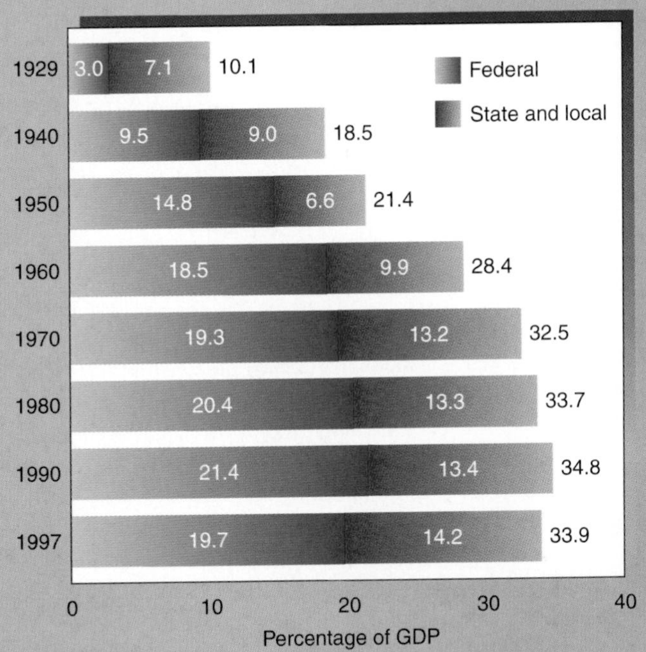

SOURCE: Economic Report of the President, *1998, Tables B-1, B-20, B-83, B-84. Grants to state and local governments are included in federal expenditures.*

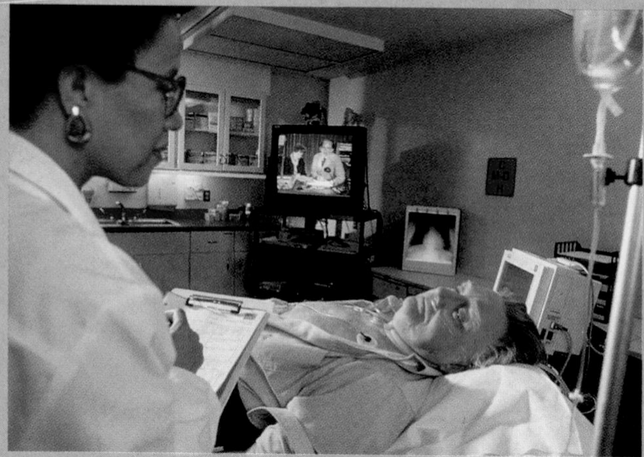

During the past four decades, government spending on defense has declined substantially as a share of the economy, while that for income transfers and health care has increased sharply.

than triple the level of 1929. Most of this growth of government took place at the federal level. *As a share of our economy,* federal expenditures in 1970 were more than six times the level of 1929. Since 1970 the size of government as a proportion of the economy has grown at a much slower rate. ***In 1997 total government expenditures comprised 33.9 percent of GDP, only slightly higher than the figure for 1970.***

SIZE OF GOVERNMENT: UNITED STATES COMPARED TO OTHER COUNTRIES

The size of government varies substantially across countries. As **Exhibit 5A–2** shows, government expenditures constitute 50 percent or more of GDP in Sweden, Denmark, France, Belgium, and Italy. In contrast, government spending amounts to only about one-third of GDP in the United States, Australia, and Japan. In Singapore, South Korea, Thailand, and Hong Kong, the size of government is still smaller.

CHANGING COMPOSITION—LESS SPENDING ON DEFENSE, MORE ON INCOME TRANSFERS AND HEALTH CARE

Government purchases
Current expenditures on consumption and investment goods provided by federal, state, and local governments; they exclude transfer payments.

Transfer payments
Payments to individuals or institutions that are not linked to the current supply of a good or service by the recipient.

It is important to distinguish between (1) government purchases of goods and services and (2) transfer payments. **Government purchases** occur when either consumption or investment goods are supplied through the public sector. Government-supplied consumption goods would include government expenditures on such items as police and fire protection, medical services, and administration. Government investments would include the provision of long-lasting goods, such as highways, jet planes, and buildings. **Transfer payments** are transfers of income from taxpayers to recipients who do not provide current goods and services in exchange for these payments. Simply put, transfer payments take income from some to provide additional income to others. By far, social security is the largest income transfer program. Pensions of retired government employees, along with income transfers to the unemployed, the disabled, and welfare recipients are also included in the income transfer category.

EXHIBIT 5A–2

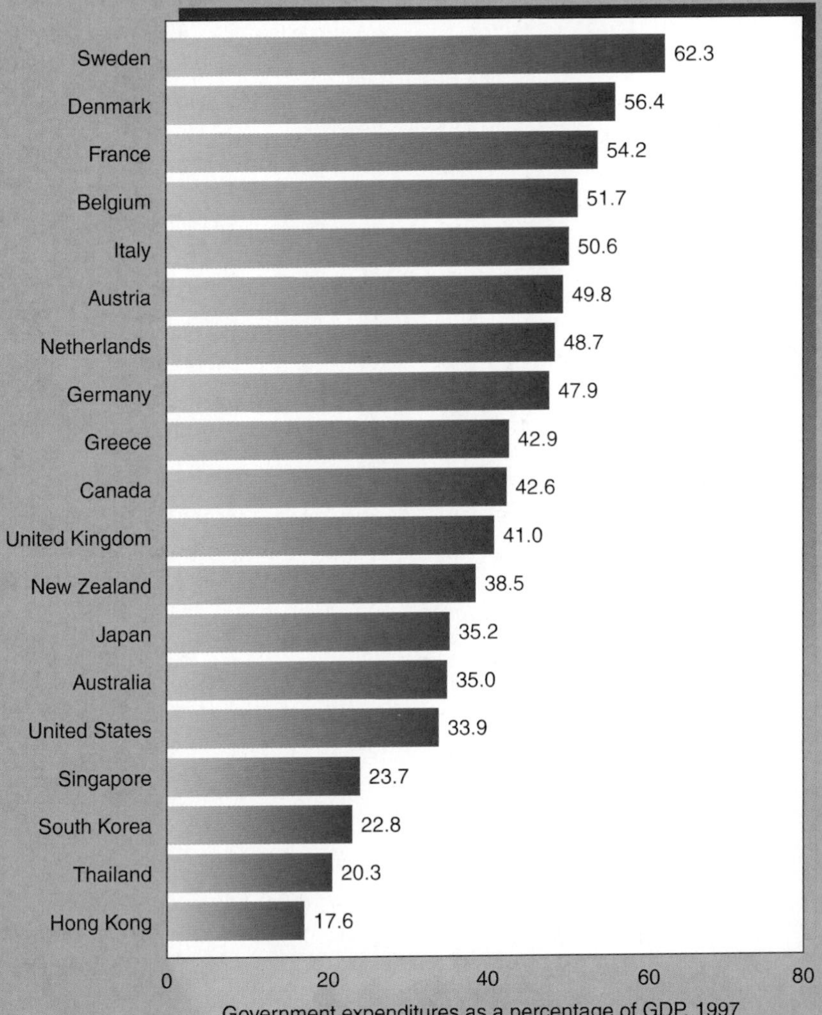

SOURCES: Organization for Economic Cooperation and Development, Economic Outlook, *Dec. 1997;* Economic Report of the President, *1998; and International Monetary Fund,* Government Finance Statistics Yearbook, *1997.*

Even though government spending as a share of the economy in the United States has changed only modestly since 1970, there has been a dramatic shift in the composition of government spending during the past four decades. Spending on defense has fallen as a share of the economy, while expenditures on transfer payments (income transfers) and health care have soared.

As Exhibit 5A–3 shows, in 1960, defense expenditures comprised 10.4 percent of GDP, more than half of the total spending of the federal government. By 1997, defense spending was only 4.3 percent of GDP (and less than 20 percent of the federal budget). In contrast, government expenditures on income transfers rose from 5.6 percent of

EXHIBIT 5A-3

CHANGES IN EXPENDITURES ON DEFENSE, INCOME TRANSFERS, AND HEALTH CARE: 1960–1997

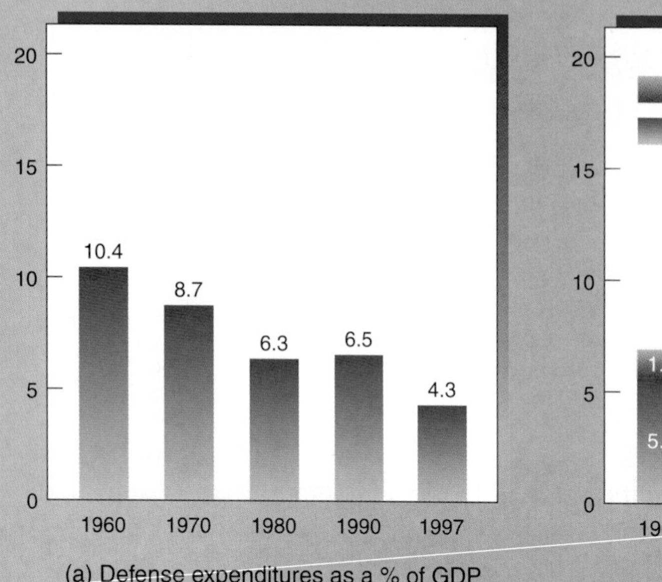

(a) Defense expenditures as a % of GDP

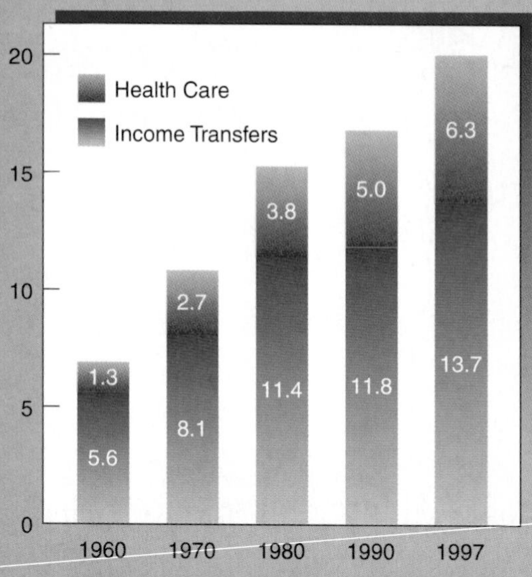

(b) Expenditures as a % of GDP

Note: The 1997 figure for health care expenditures was based on 1996 data.

SOURCES: Economic Report of the President, *1998, Tables B-1 and B-84, and* Health Care Financing Review, *Fall 1997, Table 9, p. 187.*

GDP in 1960 to 13.7 percent in 1997. During this same period, government spending on health care, primarily Medicare for the elderly and Medicaid for those with low incomes, rose from 1.3 percent of GDP in 1960 to 6.3 percent in 1997. Spending on income transfers and health care now constitutes 20 percent of GDP, substantially more than half of total government expenditures.

PRIMARY FUNCTIONS OF GOVERNMENT: FEDERAL COMPARED TO STATE AND LOCAL

Exhibit 5A–4 indicates the primary categories of government spending for both the federal and state and local levels. The figures reveal a great deal about the nature of the federal government in the mid-1990s. As part a of Exhibit 5A–4 shows, federal expenditures for just three things—(1) income transfers (including social security and other income security programs), (2) health care, and (3) net interest on the national debt—accounted for 72 percent of federal spending in 1997. Of course, the federal government is solely responsible for national defense and international affairs, which accounted for an additional 18 percent of the federal budget. This means that expenditures on everything else—the federal courts, national parks, highways, education,

EXHIBIT 5A–4

WHAT GOVERNMENTS BUY

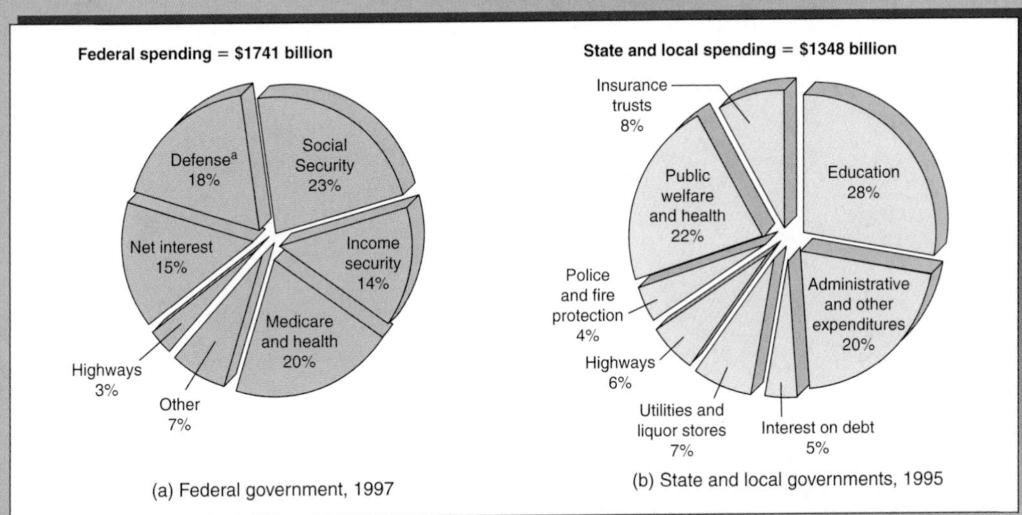

[a]*Including international affairs.*

SOURCES: Economic Report of the President, *1998, Table B-81, and* Statistical Abstract of the United States, *1998, Table 506.*

job training, agriculture, energy, natural resources, federal law enforcement, and numerous other programs—were only 10 percent of the federal budget.

Part b of Exhibit 5A–4 highlights the functional responsibilities of state and local governments. In the United States, public education has traditionally been the responsibility of state and local governments. Education is the largest spending category for state and local governments. Administration, public welfare and health, highways, utilities, insurance trust funds, law enforcement, and fire protection are other major areas of expenditure at the state and local levels.

Education constitutes the largest category of spending at the state and local levels of government.

EXHIBIT 5A-5

SOURCES OF GOVERNMENT REVENUE

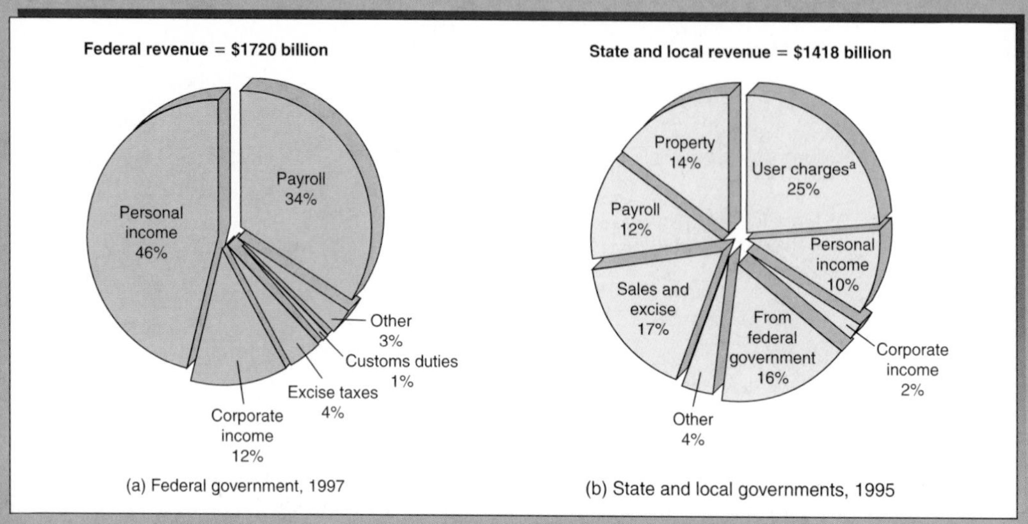

[a]*Revenues from government-operated utilities and liquor stores are included in this category.*

SOURCES: Economic Report of the President, *1998, Table B-81, and* Statistical Abstract of the United States, *1998, Table 506.*

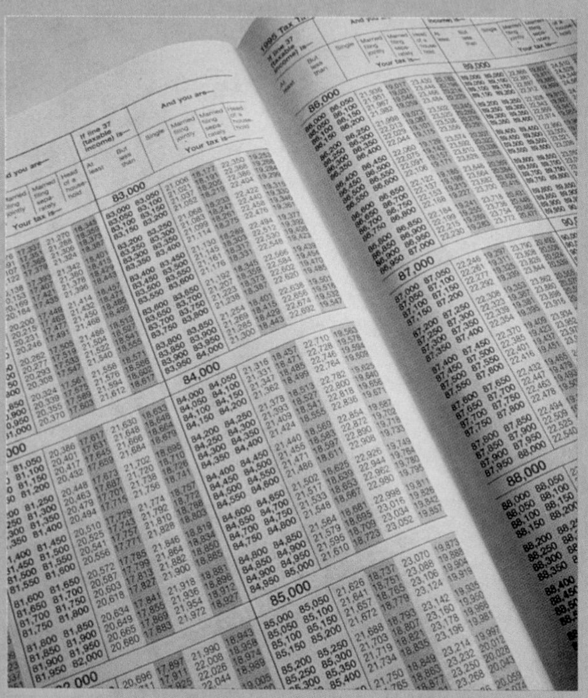

TAXES AND OTHER SOURCES OF GOVERNMENT REVENUES

Exhibit 5A–5 indicates the major revenue sources for both the federal and state and local levels of government. At the federal level, the personal income tax and payroll tax account for 80 percent of federal revenue. At the state and local level, **user charges,** sales taxes, property taxes, and grants from the federal government provide the primary sources of revenue.

User charges
Payments that users (consumers) are required to make if they want to receive certain services provided by the government.

The personal income and payroll taxes account for 80 percent of federal revenue.

CHAPTER 6

[Public choice] analyzes the motives and activities of politicians, civil servants and government officials as people with personal interests that may or may not coincide with the interest of the general public they are supposed to serve. It is an analysis of how people behave in the world as it is.

Arthur Seldon[1]

It does not follow that whenever laissez faire falls short government interference is expedient; since the inevitable drawbacks of the latter may, in any particular case, be worse than the shortcomings of private enterprise.

Harry Sidgwick, 1887[2]

The Economics of Collective Decision Making

CHAPTER FOCUS

- What are the major forces that determine outcomes under representative democracy?
- Can government action be mutually advantageous to all citizens?
- Does democratic decision making lead to economic efficiency? Is there sometimes a conflict between good economics and good politics? Why?
- Why does representative democracy often tax some people in order to provide benefits to others? What types of income transfers are attractive to politicians?
- Can government action sometimes improve on the efficiency of the market? When is it most likely to do so?

[1]Preface to Gordon Tullock, *The Vote Motive* (London: Institute of Economic Affairs, 1976), p. x.

[2] Quoted in Charles Wolf, Jr., *Markets or Government* (Cambridge: MIT Press, 1988), p. 17.

As we stressed in the previous chapter, the economic role of government is pivotal. The government sets the rules of the game. Its performance with regard to the protection of property rights and establishment of a stable monetary environment affects the efficiency of market allocation. Governments may also contribute positively through the efficient production of public goods. In addition to these basic functions, modern governments are also often involved in the operation of enterprises, provision of essentially private goods, regulation, and, most significantly, income transfer activities. (See prior special section, Facts and Figures of Government.)

Given the size and breadth of government economic activity, it is vitally important to understand how it works. Government decisions are collective, or political, decisions. In most industrialized nations, political control is exercised through a representative democracy. In this chapter, we will use the economic way of thinking to study collective decision making and learn more about how a representative democracy functions and what we can expect from it.

AN OVERVIEW OF COLLECTIVE DECISION MAKING

It is important to recognize that government, including one that is controlled democratically, is not a corrective device that will always do the right thing or necessarily undertake policies that promote the general welfare. It is, instead, an alternative method of social organization—an institutional process through which individuals collectively make choices and carry out activities.

Public-choice analysis
The study of decision making as it affects the formation and operation of collective organizations, such as governments. In general, the principles and methodology of economics are applied to political science topics.

Public-choice analysis is a branch of economics that applies the principles and methodology of economics to the operation of the political process. In analyzing the behavior of people in the marketplace, economists develop a logically consistent theory of behavior that can be tested against reality. Public choice applies this same methodology to collective decision making. It develops a logically consistent theory linking individual behavior to political action, analyzes the implications of the theory, and tests them against events in the real world. Since the theory of collective decision making is not as well developed as our theory of market behavior, our conclusions will not be as well defined. During the past 40 years, however, social scientists have made great strides, enhancing our understanding of public sector resource allocation.[3]

Economists use the self-interest postulate to enhance our understanding of decisions in the market. Likewise, public-choice economists apply the self-interest postulate to political decision making. They assume that, just as people are motivated by narrow interests and the desire for personal wealth, power, and prestige in the market sector, so, too, will these factors influence them when they make decisions in the political arena.

[3]The contributions of Kenneth Arrow, James Buchanan, Duncan Black, Anthony Downs, Mancur Olson, Robert Tollison, and Gordon Tullock have been particularly important. Public choice is something of a cross between economics and political science. Thus, advanced courses are generally offered in both departments.

OUTSTANDING ECONOMIST

James Buchanan (1919-)

James Buchanan is a key figure in the "public choice revolution." His most famous work, *The Calculus of Consent* (1962), coauthored with Gordon Tullock, argues that unless rules bring the self-interests of the political players into harmony with the wise use of resources, government will go awry.[1] This and related contributions won him the 1986 Nobel Prize in economics.

[1]J. M. Buchanan and G. Tullock, *The Calculus of Consent* (Ann Arbor: University of Michigan Press, 1962).

Closely related to self-interest as a motivator for politicians and bureaucrats are the concepts of survival and expansion. In the private sector, even if some managers are not primarily seeking profits, the profit-making firms are most likely to survive, prosper, and expand; and they are the firms that will be imitated. Similarly, in the public sector, politicians and the bureaucrats they hire must often act in the narrow self-interest of their constituents (and not incidentally in their own career self-interests) if they hope to survive. Those who cooperate most closely with powerful constituency groups will obtain more political clout and have the opportunity to lead larger government agencies.

As we illustrated in Exhibit II-B (Introduction to Part II), the collective decision process can be thought of as a complex interaction among voters, legislators, and bureaucrats. Citizen-voters elect a legislative body, which levies taxes and allocates budgets to various government agencies and bureaus. Directed by legislators, civil servants utilize the funds to supply government services and income transfers to the voters. In a representative democracy, voter support determines the composition of the legislative body, and a majority vote of the legislature is generally required for the passage of taxes, budget allocations, and regulatory activities. Let us take a closer look at the incentive structure confronting the three primary political players—voters, legislators, and bureaucrats—and consider the implications with regard to the operation of the political process.

THE VOTER-CONSUMER

How do voters decide whom to support? No doubt many factors influence their decision. Since voters must choose a candidate to represent them on a great many issues, they cannot know in detail how (and how effectively) the candidate will try to influence each issue in the future. Of necessity, the criteria they use must be very general. Which candidate appears to be the most persuasive, so as to represent best the voters back home? Who appears to be honest, sincere, and competent? Most voters do not know the candidates personally, so several such questions may come down to this: Which one presents the best television image?

The self-interest postulate indicates that voters, like market consumers, will ask, "What can you do for me, and for my goals, and how much will it cost me?" The greater the voter's perceived net personal gain from a particular candidate's election, the more likely it is that the voter will favor that candidate. In contrast, the greater the perceived net economic cost imposed on the voter by the positions of a candidate, the less inclined the voter will be to support the candidate. Other things equal, voters will tend to support those candidates whom they believe will provide them the most government services and transfer benefits, net of personal costs.

Unfortunately, rational voters frequently lack the detailed information needed to cast their ballots in a truly knowledgeable fashion. As we discussed in Chapter 5, collective decisions break the direct link between the individual voter's choice and the outcome of the issue. ***Most citizens recognize that their vote is unlikely to determine the outcome of an election. So they have little incentive to spend much effort seeking the information needed to cast an informed ballot. Economists refer to this lack of incentive as the* rational ignorance effect.**

Rational ignorance effect
Voter ignorance resulting from the fact that people perceive their individual votes as unlikely to be decisive. Therefore, they rationally have little incentive to seek the information needed to cast an informed vote.

Most voters simply rely on information that is supplied to them freely by candidates (via political advertising) and the mass media, as well as conversations with friends and coworkers. The rational ignorance effect explains why the majority of individuals of voting age cannot accurately identify their congressional representatives, much less identify and understand those representatives' positions on such issues as minimum wage legislation, tariffs, and agricultural policy. The fact that voters acquire scanty information merely indicates that they are responding rationally to economic incentives.

To see in a more personal way why citizens are likely to make better-informed decisions as consumers than as voters, imagine that you are planning to buy a car next week and also to vote for one of two Senate candidates. You have narrowed your choice of a car to either a Ford or a Honda. In the voting booth, you will choose between candidates Smith and Jones. Both the auto purchase and the Senate vote involve complex trade-offs for you. The two cars come with many options, and you must choose among dozens of different combinations; the winning Senate candidate will represent you on hundreds of issues, although you are limited to voting for only one of the two choices.

Which decision will command more of your scarce time for research and thinking about the best choice? Because your choice with regard to the car is decisive, and you must pay for what you choose, an uninformed car purchase could be very costly for you. But if you mistakenly vote for the wrong Senate candidate out of ignorance, the probability is virtually zero that your vote will decide who wins. Because your vote will not swing the election, a mistake or poorly informed choice will have little consequence. It would not be surprising, then, if you spent substantial time considering the car purchase and very little time becoming informed about either the candidates or the political issues at election time. The evidence is consistent with this view. For example, citizens in modern democracies support a great many profitable

Voters, politicians, and bureaucrats are the primary decision makers in the political arena.

auto magazines, while even the very best of the magazines focusing on politics and policy cannot operate without donated funds. Citizens simply will not pay enough for even a single political magazine in the United States to earn a profit.

The fact that one's vote is unlikely to be decisive explains more than lack of information on the part of voters. It also helps to explain why many citizens fail to vote. Even in a presidential election, only about half of all voting-age Americans take the time to register and vote. Given the low probability that one's vote will be decisive, this low voter turnout should not be surprising. The rationality of voters is further indicated by the fact that, when voters perceive that the election is close, voter turnout is larger. A vote in a close election has a greater chance of actually making a difference.

The Politician-Supplier

Public-choice theory postulates that pursuit of votes is the primary stimulus shaping the behavior of political suppliers. In varying degrees, such factors as pursuit of the public interest, compassion for the poor, and the achievement of fame, wealth, and power may influence the behavior of politicians. But regardless of ultimate motivation, the ability of politicians to achieve their objectives is sorely dependent upon their ability to get elected and reelected.

Rationally uninformed voters often must be convinced to "want" a candidate. Voter perceptions may be based on realities, but it is always perceptions, not the realities themselves, that influence decisions. This is true regardless of whether the decisions are private or political. As a result, a candidate's positive attributes must be brought to the attention of the rationally ignorant voters, whose attention is likely to be focused on their jobs, various civic activities, and local sports teams (which are probably more entertaining). An expert staff, sophisticated polling to ferret out which issues and which positions will be favored by voters, and high-quality advertising to shape a favorable image for the candidate are vitally important for a successful campaign. Thus, political campaigns are costly. For example, it is not unusual for an incumbent candidate for the U.S. Senate to spend more than $10 million during the two years prior to each election.

Are we implying that politicians are selfish, caring only for their pocketbooks and reelection chances? The answer is no. When people act in the political sphere, they may genuinely want to help their fellow citizens. Factors other than personal political gain, narrowly defined, may influence their actions. On certain issues, political officials may feel strongly that their position is best for the nation, even though it may not be currently popular. The national interest as perceived by the political supplier may conflict with the position that would be most favorable to reelection prospects. Some politicians may opt for the national interest even when it means political defeat. None of this is inconsistent with an economic view of public choice.

However, the existence of political suicide does not change the fact that most politicians prefer political survival. There is a strong incentive for political suppliers to stake out positions that will increase their vote total in the next election. In fact, competition more or less forces politicians to make decisions in light of political considerations. ***Regardless of ultimate motivation, the ability of politicians to achieve their objectives depends on their ability to get elected and reelected. Just as profits are the lifeblood of the market entrepreneur, votes are the lifeblood of the politician.*** Many factors undoubtedly influence political suppliers. Political competition, however, limits their options. In the same way that neglect of economic profit is the route to market oblivion, neglect of potential votes is the route to political oblivion.

Just as the general does not want his Camp Swampy budget cut, most heads of agencies want expanded budgets to help them do more, and to do it more comfortably.

Civil Servants: Government Bureaucrats as Political Participants

Bureaucratic interests can be an additional factor in politics. The interests of bureaucrats are often complementary with those of special interest groups. The bureaucrats who staff an agency usually want to see their agency's goals furthered, whether the goals are to protect more wilderness, increase the number and the pay of public school teachers, or provide additional subsidized irrigation projects. Like other people, bureaucratic decision makers have narrowly focused interests. Many believe strongly in what they are trying to do. To further those interests usually requires larger budgets for the support of favored constituents' interests. Importantly, the larger budgets also provide bureaucrats with expanded career opportunities. Bureaus, therefore, usually work to expand their programs to deliver benefits to their constituencies who, in turn, work with politicians to expand their bureau budgets and programs.

The political process, which begins with election races and proceeds to legislative decisions and bureaucratic actions, brings about results that please some voters and displease others. In any case, these results help to fuel the next round of activities in the process. The goals of the three major categories of participants—voters, politicians, and bureaucrats—sometimes conflict. Each wants more from the limited supply of resources. But coalitions form among individuals and groups from the three categories, with members of each coalition hoping to enhance their ability to gain more from the government.

WHEN VOTING WORKS WELL

Will voting and representative government provide support for productive projects while rejecting unproductive (and counterproductive) ones? People have a tendency to believe that support by a majority makes a political action productive or legitimate. Perhaps surprising to some, if a government project is really productive, it will always be possible to allocate the project's cost so that *all* voters will gain. **Exhibit 6–1** illustrates this point. Column 1 presents hypothetical data on the distribution of benefits from a government road-construction project. These benefits sum to $40, which exceeds the $25 cost of the road. Because voter benefits exceed costs, the project is indeed productive. If the project's $25 cost were allocated equally among the voters (Plan A), Adams and Chan gain substantially, but Green, Lee, and Diaz will lose. The value of the project to the latter three voters is less than their $5 cost. If the fate of the project were decided by direct majority vote, the project would be defeated by the "no" votes of Green, Lee, and Diaz.

EXHIBIT 6-3

VOTE TRADING AND PASSING COUNTERPRODUCTIVE LEGISLATION

	Net Benefits (+) or Costs (−) to Each Voter in District			
Voters of District[a]	Construction of Post Office in A	Dredging Harbor in B	Construction of Military Base in C	Total
A	+$10	−$ 3	−$ 3	+$4
B	−$ 3	+$10	−$ 3	+$4
C	−$ 3	−$ 3	+$10	+$4
D	−$ 3	−$ 3	−$ 3	−$9
E	−$ 3	−$ 3	−$ 3	−$9
Total	−$ 2	−$ 2	−$ 2	−$6

[a]*We assume the districts are of equal size.*

years. The residents of many western states are the recipients of federally subsidized electricity. Every senator west of Missouri voted to continue the subsidized rates for electricity generated by Hoover Dam. In turn, they can expect senators and representatives from California, Arizona, and Nevada to support subsidized electricity rates in their states. In contrast, residents of other states will pay higher taxes so that many residents in western states can enjoy cheap electricity.

A unique form of special-interest lobbying is the monopoly held by Crane & Company for supplying the Bureau of Engraving and Printing with the paper on which U.S. currency is printed. The firm has been the sole supplier of paper for U.S. currency since 1879. Legislation was introduced in 1998 to provide for competition in the bidding, but the Massachusetts Congressional delegation fought off the legislation. Crane is located in Dalton, Massachusetts. The four-year contract is expected to total $400 million.

Why don't representatives oppose measures that force their constituents to pay for projects that benefit others? There is some incentive to do so, but the constituents of any one elected representative can capture only a small portion of the benefits of tax savings from improved efficiency, since they would be spread nationwide among all taxpayers. We would not expect the president of a corporation to devote the firm's resources to projects not primarily benefiting stockholders. Neither should we expect an elected representative to devote political resources to projects such as defeating pork-barrel programs, when the benefits of greater efficiency would not go primarily to that representative's constituents. Instead, each representative has a strong incentive to work for programs whose benefits are concentrated among his or her constituents—especially the organized interest groups that can help the representative be reelected. Heeding such incentives is a survival (reelection) characteristic.

The bottom line is clear: Public-choice analysis indicates that majority voting and representative democracy do not work so well when concentrated interests benefit at the expense of widely dispersed interests. This special-interest bias of the political process helps to explain the presence of many programs that reduce the size of the economic pie.

The analysis is symmetrical. When the benefits of a government action are widespread and the costs highly concentrated (Type 4 of Exhibit 6–2), the concentrated interests will strongly oppose the proposal. Most others will be largely uninformed and uninterested. Once again, politicians will have an incentive to respond to the views of the concentrated interests. Projects of this type will tend to be rejected even when they are productive—that is, when they would generate larger benefits than costs.

Shortsightedness Effect

The complexity of many issues makes it difficult for voters to identify the future benefits and costs. Will a reduction in tariff rates lead to more rapid economic growth? Is global warming a future threat and, if so, what might be done about it? What impact will an increase in the national debt have on future prosperity? These questions are hard to answer. The difficulty of predicting the future results of current policies acts to reinforce the rational ignorance effect. Few voters will seriously research and analyze the implications of complex policy alternatives having impacts mainly in the future. Instead, they rely on current conditions when judging the performance of incumbents. To the voter, the most easily seen indicator of performance is, "How are things now?"

Accordingly, politicians seeking reelection have a strong incentive to support policies that generate current benefits in exchange for future costs, particularly if the future costs will be difficult to identify on election day. Public-sector action will therefore be biased in favor of legislation that offers immediate (and easily identifiable) current benefits in exchange for future costs that are complicated and difficult to identify. Simultaneously, there is a bias against legislation that involves immediate and easily identifiable costs (for example, higher taxes) while yielding future benefits that are complex and difficult to identify. Economists refer to this bias inherent in the collective decision-making process as the **shortsightedness effect.**

Shortsightedness effect
Misallocation of resources that results because public-sector action is biased (1) in favor of proposals yielding clearly defined current benefits in exchange for difficult-to-identify future costs and (2) against proposals with clearly identifiable current costs but yielding less concrete and less obvious future benefits.

The shortsightedness effect is compounded by the lack of tradable property rights—the lack of a capital market—in government enterprises. For comparison with the private sector, consider the problem of choosing programs and strategies for a large corporation, such as General Motors. Its stockholders elect a board of directors to set policy and select professional management leadership. The corporation, like a government, faces complex choices of programs that are difficult for the individual stockholder to understand fully and evaluate. However, when evaluating the business programs and strategy of the corporation, the stockholder has an incentive very different from that of a voter. Why? Any stockholder who senses trouble before others do can sell out before the stock price falls. Similarly, the stockholder (or other observer) who recognizes a good program choice by a firm before others do can profit individually by buying stock in the firm. (Remember our reference to the many profitable auto magazines and the complete lack of profitable political magazines? There are dozens of highly profitable magazines and newsletters for those who follow corporate stocks!)

The choices of informed, quick-to-act stockholders are registered in stock markets and passed on almost instantly. Investor decisions to buy or sell stock cause the stock price to rise or fall, signaling whether trouble or a winning program is forecast by the most attentive buyers and sellers of the stock. A strategy choice or a new program that investors like will quickly be signaled by a rising share price that rewards management choices well ahead of actual changes in profits and losses. No such advanced market signals, complete with incentives, exist in the collective decision-making processes of government. The result is the restriction of the planning horizon of elected officials. ***As a result of the shortsightedness effect, politicians have a strong incentive to promote programs providing easily observable benefits prior to the next***

election, even when the true cost of these programs outweighs the benefits for citizens as a group.

It is easy to think of instances where positive short-term effects have increased the political attractiveness of policies that exert a long-term detrimental impact. For example, budget deficits allow politicians to finance current benefits for constituents with future taxes. This strategy has political attractiveness even though it will probably result in higher interest rates and less capital formation. Rent controls that reduce the current price of rental housing provide another example. As we noted in Chapter 4, the short-term results will be far more positive than the effects in the long run (housing shortages, black markets, and deterioration in the quality of housing).

Rent Seeking

There are two ways individuals can acquire wealth: production and plunder. When individuals produce goods or services and exchange them for income, they not only enrich themselves but they also enhance the wealth of the society. Sometimes the rules—or lack of rule enforcement—also allow people to get ahead by plundering what others have produced. Such activities enrich some at the expense of others, usually after a strenuous political struggle that consumes additional resources and reduces the wealth of the society.

Rent seeking is the term used by economists when referring to actions taken by individuals and groups seeking to use the political process to plunder the wealth of others.[6] The incentive to engage in rent seeking is directly proportional to the ease with which the political process can be used for personal (or interest group) gain at the expense of others. When the effective law of the land makes it difficult to take the property of others or force others to pay for projects favored by you and your interest group, rent seeking is unattractive. Under such circumstances, its benefits are relatively low, and few resources flow into rent-seeking activities. In contrast, when government fails to levy user fees or similar forms of financing to allocate the cost of its projects to the primary beneficiaries, or when it becomes heavily involved in tax-transfer activities, the payoff for rent seeking expands.

Rent seeking
Actions by individuals and interest groups designed to restructure public policy in a manner that will either directly or indirectly redistribute more income to themselves.

Rent seeking—perhaps "favor seeking" would be more descriptive—will also increase when governments become more heavily involved in erecting trade barriers, mandating employment benefits, providing subsidies, fixing prices, and levying discriminatory taxes (taxes unrelated to the provision of public services to the taxpayer). Interests seeking special favors include bureaucratic leaders searching for ways to enlarge their agency budgets and regulatory authority. The narrow interests of government bureaucracies are strongly represented in the political process.

When a government, rather than acting as a neutral force protecting property rights and enforcing contracts, attempts to favor some at the expense of others, counterproductive activities will expand while positive-sum productive activities will shrink. People will spend more time organizing and lobbying politicians and less time producing goods and services. Since fewer resources will be utilized to create wealth (and more utilized in rent-seeking activities), economic progress will be retarded.

Inefficiency of Government Operations

Will government goods and services be produced efficiently? Professional pride, and pride in doing a job well, are likely to be present in the public sector as well as the

[6]See the classic work of Charles K. Rowley, Robert D. Tollison, and Gordon Tullock, *The Political Economy of Rent-Seeking* (Boston: Kluwer Academic Publishers, 1988), for additional details on rent seeking.

private. However, the incentive to operate efficiently differs in the two sectors. In the private sector, there is a strong incentive to produce efficiently because lower costs mean higher profits, and high costs mean losses and even business failure. This index of performance (profit rate) is unavailable in the public sector. Missing also are signals from the capital market. When a corporation announces a strategy or a plan that investors believe to be faulty, the price of the corporation's stock will drop. There is no mechanism similar to the stock market in the public sector. This makes inefficiency more difficult to detect. In addition, direct competition in the form of other firms trying to take an agency's customers is typically absent in the public sector. As a result, bureaucratic leaders are more free to pursue their narrow goals and interests without a strong regard for the control of costs relative to benefits. (See cartoon below.)

While bankruptcy weeds out inefficiency in the private sector, there is no parallel mechanism to eliminate inefficiency in the public sector. In fact, poor performance and failure to achieve objectives are often used as an argument for *increased* funding in the public sector. Furthermore, public-sector managers are seldom in a position to gain personally from measures that reduce costs. The opposite is often true. If an agency fails to spend this year's allocation, its case for a larger budget next year is weakened. Agencies typically go on a spending spree near the end of the budget period if they discover that they have failed to spend all the current year's appropriation.

It is important to note that the argument of internal inefficiency is not based on the assumption that employees of a bureaucratic government are necessarily lazy or incapable. Rather, the emphasis is on the information and incentives under which managers and other workers toil. No individual or relatively small group of individuals has much incentive to ensure economic efficiency. Their performances cannot readily be judged, and, without private ownership, their personal wealth cannot be significantly altered by changes in the level of efficiency. Because public officials and bureau

THE FAMILY CIRCUS
By Bil Keane
1-26
©1998 Bil Keane, Inc.
Dist. by Cowles Synd., Inc.
BIL KEANE
"Daddy, could you buy a new metal detector? I dropped my quarter in the snow."

Just as the boy considers the quarter more important than the far greater cost of the metal detector, so too does the leader of a bureau often consider the bureau's goals more important than the costs, even if the latter are far greater.

managers spend other people's money, they are likely to be less conscious of cost than they would be with their own resources. Without a need to compare sales revenues to costs, there is no test with which to define economic inefficiency or measure it accurately, much less to eliminate it. The perverse incentive structure of a bureaucracy and the fact that market signals are missing are bound to affect its internal efficiency.

The empirical evidence is consistent with this view. Economies dominated by government control, like those of the former Soviet bloc, India, Syria, Nicaragua, and Nigeria (and many other African countries) have performed poorly. The level of output per unit of resource input in countries with numerous government enterprises is low. Similarly, when private firms are compared with government agencies providing the same goods or services, the private firms generally have been shown to provide them more economically.

Competition is a key to efficient production and low cost. Units of government can sometimes provide services on a more competitive basis by contracting with private firms or even with other units of government. For example, many cities contract with private firms to provide trash removal services. The city continues to finance the activity through taxes and to specify the level of service. But operational efficiency is greater because competition among potential contractors keeps the cost of the trash removal contracts down. This sort of competitive contracting has increased in recent decades. In the state of Illinois, more than 90 percent of municipalities contracted out their trash removal services. In the United States, 7 state governments were contracting out more than 100 services in 1998, while 14 states contracted out more than 50 services. Even the federal Internal Revenue Service has moved in this direction. The IRS recently awarded a $30.9 million contract to a private partnership to manage its inventory of office equipment and other supplies. Private, competitive firms can typically reduce costs, relative to government agency production.

ECONOMICS OF THE TRANSFER SOCIETY

As **Exhibit 6–4** illustrates, direct income transfers through the public sector have increased sharply during the past seven decades. In 1929 cash income transfers accounted for only 1.8 percent of national income; by 1997 the figure had risen to 16.8 percent. If in-kind benefits, such as food stamps, medical care, and housing, were included, the size of the transfer sector would have constituted well over 20 percent of national income.

The ideal distribution of income is largely a matter of personal preference. There is nothing in positive economics that tells us that one distribution of income is better than another. Some people may desire to enhance the living standards of those with low incomes. However, in some respects, income transfers to the poor are a public good. The contributions of any one individual will exert an insignificant impact on the living standards of the poor. Recognizing this point, even those who would willingly contribute to reduce the general level of poverty, have an incentive to become *free riders*. When many people become free riders, however, less than the desired amount of antipoverty effort will be voluntarily supplied. If everyone is required to contribute through the tax system, then the free-rider problem can be overcome. Under these circumstances, transfers directed to the poor may be consistent with economic efficiency.

However, there is also reason to believe that the rent-seeking model underlies a substantial portion of income transfers. In the United States, *means-tested transfers,* those directed toward the poor, constitute only about one-sixth of all transfers. No

EXHIBIT 6-4

THE GROWTH OF GOVERNMENT TRANSFER PAYMENTS

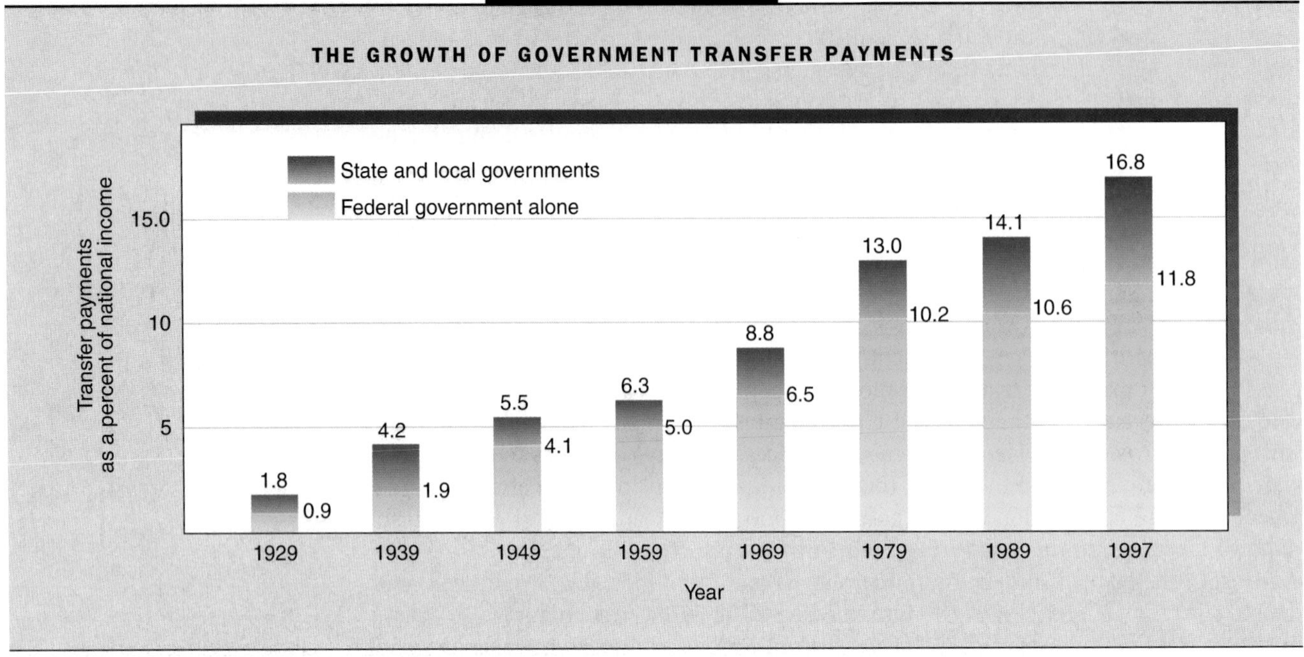

The government now taxes approximately 17 percent of national income away from some people and transfers it to others. Means-tested income transfers—those directed toward the poor—account for only about one-sixth of all income transfers.

SOURCE: Economic Report of the President, *1998, Tables B-83, B-84.*

income test is applied to the other five-sixths, and they are generally directed toward groups that are either well organized (like businesses and labor union interests) or easily identifiable (like the elderly and farmers). The recipients of these transfers often have incomes well above the average.

Within the framework of public-choice analysis, the relatively small portion of income transfers directed toward the poor is not surprising. There is little reason to believe that transfers to the poor will be particularly attractive to vote-seeking politicians. After all, in the United States, the poor are less likely to vote than middle- and upper-income recipients. They are also less likely to be well informed on political issues and candidates. They are not united. Neither are they a significant source of financial resources that exert a powerful influence on the political process.

Whatever the motivation for the income transfers, there are three major reasons why redistribution through the public sector will reduce the size of the economic pie. First, income redistribution weakens the link between productive activity and reward. When taxes take a larger share of one's income, the individual reward derived from hard work and productive service is reduced. The basic economic postulate suggests that when benefits allocated to producers are reduced (and benefits to nonproducers are raised), less productive effort will be supplied.

Second, as public policy redistributes a larger share of income, more resources will flow into wasteful rent-seeking activities. Resources used for lobbying and other means of rent seeking will not be available to increase the size of the economic pie.

Third, higher taxes to finance income redistribution and an expansion in rent seeking will induce taxpayers to focus less on income-producing activities, and more on actions to protect their income. More accountants, lawyers, and tax-shelter experts will be retained as people seek to limit the amount of their income that is redistributed to others. Like the resources allocated to rent seeking, resources allocated to protecting one's wealth from the reach of public policy will also be unavailable for productive activity. Therefore, the incentives generated by large-scale redistribution policies can be expected to reduce the size of the economic pie.

PUBLIC SECTOR VERSUS THE MARKET: A SUMMARY

Economic theory helps explain why both market forces and public-sector action sometimes break down—that is, why they sometimes fail to meet the criteria for ideal efficiency. The deficiencies of either sector will often be more or less decisive, depending on the type of economic activity. Nobel laureate Paul Samuelson has stated, "There are not rules concerning the proper role of government that can be established by *a priori* reasoning."[7] This does not mean, however, that economics has nothing to say about the *strength* of the case for either the market or the public sector in terms of specific classes of activities. Nor does it mean that social scientists have nothing to say about institutional arrangements for conducting economic activity. It merely indicates that each issue and type of activity must be considered individually.

When we consider the usefulness of government and the private sector in specific cases, it will help to remember two things. The first is the basic characteristic of government: its monopoly on the use of coercive force. It is a powerful tool indeed, for better and for worse. The second thing to remember is that individuals have two fundamental ways to inform and possibly influence an institution such as government or a private firm: exit and voice. Both exit and voice are quite useful in dealing with individuals, firms, and other groups in the private sector. We can speak, and if that doesn't work we can exit from a private arrangement by failing to renew it or by shifting to another alternative. Other buyers and sellers are available even if they do not have identical products in identical locations.

With government, we may be largely limited to voice. In a representative democracy, we can use voice to communicate our displeasure with a new tax or regulation, but exit is usually difficult. We have to move physically from the area of the government's authority. When government is at the local level, of course, exit is less costly. That is one reason why giving local government more powers is less dangerous than giving the same powers to a national government. Nonetheless, the ability to exit easily and shift to competing entities almost always gives individuals more control in the market than in the public sector.

When we make the necessary comparisons in individual situations, the case for government intervention is obviously stronger for some activities than for others. For example, if property rights cannot be well enforced so that an activity involves substantial external effects, market arrangements often result in economic inefficiency, and public-sector action should be considered; it may allow for greater efficiency. Similarly, when competitive pressures are weak and exit is more difficult for one party or the other, or when there is reason to expect consumers to be poorly informed, market failure may result. And again, government action should be examined. (See the Thumbnail Sketch for a summary of factors that influence the case for market or for public-sector action.)

---

[7]Paul A. Samuelson, "The Economic Role of Private Activity," in *The Collected Scientific Papers of Paul A. Samuelson,* vol. 2, ed. J. E. Stiglitz (Cambridge: MIT Press, 1966), p. 1423.

THUMBNAIL SKETCH

What Weakens the Case for Market-Sector Allocation versus Public-Sector Intervention, and Vice Versa?

These factors weaken the case for market-sector allocation:

1. Lack of competition
2. External costs and benefits
3. Public goods
4. Poor information

These factors weaken the case for public-sector intervention:

1. The power of special interests
2. The shortsightedness effect
3. Rent-seeking costs
4. Lack of signals and incentives to promote operational efficiency

The same analysis holds for the public sector. When there is a good reason to believe that special-interest influence will be strong, the case for government action to correct market failures is weakened. Similarly, the lack of a means to identify and weed out public-sector inefficiency weakens the case for government action. In many cases, the choice of proper institutions may be a choice among evils. For example, we might expect a lack of private-sector competition if a particular activity is left to the market, or perverse regulation due to the special-interest effect if it is turned over to the public sector. Understanding the shortcomings of both the market and the public sectors is important if we are to improve our current economic institutions.

IMPLICATIONS OF PUBLIC CHOICE: GETTING MORE FROM GOVERNMENT

It is important to distinguish between ordinary politics and constitutional rules. Constitutions establish the procedures that will be utilized to make political decisions. They also may reduce the negative results from the problems just discussed, by limiting the reach of the majority. They do so by placing certain matters (for example, the taking of private property without compensation, restrictions on freedom of speech or worship, and various restrictions on voting) beyond the reach of majority rule or normal legislative procedures.

Both bad news and good news flow from public-choice analysis. The bad news is that, for certain classes of economic activity, unconstrained democratic government will predictably be a source of economic waste and inefficiency. Not only does the invisible hand of the market sometimes fail to meet our ideal efficiency criteria; so, too, does political decision making. That makes the growth of government worrisome. But there is also some good news arising from public-choice theory: Properly structured constitutional rules can improve the expected result from government. So the study of how people behave when they make collective choices "in the world as it really is" suggests constructive alternatives for improving the government process.

Whether political organization leads to desirable or undesirable economic outcomes is dependent upon the structure of the political (constitutional) rules. In government as elsewhere, proper incentives are critical to good decision making. When the structure of the political rules harmonizes the self-interest of individual voters, politicians, and bureaucrats with the general welfare, government will promote economic prosperity. On the other hand, if the rules fail to bring about this harmony, political allocation will lead to both waste of resources and conflict among citizens. The challenge before us is to develop political economy institutions that are more consistent with economic efficiency and prosperity. Public-choice theory provides us with insight concerning how this objective might be achieved. Needless to say, this topic is one of the most exciting and potentially fruitful areas of study in economics.

LOOKING *Ahead*

Democratic governments are a creation of the interactions of human beings. Public-choice analysis helps us better understand these interactions and possible modifications of the rules that would improve the results achieved from government. Issues involving comparisons between market- and public-sector organization will be discussed repeatedly throughout this book. Public choice—the study of how the public sector works—is an integral and exciting aspect of economic analysis. It helps us to understand the "why" behind many of today's current events. Who said economics is the dismal science?

KEY POINTS

➤ In a representative democracy, government is controlled by voters who elect politicians to set policy and hire bureaucrats. All three classes of participants influence political outcomes.

➤ Other things constant, voters have a strong incentive to support the candidate who offers them the greatest gain relative to personal costs. But it is costly to obtain information. Because collective decisions break the link between the choice of the individual and the outcome of the issue, it is rational for voters to remain uninformed on many issues.

➤ Politicians have a strong incentive to follow a strategy that will enhance their chances of getting elected (and reelected). Political competition more or less forces them to focus on how their actions influence their support among voters.

➤ The distribution of the benefits and costs among voters influences how the political process works. When voters pay in proportion to the benefits they receive from a public-sector project, democratic decision making works quite well. Productive projects tend to be approved and counterproductive ones rejected.

➤ There is a strong incentive for politicians to support special-interest issues. Special-interest groups supply both financial and direct elective support to the politicians, while most other voters tend to be uninformed on special-interest issues.

➤ The shortsightedness effect is another potential source of conflict between good politics and sound economics. Both voters and politicians tend to support projects that promise substantial current benefits at the expense of difficult-to-identify future costs.

➤ Rent seeking moves resources away from productive activities. Widespread use of the taxing, spending, and regulating powers of government will encourage rent seeking. The output of economies with substantial amounts of rent seeking will fall below their potential.

➤ The economic incentive for operational efficiency is weak in the public sector. No individual or relatively small group of individuals can capture the gains derived from improved operational efficiency.

➤ A large and growing part of government is devoted to transferring income, most of which does not go to poor people. Transfers tend to reduce the size of the economic pie.

CRITICAL ANALYSIS QUESTIONS

1. Do you think that people who participate in the political process are motivated differently than when they participate in the private sector? Why or why not?

*2. "Government can afford to take a long view when it needs to, while a private firm has a short-term outlook. Corporate officers, for example, typically care about the next three to six months, not the next 50 to 100 years. Government, not private firms, should own things like forests, that take decades to develop." Evaluate this view.

3. "A democratic government is a corrective device used to remedy inefficiencies that arise when market allocation is not working well." Is this statement true or false? Explain.

4. What is rent seeking? When is it likely to be widespread? How does it influence economic efficiency? Explain.

*5. Does the democratic political process incorporate the invisible hand principle? Is the presence or absence of the invisible hand principle important? Why or why not?

*6. "The average person is more likely to make an informed choice when he or she purchases a personal computer than when he or she votes for a congressional candidate." Evaluate this statement.

7. Do you think special-interest groups exert much influence on local government? Why or why not? As a test, check the composition of the local zoning board in your community. How many real-estate agents, contractors, developers, and landlords are on the board? Are there any citizens without real-estate interests on the board?

*8. "Voters should simply ignore political candidates who play ball with special-interest groups, and vote instead for candidates who will represent all the people when they are elected. Government will work far better when this happens." Evaluate this view.

9. Do you think that advertising exerts more influence on the type of car chosen by a consumer than on the type of politician chosen by the same person? Explain your answer.

*10. "When an economic function is turned over to the government, social cooperation replaces personal self-interest." Is this statement true? Why or why not?

*11. What's wrong with this way of thinking? "Public policy is necessary to protect the average citizen from the power of vested interest groups. In the absence of government intervention, regulated industries, such as airlines, railroads, and trucking, would charge excessive prices, products would be unsafe, and the rich would oppress the poor. Government curbs the power of special-interest groups."

12. Do you think that the political process works to the advantage of the poor? Why or why not?

13. "Since government-operated firms do not have to make a profit, they can usually produce at a lower cost and charge a lower price than privately owned enterprises." Evaluate this view.

---

*Asterisk denotes questions for which answers are given in Appendix B.

Core microeconomics

CONSUMERS ARE SPENDING LESS ON FOOD, BUT MORE ON MEDICAL CARE AND RECREATION

Compared to 1965, consumers now spend a smaller portion of their income on food, but larger amounts on medical care and recreation. As a share of total consumption, expenditures on housing, transportation, and clothing have been relatively constant during recent decades.

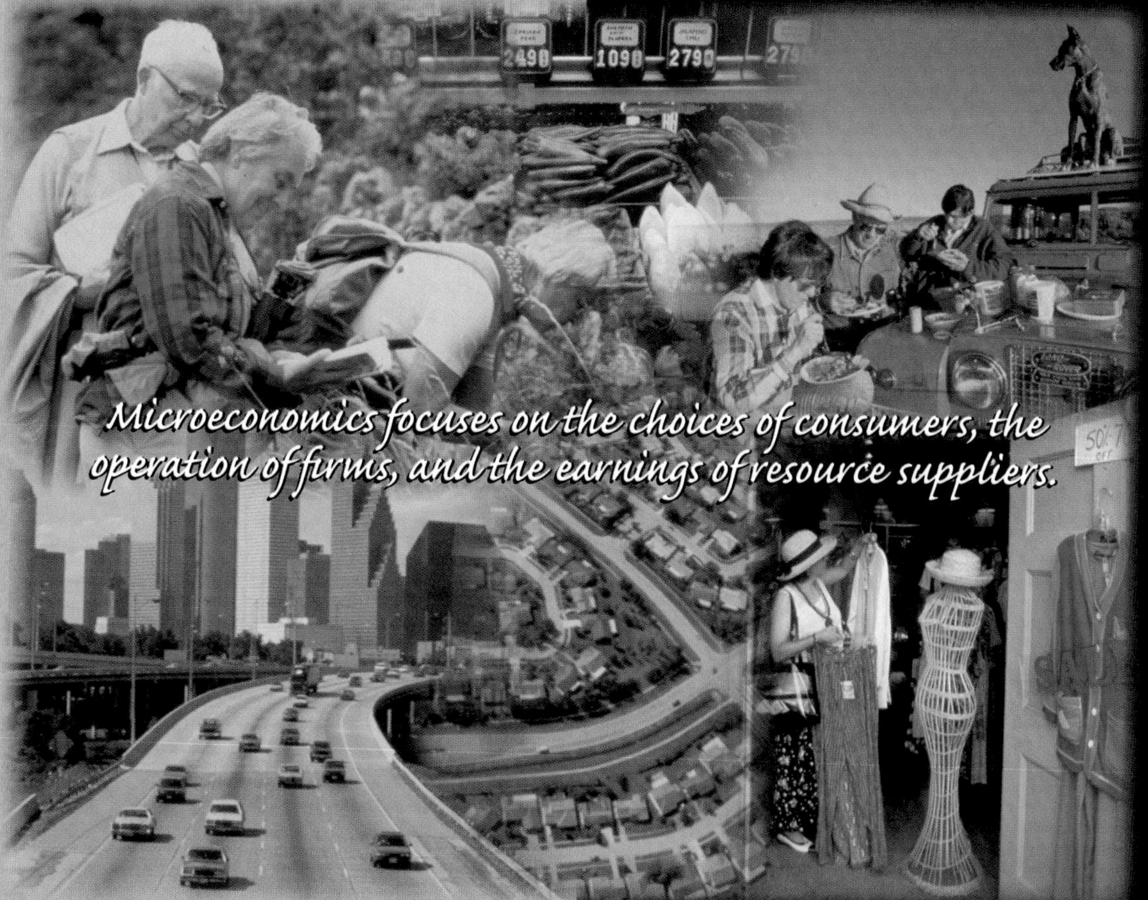

Microeconomics focuses on the choices of consumers, the operation of firms, and the earnings of resource suppliers.

THE SIZE OF FIRMS IS DIVERSE

Most firms are small. In 1995, 87 percent of all business firms employed fewer than 20 workers. These small firms employed 25.7 percent of those directly employed by a business firm. At the other end of the spectrum, firms with 500 or more workers employed 19.9 percent of the total. Between 1980 and 1995, there was a slight decline in the proportion of workers employed by large firms.

EXHIBIT III-A

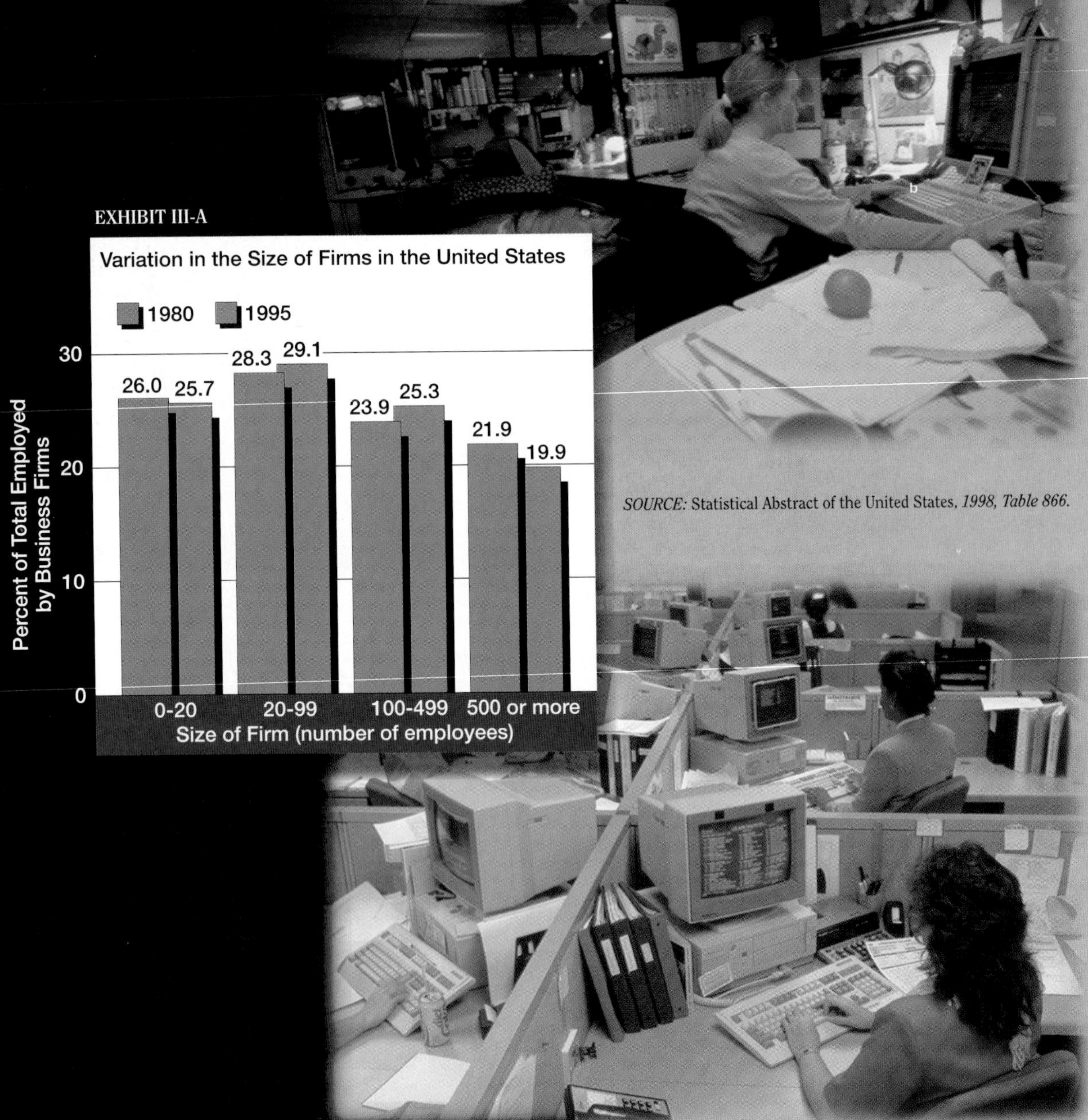

SOURCE: Statistical Abstract of the United States, *1998, Table 866.*

BUSINESS FIRMS EARN ABOUT 5 CENTS PER DOLLAR OF SALES AND 14 CENTS PER DOLLAR OF EQUITY CAPITAL INVESTED BY OWNERS

Public opinion surveys indicate that people believe that the profits of business firms average approximately 25 cents out of every dollar of sales. The actual figure is much less. During recent decades, the accounting profit of manufacturing firms has averaged approximately 5 cents per dollar of sales and 14 cents per dollar of stockholder equity invested. The profit rates of nonmanufacturing firms are generally lower than the rates shown here.

EXHIBIT III-B

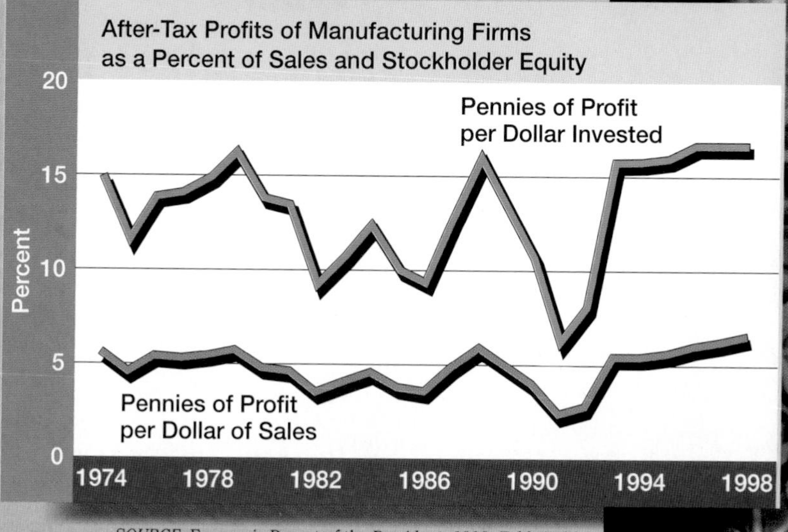

SOURCE: Economic Report of the President: 1998, *Table B-94.*

BUSINESS COMPETITION IS HIGHLY DYNAMIC

Numerous businesses come and go. Each year, newly incorporated businesses account for proximately 10 percent of the total. Approximately percent of businesses file for bankruptcy during a typical year. In addition, many others close their doors or sell their assets to other, more successful (or more optimistic) operators.

XHIBIT III-C

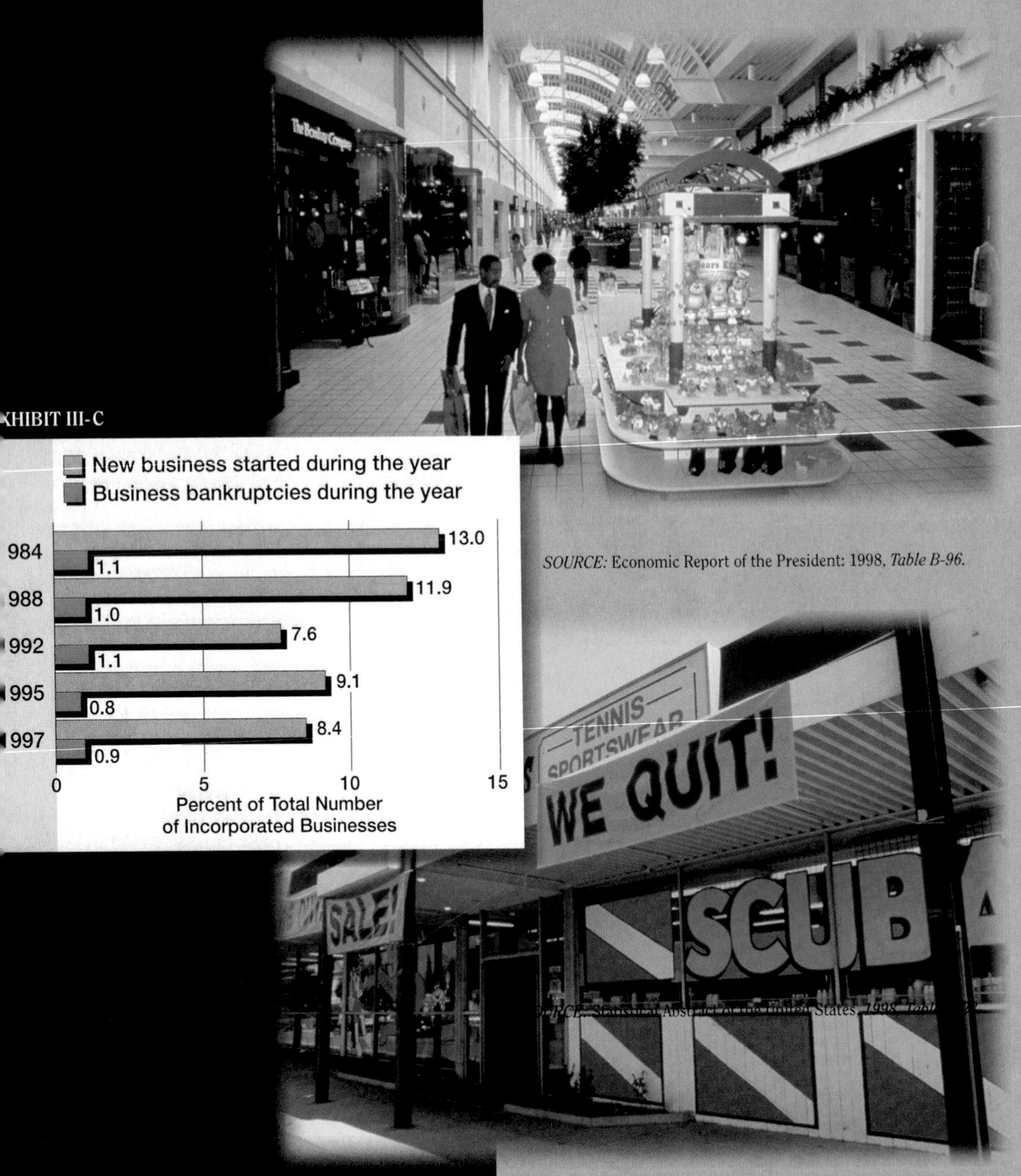

SOURCE: Economic Report of the President: 1998, *Table B-96.*

RCE: Statistical Abstract of the United States, *1998, Tabl*

TYPICAL DIVISION OF NATIONAL INCOME: FOUR-FIFTHS TO HUMAN CAPITAL AND ONE-FIFTH TO PHYSICAL CAPITAL

As the accompanying graphic shows, employee compensation and income of self-employed workers account for approximately 80 percent of national income. These earnings are primarily returns to human capital (the education, skill, and experience of workers). Rents, interest, and corporate profits—which reflect returns physical capital—earn approximately 20 percent of na tional income. This division of national income has bee relatively constant for several decades.

EXHIBIT III-D

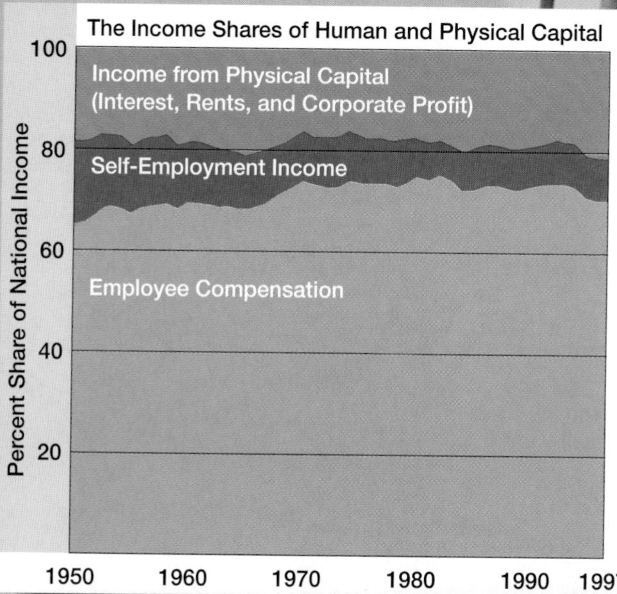

SOURCE: Economic Report of the President *(various issues).*

THE LIFE-CYCLE PATTERN OF INCOME

Both younger, less-experienced workers and older workers (as they move toward retirement) have wer earnings than workers in the prime working-age oup (35–64 years). This pattern is illustrated here. In cent years, the proportion of the workforce in the ime working-age categories has increased as the baby-boom generation has moved into this age group. Think how this is currently influencing the growth of income and rate of unemployment. Also consider how income growth and employment will be affected when the large baby-boom generation moves into the retirement phase of life.

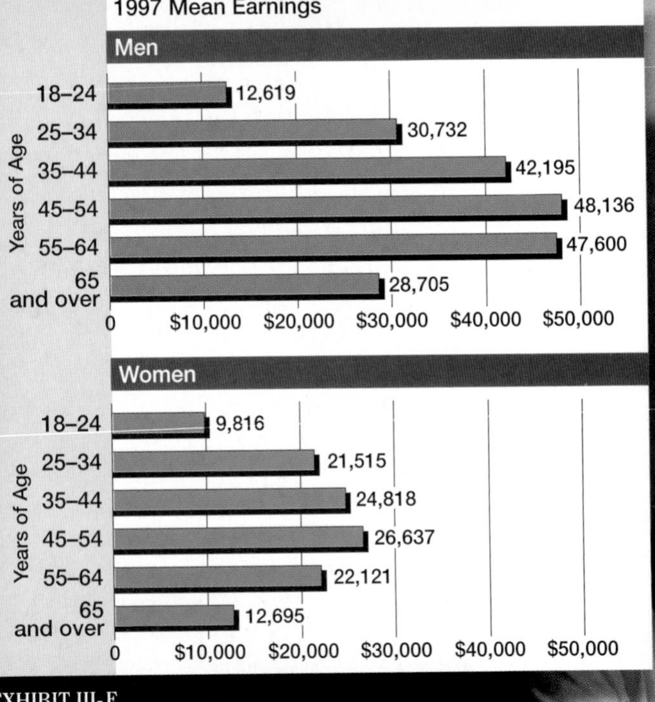

XHIBIT III-E

OURCE: Department of Commerce, Current Population Reports, *P-60 series, "Money Income in the United States: 1997", Table 9.*

Experienced, prime working-age persons tend to earn more than youthful and elderly workers.

CHAPTER 7

The most famous law in economics, and the one economists are most sure of, is the law of demand. On this law is built almost the whole edifice of economics.

David R. Henderson[1]

A thing is worth whatever a buyer will pay for it.

Publilius Syrus, first century B.C.[2]

Demand and Consumer Choice

CHAPTER FOCUS

- What are the fundamental postulates undergirding consumer choice?
- How does the law of diminishing marginal utility help explain the law of demand?
- How do the demand curves of individuals translate into a market demand curve?
- What determines consumer preferences for a specific item? How important are product quality, advertising, time, and risk?
- What is demand elasticity? What factors determine it and how is it used to analyze consumer spending and a firm's revenue?

---

[1]David R. Henderson, "Demand," in *The Fortune Encyclopedia of Economics,* ed. David R. Henderson (New York: Warner Books, Inc., 1993), p. 7.

[2]Quoted in Michael Jackman, ed., *Macmillan Book of Business and Economic Quotations* (New York: Macmillan, 1984), p. 150.

The statement of David Henderson highlights the central position of the law of demand in economics. As Publilius Syrus noted more than 2,000 years ago, demand reflects the willingness of individuals to pay for what is offered in the market. In this section, we begin our examination of microeconomic markets for specific products with an analysis of the demand side of markets. In essence we will be going "behind" the market demand curve to see how it is made up of individual consumer demands, and what factors determine the choices of individual consumers.[3]

THE FUNDAMENTALS OF CONSUMER CHOICE

Each of us must decide how to allocate our limited income among the many possible things we could purchase. The prices of goods, *relative to each other,* are very important determining factors. If your favorite cereal doubled in price, would you switch to a different brand? Would your decision be different if all cereals, not just yours, doubled in price? Your choice *between* brands of cereal will be affected only by the change in relative prices. If all cereal prices rose, you might quit purchasing cereal, but this will not give you a strong reason to switch to a different brand. Relative prices measure opportunity cost. If cereal is $2.50 per box when movie tickets are $5, you must give up two boxes of cereal to purchase a movie ticket.

There have been some substantial changes during the past few decades in the way American consumers allocate their income. As a share of total consumption, spending on food (including beverages and tobacco) fell from 26 percent in 1963 to less than 16 percent in 1996. In contrast, medical expenditures rose from 10 percent of the total to 15 percent during the same period. On the other hand, spending on housing remained about the same.

To understand what accounts for these changes, as well as consumer choice more generally, it is important to outline several fundamental principles underlying consumer behavior.

1. *Limited income necessitates choice.* Because of scarcity we all have limited incomes. The limited nature of our income requires us to make choices about which goods we will and will not purchase. To stay within our budget, when more of one good or service is purchased, we must purchase less of some other goods. This is precisely the meaning of the "cost" of purchasing something.

2. *Consumers make decisions purposefully.* The goals that underpin the choices of a consumer can usually be met in alternative ways. If two products have an equal cost, a

[3]You may want to review the section on demand in Chapter 3 before proceeding with this chapter.

consumer would choose to purchase the one expected to have the higher benefit. On the other hand, if two products yield equal benefits, the consumer would choose to purchase the cheaper one. Fundamentally, we assume that consumers are rational—they are able to weigh the costs and benefits of their choices.

3. *One good can be substituted for another.* Consumers can achieve *utility*—that is, satisfaction—from many different alternatives. Either a hamburger or a taco might satisfy your hunger, while going either to a movie or to a football game might satisfy your desire for entertainment. With $300, you might either buy a new TV set or take a vacation. No single good is so precious that some of it will not be given up in exchange for a large enough quantity of other goods. There are many alternative ways to satisfy individual wants.

We have been discussing "wants," but how about our "need" for basic commodities such as water or energy? The need of a person for an item is closely related to its cost—what must be given up to obtain the item. Do southern California residents need water from the north? When water becomes more expensive, individual residents faced with a high water bill will plant cactus instead of grass, pay a plumber to fix leaking faucets, and use flow constrictors on shower heads. The need for water thus depends on its cost to the user. People living in Montana, where household electricity costs nearly twice as much as in nearby Washington, use about half as much electricity per household. Montanans reduce their "need" for electricity by substituting gas, fuel oil, insulation, and wool sweaters for the relatively more expensive electricity. Each of the things we purchase has substitutes.

4. *Consumers must make decisions without perfect information, but knowledge and past experience will help.* In Chapter 1 we noted that information is costly to acquire. Asking family and friends, searching through magazines such as *Consumer Reports,* and contacting the local Better Business Bureau are all ways of gathering information about products and potential sellers. The likelihood that a consumer will spend the necessary time, effort, and money to gather this information is directly related to its value to the consumer. Many people will collect this information when deciding on the purchase of a new automobile, but very few would do the same for a purchase of a pencil or a roll of paper towels. When making a bad decision is not very costly, consumers will rationally choose to be less informed.

No human being has perfect foresight. Consumers will not always correctly anticipate the consequences of their choices. They will, however, have a good chance of doing so in areas of common knowledge and experience. You have a pretty good idea of what to expect when you buy a cup of coffee, five gallons of gasoline, or a box of your favorite cereal. Why? Because you have learned from experience—your own and that of others—what to expect. Your expectations may not always be fulfilled precisely (for example, the coffee may be stronger than expected or the gasoline may make your car's engine knock), but even then, you will gain valuable information that will help you project the outcome of future choices more accurately. Being a good consumer is a process of learning through previous choices.

5. *The law of diminishing marginal utility applies: As the rate of consumption increases, the marginal utility derived from consuming additional units of a good will decline.* *Utility* is a term economists use to describe the subjective personal benefits that result from an action. The **law of diminishing marginal utility** states that the **marginal** (or additional) **utility** derived from consuming successive units of a product will eventually decline as the rate of consumption increases. For example, the law says that even though you might like ice cream, your marginal satisfaction from additional ice

Law of diminishing marginal utility
The basic economic principle that, as the consumption of a commodity increases, the marginal utility derived from consuming more of the commodity (per unit of time) will eventually decline.

Marginal utility
The additional utility received from the consumption of an additional unit of a good.

cream will eventually decline. Ice cream at lunchtime might be great. An additional helping for dinner might also be good. However, after you have had it for lunch and dinner, having another serving for a midnight snack will have lost some attraction. The law of diminishing marginal utility will have set in, and thus the marginal utility derived from the consumption of additional units of ice cream will decline.

The law of diminishing marginal utility explains why, even if you really like a certain product, you will not spend your entire budget on it. Consumers would be unlikely to stop purchasing a good if an additional unit yielded more satisfaction than the previous one. Failure to purchase an additional unit indicates that the buyer has reached the point where additional units provide less and less marginal utility. Utility-seeking buyers will not operate in the range of increasing marginal utility, but in the range where their marginal utility is declining.

Marginal Utility, Marginal Benefit, and the Demand Curve

Marginal benefit
The maximum price a consumer would be willing to pay for an additional unit. It is the dollar value of the consumer's marginal utility from the additional unit, and thus falls as consumption increases.

The law of diminishing marginal utility helps us to understand the law of demand and the shape of the demand curve. The height of an individual's demand curve at any specific unit is equal to the maximum price the consumer would be willing to pay for that unit—its **marginal benefit** to the consumer. Although marginal benefit is measured in dollars, it is really a reflection of the opportunity cost in terms of other goods forgone. If a consumer is willing to pay, at most, $5 for a product, this indicates a willingness to give up, at most, $5 worth of other goods. ***Because a consumer's willingness to pay for a unit of a good is directly related to the utility derived from consumption of the unit, the law of diminishing marginal utility implies that a consumer's marginal benefit, and thus the height of the demand curve, falls with the rate of consumption.***

Exhibit 7-1 shows this relationship for a hypothetical consumer Jones related to her weekly consumption of frozen pizza. The law of diminishing marginal utility applies—each additional pizza consumed per week will generate less marginal utility for Jones than the previous pizza. For this reason, Jones's maximum willingness to pay—her marginal benefit—will fall as the quantity consumed increases. In addition, the steepness of Jones's demand curve—its elasticity—is a reflection of how rapidly marginal utility diminishes with additional consumption. An individual's demand curve for a good whose marginal value declines rapidly will be very steep.

Given knowledge about a consumer's maximum willingness to pay for additional units of a good, we are now in a position to discuss the choice of how many units a consumer will choose to purchase. ***At any given price, consumers will purchase all units of a good for which their maximum willingness to pay—their marginal benefit—is greater than the price.*** They will stop at the point where the next unit's marginal benefit would be less than the price. Although there are some problems with divisibility (it is hard to purchase half a car), we can generally say that a consumer will purchase all units of a good up to the point where the marginal benefit equals the price of the good ($MB = P$).

Returning to Exhibit 7-1, if the price of frozen pizza were $2.50, Jones would choose to purchase three frozen pizzas per week.[4] Remember from Chapter 3 that consumer surplus is defined as the difference between the maximum price the

---

[4]Jones would certainly purchase the second unit because $MB > P$. For the third unit, $MB = P$, so Jones would be indifferent between buying the unit and not purchasing it. For a good that is easily divisible, say, pounds of roast beef, the consumer would continue purchasing up to 2.9999 pounds. Thus, economists are comfortable with simply concluding that the consumer will purchase this final unit, implying that Jones will purchase three frozen pizzas.

EXHIBIT 7-1

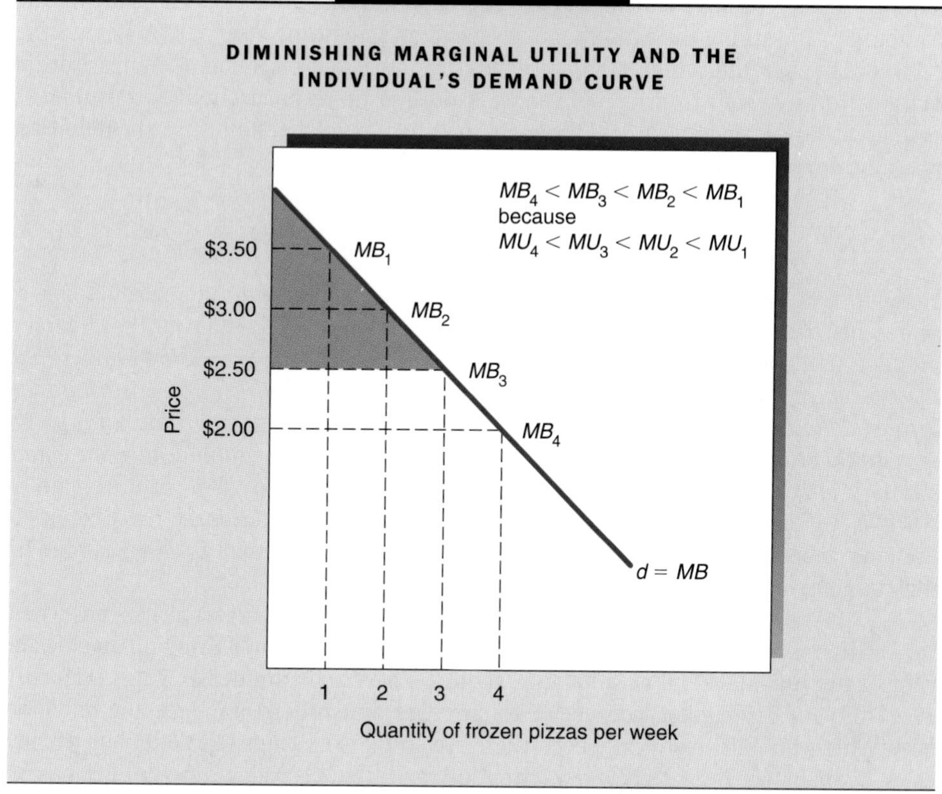

An individual's demand curve, Jones's demand for frozen pizza in this case, reflects the law of diminishing marginal utility. Because marginal utility (MU) *falls with increased consumption, so does the consumer's maximum willingness to pay—marginal benefit* (MB). *A consumer will purchase until* MB = Price, *so at $2.50 Jones would purchase 3 pizzas and receive a consumer surplus shown by the shaded triangle.*

consumer would be willing to pay and the price actually paid. Jones's maximum willingness to pay for the first unit is $3.50, which, at a price of $2.50, generates $1.00 of consumer surplus for Jones. When a consumer has purchased all units to the point where $MB = P$, total consumer surplus is the total triangular area under the demand curve, but above the price. Total consumer surplus for Jones is shown as the shaded area in Exhibit 7-1.

Within this framework, how would a consumer respond to a decline in the price of a good? Answer: Purchases will be increased to the point where marginal benefit diminishes to the level of the new lower price. If marginal utility declines rapidly with consumption, the consumer will expand purchases only slightly. If marginal utility declines less rapidly, it will take a larger expansion in purchases to reach this point. If the price were to rise, the consumer would cut back purchases, eliminating those for which marginal benefit was now less than the price. It is through this linkage with marginal benefit and maximum willingness to pay that the law of diminishing marginal utility underlies an individual demand curve.

Consumer Equilibrium with Many Goods

The last time you were at the mall, you probably saw something you liked. After all, there are many things we would like—many different alternatives that would give us utility. Next, you looked at the price tag: "$40, wow! That's too much." What you were really saying was "I like this item, but my willingness to pay is less than $40 so I won't buy it," or, even more precisely, "I like this item, but not as much as the $40 worth of other goods that I would have to give up." Consumer choice is a constant comparison of value *relative* to price. Although you might like steak better than hamburger, steak is more costly. You may conclude that your happiness is better served by buying the hamburger, and saving the extra money to spend on something else.

The idea that choices across goods are based upon a relative comparison of marginal utility (MU) to price (P) can be expressed more precisely. If a consumer is spending a limited income across products so as to maximize total utility, the following relationship will be present:

$$\frac{MU_A}{P_A} = \frac{MU_B}{P_B} = \ldots = \frac{MU_n}{P_n}$$

Here MU represents the marginal utility derived from the last unit of a product, and P represents the price of the good. The subscripts $_{A}, _{B}, \ldots, _{n}$ indicate the different products available to the consumer. ***In the continuous case, this expression implies that the consumer will maximize his or her satisfaction (or total utility) by ensuring that the last dollar spent on each commodity yields an equal degree of marginal utility. Alternatively stated, the last unit of each commodity purchased should have an equal marginal utility per dollar spent on it.*** Thus, if the price of a gallon of ice cream is twice as high as the price of a liter of Coke, a consumer will purchase these items to the point where the marginal utility of the last gallon of ice cream is twice as high as the marginal utility of the last liter of Coke.

Perhaps the best way to grasp this point is to think about what happens when the relation is absent. Suppose that you are at a local restaurant eating buffalo chicken wings and drinking beer. For simplicity, assume a beer and an order of wings each cost $1. With your $10 budget, you decide to purchase nine orders of wings, and only one beer. When you finish your only beer, there are still lots of wings left. You have already eaten so many wings that you are getting full, and the ones remaining do not look as

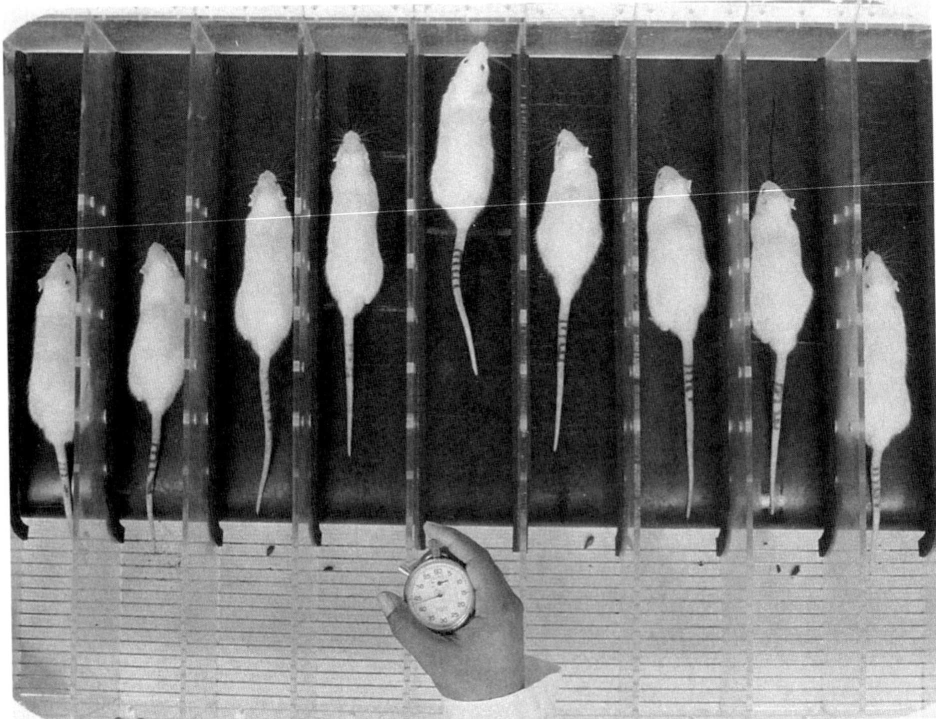

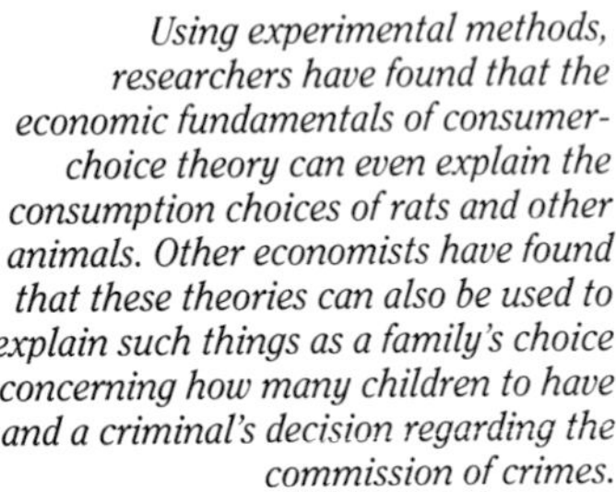

Using experimental methods, researchers have found that the economic fundamentals of consumer-choice theory can even explain the consumption choices of rats and other animals. Other economists have found that these theories can also be used to explain such things as a family's choice concerning how many children to have and a criminal's decision regarding the commission of crimes.

attractive. However, you would really like another beer, but you are out of money. You have not spent your $10 in a way that maximizes your utility because you failed to satisfy the above condition. You are at a point where the marginal utility of wings is lower than the marginal utility of beer, and because they both have the same price ($1), this implies

$$\frac{MU_{wings}}{P_{wings}} < \frac{MU_{beer}}{P_{beer}}$$

If you were able to reallocate your money by purchasing fewer wings and more beer, you could increase your total utility. As you spend more on beer, the marginal utility of beer will decrease, lowering the value of the right side of the equation. Simultaneously, as you spend less on wings, the marginal utility of wings will rise, increasing the value of the left side of the equation. You will have optimally allocated your budget when these values (ratios) are equal.

The equation can also be used to derive the law of demand. Beginning from a situation where the two sides were equal, suppose the price of wings increased. It would lower the value of *MU/P* for wings below the *MU/P* for beer. In response you would reallocate your budget, purchasing fewer wings and more beer. Thus we have the law of demand—as the price of wings rises you will purchase less. If people really attempt to spend their money in a way that yields the greatest amount of satisfaction, the usefulness of the consumer decision-making theory outlined here is difficult to question.

Price Changes and Consumer Choice

The demand curve or schedule shows the amount of a product that consumers would be willing to purchase at alternative prices during a specific time period. The law of demand states that the amount of a product purchased is inversely related to its price. We have seen how the law of demand can be derived from some fundamental principles of consumer behavior and preferences. However, it is possible to go farther and distinguish two different phenomena underlying a consumer's response to a price change. First, as the price of a product declines, the lower opportunity cost will induce consumers to buy more of it—even if they have to give up other products. Economists refer to this tendency to substitute a product that has become relatively cheaper for goods that are now relatively more expensive as the **substitution effect.**

Substitution effect
That part of an increase (decrease) in amount consumed that is the result of a good being cheaper (more expensive) in relation to other goods because of a reduction (increase) in price.

Second, with a fixed amount of money income, a reduction in the price of a product will increase a consumer's real income—the amount of goods and services consumers are able to purchase with their fixed amount of money income. If your rent or mortgage payment fell by $100 per month, it would allow you to afford more of numerous other goods. This increase in your real income has the same effect as if the rent had remained the same, but your income had risen by $100 per month. Because of the equivalence, this second way in which a price change affects consumption is referred to as the **income effect.** Typically, consumers will respond by purchasing more of the cheaper product (as well as other products) because they can now better afford to do so. (Both the income and substitution effects are derived graphically in the addendum to this chapter, titled "Consumer Choice and Indifference Curves".) The substitution and income effects will generally work in the same direction, causing consumers to purchase more as the price falls and less as the price rises.[5]

Income effect
That part of an increase (decrease) in amount consumed that is the result of the consumer's real income (the consumption possibilities available to the consumer) being expanded (contracted) by a reduction (rise) in the price of a good.

[5]The substitution effect will always work in this direction. The income effect, however, may work in the reverse direction for some types of goods known as inferior goods. These will be addressed later in this chap-

Time Cost and Consumer Choice

You may have heard the saying that "time is money." It is certainly true that time has value, and this value can be measured in dollars. We might begin by asking how much a person would be willing to pay to save an hour (perhaps for a nonstop airline flight that takes one hour less travel time, or for a house with a shorter commute to work). In practice, we frequently measure the value people place on their time by their wage rate.

The monetary price of a good is not always a complete measure of its cost to the consumer. Consumption of most goods requires time as well as money; and time, like money, is scarce to the consumer. So a lower time cost, like a lower money price, will make a product more attractive. Indeed, some commodities are demanded primarily because of their ability to save valuable time for consumers. People are often willing to pay relatively high money prices for such goods. The popularity of automatic dishwashers, prepared foods, air travel, and taxi service is based partly on the time savings they offer.

Time costs, unlike money prices, differ among individuals. They are higher for persons with greater earning power. Other things being equal, high-wage consumers choose fewer time-intensive (and more time-saving) commodities than persons with a lower time cost. High-wage consumers are overrepresented among air and taxicab passengers but underrepresented among television watchers, chess players, and long-distance bus travelers. Can you explain why? You can, if you understand how both money and time costs influence the choices of consumers.

Failure to account for time costs can lead to bad decisions. For example, which is cheaper for consumers: (a) waiting in line three hours to purchase a $25 concert ticket or (b) buying the same ticket for $40 without standing in line? For a consumer who values his time more than $5 per hour, the $40 without the wait in line is less costly. As another example, when government-imposed price ceilings (discussed in Chapter 4) create shortages, rationing by waiting in line is frequently used. In many cases, the benefit of the lower price to consumers will be largely, if not entirely, offset by increased time cost.

MARKET DEMAND REFLECTS THE DEMAND OF INDIVIDUAL CONSUMERS

The market demand schedule is the relationship between the market price of a good and the amount demanded by all the individuals in the market area. Because individual consumers purchase less at higher prices, the amount demanded in a market area as a total is also inversely related to price.

Exhibit 7-2 illustrates the relationship between individual demand and market demand for a hypothetical two-person market. The individual demand curves for both Jones and Smith are shown. Jones and Smith each consume three frozen pizzas per week at a price of $2.50. The amount demanded in the two-person market is six pizzas. If the price rises to $3.50 per pizza, the amount demanded in the market will fall to three pizzas, one demanded by Jones and two by Smith. ***The market demand is simply the horizontal sum of the individual demand curves.***

Market demand reflects individual demand. Individuals buy less as price increases. Therefore, the total amount demanded in the market declines as price increases.

EXHIBIT 7-2

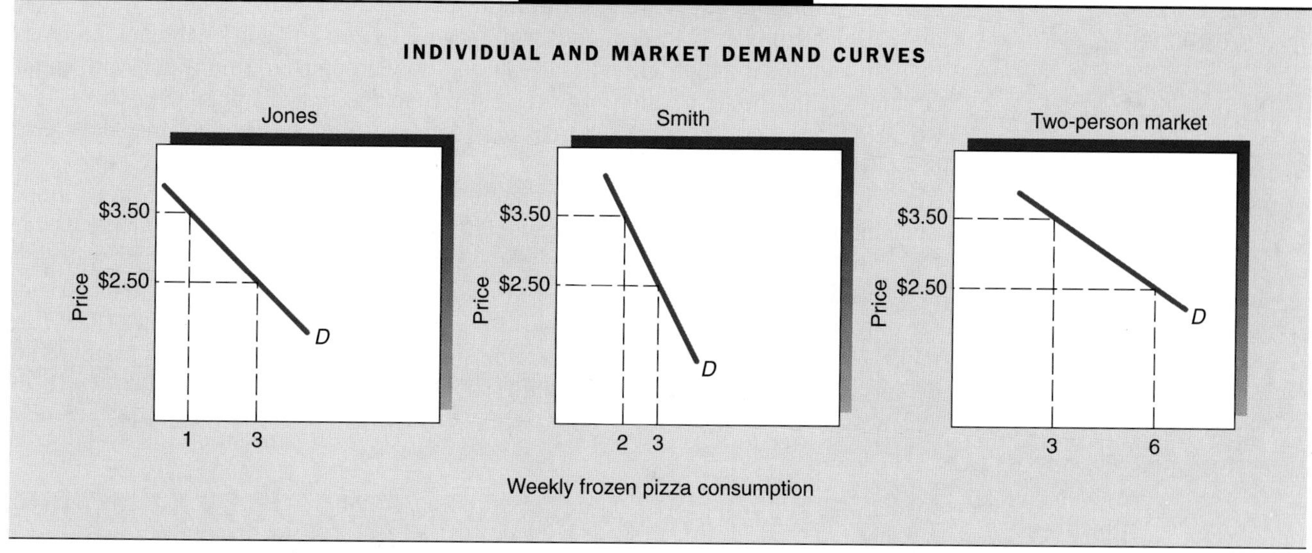

The market demand curve is merely the horizontal sum of the individual demand curves. It will slope downward to the right just as the individual demand curves do.

TOTAL VERSUS MARGINAL VALUE

> *Nothing is more useful than water; but it will purchase scarce anything. . . . A diamond, on the contrary, has scarce any value in use; but a very great quantity of other goods may frequently be had in exchange for it.*
>
> *Adam Smith*[6]

The classical economists, including Adam Smith, were puzzled that water, which is necessary for life, sells so cheaply, while diamonds have a far greater price. Does this mean that people value diamonds more than water? This same confusion can be found in everyday life: "You are going out to play golf? Is golf more important to you than I am?"

A century after Smith's time, economists solved this puzzle when they discovered the importance of the *marginal* analysis we have been discussing. The total value of a good includes consumer surplus; thus, total value can be quite large even though the price (which reflects the marginal value) is quite low. These factors provide the explanation for why market price has so little to do with the total contribution that a good makes to the welfare of users.

It is possible for something to have a large total value, but a very small marginal value, and also for something that has high marginal value to have a low total value. Spending time with family or friends can be more valuable in total than playing golf, but it can simultaneously be true that one *additional* hour spent with them is less valuable than an *additional* hour of golf.

[6]Adam Smith, *An Inquiry into the Nature and Causes of the Wealth of Nations,* 1776, ed. Edwin Cannan (Chicago: University of Chicago Press, 1976), p. 33.

The willingness to pay for additional units depends on one's valuation of the *marginal* unit, not the value of all units taken together. While, in total, water is far more valuable to you than diamonds, you may well value an additional diamond more than an additional gallon of water. If you had no diamonds and no water, you would certainly value the first gallon of water more than the first diamond. But this is not where you are. You consume hundreds of gallons of water per year, but may only have one or two diamonds.

When additional units are available at a low cost, they will be consumed until their marginal value is also low. Because the supply of water is relatively large, water has a low price. At this low price people begin to use water for fish tanks, watering lawns, and many other low-valued uses. If diamonds were as plentiful as water, and sold for only pennies per pound, we would use them for gravel in the bottom of our fish tanks. On the other hand, if water became significantly less abundant, its price would be very high and we might quit taking showers because they cost $1,000 worth of water.

DETERMINANTS OF SPECIFIC PREFERENCES—WHY CONSUMERS BUY WHAT THEY BUY

Did you ever wonder why a friend spent hard-earned money on something that you would not want even if it were free? People have different tastes and preferences, but what determines these preferences? Economists have not been able to explain very much about how preferences are determined. The best strategy has generally been to take preferences as given, using price and other demand-related factors to explain and predict human behavior. Still, several observations about what influences consumer preferences have been made:

1. *The determining factors in consumer preferences are frequently complex.* People looking for a house want far more than just a shelter: They want an attractive setting, a convenient location, higher-quality public services, and a great many other things. Moreover, each person may evaluate the same housing attribute differently. For example, living near a school may be a high priority for a family with children but a nuisance to a retired couple.

2. *Consumer preferences are shaped by attitudes toward time and risk.* A consumer would nearly always prefer to receive a good now rather than later. The degree of this difference, however, differs across consumers. Those who have a higher rate of time preference will be willing to pay extra (perhaps by borrowing and paying interest) to make goods available earlier, while others will save and let their money grow in the bank with interest until they can make their desired purchase. This interest is the reward earned for delaying current consumption. In addition to time preference, consumers also differ in the degree of risk they are willing to take (or more precisely how much they are willing to pay to reduce risk). Would you prefer to pay $20 more for a brand-name product, or take a gamble on a unknown product that costs less? Buying insurance is another way to reduce risk. Some consumers will decide to purchase flood insurance for their homes, or dental insurance, while others will not. They will prefer to save the money from the premiums and pay out-of-pocket for any expenses incurred. With regard to risk preference, a person may be either *risk loving, risk neutral,* or *risk averse.* Suppose you could have either $50 cash or a chance to flip a fair coin where heads wins $100 and tails wins nothing. Which would you choose—the certain $50 or the 50 percent chance at winning $100? A risk-loving person would prefer to take the gamble at winning $100, a risk-averse person would take the cash, and a risk-neutral person would be indifferent between the two alternatives.

3. ***Advertising influences consumer choice and preferences.*** Advertisers would not spend more than $100 billion in the United States each year if they did not get results. But exactly how does advertising affect consumers? Does it simply provide valuable information about product quality, price, and availability? Or does it use repetition and misleading information to manipulate consumers? Economists are not of one opinion. Let us take a closer look at this important issue.

Advertising—How Useful Is It?

Does advertising benefit consumers? Advertising is often used as a sponsoring medium, reducing the purchase price of newspapers, magazines, and television viewing. But since the consumers of the advertised products indirectly pay for these benefits, advertising cannot be defended solely on the basis of its sponsorship role.

Advertising does convey information about product price, quality, and availability. New firms or those with new products, new hours, new locations, or new services can use advertising to keep consumers informed, thus facilitating trade and increasing efficiency. After all, people who do not know the advantages of the newly available product or service, or the details of its availability, are not likely to become customers.

Is Advertising Wasteful? What about those repetitious television commercials that offer little or no new information? A great deal of media advertising simply seems to say "We are better," without providing supportive evidence. An advertiser may wish to take customers from a competitor or establish a brand name for a product. A multimillion-dollar media campaign by a soap, soft drink, or automobile manufacturer designed to capture a larger market share may be offset by a similar campaign waged by a competitor. The consumers of these products end up paying the costs of these battles for their attention and their dollars. We must remember, though, that consumers are under no obligation to purchase advertised products. If advertising results in higher prices with no compensating benefits, consumers can turn to cheaper, unadvertised products. And this fact leads to another question: How can brand names, especially when they are created by competing advertising campaigns, possibly benefit consumers?

A brand name in which people have confidence, even if it has been established by advertising, has a function beyond gaining the attention of consumers. It is an asset at risk for the seller. People value buying from sellers in whom they have confidence, and will pay a premium to do so. That premium makes a brand name valuable. If something happens to damage the reputation of a brand name, the willingness of consumers to purchase the product falls. In a very real sense, the brand name is hostage to consumer satisfaction.

When brand names are not allowed, as in the case of alcoholic beverages during Prohibition, consumers often suffer. For example, with no brand-name reputations to protect, anonymous moonshiners sometimes were careless and allowed dangerous impurities into the brew. Some consumers were blinded, and others died. Today the situation is different. Those who buy Johnnie Walker scotch know that the distiller has an enormous sum of money tied up in the brand.[7] The Guinness Corporation, owner of

[7]*Financial World* magazine estimated that, in 1992, the Johnnie Walker Red brand name was worth $2.6 billion.

the brand, would spend a large amount of money to avoid even one death from an impure batch. And this brand's value is dwarfed by many others. The Marlboro brand had an estimated value of $31.2 billion at one time, and Coca-Cola's brand value has been estimated at $24.4 billion. Is a brand name, promoted by costly advertising, worthwhile to the customer? In a market, each customer decides whether to pay the premium for the brand name.

Is Advertising Misleading and Manipulative? Unfair and deceptive advertising—including false promises, whether spoken by a seller or packaged by an advertising agency—is illegal under the Federal Trade Commission Act. A publicly advertised false claim is easier to establish and prosecute than the same words spoken in private. What about general, unsupported claims that a product is superior to the alternatives or that it will help a person enjoy life more? Does advertising of this type shape the preferences of people? In evaluating the manipulative effect of advertising, two things should be kept in mind. First, business decision makers are likely to choose the simplest route to economic gain. Generally, it is easier for business firms to cater to the actual desires of consumers than to attempt to reshape their preferences or persuade them to purchase an undesired product. Second, even if advertising does influence preferences, does it follow that this is bad? College classes in music and art appreciation, for example, may also change preferences for various forms of art and music. Does this make them bad? Economic theory is neutral. It neither condemns nor defends advertising—or college classes—as they try to change the tastes of target audiences.

ELASTICITY OF DEMAND

Buyers will predictably demand fewer units when the price rises, while sellers will predictably be willing to sell more. But these responses might be large or small, depending on the choices available to them. Such factors as the availability of substitutes for buyers (and the cost of production for sellers), as well as the time available for adjustments, will influence the size of the change in quantity in response to a change in price. How responsive will consumers be to a specific change in the price of a good? How many more units will producers supply if the price of a good increases? The answers to these questions are important for predicting the changes in a market when a price changes. To find answers, we must estimate the responses of buyers and sellers to the change that is being examined. Economists have developed a concept called *elasticity* for this purpose. In fact, the term *elasticity* means "responsiveness." We begin with the responsiveness of buyers to a change in price. It is measured by the **price elasticity of demand,** defined as:

Price elasticity of demand
The percent change in the quantity of a product demanded divided by the percent change in the price causing the change in quantity. Price elasticity of demand indicates the degree of consumer response to variation in price.

$$\text{Price elasticity of demand} = \frac{\text{percentage change in quantity demanded}}{\text{Percentage change in price}} = \frac{\%\Delta Q}{\%\Delta P}$$

This ratio is often called the *elasticity coefficient.* It can be expressed more briefly using the notation $\%\Delta Q$ to represent percent change in quantity and $\%\Delta P$ to represent percent change in price, where the Greek letter delta (Δ) means "change in." The law of demand states that an increase in price lowers quantity purchased, while a decrease in price increases quantity purchased. Because a change in price causes the quantity demanded to change in the opposite direction, the price elasticity coefficient is always negative, although economists often ignore the sign and simply use the absolute value of the coefficient.

To see how the concept of elasticity works, suppose that the price of the Ford Taurus rose 10 percent, while other prices remained the same. Ford could expect Taurus sales to fall substantially—perhaps 30 percent—as car buyers respond by switching to the many competing cars whose price had not changed. The strong responsiveness of buyers means that the demand for the Taurus is elastic. Now consider a different situation. Suppose that because of a new tax, the price of not only the Taurus but *all new cars* rises 10 percent. Consumer options in responding to *this* price increase are much more limited. They can't simply switch to a close substitute, as they could if the price of the Taurus alone rose. They must either pay the extra money for a new car, or buy a used car instead, which probably will need repairs more quickly and will have fewer safety and other features. This 10 percent rise in the price of all new cars will lead to a smaller response, perhaps a 5 percent decline in sales of new cars.

To calculate the elasticity coefficient for the Taurus in our example above, we begin with the 30 percent decline in quantity demanded, and divide by the 10 percent rise in the price that caused the decline. Thus, the elasticity of demand for the Taurus would be:

$$\frac{\%\Delta \text{Quantity}}{\%\Delta \text{Price}} = \frac{-30\%}{+10\%} = -3$$

or 3.0 (ignoring the minus sign), implying that the percentage change in quantity is three times the percentage change in price. To calculate the demand for all cars in our example, we see that the percentage change in quantity, -5 percent, divided by the percentage change in price, $+10$ percent, gives us $-\frac{1}{2}$, or -0.5. Again ignoring the sign, the price elasticity of demand for all cars of 0.5 implies that the percentage change in quantity is half the percentage change in price, using our hypothetical numbers.

Usually to calculate elasticity, we are only given actual numbers regarding the quantities purchased at different prices and must first compute the percentage changes. Suppose we begin with a price change, say from P_0 to P_1, which causes a change in quantity demanded, from Q_0 to Q_1. The change in quantity demanded is $Q_0 - Q_1$. To calculate the *percentage* change in quantity we divide the actual change by the midpoint (or average) of the two quantities.[8] Although it is usually easy to figure the midpoint without a formula (halfway between \$4 and \$6 is \$5), it can also be found as $(Q_0 + Q_1)/2$. Finally, because 0.05 is simply 5 percent, we multiply by 100. Thus, we may express the percentage change in quantity demanded as:

$$\frac{Q_0 - Q_1}{(Q_0 + Q_1)/2} \times 100$$

Similarly, when the change in price is $P_0 - P_1$, the *percentage* change in price is

$$\frac{P_0 - P_1}{(P_0 + P_1)/2} \times 100$$

We may divide the resulting percentage change in quantity by the percentage change in price to arrive at the elasticity.

Using these expressions for the percentage changes, however, it is possible to come up with a more direct method of computing elasticity from the numbers.

[8]This formula uses the average of the starting point and the ending point of the change so that it will give the same result whether we start from the lower or the higher price. This *arc* elasticity formula is not the only way to calculate elasticity, but it is the most frequently used.

Dividing the percentage change in quantity by the percentage change in price and simplifying gives

$$\frac{(Q_0 - Q_1)/(Q_0 + Q_1)}{(P_0 - P_1)/(P_0 + P_1)}$$

(Because each term is multiplied by 100 and the denominator of each term contains a 2, these factors cancel out of the final expression.)

A numerical example may help to illustrate. Suppose that Trina's Cakes can sell 50 specialty cakes per week at \$7 each, or 70 of the cakes at \$6 each. The percentage difference in quantity is the difference in the quantity ($50 - 70 = -20$), divided by the midpoint (60), times 100. The result is a -33.33 percent change in quantity ($-20 \div 60 \times 100 = -33.33$). The percentage change in price is the difference in price (\$7 − \$6 = \$1) divided by the midpoint price (\$6.50) times 100, or a 15.38 percent change in price ($1 \div 6.5 \times 100 = 15.38$). Dividing the percentage change in quantity by the percentage change in price ($-33.33 \div 15.38$) gives an elasticity coefficient of -2.17. Alternatively, we could have used the formula that included all of these directly as:

$$\frac{[(50 - 70)/(50 + 70)]}{[(7 - 6)/(7 + 6)]} = \frac{-20/120}{1/13} = \frac{-1/6}{1/13} = \frac{-13}{6} = -2.17$$

The same result is obtained either way. The elasticity of 2.17 indicates that the percentage change in quantity is just more than twice the percentage change in price.

The elasticity coefficient permits us to make a precise distinction between elastic and inelastic. When the elasticity coefficient is greater than 1 (ignoring the sign), as it was for the demand for Trina's Cakes, demand is elastic. When it is less than 1, demand is inelastic. Demand is said to be *unitary elastic* if the price elasticity is exactly 1.

Graphic Representation of Price Elasticity of Demand

Exhibit 7-3 presents demand curves of varying elasticity. A demand curve that is completely vertical is termed *perfectly inelastic.* In the real world, such a demand is nonexistent. Since there are substitutes for each good that become more attractive as the price of that good rises, and since the income effect is also present, we should expect that a higher price will always reduce quantity demanded, other things the same. Still, the (mythical) perfectly inelastic demand curve is shown in part a of Exhibit 7-3.

The more inelastic the demand, the steeper the demand curve *over any specific price range.* Inspection of the demand for cigarettes (part b of Exhibit 7-3), which is highly inelastic, and the demand for apples (part d), which is relatively elastic, indicates that the inelastic curve tends to be steeper. When demand elasticity is unitary, as part c illustrates, a demand curve that is convex to the origin will result. When a demand curve is completely horizontal, an economist would say that it is *perfectly elastic.* Demand for the wheat of a single wheat farmer, for example, would approximate perfect elasticity (part e).

Because elasticity is a relative concept, the elasticity of a straight-line demand curve will differ at each point along the demand curve. As Exhibit 7-4 illustrates, the elasticity of a straight-line demand curve (one with a constant slope) will range from highly elastic to highly inelastic. Here, when the price rises from \$10 to \$11, sales decline from 20 to 10. According to the formula, the price elasticity of demand is -7.0. Demand is very elastic in this region. In contrast, demand is quite inelastic in the \$1 to \$2 price range. As the price increases from \$1 to \$2, the amount demanded declines from 110 to 100. The elasticity of demand in this range is only -0.14; demand is highly inelastic.

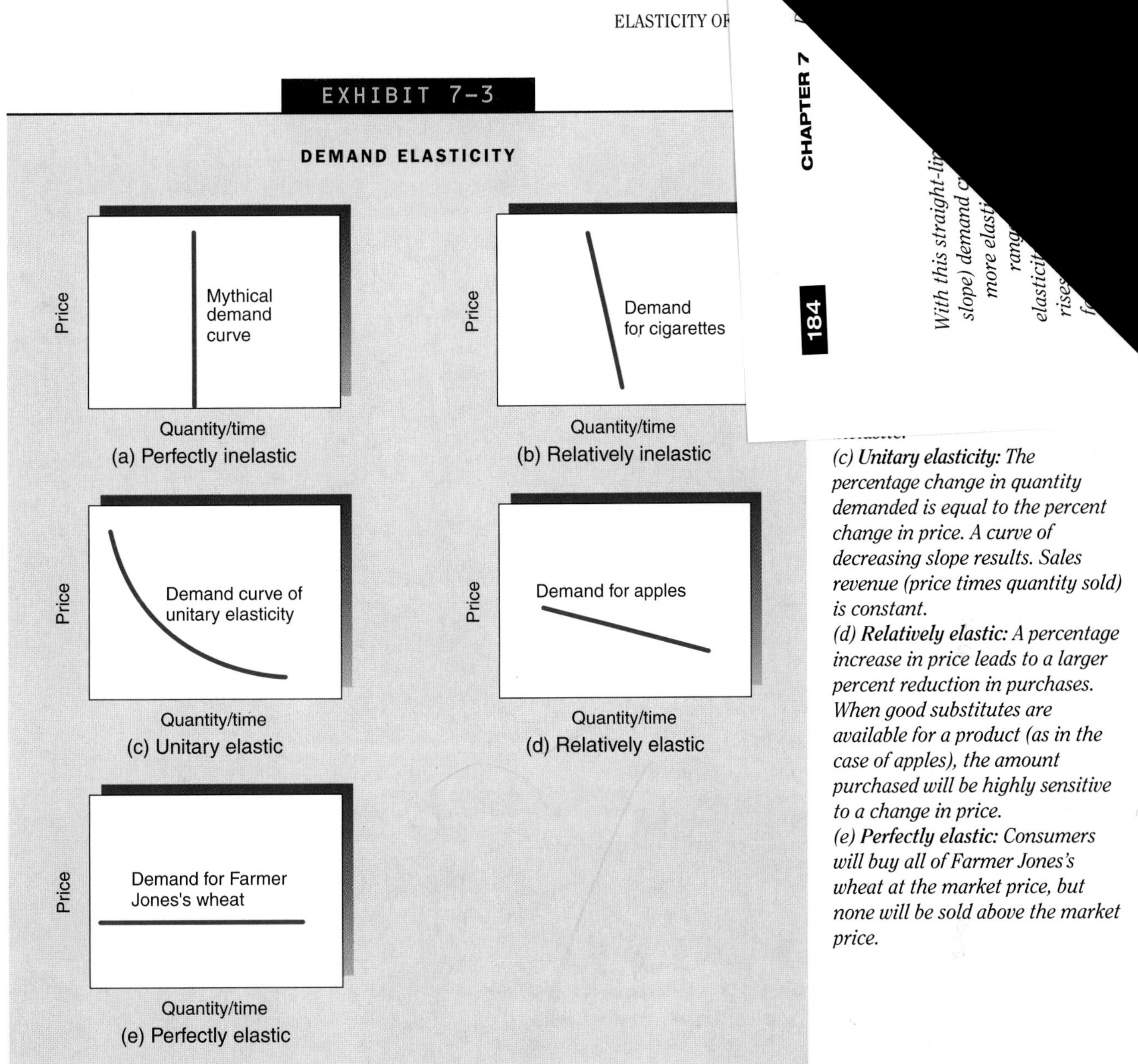

EXHIBIT 7-3

DEMAND ELASTICITY

*(c) **Unitary elasticity:** The percentage change in quantity demanded is equal to the percent change in price. A curve of decreasing slope results. Sales revenue (price times quantity sold) is constant.*
*(d) **Relatively elastic:** A percentage increase in price leads to a larger percent reduction in purchases. When good substitutes are available for a product (as in the case of apples), the amount purchased will be highly sensitive to a change in price.*
*(e) **Perfectly elastic:** Consumers will buy all of Farmer Jones's wheat at the market price, but none will be sold above the market price.*

Why do we bother with elasticity? Why not talk only about the slope of a demand curve? We use elasticities because they are independent of the units of measure. Whether we talk about dollars per gallon or cents per liter, the elasticities, given in percentages, remain the same. This is appropriate because people do not care what units of measurement are used; their response depends on the actual terms of exchange.

Determinants of Price Elasticity of Demand

Economists have estimated the price elasticity of demand for many products. As the estimates of **Exhibit 7-5** illustrate, the elasticity of demand among products varies substantially. The demand for several products—salt, toothpicks, matches, light bulbs, and newspapers, for example—is highly inelastic. On the other hand, the demand curves for fresh tomatoes, Chevrolet automobiles, and fresh green peas are highly

EXHIBIT 7-4

SLOPE OF DEMAND CURVE VERSUS PRICE ELASTICITY

...e (constant-...urve, demand is ...c in the high-price ...e. The formula for arc ...y shows that, when price ... from $1 to $2 and quantity ...alls from 110 to 100, demand is inelastic. A price rise of the same magnitude (but of a smaller percentage), from $10 to $11, leads to a decline in quantity of the same size (but of a larger percentage), so that elasticity is much greater. (Price elasticities are negative, but we typically ignore the sign and look only at the absolute value.)

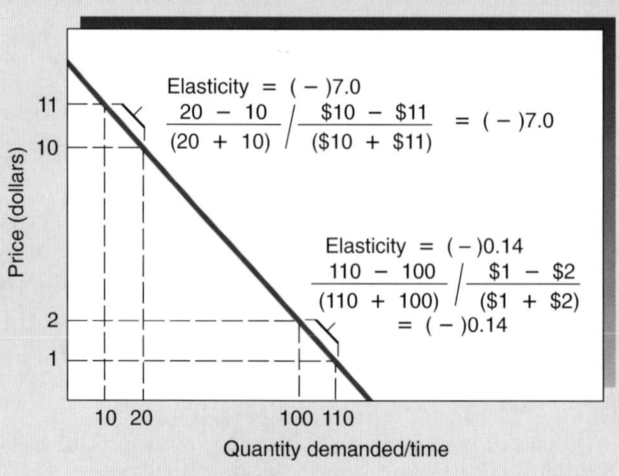

EXHIBIT 7-5

ESTIMATED PRICE ELASTICITY OF DEMAND FOR SELECTED PRODUCTS

SOURCES: *Hendrick S. Houthakker and Lester D. Taylor,* Consumer Demand in the United States, 1929–1970 *(Cambridge: Harvard University Press, 1966, 1970); Douglas R. Bohi,* Analyzing Demand Behavior *(Baltimore: Johns Hopkins University Press, 1981); Hsaing-tai Cheng and Oral Capps Jr., "Demand for Fish,"* American Journal of Agriculture Economics, *August 1988; and U.S. Department of Agriculture.*

INELASTIC		APPROXIMATELY UNITARY ELASTICITY	
Salt	0.1	Movies	0.9
Matches	0.1	Housing, owner occupied, long run	1.2
Toothpicks	0.1	Shellfish, consumed at home	0.9
Airline travel, short run	0.1	Oysters, consumed at home	1.1
Gasoline, short run	0.2	Private education	1.1
Gasoline, long run	0.7	Tires, short run	0.9
Residential natural gas, short run	0.1	Tires, long run	1.2
Residential natural gas, long run	0.5	Radio and television receivers	1.2
Coffee	0.25	**ELASTIC**	
Fish (cod), consumed at home	0.5	Restaurant meals	2.3
Tobacco products, short run	0.45	Foreign travel, long run	4.0
Legal services, short run	0.4	Airline travel, long run	2.4
Physician services	0.6	Fresh green peas	2.8
Taxi, short run	0.6	Automobiles, short run	1.2–1.5
Automobiles, long run	0.2	Chevrolet automobiles	4.0
		Fresh tomatoes	4.6

elastic. What factors explain this variation? Why is demand for some products, but not for others, highly responsive to changes in price? The answer lies primarily in the availability of good substitutes and also to some extent on the share of the typical consumer's total budget expended on a product.

Availability of Substitutes. ***The most important determinant of the price elasticity of demand is the availability of substitutes. When good substitutes for a product are available, a price rise induces many consumers to switch to other products. Demand is elastic.*** For example, if the price of felt-tip pens increased, many consumers would simply switch to pencils or ballpoint pens. If the price of apples increased, consumers would substitute oranges, bananas, peaches, or pears.

When good substitutes are unavailable, the demand for a product tends to be inelastic. Medical services are an example. When we are sick, most of us find witch doctors, faith healers, palm readers, and cod-liver oil to be highly imperfect substitutes for the services of a physician. Not surprisingly, the demand for physician services is inelastic.

The availability of substitutes increases as the product class becomes more specific, thus increasing price elasticity. For example, as Exhibit 7-5 shows, the price elasticity of Chevrolets, a narrow product class, exceeds that of the broad class of automobiles in general. If the price of Chevrolets alone rises, many substitute cars are available. But if the prices of all automobiles rise together, consumers have fewer good substitutes.

Share of Total Budget Expended on Product. If the expenditures on a product are quite small relative to the consumer's budget, the income effect will be small even if there is a substantial increase in the price of the product. This will make demand less elastic. Compared to one's total budget, expenditures on some commodities are almost inconsequential. Matches, toothpicks, and salt are good examples. Most consumers spend only $1 or $2 per year on each of these items. A doubling of their price would exert little influence on the family budget. Therefore, even if the price of such a product were to rise sharply, consumers would still not find it in their interest to spend much time and effort looking for substitutes.

Exhibit 7-6 provides a graphic illustration for both elastic and inelastic demand curves. In part a, the demand curve for ballpoint pens is elastic, because there are good substitutes—for example, pencils and felt-tip pens. Therefore, when the price of the pens increases from $1.00 to $1.50, the quantity purchased declines sharply from 100,000 to only 25,000. The calculated price elasticity equals -3.0. The fact that the absolute value of the coefficient is greater than 1 confirms that the demand for ballpoint pens is elastic over the price range illustrated. Part b of Exhibit 7-6 illustrates the demand curve for cigarettes. Because most consumers do not find other products to be a good substitute, the demand for cigarettes is highly inelastic. In the case of cigarettes, a substantial (from $1.00 to $1.50) increase in price leads to only a small reduction in quantity demanded. The price elasticity coefficient is -0.26, substantially less in absolute value than 1, confirming that the demand for cigarettes is inelastic (Exercise: Use the price elasticity formula to verify the values of these elasticity coefficients).

TIME AND DEMAND ELASTICITY

As changing market conditions raise or lower the price of a product, both consumers and producers will respond. However, their response will not be instantaneous, and it is likely to become larger over time. ***In general, when the price of a product increases, consumers will reduce their consumption by a larger amount in the long run than in the short run. Thus, the demand for most products will be more elastic in the***

EXHIBIT 7-6

INELASTIC AND ELASTIC DEMAND

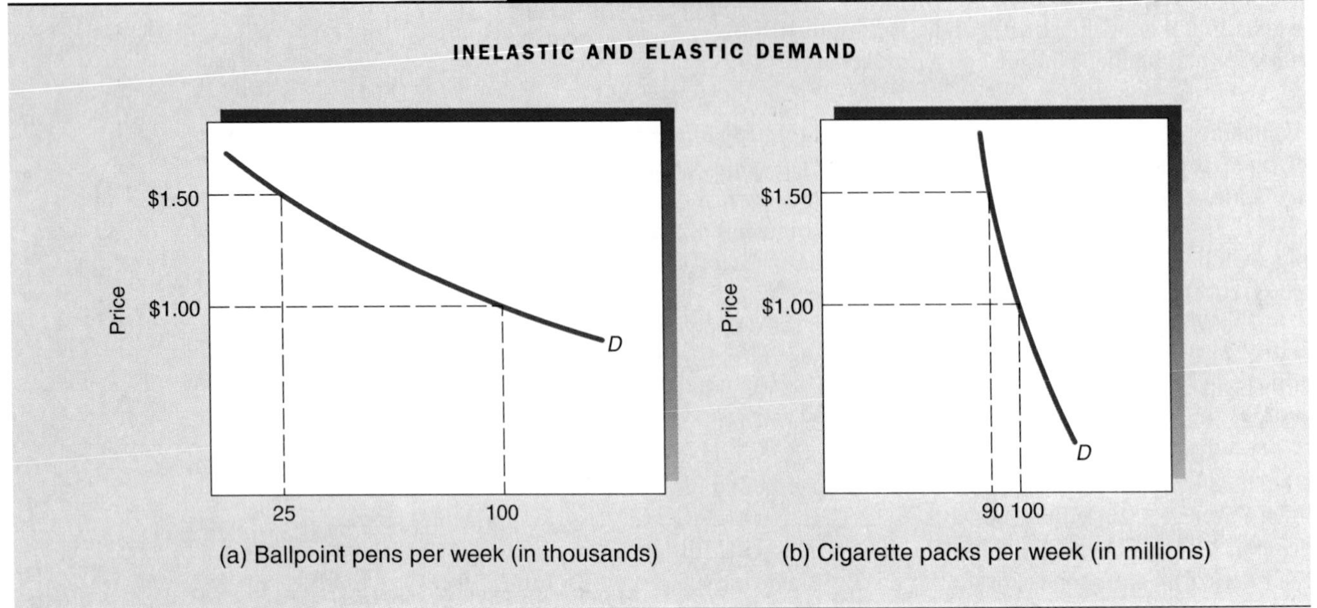

As the price of ballpoint pens (a) rose from $1.00 to $1.50, the quantity purchased plunged from 100,000 to 25,000. The percent reduction in quantity is larger than the percent increase in price. Thus, the demand for the pens is elastic. In contrast, an increase in the price of cigarettes from $1.00 to $1.50 results in only a small reduction in the number purchased (b). Reflecting the inelasticity of demand for cigarettes, the percent reduction in quantity is smaller than the percent increase in price.

long run than in the short run. This relationship between the elasticity coefficient and the length of the adjustment period is often referred to as the second law of demand.

The first law of demand says that buyers will respond predictably to a price change, purchasing more when the price is lower than when the price is higher, if other things remain the same. The second law of demand says that the buyers' response will be greater after they have had time to adjust more fully to a price change.

TOTAL REVENUE, TOTAL EXPENDITURE, AND THE PRICE ELASTICITY OF DEMAND

One of the most important applications of price elasticity is to determine how total consumer expenditure (that is, total consumer spending) on a product changes when the price changes. This can be done either (1) for an individual's total spending on a product using the elasticity of demand from an individual's demand curve for a product, (2) for the total combined expenditures of all consumers on a product using the elasticity from the total market demand curve for a product, or (3) for total consumer expenditures on the product produced by an individual business firm using the demand curve facing the firm. In this final case the issue takes on added meaning because it is equivalent to the firm's total revenue.

Returning to part a of Exhibit 7-6, consumers purchase 25,000 ballpoint pens at a price of \$1.50. Total consumer expenditures on ballpoint pens are thus the price paid times the quantity purchased, which is \$37,500 (\$1.50 per pen × 25,000 pens). Had this been a particular firm's demand curve, say, the demand for Bic ballpoint pens, total consumer expenditures would be equal to Bic's total revenue. Thus, the elasticity of demand can also be used to determine how a firm's total revenue will change if it changes its price. We begin with the application to total consumer expenditures.

Total Expenditures and Demand Elasticity

If the price of a product rises, total consumer expenditures on it can either rise, fall, or stay the same. Which will happen depends on the elasticity of demand. According to the law of demand, as the price rises the quantity purchased will fall, and as price falls the quantity purchased will rise:

$$\text{Total Expenditures} = \textit{Price} \times \textit{Quantity}$$
$$? = \uparrow \times \downarrow$$
$$? = \downarrow \times \uparrow$$

Because total expenditures are equal to price times quantity, and because price and quantity move in opposite directions, what happens to total expenditures depends upon whether the effect of the change in price or the effect of the change in quantity is greater. Price elasticity determines this because it is the ratio of the percentage change in quantity to the percentage change in price. When demand is inelastic, the price elasticity coefficient is less than one. This means the bottom of this fraction (the percentage change in price) is greater than the top (the percentage change in quantity). Thus, the effect of the change in price will be greater than the effect of the change in quantity. ***Therefore, when demand is inelastic, a change in price will cause total expenditures to change in the same direction.***

When demand is elastic, the effect of the change in quantity will be greater than the effect of the change in price. ***Therefore, a change in price will cause total expenditures to move in the opposite direction when demand is elastic.***

When demand is of unitary elasticity, the effect of the change in quantity will be equal in magnitude to the effect of the change in price on total expenditures—they will completely offset each other. ***Thus, when demand elasticity is unitary, total expenditures will remain unchanged as price changes.***

The demand curves shown in Exhibit 7-6 can be used to illustrate the linkage between elasticity of demand and changes in total revenue. In the case of cigarettes (part b), the price elasticity of demand for the price increase from \$1.00 to \$1.50 is 0.26, indicating that demand is inelastic. (Exercise: Use the price elasticity formula to verify this coefficient.) This increase in cigarette prices leads to an increase in expenditures on the product from \$100 million (\$1.00 × 100 million packs) to \$135 million (\$1.50 × 90 million packs). If the change had occurred in the opposite direction, with the price falling from \$1.50 to \$1.00, total expenditures would have declined.

The price elasticity of demand for ballpoint pens for a price increase from \$1.00 to \$1.50 (part a of Exhibit 7-6) is 3.0, indicating that demand is elastic. This increase in the price of ballpoint pens leads to a reduction in total consumer expenditures from \$100,000 (\$1.00 × 100,000 pens) to \$37,500 (\$1.50 × 25,000 pens). If the change had occurred in the opposite direction, with the price falling from \$1.50 to \$1.00, total expenditures would have risen.

EXHIBIT 7-7

DEMAND ELASTICITY AND HOW CHANGES IN PRICE AFFECT TOTAL CONSUMER EXPENDITURES OR A FIRM'S TOTAL REVENUE

Price Elasticity of Demand	Numerical Elasticity Coefficient (in absolute value)	Impact of Raising Price on Total Consumer Expenditures or a Firm's Total Revenue	Impact of Lowering Price on Total Consumer Expenditures or a Firm's Total Revenue
Elastic	1 to ∞	decrease	increase
Unitary Elastic	1	unchanged	unchanged
Inelastic	0 to 1	increase	decrease

Because of the different price elasticities, a price increase results in higher total consumer expenditures on cigarettes but lower total consumer expenditures on ballpoint pens. **Exhibit 7-7** summarizes the relationship between changes in price and total expenditures, for demand curves of varying elasticity.

Total Revenues and Demand Elasticity

This same analysis can be performed using a particular firm's demand curve, rather than the total market demand curve for the product. Here, total consumer expenditures from the firm's perspective are simply the firm's total revenues, the price per unit times the quantity sold. As we discussed earlier in this chapter, the demand curve facing one specific firm in an industry will be substantially more elastic than the demand curve for the entire market. (Remember the demand elasticity comparison between the Ford Taurus and all automobiles.)

Because of the relationship between price and quantity sold, a firm's total revenue can either rise, fall, or stay the same in response to a change in price. Again, the outcome will be determined by price elasticity of demand. When the firm's demand curve is inelastic, its total revenues will rise if it increases its price and fall if it lowers its price. When demand is elastic, however, revenue will fall if price is increased, and will rise if price is reduced. When demand is of unitary elasticity, a change in price will leave total revenue unaffected. **Exhibit 7-8** gives a numerical example to illustrate this point.

Part a of the exhibit shows how a firm's total revenue is calculated from data on price and quantity sold. In addition, the price elasticity has been computed using the formula. These same data are shown graphically along with the firm's demand curve in part b of the exhibit. As the firm lowers its price from $9 to $8 to $7, the firm's revenues expand from $0 to $8 to $14. In this range, the firm's demand curve is elastic, so total revenue is rising as price is lowered. Intuitively, as the firm lowers its price, it is losing revenue from the current customers because they are paying a lower price, but gaining revenue from new customers who are now buying at the lower price. When demand is elastic, the expansion in revenue from additional sales is more than enough to offset the reductions in revenue from the lower price. An example of this is shown by the shaded areas in part b of the exhibit. At a price of $7, the firm sells 2 units. Total revenue is $14, which is shown by the red shaded area. When price is lowered to $6, sales increase to 3 units, and total revenue is $18, shown by the blue shaded area. The small part of the red shaded area above the blue area is lost revenue on existing sales,

EXHIBIT 7-8

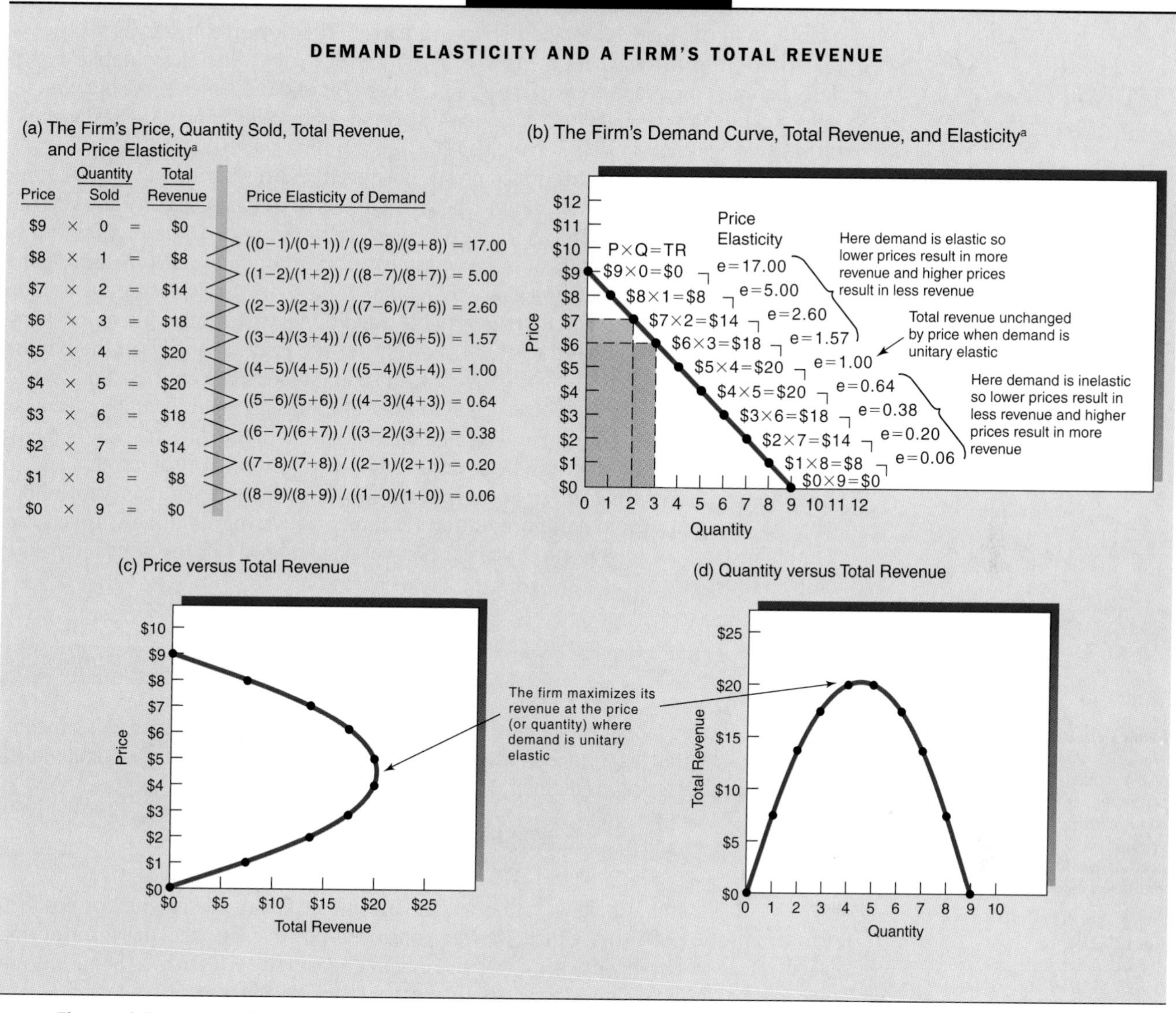

[a]*The sign of all elasticity coefficients is negative.*

while the small part of the blue area to the right of the red area is the gain in revenue on new sales. Because the gain is greater than the loss, revenue increases.

This process continues until demand reaches unitary elasticity between a price of $4 and $5. In this range total revenue is unchanged at $20 regardless of whether price is $4 or $5. Here, as price is lowered, the revenue from new sales exactly offsets the loss in revenue from existing sales.

As price falls farther from $4 to $3 to $2, the firm's total revenues begin to fall. Here, price reductions result in lower revenue because demand becomes inelastic. The revenue from the new sales is not enough to offset the losses in revenue due to the lowered price.

Of course, this example could be viewed in reverse. As the firm raises its price up from $1, revenues expand until demand is unitary elastic, and, above this, revenues fall with further price increases as demand becomes elastic. The issue is whether the higher revenue from the sales that remain is sufficient to offset the lower revenue from the lost sales.

This relationship between the firm's total revenue and its price is shown in part c of the exhibit. Alternatively, one may view this as a relationship between the quantity and the total revenue, as shown in part d. The firm maximizes its revenue at the price (or quantity) where demand is of unitary elasticity.[9] One might notice a similarity between the graph shown in part c of the exhibit and the Laffer curve between tax rates and total tax revenue from Chapter 4. It is indeed the elasticity of the tax base to a tax rate change that underlies the Laffer curve in a similar manner.

Firms attempt to maximize profit, not revenue. Profit is simply total revenue minus total cost. The price or output where demand is of unitary elasticity and revenue is maximized is not the same as the one where total profit is maximized. They will be close, however, for some types of firms whose costs are mostly upfront (or "fixed") with little marginal cost of producing additional units. For a concert or sporting event, most of the cost is of this type, and there is very little additional cost of allowing more people into the event. Suppose that the exhibit shown is for the price, quantity (in thousands), and total revenue (also in thousands) for a firm selling tickets to a concert. Can you explain why even if the capacity of the stadium was 10 thousand that they might decide to set the ticket price at a level that does not sell out the stadium? Alternatively, suppose the exhibit was the relationship between a university's tuition (in thousands) and its enrollment (also in thousands). If current tuition was $6 thousand, can you explain why the university could get more tuition revenue by lowering its tuition? If you can, you understand the importance price elasticity of demand plays in the decision making of the business firm.

INCOME ELASTICITY

Income elasticity
The percentage change in the quantity of a product demanded divided by the percentage change in consumer income causing the change in quantity demanded. It measures the responsiveness of the demand for a good to a change in income.

Normal good
A good that has a positive income elasticity, so that, as consumer income rises, demand for that good rises also.

Increases in consumer income will increase the demand for most goods. **Income elasticity** indicates the responsiveness of the demand for a product to a change in income. Income elasticity is defined as:

$$\frac{\text{Percentage change in quantity demanded}}{\text{Percentage change in income}}$$

As **Exhibit 7-9** shows, although the income elasticity coefficients for products vary from one good to another, they are normally positive. In fact, the term **normal good** refers to any good with a positive income elasticity of demand. Some normal goods have lower income elasticities than others, however. In general, goods that people regard as "necessities" will have low income elasticities (between 0 and 1). Significant quantities are purchased even at low incomes, and, as income increases, spending on these items will increase by less than a proportional amount. It is understandable that such items as fuel, electricity, bread, tobacco, economy clothing, and potatoes have a low income elasticity.

Goods that consumers regard as "luxuries" generally have a high (greater than 1) income elasticity. For example, private education, new automobiles, recreational activities, donations to environmental groups, swimming pools, and vacation air travel are all highly income elastic. As income increases, the demand for these goods expands even more rapidly, and therefore spending on these items increases as a proportion of income.

[9]An astute student might note that total revenue is really maximized at a price of $4.50 and a quantity of 4.5 (if possible, say, 4.5 pounds of roast beef). Here total revenue is $20.25. Because the elasticity formula uses the midpoint as a basis, the elasticity shown for the price change from $4 to $5 is really the elasticity at the midpoint between these two prices, or $4.50.

EXHIBIT 7-9

ESTIMATED INCOME ELASTICITY OF DEMAND FOR SELECTED PRODUCTS

Low income elasticity		High income elasticity	
Margarine	−0.20	Private education	2.46
Fuel	0.38	New cars	2.45
Electricity	0.20	Recreation and amusements	1.57
Fish (haddock)	0.46	Alcohol	1.54
Food	0.51		
Tobacco	0.64		
Hospital care	0.69		

SOURCES: *Hendrick S. Houthakker and Lester D. Taylor,* Consumer Demand in the United States, 1929–1970 *(Cambridge: Harvard University Press, 1966); L. Taylor, "The Demand for Electricity: A Survey,"* Bell Journal of Economics *(Spring 1975); and F. W. Bell, "The Pope and the Price of Fish,"* American Economic Review 58, *(December 1968).*

A few commodities, such as margarine, low-quality meat cuts, and bus travel, actually have a negative income elasticity. Economists refer to goods with a negative income elasticity as **inferior goods.** As income expands, the demand for inferior goods will decline. Conversely, as income declines, the demand for inferior goods will increase.

Inferior good
A good that has a negative income elasticity, so that, as consumer income rises, the demand for that good falls.

THE PRICE ELASTICITY OF SUPPLY

We may also define the **price elasticity of supply,** which is the percentage change in quantity supplied, divided by the percentage change in the price causing the supply response. Because this measures the responsiveness of sellers to a change in price, it is analogous to the price elasticity of demand. However, the price elasticity of supply will be positive because the quantity producers are willing to supply is directly related to price. As in the case of demand elasticity, time plays a role. Supply elasticities will be greater when suppliers have a longer time to respond to a price change. In the next two chapters we will discuss more fully the factors that determine supply elasticity. For now, it is important simply to recognize the concept of supply elasticity and the fact that suppliers (like buyers) will be more responsive to a price change when they have had more time to adjust to it.

Price elasticity of supply
The percentage change in quantity supplied, divided by the percentage change in the price causing the change in quantity supplied.

LOOKING *Ahead*

The market demand indicates how strongly consumers desire each good or service. In the following chapter, we turn to a firm's costs of production that arise because resources have alternative uses. In fact, the cost of producing a good is precisely consumers' value of the alternative goods that could have been produced with those same resources. An understanding of these two topics—consumer demand and cost of production—is essential if we are to understand how market prices result in resources being allocated toward the production of goods most highly valued by consumers.

KEY POINTS

➤ Consumer choice is a process of allocating limited income among goods and services in a way that maximizes utility. The role of relative prices, information, preferences for risk and time, and the law of diminishing marginal utility help explain these choices. These ideas underlie the position and shape of an individual's demand curve for a product.

➤ The market demand curve reflects the demand of individuals. It is simply the horizontal sum of the demand curves of individuals for the product.

➤ A good with high total value can have low marginal value, and vice versa. Because market price is a marginal valuation, it does not have to correlate with the total value of the good.

➤ The advertising budgets of profit-seeking business firms indicate that advertising influences the choices of consumers. Advertising can reduce the search time of consumers, help them make more informed choices, and provide assurances with regard to quality (through brand names).

➤ Price elasticity reveals the responsiveness of the amount purchased to a change in price. When there are good substitutes available and the item forms a sizable component of the consumer's budget, its demand will tend to be more elastic. Typically, the price elasticity of a product will increase as more time is allowed for consumers to adjust to a change in price. This direct relationship between size of the elasticity coefficient and the length of the adjustment period is often referred to as the *second law of demand.*

➤ The concept of elasticity is useful in determining how a change in price will affect total consumer expenditures on an item or a firm's total revenue. An increase in price will lower total revenue (or expenditure) when demand is elastic, but increase it when demand is inelastic. A decrease in price will raise total revenue (or expenditure) when demand is elastic, but decrease it when demand is inelastic. When demand is unitary elastic, total revenue (or expenditure) is unaffected by a change in price.

➤ The concept of elasticity can also be applied to consumer income (income elasticity) and supply (the price elasticity of supply).

CRITICAL ANALYSIS QUESTIONS

*1. Suppose that in an attempt to raise more revenue, Nowhere State University (NSU) increases its tuition. Will this necessarily result in more revenue? Under what conditions will revenue (a) rise, (b) fall, or (c) remain the same? Explain this in words, focusing on the relationship between the increased revenue from the students who enroll despite the higher tuition and the lost revenue from lower enrollment. If the true price elasticity were 1.2, what would you suggest the university do to expand revenue?

2. A bus ticket between two cities costs $50 and the trip will take 56 hours while an airplane ticket costs $300 and takes 6 hours. Mary values her time at $6 per hour, and Michele values her time at $4 per hour. Will Mary take the bus or the plane? Which will Michele take?

*3. The accompanying chart presents data on the price of fuel oil, the amount of it demanded, and the demand for insulation.

a. Calculate the price elasticity of demand for fuel oil as its price rises from 30 cents to 50 cents; from 50 cents to 70 cents.

b. Are fuel oil and insulation substitutes or complements? How can you tell from the figures alone?

Fuel Oil		Insulation
Price per Gallon (cents)	Quantity Demanded (millions of gallons)	Quantity Demanded (millions of tons)
30	100	30
50	90	35
70	60	40

4. A consumer is currently purchasing 3 pairs of jeans and 5 t-shirts per year. The price of jeans is $30, and t-shirts cost $10. At the current rate of consumption, the marginal utility of jeans is 60 and the marginal utility of t-shirts is 30. Is this consumer maximizing his utility? Would you suggest he buy more jeans and fewer t-shirts, or more t-shirts and fewer jeans?

5. Residential electricity in the state of Washington costs about half as much as in nearby Montana. A study showed that in Washington, the average household used about 1,200 kilowatt-hours per month, whereas Montanans used about half that much per household. Do these

data provide us with two points on the average household's demand curve for residential electricity in this region? Why or why not?

*6. *What's wrong with this way of thinking?* "Economics is unable to explain the value of goods in a sensible manner. A quart of water is much cheaper than a quart of oil. Yet water is essential to both animal and plant life. Without it, we could not survive. How can oil be more valuable than water? Yet economics says that it is."

*7. The wealthy are widely believed to have more leisure time than the poor. However, even though we are a good deal wealthier today than our great-grandparents were 100 years ago, we appear to live more hectic lives and have less free time. Can you explain why?

8. What are the major determinants of a product's price elasticity of demand? Studies indicate that the demand for Florida oranges, Bayer aspirin, watermelons, and airfares to Europe are elastic. Why?

9. Most systems of medical insurance substantially reduce the costs to the consumer of using additional units of physician services and hospitalization. Some reduce these costs to zero. How does this method of payment affect the consumption levels of medical services? Might this method of organization result in "too much" consumption of medical services? Discuss.

*10. Are the following statements true or false? Explain your answers.

a. A 10 percent reduction in price that leads to a 15 percent increase in amount purchased indicates a price elasticity of more than 1.
b. A 10 percent reduction in price that leads to a 2 percent increase in total expenditures indicates a price elasticity of more than 1.
c. If the percentage change in price is less than the resultant percentage change in quantity demanded, demand is elastic.

*11. Respond to the following questions: If you really like pizza, should you try to consume as much pizza as possible? If you want to succeed, should you try to make the highest possible grade in your economics class?

*12. Sue loves ice cream but cannot stand frozen yogurt desserts. In contrast, Carole cannot tell the difference between ice cream and frozen yogurt desserts. Who will have the more elastic demand for yogurt?

*13. "If all the farmers reduced their output to one-half the current rate, farm incomes would increase, the total utility derived from farm output would rise, and the nation would be better off." Is this statement true or false? Explain your answer.

*14. "Market competition encourages deceitful advertising and dishonesty." Is this statement true or false? Explain your answer.

---

*Asterisk denotes questions for which answers are given in Appendix B.

ADDENDUM: CONSUMER CHOICE AND INDIFFERENCE CURVES

ADVANCED MATERIAL

In the text of this chapter, we used marginal utility analysis to develop the demand curve of an individual. In developing the theory of consumer choice, economists usually rely on a more formal technique—*indifference curve* analysis. Because this technique is widely used at a more advanced level, many instructors like to include it in their introductory course. In this addendum, we use indifference curve analysis to develop the theory of demand in a more formal—some would say more elegant—manner.

What Are Indifference Curves?

There are two elements in every choice: (1) preferences (the desirability of various goods) and (2) opportunities (the attainability of various goods). The **indifference curve** relates to the former: preferences. It separates better (more preferred) bundles of goods from inferior (less preferred) bundles, providing a diagrammatic picture of how an individual ranks alternative consumption bundles.

In **Exhibit 7A-1**, we assume that Robinson Crusoe is initially consuming 8 fish and 8 breadfruit per week (point *A*). This initial bundle provides him with a certain level of satisfaction (utility). He would, however, be willing to trade this initial bundle for certain other consumption alternatives if the opportunity presented itself. Since he likes both fish and breadfruit, he would especially like to obtain bundles to the northeast of point *A*, since they represent more of both goods. However, he would also be willing to give up some breadfruit if in return he received a compensatory amount of fish. Similarly, if the terms of trade were right, he would be willing to exchange fish for breadfruit. The trade-offs he is just willing to make—those that would make him no better and no worse off—

EXHIBIT 7A-1

THE INDIFFERENCE CURVE OF ROBINSON CRUSOE

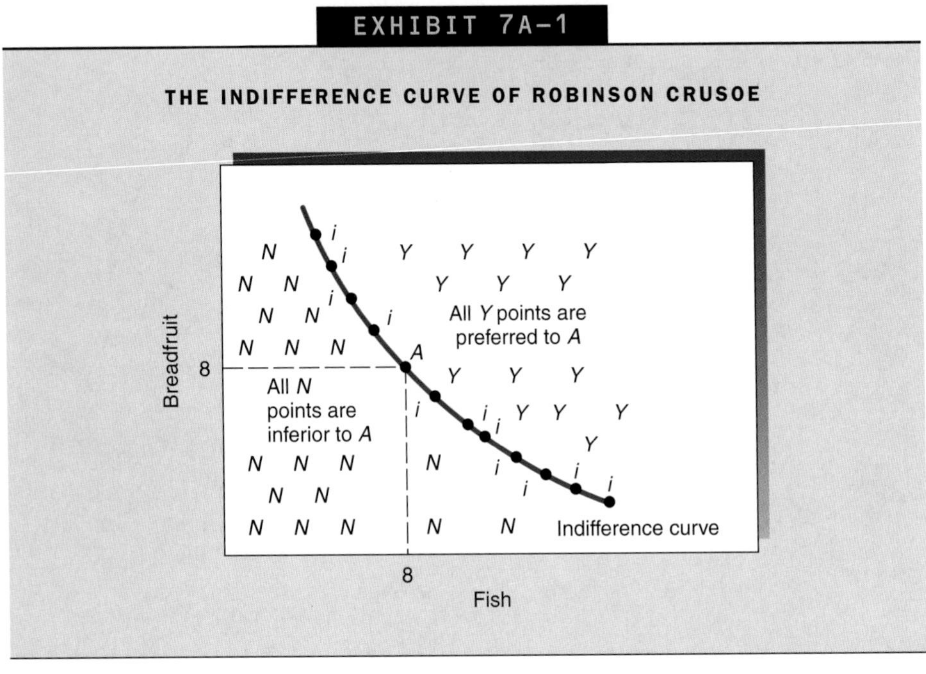

The curve generated by connecting Crusoe's "I do not care" answers separates the combinations of fish and breadfruit that he prefers to the bundle A from those that he judges to be inferior to A. The i points map out an indifference curve.

lie *along* the indifference curve. Of course, he is happy to move to any bundle on a higher indifference curve.

Starting from point A (8 fish and 8 breadfruit), we ask Crusoe if he is willing to trade that bundle for various other bundles. He answers "Yes" (Y), "No" (N), or "I do not care" (i). Exhibit 7A-1 illustrates the pattern of his responses. Crusoe's "I do not care" answers indicate that the original bundle (point A) and each alternative indicated by an i are valued equally by Crusoe. These i points, when connected, form the indifference curve. This line separates the preferred bundles of fish and breadfruit from the less-valued combinations. Note that such a curve is likely to be entirely different for any two people. The preferences of individuals vary widely.

We can establish a new indifference curve by starting from any point not on the original curve and following the same procedure. If we start with a point (a consumption bundle) to the northeast of the original indifference curve, all points on the new curve will have a higher level of satisfaction for Crusoe than any on the old curve. The new curve will probably have about the same shape as the original.

Characteristics of Indifference Curves

In developing consumer theory, economists assume that the preferences of consumers exhibit certain properties. These properties enable us to make statements about the general pattern of indifference curves. What are these properties, and what do they imply about the characteristics of indifference curves?

1. *More goods are preferable to fewer goods—thus, bundles on indifference curves lying farthest to the northeast of a diagram are always preferred.* Assuming the consumption of only two commodities that are both desired, the individual will always prefer a bundle with more of one good (without loss of the other) to the original bundle. This means that combinations to the northeast of a point on the diagram will always be preferred to points lying to the southwest.

2. *Goods are substitutable—therefore, indifference curves slope downward to the right.* As we indicated in the text of this chapter, individuals are willing to substitute one good for another. Crusoe will be willing to give up some breadfruit if he is compensated with enough fish. Stated another way, there will be some amount of additional fish such that Crusoe will stay on the same indifference curve, even though his consumption of breadfruit has declined. However, in order to remain on the same indifference curve, Crusoe must always acquire more of one good to compensate for the loss of the other. The indifference curve for goods thus will always slope downward to the right (run northwest to southeast).

3. *The valuation of a good declines as it is consumed more intensively—therefore, indifference curves are always convex when viewed from below.* The slope of the indifference curve represents the willingness of the individual to substitute one good for the other. Economists refer to the amount of one good that is just sufficient to compensate the consumer for the loss of a unit of the other good as the **marginal rate of substitution.** It is equal to the slope of the indifference curve. Reflecting the principle of diminishing marginal utility, the marginal rate of substitution of a good will decline as the good is consumed more intensively relative to other goods. Suppose Crusoe remains on the same indifference curve while continuing to expand his consumption of fish relative to breadfruit. As his consumption of fish increases (and his consumption of breadfruit declines), his valuation of fish relative to breadfruit will decline. It will take more and more units of fish to compensate for the loss of still another unit of breadfruit. The indifference curve will become flatter, reflecting the decline in the marginal rate of substitution of fish for breadfruit as Crusoe consumes more fish relative to breadfruit.

Of course, just the opposite will happen if Crusoe's consumption of breadfruit increases relative to that of fish—if he moves northwest along the same indifference curve. In this case, as breadfruit is consumed more intensively, Crusoe's valuation of it will decline relative to that of fish, and the marginal rate of substitution of fish for breadfruit will rise (the indifference curve will become steeper and steeper). Therefore, since the valuation of each good declines as it is consumed more intensively, indifference curves must be convex when viewed from the origin.

4. *Indifference curves are everywhere dense.* We can draw an indifference curve through any point on the diagram. This simply means that any two bundles of goods can be compared by the individual.

5. *Indifference curves cannot cross—if they did, rational ordering would be violated.* If indifference curves crossed, our postulate that more goods are better than fewer goods would be violated. **Exhibit 7A-2** illustrates this point. The crossing of the indifference curves implies that points Y and Z are equally preferred, since they both are on the same indifference curve as X. Consumption bundle Y, though, represents more of both fish and breadfruit than bundle Z, so Y must be preferred to Z. Whenever indifference curves cross, this type of internal

EXHIBIT 7A-2

INDIFFERENCE CURVES CANNOT CROSS

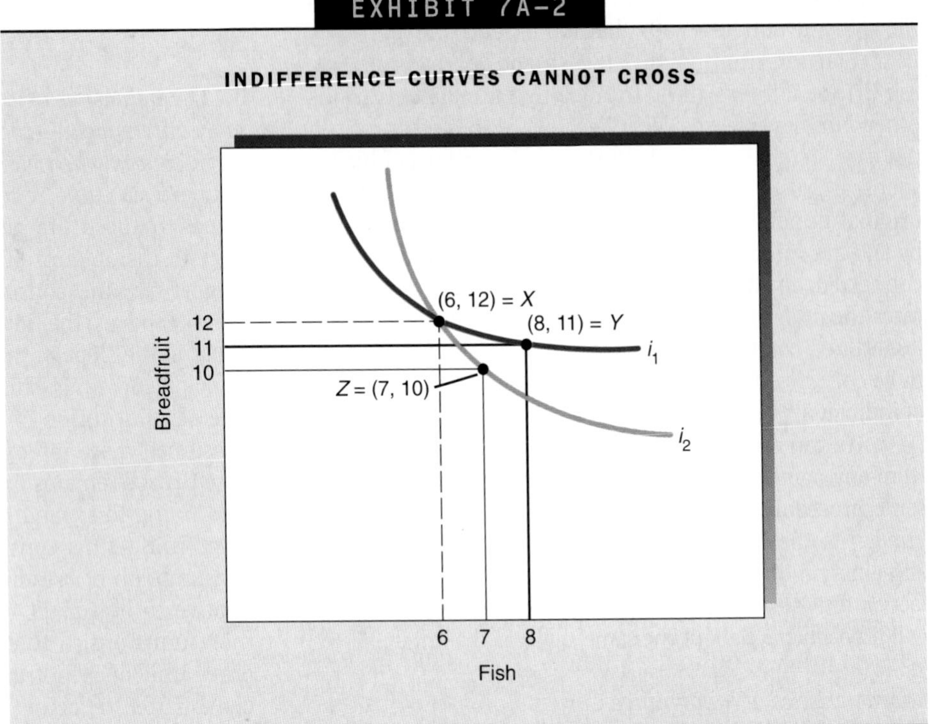

If the indifference curves of an individual crossed, it would lead to the inconsistency pictured here. Points X and Y must be equally valued, since they are both on the same indifference curve (i_1). Similarly, points X and Z must be equally preferred, since they are both on the indifference curve (i_2). If this is true, Y and Z must also be equally preferred, since they are both equally preferred to X. However, point Y represents more of both goods than Z, so Y has to be preferred to Z. When indifference curves cross, this type of internal inconsistency always arises.

inconsistency (irrational ranking) will arise. So, the indifference curves of an individual must not cross.

The Consumer's Preferred Bundle

Together with the opportunity constraint of the individual, indifference curves can be used to indicate the most preferred consumption alternatives available to an individual. The **consumption-opportunity constraint** separates consumption bundles that are attainable from those that are unattainable.

Assuming that Crusoe could produce only for himself, his consumption-opportunity constraint would look like the production-possibilities curves discussed in Chapter 2. What would happen if natives from another island visited Crusoe and offered to make exchanges with him? If a barter market existed that permitted Crusoe to exchange fish for breadfruit at a specified exchange rate, his options would resemble those of the market constraint illustrated by **Exhibit 7A-3**. First, let us consider the case where Crusoe inhabits a barter economy in which the current market exchange rate is 2 fish to 1 breadfruit. Suppose as a result of his expertise as a fisherman, Crusoe specializes in this activity and is able to bring 16 fish to the market per week. What consumption alternatives will be open to him? Since 2 fish can be bartered in the market for 1 breadfruit, Crusoe will be able to consume 16 fish, or 8 breadfruit, or any combination on the market constraint indicated by the line between these two points. For example, if he trades 2 of his 16 fish for 1 breadfruit, he will be able to consume a bundle consisting of 14 fish and 1 breadfruit. Assuming that the set of indifference curves of Exhibit 7A-3 outlines Crusoe's preferences, he will choose to consume 8 fish and 4 breadfruit. Of course, it will be possible for Crusoe to choose many other combinations of breadfruit and fish, but none of the other attainable combinations would enable him to reach as high a level of satisfaction. Because he is able to bring only 16 fish to the market, it would be impossible for him to attain an indifference curve higher than i_2.

Crusoe's indifference curve and the market-constraint curve will coincide (they will be tangent) at the point at which his attainable level of satisfaction is maximized. At that point (8 fish and 4 breadfruit), the rate at which Crusoe is willing to exchange fish for breadfruit (as indicated by the slope of the indifference curve) will be just equal to the rate at which the market will *permit* him to exchange the two (the slope of the market constraint).

EXHIBIT 7A-3

CONSUMER MAXIMIZATION — BARTER ECONOMY

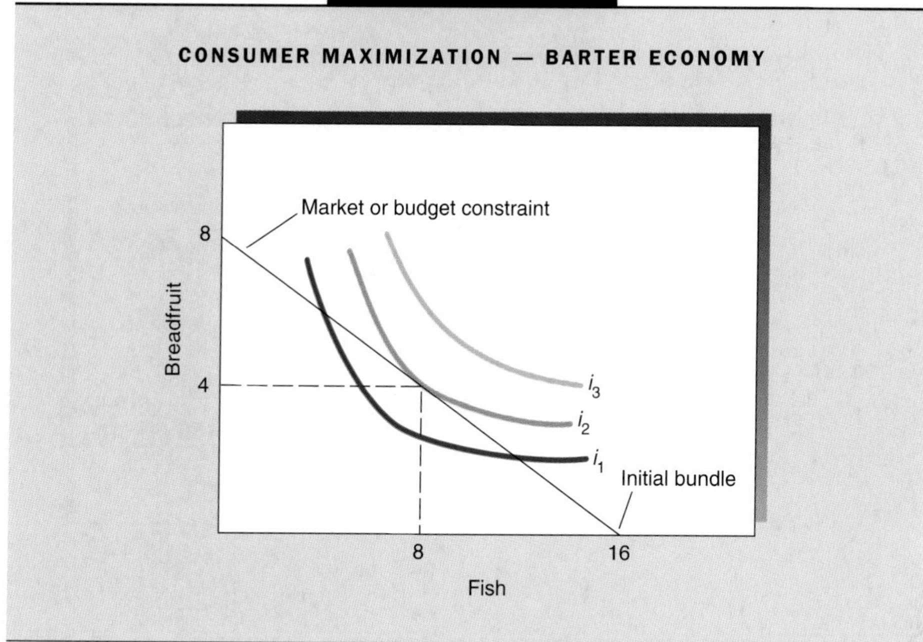

Suppose that the set of indifference curves shown here outlines Crusoe's preferences. The slope of the market (or budget) constraint indicates that 2 fish trade for 1 breadfruit in this barter economy. If Crusoe produces 16 fish per week, he will trade 8 fish for 4 breadfruit in order to move to the consumption bundle (8 fish and 4 breadfruit) that maximizes his level of satisfaction.

If the two slopes differ at a point, Crusoe will always be able to find an attainable combination that will permit him to reach a *higher* indifference curve. He will always move down the market constraint when it is flatter than his indifference curve, and up if the market constraint is steeper.

Crusoe in a Money Economy

As far as the condition for maximization of consumer satisfaction is concerned, moving from a barter economy to a money-income economy changes little. **Exhibit 7A-4** illustrates this point. Initially, the price of fish is $1, and the price of breadfruit is $2. The market therefore permits an exchange of 2 fish for 1 breadfruit, just as was the case in Exhibit 7A-3. In Exhibit 7A-4, we assume that Crusoe has a fixed money income of $16. At this level of income, he confronts the same market constraint (usually called a **budget constraint** in an economy with money) as in Exhibit 7A-3. Given the product prices and his income, Crusoe can choose to consume 16 fish, or 8 breadfruit, or any combination indicated by a line (the budget constraint) connecting these two points. Given his preferences, Crusoe will again choose the combination of 8 fish and 4 breadfruit if he wishes to maximize his level of satisfaction. As was true for the barter economy, when Crusoe maximizes his satisfaction (moves to the highest attainable indifference curve), the rate at which he is willing to exchange fish for breadfruit will just equal the rate at which the market will permit him to exchange the two goods. Stated in more technical terms, when his level of satisfaction is at a maximum, Crusoe's marginal rate of substitution of fish for breadfruit, as indicated by the slope of the indifference curve at E_1, will just equal the price ratio (P_F/P_b, which is also the slope of the budget constraint).

What will happen if the price of fish increases? Exhibit 7A-4 also answers this question. Since the price of breadfruit and Crusoe's *money* income are constant, a higher fish price will have two effects. First, it will make Crusoe poorer, even though his money income will be unchanged. His budget constraint will turn clockwise around point A, illustrating that his consumption options are now more limited—that is, his real income has declined. Second, the budget line will be steeper, indicating that a larger number of breadfruit must now be sacrificed to obtain an additional unit of fish. It will no longer be possible for Crusoe to attain indifference curve i_2. The best he can do is indifference curve i_1, which he can attain by choosing the bundle of 5 fish and 3 breadfruit.

Using the information supplied by Exhibit 7A-4, we can now locate two points on Crusoe's demand curve for fish. When the price of fish was $1, Crusoe chose 8 fish; when the price rose to $2, Crusoe reduced his consumption to 5 (see **Exhibit 7A-5**). Of course, other points on

Suppose that Crusoe's income is \$16 per day, the price of fish (P_F) is \$1, and the price of breadfruit (P_b) is \$2. Thus, Crusoe confronts exactly the same price ratio and budget constraint as in Exhibit 7A-3. Assuming that his preferences are unchanged, he will again maximize his satisfaction by choosing to consume 8 fish and 4 breadfruit. What will happen if the price of fish rises to \$2? Crusoe's consumption opportunities will be reduced. His budget constraint will turn clockwise around point A, reflecting the higher price of fish. His fish consumption will decline to 5 units. (Note: Because Crusoe's real income has been reduced, his consumption of breadfruit will also decline.)

EXHIBIT 7A-4

CONSUMER MAXIMIZATION — MONEY-INCOME ECONOMY

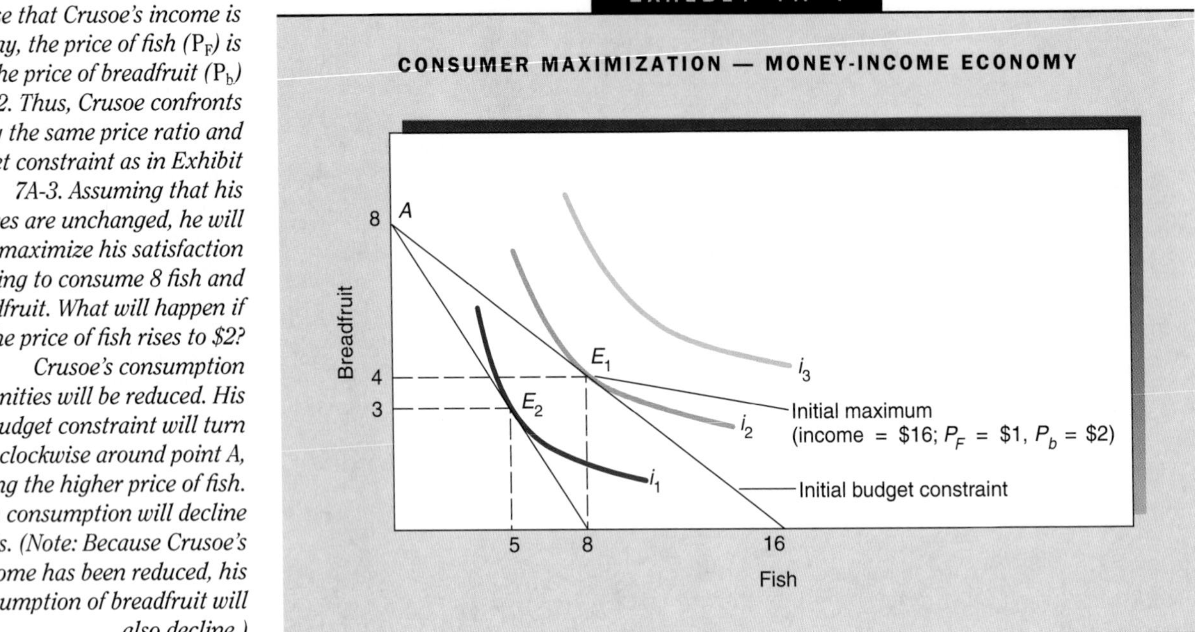

EXHIBIT 7A-5

CRUSOE'S DEMAND FOR FISH

As Exhibit 7A-4 illustrates, when the price of fish is \$1, Crusoe chooses 8 units. When the price of fish increases to \$2, he reduces his consumption to 5 units. This gives us two points on Crusoe's demand curve for fish. Other points on the demand curve could be derived by confronting Crusoe with still other prices of fish. (Note: Crusoe's money income [\$16] and the price of breadfruit [\$2] are unchanged in this analysis.)

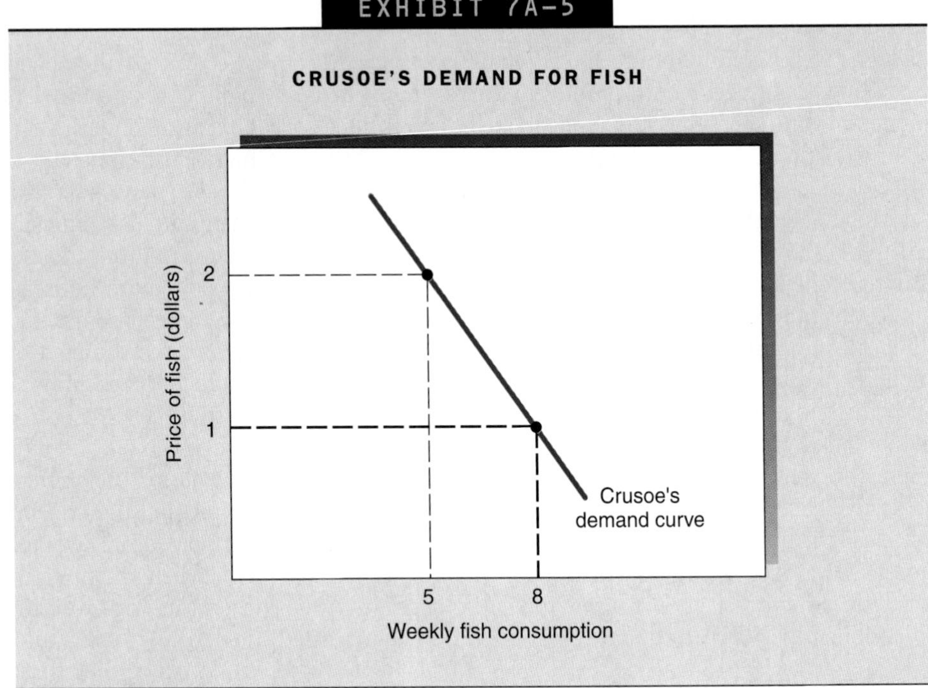

Crusoe's demand curve could also be located if we considered other prices for fish.

The demand curve of Exhibit 7A-5 is constructed on the assumption that the price of breadfruit remains $2 and that Crusoe's money income remains constant at $16. If either of these factors were to change, the entire demand curve for fish, illustrated by Exhibit 7A-5, would shift.

The indifference curve is a useful way to illustrate how a person with a fixed budget chooses between two goods. In the real world, of course, people have hundreds, or even thousands, of goods to choose from, and the doubling of only one price usually has a small impact on a person's overall consumption and satisfaction possibilities. In our simple example, the twofold increase in the price of fish makes Crusoe much worse off, because he spends a large portion of his budget on the item.

The Income and Substitution Effects

In the text, we indicated that, when the price of a product rises, the amount consumed will change as a result of both an *income effect* and a *substitution effect.* Indifference curve analysis can be used to separate these two effects. **Exhibit 7A-6** is similar to Exhibit 7A-4. Both exhibits illustrate Crusoe's response to an increase in the price of fish from $1 to $2 when money income ($16) and the price of breadfruit ($2) are held constant. Exhibit 7A-6, however, breaks down his total response into the substitution effect and the income effect. The reduction in the consumption of fish solely because of the substitution (price) effect, holding Crusoe's real income (level of utility) constant, can be found by constructing a line tangent to Crusoe's original indifference curve (i_2), and having a slope indicating the higher price of fish. This line (the broken line in Exhibit 7A-6), which is parallel to Crusoe's actual budget constraint (the line containing point E_2), reflects the higher price of fish. It is tangent to the original indifference curve i_2, so Crusoe's real income is held constant. As this line indicates, Crusoe's consumption of fish would fall from 8 to 7, due strictly to the fact that fish are now more expensive. This move from E_1 to F is a pure substitution effect.

Real income, though, has actually been reduced. As a result, Crusoe will be unable to attain point F on indifference curve i_2. The best he can attain is point E_2, which decreases his consumption of fish by another 2 units to 5. Since the broken line containing F and the budget constraint containing E_2 are parallel, the relative price of fish and breadfruit is held constant as Crusoe moves from F to E_2. This move from F to E_2 is thus a pure income effect. (Note: Because the consumption of both goods drops in this move, when income falls but the prices do not change, both goods must be normal goods.) This reduction in the consumption of fish (and breadfruit) in the

EXHIBIT 7A-6

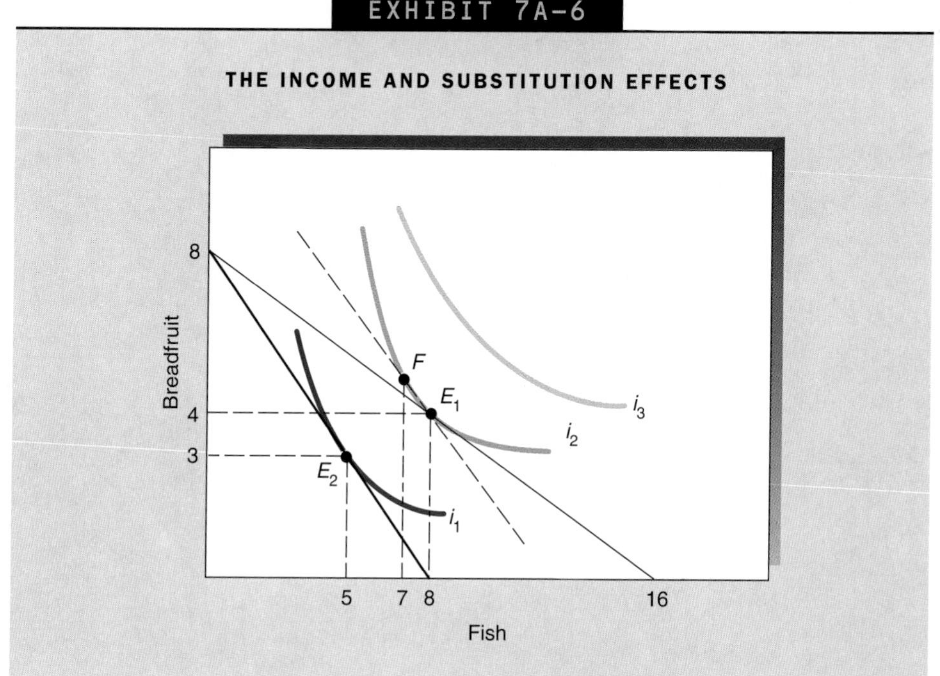

Here we break down Crusoe's response to the rise in the price of fish from $1 to $2 (see Exhibit 7A-4) into the substitution and income effects. The move from E_1 *to* F *illustrates the substitution effect, whereas the move from* F *to* E_2 *reflects the income effect.*

move from F to E_2 is due entirely to the decline in Crusoe's real income.

Indifference curve analysis highlights the assumptions and considerations that enter into consumer decisions. The logic of the proof that there is an inverse relationship between the price and the amount demanded is both elegant and reassuring. It is elegant because of the internal consistency of the logic and the precision of the analysis. It is reassuring because it conforms with our expectations, which are based on the central postulate of economics—that incentives matter in a predictable way.

Indifference curve
A curve, convex from below, that separates the consumption bundles that are more preferred by an individual from those that are less preferred. The points on the curve represent combinations of goods that are equally preferred by the individual.

Marginal rate of substitution
The change in the consumption level of one good that is just sufficient to offset a unit change in the consumption of another good without causing a shift to another indifference curve. At any point on an indifference curve, it will be equal to the slope of the curve at that point.

Consumption-opportunity constraint
The constraint that separates consumption bundles that are attainable from those that are unattainable. In a money-income economy, this is usually a budget constraint.

Budget constraint
The constraint that separates the bundles of goods that the consumer can purchase from those that cannot be purchased, given a limited income and the prices of the products.

CHAPTER 8

[A] supply curve traces out the quantity of a good that sellers will produce at various prices. As the price falls, so does the number of units supplied.

Al Ehrbar[1]

The supply curve of any commodity or service reflects opportunity costs which are determined indirectly by consumers clamoring for a myriad of goods.

Marshall Colberg[2]

Costs and the Supply of Goods

CHAPTER FOCUS

- Why are business firms used by societies everywhere to organize production?
- How are firms organized in market economies?
- What are explicit and implicit costs, and how do they guide the behavior of the firm?
- How does economic profit differ from accounting profit, and what role does it play?
- How do short-run costs differ from long-run costs, and what factors shift the firm's cost curves?

---

[1]Al Ehrbar, "Supply," in *The Fortune Encyclopedia of Economics* (New York: Warner Books, 1993), p. 87.

[2]Marshall R. Colberg, Dascomb R. Forbush, and Gilbert R. Whitaker, *Business Economics* (Homewood, Ill.: Irwin, 1980), p. 12.

Demand and supply interact to determine the market price of a product. In the preceding chapter, we illustrated that the demand for a product reflects the strength of consumer desire for that product. In this chapter, we focus on the cost of production. The resources needed for production of a good could be used to produce other goods instead. Therefore, as Professor Colberg points out (see quotation at the beginning of this chapter), the cost of resources to produce one product reflects consumer demands for other items that could be produced with the same resources. If the cost of producing a good exceeds its price, the market is signaling that, although the good may be desired, other goods that could be produced with the same resources are more urgently desired. Producers suffer losses when the per-unit cost of a good exceeds its price. In a market economy, they are unlikely to continue supplying the good under such conditions. Thus, supply and cost of production are closely linked. For example, a producer who faces a cost of $1,500 to produce a large-screen TV set is unlikely to continue supplying the sets for very long if their market price is $1,000. In the long run, sets that cost $1,500 will be supplied only if their market price is at least that amount.

In this chapter, we lay the foundation for a detailed investigation of the link between costs and market supply. What do economists mean by costs? Why are costs so important? What is the function of costs in a market economy? We discuss these and related questions in this chapter.

ORGANIZATION OF THE BUSINESS FIRM

The business firm is an entity designed to organize raw materials, labor, and machines with the goal of producing goods and/or services. Firms (1) purchase productive resources from households and other firms, (2) transform them into a different commodity, and (3) sell the transformed product or service to consumers.

Economies differ in the amount of freedom they allow business decision makers. They differ also in the incentive structure used to stimulate and guide business activity. Nevertheless, every society relies on business firms to organize resources and transform them into products. In market economies, most business firms choose their own price, output level, and methods of production. They reap the benefits of sales revenues, but they are also fully responsible for their costs. In socialist countries, government policy often establishes the selling price and constrains the actions of business firms in various other ways. Firms typically are not expected to pay all their bills from their revenues, and they are often not allowed to keep the proceeds if revenues exceed costs. In any case, the central position of the business firm as the entity used to organize production is universal to capitalist and socialist economies alike. In this chapter we focus on the organization and behavior of firms in a market economy.

Incentives, Cooperation, and the Nature of the Firm[3]

Most firms are privately owned in capitalist countries. Owners risk their wealth on the success of the business. If the firm is successful and makes profits, these financial gains go to the owners. Conversely, if the firm suffers losses, the owners must bear the consequences. Because the owners receive what remains after the revenue of the firm is used to pay the contractual costs, they are called **residual claimants.**

Residual claimants
Individuals who personally receive the excess, if any, of revenues over costs. Residual claimants gain if the firm's costs are reduced or revenues increased.

In a market economy, the property right of owners to the residual income of the firm plays a very important role: It provides owners with a strong incentive to organize and structure their business in a manner that will keep their cost of producing output low (relative to the value of the output). The wealth of these residual claimants is directly influenced by the success or failure of the firm. Thus, they have a strong incentive to see that resources under their direction are used efficiently.

There are two ways of organizing productive activity: contracting and **team production,** in which workers are hired by a firm to work together under the supervision of the owner, or the owner's representative. Most business firms use both contracting and team production.

Team production
A process of production wherein employees work together under the supervision of the owner or the owner's representative.

In principle, all production could be accomplished solely through individual contracting. For example, a builder might have a house built by contracting with one person to pour the concrete, another to construct the wooden part of the house, a third to install the roofing, a fourth to do the electrical wiring, and so on. No employees would have to be involved in such a project. More commonly though, goods and services are produced with some combination of contracting and the use of team production by employees of a firm.

Why do firms use team production? If contracting alone is used to produce something, the producer must, for each project (1) determine what is required to produce the desired result in the best way, given the circumstances and the current technology and prices, (2) search out reliable suppliers, and (3) negotiate and enforce the contracts. The entrepreneur who wants to produce by this method must have specialized knowledge in a variety of areas and must devote a great deal of time and effort to the planning and contracting processes. Not many people have the expertise or the time to take care of all these tasks by themselves except on a small scale. Team production for certain tasks may be more practical and less costly.

Accordingly, a builder is likely to hire knowledgeable, experienced workers to plan the construction process, to purchase materials, and to build such structures as houses and office buildings. The firm itself will then contract with others to obtain materials and specialized labor services.

A firm, then, is a business organization that may use team production to reduce many of the transaction costs associated with contracting. Team production, however, raises another set of problems. Team members—that is, the employees working for the firm—must be monitored and provided with an incentive system that discourages **shirking,** or working at less than a normal rate of productivity. Taking long work breaks, paying more attention to their own convenience than to work results, and wasting time when diligence is called for are examples of shirking. A worker will shirk more when the costs of doing so are shifted to other team members, including the owners of

Shirking
Working at less than a normal rate of productivity, thus reducing output. Shirking is more likely when workers are not monitored, so that the cost of lower output falls on others.

[3]A classic article on this topic is Ronald Coase, "The Nature of the Firm," *Economica* (1937): 386–405. See also Armen Alchian and Harold Demsetz, "Production, Information Costs, and Economic Organization," *American Economic Review* (December 1972): 777–795.

APPLICATIONS IN ECONOMICS

The Principal-Agent Problem

In recent years, economists have focused a great deal of attention on a class of problems in which one individual is hired to act on behalf of another. This *principal-agent problem* arises when the purchaser of services (the principal) lacks full information about the circumstances faced by the seller (the agent), and thus cannot know how well the agent performs the purchased services. As a result, the agent may to some extent work toward objectives other than those sought by the principal, who is paying for the services. Because agents exercise their own judgment in performing the work and cannot be completely monitored, they have opportunities to shirk, and, in general, to serve their own ends rather than those of the principal.

We all run into the principal-agent problem when we pay a dentist, a mechanic, or a lawyer to perform services for us. These agents we hire know more than we do about their work and about the circumstances of the specific job we pay them to do. We cannot be sure that they are doing the best possible job for us. The owner of a business firm faces similar incentive problems with every employee hired. A large firm has many managers who spend a good deal of time monitoring the work of employees and providing them with the incentive to work efficiently. But they cannot monitor perfectly and, in any case, who will monitor the monitors?

Even top-level executives hired to manage a firm do not have the same objectives as owners—primarily profit maximization—unless, of course, the managers are the owners. So the judgments of executives, too, are influenced by what is in their personal best interests. They want perks, personal job security, and other benefits that may not be consistent with profit maximization for the firm. The problem becomes more serious as firms grow larger and acquire more managers and employees. Ultimately it is the job of the owners, as residual claimants, to develop an incentive structure that minimizes the principal-agent problem. For the owner, the saying "the buck stops here" always applies.

the firm. Hired managers, even including those at the top, must be monitored and provided with the incentive to avoid shirking.

When team production is utilized, the problem of imperfect monitoring and imperfect incentives is always present. It is part of a larger class of what economists call **principal-agent problems** (see the Applications in Economics feature on this subject). Any person who has taken a car to an auto mechanic has experienced such a problem. The mechanic wants to get the job done quickly and to make as much money on it as possible. The car owner wants to get the job done quickly also, but in a way that permanently fixes the problem, at the lowest possible cost. Because the mechanic typically knows far more about the job than the customer, it is hard for the customer to monitor the mechanic's work. There is a possibility, therefore, that the mechanic may charge a large amount for a "quick fix" that will not last.

Principal-agent problem
The incentive problem arising when the purchaser of services (the principal) lacks full information about the circumstances faced by the seller (the agent) and thus cannot know how well the agent performs the purchased services. The agent may to some extent work toward objectives other than those sought by the principal paying for the service.

The owner of a firm is in a similar situation. It is often difficult to monitor the performance of individual employees and provide them with an incentive structure that will encourage high productivity. Nonetheless, the ability of the firm to use resources effectively, and to succeed in a competitive market, depends crucially upon resolving these problems. If a firm is going to keep costs low and the value of output high, it must discover and use an incentive structure that motivates managers and workers, and discourages shirking.

THREE TYPES OF BUSINESS FIRMS

Business firms can be organized in one of three ways: as a proprietorship, a partnership, or a corporation. The structure chosen determines how the owners share the risks and liabilities of the firm and how they participate in the making of decisions.

A **proprietorship** is a business firm that is owned by a single individual who is fully liable for the debts of the firm. In addition to assuming the responsibilities of ownership, the proprietor often works directly for the firm, providing managerial and

Proprietorship
A business firm owned by an individual who possesses the ownership right to the firm's profits and is personally liable for the firm's debts.

EXHIBIT 8-1

HOW BUSINESS FIRMS ARE ORGANIZED

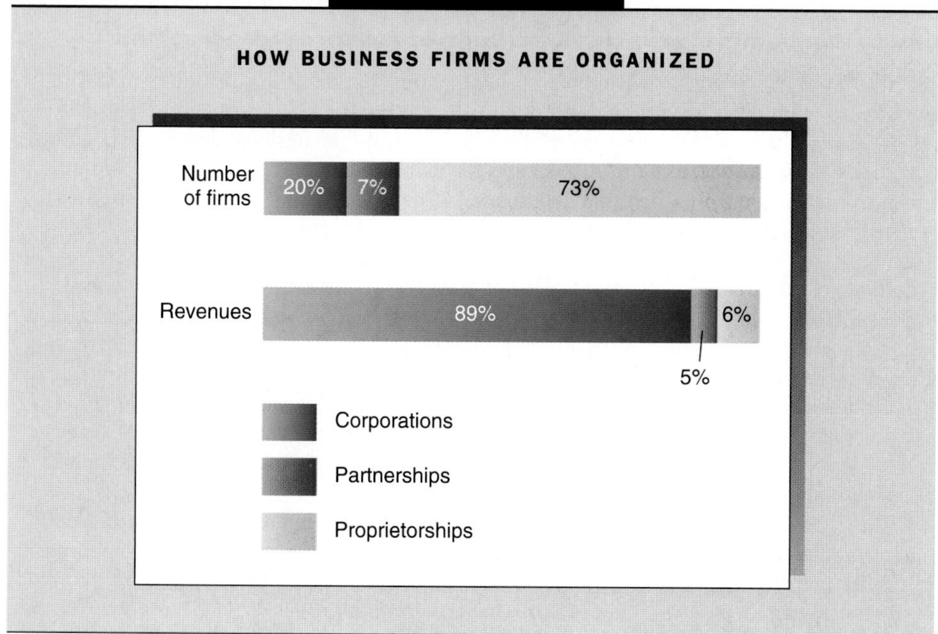

Nearly three out of every four firms are proprietorships, but only 6 percent of all business revenue is generated by proprietorships. Corporations account for only one out of every five firms, but generate 89 percent of all revenues.

SOURCE: Statistical Abstract of the United States, 1997, *Table 834. (Data are for 1994.)*

other labor services. Many small businesses, including neighborhood grocery stores, barbershops, and farms, are business proprietorships. As **Exhibit 8-1** shows, proprietorships account for 73 percent of the business firms in the United States. Because most proprietorships are small, however, they account for only 6 percent of all business revenues.

A **partnership** consists of two or more persons acting as coowners of a business firm. The partners share risks and responsibilities in some prearranged manner. There is no difference between a proprietorship and a partnership in terms of owner liability. In both cases, the owners are fully liable for all business debts incurred by the firm. Many law, medical, and accounting firms are organized along partnership lines. This form of business structure accounts for only 7 percent of the total number of firms and 5 percent of all business revenues.

Partnership
A business firm owned by two or more individuals who possess ownership rights to the firm's profits and are personally liable for the debts of the firm.

Even though **corporations** composed only 20 percent of all business firms, they accounted for 89 percent of total business revenue. What accounts for the attractiveness of the corporate structure? First, although the stockholders of the corporation are the legal owners, their liability is limited to the extent of their explicit investment. If a corporation owes you money, you cannot directly sue the stockholders. Of course, you can sue the corporation. However, if a corporation goes bankrupt, you and others to whom the firm owes money will simply be out of luck. This limited liability makes it possible for corporations to attract investment funds from a large number of "owners" who do not participate in the day-to-day management of the firm.

Corporation
A business firm owned by shareholders who possess ownership rights to the firm's profits, but whose liability is limited to the amount of their investment in the firm.

Second, ownership can easily be transferred under the corporate structure. The shares, or ownership rights, of an owner who dies can be sold by the heirs to another owner without disrupting the business firm. Because of this, the corporation is an ongoing concern. Similarly, stockholders who become unhappy with the way a corporation is run can bail out merely by selling their stock.

The stockholders of many large corporations simply hire managers—trained experts—to operate the firm. The decisions of stockholders to buy and sell shares of stock mirror the confidence of investors in the management of the firm. If current

APPLICATIONS IN ECONOMICS

Costs, Sensitivity to Consumers, and the Structure of Modern Corporations

Will business firms operate efficiently and respond to the interests of customers? Offering consumers value at a low cost is the ticket to profitability. In the case of owner-managed firms, the owner' s property right to the residual income provides a strong incentive for cost-effective production and sensitivity to the preferences of consumers.

For a large corporation with millions of stockholders, however, the situation is more complex. Although the stockholders hold the legal claim to residual income, professional managers direct the operation of the firm. The objectives of managers may conflict with those of stockholders. For example, managers may prefer high salaries, large offices, and first-class travel. They may also prefer the power and prestige of business expansion, even if it reduces profitability.

Can the stockholders control the actions of managers and direct them toward the pursuit of profitability? Direct control is unlikely. Most stockholders of large corporations own only a tiny fraction of the firm's outstanding shares. Although they elect a board of directors, which in turn appoints high-level managers, few individual stockholders have either the incentive or the information to exercise direct control. Most find it too expensive even to attend the annual shareholder' s meeting.

Despite this problem, there are three major factors that promote cost efficiency and limit the power of corporate managers. Let us consider each.

Competition for Investment Funds and Customers Even without the ability to exercise control of the corporation, stockholders have an incentive to monitor management in order to anticipate problems or constructive innovations. Investors who are the first to spot a good, new management strategy can buy stock early, before others realize the opportunity and bid the price up. Stockholders who are the first to spot a problem can "bail out" by selling their stock before others see the problem and dump their stock, thus depressing the price. So managers get constant feedback via the stock price, which can be just as important as current profits to stockholders and boards of directors.

Similarly, consumers have an incentive to monitor the quality and price of the firm's output. No one forces them to buy the corporation's product; so, if other firms supply superior products or offer a lower price, consumers can take their business to rival firms.

The corporation's need to meet the competition limits the ability of managers to pursue their personal objectives at the expense of either stockholders or customers.

Compensation and Management Incentives The compensation of managers can be structured in a manner that will bring the interests of managers into harmony with those of shareholders. Market determination of managerial salaries will help achieve this objective. Those managers who establish a track record of business profitability and rising stock prices will command higher-paying positions in the job market. The demand for managers associated with losing enterprises and business failures will be weak. And internally, corporate firms can, and often do, tie the compensation of managers to the market success of the business. Salary increases and bonuses may be directly related to the firm's profitability. A large portion of the compensation of high-level managers may be in the form of stock options-to-buy that are extremely valuable if the market value of the firm's shares rises but worthless if it falls. Such policies will encourage corporate managers to maximize the flow of the firm's profits (and the value of the shares), reducing the conflict between the interests of managers and shareholders.[1]

Threat of Corporate Takeover Managers who do not serve the interests of their shareholders are vulnerable to a *takeover,* a move by an outside person or group to gain control of the firm. As we previously noted, shareholders who lose confidence in management can "fire" management by selling their shares. When a significant number of shareholders follow this course of action, the market value of the firm's stock will decline. This will increase the attractiveness of the firm to takeover specialists shopping for a poorly run business, the value of which could be substantially increased by a new management team.[2]

Consider a firm currently earning $1.50 per share. Reflecting current earnings that are expected to continue, the market value of the firm's stock might be $15 per share (assuming a 10 percent interest rate). If the earnings of the firm are reduced because the current management team is pursuing its own objectives at the expense of profitability, then a corporate takeover could lead to substantial gain. Suppose some outside persons believe that they could restructure the firm, improve the management, and thereby increase the firm's earnings to $3 per share. Therefore, they tender a takeover bid—an offer to buy shares of the firm's stock—for $20 per share. If the takeover team is correct and it increases the firm's earnings to $3 per share, then the stock value of the firm will rise accordingly (to $30 per share).

Of course, the current management has an incentive to resist the takeover. After all, they are likely to lose their jobs if the potential new owners are successful. Thus, outsiders are seldom welcomed with open arms. Still, the presence of large inefficiencies is a powerful attraction for an effective takeover. Managers who pursue their own interests at the expense of stockholders make themselves vulnerable. The mere potential of the takeover reduces the likelihood that managers will stray too far from the profit-maximization strategy.

(continued)

Concluding Thought How efficient is the corporate business structure? Perhaps history provides the best answer. If the corporate structure were not an efficient form of business organization, it would not have continued to survive, nor would it be so prevalent. Rival forms of business organization, including proprietorships, partnerships, consumer cooperatives, employee ownership, and mutually owned companies can and do compete in the marketplace for investment funds. In certain industries, some of these alternative forms of business organization are dominant. Nonetheless, in most industries, the corporate structure is the dominant form of business organization (see Exhibit 8-1). This is strong evidence that, despite its defects, it is generally a cost-efficient, consumer-sensitive form of organization.

---

[1]A number of articles covering executive compensation and the effects of various plans appeared in a special section on "Executive Pay" in *The Wall Street Journal,* April 12, 1995, pp. R1–R14.

[2]For a discussion of corporate takeovers from various points of view, see Hal R. Varian et al., "Symposium on Takeovers," *Journal of Economic Perspectives* 2, no. 1 (winter 1988): 3–81. See also John R. Coffee Jr., et al., "Corporate Takeovers: Who Wins; Who Loses; Who Should Regulate?" *Regulation* 12, no. 1 (1988): 23.

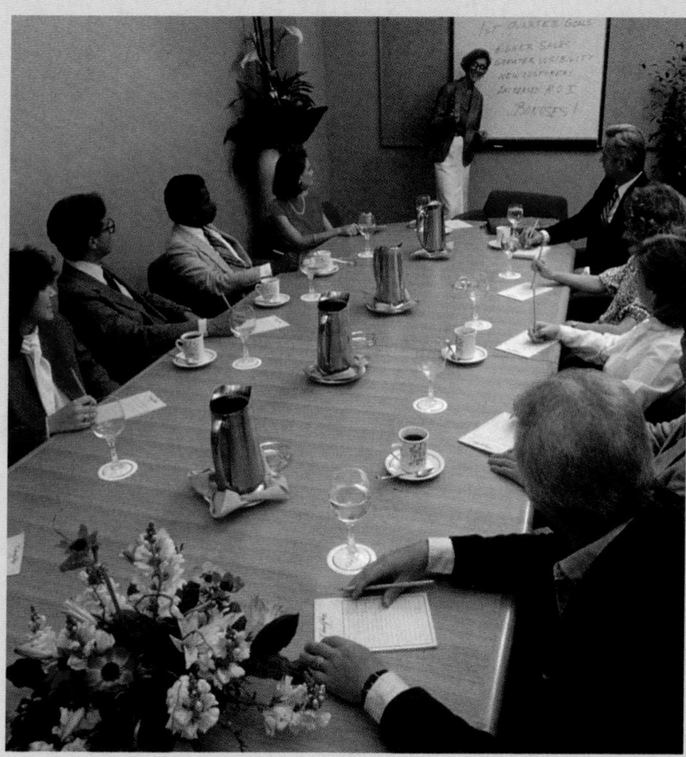

Competition for investment funds and consumers, management compensation in the form of stock options, and the threat of a takeover increase the incentive of corporate managers to serve the interests of customers and stockholders.

stockholders and prospective investors believe that the managers are doing a good job, the demand for the firm's stock will be strong and its price is likely to rise. Conversely, when a substantial number of stockholders are selling shares because they are dissatisfied with a corporation's management, the stock's price will tumble. In turn, falling stock prices will often lead to a management shake-up. The price of a firm's stock provides one of several forms of discipline placed on corporate management in a market economy. (See the Applications in Economics box on modern corporate structure.)

ECONOMIC ROLE OF COSTS

Consumers would like to have more economic goods, but resources to produce them are scarce. The use of resources to make one commodity takes resources from the production of other desired goods. Therefore, the desire for a given product must be balanced against the desire for other items that must be sacrificed to produce it. Every economic system must make these balancing judgments. When decisions are made in the political arena, the budget process performs this balancing function. Congress (or the central committee, or the king) decides which goods will be purchased or produced by government agencies and which will be forgone. Taxes and budgets are set accordingly.

In a market economy, consumer demand and cost of production are central to the performance of this balancing function. Production of one good necessitates a reduction in the output of others. Resources have alternative uses. Costs are incurred as the resources required for the production of a good are bid away from employment alternatives elsewhere. Thus, the production cost of a good reveals the value of the resources used to produce it. The price consumers are willing to pay for the good reveals the value they place on it.

The demand for a product can be thought of as the voice of consumers instructing firms to produce a good. On the other hand, costs of production represent the voice of consumers saying that other items that could be produced with the resources are also desired. The demand for a product indicates the intensity of consumers' desires for the item. The cost of producing a product indicates the desire of consumers for other goods that must now be forgone because the resources have been employed in the production of the first item. A profit-seeking firm will try to produce only those units of output for which buyers are willing to pay the full cost.

CALCULATING ECONOMIC COSTS AND PROFITS

Business firms, regardless of their size, are primarily concerned with profit. Profit, of course, is the firm's total revenue minus its total costs. But to state profit correctly, costs must be measured properly. Most people, including some who are in business, think of costs as amounts paid for raw materials, labor, machines, and similar inputs. However, this concept of cost, which stems from accounting procedures, may exclude some important components of the firm's costs. When cost is miscalculated, so, too, is profit because it is merely revenue minus cost. Bad economic decisions may result from a miscalculation of cost and profit.

Explicit costs
Payments by a firm to purchase the services of productive resources.

Implicit costs
The opportunity costs associated with a firm's use of resources that it owns. These costs do not involve a direct money payment. Examples include wage income and interest forgone by the owner of a firm who also provides labor services and equity capital to the firm.

Total cost
The costs, both explicit and implicit, of all the resources used by the firm. Total cost includes an imputed normal rate of return for the firm's equity capital.

The key to understanding the economist's concept of profit is remembering the idea of *opportunity cost.* The firm incurs a cost whenever it uses a resource, thereby requiring the resource owner to forgo the highest valued alternative. These costs may either be explicit or implicit. **Explicit costs** result when the firm makes a monetary payment to resource owners. Money wages, interest, and rental payments are a measure of what the firm gives up to employ the services of labor and capital resources. Firms may also incur **implicit costs**—those associated with the use of resources owned by the firm. Since implicit costs do not involve a direct money or contractual payment, they are sometimes excluded from accounting statements. For example, the owners of small proprietorships often work for their own business. There is an opportunity cost associated with the use of this resource (the owner's labor services); other opportunities for the owner's time have to be given up because of the time spent in the operation of the business. The highest valued alternative forgone is the opportunity cost of the labor service provided by the owner. The **total cost** of production is the sum of the explicit and implicit costs incurred by the employment of all resources involved in the production process.

Accounting statements generally omit the implicit cost of equity capital—the cost of funds supplied by owners. If a firm borrows financial capital from a bank or other private source, it will have to pay interest. Accountants properly record this interest expense as a cost. In contrast, when the firm acquires financial capital through the issuance of stock, accountants make no allowance for the cost of this financial capital. Regardless of whether it is acquired by borrowing or stock (equity capital), the use of financial capital involves an opportunity cost. Persons who supply equity capital to a firm expect to earn at least a normal rate of return—a return comparable to what they could earn if they chose other investment opportunities (including bonds). If they do not earn this normal rate of return, investors will not continue to supply financial capital to the business.

When calculating costs, economists use the normal return on financial capital as a basis for determining the implicit **opportunity cost of equity capital.** If the normal rate of return on financial capital is 10 percent, equity investors will refuse funds to firms that persistently fail to earn a 10 percent rate of return on capital assets. As a result, earning the normal rate of return—that is, covering the opportunity cost of all its capital—is vital to the survival of a business firm.

Opportunity cost of equity capital
The implicit rate of return that must be earned by investors to induce them to continue to supply financial capital to the firm.

Accounting Profit and Economic Profit

Because economists seek to measure the opportunities lost due to the production of a good or service, they include both explicit and implicit costs in total cost. **Economic profit** is equal to total revenues minus total costs, including both the explicit and

Economic profit
The difference between the firm's total revenues and total costs.

APPLICATIONS IN ECONOMICS

Economic and Accounting Costs—A Hypothetical Example

The revenue-cost statement for a corner grocery store owned and operated by Terry Smith is presented here.

Terry works full-time as the manager, chief cashier, and janitor. Terry has $30,000 worth of refrigeration and other equipment invested in the store. Last year, Terry's total sales were $85,000; suppliers and employees were paid $50,000. Terry's revenues exceeded explicit costs by $35,000. Did Terry make a profit last year? The accounting statement for the store will probably show a net profit of $35,000. However, if Terry did not have a $60,000 personal investment in equipment, these funds could be earning 5 percent interest. Thus, Terry is forgoing $3,000 of interest each year. Similarly, if the building that Terry owns were not being used as a grocery store, it could be rented to someone else for $500 per month. Rental income thus forgone is $6,000 per year. In addition, since Terry is tied up working in the grocery store, a $28,000 managerial position with the local Safeway is forgone. Considering the interest, rental, and salary income that Terry had to forgo in order to operate the grocery store last year, Terry's implicit costs were $37,000. The total costs were $87,000. The total revenue of Terry's grocery store was less than the opportunity cost of the resources utilized. Terry incurred an economic loss of $2,000, despite the accounting profit of $35,000.

TOTAL REVENUE	
Sales (groceries)	$85,000
Costs (explicit)	
Groceries, wholesale	$38,000
Utilities	2,000
Taxes	3,000
Advertising	1,000
Labor services (employees)	6,000
Total (explicit) costs	$50,000
Net (accounting) profit	$35,000
Additional (implicit) costs	
Interest (personal investment)	$ 3,000
Rent (Terry's building)	6,000
Salary (Terry's labor)	28,000
Total(implicit) costs	$37,000
TOTAL EXPLICIT AND IMPLICIT COSTS	$87,000
ECONOMIC PROFIT (TOTAL REVENUE MINUS EXPLICIT AND IMPLICIT COSTS)	−$ 2,000

implicit cost components. Economic profits will be present only if the earnings of the business exceed the opportunity cost of all resources used by the firm, *including the opportunity cost of the assets owned by the firm.* Economic losses result when the earnings of the firm are insufficient to cover explicit and implicit costs. When the firm's revenues are just equal to its costs, both explicit and implicit, economic profits will be zero.

Remember that zero economic profits do not imply that the firm is about to go out of business. On the contrary, they indicate that the owners are receiving exactly the market (normal) rate of return on their investment (assets owned by the firm).

Accounting profits
The sales revenues minus the expenses of a firm over a designated time period, usually one year. Accounting profits typically make allowances for changes in the firm's inventories and depreciation of its assets. No allowance is made, however, for the opportunity cost of the equity capital of the firm's owners, or other implicit costs.

Because accounting procedures often omit implicit costs, such as those associated with owner-provided labor services or capital assets, the accounting costs of the firm generally understate the opportunity costs of production. This understatement of cost leads to an overstatement of profits. Therefore, the **accounting profits** of a firm are generally greater than the firm's economic profits (see the Applications in Economics box on accounting costs). When the omission of the costs of owner-provided services is unimportant, as is the case for most large corporations, accounting profits approximate the returns to the firm's equity capital. High accounting profits (measured as a rate of return on a firm's assets), relative to the average for other firms, suggest that a firm is earning an economic profit. Correspondingly, a low rate of accounting profit implies economic losses.

SHORT RUN AND LONG RUN

Short run (in production)
A time period so short that a firm is unable to vary some of its factors of production. The firm's plant size typically cannot be altered in the short run.

A firm cannot instantaneously adjust its output. Time plays an important role in the production process. All of a firm's resources can be expanded (or contracted) over time, but for specialized or heavy equipment, expanding (and contracting) availability quickly may be very expensive or even impossible. Economists often speak of the **short run** as a time period so short that the firm is unable to alter its present plant size. In the short run, the firm is "stuck" with its existing plant and heavy equipment. They are "fixed" for a given time period. The firm can alter output, however, by applying larger or smaller amounts of "variable" resources, such as labor and raw materials. Existing plant capacity can thus be used more or less intensively in the short run.

In sum, we can say that the short run is that period of time during which at least one factor of production, usually the size of the firm's plant, cannot be varied. How long is the short run? The length varies from industry to industry. In some industries, substantial changes in plant size can be accomplished in a few months. In other industries, particularly those that use assembly lines and mass-production techniques (for example, aircraft and automobiles), the short run might be a year or even several years.

Long run (in production)
A time period long enough to allow the firm to vary all factors of production.

The **long run** is a time period of sufficient length to allow a firm the opportunity to alter its plant size and capacity and all other factors of production. All resources of the firm are variable in the long run. In the long run, from the viewpoint of an entire industry, new firms may be established and enter the industry; other firms may dissolve and leave the industry. Thus, the short run may be alternatively viewed as a time period during which the number of firms in the industry is fixed.

Perhaps an example will help to clarify the distinction between the short- and long-run time periods. If a battery manufacturer hired 200 additional workers and ordered more raw materials to squeeze a larger output from the existing plant, this would be a short-run adjustment. In contrast, if the manufacturer built an additional plant (or expanded the size of its current facility) and installed additional heavy equipment, this would be a long-run adjustment.

OUTPUT AND COSTS IN THE SHORT RUN

We turn now to definitions of various aspects of the firm's costs and to what we can say about the relationship of those costs to the level of output, even without detailed knowledge of the production process. We have emphasized that in the short run some of a firm's factors of production, such as the size of the plant, will be fixed. Other productive resources will be variable. In the short run, then, we can break the firm's costs into these two categories—fixed and variable. Examining how each category of costs behaves, and seeing that behavior graphically, will illustrate characteristics of the profit-maximizing level of output for a firm. It will be important to distinguish between a firm's total costs and its per-unit costs, which will be called "average" costs.

Each of the firm's fixed costs, and their sum, **total fixed cost *(TFC)*,** will remain unchanged when output is altered in the short run. For example, a firm's insurance premiums, its property taxes, and, most significantly, the opportunity cost of using its fixed assets will be present whether the firm produces a large or small rate of output. These costs will not vary with output. They are "fixed" as long as the firm remains in business. Fixed costs will be present at all levels of output, including zero. They can be avoided only if the firm goes out of business.

Total fixed cost
The sum of the costs that do not vary with output. They will be incurred as long as a firm continues in business and the assets have alternative uses.

What will happen to **average fixed cost *(AFC)*,** fixed costs per unit, as output expands? Remember that the firm's fixed cost will be the same whether output is 1, 100, or 1,000. The *AFC* is simply fixed cost divided by output. As output increases, *AFC* declines because the fixed cost will be spread over more and more units (see part a of Exhibit 8-2).

Average fixed cost
Total fixed cost divided by the number of units produced. It always declines as output increases.

Some costs vary with output. For example, additional output can usually be produced by hiring more workers and buying more raw materials. The sum of those and other costs that rise as output increases comprise the firm's **total variable cost *(TVC)*.** At any given level of output, the firm's **average variable cost *(AVC)*** is the total variable cost divided by output.

Total variable cost
The sum of those costs that rise as output increases. Examples of variable costs are wages paid to workers and payments for raw materials.

Average variable cost
The total variable cost divided by the number of units produced.

We have noted that total cost *(TC)* includes explicit and implicit costs. The total cost of producing a good is also the sum of the fixed and variable costs at each output level. At zero output, total cost will equal total fixed cost. As output expands from

EXHIBIT 8-2

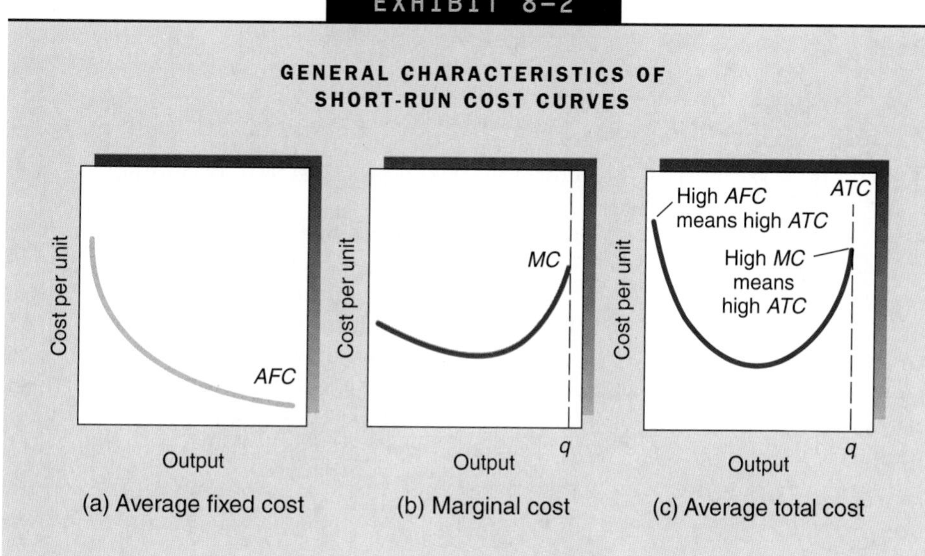

Average fixed costs (a) will be high for small rates of output, but they will always decline as output expands. Marginal cost (b) will rise sharply as the plant's production capacity q *is approached. As graph (c) illustrates,* ATC *will be a U-shaped curve, since* AFC *will be high for small rates of output and* MC *will be high as the plant's production capacity is approached.*

Average total cost
Total cost divided by the number of units produced. It is sometimes called per unit cost.

Marginal cost
The change in total cost required to produce an additional unit of output.

zero, variable cost and fixed cost must be added to obtain total cost. **Average total cost *(ATC)*,** sometimes referred to as *unit cost,* can be found by dividing total cost by the total number of units produced. *ATC* is also equal to the sum of the average fixed and average variable costs. It indicates the amount per unit of output that must be gained in revenue if total cost is to be covered.

The economic way of thinking emphasizes the importance of what happens "at the margin." How much does it cost to produce an additional unit? **Marginal cost *(MC)*** is the change in total cost that results from the production of one additional unit. The profit-conscious decision maker recognizes *MC* as the addition to cost that must be covered by additional revenue if producing the marginal unit is to be profitable. In the short run, as illustrated by Exhibit 8-2b, *MC* will generally decline if output is increased, then eventually reach a minimum, and then increase. The rising *MC* simply reflects the fact that it becomes increasingly difficult to squeeze additional output from a plant as the facility's maximum capacity (the dotted line of part b of Exhibit 8-2) is approached. The accompanying Thumbnail Sketch summarizes the interrelationships among a firm's various costs.

As a firm alters its rate of output in the short run, how will unit cost be affected? First, let us look at this question intuitively. In the short run, the firm can vary output by using its fixed plant size more (or less) intensively. As Exhibit 8-2 illustrates, there are two extreme situations that will result in a high unit cost of output. First, when the output rate of a plant is small relative to its capacity, it is obviously being underutilized. Under these circumstances, *AFC* will be high, and therefore *ATC* will also be high. It will be costly and inefficient to operate a large plant substantially below its production capacity. At the other extreme, overutilization can also result in high unit cost. An overutilized plant will mean congestion, time spent by workers waiting for machines, and similar costly delays. As output approaches the maximum capacity of a plant, overutilization will lead to high *MC* and therefore to high *ATC*.

THUMBNAIL SKETCH

Compact Glossary on Cost

Term	Symbol	Equation	Definition
Fixed cost			Cost that is independent of the output level
Variable cost			Cost that varies with the output level
Total fixed cost	*TFC*		Cost of the fixed inputs (equals sum of quantity times unit price for each fixed input)
Total variable cost	*TVC*		Cost of the variable inputs (equals sum of quantity times unit price for each variable input)
Total cost	*TC*	$TC = TFC + TVC$	Cost of all inputs (equals fixed costs plus variable costs)
Marginal cost	*MC*	$MC = \Delta TC \div \Delta q$	Change in total cost resulting from a one-unit rise in output (q) [equals the *change* in total cost divided by the *change* in output]
Average fixed cost	*AFC*	$AFC = TFC \div q$	Total fixed cost per unit of output (equals total fixed cost divided by total output)
Average variable cost	*AVC*	$AVC = TVC \div q$	Total variable cost per unit of output (equals total variable cost divided by total output)
Average total cost	*ATC*	$ATC = AFC + AVC$	Total cost per unit of output (equals average fixed cost plus average variable cost)

Thus, the ATC *curve will be U-shaped, as pictured in part c of Exhibit 8-2.* ATC *will be high for both an underutilized plant (because* AFC *is high) and an overutilized plant (because* MC *is high).*

Diminishing Returns and Production in the Short Run

Our analysis of the changes in unit cost as the output rate rises is consistent with a long-established economic law. This **law of diminishing returns** states that, as more and more units of a variable factor are applied to a fixed amount of other resources, output will eventually increase by smaller and smaller amounts. Therefore, in terms of their impact on output, the returns to the variable factor will diminish. The impact on costs is clear: When the returns to the variable factor are rising, marginal costs (the additions to total variable cost from adding a unit of output) are falling. Similarly, when the returns to the variable factor are falling, marginal cost is increasing.

Law of diminishing returns
The postulate that, as more and more units of a variable resource are combined with a fixed amount of other resources, employment of additional units of the variable resource will eventually increase output only at a decreasing rate. Once diminishing returns are reached, it will take successively larger amounts of the variable factor to expand output by one unit.

The law of diminishing returns is as famous in economics as the law of gravity is in physics. It is based on common sense and real-life observation. Have you ever noticed that, as you apply a single resource more intensively, the resource eventually tends to accomplish less and less? Consider a farmer who applies fertilizer (a resource) more and more intensively to an acre of land (a fixed factor). At some point, the application of additional 100-pound units of fertilizer will expand the wheat yield by successively smaller amounts.

Essentially, the law of diminishing returns is a constraint imposed by nature. If it were not valid, it would be possible to raise all the world's food on an acre of land, or even in a flowerpot. Logically, then, there would be no point in cultivating any of the less-fertile land. We would be able to increase output simply by applying another unit of labor and fertilizer to the world's most fertile flowerpot! In the real world, of course, this is not the case; the law of diminishing returns is valid and it restricts our options.

Exhibit 8-3 illustrates the law of diminishing returns numerically. Column 1 indicates the quantity of the variable resource, labor in this example, that is combined with a specified amount of the fixed resource. Column 2 shows the **total product** that will result as the utilization rate of labor increases. Column 3 provides data on the **marginal product,** the change in total output associated with each additional unit of labor. Without the application of labor, output would be zero. As additional units of labor are applied, total product (output) expands. As the first three units of labor are applied, total product increases by successively larger amounts (8, then 12, then 14). Beginning with the fourth unit, however, diminishing returns are confronted. When the fourth unit is added, marginal product—the change in the total product—declines to 12 (down from 14, when the third unit was applied). As additional units of labor are applied, marginal product continues to decline. It is increasingly difficult to squeeze a larger total product from the fixed resources (for example, plant size and equipment). Eventually, marginal product becomes negative (beginning with the tenth unit).

Total product
The total output of a good that is associated with alternative utilization rates of a variable input.

Marginal product
The increase in the total product resulting from a unit increase in the employment of a variable input. Mathematically, it is the ratio of the change in total product to the change in the quantity of the variable input.

Column 4 of Exhibit 8-3 provides data for the **average product** of labor, which is simply the total product divided by the units of labor applied. Note the average product increases as long as the marginal product is greater than the average product. Whenever the marginal unit's contribution is greater than the average, it must cause the average to rise. Here, this is true through the first four units. The marginal product of the fifth unit of labor, though, is 10, less than the average product for the first four units of labor (11.5). Therefore, beginning with the fifth unit, the average product declines as additional labor is applied. When marginal productivity is below the average, it brings down the average product.

Average product
The total product (output) divided by the number of units of the variable input required to produce that output level.

EXHIBIT 8-3

LAW OF DIMINISHING RETURNS (HYPOTHETICAL DATA)

(1) Units of the Variable Resource, Labor (per day)	(2) Total Product (output)	(3) Marginal Product	(4) Average Product
0	0		—
		8	
1	8		8.0
		12	
2	20		10.0
		14	
3	34		11.3
		12	
4	46		11.5
		10	
5	56		11.2
		8	
6	64		10.7
		6	
7	70		10.0
		4	
8	74		9.3
		1	
9	75		8.3
		−2	
10	73		7.3

Using the data from Exhibit 8-3, **Exhibit 8-4** illustrates the law of diminishing returns graphically. Initially, the total product curve (part a) increases quite rapidly. As diminishing marginal returns are confronted (beginning with the fourth unit of labor), total product increases more slowly. Eventually, a maximum output (75) is reached with the application of the ninth unit of labor. The marginal product curve (part b) reflects the total product curve. Geometrically, marginal product is the slope—the rate of increase—of the total product curve. That slope, the marginal product, reaches its maximum with the application of three units of labor. Beyond three units, diminishing returns are present. Eventually, at ten units of labor, the marginal product becomes negative. When marginal product becomes negative, total product is necessarily declining. The average product curve rises as long as the marginal product curve is above it, since each added unit of labor is raising the average. The average product reaches its maximum at four units of labor. Beyond that, each additional unit of labor brings down the average product, and the curve declines.

DIMINISHING RETURNS AND COST CURVES

What impact will diminishing returns have on a firm's costs? Once a firm confronts diminishing returns, larger and larger additions of the variable factor are required to expand output by one unit. This will cause marginal costs (MC) *to rise. As* MC *continues to increase, eventually it will exceed average total cost. Until that point,* MC *is below* ATC, *bringing* ATC *down. When* MC *is greater than* ATC, *the additional units cost more than the average, and* ATC *must increase.* To make the point clear, consider a similar case in another setting. What happens when you make an additional exam grade above your current class average? Your class average goes up. What happens if a

EXHIBIT 8-4

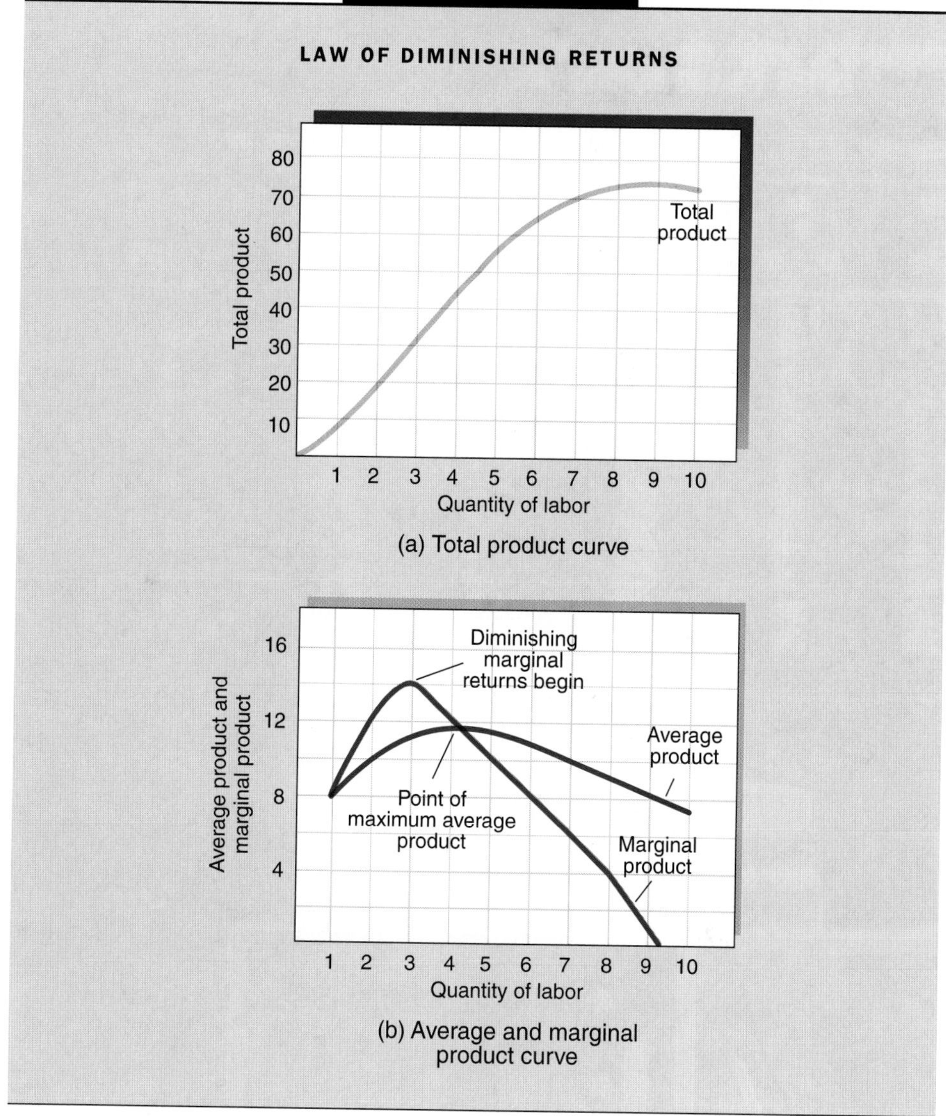

As units of variable input (labor) are added to a fixed input, total product will increase, first at an increasing rate and then at a declining rate (a). This will cause both marginal and average product curves (b) to rise at first and then decline. Note that the marginal product curve intersects the average product curve at its maximum (when 4 units of labor are used). The smooth curves indicate that labor can be increased by amounts of less than a single unit.

unit of above-average cost is added to output? Average total cost rises. The firm's *MC* curve therefore crosses the *ATC* curve at the *ATC*'s lowest point. For output rates beyond the minimum *ATC*, the rising *MC* causes *ATC* to increase.

Exhibit 8-5 numerically illustrates the implications of the law of diminishing returns for a firm's short-run cost curve. Here, we assume that Royal Roller Blades, Inc., combines units of a variable input with a fixed factor to produce units of output (pairs of the popular inline skates). Columns 2, 3, and 4 indicate how the total cost schedules vary as output is expanded. Total fixed costs *(TFC)*, representing the opportunity cost of the fixed factors of production, are $50 per day. Total fixed costs are constant, $50 per day at all levels of output. For the first four units of output, total variable costs *(TVC)* increase at a *decreasing rate.* Why? In this range, there are increasing returns to the variable input. Beginning with the fifth unit of output, however, diminishing marginal returns are present. From this point on, *TVC* and *TC* increase by successively larger amounts as output is expanded.

EXHIBIT 8-5

NUMERICAL SHORT-RUN COST SCHEDULES OF ROYAL ROLLER BLADES, INC.

Total Cost Data (per day)				Average/Marginal Cost Data (per day)			
(1) Output per Day	(2) *TFC*	(3) *TVC*	(4) *TC* (2) + (3)	(5) *AFC* (2) ÷ (1)	(6) *AVC* (3) ÷ (1)	(7) *ATC* (4) ÷ (1)	(8) *MC* Δ(4) ÷ Δ(1)
0	$50	$ 0	$ 50	—	—	—	—
1	50	15	65	$50.00	$15.00	$65.00	$15
2	50	25	75	25.00	12.50	37.50	10
3	50	34	84	16.67	11.33	28.00	9
4	50	42	92	12.50	10.50	23.00	8
5	50	52	102	10.00	10.40	20.40	10
6	50	64	114	8.33	10.67	19.00	12
7	50	79	129	7.14	11.29	18.43	15
8	50	98	148	6.25	12.25	18.50	19
9	50	122	172	5.56	13.56	19.11	24
10	50	152	202	5.00	15.20	20.20	30
11	50	202	252	4.55	18.36	22.91	50

EXHIBIT 8-6

COSTS IN THE SHORT RUN

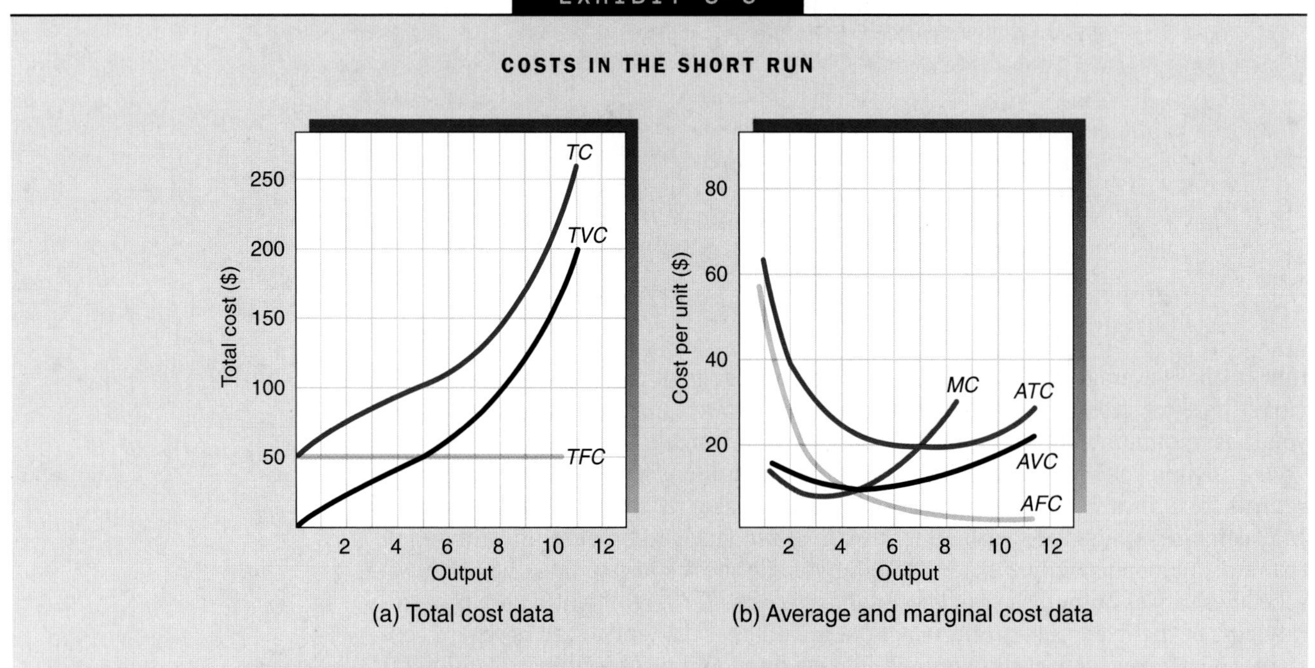

(a) Total cost data

(b) Average and marginal cost data

Using data from Exhibit 8–5, this exhibit illustrates the general shape of the firm's short-run total cost curves (a), and average and marginal cost curves (b). Note that when output is small (for example, 2 units), ATC *will be high because the* AFC *is so high. Similarly, when output is large (for example, 11 units), per-unit cost* (ATC) *will be high because it is extremely costly to produce the marginal units. Thus, the short-run* ATC *curve will be U-shaped.*

Columns 5 through 8 of Exhibit 8-5 reveal the general pattern of the average and marginal cost schedules. For small output rates, the *ATC* of producing roller blades is high, primarily because of the high *AFC*. Initially, *MC* is less than *ATC*. When diminishing returns set in for output rates beginning with five units, however, *MC* rises. Beginning with the sixth unit of output, *MC* exceeds *AVC*, causing *AVC* to rise. Beginning with the eighth unit of output, *MC* exceeds *ATC*, causing it also to rise. *ATC* thus reaches a minimum at seven units of output. Look carefully at the data of Exhibit 8-5 to be sure that you fully understand the relationships among the various cost curves.

Using the numeric data of Exhibit 8-5, **Exhibit 8-6** graphically illustrates both the total and the average (and marginal) cost curves. Note that the *MC* curve intersects both the *AVC* and *ATC* curves at the minimum points (part b). As *MC* continues to rise above *ATC*, unit costs rise higher and higher as output increases beyond seven units.

In sum, the firm's short-run cost curves reflect the law of diminishing marginal returns. Assuming that the price of the variable resource is constant, *MC* declines so long as the marginal product of the variable input is rising. This results because, in this range, smaller and smaller additions of the variable input are required to produce each extra unit of output. The situation is reversed, however, when diminishing returns are confronted. Once diminishing returns set in, more and more units of the variable factor are required to generate each additional unit of output. *MC* will rise, because the marginal product of the variable resource is declining. Eventually, *MC* exceeds *AVC* and *ATC*, causing these costs also to rise. A U-shaped short-run average total cost curve results.

OUTPUT AND COSTS IN THE LONG RUN

The short-run analysis relates costs to output *for a specific size of plant*. Firms, though, are not committed forever to their existing plant. In the long run, a firm can alter its plant size and all other factors of production. All resources used by the firm are variable in the long run.

How will the firm's choice of plant size affect production costs? **Exhibit 8-7** illustrates the short-run *ATC* curves for three plant sizes, ranging from small to large. If these three plant sizes were the only possible choices, which one would be best? The answer depends on the rate of output the firm expects to produce. The smallest plant would have the lowest cost if an output rate of less than q_1 were produced. The medium-sized plant would provide the least-cost method of producing output rates between q_1 and q_2. For any output level greater than q_2, the largest plant would be the most cost-efficient.

The long-run* ATC *curve shows the minimum average cost of producing each output level when the firm is free to choose among all possible plant sizes. It can best be thought of as a planning curve, because it reflects the expected per-unit cost of producing alternative rates of output while plants are still in the blueprint stage.

Exhibit 8-7 illustrates the long-run *ATC* curve when only three plant sizes are possible, and the planning curve *ABCD* is thus mapped out. Of course, given sufficient time, firms can usually choose among many plants of various sizes. **Exhibit 8-8** presents the long-run planning curve under these circumstances. It is a smooth curve, with each short-run *ATC* curve tangent to it.[4]

[4]The tangency, though, will occur at the least-cost output level for the short run only when the long-run curve is parallel to the x-axis, as in q_n, Exhibit 8-8.

EXHIBIT 8-7

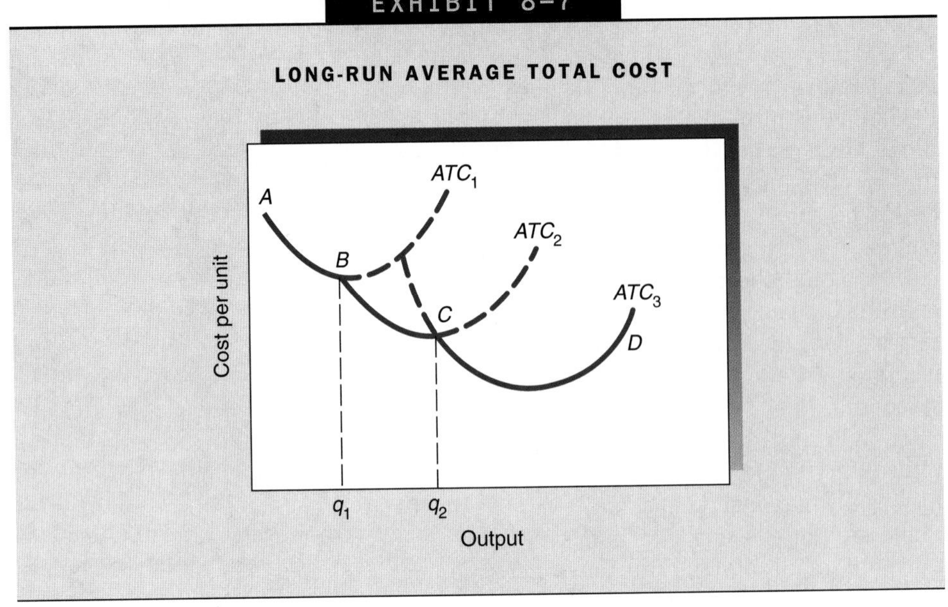

The short-run average total cost curves are shown for three alternative plant sizes. If these three were the only possible plant sizes, the long-run average total cost curve would be ABCD.

It is important to keep in mind that no single plant size could produce the alternative output rates at the costs indicated by the planning curve* LRATC *in Exhibit 8-8. Any of the planning-curve options are available before a plant size is chosen and the plant is built; however, although the firm can plan for the long run, choosing among many options, it can *operate* only in the short run. The *LRATC* curve outlines the possibilities available in the planning stage, indicating the expected average total costs of production for each of a large number of plants, which differ in size.

EXHIBIT 8-8

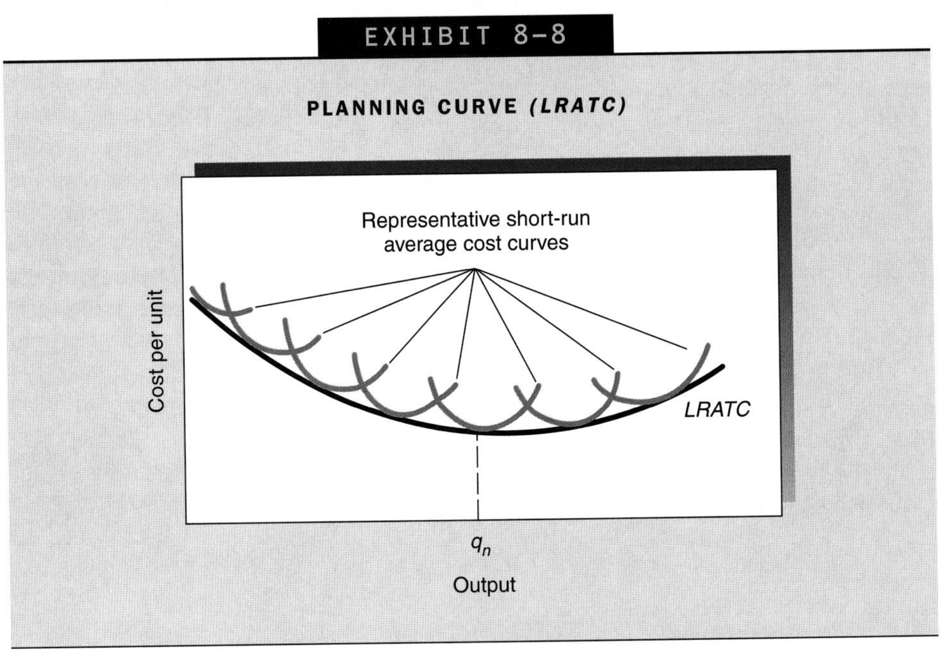

When many alternative plant sizes are possible, the long-run average total cost curve (LRATC) *is mapped out.*

When firms are able to plan large volumes of output, the use of mass-production methods will generally lead to lower per-unit costs. This helps explain why the LRATC *has a downward-sloping portion.*

Size of Firm and Unit Cost in the Long Run

Do larger firms have lower minimum unit costs than smaller ones? The answer to this question depends on which industries are being considered. There is a sound basis, though, for expecting some initial reductions in per-unit cost from large-scale production methods. Why? Large firms typically produce a large total volume of output.[5] Volume of output denotes the total number of units of a product that the firm expects to produce.[6] There are three major reasons why planning a larger volume generally reduces, at least initially, unit costs: (1) mass production, (2) specialization,

[5]Throughout this section, we assume that firms with larger plants necessarily plan a larger volume of output than do their smaller counterparts. Reality approximates these conditions. Firms choose large plants because they are planning to produce a large volume.

[6]Note the distinction between rate and volume of output. Rate of output is the number of units produced during a specific period (for example, the next six months). Volume is the total number of units produced during all time periods. For example, Boeing might produce two 767 airplanes per month (rate of output) while planning to produce a volume of two hundred 767s during the expected life of the model. Increasing the rate (reducing the time period during which a given output is produced) tends to raise costs, whereas increasing the volume (total amount produced) tends to lower costs. For additional information on production and costs, see Armen Alchian, "Costs," in *International Encyclopedia of the Social Sciences* (New York: Macmillan, 1968), pp. 404–415; and Jack Hirshleifer, "The Firm's Cost Function: A Successful Reconstruction," *Journal of Business* (July 1962): 235–255.

and (3) improvements in production as a result of experience, or "learning by doing." Let us consider each of these factors.

Mass-production techniques usually are economical only when large volumes of output are planned, since they tend to involve large development and setup costs. Once the production methods are established, though, marginal costs are low. For example, the use of molds, dies, and assembly-line production methods reduce the per-unit cost of automobiles only when the planned volume is in the millions. High-volume methods, although cheaper to use for high rates of output and high volumes, will typically require high fixed costs, and therefore will cause unit costs to be far higher for low volumes of production.

Large-scale operation also permits specialized use of labor and machines. Adam Smith noted 200 years ago that the output of a pin factory is much greater when one worker draws the wire, another straightens it, a third cuts it, a fourth grinds the point, a fifth makes the head of the pin, and so on.[7] In economics, the whole can sometimes be greater than the sum of the parts. Specialization provides the opportunity for people to become exceptionally proficient at performing small but essential functions. The result is more output per unit of labor.

Workers and managers in a firm that has made more units have probably learned more from their experience than their counterparts in smaller firms that have produced less output. Improvements in the production process result. Baseball players improve by playing baseball, and pianists by playing the piano. Similarly, the employees of a firm improve their skills as they "practice" productive techniques. This factor of "learning by doing" has been found to be tremendously important in the aircraft and automobile industries, among others. As managers and workers learn and develop skills producing the first 50 airplanes, for example, they are able to use these resources to produce the next batch of 50 airplanes more economically. Thus, firms that produce a large volume of output are able to achieve lower per-unit costs because of their prior production experience.

Economies and Diseconomies of Scale

Economies of scale
Reductions in the firm's per-unit costs that are associated with the use of large plants to produce a large volume of output.

Economic theory suggests that, at least initially, larger firms have lower unit costs than comparable smaller firms. When unit costs decline as output expands, **economies of scale** are present over the initial range of outputs. The long-run *ATC* curve is falling.

Are *diseconomies of scale* possible—that is, are there ever situations in which the long-run average total costs are greater for larger firms than they are for smaller ones? The economic justification for diseconomies of scale is less obvious (and less tenable) than that for economies of scale. However, as a firm gets bigger and bigger, bureaucratic inefficiencies *may* result. Code-book procedures tend to replace managerial genius. Motivating the workforce and carrying out managerial directives are also more complex when the firm is larger, and principal-agent problems grow as the number of employees increases and more levels of monitoring need to be done. Coordinating more people and conveying information to them is more difficult. These factors combine to cause rising long-run average total costs in some, though certainly not all, industries.

It is important to note that scale economies and diseconomies stem from sources different from those of increasing and diminishing returns. ***Economies and***

[7]Smith went on to state, "I have seen a small manufactory of this kind where ten men only were employed, and where some of them consequently performed two or three distinct operations. Those ten persons, therefore, could make among them upwards of forty-eight thousand pins in a day. But if they had all wrought separately and independently, and without any of them having been educated to this particular business, they certainly could not each of them have made twenty, perhaps not one pin in a day." Adam Smith, *An Inquiry into the Nature and Causes of the Wealth of Nations,* 1776, edited by Edwin Cannan (Univ. of Chicago Press, 1976), pp.

EXHIBIT 8-9

THREE DIFFERENT TYPES OF LONG-RUN AVERAGE TOTAL COST CURVES

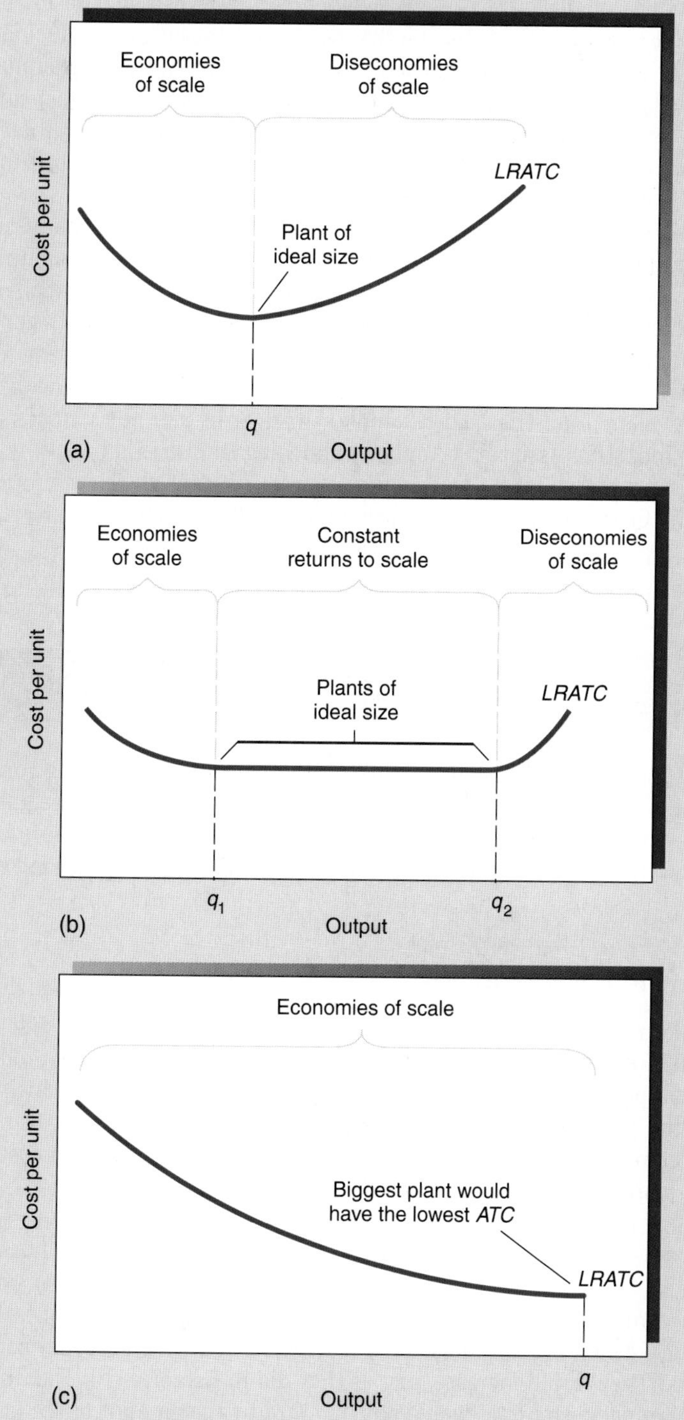

For one type of LRATC *curve, economies of scale are present for output levels less than* q, *but immediately beyond* q, *diseconomies of scale dominate (a). In another instance, economies of scale are important until some minimum output level* (q_1) *is attained. Once the minimum has been attained, there is a wide range of output levels* (q_1 *to* q_2) *that are consistent with the minimum* ATC *for the industry (b). In a third situation, economies of scale exist for all relevant output levels (c). As we will see later, this type of* LRATC *curve has important implications for the structure of the industry.*

diseconomies of scale are long-run concepts. They relate to conditions of production when all factors are variable. In contrast, increasing and diminishing returns are short-run concepts, applicable only when the firm has a fixed factor of production.

Exhibit 8-9 outlines three different long-run average total cost *(LRATC)* curves that describe real-world conditions in differing industries. For part a, both economies and diseconomies of scale are present. Higher per-unit costs will result if the firm chooses a plant size other than the one that minimizes the cost of producing output q. If each firm in an industry faces the same cost conditions, we can generalize and say that all plants larger or smaller than this ideal size will experience higher unit costs. A very narrow range of plant sizes would be expected in industries with the *LRATC* depicted by part a. Some lines of retail sales and agriculture might approximate these conditions.

Part b demonstrates the general shape of the *LRATC* that economists believe is present in most industries. Initially, economies of scale exist, but once a minimum efficient scale is reached, wide variation in firm size is possible. Firms smaller than the minimum efficient size would have higher per-unit costs, but firms larger than that would not gain a cost advantage. **Constant returns to scale** are present for a broad range of output rates (between q_1 and q_2). This situation is consistent with real-world conditions in many industries. For example, small firms can be as efficient as larger ones in such industries as apparel, lumber, publishing, and several lines of retailing.

Constant returns to scale
Unit costs that are constant as the scale of the firm is altered. Neither economies nor diseconomies of scale are present.

In part c of Exhibit 8-9, economies of scale exist for all relevant output levels. The larger the firm size, the lower the per-unit cost. The *LRATC* in the local telephone service industry may approximate the curve shown here.

WHAT FACTORS CAUSE COST CURVES TO SHIFT?

In outlining the general shapes of a firm's cost curves in both the long run and short run, we assumed that certain other factors—resource prices, taxes, regulations, and technology—remained constant as the firm altered its rate of output. Let us now consider how these other factors would affect production costs if they did not remain constant.

Prices of Resources

If the price of resources used should rise, the firm's cost curves will shift upward, as **Exhibit 8-10** illustrates. Higher resource prices will increase the cost of producing each alternative output level. For example, what happens to the cost of producing automobiles when the price of steel rises? The cost of producing automobiles also rises. Conversely, lower resource prices will result in cost reductions. Thus, the cost curves for any specific plant size will shift downward.

Taxes

Taxes are a component of a firm's cost. Suppose that an excise tax of 20 cents were levied on each gallon of gasoline sold by a service station. What would happen to the seller's costs? They would increase, just as they did in Exhibit 8-10. The firm's average total and marginal cost curves would shift upward by the amount of the tax. If the tax were an annual business license fee instead, it would raise the average cost, but not the variable cost.

EXHIBIT 8-10

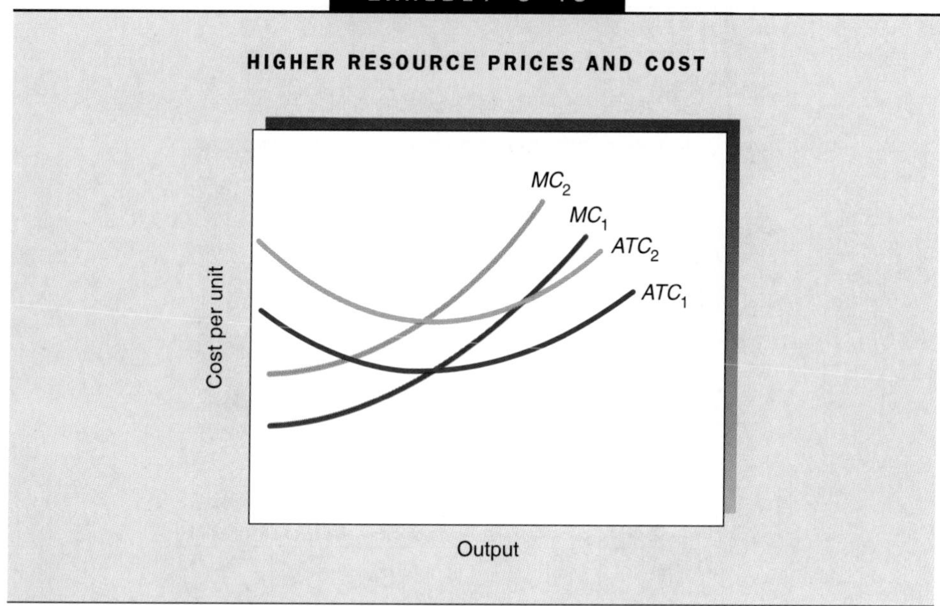

An increase in resource prices will cause the firm's cost curves to shift upward.

Regulations

The government often imposes health, safety, environmental, and production regulations on business firms. Regulations may require businesses to provide a certain number of water fountains and rest rooms for customers and workers. The Americans With Disabilities Act forces many firms to make their facilities accessible for persons in wheelchairs. Regulations may force firms to include certain features in a product (for example, strong bumpers and air bags for automobiles). Although regulations yield benefits, they are also costly. Like tax increases, increases in regulatory compliance costs will shift cost curves upward. In some cases, only fixed costs will be affected,

"OF COURSE YOU MAY REGISTER A COMPLAINT ABOUT ALL THE GOVERNMENT PAPERWORK, SIR... BUT IT HAS TO BE IN WRITING."

Suppose that an egg producer discovers (or develops) a "super" mineral water that makes it possible to get more eggs from the same number of chickens. Because of this technological improvement, various output levels of eggs can now be produced with less feed, space, water, and labor. Costs will be reduced. The egg producer's ATC *and* MC *curves will shift downward.*

EXHIBIT 8-11

EGG-PRODUCTION COSTS AND TECHNOLOGICAL CHANGE

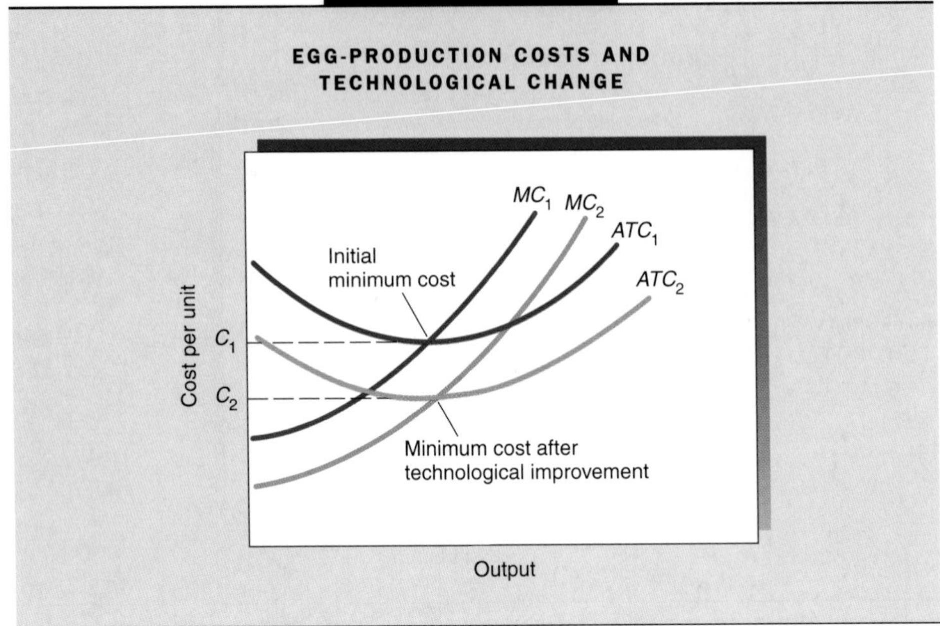

while in other instances variable costs will be altered as well. In both cases, the firm's *ATC* will be higher.

TECHNOLOGY

Technological improvements often make it possible to produce a specific output with fewer resources. For example, the printing press drastically reduced the number of labor-hours required to print newspapers and books. The spinning wheel reduced the labor-hours necessary to weave cotton into cloth. More recently, computers and robots have reduced costs in many industries. As **Exhibit 8-11** shows, a technological improvement will shift the firm's cost curves downward, reflecting the reduction in the amount of resources used to produce alternative levels of output.

ECONOMIC WAY OF THINKING ABOUT COSTS

When analyzing the firm's costs, economists often present a highly mechanical—some would say unrealistic—view. The role of personal choice in a world of uncertainty is often glossed over.

It is important to keep in mind that costs are incurred when choices are made. When business decision makers choose to purchase raw materials, hire new employees, or renew the lease on a plant, they incur costs. All these decisions, like other choices, must be made under conditions of uncertainty. Of course, past experience can help business decision makers to anticipate the likely costs of various decisions. But the world is constantly changing; the future may differ substantially from the past.

Opportunity costs are expected costs—they represent the highest valued option that the decision maker expects to give up as the result of a choice. Think for a moment of what the cost curves developed in this chapter really mean. The firm's short-run *MC* curve represents the opportunity cost of expanding output, *given the* *firm's current plant size.* The firm's long-run *ATC* curve represents the opportunity cost per-unit of output associated with varying plant sizes and rates of output, *given that the alternative plants are still on the drawing boards.* Opportunity costs look forward, reflecting expectations as to what will be forgone as a result of current decisions. At the time decisions must be made, neither the short-run *MC* nor the long-run *ATC* can be determined from accounting records, since accounting costs look backward. Accounting figures yield valuable information about historical costs, but, as the following discussion will show, they must be interpreted carefully when forecasting future costs.

Sunk Costs

Sunk costs are historical costs associated with past decisions that cannot be reversed. While sunk costs provide knowledge relevant to current decisions, the specific costs themselves are no longer relevant. When past choices cannot be reversed, money that has been spent is gone for good. Current choices must be based on the costs and benefits expected in relation to *current and future* market conditions, if mistakes are to be avoided (see the Myths of Economics box).

Sunk costs
Costs that have already been incurred as a result of past decisions. They are sometimes referred to as historical costs.

If they are to minimize costs, business decision makers must recognize the irrelevance of sunk costs. Let us consider a simple example that emphasizes this point. Suppose that the firm of Exhibit 8-5 pays $100,000 to purchase and install a roller blade–producing machine. The machine is expected to last ten years. The company's books record the cost of the machine as $10,000 each year under the heading of depreciation. The machine can be used only to make roller blades. Since dismantling and reinstallation costs are high, it cannot be leased or sold to another firm. Also, it has no scrap value. In other words, there are no alternative uses for the machine. The machine's annual production of roller blades will generate $50,000 of revenues for the firm when it is employed with raw materials and other factors of production that cost $46,000. Thus, the net revenue generated by the machine is $4,000.

MYTHS OF ECONOMICS

"A good business decision maker will never sell a product for less than its production costs."

This statement contains a grain of truth. A profit-seeking entrepreneur would not *undertake* a project knowing that the costs could not be covered. However, this view fails to emphasize (1) the time dimension of the production process and (2) the uncertainty associated with business decisions. The production process takes time. Raw materials must be purchased, employees hired, and plants equipped. Retailers must contract with suppliers. As these decisions are made, costs result. Many of the firm's costs of production are incurred long before the product is ready for marketing.

Even a good business decision maker is not always able to predict the future. Market conditions may change in an unexpected manner. At the time the product is ready for sale, buyers may be unwilling to pay a price that will cover the seller's past costs of production. These past costs, however, are now sunk costs and no longer relevant. Current decisions must be made on the basis of current cost and revenue considerations.

Should a grocer refuse to sell oranges that are about to spoil because their wholesale cost cannot be covered? The grocer's current opportunity cost of selling the oranges may be nearly zero. The alternative may be to throw them in the garbage next week. Almost any price, even one far below past costs, would be better than letting the oranges spoil.

Consider another example. Suppose a couple who own a house plan to relocate temporarily. Should they refuse to rent their house for $500 (if this is the best offer available) because their monthly house payment is $800? Of course not. The house payment will go on, regardless of whether they rent the house. If the homeowners can cover their opportunity costs (perhaps wear and tear plus a $60 monthly fee for a property management service), they will gain by renting rather than leaving the house vacant.

Past mistakes provide useful lessons for the future, but they cannot be reversed. Bygones are bygones, even if they resulted in business loss. There is no need to fret over spilt milk, burnt toast, or yesterday's business losses.

Should the firm continue to use the machine? Its annual depreciation cost suggests that the machine cost the firm $10,000, compared to the $4,000 of net revenue it generates. Thus, the accounting records indicate that the machine reduces the firm's profit by $6,000 annually. The machine's depreciation cost, however, is a sunk cost. It was incurred when the machine was installed. The current opportunity cost of the machine is precisely zero. The firm is not giving up anything by continuing to use it. Since use of the machine generates $4,000 of additional net revenue, the firm can gain from its continued operation. Of course, if current market conditions are not expected to improve, the firm will not purchase a similar machine or replace the machine when it wears out, but this should not influence the decision of whether to continue operating the current one. The irrelevance of sunk costs helps explain why it often makes sense to continue using older equipment (it has a low opportunity cost), even though it may not be wise to purchase similar equipment again.

COST AND SUPPLY

Economists are interested in cost because they seek to explain the supply decisions of firms. A strictly profit-maximizing firm will compare the expected revenues derived from a decision or a course of action with the expected costs. If the expected revenues exceed costs, the course of action will be chosen because it will expand profits (or reduce losses).

In the short run, when making supply decisions, the marginal cost of producing additional units is the relevant cost consideration. A profit-maximizing decision maker will compare the expected marginal costs with the expected additional revenue from larger sales. If the latter exceeds the former, output (the quantity supplied) will be expanded.

Whereas marginal costs are central to the choice of short-run output, the expected average total cost is vital to a firm's long-run supply decision. *Before entering an industry* (or purchasing capital assets for expansion or replacement), a profit-maximizing decision maker will compare the expected market price with the expected long-run average total cost. Profit-seeking potential entrants will supply the product if, and only if, they expect the market price to exceed their long-run average total cost. Similarly, existing firms will continue to supply a product only if they expect that the market price will enable them at least to cover their long-run average total cost.

LOOKING *Ahead*

In this chapter, we outlined several basic principles that affect costs for business firms. We will use these basic principles when we analyze the price and output decisions of firms under alternative market structures in the chapters that follow.

KEY POINTS

➤ The business firm is used to organize productive resources and transform them into goods and services. There are three major types of business structure—proprietorships, partnerships, and corporations.

➤ To solve the principal-agent problem, which tends to reduce worker efficiency in team production, every firm must provide work incentives and monitoring.

➤ The demand for a product indicates the intensity of consumers' desires for the item. The (opportunity) cost of producing the item indicates the desire of consumers for other goods that could have been produced instead.

➤ In economics, total cost includes not only explicit payments for resources employed by the firm, but also the implicit costs associated with the use of productive resources owned by the firm (such as the opportunity cost of the firm's equity capital or owner-provided services).

➤ Because accounting methods omit the cost of equity capital (and sometimes other implicit costs), they generally understate the opportunity cost of producing a good and overstate the firm's economic profit.

➤ Economic profit (loss) results when a firm's sales revenues exceed (are less than) its total costs, both explicit and implicit. Firms that are making the market (or "normal") rate of return on their assets will therefore make zero economic profit.

➤ The firm's short-run average total cost *(ATC)* curve will tend to be U-shaped.

➤ The law of diminishing returns explains why a firm's short-run marginal and average total costs will eventually rise. When diminishing marginal returns are present, successively larger amounts of the variable input will be required to increase output by one more unit.

➤ The long-run *ATC (LRATC)* reflects the costs of production for plants of various sizes. When economies of scale are present, *LRATC* will decline. When constant returns to scale are experienced, *LRATC* will be constant. When diseconomies of scale are present, *LRATC* will rise.

➤ Changes in: (a) resource prices, (b) taxes, (c) regulations, and (d) technology will cause the cost curves of a firm to shift.

➤ Sunk costs are costs that have already been incurred and cannot be recovered. While they may provide information helpful for future decisions, sunk costs are no longer directly relevant for decision making.

CRITICAL ANALYSIS QUESTIONS

*1. What is economic profit? How might it differ from accounting profit? Explain why firms that are making zero economic profit are likely to continue in business.

*2. Which of the following statements do you think reflect sound economic thinking? Explain your answer.

a. "I paid $200 for this economics course. Therefore, I'm going to attend the lectures even if they are useless and boring."
b. "Because we own rather than rent, and the house is paid for, housing doesn't cost us anything."
c. "I own 100 shares of stock that I can't afford to sell until the price goes up enough for me to get back at least my original investment."
d. "It costs to produce private education, whereas public schooling is free."

3. Suppose a firm produces bicycles. Will the firm's accounting statement reflect the opportunity cost of the bicycles? Why or why not? What costs would an accounting statement reveal? Should current decisions be based on accounting costs? Explain.

4. What is the principal-agent problem? When will the principal-agent problem be most severe? Why might there be a principal-agent problem between the stockholder-owners and the managers of a large corporation?

5. Suppose that Ajax, Inc., is the target of a takeover attempt by the management of Beta Corporation, which is offering to buy stock from any Ajax stockholder who wants to sell at 20 percent above the current price. Explain how the resistance of Ajax management to the takeover attempt might illustrate the principal-agent problem. Is it possible that the Beta Corporation management's action is itself an illustration of the principal-agent problem? Explain.

6. What are some of the advantages of the corporate business structure of ownership for large business firms? What are some of the disadvantages? Is the corporate form of business ownership cost-efficient? In a market economy, how would you tell whether the corporate structural form was efficient?

7. Explain the factors that cause a firm's short-run average total costs to decline initially, but eventually to increase as the rate of output rises.

*8. Which of the following are relevant to a firm's decision to increase output: (a) short-run average total cost, (b) short-run marginal cost, (c) long-run average total cost? Justify your answer.

9. Economics students often confuse (a) diminishing returns to the variable factor and (b) diseconomies of

scale. Explain the difference between the two, and give one example of each.

10. "Firms that make a profit have increased the value of the resources they used; their actions created wealth. In contrast, the actions of firms that make losses reduce wealth. The discovery and undertaking of profit-making opportunities are key ingredients of economic progress." Evaluate the statement.

*11. Is profit maximization consistent with the self-interest of corporate owners? Is it consistent with the self-interest of corporate managers? Is there a conflict between the self-interest of owners and that of managers?

*12. What is the opportunity cost of (a) borrowed funds and (b) equity capital? Under current tax law, firms can take the opportunity cost of borrowed funds, but not equity capital, as an expense. How does this tax feature affect the debt/equity ratio of business firms?

*13. "If a firm maximizes profit, it must minimize the cost of producing the profit-maximum output." Is this statement true or false? Explain your answer.

14. Why do economists consider normal returns to capital as a cost? How does economic profit differ from normal returns (or "normal profit")?

*15. Draw a U-shaped short-run *ATC* curve for a firm. Construct the accompanying *MC* and *AVC* curves.

16. What is shirking? If the managers of a firm are attempting to maximize the profits of the firm, will they have an incentive to limit shirking? How might they go about doing so?

17. What are implicit costs? Do implicit costs contribute to the opportunity cost of production? Should an implicit cost be counted as cost? Give three examples of implicit costs. Does the firm's accounting statement take implicit costs into account? Why or why not?

*18. Consider a machine purchased one year ago for $12,000. The machine is being depreciated $4,000 per year over a three-year period. Its current market value is $5,000, and the expected market value of the machine one year from now is $3,000. If the interest rate is 10 percent, what is the expected cost of holding the machine during the next year?

*19. Investors seeking to take over a firm often bid a positive price for the business even though it is currently experiencing losses. Why would anyone ever bid a positive price for a firm operating at a loss?

20. Fill in the blanks in the following table:

Units of Variable Input	Total Product	Marginal Product	Average Product	Price of Input	Total Variable Cost	Average Variable Cost	Total Fixed Cost	Total Cost	Average Total Cost	Marginal Cost
0	0	______	______	$1	______	______	$2	______	______	______
1	6	______	______	$1	______	______	$2	______	______	______
2	15	______	______	$1	______	______	$2	______	______	______
3	27	______	______	$1	______	______	$2	______	______	______
4	37	______	______	$1	______	______	$2	______	______	______
5	45	______	______	$1	______	______	$2	______	______	______
6	50	______	______	$1	______	______	$2	______	______	______
7	52	______	______	$1	______	______	$2	______	______	______
8	50	______	______	$1	______	______	$2	______	______	______

a. What happens to total product when marginal product is negative?
b. What happens to average product when marginal product is greater than average product?
c. What happens to average product when marginal product is less than average product?
d. At what point does marginal product begin to decrease?

*Asterisk denotes questions for which answers are given in Appendix B.

e. At what point does marginal cost begin to increase?
f. Summarize the relationship between marginal product and marginal cost.
g. What happens to marginal costs when total product begins to fall?
h. What is happening to average variable costs when they equal marginal costs?
i. Marginal costs equal average variable costs between what output levels?
j. What is happening to average total costs when they equal marginal costs?
k. Marginal costs equal average total costs between what output levels?

CHAPTER 9

Competition means decentralized planning by many separate persons.

Friedrich A. von Hayek[1]

[I]t is competition that drives down costs and prices, induces firms to produce the goods consumers want, and spurs innovation and the expansion of new markets . . .

President's Council of Economic Advisers[2]

Price Takers and the Competitive Process

CHAPTER FOCUS

- ▲ How do firms that are price takers differ from those that are price searchers?
- ▲ What determines the output of a price taker?
- ▲ How do price takers respond when price changes in the short run? In the long run?
- ▲ How does time influence the elasticity of supply?
- ▲ What must firms do in order to make profits? How do profits and losses influence the supply and market price of a product?
- ▲ How does competition provide an incentive for producers to supply goods that consumers want at a low cost?

---

[1]F. A. Hayek, "The Use of Knowledge in Society," *American Economic Review* 35 (September 1945): 521.

[2]President's Council of Economic Advisers, *Economic Report of the President, 1996* (Washington, D.C.: U.S. Government Printing Office, 1996), p. 155.

In the previous chapters we saw how firms make production decisions and how costs affect those decisions. In this and the next two chapters, we take a closer look at how the product prices and profit levels that emerge from market trading will influence production. How much will be produced in a given market? What determines the profitability of firms, and how does the level of profit influence market supply over time? When goods and services are allocated by markets, will resources be allocated efficiently? Is there any reason to believe that there will be a linkage between market allocation and economic prosperity? These are the major questions that we will address in the next several chapters.

PRICE TAKERS AND PRICE SEARCHERS

Price takers
Sellers who must take the market price in order to sell their product. Because each price taker's output is small relative to the total market, price takers can sell all their output at the market price, but they are unable to sell any of their output at a price higher than the market price.

This chapter will focus on markets where the firms are **price takers:** They simply take the price that is determined in the market. ***In a price-taker market, the firms all produce identical products (for example, wheat, eggs, or regular unleaded gasoline) and each seller is small relative to the total market. Thus, the output supplied by any single firm exerts little or no effect on the market price. Each firm can sell all its output at the market price, but it is unable to sell any of its output at a price higher than the market price.*** When a firm is a price taker, there is no price decision to be made. Price takers will merely attempt to choose the output level that will maximize profit, given their costs and the price determined by the market.

Price searchers
Firms that face a downward sloping demand curve for their product. The amount that the firm is able to sell is inversely related to the price that it charges.

In the real world, most firms are not price takers. If the firm lowers its price, it will generally attract additional customers. Correspondingly, firms are usually able to increase their price, at least a little, without losing all their customers. For example, if Nike increased the price of its athletic shoes by 10 percent, the number of shoes sold would decline, but it would not fall to zero. Firms like Nike are **price searchers:** They can choose what price they will charge for their product, but the quantity that they are able to sell is very much related to that price. As price searchers seek maximum profit, they must not only decide how much to produce, but also what price to charge. We will examine markets where the firms are price searchers in the following two chapters.

Competition as a dynamic process
A term that denotes rivalry or competitiveness between or among parties (for example, producers or input suppliers), each of which seeks to deliver a better deal to buyers when quality, price, and product information are all considered. Competition implies a lack of collusion among sellers.

If most real-world firms are price searchers rather than price takers, why take the time to analyze the latter? There are several reasons to do so. First, although most firms are not price takers, there are a number of important markets, particularly in agriculture, where the firms do essentially take the price determined in the market. Second, the price-taker model helps clarify the relationship between the decision making of individual firms and market supply in both price-taker and price-searcher markets. Finally, and perhaps most important, the study of markets where firms are price takers enhances our knowledge of **competition as a dynamic process.** Understanding how the competitive process works when firms are price takers will also contribute to our understanding of the process as it applies to many price searchers.

Historically, almost all economists have referred to markets where firms are price takers as **purely competitive markets.** Increasingly, however, these markets are referred to as price-taker markets because this expression is more descriptive. Furthermore, it avoids the implication that competitive forces are necessarily less pure or less intense in price-searcher markets. Clearly, this is not always the case. In fact, price searchers often use a broad array of competitive weapons—for example, quality of product, style, convenient location, advertising, and price—all in an effort to attract consumers. When **barriers to entry** are low, the competitive process is just as important in price-searcher markets as it is when the firms are price takers.

Purely competitive markets
Markets characterized by a large number of small firms producing an identical product in an industry (market area) that permits complete freedom of entry and exit. Also called price-taker markets.

Barriers to entry
Obstacles that limit the freedom of potential rivals to enter and compete in an industry or market.

Nonetheless, it should be noted that price-taker markets and purely competitive markets are merely alternative names for the same thing. Thus, if you hear someone speak of pure competition or a purely competitive market, the person is referring to markets that have characteristics like those analyzed in this chapter.

MARKETS WHEN FIRMS ARE PRICE TAKERS

Consider the situation of Les Parrot, a Texas cattle rancher. As Parrot consults the financial pages of the local newspaper, he finds that the current market price of quality steers is 88 cents per pound. Even if his ranch is quite large, there is little that Parrot can do to change the market price of beef cattle. After all, there are tens of thousands of farmers who raise cattle. Thus, Parrot supplies only a small portion of the total cattle market. The amount that he sells will exert little or no impact on the market price of cattle. Parrot is a price taker.

The firms in a market will be price takers when the following four conditions are met:

1. All the firms in the market are producing an identical product (for example, beef cattle of a given grade).
2. A large number of firms exist in the market.
3. Each firm supplies only a very small portion of the total amount supplied to the market.
4. No barriers limit the entry or exit of firms in the market.

When these conditions are met, the firms in the market must accept the market price. This is why they are called price takers. **Exhibit 9–1** illustrates the relationship between the market forces (frame b) and the demand curve facing the price-taking

Producers in the wheat farming and beef cattle markets are price takers. If they are going to sell their output, they must do so at the price determined by the market. Because individual producers are small relative to the total market, they can sell as many units as they like at the market price.

EXHIBIT 9-1

PRICE TAKER'S DEMAND CURVE

The market forces of supply and demand determine price (b). Price takers have no control over price. Thus, the demand for the product of the firm is perfectly elastic (a).

firm (frame a). If the firm sets a price above the market level, consumers will simply buy from other sellers. Why pay the higher price when the identical good is available elsewhere at a lower price? For example, if the price of wheat were $5.00 per bushel, a farmer would be unable to find buyers for wheat at $5.50 per bushel. A firm could set its price below the market level. However, since it is small relative to the total market, the firm can already sell as much as it wants at the market price. A price reduction would merely reduce revenues. A firm that is a price taker thus confronts a perfectly elastic demand for its product. (Note in the exhibit, that a lowercase *d* is used to denote the demand curve faced by the *firm* while a capital *D* indicates the *market* demand curve.)

OUTPUT IN THE SHORT RUN

The firm's output decision is based on comparison of benefits with costs. If a firm produces at all, it will expand output as long as the benefits (additional revenues) from the production and sales of the additional units exceed their marginal costs. How will changes in output influence the firm's costs? In the preceding chapter, we discovered that the firm's short-run marginal costs will eventually increase as the firm expands its output by working its fixed plant facilities more intensively. The law of diminishing marginal returns assures us that this will be the case. Eventually, both the firm's short-run marginal and average total cost curves will turn upward.

Marginal revenue (*MR*)
The incremental change in total revenue derived from the sale of one additional unit of a product.

What about the benefits or additional revenues from output expansion? **Marginal revenue (*MR*)** is the change in the firm's total revenue per unit of output. It is the additional revenue derived from the sale of an additional unit of output. Mathematically,

$$MR = \text{Change in total revenue/Change in output}$$

The price taker sells all units at the same price; therefore, its marginal revenue will be equal to the market price.

In the short run, the price taker will expand output until marginal revenue (its price) is just equal to marginal cost. This decision-making rule will maximize the firm's profits (or minimize its losses).

Exhibit 9–2 helps explain why. Since the firm can sell as many units as it would like at the market price, the sale of one additional unit will increase revenue by the price of the product. Does the firm gain by producing an extra unit? The answer is yes, as long as the marginal revenue (price, for the price taker) is greater than or equal to the marginal cost of that unit. Profit is simply the difference between total revenue and total cost. Profit will increase as long as production and sale of a unit add more to revenue than to cost. Thus, the firm will gain from an increase in output as long as marginal revenue exceeds marginal cost. Eventually, however, as the firm produces a larger and larger quantity from its fixed size of plant, marginal costs will rise and exceed price and marginal revenue. When production of an additional unit adds more to cost than it adds to revenue, profit will be reduced if the unit is produced. Thus, the profit of the price taker is maximized at the output rate where $P = MR = MC$. In Exhibit 9–2, this occurs at output level q.

A profit-maximizing firm with the cost curves indicated by Exhibit 9–2 would produce exactly q. The total revenue of the firm would be the sales price P multiplied by output sold q. Geometrically, the firm's total revenues would be $P0qB$. The firm's total cost would be found by multiplying the average total cost (ATC) by the output level. Geometrically, total costs are represented by $C0qA$. The firm's total revenues exceed total costs, and the firm is making short-run economic profit (the shaded area).

In the real world, of course, decisions are not made by entrepreneurs who spend time drawing demand and marginal cost curves. Many have not even heard of these concepts. A business decision maker who has never heard of the $P = MC$ rule for profit maximization, however, probably has another rule that yields approximately the same outcome. For example, the rule might be to produce those units, and only those units, that add more to revenue than to cost. This ensures maximum profit (or minimum loss). It also takes the firm to the point at which $P = MC$. Why? To stop short of that point would mean not producing some profitable units—units that would add more to revenue than to cost. Similarly, the decision maker would not go beyond that point because production of such units would add more to cost than to revenue. This commonsense rule thus leads to the same outcome as our model, even when the

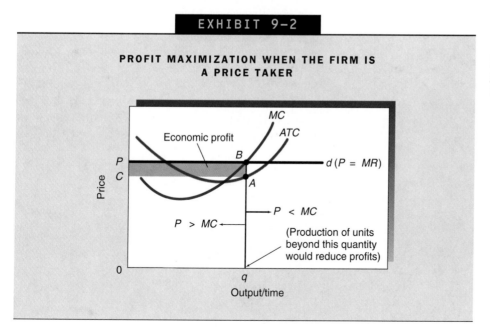

EXHIBIT 9–2

PROFIT MAXIMIZATION WHEN THE FIRM IS A PRICE TAKER

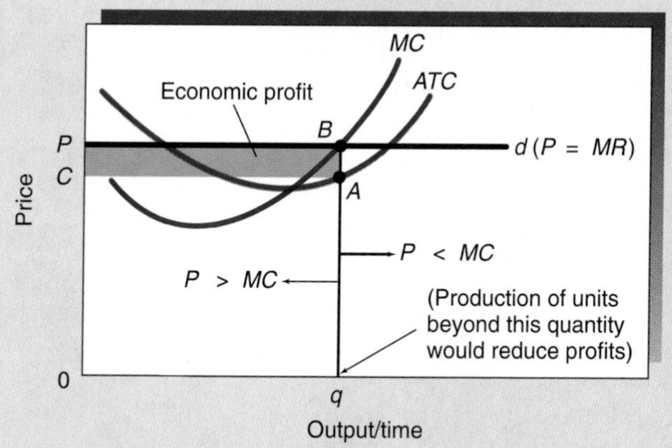

The price taker would maximize profits by producing the output level q, *where* P = MC.

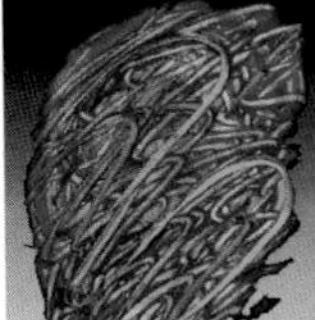

APPLICATIONS IN ECONOMICS

Experimental Economics—The Significance of Competition

Do individual decision makers, without any economics training, behave as if they understand marginal costs? Do they act as price takers, even though not all the assumptions of that model are satisfied? Or, when there are only a few sellers, do they collude successfully so as to raise price above marginal cost?

Verifying economic principles and comparing alternative economic models by scientific testing is not an easy task. Simply observing people to see whether they behave as economic principles suggest is not completely satisfactory. A normal economic event that we can observe may be the result of more than one cause; therefore, the economist seeking to isolate the impact of one causal factor must try to be sure that other factors influencing the outcome do not vary, or else try to take them into account in the analysis. To isolate the impact of a change in the price of a product on consumer behavior, for example, the economist must somehow account for the impact of all other price changes, income changes, and so on, that may have occurred. In other disciplines, scientists use experiments in the laboratory, with all factors controlled, to tackle a problem. They test the principles on which their science is built, using carefully detailed methods, so that other scientists can replicate the experiment.

Beginning about the middle of the twentieth century, economists also began to conduct laboratory experiments. A good many experiments have been conducted to investigate the predictive power of the price-taker model. In one of the earliest, conducted in 1956 by leading experimental economist Vernon Smith of the University of Arizona, individuals were brought into a laboratory setting and arbitrarily assigned roles as buyers and sellers, in a game-like setting. Each buyer was given a different "limit price" (that is, a maximum price he or she was allowed to pay) for a paper asset. Any buyer who could purchase the paper commodity for less than the limit price received a cash payment equal to the difference between the limit price and the amount actually paid. Therefore, as in other markets, each buyer gained financially by purchasing at lower prices. The sellers were treated in a parallel fashion. Each had a "limit price" (a minimum selling price) and received in cash any extra revenue above that price.

Buyers and sellers were free to make verbal offers to buy or sell. How did markets develop? Did the outcomes resemble a market where sellers compete, or did sellers collude, controlling the market price for their own benefit and controlling entry into the market?

The price-taker model predicts that all mutually advantageous trades among buyers and sellers will occur and that the price of the good will converge toward a single price—the market price. Prior to the work in experimental economics, many economists thought this model was relevant only under highly restrictive conditions. By changing the number of sellers, the type of trading rules, and so on, experimental researchers have generated similar results under a wide variety of conditions. Their findings suggest that outcomes approximating those of the price-taker model often emerge even when the strict assumptions of the model are absent. For example, even if the number of sellers is relatively small, say ten to fifteen, outcomes similar to those predicted by the price-taker model generally occur.

Participants in these experiments are often startled to discover that their competitive trading generated the largest possible joint income gain and, furthermore, that the competitive model presented in this chapter predicted this occurrence. Vernon Smith cites cases where, after the experiment, participants describe the experimental market as "unorganized, unstable, chaotic, and confused." Generally, they are amazed when shown that their actions (trades) achieved the maximum income for the group, and that a sealed envelope, given to them prior to the experiment, predicted the approximate amount of their (maximum) joint gain.

Smith himself was at first surprised at the efficient outcomes resulting from economic experiments. He had not been prepared to believe Adam Smith's principle that markets cause individual traders to reach efficient outcomes, even though this is not their intention. These results are achieved even when the individual participants are far from proficient traders. After numerous experiments, the modern Smith stated:

> In many experimental markets, poorly informed, error-prone, and uncomprehending human agents interact through the trading rules to produce social algorithms which demonstrably approximate the wealth maximizing outcomes traditionally thought to require complete information and cognitively rational actors.[1]

Experimental economics has confirmed that Adam Smith was right in 1776 when he described the invisible hand of the market at work. It has also established that the invisible hand does not require very much beyond the desire of each individual to better his or her own situation. Perfect information, perfect traders, and perfect markets are not necessary for traders to reach efficient solutions, when they can trade freely.

Experimental economics has researched many additional economic questions. Vernon Smith and his colleague Arlington Williams, another leading researcher in this area, summarize the findings of their work in the following manner:

---

[1]Vernon L. Smith, "Economics in the Laboratory," *Journal of Economic Perspectives* 8, no. 1 (winter, 1994): 118.

(continued)

Experimental market research has provided an empirical foundation for tenets of economic theory that were already well established, and it has also yielded insight into the details of how particular rules affect the outcome of the trading process. Thirty years of experiments have also brought good news: under most circumstances, markets are extremely efficient in facilitating the movement of goods from the lowest-cost producers to the consumers who place the highest value on them. Organized exchange thus effectively advances human welfare.[2]

[2]Vernon L. Smith and Arlington W. Williams, "Experimental Market Economics," *Scientific American* 267 (December 1992): 121. See also Smith, "Economics in the Laboratory," 113–132.

decision maker knows none of the technical jargon of economics. No wonder economics is sometimes thought of as "organized common sense."

Just how accurate is the price taker's competitive model in predicting behavior in real markets? Do other models, which assume that sellers collude to eliminate competition, yield better predictions? Direct scientific evidence bearing on such questions is highly desirable. As the Applications in Economics box on the significance of competition indicates, such evidence has been produced repeatedly in recent decades by the relatively new subdiscipline of experimental economics. The evidence indicates that the general implications of the price-taker model are valid under a variety of circumstances.

Profit Maximizing—A Numeric Example

Exhibit 9–3 uses numeric data to illustrate profit-maximizing decision making for a firm that is a price taker. Put yourself in the place of the owner of this firm. Your short-run total and marginal cost schedules have the general characteristics we discussed in the previous chapter. Since the firm confronts a market price of $5 per unit, its marginal revenue is $5. Total revenue thus increases by $5 per additional unit of output. You will maximize your profit when you supply an output of 15 units.

There are two ways of viewing this profit-maximizing output rate. First, profit is equal to the difference between total revenue and total cost. Thus, profit will be maximized at the output rate at which this difference (*TR* minus *TC*) is greatest. Column 6 of Exhibit 9–3 provides this information. For small output rates (less than 11), you and your firm would actually experience losses. But at 15 units of output, an $11 profit is earned ($75 total revenue minus $64 total cost). A look at the profit figures of column 6 indicates that it would be impossible to earn a profit larger than $11 at any other rate of output.

Exhibit 9–4 presents in part a the total revenue and total cost approach in graph form. (However, the curves are drawn smoothly, as though output could be increased by tiny amounts, not just in whole-unit increments as shown in Exhibit 9–3.) Profits will be greatest when the total revenue line exceeds the total cost curve by the largest vertical amount. That takes place, of course, at 15 units of output.

You can also use the marginal approach to determine the profit-maximizing rate of output for this competitive firm. Remember, as long as price (marginal revenue) exceeds marginal cost, production and sale of additional units will add to the firm's profit (or reduce its losses). A look at columns 4 and 5 of Exhibit 9–3 reveals that *MR* is greater than *MC* for the first 15 units of output. Producing these units will expand

EXHIBIT 9–3

PROFIT MAXIMIZATION FOR A PRICE TAKER: A NUMERIC ILLUSTRATION

(1) Output (per day)	(2) Total Revenue (*TR*)	(3) Total Cost (*TC*)	(4) Marginal Revenue (*MR*)	(5) Marginal Cost (*MC*)	(6) Profit (*TR* – *TC*)
0	$ 0.00	$ 25.00	$0.00	$ 0.00	$–25.00
1	5.00	29.80	5.00	4.80	–24.80
2	10.00	33.75	5.00	3.95	–23.75
3	15.00	37.25	5.00	3.50	–22.25
4	20.00	40.25	5.00	3.00	–20.25
5	25.00	42.75	5.00	2.50	–17.75
6	30.00	44.75	5.00	2.00	–14.75
7	35.00	46.50	5.00	1.75	–11.50
8	40.00	48.00	5.00	1.50	– 8.00
9	45.00	49.25	5.00	1.25	– 4.25
10	50.00	50.25	5.00	1.00	– 0.25
11	55.00	51.50	5.00	1.25	3.50
12	60.00	53.25	5.00	1.75	6.75
13	65.00	55.75	5.00	2.50	9.25
14	70.00	59.25	5.00	3.50	10.75
15	75.00	64.00	5.00	4.75	11.00
16	80.00	70.00	5.00	6.00	10.00
17	85.00	77.25	5.00	7.25	7.75
18	90.00	85.50	5.00	8.25	4.50
19	95.00	95.00	5.00	9.50	0.00
20	100.00	108.00	5.00	13.00	– 8.00
21	105.00	125.00	5.00	17.00	–20.00

the firm's profit. In contrast, producing any unit beyond 15 adds more to cost than to revenue. Profit will therefore decline if you expand output beyond 15 units. Given the firm's cost and revenue schedule, you will maximize profit by producing 15, and only 15, units per day.

Part b of Exhibit 9–4 graphically illustrates the marginal approach. Note here that the output rate (15 units) at which the marginal cost and marginal revenue curves intersect coincides with the output rate in part a at which the total revenue curve exceeds the total cost curve by the largest amount.

Losses and Going Out of Business

Suppose changes take place in the market that depress the price below a firm's average total cost. How will a profit maximizer (or loss minimizer) respond to this situation? The answer to this question depends both on the firm's current sales revenues relative to its variable cost and on its expectations about the future. The firm's owner has three options: (1) continue to operate in the short run, (2) shut down temporarily, or (3) go out of business.

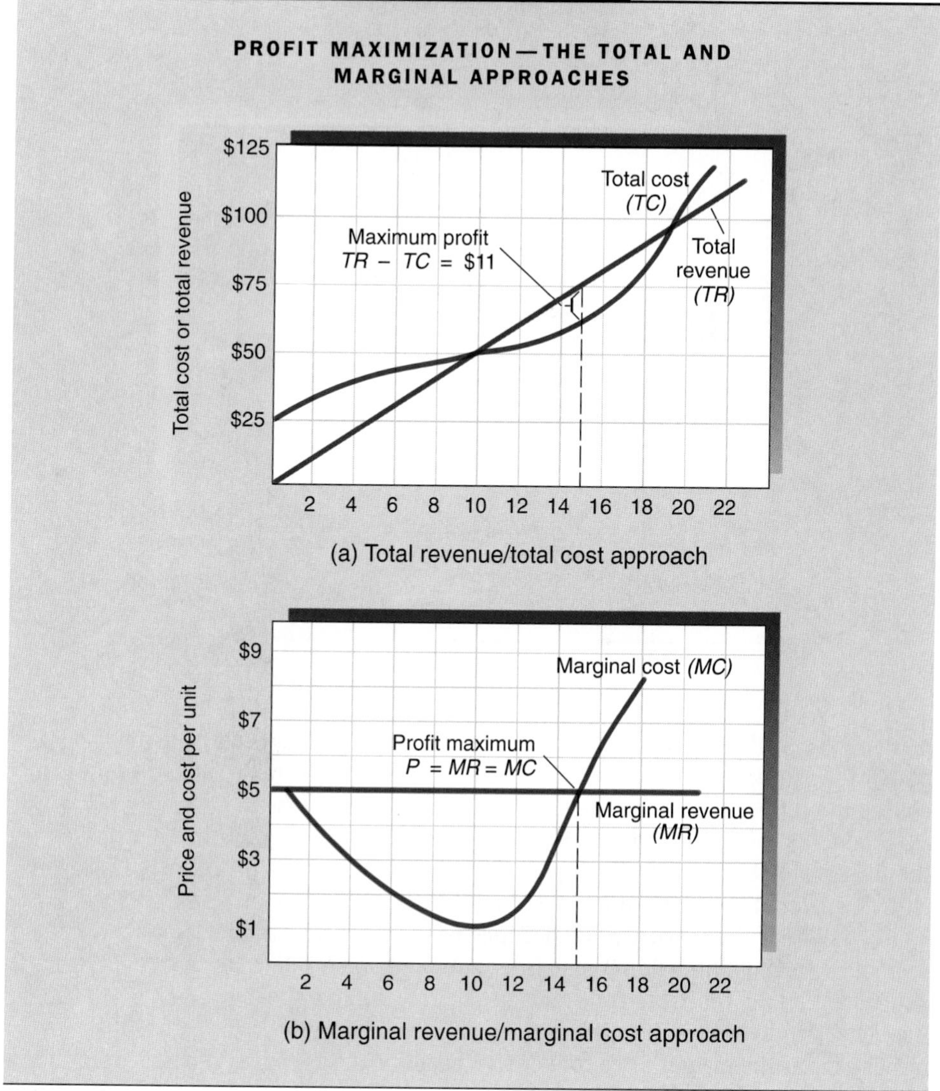

Using the data of Exhibit 9–3, here we provide two ways of viewing profit maximization. In the first, the profits of the price taker are maximized at the output level at which total revenue exceeds total cost by the maximum amount (a). In the second, the maximum-profit output is identified by comparing marginal revenue and marginal cost (b).

If the firm anticipates that the lower market price is temporary, it may want to continue operating in the short run as long as it can cover its variable cost.[3] **Exhibit 9–5** illustrates why. The firm shown in this exhibit would minimize its loss at output level q, where $P = MC$. But at q, total revenues ($OqBP_1$) are less than total costs ($OqAC$). The firm faces short-run economic losses. Even if it shuts down completely, it will still incur fixed costs, *unless the firm goes out of business.* If it anticipates that the

[3]Keep in mind the opportunity-cost concept. The firm's fixed costs are *opportunity costs* that do not vary with the level of output. They can be avoided if, and only if, the firm goes out of business. To specify fixed costs, we need to know (1) how much the firm's fixed assets would bring if they were sold or rented to others and (2) any other costs, such as operating license fees and debts, that could be avoided if the firm declared bankruptcy and/or went out of business. Since fixed costs can be avoided if the firm goes out of business, the firm will foresee greater losses from operating even in the short run if it does not expect conditions to improve.

A firm making losses will operate in the short run if it (1) can cover its variable costs now and (2) expects price to be high enough in the future to cover all its costs.

EXHIBIT 9-5

OPERATING WITH SHORT-RUN LOSSES

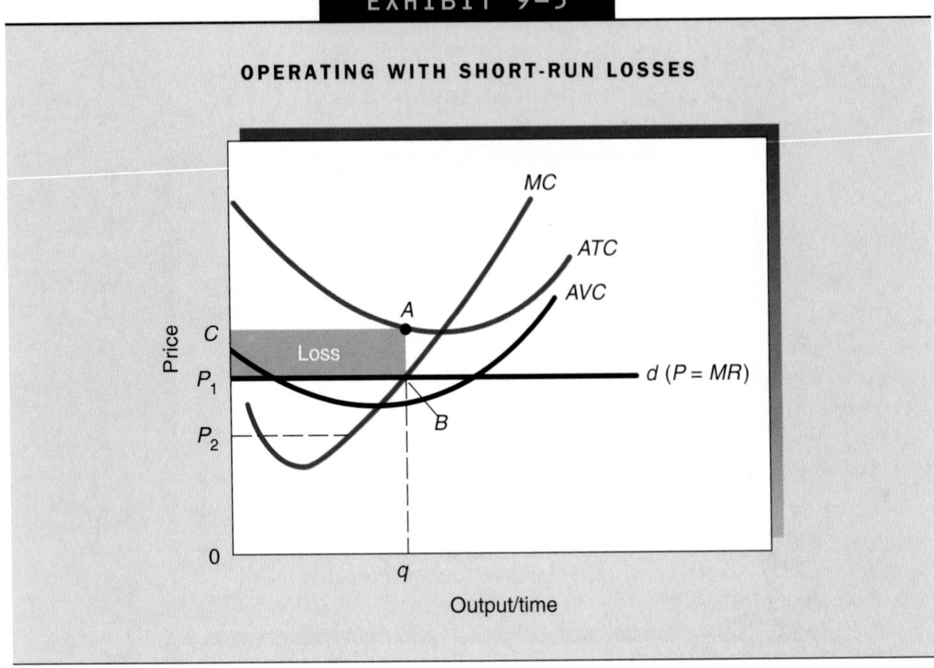

market price will increase enough that the firm will be able to cover its average total costs in the future, it may not want to sell its assets and terminate operations. It may choose to produce q units in the short run, even though losses are incurred. At price P_1, production of output q is clearly more advantageous than shutting down, because the firm is able to cover its variable costs and pay some of its fixed costs. If it were to shut down, *but not sell out,* the firm would lose the entire amount of its fixed cost.

What if the market price declines below the firm's average variable cost (for example, P_2)? Under these circumstances, a temporary **shutdown** is preferable to short-run operation. If the firm continues to operate in the short run, operating losses merely add to losses resulting from the firm's fixed costs. Therefore, even if the firm's owner expects the market price to increase, enabling it to survive and prosper in the future, shutting down in the short run when the market price falls below its average variable cost (*AVC*) will reduce losses. Temporary shutdowns are actually planned on a regular basis in some markets. For example, restaurants and motels in some areas shut down in slow seasons, operating only when tourists or other seasonal purchasers provide enough demand. The price-taker model predicts that these firms will operate only when they expect to cover at least their variable costs.

Shutdown
A temporary halt in the operation of a business firm. Because the firm anticipates returning to the market in the future, it does not sell its assets and go out of business. The firm's variable cost is eliminated by the shutdown, but its fixed costs continue.

The firm's third option is **going out of business** immediately. After all, even the losses resulting from the firm's fixed costs can be avoided if the firm sells out. When market conditions are not expected to change for the better, going out of business is the preferred option.

Going out of business
The sale of a firm's assets and its permanent exit from the market. By going out of business, a firm is able to avoid fixed costs, which would continue during a shutdown.

Firm's Short-Run Supply Curve

The price taker that intends to stay in business will maximize profits (or minimize losses) when it produces the output level at which P = MC *and variable costs are covered. Therefore, the portion of the firm's short-run marginal cost curve that lies above its average variable cost is the short-run supply curve of the firm.*

This ice cream store in Morgantown, West Virginia, closes for several months each winter and reopens during the summer. During these short-run shutdowns, the store still pays fixed costs, such as rent, taxes, and insurance. Only variable costs are avoided during the winter months.

Exhibit 9–6 illustrates that, as the market price increases, the firm will expand output along its *MC* curve. If the market price were less than P_1, the firm would shut down immediately because it would be unable to cover even its variable costs. If the market price is P_1, however, a price equal to the firm's average variable cost, the firm may supply output q_1 in the short run. Economic losses will result, but the firm would incur similar losses if it shut down completely. As the market price increases to P_2, the firm will happily expand output along its *MC* curve to q_2. At P_2, price is also equal to average total costs. The firm is making a "normal rate of return," or zero economic profits. Higher prices will result in a still larger short-run output. The firm will supply q_3 units at market price P_3. At this price, economic profits will result. At still higher prices, output will be expanded even more. As long as price exceeds average variable cost, higher prices will cause the firm to expand output along its *MC* curve, which therefore becomes the firm's short-run supply curve.

Short-Run Market Supply Curve

The short-run market supply curve corresponds to the total amount supplied by all the firms in the industry. ***When the firms are price takers, the short-run market supply curve is the horizontal summation of the marginal cost curves (above the level of average variable cost) for all firms in the industry. Since individual firms will supply a larger amount at a higher price, the short-run market supply curve will slope upward to the right.***

As price increases, firms will expand output along their MC *curve. Thus, the firm's* MC *curve is also its supply curve (a). When resource prices are constant, the short-run market supply (a) is merely the sum of the supply produced by all the firms in the market area (b).*

EXHIBIT 9-6

SHORT-RUN SUPPLY CURVE FOR THE FIRM AND THE MARKET

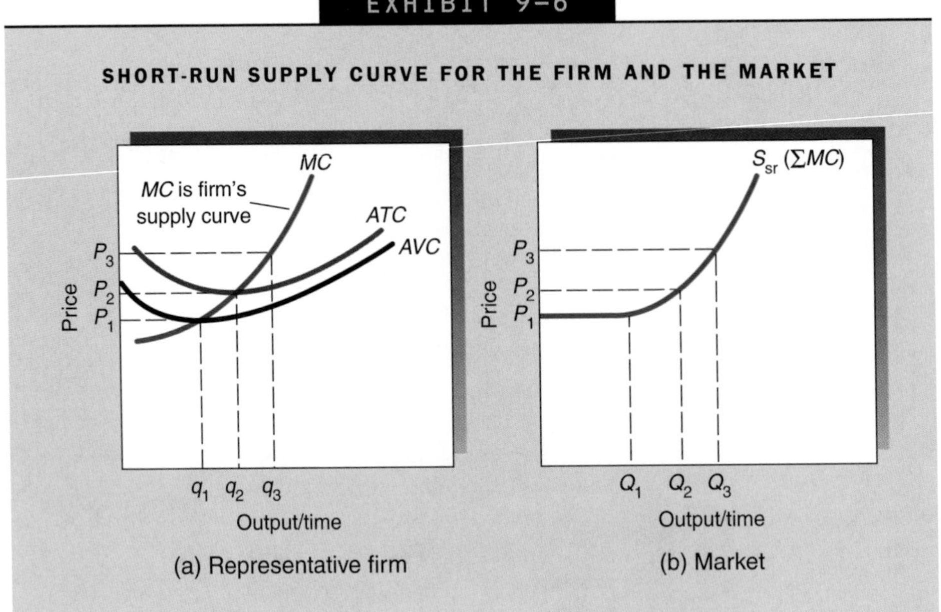

Exhibit 9–6 illustrates this relationship. As the price of the product rises from P_1 to P_2 to P_3, the individual firms expand their output along their marginal cost curves. Since the individual firms supply a larger output as the market price increases, the total amount supplied to the market also expands.

Our construction of the short-run market supply curve assumes that the prices of the resources used by the industry are constant. When the entire industry (rather than just a single firm) expands output, resource prices may rise. If so, the short-run market supply curve (reflecting the higher prices of purchased inputs) will be slightly more inelastic (steeper) than the sum of the supply curves of the individual firms. The reason, of course, is that when just one firm expands, it has a minuscule effect on the market for resources, but when the entire industry expands output, the rise in resource demand is larger, so resource prices are more likely to rise.

The short-run market supply curve, together with the demand curve for the industry's product, will determine the market price. At the short-run equilibrium market price, each firm will have expanded output until marginal costs have risen to the market price. Firms will have no desire to change output, *given their current size of plant.*

OUTPUT ADJUSTMENTS IN THE LONG RUN

In the long run, firms have the opportunity to alter their plant size and enter or exit an industry. As long-run adjustments are made, output in the whole industry may either expand or contract.

LONG-RUN EQUILIBRIUM

In addition to the balance between quantity supplied and quantity demanded necessary for short-run equilibrium, firms that are price takers must earn the normal rate of

EXHIBIT 9–7

LONG-RUN EQUILIBRIUM IN A PRICE-TAKER MARKET

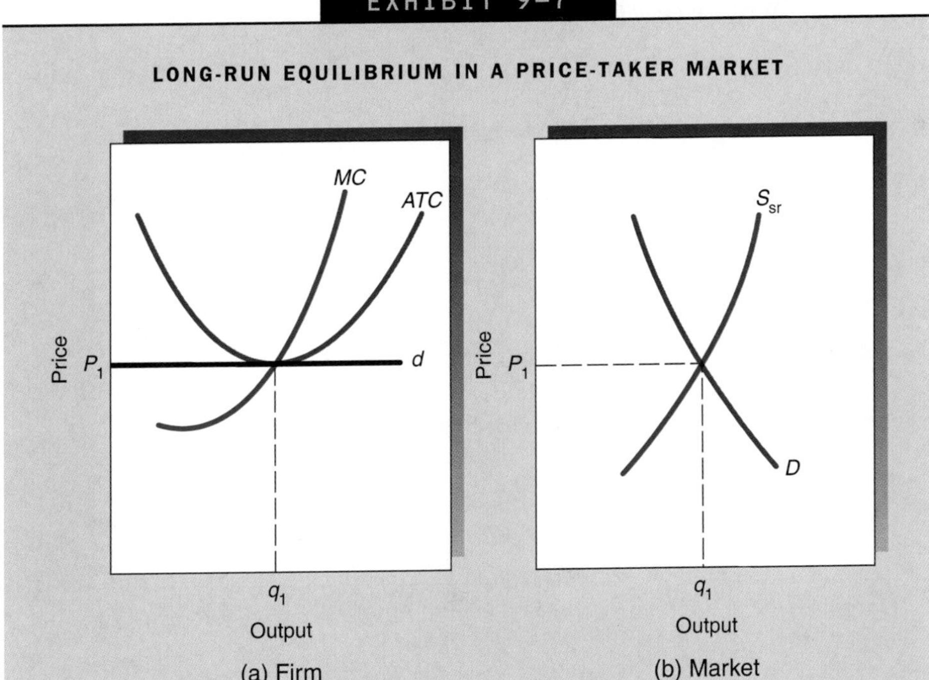

The two conditions necessary for equilibrium in a price-taker market are depicted here. First, quantity supplied and quantity demanded must be equal in the market (b). Second, the firms in the industry must earn zero economic profit (that is, the "normal rate of return") at the established market price (a).

return, and only the normal rate, before long-run equilibrium can be attained. ***If economic profit is present, new firms will enter the industry, and the current producers will have an incentive to expand the scale of their operations. This will lead to an increase in supply, placing downward pressure on prices. In contrast, if firms in the industry are suffering economic losses, they will leave the market. Supply will decline, placing upward pressure on prices.***

Therefore, as **Exhibit 9–7** illustrates, when a price-taker market is in long-run equilibrium (1) the quantity supplied and the quantity demanded will be equal at the market price, and (2) the firms in the industry will be earning normal (zero) economic profit (that is, their minimum *ATC* will just equal the market price).

ADJUSTING TO EXPANSION IN DEMAND

Suppose a price-taker market is in equilibrium. What will happen if there is an increase in demand? **Exhibit 9–8** presents an example. An entrepreneur introduces a fantastic new candy product. Consumers go wild over it. However, since it sticks to one's teeth, the market demand for toothpicks increases from D_1 to D_2. The price of toothpicks rises from P_1 to P_2. What impact will the higher market price have on the output level of toothpick-producing firms? It will increase (from q_1 to q_2 in part a of the exhibit) as the firms expand output along their *MC* curves. In the short run, the toothpick producers will make economic profits. The profits will attract new toothpick producers to the industry and cause the existing firms to expand the scale of their plants. Hence, the market supply will increase (shift from S_1 to S_2) and eventually eliminate the short-run profits. If cost conditions are unchanged in the industry, the market price for toothpicks will return to its initial level, even though output has expanded to Q_3.

EXHIBIT 9-8

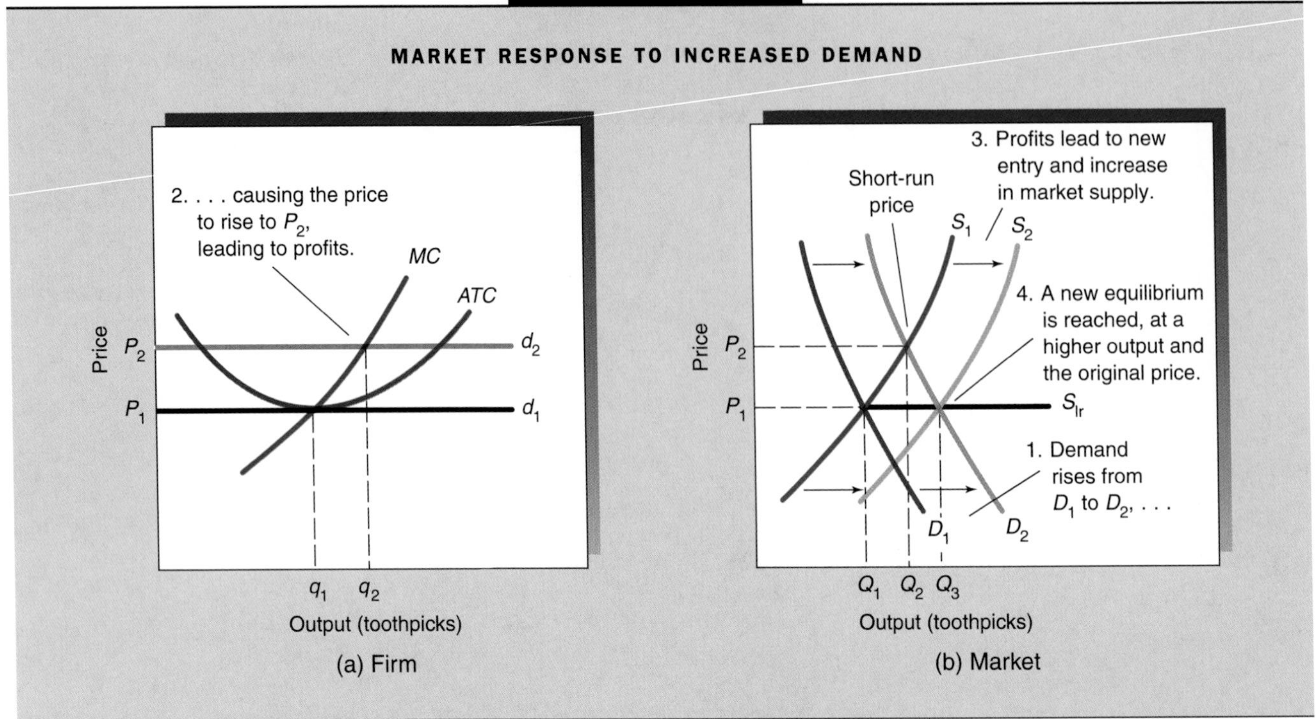
MARKET RESPONSE TO INCREASED DEMAND
2. . . . causing the price to rise to P_2, leading to profits.
MC
ATC
Price
P_2
P_1
d_2
d_1
q_1 q_2
Output (toothpicks)
(a) Firm
3. Profits lead to new entry and increase in market supply.
Short-run price
S_1
S_2
4. A new equilibrium is reached, at a higher output and the original price.
S_{lr}
1. Demand rises from D_1 to D_2, . . .
D_1
D_2
Q_1 Q_2 Q_3
Output (toothpicks)
(b) Market

The introduction of a new candy product that sticks to one's teeth causes the demand for toothpicks to increase to D_2 *(b). Toothpick prices rise to* P_2*, inducing firms to expand output. Toothpick firms make short-run profits (a), which draw new competitors into the industry. Thus, the toothpick supply expands (shifts from* S_1 *to* S_2*). If cost conditions are unchanged, the expansion in supply will continue until the market price of toothpicks has declined to its initial level of* P_1*.*

When the demand for a firm's product rises, one response is to expand the size of the factory. This will shift the cost curve for the firm to the right, allowing a larger output at minimum cost.

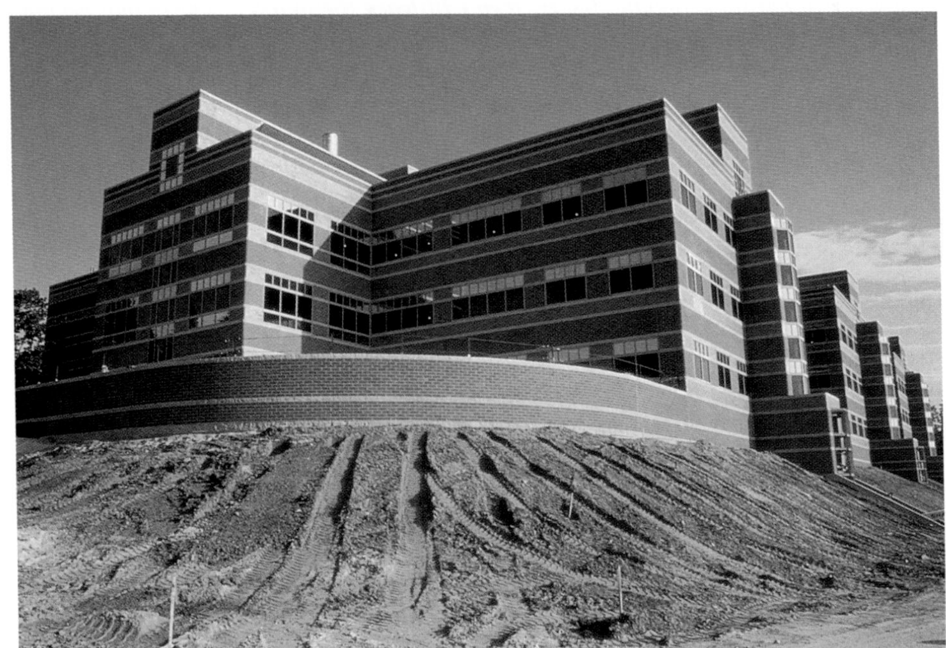

Adjusting to Decline in Demand

Economic profits attract new firms to an industry. In contrast, economic losses (when they are expected to continue) encourage capital and entrepreneurship to move out of the industry and into other areas where the profitability potential is more favorable. Economic losses mean that the owners of capital in the industry are earning less than the market rate of return. The opportunity cost of continuing in the industry exceeds the gain.

Exhibit 9–9 illustrates how market forces react to economic losses. Initially, an equilibrium price exists in the industry. The firms are able to cover their average costs of production. Now suppose there is a reduction in consumer income, causing the market demand for the product to decrease and the market price to decline. At the new, lower price, firms in the industry will not be able to cover their costs of production. In the short run, they will reduce output along their *MC* curve. This reduction in output by the individual firms results in a reduction in the quantity supplied in the market. For an illustration of demand reduction from a different source, see the Applications in Economics boxed feature on a shift in demand.

In the face of short-run losses, the inflow of capital will decline and the industry's capital assets will shrink as firms fail to replace equipment when it wears out. Some firms will leave the industry as their fixed costs become variable and they are no

EXHIBIT 9–9

IMPACT OF DECLINE IN DEMAND

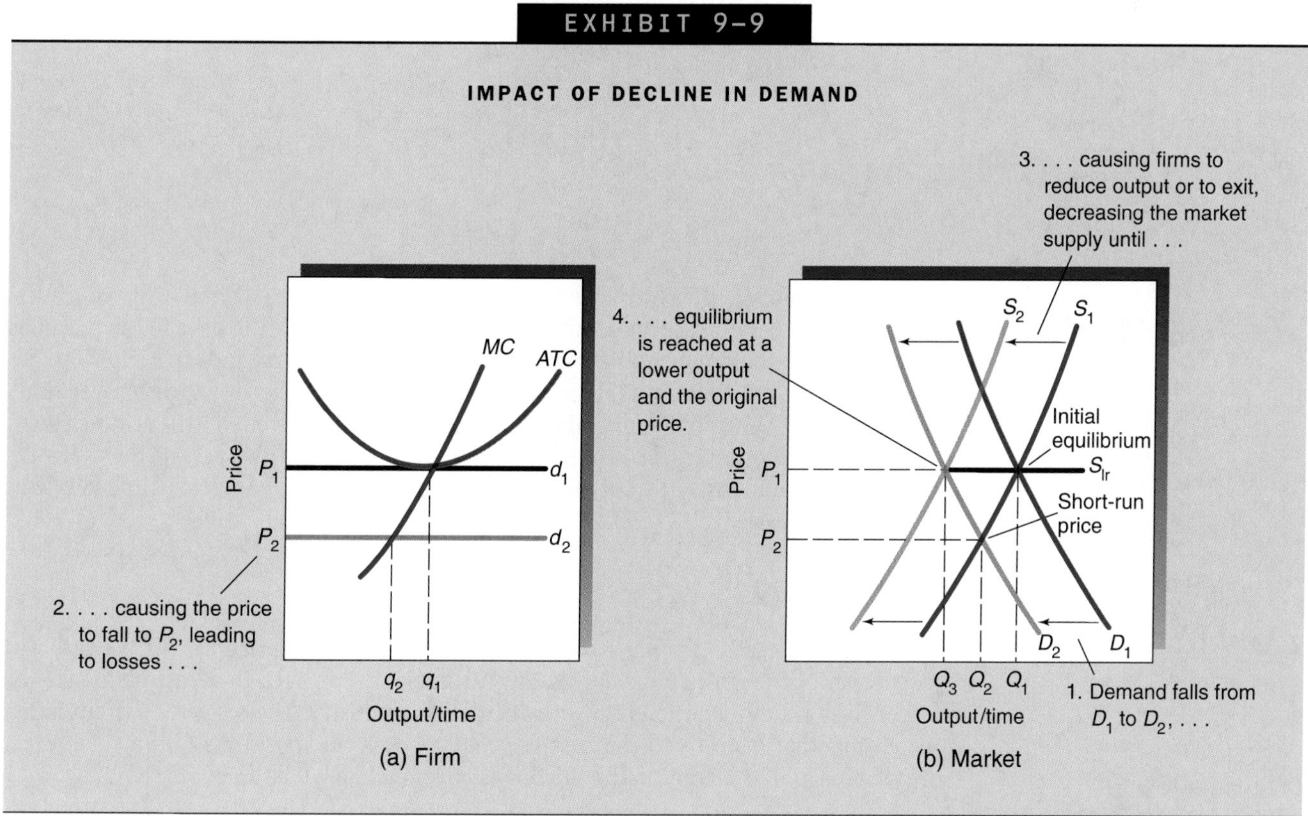

Price
P1
P2
MC
ATC
d1
d2
2. . . . causing the price to fall to P2, leading to losses . . .
q2 q1
Output/time
(a) Firm
4. . . . equilibrium is reached at a lower output and the original price.
3. . . . causing firms to reduce output or to exit, decreasing the market supply until . . .
S2
S1
Initial equilibrium
Slr
Short-run price
D2
D1
Q3 Q2 Q1
Output/time
1. Demand falls from D1 to D2, . . .
(b) Market

A reduction in market demand will cause price to fall and short-run losses to occur. The losses will cause some firms to go out of business and others to reduce their scale. In the long run, the market supply will fall, causing the market price to rise. The supply will continue to decline and price will continue to rise until the short-run losses have been eliminated.

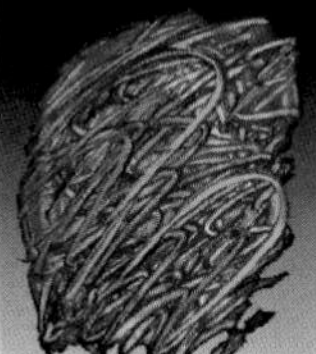

APPLICATIONS IN ECONOMICS

A Shift in Demand—Impact of a Papal Decree on the Price of Fish

Sometimes changes in institutions, legal restrictions, or regulatory policies influence the demand for a product. One classic case that illustrates this point has been carefully researched and documented. The 1966 papal decree lifting the Roman Catholic church's ban on the eating of meat on Fridays provides the illustration. Before the ban was lifted, most of the nearly 600 million Roman Catholics consumed fish on Fridays. After the decree, many substituted beef, pork, and chicken in their Friday meals. The market demand for fish therefore declined. As our analysis indicates, a decline in demand will lead to a lower market price in the short run.

Economist Frederick Bell of Florida State University estimated the impact of the reduction in demand on the market price of fish in the Northeastern United States, an area where Catholics compose a large proportion of the total population.[1] As we discussed earlier, changes in personal income and the price of related commodities (beef, pork, and poultry in this case) will influence the demand for a good. Bell utilized statistical techniques to adjust for these factors. This permitted him to isolate the independent effect of the papal decree on the demand for and price of fish.

The prices of seven different species of fish were considered. As the accompanying exhibit illustrates, Bell's analysis showed that the price of each variety fell. The price of large haddock was 21 percent lower after the papal decree than for the previous ten years. In other instances, the decline in price was smaller. On average, Bell estimated, the price of fish in the Northeastern United States fell by 12.5 percent as a result of the pope's edict. Just as economic theory indicates, a reduction in demand for a product leads to a lower price in the short run.

Species	Percent Change in Price of Fish after Papal Decree
Sea scallops	−17
Yellowtail flounder	−14
Large haddock	−21
Small haddock (scrod)	−2
Cod	−16
Ocean perch	−10
Whiting	−20
All species (average)	−12.5

[1] Frederick W. Bell, "The Pope and the Price of Fish," *American Economic Review* 58 (December 1968): 1346–1350.

longer able to cover their variable costs at the prevailing price. Others will reduce the scale of their operations, producing only those units for which the new, lower revenues can still justify the production costs. These factors will cause the industry supply to decline, to shift from S_1 to S_2. What impact will this have on price? It will rise. Over time, given no other shifts in demand, the short-run market supply curve will decline—will continue shifting to the left—until the price rises sufficiently to permit the firms remaining in the industry to earn once again "normal profits." At that point, long-run equilibrium is reached.

Long-Run Supply

The *long-run market supply curve* indicates the minimum price at which firms will supply various market output levels, given sufficient time both to adjust plant size (or other fixed factors) and to enter or exit from the industry. The shape of the curve depends on what happens to the cost of production as the *industry's* output is altered. Three possibilities emerge, although one is far more likely than the other two.

Constant-cost industry
An industry for which factor prices and costs of production remain constant as market output is expanded. Thus, the long-run market supply curve is horizontal.

Constant-Cost Industries. If factor prices remain unchanged, the long-run market supply curve will be perfectly elastic. In terms of economics, this describes a **constant-cost industry.** Exhibits 9–8 and 9–9 both picture constant-cost industries. As

Exhibit 9–8 illustrates, an expansion in demand causes prices to increase *temporarily.* With time, however, the higher prices and profits will stimulate expansion and additional production, which will push the market price down to its initial level (and profitability to its normal rate). In the long run, the larger supply will not require a permanent price increase. Similarly, Exhibit 9–9 illustrates the impact of a decline in demand in a constant-cost industry. The *long-run supply curve* (S_{lr}) is perfectly elastic, reflecting the basically unchanged cost at the lower rate of industry output.

A constant-cost industry is most likely to arise when the industry's demand for resource inputs is quite small relative to the total demand for these resources. For example, the demand of the matches industry for wood, chemicals, and labor is very small relative to the total demand for these resources. Thus, doubling the output of matches would exert very little impact on the price of the resources used by this industry. Matches therefore approximate a constant-cost industry.

Increasing-Cost Industries. In most industries, an increase in market demand and *industry* output will lead to higher per-unit production costs for all the firms in the industry. Economists refer to such industries as **increasing-cost industries.** The rising output and expanded resource demand in such industries result in higher prices for at least some resources, causing the firms' cost curves to shift upward. For example, a rising demand for housing places upward pressure on the prices of lumber, window frames, building sites, and construction labor, causing the cost of housing to rise. Similarly, an increase in demand (and market output) for beef may cause the prices of feed grains, hay, and grazing land to rise. Thus, the production costs of beef rise as more of it is produced.

Increasing-cost industry
An industry for which costs of production rise as output is expanded. Thus, even in the long run, higher market prices will be required to induce the firms to expand the total output in such industries. The long-run market supply curve in such industries will slope upward to the right.

For an increasing-cost industry, an expansion in market demand will bid up resource prices, causing the per-unit cost of the firms to rise. As a result, a larger market output will be forthcoming only at a higher price. The long-run market supply curve for the product will therefore slope upward.

In central areas of large cities, the supply of parking spaces can be expanded only by using higher-cost space and higher-cost techniques, such as taller parking garages that use a large portion of the building for access ramps. As a result, the unit cost of parking spaces increases as the total number is expanded. Thus, provision of parking space is an increasing-cost industry.

EXHIBIT 9–10

INCREASING COSTS AND LONG-RUN SUPPLY

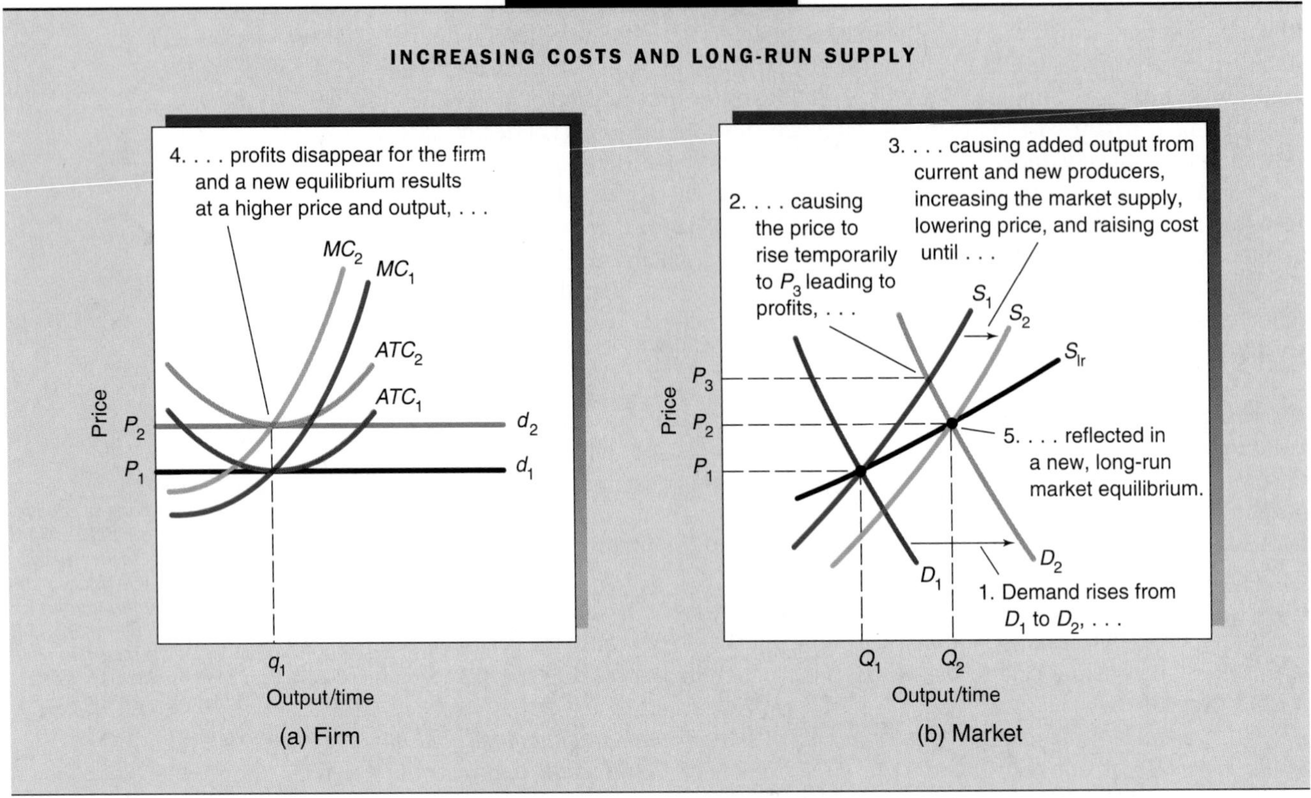

Most often, higher factor prices will cause costs to rise as the market output increases. For such increasing-cost industries, the long-run supply curve (S_{lr}) will slope upward to the right (b).

Exhibit 9–10 depicts an increasing-cost industry. Greater demand causes higher prices and a larger market output. *As the industry expands,* factor prices rise and costs increase. What happens to the firm's cost curves? Both the average and marginal cost curves rise (shift to ATC_2 and MC_2). Greater production cost necessitates a higher long-run price (P_2), so the long-run supply curve slopes upward to the right.

Decreasing-cost industry
An industry for which costs of production decline as the industry expands. The market supply is therefore inversely related to price. Such industries are atypical.

Decreasing-Cost Industries. Sometimes, factor prices will decline when the market output of a product is expanded. The lower resource prices will reduce the unit costs of the firms, placing them in a position to supply a larger market output at a lower price. In such **decreasing-cost industries,** the long-run (but not the short-run) market supply curve will slope downward to the right. For example, as the electronics industry expands, suppliers of certain components may be able to adopt large-scale production techniques that will lead to lower component prices. If rising electronics demand leads to reduced component cost (and if other resource prices do not rise to offset the reductions), then the cost curves of the electronics firms will shift downward. Under these circumstances, the industry supply curve for electronics products—reflecting the lower cost—will slope downward to the right.

In most industries, however, increases in demand and expansion in market output cause higher rather than lower input prices. Thus, increasing-cost industries are the norm, and decreasing-cost industries are quite rare.

Supply Elasticity and the Role of Time

It takes time for firms to adjust to a change in the price of a product. In the short run, firms are stuck with the existing size of their plant. If price increases in the short run, they can expand output only by utilizing their existing plant more intensely. Thus, their output response will be limited. In the long run, however, they will have time to build new plants. This will allow them to expand output by a larger amount in response to an increase in price. Thus, the market supply curve will be more elastic in the long run than in the short run.

The short- and long-run distinction offers a convenient two-stage analysis, but in the real world there are many intermediate production "runs." Some factors that could not be easily varied in a one-week time period can be varied over a two-week period. Economical expansion of other factors might require a month, and still others, six months. To be more precise, the cost penalty for quicker availability is greater for some production factors than for others. In any case, a faster expansion usually means that greater cost penalties are necessary to provide for an earlier availability of productive factors.

When a firm has a longer time period to plan output and adjust all its productive inputs to the desired utilization levels, it will be able to produce any specific rate of output at a lower cost. ***Because it is less costly to expand output slowly in response to a demand increase, the expansion of output by firms will increase with time, as long as price exceeds cost. Therefore, the elasticity of the market supply curve will be greater when more time is allowed for firms to adjust output.***

Exhibit 9–11 illustrates the impact of time on the response by producers to an increase in price resulting from an expansion in demand. When the price of a product increases from P_1 to P_2, the immediate supply response of the firms is small, reflecting the high cost of hasty expansion. After one week, firms are willing to expand output only from Q_1 to Q_2. After one month, because of cost reductions made possible by the longer production planning period, firms are willing to offer Q_3 units at the

EXHIBIT 9–11

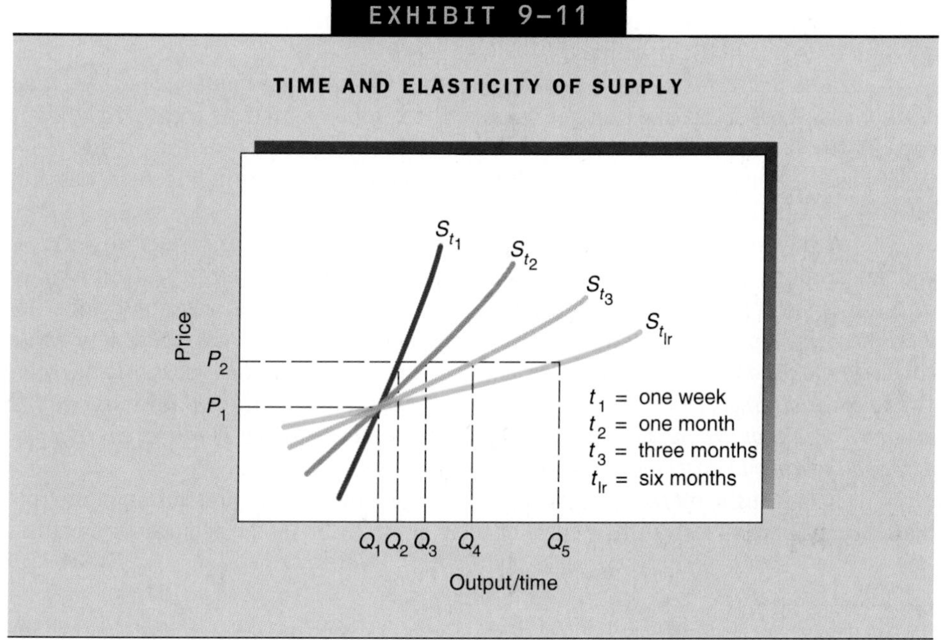

The elasticity of the market supply curve usually increases as more time is allowed for adjustment to a change in price.

price P_2. After three months, the rate of output expands to Q_4. In the long run, when it is possible to adjust all inputs to the desired utilization levels (after a six-month time period, for example), firms are willing to supply Q_5 units of output at the market price of P_2. ***The supply curve for products is typically more elastic over a longer time period than over a shorter period.***

ROLE OF PROFITS AND LOSSES

The price-taker model highlights the role of profits and losses: They are signals sent to producers by consumers. Economic profits will be largest in those areas where the value of additional units to consumers is highest relative to their production costs. Profit-seeking entrepreneurs will guide additional resources into these areas. Supply will increase, driving prices down and eliminating the profits. ***Free entry and the competitive process will protect the consumer from arbitrarily high prices. In the long run, competitive prices will reflect costs of production.***

Economic profits result because a firm or an entrepreneur acts to increase the value of resources. Business firms purchase resources and use them to produce a product or service that is sold to consumers. Costs are incurred as the business pays workers and other resource owners for their services. If the sales of the business firm exceed the costs of employing all the resources required to produce the firm's output, then the firm will make a profit. ***In essence, profit is a reward that business owners will earn if they produce a good that consumers value more (as measured by their willingness to pay) than the resources required for the good's production (as measured by the cost of bidding the resources away from their alternative employment possibilities).***

For example, suppose that it costs a shirt manufacturer \$20,000 per month to lease a building, rent the required machines, and purchase the labor, cloth, buttons, and other materials necessary to produce and market 1,000 shirts per month. Thus, the average cost of the shirts is \$20 (the \$20,000 monthly cost divided by the 1,000 monthly output). If the manufacturer sells the 1,000 shirts for \$22 each, its actions create wealth. Consumers value the shirts more than they value the resources required for their production. The manufacturer's \$2 profit per shirt is a reward received for increasing the value of the resources.

In contrast, losses are a penalty imposed on businesses that reduce the value of resources. Losses indicate that the value of the resources used (as measured by their cost) by the firm exceeds the price consumers are willing to pay for the product supplied. Losses, along with bankruptcies, are the market's way of bringing such wasteful activities to a halt.

We live in a world of changing tastes and technology, imperfect knowledge, and uncertainty. Business decision makers cannot be sure of either future market prices or costs of production. Their decisions must be based on expectations. Nonetheless, the reward-penalty structure of a market economy is clear. ***Firms that anticipate correctly the products and services for which future demand will be most urgent (relative to production cost), and produce and market them efficiently will make economic profits. Those that are inefficient and allocate resources incorrectly into areas of weak demand (relative to cost) will be penalized with losses.***

A look at the market for videotape rental provides a vivid illustration of the role played by profits and losses when entry barriers are low.[4] In 1982 videotape rental stores

[4]Data in this example are taken from Tim Tregarthen, "Supply, Demand, and Videotape," *The Margin* 6 (September–October 1990): 29.

Expanding demand made the video rental business very profitable in the mid-1980s. Many new stores entered the market, supply expanded, and eventually price reductions eliminated the abnormally high profits. This illustrates the competitive market process at work.

were new, and there were only an estimated 5,000 stores in the United States. They could charge $5 and more per 24-hour rental. The availability of rentals and the falling prices of home video players meant that profits could at times reach 80 percent of rental revenues. More important, expected profits were very high. This optimism led to the rapid entry of many new stores, which increased competition and forced prices down. By 1990 there were about 25,000 video rental stores. Prices had fallen dramatically. Even new releases were typically renting for $1.99, and most videos rented for even less. Prices are even lower now. At times, video rental supply expanded faster than the demand for rentals, and some of the firms had to leave the business. Even for those who were efficient and stayed in the business, profits were slim. Consumers, however, benefited tremendously from the highly competitive nature of the video rental business.

PRICE TAKERS, COMPETITION, AND PROSPERITY

Our analysis indicates that market forces provide price takers with a strong incentive to use resources wisely. Each firm will have a strong tendency to produce its output as cheaply as possible. Holding quality constant, the price taker can maximize profits only by minimizing the cost of production—using the least valued set of resources needed to produce the desired output.

Firms have a strong incentive to produce goods that are valued more highly than the resources required for their production. Thus, resources are drawn to those uses where they are most productive, as judged by the consumers' willingness to pay for the various goods produced. The ability of firms freely to expand or contract their businesses, and to enter or exit the market, means that resources that could be more valuable elsewhere will not be trapped unproductively in a particular industry. Resource owners can move them to where they are most highly valued in production.

OUTSTANDING ECONOMIST

Friedrich A. von Hayek (1899–1992)

Remarkably, the writings of this 1974 Nobel Prize recipient spanned seven decades. His work on knowledge and markets both enhanced our understanding of the competitive process and highlighted the fatal defects of central planning. He also made major contributions in areas as diverse as monetary theory, law and economics, business cycles, and capital theory.

The price-taker model highlights the more general importance of the competitive process. Competition places pressure on producers to operate efficiently and to avoid waste. It weeds out the inefficient—those who fail to provide consumers with quality goods at low prices. Competition also keeps producers on their toes in other areas. The production techniques and product offerings that lead to success today will not necessarily pass the competitive market test tomorrow. Producers who survive in a competitive environment cannot be complacent. As the chapter-opening quotation from the President's Council of Economic Advisers indicates, competition forces firms to be forward-looking and innovative. They must be willing to experiment and quick to adopt improved methods.

In competitive markets, business firms must serve the interests of consumers. As Adam Smith noted more than 200 years ago, competition harnesses personal self-interest and puts it to work, elevating our standard of living and directing our resources toward the production of those goods that we desire most intensely relative to their cost. Smith stated:

> It is not from the benevolence of the butcher, the brewer, or the baker, that we expect our dinner, but from their regard to their own self-interest. We address ourselves, not to their humanity but to their self-love, and never talk to them of our own necessities, but of their advantages.[5]

In a competitive environment, even self-interested individuals and profit-seeking business firms have a strong incentive to recognize and serve the interests of others, and to supply products that are valued more highly than the resources required for their production. This is the path to greater income and larger profits. Paradoxical as it may seem, personal self-interest—a characteristic many view as less than admirable—is a powerful source of economic progress when it is directed by competition.

---

[5]Adam Smith, *An Inquiry into the Nature and Causes of the Wealth of Nations* (1776; Cannan's ed., Chicago: University of Chicago Press, 1976), p. 18.

LOOKING *Ahead*

In the real world, consumers often seek variety in product design, style, durability, service, and location. As a result, the products of one firm are not perfect substitutes for those of another. In such cases, not all consumers switch to other suppliers when the price of one firm's output changes. Most firms are price searchers rather than price takers. In addition, barriers to entry sometimes limit competition. In the next two chapters, we will examine markets where the firms are price searchers and will consider the importance of entry barriers into such markets.

KEY POINTS

➤ A firm that confronts a perfectly elastic demand for its product is a price taker. A firm that can raise its price without losing all its customers (and which must lower its price in order to sell more units) is a price searcher.

➤ To maximize profit, a price taker will expand output as long as the sale of additional units adds more to revenues than to costs. Therefore, the profit-maximizing price taker will produce the output level at which marginal revenue (and price) equals marginal cost.

➤ The price taker's short-run marginal cost curve (above its average variable cost) is its supply curve. The short-run market supply curve is the horizontal summation of the marginal cost curves (above *AVC*) of the firms in the industry.

➤ A firm experiencing losses, but anticipating that it will be able to cover its costs in the long run, will operate in the short run if it can cover its average variable costs. Conversely, the firm will shut down if it cannot cover average variable cost. A firm that does not anticipate being able to cover its average total cost even in the long run will minimize losses by immediately going out of business.

➤ When price exceeds average total cost, a firm will make economic profit. When entry barriers are absent, profits will attract new firms into the industry and stimulate the existing firms to expand. As the market supply increases, price will eventually fall to the level of average total cost, eliminating the economic profit.

➤ When the market price is less than the firm's average total cost, the resulting losses imply that the resources could be used to produce more value elsewhere. Losses will cause firms to leave the industry or to reduce the scale of their operations. As market supply declines, price will increase and eventually the firms remaining in the market will be able to earn normal returns (zero economic profit).

➤ As the output of an industry expands, marginal costs will increase in the short run, causing the short-run market supply curve to slope upward to the right. Normally, as industry output expands, rising factor prices will push the costs of each firm upward, causing the long-run market supply curve to slope upward to the right.

➤ In the short run, "fixed" resources like the size of the firm's plant will limit the ability of firms to expand output quickly. In the long run, firms can alter the size of their plants and other resources that are fixed in the short run. As a result, the market supply curve will generally be more elastic in the long run.

➤ Firms earn economic profit by producing goods that can be sold for more than the cost of the resources required for their production. Profit is a reward for actions that increase the value of resources. Conversely, losses are a penalty imposed on those who reduce the value of resources.

➤ The competitive process provides strong pressure for producers to operate efficiently and heed the views of consumers. Competition and the market process harness self-interest and use it to direct producers toward wealth-creating activities.

CRITICAL ANALYSIS QUESTIONS

*1. Farmers are often heard to complain about the high costs of machinery, labor, and fertilizer, suggesting that these costs drive down their profit rate. Does it follow that if, for example, the price of fertilizer fell by 10 percent, farming (a highly competitive industry with low barriers to entry) would be more profitable? Explain.

*2. If the firms in a price-taker market are making short-run profits, what will happen to the market price in the long run? Explain.

3. "In a price-taker market, if a business operator produces efficiently—that is, if the cost of producing the good is minimized—the operator will be able to make at least a normal profit." True or false? Explain.

4. Suppose that the government of a large city levies a 5 percent sales tax on hotel rooms. How will the tax affect (a) prices of hotel rooms, (b) the profits of hotel owners, and (c) gross (including the tax) expenditures on hotel rooms?

*5. Within the framework of the price-taker model, how will an unanticipated increase in demand for a product affect each of the following in a market that was initially in long-run equilibrium?

a. The short-run market price of the product
b. Industry output in the short run
c. Profitability in the short run
d. The long-run market price in the industry
e. Industry output in the long run
f. Profitability in the long run

*6. Suppose that the development of a new drought-resistant hybrid seed corn leads to a 50 percent increase in the average yield per acre without increasing the cost to the farmers who use the new technology. If the producers in the corn production industry are price takers, what will happen to the following?

a. The price of corn
b. The profitability of corn farmers who quickly adopt the new technology
c. The profitability of corn farmers who are slow to adopt the new technology
d. The price of soybeans, a substitute product for corn

7. "When the firms in the industry are just able to cover their cost of production, economic profit is zero. Therefore, if there is a reduction in demand causing prices to go down even a little bit, all of the firms in the industry will be driven out of business." True or false? Explain.

8. Why does the short-run market supply curve for a product slope upward to the right? Why does the long-run market supply curve generally slope upward to the right? Why is the long-run market supply curve generally more elastic than the short-run supply curve?

9. How does competition among firms affect the incentive of each firm to (a) operate efficiently (produce at a low per-unit cost) and (b) produce goods that consumers value? What happens to firms that fail to do these two things?

10. Will firms in a price-taker market be able to earn profits in the long run? Why or why not? What are the major determinants of profitability for a firm? Discuss.

*11. During the summer of 1988, drought conditions throughout much of the United States substantially reduced the size of the corn, wheat, and soybean crops, three commodities for which demand is inelastic. Use the price-taker model to determine how the drought affected (a) grain prices, (b) revenue from the three crops, and (c) the profitability of farming.

12. Why is competition in a market important? Is there a positive or negative impact on the economy when strong competitive pressures drive various firms out of business? Discuss.

*13. The accompanying table presents the expected cost and revenue data for the Tucker Tomato Farm. The Tuckers produce tomatoes in a greenhouse and sell them wholesale in a price-taker market.

a. Fill in the firm's marginal cost, average variable cost, average total cost, and profit schedules.
b. If the Tuckers are profit maximizers, how many tomatoes should they produce when the market price is $500 per ton? Indicate their profits.
c. Indicate the firm's output level and maximum profit if the market price of tomatoes increases to $550 per ton.
d. How many units would the Tucker Tomato Farm produce if the price of tomatoes declined to $450? Indicate the firm's profits. Should the firm continue in business? Explain.

COST AND REVENUE SCHEDULES—TUCKER TOMATO FARM, INC.

OUTPUT (TONS PER MONTH)	TOTAL COST	PRICE PER TON	MARGINAL COST	AVERAGE VARIABLE COST	AVERAGE TOTAL COST	PROFITS (MONTHLY)
0	$1,000	$500				
1	1,200	500				
2	1,350	500				
3	1,550	500				
4	1,900	500				
5	2,300	500				
6	2,750	500				
7	3,250	500				
8	3,800	500				
9	4,400	500				
10	5,150	500				

14. In the accompanying table, you are given information about two firms that compete in a price-taker market. Assume that fixed costs for each firm are $20.

a. Complete the table.

b. What is the lowest price at which firm A will produce?

c. How many units of output will it produce at that price? (Assume that it cannot produce fractional units.)

d. What is the lowest price at which firm B will produce?

e. How many units of output will it produce?

f. How many units will firm A produce if the market price is $20?

g. How many units will firm B produce at the $20 price? (Assume it cannot produce fractional units.)

h. If each firm's total fixed costs are $20 and the price of output is $20, which firm would be receiving a higher net profit or smaller loss?

i. How much would that net profit or loss be?

FIRM A				FIRM B			
QUANTITY	TOTAL VARIABLE COST	MARGINAL COST	AVERAGE VARIABLE COST	QUANTITY	TOTAL VARIABLE COST	MARGINAL COST	AVERAGE VARIABLE COST
1	$ 24			1	$ 8		
2	30			2	10		
3	38			3	16		
4	48			4	24		
5	62			5	36		
6	82			6	56		
7	110			7	86		

*Asterisk denotes questions for which answers are given in Appendix B.

CHAPTER 10

[T]he price to the price-searcher is not determined for him as if by some impersonal market mechanism. Instead he must search out the optimal (wealth-maximizing) price. And, not knowing the demand schedule exactly, he will have to resort to retrial-and-error search processes.

Armen A. Alchian and William R. Allen[1]

Price-Searcher Markets with Low Entry Barriers

CHAPTER FOCUS

- Why do firms engage in competitive advertising and price cutting?
- How do price searchers act when entry barriers are low? How do consumers fare in such markets?
- What do entrepreneurs do? Why is the important role of the entrepreneur left out of economic models?
- What are contestable markets? Can contestable markets be competitive when there is room for only one or two rival firms?
- Why do some economists criticize price-searcher behavior when entry barriers are low, while others like the results?
- Why is competition critical to a prosperous, innovative economy?

[1]Armen A. Alchian and William R. Allen, *University Economics*, 2d ed. (Belmont, Calif.: Wadsworth Publishing Co., 1967), p. 113.

In the previous chapter we learned that price takers must accept the market price. They merely adjust their output to supply more units if they expect the cost of the additional units to be less than the market price. Price searchers have a more complex set of decisions to make in their search for profit. (See the chapter opening quotation from Professors Alchian and Allen.) In this chapter we consider the choices facing price searchers in markets where entry barriers are low. Low entry barriers are the key to competitive markets. When the restraints limiting entry are minimal, any opportunity for profit will attract competitors. Markets with low entry barriers, but where firms can raise their prices without losing all their customers, are descriptively referred to as **competitive price-searcher markets.**

Competitive price-searcher market
A market where the firms have a downward-sloping demand curve, and entry into and exit from the market are relatively easy.

How do firms that are price searchers choose price and output combinations? Are the business practices of price searchers inefficient? How important is competition to the performance of the economy? These are some of the important questions we will examine in this chapter.

COMPETITIVE PRICE-SEARCHER MARKETS

Competitive price-searcher markets are characterized by (1) low entry barriers and (2) *firms* that face a downward-sloping demand curve.[2] In contrast with price-taker markets where the firms produce identical products, price searchers produce **differentiated products.** The products supplied by the alternative sellers may differ in their design, dependability, location, ease of purchase, and a multitude of other factors. Sometimes economists use the term **monopolistic competition** to describe markets quite similar to those of the competitive price-searcher model. Since there is nothing "monopolistic" about these markets, we believe that this term is misleading. *Competitive price searcher* is much more descriptive of conditions in these markets. However, students should be aware that the expression "monopolistic competition" is often used to describe markets very much like those analyzed in this chapter.

Differentiated products
Products distinguished from similar products by such characteristics as quality, design, location, and method of promotion.

Monopolistic competition
Term often used by economists to describe markets characterized by a large number of sellers that supply differentiated products to a market with low barriers to entry. Essentially, it is an alternative term for competitive price-searcher markets.

Product differentiation explains why firms in price-searcher markets confront a downward-sloping demand curve. Ice cream from Häagen-Dazs is not identical to ice cream from Ben and Jerry's, Breyers, or Baskin-Robbins. Since some consumers are willing to pay more in order to get the specific product they like best, the *firm* will not lose all its customers to rivals if it raises its price. Rival firms, however, supply products that are quite similar to that supplied by the price searcher, so if the firm raises its price too much, many of its consumers will switch to the substitutes. ***Thus, the demand curve faced by the firm in a competitive price-searcher market will be highly elastic, because good substitutes for its output are readily available from other suppliers.***

[2]Note that the *firm* faces a downward-sloping demand curve in a price-searcher market. In price-taker markets, the *firm* will confront a perfectly elastic demand. Of course, the *market* demand curve will be downward sloping in a price-taker market.

In the highly competitive desktop computer market, firms use style, service, ease of operation, flexibility, and product dependability as competitive weapons. Firms in this market are price searchers.

The price searcher must choose between lower prices with larger quantities sold, and higher prices with smaller sales. ***Although a price searcher can set the price for its products, market forces will determine the quantity sold at alternative prices.*** In trying to find the profit-maximizing price and quantity combination, therefore, price searchers must try to estimate not just one market price, but how buyers will respond to the various prices that might be charged. In effect, price searchers must estimate the relationship between price and quantity demanded for their product. And the complexity does not end there.

Demand is not simply a given for a price searcher. The firm, by changing product quality, location, and service (among many other factors) and by advertising, can alter the demand for its products. It can increase demand by drawing customers from rivals if it can convince consumers that its products provide more value. When an airline adopts a more generous frequent-flier program or a soap manufacturer provides "cents-off" coupons, each is trying to make its product a little more attractive than rival products. The precise effects of such decisions cannot easily be predicted, but they can make the difference between profit and loss for the firm. In the real world, most firms occupy this complex and risky territory of the price searcher.

Sellers in competitive price-searcher markets face competition both from firms already producing in the market and from potential new entrants into the market. If profits are present, firms can expect that new rivals will be attracted. Because of the low entry barriers, competitive forces will be strong in price-searcher markets.

PRICE AND OUTPUT IN COMPETITIVE PRICE-SEARCHER MARKETS

How does a price searcher decide what price to charge and what level of output to produce? As the price searcher reduces price in order to expand output and sales, there will be two conflicting influences on total revenue. As **Exhibit 10–1** illustrates, the increase in sales (from q_1 to q_2) due to the lower price will, by itself, add to the revenue of the price searcher. The price reduction, however, also applies to units *that would otherwise have been sold at a higher price* (P_1, rather than the lower price, P_2). This factor by itself will cause a reduction in total revenue. As price is reduced in order to sell additional units, these two conflicting forces will result in marginal revenue—that is, change in total revenue—that is less than the sales price of the additional units. Since the price of units that could have been sold at the higher price must also be reduced, the price searcher's marginal revenue will be less than price. As Exhibit 10–1 shows, the marginal revenue curve of the price searcher will always lie below the firm's demand curve.[3] (Remember, the lowercase *d* is used when the reference is to the *firm's* demand curve.)

Any firm can increase profits by expanding output as long as marginal revenue exceeds marginal cost. Therefore, a price searcher will lower price and expand output until marginal revenue is equal to marginal cost.

Exhibit 10–2 illustrates the profit-maximizing price and output. The price searcher will increase profit by expanding output to q, where marginal revenue is equal

When a firm faces a downward-sloping demand curve, a price reduction that increases sales will exert two conflicting influences on total revenue. First, total revenue will rise because of an increase in the number of units sold (from q_1 to q_2). However, revenue losses from the lower price (P_2) on units that could have been sold at a higher price (P_1) will at least partially offset the additional revenues from increased sales. Therefore, the marginal revenue curve will lie inside the firm's demand curve.

EXHIBIT 10–1

MARGINAL REVENUE OF A PRICE SEARCHER

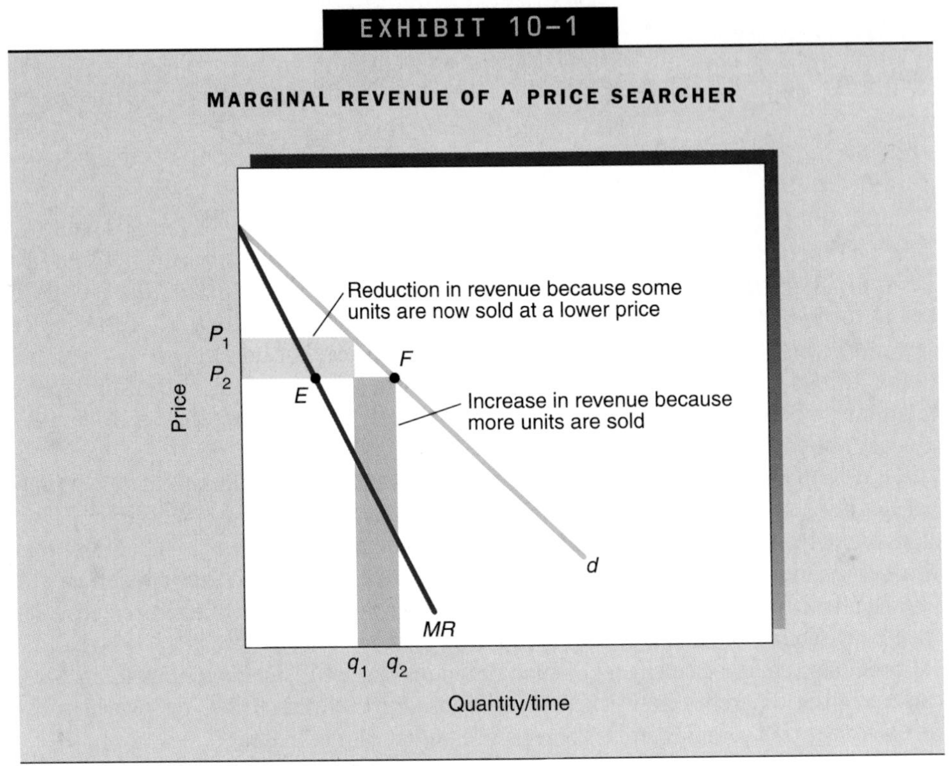

[3]For a straight-line demand curve, the marginal revenue curve will bisect any line parallel to the x-axis. For example, the MR curve will divide the line P_2F into two equal parts, P_2E and EF.

EXHIBIT 10–2

THE PRICE SEARCHER'S PRICE AND OUTPUT

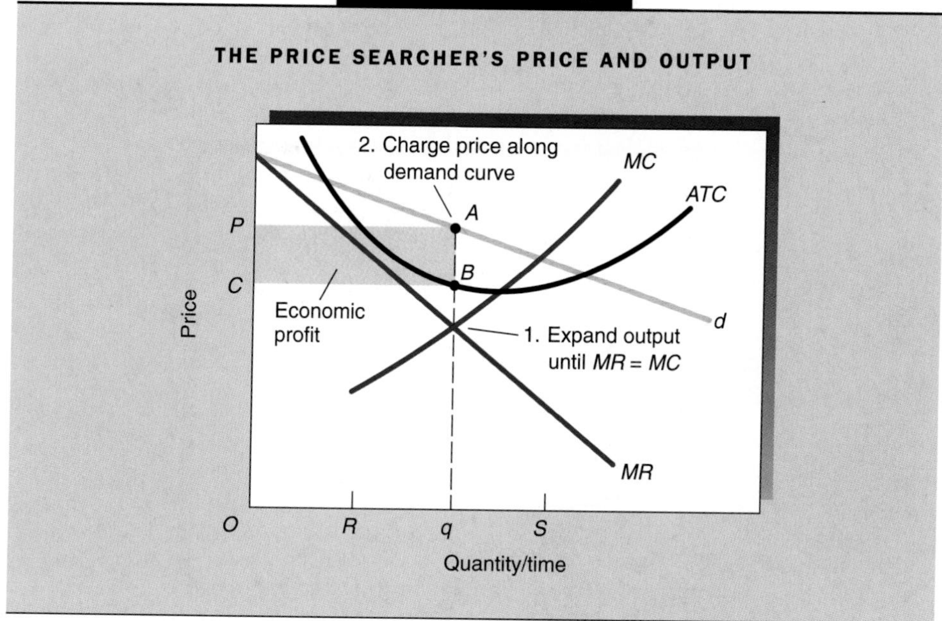

A price searcher maximizes profits by producing output q, *for which* MR = MC, *and charging price* P. *The firm is making economic profits. What impact will they have, if this is a typical firm?*

to marginal cost and price *P* can be charged. Beyond *q*, the price reduction required for the sale of additional output would reduce the firm's profit. For any output level less than *q* (for example, *R*), a price reduction and sales expansion will add more to total revenues than to total costs. At output *R*, marginal revenues exceed marginal costs. Thus, profits will be greater if price is reduced so output can be expanded. On the other hand, if output exceeds *q* (for example, *S*), sale of additional units beyond *q* will add more to costs (*MC*) than to revenues (*MR*). The firm will therefore gain by raising the price to *P*, even though the price rise will result in the loss of some customers. Profits will be maximized by charging price *P* and producing the output level *q*, where $MC = MR$.

The firm pictured in Exhibit 10–2 is making an economic profit. Total revenues *PAqO* exceed the firm's total costs *CBqO* at the profit-maximizing output level. Given the low barriers to entry, profits will attract rivals. Other firms will enter the market and attempt to produce a similar product (or service).

What will the entry of new rivals do to the demand for the products of the firms already in the market? These new rivals will draw customers away from existing firms, reducing their demand. As long as new entrants expect to make economic profits, additional competitors will be attracted to the market. This pressure will continue until the competition among rivals has shifted the demand curve of the typical price searcher inward far enough to eliminate economic profits. In the long run, as illustrated by **Exhibit 10–3**, a price searcher in a market with low entry barriers will just be able to cover its production costs. It will produce at the $MR = MC$ output level. The entry of the new competitors will force the price of the typical firm down to the level of average per-unit cost. Once economic profit has been eliminated for a firm so that its costs are just equaled by its revenues, potential competitors are likely to seek other, greener pastures.

If losses are present in a specific market, with time, some of the firms in the market will go out of business. Losses are the market's way of saying that some of the resources currently being used by a firm are more valuable in other uses. (See Applications in Economics: The Positive Side of Business Failure.) As firms leave, some of

Since entry and exit are free, competition will eventually drive prices down to the level of average total cost for the representative price searcher.

EXHIBIT 10-3

COMPETITIVE PRICE SEARCHER AND LONG-RUN NORMAL PROFIT

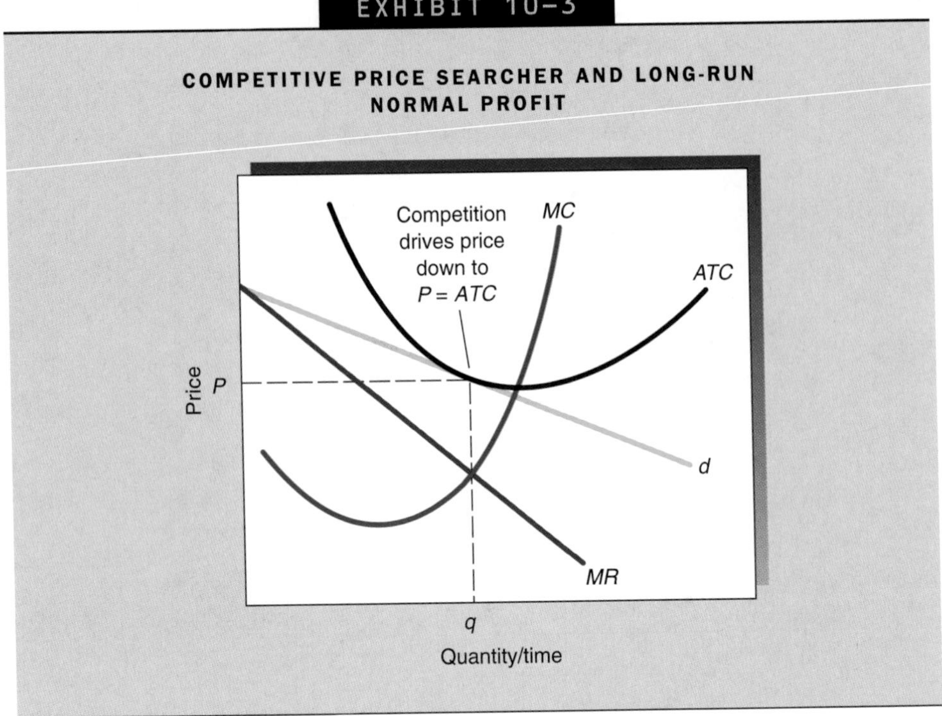

their previous customers will buy from other firms. The demand curve facing the remaining firms in the industry will be shifted outward by this process until the economic losses are eliminated and the long-run, zero-profit equilibrium illustrated by Exhibit 10–3 is restored.

Whenever firms can freely enter and exit a market, profits and losses play an important role in determining the size of the industry. Economic profits will attract new competitors to the market. The increased availability of the product (and similar products) will drive the price down until the profits are eliminated. Conversely, economic losses will cause competitors to exit from the market. The decline in the availability of the product (supply) will allow the price to rise until firms are once again able to cover their average total costs.

In the short run, a price searcher may make either economic profits or losses, depending on market conditions. After long-run adjustments have been made, however, only a normal profit (that is, zero economic profit) will be possible because of the competitive conditions caused by freedom of entry. As we will see in the following section, price adjustments are sometimes made even before entry occurs, in order to prevent that entry.

CONTESTABLE MARKETS AND THE COMPETITIVE PROCESS

Markets with few sellers are sometimes more competitive than they seem. Consider the case of the airline route between Salt Lake City, Utah, and Albuquerque, New Mexico. Only two airlines serve this route directly, since it has so little traffic. Further, there would seem to be high barriers to entry, since it takes multimillion-dollar airplanes to

APPLICATIONS IN ECONOMICS

The Positive Side of Business Failure

Each year, new businesses start up and others expand. At the same time, still other businesses will be contracting and some of them will be forced out of business and into bankruptcy. Business successes bring about the improved quality, price reductions, and increased product availability that are the core ingredients of economic progress. Each success, however, means failure elsewhere as buyers switch their purchases and resources are bid away from established businesses. So economic progress brings not only business success, but also business failure.

Economists Dwight Lee and Richard McKenzie point out that in a progressive market economy, business failure is inevitable.[1] More than that, they say, business failure is a blessing in disguise. Losses—and bankruptcy in extreme cases—provide both the information and the incentives to move resources to more highly valued, more productive uses. However, because business failure is painful for the investors, managers, and employees involved, there is constant political pressure to subsidize firms on the verge of bankruptcy, particularly if they are large.

Lee and McKenzie point out, though, that government support for failing firms is generally wasteful. The resources have a higher value elsewhere. The failure of an inefficient firm provides its employees and other suppliers with the signal and the incentive to search for the higher-valued uses for their resources, including their talents. The customers, workers, and capital of resource-wasting firms will become available for use by more-efficient, low-cost producers only if inefficient, high-cost businesses are allowed to fail. In turn, their failure will release the resources for use by more productive firms, and thereby help to promote economic growth and progress.

[1]Dwight R. Lee and Richard B. McKenzie, *Failure and Progress: The Bright Side of the Dismal Science* (Washington, D.C.: Cato Institute, 1993).

compete, as well as facilities for reservations, ticketing, baggage handling, and so on. The two airlines are well aware of the rivalry (with or without competition) between them, and they both charge a similar price. One might expect the price to be high, substantially above the cost of the service. But there is reason to believe that the two airlines, much as they would like to collude and drive up the price, will not be able to do so, as long as other airlines are free to enter this market.

To compete on an airline route may require millions of dollars in equipment, but if there is no problem with renting access to airport facilities, then the barriers to entry are much lower than equipment costs suggest. The Salt Lake City–Albuquerque market, for example, can be entered simply by shifting aircraft, personnel, and equipment from other locations. The aircraft can even be rented or leased. By the same token, if a new entrant (or an established firm) wants to leave that market, nearly all the invested capital values can be recovered, through shifting the aircraft and other capital equipment to other routes, or leasing them to other firms.

When there are no legal barriers restricting entry, an airline route is a classic case of a **contestable market:** The costs of entry and exit are low, so a firm risks little by entering.[4] If entry is later judged to be a mistake, exit is relatively easy because large components of the capital costs are recoverable. Entry into a contestable market may require substantial amounts of financial capital, but so long as it is largely recoverable, the large capital requirement is not a major deterrent (barrier) to entry.

Contestable market
A market in which the costs of entry and exit are low, so a firm risks little by entering. Efficient production and zero economic profits should prevail in a contestable market. A market can be contestable even if capital requirements are high.

In a contestable market, potential competition, as well as actual entry, can discipline firms selling in the market. When entry and exit are not expensive, even a single seller in a market faces the serious prospect of competition. Contestable markets yield

[4]The classic article on this topic is William J. Baumol's "Contestable Markets: An Uprising in the Theory of Industry Structure," *American Economic Review* 72 (March 1982): 1–15.

Airliners are extremely expensive and their cost might be a barrier to entry. But airplanes can be leased and are highly mobile among markets, as are pilots, flight attendants, and office workers. These highly mobile resources allow firms to enter into a given air transport market, and to leave it, with relative ease. Such a market is contestable.

two important results: (1) prices will not for long be higher than the level necessary to achieve zero economic profits, and (2) minimum cost of production will occur. This is true because both prices above costs and inefficiency in production present a profitable opportunity to new entrants. Potential competitors who see an opportunity for economic profit can be expected to enter and drive the price down to the level of per-unit costs.

These results do have a policy implication: If policy makers are concerned that a market is not sufficiently competitive, they should consider what might be done to make the market in question contestable. Much of the enthusiasm of economists for deregulation can be traced to the fact that regulation often is the primary restraint to entry. Many economists believe that deregulation permitting new entry can make many markets contestable, achieving lower prices and more efficiency than can direct regulation of producers.

Our model of price and output for price-searcher markets with low entry barriers is, of course, a very much simplified view of the real world. It is important to recognize that since this ongoing competitive process is at work, the experience of a specific market participant may differ considerably from that of the "typical firm" being discussed. The market process is complex, and competition is ongoing and dynamic. How much advertising should a seller purchase? Should a new model, with slightly different features, be produced? Would more or fewer places of business add to the firm's profits? Decisions on each of these changes must, if more profit is being sought, be made according to the marginal principle. That is, if the change adds more to revenue than to cost, it should be made. How much of a change? Up to the point where $MC = MR$! But identifying that point for each potential change is difficult, since it involves predictions about what would happen if the change is made. The principles to apply are clear, but estimating the impact of various changes is fraught with uncertainty. Complex judgments about potential costs and potential benefits are required before an entrepreneur can hope to match MC with MR. With this in mind, we turn now to a brief discussion of the important variable not found in economic models: entrepreneurship.

THE LEFT-OUT VARIABLE: ENTREPRENEURSHIP

To help us understand facts and make predictions, a scientific model must simplify what it describes, and draw attention to the most important relationships. Economic models are no exception. The model of decision making within business firms is

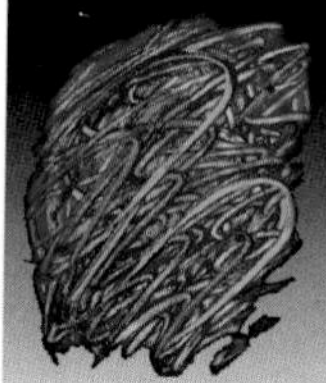

APPLICATIONS IN ECONOMICS

Entrepreneurs at the Helm of Some Bizarre Occupations

These innovative people see a need and find a niche in the market

By David Young
(CHICAGO TRIBUNE)

Mike Turk lost a coin toss and wound up with a thousand teak trophy bases he couldn't get rid of. So he bolted Army surplus hand grenades to them and sold them for $15 apiece as desk ornaments.

Joseph Tokarski, a postal worker contemplating a post-retirement business, found something of an aftermarket—cleaning up Canada goose droppings.

"There are two important dimensions to being an entrepreneur: "The first is risk and the second is innovation," said Sumaria Mohan-Neill, professor of entrepreneurship at Roosevelt University's College of Business Administration.

"To succeed, a person has to be innovative. Some would call it bizarre," she added.

Turk and Tokarski are among what may be scores of entrepreneurs around Chicago who have found unusual business niches and somehow make their livings at bizarre occupations. They manufacture odd products, they provide unusual services and some sell the grotesque.

Sometimes these entrepreneurs accidentally find their callings; sometimes out of desperation they gravitate to odd occupations after losing their regular jobs; and in some cases, they are able to turn their hobbies into going business concerns.

"People leverage their knowledge," said Steven C. Michael, business administration professor at the University of Illinois' College of Commerce in Urbana.

According to Michael, entrepreneurs have a vision of their mission and are able to sell that to other people, but they also have to be flexible enough to change course.

"Entrepreneurs don't spot markets. They spot needs and assemble the skills to fill them," says Michael, and that's the genesis of Magic Mound Mover, Joseph Tokarski's business.

Tokarski said he developed a vacuum system to clean up the backyard scat from his own dogs because no one else in the family would do the chore. The device worked so well that he decided to mount it on a golf cart and go after a problem common in Midwestern open spaces: Canada goose droppings.

A little advertising in local newspapers and by word of mouth has resulted in jobs with apartment complexes, park districts and school systems cleaning up after the ubiquitous geese.

Similarly, coming up with a clever idea to solve a problem played a big role for Turk, who was working in the family-owned surplus business Surplus Trading Corp. in Benton Harbor, Mich. Only for Turk, the problem was what to do with 1,000 teak trophy bases he acquired on the toss of coin that determined their price.

"We have all kinds of ways of doing deals in the surplus business," concedes Turk, who over the years has bought and sold 85 dozen women's panties from Victoria's Secret, 60 cases of olive oil and 500 pounds of hard candy.

But he couldn't unload the teak at any price, so he decided to turn them into novelty items. He bolted Army surplus hand grenades to the bases and attached plaques that read, "Complaint Department: Take a number." The number is attached to the detonating pin. He has sold hundreds of them.

Turk and Tokarski are lucky ones; the failure rate for entrepreneurs is high, possibly as much as 70 to 80 percent, according to business scholars.

"Complaint Department: Take a number."

designed to highlight the choices common to all firms, and it performs this job quite well. But it leaves out some important elements of the business decision-making process. Furthermore, it glosses over the complexity of other decisions that must be made by real-world entrepreneurs.

Would profits increase if prices were raised, or would lower prices lead to larger profits? Real-world decision makers cannot go into the back room and look at their demand-cost diagram to answer these questions. They must search for clues, experiment with actual price changes, and interpret what they see, often using a great deal of "seat-of-the-pants" judgment. The successful entrepreneur will search and find (or at least approximate) the profit-maximizing price—the $MR = MC$ price-and-output combination that our model shows so simply.

Our models indicate how entrepreneurs will react to profit and loss in a specific market and explain why their reactions will tend to direct markets toward equilibrium. They do not, however, explain how and when new products will be developed or new production techniques applied. Decisions in these areas involve entrepreneurial judgment and discovery in an uncertain world. How will consumers react to a potential new product? Can it be produced profitably? How can the necessary finances for additional capital assets or a new business venture be obtained? Would adoption of a new production process or alternative technology reduce cost? Could per-unit costs be reduced if the firm offered a different combination of products and services? Could a successful business activity in one area be expanded to other locations? If so, what would be the best way to expand? All these questions and many more require entrepreneurial judgment.

Entrepreneurial judgment is necessary when there is no decision rule that can be applied using only information that is freely available. For this reason, we are unable to incorporate fully the function of the entrepreneur into economic models. There simply is no way to model these complex decisions that involve uncertainty, discovery, and business judgment. All we can do is note the importance of entrepreneurial judgment and recognize that our models are limited because they are unable to capture this critical element of both business success and economic progress.

APPLICATIONS IN ECONOMICS

Three Entrepreneurs Who Have Changed Our Lives

Unlike movie stars and athletes, business entrepreneurs seldom command great respect in our society. Often, their contributions are either overlooked or misunderstood. In a competitive economy, entrepreneurs get ahead by discovering better ways of doing things, such as new production techniques that reduce cost or new products that are highly valued (relative to their cost). An interesting aspect of entrepreneurship is that it often comes from unusual sources—people who have an ability to think about and institute unconventional ideas.

Of course, highly successful entrepreneurs make a lot of money. Remember, however, that trade helps both the buyer and the seller. To be successful, entrepreneurs must provide their customers with value—a better deal than they can get elsewhere. Thus, they are an important source of economic progress. Highly successful entrepreneurs often exert enormous impact on our lives, far more than most of us realize. Consider how three key entrepreneurs of our age have affected our lives.[1]

Samuel M. Walton (1917–1992) Sam Walton worked his way through the University of Missouri with odd jobs, including delivering newspapers, waiting tables, and life guarding. After college, he first became a management trainee with JCPenney department stores, the second-largest retailer in the United States at the time. He stayed with Penney's for less than two years. After two years in the military, Walton

(continued)

purchased a Ben Franklin department store franchise in Arkansas. Over the next decade, he was able to open several new stores. Because each Ben Franklin store was an independently owned franchise, Walton had little influence on the overall direction of the company.

Frustrated with some of the corporate policies, he opened up his own store called Discount City in 1962. The business was not even incorporated until 1969. Soon the name was changed to Wal-Mart and, beginning with two stores in Arkansas, Sam Walton developed it into the largest retail chain in America. Today there are more than 2,800 Wal-Mart stores, and in 1998, its sales were more than $115 billion.

What accounts for the success of Wal-Mart? Initially, Walton did not attempt to compete with the big stores, such as Sears or Montgomery Ward. Instead, he focused on smaller towns without a major department store. His cost-saving distribution warehouse centers and innovative use of inventory control technology allowed Walton to provide consumers with brand-name goods at prices below those of his competitors. The firm spends about $500 million per year in information technology, utilizing its daily sales data to track and predict where inventory flows will be needed. Low cost, volume sales, great prices, and convenience of location—Walton used this recipe to provide consumers with more value than they could get elsewhere. It made Walton one of the richest men in America and Wal-Mart the nation's leading retailer.

Ted Turner (1938–) Rejected by Harvard, Ted Turner went to Brown University. Originally enrolled as a humanities major, he eventually shifted his major to economics. His studies in economics, however, did not occupy enough of his time to keep him out of trouble while in college. After being thrown out of his fraternity, Kappa Sigma, he was later expelled from college during his senior year.

After his failed attempt at college, Turner worked in his father's outdoor billboard business and eventually took over the company. In 1970 he risked his assets in the billboard business to acquire an unprofitable TV station, WTCG, in Atlanta. He renamed the station WTBS, the "Superstation," and managed to get it on many of the local cable systems around the country. The station offered mostly movies and major league baseball after Turner purchased the Atlanta Braves.

In 1980, Turner risked all his assets and arranged for additional financing through the "junk bond" market in order to launch a 24-hour news network, a network that is now known to the world as CNN (Cable News Network). Most experts in the TV industry predicted the venture would fail. Prior to his final decision to start CNN, Turner's own employees gave him the following message: "Please, Ted! Don't do this to us! If you commit to a venture of this size you'll sink the whole company!"

Of course, risk taking is an integral part of entrepreneurship. Few, however, have risked so much on ideas that were so widely viewed as long shots. Propelled by Turner's determination and confidence concerning what Americans wanted to watch on television, the venture succeeded. The market has verified his judgment. By 1991 Turner's cable TV operations (WTBS, CNN, TNT, and Headline News) attracted one-third of the cable TV listening audience. Turner's news stations are now widely viewed around the world. In 1995, he sold his broadcasting businesses to media giant Time Warner, receiving $7.5 billion in the bargain and becoming vice chairman of that firm. Who would have predicted that a college dropout who obtained his business experience in billboard advertising would change the way the world watches television, and become a billionaire in the process?

William "Bill" Gates III (1955–) Even as a child, Bill Gates loved computers. At the early age of 15 he earned $20,000 by writing a computer program to help manage traffic. He entered Harvard at the age of 17, and while still an undergraduate, developed BASIC for the first microcomputer, the MITS Altair. Convinced that eventually most offices and homes would have a microcomputer, Gates, along with his friend Paul Allen, created Microsoft in 1975. The focus of the business was the development of software designed to make microcomputers both more useful and more user friendly.

Gates quickly earned a reputation as a programming genius. When IBM decided to enter the personal computer (PC) market in 1980, they contracted with Gates to provide the basic operating software for their computers, a system now known as MS-DOS. Gates reserved the rights to sell his MS-DOS software to other firms. As IBM (and IBM clones) grew to dominate the PC market during the 1980s, Gates's fortune rose as well. Microsoft developed into the dominant firm in the computer software industry. Gates's programs are now used to run more than 90 percent of the world's computers. Gates's MS-DOS–based software programs, Windows 95 and Windows 98, are among the most popular in the world. By the end of 1998, Bill Gates's personal fortune was estimated at more than $50 billion.

Gates attributes his success to his workaholic nature. He continues to work long hours and is still actively involved in the operation and strategic decision making of Microsoft. If you have ever used a computer, you have almost certainly benefited from programs that Gates created. His remarkable programming genius has changed the way we use personal computers both at home and in the workplace.

---

[1]See Gene N. Landrum, *Profiles of Genius* (Buffalo: Prometheus Books, 1993); and Robert F. Hartley, *Management Mistakes and Successes* (New York: John Wiley and Sons, Inc., 1994), for additional information on entrepreneurship and the personalities of this feature.

The Entrepreneur: A Job Description

If we cannot put entrepreneurship into our models, what can we say about its function? One way to answer this question is to consider a generalized job description for an entrepreneurial position. An investor who lacks the desire, or perhaps the skill, to be an entrepreneur, but nonetheless wants to be in business, may seek someone to act as the business entrepreneur, while the investor provides some of the capital. A newspaper ad to find such a person (though perhaps not the usual way for the investor to search) might read as follows:

> *Wanted: Entrepreneur.* Diverse skills required. Must be (1) alert to new business opportunities and to new problems before they become obvious; (2) willing to back judgments with investments of hard work and creative effort before others recognize correctness of judgments; (3) able to make correct decisions and to convince others of their validity, so as to attract additional financial backing; and (4) able to recognize own inevitable mistakes and to back away from incorrect decisions without wasting additional resources. Exciting, exhausting, high-risk position. Pay will be very good for success, and very poor for failure.

Entrepreneurship is not for the faint-hearted or the lazy. Entrepreneurs are at the center of the action in the real world, even if they do not have a place in most economic models.[5]

An Evaluation of Competitive Price-Searcher Markets

As we saw earlier, determination of price and output for price searchers is in some ways similar to that for price takers. Because the long-run, equilibrium conditions in price-taker markets are consistent with ideal economic efficiency, it is useful to compare and contrast them with conditions in price-searcher markets when entry barriers are low. There are both similarities and differences.

Neither price takers nor price searchers in markets with low entry barriers will be able to earn long-run economic profit. Competing firms drawn by economic profits—that is, returns greater than opportunity costs—will enter until, in the long run, competition has driven the market price down to the level of average total cost. In each case, entrepreneurs have a strong incentive to manage and operate their businesses efficiently. Inefficient operation will lead to higher costs, losses, and forced exit from the market. Price takers and competitive price searchers alike will be motivated to develop and adopt new cost-reducing procedures and techniques because lower costs will mean higher short-run profits (or at least smaller losses).

The response to changing demand conditions in price-taker and price-searcher markets with low entry barriers is similar. In both cases, an increase in market demand leads to higher prices, short-run profits, expansion of the existing producers, and the entry of new firms. With the entry of new producers, and the concurrent expansion of existing firms, the market supply will increase, placing downward pressure on price. The process will continue until the market price falls to the level of average total cost, squeezing out all economic profit.

---

[5]For a more complete overview of entrepreneurship and references on the topic, see Mark Crosson, "Entrepreneurship," in *The New Palgrave: A Dictionary of Economics*, ed. John Eatwell et al. (New York: Stockton Press, 1987), pp. 151–153.

Retail stores usually have location, selection, and other differences to protect them from direct competition. But profits draw close substitutes, while losses dictate exit from the market in the highly competitive retail sector.

Similarly, a reduction in demand will lead to lower prices and short-run losses, causing output to fall and some firms to exit. As the market supply declines, prices will rise and eventually the short-run losses will be eliminated and the firms remaining in the industry will once again be able to cover their costs. Regardless of whether the firms are price takers or price searchers, profits and losses will direct their output decisions when barriers to entry are low.

As **Exhibit 10–4** illustrates, while the price taker confronts a horizontal demand curve, the demand curve faced by a price searcher is downward sloping. This is important because it means that the marginal revenue of the price searcher will be less than, rather than equal to, the price charged for the quantity sold. So, when the profit-maximizing price searcher expands output until $MR = MC$, price will still exceed marginal cost (panel b). In contrast, the price charged by a profit-maximizing price taker will equal marginal cost (panel a). In addition, when a price searcher is in long-run equilibrium, the firm's output rate will be less than the rate that would minimize average total cost. The price searcher would have a lower per-unit cost (97 cents rather than $1) if a larger output were produced.

Allocative Efficiency in Price-Searcher Markets with Low Entry Barriers

Are resources allocated efficiently in a price-searcher market with low barriers to entry? **Allocative efficiency** is achieved when the goods and services most desired by consumers are produced at the lowest possible cost. The efficiency of price searchers in markets with low entry barriers has been the subject of debate among economists for years.

Allocative efficiency
The allocation of resources to the production of goods and services most desired by consumers, at the lowest possible cost.

At one time, the dominant view seemed to be that allocative inefficiency results because price searchers fail to operate at an output level that minimizes their long-run average total cost. As a result of the proliferation in the number of firms, the sales of each competitor fall short of their least-cost capacity level. The potential social gain associated with the expansion of production to the $P = MC$ output rate is therefore lost. The advocates of this view argue that if there were fewer producers, each would be able to operate at the minimum-cost output rate. They see inefficiency resulting from costly duplication—too many producers operating below their minimum-cost output capacity. Two or more filling stations, restaurants, grocery stores, or similar establishments operating side by side are given as examples of the economic waste generated by price-searcher markets.

EXHIBIT 10-4

COMPARING PRICE-TAKER AND PRICE-SEARCHER MARKETS

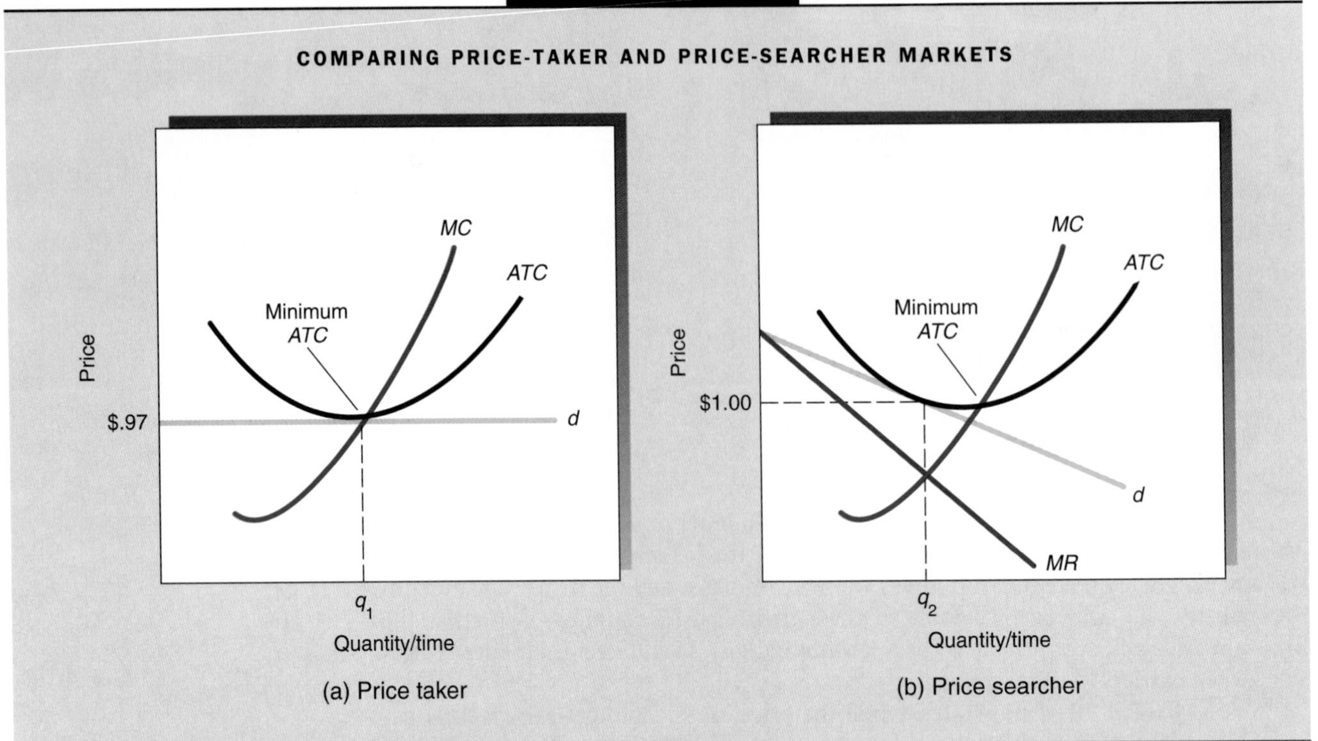

Here we illustrate the long-run equilibrium conditions of a price taker and a price searcher when entry barriers are low. In both cases, price is equal to average total cost, and economic profit is zero. However, since the price searcher confronts a downward-sloping demand curve for its product, its profit-maximizing price exceeds marginal cost, and output is not large enough to minimize average total cost when the market is in long-run equilibrium. For identical cost conditions, *the price of the product in a price-searcher market will be slightly higher than in a price-taker market. This slightly higher price is considered by some to be indicative of inefficiency, while others perceive it to be the premium a society pays for variety and convenience (product differentiation).*

In addition, the various price searchers' efforts to inform and convince consumers that their differentiated products are better than others also bring criticism. Their competitive advertising campaigns are charged with being self-defeating and wasteful. Firms have an incentive, critics say, to use advertising to promote artificial distinctions between similar products, and firms that do not engage in such advertising can expect their sales to decline. Advertising, though, consumes resources—thus it is costly from society's point of view—and it may lead to higher prices.

In recent years, this traditional view has been seriously challenged. Many economists now believe that it is mechanistic and fails to take into account the significance of dynamic competition. Most important, the traditional view assumes that consumers place no value on the wider variety of qualities and styles that result. Prices might very well be slightly lower if there were fewer gasoline stations, if they were located farther apart, and if they offered a more limited variety of service and credit plan options. Similarly, the prices of sandwiches and drinks might well be slightly lower if there were fewer fast-food restaurants, each a bit more congested and located less conveniently for some customers. However, customers value convenience, product diversity, and "having it their way," as well as lower prices. Thus, many economists now argue that consumers are served quite well by price-searcher markets. In this view, the higher prices (and costs) are simply the premium consumers pay for ease of purchase, variety, and personalized products.

When consumers enjoy differentiated products, one cannot conclude that uniform products with a lower price, but less variety from which to select, would be preferable to products of greater diversity with slightly higher prices. In fact, consumers often pay more for various unique products, rather than all flocking to a single, cheaper version when available. For example, many consumers purchase designer jeans and specialty shirts even when they are aware that equally durable, more standardized versions are available at a lower price.

The defenders of product diversity also deny that price-searcher markets lead to excessive, wasteful advertising. They point out that advertising often reduces the consumer's search time and provides valuable information about prices, new products, and new firms entering the market. Furthermore, if advertising results in higher prices with no compensating benefits, people can turn to cheaper, unadvertised products. After all, consumers are under no obligation to purchase advertised products. In fact, some price searchers use higher-quality service and lower prices to compete with rivals who advertise heavily. When consumers really prefer lower prices and less advertising, firms offering that combination will prosper.

A SPECIAL CASE: PRICE DISCRIMINATION

Thus far, we have assumed that all sellers of a product will charge each customer the same price. Sometimes, though, price searchers can increase their revenues (and profits) by charging different prices to different groups of consumers. Such businesses as hotels, restaurants, and drugstores often charge senior citizens less than other customers. Students and children are often given discounts at movie theaters and athletic events. Grocery stores commonly give discounts to customers who clip "cents off" coupons from newspapers or magazines. Colleges often give financial aid (reduced tuition) to students from less-wealthy families. These practices are called **price discrimination.** *To gain from such a practice, price searchers must be able to do two things: (1) identify and separate at least two groups with differing elasticities of demand, and (2) prevent those who buy at the low price from reselling to the customers charged higher prices.* Let us take a closer look at why sellers may find price discrimination advantageous. Suppose that a seller has two groups of customers: one with an inelastic demand for its product and the other with an elastic demand. An increase in the price charged the first group will increase the total revenue derived from that group. On the other hand, a reduction in price will increase revenues derived from the latter. Thus, a seller may be able to increase total revenue and profit by charging the first group a higher price than the second.

Price discrimination
A practice whereby a seller charges different consumers different prices for the same product or service.

The pricing of airline tickets illustrates the potential of price discrimination. The airline industry has found that the demand of business fliers is substantially more inelastic than the demand of vacationers, students, and other travelers. Thus, airlines usually charge high fares to persons who are unwilling to stay over a weekend, who spend only a day or two at their destination, and who make reservations a short time before their flight. These high fares fall primarily on business travelers who are less sensitive to price. In contrast, discount fares are offered to fliers willing to make reservations well in advance, travel during off-peak hours, and stay at their destinations over a weekend before returning home. Such travelers are likely to be vacationers and students, who are highly sensitive to price.

Exhibit 10–5 illustrates the logic of this policy. Panel a shows what would happen if a single price were charged to all customers. Given the demand, the profit-maximizing firm expands output to 100, where *MR* equals *MC*. The profit-maximizing price on coast-to-coast flights is $400, which generates $40,000 of revenue per flight. Since the marginal cost per passenger is $100, this provides the airline with net operating revenue of $30,000 with which to cover other costs.

However, as panel b shows, although the market demand schedule is unchanged, the airline can do even better if it uses price discrimination. When it charges business travelers $600, most of these passengers continue to travel since their demand is highly inelastic. On the other hand, a $100 price cut generates substantial additional ticket sales from vacationers, students, and others whose demands are more elastic. Therefore, with price discrimination, the airline can sell 60 tickets (primarily to business travelers) at $600 and 60 additional tickets to others at $300. Total revenue jumps to $54,000 and leaves the airline with $42,000 ($54,000 minus 120 times the $100 marginal cost per passenger) of revenue in excess of variable cost. Compared to the single-price outcome (panel a), the price discrimination strategy expands profit by $12,000.

When sellers can segment their market (at a low cost) into groups with differing price elasticities of demand, price discrimination can increase profits. *For each group,* the seller will maximize profit by equating marginal cost and marginal revenue.

EXHIBIT 10–5

PRICE DISCRIMINATION

Price (coast-to-coast flights)
$400
Net operating revenue
$30,000
MC
MR
d
100
Output

(a) Seller charges a single price

Price (coast-to-coast flights)
$600
$300
Net operating revenue from business travelers
Net operating revenue from others
$30,000
$12,000
MC
d
60
120
Output

(b) Seller uses price discrimination

As panel a illustrates, a $400 ticket price will maximize profits on coast-to-coast flights if an airline charges a single price. *However, the airline can do still better if it raises the price to $600 for passengers (business travelers) with a highly inelastic demand and* reduces *the price to $300 for travelers (for example, students and vacationers) with a more elastic demand. When sellers can segment their market, they can gain by (a) charging a higher price to consumers with a less elastic demand and (b) offering discounts to customers whose demand is more elastic.*

This rule will lead to higher prices for groups with the most inelastic demand and lower prices for the groups with the most elastic demand. Compared to the single-price situation, price discrimination increases profitability because a higher price increases the net revenue from groups with an inelastic demand, while a lower price increases the net revenue from price-sensitive customers. With price discrimination, the number of units sold also increases (compare panel a with panel b) because the discounts provided to price-sensitive groups increase the quantity sold more than the higher prices charged the less price-sensitive groups reduce sales.

Sometimes price discrimination is subtle. Colleges engage in price discrimination by charging a high standard tuition to get additional revenue from high-income students with a more inelastic demand, while providing low-income students with scholarships based on need (tuition "discounts"). The partial-tuition scholarships given to students whose parents are less wealthy enable the college to attract students who have a more elastic demand. Low-income students thus are not priced out of the market by the high standard tuition.

How do buyers fare when a seller can price discriminate? Some buyers pay more than they would if a single intermediate price were offered. They purchase fewer units, and they are worse off. In contrast, those for whom the price discrimination process lowers the price are better off. Of course, with some products, such as airline transportation, a single buyer might be better off with some purchases and worse off with others.

On balance, however, we can expect that output will be greater with price discrimination than it would be with a single price. The market is not as understocked as it would have been in the absence of the price discrimination. Thus, from an allocative

Giving financial aid, in the form of lower tuition charges, to students from families with lower incomes—and who thus are likely to be more price sensitive—allows a college to practice price discrimination, charging a higher tuition price to those who are expected to be less price sensitive.

standpoint, price discrimination gets high marks; it allows more trades, reducing the allocative inefficiency due to price being set above marginal cost. Some of the gains that would accrue to consumers with an inelastic demand are transferred to the price searcher as increased revenue, but additional gains from trade are created by the increased output of goods that would be lost if the price searcher did not (or could not) price discriminate.

In some markets, there is an additional gain emanating from price discrimination: Production may occur that would be lost entirely if only a single price could be charged. With price discrimination, some otherwise unprofitable firms may be able to generate enough additional revenue to operate successfully in the marketplace. For example, some small towns in Montana might not provide enough revenue at a single price to enable a local physician to cover her opportunity costs. However, if she is able to discriminate on the basis of income, charging higher-income patients more than normal rates and lower-income patients less, the resulting revenues from practice in the small town may enable the physician to stay in the community. In this case, all residents of the town may be better off as the result of the price discrimination, because it makes it possible for them to access a local physician. After all, even those being charged the highest prices are not disadvantaged if the price discrimination keeps the physician in town. They are just as able to seek physician services elsewhere as they would have been in the absence of the price-discriminating local doctor. With or without price discrimination, access to competing sellers (or buyers) protects market participants from unfair treatment.

In summary, if potential customers can be segmented into groups with different elasticities of demand and retrading can be controlled at a low cost, sellers can often gain by charging higher prices to those with the more inelastic demand (and lower prices to those with an elastic demand). Price discrimination can also increase the total gains from trade and thereby reduce allocative inefficiency. Sometimes it even allows production where none would have otherwise occurred.

COMPETITION AMONG FIRMS: HOW IT INCREASES PROSPERITY

When barriers to entry are low, businesses must compete for the loyalty of customers. This is true for price takers and price searchers alike, for small-scale or large-scale firms, in local, regional, national, or even global markets. There are three major reasons why firms operating in a competitive environment will be a force promoting economic progress.

1. Competition places pressure on producers to operate efficiently and cater to the preferences of customers.
2. Competition provides firms with a strong incentive to develop improved products and discover lower-cost methods of production.
3. Competition causes firms to discover the type of business structure and size of business that can best keep the per-unit costs of production low.

EFFICIENT OPERATION AND CONSUMER SATISFACTION

First, competition weeds out the inefficient. An efficient firm will seek ways to cut costs by adopting lower-cost production techniques or figuring out how to produce a given output with fewer resources. In some cases, this will involve "downsizing," to use the terminology of the news media. Firms that fail to provide consumers with quality goods at competitive prices will experience losses and eventually be driven out of business, making the labor and capital they had employed available to other firms. Successful competitors have to outperform rival firms. They may do so through a variety of methods—quality of product, style, service, convenience of location, advertising, and price—but they must consistently offer consumers as much or more value than they can get elsewhere.

What keeps McDonald's, Wal-Mart, General Motors, or any other business firm from raising prices, selling shoddy products, and providing lousy service? Competition is the answer. If McDonald's fails to provide an attractively priced, tasty sandwich with a smile, people will turn to Burger King, Wendy's, Dairy Queen, and other rivals. If Wal-Mart does not provide convenience and value, people will turn to Sears, Kmart, and other retailers. Similarly, as recent experience has shown, even a firm as large as General Motors will lose customers to Ford, Honda, Toyota, Chrysler, Volkswagen, Mazda, and other automobile manufacturers if it fails to please the customer as much as rival suppliers.

Incentive for Innovation

When markets are competitive, suppliers have a strong incentive to be innovative. An entrepreneur who figures out how to produce a good more efficiently or who develops a new product that is highly valued relative to its cost gains an advantage over rivals. Such producers will earn larger profits.

Think of the new products that have been introduced during the last 50 years: microwave ovens, videocassette recorders, color television sets, personal computers, compact disc players, fax machines, cellular telephone service, drive-through food service, and coronary artery bypass devices come to mind. New, improved products are constantly upgrading the way that we live and work.

Since no one knows precisely what products consumers will want next or which production techniques will minimize per-unit costs, competition is necessary to motivate an attempt to discover the answers. Is that new visionary idea the greatest

Firms in the computer industry spend millions of dollars trying to differentiate their products in the eyes of consumers, but innovation is required for survival. The industry is highly competitive and innovations come at a rapid pace.

thing since the development of the fast-food chain? Or is it simply another dream that will soon turn to vapor? In a market economy, it is relatively easy to try new business ideas. One only needs to win the support of investors willing to finance the innovative new product or production technology. However, competition holds entrepreneurs and the investors who support them accountable: Their ideas must face a "reality check" imposed by consumers. Consumers must value the innovative idea enough to cover its cost. When competition is present, consumers are the ultimate judge and jury of business innovation and performance.

Since today's successful product may not pass tomorrow's competitive test, businesses in a competitive market must be good at anticipating, identifying, and quickly adopting improved ideas, whether their own or others'. Again, the ongoing, dynamic characteristic of competition must continually be considered.

Appropriate Structure, Size, and Scope

Competition also demands that a firm discover the type of business structure that best keeps the per-unit cost of its product or service low. Unlike other economic systems, a market economy does not mandate or limit the types of firms that are permitted to compete. Any form of business organization is permissible. An owner-operated firm, a partnership, a corporation, an employee-owned firm, a consumer cooperative, a commune, or any other form of business is free to enter the market. In order to be successful, however, a business structure must be cost-effective. A form of business organization that results in high per-unit cost will be driven from a competitive market by lower-cost rivals.

The same is true for the size of a firm. For some products, a business must be quite large to take full advantage of economies of scale. When per-unit costs decline as output increases, small businesses tend to have higher production costs (and therefore higher prices) than their larger counterparts. When this is the case, consumers interested in maximum value for their money will tend to buy from the lower-priced larger firm. Consequently, only large firms, generally organized as corporations, are able to survive in such markets. The auto and airplane manufacturing industries provide examples.

In other instances, small firms, often organized as individual proprietorships or partnerships, will be more cost-effective. When personalized service and individualized products are valued highly by consumers, it may be difficult for large firms to compete. Under these circumstances, mostly small firms will survive. For example, this is generally true for law and medical practices, printing shops, and hair-styling salons. A market economy permits cost considerations and the interaction between producers and consumers to determine the type and size of firm in each market.

The scope of a business is another variable determined in the market. Should a gasoline station stand alone, or should its scope be expanded to include auto repair services? Or should it instead be combined with a convenience store, or would a different combination create more value relative to cost? Numerous alternative combinations of business activities are possible. Differences in locations and other circumstances will often influence how well each is received. A new and better combination of products and services in the right place can generate a profit, at least temporarily until others catch on and provide close substitutes. In contrast, a business choosing the wrong scope of operation for the situation will earn less and it could be driven from the market by rivals offering a more appropriate scope of activities. Once again, consumer choices and market forces will determine the scope of operation that best fits the circumstances.

Rival firms struggle for the dollar votes of consumers. In order to succeed in a competitive environment, business entrepreneurs must figure out how to provide buyers with more attractive options—how to supply consumers with goods and services

that are valued highly relative to their costs. As they do so, they create wealth, increase the value of resources, and promote economic progress.

LOOKING *Ahead*

In this chapter we have analyzed the choices facing price searchers, and their behavior when barriers to entry are low. Next, we will see how barriers to entry might be formed, how price searchers react, and how the results differ when entry barriers are high rather than low.

KEY POINTS

➤ Firms in price-searcher markets with low barriers to entry face a downward-sloping demand curve. They are free to set the prices for the products that they sell, but face strong competitive pressure from existing and potential rivals.

➤ The mark of the price-searcher market with low barriers to entry is product differentiation. Price searchers use product quality, style, convenience of location, advertising, and price as competitive weapons. Because each firm competes with rivals offering similar products, each confronts a highly elastic demand curve for its products.

➤ A profit-maximizing price searcher will expand output as long as marginal revenue exceeds marginal cost, lowering its price in the process, until $MR = MC$. The price charged by the profit-maximizing price searcher will be greater than its marginal cost.

➤ If firms in a price-searcher market with low barriers to entry are making economic profits, rival firms will be attracted to the market. Their entry will expand the supply of the product (and similar products), lowering price and enticing some customers away from established firms. The demand curve faced by each firm will fall (shift inward) until the economic profits have been eliminated.

➤ Economic losses will cause price searchers to exit from the market, raising the demand for each remaining firm (shifting it outward) until the losses have been eliminated, ending the incentive to exit.

➤ When barriers to entry are low, firms in a market will make only normal profits in the long run. In the short run, they may make either economic profits or losses, depending on market conditions.

➤ Competition can come from potential as well as actual rivals. If entry and exit can be arranged at low cost, and if there are no legal barriers to entry, the theory of contestable markets indicates that competitive results will be approximated even if there are only a few firms actually in the market.

➤ Although standard economic models do not include the central role of entrepreneurial decision making in a world of uncertainty, economists recognize its importance. Entrepreneurs who discover and introduce lower-cost production methods and new products that are highly valued relative to cost promote economic progress.

➤ Traditional economic theory has criticized competitive price-searcher markets because (a) price exceeds marginal cost at the profit-maximizing output level; (b) long-run average cost is not minimized; and (c) excessive advertising is sometimes encouraged. More recently, economists stress that when barriers to entry are low, price searchers have an incentive to (a) produce efficiently; (b) undertake production if and only if their actions will increase the value of resources used; and (c) be innovative in offering new product options.

➤ When a price searcher can (a) identify groups of customers that have different price elasticities of demand and (b) prevent customers from retrading the product, price discrimination may emerge. Sellers may be able to gain by charging higher prices to groups with a more inelastic demand and lower prices to those with a more elastic demand. The practice generally leads to a larger output and more gains from trade than would otherwise occur.

➤ When barriers to entry are low, competition gives each firm a strong incentive to (a) operate efficiently and cater to the preferences of consumers, (b) improve products and discover lower-cost methods of production, and (c) discover the type of business structure, size of firm, and scope of operation that can best keep the per-unit cost of products or services low. These factors are a key to economic progress.

CRITICAL ANALYSIS QUESTIONS

1. Street-corner vendors using pushcarts have sometimes engaged in price wars at popular locations within Washington, D.C. Explain why a strategy of cutting price below cost in order to drive out other vendors from a given location would not make sense if there were no legal barriers to entry.

2. Price searchers can set the price of their product. Does this mean that price searchers will charge the highest possible price for their product? What price will maximize the profits of a price searcher? How will the firm's marginal cost compare with price at the profit-maximum output?

*3. What determines the *variety* of styles, designs, and sizes of different products? Why do you think there are only a few different varieties of toothpicks but lots of different types of napkins on the market?

*4. How would the imposition of a fixed, per-unit tax of $2,000 on new automobiles affect the average *quality* of automobiles, if the proceeds of the tax were used to subsidize a government-operated lottery?

5. What is the primary function of the entrepreneur? Some economists have charged that the major market-structure models of economic theory assume away the function of the entrepreneur. In what sense is this true? Is the function of the entrepreneur important? Discuss.

6. Is quality and style competition as important as price competition? Would you like to live in a country where government regulation restricted the use of quality and style competition? Why or why not? Do you think you would get more or less for your consumer dollar if quality and style competition were restricted? Discuss.

*7. Suppose that a price searcher is currently charging a price that maximizes the firm's total revenue. Will this price also maximize the firm's profit? Why or why not? Explain.

8. Since price searchers can set their prices, does this mean that their prices are unaffected by market conditions? In price-searcher markets with low barriers to entry, will the firms be able to make economic profit in the long run? Why or why not? What do competitive price searchers have to do in order to make economic profit?

*9. Suppose that a group of investors wants to start a business operated out of a popular Utah ski area, and the group is considering either building a new hotel complex or starting a new local airline serving that market. Each new business would require about the same amount of capital and personnel hiring. The group believes each to have the same profit potential. Which is the safer (less likely to result in a substantial capital loss) investment? Why? Is there an offsetting advantage to the other investment?

10. "Really tough competition is deadly to innovation. Producers have no profits to plow back into innovation." Evaluate. (*Hint:* Investments are made in search of future profit.)

*11. "When competition is really severe, only the big firms survive. The little guy has no chance." True or false? Explain.

12. Is price discrimination harmful to the economy? How does price discrimination affect the total amount of gains from exchange? Explain. Why do colleges often charge students different prices, based on their family income?

13. What is the primary requirement for a market to be competitive? Is competition necessary for markets to work well? Why or why not? How does competition influence the following: (a) the cost efficiency of producers, (b) the quality of products, and (c) the discovery and development of new products? Explain your answers.

14. The accompanying graph shows the short-run demand and cost situation for a price searcher in a market with low barriers to entry.

a. What level of output will maximize the firm's profit level?
b. What price will the firm charge?
c. How much revenue will the firm receive in this situation? How much is total cost? Total profit?
d. How will this situation change with the passage of time?

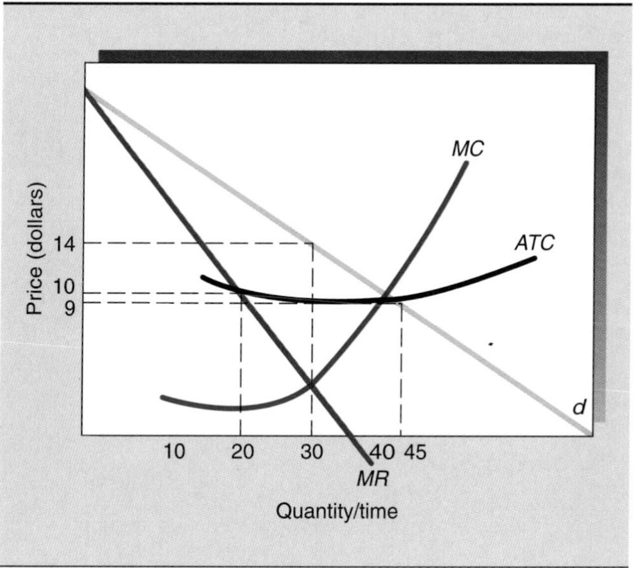

*15. Rod N. Reel owns a dealership that sells fishing boats in an open price-searcher market. In developing his pricing strategy, Rod hired an economist to estimate his demand curve. Columns (1) and (2) of the following chart provide the data for the expected weekly quantity demanded for Rod's fishing boats at alternative prices. Rod's marginal (and average) cost of supplying each boat is constant at $5,000 per boat no matter how many boats he sells per week in this range. This cost includes all opportunity costs and represents the economic cost per boat.

a. Find Rod's economic profits at each alternative price by calculating the difference between total revenue and total cost.
b. Find Rod's marginal revenue and marginal cost from the sale of each additional boat.
c. If Rod wants to maximize his profits, what price should he charge per boat?
d. How many boats will Rod sell per week at the profit-maximizing price?
e. What will Rod's profits be per week at this price and sales volume?
f. At the price and sales level where profits are maximized, has Rod sold all boats that have higher marginal revenue than marginal cost?
g. If Rod's profits are typical of all firms in the boat sales business, what might be expected to happen in the future? Will more boat dealers open in the area or will some of the existing ones go out of business? What will happen to the profitability of the boat dealers in the future once the entry/exit has occurred?
h. *Challenge Question:* Recall the relationship between elasticity of demand, price changes, and their impact on total revenues. As Rod lowers his price from $9,000 down to $5,000, his total revenues keep increasing. Is demand in this price range elastic, inelastic, or unitary elastic? When Rod lowers his price from $5,000 to $4,000, his total revenues stay the same. Is demand in this price range elastic, inelastic, or unitary elastic? Can you guess what might happen at prices below $4,000? Explain.

*Asterisk denotes questions for which answers are given in Appendix B.

Price of Fishing Boats (1)	Number of Fishing Boats Sold per Week (2)	Total Revenues per Week (3)	Total Cost per Week (4)	Economic Profit per Week (5)	Marginal Revenue (6)	Marginal Cost (7)
$9,000	0	______	______	______	—	—
8,000	1	______	______	______	______	______
7,000	2	______	______	______	______	______
6,000	3	______	______	______	______	______
5,000	4	______	______	______	______	______
4,000	5	______	______	______	______	______

CHAPTER 11

If there are economies of scale throughout the region of possible industry outputs, only one or a few firms may be able to exist in the industry.

George Stigler[1]

Price-Searcher Markets with High Entry Barriers

CHAPTER FOCUS

- What are the barriers to entry that protect some firms against competition from potential rivals?
- What is a monopoly? Does it guarantee the ability to make a profit?
- What is an oligopoly? When are oligopolists likely to collude? Why is it impossible to construct a general theory of output and price for an oligopolist?
- Why are economists critical of high barriers to entry?
- What policy alternatives do economists suggest to reduce the problems associated with high barriers to entry?
- Is competition able to discipline large firms in markets with high barriers to entry?

[1]George J. Stigler, *The Theory of Price* (New York: Macmillan, 1987), p. 204.

In the previous two chapters, we analyzed the way firms behave in competitive markets, characterized by low barriers to entry. We now turn to the analysis of firm behavior when entry barriers are high and there are few, if any, rival firms offering the same or similar products. This chapter focuses on factors that increase the difficulty of entry into a market and analyzes how they influence the ability of markets to discipline business firms. The potential of various policy alternatives that might improve the efficiency of resource allocation in these markets will also be considered.

WHY ARE ENTRY BARRIERS SOMETIMES HIGH?

What makes it difficult for potential competitors to enter a market? Four factors can be important: economies of scale, government licensing, patents, and control over an essential resource.

Economies of Scale

In some industries, firms experience declining average total costs over the full range of output that consumers are willing to buy. When this is the case, the larger firm will always have lower unit costs. Because the unit costs of smaller firms are higher than those of their larger rivals, it will be difficult for small firms to enter the market, build a reputation, and compete effectively. Under these circumstances, a single firm will tend to emerge in the industry, and the cost advantage resulting from its size will provide the firm with protection from potential rivals.

Government Licensing

Legal barriers are the oldest and most effective method of protecting a business firm from potential competitors. Kings once granted exclusive business rights to favored citizens or groups. Today, governments continue to establish barriers, restricting the right to buy and sell goods. To compete in certain parts of the communications industry in the United States (for example, to operate a radio or television station), one must obtain a government franchise. Similarly, local governments often grant exclusive franchises for the operation of cable television systems.

Licensing
A requirement that one obtain permission from the government in order to perform certain business activities or work in various occupations.

Licensing limits entry. States and cities often require persons to obtain a license before they are permitted to operate various businesses—including liquor stores, hair styling shops, taxicabs, funeral homes, and drugstores—just to list a few. Sometimes these licenses cost little and are designed to ensure certain minimum standards. In other cases, they are expensive and designed primarily to limit competition.

PATENTS

Most countries have established patent laws designed to provide inventors with a property right to their inventions. Patent laws grant the owner the exclusive legal right to the commercial use of a newly invented product or process for a limited period of time, 17 years in the United States. Once a patent is granted, others are not allowed to copy the product or procedure without the permission of the patent holder. For example, when a pharmaceutical company is granted a patent for a newly developed drug, other potential suppliers must obtain permission from the patent holder before producing and selling the product. Others might be able to supply the drug more economically. If they want to do so, however, they will have to purchase the production and marketing rights from the originating firm as long as the patent is in effect.

Costs, as well as benefits, come with a patent system. The entry barrier created by the grant of a patent generally leads to higher consumer prices for products that have already been developed. On the positive side, however, patents increase the potential returns to inventive activity, thus encouraging scientific research and technological improvements. It typically costs tens of millions of dollars to develop and test a new drug, for example. Without the profit potential emanating from the patent system, less research would be undertaken by drug firms. Thus, the absence of patent protection might well lead to a slowdown in the pace of technological innovation.

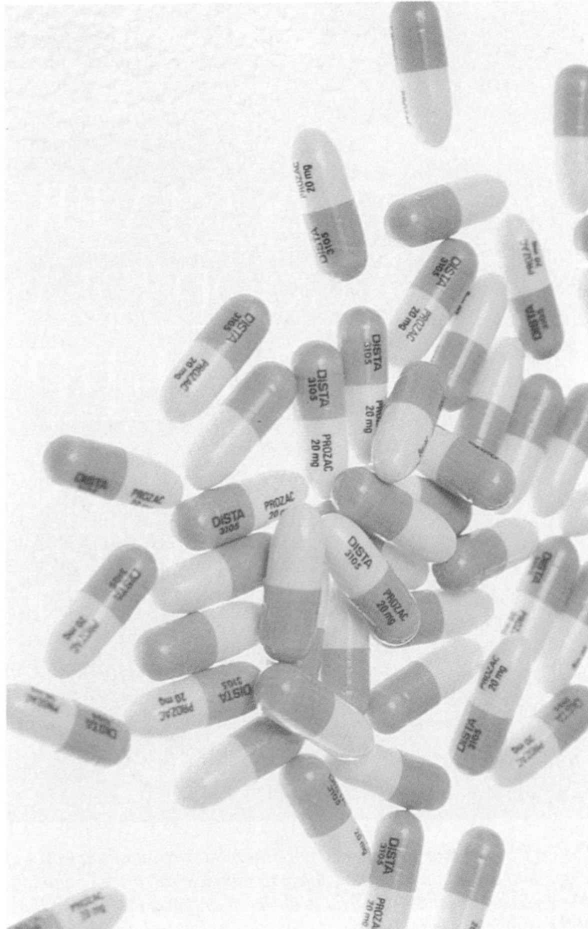

A firm that develops a new drug can use patent protection to restrain production by others for 17 years. Although consumers will pay higher prices than if open competition were permitted, they may benefit from additional investment in research and more rapid development of new products than would be the case in the absence of patent protection.

Control over an Essential Resource

If a single firm has sole control over a resource essential for entry into an industry, it can eliminate potential competitors. An example often cited is the Aluminum Company of America, which before the Second World War controlled the known supply of bauxite conveniently available to American firms. Without this critical raw material, potential competitors could not produce aluminum. With time, however, other supplies of bauxite were found, and this source of monopoly was lost to the company.

Resource monopolies seldom are complete, and profits constantly draw new challengers. New technology, mineral exploration, and other ways to exploit profitable price situations are always sought. Over time, they are usually found.

Barriers to entry are often temporary, but they do exist. Let us move on to see what happens when, at least temporarily, there is a barrier to entry high enough to limit the market to only one seller.

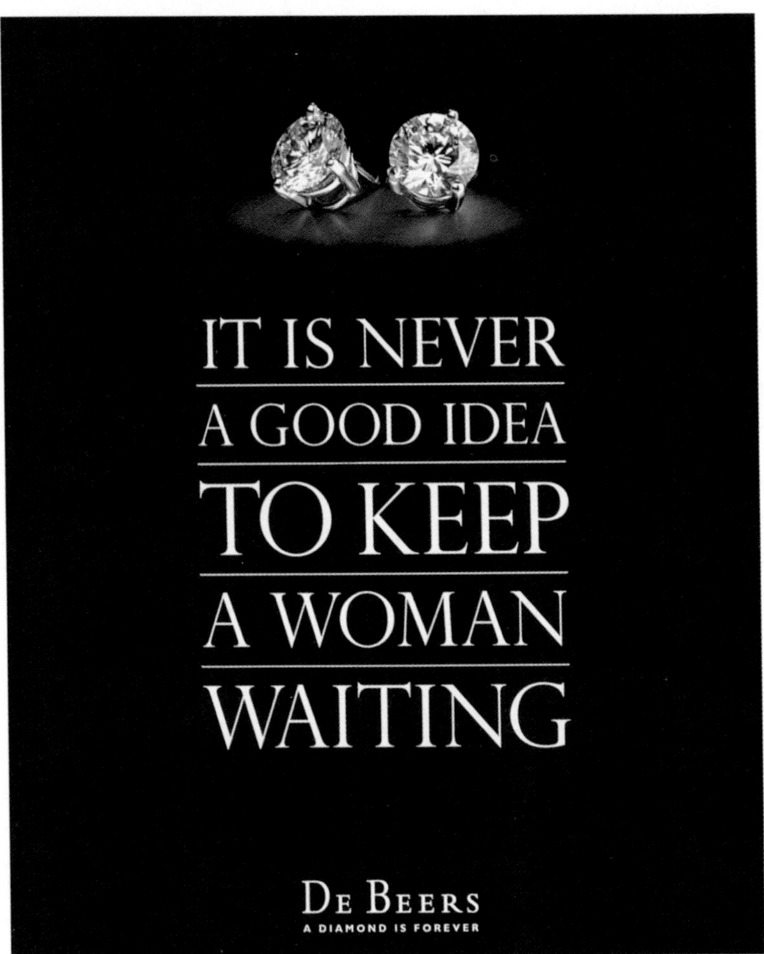

The De Beers company controls more than 80 percent of the world's known supply of diamonds. If De Beers is going to use its large market share to increase the price of diamonds, it needs to convince consumers that diamonds are special—the way to show an undying love—and that other gems are a poor substitute. Much of the company's advertising is designed to achieve these objectives.

THE CASE OF MONOPOLY

The word *monopoly,* derived from two Greek words, means "single seller." We will define **monopoly** as a market characterized by (1) high barriers to entry and (2) a single seller of a well-defined product for which there are no good substitutes. Even this definition is ambiguous, because "high barriers" and "good substitutes" are both relative terms. Are the barriers to entry into the automobile or steel industries high? Many observers would argue that they are. After all, economies of scale are important in these industries and it would take a great deal of financial capital to operate at the least-cost scale of output. However, there are no *physical* or *legal* restraints that prevent an entrepreneur from producing automobiles or steel. If price is well above cost and profit potential is present in these industries, it should not be too difficult to find the necessary investment capital. Thus, some would argue that entry barriers into these industries are not particularly high.

Monopoly
A market structure characterized by (1) a single seller of a well-defined product for which there are no good substitutes and (2) high barriers to the entry of any other firms into the market for that product.

"Good substitute" is also a subjective term. There is always some substitutability among products, even those produced by a single seller. Is a letter a good substitute for telephone communication? For some purposes—correspondence between law firms, for example—a letter delivered by mail is a very good substitute. In other cases, when the speed of communication and immediacy of response are important, telephone communication can have a tremendous advantage over letter writing. Are there any good substitutes for electricity? Most of the known substitutes for electric lighting (candles, oil lamps, and battery lights, for example) are inferior to electric lights in most uses. Natural gas, fuel oil, and wood, though, are often excellent substitutes for electric heating.

Monopoly, then, is always a matter of degree. Only a small fraction of all markets are served by only one seller. Nevertheless, there are two reasons why it is important to understand how such markets work. First, the monopoly model will help us understand markets in which there are few sellers and little active rivalry. When there are only two or three producers in a market, rather than competing with each other, firms may seek to collude and thus together behave like a monopoly. Second, in a few important industries there is by law often only a single producer in each market. Local telephone and electricity services are examples. The monopoly model will illuminate the operation of such markets.

PRICE AND OUTPUT UNDER MONOPOLY

Suppose you invent, patent, and produce a microwave device that locks the hammer of any firearm in the immediate area. This fabulous invention can be used to immobilize potential robbers or hijackers. Since you own the exclusive patent right to the firearm lock device, you are not concerned about a competitive supplier in the foreseeable future. Although other products are competitive with your invention, they are poor substitutes. In short, you are a monopolist.

What price should you charge for your product? Since you are the only seller of this device, the demand for your product is also the market demand curve. It will be downward sloping because consumers will cut back on their purchases as the price of the firearm lock increases. Like other price searchers, you will have to search to determine the most profitable price to charge. An expansion in output will increase profit as long as the production and sale of additional units add more to revenue than to cost. ***Like other price searchers, the monopolist will expand output until marginal revenue equals marginal cost. This profit-maximizing output rate can be sold at a price indicated on the firm's demand curve.***

Exhibit 11–1 provides a graphic illustration of profit maximization for a price searcher—in this case a monopolist.[2] The firm will continue to expand output as long as marginal revenue exceeds marginal cost. Therefore, output will be expanded to *Q*, where *MR* = *MC*. The monopolist will be able to sell the profit-maximizing output *Q* at price *P*, the height of the demand curve at *Q*. At any output less than *Q*, the benefits (marginal revenue) of producing the *additional* units will exceed their costs. In this range, the monopolist will gain by reducing price and expanding output toward *Q*. For any output greater than *Q*, the monopolist's costs of producing additional units will be greater than the benefits (marginal revenue). Production of such units would reduce profits. Thus, output rate *Q* and price *P* will maximize the firm's profit.

Exhibit 11–1 also depicts the profits of a monopolist. At output *Q* and price *P* the firm's total revenue is equal to *PAQO*, the price times the number of units sold. The firm's total cost would be *CBQO*, the average per-unit cost multiplied by the number of units sold. The firm's profits are merely total revenue less total cost, the shaded area of Exhibit 11–1.

Exhibit 11–2 provides a numeric illustration of profit-maximizing decision making. At low output rates, marginal revenue exceeds marginal cost. The monopolist will continue expanding output as long as *MR* is greater than *MC*. Thus, an output rate of eight units per day will be chosen. (Note: If tiny portions of a unit could be produced and sold, then production would increase to where *MR* = *MC*.) Given the demand for the product, the monopolist can sell eight units at a price of $17.25 each. Total revenue will be $138, compared to a total cost of $108.50. The monopolist will make a profit of $29.50. The profit rate will be smaller at all other output rates. For example, if the monopolist reduces the price to $16 in order to sell nine units per day, revenue will in-

The monopolist will reduce price and expand output as long as MR *exceeds* MC. *Output* Q *will result. When price exceeds average total cost at any output level, profit will accrue at that output level.*

EXHIBIT 11–1

SHORT-RUN PRICE AND OUTPUT OF A MONOPOLIST

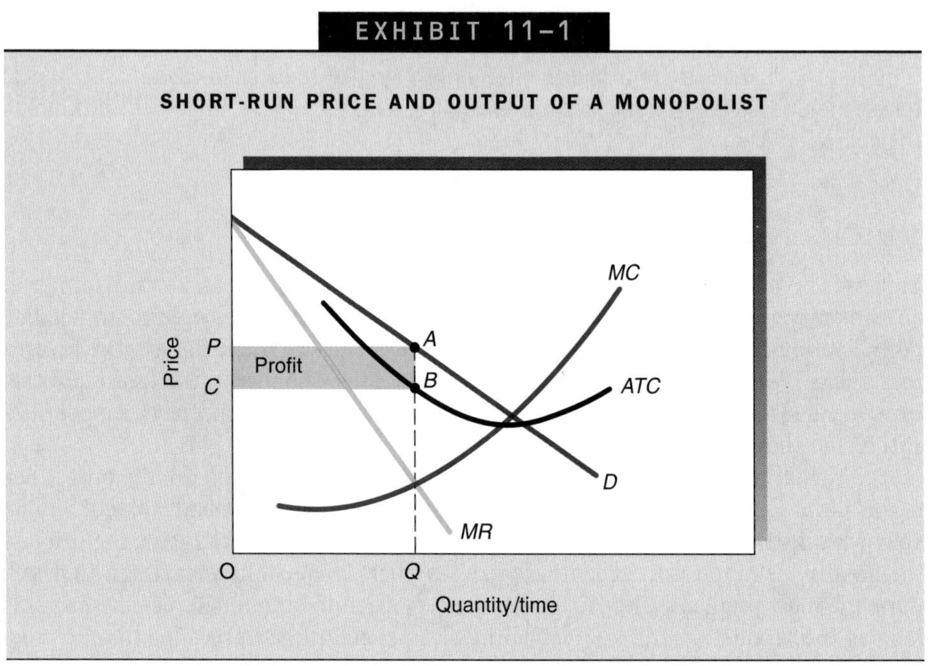

[2]In this chapter we assume that firms are unable to use price discrimination to increase their revenues. If they could, the analysis of price discrimination from the previous chapter would help to describe their decisions.

EXHIBIT 11–2

PROFIT MAXIMIZATION FOR A MONOPOLIST

RATE OF OUTPUT (PER DAY) (1)	PRICE (PER UNIT) (2)	TOTAL REVENUE (1) × (2) (3)	TOTAL COST (PER DAY) (4)	PROFIT (3) − (4) (5)	MARGINAL COST (6)	MARGINAL REVENUE (7)
0	—	—	$ 50.00	$−50.00	—	—
1	$25.00	$ 25.00	60.00	−35.00	$10.00	$25.00
2	24.00	48.00	69.00	−21.00	9.00	23.00
3	23.00	69.00	77.00	−8.00	8.00	21.00
4	22.00	88.00	84.00	4.00	7.00	19.00
5	21.00	105.00	90.50	14.50	6.50	17.00
6	19.75	118.50	96.75	21.75	6.25	13.50
7	18.50	129.50	102.75	26.75	6.00	11.00
8	17.25	138.00	108.50	29.50	5.75	8.50
9	16.00	144.00	114.75	29.25	6.25	6.00
10	14.75	147.50	121.25	26.25	6.50	3.50
11	13.50	148.50	128.00	20.50	6.75	1.00
12	12.25	147.00	135.00	12.00	7.00	−1.50
13	11.00	143.00	142.25	.75	7.25	−4.00

crease by $6. However, the marginal cost of producing the ninth unit is $6.25. Since the cost of producing the ninth unit is greater than the revenue it brings in, profits will decline.

When high barriers to entry are present, they will insulate the monopolist from direct competition with rival firms producing a similar product. In markets with high entry barriers, monopoly profits will not attract—at least not quickly—rivals who will expand supply, cut prices, and spoil the seller's market.

Protected by high entry barriers, a monopolist may be able to continue earning a profit, even in the long run. Does this mean that monopolists can charge as high a price as they want? Monopolists are often accused of price gouging. In evaluating this charge, however, it is important to recognize that, like other sellers, monopolists will seek to maximize *profit,* not *price.* Consumers will buy less as price increases. Thus, a higher price is not always best for monopolists. Exhibit 11–2 illustrates this point. What would happen to the profit of the monopolist if price were increased from $17.25 to $18.50? At the higher price, only seven units would be sold, and total revenue would equal $129.50. The cost of producing seven units would be $102.75. Thus, when price is $18.50 and output seven units, profit is only $26.75, less than could be attained at the lower price ($17.25) and larger output (eight units). The highest price is not always the best price for the monopolist. Sometimes a price reduction will increase the firm's total revenue more than its total cost.

Will a monopolist always be able to make an economic profit? The profitability of a monopolist is limited by the demand for the product that it produces. In some cases, a monopolist—even one protected by high barriers to entry—may be unable to sell for a profit. For example, there are thousands of clever, patented items that are never produced because demand-cost conditions are not favorable. **Exhibit 11–3**

Even a monopolist will incur losses if the average total cost curve lies above the demand curve.

EXHIBIT 11–3

WHEN A MONOPOLIST INCURS LOSSES

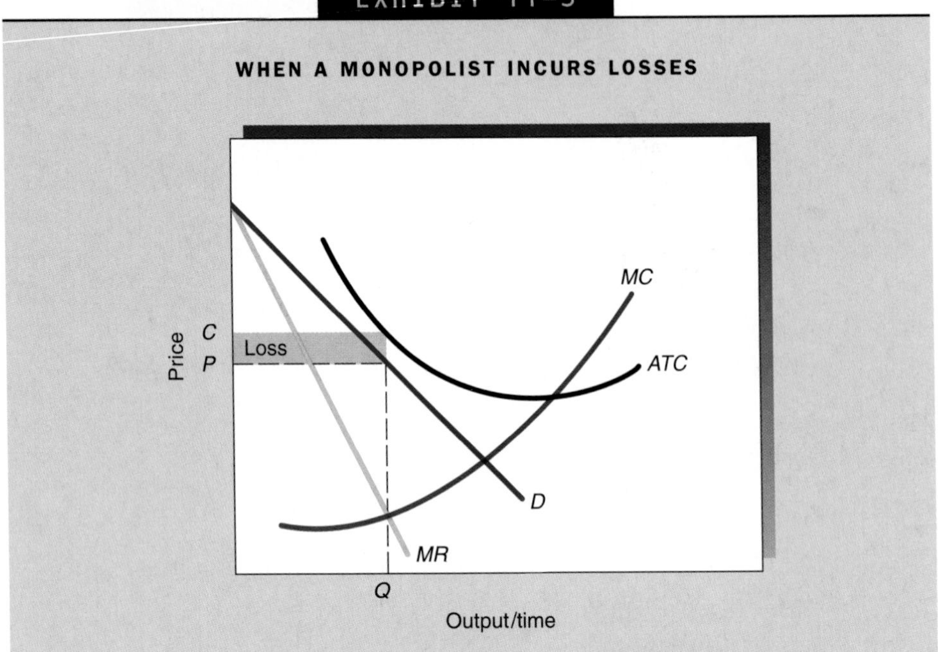

illustrates this possibility. In this case, the monopolist's average total cost curve is above its demand curve at every level of output. Even when operating at the $MR = MC$ rate of output, economic losses (shaded area) will occur. While output Q could be sold at price P, this price is insufficient to cover the per-unit cost of the monopolist. Under these circumstances, not even a monopolist would want to operate, at least not for long.

The Monopoly Model and Decision Making in the Real World

Until now, we have proceeded as if monopolists always knew exactly what their revenue and cost curves looked like. Of course, this is not true in the real world. Like other price searchers, a monopolist cannot be sure of the demand conditions for a product. Demand curves frequently shift, and choices must be made without the benefit of perfect knowledge. How many sales will be lost if the price is raised? How many sales will be added if the price is lowered? Like other price searchers, monopolists often experiment with price changes, attempting to find the price at which profit will be maximized. Price will be set on the basis of what the price searching monopolist *expects* to happen when price is changed. Thus, the revenue and cost data illustrated in Exhibits 11–1, 11–2, and 11–3 might be thought of as representing *expected* revenues and costs associated with various output levels. To complicate matters further in real life, quality changes of various sorts can be undertaken by the monopolist searching for additional profits. Buyer reactions to potential quality changes, and resulting shifts in demand and cost, must also be considered by the profit-seeking monopolist.

A monopolist, like other business decision makers, seldom calculates what we have called demand, marginal revenue, and cost curves. Given imperfect information, the profit-maximizing price may be only approximated. Like other price searchers, however, the monopolist has a strong incentive to find the profit-maximizing price and output rate and, when it does, the outcome will be *as if the MR = MC* rule had been used to maximize profit.

It is difficult for a monopolist to predict the demand conditions it will face, and thus consumer response to alternative prices (and quality) changes. But life is even more complex for the next class of price searchers we consider: large firms with few rivals in a market protected by high barriers to entry.

CHARACTERISTICS OF OLIGOPOLY

In the United States, the great majority of output in such industries as automobiles, steel, cigarettes, and aircraft is produced by five or fewer dominant firms. These industries are characterized by **oligopoly.** *Oligopoly means* "few sellers." *The distinguishing characteristics of an oligopolistic market are (1) a small number of rival firms, (2) interdependence among the sellers because each is large relative to the size of the market, (3) substantial economies of scale, and (4) high entry barriers into the market.*

Oligopoly
A market situation in which a small number of sellers compose the entire industry. It is competition among the few.

INTERDEPENDENCE AMONG OLIGOPOLISTIC FIRMS

Since the number of sellers in an oligopolistic industry is small, the decisions of a firm often influence the demand, price, and profit of rivals. This adds to the complexity of the firm's decision making. When a firm is deciding what price to charge, output to produce, or quality of product to offer, the potential reactions of rivals must be taken into account. The business decisions of the firms are interrelated. Thus, the welfare of each seller is dependent on the policies followed by major rivals.

SUBSTANTIAL ECONOMIES OF SCALE

In an oligopolistic industry, large-scale production (relative to the total market) is generally required to achieve minimum per-unit cost. Economies of scale are significant. When the firms operate at the least-cost rate of output, a small number of large-scale firms will be able to produce the entire market demand for the product. Using the automobile industry as an example, Exhibit 11–4 illustrates the importance of economies of scale as a source of oligopoly. It has been estimated that each firm must produce approximately 1 million automobiles annually before its per-unit cost of production is minimized. However, when the selling price of automobiles is barely sufficient for firms to cover their costs, the total quantity demanded from these producers is only 6 million. To minimize costs, then, each firm must produce at least one-sixth (1 million of the 6 million) of the output demanded. In other words, the industry can support no more than five or six domestic firms of cost-efficient size.

SIGNIFICANT BARRIERS TO ENTRY

As with monopoly, barriers to entry limit the ability of new firms to compete effectively in oligopolistic industries. Economies of scale are probably the most significant entry barrier protecting firms in an oligopolistic industry.[3] A potential competitor may be

---

[3]Economies of scale will not be a barrier to entry in the industry, of course, if resources can be freely moved into and out of the industry at a low cost. Such resource mobility would render the market contestable, as we learned in the previous chapter, removing scale economies as a barrier to entry in this special case.

Oligopoly exists in the automobile industry because firms do not fully realize the cost reductions from large-scale output until they produce approximately one-sixth of the total market.

EXHIBIT 11-4

ECONOMIES OF SCALE AND OLIGOPOLY

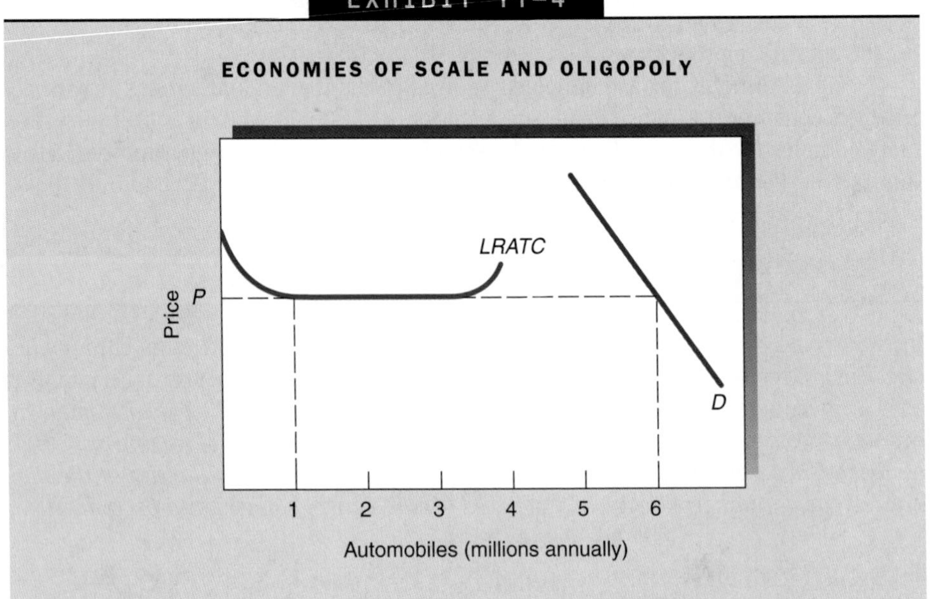

unable to start out small and gradually grow to the optimal size, since it must gain a large share of the market before it can minimize per-unit cost. The manufacture of refrigerators and diesel engines, as well as automobile production, seems to fall into this category. Other factors, including patent rights, control over an essential resource, and government-imposed entry restraints, may also prevent new competitors from entering profitable oligopolistic industries. The presence of high entry barriers is what distinguishes oligopoly from a competitive price-searcher market.

Products May Be Either Identical or Differentiated

The products of sellers in an oligopolistic industry may be either similar or differentiated. When firms produce identical products, such as milk or gasoline, there is less opportunity for nonprice competition. On the other hand, rival firms producing differentiated products are more likely to use style, quality, and advertising as competitive weapons.

PRICE AND OUTPUT IN THE CASE OF OLIGOPOLY

Unlike a monopolist or a price taker, an oligopolist cannot determine the product price that will deliver maximum profit simply by estimating market demand and cost conditions. A key factor in determining the demand facing an oligopolistic firm is the pricing behavior of close rivals. Thus, an oligopolist must predict not only how buyers will react to options, but also how rival firms (that is, the rest of the industry) will react to alternative price (and quality) adjustments. Because economics cannot specify the reaction of an oligopolistic firm to the actions of a rival, the precise price and output that will emerge under oligopoly cannot be determined. Economics does, however, indicate a potential range of prices, and the factors that will determine whether prices in the industry will be high or low relative to costs of production.

Consider an oligopolistic industry in which seven or eight rival firms produce the entire market output because substantial economies of scale are present. The firms produce nearly identical products and have similar costs of production. **Exhibit 11–5** depicts the market demand conditions and long-run costs of production of the individual firms for such an industry.

What price will prevail? We can answer this question for two extreme cases. First, suppose that each firm sets its price independently of the other firms. There is no collusion (no agreement among the firms to keep the price high), and each competitive firm acts independently, seeking to maximize profits by offering consumers a better deal than its rivals. Under these conditions, the market price would be driven down to P_c. Firms would be just able to cover their per-unit costs of production. What would happen if a single firm raised its price? Its customers would switch to rival firms, which would now expand to accommodate the new customers. The firm that raised its price would lose out. It would be self-defeating for any one firm to raise its price if the other firms did not raise theirs.

What happens if supply conditions are such that the current market price was greater than P_c? Any *individual firm* that reduces its price slightly, by 1 or 2 percent, for example, will gain numerous customers if the other firms maintain the higher price. The price-cutting firm will attract some new buyers to the market, but more important, it will also lure many buyers away from rival firms charging higher prices. Thus, if the rival sellers act independently, each will have a strong incentive to reduce price in order to increase sales and gain a larger share of the total market. But what happens when each firm attempts to undercut its rivals? Price is driven down to P_c, and the economic profit of the firms is eliminated.

When rival oligopolists compete (on the basis of price) with one another, they drive the market price down to the level of costs of production. They do not always compete, however. There is a strong incentive for oligopolists to collude, agreeing to raise price and to restrict output.

EXHIBIT 11–5

RANGE OF PRICE AND OUTPUT UNDER OLIGOPOLY

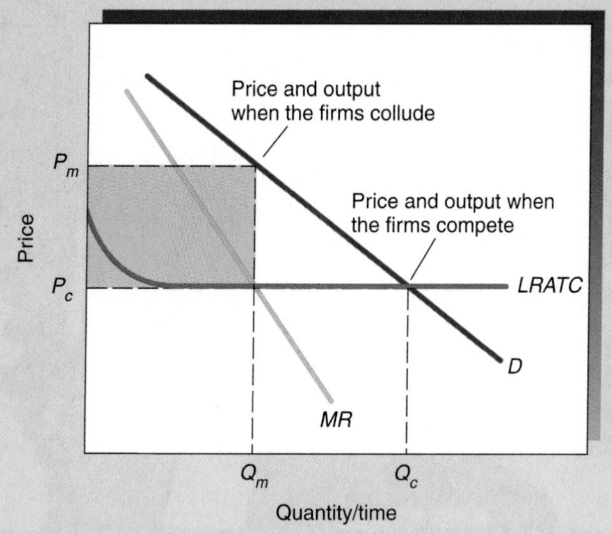

If oligopolists competed with one another, price cutting would drive price down to P_c*. In contrast, perfect cooperation among firms would lead to a higher price of* P_m *and a smaller output (*Q_m *rather than* Q_c*). The shaded area shows profit if firms collude. Demand here is the market demand.*

Cartel
An organization of sellers designed to coordinate supply decisions so that the joint profits of the members will be maximized. A cartel will seek to create a monopoly in the market.

Suppose the oligopolists, recognizing their interdependence, acted cooperatively to maximize their joint profit. They might form a **cartel** to accomplish this objective. Probably the world's best-known cartel is the Organization of Petroleum Exporting Countries (OPEC), a group of 13 oil-producing nations that succeeded in limiting their combined production, and thus raising prices beginning in 1973. Since the mid-1980s, however, disagreements on production quotas and failure of individual OPEC members to stay within their quotas, along with the increased production in other nations encouraged by the higher prices, has reduced world oil prices. Cartel agreements are difficult to arrange and to enforce.

Instead of forming a cartel, oligopolists might collude without the aid of a formal organization. Under federal antitrust laws in the United States, collusive action to raise price and expand the joint profit of the firms would, of course, be illegal. Nevertheless, let us see what would happen if oligopolists followed this course. Exhibit 11–5 shows the marginal revenue curve that would accompany the market demand D for the product. Under perfect cooperation, the oligopolists would refuse to produce units for which marginal revenue was less than marginal cost. Thus, they would restrict joint output to Q_m where $MR = MC$. Market price would rise to P_m. With collusion, substantial joint profits (the shaded area of Exhibit 11–5) could thus be attained. The case of perfect cooperation would be identical with the outcome under monopoly.

In the real world, however, the outcome is likely to fall between the extremes of price competition and perfect cooperation. Oligopolists generally recognize their interdependence and try to avoid vigorous price competition, which would drive price down to the level of per-unit costs. But there are also obstacles to collusion, which is why prices in oligopolistic industries do not rise to the monopoly level. Oligopolistic prices are typically above per-unit cost but below those a monopolist would set.

Collusive agreements among oligopolists and cartels like OPEC are difficult to maintain because each cartel member would be better off if it could cheat on the agreement and charge a slightly lower price, especially if other members do not.

The Incentive to Collude and to Cheat

Collusion is the opposite of competition. It involves cooperative actions by sellers to turn the terms of trade in favor of the group, and against buyers. Since oligopolists can profit by colluding to restrict output and raise price, economic theory suggests that they will have a strong incentive to do so. To accomplish this, however, the firms must also agree on production shares for each firm, or a division of the market so that production is limited to the level that will be purchased at the chosen cartel price.

Collusion
Agreement among firms to avoid various competitive practices, particularly price reductions. It may involve either formal agreements or merely tacit recognition that competitive practices will be self-defeating in the long run. Tacit collusion is difficult to detect. In the United States, antitrust laws prohibit collusion and conspiracies to restrain trade.

Each individual oligopolist, though, also has an incentive to cheat on collusive agreements. **Exhibit 11–6** explains why. An undetected price cut will enable a firm to attract (1) customers who would not buy from any firm at the higher price *and* (2) those who would normally buy from other firms. Thus, the demand facing each *individual firm* will be considerably more elastic than the market demand curve. As Exhibit 11–6 shows, the price P_i that maximizes the industry's profits will be higher than the price P_F that is best for a single oligopolist when the others stay with the higher price. If a firm can find a way to undercut the price set by the collusive agreement, while other sellers maintain the higher price, the firm's expanded sales (beyond the level agreed upon by the cartel) will more than make up for the reduction in per-unit profit margin.

In oligopolistic industries, there are two conflicting tendencies. An oligopolistic firm has a strong incentive to cooperate with its rivals so that joint profit can be maximized. However, it also has a strong incentive to cheat secretly on any collusive agreement in order to increase its share of the joint profit. Oligopolistic agreements, therefore, tend to be unstable. This instability exists whether the cooperative behavior is formal, as in the case of a cartel, or informal.

Obstacles to Collusion

There are certain situations in which it is difficult for oligopolists to collude. Five major obstacles limit collusive behavior.

EXHIBIT 11–6

GAINING FROM CHEATING

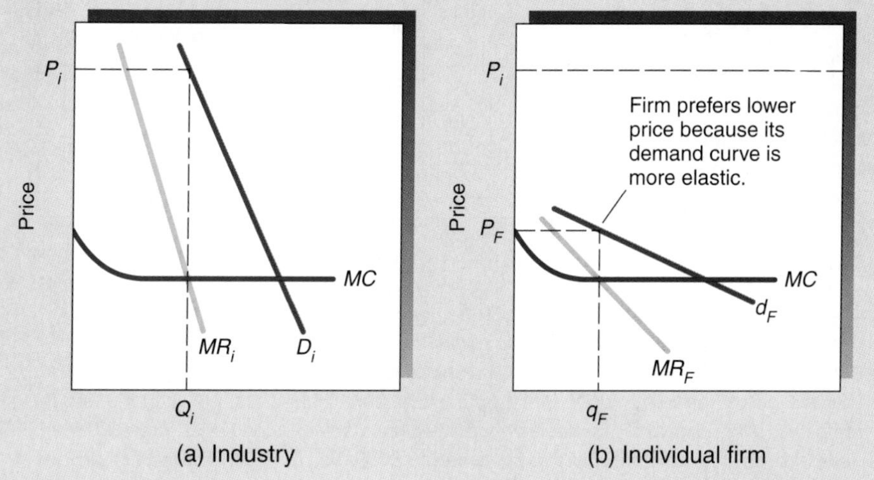

The industry demand (D_i) and marginal revenue (MR_i) curves show that the joint profits of oligopolists would be maximized at Q_i where $MR_i = MC$. Price P_i would be best for the industry as a whole (a). However, the demand curve (d_F) facing each firm (under the assumption that no other firms cheat) would be much more elastic than D_i. Given the greater elasticity of its demand curve, an individual firm (b) would maximize its profit by cutting its price to P_F and expanding output to q_F, where $MR_F = MC$. Thus, individual oligopolists could gain by secretly shaving price and cheating on the collusive agreement.

1. *As the number of firms in an oligopolistic market increases, the likelihood of effective collusion declines.* Other things constant, an increase in the number of major firms in an industry will make it more difficult for the oligopolists to communicate, negotiate, and enforce agreements among themselves. In addition, the greater the number of firms, the more likely it is that the objectives of individual firms will conflict with those of the industry. Each firm will want a bigger slice of the pie. Opinions about the best collusive price arrangement will differ because marginal costs, unused plant capacity, and estimates of market demand elasticity

APPLICATIONS IN ECONOMICS

The Prisoner's Dilemma and Game Theory

In an oligopoly, a few firms compete by selling into the same market, and the actions of each influence the demand faced by rival sellers. Because they sell similar products and compete for the same customers, the interests of each firm are in conflict with the interests of the others. One firm can gain customers, at the expense of the others, by reducing its price or increasing its advertising. But if the other firms react competitively by doing the same, then all the firms may lose. Yet if rivals cut price or take other steps to offer consumers a better deal, firms that fail to follow suit will lose customers to their more aggressive competitors. Thus, each firm finds itself on the horns of a dilemma—in this case a variant of the classic "prisoner's dilemma."

Economists have increasingly used game theory, as in the analysis of the prisoner's dilemma, to analyze strategic choices made by competitors in a conflict situation, such as members of an oligopoly. Such choices depend on the anticipated actions of others.

To understand the prisoner's dilemma, consider the hypothetical case of Al and Bob, two touring Americans who just met at a train station in a small foreign country. They are taken prisoner and hauled into the local police station to be questioned separately. They are suspected of being the two men who robbed a local merchant, and each is told that if he makes the job of the police easier by confessing immediately, he will get only a 6-month sentence. But each is also told that if he says nothing while the other confesses, then the one who did not confess immediately will get a 12-month sentence. If neither confesses, both will be held for 3 months while the investigation continues. Al and Bob will not be allowed to communicate with each other. Will they confess?

To analyze such situations, the game theorist begins by laying out the alternative outcomes and showing how they are related to choices made by the players of the game, as we do in **Exhibit 11–7**. For each man individually, in this version of the dilemma, the box reveals that the best choice depends on what the other does. If Al confesses, then Bob can save 6 months of jail time by also confessing. The same holds for Al, if he thinks Bob will confess. But if neither confesses, both serve only three months in jail.[1] The proper strategy for each prisoner depends heavily on his estimate of the likelihood that the other will confess. The problem becomes more complex if we consider prisoners who face a series of such decisions over time, each prisoner learning the other's previous choice before the next set of choices must be made.

Firms in an oligopoly must make decisions somewhat like those of the prisoners: Should a firm cut its price, luring more customers, some from competitors, or should it keep its price high and risk losing customers to competitors who

EXHIBIT 11–7

THE PRISONER'S DILEMMA

		Al's Choice: Confess	Al's Choice: Not Confess
Bob's Choice	Confess	6 months each	Al: 12 months Bob: 6 months
	Not Confess	Al: 6 months Bob: 12 months	3 months each

Al and Bob must each decide, without communicating with each other, whether to confess. Al knows that if Bob does not confess, *then Al can either confess and spend 6 months in jail, or not confess and spend 3 months. But* if Bob does confess, *then Al's failure to confess would cost him an additional 6 months in jail. Bob is in a similar situation, facing the same options under the same assumptions about whether Al confesses. Each has the incentive to confess if he thinks the other one will, but to not confess if he thinks the other will also remain silent.*

are likely to differ among firms. Aggressive, less-mature firms may be especially interested in expanding their share of total output. Exactly these problems have contributed to the inability of OPEC to maintain high oil prices. When they met in November 1998, for example, they were simply unable to agree on production quotas. Conflicting interests will always make it more difficult to reach a collusive agreement, and will contribute to the breakdown of any agreement that is made.

2. ***When it is difficult to detect and eliminate price cuts, collusion is less attractive.*** Unless a firm has a way of policing the pricing activities of rivals, it may be the

(continued)

cut prices? If all firms keep the price high, then as a group they will reap more profit. If all cut prices, then as a group they will reap less profit. But the firm that fails to cut price when others do so will lose many customers to the other competing firms. The decision about whether to spend large amounts on advertising has similar characteristics.

For example, consider the pricing policy or advertising strategy of large automakers, such as Ford, General Motors, and Chrysler. Suppose the profit rate of each would be 15 percent if all the major automobile producers raised their prices (or cut their advertising expenditures) by a similar amount. In contrast, each would have a profit rate of only 10 percent if intense competition leads to lower prices and/or larger advertising expenditures. Industry profits are highest when all firms decide to charge high prices. However, if one automaker reduces its price or advertises more heavily, it will be able to win customers away from rivals and increase its profit rate to 20 percent. Thus, if the firm thinks its rivals will continue to charge higher prices (or fail to match its advertising expenditures), it will be able to gain from cutting its prices (and increasing its advertising). If the other firms follow a similar course, however, this strategy will backfire and the profit rate of all the firms in the industry will be less than the level that would have been achieved had they all charged higher prices (or spent less on advertising).

While our simplified analysis highlights the interdependence among the firms and the importance of probability estimates concerning the strategy of rivals, the real world is much more complex. The choices of the rival firms will be repeated over and over again, although often in modified forms. A prior strategy may be modified in light of previous reactions on the part of rivals. The attractiveness of a strategy will be influenced by the likelihood it will be detected by rivals and the speed with which they might be able to react effectively. In addition, the strategies of oligopolistic firms will be influenced by market conditions and the threat of foreign competition, factors that change with the passage of time. Within the framework of game theory models, additional assumptions must be made in order to account for these and other complex factors—factors that often change in the real world. In turn, if the assumptions incorporated into game theory models are not consistent with real-world conditions, the implications of the game theory analysis may well be invalid.

Economists have used game theory extensively to show how results change when the "rules of the game" change for the firms in an oligopolistic market, as well as for auction-bidding markets and other business decision-making situations. When the rules of the game are carefully defined and enforced, as in the case of economic experiments in laboratories, game theory has yielded interesting and important testable conclusions. But in open markets in the real world, empirical work using game theory has been less successful. The use of models is always difficult when the problem to be solved is complex, and human expectations about the changing strategy choices of other human beings must be taken into account. There is no question, however, that game theory can be useful for scholars and business practitioners alike, in helping them to frame the issues involved in strategic decision making.[2]

[1]If the numbers were slightly different from those in the accompanying chart, both Al and Bob would have an incentive to confess regardless of what they thought the other would do. For example, if each were told that he would get only a 1-month sentence if he confessed and the other party did not, then confession would become the dominant strategy for both Bob and Al. Under these circumstances, if Bob thought Al would remain silent, then Bob would spend only 1 month in jail if he confessed (compared to 3 months if he also remained silent). Al would be in a similar situation if he believed Bob would remain silent. On the other hand, if Bob thought Al would confess, then Bob's best option would be to also confess since confession would lead to only a 6-month sentence while silence would result in a 12-month jail term. The same would also be true for Al if he thought Bob would confess. Thus, in this classic prisoner's dilemma case, both have an incentive to confess even though confession leads to more jail time for both of them—6 months rather than 3 months. What is best for the individual (or firm) does not always lead to the best outcome from the viewpoint of the group (or industry).

[2]For a further explanation of game theory and the prisoner's dilemma, see Avinash Dixit and Barry Nalebuff, "Game Theory," in *The Fortune Encyclopedia of Economics* (New York: Warner Books, 1993), pp. 640–643.

"sucker" in a collusive agreement. Firms that secretly cut prices may gain a larger share of the market, while those maintaining higher prices are losing customers and profits. OPEC provides a good example. Cheating by members on production and sales quota agreements has been widely reported.

Price cutting can sometimes be accomplished in ways that are difficult for the other firms to identify. For example, a firm might provide better credit terms, faster delivery, and other related services "free" to improve slightly the package offered to the buyer. In industries where differentiated products are supplied, oligopolists can hold money prices constant and still use improvements in quality and style to provide consumers with more value. "Price cuts" like this are particularly attractive to oligopolists because they cannot be easily and quickly duplicated by rivals. Competitors can quickly match a reduction in money price, but it will take time for them to match an improvement in quality. Collusive agreements on price are of limited value in situations where quality and style are important competitive weapons. The bottom line is this: When cheating (price cutting) is profitable and difficult for rivals to detect and police, collusive agreements—both formal and informal—will be difficult to maintain.

3. ***Low entry barriers are an obstacle to collusion.*** Unless potential new rivals can be excluded, oligopolists will be unable to sustain economic profits. Profitable collusion will merely attract competitors into the industry until the profits drawing the entrants are eliminated. Once again, OPEC provides a case in point. OPEC's 13 member nations produced more than half the world's oil in 1973, when they began to reduce output and raise oil prices. But higher prices led firms in other nations to seek, find, and produce more oil. By 1985, world oil output had risen and OPEC's production represented only 30 percent of the total. Prices began to fall as more and more production came onto the market. Even with collusion, long-run profits will not be possible unless entry into the industry can be blocked.

   Local markets are sometimes dominated by a few firms. For example, many communities have only a small number of ready-mix concrete producers, bowling alleys, accounting firms, and furniture stores. In the absence of government restrictions, however, entry barriers into these markets are generally low. The threat of potential rivals reduces the gains from collusive behavior under these conditions. Even if the number of rival firms is small, the firms will be unable to maintain above-normal profit rates when entry barriers are low. Under these circumstances, the competitive price-searcher model, rather than oligopoly, is more applicable.
4. ***Unstable demand conditions are an obstacle to collusion.*** Demand instability leads to honest differences of opinion among oligopolists about what is best for the industry. One firm may want to expand because it anticipates a sharp increase in future demand, while a more pessimistic rival may want to hold the line on existing industrial capacity. The larger the differences in expectations about future demand, the greater the potential for conflict among oligopolistic firms. Successful collusion is more likely when demand is relatively stable.
5. ***Vigorous antitrust action increases the cost of collusion.*** Under existing antitrust laws, collusive behavior is prohibited. Secret agreements are, of course, possible. Simple informal cooperation might be conducted without discussions or collusive agreements. However, like other illegal behavior, such agreements are not legally enforceable by any firm. Vigorous antitrust action can discourage firms from making such illegal agreements. As the threat of getting caught increases, participants will be less likely to attempt collusive behavior.

UNCERTAINTY AND OLIGOPOLY

Uncertainty and imprecision characterize the theory of oligopoly. We know that firms will gain if they successfully restrict output and raise price. However, collusion is fraught with conflicts and difficulties. In some industries, these difficulties are so great that the **market power** of the oligopolists is relatively small. In other industries, oligopolistic cooperation, although not perfect, may raise prices significantly, indicating a higher degree of market power, which is, in effect, a degree of monopoly power. Analysis of the costs and benefits of collusive behavior, under varying degrees of cooperation and conflict, has become an important part of economics over the last two decades. (See the Applications in Economics feature on **game theory.**) Although this developing field of economics does not yield precise predictions on oligopoly pricing and output, it does suggest the conditions that make it more likely that an oligopolist will face discipline from competitive pressures.

Market power
The ability of a firm that is not a pure monopolist to earn unusually large profits, indicating that it has some monopoly power. Because the firm has few (or weak) competitors, it has a degree of freedom from the discipline of vigorous competition.

Game theory
Analyzes the strategic choices made by competitors in a conflict situation, such as decisions made by members of an oligopoly.

MARKET POWER AND PROFIT—THE EARLY BIRD CATCHES THE WORM

Our analysis of both monopoly and oligopoly indicates that because entry barriers into these markets are often high, firms may be able to earn economic profit over lengthy periods of time. Suppose a well-established firm, such as Exxon or IBM, is able to use its market power to persistently earn above-normal returns. Do the current stockholders gain? Surprisingly, the answer is no. The ownership value of a share of corporate stock for such corporations began long ago to reflect their market power and expected future profitability. Many of the present stockholders paid high prices for their stock because they expected these firms to be highly profitable. In other words, they paid for the above-normal economic profits that the firm was expected to earn because of its market power.

Do not expect to get rich buying the stock of monopolistic or oligopolistic firms known to be highly profitable. You are already too late. The early bird catches the worm. Those who owned the stock when these firms initially developed their market position have already captured the gain. The value of their stock increased at that time. After a firm's future prospects are widely recognized, subsequent stockholders fail to gain a higher-than-normal rate of return on their financial investment.

DEFECTS OF MARKETS WITH HIGH ENTRY BARRIERS

Monopolists, by keeping the market constantly understocked, by never fully supplying the effectual demand, sell their commodities much above the natural price, and raise their emoluments, whether they consist of wages or profit, greatly above their natural rate.

Adam Smith[4]

What types of problems arise when entry barriers limit the number of firms in an industry to a single monopolist or a small group of oligopolists? From Adam Smith's

[4]Adam Smith, *An Inquiry into the Nature and Causes of the Wealth of Nations* (1776; Cannan's ed., Chicago: University of Chicago Press, 1976), p. 69.

time to the present, economists have generally considered monopoly a necessary evil at best. The attitude toward markets with only a few sellers and high entry barriers is only slightly more tolerant. Open competition, unfettered by high barriers to entry, has been recognized as a key form of market discipline restraining the behavior of producers and encouraging innovation. There are four major reasons for this view.

1. ***A reduction in the competitiveness of a market limits the options available to consumers.*** If you do not like the food at a local restaurant, you can go to another restaurant. If you do not like the wares of a local department store, you can buy good substitutes from other retailers. The competition of rivals, both existing and potential, protects the consumer from the arbitrary behavior of any seller. But consider your alternatives if you do not like the local telephone service. The entry of competitors is typically forbidden in that market. What can you do when the service is bad? You can voice a complaint to the company or your legislative representative, but unlike a competitive situation, you have no exit option other than sacrificing your phone service. When consumers do not have good exit options—when they must either take what the seller offers or do without—their ability to discipline sellers is greatly reduced.
2. ***Reduced competition results in allocative inefficiency.*** Allocative efficiency requires that additional units be produced when they are valued more highly than what it costs to produce them. When barriers to entry are low, production of each good will be expanded until its price is driven down to the level of per-unit costs. With high barriers to entry, however, this will not generally be the case. A monopolist or cartel that does not have to worry about rivals entering the market can often gain by restricting output and raising price. That is, output may not be produced even though consumers value it more than its costs of production. Prices may exceed not only marginal costs, but also average total cost for a long period of time when entry barriers into a market are high. As Adam Smith noted more than 200 years ago, monopolists (and cartels) will understock the market and charge a higher price than would prevail if the producers were disciplined by independent rivals and the threat of new entrants.
3. ***When barriers to entry are high, consumers are less able to direct producers to serve their interests.*** With low barriers to entry, producers have little choice but to serve the interests of consumers. Producers that do not operate efficiently will lose customers to lower-cost rivals. Firms that fail to produce goods that consumers value highly relative to their costs will experience losses. Thus, if producers want to make profits when entry barriers are low, they will have to provide consumers what they want at an attractive price.

   In contrast, when entry barriers are high and there are few, if any, alternative suppliers, the discipline of market forces is weakened. Protected from potential new competitors, inefficient firms may be able to earn a normal return or even a profit.
4. ***Government grants of monopoly power will encourage rent seeking; resources will be wasted by firms attempting to secure and maintain grants of market protection.*** Grants of special favor by the government will lead to costly activities seeking those favors. As we noted in Chapter 6, economists refer to such activities as *rent seeking.* When government licenses or the imposition of other entry barriers enhance profitability and provide protection from the rigors of market competition, people will expend scarce resources attempting to secure and maintain these political favors. From an efficiency standpoint, such rent-seeking activities are wasteful; they consume valuable resources without contributing to output. In aggregate, output is reduced as the result of these wasteful activities. These

"Last year, as in previous years, your company had to contend with spiralling labor costs, exorbitant interest rates, and unconscionable government interference. Management was able once more, through a combination of deceptive marketing practices, false advertising, and price fixing, to show a profit which, in all modesty, can only be called excessive."

rent-seeking costs from grants of monopoly power add to the welfare losses resulting from the allocative inefficiency mentioned above.

By way of illustration, suppose the government issues a license providing a seller with the exclusive right to sell liquor in a specific market. If this grant of monopoly power permits the licensee to earn monopoly profit, potential suppliers will expend resources trying to convince government officials that they should be granted the license. The potential monopolists will lobby government officials, make political contributions, hire representatives to do consulting studies, and undertake other actions designed to convince politicians and their appointees that they can best "serve the public interest" as a monopoly supplier. Any firm that expects its rent-seeking activities to be successful will be willing to spend up to the present value of the future expected monopoly profits, if necessary, to obtain the monopoly protection. Other suppliers, of course, may also be willing to invest in rent-seeking activities. When several suppliers believe they can win, the total expenditures of all firms on rent-seeking activities may actually consume resources worth more than the economic profit expected from the monopoly enterprise.

POLICY ALTERNATIVES WHEN ENTRY BARRIERS ARE HIGH

What government policies might be used to counteract the problems that result from high barriers to entry? Economists suggest four policy options:

1. Control the structure of the industry in order to assure the presence of rival firms.
2. Reduce tariffs and other artificial barriers that limit competition.

3. Regulate the price and output of firms in the market.
4. Supply the market with goods produced by a government firm.

Each of these policies has been used to either reduce entry barriers or to counteract their negative results. We will briefly discuss each in turn.

Antitrust Policy and Controlling the Structure of an Industry

The major problems raised by high barriers to entry and monopoly power are avoided when rival sellers are present. A firm will be unable to restrict output and raise price when it confronts rivals producing the same product or close substitutes. The United States, to a greater degree than most Western countries, has adopted antitrust laws designed to prevent monopoly and promote competition. Antitrust legislation began in 1890 with the passage of the Sherman Antitrust Act. Additional legislation, including the Clayton Act and the Federal Trade Commission Act of 1914, has buttressed policy in this area. Antitrust laws provide the U.S. Department of Justice with the power to prosecute firms engaging in collusive behavior or other actions designed to create a monopoly or cartel. They also provide the government with the power to break up an existing monopoly and prevent mergers that significantly reduce competition.

Antitrust laws have been used to both prevent and discourage mergers, particularly those involving large firms in oligopolistic industries. When the Exxon and Mobil corporations proposed a merger in 1998, the Federal Trade Commission (FTC) announced that it would spend several months studying the proposal to determine whether the merger violated antitrust laws. Would this merger reduce competition in the energy market? The answer to this question is not obvious. There are other strong producers in this market. If the merger generates sufficient economies of scale, it might actually lower prices and increase the competitiveness of the industry. However, Exxon and Mobil are the two largest U.S. firms in the oil market. Their merger will create a dominant firm in the industry and reduce the number of competitors by one, perhaps making tacit collusion more likely.

In recent years, the Justice Department has been less likely to oppose mergers, including those increasing a firm's market share, if the merger is expected to reduce prices. Nonetheless, the Exxon-Mobil merger is worrisome to some. Thus, the FTC is analyzing its potential impact on both costs and the future competitiveness of the industry. As this book goes to press, the study continues.

Government has also acted to break up existing monopolies. The case involving AT&T, the giant telecommunications company, provides a recent example. In 1984 the Department of Justice obtained a court decree forcing AT&T to split into eight separate firms. Until then, the firm had a monopoly on long-distance telephone service in the United States. The decree also allowed other firms, such as MCI and Sprint, to enter and compete in the long-distance telephone market. Previously, provision of long-distance telephone service was thought to have economies of scale so important that low costs could be attained only with a single, large firm. The rates charged by AT&T were regulated by the government. New technologies appeared, however, convincing the government that competition would provide lower costs than the regulated monopoly.

When analyzing the attractiveness of antitrust actions designed to maintain or increase the number of firms in an industry, the potential importance of economies of scale must be considered. When economies of scale are unimportant, maintaining and/or expanding the number of rivals in an industry is a good strategy. However, when substantial economies of scale are present, larger firms will have lower per-unit cost than smaller ones. Sometimes economies of scale can be so important that per-unit cost of production will be lowest when the entire output of the industry is produced by a few firms (an oligopoly) or even a single firm (a monopoly). In the latter case, the "natural" tendency will be toward a **natural monopoly**—the situation where economies of scale are such that unit cost will be minimized only if the entire industry output is produced by a single firm. Under these circumstances, increasing the number of firms in the industry would also prevent low-cost production. Because their costs are higher, the prices charged by the smaller firms might even exceed those of a monopolist. Furthermore, it will be difficult to maintain the larger number of rivals because the firms will have a strong incentive to grow and/or merge in order to achieve the lower unit costs accompanying a larger scale of operation. Thus, increasing the number of firms is not an attractive option when the industry is a natural monopoly.

Natural monopoly
A market situation in which the average costs of production continually decline with increased output. Therefore, average costs of production will be lowest when a single, large firm produces the entire output demanded.

Reduce Artificial Barriers to Trade

A second strategy would be to reduce tariffs, quotas, licensing requirements, and other restraints that limit the entry in a market. Government-imposed entry restraints are often the source of monopoly power. When this is the case, removal of these restraints is the most effective way to strengthen the forces of competition.

When a few firms dominate a domestic market, competition from foreign suppliers can help keep the domestic firms on their toes. The foreign competition will help assure that the domestic firms seek to improve quality and keep their costs low. For example, most observers believe that foreign competition in the U.S. auto industry has played precisely this role. Profits for U.S. producers in the highly competitive automobile segment of the industry have been low. In contrast, a 25 percent tariff on imported trucks protects the same U.S. producers in the truck segment of the industry. There, profits per vehicle are much higher. When General Motors began selling their newly designed line of full-sized pickups in 1998 (the first full updating of those models in 10 years), the profit on a well-equipped $30,000 unit was reported to be $8,000. The tariff keeps the price of foreign imports high, so the level of competition is lower in the U.S. market for new trucks than in the market for cars.

Not all goods are traded in international markets. Thus, competition from abroad is not always a realistic alternative. In addition, political obstacles often undermine this option. Trade restraints protecting an industry against competition from abroad are generally a special interest issue. The beneficiaries of the restraints—primarily the owners, managers, and workers in the protected industries—are highly concentrated and generally well organized. In contrast, the costs of the restraints are nearly always thinly spread among poorly organized consumers. The better organized, concentrated interests are likely to prevail. Therefore, even when lower trade barriers are needed to increase the competitiveness of an industry, political factors may reduce the likelihood they will be adopted.

Regulate the Protected Producer

Can government regulation improve the allocative efficiency of a monopoly or an oligopoly? In theory, the answer to this question is clearly yes. Exhibit 11–8 illustrates why ideal government price regulation, in the case of a monopolist, would improve resource allocation. The profit-maximizing monopolist sets price at P_0 and produces output Q_0, where $MR = MC$. Consumers, however, would value additional units more than the opportunity cost. There are steps that the regulatory agency can take to improve resource allocation in the presence of a monopoly.

If unregulated, a profit-maximizing monopolist with the costs indicated here would produce Q_0 units and charge P_0. If a regulatory agency forced the monopolist to reduce price to P_1, the monopolist would expand output to Q_1. Ideally, we would like output to be expanded to Q_2, where P = MC, but regulatory agencies usually do not attempt to keep prices as low as P_2. Can you explain why?

EXHIBIT 11-8

REGULATION OF A MONOPOLIST

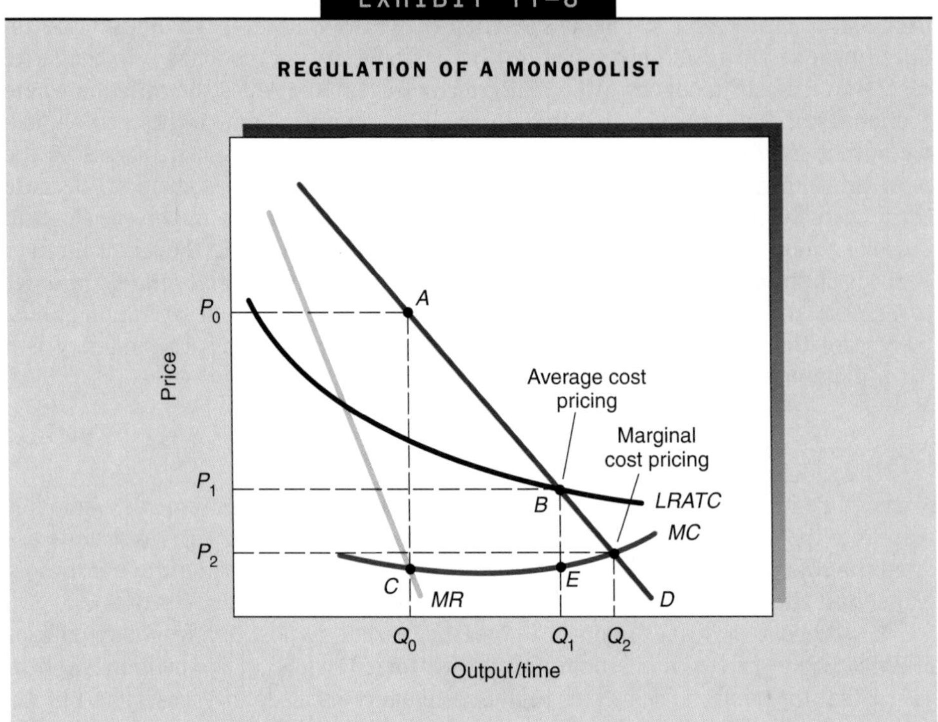

Average Cost Pricing. If a regulatory agency forces the firm in Exhibit 11–8 to reduce price to P_1, at which the *ATC* curve intersects with the market (and firm) demand curve, the firm will expand output to Q_1. Since it cannot charge a price above P_1, the firm cannot increase revenues by selling a smaller output at a higher price. Once the price ceiling is instituted, the firm can increase revenues by P_1, and by only P_1, for each unit it sells. The regulated firm's *MR* is constant at P_1 for all units sold until output is increased to Q_1. Since the firm's *MC* is less than P_1 (and therefore less than *MR*), the profit-maximizing regulated firm shown here will expand output from Q_0 to Q_1. The benefits from the consumption of these units (ABQ_1Q_0) clearly exceed their costs (CEQ_1Q_0). Social welfare has improved as a result of the regulatory action (we will ignore the impact on the distribution of income). At that output level, revenues are sufficient to cover costs. The firm is making zero economic profit (or "normal" accounting profit).

Marginal Cost Pricing. Even at the Q_1 output level, marginal cost is still less than price. Additional welfare gains could be achieved if output were increased to Q_2. However, if a regulatory agency forced the monopolist to reduce price to P_2 (so that price would equal marginal cost at the output level Q_2), economic losses would result. Even a monopolist, unless subsidized, would not undertake production if the regulatory agency set the price at P_2 or any price below P_1. Usually, problems associated with determining and allocating the necessary subsidy would make this option unfeasible.

Problems with Regulation. Even though government regulation of monopoly seems capable of improving market results, as in the preceding average cost pricing example, economic analysis suggests that regulation will usually not be an ideal solution. Why? Three factors tend to reduce both the effectiveness of regulation and the probability that the regulators will act on behalf of all citizens to control monopoly. Let us look at each of these factors.

1. ***Lack of Information.*** In discussing ideal regulation, we assumed that we knew what the firm's *ATC, MC,* and demand curves looked like. In reality, of course, this would not be the case. The firms themselves have difficulty knowing their costs, and especially their demand curves, with any precision.

   Because estimates of demand and marginal costs are difficult to obtain, regulatory agencies usually use profits (or rate of return) as a gauge to determine whether the regulated price is too high or too low. The regulatory agency, guarding the public interest, seeks to impose a "fair" or "normal" rate of return on the firm. If the firm is making profits (that is, an abnormally high rate of return), the price must be higher than P_1 and should be lowered. If the firm is incurring losses (less than the fair or normal rate of return), the regulated price must be less than P_1, and the firm should be allowed to increase price.

   The actual existence of profits, though, is not easily identified. Accounting profit, even allowing for a normal rate of profit, is not the same as economic profit. In addition, regulated firms have a strong incentive to adopt reporting techniques and accounting methods that conceal profits. This will make it difficult for a regulatory agency to identify and impose a price consistent with allocative efficiency.
2. ***Cost Shifting.*** As long as demand is sufficient, the owners of the regulated firm can expect the long-run rate of profit to be essentially fixed, regardless of whether efficient management reduces costs or inefficient management allows costs to increase. If costs decrease, the "fair return" rule imposed by the regulatory agency will force a price reduction; if costs increase, the "fair return" rule will allow a price increase. Compared to the managers of unregulated firms, managers of regulated firms have more freedom to pursue personal objectives and less incentive to seek lower costs. Predictably, they will often fly first-class, entertain lavishly at company expense, give their relatives and friends good jobs, grant unwarranted wage increases, and so on. Actions like these will make managerial life more comfortable and they may well keep the regulators from imposing a lower price ceiling in the near future. As the result of the firm's monopoly position, consumers are unable to switch to substitute products (and rival firms) and thereby help to control managerial inefficiency. Normally, wasteful activities would be policed by the owners, but since the firm's rate of return is set by the regulatory agency, the owners have little incentive to be concerned. Thus, to a large degree, the incentive structure accompanying price regulation is inconsistent with low-cost production.
3. ***Special-Interest Influence.*** The difficulties of government regulation discussed thus far are practical limitations that a regulatory agency would confront in seeking to perform its duties efficiently. But, in the political arena, regulatory authorities cannot necessarily be expected to pursue only efficiency. Regulated firms have a strong incentive to see that "friendly," "reasonable" people serve as regulators, and they will invest political and economic resources to this end. Just as rent-seeking activities designed to gain monopoly privileges can be expected, so can activities to influence regulatory decisions.

   Each competing segment of a regulated industry will try to use the regulatory mechanism for its own competitive advantage. What services and specialized programming should a regulated cable television firm be allowed to offer, at each price? Alternative providers of TV services, such as satellite companies, will work to see that regulated prices and services of the cable firms are set to minimize the ability of cable firms to compete with the providers of satellite video services.

Consumer interests, in contrast to those of industry, are widely dispersed and disorganized. Ordinarily, consumers cannot be expected to invest time, resources, votes, and political contributions to ensure that a particular regulatory commission represents their views. The firms that are regulated can, however, be expected to make such investments. Even though the initial stimulus for a regulating agency might come from consumer interests, economic theory suggests that such agencies will eventually reflect the views of the business and labor interests they are supposed to regulate.

Supply Market with Government Production

Government-operated firms—socialized firms such as the U.S. Postal Service, the Tennessee Valley Authority, and many local public utilities—present an alternative to both private monopoly and regulation. However, both theory and experience indicate that socialized firms will fail to counteract fully the problems that stem from high barriers to entry. The same perverse managerial incentives—incentives to ignore efficiency and pursue personal or professional objectives at the firm's expense—that regulated firms confront also tend to plague the government-operated firm. In addition, the rational ignorance effect comes into play here. Individual voters have little incentive to acquire information about the operation of government firms because their choices will not be decisive. Predictably, the "owners" of a socialized firm (voters) will be uninformed about how well the firm is run, or how it might be run better. This is especially true when there are no direct competitors against which the firm's performance might easily be compared.

Government-operated firms do not provide an environment that rewards efficient management and reductions in cost. Unlike investors in the private sector, no small group of voters normally is in a position to gain substantial wealth by taking over the socialized firm and improving its management. Even more than with monopoly or oligopoly in the private sector, customers of the socialized monopoly (voter-taxpayers) cannot easily switch their business to other sellers. Even those voter-taxpayers who do not consume the product often have to pay taxes to support its provision. When the government operates a business—particularly one with monopoly power—there is typically less investor scrutiny, less reward for efficiency, and less penalty for inefficiency. Higher costs are an expected result.

Government ownership, like unregulated monopoly and government regulation, is a less than ideal solution. Thus, it should not be surprising that those who denounce monopoly in, for instance, the telephone industry seldom point to a government-operated monopoly—such as the postal service—as an example of how an industry should be run.

Pulling It Together

The policy implications that can legitimately be drawn from an analysis of high barriers to entry are less than fully satisfying. We may not like the reduction in competition or its effects, but economic analysis suggests important qualifications to the "solutions" usually put forth.

Most of the policy alternatives are not terribly attractive. Economies of scale often reduce the attractiveness of antitrust actions. When larger firms have lower per-unit costs, restructuring the industry to increase the number of firms will be both costly and difficult to maintain. Government measures, such as tariff reductions and removal of entry barriers into markets, are perhaps the surest recommendation for increasing competition. Such policies, however, will certainly face political opposition, primarily from owners and workers in protected industries.

Regulation is also a less than ideal solution. Regulators do not possess the information necessary to impose an efficient outcome, and they may be susceptible to manipulation by industrial and labor interests. Moreover, since public-sector managers are likely to pursue political objectives at the expense of economic efficiency, public ownership also has shortcomings. Thus, economic theory indicates that there are no ideal solutions when substantial economies of scale are present. Choices must be made among alternatives, all of which are imperfect.

THE COMPETITIVE PROCESS IN THE REAL WORLD

How competitive are markets? This question is difficult to answer. In a very real sense, every firm competes with every other firm for the consumer's additional dollar of spending. Competition is everywhere; the seller of compact discs, for example, competes with the bookstore and the local restaurant for our entertainment budgets. The sellers of swimming pools compete with airlines, hotels, casinos, and automobile rental companies for the vacation and leisure time expenditures of consumers.

Moreover, price competition is only one element of the competitive process. Even though they are difficult for our models to capture fully, nonprice factors like quality, design, convenience, and terms of credit are important competitive weapons firms use as they seek to increase profitability and market share. These nonprice competitive weapons are generally more important in concentrated industries because, unlike a reduction in price, it is more difficult for rivals to quickly duplicate improvements in these areas. Like price reductions, however, improvements in the various dimensions of product quality provide consumers with more value per dollar of expenditure. Furthermore, competition of this type makes collusion more difficult and erodes profits even in industries with few rival firms. Perhaps this helps explain why profit levels, even in manufacturing industries, are considerably lower than is generally thought to be the case. For example, a national sample poll of adults conducted by Opinion Research of Princeton found that the average person thought profits comprised 29 percent of every dollar of sales in manufacturing. In reality, the after-tax accounting profits of manufacturing corporations are about 4 cents to 5 cents per dollar of sales. Competition among manufacturers is generally strong.

Over time, technological change and the development of new products is also an integral part of the competitive process. No firm can be assured that customers will continue to purchase its product or service. Dynamic change can threaten the market position of even well-entrenched firms with monopoly power. For example, the development of fax machines and growth of e-mail pose a substantial threat to the market power of the U.S. Postal Service, a legally protected monopoly. Profitability and high prices will hasten the development of substitutes. The high price of natural rubber spurred the development of synthetic rubber. High rail-shipping rates accelerated the development of long-distance trucking. More recently, the output reductions and price increases achieved by the Organization of Petroleum Exporting Countries (OPEC) subjected oil to vastly intensified competition from coal, solar energy, and other nonpetroleum energy sources, as well as from greatly expanded exploration efforts in non-OPEC nations. The result was a long tumble in the price the OPEC cartel was able to charge for its oil. What seemed to be a secure monopoly position for OPEC in the 1970s turned out to be something very different. By the end of 1998, oil prices, corrected for inflation, were lower than they had been prior to the beginning of OPEC's cartel activities in 1973.

The patent system is based on the premise that the expectation of monopoly profit for a period of time will stimulate technological change and the discovery of new, improved products. This is why new products or production methods are granted a patent—that is, a monopoly—for a period of 17 years. Others are prohibited from copying the product or technique. If this "reward" of temporary monopoly power and profit did not exist, businesses would be less inclined to undertake research designed to reduce costs and improve product quality. Of course, dynamic competitive forces may operate slowly in response to price changes. Nonetheless, they are often able to erode the dominant market position of even giant firms.

The dynamic nature of competitiveness in the U.S. economy is shown by the fact that the firms composing the largest 100 or 200 corporations are different from one another and are constantly changing. As successful management and the vagaries of business fortune exert their influences, some firms are pushed out of the top group and others enter. Following the fate of various firms over time is not easy, since mergers occur and names change, but historical research indicates that, of the largest 100 manufacturing corporations in 1909, only 36 remained on the list in 1948. Of the 50 largest in 1947, only 25 remained on the list in 1972, and 5 failed to make even the top 200. Of the firms on the *Fortune* 500 list in 1980, only about half were able to make the list in 1990.

The competitiveness of markets is complex and difficult to measure. However, economists generally agree that the U.S. economy has become more competitive over the past several decades. Better communications, reductions in transportation costs, increased competition from imports, and deregulation of several key markets have all tended to enhance the competitiveness of markets in the United States.

LOOKING *Ahead*

The last several chapters have focused on product markets. Of course, resources are required to produce products. The following chapter will focus on the resources market and the employment decisions of both business firms and resource suppliers.

KEY POINTS

➤ The four major barriers to entry into a market are economies of scale, government licensing, patents, and control of an essential resource.

➤ Monopoly is present when there is a single seller of a well-defined product for which there are no good substitutes and the entry barriers into the market are high. While there are only a few markets for which the entire output is supplied by a single seller, the monopoly model also helps one better understand the operation of markets dominated by a small number of firms.

➤ The market demand curve is also the monopolist's demand curve. Like other price searchers, a profit-maximizing monopolist will lower price and expand output as long as marginal revenue exceeds marginal cost. At the maximum-profit output, *MR* will equal *MC*. The monopolist will charge the price on its demand curve consistent with that output.

➤ If profit is present, high barriers to entry will shield a monopolist from competitive pressures and, in such cases, monopolists can earn long-run economic profits. Sometimes demand and cost conditions will be such that even a monopolist will be unable to earn economic profit.

➤ An oligopolistic market is characterized by (1) a small number of rival firms, (2) interdependence among the sellers, (3) substantial economies of scale, and (4) high entry barriers into the market.

➤ There is no general theory of equilibrium price and output for oligopolistic markets. If rival oligopolists acted totally independent of their competitors, they would drive price down to the per-unit cost of production. Alternatively, if they colluded perfectly, price would rise to the level a monopolist would charge. The actual outcome will generally fall between these two extremes.

➤ Oligopolists have a strong incentive to collude and raise their prices. However, each firm will be able to gain if it can cut its price (or raise the quality of its product) because the demand curve confronted by the firm is more elastic than the industry demand curve. This introduces a conflict between the interests of individual firms and the industry as a whole. This conflict makes collusive agreements difficult to maintain.

➤ Oligopolistic firms are less likely to collude successfully against the interests of consumers if (a) the number of rival firms is large; (b) it is costly to prohibit competitors from offering secret price cuts (or quality improvements) to customers; (c) entry barriers are low; (d) market demand conditions tend to be unstable; and/or (e) the threat of antitrust action is present.

➤ Economists criticize high barriers to market entry because (a) the ability of consumers to discipline producers is weakened, (b) the unregulated monopolist or oligopolist can often gain by restricting output and raising price, (c) profits are less able to stimulate new entry, and (d) legal barriers to entry will encourage firms to "invest" resources in seeking additional protective barriers and maintaining existing ones.

➤ A natural monopoly exists when long-run average total costs continue to decline as firm size increases, over the entire range of market demand. Thus, a larger firm always has lower costs.

➤ When entry barriers are high and competition among rival firms weak, the major policy alternatives are: (a) antitrust action designed to maintain or increase the number of firms in the industry, (b) relaxation of regulations that limit entry and trade, (c) price regulation, and (d) provision of output by government firms. When feasible, option b is the most attractive alternative. Under most circumstances, all the other options have shortcomings.

➤ Competitive forces are present even in markets with high barriers to entry. Quality competition is an important element of the competitive process. Profitability and high prices encourage technological change and the development of substitute products.

CRITICAL ANALYSIS QUESTIONS

*1. "Barriers to entry are crucial to the existence of long-run profits, but they cannot guarantee the existence of profits." Evaluate.

2. "Monopoly is good for producers but bad for consumers. The gains of the former offset the losses of the latter. On balance, there is no reason to think that monopoly is bad for the economy." Evaluate.

*3. Do monopolists charge the highest prices for which they can sell their products? Do they maximize their average profit per sale? Are monopolistic firms always profitable? Why or why not?

4. The retail liquor industry is potentially a competitive industry. However, the liquor retailers of a southern state, with the cooperation of the state legislature, organized a trade association that sets prices for all firms. For all practical purposes, a competitive industry became a monopoly. Compare the price and output policy for a purely competitive industry with the policy that would be established by a profit-maximizing monopolist or trade association. Who benefits and who is hurt by the formation of the monopoly?

5. Does economic theory indicate that an ideal regulatory agency that forces a monopolist to charge a price equal to either marginal or average total cost would improve economic efficiency? Explain. Does economic theory suggest that a regulatory agency will in fact follow a proper regulation policy? What are some of the factors that complicate the regulatory function?

6. Is a monopolist subject to any competitive pressures? Explain. Would an unregulated monopolist have an incentive to operate and produce efficiently? Why or why not?

7. How will high entry barriers into a market influence (a) the long-run profitability of the firms, (b) the cost efficiency of the firms in the industry, (c) the likelihood that some inefficient (high-cost) firms will survive, and (d) the incentive of entrepreneurs to develop substitutes for the

product supplied by the firms? Are competitive pressures present in markets with high barriers to entry? Discuss.

*8. Why is oligopolistic collusion more difficult when there is product variation than when the products of all firms are identical?

9. In large cities, taxi fares are often set above the market equilibrium rate. Sometimes the number of licenses is limited in order to maintain the above-market price. Other times licenses are automatically granted to anyone wanting to operate a taxi. When taxi fares are set above market equilibrium, compare and contrast resource allocation under the restricted license system (assume the licenses are tradable) and the free-entry system. In which case will it be easier for customers to get a taxi? In which case will the amount of capital required to enter the taxi business be greater?

10. We have a theory to explain the equilibrium price and output for monopoly, but not for oligopoly. Why? What role can game theory play in helping us to understand decisions made by oligopolists?

*11. Historically, the real cost of transporting both goods and people has declined substantially. What impact does a reduction in transportation cost have on the market power of individual producers? Do you think the U.S. economy is more or less competitive today than it was 100 years ago? Explain.

*12. "My uncle just bought 1,000 shares of Mammoth Manufacturing, one of the largest and most profitable companies in the United States. Given the high profit rate of this company, he will make a bundle from this purchase." Evaluate this statement. Is it necessarily true? Explain.

*13. Gouge-em Cable Company is the only cable television service company licensed to operate in Backwater County. Most of its costs are access fees and maintenance expenses. These fixed costs total $640,000 monthly. The marginal cost of adding another subscriber to its system is constant at $2 per month. Gouge-em's demand curve can be determined from the data in the accompanying table.

Subscription Price (per momth)	Number of Subscribers
$25	20,000
20	40,000
15	60,000
10	80,000
5	100,000
1	150,000

a. What price will Gouge-em charge for its cable services? What are its profits at this price?
b. Now suppose the Backwater County Public Utility Commission has the data and feels that cable subscription rates in the county are too expensive and that Gouge-em's profits are unfairly high. What regulated price will it set so that Gouge-em makes only a normal rate of return on its investment?

14. Suppose that you produce and sell children's tables in a localized market. Past experience permits you to estimate your demand and marginal cost schedules. This information is presented in the accompanying table.

a. Fill in the missing revenue and cost schedules.
b. Assuming you are currently charging $55 per table set, what should you do if you want to maximize profits?
c. Given your demand and cost estimates, what price should you charge if you want to maximize weekly profit? What output should you produce? What is your maximum weekly profit?

Price	Quantity Demanded (per week)	Marginal Cost	Total Revenue	Marginal Revenue	Fixed Cost	Total Cost
$60	1	$50	____	____	$40	____
55	2	20	____	____	____	____
50	3	24	____	____	____	____
45	4	29	____	____	____	____
40	5	35	____	____	____	____
35	6	45	____	____	____	____

15. The diagram below shows demand and long-run cost conditions in an industry.

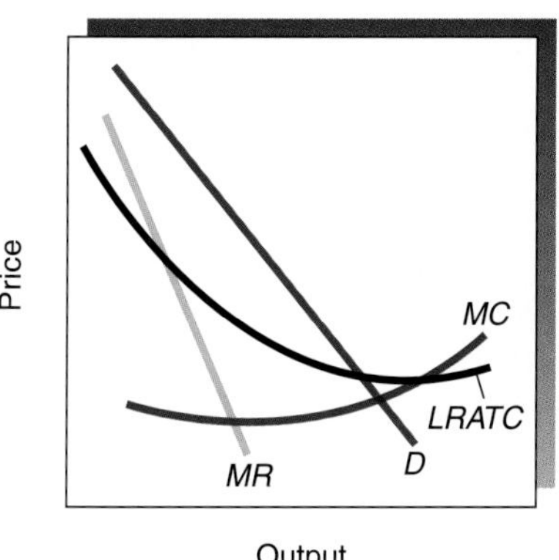

a. Explain why the industry is likely to be monopolized.
b. Indicate the price that a profit-maximizing monopolist would charge, and label it *P*.
c. Indicate the monopolist's output level, and label it *Q*.
d. Indicate the maximum profits of the monopolist.
e. Will the profits attract competitors to the industry? Why or why not? Explain.

---

*Asterisk denotes questions for which answers are given in Appendix B.

CHAPTER 12

It is . . . necessary to attach price tags to the various factors of production . . . in order to guide those who have the day-to-day decisions to make as to what is plentiful and what is scarce.

Professor James Meade[1]

The Supply of and Demand for Productive Resources

CHAPTER FOCUS

- What are the types of resource markets and what important roles do they play?
- Why do business firms demand labor, machines, and other resources? Why is the demand for a productive resource inversely related to its price?
- How do business firms decide how many skilled laborers, unskilled laborers, machines, and other factors of production to employ?
- How is the quantity supplied of a resource related to its price in the short run? In the long run?
- What determines the market price of a resource? How do resource prices help to allocate efficiently a society's resources across competing uses?

[1]James E. Meade, "Economic Efficiency and Distributional Justice," in *Contemporary Issues in Economics*, ed. Robert W. Crandall and Richard S. Eckaus (Boston: Little, Brown, 1972), p. 319.

In previous chapters we focused on product markets in which consumers purchase goods and services that are supplied by business firms. To produce these products, firms must hire productive resources, such as machines and workers. How do businesses decide which resources to employ and the quantity of each that will be used? What encourages them to conserve on their use of scarce resources? What factors influence the availability of resources both now and in the future? Analysis of **resource markets** will help us answer these questions and related issues. (*Note:* Because resources are also referred to as *factors* or *inputs,* these markets are also known as *factor markets* or *input markets.*)

Resource markets
Markets in which business firms demand factors of production (for example, labor, capital, and natural resources) from household suppliers. The resources are then used to produce goods and services. These markets are sometimes called factor markets *or* input markets.

EXHIBIT 12-1

THE MARKET FOR RESOURCES

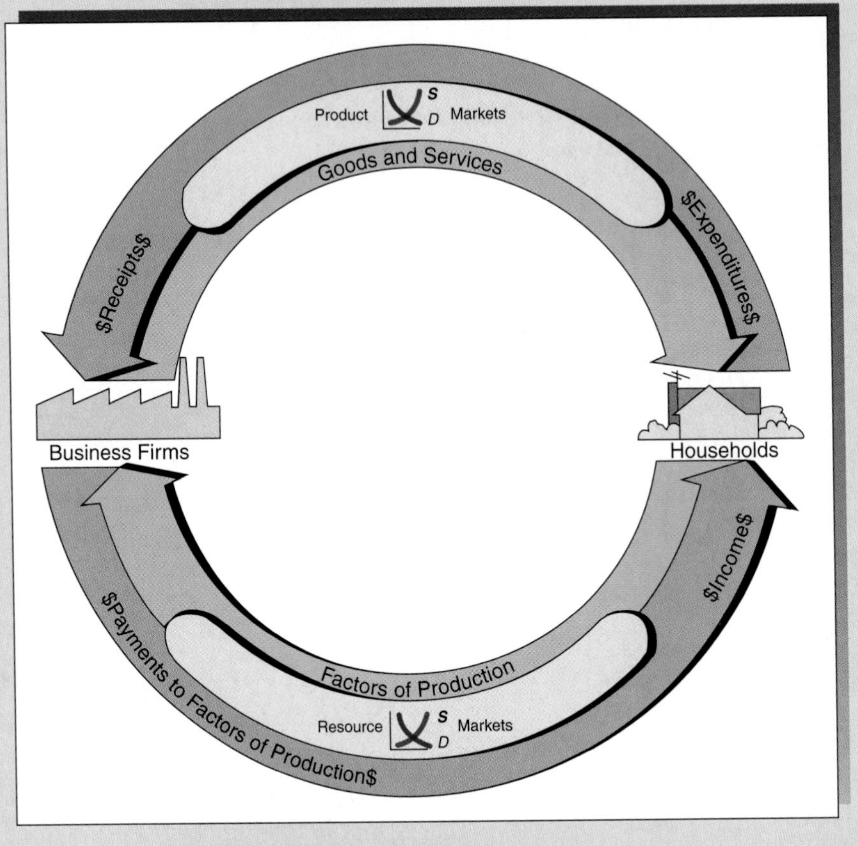

Until now, we have focused on product markets, where households demand goods and services that are supplied by firms (upper loop). We now turn to resource markets, where firms demand factors of production—human capital (for example, skills and knowledge of workers) and physical capital (for example, machines, buildings, and land)—which are supplied by households in exchange for income (bottom loop). In resource markets, firms are buyers and households are sellers, just the reverse of the case for product markets.

Just as in product markets, the forces of supply and demand combine to determine price in resource markets. The buyers and sellers in resource markets are just the reverse of what they are in product markets. In resource markets, business firms are the purchasers; they demand resources that are used to produce goods and services. Households are the sellers; they supply resources in exchange for income. The income derived from supplying productive resources, such as the wages received from the sale of labor services, provides the major source of income for most of us. Prices in resource markets coordinate the choices of buyers and sellers and bring the amount of each resource demanded into harmony with the amount supplied. Resource prices also help to allocate factors of production efficiently and channel them into the areas in which they are most productive. This enables us to have higher incomes and a larger supply of consumer goods than would otherwise be the case.

As the circular flow diagram of **Exhibit 12–1** illustrates, there is a close relationship between product and resource markets. Households earn income by selling factors of production—for example, the services of their labor and capital—to business firms. Their offers to sell form the supply curve in resource markets (bottom loop). The income households derive from the sale of resources provides them with the buying power required to purchase goods and services in product markets. These household expenditures for products generate revenues that provide business firms with the incentive to produce goods and services (top loop). In turn, the business firms demand resources because they contribute to the production of goods and services that can be sold in product markets.

HUMAN AND NONHUMAN RESOURCES

Broadly speaking, there are two different types of productive inputs—nonhuman and human. **Nonhuman resources** can be further broken down into the categories of physical capital, land, and natural resources. *Physical capital* consists of human-made resources, such as tools, machines, and buildings, that are used to produce other things.

Nonhuman resources
The durable, nonhuman inputs that can be used to produce both current and future output. Machines, buildings, land, and raw materials are examples. Investment can increase the supply of nonhuman resources. Economists often use the term physical capital *when referring to nonhuman resources.*

Net investment can increase the supply of nonhuman resources. Investment, however, involves a cost. Resources that are used to produce machines, upgrade the quality of land, or discover natural resources could be used directly to produce goods and services for current consumption. Why take the roundabout path? The answer is that sometimes indirect methods of producing goods are less costly in the long run. For example, Robinson Crusoe found he could catch more fish by taking some time off from hand-fishing to build a net. Even though his initial investment of time in making the net reduced his current catch, once the net was completed he was able to more than make up for this loss. Benefits and costs will influence investment choices ranging from fishing nets to complex machines. These investments will be undertaken only when decision makers expect the benefits of a larger future output to more than offset the current reduction in the production of consumption goods. Just as the supply of machines can be increased, so, too, can wise land development and soil-conservation practices be used to upgrade both the quantity and quality of land. Similarly, the supply of natural resources can be increased (within limits) by the application of more resources to discovery and development.

Human resources are composed of the skills and knowledge of workers. Investment in such things as education, training, health, and experience can enhance the skill, ability, and ingenuity of individuals, and thereby increase their productivity.

Human resources
The abilities, skills, and health of human beings that can contribute to the production of both current and future output. Investment in training and education can increase the supply of human resources.

OUTSTANDING ECONOMIST

Gary Becker (1930–)

This 1992 Nobel Prize recipient is best known for his role in the development of human-capital theory and his innovative application of that theory to areas as diverse as employment discrimination, family development, and crime. In his widely acclaimed book *Human Capital,** he developed the theoretical foundation for human investment decisions in education, on-the-job training, migration, and health. Becker is a past president of the American Economic Association and a longtime professor at the University of Chicago.

*Gary Becker, *Human Capital* (New York: Columbia University Press, 1964).

Investment in human capital
Expenditures on training, education, skill development, and health designed to increase human capital and the productivity of an individual.

Economists refer to such activities as **investment in human capital.**[2] Like physical capital, human capital also depreciates (human skills decline with age or lack of use). During any given year, education and training will add to the stock of human capital while depreciation detracts from it.

Decisions to invest in human capital involve all the basic ingredients of other investment decisions. Consider the decision of whether to go to college. As you know, an investment in a college education requires the sacrifice of current earnings as well as payments for direct expenses, such as tuition and books. The investment is expected to lead to a better job (when both monetary and nonmonetary aspects are considered) and other benefits. The rational investor will weigh the current costs against the expected future benefits. College will be chosen only if the benefits outweigh the costs.

Human resources differ from nonhuman resources in two important respects. First, human capital is embodied in the individual. Individuals cannot be separated from their knowledge, skills, and health conditions in the same way that they can be separated from physical capital, such as buildings or machines that they might own. As a result, choices concerning the use of human resources are vitally affected by working conditions, location, job prestige, and similar nonpecuniary factors. Although monetary factors influence human-capital decisions, individuals will often choose to trade off some money income for better working conditions.

Second, human resources cannot be bought and sold in nonslave societies. Workers sell only the *services* of their labor, not the ownership to the human resource itself. Individuals have the option of quitting, selling their labor services to another employer, or using them in an alternative manner. Thus, we usually speak of the worker as selling (and the firm as buying) labor services.

In competitive markets, the price of resources, like the price of products, is determined by supply and demand. We will begin our analysis of resource markets by focusing on the demand for resources, both human and nonhuman.

DEMAND FOR RESOURCES

Profit-seeking producers employ laborers, machines, raw materials, and other resources because they help produce goods and services. ***The demand for a resource***

[2]The contributions of T. W. Schultz and Gary Becker to the literature on human capital have been particularly significant. See Daniel S. Hamermesh and Albert Rees, *The Economics of Work and Pay* (New York: Harper & Row, 1988), Chapter 3, for additional detail on human-capital theory.

exists because there is a demand for goods that the resource helps to produce. The demand for each resource is thus a **derived demand;** *it is derived from the demand of consumers for products.*

Derived demand
The demand for a resource; it stems from the demand for the final good the resource helps to produce.

For example, a service station hires mechanics because customers demand repair service, not because the service station owner receives benefits simply from having mechanics around. If customers did not demand repair service, mechanics would not be employed for long. Similarly, the demand for such inputs as carpenters, plumbers, lumber, and glass windows is derived from the demand of consumers for houses and other consumer products these resources help to make. Most resources contribute to the production of numerous goods. For example, glass is used to produce windows, ornaments, dishes, light bulbs, and mirrors, among other things. The total demand for a resource is the sum of the derived demand for it in each of its uses.

The demand curve for a resource shows the amount of the resource that will be used at different prices. As Exhibit 12–2 illustrates, there will be an inverse relationship between the price of a resource and the amount demanded of it. There are two major reasons why less of a resource will be demanded as its price increases: (1) producers will turn to substitute resources and (2) consumers will buy less of goods that become more expensive as the result of higher resource costs. Let us take a closer look at each of these factors.

Substitution in Production. *Firms will use the input combination that minimizes their cost. When the price of a resource goes up, firms will turn to lower-cost substitute inputs and cut back on their use of a more expensive resource.*

Typically, there are many ways producers can reduce their use of a more expensive resource. For example, if the price of oak lumber increases, furniture manufacturers will use other wood varieties, metals, and plastics more intensely. Similarly, if the price of copper tubing increases, construction firms and plumbers will substitute plastic pipe for the more expensive tubing. Sometimes producers will alter the style

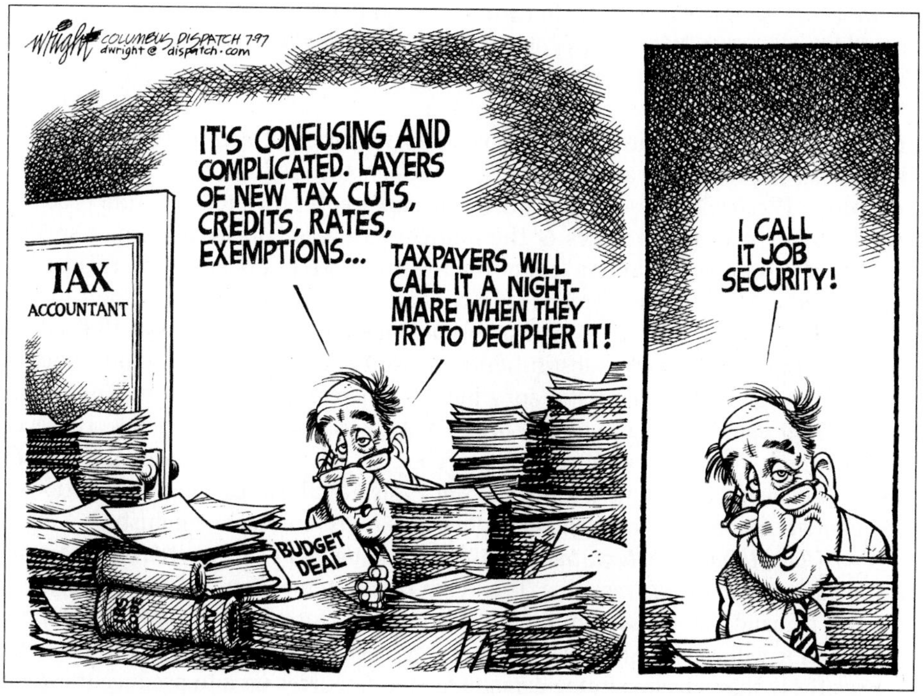

The demand for resources is a derived demand. A more complex tax code would increase the demand for (and thus the wages of) accountants, while a simpler tax code would lower the demand for (and wages of) accountants.

As the price of a resource increases, producers that use the resource intensely will (1) turn to substitute resources and (2) face higher costs, which will lead to higher prices and reduction in output. At the lower rate of output, producers will use less of the resource that increased in price. Both of these factors contribute to the inverse relationship between the price and amount demanded of a resource.

EXHIBIT 12-2

THE DEMAND CURVE FOR A RESOURCE

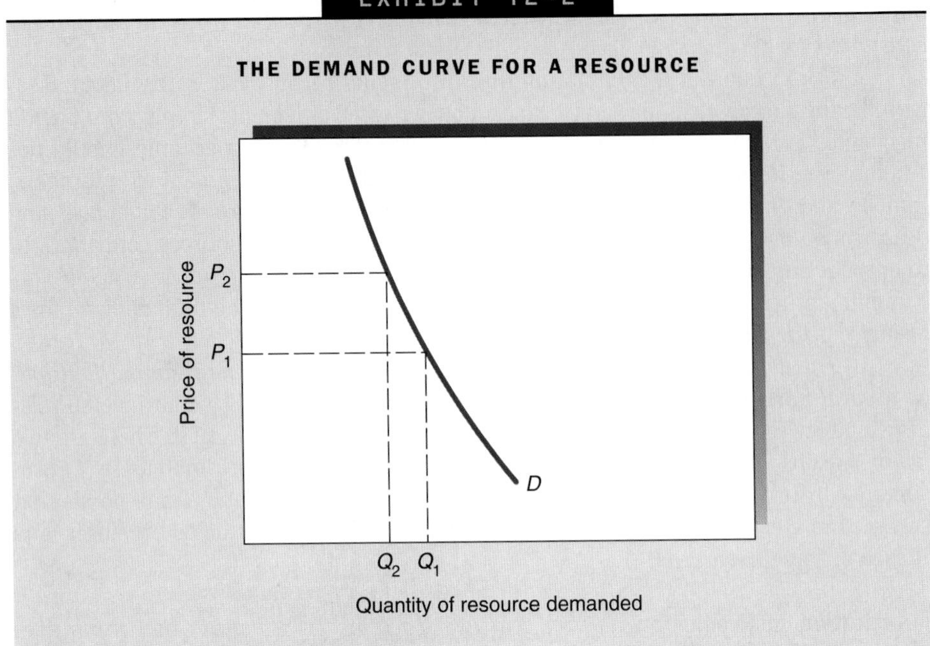

and dimensions of a product in order to conserve on the use of a more expensive resource. In other cases, a shift in location may play a role in the substitution process. For example, if prices of office space and land increase in the downtown area of a large city, firms may move to the suburbs in order to cut back on their use of the more expensive resource.

The degree to which firms will be able to reduce their use of a more expensive resource will vary. The easier it is to turn to substitute factors, the more elastic the demand for a resource. ***Other things constant, the more (and better) substitute resources that are available, the more elastic the demand for the resource.***

Substitution in Consumption. An increase in the price of a resource will lead to higher costs of production and thus higher prices for the products that the input helps to produce. Faced with these higher prices, *consumers* will turn to substitute products and cut back on their purchases of the more expensive products. In turn, a smaller quantity of resources (including less of the one that rose in price) will be required to produce the smaller amount demanded by consumers at the now higher price.

The experience of the American automobile industry in the early 1980s illustrates the importance of this substitution-in-consumption effect. Throughout much of the 1970s, wages in the domestic auto industry increased quite rapidly. The higher wages placed upward pressure on the prices of American-made automobiles. However, as auto prices rose, many consumers switched to substitute products, particularly foreign-produced automobiles. American auto sales declined, causing a reduction in the quantity of labor demanded (and employment) in the automobile industry.

Other things constant, the more elastic the demand for the product, the more elastic the demand for the resource. This relationship stems from the derived nature of resource demand. An increase in the price of a product for which consumer demand is highly elastic will cause a sharp reduction in the sales of the good. There will thus also be a relatively sharp decline in the demand for the resources used to produce the good.

Time and the Demand for Resources

The elasticity of the demand for a resource is influenced by the ease of substitution in both production and consumption, as well as the length of time under consideration. It takes time for producers to adjust fully to a change in the price of a resource. Typically, a producer will be unable to alter a production process or the design of a product immediately in order to conserve on the use of a more expensive input or to make better use of an input whose price has declined. Consumers may also find it difficult to alter their consumption patterns quickly in response to price changes. Thus, the demand for a resource generally becomes more elastic with the passage of time.

Exhibit 12–3 illustrates the impact of time on the elasticity of resource demand. Because it is generally difficult to substitute quickly away from a more expensive resource, demand is relatively inelastic in the short run. Thus, an increase in price from P_1 to P_2 will lead to only a small reduction in quantity of the resource used (from Q_1 to Q_2). Given more time, however, producers will be able to make a larger substitution away from the more expensive resource. Therefore, the P_2 price increase elicits a larger reduction in quantity demanded (to Q_3) with the passage of time. In the long run, the demand for a resource is nearly always more elastic than in the short run.

Shifts in the Demand for Resources

Like the demand schedule for a product, the entire demand curve for a resource may shift. There are three reasons why this may occur.

1. ***A change in the demand for a product will cause a similar change in the demand for the resources used to make the product.*** Anything that increases the demand for a consumer good simultaneously increases the demand for resources required to make

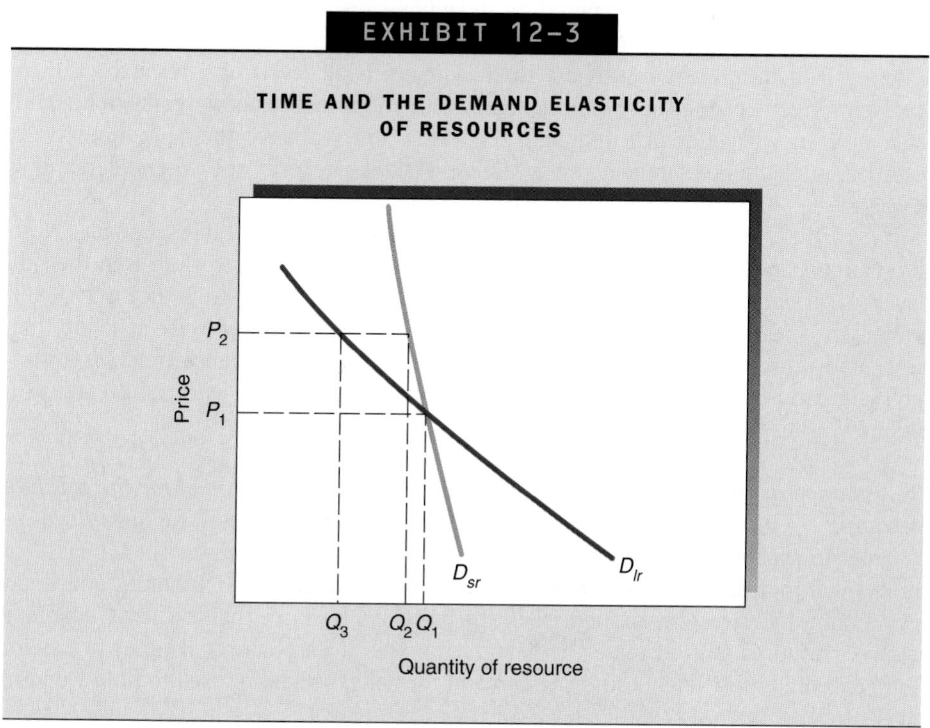

The demand for a resource will be more elastic (1) the easier it is for firms to switch to substitute inputs and (2) the more elastic the consumer demand for the products the resource helps to produce. As we illustrate here, demand for a resource in the long run (D_{lr}) is nearly always more elastic than demand in the short run (D_{sr}).

it. Conversely, a decline in product demand will reduce the demand for resources embodied in the product.

Changes in the music recording industry provide a good example of the linkage between product and resource demand. During the late 1980s and early 1990s, the demand for compact discs increased sharply, driven by the rapidly falling prices of compact disc players. This increase in demand for compact discs led to an increase in demand for workers to produce them. Employment at plants producing the laser optic encoding devices and the types of plastics and metals used to produce the discs expanded rapidly. Similarly, the higher consumer demand for compact discs meant falling demand for vinyl records and tapes. Workers were being laid off at plants producing raw vinyl and related items, such as diamond record player needles. Reflecting the changing demand in product markets, employment in industries related to compact discs expanded, while employment in industries related to records and tapes fell. This reallocation of resources is a natural and integral part of how markets respond to changing consumer demands.

2. ***Changes in the productivity of a resource will alter demand—the higher the productivity of a resource, the greater will be the demand for it.*** The productivity of a resource will depend on the amount of other resources with which it is working. In general, additional capital will tend to increase the productivity of labor. For example, someone with a dump truck can haul more material than the same person with a wheelbarrow. The quantity and quality of the tools with which we work significantly affect our productivity.

Technological advances can also improve the productivity of resources, including labor. Advances in the computer industry illustrate this point. Working with computer technology, an accountant and a data-entry person can maintain business records and create bookkeeping reports that previously would have required 10 to 15 workers. Improvements in word-processing equipment have vastly increased the productivity of typists, journalists, lawyers, and writers. Similarly, computers have substantially increased the productivity of typesetters, telephone operators, quality-control technicians, and workers in many other occupations.

In addition, improvements in the quality (skill level) of a resource will increase productivity and therefore the demand for the resource. As workers obtain valuable new knowledge and/or upgrade their skills, they enhance their productivity. In essence, such workers move into a different skill category, one where demand is greater.

These factors help explain why wage rates in the United States, Canada, Western Europe, and Japan are higher than in most other areas of the world. Given the skill level of workers, the technology, and the capital equipment with which they work, individuals in these countries produce more goods and services per hour of labor than workers in most other countries. In turn, the demand for their labor (relative to supply) is greater because of their high productivity. Essentially, the workers' greater productivity leads to their higher wage rates.

3. ***A change in the price of a related resource will affect the demand for the original resource.*** A rise in the price of a resource will cause the demand for *substitute* resources to expand. For example, when the price of lumber increases, the demand for bricks will increase as home builders switch to building more brick homes and fewer wood homes. Conversely, an increase in the price of a resource that is a *complement* to a given resource will decrease the demand for the given resource. Higher prices for lumber would most likely cause the demand for nails, which are used to hold wood in place, to fall.

MARGINAL PRODUCTIVITY AND THE FIRM'S HIRING DECISION

How does a producer decide whether to employ additional units of a resource? Like other decisions, the marginal benefit relative to the marginal cost is the determining factor. Because firms are mostly price takers in resource markets (meaning they can hire as many units of the resource as they wish without affecting the market price of the resource), the marginal cost of hiring one more worker is simply the relevant wage cost, while the marginal cost of purchasing a machine is its price. These represent the increase in the firm's costs that results from employing one more unit of the resource. But what about the marginal benefit of the resource to the firm? It is measured by the increase in the firm's revenue that results from employing one more unit of the resource, the resource's **marginal revenue product (MRP).** A profit-maximizing firm will hire an additional unit of the resource only if the marginal revenue product exceeds the cost of employing the resource.

Marginal revenue product (MRP)
The change in the total revenue of a firm that results from the employment of one additional unit of a resource. The marginal revenue product of an input is equal to its marginal product multiplied by the marginal revenue of the good or service produced.

Suppose a retail store was considering hiring a security guard at a wage rate of $25 per hour to help reduce shoplifting. If the security guard could prevent $20 worth of shoplifting per hour, should the profit-maximizing firm hire the guard? Because the marginal cost of employing the security guard (the wage of $25) is higher than the guard's marginal revenue product (the $20 reduction in shoplifting per hour), the wise decision is for the firm not to hire the security guard. Hiring the guard would result in a reduction in the firm's profit of $5 per hour. The guard would be employed only if the reduction in shoplifting would exceed the wage cost. In most situations, the direct impact of hiring an additional resource on a firm's revenue is not as clear, so let's take a closer look at the firm's decision and how marginal revenue product is determined.

EMPLOYMENT OF A VARIABLE RESOURCE WITH A FIXED RESOURCE

When an additional unit of the resource is employed relative to a fixed amount of other resources, the direct result is that the firm's output will increase by an amount equal to the resource's **marginal product (MP).** Because this is measured in units of physical output, it is sometimes referred to as *marginal physical product.* In turn, the firm will sell each of these additional units of output. Recall that **marginal revenue (MR)** is the increase in the firm's revenue that results from the sale of each additional unit of output. Thus, a resource's marginal revenue product is equal to the marginal product of the resource multiplied by the marginal revenue of the good or service produced. ***Because of the law of diminishing returns, the marginal product of a resource will fall as employment of the resource expands, and thus the marginal revenue product of a resource will also fall as employment expands.***

Marginal product (MP)
The change in total output that results from the employment of one additional unit of a resource—one workday of skilled labor, for example.

Marginal revenue (MR)
The change in a firm's total revenue that results from the production and sale of one additional unit of output.

The relationship between the marginal revenue a firm derives from selling an additional unit of output and the price for which it is sold is different for *price taker* firms than for *price searcher* firms, however. Because a price taker firm sells all units produced at the same price, the price taker's marginal revenue will be equal to the market price of the product. The price searcher, however, must reduce price (for all units) in order to expand the number of units sold. Thus, the price searcher's marginal revenue will be less than the sales price of the units. The marginal product of a resource multiplied by the selling price of the product is called the resource's **value of marginal product (VMP).** ***For a price taker firm, the MRP of a resource is equal to its VMP because price and marginal revenue are equal. For a price searcher firm, however, the MRP of a resource will be lower than its VMP because marginal revenue is less than price.***

Value of marginal product (VMP)
The marginal product of a resource multiplied by the selling price of the product it helps to produce. For a price taker firm, marginal revenue product (MRP) will be equal to the value marginal product (VMP).

Using these measures, **Exhibit 12–4** illustrates how a firm decides how much of a resource to employ. Compute-Accounting, Inc., uses computer equipment and data-entry operators to supply clients with monthly accounting statements. The firm is a price taker: It sells its service in a competitive market for $200 per statement. Given the fixed quantity of computer equipment owned by Compute-Accounting, column 2 relates the employment of data-entry operators to the expected total output (quantity of accounting statements). One data-entry operator can process five statements per week. When two operators are employed, nine statements can be completed. Column 2 indicates how total output is expected to change as additional data-entry operators are employed. Column 3 presents the marginal product schedule for data-entry operators. Column 6, the MRP schedule, shows how the employment of each additional operator affects total revenue. Both fall as additional operators are employed due to the law of diminishing returns.

Since Compute-Accounting is a price taker, the marginal revenue product and the value marginal product of labor are equal. Thus, the marginal revenue product of labor (column 6) can be calculated by multiplying the marginal product (column 3) times the sales price of an accounting statement (column 4).

How does Compute-Accounting decide how many operators to employ? As additional operators are employed, the output of processed statements (column 2) will increase, which will expand total revenue (column 5). Employment of additional operators, though, will also add to production costs because the operators must be paid. Applying the profit-maximization rule, Compute-Accounting will hire additional operators as long as their employment adds more to revenues than to costs. This will

EXHIBIT 12–4

SHORT-RUN DEMAND SCHEDULE OF A FIRM

Units of Variable Factor (Data-Entry Operators) (1)	Total Output (Accounting Statements Processed per Week) (2)	Marginal Product (Change in Column 2 Divided by Change in Column 1) (3)	Sales Price per Statement (4)	Total Revenue (2) × (4) (5)	MRP (3) × (4) (6)
0	0.0	—	$200	$ 0	—
1	5.0	5.0	200	1,000	1,000
2	9.0	4.0	200	1,800	800
3	12.0	3.0	200	2,400	600
4	14.0	2.0	200	2,800	400
5	15.5	1.5	200	3,100	300
6	16.5	1.0	200	3,300	200
7	17.0	0.5	200	3,400	100

Compute-Accounting, Inc., uses computer technology and data-entry operators to provide accounting services in a competitive market. For each accounting statement processed, the firm receives a $200 fee (column 4). Given the firm's current fixed capital, column 2 shows how total output changes as additional data-entry operators are hired. The marginal revenue product (MRP) schedule (column 6) indicates how hiring an additional operator affects the total revenue of the firm. Since a profit-maximizing firm will hire an additional employee if, and only if, the employee adds more to revenues than to costs, the marginal revenue product curve is the firm's short-run demand curve for the resource (see Exhibit 12–5).

be the case as long as the MRP (column 6) of the data-entry operators exceeds their wage rate. At a weekly wage of $1,000, Compute-Accounting would hire only one operator. If the weekly wage dropped to $800, two operators would be hired. At still lower wage rates, additional operators would be hired. ***Thus, profit-maximizing firms will expand their employment of each variable resource until the MRP of the resource (the firm's additional revenue generated by the resource) is just equal to the price of the resource (the firm's marginal cost of employing the resource). This profit-maximization rule applies to all firms, price takers and price searchers alike.***

MRP AND THE FIRM'S DEMAND CURVE FOR A RESOURCE

Using the data in Exhibit 12–4, one can construct Compute-Accounting's demand curve for data-entry operators. Recall that the height of a demand curve shows the maximum price (here the wage) the buyer (here the firm) would be willing to pay for the unit. Because the marginal revenue product of the first data-entry operator is $1,000, the firm would be willing to hire this worker only up to a maximum price of $1,000. Because of this relationship, as **Exhibit 12–5** illustrates, a firm's short-run demand curve for a resource is precisely the *MRP* curve for the resource.[3] Using this demand curve yields the identical solutions as the table. At a weekly wage of $1,000, Compute-Accounting would hire only one operator. If the weekly wage dropped to $800, two operators would be hired. At still lower wage rates, additional operators would be hired.

EXHIBIT 12–5

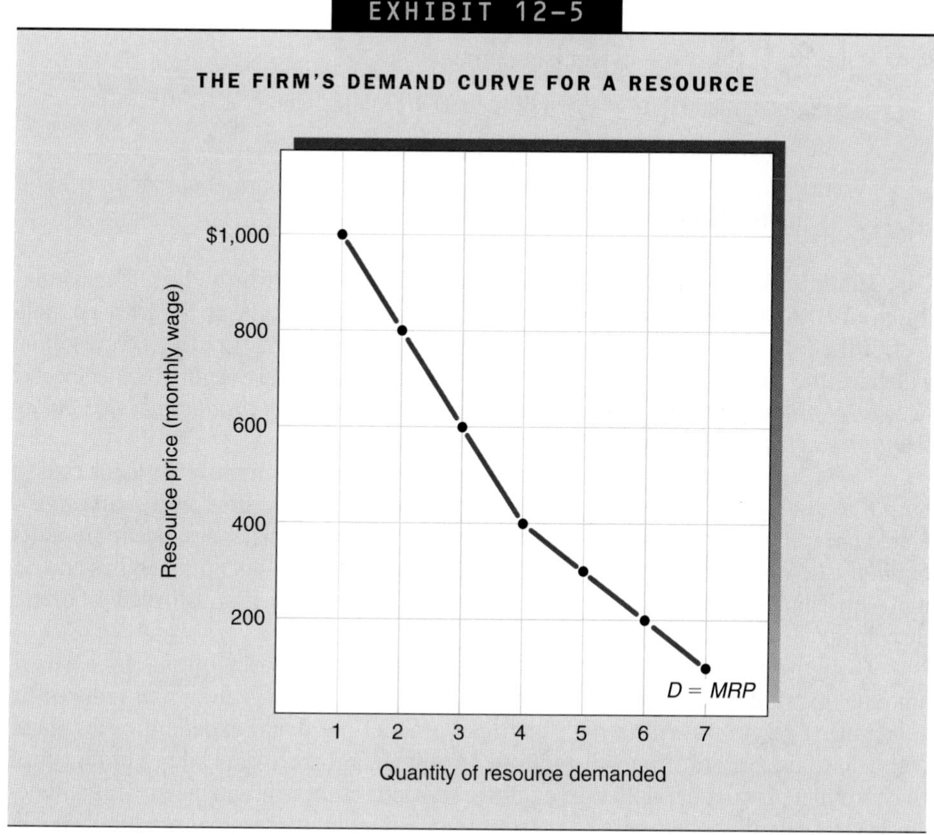

The firm's demand curve for a resource will reflect the marginal revenue product (MRP) *of the resource. In the short run, it will slope downward because the marginal product of the resource will fall as more of it is used with a fixed amount of other resources. The location of the* MRP *curve will depend on (1) the price of the product, (2) the productivity of the resource, and (3) the quantity of other factors working with the resource.*

[3]Strictly speaking, this is true only for a variable resource that is employed with a fixed amount of another factor.

Underlying the downward-sloping demand curve is the law of diminishing returns causing MP, and thus MRP, to fall as employment of the resource expands.

The location of the firm's MRP curve depends on (1) the price of the product, (2) the productivity of the resource, and (3) the amount of other resources with which the resource is working. Changes in any one of these three factors will cause the MRP curve to shift. For example, if Compute-Accounting obtained additional computer equipment that made it possible for the operators to complete more statements each week, the MRP curve for labor would increase (shift outward). This increase in the quantity of the other resources working with labor would increase labor's productivity.

Employment Levels When There Are Numerous Factors of Production

Thus far, we have analyzed the firm's hiring decision assuming that it employed one variable resource (labor) and one fixed resource. Production, though, usually involves the use of many resources. How should these resources be combined to produce the product? We can answer this question by considering either the conditions for profit maximization or the conditions for cost minimization.

Profit Maximization When Multiple Resources Are Employed. The same decision-making considerations apply when the firm employs several factors of production. The profit-maximizing firm will expand its employment of a resource as long as the MRP of the resource exceeds its employment cost. If we assume that resources are perfectly divisible, the profit-maximizing decision rule implies that, in equilibrium, the MRP of each resource will be equal to the price of the resource. Therefore, the following conditions will exist for the profit-maximizing firm:

MRP of skilled labor = Price (wage rate) of skilled labor

MRP of unskilled labor = Price (wage rate) of unskilled labor

MRP of machine A = Price (explicit or implicit rental price) of machine A and so on, for all other factors.

Cost Minimization When Multiple Resources Are Employed. If the firm is maximizing profits, clearly it must produce the profit-maximizing output at the least possible cost. If the firm is minimizing costs, the marginal dollar expenditure for each resource will have the same impact on output as every other marginal resource expenditure. ***Factors of production will be employed such that the marginal product per last dollar spent on each factor is the same for all factors.***

To see why, consider a situation in which a dollar expenditure on labor caused output to rise by ten units, whereas an additional dollar expenditure on machines generated only a five-unit expansion in output. Under these circumstances, five more units of output (at no added cost) would result if the firm spent $1 less on machines and $1 more on labor. The firm's *per-unit* cost would be reduced if it substituted labor for machines.

If the marginal dollar spent on one resource increases output by a larger amount than a dollar expenditure on other resources, costs can always be reduced by substituting resources with a high marginal product per dollar expenditure for those with a low one. Substitution will continue to reduce unit costs (and add to profit) until the marginal product per dollar expenditure on each resource is equalized. This will occur because as additional units of a resource are hired, their marginal product will fall. Thus, the proportional relationship between the price of each resource and its marginal product will eventually be achieved.

Therefore, the following condition exists when per unit costs are minimized:

$$\frac{\textit{MP of skilled labor}}{\textit{Price of skilled labor}} = \frac{\textit{MP of unskilled labor}}{\textit{Price of unskilled labor}} = \frac{\textit{MP of machine A}}{\textit{Price (rental value) of machine A}}$$

and so on, for the other factors.

This relationship, which will be present if a firm is minimizing its per-unit cost of production, indicates why wage differences across skill categories will tend to reflect productivity differences. If skilled workers are twice as productive as unskilled workers, their wage rates will tend toward twice the wage rates of unskilled workers. For example, suppose that a construction firm hiring workers to hang doors is choosing among skilled and unskilled workers. If skilled door hangers can complete four doors per hour, while unskilled workers can hang only two doors per hour, a cost-minimizing firm would hire only skilled workers—as long as their wages are less than twice the wages of unskilled workers. On the other hand, only unskilled workers would be hired if the wages of skilled workers are more than twice that of unskilled workers. With competition, wages across skill categories will tend to mirror productivity differences. (The Addendum to this chapter provides advanced material on the relationship between resource use and cost minimization.)

Low wages do not necessarily mean low cost; it is not always cheaper to hire the lowest wage workers. It is not just wages, but rather wages *relative to productivity* that matter. If the wages of skilled workers are twice those of unskilled workers, it will still be cheaper to hire additional skilled workers if their marginal productivity (output per hour) is more than twice that of the unskilled workers.

The importance of wages relative to productivity explains why relatively few firms moved to Mexico following the passage of the North American Free Trade Agreement (NAFTA). Remember the forecast by some of a "giant sucking sound" indicating the movement of both firms and jobs to Mexico? Why didn't the low wages of Mexico cause firms to relocate? Answer: While wages are low in Mexico, so, too, is productivity. Given this factor, many firms are able to achieve lower production costs in the high-wage United States than in low-wage Mexico. Suppose that the average wage rate of a U.S. worker is $12 per hour and average hourly productivity is 36 units, while the average wage is $4 per hour in Mexico and average productivity is 8 units. To maximize profits (or minimize costs) a firm should locate wherever MP/P is greatest. In the United States the firm would get 3 units of output (36/12) per dollar spent on labor. In Mexico, the firm would get only 2 units of output (8/4) per dollar spent on labor. Thus, a cost-minimizing firm would want to locate in the United States despite the higher wages, because the productivity difference more than makes up for the wage difference. Although U.S. wages are 3 times higher, U.S. productivity is 4.5 times higher. The higher productivity more than compensates for the higher wage cost.

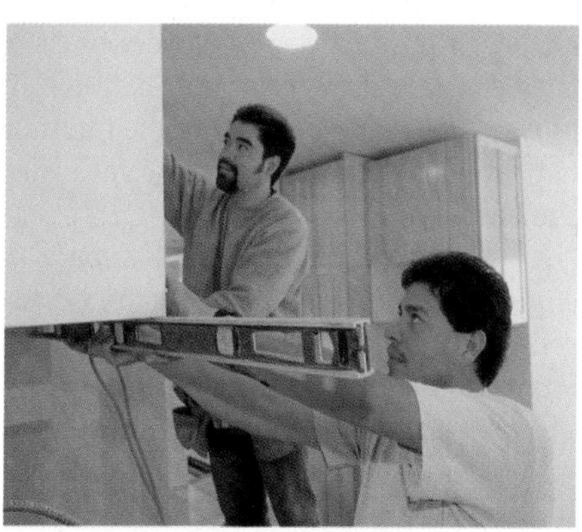

Wage differentials reflect skill differentials. If a high-skill worker is twice as productive as a low-skill worker, the high-skill worker will be able to command twice the wage rate.

The Central Proposition of the Marginal Productivity Theory of Employment

The central proposition of the marginal productivity theory of resource employment is that firms minimize their per-unit costs of production when they hire additional units of each resource as long as the units' marginal productivity generates revenues in excess of costs. Firms that minimize per-unit costs and maximize profit will never pay more for a unit of input, whether it is skilled labor, a machine, or an acre of land, than the input is worth to them. The worth of a unit of input to the firm is determined by how much additional revenue (marginal revenue product) is expected from its employment.

In the real world, it is sometimes difficult to measure the marginal product of a factor. And, as we have indicated, the marginal product of a resource is influenced by the other factors with which it is employed. Production is a team effort involving interdependent use of resources. We do not mean to imply that business decision makers will necessarily think in terms of equating the marginal product/price ratio (MP/P) for each factor of production. Their thought process may well be something like this: "Can we reduce costs by using more of one resource and less of another?" Real-world business decision makers may use experience, trial and error, and intuitive rules as they seek to minimize costs.

Regardless of the methods and procedures used, however, when a firm maximizes profits and minimizes costs, the marginal product/price ratio will be equal for all factors of production. The results will be *as if* the firms had followed the cost-minimization decision-making rules presented earlier. Furthermore, competitive forces will more or less force firms to approximate these minimum cost conditions. Firms that fail to do so will be unable to compete successfully with rivals achieving lower per-unit costs.

The marginal-productivity theory explains the conditions underlying the demand for resources. Of course, resource prices will also be influenced by the supply of resources. We now turn to that topic.

SUPPLY OF RESOURCES

In essence, our analysis of resource demand concludes that employers will hire a resource so long as they can gain by doing so. The same basic postulate also applies to resource suppliers. Resource owners will supply their services to an employer only if they perceive that the benefits of doing so exceed their costs (the value of the other things they could do with their time or resources). Thus, in order to attract factors of production, employers must offer resource owners at least as good a deal as they can get elsewhere. For example, if an employer does not offer a potential employee a package of income payments and working conditions that is as good as or better than the employee can get elsewhere, the employer will be unable to attract the employee.

Resource owners will supply their services to those who offer them the best employment alternative, all factors considered. Other things constant, as the price of a specific resource (for example, engineering services, craft labor, or wheat farmland) increases, the incentive of potential suppliers to provide the resource increases.

An increase in the price of a resource will attract potential resource suppliers into the market. A decrease will cause them to shift into other activities. Therefore, as

Exhibit 12–6 illustrates, the supply curve for a specific resource will slope upward to the right.[4]

Short-Run versus Long-Run Resource Supply

As in the case of demand, the supply response in resource markets may vary between the short run and long run. If the wage rate for CPAs rose, for example, we would expect more workers supplying services as CPAs. But where do these additional CPAs come from? In the short run, the additional supply must come from individuals who possess the necessary skills, but are currently employed elsewhere. The higher wages might induce some college accounting professors and some stay-at-home spouses with accounting credentials to move into private-sector employment as CPAs. In the short run, there is insufficient time to alter the availability of a resource through investment in human and physical capital. In contrast, in the long run, resource suppliers have time to adjust their investment choices in response to a change in resource prices. With time, the higher wages for CPAs would cause more students to major in accounting, and others to pursue the necessary additional courses to become CPAs. Higher resource prices will increase the quantity supplied in both the short run and the long run, but the response will be greater in the long run. Therefore, as **Exhibit**

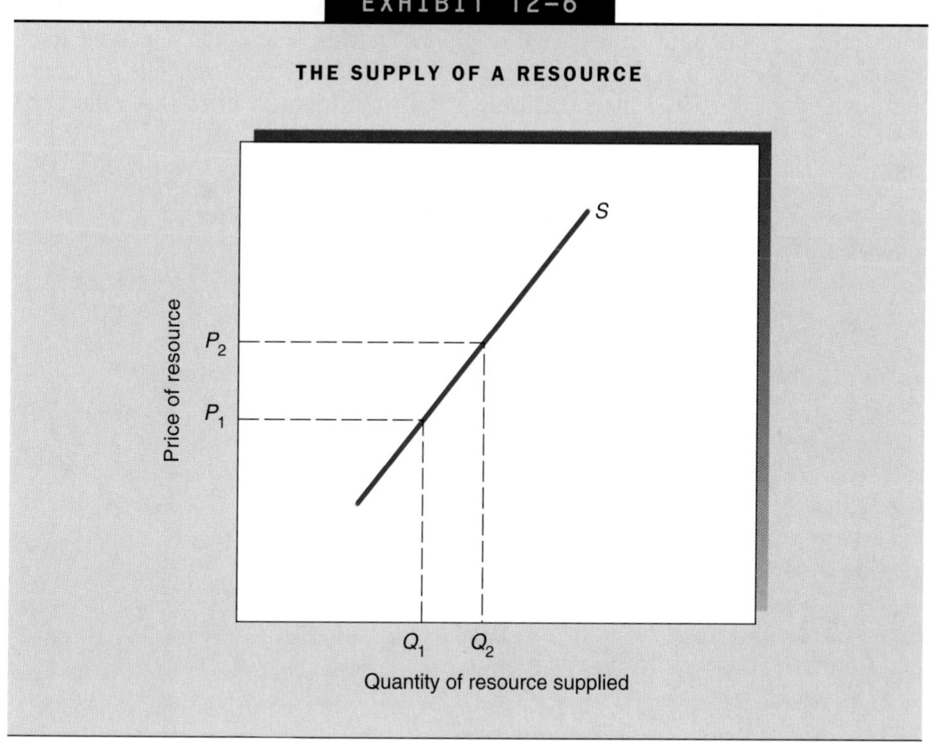

As the price of a resource increases, individuals have a greater incentive to supply it. Therefore, a direct relationship will exist between the price of a resource and the quantity supplied.

[4]Although the supply for nonhuman resources will always slope upward, the supply of labor at very high wage rates can become backward bending. As wages rise, individuals will substitute toward more work, but simultaneously the higher income will cause them to desire more leisure. At very high wage rates the income effect might dominate, causing a negative relationship between wage rates and quantity of labor supplied in this range. For example, at a wage of $10,000 per hour, many individuals would probably supply fewer hours of work than at $500 per hour!

12–7 illustrates, the long-run supply of resources will be more elastic than the short-run supply.

Resource mobility
The ease with which factors of production are able to move among alternative uses. Resources that can easily be transferred to a different use or location are said to be highly mobile. Resources with few alternative uses are immobile.

Short-Run Supply. The short-run supply response to a change in price is determined by how easily the resource can be transferred from one use to another—that is, **resource mobility.** The supply of resources with high resource mobility will be relatively elastic even in the short run. Resources that have few alternative uses (or are not easily transferable) are said to be immobile. The short-run supply of immobile resources will be highly inelastic.

Consider the mobility of labor. Within a skill category (for example, plumber, store manager, accountant, or secretary), labor will be highly mobile within the same geographic area. Movements between geographic areas and from one skill category to another are more costly to accomplish. Labor will thus be less mobile for movements of this variety. In addition, because it is easier for a high-skilled person to perform effectively in a lower-skill position than vice versa, short-run mobility will tend to decline as the skill level of the occupation rises. Thus, the short-run supply curve in high-skill occupations is usually quite inelastic.

What about the mobility of land? Land is highly mobile among uses when location does not matter. For example, the same land can often be used to raise corn, wheat, soybeans, or oats. Thus, the supply of land allocated to production of each of these commodities will be highly responsive to changes in their relative prices. Undeveloped land on the outskirts of cities is particularly mobile among uses. In addition to its value in agriculture, such land might be quickly subdivided and used for a housing development or a shopping center. Because land is totally immobile physically, one might think that its supply is unresponsive to changes in price that reflect the

EXHIBIT 12–7

TIME AND THE ELASTICITY OF SUPPLY FOR RESOURCES

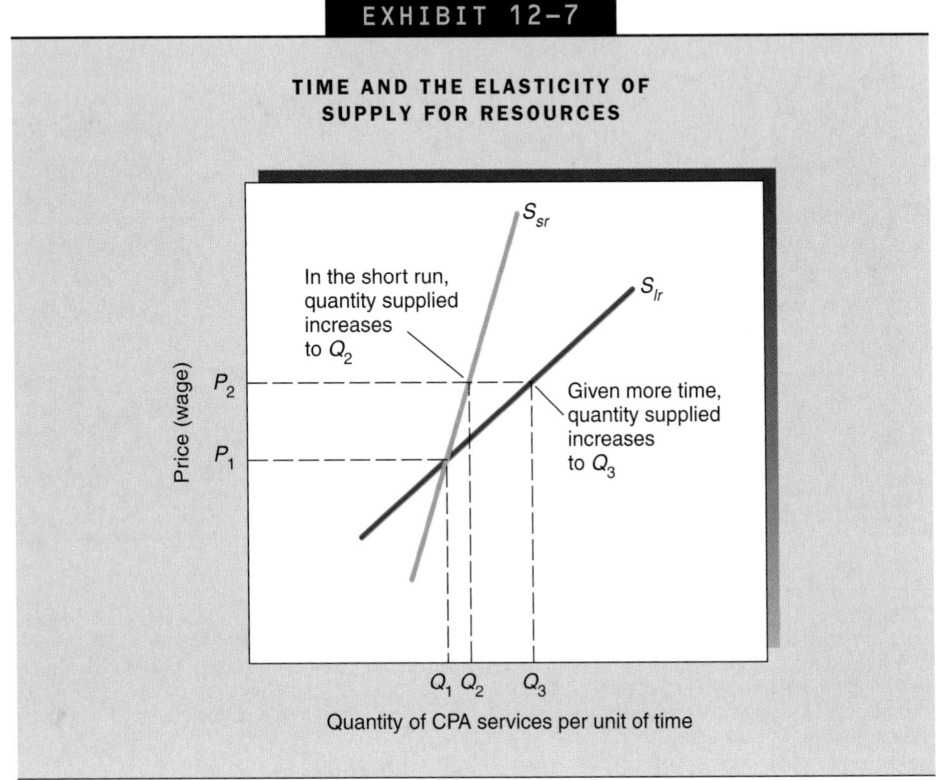

The supply of certified public accountant (CPA) services and other resources that require a substantial period of time between current investment and expansion in the future quantity supplied will be more elastic in the long run than in the short run.

EXHIBIT 12–9

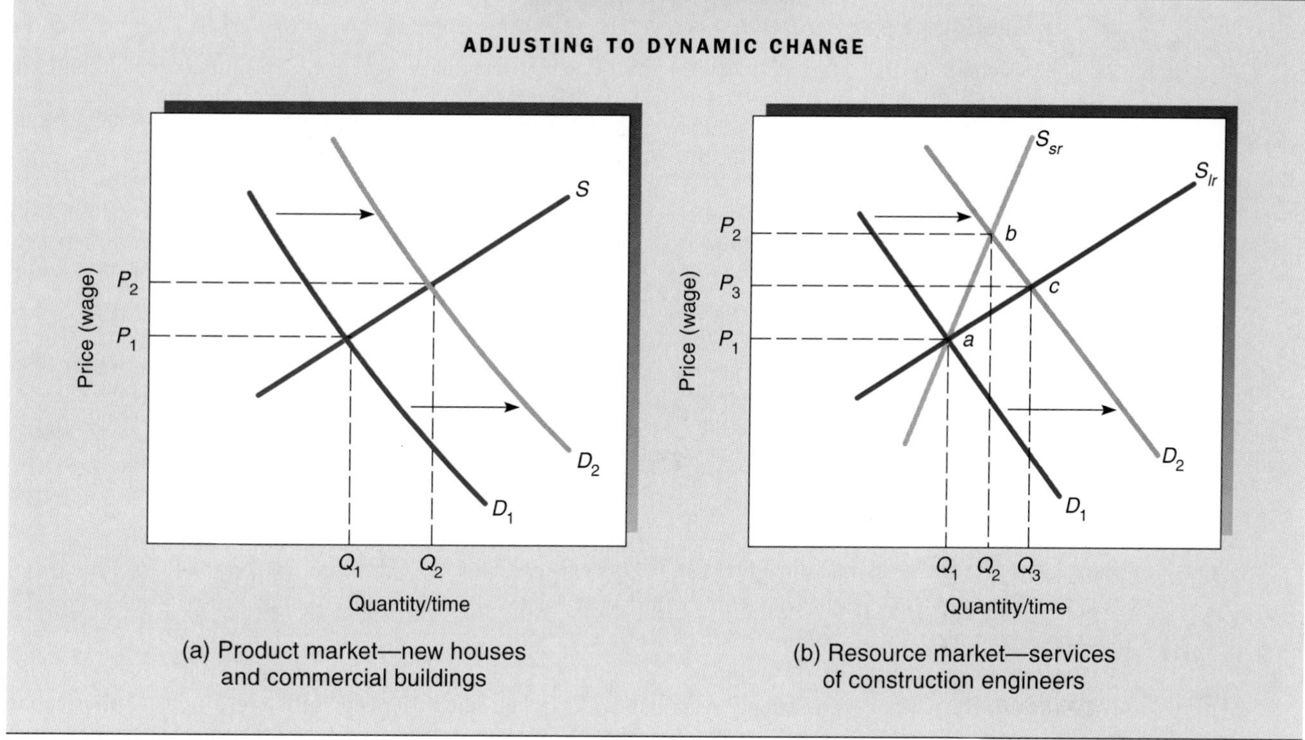

(a) Product market—new houses and commercial buildings

(b) Resource market—services of construction engineers

An increase in demand for housing and commercial buildings (frame a) will lead to an increase in demand for the services of construction engineers (frame b) and other resources used in the construction industry. Initially, the increase in the resource price will be substantial (move from a *to* b*), particularly if the supply of the resource is highly inelastic in the short run. The higher resource price will attract additional human capital investment and, with time, the resource supply curve will become more elastic, which will moderate the price (or wage) increase of the resource (move from* b *to* c*).*

amount of engineering services at a below-equilibrium resource price. Rather than doing without the resource, employers will attempt to hire engineers away from other firms by bidding the price up to P_1 and thereby eliminating the excess demand.

How will a resource market adjust to an unexpected change in market conditions? Suppose that there is a sharp increase in the demand for houses, apartments, and office buildings. The increase in demand for these products will also increase the demand for resources required for their construction. Thus, the demand for such resources as steel, lumber, brick, and the labor services of carpenters, architects, and construction engineers will increase. **Exhibit 12–9** provides a graphic illustration of both the increase in demand for new houses and buildings (frame a) and the accompanying increase in demand for construction engineers. The market demand for the services of construction engineers increases from D_1 to D_2 (frame b) and initially there is a sharp rise in their wages (price increases from P_1 to P_2). The higher wages will induce additional people to undertake the education and training necessary to become a construction engineer. With the passage of time, the entry of the newly trained construction engineers will increase the elasticity of the resource supply curve. As these new construction engineers eventually enter the occupation, the supply curve will become more elastic (S_{lr} rather than S_{sr}), which will place downward pressure on wages in the occupation (the move from *b* to *c*). Therefore, as part b of Exhibit 12–9 illustrates, the long-run price increase (to P_3) will be less than the short-run increase (to P_2).

APPLICATIONS IN ECONOMICS

The Importance of Factor Markets—The Case of Energy

Our analysis indicates that resource markets encourage conservation and direct users away from more expensive resources. Could these functions be accomplished as well without the use of price incentives? Examination of energy use under central planning indicates that it would be difficult to achieve a similar response without the information and incentives generated by prices in markets.

Economist Mikhail Bernstam, in a book written for London's Institute of Economic Affairs, examined the efficiency of energy use under both central planning and market allocation. He used data from the 1980s, before the fall of socialist regimes in Europe, and the results of his research are striking. On average, centrally planned socialist economies used nearly three times as much energy per unit of GDP as economies employing factor markets. This relationship also held for countries that were similar except for their use of markets. Centrally planned North Korea used three times as much energy per unit of GDP as South Korea, where factor markets and resource prices distributed energy. And centrally planned East Germany consumed 3.5 times as much energy per unit of output as West Germany.*

Energy prices rose sharply during the 1973–1980 period. Bernstam found that in North America and Europe, per-capita energy consumption (which had been increasing) began to decline following the price increases of the 1970s. Resource markets in these areas directed users toward substitutes and away from the more expensive energy resources during the post-1973 period. In contrast, there was no evidence of a similar response on the part of central planners in the former Soviet Union. Per-capita energy consumption continued to rise in the former Soviet Union throughout the 1970s and 1980s.

---

*Mikhail S. Bernstam, *The Wealth of Nations and the Environment* (London: Institute of Economic Affairs, 1991).

The supply response and market adjustment for other resources—physical as well as human—will be similar. For example, an unexpected construction boom will generally cause sharp initial increases in the prices of lumber, bricks, and other building materials. With time, however, additional investment will increase the availability of these resources and moderate the increase in their price, just as additional investment in human capital eventually moderated the wage increases of the construction engineers.

The market adjustment to an unexpected reduction in demand for a resource is the same. The price falls farther in the short run than in the long run. At the lower price, some resource suppliers will use their talents in other areas, and the incentive for potential new suppliers to offer the resource will be reduced. Thus, with time, the quantity of the resource supplied will decline, making the decline in price more moderate. Those with the poorest alternatives (that is, lowest opportunity cost) will continue to provide the resource at the lower prices. Those with better alternatives will move to other areas.

Pulling things together, our analysis indicates that prices in resource markets play a vitally important role. These prices coordinate the actions of the firms demanding factors of production and the households supplying them. Resource prices provide users with both information on scarcity and the incentive to economize on resource use when producing output. They also provide suppliers with an incentive to learn skills and provide resources—particularly those that are intensely demanded by users. Without the use of resource markets and the price incentives they provide, efficient use and wise conservation of resources is unlikely. (See the Applications in Economics feature for evidence on this point.)

THE COORDINATING FUNCTION OF RESOURCE PRICES

Throughout this text we have stressed that profit is a reward earned by producers who increase the value of resources, while loss is a punishment imposed on producers who reduce the value of resources to society. The key links in this process are the prices of the products being sold and the prices of the resources used in production. A firm's profits are its revenues (which are determined by the product price) minus its costs (which are determined by the prices of the resources it uses). The price of the product measures the value that consumers place on that product. The price of the resources, however, measures the value that consumers place on *other products* that could be produced with those same resources. This is the linkage we are now ready to explore further.

As we have shown, the price of a resource will equal the resource's marginal revenue product when the resource market is in equilibrium. The resource's marginal revenue product depends upon the price consumers are willing to pay for (and thus their value of) the output produced by the resource. When a firm wishes to hire a resource, it must offer that resource a payment at least as attractive as what the resource could have earned elsewhere—that is, the resource's MRP in its next best alternative employment. Thus, the price a firm pays for a resource is equal to the resource's value (as measured by consumer valuation) in the alternative use. If the output the firm produces with that resource can be sold at a higher price than the price of the alternative outputs, then and only then will the firm earn a profit. Thus, profit is a reward to those entrepreneurs who are able to see and act on opportunities to put resources to higher-valued uses. Because consumer tastes and preferences continuously change, so do product and resource prices, and thus these opportunities are created and destroyed on a daily basis in a dynamic market economy.

The ability of resource prices to adjust is essential for a properly functioning market system. They determine the reallocations of resources between industries that allow an economy to satisfy the changing preferences of consumers. The way in which market prices provide an incentive for resources to flow continuously to their highest-valued social uses is indeed the essence of Adam Smith's *invisible hand principle.*

LOOKING *Ahead*

In this chapter we presented the theoretical underpinnings of factor markets. This analysis can be applied to a broad range of economic issues. The next chapter will focus on the labor market and earnings differences among workers. Later, we will focus on the capital market and the allocation of resources over time. The operation of these two markets plays an important role in determining the distribution of income, a topic that will also be analyzed in detail in a subsequent chapter.

KEY POINTS

➤ Productive assets and services are bought and sold in resource markets. These markets help to determine what is produced, how it is produced, and the distribution of income. There are two broad classes of productive resources: (1) nonhuman capital and (2) human capital.

➤ The demand for resources is derived from the demand for products that the resources help to produce. The quantity of a resource demanded is inversely related to its price because of substitutions made by both producers and consumers.

➤ The demand curve for a resource, like the demand for a product, may shift. The major factors that can increase the demand for a resource are (a) an increase in demand for products that use the resource, (b) an increase in the productivity of the resource, and (c) an increase in the price of substitute resources.

➤ Profit-maximizing firms will hire additional units of a resource up to the point where the marginal revenue product (MRP) of the resource equals its price. With multiple inputs, firms will expand their usage of each until marginal product divided by price (MP/P) is equal across all inputs. When real-world decision makers minimize per-unit costs, the outcome will be as if they had followed these mathematical procedures, even though they may not consciously do so.

➤ The amount of a resource supplied will be directly related to its price. The supply of a resource will be more elastic in the long run than in the short run. In the long run, investment can increase the supply of both physical and human resources.

➤ The prices of resources are determined by supply and demand. Changes in the market prices of resources will influence the decisions of both users and suppliers. Higher resource prices give users a greater incentive to turn to substitutes and suppliers a greater incentive to provide more of the resource.

➤ Changes in resource prices in response to changing market conditions are essential for the efficient allocation of resources in a dynamic world. Profit is a reward to the entrepreneur who is able to see and act on opportunities to put resources to higher-valued uses.

CRITICAL ANALYSIS QUESTIONS

1. What is the meaning of the expression "invest in human capital?" In what sense is the decision to invest in human capital like the decision to invest in physical capital? Is human capital investment risky? Explain.

2. "The demand for resources is a derived demand." What is meant by that statement? Why is the employment of a resource inversely related to its price?

*3. Use the information of Exhibit 12–4 to answer the following:

a. How many employees (operators) would Compute-Accounting hire at a weekly wage of $250 if it were attempting to maximize profits?

b. What would the firm's maximum profit be if its fixed costs were $1,500 per week?

c. Suppose there was a decline in demand for accounting services, reducing the market price per monthly statement to $150. At this demand level, how many employees would Compute-Accounting hire at $250 per week in the short run? Would Compute-Accounting be able to stay in business at the lower market price? Explain.

*4. Are productivity gains the major source of higher wages? If so, how does one account for the rising real wages of barbers, who by and large have used the same technique for a half-century? (Hint: Do not forget opportunity cost and supply.)

5. Are the following statements both correct? Are they inconsistent with each other? Explain.

a. "Firms will hire a resource only if they can make money by doing so."

b. "In a market economy, each resource will tend to be paid according to its marginal product. Highly productive resources will command high prices, whereas less productive resources will command lower prices."

6. "However desirable they might be from an equity viewpoint, programs designed to reduce wage differentials will necessarily reduce the incentive of people to act efficiently and use their productive abilities in those areas where demand is greatest relative to supply." Do you agree or disagree? Why?

7. Suppose that you were the manager of a large retail store that was currently experiencing a shoplifting problem. Every hour, approximately $15 worth of merchandise was being stolen from your store. Suppose that a security guard would completely eliminate the shoplifting in your store. If you were interested in maximizing your profits, should you hire a security guard if the wage rate of security guards was $20 per hour? Why or why not? What does this imply about the relationship between average shoplifting per hour in the economy and the wage rates of security guards?

*8. A dressmaker uses labor and capital (sewing machines) to produce dresses in a competitive market. Suppose the last unit of labor hired cost $1,000 per month and increased output by 100 dresses. The last unit of capital hired (rented) cost $500 per month and increased output by 80 dresses. Is the dressmaker minimizing cost? If not, what changes need to be made?

9. A firm is considering moving from the United States to Mexico. The firm pays its U.S. workers $12 per hour. Current U.S. workers have a marginal product of 40, while the Mexican workers have a marginal product of 10. How

low would the Mexican wage have to be to make this move a profitable opportunity?

*10. "The earnings of engineers, doctors, and lawyers are high because lots of education is necessary to practice in these fields." Evaluate this statement.

11. Other things constant, what impact will a highly elastic demand for a product have on the elasticity of demand for the resources used to produce the product? Explain.

*12. The following chart provides information on a firm that hires labor competitively and sells its product in a competitive market:

Units of Labor	Total Output	Marginal Product	Product Price	Total Revenue	MRP
1	14	___	$5	___	___
2	26	___	$5	___	___
3	37	___	$5	___	___
4	46	___	$5	___	___
5	53	___	$5	___	___
6	58	___	$5	___	___
7	62	___	$5	___	___

a. Fill in the missing columns.
b. How many units of labor would be employed if the market wage rate were $40? Why?
c. What would happen to employment if the wage rate rose to $50? Explain.

13. Leisure Times, Inc., employs skilled workers and capital to install hot tubs. The capital includes the tools and equipment that the workers use to construct and install the tubs. The installation services are sold in a competitive market for $1,200 per hot tub. Leisure Times is able to hire workers for $2,200 per month, including the cost of wages, fringe benefits, and employment taxes. As additional workers are hired, the increase in the number of hot tubs installed is indicated in the table.

Number of Workers Employed	Number of Hot Tubs Installed (per month)
1	5
2	12
3	18
4	23
5	27
6	30
7	32
8	33
9	34

a. Indicate the marginal product and MRP schedules of the workers.
b. What quantity of workers should Leisure Times employ if it is maximizing profit?
c. If a construction boom pushes the wages of skilled workers up to $2,500 per month, how many workers would Leisure Times employ if it is maximizing profit?
d. Suppose that strong demand for hot tubs pushes the price of installation services up to $1,500 per month. How would this affect employment of the skilled workers if the wage rate of the workers remained at $2,500 per month?

14. A recent flyer on a university campus stated that consumers should boycott sugar due to the low wages earned by laborers on sugar cane farms in Florida. Using the notion of derived demand, what impact would a boycott on sugar have on the wages of the farm laborers in the short run? In the long run?

*Asterisk denotes questions for which answers are given in Appendix B.

ADDENDUM: PRODUCTION THEORY AND ISOQUANT ANALYSIS

ADVANCED MATERIAL

When analyzing production theory and input utilization, economists often rely on isoquant analysis. Since the technique is widely used at the intermediate level, some instructors explain the concept in their introductory course.

WHAT ARE ISOQUANTS?

Generally, several alternative input combinations can be used to produce a good. For example, 100 bushels of wheat might be produced with 2 acres of land, 5 bushels of seed, and 100 pounds of fertilizer. Alternatively, the wheat could be produced with more land and less fertilizer, or more seed and less land, or more fertilizer and less seed. Many input combinations could be used to produce 100 bushels of wheat.

The word "isoquant" means "equal quantity." An **isoquant** is a curve that indicates the various combinations of two inputs that could be used to produce an equal quantity of output. **Exhibit 12A-1** provides an illustration. The isoquant labeled "100 units of cloth" shows the various combinations of capital and labor that a technically efficient producer could use to produce 100 units of cloth. Every point on an isoquant is technically efficient. By that, we mean that it would not be possible, given the current level of technology, to produce a larger output with the input combination. If a producer wanted to produce a larger output, 140 units of cloth, for example, it would be necessary to use more of at least one of the resources. Since larger output levels require additional resources, isoquants representing larger levels of output always lie to the northeast in an isoquant diagram.

Characteristics of Isoquants

Isoquant analysis must be consistent with the laws of production. What do the laws of production imply about the characteristics of isoquants?

EXHIBIT 12A-1

THE ISOQUANT

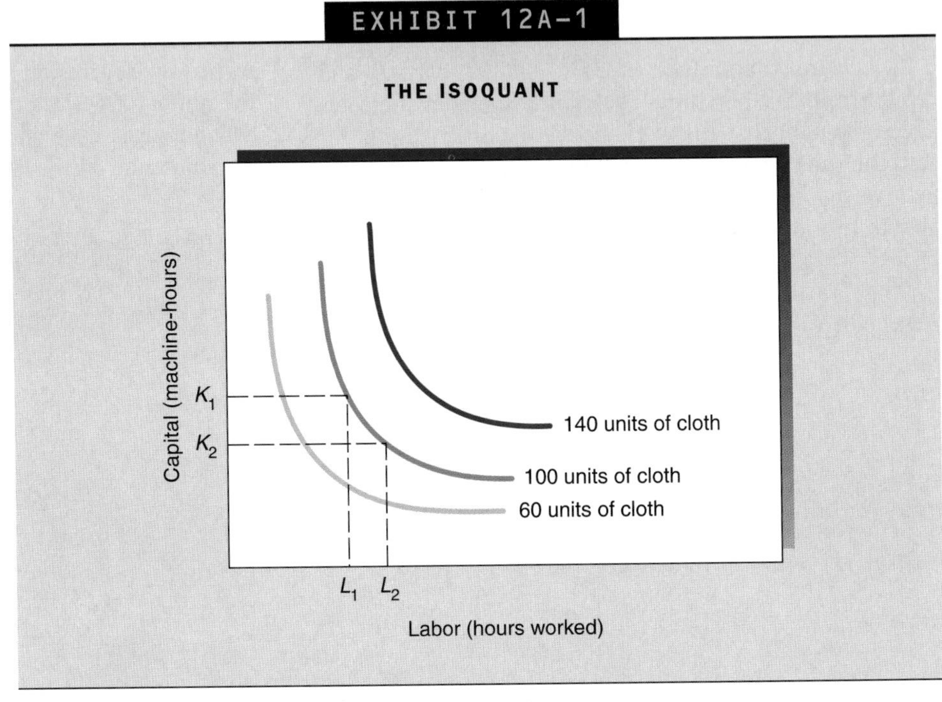

An isoquant represents all input combinations that, if used efficiently, will generate a specific level of output. As illustrated here, 100 units of cloth could be produced with the input combinations L_1K_1 *or* L_2K_2 *or any other combination of labor and capital that lies on the isoquant representing 100 units of cloth.*

1. *Isoquants Slope Downward to the Right.* Within the relevant range of utilization, an increase in the usage level of an input makes it possible to expand output. If, for example, the use of the labor input is expanded, it is possible to produce the same output level (stay on the same isoquant) with a smaller quantity of capital. Since both labor and capital can be used to increase production, they can be substituted for each other. Constant output can be maintained either by (a) using more labor and less capital or (b) by using more capital and less labor. Thus, every isoquant runs from the northwest to the southeast, as illustrated by Exhibit 12A-1.

2. *Isoquants Are Convex When Viewed from the Origin.* The convexity of isoquants stems from the fact that as one continues to substitute labor for capital, larger and larger amounts of labor are required to maintain output at a constant level. As labor is used more intensively, it becomes increasingly difficult to substitute labor for each additional unit of capital. Since larger and larger amounts of labor are required to compensate for the loss of each additional unit of capital (and thus maintain the constant level of output), the isoquant becomes flatter as labor is used more intensively (see **Exhibit 12A-2**, point *B*).

On the other hand, when capital is used more and more intensively, larger and larger amounts of capital are required to compensate for the loss of a unit of labor. Thus, an isoquant becomes steeper as capital (the *y* factor) is used more intensively (see Exhibit 12A-2, point *A*). It is convex when viewed from the origin.

3. *The Slope of the Isoquant Is the Marginal Product of Labor Divided by the Marginal Product of Capital.* The slope of the isoquant is determined by the amount of labor that must be added to maintain a constant level of output when one less unit of capital is used. This slope is dependent on the marginal productivity of labor relative to capital. When labor is used intensively relative to capital, its marginal product is low, relative to capital. Under these circumstances, as Exhibit 12A-2 (point *B*) illustrates, the slope of the isoquant is small (the isoquant is relatively flat). In contrast, when capital is used intensively (Exhibit 2, point *A*), the marginal product of labor is high, relative to capital. The steepness of the isoquant reflects this fact. At any point on the isoquant, the slope of the isoquant is equal to MP_L/MP_K.

THE ISOCOST LINE

A set of isoquants outlines the technically efficient input combinations that could be used to produce alternative levels of output. Before we can determine the economically efficient input combinations for producing a level of output, we must also incorporate information about cost and resource prices.

Firms generally can purchase inputs at a fixed price per unit. The **isocost line** shows the alternative

EXHIBIT 12A-2

CONVEXITY AND THE SLOPE OF THE ISOQUANT

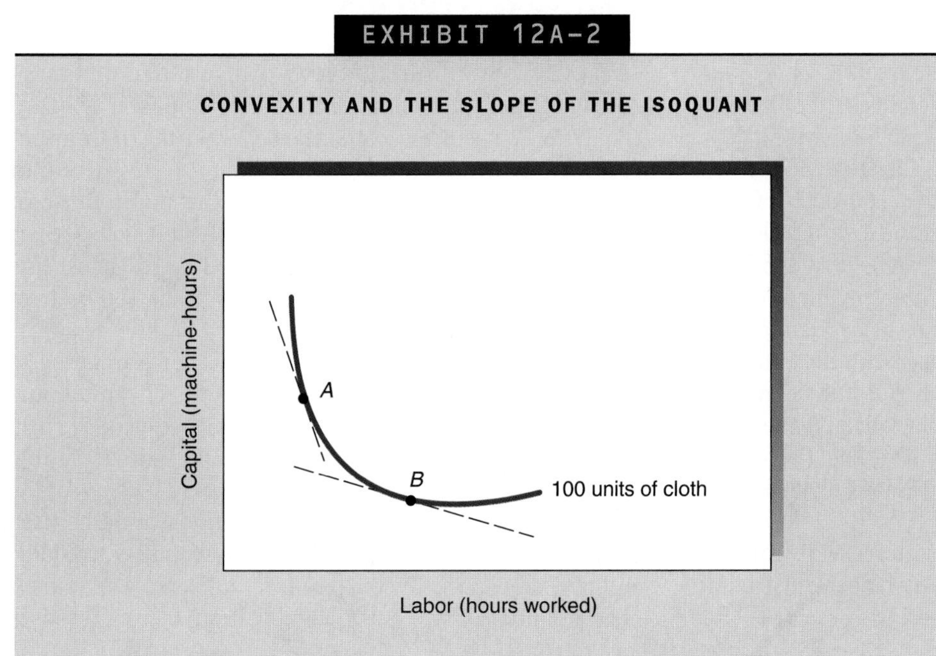

When labor is used intensively relative to capital (point B*), the slope of the isoquant is much flatter than it is when capital is used more intensively (point* A*). The slope of an isoquant is the ratio of the marginal products of the two factors (*MP_L *divided by* MP_K*). When labor is used more intensively relative to capital, its marginal product falls (and that of capital increases). Since the marginal product of labor is low (and the marginal product of capital is high) when labor is used intensively (as at point* B*), the isoquant is relatively flat.*

EXHIBIT 12A-3

THE ISOCOST LINE

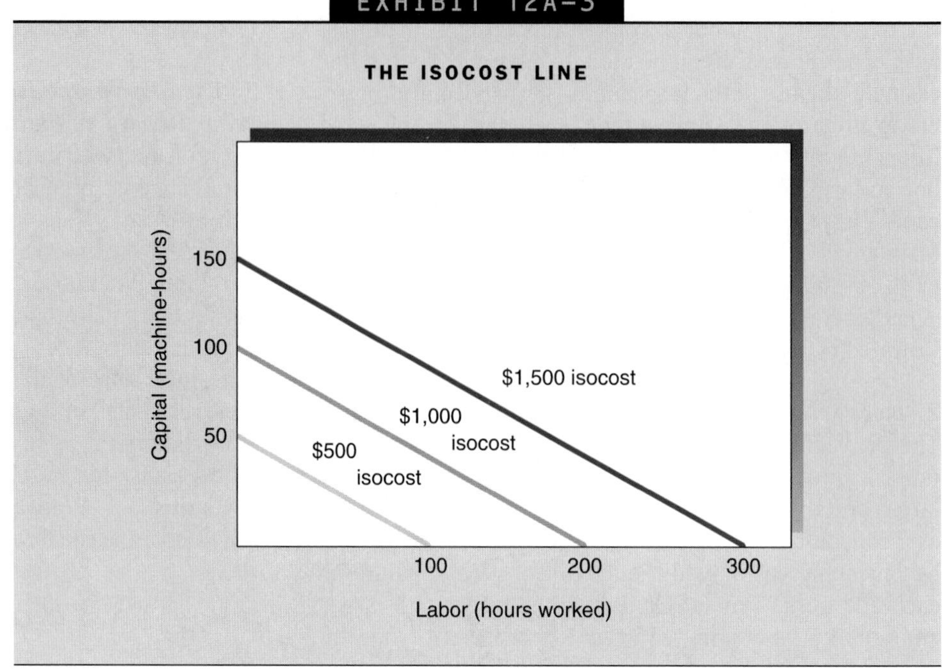

The isocost line indicates the alternative combinations of the resources that can be purchased with a given outlay of funds. When the price of a unit of labor is $5 and that of a unit of capital is $10, the three isocost lines shown here represent the alternative combinations of labor and capital that could be purchased at costs of $500, $1,000 and $1,500. The slope of the isocost line is equal to P_L/P_K *($5/$10 = 1/2 in this case).*

combinations of inputs that can be purchased with a given outlay of funds. As the term implies, the cost of purchasing an input combination on the isocost line is equal to the cost of purchasing any other input combination on the same line. To construct an isocost line, two pieces of information are required: (a) the prices of the resources and (b) the specific outlay of funds. **Exhibit 12A-3** illustrates the construction of three different isocost lines, assuming that the price of labor is $5 per unit and that the price of capital is $10 per unit. Consider the $500 isocost line. If all funds were spent on labor, 100 units of labor could be purchased. Alternatively, if the entire $500 were expended on capital, 50 units of capital could be purchased. It would be possible to purchase any input combination between these two extremes—for example, 80 units of labor and 10 units of capital—with the $500. The input combinations are represented by a line connecting the two extreme points, 100 units of labor on the x-axis and 50 units of capital on the y-axis. Note that the slope of the isocost line is merely the price of labor divided by the price of capital (P_L/P_K).

If the outlay of funds were to increase, it would be possible to purchase more of both labor and capital. Thus, as Exhibit 12A-3 illustrates, the isocost lines move in a northeast direction as the size of the outlay of funds increases.

MINIMIZING THE COST OF PRODUCTION

A profit-seeking firm will want to choose the minimum-cost method of production. We can combine isoquant analysis and the isocost line to derive the minimum-cost input combination for producing a given output level. As **Exhibit 12A-4** illustrates, the minimum-cost input combination for producing 100 units of cloth is represented by the point at which the lowest isocost line just touches (is tangent to) the isoquant for 100 units of cloth. At that point (A of Exhibit 12A-4), the producer will be able to combine 120 units of labor purchased at a cost of $600 ($5 per unit) with 40 units of capital purchased at a cost of $400 ($10 per unit) to produce 100 units of cloth. The total cost of the 100 units is $1,000 ($10 per unit).

Of course, other input combinations could be used to produce the 100 units of cloth. However, they would be more costly, given the current prices of labor and capital. For example, if the input combination B were used to

EXHIBIT 12A-4

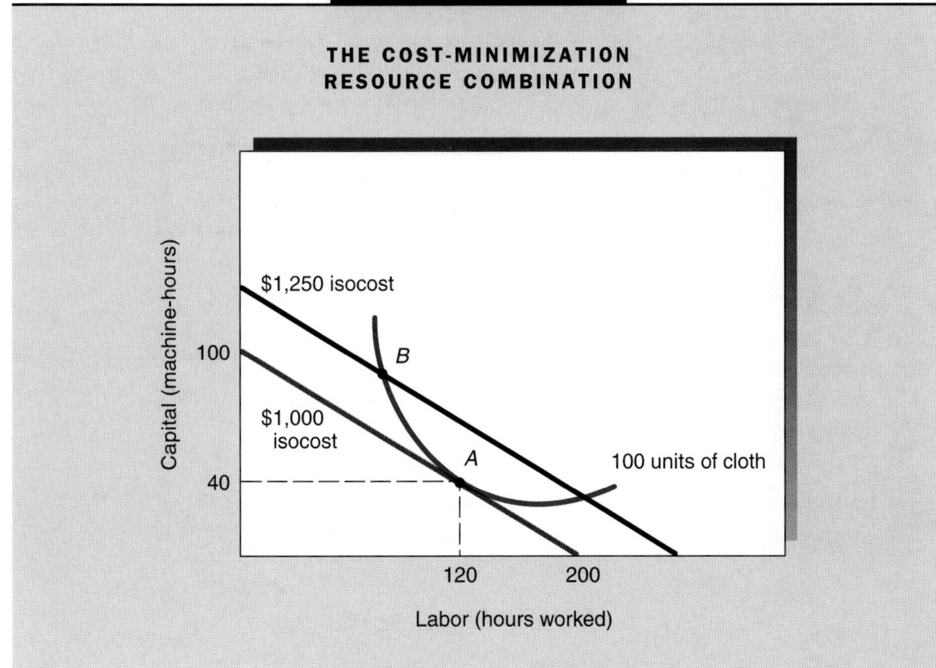

When the cost of producing an output level (for example, 100 units of cloth) is minimized, the isoquant is tangent to the isocost line. At that point (A), $MP_L/MP_K = P_L/P_K$.

produce the 100 units, the total cost would be $1,250 ($12.50 per unit).

When costs are at a minimum, the isoquant is tangent to the isocost line. The slopes of the two are equal at that point. In other words, when the cost of producing a specific output is at a minimum, the MP_L/MP_K (the slope of the isoquant) will be equal to P_L/P_K (the slope of the isocost line). Since:

$$\frac{MP_L}{MP_K} = \frac{P_L}{P_K}$$

then:

$$\frac{MP_L}{P_L} = \frac{MP_K}{P_K}$$

The latter equation represents precisely the condition that our earlier analysis indicated would be present if the cost of production were at a minimum.

The isoquant analysis indicates that when a firm chooses the minimum-cost method of production, the ratio of the price of labor to the price of capital will equal the ratio of the marginal productivities of the factors. This makes good economic sense. It implies, for example, that if capital is twice as expensive per unit as labor, the firm will want to substitute the cheaper labor for capital until the marginal product of capital is twice that of labor.

Cost Minimization and Changes in Resource Prices

The minimum-cost input combination is dependent on both (a) the technical relationship between the productive inputs and output, as illustrated by the isoquant, and (b) the price of the factors, represented by the isocost line. If the ratio of the price of labor to the price of capital changes, the minimum-cost input combination will be altered.

Exhibit 12A-5 illustrates this point. Exhibit 12A-4 shows that if the price of labor were $5 and the price of capital were $10, the minimum-cost input combination to produce 100 units of cloth would be 120 units of labor and 40 units of capital. The total cost of the 100 units would be $1,000. Exhibit 12A-5 indicates what would happen if the price of labor increased from $5 to $10. At the higher price of labor, a $1,000 outlay of funds would now purchase only 100 units of labor (rather than 200). As a result of the increase in the price of labor, the iso-

EXHIBIT 12A-5

The slope of the isocost line increases as the price of a unit of labor rises from $5 to $10. As a result of the increase in the price of labor, (a) cost-minimizing producers substitute capital for the more expensive labor, and (b) the minimum cost of producing 100 units of cloth rises.

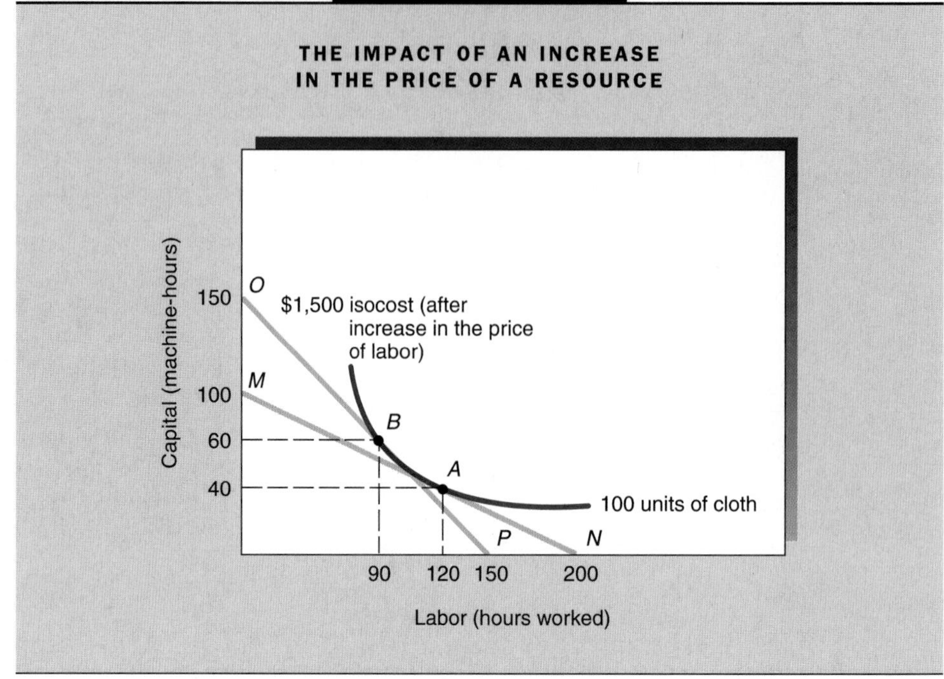

cost line would become steeper, as indicated by the change in isocost lines from *MN* to *OP*. The lowest isocost line that is tangent to the isoquant for 100 units would now be *OP*. The new minimum-cost input combination would be 90 units of labor and 60 units of capital. Cost-minimizing producers would substitute capital for labor. The cost of producing the 100 units would rise (from $1,000 to $1,500).

The Significance of Isoquant-Isocost Analysis

Isoquant-isocost analysis is most applicable in the long run, when all factors are variable and the possibilities for substitution are greatest. It is a conceptual tool, more suitable for illustrating principles than for solving management problems. Few firms would try to design their production activities by drawing isoquants, although some managers might make mental use of the model when analyzing and developing alternative manufacturing processes designed to minimize costs. In any case, firms that do maximize profits behave as though they were using the analysis.

Isoquant-isocost analysis helps clarify the production conditions that must be met if a firm is to minimize its production cost and get the largest possible output from a specific outlay of funds.

Isoquant
A curve representing the technically efficient combinations of two inputs that can be used to produce a given level of output.

Isocost line
A line representing the various combinations of two factors that can be purchased with a given money budget (cost).

CHAPTER 13

A fair day's-wages for a fair day's-work; it is as just a demand as governed men ever made of governing. It is the everlasting right of man.
Thomas Carlyle[1]

Earnings, Productivity, and the Job Market

CHAPTER FOCUS

- Why do some people earn more than others?
- Are earnings differences according to race and gender the result of employment discrimination?
- Who pays for fringe benefits? Do government-mandated fringe benefits increase employee compensation?
- Why are wages higher in the United States than in India or China?
- Why do wages increase? Why has the growth of wages and income per capita slowed during the past 25 years?
- Does automation destroy jobs?

[1]Thomas Carlyle, *Past and Present*, Book 1, Chapter 3 (Boston: Little, and Brown, 1843).

The earnings of workers reflect the availability of tools (physical capital) and the skills and abilities of individual workers (human capital). Approximately four-fifths of the national income in the United States is earned by employees and self-employed workers. The earnings in these two categories primarily reflect a return to human capital. The other one-fifth—income in the form of interest, rents, and corporate profits—reflects mostly returns to physical capital. These shares to human and physical capital have been relatively constant for several decades.

The earnings of U.S. workers are among the highest in the world. However, they vary widely. An unskilled laborer may earn $6.00 per hour, or even less. Lawyers and physicians often earn $100 per hour and more. Dentists and even economists might receive $60 per hour. What accounts for these differences in earnings? Compared to other countries, why are the earnings of American workers so high? How have earnings changed in recent years? This chapter addresses these topics and related issues.

WHY DO EARNINGS DIFFER?

The earnings of individuals in the same occupation or with the same amount of education often differ substantially. The earnings of persons with the same family background also vary widely. For example, one researcher found that the average annual earnings differential between brothers was $26,190, compared with $29,005 for men paired randomly.[2] The earnings of persons with the same intelligence quotient, level of training, or amount of experience typically differ. How do economists explain these variations? Several factors combine to determine the earning power of an individual. Some seem to be the result of good or bad fortune. Others are clearly the result of conscious decisions made by individuals. In the previous chapter, we analyzed how the market forces of supply and demand operate to determine resource prices. The subject of earnings differentials can be usefully approached within the framework of the supply and demand model because the wages earned by workers are simply market-determined resource prices.

The earnings of all employees in a competitive market economy would be equal if: (1) all individuals were identical in preferences, skills, and background, (2) all jobs were equally attractive, and (3) workers were perfectly mobile among jobs. If, given these conditions, higher wages existed in any area of the economy, the supply of workers to that area would expand until the wage differential was eliminated. Similarly, low wages in any area would cause workers to exit until wages in that area returned to normal. However, the conditions necessary for earnings equality do not exist in the real world. Thus, earnings differentials are present. The observed differentials can be explained by the absence of the three conditions that would lead to equality of wages.

[2]Christopher Jencks, *Inequality* (New York: Basic Books, 1972), p. 220. Salary figures are in 1998 dollars.

Earnings Differentials Due to Nonidentical Workers

Workers differ in several important respects that influence both the supply of and demand for their services, and thus create differences in their wage rates.

Worker Productivity and Specialized Skills. The demand for employees who are highly productive is greater than the demand for those who are less productive. Persons who can operate a machine more skillfully, hit a baseball more consistently, or sell life insurance policies with greater regularity will be more valuable to employers. Such employees will contribute more to the firm's revenue—that is, their marginal revenue product (*MRP*) will be higher—than that of their less-skillful counterparts. In competitive labor markets, workers earn a wage equal to their marginal revenue product. As a result, the labor services of more productive workers will command higher wages in the marketplace.

Worker productivity is the result of a combination of factors, including native ability, parental training, hard work, and investment in human capital. The link between higher productivity and higher earnings provides individuals with the incentive to invest in themselves and thereby upgrade their knowledge and skills. If additional worker productivity did not lead to higher earnings, individuals would have little incentive to incur the direct and indirect costs of productivity-enhancing educational and training programs.

Exhibit 13–1 illustrates the impact of worker productivity and the cost of investment in human capital on the wages of skilled and unskilled workers. Because the productivity of skilled workers exceeds that of unskilled workers, the demand for skilled workers (D_s) exceeds the demand for unskilled workers (D_u). The vertical distance between the two demand curves reflects the higher marginal product (*MP*) of

EXHIBIT 13–1

DEMAND, SUPPLY, AND WAGE RATES FOR SKILLED AND UNSKILLED WORKERS

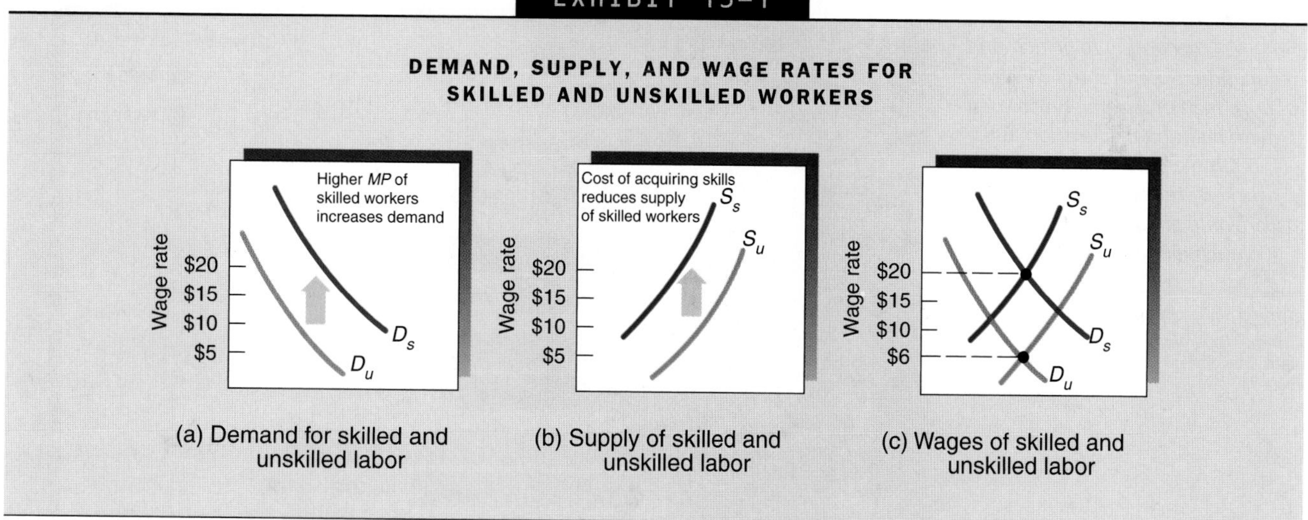

The productivity—and therefore marginal product (MP) *—of skilled workers is greater than that of unskilled workers. Therefore, as part a illustrates, the demand for skilled workers* (D_s) *will exceed the demand for unskilled workers* (D_u)*. Education and training generally enhance skills. Since upgrading skills through investments in human capital is costly, the supply of skilled workers* (S_s) *is smaller than the supply of unskilled workers at any given wage (part b). As part c illustrates, the wages of skilled workers are high relative to unskilled workers due to the strong demand and small supply of skilled workers relative to unskilled workers. (Note: The quantity of skilled labor employed may be far smaller, far larger, or by accident equal to the quantity of unskilled labor hired.)*

skilled workers relative to the unskilled workers (part a). Since investments in human capital (for example, education or training) are costly, the supply of skilled workers (S_s) will be smaller than the supply of unskilled workers (S_u). The vertical distance between the two supply curves indicates the wage differential that is necessary to compensate workers for the costs incurred in the acquisition of their skills (part b). Wages are determined by demand relative to supply (part c). Since the demand for skilled workers is large while their supply is small, the equilibrium wage of skilled workers will be high ($20 per hour). In contrast, since the supply of unskilled workers is large relative to the demand, the wages of unskilled workers will be substantially lower ($6 per hour).

Of course, native ability and motivation will influence the rate at which an individual can transform education and training into greater productivity. Individuals differ in the amount of valuable skills they develop from a year of education, vocational school, or on-the-job training. We should not expect, therefore, a rigid relationship to exist between years of education (or training) and skill level. On average, however, there is a strong positive relationship between investment in education and earnings. **Exhibit 13–2** presents annual earnings data according to educational level for year-round, full-time workers in 1997. The earnings of both men and women increased consistently with additional schooling. High school graduates earned about 50 percent more than their counterparts with less than a ninth grade education. Men college graduates working full-time, year-round earned $55,832 compared to $32,611 for men with only a high school education. In the case of women, college graduates earned $37,319 compared to $22,656 for those who only graduated from high school. The earnings of both men and women continued to increase as they earned master's and doctoral degrees.

EXHIBIT 13–2

The accompanying graph presents data for mean annual earnings of year-round, full-time workers according to gender and education. Note that the earnings of both men and women increased with additional education. Even though the data are for full-time workers, the earnings of women were only about two-thirds those of men with similar education.

SOURCE: U.S. Department of Commerce, Current Population Reports, P-60 Series. Money Income in the United States: 1997, *Table 9.*

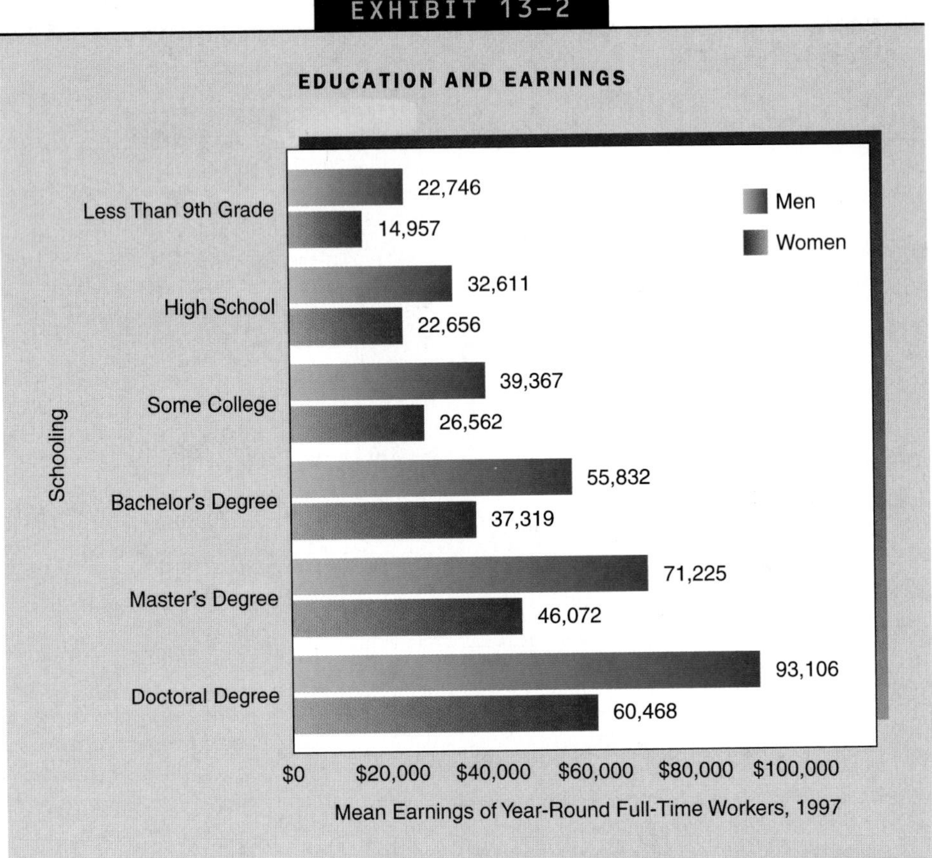

Some of the additional earnings of those with more education may merely reflect their greater native ability, intelligence, and motivation. (See Applications in Economics box, "A College Degree as a Job Market Signal.") Research, however, indicates that a large proportion of the additional earnings is in fact the result of knowledge and skills acquired from investment in additional education. Economic research has also shown that on-the-job training enhances the earnings of workers.

Investment in human capital and development of specialized skills can protect high-wage workers from the competition of others willing to offer their services at a lower price. Few persons could develop the specialized skills of a Julia Roberts, Mark McGuire, or Larry King. Similarly, the supply of heart surgeons, trial lawyers, engineers, business entrepreneurs, and many other specialized workers is limited in occupations where specific skills, knowledge, and human-capital investments contribute to job performance.

The annual earnings of star athletes, entertainers, and television personalities often run into the millions of dollars. What is the marginal revenue product of a superstar entertainer like Julia Roberts? How many more people will go see a movie in which Roberts is the star compared to the number who would attend if the lead actress were less known or less talented? If an additional two million or three million people spend five dollars to attend a movie, this would generate $10 million or $15 million of additional revenue. It is easy to see how a star "box office" attraction would provide the company producing the movie with substantial additional revenues. In turn, competitive labor markets will ensure that big stars get paid their marginal revenue product.

What about the large salaries received by CEOs of major corporations? Decisions made by the CEOs of large corporations can and do exert a huge financial impact

APPLICATIONS IN ECONOMICS

A College Degree as a Job Market Signal: Why You Should Take More Math

"Why should I take *this* difficult course?" "When will I ever use *this?*" Students often complain about taking courses not directly related to their future career. This complaint often reflects an incomplete understanding of exactly why college graduates do better in the job market than those without a college degree. A college degree increases earnings because of both (1) *human capital*—knowledge that will directly increase job productivity and (2) *signaling*—factors that indicate an individual's attitude and motivational characteristics, as well as his or her general analytical skills.

Suppose an employer is looking for an employee who is a very good analytical problem solver. Without a way to directly observe this ability, the employer may look for indicators that are likely to signal this attribute. For example, even if a job does not directly require calculus, persons with a good calculus grade are likely to possess better problem-solving skills than those with a poor grade (or those who dodged the subject). Thus, employers may favor job applicants with good calculus grades, even if the subject is not directly used on the job.

Persons who attend college and earn a degree are likely to possess greater intellectual ability than those who do not. Even if college provided no additional direct human capital, a degree could still help employers identify individuals with abilities that are difficult to observe. Similarly, students who are admitted to and graduate from elite universities like Harvard and Yale are likely to have superior abilities relative to those attending lower-level schools. Because of this signaling device, even mediocre graduates from top universities often have better entry-level job market prospects than exceptional students from lesser-known schools. The signaling function also explains why students who choose majors *perceived by others* as "hard" (such as engineering, economics, or finance) generally do better in the job market than those choosing "easy" majors (such as physical education, marketing, or social work).

"When will I ever use this stuff?" "When will a good grade in challenging courses like math and economics matter?" The answer to these questions is soon. These devices that signal prospective employers about your work habits, motivation, and ability to handle demanding jobs will matter most at the time you enter the job market. It is at the beginning stage of your career when it is difficult for employers to judge your true abilities. As you spend additional years on the job, however, your revealed productivity—and the enhancement of that productivity by your college education—will become more and more important.

on the profitability of their companies. A CEO may be particularly valuable when a company is in trouble, faces new competition, or confronts a changing technological or regulatory environment.

Economic studies have found that many sports and entertainment superstars have marginal revenue products pretty much in line with their salaries.[3] However, there may be another factor at work here. The earnings in some markets resemble tournaments. Only the top-ranked person receives the big payoff, while those who finish second receive much less. This type of compensation is called **tournament pay.**[4] This name refers to reward systems structured like golf tournaments, in which a slight difference in productivity (perhaps one or two shots) is associated with a difference in pay of several hundred thousand dollars.

Tournament pay
A form of compensation where the top performer (or performers) receives much higher rewards than other competitors, even if the others perform at only a slightly lower level.

In this type of environment, workers basically subject themselves to a lottery where the winner (the person with the highest productivity) receives compensation higher than his or her marginal revenue product, while the losers receive less than their marginal revenue product. There are some constraints against how low the compensation of the losers can be, however, because they could find alternative jobs that would pay a salary equal to their marginal revenue product. Theory suggests that tournament pay environments can work to increase the effort of those in the second tier as they compete to move to the top.

Because there is such a large bonus associated with having higher productivity than others in the field, the tournament pay environment creates a strong incentive for

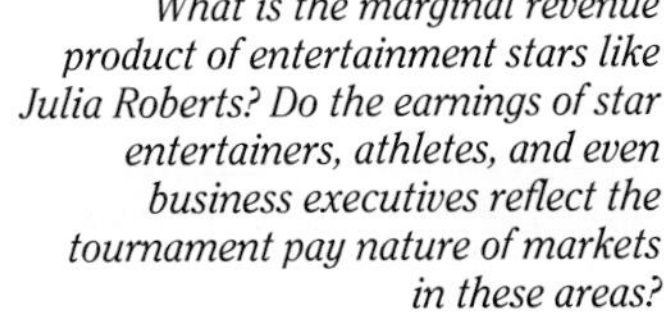

What is the marginal revenue product of entertainment stars like Julia Roberts? Do the earnings of star entertainers, athletes, and even business executives reflect the tournament pay nature of markets in these areas?

[3]Paul M. Sommers and Noel Quinton, "Pay and Performance in Major League Baseball: The Case of the First Family of Free Agents," *Journal of Human Resources* (summer 1982): 426–435.

[4]Edward Lazear and Sherwin Rosen, "Rank Order Tournaments as an Optimum Labor Contract," *Journal of Political Economy* 89 (October 1981): 841–864; and Robert Frank and Phillip Cook, *The Winner-Take-All Society* (New York: The Free Press, 1995).

potential superstars to expend considerable effort attempting to become the best (or one of only a few top performers). As a result, many people spend long hours developing skills that will increase their chances of becoming a "star" in athletics, entertainment, professions, and business. Is this good or bad? Economics does not answer that question; it merely explains how these markets work.

Worker Preferences. An important source of earnings differentials that is sometimes overlooked is worker preferences. People have different objectives in life. Some want to make a great deal of money. Many are willing to work two jobs, or very long hours, undergo agonizing training and many years of education, and sacrifice social and family life to make money. Others may be "workaholics" because they enjoy their jobs. Still others may be satisfied with enough money to get by, preferring to spend more time with their family, with the Boy Scouts, in front of the television, on vacation, or at the local tavern.

Economics does not indicate that one set of worker preferences is more desirable than another, any more than it suggests that people should eat more spinach and less pastrami. Economics does indicate, however, that worker preferences toward money, work, and skill development will contribute to differences in earnings. Other things constant, persons who are more highly motivated by monetary objectives will be more likely to do the things necessary to command higher wage rates.

Race and Gender. Discrimination on the basis of race or gender contributes to earnings differences among individuals. **Employment discrimination** may directly limit the earnings opportunities of minorities and women. Employment discrimination exists when minority or women employees are treated in a manner different from similarly productive whites or men. Of course, the earnings of minorities or women may differ from those of whites or men, respectively, for reasons other than employment discrimination. Nonemployment discrimination may limit the opportunity of minority groups and women to acquire human capital (for example, access to high-quality education or specialized training) that would enhance both productivity and earnings. Limited opportunities as the result of growing up in a low-income or a single-parent family may also influence skill development and educational achievement. Thus, factors other than employment discrimination will influence earnings differences among individuals according to race or ethnic status. A later section in this chapter will analyze the impact of employment discrimination in greater detail.

Employment discrimination
Unequal treatment of persons on the basis of their race, sex, or religion, restricting their employment and earnings opportunities compared to others of similar productivity. Employment discrimination may stem from the prejudices of employers, customers, fellow employees, or all three.

Earnings Differentials Due to Nonidentical Jobs

When individuals evaluate employment alternatives, they consider working conditions as well as wage rates. Is a job dangerous? Does it offer the opportunity to acquire the experience and training that will enhance future earnings? Is the work strenuous and nerve-racking? Are the working hours, job location, and means of transportation convenient? These factors are what economists call **nonpecuniary job characteristics.** People will accept jobs with undesirable working conditions if the wages are high enough, compared to potential job alternatives with better working conditions. Because the higher wages, in essence, compensate workers for the unpleasant nonpecuniary attributes of a job, economists refer to wage differences stemming from this source as **compensating wage differentials.**

Nonpecuniary job characteristics
Working conditions, prestige, variety, location, employee freedom and responsibilities, and other nonwage characteristics of a job that influence how employees evaluate the job.

Compensating wage differentials
Wage differences that compensate workers for risk, unpleasant working conditions, and other undesirable nonpecuniary aspects of a job.

Examples of higher wages that compensate various workers for less-attractive working conditions abound. Because of the dangers involved, aerial window washers (those who hang from windows 20 stories up) earn higher wages than other window washers. Sales jobs involving a great deal of out-of-town travel typically pay more than similar jobs without such inconvenience. Coal miners and sewer workers accept these jobs because they generally pay more than the alternatives available to low-skill workers. Jobs in attractive locations within the United States pay less than similar jobs in less-attractive areas.

Compensating factors even influence the earnings of economists. When economists work for colleges or universities, they generally enjoy a more independent work environment and stimulating intellectual climate than when they are employed in the business sector. Unsurprisingly, the earnings of economists in academia are typically lower than those of economists in business. However, it is important to remember that the academic economist with the lower earnings has chosen this job over business sector employment. The lower earnings do not imply the worker is worse off. As we mentioned previously, differences in worker preferences also play an important role in earnings differences.

Earnings Differentials Due to Immobility of Labor

It is costly to move to a new location or train for a new occupation in order to obtain a job. Such movements do not take place instantaneously. In the real world, labor, like other resources, does not possess perfect mobility. Some wage differentials thus result from an incomplete adjustment to change.

Since the demand for labor resources is a derived demand, it is affected by changes in product markets. An expansion in the demand for a product causes a rise in the demand for specialized labor to produce the product. Since resources are often highly immobile (that is, the supply is inelastic) in the short run, the expansion in demand may cause the wages of the specialized laborers to rise sharply. This happened in the oil-drilling industry in the late 1970s. An expansion in demand triggered a rapid increase in the earnings of petroleum engineers, oil rig operators, and other specialized personnel. Falling oil prices caused the opposite effect in the mid-1980s. The demand for and employment opportunities of specialized resources declined substantially as output in the oil industry fell during the period 1985–1986. Demand shifts in the product market favor those in expanding industries but work against those in contracting industries.

Institutional barriers may also limit the mobility of labor. Licensing requirements, for example, limit the mobility of labor into many occupations—medicine, taxicab driving, architecture, and mortuary science among them. Unions may also follow policies that limit labor mobility and alter the free-market forces of supply and demand. Minimum wage rates may retard the ability of low-skill workers to obtain employment in certain sectors of the economy. These restrictions on labor mobility will influence the size of wage differentials among workers.

Summary of Wage Differentials

As the accompanying Thumbnail Sketch shows, wage differentials stem from many sources, which can be categorized in three main ways: differences in workers, differences in jobs, and immobility of resources. Many of these factors play an important allocative role, compensating people for (1) human-capital investments that increase their productivity or (2) unfavorable working conditions. Other wage differentials reflect, at least partially, locational preferences or the desires of individuals for higher money income rather than nonmonetary benefits. Still other differentials, such as

THUMBNAIL SKETCH

What Are the Sources of Earnings Differentials?

Differences in Workers

1. Productivity and specialized skills (reflects native ability, parental training, and investment in human capital)
2. Worker preferences (trade-off between money earnings and other things)
3. Race and gender discrimination

Differences in Jobs

1. Location of job
2. Working conditions (for example, job safety, likelihood of temporary layoffs, and comfort of work environment)
3. Opportunity for training and skill-enhancing work experience

Immobility of Resources

1. Temporary disequilibrium resulting from dynamic change
2. Institutional restrictions (for example, occupational licensing and union-imposed restraints)

those related to discrimination and occupational restrictions, are unrelated to worker productivity or preferences and do not promote efficient production.

THE ECONOMICS OF EMPLOYMENT DISCRIMINATION

How does employment discrimination affect the job opportunities available to women and minorities? Do employers gain from discrimination? Economics sheds light on both these questions. There are two outlets for labor-market discrimination: wage rates and employment restrictions. **Exhibit 13–3** illustrates the impact of wage discrimination. When majority employees are preferred to minority workers (or men to women

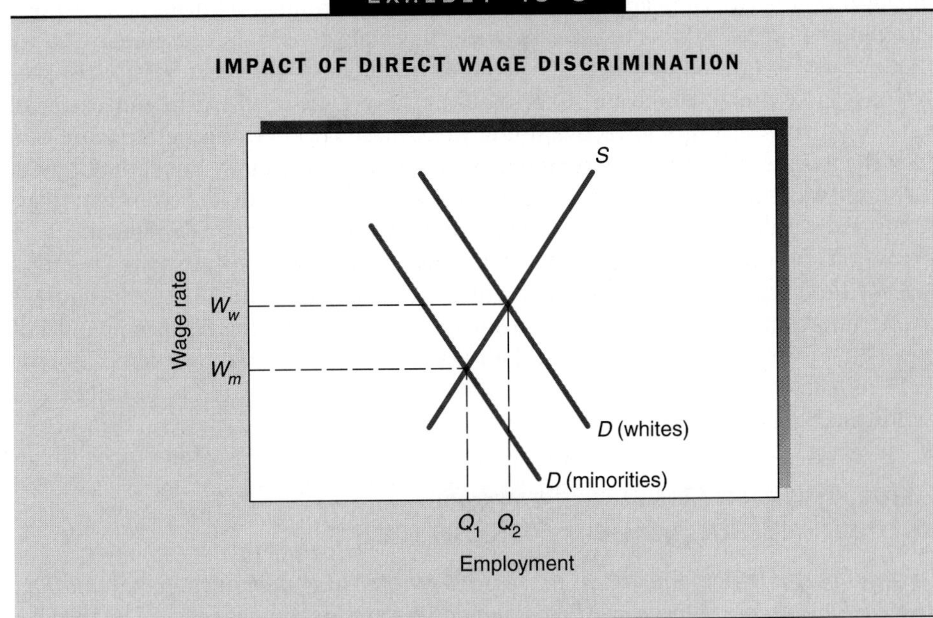

If there is employment discrimination against minorities or women, the demand for their services will decline, and their wage rate will fall from W_w *to* W_m.

workers), the demand for the latter groups is reduced. Consequently, the wages of minorities and women decline relative to those of white men.

Essentially, there is a dual labor market—one market for the favored group and another for the group against which the discrimination is directed. The favored group, such as whites, is preferred, but the less-expensive labor of minority workers is a substitute productive resource. Both white and minority employees are employed, but the whites are paid a higher wage rate.

Exclusionary practices may also be an outlet for employment discrimination. Either in response to outside pressure or because of their own views, employers may primarily hire whites and males for certain types of jobs. When minority and female workers are excluded from a large number of occupations, they are crowded into a smaller number of remaining jobs and occupations. If entry restraints prevent people from becoming supervisors, plumbers, electricians, and truck drivers, they will be forced to accept alternatives. Thus, the supply of labor in the unrestricted occupations increases, causing wage rates to fall. In turn, the exclusionary practices reduce supply and push wages up in occupations and industries dominated by white males.

Although employment discrimination undoubtedly influences earning opportunities available to minorities and women, economic theory indicates that discrimination is costly to employers when they are merely reflecting their own prejudices. ***If employers can hire equally productive minority employees (or women) at a lower wage than whites (or men), the profit motive gives them a strong incentive to do so. Hiring the higher-wage whites when similar minority employees are available will increase the costs of firms that discriminate.*** Employers who hire employees regardless of their race or gender will have lower costs and higher profits than rival firms who try to fill positions with (mostly) white males. Thus, competitive forces tend to reduce the profitability of firms that discriminate.

Discriminatory hiring practices may stem from factors other than employer prejudice, however. If either the firm's employees or its customers have a preference for or against various groups, this may lead to discriminatory hiring even if the employer is totally unbiased. When we think about discrimination, and possible solutions, it is important to consider the source of the discrimination. If discrimination reflects only employer prejudices, competitive markets will place discriminating firms at a cost disadvantage. However, this is not the case when the employer is simply responding to the biases of customers and employees. When discrimination is customer based, a worker from a favored group will be able to bring in more revenue for the firm. For example, adult nightclubs that hire attractive young women as dancers will generate more revenue than those that hire dancers from all age and gender groups. Similarly, Chinese restaurants that hire all (or most all) Chinese servers are likely to do better than if the ethnic and racial composition of their employees mirrors that of the labor force.

Historically, customer-based discrimination has often gone unchallenged. This appears to be changing. In a recent highly publicized case, the Hooters restaurant chain was charged with discrimination against males. Although the Equal Employment Opportunity Commission dropped its four-year investigation, Hooters agreed to pay $3.75 million in damages and begin hiring male servers as the result of privately filed lawsuits in Illinois and Maryland.

Employment Discrimination and the Earnings of Minorities

Earnings may differ among groups for reasons other than employment discrimination. If we want to isolate the impact of employment discrimination, we must (1) adjust for differences between groups in education, experience, and other productivity-related

EXHIBIT 13–4

THE ACTUAL AND PRODUCTIVITY-ADJUSTED WAGES OF MINORITIES COMPARED TO WHITES: 1994–1997

	Men		Women	
	Actual	Adjusted	Actual	Adjusted
White	100	100	100	100
African-American	78	85	90	92
American Indian	84	95	89	97
Asian-American[a]	97	91	103	97
Mexican-American	66	91	76	96
Other Hispanic	79	91	86	95

[a]*Primarily Chinese Americans and Japanese Americans.*

SOURCE: These data were supplied by David MacPherson. They were derived from the 1994–1997 Current Population Surveys. The data were adjusted for years of schooling, work experience, region, industry, sector of employment, union status, and marital status.

factors and (2) then make comparisons between similarly qualified groups of employees who differ only with regard to race (or gender).

How do the earnings of minorities compare with those of similarly productive whites? **Exhibit 13–4** presents data on this topic. Both the actual wages of minorities relative to whites and the "productivity-adjusted" minority/white wage ratio are presented. In essence, the adjusted ratio is an estimate of how the wages of minorities would compare with those of whites if the two groups had the same productivity characteristics (schooling, work experience, marital status, regional location, and union and industry status). The actual wages of black men were 78 percent of the wages of white men in 1994–1997. However, when the workforce characteristics of black men were taken into account, the adjusted hourly earnings of black men rose to 85 percent of the white male earnings. This implies that productivity-related factors accounted for one-quarter of the wage differential between the two groups. A 15 percent differential, that may well be the result of employment discrimination, remained after adjustment for the productivity characteristics.[5]

Mexican Americans constitute the second-largest minority group in the United States. Even though the actual wages of Mexican-American men were only 66 percent of the wages of white men, their "adjusted" earnings were equal to 91 percent of the white wages. These data were not adjusted for language—inability to speak English. Adjustment for this factor would almost certainly further narrow the differential. This suggests that when Mexican-American men possess the same worker characteristics as white men, their earnings are pretty close to parity with their white counterparts. The actual and corrected earnings for other minority groups are also presented in Exhibit

[5]Other researchers using more refined data have found that productivity factors account for a larger share of the earnings differential between whites and blacks. For evidence on this point, see Francine D. Blau and Lawrence M. Kahn, "Race and Gender Pay Differentials," in *Research Frontiers in Industrial Relations and Human Resources*, ed. David Lewin, Olivia S. Mitchell, and Peter D. Scherer (Madison, Wisc.: Industrial Relations Research Association, 1992), pp. 381–416; Derek A. Neal and William R. Johnson, "The Role of Premarket Factors in Black-White Wage Differences," *Journal of Political Economy* (October 1996): 869–895; and June O'Neill, "The Role of Human Capital in Earnings Differences between Black and White Men," *Journal of Economic Perspectives* (fall 1990): 25–45. For a detailed explanation of how the adjusted ratios of Exhibit 13–4 were derived and information on the significance of productivity differences and employment discrimination on the basis of gender, see David A. Macpherson and Barry T. Hirsch, "Wages and Gender Composition: Why Do Women's Jobs Pay Less?" *Journal of Labor Economics* (July 1995).

13–4. Interestingly, adjustment for productivity factors reduces the wages of Asian Americans relative to whites. This occurs because the productivity characteristics—particularly the average level of education—of Asian Americans are higher than those of whites.

Turning to the data for women, the productivity-adjusted wage rates of minority women relative to white women are between 92 percent and 97 percent for each of the groups included in Exhibit 13–4. This implies that the independent effect of racial discrimination is relatively small.

Employment Discrimination and the Earnings of Women

During the last several decades, there has been a dramatic shift in the household versus market work choices of women. As **Exhibit 13–5** shows, the labor force participation rate of women rose from 37.6 percent in 1960 to 60.5 percent in 1997. Increased labor force participation by married women accounted for most of this increase.

Exhibit 13–5 also shows that the female/male (F/M) earnings ratio for full-time workers was approximately 60 percent throughout the 1960–1980 period. Since the early 1980s, the earnings of women have steadily increased relative to men. Nevertheless, women working full time earned only 73.8 percent as much as their male counterparts in 1997. (Note: Women employed full time still worked approximately 10 percent fewer hours than men who were employed full time. Therefore, the hourly

EXHIBIT 13–5

LABOR-FORCE EXPERIENCE OF WOMEN, 1960–1997

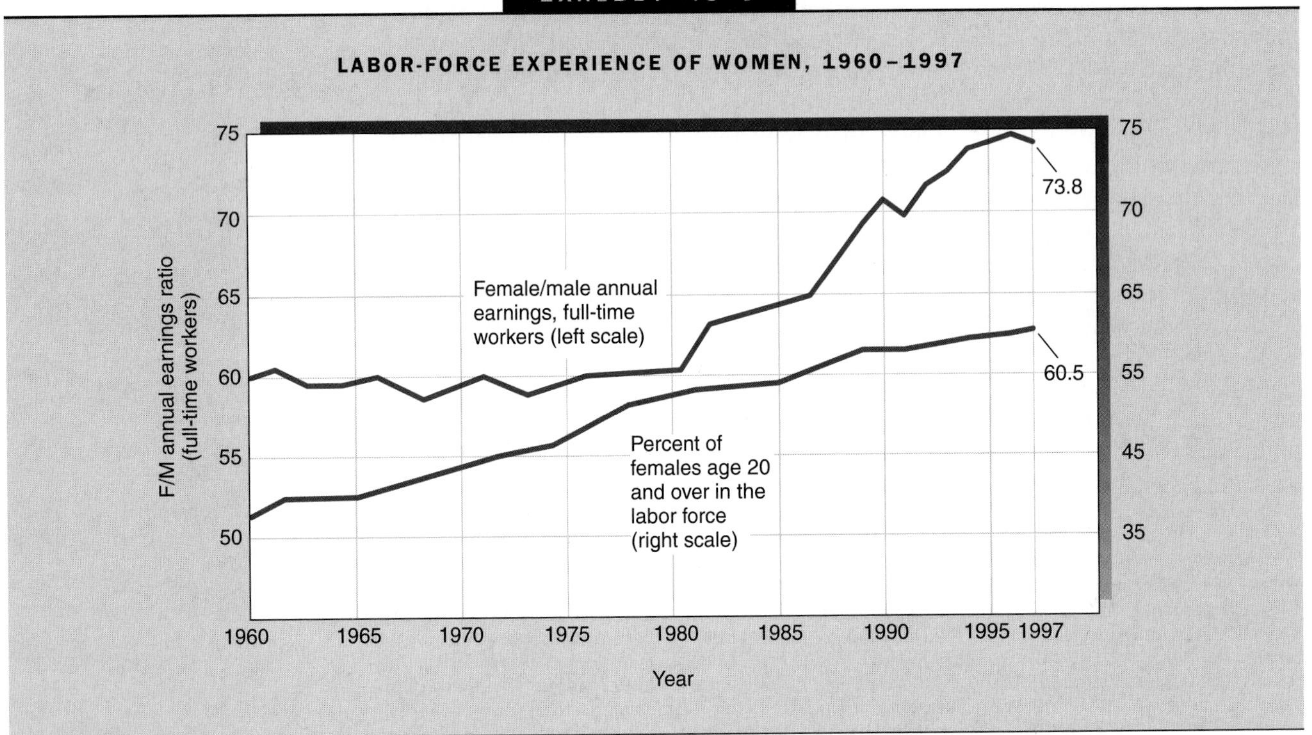

Between 1960 and 1997, the labor-force participation of females rose from 37.6 to 60.5 percent. However, the F/M earnings ratio fluctuated around 60 percent during the 1960–1980 period, before climbing throughout the 1980s. By 1997, the F/M earnings ratio had risen to 73.8 percent.

earnings of full-time working women were approximately 80 percent as high as those of their male counterparts in 1997.)

Is Employment Discrimination the Cause of Earnings Differentials According to Gender? Why are the earnings of women so low compared to those of men? Most people blame employment discrimination. There is substantial evidence that appears to support this view. As we noted in Exhibit 13–2, the earnings of women working full time, year-round are substantially less than those of men with similar amounts of education. In contrast with minorities relative to whites, the age, education, marital status, language, and locational characteristics of men and women are similar. Thus, correcting for these factors does little to reduce the earnings differential between men and women. Occupational data are also consistent with the view that women are crowded into a few low-paying jobs. Until recently, more than half of all women were employed in just four occupations—clerical workers, teachers, nurses, and food-service workers.

Despite this evidence, the case that employment discrimination is the sole or even the primary source of the earnings differential between men and women is less than airtight. For one thing, the size of even the adjusted differential should cause one to pause. If an employer could really hire women who are willing and able to do the same work as men for 25 percent less, the profit motive would provide the employer with a strong incentive to do so. If an employer could really cut labor costs 25 percent merely by hiring women (primarily) rather than men, surely many less "sexist" employers (both men and women) would jump at the chance. Of course, as more and more employers substituted women for men workers, the F/M earnings ratio would move toward parity.

In addition, it is important to recognize that, historically, married men and women have had different areas of specialization within the family. Until quite recently, married men typically pursued paid employment aggressively because they were expected to be the family's primary breadwinner. Given this traditional responsibility for monetary earnings, men were more likely to (1) have continuous labor-force participation, (2) move in order to get a higher-paying job, and (3) accept jobs with long hours, uncertain schedules, and out-of-town travel.

In contrast, married women traditionally had the primary responsibility for operating the household and caring for children. Given these areas of specialization, many women sought jobs with more flexible hours and other characteristics complementary with household responsibilities.[6] Because women expected to have temporary spells out of the labor force (for example, when children were small or financial requirements less demanding), jobs requiring skills and credentials that were easily transportable among employers were particularly attractive. Considering these factors, an overrepresentation of women in nursing, teaching, and secretarial positions is not surprising.

How important are gender differences in specialization within the family? Since preferences cannot be directly observed, the family specialization theory is difficult to test. However, **Exhibit 13–6** sheds some light on its importance. Here we illustrate the median annual earnings of women relative to men, according to marital status. Clearly, married women earn substantially less than married men. Even when working full time, year-round, married women earn only 66 percent as much as men. However, the earnings gap between men and women is substantially less for singles,

[6]For an analysis of how family specialization influences the employment and earnings of women, see James P. Smith and Michael P. Ward, "Women in the Labor Market and in the Family," *Journal of Economic Perspectives* (winter 1989): 9–23; and Solomon Polachek, "Discontinuous Labor Force Participation and Its Effect on Women's Market Earnings," in *Sex Discrimination and the Division of Labor*, ed. Cynthia B. Lloyd (New York: Columbia University Press, 1975).

EXHIBIT 13–6

Although the female/male earnings ratio varies considerably according to marital status and time worked, the earnings of single women relative to the earnings of single men are much higher than the earnings of women in other marital status groupings.

SOURCE: U.S. Department of Commerce, "Money Income in the United States: 1997," Current Population Reports, *Series P60-200, Table 8.*

FEMALE/MALE EARNINGS ACCORDING TO MARITAL STATUS, 1997

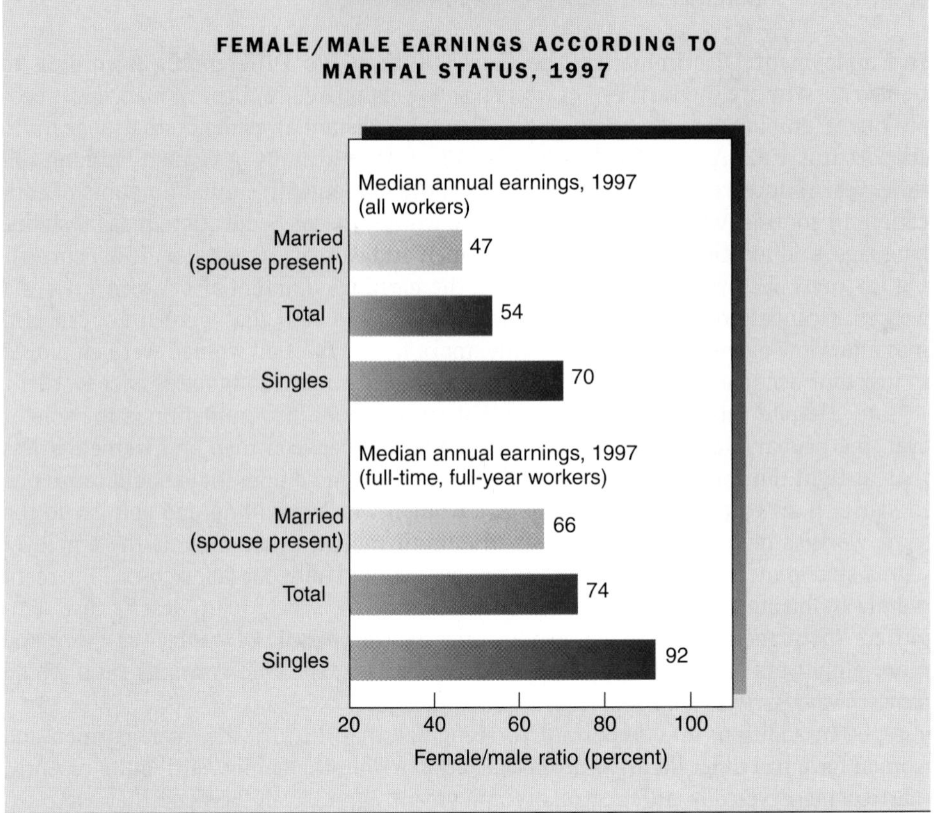

the group least influenced by actual and potential differences in specialization within the traditional family. In fact, in 1997 the female/male annual earnings ratio for full-time, full-year workers was 92 percent for singles. Thus, the earnings of single women were only 8 percent less than those of single men. This pattern of earnings differences according to marital status implies that, although employment discrimination may well be a contributing factor, family specialization is also an important determinant of the overall earnings differential between men and women.

The Changing Workforce Objectives of Women. Although the career objectives of men and women have differed substantially in the past, the differences have narrowed in recent years. In 1968 a national sample of women 14 to 24 years of age found that only 27 percent expected to be working at age 35. In contrast, a similar sample of young women in 1979 found that 72 percent expected to be working at that age.[7] These figures indicate that there was a dramatic increase during the 1970s in the proportion of young women preparing for a career and planning for a lifetime of labor-force participation. As the proportion of women planning for a workforce career rose, the educational choices also changed dramatically. In the early 1970s, women were much less likely than men to study mathematics, engineering, medicine, law, and similar fields leading to high-paying professional jobs. But as **Exhibit 13–7** shows, the proportion of women earning degrees in accounting, veterinary medicine, dentistry, medicine, law,

[7]See Chapter 7 of the *Economic Report of the President, 1987*. The numbers presented here are from Table 7-3 of the report.

EXHIBIT 13-7

WOMEN AS A PROPORTION OF PERSONS EARNING SELECTED PROFESSIONAL DEGREES, 1970-71, 1987-88, AND 1994-95

Field of Study	1970–71	1987–88	1994–95
Engineering	0.8	15.3	16.5
Dentistry	1.2	26.1	36.4
Optometry	2.4	34.3	54.6
Law	7.3	40.4	42.6
Veterinary Medicine	7.8	50.0	64.5
Medicine	9.2	33.0	38.8
Accounting	10.1	52.6	55.4
Economics	11.2	32.8	30.5
Architecture	12.0	38.7	36.5
Pharmacy	25.2	59.7	65.3

SOURCE: Commission of Professionals in Science and Technology, Professional Women and Minorities *(Washington, D.C.: CPST, 1987); and U.S. Department of Education,* Digest of Education Statistics, *1990 and 1997, (Washington, D.C.: U.S. Government Printing Office).*

architecture, pharmacy, and economics increased dramatically in the 1970s and 1980s. By the 1990s, parity was achieved in several of these areas.

It is interesting to reflect on the importance of employment discrimination, traditional household responsibilities, and educational choices in light of the changes during the last four decades. In 1962 equal pay legislation was passed requiring employers to pay equal wage rates to men and women working on the same job. In 1964 the historic Civil Rights Act prohibiting employment discrimination on the basis of both race and gender was passed. Despite these actions, there was little change in the earnings of women relative to men during the 1960s and 1970s. However, as the career

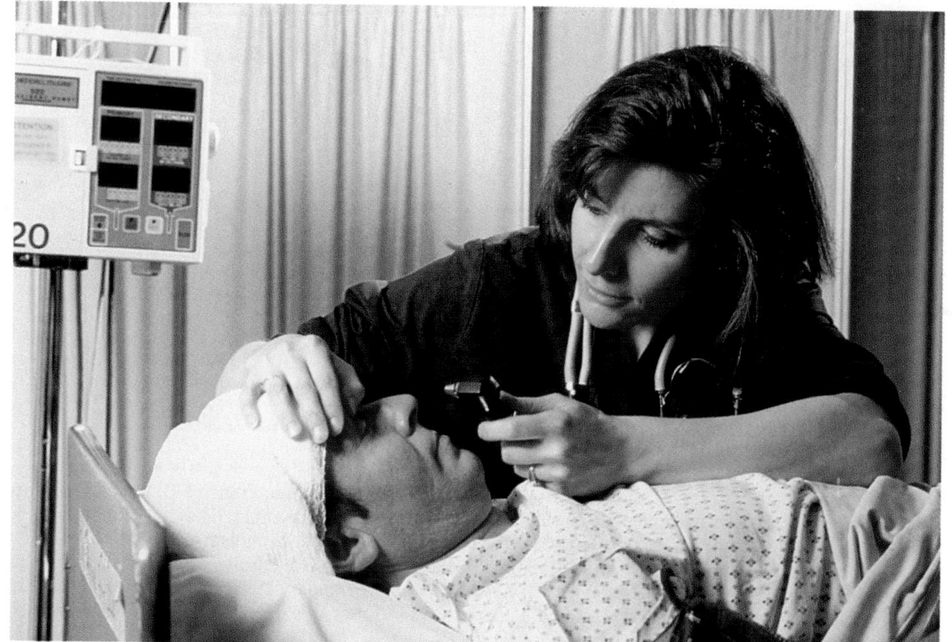

The female/male earnings ratio hovered around 60 percent throughout the 1950–1980 period. During the 1970s, an increasing proportion of women began to plan for full-time, long-term labor force participation. Reflecting this commitment, the career and educational choices of women shifted toward the professions (see Exhibit 13–7). As this happened, the earnings of women began to increase steadily relative to men (see Exhibit 13–6).

objectives of women—perhaps pushed along by earlier legislative actions—began to change during the 1970s, the educational choices of men and women started to become more similar (see Exhibit 13–7).[8] Soon thereafter, the earnings of women began to rise relative to men (see Exhibit 13–5). As more and more women plan and prepare educationally for a workforce career, the upward trend in the F/M earnings ratio will almost surely continue.

THE ECONOMICS OF FRINGE AND MANDATED BENEFITS

Fringe benefits
Benefits other than normal money wages that are supplied to employees in exchange for their labor services. Higher fringe benefits come at the expense of lower money wages.

When referring to wages or compensation, we have proceeded as if employees were compensated only with money payments. Of course, this is an oversimplification. There are generally two components of employee compensation: (1) money wages and (2) **fringe benefits,** which include such items as health-care insurance, layoff benefits, pension benefits, on-the-job training, on-the-premises child-care services, severance benefits, use of an automobile, discounts on life and auto insurance, parental-leave benefits, and paid time off for sickness, personal business, vacation, jury duty, and holidays.

As **Exhibit 13–8** illustrates, fringe benefits compose a sizable and increasing share of employee compensation. In 1996, fringe benefits accounted for approximately

EXHIBIT 13–8

WAGES AND FRINGE BENEFITS: 1980–1996

Fringe benefits are an increasingly important component of employee compensation. These benefits accounted for 28 percent ($4.91 out of the $17.49 total) of employee compensation per hour in 1996, up from 24 percent in 1980.

SOURCE: Statistical Abstract of the United States, *various issues.*

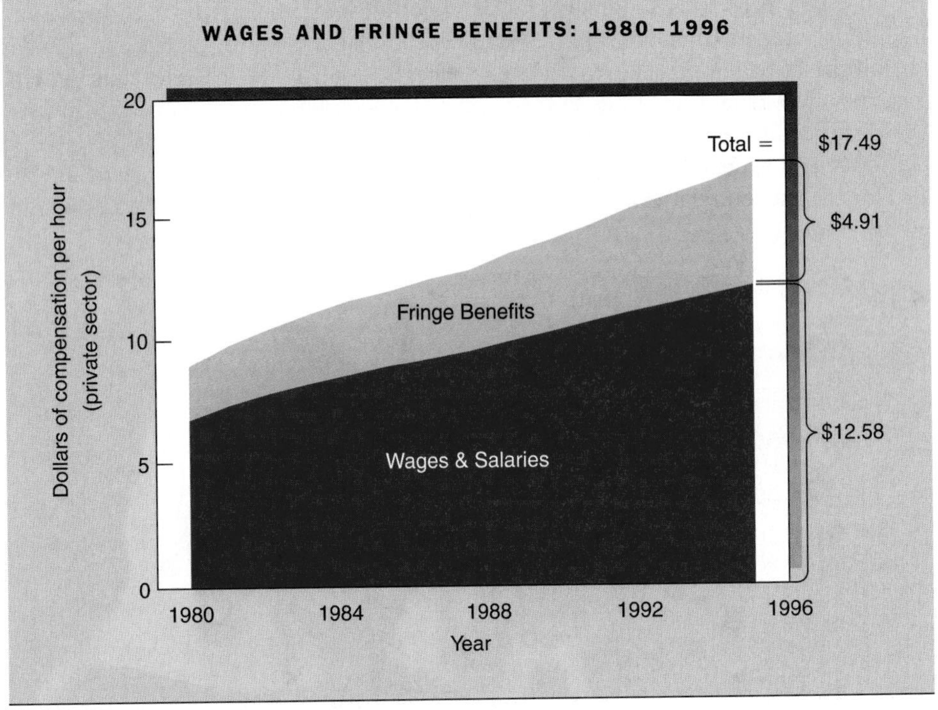

[8]For additional details on recent changes in the male/female earnings gap, see Francine D. Blau, "Trends in the Well-Being of American Women, 1970–95," *Journal of Economic Literature* (March 1998): 112–165; William E. Even and David A. Macpherson, "The Decline of Private Sector Unionism and the Gender Wage Gap," *Journal of Human Resources* (spring 1993): 279–296; June O'Neill and Solomon Polachek, "Why the Gender Gap Narrowed in the 1980s", *Journal of Labor Economics* (January 1993): S205–228; and Claudia Goldin, "Gender Gap," *Fortune Encyclopedia of Economics,* ed. David R. Henderson (New York: Warner Books, 1993).

28 percent of the total compensation of employees in the United States, up from 24 percent in 1980. In the manufacturing sector, the fringe benefit component was even larger; it accounted for just over one-third of total employee compensation in 1996.

Like money wages, provision of fringe benefits is costly to employers. When deciding whether to employ a worker, the employer must consider the total cost of the compensation package. Employment will be expanded as long as the employee's *MRP* exceeds the cost of the employee's total compensation package, including the cost of the fringe benefits. Conversely, workers will not be hired if their employment adds more to cost than to revenue.

In a competitive situation, employers will have to pay a compensation package equal to that prevailing in the market for workers in each skill category. If they do not, they will lose employees to rival firms. ***Fringe benefits are nothing more than a component of the market-determined compensation package. Employers who offer more attractive fringe benefits will be able to attract workers with a lower money wage.*** Those who offer little in the way of fringe benefits will have to pay higher wages. In essence, employees pay for fringe benefits in the form of lower money wages. Contrary to the view of some, fringe benefits are not a "gift" from the employer. Rather, they are earned by the employees as a component of their total compensation package.

Why might employers and employees find a compensation package that includes fringe benefits mutually advantageous? There are two major reasons. First, it may be cheaper for the employees of a firm to purchase certain benefits as a group rather than separately as individuals. When this is the case, employees may prefer the group-purchased benefit rather than additional money wages of equal cost. Life and health-care insurance is an example. It is often cheaper for an insurance company to provide a single policy covering 100 employees (and their families) than it would be for workers to buy 100 separate policies. Therefore, group-purchased life and health insurance is often cheaper than the same coverage purchased as an individual.

Second, compensation in the form of fringe benefits may lead to a tax savings. For example, employer-provided health insurance, child-care services, or use of company-purchased football tickets generate "income" to the employee, but such in-kind benefits are usually not taxable. Therefore, compensation in this form may increase the employee's after-tax compensation more than an equivalent amount of money earnings. Thus, current tax law often makes it more attractive for employees to obtain these benefits through their employers.

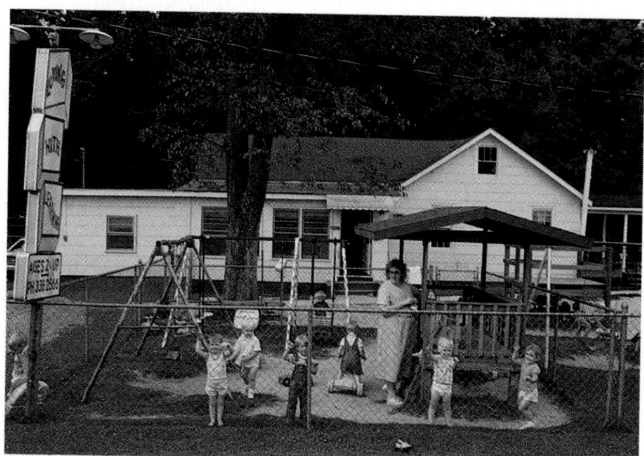

Fringe benefits, such as employer-provided medical insurance and child-care service, are, in fact, part of the employee's compensation package. They are earned and paid for by the employee. The employee's productivity (MRP) must be sufficient to cover all compensation costs, including fringe benefits. Otherwise, the employee will not be hired.

The cost of providing fringe benefits will vary among employers. Large firms may be able to provide some fringe benefits—health-care insurance and child-care services, for example—much more cheaply than small firms. Moreover, employees will vary in their personal valuation of various fringe benefits. For example, parental-leave benefits or child-care services may be highly valued by one employee while yielding little or no utility to another.

In the absence of legislation, agreements between employers and employees (and their representatives) determine the proportion of money wages and fringe benefits in the total compensation package. ***Employers and employees have an incentive to structure the compensation package so that it will transfer the maximum amount of value to employees for any given cost to the employer. Compensation packages of this type will attract employees and thereby minimize the employer's labor costs.***

It will cost an employer the same to pay an employee $1,000 per month as it will to pay $800 per month plus a fringe-benefit package that costs $200 per month. In both cases, the employer's monthly cost is $1,000. When the employer's cost of providing a fringe benefit is low (relative to its cost if purchased directly by the employee) and the employee's valuation of the benefit is high, employers and employees will find it mutually advantageous to substitute the fringe benefits for higher money wages. Conversely, when there is little or no advantage derived from employer-coordinated group provision, or when employees value a fringe benefit less than its cost, employees will prefer higher money wages rather than the fringe benefit. ***In fact, failure to include a fringe benefit in a wage package is strong evidence that it costs more than the value it provides to employees (or that the employee could purchase the benefit just as cheaply without assistance from the employer).***

Impact of Mandated Benefits

Mandated benefits
Fringe benefits that the government forces employers to include in their total compensation package paid to employees.

In recent years several states, and in some cases the federal government, have mandated that employers supply their employees with various fringe benefits, including health-care insurance, parental leave, and child-care services. Proponents of **mandated benefits** argue that they provide protection for employees who work for employers who are unwilling to provide various fringe benefits. Critics charge that mandated benefits (1) force employees to purchase (in the form of lower money wages) benefits valued less than their cost, and (2) push up labor costs for firms, thus reducing employment.

In analyzing the full impact of mandated benefits, there are three key points to keep in mind. First, a mandated benefit is only one component of the total compensation package. Increasing a single component of the package will not necessarily increase the size of the overall package. The parties will adjust. As they adjust, money wages and other fringe benefits will be reduced below what they would have been in the absence of the mandated benefits. Legislation mandating benefits thus reduces flexibility. It forces employers and employees to include a specific item in the total compensation package even when the parties would have preferred to structure the compensation package differently. In many cases, employer-provision of a benefit—particularly provision by small firms—will cost more than the benefit is valued by employees. When this is the case, mandated benefits will increase labor costs without providing a proportional increase in value to employees.

Second, employees earn and ultimately pay for all components of their compensation package—including any benefits mandated by government. Workers will not be hired if their employment adds more to costs than to revenues. The view that fringe benefits are a gift from the employer, and that the size of the benefits package can be increased by requiring employers to include various government-mandated benefits, is purely and simply wrong.

Third, fringe benefits are often an inefficient form of compensating employees. When neither savings from group purchase nor tax advantages exist, employees will prefer money wages to in-kind benefits. When in-kind compensation is efficient—when employees value a fringe benefit more than the additional money that it costs—an employer has a strong incentive to adopt (and employees have a strong incentive to bargain for) this form of compensation. Failure of a fringe benefit to emerge in a given employment setting is strong evidence that it is inefficient—that employees would prefer additional money wages rather than the fringe benefit (given its cost of provision).

How do mandated benefits affect the welfare of workers? Our analysis indicates that adjustments in other dimensions of employment contracts will erode much of their impact. Even when they alter the structure of compensation, mandated benefits are unlikely to increase the overall level of employee compensation. In cases where employees would prefer additional money wages rather than the benefits, forcing the mandated benefits into the compensation package will reduce the welfare of employees because, as labor markets adjust, losses from reductions in other components of the compensation package will more than offset the gains derived from the mandated benefits. Even if specific employees value the benefits more than their costs, lower money wages will partially offset the positive effects of the mandated benefits. Thus, any positive impact of mandated benefits on the total compensation of employees will generally be substantially less than the proponents believe. While we have focused on the net benefits derived by employees, parallel arguments apply to the employer's net cost. Just as the secondary effects erode much of the positive impact on employee benefits, so too do they erode much of the negative impact on the labor costs of employers.

THE LINK BETWEEN PRODUCTIVITY AND EARNINGS

Output and income are closely linked. In fact, they are opposite sides of the same coin. Output is the value of the goods and services produced as measured by the amount purchasers pay for these items. Income is the payments to the resource suppliers, including the profits and losses of the entrepreneurs, who generated the output. This, too, is equal to the amount purchasers pay for the goods and services produced.

Productivity—that is, output per worker—and wages are also closely linked. When workers are more productive, the demand for their services will be higher and therefore they will be able to command higher wage rates. ***High productivity is the source of high wages. When the output per hour of workers is high, the real wages of the workers will also be high.***

Differences in output per worker are the major source of variations in earnings across countries. For example, the earnings per worker are vastly greater in the United States than they are in India or China, because the output of U.S. workers is much greater than the output of their counterparts in those countries. The average worker in the United States is better educated, works with more productive machines, and benefits from more efficient economic organization than the average person in India or China. Thus, the value of the output produced by the average U.S. worker is approximately 15 times that produced by the average worker in India or China. American workers earn more because they produce more. If they did not produce more, they would not be able to earn more.

The *growth* of productivity provides the source for the growth of real earnings. Average real earnings (total compensation) per hour in the United States in 1997 were approximately double the earnings of U.S. workers in the mid-1950s. Similarly, the output of goods and services per hour of U.S. workers in 1997 was approximately twice the level of 40 years ago. Earnings rose because productivity increased. If productivity had not increased, the increase in earnings would not have been possible.

Increased availability of physical capital, improvements in the skill level of the labor force, and advances in technology provide the impetus for the growth of both productivity and earnings. For several decades, the educational level of members of the workforce in the United States (representing investment in human capital) has steadily increased. Simultaneously, the physical capital per worker has expanded. Technological advances have also enhanced productivity and thereby contribute to the growth of output and income. Some observers argue that technology and **automation** adversely affect workers (see the accompanying Myth of Economics box). In fact, just the opposite is true. ***Once you recognize that expansion in output is the source of higher earnings, the positive impact of improvements in technology is apparent: Better technology makes it possible for workers to produce more and thus to earn more.*** For example, accountants can handle more business accounts using microcomputers rather than a pencil and calculator. A secretary can prepare more letters when working with a word processor rather than a typewriter.

Automation
A production technique that reduces the amount of labor required to produce a good or service. It is beneficial to adopt the new labor-saving technology only if it reduces the cost of production.

Improvements in equipment and technology increase worker productivity. In turn, higher productivity is the source of higher earnings.

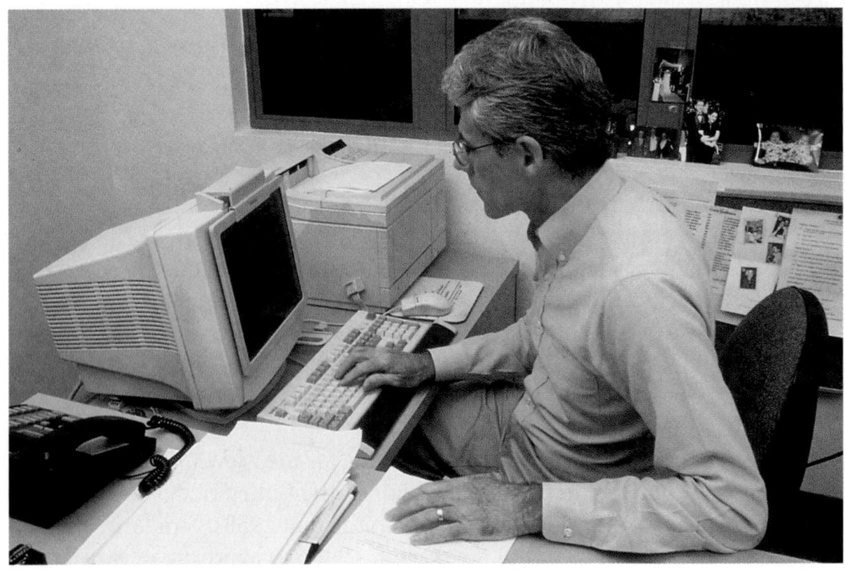

MYTHS OF ECONOMICS

"Automation Is the Major Cause of Unemployment. If We Keep Allowing Machines to Replace People, We Are Going to Run Out of Jobs."

Machines are substituted for people if, and only if, the machines reduce costs of production. Why has the automatic elevator replaced the operator or the power shovel replaced the ditch digger? Because each is a cheaper method of accomplishing a task.

When automation and technological improvements reduce the cost of producing a good, they allow us to obtain each unit of the product with fewer resources. If the demand for the product is inelastic, consumers will spend less on the good and therefore have more of their income available for spending on other things.

Consider the following example. Suppose that someone develops a new toothpaste that really prevents cavities and sells it for half the price of the current brands. If the demand for toothpaste is inelastic, at the lower price, consumers will spend less on this product than was previously the case. Furthermore, the decline in cavities will reduce the demand for and expenditures on dental services. Lower dental care expenditures, however, will increase the income available for consumers to spend on other goods and services. As a result, they will spend more on clothes, recreation, vacations, personal computers, education, and numerous other items. This additional spending, which would not have taken place if dental costs had not been reduced, will generate additional demand and employment in these sectors.

When the demand for a product is elastic, a cost-saving invention can even generate an increase in employment in the industry affected by the invention. This was essentially what happened in the automobile industry when Henry Ford's mass-production techniques reduced the cost (and price) of cars. When the price of automobiles fell 50 percent, consumers bought three times as many cars. Even though the worker-hours *per car* fell by 25 percent between 1920 and 1930, employment in the industry increased by approximately 50 percent during the decade.

Of course, technological advances may diminish the earnings of specific individuals or groups. Home appliances, such as automatic washers and dryers, dishwashers, and microwave ovens, reduced the job opportunities of maids. Computer technology has reduced the demand for telephone operators. In the future, videotaped lectures may even reduce the earnings and job opportunities of college professors. It is understandable why groups directly affected in this manner often fear and oppose automation.

Focusing on the loss of specific jobs, though, conceals the overall impact of technological improvements. Cost-reducing improvements in technology release scarce resources for the expansion of output and employment in other areas. As a result, we are able to produce more and achieve a higher standard of living than would have otherwise been possible.

Furthermore, running out of jobs is not a problem. Jobs represent obstacles, tasks that must be accomplished if we desire to loosen the bonds of scarcity. As long as our ability to produce goods and services falls short of our consumption desires, there will be jobs. A society running out of jobs would be in an enviable position: It would be nearing the impossible goal—victory over scarcity!

Profit-maximizing firms will adopt automated production methods only when they reduce costs. Cost-effective automation releases labor and other resources so they can be used to expand production in other areas. In turn, the expansion in production provides the source for higher earnings.

The Great Productivity Slowdown

What has happened to productivity in recent decades? As **Exhibit 13–9** shows, the rate of increase in output per hour worked in the United States has fallen sharply, particularly since 1973. Predictably, the rise in real compensation per hour has followed a similar path. Between 1948 and 1959, both productivity and real compensation per hour grew at an average annual rate of slightly more than 3 percent. During the 1960–1973 period, both of these growth rates declined to slightly less than 3 percent. Since 1973 the growth of both productivity and real hourly compensation has sagged badly. During the 1974–1997 period, the annual growth of hourly worker productivity fell to 1.2 percent. Real compensation per hour grew at an annual rate of only 0.4 percent during this period. The slowdown in productivity growth is also reflected in the total output figures. The average annual growth of per capita GDP in the United States fell from 2.7 percent during 1955–1973 to 1.6 percent during 1974–1998. In fact, the growth of output (real gross domestic product) has declined during every decade since the 1960s.

As **Exhibit 13–10** shows, the United States is not alone with regard to this slowdown in growth rate. If anything, the reductions in the growth rates of the other major industrial economies have been even greater than that of the United States. For example, the growth rate of per capita GDP of Japan fell from 8.7 percent during 1955–1973 to 2.4 percent during 1974–1998. In Germany, growth of per capita real GDP declined from 4.2 percent during the earlier period to 2.2 percent during the later period. France's growth rate fell from 4.4 percent during 1955–1973 to 1.9 percent during 1974–1998. Italy, Canada, and the United Kingdom have also experienced substantial reductions in growth during the last two decades.

What accounts for this decline in the growth of the major industrial economies during the last 25 years? Research in this area indicates that at least five major factors contributed to the slowdown in productivity.

1. ***A slowdown in the rate of capital formation has retarded the growth of productivity.*** As we have previously noted, more and better equipment and tools enhance the

EXHIBIT 13–9

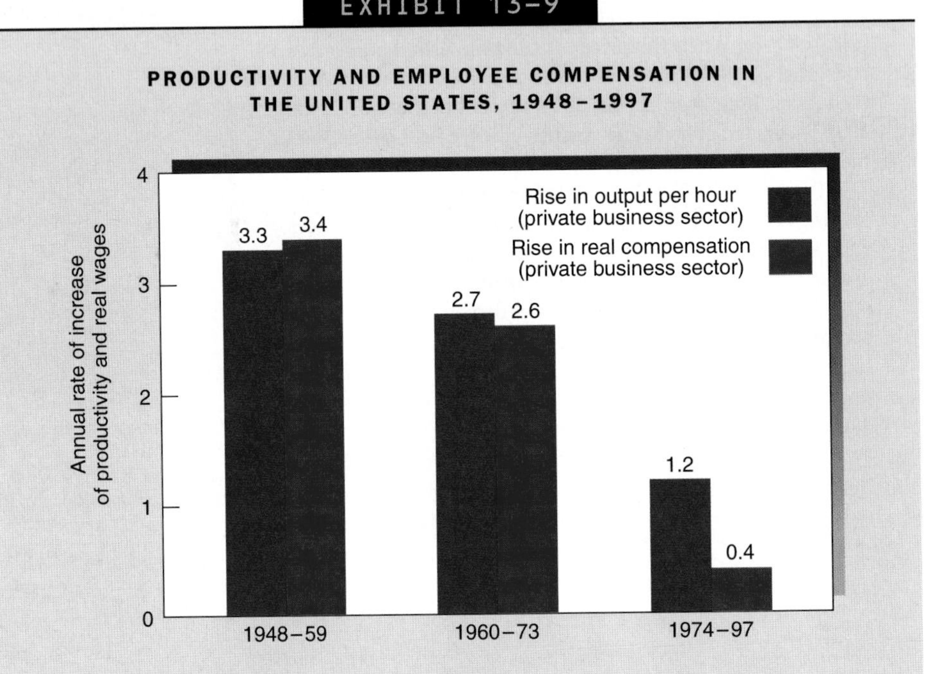

As illustrated in the graph, worker productivity and employee compensation per hour are closely linked. Since 1973, growth of both productivity and real compensation per hour has slowed substantially compared to the growth figures achieved during the 1948–1973 period.

SOURCE: U.S. Department of Labor, Monthly Labor Review *(September 1998), Table 41.*

EXHIBIT 13-10

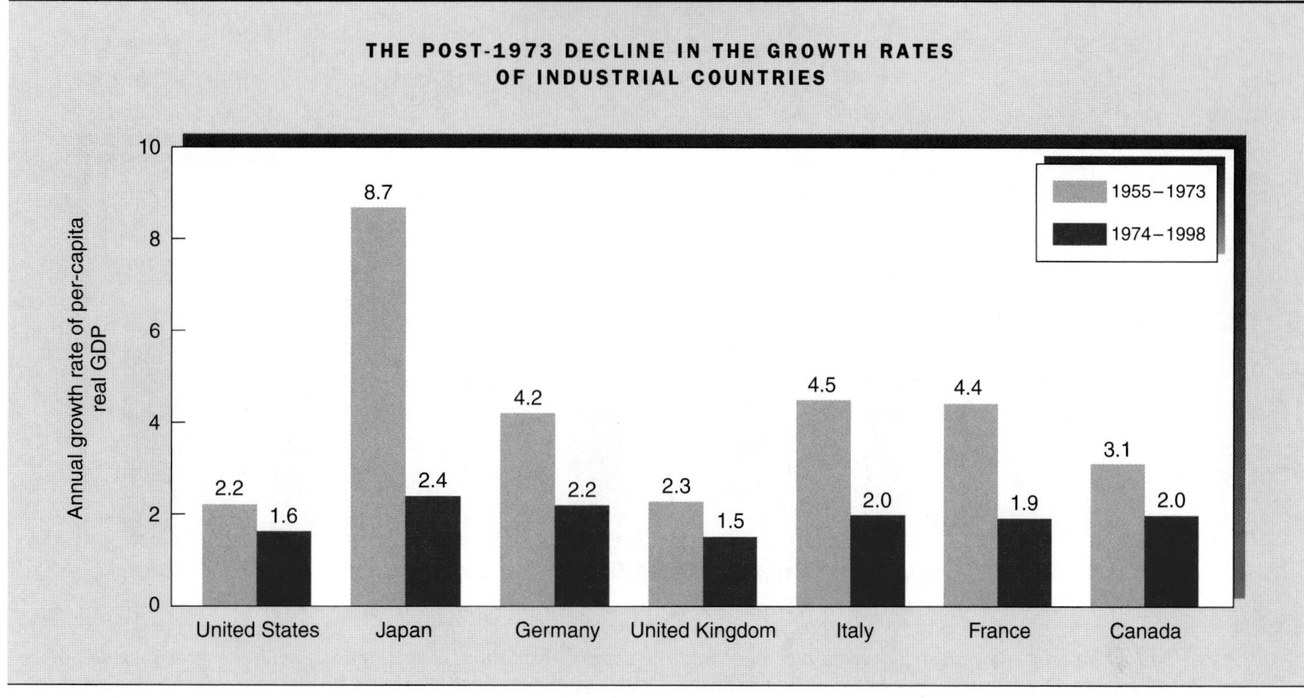

Here we present the growth rates of real per-capita GDP for 1955–1973 and 1974–1998 for industrial economies. In every case, the growth rate for the more recent period was substantially less than that for the earlier period.

SOURCE: World Bank, World Tables, 1980 *and International Monetary Fund,* International Financial Statistics Yearbook *(various issues).*

productivity of workers. Other things constant, workers are able to produce more when they are working with more physical capital. When the supply of productivity-enhancing capital assets grows more slowly, the growth of labor productivity also tends to slow. This is precisely what has happened. **Exhibit 13–11** presents the figures for investment as a share of GDP for the most recent decade and the decade prior to 1973. In every case, the investment rate of the major industrial countries during the more recent period was lower than that for the period prior to 1973.

2. ***Both sharply higher energy prices and an increase in environmental regulations have reduced the productivity of capital during the last two decades.*** The sharply higher oil prices of the 1973–1981 period substantially reduced the efficiency of vast amounts of capital. Machines and structures designed for cost effectiveness at pre-1973 energy prices were suddenly rendered obsolete. They were too costly to operate at the higher level of energy prices. At the same time, regulations designed to improve the environment and reduce the level of pollution also reduced the effectiveness of capital. Many firms were forced either to terminate their use of various equipment or to undertake costly modifications in order to meet the more rigid regulatory standards of the 1970s and 1980s.[9]
3. ***During the 1970s and 1980s, youthful, less-experienced workers composed a large share of the U.S. labor force.*** Beginning in the latter half of the 1960s, the United

[9]See Edward F. Denison, *Trends in American Economic Growth, 1929–1982* (Washington, D.C.: Brookings Institution, 1985); and the articles in the *Journal of Economic Perspectives* (fall 1988) for additional details on this topic.

EXHIBIT 13-11

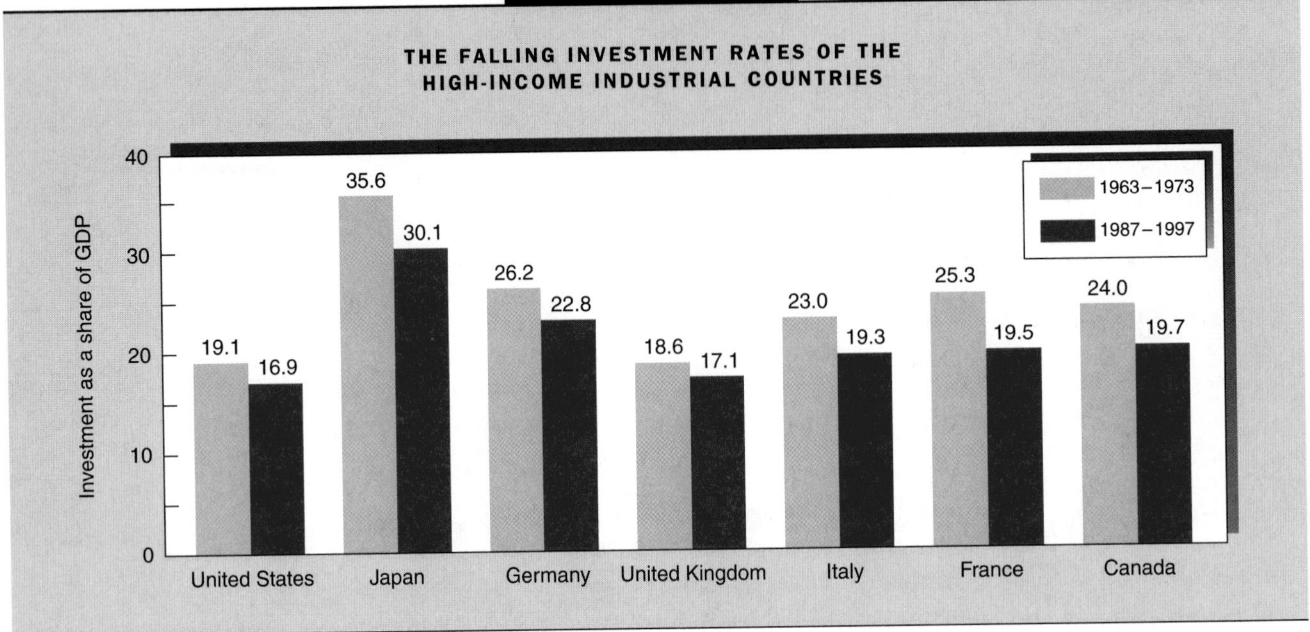

During the last decade, the industrial economies allocated less of their total output to investment than was true during the 1963–1973 period. This reduction in the rate of capital formation is one reason why the growth rates of these economies have declined.

SOURCE: Derived from International Monetary Fund, International Financial Statistics Yearbook: 1998, *p. 163.*

States experienced a sharp influx of less-experienced workers into the workforce as the labor-force participation of women increased and the children of the post–Second World War baby boom came of working age. Economics indicates that a rapid growth of the labor force—particularly the increased number of inexperienced and less-skilled workers—will reduce productivity. However, this situation has now changed and the baby-boomers have moved into their prime-age working years. Nonetheless, there is little sign of an increase in the rate of growth.

4. ***A reduction in the average achievement level of the new labor-force entrants may have retarded growth.***[10] As we have previously noted, educational levels as measured by years of school have increased throughout the post–Second World War period. However, additional schooling may not necessarily mean a more knowledgeable and skillful workforce. The SAT scores of high school graduates and other measures of basic skills declined during the 1970s and have failed to rebound to their previous highs. Prior to that time, these basic-skills test scores had been improving for at least 50 years. Thus, compared with the 1950s and 1960s, the improvement in the quality of the labor force may have slowed during the last two decades. Furthermore, the amount of human capital possessed by the more recent labor-force entrants may be less than the schooling figures imply.
5. ***The growth of government expenditures is associated with the slowdown in economic growth.*** Economic theory indicates that government's protective function and provision of various public goods, such as national defense and a stable monetary

[10]See John H. Bishop, "Is the Test Score Decline Responsible for the Productivity Decline?" *American Economic Review* (March 1989): 178–197.

regime, will enhance productivity and economic growth. However, as government grows and becomes involved in more and more activities for which it is ill-suited, diminishing returns will be confronted. Beyond some point, the distortions accompanying higher taxes (and/or additional borrowing) and disadvantages of government compared to market allocation will exert a negative impact on economic growth.

There is evidence that the size of government in the high-income industrial economies, particularly those of Western Europe, now exceeds the growth-maximizing level. Among the 23 long-standing members of the Organization for Economic Cooperation and Development (OECD), government expenditures as a share of the economy rose from 27 percent in 1960 to 48 percent in 1996. The growth of government during the last several decades has been astonishing for several OECD countries. For example, *as a share of the economy,* government expenditures in Denmark rose from 24.8 percent in 1960 to 60.8 percent in 1996. During the same period, government spending rose from 31 percent to 66 percent of the economy in Sweden and from 26.6 percent to 59.4 percent in Finland. The growth of government in OECD countries has been associated with the falling growth rates. More significantly, the OECD countries (Denmark, Finland, Greece, Portugal, Spain, and Sweden) with the largest increases in size of government during the 1960–1996 period experienced the largest growth rate reductions. In contrast, the OECD members (Iceland, Ireland, New Zealand, United Kingdom, and the United States) with the least expansion in size of government as a share of the economy experienced the smallest reductions in economic growth.[11]

Perspective on the Productivity Slowdown

Clearly, the lagging growth rate of productivity is a serious matter. Unless it is reversed, the future growth of income will be quite slow compared with the 25 years following World War II. Some of the unfavorable factors—for example, the oil price increases and the rapid growth of inexperienced workers—have reversed. Perhaps these changes will lead to an increase in the growth rate in the near future. In addition, some would argue that the recent growth figures should be viewed in a longer-term historical context. Perhaps the 1948–1973 period was an aberration. Most researchers place the annual per-capita growth rate of the United States, Germany, France, and the United Kingdom at approximately 1 percent throughout most of the century prior to 1950. Maybe this is the proper benchmark against which the growth of the last two decades should be measured.[12]

[11]For additional evidence on the linkage between larger government expenditures and slower growth, see James Gwartney, Robert Lawson, and Randall Holcombe, *The Size and Functions of Government and Economic Growth,* Joint Economic Committee (April 1998).

[12]See Claudia Goldin, *Labor Markets in the Twentieth Century,* National Bureau of Economic Research Historical Working Paper No. 58 (June 1994), for evidence on the long-term growth rate of labor productivity.

LOOKING *Ahead*

While this chapter focused on the labor market, the following chapter will analyze the capital market. Real income and output are strongly influenced by the amount of both the physical and human capital with which people work. The next chapter analyzes the factors that underlie the availability of capital and the investment choices of decision makers.

KEY POINTS

➤ Wage differentials exist because of differences in workers (productivity, personal preferences, race, and gender), differences in jobs (location, risk, and working conditions), and degree of labor mobility (institutional restrictions, such as licensing).

➤ Economic research indicates that approximately one-third of the earnings disparity between whites and blacks is due to differences in employability characteristics (education, productivity, etc.) rather than employment discrimination.

➤ The annual earnings of women working full time are approximately 75 percent of the figure for males. In addition to employment discrimination, differences in career goals and educational choices have contributed to earnings differentials according to gender. As the career and educational choices of women have become more like those of men during the last two decades, the female/male earnings ratio has steadily increased.

➤ Fringe benefits are a component of employee compensation. When the employer's cost of providing a fringe benefit is low, and the employee's personal valuation of the benefit is high, employers and employees will find it mutually advantageous to *substitute* fringe benefits for money wages in the total compensation package. When fringe benefits are mandated by government, other forms of compensation will be scaled back. The fact that these benefits were not already being provided suggests that many employees valued the other forms of compensation that are now cut back more than the mandated benefit.

➤ Productivity is the ultimate source of high wages and earnings. Workers in the United States (and other high-income industrial countries) earn high wages because their output per hour is high as the result of (a) greater worker knowledge and skills (human capital) and (b) the use of modern machinery (physical capital).

➤ During the last 25 years, the growth of productivity in the United States and other major industrial nations has lagged well below the growth rate achieved during the 25 years following the Second World War. A slowdown in the growth of capital per worker, higher energy prices, environmental regulations, an influx of inexperienced younger workers, a decline in the basic skill levels of new labor-force entrants, and growth in the size of government contributed to this slowdown in productivity. If the slowdown in productivity continues, future improvements in our standard of living will come about more slowly.

➤ Automated methods of production will be adopted only if they reduce costs. Although automation might reduce employment in a specific industry, it also releases resources that can be employed in other areas. Improved technology permits us to achieve larger output and income levels than would otherwise be possible.

CRITICAL ANALYSIS QUESTIONS

1. What are the major reasons for the differences in earnings among individuals? Why are wages in some occupations higher than in others? How do wage differentials influence the allocation of resources? Explain.

*2. Why are real wages in the United States higher than in other countries? Is the labor force itself responsible for the higher wages of American workers? Explain.

3. What are the major factors that would normally explain earnings differences between (a) a lawyer and a minister, (b) an accountant and an elementary school teacher, (c) a business executive and a social worker, (d) a country lawyer and a Wall Street lawyer, (e) an experienced, skilled craftsperson and a 20-year-old high school dropout, and (f) an upper-story and a ground-floor window washer?

4. Is employment discrimination the only important cause of earnings differences between whites and blacks or men and women? Carefully justify your answer.

5. During the last three decades, the labor-force participation of married females approximately doubled. What impact did this influx of married workers into the labor force have on (a) the average years of work experience of women relative to men, (b) the mean hours of work time of women relative to men, and (c) the female/male earnings ratio?

*6. "Jobs are the key to economic progress. Unless we create more jobs, our standard of living will fall." Is this statement true or false? Explain.

7. "If Jones has a skill that is highly valued, she will be able to achieve high market earnings. In contrast, Smith may work just as hard or even harder, and still earn only a low income."

a. Does hard work necessarily lead to a high income?

b. Why are the incomes of some workers high and others low?

c. Do you think the market system of wage determination is fair? Why or why not?

d. Can you think of a more equitable system? If so, explain why it is more equitable.

*8. People who have invested heavily in human capital (for example, lawyers, doctors, and even college professors) generally have higher wages, but they also generally work more hours than other workers. Can you explain why?

9. Does it sometimes make sense for employers to pay workers with in-kind benefits (health-care insurance, child-care services, termination payments, and the like) rather than higher money wages? Why? Discuss.

*10. "If individuals had identical abilities and opportunities, earnings would be equal." Is this statement true or false?

11. "If it were not for employment discrimination against women, the average earnings of men and women would be equal." Is this statement true or false?

*12. Other things being constant, how will the following factors influence hourly earnings? Explain your response.

a. The employee must work the midnight to 8:00 A.M. shift.

b. The job involves broken intervals (work 3 hours, off 2 hours, work 3 additional hours, and so on) of employment during the day.

c. The employer provides low-cost child-care services on the premises.

d. The job is widely viewed as prestigious.

e. The job requires employees to move often from city to city.

f. The job requires substantial amounts of out-of-town travel.

*13. In addition to money-wage compensation, some employers provide employees with health-care benefits; paid time off for sickness, vacation, and jury duty; on-the-premises child-care services; and severance benefits in case of termination.

a. How do these benefits affect the employer's cost of employment? Do you think employers offering the benefits would be willing to pay higher wages if the benefits were not offered?

b. Would you be willing to work for an employer who did not offer any of these benefits if the money-wage payments were high enough?

c. Are these benefits "gifts" from employers offering them? Who really pays for the benefits?

14. Part-time jobs held by college students rarely provide fringe benefits, such as health insurance. Do you think the typical college student would prefer a job that paid $8.00 per hour with no health insurance benefits or a job that paid $6.00 per hour with health insurance benefits? Suppose the government were to mandate that all employers must provide health-care benefits to all employees, including those who are working only part time. What impact would this have on the welfare of college students who hold part-time jobs?

*15. Consider two occupations (A and B) that employ persons with the same skill and ability. When employed, workers in the two occupations work the same number of hours per day. In occupation A, employment is stable throughout the year, while employment in B is characterized by seasonal layoffs. In which occupation will the hourly wage rate be highest? Why? In which occupation will the annual wage be highest? Why?

*16. In 1994 the median earnings of single men working full time, year-round were only 75 percent of their married counterparts. Does this indicate that employment discrimination existed against single men and in favor of married men?

---

*Asterisk denotes questions for which answers are given in Appendix B.

CHAPTER 14

To produce capital, people must forgo the opportunity to produce goods for current consumption. People can choose whether to spend their time picking apples or planting apple trees. In the first case there are more apples today; in the second, more apples tomorrow.

Steven Landsburg[1]

Investment, the Capital Market, and the Wealth of Nations

CHAPTER FOCUS

- Why do people invest? Why are capital resources often used to produce consumer goods?
- Why are investors willing to pay interest to acquire loanable funds? Why are lenders willing to loan funds?
- What is the interest rate? How is the nominal interest rate influenced by the inflation rate and the riskiness of a loan?
- Why is the interest rate so important when evaluating costs and revenues across time periods?
- When is an investment profitable? How do profitable and unprofitable investments influence the wealth of nations?
- How important are investment and the efficient use of capital to the wealth of a nation?

[1]Steven E. Landsburg, *Price Theory and Applications* (Fort Worth, Tex.: The Dryden Press, 1992), p. 581.

In the previous chapter we noted that the income of both individuals and nations is closely related to their productivity—their ability to supply goods and services that are highly valued by others. In turn, productivity is influenced by investment choices. Consider such choices as whether to construct an office building, purchase a harvesting machine, or go to law school. The returns derived from investments such as these are generally spread over several years (or even decades). Some costs of investments, such as maintenance expenses, may also be incurred over a lengthy time period. Why should we expect profit-seeking individuals and corporate decision makers to pay now to create benefits later—sometimes much later? How can people compare the benefits and costs of an activity when both are spread across lengthy periods of time? How can investment funds be channeled toward projects that have the greatest likelihood to increase the wealth of people and nations? Will market decisions made by profit-seeking individuals be short-sighted, providing too little conservation and too few investments for the future? As we explain the investment process and capital markets, this chapter will help you answer these questions.

WHY PEOPLE INVEST

Capital
Resources that enhance our ability to produce output in the future.

Investment
The purchase, construction, or development of capital resources, including both nonhuman capital and human capital. Investments increase the supply of capital.

Saving
Current income that is not spent on consumption goods.

Capital is a term used by economists to describe long-lasting resources that are valued because they can help us produce goods and services in the future. As we previously discussed, there are two broad categories of capital: (1) *physical capital:* nonhuman resources, such as buildings, machines, tools, and natural resources, and (2) *human capital:* human resources, that is, the knowledge and skills of people. **Investment** is the purchase, construction, or development of a capital resource. Thus, investment expands the availability of capital resources.

Saving is income not spent on current consumption. ***Investment and saving are closely linked. In fact, the two words describe different aspects of the capital formation process. Saving applies to the nonconsumption of income, while investment applies to the use of the unconsumed income to produce a capital resource.*** Sometimes saving and investment are conducted by the same person, as when a farmer saves current income (refrains from spending it on consumption goods) in order to purchase a new tractor (an investment good).

It is important to recognize that saving is required for investment. Someone must save—refrain from consumption—in order to provide the resources for investment. When investors finance a project with their own funds, they are also saving (refraining from current consumption). Investors, however, do not always use their own funds to finance investments. Sometimes they will borrow funds from others. When this is the case, it is the lender rather than the investor that is doing the saving.

Considering the alternative use of resources also highlights the linkage between investment and saving. Resources used to produce capital will be unavailable for the direct production of consumption goods. The opportunity cost of investing more

Savings deposited by some individuals allow resources to be devoted to investments, such as the making of tractors.

and using more of our resources to produce capital resources today, is that fewer current resources will be available to produce consumption goods. To invest more, we have to reduce our current consumption.

Why would anyone want to delay consumption in order to undertake an investment? Consumption is the ultimate objective of all production. However, we can sometimes produce more consumption goods by first using resources to produce capital resources and then utilizing these resources to produce the desired consumer goods. Using capital to produce consumption goods makes sense only when it allows us to produce more consumption goods than we otherwise could.

Perhaps a simple illustration can highlight the potential gains from using capital to produce consumption goods. Suppose that Robinson Crusoe can catch fish by either (1) combining his labor with natural resources (direct production) or (2) constructing a net and eventually combining his labor with this capital resource (indirect production). Let us assume that Crusoe could catch 2 fish per day by hand fishing, but could catch 3 fish per day if he constructed and used a net that would last for 310 days. Suppose it would take Crusoe 55 days to build the net. The opportunity cost of constructing the net would be 110 fish (2 per day not caught, for each of the 55 days Crusoe spent building the net). As the accompanying chart indicates, if Crusoe invested in the capital resource (the net), his output during the next year (including the 55 days required to build the net) would be 930 fish (3 per day for 310 days). Alternatively, hand-fishing during the year would lead to an output of only 730 fish (2 fish per day for 365 days).

NUMBER OF FISH CAUGHT		
	WITHOUT NET	WITH NET
Per day	2	3
Annual	730	930

Crusoe's investment in the net will enhance his productivity. With the net, his total output during the year will increase by 200 fish. In the short term, however, investing in the net will impose a sacrifice. During the 55 days it takes to construct the net, Crusoe's production of consumption goods will decline.

How can Crusoe or any other investor know if the value of the larger future output is worth the short-term cost? Most of us have a preference for goods now rather than later. For example, if you are typical, you would prefer a sleek new sports car now rather than the same car 10 years from now. On average, individuals possess a **positive rate of time preference.** By this we mean that, other things the same, people subjectively value goods obtained sooner more highly than goods obtained later.

Positive rate of time preference
The desire of consumers for goods now rather than in the future.

When only Crusoe is involved, the attractiveness of the investment in the fishing net is dependent upon his time preference. If he places a high value on a couple of fish per day during the next 55 days, as indeed he may if he is on the verge of starvation, the cost of the investment may well exceed the value of the larger future output. If Crusoe could find someone who would loan him fish while he built the net, however, he could consume the borrowed fish now, even while building the net, and pay later from the increase in fish production made possible by the net. If such a loan is available, the attractiveness of the investment (building the net instead of hand fishing now) would be influenced by the price of borrowing fish. Is the payment of additional fish, in order to maintain consumption while investing in the net, worth the extra cost? To answer this question, Crusoe must consider the cost of paying for earlier availability—he must consider, in effect, the interest rate.

INTEREST RATES

The interest rate links the future to the present. It allows individuals to evaluate the value today—the present value—of future income and costs. In essence, it is the market price of earlier availability. From the viewpoint of a potential borrower, the interest rate is the premium that must be paid in order to acquire goods early and pay for them later. From the lender's viewpoint, it is a reward for waiting—a payment for supplying others with current purchasing power. The interest rate allows the lender to calculate the future benefit (future payments earned) derived from extending a loan or saving funds today.

In a modern economy, people often borrow funds in order to finance current investments and consumption. Because of this, the interest rate is often defined as the price of loanable funds. This definition is proper. But we should remember that it is the earlier availability of goods and services purchased, not the money itself, that is desired by the borrower.

DETERMINATION OF INTEREST RATES

Interest rates are determined by the demand for and supply of loanable funds. Investors demand funds in order to finance capital assets that they believe will increase output and generate profit. Simultaneously, consumers demand loanable funds because they have a positive rate of time preference: They prefer earlier availability.

The demand of investors for loanable funds stems from the productivity of capital. Investors are willing to borrow in order to finance the use of capital in production because they expect that an expansion in future output will provide them with more than enough resources to repay both the amount borrowed—the principal—and interest on the loan. Our prior example of Robinson Crusoe illustrates this point. Remember, Crusoe could increase his output by 200 fish this year if he could take off 55 days from hand fishing in order to build a net. Doing so would reduce Crusoe's fish production by 2 fish per day during the time he was constructing the net. Suppose a fishing crew from a neighboring island visited Crusoe and offered to lend him 110 fish so that he could undertake the capital investment project (building the net). If Crusoe could borrow the 110 fish (the principal) in exchange for, say, 165 fish one year later (110 fish to repay the principal and 55 as interest on the loan), the investment project would be highly profitable. Crusoe could repay the funds borrowed, plus the 50 percent interest rate, and still have 145 additional fish (the 200 additional fish caught minus the 55 fish paid in interest).

Crusoe's demand for loanable fish—and, more generally, the demand of investors for loanable funds—stems directly from the productivity of the capital investment. Crusoe can gain by borrowing to finance the construction of a fishing net only because the net enables him to expand his total output during the year. Similarly, investors can gain by borrowing funds to undertake investment projects only when the capital assets they purchase permit them to expand output (or reduce costs) by enough to make the interest payments and still have more output than they would have without the investment.

As **Exhibit 14–1** illustrates, the interest rate brings the choices of investors and consumers wanting to borrow funds into harmony with the choices of lenders willing to supply funds. Higher interest rates make it more costly for investors to undertake capital spending projects and for consumers to buy now rather than later. Both investors and consumers will therefore curtail their borrowing as the interest rate rises. Investors will borrow less because some investment projects that would be

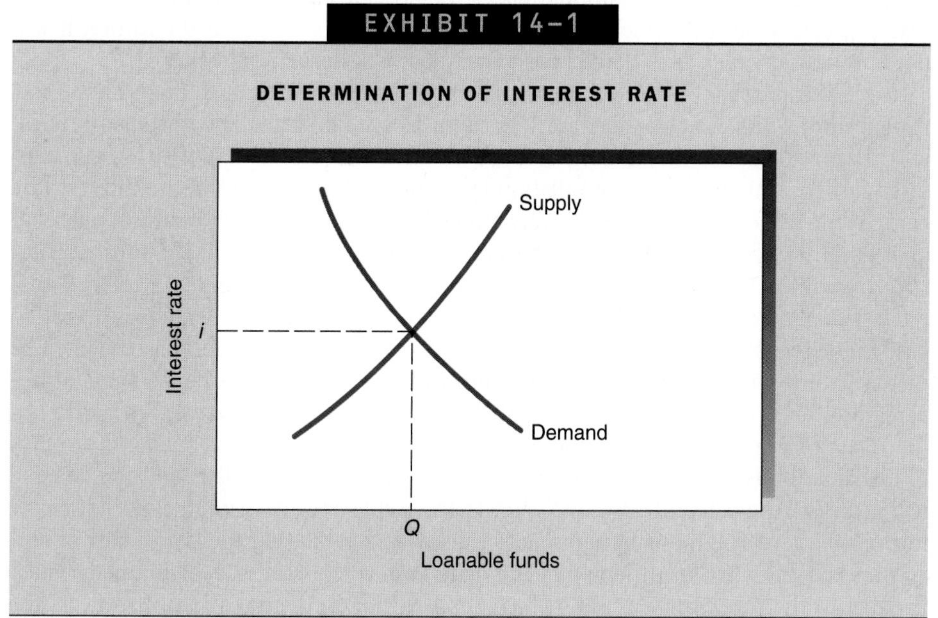

The demand for loanable funds stems from the consumer's desire for earlier availability and the productivity of capital. As the interest rate rises, current goods become more expensive in comparison with future goods. Therefore, borrowers will demand less loanable funds. On the other hand, higher interest rates will stimulate lenders to supply additional funds to the market.

profitable at a low interest rate will be unprofitable at higher rates. Some consumers will reduce their current consumption rather than pay the high interest premium, when the interest rate increases. Therefore, the amount of funds demanded by borrowers is inversely related to the interest rate.

The interest rate also provides a reward to persons (lenders) willing to reduce their current consumption in order to provide loanable funds to others. If some individuals are going to borrow in order to undertake an investment project (or consume more than their current income), others must curtail their current consumption by an equal amount. In essence, the interest rate provides lenders with the incentive to reduce their current consumption so that borrowers can either invest or consume beyond their current income. Higher interest rates provide persons willing to save (willing to supply loanable funds) with the ability to purchase more goods in the future, in exchange for the sacrifice of current consumption. Even though people have a positive rate of time preference, they will give up current consumption to supply funds to the loanable funds market if the price is right—that is, if the interest rate is attractive enough. In a market economy, it is often those who are in their peak earning years who are most attracted to saving. By saving now, they can provide for a larger income later, perhaps during their retirement years. But like everyone else, they will tend to save more at higher interest rates. Therefore, as the interest rate rises, the quantity of funds supplied to the loanable funds market expands.

As Exhibit 14–1 illustrates, the interest rate will bring the quantity of funds demanded into balance with the quantity supplied. ***At the equilibrium interest rate, the quantity of funds borrowers demand for investment and consumption now (rather than later) will just equal the quantity of funds lenders save. So the interest rate brings the choices of borrowers and lenders into harmony.***

Money Rate versus Real Rate of Interest

We have emphasized that the interest rate is a premium paid by borrowers for earlier availability and a reward received by lenders for delaying consumption. However, during a period of inflation—a general increase in prices—the nominal interest rate, or **money rate of interest,** is a misleading indicator of how much borrowers are paying and lenders are receiving. Inflation reduces the purchasing power of a loan's principal. Rising prices mean that when the borrower repays the principal in the future, it will not purchase as much as it would have when the funds were initially loaned.

Money rate of interest
The rate of interest in monetary terms that borrowers pay for borrowed funds. During periods when borrowers and lenders expect inflation, the money rate of interest exceeds the real rate of interest.

Recognizing the declining purchasing power of the dollars to be repaid by borrowers during inflation, lenders are less eager to provide loans at a specified interest rate. They will reduce the amount of loanable funds supplied unless they are compensated for the anticipated rate of inflation by an upward adjustment of the interest rate paid. At the same time, when borrowers anticipate inflation, they will want to purchase goods and services now before they become even more expensive in the future. Thus, they are willing to pay an **inflationary premium,** an additional amount of interest that reflects the expected rate of future price increases. If borrowers and lenders fully anticipate a 5 percent rate of inflation during the life of the loan, for example, they will be just as willing to agree on a 9 percent interest rate as they were earlier to agree on a 4 percent interest rate when both anticipated stability in the general level of prices.

Inflationary premium
A component of the money interest rate that reflects compensation to the lender for the expected decrease, due to inflation, in the purchasing power of the principal and interest during the course of the loan. It is determined by the expected rate of future inflation.

Real rate of interest
The money rate of interest minus the expected rate of inflation. The real rate of interest indicates the interest premium, in terms of real goods and services, that one must pay for earlier availability.

Compared to the situation when the general price level is stable, the supply of loanable funds will decline (the supply curve will shift to the left) and the demand will increase (the demand curve will shift to the right) once decision makers anticipate future inflation. The money interest rate thus rises, overstating the "true" cost of borrowing and the yield from lending. This true cost is the **real rate of interest,** which is equal to the money rate of interest minus the inflationary premium. It reflects the real burden to borrowers and payoff to lenders in terms of command over goods and services.

Our analysis indicates that high rates of inflation will push up the money rate of interest. The real world is consistent with this view. Money interest rates rose to historical highs in the United States as inflation soared to double-digit rates during the 1970s. These same nominal rates fell to the 5 percent range as inflation fell below 2 percent in the late 1990s. Cross-country comparisons also illustrate the linkage between inflation and high interest rates. The lowest money interest rates in the 1990s were found in nations such as Germany, Switzerland, and Japan, all with low rates of inflation. In contrast, the highest money interest rates were observed in Russia, Brazil, Turkey, and other countries with high rates of inflation during the period.

Interest Rates and Risk

We have proceeded as though there were only a single interest rate present in the loanable funds market. In the real world, of course, there are many interest rates. There is the mortgage rate, the prime interest rate (the rate charged to business firms with strong credit ratings), the consumer loan rate, and the credit card rate, to name only a few.

Interest rates in the loanable funds market will differ primarily as the result of differences in the risk associated with the loan. It is riskier to loan funds to an unemployed worker than to a well-established business with substantial assets. Similarly, extending an unsecured loan like that accompanying purchases on a credit card is riskier than extending a loan that is secured by an asset, such as a mortgage loan on a house. The risk also increases with the duration of the loan. The longer the time period, the more likely that the financial standing of the borrower will deteriorate or that market conditions will change unfavorably.

As **Exhibit 14–2** illustrates, the money rate of interest on a loan has three components. The pure-interest component is the real price one must pay for earlier availability. The inflationary-premium component reflects the expectation that the loan will be repaid with dollars of less purchasing power as the result of inflation. The risk-premium component reflects the probability of default—the risk imposed on the lender by the possibility that the borrower may be unable to repay the loan.

EXHIBIT 14–2

THREE COMPONENTS OF MONEY INTEREST

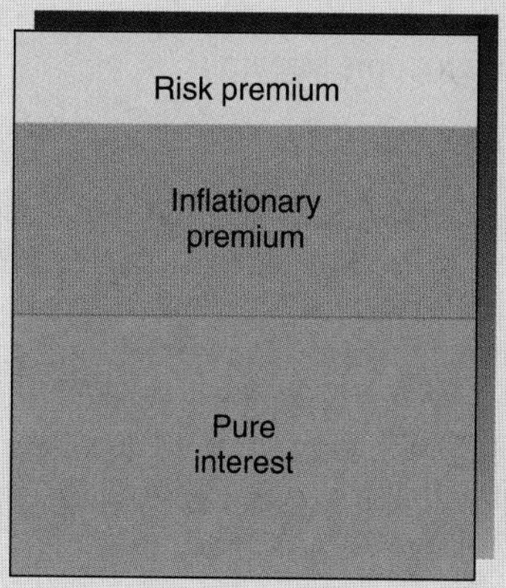

The money interest rate reflects three components: pure interest, inflationary premium, and risk premium. When decision makers expect a high rate of inflation during the period in which the loan is outstanding, the inflationary premium will be substantial. Similarly, the risk premium will be large when the probability of default by the borrower is substantial.

PRESENT VALUE OF FUTURE INCOME AND COSTS

If you deposited \$100 today in a savings account earning 6 percent interest, you would have \$106 one year from now. To put it another way, the present value of \$106 one year from now is equal to the amount (\$100) that you would have to invest today in order to have that amount at that time. The interest rate allows us to make this calculation. ***The interest rate connects the value of dollars (and capital assets) today with the value of dollars (expected income and receipts) in the future. It is used to discount the value of a dollar in the future so that its present worth can be determined today.***

Present value (PV)
The current worth of future income after it is discounted to reflect the fact that revenues in the future are valued less highly than revenues now.

The **present value (PV)** of a payment received one year from now can be expressed as follows:

$$PV = \frac{\text{Receipts One Year from Now}}{1 + \text{Interest Rate}}$$

If the interest rate is 6 percent, the current value of \$100 to be received one year from now is

$$PV = \frac{\$100}{1.06} = \$94.34$$

If you placed \$94.34 in a savings account yielding 6 percent interest, during the year the account would earn \$5.66 interest (6 percent of \$94.34) and therefore grow to \$100 one year from now. Thus, the present value of \$100 to be received a year from now is \$94.34.

Discounting
The procedure used to calculate the present value of future income, which is inversely related to both the interest rate and the amount of time that passes before the funds are received.

Economists use the term **discounting** to describe this procedure of reducing the value of a dollar to be received in the future to its present worth. Clearly, the value of a dollar in the future is inversely related to the interest rate. For example, if the interest rate is 10 percent, the present value of \$100 received one year from now would be only \$90.91 (\$100 divided by 1.10).

The present value of \$100 received two years from now is

$$PV = \frac{\$100}{(1 + \text{Interest Rate})^2}$$

If the interest rate is 6 percent, \$100 received two years from now would be equal to \$89 today (\$100 divided by 1.06^2). In other words, \$89 invested today would yield \$100 two years from now.

The present-value procedure can be used to determine the current value of any future income (or cost) stream. If R represents receipts received at the end of various years in the future (indicated by the subscripts) and i represents the interest rate, the present value of the future income stream is

$$PV = \frac{R_1}{(1+i)} + \frac{R_2}{(1+i)^2} + \dots\dots + \frac{R_n}{(1+i)^n}$$

Exhibit 14–3 shows the present value of \$100 received at various times in the future at several different discount rates. The chart clearly illustrates two points. First, the present value of income received at a date in the future declines with the interest rate. The present value of the \$100 received one year from now, when discounted at a 4 percent interest rate, is \$96.15, compared to \$98.04 when a 2 percent discount rate is applied. Second, the present value of the \$100 also declines as the date of its receipt is set farther into the future. If the applicable discount rate is 6 percent, the present value of \$100 received one year from now is \$94.34, compared to \$89 if the \$100 is received two years from now. If the \$100 is received five years from now, its current worth is

EXHIBIT 14-3

PRESENT VALUE OF $100 TO BE RECEIVED IN THE FUTURE

The columns indicate the present value of $100 to be received a designated number of years in the future at alternative discount (interest) rates. For example, at a discount rate of 2 percent, the present value of $100 to be received five years from now is $90.57. Note that the present value of the $100 declines as either the interest rate or the number of years in the future increases.

YEARS IN THE FUTURE	PRESENT VALUE OF $100 TO BE RECEIVED A DESIGNATED NUMBER OF YEARS IN THE FUTURE AT ALTERNATIVE DISCOUNT RATES					
	2 PERCENT	4 PERCENT	6 PERCENT	8 PERCENT	12 PERCENT	20 PERCENT
1	98.04	96.15	94.34	92.59	89.29	83.33
2	96.12	92.46	89.00	85.73	79.72	69.44
3	94.23	88.90	83.96	79.38	71.18	57.87
4	92.39	85.48	79.21	73.50	63.55	48.23
5	90.57	82.19	74.73	68.06	56.74	40.19
6	88.80	79.03	70.50	63.02	50.66	33.49
7	87.06	75.99	66.51	58.35	45.23	27.08
8	85.35	73.07	62.74	54.03	40.39	23.26
9	83.68	70.26	59.19	50.02	36.06	19.38
10	82.03	67.56	55.84	46.32	32.20	16.15
15	74.30	55.53	41.73	31.52	18.27	6.49
20	67.30	45.64	31.18	21.45	10.37	2.61
30	55.21	30.83	17.41	9.94	3.34	0.42
50	37.15	14.07	5.43	2.13	0.35	0.01

only $74.73. ***So the present value of a future dollar payment is inversely related both to the interest rate and to how far in the future the payment will be received.***

To see in a more personal way the importance of interest and the value of saving, consider what you could gain by saving just $1,000 per year ($83.33 per month) for 10 years in a tax-free individual retirement account. If you begin at age 25 and continue only until age 35 (putting nothing into the account after that), and the account returns 8 percent annually, the account will be worth $168,627 when you reach age 65. In contrast, if you wait until age 35 and then save the same $1,000 per year for 30 years (not 10 years of saving as before) with the same 8 percent annual return, by age 65 your account will be worth only $125,228. Ten years of saving, starting at age 25, yields far more than 30 years of saving the same amount each year but waiting until age 35 to start. Which savings plan is more attractive to you?

PRESENT VALUE, PROFITABILITY, AND INVESTMENT

Investment decisions, like saving decisions, require comparisons of costs and benefits over time. Investment involves an up-front cost of acquiring a machine, skill, or other asset that is expected to generate additional output and revenue in the future. How can an investor know if the expected future revenues will be sufficient to cover the costs? The discounting procedure helps provide the answer. It permits the investor to place both the costs and the expected future revenues of an investment project into present-value terms. If the present value of the revenue derived from the investment exceeds

EXHIBIT 14–4

DISCOUNTED PRESENT VALUE OF $12,000 OF TRUCK RENTAL FOR FOUR YEARS (INTEREST RATE = 8 PERCENT)

Year (1)	Expected Future Income Received at Year-End (2)	Discounted Value (8 Percent Rate) (3)	Present Value of Income (4)
1	$12,000	0.926	$11,112
2	12,000	0.857	10,284
3	12,000	0.794	9,528
4	12,000	0.735	8,820
			$39,744

the present value of the cost, it makes sense to undertake the investment. If revenues and costs of such an investment turn out as expected, the investor will reap economic profit. In turn, profitable investments will increase the value of resources, and thereby create wealth.

On the other hand, if the cost of the project exceeds the discounted value of the future receipts, losses will result. The losses indicate that the resources used to undertake the investment would have more value elsewhere. Investments that result in losses reduce the value of resources and thereby diminish wealth. Such investments are counterproductive.

Let's look at a hypothetical investment option to "see how it pencils" and thus whether it would be a good investment. Suppose a truck rental firm is contemplating the purchase of a new $40,000 truck. Past experience indicates that after making allowances for operational and maintenance expenses, the firm can rent out the truck for net revenues of $12,000 per year (received at the end of each year) for the next four years, the expected life of the vehicle.[2] Since the firm can borrow and lend funds at an interest rate of 8 percent, we will discount the future expected income at an 8 percent rate. **Exhibit 14–4** illustrates the calculation. Column 4 shows how much $12,000, available at year-end for each of the next four years, is worth today. In total, the present value of the expected rental receipts is $39,744—less than the purchase price of the truck. Therefore, the project should not be undertaken.

If the interest rate in our example had been 6 percent, using the pencil would yield a different result: The present value of the future rental income would have been $41,580.[3] Because it pays to purchase a capital good whenever the present value

[2]For the sake of simplicity, we assume that the truck has no scrap value at the end of four years.

[3]The derivation of this figure is shown in the following tabulation:

Year	Expected Future Income (dollars)	Discounted Value per Dollar (6% rate)	Present Value of Income (dollars)
1	12,000	0.943	11,316
2	12,000	0.890	10,680
3	12,000	0.840	10,080
4	12,000	0.792	9,504
			41,580

of the income generated exceeds the purchase price of the capital good, the project would have been productive (and thus profitable) at the lower interest rate. A lower market interest rate indicates that the alternative projects competing for funds are less profitable.

EXPECTED FUTURE EARNINGS AND ASSET VALUES

The present value of the expected revenue minus the cost of an investment reveals whether the project should be undertaken. However, *once an investment project has been completed,* the present value of the expected future net earnings will determine the market value of the asset. If the present value of the expected net earnings rises (or falls), so too will the value of the asset.

The value of an asset is equal to the present value of the expected net revenues that can be earned by the asset. If the asset is expected to generate a constant annual net income each year in the future, its value would be equal to:

$$\text{Asset Value} = \frac{\text{Annual Net Income from the Asset}}{\text{Interest Rate}}$$

What is the market value of a tract of land if it is expected to generate $1,000 of rental income net of costs each year indefinitely into the future? If the market interest rate is 10 percent, investors would be willing to pay $10,000 for the land. When purchased at this price, the land would provide an investor with the 10 percent market rate of return. Correspondingly, if an asset generates $2,500 of net earnings annually and the market interest rate is 10 percent, the asset would be worth $25,000. There is a direct relationship between the expected future earnings generated by an asset and the asset's market value. ***As the present value of the future earnings derived from the ownership of an asset increases, so too does the market value of the asset.***

This linkage between expected future earnings and the price of an asset provides a strong incentive for the owners of business assets to make sure that the assets are being used wisely. Some entrepreneurial investors are particularly good at (1) identifying a business that is poorly operated, (2) purchasing the business at a depressed price, (3) improving the operational efficiency of the firm, and then (4) reselling the

The value of this farmland will be seriously reduced by the erosion. As soon as an appraiser can see the erosion and estimate the loss of future income, the present value of the farmland (and its market price) will decline and thereby reduce the wealth of the farm owner.

business at a handsome profit. Suppose that a poorly run business currently has net earnings of $1 million per year. What is the market value of the business? If the firm is expected to continue earning $1 million per year, the market value of the firm would be $10 million if the interest rate is 10 percent. Suppose that an alert entrepreneur buys the business for $10 million, hires new management, and improves the operational efficiency of the firm. As the result of these changes, the annual net earnings of the firm increase to $2 million per year. Now how much is the firm worth? If the $2 million annual earnings are expected to continue into the future, the net present value of the firm would rise to $20 million. Thus, the entrepreneur who improved the performance of the firm would be able to sell the firm for a very substantial profit.

In a competitive environment, there is a strong incentive for business managers and asset owners to use the resources under their control efficiently. If they do not, the value of the assets will decline, and the business will be vulnerable to a takeover by alert entrepreneurs capable of operating the firm more efficiently (and using the assets more profitably).

Investors and Corporate Investments

In modern market economies, investors typically are not entrepreneurs who personally decide which factories to expand, which machine tools to build, and which research investments to undertake. Instead corporate officers, under the scrutiny of corporate boards of directors, make the entrepreneurial capital investment choices. Nevertheless, individual investors (buyers and sellers of stock) influence that process through the stock market itself. Stock-market investors who first believe that a corporation is currently making decisions that are likely to increase future profits will buy more of the corporation's stock, driving up its price. Similarly, stockholders who believe that the corporation's current investment decisions will reduce future profits have an incentive to "bail out" by selling their stock holdings, reducing the market value of the stock. Either way, the price of a corporation's stock shares gives corporate officers very fast feedback on how market investors evaluate their decisions.

Do corporate officers respond to stock price changes? Normally they do. Often they own stock and the value of their pay package depends on the stock price. Also, the members of the corporate board (which hires and fires the officers) are typically large shareholders. Thus, the corporate officers have a strong incentive to act on the feedback provided from the stock market. The choices of individual buyers (and nonbuyers) of the firm's products provide the ultimate judgments on business performance. However, the choices of investors and their fund managers provide early returns on the expected success of business ventures.

INVESTING IN HUMAN CAPITAL

In principle, investments in human capital—an individual's choice to continue in school, for example—involve all the ingredients of other investment decisions. And since the returns and some of the costs normally accrue in the future, the discounting procedure is as helpful here as in decisions about physical capital.

Exhibit 14–5 is a simplified illustration of the human-capital decision confronting Juanita, an 18-year-old high school graduate contemplating the pursuit of a bachelor's degree in business administration. Just as an investment in a truck involves a cost in order to generate a future income, so does a degree in business administration. If Juanita does not go to college, she will be able to begin work immediately, starting at annual earnings of E_1. But if she goes to college, she will incur direct costs (C_d) in the

EXHIBIT 14-5

INVESTING IN HUMAN CAPITAL

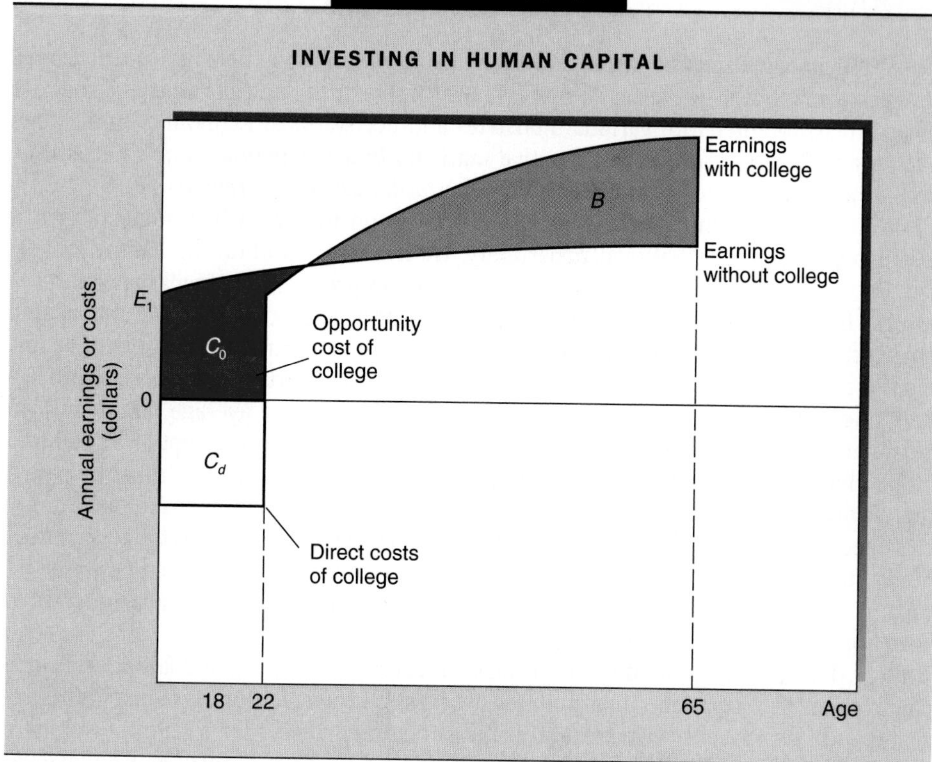

Here we provide a simplified illustration of the human-capital investment decision confronting Juanita, an 18-year-old who has just finished high school. If Juanita goes to college and majors in business administration, she will incur the direct cost (C_d) *of the college education (tuition, books, transportation, and so on) plus the opportunity cost* (C_0) *of earnings forgone while in college. However, with a business degree, she can expect additions to future earnings* (B) *during her career. If the discounted present value of the additional future earnings exceeds the discounted value of the direct and indirect costs of a college education, the business degree will be a profitable investment for Juanita.*

form of tuition, books, transportation, and related expenses. She will also bear the opportunity cost (C_o) of lower earnings while in college. However, the study of business will expand Juanita's knowledge and skills, and thereby enable her to earn a higher future stream of income ("Earnings with college" rather than "Earnings without college").

Will the higher future income be worth the cost? To answer this question, Juanita must project her additional income stemming from completion of the business degree, discount each year's additional income, and compare the total with the discounted value of the cost, including the opportunity cost of earnings lost during the period of study. If the discounted present value of the additional future income exceeds the discounted present value of the cost, acquiring the degree is a worthwhile human-capital investment.

Of course, nonmonetary considerations may also be important, particularly for human-capital investment decisions, since human capital is embodied in the individual. For example, Juanita might prefer working as a college graduate in the business world (rather than in the jobs available to high school graduates) even if she did not make more money. Thus, the nonmonetary attractiveness of business may induce her to pursue the business degree even if the monetary rate of return is low (or even negative).

Although nonmonetary factors are more important in human-capital decision making, opportunity cost and the pursuit of profit influence human-capital investors just as they do physical-capital investors. As with choosing to purchase a new machine, choosing a human-capital investment project such as Juanita's degree involves cost, the possibility of profit, and uncertainty. The same principles apply to both types of decisions. Giving due consideration to nonmonetary factors as a potential "benefit," human-capital investors, like physical-capital investors, seek to undertake only those projects that they anticipate will yield benefits greater than their costs.

PROFIT AND PROSPERITY

As we previously discussed, firms and individual investors may be able to earn persistent economic profit—a return in excess of the opportunity cost of funds—if they are able to restrict entry into various industries and occupations. Economic profit, however, may also be present in competitive markets. ***In a competitive market economy, there are two sources of economic profit: uncertainty and entrepreneurship.***

While investment places people in a position to earn a handsome return, it also exposes them to additional uncertainty. We live in a world of uncertainty, imperfect information, and dynamic change. No one knows precisely what will happen in the future. In such a world, investing has elements of a game of chance. Unanticipated changes, changes that no one could have foreseen, create winners and losers. If people did not care whether their income experienced substantial variability or not, the uncertainty accompanying investment projects would not affect the average rate of return. Most people, though, dislike uncertainty. They prefer the certain receipt of $1,000 to a 50-50 chance of receiving either nothing or $2,000. Therefore, people must be paid a premium—an economic profit—if they are going to accept willingly the uncertainty that necessarily accompanies investments. For example, compared to government bonds, the returns to stocks are considerably more uncertain. This uncertainty of return is one reason why stocks have historically yielded a higher average return than bonds.

The market value of stocks displays uncertainty by rising and falling from one day to the next. But in the United States over the past two centuries, owners of representative stocks have received a return of 7 percent, corrected for inflation.[4] Compare that 7 percent return to the 3.5 percent return on long-term government bonds over the same time period, again corrected for inflation. Thus, equity ownership has yielded twice the rate of return of government bonds. How important is this 3.5 percent differential rate of return? If $100 had been invested in 1801, in representative stocks with the untaxed returns reinvested (as returns often are today in individual retirement accounts), the value of the $100 investment would have been more than $56 million in 1998. The same investment at the bond rate of 3.5 percent would have yielded roughly 1,000 times less, or less than $100,000, by 1998. This example, based on observed rates of return, illustrates the value to savers of less uncertainty. At the same time, it highlights both the time value of money and the importance, over a long period of time, of a seemingly small difference in interest rates.

In a world of uncertainty, discovery of potential opportunities to combine resources in a manner that increases their value provides a second source of economic profit. Some are better than others at identifying such opportunities. ***At any given time, there is virtually an infinite number of potential investment projects. Some will increase the value of resources and therefore lead to a handsome rate of return on capital. Others will actually reduce the value of resources, generating economic losses. Entrepreneurship involves the ability to recognize and undertake economically beneficial projects that have gone unnoticed by others.*** Originality, quickness to act, and imagination are important aspects of entrepreneurship. Successful entrepreneurship also involves leadership—new buyers must be enticed and financial backers must be convinced to invest. Discovery is vitally important—most profits will be gone by the time the concept is proven and imitators arrive on the scene. Naturally, risk is involved. All too frequently, the entrepreneur's vision turns out to have been a mirage. What appeared to be a profitable opportunity is seen later as an expensive illusion.

---

[4]These estimates are from Jeremy Siegel, *Stocks for the Long Run* (New York: McGraw-Hill, 1998).

OUTSTANDING ECONOMIST

Joseph Schumpeter (1883–1950)

Born in Austria, Schumpeter was a long-time professor of economics at Harvard University. Generally recognized as one of the top five economists of this century, he is perhaps best known for his views on entrepreneurship and the future of capitalism. He believed that the creative and innovative behavior of business entrepreneurs was the primary fuel of economic progress.

The great Harvard economist Joseph Schumpeter believed that entrepreneurship and innovative behavior were the moving forces behind capitalism. According to Schumpeter, this entrepreneurial discovery of new, improved ways of doing things is a central engine of economic progress and improvements in living standards. As Schumpeter put it:

> The fundamental impulse that sets the capitalist engine in motion comes from the new consumer's goods, the new methods of production or transportation, and new markets, and the new forms of industrial organization that capitalist enterprise creates.[5]

Potential entrepreneurs are confined to using their own wealth and that of coventurers, in addition to whatever can be borrowed. Entrepreneurs with a past record of success will be able to attract funds more readily for investment projects. Therefore, in a market economy, previously successful entrepreneurs will exert a disproportionate influence over decisions as to which projects will be undertaken and which will not.

THE CAPITAL MARKET AND THE WEALTH OF NATIONS

Both interest and profit perform important allocative functions.[6] Interest induces people to give up current consumption, a sacrifice that is a necessary ingredient for capital formation. Economic profit provides both human- and physical-capital decision makers with the incentive to (1) undertake investments yielding an uncertain return and (2) discover and undertake beneficial (wealth-creating) investment opportunities.

For a nation to realize its potential, it must have a mechanism capable of attracting savings and channeling them into investment projects that create wealth. In a market economy, the capital market performs this function. This highly diverse market

[5]Joseph A. Schumpeter, *Capitalism, Socialism, and Democracy* (New York: Harper Torchbooks, 1950), p. 83.

[6]In addition to wages, interest, and profits, economists often discuss rent as a return to a factor of production, the supply of which is perfectly inelastic. We have not included this discussion for two reasons. First, one can legitimately argue that the supply of all factors of production has some elasticity. After all, even the supply of usable land can be expanded through drainage, clearing, and conservation. Therefore, rent is always a matter of degree. Second, the term *rent* is used in a variety of ways, even by economists. The macroeconomic usage differs substantially from the usage in microeconomics. The term is sometimes used to define the returns to a specialized resource, such as an actor's talent, even though training plays an integral part in the supply of the resource. *Rent* is also sometimes applied to a factor the supply of which is temporarily fixed, even though it can clearly be expanded in the future. Since the returns to capital can be adequately discussed without introducing rent, we concluded that the cost of the ambiguity of the term exceeded the benefits of an extended discussion.

includes markets for stocks, real estate, and businesses, as well as the loanable funds market.

The capital market brings together people who are willing to save with those willing to invest. Savers and investors may have widely differing plans and goals. A person who is saving for retirement in only 10 years may be willing to buy a new bond from General Motors, knowing that the bond will not be repaid for 30 years, because the bond market will allow the bondholder to sell the bond to another saver in 10 years. Capital markets allow individuals with widely differing time horizons to gain nonetheless from trading with one another.

Risk preferences also differ. Some people save and supply funds to the capital market in exchange for a fixed rate of return. People who purchase bonds and maintain savings deposits are examples. Other people supply funds in exchange for an uncertain return linked to the success or failure of a business or investment project. Stockholders and partnership investors fall into this category. Still others supply funds to the capital market when they use their own funds to purchase a business or acquire additional schooling.

The key attribute of the capital market is its ability to direct funds toward wealth-creating projects. When investment in a capital asset generates additional output (and revenue) that is valued more highly than the value of the resources required for its production, the investment will create wealth. When property rights are securely defined and enforced, wealth-creating investments will also be profitable.

Private ownership and a competitive capital market provide investors with a great deal of freedom. Nonetheless, because they are investing their own funds, private investors have a strong incentive to evaluate potential projects carefully and undertake those expected to yield the most profit. In an uncertain world, of course, mistakes will occur. Sometimes projects will be undertaken that prove unprofitable. If investors were unwilling to take chances, many innovative ideas and worthwhile but risky projects would never be tested. In a world of uncertainty, mistaken investments are a necessary price that must be paid for fruitful innovations in new technologies and products. The capital market will at least assure that the mistakes are self-correcting. Unexpected losses will signal investors to terminate unprofitable and unproductive projects, and investors whose own wealth is at stake will be very sensitive to such signals.

Without a private capital market, it is virtually impossible to attract funds and to channel them consistently into wealth-creating projects. When investment funds are allocated by the government rather than by the market, an entirely different set of criteria comes into play. The individual voter, unlike a partner or an owner of stock, has little incentive to be alert for new opportunities or wary of mistaken investments undertaken by government officials. Furthermore, the citizen-voter can neither (1) invest more upon discovery of an attractive project nor (2) opt out (sell) when problems are detected. Thus, voters are in a weak position to monitor and direct government investment effectively. Most simply remain on the sidelines. As they do so, the political clout of special interests replaces market return as the basis for allocating the funds. Predictably, investment projects that reduce wealth rather than enhance it become more likely.

The experience of Eastern Europe and the former Soviet Union illustrates what happens when political factors replace economic considerations in the allocation of investment. The investment rates of these countries were among the highest in the world. Their central planners channeled approximately one-third of the national output into capital formation. But even these high rates of investment did little to improve living standards. Funds were often wasted on political boondoggles and high-visibility projects favored by important political leaders.

Compared to Latin American countries with similar levels of per-capita income in 1970, the economies of Singapore, Hong Kong, South Korea, Taiwan, Malaysia, and Thailand have expanded very rapidly during the last three decades. High investment rates contributed to their growth. Of course, investment does not just happen. An environment attractive for investment—for example, financial stability and a legal system that protects property rights—are particularly important. In recent years, several of these high-growth Asian economies have experienced financial instability. In some cases, counterproductive investment projects were undertaken as the result of political corruption and systematic government interference designed to help interest groups. Like the failures of central planning, the recent Asian experience also highlights the importance of a capital market that is capable of channelling funds into productive projects.

Evidence from around the world confirms what economic analysis indicates: Properly guided investment in both physical and human capital is an important source of productivity and income growth. ***Other things constant, countries that invest more and channel more of their investments into productive projects today will tend to have a higher income tomorrow.***

LOOKING *Ahead*

As the preceding two chapters have stressed, investment in physical and human capital will influence the wealth and income of both individuals and nations. Differences among individuals in these factors will also contribute to income inequality. In the next chapter, we will consider the issue of income inequality in some detail.

KEY POINTS

➤ We can often produce more consumption goods by first using our resources to produce physical- and human-capital resources and then using these capital resources to produce the desired consumption goods. Because resources used to produce capital goods will be unavailable for the direct production of consumption goods, saving is necessary for investment.

➤ People have a positive rate of time preference; they generally value present consumption more highly than future consumption.

➤ The interest rate is the price of earlier availability. It is the premium that borrowers must pay to lenders to acquire goods now rather than later.

➤ Interest rewards lenders who curtail current consumption and supply loanable funds in the market. The demand for loanable funds by investors stems from the productivity of capital resources and the demand by consumers stems from the positive rate of time preference. The market interest rate will bring the quantity of funds demanded by borrowers into balance with the quantity supplied by lenders.

➤ During inflationary times, the money rate of interest incorporates an inflationary premium reflecting the expected future increase in the price level. When inflation is expected, the money rate of interest exceeds the real rate of interest.

➤ The money rate of interest on a specific loan reflects three basic factors—the pure interest rate, an inflationary premium, and a risk premium that is directly related to the probability of default by the borrower.

➤ The interest rate allows individuals to place a current valuation on future revenues and costs. The discounting procedure can be used to calculate the present value of an expected net income stream from a potential investment project. If the present value of the expected revenues exceeds the present value of the expected costs—and if things turn out as expected—the project will be profitable.

➤ The present value of expected future net earnings will determine the market value of existing assets. An increase (decline) in the expected future earnings derived from an asset will increase (reduce) the market value of the asset.

➤ Economic profit plays a central role in the allocation of capital and the determination of which investment projects will be undertaken. In a competitive environment, economic profit reflects uncertainty and entrepreneurship—the ability to recognize and undertake profitable projects that have gone unnoticed by others.

➤ To grow and prosper, a nation must have a mechanism that will attract savings and channel them into investment projects that create wealth. The capital market performs this function in a market economy. When property rights are defined and securely enforced, productive investments will also be profitable.

➤ Investment in both physical and human capital is an important source of productivity growth. The economies of countries that invest more and channel their investment funds into more productive projects generally grow more rapidly.

CRITICAL ANALYSIS QUESTIONS

*1. How would the following changes influence the rate of interest in the United States?
   a. An increase in the positive time preference of lenders
   b. An increase in the positive time preference of borrowers
   c. An increase in domestic inflation
   d. Increased uncertainty about a nuclear war
   e. Improved investment opportunities in Europe

2. "Any return to capital above the pure-interest yield is unnecessary. The pure-interest yield is sufficient to provide capitalists with the earnings necessary to replace their assets and to compensate for their sacrifice of current consumption. Any return above that is pure gravy; it is excess profit." Do you agree with this view? Why or why not?

3. How are human- and physical-capital investment decisions similar? How do they differ? What determines the profitability of a physical-capital investment? Do human-capital investors make profits? If so, what is the source of the profit? Explain.

*4. A lender made the following statement to a borrower: "You are borrowing $1,000, which is to be repaid in 12 monthly installments of $100 each. Your total interest charge is $200, which means your interest rate is 20 percent." Is the effective interest rate on the loan really 20 percent? Explain.

5. In a market economy, investors have a strong incentive to undertake profitable investments. What makes an investment profitable? Do profitable investments create wealth? Why or why not? Do all investments create wealth? Discuss.

*6. Over long periods of time, the rate of return of an average investment in the stock market has exceeded the return on high-quality bonds. Is the higher return on stocks surprising? Why or why not?

7. The interest rates charged on outstanding credit card balances are generally higher than the interest rate that banks charge customers with a good credit rating. Why do you think the credit card rate is so high? Should the government impose an interest rate ceiling of, say, 10 percent? If it did, who would be hurt and who would be helped? Discuss.

*8. If the money rate of interest on a low-risk government bond is 10 percent and the inflation rate for the last several years has been steady at 4 percent, what is the estimated real rate of interest?

9. Suppose you are contemplating the purchase of a minicomputer at a cost of $1,000. The expected lifetime of the asset is three years. You expect to lease the asset to a business for $400 annually (payable at the end of each year) for three years. If you can borrow (and lend) money at an interest rate of 8 percent, will the investment be a profitable undertaking? Is the project profitable at an interest rate of 12 percent? Provide calculations in support of your answer.

*10. Alicia's philosophy of life is summed up by the proverb "A penny saved is a penny earned." She plans and saves for the future. In contrast, Mike's

view is "Life is uncertain; eat dessert first." Mike wants as much as possible now.
a. Who has the highest rate of time preference?
b. Do people like Alicia benefit from the presence of people like Mike?
c. Do people like Mike benefit from the presence of people like Alicia? Explain.

*11. Some countries with very low incomes per capita are unable to save very much. Are people in these countries helped or hurt by people in high-income countries with much higher rates of saving?

*12. According to a news item, the owner of a lottery ticket paying $3 million over 20 years is offering to sell the ticket for $1.2 million cash now. "Who knows?" the ticket owner explained. "We might not even be here in 20 years, and I do not want to leave it to the dinosaurs."
a. If the ticket pays $150,000 per year at the end of each year for the next 20 years, what is the present value of the ticket when the appropriate rate for discounting the future income is thought to be 10 percent?
b. If the discount rate is in the 10 percent range, is the sale price of $1.2 million reasonable?
c. Can you think of any disadvantages of buying the lottery earnings rather than a bond?

13. Suppose you decide to rent an apartment for five years. Further suppose that the owner offers to provide you with a used refrigerator for free and promises to maintain and repair the refrigerator during the next five years. You also have the option of buying a new energy-efficient refrigerator (with a five-year free maintenance agreement) for $700. The new refrigerator will reduce your electric bill by $150 per year and will have a market value of $200 after five years. If necessary, you can borrow money from the bank at an 8 percent rate of interest. Which option should you choose?

*14. Suppose that you are considering whether to enroll in a summer computer training program that costs $2,500. If you take the program, you will have to give up $1,500 of earnings from your summer job. You figure that the program will increase your earnings by $500 per year for each of the next 10 years. Beyond that, it is not expected to affect your earnings. If you take the program, you will have to borrow the funds at an 8 percent rate of interest. From a strictly monetary viewpoint, should you enroll in the program?

---

*Asterisk denotes questions for which answers appear in Appendix B.

CHAPTER 15

All animals are equal, but some animals are more equal than others.

George Orwell[1]

Income Inequality and Poverty

CHAPTER FOCUS

- How do resource prices and income differences influence the incentive of people to develop resources and use them productively?
- How much income inequality is there in the United States? Has the degree of inequality changed in recent years?
- How does income inequality in the United States compare with that in other countries?
- How much income mobility exists—do the rich remain rich while the poor remain poor?
- How widespread is poverty? How has the poverty rate changed in recent decades? Did the War on Poverty help reduce the poverty rate?

[1]George Orwell, *Animal Farm* (New York: Harcourt Brace and Company, 1946), p. 112.

In a market economy, individuals receive income from selling their resources, such as their labor, at market-determined prices. Resource prices thus play an important role in determining the distribution of income. Differences in resource prices and the productivity of individuals will cause market incomes to vary. Of course, economic inequality is present in all societies. Substituting politics and central planning for markets does not eliminate inequality. Nonetheless, most of us are troubled by the extremes of inequality—extravagant luxury on the one hand and grinding poverty on the other. How much inequality is there in the United States? Do the same families continually enjoy high incomes, while those in poverty are unable to escape that condition? What impact have income transfer programs had on the welfare of the poor? This chapter focuses on these questions and related issues.

RESOURCE PRICES AND INCOME DIFFERENCES

In the United States, approximately 80 percent of national income is derived from the productive skills and knowledge of individual workers. People differ with regard to their productive abilities, opportunities, preferences, and intestinal fortitude. Some will be able to hit a baseball, perform a rock concert, design a computer, or operate a restaurant so effectively that people will pay millions to consume the product or service that they supply. There will be others with disabilities and/or few skills who may be unable even to support themselves. Thus, incomes vary substantially.

Incomes not only determine how much individuals can spend on goods and services, they also affect the individual's incentive to supply the resources required to produce goods and services. Market participants prosper by supplying resources that are highly valued *by others*. After all, the price at which you can sell a productive resource or service depends on how much others are willing to pay for it. Individuals who supply large amounts of physical and human resources highly valued by others will earn large incomes. The close link between personal prosperity and provision of productive resources provides individuals with a strong incentive to develop those skills, talents, and resources that others value highly.[2]

[2]Adam Smith makes this point in a very famous passage:

> *Every individual is continually exerting himself to find out the most advantageous employment for whatever capital [and other resources] he can command. It is his own advantage, indeed, and not that of the society which he has in view. But the study of his own advantage naturally, or rather necessarily, leads him to prefer that employment which is most advantageous to society. . . . He intends only his own gain, and he is in this, as in many other cases, led by an invisible hand [competitive markets] to promote an end which was not part of his intention.*

See Smith, *An Inquiry into the Nature and Causes of the Wealth of Nations* (New York: Modern Library, 1937), p. 423.

A market economy does not have a central distributing agency that carves up the economic pie and allocates slices to various individuals. In fact, this fallacious view—the idea that there is a fixed-size economic pie to be divided among individuals—reflects a misunderstanding of the nature of income. Income and wealth are *created* by individuals. The amount of income individuals create is influenced by the incentive structure that they confront. Individuals are motivated to create income precisely because it enhances their personal welfare and that of those about whom they care. When the link between work effort and reward is broken, individuals have less incentive to create income.

Differences in resource prices reflect relative scarcity. They also provide individuals with the incentive to supply those resources that others value most (relative to cost). Income is created when individuals supply productive resources to others. Thus, it is a mistake to view income as if it were manna from heaven. Taxes and transfers that alter incomes also alter the incentive to supply scarce resources and thereby expand the size of the economic pie. Therefore, while focusing on the distribution of income, we must not forget the role that differences in resource prices and incomes play in the allocation of resources.

INCOME INEQUALITY IN THE UNITED STATES

Money income is only one component of economic well-being. Such factors as leisure, noncash transfer benefits, the nonpecuniary advantages and disadvantages of a job, and the expected stability of future income are also determinants of economic welfare. Money income is quite important, however, because it represents command over market goods and services. Moreover, it is readily observable. Consequently, it is the most widely used measure of economic well-being and of the degree of inequality prevailing in society.

Exhibit 15–1 presents data on money income in the United States. First, consider the data on the share of *before-tax* annual money income by quintile—that is, each fifth of families—ranked from the lowest to the highest. If there were total equality of family annual income, each quintile (20 percent) of families would generate 20 percent of the aggregate income. Given differences in education, skill, ability, work effort, age, family size, and numerous other factors, clearly we would not expect this to be the case. Due to these differences, some families will be able to generate—and thus receive—more income than others. It is, however, informative to observe the shares of income by quintile.

The data indicate that a reduction in before-tax income inequality occurred throughout the 1950s and 1960s. In 1970 the top quintile earned 40.9 percent of the aggregate money income, down from 42.7 percent in 1950. During the same period, the share of income earned by the lowest quintile rose from 4.5 percent in 1950 to 5.4 percent in 1970. Thus, between 1950 and 1970, the income share earned by the top quintile of families declined, while that earned by the bottom quintile rose. Beginning in the 1970s, this trend reversed. During the last two decades, the share of income earned by the top quintile has steadily risen, while that earned by the bottom group has fallen.[3] By 1997, the share of before-tax money income of the top group had risen to

[3]A reduction in the *share* of income earned by the bottom quintile income group does not imply that their income level fell. It merely indicates that their income did not grow as rapidly as that of other groups—particularly the top quintile. In fact, the inflation-adjusted income of the bottom quintile of earners increased during the last two decades.

EXHIBIT 15–1

INEQUALITY IN MONEY INCOME DURING SELECTED YEARS, 1950–1997

	Lowest 20 Percent of Recipients	Second Quintile	Third Quintile	Fourth Quintile	Top 20 Percent of Recipients
Family Income Before Taxes					
1950	4.5	12.0	17.4	23.4	42.7
1960	4.8	12.2	17.8	24.0	41.3
1970	5.4	12.2	17.6	23.8	40.9
1980	5.1	11.6	17.5	24.3	41.6
1990	4.6	10.8	16.6	23.8	44.3
1997	4.2	9.9	15.7	23.0	47.2
Family Income After Taxes and Transfers					
1979	6.4	12.6	17.8	24.2	39.0
1992	5.5	11.3	17.0	24.2	42.0
1997	5.4	10.7	16.2	23.2	44.5
Household Expenditures					
1961	7.1	13.2	18.2	24.1	37.4
1972	7.1	12.9	18.0	23.9	38.1
1980	6.8	12.8	18.1	24.1	38.2
1991	7.0	12.5	17.4	23.4	39.7

SOURCES: Bureau of the Census, Current Population Reports, *Series P-60;* Statistical Abstract of the United States: 1995, *Table 733; Congressional Budget Office,* 1994 Green Book, *p. 1191; Bureau of the Census,* Money Income in the United States: 1997; *and Daniel T. Slesnick, "Consumption, Needs, and Inequality,"* International Economic Review *(August 1994).*

47.2 percent, while that earned by the bottom 20 percent of families had fallen to 4.2 percent of the total. Thus, the top quintile of families earned approximately 11 times as much before-tax money income as the bottom quintile of families in 1997.

Low-income families are the primary beneficiaries of noncash transfer programs that provide people with food (food stamps), health care, and housing. Correspondingly, under a system of progressive taxation, taxes take a larger share of income as one's income increases. Therefore, one would expect *after-tax and transfer* income to be less unequal than before-tax income. Indeed, this is the case. After taxes and transfers, the bottom quintile of families received 5.4 percent of the total income in 1997 (compared to 4.2 percent of the before-tax income). At the same time, the after-tax and transfer share of the top quintile of families was 44.5 percent in 1997 (compared to 47.2 percent before taxes). In fact, taking into account taxes and transfers increases the income share of every quintile except the top group. However, like the before-tax figures, the income data after taxes and transfers suggest that there has been an increase in income inequality in recent years.

A Closer Look at Factors Influencing Income Distribution

How meaningful are the data of Exhibit 15–1? If all families were similar except in the amount of income earned, the use of annual income data as an index of inequality would be more reasonable. However, the fact is that the aggregate data lump together (1) small and large families, (2) prime-age earners and elderly retirees, (3) multi-earner families and families without any current earners, and (4) husband-wife families and single-parent families.

Consider just one factor: the impact of age and the pattern of lifetime income. Typically, the annual income of young people is low, particularly if they are going to school or are acquiring training. Many persons under 25 years of age studying to be lawyers, doctors, engineers, and economists will have a low annual income during this phase of their life. But this does not mean they are poor, at least not in the usual sense. After completing their formal education and acquiring work experience, such individuals move into their prime working years, when annual income is generally quite high, particularly for families where both husband and wife work. Remember, though, that this is also a time when families are purchasing houses and providing for children. Consequently, all things considered, annual income during the prime working years may overstate the economic well-being of most households. Finally, there is the retirement phase, characterized by less work, more leisure, and smaller family size. Even families who are quite well-off tend to experience income well below the average for the entire population during the retirement phase. ***Given the life cycle of income, lumping together families of different ages (phases of their life-cycle earnings) results in substantial inequality in the annual income figures even if incomes over a lifetime were approximately equal.***

Exhibit 15–2 highlights major differences between high- and low-income families that underlie the distributional data of Exhibit 15–1. The typical high-income family (top 20 percent) is headed by a well-educated person in the prime working-age

EXHIBIT 15–2

DIFFERING CHARACTERISTICS OF HIGH- AND LOW-INCOME FAMILIES, 1997

	Bottom 20 Percent of Income Recipients	Top 20 Percent of Income Recipients
Education of Householder		
Percent with less than high school	35	4
Percent with college degree or more	6	54
Age of Householder (percent distribution)		
Under 35	34	12
35–64	44	79
65 and over	22	9
Family Status		
Married-couple family (percent of total)	48	94
Single-parent family (percent of total)	52	6
Persons per Family	3.0	3.4
Earners per Family	0.83	2.2
Percent of married-couple families in which wife works full time	4	51
Percent of Total Weeks Worked Supplied by Group	7	32

SOURCE: U.S. Department of Commerce, Money Income in the United States: 1997 *(Washington, D.C.: Government Printing Office, 1998).*

phase of life whose income is supplemented with the earnings of other family members, particularly working spouses. In contrast, persons with little education, nonworking retirees, younger workers (under age 35), and single-parent families are substantially overrepresented among low-income families (bottom 20 percent of income recipients). In 1997, 35 percent of the householders in the lowest income quintile failed to complete high school, compared to only 4 percent for the highest income quintile. While only 6 percent of the household heads in the bottom quintile completed college, 54 percent of the householders in the top group did so. Seventy-nine percent of the high-income families had household heads in the prime working-age category (age 35 to 64), compared with only 44 percent of the low-income families. Only one parent was present in 52 percent of the low-income families, whereas 94 percent of the high-income group were husband-wife families. Contrary to the views of some, high-income families are larger than low-income families. In 1997 there were 3.4 persons per family in the top income quintile, compared to only 3.0 family members among the bottom quintile of income recipients.

There was a striking difference in the work time between low- and high-income families. No doubt, much of this difference reflected such factors as family size, age, working spouses, and the incidence of husband-wife families. In high-income families, the average number of workers per family was 2.2, compared with 0.83 for low-income families. Among married couple families, a wife working full time was present only 4 percent of the time in low-income families, compared to 51 percent of the time among the top income group. As we would expect, couples who decide not to have the wife work full time pay for this choice by falling down the income distribution.

In terms of their work effort supplied to the economy, the top 20 percent of income recipients contributed 32 percent of the total number of weeks worked, while the low-income group contributed only 7 percent of the total work time. Thus, high-income families worked 4.6 times as many weeks as low-income families and earned approximately 11 times as much before-tax income. This implies that the earnings per week worked by the top income recipients were only a little more than twice the earnings per week worked by the low-income recipients. Clearly, differences in the amount of time worked were a major factor contributing to the income inequality of Exhibit 15–1.

In summary, Exhibit 15–2 sheds substantial light on the distributional data of Exhibit 15–1. ***Those with high incomes are far more likely to be well-educated, husband-wife families with dual earners in their prime working years. In contrast, those with low incomes are often single-parent families headed by a poorly educated adult who is either youthful or elderly. The household heads of those families with little income are often either out of the labor force or working only part-time.*** Given these factors, it is not surprising that the top 20 percent of recipients have substantially higher incomes, both before and after taxes, than the bottom quintile of family income recipients.[4]

Why Has Income Inequality Increased?

Exhibit 15–1 indicates that there has been an increase in income inequality in the United States during the last couple of decades. Why has the gap between the rich and the poor been growing? The answer to this question is a point of controversy among

[4]For additional information on income inequality, see: Frank Levy and Richard J. Murnane, "U.S. Earnings Levels and Earnings Inequality: A Review of Recent Trends and Proposed Explanations," *Journal of Economic Literature* (September 1992): 1333–1381; Symposium on "Wage Inequality," *Journal of Economic Perspectives* (spring 1997); and *Economic Report of the President, 1997* (Washington, DC: U.S. Government Printing Office, 1997), Chapter 5.

social scientists. Research in this area, however, indicates that at least four factors contributed substantially to the recent shift toward greater inequality.

1. ***The increasing proportion of single-parent and dual-earner families has contributed to the increase in the inequality of family income.*** The nature of the family and the allocation of work responsibilities within the family have changed dramatically in recent decades. In 1997 almost one-fourth (23 percent) of all families were headed by a single parent, double the figure of the mid-1960s. At the same time, the labor-force participation rate of married women increased from 40 percent in 1970 to 61 percent in 1997.

   By way of comparison with the late 1960s and early 1970s, we now have both more single-parent families *and* more dual-earner families. Both of these changes tend to promote income inequality. Perhaps an example will illustrate why. Consider two hypothetical families, the Smiths and the Browns. In 1970 both were middle-income families with two children and one market worker earning $35,000 (in 1999 dollars). Now consider their 1999 counterparts. The Smiths of 1999 are divorced and one of them, probably Mrs. Smith, is trying to work part-time and take care of the two children. The probability is very high that the single-parent Smith family of 1999 will be in the low-, rather than the middle-, income category. They may well be in the bottom quintile of the income distribution. In contrast, the Browns of 1999 both work outside the home, and each earns $35,000 annually. Given their dual incomes, the Browns are now a high-, rather than a middle-, income family. Along with many other dual-income families (see Exhibit 15–2), the Browns' 1999 family income will probably place them in the top quintile of income recipients.

   Even if there were no changes in earnings between skilled and less-skilled workers, the recent changes within the family would enhance income inequality among families and households. More single-parent families like the Smiths increase the number of families with low incomes, while more dual-earner families like the Browns increase the number of high-income families. Both will promote income inequality.
2. ***Earnings differentials between skilled and less-skilled workers have increased in recent years, further magnifying income inequality.*** In 1970 workers with little education who were willing to work hard, often in a hot and sweaty environment, were able to command high wages. This is less true today. Throughout the 1950s and 1960s, guidance counselors told high school students that a college education was essential for economic success. For a long time, it appeared that they were wrong. In 1974 the annual earnings of men who graduated from college were only 27 percent higher than the earnings of male high school graduates, hardly a huge pay-off for the time and cost of a college degree. Since 1974, however, things have changed dramatically. By the mid-1980s, the earnings premium of male college graduates relative to male high school grads had risen to the 50–60 percent range, approximately twice the premium of 1974. By 1997, the income premium of male college graduates relative to high school graduates had risen to 71 percent. Similarly, the earnings of women college graduates have increased sharply during the last two decades relative to women with only a high school education.

   Why have the earnings of persons with more education (and skill) risen relative to those with less education (and skill)? Deregulation of the transport industry and the waning power of unions may have reduced the number of high-wage, blue-collar jobs available to workers with little education. International competition has also played a role. As we mentioned at the very beginning of the book, the international trade sector has grown substantially during the last two decades. Increasingly, American workers compete in a global economy. Furthermore, innovations and cost reductions in both communications and transportation provide firms with greater flexibility with regard to location. Firms producing goods that require substantial amounts of low-skill labor are now better able to move to such places as Korea, Taiwan, and Mexico, where low-skill labor is cheaper. In contrast, the United States is more attractive than most other countries to firms requiring substantial amounts of high-skill, well-educated workers. Thus, globalization tends to reduce the demand for American workers with few skills and little education, while increasing the demand for high-skill workers with college degrees. This widens earnings differentials and increases earnings inequality. (However, it is worth noting that this process reduces *worldwide* income inequality.[5])

3. ***Reductions in communication and transportation costs may have increased the number of markets characterized by a few people at the top with very high earnings.*** As we noted in Chapter 13, the market compensation of star entertainers and athletes, the most talented professionals, and top business executives is often like that of winner-take-all tournaments. At any point in time, a few people at the top command huge earnings, while most others in these areas have modest or even low incomes. As transport and communication costs have declined, markets have increasingly become national and even global, rather than local. This increases the incomes of a few people at the top, but it also increases the degrees of income inequality.
4. ***The reported incomes of high-income Americans increased sharply because of changes in the tax code.*** Prior to 1981, high-income Americans confronted top marginal tax rates of up to 70 percent (50 percent on earnings). Such high marginal tax rates encouraged high-income earners to undertake investments and structure their business affairs in a manner that sheltered much of their income from the Internal Revenue Service. As we indicated in Chapter 4 (see Exhibit 4–12), the taxable incomes of the top 10 percent of earners expanded sharply when the top marginal tax rates were reduced to the 30 percent range during the 1980s. Some of this increase in income reflected greater work effort due to the increased incentive to earn. Much of it, however, merely reflected a reduction in tax-shelter activities in response to the lower marginal tax rates. The flip side of the reduction in tax-shelter activities accompanying the lower marginal tax rates of the 1980s was an increase in the visible income of the rich. To the extent this factor contributed to the increase in the measured income of wealthy Americans, the increase in income inequality was more imaginary than real.

INCOME INEQUALITY IN OTHER COUNTRIES

How does income inequality in the United States compare to that in other nations? **Exhibit 15–3** presents summary data compiled by the World Bank. These data indicate that the degree of income inequality in the United States exceeds that of the other

[5]For additional information on the relationship between international trade and income inequality, see Gary Burtless, "International Trade and the Rise in Earnings Inequality," *Journal of Economic Literature* (June 1995): 800–816; and Symposium on "Income Inequality and Trade," *Journal of Economic Perspectives* (summer 1995).

EXHIBIT 15–3

INCOME INEQUALITY AROUND THE WORLD

Country	Year	Percent Share of Income Earned By: Bottom 20 Percent	Middle Three Quintiles	Top 20 Percent
Less-Developed Economies				
India	1994	9.2	51.5	39.3
Indonesia	1995	8.4	48.5	43.1
Costa Rica	1996	4.0	44.2	51.8
Venezuela	1995	4.3	43.9	51.8
Nicaragua	1993	4.2	40.6	55.2
Mexico	1992	4.1	40.6	55.3
Chile	1994	3.5	35.5	61.0
Colombia	1995	3.1	35.4	61.5
Kenya	1992	3.4	34.5	62.1
Paraguay	1995	2.3	35.3	62.4
Brazil	1995	2.5	33.3	64.2
High-Income Industrial Nations				
Germany	1989	9.0	53.9	37.1
Italy	1991	7.6	53.5	38.9
Canada	1994	7.5	53.2	39.3
United Kingdom	1986	7.1	53.1	39.8
France	1989	7.2	52.7	40.1
Spain	1990	7.5	52.2	40.3
Australia	1989	7.0	52.1	40.9
United States	1994	4.8	50.0	45.2

SOURCE: The World Bank, World Development Report, 1998.

large industrial economies. For example, the bottom quintile of income recipients earn a larger share (and the top quintile a smaller share) of the total income in Germany, Italy, Canada, the United Kingdom, France, Spain, and Australia than is the case for the United States. The lesser degree of inequality in these countries is not surprising. Compared to the United States, the other large industrial economies are characterized by a more homogeneous population and more extensive use of income transfer policies.

The share of income generated by the wealthy is usually greater in less-developed countries. The top 20 percent of income recipients earned 60 percent or more of the aggregate income in Brazil, Paraguay, Kenya, Colombia, and Chile. The top quintile earned approximately 55 percent of the total in Mexico and Nicaragua. Among the developing nations of Exhibit 15–3, only Indonesia and India were marked by a degree of inequality similar to that of most developed countries.[6]

[6]The data of Exhibit 15–3 are not adjusted for cross-country differences in either size of household or the demographic composition of the population. In addition, procedures used to make the estimates and the reliability of the data vary across countries. Thus, these data should be interpreted with a degree of caution.

INCOME MOBILITY AND INEQUALITY IN ECONOMIC STATUS

Income mobility
Movement of individuals and families either up or down income-distribution rankings when comparisons are made at two different points in time. When substantial income mobility is present, one's current position will not be a very good indicator as to what one's position will be a few years in the future.

Statistics on the distribution of annual income fail to reveal **income mobility**—the degree of movement across income groupings—and thus they may be misleading. Consider two countries with identical distributions of annual income. In both cases, the annual income of the top quintile of income recipients is eight times greater than that of the bottom quintile. Now, suppose that in the first country—we will refer to it as Static—the same people are at the top of the income distribution, year after year. Similarly, the poor people of Static remain poor year after year. Static is characterized by an absence of income mobility. In contrast, earners in the second country, which we will call Dynamic, are constantly changing places. Indeed, during every five-year period, each family spends one year in the upper-income quintile, one year in each of the three middle-income quintiles, and one year in the bottom-income quintile. In Dynamic, no one is rich for more than one year (out of each five), and no one is poor for more than a year. Obviously, the nature of economic inequality in Static is vastly different from that in Dynamic. You would not know it, though, by looking at their identical annual income distributions.

The contrast between Static and Dynamic indicates why it is important to consider income mobility when addressing the issue of economic inequality. Until recently, detailed data on income mobility were sparse. This is now beginning to change.[7] **Exhibit 15–4** presents data on the mobility of household income between 1968 and 1991. These data compare the relative income positions of the *same households* at two different points in time. Based on their 1968 income, each household was placed into income quintiles ranked from highest to lowest. Later, the 1991 income level of the

EXHIBIT 15–4

INCOME MOBILITY—INCOME RANKING, 1968 AND 1991

	Income Status of Household in 1991				
Income Status of Household in 1968	Top-Paid Quintile	Next-Highest-Paid Quintile	Middle Quintile	Next-Lowest-Paid Quintile	Lowest-Paid Quintile
Top-Paid Quintile	42.0	24.5	16.1	10.8	6.7
Next-Highest-Paid Quintile	27.6	26.2	20.4	16.7	9.2
Middle Quintile	18.2	26.2	20.2	21.8	13.6
Next-Lowest-Paid Quintile	9.6	14.3	26.4	26.2	23.6
Lowest-Paid Quintile	2.7	8.7	17.3	24.5	46.0

Note: Only persons with income in both 1968 and 1991 are included.

SOURCE: Tabulation of Peter Gottschalk as reported in Lawrence Mishel, Jared Bernstein, and John Schmitt, The State of Working America 1996–97 *(New York: M. E. Sharpe, 1997).*

[7]For a review of the literature on income mobility, see Isabel V. Sawhill and Daniel P. McMurrer, *Income Mobility in the United States* (Washington, DC: Urban Institute, 1996). For an early classic work on this topic, see Greg J. Duncan et al., *Years of Poverty, Years of Plenty: The Changing Fortunes of American Workers and Families* (Ann Arbor: Institute for Social Research, University of Michigan, 1984).

same households was used to group once again the income of each by quintiles. The first row of Exhibit 15–4 indicates the relative income position in 1991 of the households that were in the top quintile of income recipients in 1968. Approximately two-fifths (42 percent) of those with incomes in the top quintile in 1968 were able to maintain this lofty position 23 years later. Nearly three-fifths (58 percent) of the top earners in 1968 had fallen to a lower income quintile by 1991. However, only one in six of the high-income households fell to one of the bottom two quintiles of the 1991 income distribution. This suggests that once households are able to achieve high-income status, dramatic reductions that push them back to a low level of income are rare.

The bottom row of Exhibit 15–4 tracks the experience of those in the lowest-income quintile in 1968. Less than half (46 percent) of the households in the lowest income quintile remained there in 1991. More than one-quarter (28.7 percent) moved up to one of the top three income quintiles in 1991. Among those in the next-to-lowest income quintile in 1968, one-half had moved up to a higher income grouping by 1991.

The income mobility data highlight a point that is concealed by the annual figures: There is considerable movement up and down the economic ladder. Relative income positions often change over time. A sizable portion of those with a high relative income during one year subsequently find themselves in a lower income position. At the same time, many of those with low relative incomes during a given year move up to higher income quintiles in subsequent years.

The data of Exhibit 15–4 are for the same group of households. If newly formed households had been included, there would have been even more income mobility, particularly in an upward direction.[8] Often, current income is low because the household is young and inexperienced or going to school while working part-time. In other cases, the low current income status is the result of a job loss or business setback during the year. In still other cases, it reflects an accident or a temporary health problem. The distribution of income in the United States is dynamic. With time, most of those with low incomes *at a point in time* move up the income ladder only to be replaced by others who are youthful, inexperienced, or victims of current misfortune. Many readers of this book (college students) currently have very low annual income and are thus currently poor and in the lower part of the income distribution. After college graduation, however, the earning power of a college degree will place many of these currently poor individuals in the upper-income brackets.

Some believe that inheritance is the primary path to riches. The empirical evidence is inconsistent with this view. In 1996, approximately 2.7 million Americans were millionaires—they had net assets of $1 million or more. Four out of five of these millionaires achieved their wealth on their own—some through success in business, others in the professions, and still others through saving and wise investment. Only one in five millionaires inherited their wealth.

HOUSEHOLD EXPENDITURES AND INEQUALITY

Given the pattern of lifetime income and the mobility up and down the income ladder, many economists argue that differences in household expenditures are a more accurate indicator of economic status than is annual income. When the current income of an individual or a household understates either their future earning prospects or their income level during an earlier period, current expenditures generally exceed current

[8]For evidence on this point, see Michael W. Cox and Richard Alm, "By Our Own Bootstraps: Economic Opportunity and the Dynamic of Income Distribution," *Federal Reserve Bank of Dallas Annual Report, 1995;* and U.S. Department of the Treasury, Office of Tax Analysis, *Household Income Mobility During the 1980s: A Statistical Analysis Based on Tax Return Data* (Washingon, DC: U.S. Department of the Treasury, 1992).

Generational Mobility: There is a weak positive correlation between the earnings of fathers and sons. If a father has lifetime earnings 20 percent above the average of his generation, a son can expect to earn about 8 percent more. There is virtually no correlation between the earnings of grandparents and their grandchildren. Apparently, there is some truth in the old saying, "From shirtsleeves to shirtsleeves in three generations."

income. On the other hand, if current income is high relative to one's prior or expected future income, more will be saved, causing expenditures to fall short of current income. To a large degree, current expenditures reflect long-term economic status.

What do expenditures indicate with regard to the degree of inequality in the United States? Daniel Slesnick of the University of Texas has studied this issue extensively. In addition to the income data, Exhibit 15–1 also presents Slesnick's calculations on share of household expenditures by quintile. In 1991, the 20 percent of households with the smallest consumer expenditure levels undertook 7 percent of the aggregate expenditures. On the other hand, the expenditures of the top quintile summed to 39.7 percent of the total. The expenditures of the top group were 5.7 times those of the bottom group. This ratio is significantly lower than the corresponding figure for annual income, both before and after taxes. Thus, the expenditure share of the bottom quintile relative to the top group is significantly greater than the income share.

In contrast with the annual income data, the distribution of household consumption expenditures does not indicate that there has been a major change in economic inequality in the United States during recent decades. Throughout the 1961–1991 period, the expenditures of the bottom quintile were approximately 7 percent of the total, while those of the top quintile were slightly less than 40 percent. This suggests that the increase in inequality as measured by the annual income data is a reflection of dynamic change, temporary fluctuations in annual income, and measurement issues rather than a true increase in economic inequality.

POVERTY IN THE UNITED STATES

In an affluent society, such as that of the United States, income inequality and poverty are related issues. Poverty could be defined in strictly relative terms—the bottom one-fifth of all income recipients, for example. However, this definition would not be very helpful, since it would mean that poverty could never decline.

The official definition of poverty in the United States is based on the perceived minimum income necessary to provide food, clothing, shelter, and basic necessities economically for a family. This **poverty threshold income level** varies with family size and composition, and it is adjusted annually for changes in prices. For purposes of determining whether income is above the poverty threshold, the official poverty rate considers only money income. (See the Measures of Economic Activity feature for additional details on how the poverty rate is measured.)

Poverty threshold income level
The level of money income below which a family is considered to be poor. It differs according to family characteristics (for example, number of family members) and is adjusted when consumer prices change.

How many people are poor? According to the official definition of poverty, there were 35.6 million poor people and 7.3 million poor families in 1997. As **Exhibit 15–5** indicates, 13.3 percent of the population and 10.3 percent of the families were officially classified as poor in 1997. During the 1950s and 1960s, the poverty rate declined substantially. By 1970 the official poverty rate for families had fallen to 10.1 percent, down from 18.1 percent in 1960 and 32.0 percent in 1947. In contrast with the 1950s and 1960s, the official poverty rate has changed by only a small amount since 1970. After rising slightly during the 1970s and 1980s, the official poverty rate has fallen modestly during the economic expansion of the 1990s. In 1997, the poverty rate of both persons and families was slightly higher than in 1970.

In recent years, the composition of the poverty population has changed substantially. As **Exhibit 15–6** indicates, elderly persons and the working poor formed the

MEASURES OF ECONOMIC ACTIVITY

Determining the Poverty Rate

Families and individuals are classified as poor or non-poor based on the poverty threshold income level originally developed by the Social Security Administration (SSA) in 1964. Since consumption survey data indicated that low- and median-income families of three or more persons spent approximately one-third of their income on food, the SSA established the poverty threshold income level at three times the cost of an economical, nutritionally adequate food plan. A slightly larger multiple was used for smaller families and individuals living alone. The poverty threshold figure varies according to family size, because the food costs vary by family size and composition. It is adjusted annually to account for rising prices. The following chart illustrates how the poverty threshold for a family of four has increased as prices have risen from 1959 to 1997:

1959	$ 2,973
1970	3,968
1980	8,414
1990	13,359
1995	15,570
1997	16,400

Even though the poverty threshold income level is adjusted for prices, it is actually an absolute measure of economic status. As real income increases, the poverty threshold declines relative to the income of the general populace.

The official poverty rate is the number of persons or families living in households with a money income below the poverty threshold as a proportion of the total. Only money income is considered. Income received in the form of noncash benefits, such as food stamps, medical care, and housing subsidies, is completely ignored in the calculation of the official poverty rate.

Since noncash benefits targeted for low-income households have grown rapidly since the late 1960s, the failure of the official poverty rate to count this "income" reduces its accuracy as a measurement tool. To remedy this deficiency, the Bureau of the Census has developed several alternative measures of poverty that count the estimated value of noncash benefits as income. In addition to the official poverty rate, the bureau now publishes annual data for the "adjusted" poverty rates that include a valuation for various noncash benefits (for example, food stamps, medical care, school lunches, and housing benefits). Of course, inclusion of these benefits reduces the poverty rate. For example, while the official poverty rate for persons was 13.3 percent in 1997, the adjusted poverty rate that included the value of the noncash food, housing, and medical benefits was only 10.0 percent.

The poverty rate is calculated each year based on a current population survey of nearly 50,000 households designed to reflect the population of the United States. The two major sources for comprehensive data on this topic are the Bureau of the Census annual publications, *Money Income in the United States* and *Poverty in the United States.*

EXHIBIT 15-5

SOURCES: Bureau of the Census, Current Population Reports, *Series P60-201;* Poverty in the United States: 1997; *and* Economic Report of the President, 1964, *Table 7.*

POVERTY RATE OF PERSONS AND FAMILIES IN THE UNITED STATES, 1947–1997

	Poverty Rate (Percent)	
Year	Persons	Families
1947	n.a.	32.0
1960	22.2	18.1
1970	12.6	10.1
1980	13.0	10.3
1990	13.5	10.7
1997	13.3	10.3

core of the poverty population in 1959. Twenty-two percent of the poor families were headed by an elderly person in 1959. Most poor people (70 percent) worked at least some hours during the year. In 1997, the picture was dramatically different: Only 9 percent of the poor families were headed by an elderly person and only 50 percent of the heads of poor households worked at all during the year.

There has also been a substantial growth in the proportion of female-headed families and an accompanying decline in the proportion of husband-wife families in the

EXHIBIT 15-6

SOURCES: U.S. Department of Commerce, Characteristics of the Population Below the Poverty Level: 1982, *Table 5; and* Poverty in the United States: 1997, *(P60-201).*

CHANGING COMPOSITION OF POOR AND POVERTY RATE OF SELECTED GROUPS: 1959, 1976, AND 1997

	1959	1976	1997
Number of Poor Families (in millions)	8.3	5.3	7.3
Percent of Poor Families Headed by a:			
Female	23	48	55
Black	26	30	27
Elderly person (age 65 and over)	22	14	9
Person who worked at least some during the year	70	55	50
Poverty Rate			
All families	18.5	10.1	10.3
Married couple families	15.8	7.2	5.2
Female-headed families	42.6	32.5	31.6
Whites	18.1	9.1	11.0
Blacks	55.1	31.1	26.5
Children (under age 18)	27.3	16.0	19.9

general population. Since the poverty rate of female-headed families is several times higher than the rate for husband-wife families (31.6 percent compared with 5.2 percent in 1997), an increase in family instability tends to push the poverty rate upward. In 1997, more than half (55 percent) of the poor families were headed by a female, compared with only 23 percent in 1959.

The poverty rate of blacks in 1997 was 26.5 percent, compared to 11.0 percent for whites. Nonetheless, 69 percent of the people in poverty were white. Perhaps the most tragic consequence of poverty is its impact on children. During the last two decades, the poverty rate among children has increased substantially. In 1997, 19.9 percent of the children in the United States lived in poverty, up from 16.0 percent in 1976.

Just as with the income distribution data, there is movement into and out of poverty. A large proportion of poor families remain so for only a brief period of time. For example, even though 14.6 percent of the population was poor during the average month in 1993–1994, only 4.8 percent of the population was poor during the entire period. In fact, the median duration of poverty spells during 1993–1994 was only 4.9 months. Many of these short-term spells of poverty were the result of such factors as medical problems or job changes. Poverty is a long-term problem for only a small number of families. During the typical 10-year period, less than 3 percent of families are poor for 8 or more years.

Transfer Payments and the Poverty Rate

In the mid-1960s, it was widely believed that an increase in income transfers directed toward the poor would substantially reduce, if not eliminate, the incidence of poverty. The 1964 *Economic Report of the President* argued that poverty could be virtually eliminated if the federal government increased its expenditures on transfer programs by approximately 2 percent of aggregate income. Following the declaration of the "War on Poverty" by the Johnson administration, expenditures in this area increased rapidly. Overall transfers, including those directed toward the elderly, approximately doubled as a proportion of personal income between 1965 and 1975. Measured in 1982–1984 dollars, **means-tested income transfers**—those limited to people with incomes below a certain cutoff point—tripled, expanding from $24 billion in 1965 to $70 billion in 1975. *As a proportion of aggregate income,* means-tested transfers jumped from 1.5 percent in 1965 to 3.0 percent in 1975. During the 1975–1990 period, both total transfers and means-tested transfers continued to increase as a percent of income, although at a much slower rate than during the previous decade. By the mid-1990s, means-tested transfers had risen to 5 percent of aggregate income.[9]

Means-tested income transfers
Transfers that are limited to persons or families with an income below a certain cutoff point. Eligibility is thus dependent on low-income status.

[9]The following chart indicates the expenditures on both total income transfers and means-tested transfers as a percentage of personal income for 1965, 1975, 1985, and 1994. Both cash and in-kind benefits are included in the figures.

PERCENT OF AGGREGATE INCOME

YEAR	TOTAL TRANSFER PAYMENTS	MEANS-TESTED TRANSFER PAYMENTS
1965	8.5	1.5
1975	17.4	3.0
1985	18.8	3.4
1994	21.8	5.2

The means-tested noncash transfers included food (food stamps, school lunch subsidies, and WIC program), housing, and energy assistance benefits, plus Medicaid payments. In addition to these benefits, Medicare payments were also included in the total transfer figures. Expenditures on job training and educational subsidies are not included. See *Statistical Abstract of the United States: 1998,* Tables 600 and 605.

Did the expansion in government income transfers reduce the poverty rate as the 1964 *Economic Report of the President* anticipated? Antipoverty programs provide both cash and noncash benefits. **Exhibit 15–7** shows the poverty rate with and without the benefits of noncash transfer programs counted as income. Continuing the trend of the post–Second World War era, the official poverty rate fell throughout the 1960s. During the 1970s, however, the rate leveled off. By 1980, it was 10.3 percent, virtually unchanged from the 1968 rate. In 1997, the official poverty rate was still 10.3 percent.

Aggregate poverty-rate data as presented in Exhibit 15–7 conceal an important difference between the experience of the elderly and nonelderly that has often been overlooked. **Exhibit 15–8** highlights this point. The poverty rate for the elderly has continued to decline throughout the 1970s, 1980s, and 1990s. By 1997, the official poverty rate of the elderly had fallen to 6.0 percent, down from 17.0 percent in 1968 and 30.0 percent in 1959 (see part a of Exhibit 15–8). The experience of working-age Americans, however, was vastly different. After falling for several decades, the official poverty rate of nonelderly families reached a low in 1968, shortly after the War on Poverty was launched. The nonelderly poverty rate rose during 1970–1985 and it has fallen slightly since. However, the 1997 poverty rate of 11.1 percent was still well above the 9 percent rate of 1968 (part b of Exhibit 15–8). Even after adjustment for the noncash benefits (part c), the poverty rate of working-age Americans was higher in 1997 than in 1968.

Clearly, the income transfer programs of the War on Poverty did not work as anticipated. The 1990s was a period of sustained economic expansion. The unemployment rate fell to a 30-year low. Even more significant, U.S. income per person *adjusted for inflation* was 83 percent higher in 1997 than in 1965. Despite all of these positive factors, the poverty rate in 1997 was virtually unchanged from that of the mid-1960s!

EXHIBIT 15–7

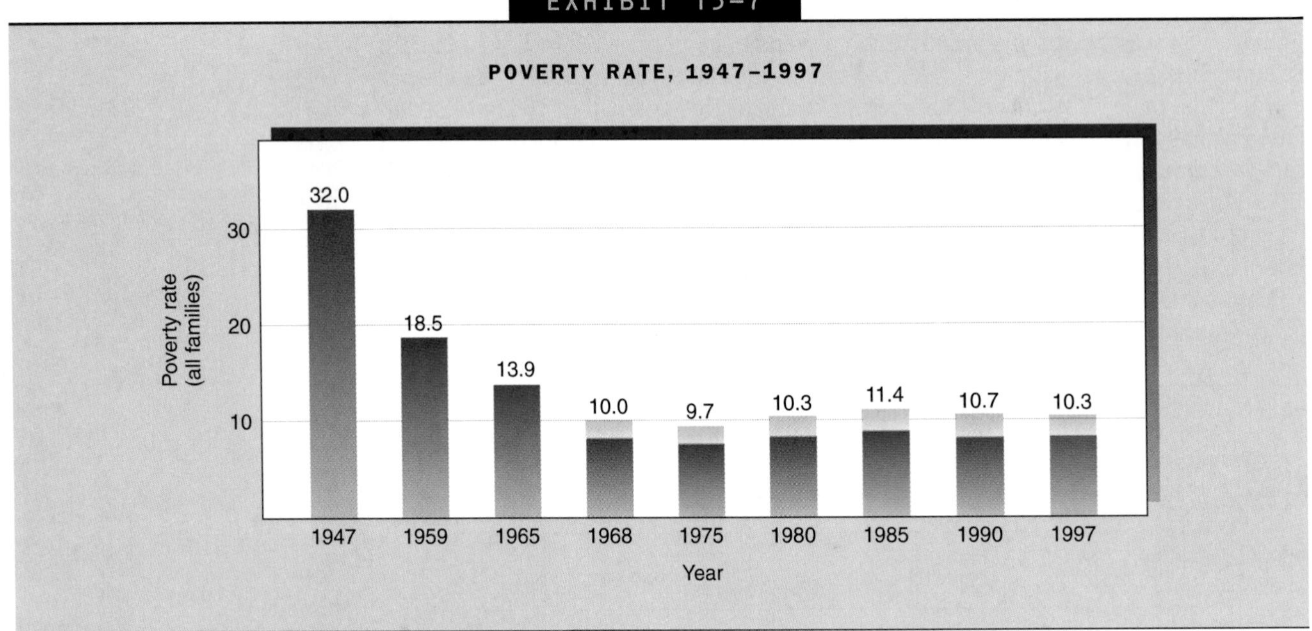

The official poverty rate of families declined sharply during the 1950s and 1960s, changed little during the 1970s, and rose during the early 1980s. The rate has fallen by only a small amount since the mid-1980s. The shaded area of the bars indicates the additional reduction in the poverty rate when noncash benefits are counted as income. In 1990, the poverty rate adjusted for noncash benefits was 8.4 percent and in 1997 it was 8.3 percent.

SOURCE: Department of Commerce, Poverty in the United States: 1997, *(P60–201).*

EXHIBIT 15-8

CHANGING POVERTY RATES FOR ELDERLY VERSUS NONELDERLY, 1959–1997

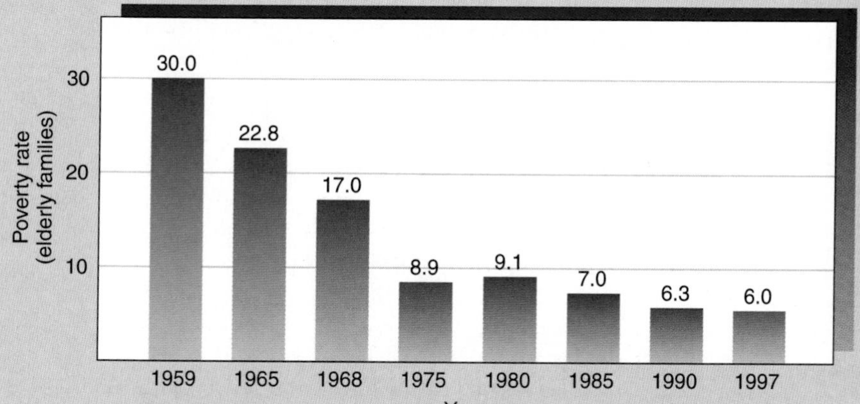

(a) The official poverty rate for elderly families has declined sharply since 1959.

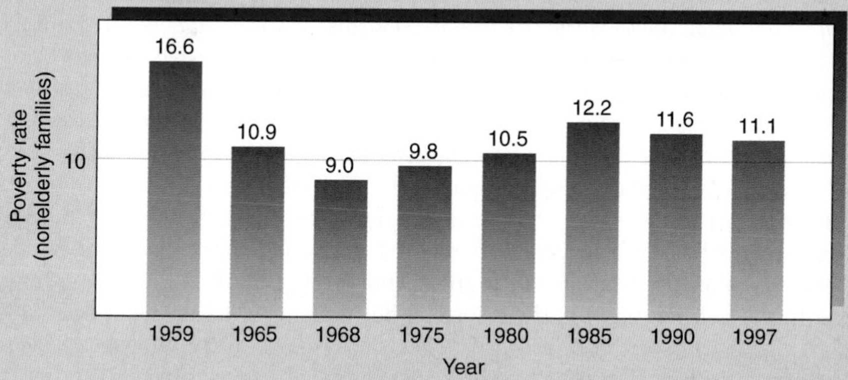

(b) In contrast, the official poverty rate for nonelderly families has risen since the late 1960s.

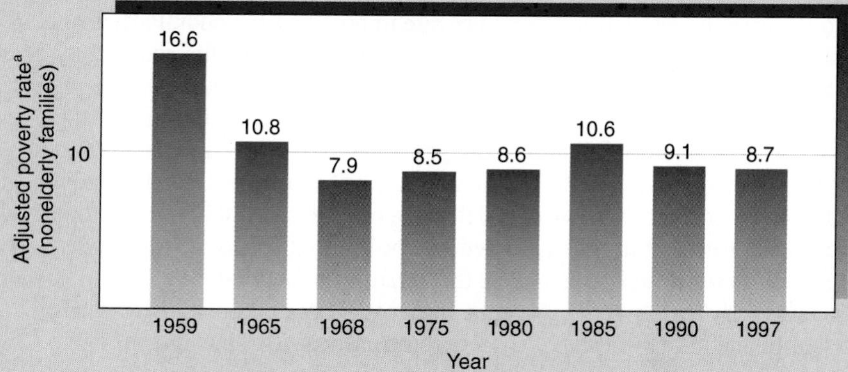

(c) Adjusting for noncash transfers reduces the poverty rate of the nonelderly but it does not alter the basic pattern.

[a]*Adjusted for food, medical, and housing benefits.*

SOURCES: Derived from Department of Commerce, Money Income in the United States: 1997; Poverty in the United States: 1990; *and* Measuring the Effects of Benefits and Taxes on Income and Poverty, 1990 *and* 1992. *See also James Gwartney and Thomas S. McCaleb, "Have Antipoverty Programs Increased Poverty?* The Cato Journal *(spring/summer, 1985)*

The poverty rate of the elderly (6.0 percent in 1997) is lower than the poverty rate of those under age 65 (11.1 percent in 1997). Furthermore, during the last three decades, the poverty rate for the elderly has persistently declined, while the rate for the nonelderly has risen slightly.

Why wasn't the War on Poverty more effective? Application 5 will consider that issue in more detail and analyze the welfare reforms that were adopted in 1996. However, a couple of points are worth noting at this time. Means-tested income transfers generate two major side effects that reduce their effectiveness as an antipoverty weapon. ***First, transfer programs that significantly reduce the adversities of poverty will also reduce the opportunity cost of choices that often lead to poverty.*** This factor is sometimes called the **Samaritan's dilemma.** To the extent that antipoverty programs reduce the negative side effects of, for example, births by unmarried mothers, abandonment of children by fathers, dependence on drugs or alcohol, or dropping out of school, they inadvertently encourage people to make choices that result in these conditions. Of course, this is not the intent of the transfers, but nonetheless it is one of their side effects. In the short run, these secondary effects may not be very important. Over the longer term, however, their negative consequences may be substantial.

Samaritan's dilemma
General assistance to those with low incomes reduces the opportunity cost of choices that lead to poverty. Thus, there is a conflict between providing income transfers to the poor and discouragement of behavior that increases the incidence of poverty.

Second, income-linked transfers reduce the incentive of low-income individuals to help themselves. When the size of transfers is linked to income, larger transfers tend to increase the **implicit marginal tax rate** imposed on the poor. Participants in the food stamp program, for example, have their food stamp benefits reduced by $30 for every $100 of income earned. Thus, every $100 of additional income leads to only a $70 increase in well-being (spendable net income) once the reduction in food stamp benefits is taken into account. When a person qualifies for several different programs, the problem is compounded, and the combined implicit marginal tax rate can frequently exceed 50 or 60 percent. In some cases, the rate may exceed 100 percent—that is, work and additional earnings may actually reduce the family's economic status. Because the high implicit marginal tax rates reduce the incentive of poor families to work and earn, the transfers may merely replace income that would have otherwise been earned. Thus, the transfers add little or nothing to *net* income of those with low incomes.

Implicit marginal tax rate
The amount of additional (marginal) earnings that must be paid explicitly in taxes or implicitly in the form of a reduction in income supplements. Since the marginal tax rate establishes the fraction of an additional dollar earned that an individual is permitted to keep, it is an important determinant of the incentive to work.

Estimating the Costs of Redistribution

Economics indicates that the use of income transfers to upgrade the status of those with low incomes is like trying to transfer water with a "leaky bucket." The increases in the marginal tax rates (either explicit or implicit) confronted by both the taxpayer-donor and the transfer recipient adversely affect work incentives and reduce the size of the economic pie. Thus, the cost of the transfers in terms of loss of output exceeds the amount of income transferred. Furthermore, much of the income received by recipients merely replaces income that they might otherwise have earned.

A study by Edgar Browning and William Johnson sought to measure the loss of output due to the reduction in the supply of labor associated with the rise in marginal tax rates accompanying income transfers.[10] Browning and Johnson estimated that it would cost $3.49 in terms of lost output for every additional dollar taxed from the top 60 percent of income recipients and transferred to the bottom 40 percent.

Transferring income from producers to nonproducers is thus an expensive undertaking. Are redistribution programs worth the cost? Economics cannot answer that question. It can only help identify and quantify the cost (in terms of lost output) and expected effectiveness of alternative programs. Hopefully, better information in these areas will help voters and policy makers to make wiser decisions.

LOOKING *Ahead*

Income transfers are the focal point of many current policy issues. Demographic changes are causing policy makers to consider the future structure of social security, which is, by far, the largest single income transfer program. There is also considerable concern and controversy about the recent increases in income inequality and the potential of public policy to deal with this issue. Important welfare reforms have recently been passed and others are under consideration. Applications 2 (Social Security) and 5 (Welfare Reform and Inequality) provide additional details on these topics.

KEY POINTS

➤ Market participants create income by supplying resources that are highly valued *by others.* The link between income and provision of productive resources provides individuals with the incentive to develop skills, talents, and resources others value. The view that there is a fixed-size economic pie that can be sliced and divided among the citizenry is fallacious.

➤ In 1997, the bottom 20 percent of families earned 4.2 percent of aggregate income, while the top 20 percent earned approximately 11 times that amount (47.2 percent). After taxes and transfers are taken into account, the top quintile of families earn a little more than eight times the income of the bottom quintile. The degree of income inequality declined during the 1950s and 1960s, but it has risen during the last 25 years.

➤ A substantial percentage of the inequality in annual income reflects differences in age, education, family size, marital status, number of earners in the family, and time worked. Young, inexperienced workers, students, single-parent families, and retirees are overrepresented among those with low incomes.

➤ While no single factor can explain the recent increase in income inequality, the following four factors probably contributed to it: (a) an increasing proportion of both single-parent *and* dual-earner families, (b) an increase in earnings differentials on the basis of skill and

[10]See Edgar K. Browning and William Johnson, "The Trade-off between Equality and Efficiency," *Journal of Political Economy* (April 1984).

education, (c) more "winner-take-all" markets, and (d) increases in the reported income of those in the top tax bracket due to lower marginal tax rates.

➤ Among the large industrial nations, there is less income inequality in Germany, Italy, Canada, the United Kingdom, France, Spain, and Australia than in the United States. In general, income is distributed more equally in the advanced industrial countries than in less-developed nations.

➤ The tracking of household income over time indicates that there is considerable movement both up and down the income spectrum. Annual income data camouflage this movement.

➤ According to the official data, 13.3 percent of the population and 10.3 percent of the families in the United States were officially classified as poor in 1997. Those living in poverty were generally younger, less educated, less likely to be working, and more likely to be living in families headed by a single parent than those who were not poor.

➤ There is considerable movement both into and out of poverty. A relatively small proportion of families comprise the long-term poor.

➤ During the last several decades, income transfers—including means-tested transfers—have expanded rapidly both in real dollars and as a share of personal income. These transfers have been largely ineffective. Even though per-capita income increased by more than 80 percent between 1965 and 1997, the poverty rate of working-age Americans was about the same during the two years.

➤ Income supplements large enough to significantly increase the economic status of poor people will (a) encourage behavior that increases the risk of poverty and/or (b) create high implicit marginal tax rates that reduce the recipient's incentive to earn.

CRITICAL ANALYSIS QUESTIONS

1. Do you think the current distribution of income in the United States is too unequal? Why or why not? What criteria do you think should be used to judge the fairness of the distribution of income? Is the final outcome more important than the process that generates the income?

*2. Is annual money income a good measure of economic status? Is a family with a $50,000 annual income able to purchase twice the quantity of goods and services as a family with $25,000 of annual income? Is the standard of living of the $50,000 family twice as high as that of the $25,000 family? Discuss.

3. What is income mobility? If there is substantial income mobility in a society, how does this influence the importance of income distribution data?

*4. Consider a table such as Exhibit 15–4 in which the family income of parents is grouped by quintiles down the rows, and that of their offspring is grouped by quintiles across the columns. If there were no intergenerational mobility in this country, what pattern of numbers would be present in the table? If the nation had attained complete equality of opportunity, what pattern of numbers would emerge? Explain.

5. Do individuals have a property right to income they acquire from market transactions? Is it a proper function of government to tax some people in order to provide benefits to others? Why or why not? Discuss.

*6. Since income transfers to the poor typically increase the marginal tax rate confronted by the poor, does a $1,000 additional transfer payment necessarily cause the income of poor recipients to rise by $1,000? Why or why not?

*7. Sue is a single parent with two children. She is considering a job that pays $800 per month. She is currently drawing monthly cash benefits of $300, plus food-stamp benefits of $100, and Medicaid benefits valued at $80. If she accepts the job, she will be liable for employment taxes of $56 per month and lose all transfer benefits. What is Sue's implicit marginal tax rate for this job?

8. What groups are overrepresented among those with relatively low incomes? Do the poor in the United States generally stay poor? Why or why not?

9. Some argue that taxes exert little effect on people's incentive to earn income. In considering this issue, suppose you were required to pay a tax rate of 50 percent on all money income you earn while in school. Would this affect your employment? How might you minimize the personal effects of this tax?

10. Large income transfers are targeted toward the elderly, farmers, and the unemployed, regardless of their

economic condition. Why do you think this is so? Does an expansion in the size of tax-transfer activities reduce income inequality?

11. "Welfare is a classic case of conflicting goals. Low welfare payments continue to leave people in poverty, but high welfare payments attract people to welfare rolls, reduce work incentives, and cause higher rates of unemployment." Is this statement true? Discuss.

12. "Means-tested transfer payments reduce the current poverty rate. However, they also create an incentive structure that discourages self-provision and self-improvement. Thus, they tend to increase the future poverty rate. Welfare programs essentially purchase a lower poverty rate today in exchange for a higher poverty rate in the future." Evaluate this statement.

---

*Asterisk denotes questions for which answers are given in Appendix B.

International economics

More than one-fifth of the worldwide output is produced in one country and exported to another country, twice the figure of 1960. In the United States, both the exports and imports have tripled *as a share of the economy* since 1960. Lower costs of both transportation and communications have contributed substantially to the growth of international trade. Lower tariffs and more liberal trade policies have also played a role.

The rapid growth of international trade is changing our lives. The world is becoming a global village.

DIFFERENCES AMONG COUNTRIES IN THE SIZE OF THE TRADE SECTOR

Here we illustrate the size of the trade sector as a share of the economy for various countries grouped by size. Data are presented for both 1970 and 1997. Smaller, less populous countries (like Singapore, Hong Kong, and Ireland) generally have larger trade sectors as a share of total output. Note the general increase in trade between 1970 and 1997.

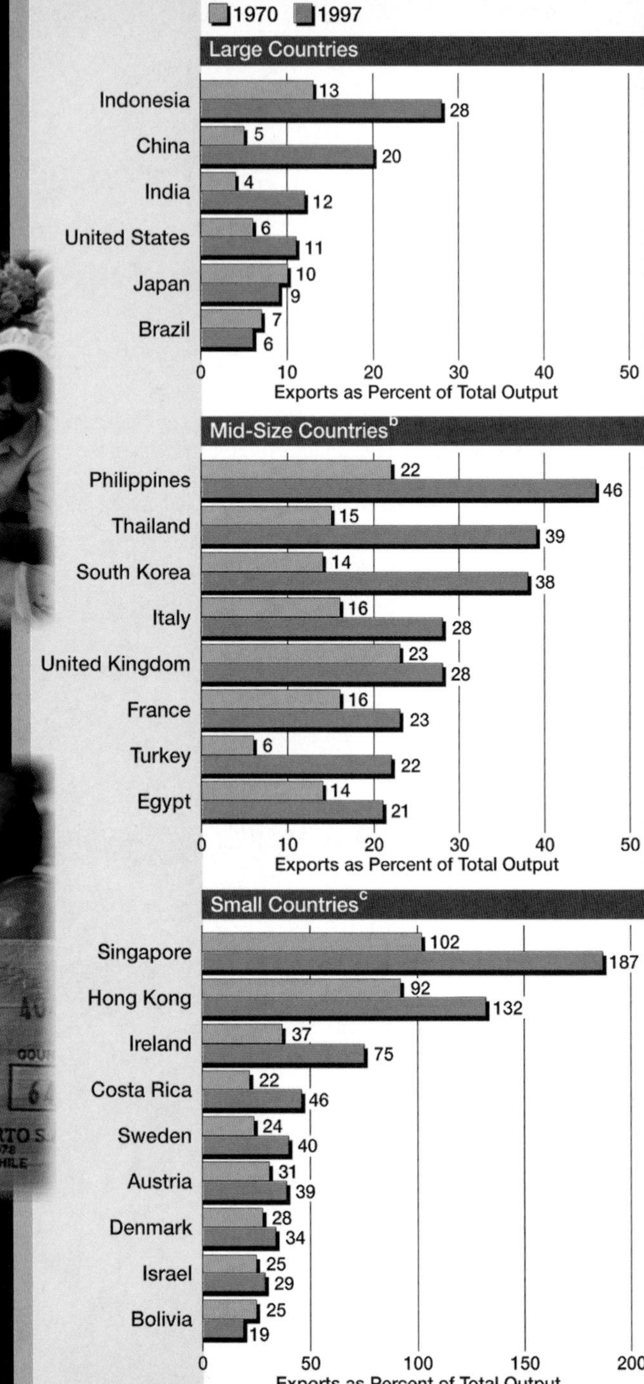

[a]Population more than 120 million.
[b]Population between 40 and 65 million.
[c]Population less than 10 million.
SOURCE: World Bank, World Development Report *(various years).*

EXHIBIT IV-A

THE MAJOR IMPORT AND EXPORT PRODUCTS OF THE UNITED STATES

Economic theory indicates that trade and specialization permit both the United States and its trading partners to achieve a larger output and a higher consumption level than would otherwise be possible. Domestic producers of export products, such as computers, aircraft, wheat, corn, and soybeans, gain from sales to foreigners at attractive prices. Domestic consumers of import products, such as petroleum, clothing, shoes, and electronic equipment, and agricultural products, such as coffee, bananas, and kiwi gain from the purchase of these goods from foreigners at low prices. Furthermore, competition in worldwide markets for automobiles, semiconductors, telecommunications equipment, and industrial machines enhances economic efficiency. International trade and competition help promote prosperity.

EXHIBIT IV-B

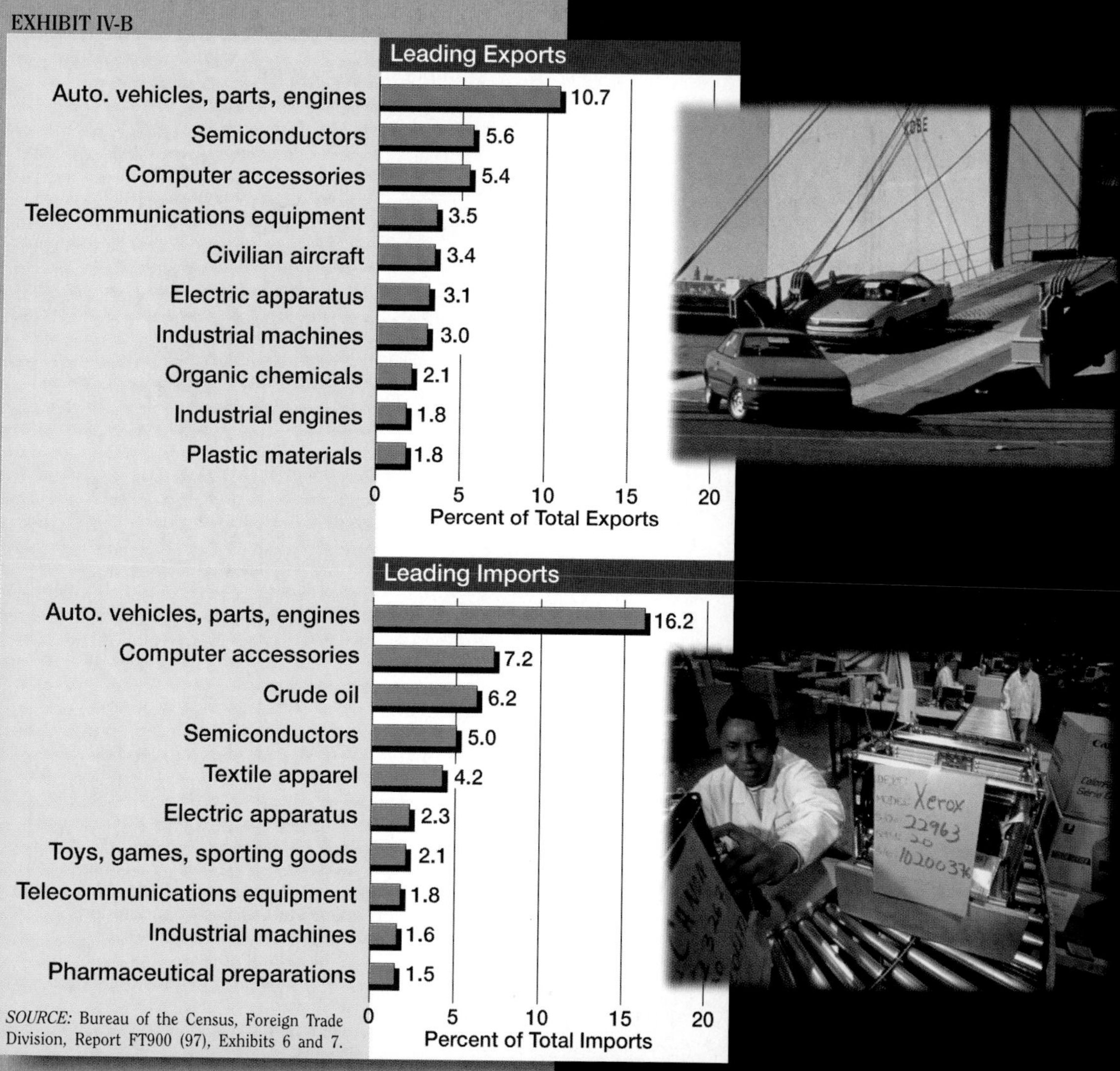

SOURCE: Bureau of the Census, Foreign Trade Division, Report FT900 (97), Exhibits 6 and 7.

Thirty percent of the new autos sold in the United States are produced by a foreign manufacturer. United States computer firms, such as Apple, Compaq, Dell, Gateway, and IBM, sell a large share of their output abroad.

THE MAJOR TRADING PARTNERS OF THE UNITED STATES

The major trading partners of the United States are Canada, Japan, and Mexico. In 1997, 42 percent of all United States trade was with these three countries. During the last decade, trade with Mexico has expanded rapidly.

EXHIBIT IV-C

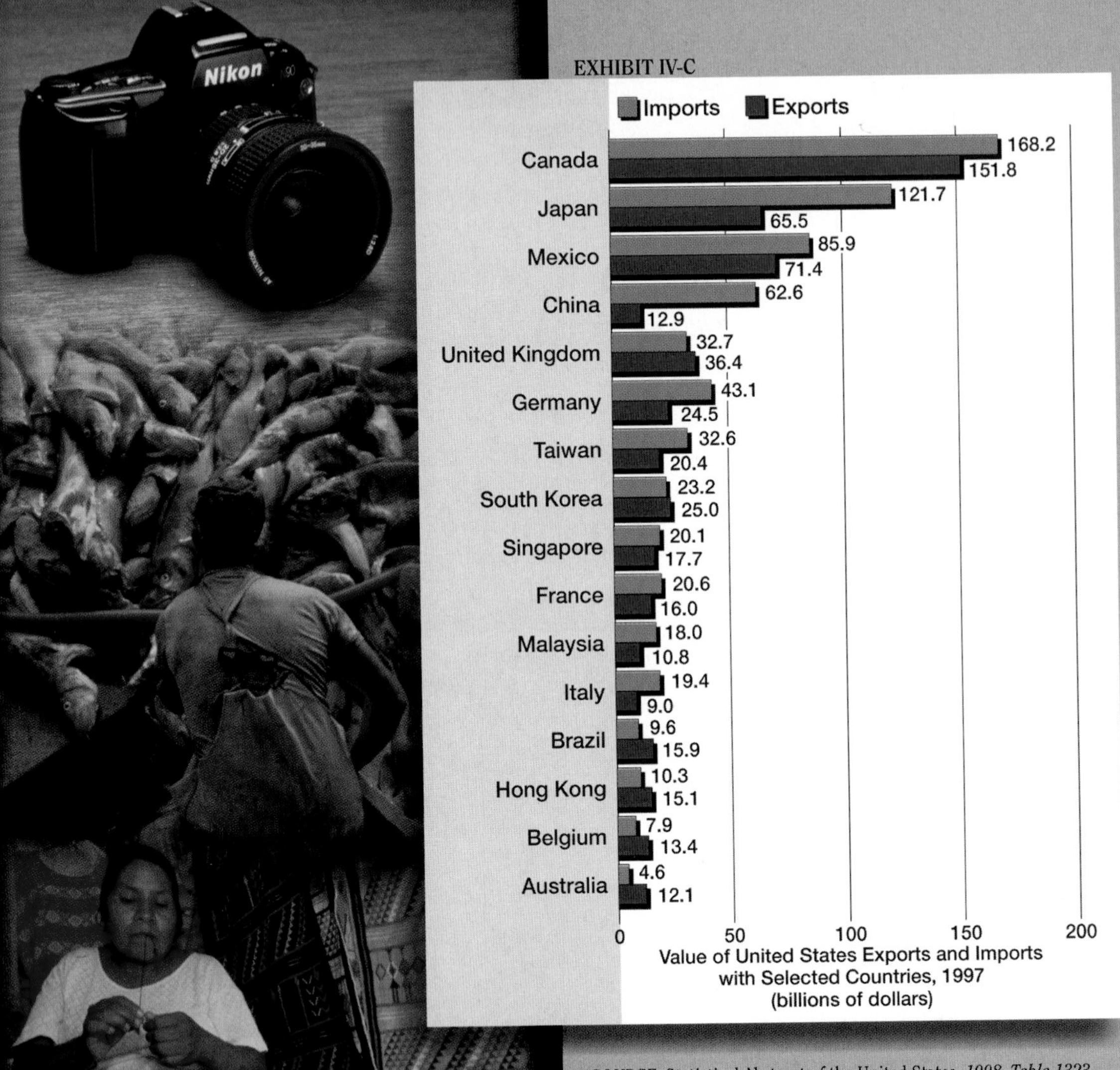

SOURCE: Statistical Abstract of the United States, *1998, Table 1323.*

TRADE GENERATES FOREIGN EXCHANGE TRANSACTIONS

Although the same general principles apply to trade among individuals, business firms, and nations, the latter generally involves the exchange of one currency for another. Thus, this section will analyze the impact of both international trade and the operation of the foreign exchange market.

CHAPTER 16

Free trade consists simply in letting people buy and sell as they want to buy and sell. It is protection [trade restrictions] that requires force, for it consists in preventing people from doing what they want to do.

Henry George[1]

Gaining from International Trade

CHAPTER FOCUS

- How has the magnitude of international trade changed in recent decades?
- Under what conditions can a nation gain from international trade?
- What impact do trade restrictions have on an economy?
- Do trade restrictions create jobs? Does trade with low-wage countries depress wage rates in high-wage countries like the United States?
- Why do nations adopt trade restrictions?
- How does the economic record of countries that impose trade restrictions compare with the record of those that follow more liberal trade policies?

---

[1]Henry George, *Protection or Free Trade* (1886; New York: Robert Schalkenbach Foundation, 1980), p. 47.

We live in a shrinking world. The breakfast of many Americans includes bananas from Honduras, coffee from Brazil, or hot chocolate made from Nigerian cocoa beans. Americans often drive a car produced by a Japanese or European manufacturer that consumes gasoline refined from petroleum extracted in Saudi Arabia or Venezuela. Similarly, many Americans work for companies that sell a substantial amount of their products to foreigners. Spurred by cost reductions in transportation and communications, the volume of international trade has grown rapidly in recent decades. Approximately 21 percent of the world's total output is now sold in a country other than that in which it was produced—double the figure of four decades ago.

Perhaps surprising to some, most international trade is not between the governments of the nations involved but rather between individuals and business firms that happen to be located in different countries. Why do people engage in international trade? The expectation of gain provides the answer. Domestic producers are often able to sell their products to foreigners at attractive prices, while domestic consumers sometimes find that the best deals are available from foreign suppliers. Like other voluntary exchange, international trade results because both the buyer and the seller expect to gain and generally do. If both parties did not expect to gain, they would not agree to the exchange.

CROSS COUNTRY DIFFERENCES IN THE SIZE OF THE TRADE SECTOR

The size of the trade sector varies substantially among nations. Some of the difference is due to size of country. For industries in which economies of scale are important, the domestic market of a less-populated country may not be large enough to support cost-efficient firms. Therefore, in small countries, firms in such industries will tend to export a larger share of their output, and consumers will be more likely to purchase goods produced abroad. As a result, the size of the trade sector as a share of the economy tends to be inversely related to the population of the country.

Even among countries of similar size, there is considerable variation in the size of the trade sector. (See Illustrated Exhibit IV-A at the beginning of this section for evidence on this point.) Among the countries with a large population (120 million or more), the trade sector is largest in Indonesia. In 1997, exports accounted for 28 percent of the Indonesian output, compared to 20 percent for China, 12 percent for India, and 11 percent for the United States. The trade sectors of Japan and Brazil were even smaller: 9 percent and 6 percent, respectively. Among the mid-size countries (population between 40 million and 65 million), the trade sectors of Thailand, Philippines, and South Korea are quite large, while those of Egypt, Turkey, and France are small. As a share of domestic output, Singapore and Hong Kong have the largest international trade sectors in the world. Both import large quantities of raw materials and unfinished goods and manufacture them into products that are often exported abroad. Therefore, the gross exports of these two vibrant trade centers actually exceed their gross domestic product.

THE TRADE SECTOR OF THE UNITED STATES

As **Exhibit 16–1** illustrates, the size of the trade sector of the United States has grown rapidly during the last several decades. In 1960, total exports of goods and services accounted for less than 4 percent of the U.S. economy, while imports summed to nearly 5 percent. By 1980, both exports and imports were approximately 7 percent of the economy. Since 1980 the size of the trade sector *as a share of the economy* has approximately doubled. In 1998, exports accounted for 13 percent of total output, while imports summed to 16.1 percent.[2]

Who are the major trading partners of Americans? Canada, Japan, and Mexico head the list. In 1997, approximately 42 percent of U.S. exports were sold to purchasers in these three countries. Canadians purchased 22 percent of U.S. exports, while Mexicans purchased 11 percent, and Japanese 10 percent. These three countries also supplied approximately 42 percent of the U.S. imports—19 percent by Canadians, 14 percent by Japanese, and 10 percent by Mexicans. The nations of the European Union (particularly Germany, the United Kingdom, France, and Italy), China (including Hong Kong), and several other smaller Asian countries (Taiwan, South Korea, Singapore, and Malaysia) are also major trading partners of the United States. (See Illustrated Exhibit IV-C for additional details.)

EXHIBIT 16–1

THE GROWTH OF THE TRADE SECTOR IN THE UNITED STATES: 1960–1998

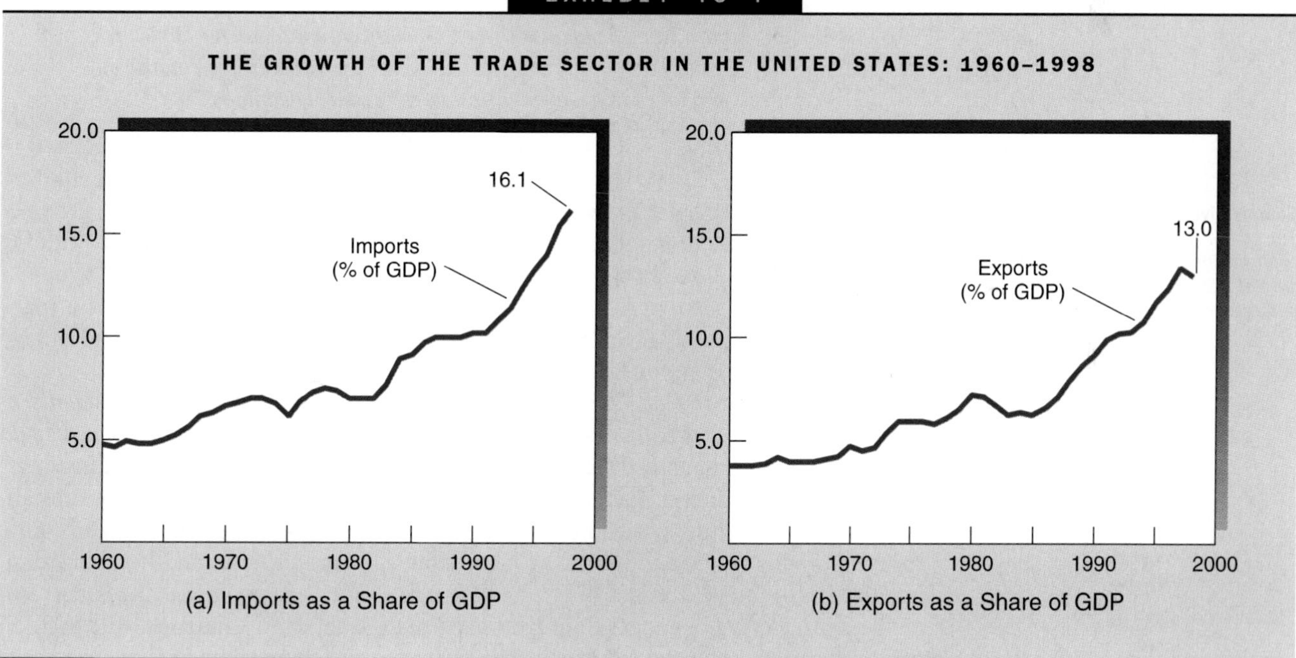

During the past several decades, international trade has grown more rapidly than total output. The growth of the trade sector has been exceedingly rapid since 1980. Imports rose from 7 percent of GDP in 1980 to 16.1 percent in 1998. During the same period, exports rose from 7 percent to 13 percent of GDP.

SOURCE: Economic Report of the President, 1998, *Table B-2. The figures are based on data for real imports, exports, and GDP.*

[2]These calculations are based on the real values of exports, imports, and GDP. If the nominal figures had been used to make the calculations, the size of the trade sector would be slightly smaller in recent years.

What are the leading imports and exports of the United States? The U.S. both imports and exports a substantial quantity of capital goods, such as automobiles, computers, semiconductors, telecommunications equipment, and industrial machines. The markets for these items are worldwide. Producers in the United States sell substantial quantities abroad, while, at the same time, many U.S. consumers purchase these goods from foreign manufacturers. Civilian aircraft, electrical equipment, chemicals, and plastics are also among the leading export products of the United States, while crude oil, textiles, toys, sporting goods, and pharmaceutical products are major imports. (See Illustrated Exhibit IV-B for additional details.)

Clearly, the impact of international trade differs across industries. In some industries, domestic producers find it very difficult to compete with their rivals abroad. For example, approximately 90 percent of the shoes purchased by Americans and nearly two-thirds of the radio and television sets, watches, and motorcycles are produced abroad. Imports also supply a high percentage of the clothing and textile products, paper, cut diamonds, and VCRs consumed in the United States. On the other hand, a large proportion of the aircraft, power-generating equipment, scientific instruments, construction equipment, and fertilizers produced in the United States is exported to purchasers abroad.

GAINS FROM SPECIALIZATION AND TRADE

If a foreign country can supply us with a commodity cheaper than we ourselves can make it, [we had] better buy it of them with some part of our own industry, employed in a way in which we have some advantage.

Adam Smith[3]

Comparative advantage
The ability to produce a good at a lower opportunity cost than others can produce it. Relative costs determine comparative advantage.

As we discussed in Chapter 2, the law of **comparative advantage** explains why a group of individuals, regions, or nations can gain from specialization and exchange. Trading partners can gain if each specializes in the production of the goods for which it is a low-opportunity-cost producer and trades for those goods for which it is a high-opportunity-cost producer. Specialization in the area of one's comparative advantage minimizes the cost of production and leads to maximum joint output.

International trade leads to mutual gain because it allows the residents of each country to: (1) specialize more fully in the production of those things that they do best, and (2) import goods when foreigners are willing to supply them at a lower cost than domestic producers. Labor-force skills and resource endowments differ substantially across countries. These differences influence costs. Therefore, a good that is quite costly to produce in one country may be economically produced in another. For example, the warm, moist climate of Brazil, Colombia, and Guatemala enhances the economical production of coffee. Countries like Saudi Arabia and Venezuela with rich oil fields can produce petroleum cheaply. Countries with an abundance of fertile land, like Canada and Australia, are able to produce products like wheat, feed grains, and beef at a low cost. In contrast, land is scarce in Japan, a nation with a highly skilled labor force. The Japanese, therefore, specialize in manufacturing, using their comparative advantage to produce cameras, automobiles, and electronic products for export. With international trade, the residents of each country can gain by specializing in the production

[3]Adam Smith, *An Inquiry into the Nature and Causes of the Wealth of Nations* (1776; Cannan's ed., Chicago: University of Chicago Press, 1976), pp. 478–479.

of goods that they can produce economically and using the proceeds to import goods that would be expensive to produce domestically.

Because failure to comprehend the principle of mutual gains from trade is often a source of "fuzzy thinking," we will take the time to illustrate the principle in detail. To keep things simple, we will consider a case involving only two countries, the United States and Japan, and two products, food and clothing. Furthermore, we will assume that labor is the only resource used to produce these products. In addition, since we want to illustrate that gains from trade are nearly always possible, we are going to assume that Japan has an **absolute advantage**—that the Japanese workers are more efficient than the Americans—in the production of both commodities. **Exhibit 16–2** illustrates this situation. Perhaps due to their prior experience or higher skill level, Japanese workers can produce three units of food per day, compared with only two units per day for U.S. workers. Similarly, Japanese workers are able to produce nine units of clothing per day, compared to one unit of clothing per day for U.S. workers.

Absolute advantage
A situation in which a nation, as the result of its previous experience and/or natural endowments, can produce more of a good (with the same amount of resources) than another nation.

Let us consider the following question: Can two countries gain from trade if one of them can produce both goods with fewer resources? Perhaps surprising to some, the answer is yes. As long as *relative* production costs of the two goods differ between Japan and the United States, gains from trade will be possible. Consider what would happen if the United States shifted three workers from the clothing industry to the food industry. This reallocation of labor would allow the United States to expand its food output by six units (two units per worker), while clothing output would decline by three units (one unit per worker). Suppose Japan reallocates labor in the opposite direction. When Japan moves one worker from the food industry to the clothing industry, Japanese clothing production expands by nine units while food output declines by three units. The exhibit shows that this reallocation of labor *within* the two countries has increased their joint output by three units of food and six units of clothing.

The source of this increase in output is straightforward: Aggregate output expands because the reallocation of labor permits each country to specialize more fully in the production of those goods that it can produce at a *relatively* low cost. Our old friend, the opportunity-cost concept, reveals the low-cost producer of each good. If Japanese workers produce one additional unit of food, they sacrifice the production of three units of clothing. Therefore, in Japan the opportunity cost of one unit of food is three units of clothing. On the other hand, one unit of food in the United States can be produced at an opportunity cost of only one-half unit of clothing. American workers

EXHIBIT 16–2

GAINS FROM SPECIALIZATION AND TRADE

	Output per Worker Day		Potential Change in Output[a]	
Country	Food (1)	Clothing (2)	Food (3)	Clothing (4)
United States	2	1	+6	−3
Japan	3	9	−3	+9
Change in Total Output			+3	+6

[a]Change in output if the United States shifts three workers from the clothing to the food industry and if Japan shifts one worker from the food to the clothing industry.

Columns 1 and 2 indicate the daily output of either food or clothing of each worker in the United States and Japan. If the United States moves 3 workers from the clothing industry to the food industry, it can produce 6 more units of food and 3 fewer units of clothing. Similarly, if Japan moves 1 worker from food to clothing, clothing output will increase by 9 units while food output will decline by 3 units. With this reallocation of labor, the United States and Japan are able to increase their aggregate output of both food (3 additional units) and clothing (6 additional units).

are therefore the low-opportunity-cost producers of food, even though they cannot produce as much food per day as the Japanese workers. Simultaneously, Japan is the low-opportunity-cost producer of clothing. The opportunity cost of producing a unit of clothing in Japan is only one-third unit of food, compared to two units of food in the United States. The reallocation of labor illustrated in Exhibit 16–2 expanded joint output because it moved resources in both countries toward areas where they had a comparative advantage.

As long as the relative costs of producing the two goods differ in the two countries, gains from specialization and trade will be possible. When this is the case, each country will find it cheaper to trade for goods that can be produced only at a high opportunity cost. For example, both countries can gain if the United States trades food to Japan for clothing at a trading ratio greater than one unit of food equals one-half unit of clothing (the U.S. opportunity cost of food) but less than one unit of food equals three units of clothing (the Japanese opportunity cost of food). Any trading ratio between these two extremes will permit the United States to acquire clothing more cheaply than it could be produced within the country and simultaneously permit Japan to acquire food more cheaply than it could be produced domestically.

How Trade Expands Consumption Possibilities

Because trade permits nations to expand their joint output, it also allows each nation to expand its consumption possibilities. The production-possibilities concept can be used to illustrate this point. Suppose that there were 200 million workers in the United States and 50 million in Japan. Given these figures and the productivity of workers indicated in Exhibit 16–2, the production-possibilities curves for the two countries are presented in **Exhibit 16–3.** If the United States used all of its 200 million workers in the food industry, it could produce 400 million units of food per day—two units per worker—and zero units of clothing (point *N*). Alternatively, if the United States used all its workers to produce clothing, daily output would be 200 million units of clothing

Here we illustrate the daily production possibilities of a U.S. labor force of 200 million workers and a Japanese labor force of 50 million workers, given the cost of producing food and clothing presented in Exhibit 16–2. In the absence of trade, consumption possibilities will be restricted to points such as U.S.$_1$ *in the United States and* J$_1$ *in Japan along the production possibilities curve of each country.*

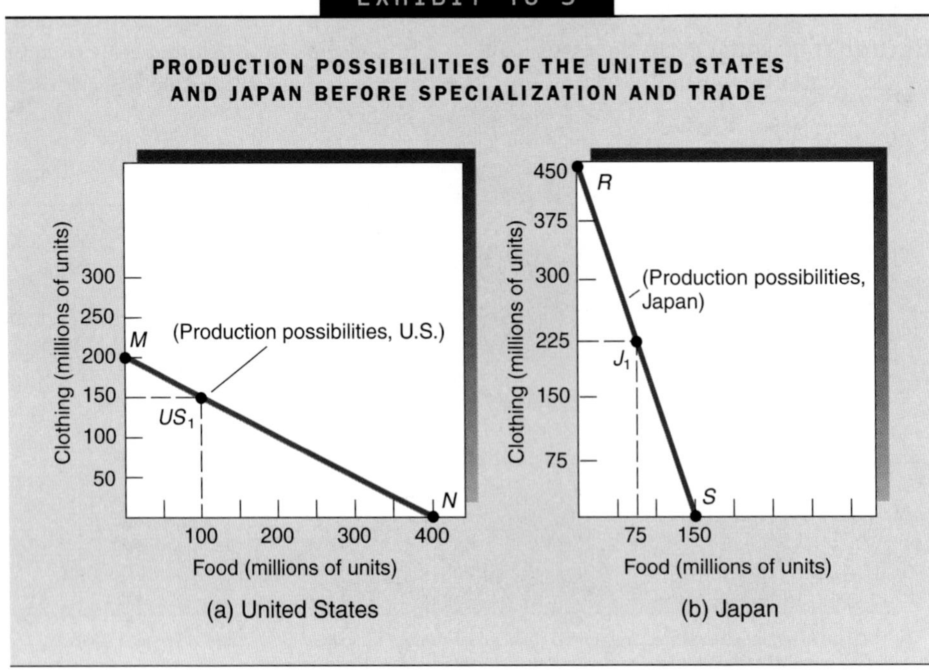

and no food (point M). Intermediate output combinations along the production-possibilities line (MN) intersecting these two extreme points also could be achievable. For example, the United States could produce 150 million units of clothing and 100 million units of food (point US_1).

Part b of Exhibit 16–3 illustrates the production possibilities of the 50 million Japanese workers. Japan could produce 450 million units of clothing and no food (R), 150 million units of food and no clothing (S), or various intermediate combinations, like 225 million units of clothing and 75 million units of food (J_1). The slope of the production-possibilities constraint reflects the opportunity cost of food relative to clothing. Because Japan is the high-opportunity-cost producer of food, its production-possibilities constraint is steeper than the constraint for the United States.

In the absence of trade, the consumption of each country is constrained by the country's production possibilities. Trade, however, expands the consumption possibilities of both. As we previously indicated, both countries can gain from specialization if the United States trades food to Japan at a price greater than one unit of food equals one-half unit of clothing but less than one unit of food equals three units of clothing. Suppose that they agree on an intermediate price of one unit of food equals one unit of clothing. As part a of **Exhibit 16–4** illustrates, when the United States specializes in the production of food (where it has a comparative advantage) and trades food for clothing (at the price ratio where one unit of food equals one unit of clothing), it can consume

EXHIBIT 16–4

CONSUMPTION POSSIBILITIES WITH TRADE

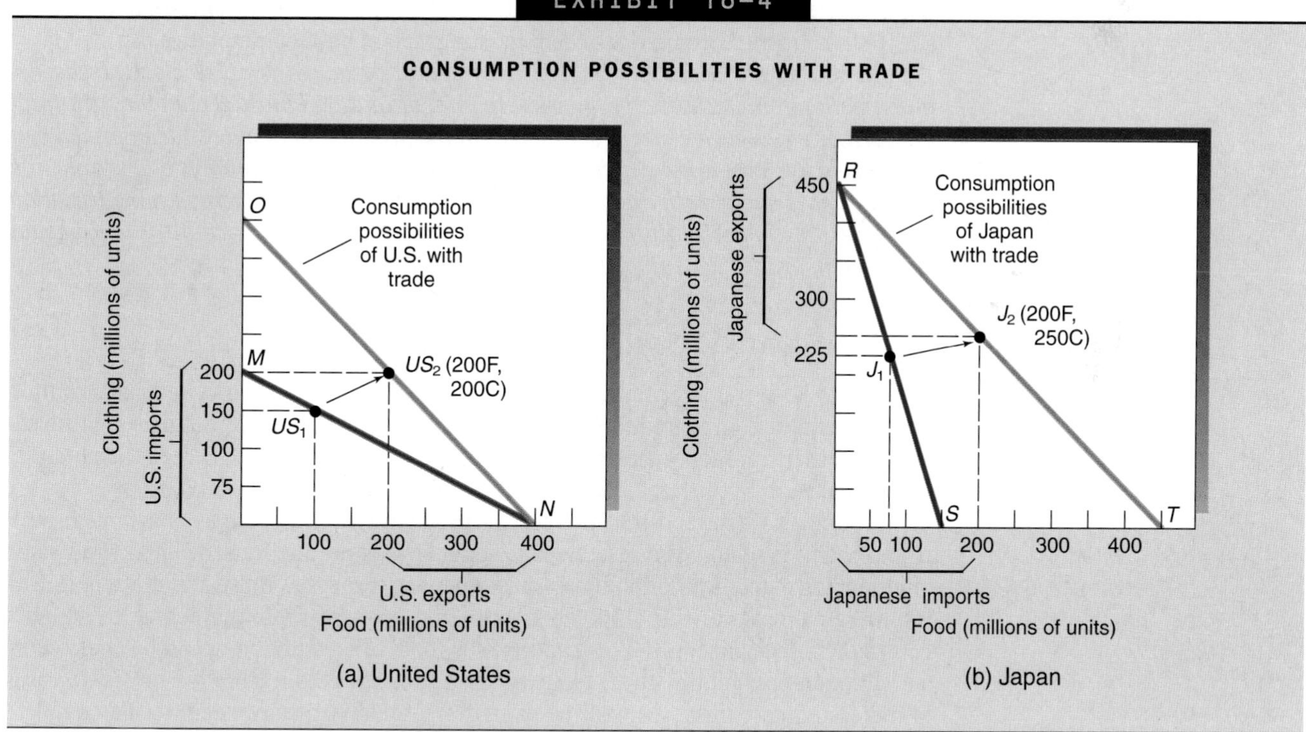

With specialization and trade, the consumption possibilities of a country can be expanded. If the United States can trade one unit of clothing for one unit of food, it can specialize in the production of food and consume along the ON *line (rather than its original production-possibilities constraint,* MN*). Similarly, when Japan is able to trade one unit of clothing for one unit of food, it can specialize in the production of clothing and consume any combination along the line* RT*. For example, with specialization and trade, the United States could increase its consumption from* US_1 *to* US_2*, gaining 50 million units of clothing and 100 million units of food. Simultaneously, Japan could increase consumption from* J_1 *to* J_2*, a gain of 125 million units of food and 25 million units of clothing.*

along the line *ON*. If the United States insisted on self-sufficiency, it would be restricted to consumption possibilities like US_1 (100 million units of food and 150 million units of clothing) along its production-possibilities constraint of *MN*. With trade, however, the United States can achieve such combinations as US_2 (200 million units of food and 200 million units of clothing) along the line *ON*. Trade permits the United States to expand its consumption of both goods.

Simultaneously, Japan is able to expand its consumption of both goods when it is able to trade clothing for food at the one-to-one price ratio. As part b of Exhibit 16–4 illustrates, Japan can specialize in the production of clothing and consume along the constraint *RT* when it can trade one unit of clothing for one unit of food. Without trade, consumption in Japan would be limited to points like J_1 (75 million units of food and 225 million units of clothing) along the line *RS*. With trade, however, it is able to consume combinations like J_2 (200 million units of food and 250 million units of clothing) along the constraint *RT*.

Look what happens when Japan specializes in clothing and the United States specializes in food. Japan can produce 450 million units of clothing, export 200 million to the United States (for 200 million units of food), and still have 250 million units of clothing remaining for domestic consumption. Simultaneously, the United States can produce 400 million units of food, export 200 million to Japan (for 200 million units of clothing), and still have 200 million units of food left for domestic consumption. After specialization and trade, the United States is able to consume at the point of US_2 and Japan at point J_2, consumption levels that would otherwise be unattainable. Specialization and exchange permit the two countries to expand their joint output, and, as a result, both countries can increase their consumption of both commodities.

The implications of the law of comparative advantage are clear: Trade between nations will lead to an expansion in total output and mutual gain for each trading partner when each country specializes in the production of goods it can produce at a relatively low cost and uses the proceeds to buy goods that it could produce only at a high cost. It is comparative advantage that matters. As long as there is some variation in the relative opportunity cost of goods across countries, each country will always have a comparative advantage in the production of some goods.

Some Real-World Considerations

In order to keep things simple, we ignored the potential importance of transportation costs, which, of course, reduce the potential gains from trade. Sometimes transportation and other transaction costs, both real and artificially imposed, exceed the potential for mutual gain. In this case, exchange does not occur.

We also assumed that the cost of producing each good was constant in each country. This is seldom the case. Beyond some level of production, the opportunity cost of producing a good will often increase as a country produces more and more of it. Rising marginal costs as the output of a good expands will limit the degree to which a country will specialize in the production of a good. This situation would be depicted by a production-possibilities curve that was convex, or bowed out from the origin. In cases of increasing cost there will still be gains from trade but there need not be complete specialization.

Additional Sources of Gain from International Trade

In addition to the gains derived from specialization in areas of comparative advantage, there are two other important sources of gains from international trade.

1. Gains from Economies of Scale and Expansion in the Size of the Market. *International trade allows both domestic producers and consumers to gain from reductions in per-unit costs that often accompany large-scale production, marketing, and distribution.* Trade expands the potential size of the market available to both domestic and foreign firms. When economies of scale are important in an industry, successful domestic firms will be able to produce larger outputs and achieve lower costs than would be possible if they were unable to sell abroad. This point is particularly important for small countries. For example, textile manufacturers in Malaysia, Taiwan, and South Korea would have much higher costs if they could not sell abroad. The domestic textile markets of these countries are too small to support large, low-cost firms in this industry. With international trade, however, textile firms in these countries operate at a large scale and compete quite effectively in the world market.

International trade also benefits domestic consumers by permitting them to purchase from large-scale producers abroad. The aircraft industry provides a vivid illustration of this point. Given the huge design and engineering costs, the domestic market of almost all countries would be substantially less than the quantity required for the efficient production of jet planes. With international trade, however, consumers around the world are able to purchase planes economically from large-scale producers like Boeing.

2. Gains from More Competitive Markets. *International trade promotes competition in domestic markets and allows consumers to purchase a wide variety of goods at economical prices.* Competition from abroad helps keep domestic producers on their toes. It forces them to improve the quality of their products and keep costs low. At the same time, the variety of goods that are available from abroad provides consumers with a much broader array of choices than would be available in the absence of international trade.

The recent experience of the U.S. automobile industry illustrates this point. Faced with stiff competition from Japanese firms, U.S. automobile manufacturers worked hard to improve the quality of their vehicles. As a result, the reliability of the

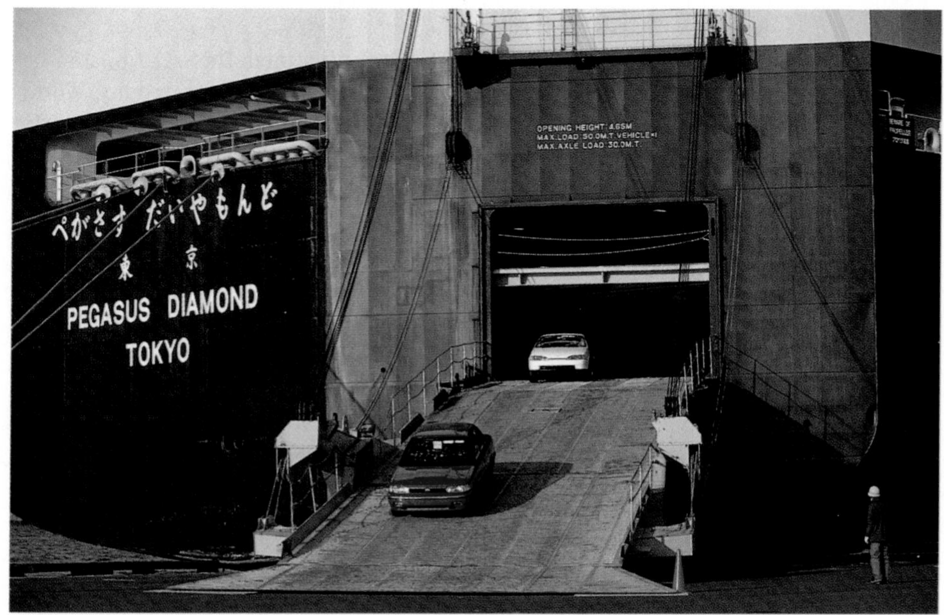

More than one-fifth of the world's output is produced in one country and sold in another. The gains from specialization, division of labor, and adoption of mass-production methods that accompany international trade allow the trading partners to achieve a larger output and higher living standards than would otherwise be the case.

automobiles and light trucks available to American consumers—including those vehicles produced by domestic manufacturers—is almost certainly higher than would have been the case in the absence of competition from abroad.

EXPORT-IMPORT LINK

Doubts about the merits of international trade often result from a failure to consider all the consequences. Why are other nations willing to export their goods to the United States? So they can obtain dollars. Yes, but why do they want dollars? Would foreigners be willing to continue exporting oil, radios, watches, cameras, automobiles, and thousands of other valuable products to Americans in exchange for pieces of paper? If so, Americans could all be semiretired, spending only an occasional workday at the dollar printing-press office! Of course, foreigners are not so naive. They trade goods for dollars so they can use the dollars to buy U.S. goods and purchase ownership rights to U.S. assets.

Exports, broadly perceived to include goods, services, and assets, provide the buying power that makes it possible for a nation to import. If a nation did not export goods, it would not have the foreign currency that is required for the purchase of imports. Similarly, if a nation did not import goods, foreigners would not have the purchasing power to buy that nation's export products. Therefore, if imports decline, so will the demand for the nation's exports. Exports and imports are closely linked.

SUPPLY, DEMAND, AND INTERNATIONAL TRADE

How does international trade affect prices and output levels in domestic markets? Supply and demand analysis will help us answer this question. Given our modern transportation and communication networks, the market for many commodities is worldwide. When a product can be transported long distances at a low cost (relative to its value), the domestic price of the product is in effect determined by the forces of supply and demand in the worldwide market.

Using soybeans as an example, **Exhibit 16–5** illustrates this relationship between the domestic and world markets for an internationally traded commodity. Worldwide market conditions determine the price of soybeans. In an open economy, domestic producers are free to sell and domestic consumers are free to buy the product at the world market price (P_w). At this price, U.S. producers will supply Q_p, while U.S. consumers will purchase Q_c. Reflecting their comparative advantage, U.S. soybean producers will export $Q_p - Q_c$ units at the world market price.

Let us compare the open-economy outcome with the situation in the absence of trade. If U.S. producers were not allowed to export soybeans, the domestic price would be determined by the domestic supply (S_d) and demand (D_d) only. A lower "no-trade" price (P_n) would emerge. Who are the winners and losers as the result of free trade in soybeans? Clearly, soybean producers gain. Free trade allows domestic producers to sell a larger quantity (Q_p rather than Q_n). As a result, the net revenues of soybean producers will rise by $P_w bcP_n$. On the other hand, domestic consumers of soybeans will have to pay a higher price under free trade. Consumers will lose (1) because they have to pay P_w rather than P_n for the Q_c units they purchase, and (2) because they lose the consumer surplus on the $Q_n - Q_c$ units now purchased at the higher price. Thus, free trade imposes a net cost of $P_w acP_n$ on consumers. As can be seen in Exhibit 16–5,

EXHIBIT 16–5

PRODUCER BENEFITS FROM EXPORTS

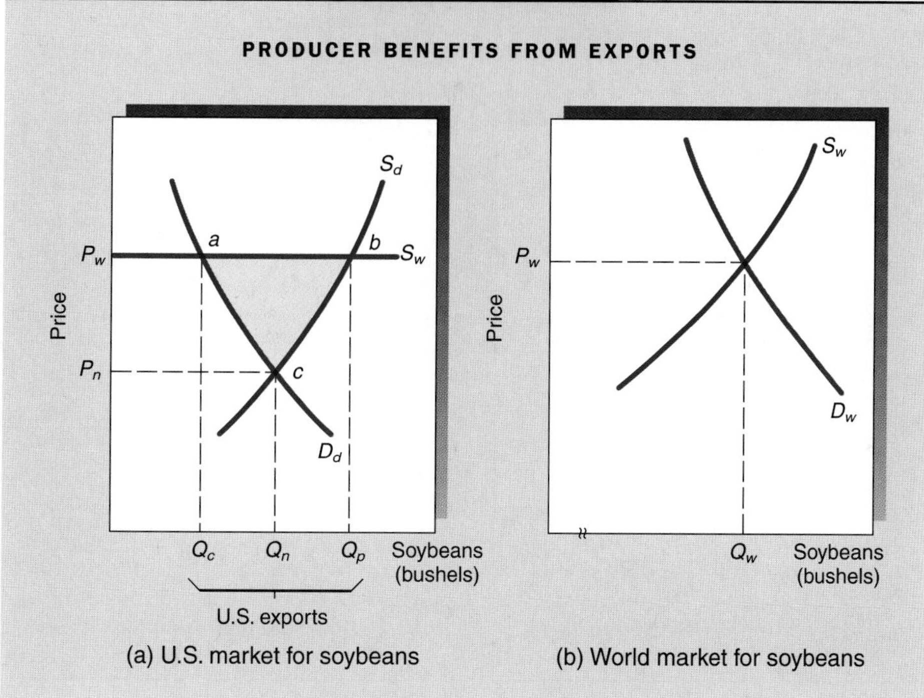

The price of soybeans and other internationally traded commodities is determined by the forces of supply and demand in the world market (b). If U.S. soybean producers were prohibited from selling to foreigners, the domestic price would be P_n *(a). Free trade permits the U.S. soybean producers to sell* Q_p *units at the higher world price (*P_w*). The quantity* $Q_p - Q_c$ *is exported abroad. Compared to the no-trade situation, the producers' gain from the higher price (*$P_w bcP_n$*) exceeds the cost imposed on domestic consumers (*$P_w acP_n$*) by the triangle* abc.

however, the gains of producers outweigh the losses to consumers by the triangle *abc*. Free trade leads to a net welfare gain.

When one focuses only on an export product, it appears that free trade benefits producers relative to consumers—but this ignores the secondary effects. How will foreigners generate the dollars they need to purchase the export products of the United States? If foreigners do not sell goods to Americans, they will not have the purchasing power necessary to purchase goods from Americans. U.S. imports—that is, the purchase of goods from low-cost foreign producers—provide foreigners with the dollar purchasing power necessary to buy U.S. exports. In turn, the lower prices in the import-competitive markets will benefit the U.S. consumers who appeared at first glance to be harmed by the higher prices (compared to the no-trade situation) in export markets.

Exhibit 16–6 illustrates the impact of imports, using shoes as an example. In the absence of trade, the price of shoes in the domestic market would be P_n, the intersection of the domestic supply and demand curves. However, the world price of shoes is P_w. In an open economy, many U.S. consumers would take advantage of the low shoe prices available from foreign producers. At the lower world price, U.S. consumers would purchase Q_c units of shoes, importing $Q_c - Q_p$ from foreign producers.

Compared to the no-trade situation, free trade in shoes results in lower prices and an expansion in domestic consumption. The lower prices lead to a net consumer gain of $P_n abP_w$. Domestic producers lose $P_n acP_w$ in the form of lower sales prices and reductions in output. However, the net gain of consumers exceeds the net loss of producers by *abc*.

For an open economy, international competition directs the resources of a nation toward the areas of competitive advantage. When domestic producers have a comparative advantage in the production of a good, they will be able to compete effectively

EXHIBIT 16-6

CONSUMER BENEFITS FROM IMPORTS

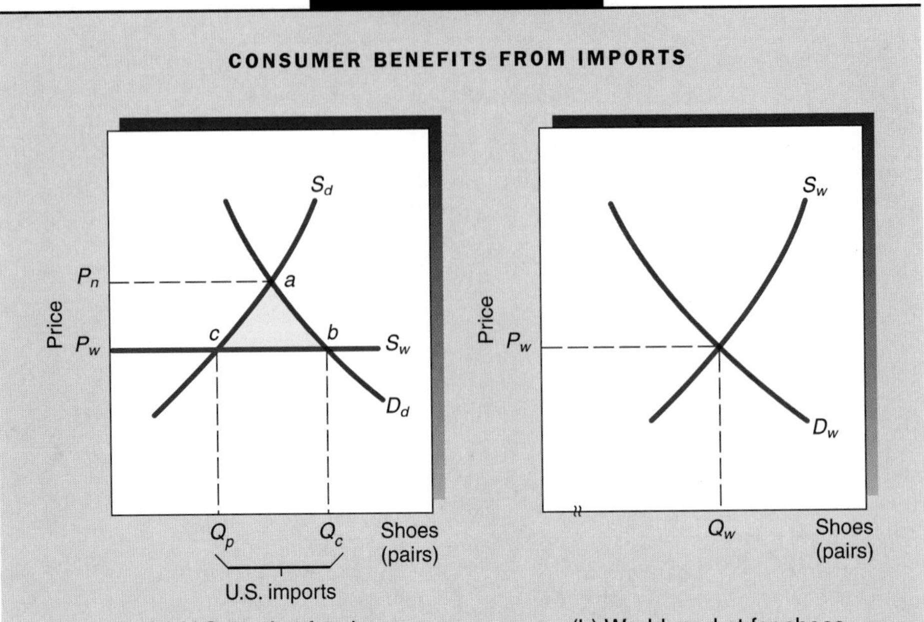

In the absence of trade, the domestic price of shoes would be P_n*. Since many foreign producers have a comparative advantage in the production of shoes, international trade leads to lower prices. At the world price* P_w*, U.S. consumers will demand* Q_c *units, of which* $Q_c - Q_p$ *are imported. Compared to the no-trade situation, consumers gain* P_nabP_w*, while domestic producers lose* P_nacP_w*. A net gain of* abc *results.*

in the world market and profit from the export of goods to foreigners. In turn, the exports will generate the purchasing power necessary to buy goods that foreigners can supply more economically.

International trade and specialization result in lower prices (and higher domestic consumption) for imported products and higher prices (and lower domestic consumption) for exported products. More important, trade permits the residents of each nation to concentrate on the things they do best (produce at a low cost), while trading for those they do least well. The result is an expansion in both output and consumption compared to what could be achieved in the absence of trade.

The pattern of U.S. exports and imports is consistent with this view. The United States is a nation with a technically skilled labor force, fertile farmland, and substantial capital formation. Thus, we export computers, aircraft, power-generating equipment, scientific instruments, and land-intensive agricultural products—items we are able to produce at a comparatively low cost. Simultaneously, we import substantial amounts of petroleum, textile (clothing) products, shoes, coffee, and diamonds—goods costly for us to produce. Clearly, trade permits us to gain by specializing in those areas in which our comparative advantage is greatest.

ECONOMICS OF TRADE RESTRICTIONS

Despite the potential benefits from free trade, almost all nations have erected trade barriers. Tariffs, quotas, and exchange-rate controls are the most commonly used trade-restricting devices. Let us consider how various types of trade restrictions influence the economy.

Economics of Tariffs

A **tariff** is nothing more than a tax on imports from foreign countries. As **Exhibit 16–7** shows, average tariff rates of between 30 percent and 50 percent of product value were often levied prior to 1945. The notorious Smoot-Hawley trade bill of 1930 pushed the average tariff rate upward to 60 percent. Many economists believe that this legislation was a major contributing factor to the length and severity of the Great Depression. During the past 50 years, the tariff rates of the United States have declined substantially. In 1997, the average tariff rate on imported goods was only 2.2 percent.

Tariff
A tax levied on goods imported into a country.

Exhibit 16–8 illustrates the impact of a tariff on automobiles. In the absence of a tariff, the world market price of P_w would prevail in the domestic market. At that price, U.S. consumers purchase Q_1 units. Domestic producers supply Q_{d1}, while foreigners supply $Q_1 - Q_{d1}$ units to the U.S. market. When the United States levies a tariff, t, on automobiles, Americans can no longer buy cars at the world price. U.S. consumers now have to pay $P_w + t$ to purchase an automobile from foreigners. At that price, domestic consumers demand Q_2 units (Q_{d2} supplied by domestic producers and $Q_2 - Q_{d2}$ supplied by foreigners). The tariff results in a higher price and lower level of domestic consumption.

The tariff benefits domestic producers and the government at the expense of consumers. Since they do not pay the tariff, domestic producers will expand their output in response to the higher (protected) market price. In effect, the tariff acts as a subsidy to domestic producers. Domestic producers gain the area S (Exhibit 16–8) in the form of additional net revenues. The tariff raises revenues equal to the area T for the government. The areas U and V represent costs imposed on consumers that do not benefit either producers or the government. Simply put, U and V represent a *deadweight loss* (loss of efficiency).

As a result of the tariff, resources that could have been used to produce goods that U.S. firms produce efficiently (compared to producers abroad) are diverted into the

EXHIBIT 16–7

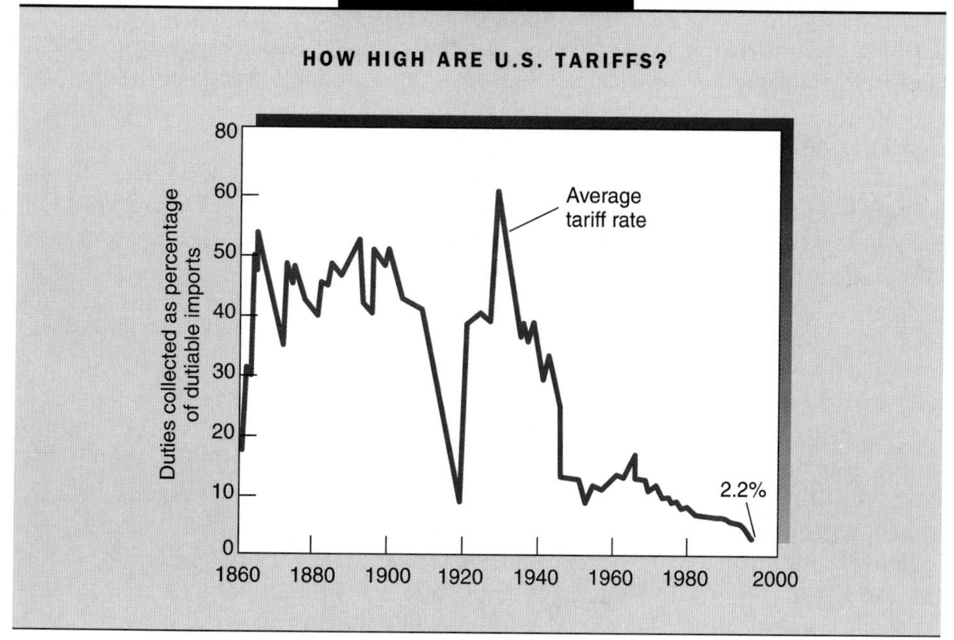

Tariff rates in the United States fell sharply during the period from 1935 to 1950. Subsequently, after rising slightly during the 1950s, they have trended downward since 1960. In 1997, the average tariff rate on merchandise imports was 2.2 percent.

EXHIBIT 16–8

IMPACT OF A TARIFF

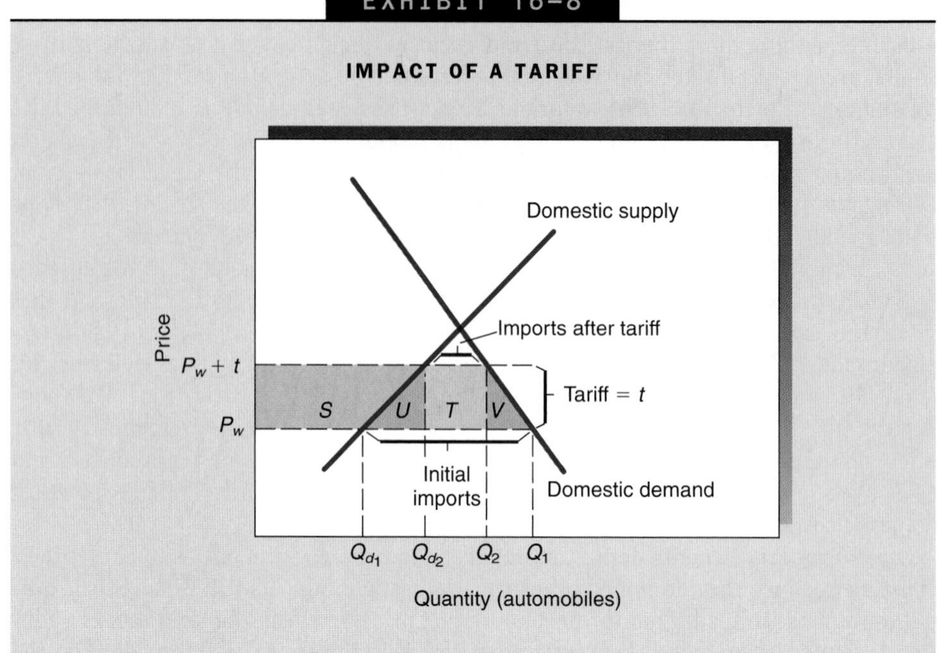

Here we illustrate the impact of a tariff on automobiles. In the absence of the tariff, the world price of automobiles is P_w*: U.S. consumers purchase* Q_1 *units (*Q_{d1}*) from domestic producers plus* $Q_1 - Q_{d1}$ *from foreign producers). The tariff makes it more costly for Americans to purchase automobiles from foreigners. Imports decline and the domestic price increases. Consumers lose the sum of the areas* S + U + T + V *in the form of higher prices and a reduction in consumer surplus. Producers gain the area* S *and the tariff generates* T *tax revenues for the government. The areas* U *and* V *are deadweight losses due to a reduction in allocative efficiency.*

production of automobiles. Thus, we end up producing less in areas where we have a comparative advantage and more in areas where we are a high-cost producer. Potential gains from specialization and trade go unrealized.

Economics of Quotas

Import quota
A specific limit or maximum quantity (or value) of a good permitted to be imported into a country during a given period.

An **import quota,** like a tariff, is designed to restrict foreign goods and protect domestic industries. A quota places a ceiling on the amount of a product that can be imported during a given period (typically a year). The United States imposes quotas on several products, including brooms, steel, shoes, sugar, dairy products, and peanuts. As in the case of tariffs, the primary purpose of quotas is to protect domestic industries from foreign competition.

Since 1953 the United States has imposed a quota to limit the importation of peanuts to 1.7 million pounds per year, approximately two peanuts per American. Using peanuts as an example, **Exhibit 16–9** illustrates the impact of a quota. If there were no trade restraints, the domestic price of peanuts would be equal to the world market price (P_w). Under those circumstances, Americans would purchase Q_1 units. At the price P_w, domestic producers would supply Q_{d1}, and the amount $Q_1 - Q_{d1}$ would be imported from foreign producers.

Now consider what happens when a quota limits imports to $Q_2 - Q_{d2}$, a quantity well below the free-trade level of imports. Since the quota reduces the foreign supply of peanuts to the domestic market, the price of the quota-protected product increases (to P_2). At the higher price, U.S. consumers will reduce their purchases to Q_2, and domestic producers will happily expand their production to Q_{d2}. With regard to the welfare of consumers, the impact of a quota is similar to that of a tariff. Consumers lose the area $S + U + T + V$ in the form of higher prices and the loss of consumer surplus. Similarly, domestic producers gain the area S, while the areas U and V represent deadweight losses from allocative inefficiency.

EXHIBIT 16–9

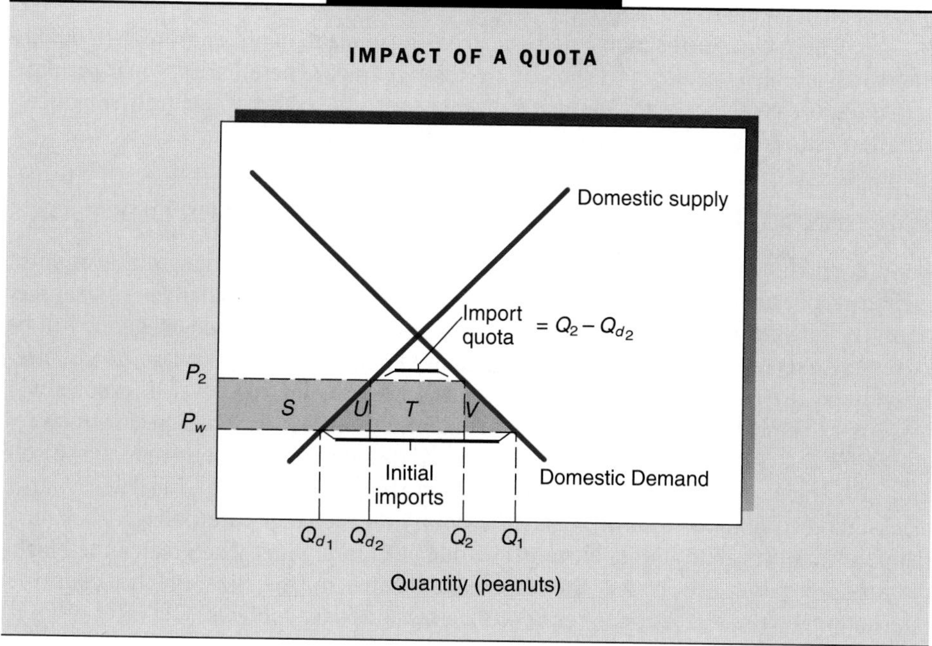

Here we illustrate the impact of a quota, such as the one the United States imposes on peanuts. The world market price of peanuts is P_w. *If there were no trade restraints, the domestic price would also be* P_w*, and the domestic consumption would be* Q_1. *Domestic producers would supply* Q_{d1} *units, while* $Q_1 - Q_{d1}$ *would be imported. A quota limiting imports to* $Q_2 - Q_{d2}$ *would push up the domestic price to* P_2. *At the higher price, the amount supplied by domestic producers increases to* Q_{d2}. *Consumers lose the sum of the area* S + U + T + V*, while domestic producers gain the area* S. *In contrast with tariffs, quotas generate no revenue for the government. The area* T *goes to foreign producers who are granted permission to sell in the U.S. market.*

However, there is a big difference between tariffs and quotas with regard to the area *T*. Under a tariff, the U.S. government would collect revenues equal to *T*, representing the tariff rate multiplied by the number of units imported. With a quota, however, these revenues will go to the foreign producers, who are granted import permits to sell in the U.S. market. Clearly, this right to sell at a premium price (since the domestic price exceeds the world market price) is extremely valuable. Thus, foreign producers will compete for the permits. They will hire lobbyists, make political contributions, and engage in other rent-seeking activities in an effort to secure the right to sell at a premium price in the U.S. market.

In many ways, quotas are more harmful than tariffs. With a quota, foreign producers are prohibited from selling additional units regardless of how much lower their costs are relative to those of domestic producers. In contrast with a tariff, a quota brings in no revenue for the government. While a tariff transfers revenue from U.S. consumers to the Treasury, quotas transfer these revenues to foreign producers. Obviously, this politically granted privilege creates a strong incentive for foreign producers to engage in wasteful rent-seeking activities. Thus, by rewarding both domestic producers with higher prices and foreign producers with valuable import permits, quotas generate two strong interest groups supportive of their continuation. As a result, removal of a quota is often even more difficult to achieve than a tariff reduction.

Other Nontariff Barriers to Trade

In order to avoid the imposition of other types of trade barriers, such as tariffs and quotas, foreign firms will sometimes agree to limit their exports to a country. Even though they are almost always the result of political pressure, agreements of this type are called **voluntary export restraints (VERs).** Japanese auto manufacturers have agreed to a VER on exports to the United States. The economic impact of a VER is similar to that of a quota. The higher selling price of the product that is caused by the VER

Voluntary export restraint (VER)
An agreement by foreign firms to limit their own exports.

creates a gain for both foreign and domestic producers, but hurts domestic consumers by more than an offsetting amount.

Other types of barriers, such as licensing requirements and product quality standards, are also used by governments to restrict trade. These barriers make it difficult and more costly for firms to import products into the country. Again these policies hurt domestic consumers but benefit domestic producers.

Exchange-Rate Controls as a Trade Restriction

Many countries, particularly less-developed countries, fix the exchange-rate value of their currency above the market rate and impose restrictions on exchange-rate transactions. At the official (artificially high) exchange rate, the country's export goods will be extremely expensive to foreigners. As a result, foreigners will purchase goods elsewhere, and the country's exports will be small. In turn, the low level of exports will make it extremely difficult for domestic residents to obtain the foreign currency required for the purchase of imports. Such exchange-rate controls both reduce the volume of trade and lead to black-market currency exchanges. Indeed, a large black-market premium indicates that the country's exchange-rate policy is substantially limiting the ability of its citizens to trade with foreigners. The greater the black-market premium, the larger the expected decline in the size of the country's international trade sector as the result of the exchange-rate controls.

WHY DO NATIONS ADOPT TRADE RESTRICTIONS?

> *Protective tariffs are as much applications of force as are blockading squadrons, and their objective is the same—to prevent trade. The difference between the two is that blockading squadrons are a means whereby nations seek to prevent their enemies from trading; protective tariffs are a means whereby nations attempt to prevent their own people from trading.*
>
> *Henry George*[4]

Physical obstacles, like bad roads and stormy weather, that increase transaction costs will retard the gains from trade. Tariffs, quotas, exchange-rate controls, and other human-made trade restrictions have similar effects. Henry George compared tariffs and other trade restrictions to a blockade (see quotation above). Both the blockade imposed by an enemy and a self-imposed blockade in the form of trade restrictions will retard the gains from specialization and exchange.

If trade restrictions promote inefficiency and reduce the potential gains from exchange, why do nations adopt them? Several factors play a role. First, there are some partially valid arguments for the protection of specific industries under certain circumstances. Second, economic illiteracy plays a role. Failing to comprehend the implications of the law of comparative advantage and the linkage between imports and exports, many people wrongly believe that trade restrictions increase employment and help keep the wages of Americans high. (See the accompanying Myths of Economics box on these topics.) Finally, and most important, trade restrictions reflect the political power of concentrated interests. We will now take a look at each of these factors.

---

[4]George, *Protection or Free Trade,* p. 47.

Partially Valid Arguments for Restrictions

There are three major, at least partially valid, arguments for protecting certain domestic industries from foreign competitors: the national-defense, infant-industry, and antidumping arguments.

National-Defense Argument. According to the national-defense argument, certain industries—aircraft, petroleum, and weapons, for example—are vital to national defense and therefore should be protected from foreign competitors so that a domestic supply of necessary materials would be available in case of an international conflict. Would we want to be entirely dependent on Arabian or Russian petroleum? Would complete dependence on French aircraft be wise? Many Americans would answer no, even if trade restrictions were required to prevent such dependence by preserving domestic industries.

Although the national-defense argument has some validity, it is often abused. Relatively few industries are truly vital to our national defense. If a resource is important for national defense, often it would make more sense to stockpile the resource during peacetime rather than follow protectionist policies to preserve a domestic industry. Furthermore, it is important to recognize that a strong economy capable of producing large volumes of the goods necessary to sustain a large war effort is itself part of a strong defense. Because the national-defense argument is often used by special interests to justify protection for their industry at the expense of the economy in general, the merits of each specific case must be carefully evaluated.

Infant-Industry Argument. Advocates of the infant-industry argument hold that new domestic industries should be protected from older, established foreign competitors. As the new industry matures, it will be able to stand on its own feet and compete effectively with foreign producers, at which time protection can be removed.

The infant-industry argument has a long and often notorious history. Alexander Hamilton used it to argue for the protection of early U.S. manufacturing. Although it is an argument for only temporary protection, the protection, once granted, is generally difficult to remove. For example, a century ago, this argument was used to gain tariff protection for the newly emerging steel industry in the United States. With time, the steel industry developed and became very powerful, both politically and economically. Despite this maturity, the tariffs remained. To this day, legislation continues to provide the steel industry with various protections that limit competition from abroad.

Anti-Dumping Argument. In some cases, **dumping,** the sale of goods abroad at a price below their cost (and below their price in the domestic market of the exporting nation), merely reflects the exporter's desire to penetrate a foreign market. In other instances, dumping may be prompted by export subsidies of foreign governments. At various times, it has been alleged that Argentina has dumped textiles, Korea has dumped steel, and Canada has dumped radial tires into the U.S. market. Dumping is illegal. The Trade Agreements Act of 1979 provides for special antidumping *duties* (tariffs) when a good is sold in the United States at a price lower than that found in the domestic market of the exporting nation.

Dumping
The sale of a good by a foreign supplier in another country at a price below that charged by the supplier in its home market.

Dumping generally benefits domestic consumers and imposes costs on domestic producers of goods for which the imports are good substitutes. The lower prices of the "dumped" goods permit consumers to obtain the goods more economically. Simultaneously, the lower prices make it more difficult for domestic producers of the goods to compete. Predictably, domestic producers (and their employees) are the major source of the charge that dumping is unfair.

MYTHS OF ECONOMICS

"Trade restrictions that prohibit foreign producers from selling their goods at lower prices than domestic producers will increase employment and protect American jobs."

Many people sincerely believe that trade restrictions increase employment and "save American jobs." This fallacious belief stems from a failure to consider the secondary effects of import restrictions on export industries. Tariffs, quotas, exchange-rate controls, and other trade restrictions may result in more employment *in industries shielded by the restraints,* but they will *destroy jobs in other industries.*

Remember, the sales from foreigners to us (our imports) provide them with the purchasing power required to buy from us (our exports). If foreigners are unable to sell as much to Americans, then they will have fewer dollars with which to buy from Americans. Therefore, a secondary effect accompanies trade restrictions: The demand for American export goods declines. As a result, output and employment in export industries will be smaller, offsetting any jobs saved in protected industries. Most noneconomists fail to recognize the link between a decline in imports due to trade restrictions and a decline in exports because foreigners have acquired fewer dollars. Thus, it is easy to see why this myth is so widely believed.

When trade restraints are lowered (or there is discussion about lowering them), predictably many workers and business officials in import-competitive industries will charge that jobs will be lost to foreign competitors. In contrast, the additional jobs in the export industries do not yet exist. No one will be saying, "I will not be employed next year if the trade restraints are not lowered." Because the jobs (and employees) in the import-competitive industries are highly visible, while the future jobs in the exporting industries are invisible, reducing trade restraints is very difficult.

Actually, the focus on jobs is misleading. After all, it is income and high productivity, not jobs, that are the sources of prosperity. The shift from less- to more-productive jobs is not without cost, but it is necessary if workers and the economy are going to reach their full potential. In essence, import restraints direct resources away from areas where domestic producers have a comparative advantage and into areas where domestic producers are relatively inefficient. Since fewer of our resources are used to produce things that we are good at (as indicated by our ability to compete effectively) and more resources are squandered attempting to produce things that we do poorly (as evidenced by our inability to compete in the world market), the per-capita output and income of Americans is lower than would be the case in the absence of the restraints.

Consider the following: If import restrictions are a good idea, why don't we use them to restrict trade among the 50 states? After all, think of all the jobs that are lost when, for example, Michigan "imports" oranges from Florida, apples from Washington, wheat from Kansas, and cotton from Georgia. All these products could be produced in Michigan. However, the residents of Michigan generally find it cheaper to "import" these commodities rather than produce them domestically. Michigan gains by using its resources to produce and "export" automobiles (and other goods it can produce economically) and then using the sales revenue to "import" goods that would be expensive to produce in Michigan.

Most people recognize that free trade among the 50 states is a major source of prosperity for each of the states. Similarly, most recognize that "imports" from other states do not destroy jobs—at least not for long. The source of gains from trade among nations is exactly the same as that from trade among people in different states. Free trade among the 50 states promotes prosperity; so, too, does free trade among nations.

Of course, sudden removal of trade barriers might harm producers and workers in protected industries. It may be costly to quickly transfer the protected resources to other, more productive activities. Gradual removal of the barriers would minimize this shock effect and the accompanying cost of relocation.

Economists generally emphasize two points with regard to dumping. First, dumping can, in a few instances, be used as a weapon to gain monopoly power. For example, if the foreign firm temporarily cuts its price below cost, it might eliminate domestic competition and later raise its price to a higher level after the domestic competitors have been driven from the market. However, this is usually not a feasible strategy. After all, domestic producers might reenter the market if the price rises in the future. In addition, alternative foreign suppliers limit the monopoly power of a producer attempting this strategy.

Second, the law of comparative advantage indicates that a country (as a whole) can gain from the purchase of foreign-produced goods when they are cheaper than domestic goods. This is true regardless of whether the low price of foreign goods reflects comparative advantage, subsidies by foreign governments, or poor business practices. Unless the foreign supplier is likely to monopolize the domestic market, there is little reason to believe that dumping harms the economy receiving the goods.

Special Interests and the Politics of Trade Restrictions

Protectionism is a politician's delight because it delivers visible benefits to the protected parties while imposing the costs as a hidden tax on the public.

Murray L. Weidenbaum[5]

Although trade restrictions arise from multiple sources, as Professor Weidenbaum points out, there is no question as to the primary reason for their adoption. ***Trade restrictions provide highly visible, concentrated benefits for a small group of people, while imposing widely dispersed costs that are often difficult to identify on the general citizenry.*** As we discussed in Chapter 6, ***politicians have a strong incentive to favor issues of this type, even if they conflict with economic efficiency.***

Trade restrictions almost always benefit producers (and resource suppliers) at the expense of consumers. In general, the former group—investors and workers in a specific industry—are well organized, and the "jobs saved" and "high wages protected" in these industries are often highly visible (refer again to the Myths of Economics box on trade restrictions). Thus, organized interest groups that benefit from trade restrictions frequently provide contributions and other resources to politicians willing to support trade restrictions favorable to their industry. In contrast, consumers, who will pay higher prices for the products of a protected industry, are an unorganized group. Most of them will not associate the higher product prices with the trade restrictions. However, it has been estimated that the average U.S. family pays at least $1,000 more per

The U.S. tariff code is complex, lengthy (the schedule fills 3,825 pages), and costly to administer. High tariffs are imposed on some products (for example, textiles, apparel, tobacco, and footwear), while low tariffs are imposed on others. Highly restrictive quotas limit the import of other goods (peanuts and sugar, for example). This system of targeted trade restrictions encourages wasteful rent-seeking. Many politicians benefit from this system because it permits them to provide protectionist policies in exchange for campaign contributions from interest groups wanting to restrict competition from foreign rivals.

[5]Personal correspondence with the authors. Professor Weidenbaum is a former chairman of the President's Council of Economic Advisers and long-time director of the Center for the Study of American Business of Washington University.

year for the products it buys because of trade restrictions. Similarly, potential workers and investors in export industries harmed by the restrictions are often unaware of their impact. Thus, most of the people harmed by trade restrictions are likely to be uninformed and thus unconcerned about trade policy.

Predictably, well-organized special interests favoring trade restrictions will generally have more political clout than those harmed by the restrictions. As a result, politicians will often be able to gain more votes by supporting trade restrictions that benefit organized interest groups than they could gain from the support of consumers and exporters. In the case of trade restrictions, sound economics often conflicts with a winning political strategy.

EMPIRICAL EVIDENCE ON THE IMPACT OF TRADE RESTRICTIONS

Our analysis indicates that countries imposing trade barriers will fail to realize their full economic potential. Countries use various means—tariffs, quotas, exchange-rate controls, and licensing requirements, for example—to restrain international trade. It is not always easy to determine the extent to which each country is restricting trade. Taxes on international trade are generally substantially lower in high-income industrial nations than in less-developed countries (LDCs). Similarly, while exchange-rate controls are a negligible restrictive factor in developed countries, they are a major factor restricting trade in several less-developed countries. Among LDCs, considerable variation exists in the height of trade barriers. Some LDCs impose exceedingly high tariffs. Others impose exchange-rate controls. When a country both imposes high tariffs and fixes the value of its currency at unrealistic rates (relative to convertible currencies like the dollar and yen), its international trade will be retarded substantially.

More than 80 less-developed countries were analyzed in a recent study. **Exhibit 16–10** presents data for the 10 with the lowest trade barriers.[6] The trade sectors of these 10 countries are large, given the size of their population. Their tariff rates are low and the exchange-rate value of their currency is pretty much in line with market forces (a low black-market exchange-rate premium provides evidence on this point). Data are also provided for the 10 LDCs that follow the most restrictive trade policies. For this latter group, the size of the trade sector is small (given the size of the country), tariffs are high, and the black-market exchange-rate premium for the conversion of the domestic currency is often high. As we previously discussed, a high black-market premium indicates that the country has imposed tight exchange-rate controls, which will restrain international trade.

The average size of the trade sector of the low-restriction countries (72.7 percent of GDP) was more than three times the average for the nations imposing substantial trade barriers. Compared to the low-restriction countries, the average tax (tariff) rate imposed on international trade was nine times higher in 1995 (and four times higher in 1980) for the high-restriction countries. Similarly, the black-market exchange-rate premium for the domestic currency was substantially higher in the high-restriction countries in both 1980 and 1995.

Look at the growth of per-capita GDP for the two groups. The average annual growth rate of per-capita GDP during the 1980–1997 period was positive for all of the countries that followed more liberal trade policies. Seven of the 10 achieved per-capita

[6] The empirical data presented in this section are part of a larger study undertaken by one of the authors. See James Gwartney and Robert Lawson, *Economic Freedom of the World: 1997 Annual Report* (Washington, D.C.: Cato Institute, 1997).

EXHIBIT 16–10

ECONOMIC GROWTH OF LESS-DEVELOPED COUNTRIES WITH LOW AND HIGH TRADE RESTRICTIONS: 1980–1997

	Size of Trade Sector as a Percentage of GDP, 1995[a]	Average Tax Rate on International Trade		Black-Market Exchange-Rate Premium		Growth of Per-Capita GDP, 1980–1997
		1980	1995	1980	1995	
Low Trade Restrictions[b]						
Singapore	166.0%	0.5	0.1	0	0	5.4
Hong Kong	148.9	0.5	0.3	0	0	4.7
Panama	94.0	3.1	1.4	0	0	0.5
Malaysia	90.6	7.7	2.1	0	0	4.0
Ireland	71.8	3.0	1.5	0	0	4.2
Taiwan	43.3	3.6	2.0	1	0	5.9
South Korea	33.7	4.1	2.0	5	0	7.5
Portugal	30.5	2.1	0.1	2	0	2.8
Indonesia	25.6	2.9	2.2	2	2	4.8
Greece	21.8	3.2	0.1	7	0	1.3
Average	72.7%	3.1	1.1	2	0	4.1
High Trade Restrictions[b]						
Rwanda	6.6%	13.3	14.6	67	105	−3.4
India	11.4	15.5	12.7	5	8	3.0
Burundi	14.8	18.1	13.6	45	44	−1.7
Iran	16.2	17.0	5.6	164	115	1.0
Bangladesh	18.3	13.4	12.1	111	28	2.4
Cameroon	20.1	11.0	7.7	2	1	−0.9
Sierra Leone	23.7	13.3	7.7	62	2	−3.5
Madagascar	27.4	8.5	8.5	51	2	−1.8
Dominican Republic	27.8	9.2	12.2	37	2	−0.4
Syria	37.5	7.1	4.0	35	301	0.4
Average	20.4%	12.6	9.9	58	61	−0.5

[a]*The size of the trade sector is equal to one-half of exports plus imports as a percentage of GDP. As Illustrated Exhibit IV-A shows, the size of the trade sector tends to be inversely related to the population of a country. Given population, the trade sector is generally large in countries with low trade restrictions and small in countries with high trade restrictions.*

[b]*More than 100 countries were rated on the basis of three international trade factors: (1) tariff rates, (2) black-market exchange rate, and (3) the actual size of the trade sectors relative to the expected size given the country's population, geographic size, and location. The less-developed countries in this table are the ten highest and ten lowest rated in the area of international trade. See James Gwartney and Robert Lawson,* Economic Freedom of the World: 1997 Annual Report *(Washington, D.C.: Cato Institute, 1997).*

growth of 4 percent or more. The average annual growth of per-capita GDP of the low-restriction countries was 4.1 percent. In contrast, the average growth rate of the 10 countries with high trade restrictions was *minus* 0.5 percent. Per-capita GDP declined during 1980–1997 in six of the ten countries that imposed substantial restrictions on international trade. Only two of the countries with high trade restrictions—Bangladesh and India—were able to achieve a growth rate in excess of 1 percent. Just as our theory implies, these data indicate that trade barriers are harmful to the economic health of a country.[7]

REDUCTIONS IN TRADE RESTRICTIONS

General Agreement on Tariffs and Trade (GATT)
An organization formed following the Second World War to set the rules for the conduct of international trade and reduce barriers to trade among nations.

World Trade Organization (WTO)
The new name given to GATT in 1994; it is currently responsible for monitoring and enforcing the multilateral trade agreements among the 133 member countries.

North American Free Trade Agreement (NAFTA)
A comprehensive trade agreement between the United States, Mexico, and Canada that went into effect in 1994. Tariff barriers will continue to be phased out under the agreement until 2004.

Although vulnerable to special-interest politics, reductions in trade restrictions have not been totally ignored. The major industrial nations established the **General Agreement on Tariffs and Trade (GATT)** organization shortly following the Second World War. For five decades, GATT played a central role in the multilateral tariff reductions and the relaxation (or elimination) of quotas. The average tariff rates of GATT members fell from approximately 40 percent in 1947 to less than 5 percent in 1997. When the most recent round of trade negotiations—the Uruguay Round—was completed at year-end 1993, GATT was given a new name: the **World Trade Organization (WTO).** This organization of 133 countries is now responsible for the monitoring and enforcement of the trade agreements developed through GATT.

In 1988, the United States and Canada negotiated a trade agreement designed to reduce barriers limiting both trade and the flow of capital between the two countries. A few years later, the United States, Canada, and Mexico finalized the **North American Free Trade Agreement (NAFTA),** which took effect in 1994. As the result of NAFTA, tariffs on the shipment of most products among the three countries will be eliminated by 2004. The agreement will also remove limits on financial investments, liberalize trade in services such as banking, and establish uniform legal requirements for the protection of intellectual property. Preliminary analysis suggests that the agreement has had significant positive effects on the trade among the three nations. Pushed along by both NAFTA and unilateral Mexican tariff reductions, trade between the United States and Mexico has increased sharply during the last decade. In 1997, U.S. exports to (and imports from) Mexico were approximately 1 percent of GDP, more than double the figure of a decade earlier. Trade between the United States and Canada has also increased as a share of the economy during the last decade.

Compared with Canada, the free trade agreement with Mexico was—and continues to be—much more controversial. As we have discussed, trade flows among nations are determined by comparative advantage, *not* relative wage rates. Nonetheless, many Americans and Canadians fear that competition from low-wage workers will adversely affect their earnings (see the Myths of Economics box on free trade with low-wage countries). Political candidate Ross Perot argued that NAFTA would lead to massive job losses because many U.S. firms would find it difficult to compete with lower-wage Mexican rivals.[8] In line with economic theory, these losses have not materialized. In fact, the growth of both output and employment in the United States has been quite strong during the post-NAFTA period. Certainly the reduced trade barriers have resulted and will continue to result in some reallocations of resources as each country adjusts and moves toward areas of comparative advantage. Although these adjustments are sometimes painful, economic theory indicates that they will lead to stronger and more prosperous North American economies.

---

[7]For additional evidence that trade restrictions retard economic growth, see Robert Barro, "Economic Growth in a Cross-Section of Countries," *Quarterly Journal of Economics* (May 1991): 407–443; David M. Gould, Roy J. Ruffin, and Graeme L. Woodbridge, "The Theory and Practice of Free Trade," *Economic Review—Federal Reserve Bank of Dallas* (fourth quarter 1993): 1–16; and Michael Michaely, Demetris Papageorgiou, and Armeane M. Choksi, eds., *Liberalizing Foreign Trade: Lessons of Experience in the Developing World* (Cambridge, Mass.: Basil Blackwell, 1991).

[8]The colorful Perot often argued his point by telling his audiences that "the sucking sound that you hear is American jobs going south."

APPLICATIONS IN ECONOMICS

Tomatoes, Regulations, and Trade Restrictions[9]

In 1995–1996, Florida tomato growers complained to the Clinton administration and Congress that the import of cheap tomatoes from Mexico was driving them out of business. Blaming the North American Free Trade Agreement (NAFTA) for their plight, they sought to have Congress declare "winter vegetables" a separate industry so they would qualify for greater protection. They also filed an antidumping suit with the Commerce Department seeking the imposition of higher tariffs on Mexican tomatoes.

When these strategies failed, the growers asked Congress to pass special package and labeling legislation. While the hard, unripe Florida tomatoes are shipped in solid-tray boxes, the Mexican tomatoes are ripened on the vine, hand-packaged, and shipped in cushioned cartons. At least some consumers believe that this procedure makes the tomatoes tastier. This issue aside, the Florida growers wanted legislation that would require all growers to use the hard-tray cartons. Of course, this would make it difficult for the riper Mexican tomatoes to be shipped without being battered or bruised. Interestingly, the problems of the Florida growers had little to do with NAFTA. The major factor contributing to the increased competitiveness of the Mexican-grown tomatoes was the sharp reduction in the exchange rate of the peso relative to the dollar during 1994–1995.

This case illustrates why it is so difficult to maintain freedom of exchange in international markets. Rather than simply argue for trade restraints, organized interest groups often support regulations that they say will be "safer," or "more convenient," or "facilitate inspection." Of course, such regulations also just happen to give the special-interest groups a competitive edge over their rivals. This is true in all countries. Japan, in particular, has been charged with the use of such diversionary tactics.

Neither is Mexico blameless. For example, the Mexican government attempted to impose cumbersome labeling and inspection procedures in an effort to reduce the competitiveness of American tires in the Mexican market. Mexico continues to prohibit American express delivery firms, such as United Parcel Service, from using large trucks south of the border. Consumers are the losers when restrictions of this type are imposed. Unfortunately, since consumers are disorganized and generally unaware they are being harmed, support of well-organized interest groups is often politically attractive.

[1]This feature is based on an article by Helene Cooper and Bruce Ingersoll, "With Little Evidence, Florida Growers Blame Tomato Woes on NAFTA," *Wall Street Journal,* April 3, 1996, p. 1.

MYTHS OF ECONOMICS

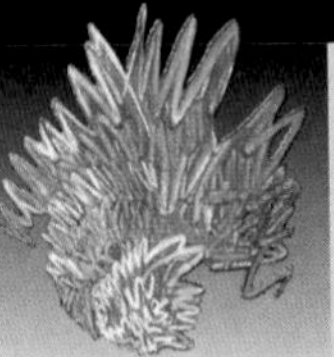

"Free trade with low-wage countries, such as China and India, would cause the wages of U.S. workers to fall."

Many Americans believe that if it were not for trade restrictions, the wages of American workers would fall to the level of workers in less-developed countries. How can U.S. labor compete with workers in China or India who are willing to work for $1 per hour or less? The fallacy of this argument stems from a misunderstanding of the source of high wages and ignorance of the law of comparative advantage. After all, average wages differ substantially between U.S. states despite more than 200 years of free trade!

High hourly wages do not necessarily mean high per-unit labor cost. Labor productivity must also be considered. For example, suppose a U.S. steel worker receives an hourly wage rate of $20 and a steel worker in India receives only $2 per hour. Given the skill level of the workers and the capital and production methods used in the two countries, however, the U.S. worker produces 20 times as many tons of steel per worker-hour as the Indian worker. Because of the higher productivity per worker-hour, labor cost per unit of output is actually lower in the United States than in India!

Labor in the United States possesses a high skill level and works with large amounts of capital equipment. These factors contribute to the high productivity per worker, which is the source of the high wages. Similarly, low productivity per worker-hour is the foundation of the low wages in such countries as India and China.

When analyzing the significance of wage and productivity differentials across countries, one must remember that gains from trade emanate from comparative advantage, not absolute advantage (see Exhibits 16–2, 16–3, and 16–4). The United States cannot produce everything cheaper than China or India merely because U.S. workers are more productive and work with more capital than workers in China and India. Neither can the Chinese and Indians produce everything cheaper merely because their wage rates are low compared to those of U.S. workers. When resources are directed by relative prices and the principle of comparative advantage, both high-wage and low-wage countries gain from the opportunity to specialize in those activities that, relatively speaking, they do best.

The comparative advantage of low-wage countries is likely to be in the production of labor-intensive goods, such as wigs, rugs, toys, textiles, and assembled manufactured products. On the other hand, the comparative advantage of the United States lies in the production of high-tech manufacturing products and other goods produced economically by a well-educated labor force. Trade permits both high- and low-wage countries to reallocate their resources away from productive activities in which they are inefficient (relative to foreign producers) toward activities in which they are highly efficient. The net result is an increase in output and consumption opportunities for both trading partners.

If foreigners, even low-wage foreigners, will sell us a product cheaper than we ourselves could produce it, we can gain by using our resources to produce other things. Perhaps an extreme example will illustrate the point. Suppose a foreign producer, perhaps a Santa Claus (who was able to hire workers at low wages), was willing to supply us with free winter coats. Would it make sense to enact a tariff barrier to keep out the free coats? Of course not. Resources that were previously used to produce coats could now be freed to produce other goods. Output and the availability of goods would expand. The real wage of U.S. workers would rise. It makes no more sense to erect trade barriers to keep out cheap foreign goods than to keep out the free coats of a friendly, foreign Santa Claus.

FALLING TRADE BARRIERS IN OTHER COUNTRIES

The reduction in trade barriers and growth of the trade sector in the United States reflects a worldwide trend. No doubt influenced by the economic success of relatively open economies like those of Hong Kong and Singapore, many LDCs unilaterally reduced their trade barriers during the late 1980s and early 1990s. Among Latin American countries, Chile began moving toward freer trade policies in the early 1980s. Spurred by the rapid economic growth of Chile during the latter half of the 1980s, other Latin American countries followed suit. Mexico cut its tariff rates by more than 50 percent during the late 1980s. In 1991 Argentina cut its average tariff level from 18 percent to 11 percent. Brazil, Bolivia, Colombia, Ecuador, Peru, and Venezuela have also made substantial cuts in their tariff rates and reduced other trade barriers in the

1990s.[9] Exchange-rate controls have also been relaxed or eliminated throughout much of Latin America during the past five years. In other parts of the world, even some of the most "protectionist" countries—including Pakistan, the Philippines, and Turkey—have cut their tariffs or relaxed restrictive quotas or both in the 1990s.

LOOKING *Ahead*

As the result of recent financial turbulence in several Asian and Latin American countries, focus has now shifted away from trade restrictions and toward the development of more stable financial arrangements. There are many similarities between trade within national borders and trade across national boundaries. However, there is also a major difference. In addition to the exchange of goods for money, trade across national borders generally involves the exchange of national currencies. The next chapter deals with the foreign exchange market and other dimensions of international finance.

KEY POINTS

➤ The volume of international trade has grown rapidly in recent decades. Over 20 percent of the world's output is sold outside the country in which it was produced. The size of the trade sector is generally larger in countries with a smaller population.

➤ Comparative advantage rather than absolute advantage is the source of gains from trade. As long as the relative production costs of goods differ among nations, all nations will be able to gain from trade. Specialization and trade allow trading partners to maximize their joint output and expand their consumption possibilities.

➤ Exports and imports are closely linked. The exports of a nation are the primary source of purchasing power used to import goods. When a nation restricts imports, it simultaneously limits the ability of foreigners to acquire the purchasing power necessary to buy the nation's exports.

➤ Relative to the no-trade alternative, international exchange and specialization result in lower prices for products that are imported and higher domestic prices for products that are exported. However, the net effect is an expansion in the aggregate output and consumption possibilities available to a nation.

➤ Import restrictions, such as tariffs and quotas, reduce foreign supply and cause the price to rise for domestic consumers. Thus, such restrictions are subsidies to producers (and workers) in protected industries at the expense of (a) consumers and (b) producers (and workers) in export industries. Jobs protected by import restrictions are offset by jobs destroyed in export industries.

➤ National-defense, infant-industry, and antidumping arguments can be used to justify trade restrictions for specific industries under certain conditions. It is clear, though, that the power of special-interest groups and voter ignorance about the harmful effects of trade restrictions are the major explanations for real-world policies.

➤ Both high-wage and low-wage countries gain from trade. If a low-wage country can supply a good to the United States cheaper than the United States can produce it, the United States can gain by purchasing the good from the low-wage country and using U.S. resources to produce other goods for which the United States has a comparative advantage. Free trade with low-wage

[9]See Susan Hickok, "Recent Trade Liberalization in Developing Countries: The Effects of Global Trade and Output," *Quarterly Review: Federal Reserve Bank of New York* (autumn 1993): 6–19.

countries does not result in wage rates equalizing or massive outflows of jobs, because these wage differences reflect productivity differences.

➤ There is substantial variation among LDCs with regard to the imposition of trade restrictions. LDCs that have low tariff rates, a freely convertible currency, and large trade sectors (relative to the size of their population) have generally outperformed those with restrictive trade policies.

CRITICAL-ANALYSIS QUESTIONS

*1. "Trade restrictions limiting the sale of cheap foreign goods in the United States are necessary to protect the prosperity of Americans." Evaluate this statement made by an American politician.

2. Suppose as the result of the Civil War that the United States had been divided into two countries and that through the years high trade barriers had grown up between the two. How might the standard of living in the "divided" United States have been affected? Explain.

*3. Can both of the following statements be true? Why or why not?

a. "Tariffs and import quotas promote economic inefficiency and reduce the real income of a nation. Economic analysis suggests that nations can gain by eliminating trade restrictions."

b. "Economic analysis suggests that there is good reason to expect that trade restrictions will exist in the real world."

4. "The average American is hurt by imports and helped by exports." Do you agree or disagree with this statement? How do imports and exports affect the welfare of and prices paid by the average American consumer? How do they affect the welfare of domestic corporations and producers producing the goods?

*5. "An increased scarcity of a product benefits producers and harms consumers. In effect, tariffs and other trade restrictions increase the domestic scarcity of products by reducing the supply from abroad. Such policies benefit domestic producers of the restricted product at the expense of domestic consumers." Evaluate this statement.

*6. The United States uses an import quota to maintain the domestic price of sugar well above the world price. Analyze the impact of the quota. Use supply-and-demand analysis to illustrate your answer. To whom do the gains and losses of this policy accrue? How does the quota affect the efficiency of resource allocation in the United States? Why do you think Congress is supportive of this policy?

7. Suppose that it costs American textile manufacturers $20 to produce a shirt, while foreign producers can supply the same shirt for $15.

a. Would a tariff of $6 per shirt help American manufacturers compete with foreign manufacturers?

b. Would a subsidy of $6 per shirt to domestic manufacturers help them compete?

c. Is there any difference between the tariff and a direct subsidy to the domestic manufacturer?

*8. "Getting more Americans to realize that it pays to make things in the United States is the heart of the competitiveness issue." (This is a quote from an American business magazine.)

a. Would Americans be better off if more of them paid higher prices in order to "buy American" rather than purchase from foreigners? Would U.S. employment be higher? Explain.

b. Would Californians be better off if they bought only goods produced in California? Would the employment in California be higher? Explain.

*9. It is often alleged that Japanese producers receive subsidies from their government that permit them to sell their products at a low price in the U.S. market. Do you think we should erect trade barriers to keep out cheap Japanese goods if the source of their low price is governmental subsidies? Why or why not?

10. How do tariffs and quotas differ? Can you think of any reason why foreign producers might prefer a quota rather than a tariff? Explain your answer.

11. What's wrong with this economic experiment? A researcher hypothesizes that higher tariffs on imported automobiles would cause total employment in the United States to increase. Automobile tariffs are raised, and the following year employment in the U.S. auto industry increases by 50,000. The researcher concludes that the higher tariffs created 50,000 jobs.

*12. Does international trade cost American jobs? Does interstate trade cost your state jobs? What is the major effect of international and interstate trade?

13. "The United States is suffering from a huge excess of imports. Cheap foreign products are driving American

firms out of business and leaving our economy in shambles." Evaluate this statement from an American politician.

14. Do you think the United States will benefit as trade barriers with Mexico are reduced? Will Mexico benefit? Will trade with a low-wage country like Mexico push wages down in a high-wage country like the United States? Why or why not?

*15. "Tariffs not only reduce the volume of imports, they also reduce the volume of exports." Is this statement true or false? Explain your answer.

16. Answer the following questions and carefully compare and contrast your answers.

a. Would the people of Europe be better off if there were dangerous rivers with no bridges that ran along the borders between countries? Why or why not?

b. Would the people of Europe be better off if there were sizable tariffs (taxes on imports), import quotas, and other regulations that limited foreigners from selling goods cheaply in the domestic market of another country? Why or why not?

c. If foreigners were "dumping" their goods—if they were selling in another country at a price below their production costs—would your answer to part b have been different?

17. Suppose that a very high tariff were placed on steel imported into the U.S. How would that affect employment in the U.S. auto industry? (Hint: Think about how higher steel prices will impact the cost of producing automobiles.)

---

*Asterisk denotes questions for which answers are given in Appendix B.

CHAPTER 17

Currencies, like tomatoes and football tickets, have a price at which they are bought and sold. An exchange rate is the price of one currency in terms of another, such as the price of a French franc in U.S. dollars or German marks.

Gary Smith[1]

International Finance and the Foreign Exchange Market

CHAPTER FOCUS

- What determines the exchange-rate value of the dollar relative to other currencies?
- What information is included in the balance-of-payments accounts of a nation? Will the balance-of-payments accounts of a country always be in balance?
- How do monetary and fiscal policies influence the exchange-rate value of a nation's currency?
- Will a healthy economy run a balance-of-trade surplus? Does a balance-of-trade deficit indicate that a nation is in financial trouble?
- How have international financial arrangements changed in recent years? How are they likely to change in the future?

[1]Gary Smith, *Macroeconomics* (New York: W. H. Freeman, 1985), p. 514.

Trade across national boundaries is complicated by the fact that nations generally use different currencies to buy and sell goods in their respective domestic markets. The British use pounds, the Japanese yen, the Mexicans pesos, and so on. Therefore, when a good or service is purchased from a seller in another country, it is generally necessary for someone to convert one currency to another. This adds to the complexity of international exchange. This complication could be avoided if the trading partners used a common currency. This is precisely what 11 European nations have decided to do. They are in the process of phasing in a common currency, the euro. If things go as planned, trade among the citizens of these nations will be conducted in euros by 2002.

Most exchanges across national boundaries, however, still involve currency conversions. If you travel in Europe, Asia, or South America, you will generally have to convert your dollars to another currency in order to purchase items. What determines the value of one currency relative to another? What is the role of the foreign exchange market? How do exchange-rate regimes differ across countries? How do these differences influence international trade? This chapter will investigate these issues and related topics.

FOREIGN EXCHANGE MARKET

Foreign exchange market
The market in which the currencies of different countries are bought and sold.

We have previously discussed the **foreign exchange market,** the market where the currencies of different countries are bought and sold. We now want to consider this market in more detail and analyze the factors that cause changes in exchange rates. Suppose you own a sporting goods shop in the United States and are preparing to place an order for athletic shoes. You can purchase them from either a domestic or foreign manufacturer. If you decide to purchase the shoes from a British firm, either you will have to change dollars into pounds at a bank and send them to the British producer, or the British manufacturer will have to go to a bank and change your dollar check into pounds. In either case, purchasing the British shoes will involve an exchange of dollars for pounds.

Exchange rate
The domestic price of one unit of foreign currency. For example, if it takes $1.50 to purchase one English pound, the dollar-pound exchange rate is 1.50.

The British producer has offered to supply the shoes for 20 pounds per pair. How can you determine whether this price is high or low? To compare the price of the British-supplied shoes with the price of those produced domestically, you must know the **exchange rate** between the dollar and the pound. ***The exchange rate is one of the most important prices of an economy because it enables consumers in one country to translate the prices of foreign goods into units of their own currency. Specifically, the dollar price of a foreign good is determined by multiplying the foreign product price by the exchange rate (the dollar price per unit of the foreign currency).*** For example, if it takes $1.50 to obtain 1 pound, then the British shoes priced at 20 pounds would cost $30 (20 times the $1.50 price of the pound).

Suppose the exchange rate is $1.50 = 1 pound and that you decide to buy 200 pairs of athletic shoes from the British manufacturer at 20 pounds ($30) per pair. You will need 4,000 pounds in order to pay the British manufacturer. If you contact an

American bank that handles foreign exchange transactions and write the bank a check for $6,000 (the $1.50 exchange rate multiplied by 4,000), it will supply the 4,000 pounds. The bank will typically charge a small fee for handling the transaction.

Where does the American bank get the pounds? The bank obtains the pounds from British importers who want dollars to buy things from Americans. ***Note that the U.S. demand for foreign currencies (such as the pound) is generated by the demand of Americans for things purchased from foreigners. On the other hand, the U.S. supply of foreign exchange reflects the demand of foreigners for things bought from Americans.***

Exhibit 17–1 presents data on the exchange rate—the cents required to purchase a German mark, Japanese yen, British pound, and Canadian dollar—during 1990–1998. An index of the exchange-rate value of the dollar against ten major currencies is also shown. Under the flexible rate system present in most industrial countries, the exchange rate between currencies changes from day to day and even from hour to hour. Thus, the annual exchange-rate data given in Exhibit 17–1 are really averages for each year.

An **appreciation** in the value of a nation's currency means that fewer units of the currency are now required to purchase one unit of a foreign currency. For example, in 1998, only 56.8 cents were required to purchase a German mark, down from 69.8 cents in 1995.[2] ***As the result of this appreciation in the value of the dollar relative to the mark, German goods became less expensive to Americans.*** The direction of change in the prices that Germans paid for American goods was just the opposite. An appreciation of the U.S. dollar relative to the mark is the same thing as a depreciation in the mark relative to the dollar.

Appreciation
An increase in the value of a domestic currency relative to foreign currencies. An appreciation increases the purchasing power of the domestic currency for foreign goods.

EXHIBIT 17–1

FOREIGN EXCHANGE RATES, 1990–1998

	U.S. Cents per Unit of Foreign Currency				Index of Exchange-Rate Value of the Dollar (Ten Currencies)[a]
Year	German Mark	Japanese Yen	British Pound	Canadian Dollar	
1990	61.9	0.690	178.41	85.7	89.1
1991	60.2	0.743	176.74	87.3	89.3
1992	64.0	0.789	176.63	82.7	86.6
1993	60.4	0.900	150.16	77.5	93.2
1994	61.7	0.979	153.19	73.2	91.3
1995	69.8	1.064	157.85	72.9	84.3
1996	66.4	0.919	156.07	73.3	87.3
1997	57.6	0.826	163.76	72.2	96.4
1998	56.8	0.763	165.73	67.4	98.8

[a]*March 1973 = 100. In addition to the currencies listed above, the index includes the Belgian franc, French franc, Italian lira, Netherlands guilder, Swedish krona, and Swiss franc.*

SOURCE: Council of Economic Advisers, Economic Report of the President *(Washington, D.C.: U.S. Government Printing Office, 1999).*

[2]Because an appreciation means a lower price of foreign currencies, some may think it looks like a depreciation. Just remember that a lower price of the foreign currency means that one's domestic currency will buy more units of the foreign currency and thus more goods and services from foreigners.

Depreciation
A reduction in the value of a domestic currency relative to foreign currencies. A depreciation reduces the purchasing power of the domestic currency for foreign goods.

When a **depreciation** occurs, it will take more units of the domestic currency to purchase a unit of foreign currency. Between 1993 and 1998, the dollar depreciated against the British pound (see Exhibit 17–1). In 1993, it took 150.16 cents to purchase a British pound; by 1998, the figure had risen to 165.73. As the number of cents required to purchase a British pound rose, British goods became more expensive for Americans.

The ten-currency index of the dollar's exchange-rate value presented in Exhibit 18–1 provides evidence on what is happening to the dollar's general exchange-rate value.[3] An increase in the index implies an appreciation in the dollar, while a decline is indicative of a depreciation in the dollar. After depreciating between 1993 and 1995, the dollar appreciated by approximately 17 percent during 1995–1998. Frequently, people will use the terms "strong" and "weak" when referring to the exchange-rate value of a currency. A strong currency is one that has appreciated substantially in value, while a weak currency is one that has declined in value on the foreign exchange market.

DETERMINANTS OF EXCHANGE RATE

Flexible exchange rates
Exchange rates that are determined by the market forces of supply and demand. They are sometimes called floating exchange rates.

What determines the exchange rate between two currencies? Under a system of **flexible exchange rates,** also called *floating exchange rates,* the value of currencies in the foreign exchange market is determined by market forces. Just as the forces of supply and demand determine other prices, so do they determine the exchange-rate value of currencies in the absence of government intervention.

The exchange-rate system in effect since 1973 might best be described as a managed flexible rate system. It is flexible because all the major industrial countries allow the exchange-rate value of their currencies to float. But the system is also "managed" because the major industrial nations have from time to time attempted to alter supply and demand in the foreign exchange market by buying and selling various currencies. Compared to the total size of this market, however, these transactions have been relatively small. Thus, the exchange-rate value of major currencies like the U.S. dollar, British pound, Japanese yen, and the new European euro is determined primarily by market forces. Several countries link their currency to major currencies, such as the U.S. dollar, English pound, or Japanese yen. As we proceed, we will investigate alternative methods of linking currencies and analyze the operation of different regimes.

DEMAND, SUPPLY, AND EQUILIBRIUM PRICE IN THE FOREIGN EXCHANGE MARKET

To simplify our explanation of how the exchange rate is determined, let us assume that the United States and Great Britain are the only two countries in the world. When Americans buy and sell with each other, they use dollars. Therefore, American sellers will want to be paid in dollars. Similarly, when the British buy and sell with each other, they use pounds. As a result, British sellers will want to be paid in pounds.

If Americans want to buy from British sellers, they will need to acquire pounds. ***In our two-country world, the demand for pounds in the exchange-rate market originates from the demand of Americans for British goods, services, and assets***

---

[3]In the construction of this index, the exchange rate of each currency relative to the dollar is weighted according to the proportion of U.S. trade with the country. For example, the index weights the U.S. dollar–Japanese yen exchange rate more heavily than the U.S. dollar–Swiss franc exchange rate because the volume of U.S. trade with Japan exceeds the volume of trade with Switzerland.

(both real and financial). For example, when U.S. residents purchase men's suits from a British manufacturer, travel in the United Kingdom, or purchase the stocks, bonds, or physical assets of British business firms, they demand pounds from (and supply dollars to) the foreign exchange-rate market to pay for these items.

The supply of foreign exchange (pounds in our two-country case) originates from sales by Americans to foreigners. When Americans sell goods, services, or assets to the British, for example, the British buyers will supply pounds (and demand dollars) in the exchange-rate market in order to acquire the dollars required to pay for the items purchased from Americans.[4]

Exhibit 17–2 illustrates the demand and supply curves of Americans for foreign exchange—British pounds in our two-country case. The demand for pounds is downward sloping because a lower dollar price of the pound—meaning a dollar will buy more pounds—makes British goods cheaper for American importers. The goods produced by one country are generally good substitutes for the goods of another country. This means that when foreign (British) goods become cheaper, Americans will increase their expenditures on imports (and therefore the quantity of pounds demanded will increase). Thus, as the dollar price of the pound declines, Americans will both buy more of the lower-priced (in dollars) British goods and demand more pounds, which are required for the purchases.

Similarly, the supply curve for pounds is dependent on the sales by Americans to the British (that is, the purchase of American goods by the British). An increase in

EXHIBIT 17–2

EQUILIBRIUM IN FOREIGN EXCHANGE MARKET

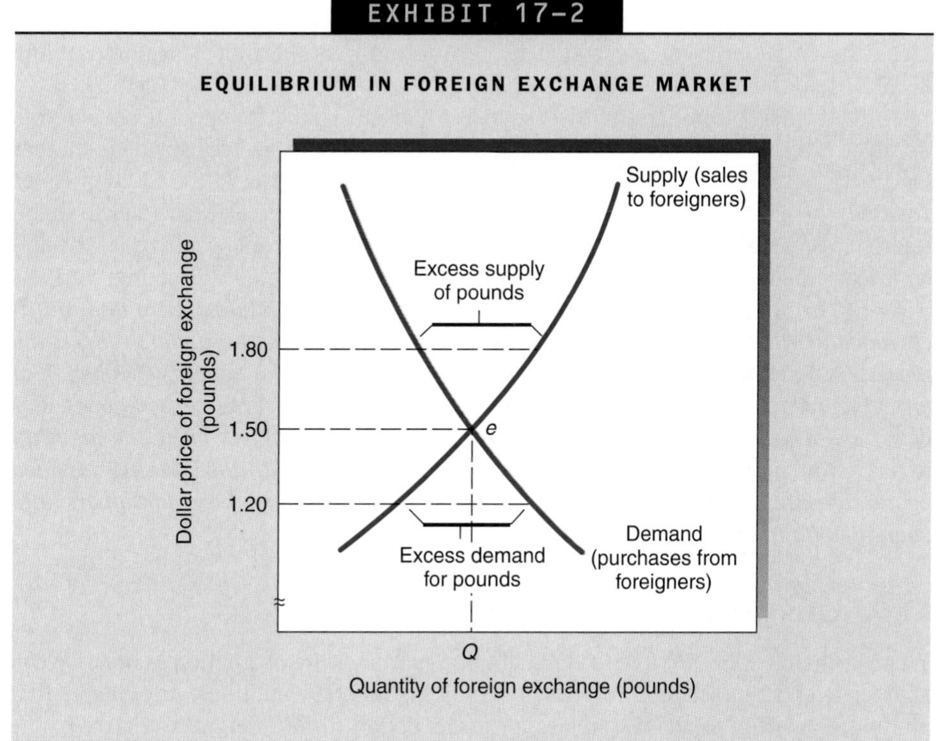

The dollar price of the pound is measured on the vertical axis. The horizontal axis indicates the flow of pounds to the foreign exchange market. The equilibrium exchange rate is \$1.50 = 1 pound. At the equilibrium price, the quantity demanded of pounds just equals the quantity supplied. A higher price of pounds, such as \$1.80 = 1 pound, would lead to an excess supply of pounds, causing the dollar price of the pound to fall. On the other hand, a lower price—for example, \$1.20 = 1 pound—would result in an excess demand for pounds, causing the pound to appreciate.

[4]We analyze the foreign exchange market in terms of the demand for and supply of foreign currencies. Alternatively, this analysis could be done in terms of the supply of and demand for dollars. Since one currency is traded for another, the same actions that generate a demand for foreign exchange simultaneously generate a supply of dollars. Correspondingly, the same exchanges that create a supply of foreign currencies simultaneously generate a demand for dollars in the foreign exchange market.

the dollar price of the pound means that a pound will purchase more dollars and more goods priced in dollars. Thus, the price (in pounds) of American goods, services, and assets to British purchasers declines. The British will purchase more from Americans and therefore supply more pounds to the foreign exchange market as the dollar price of the pound rises. Because of this, the supply curve for pounds tends to slope upward to the right.

As Exhibit 17–2 shows, equilibrium is present at the dollar price of the pound that brings the quantity demanded and quantity supplied of pounds into balance, \$1.50 = 1 pound in this case. ***The market-clearing price of \$1.50 per pound not only equates demand and supply in the foreign exchange market, it also equates (1) the value of U.S. purchases of items supplied by the British with (2) the value of items sold by U.S. residents to the British.*** Demand and supply in the currency market are merely the mirror images of these two factors.

What would happen if the price of the pound were above equilibrium—\$1.80 = 1 pound, for example? At the higher dollar price of the pound, British goods would be more expensive for Americans. Americans would cut back on their purchases of shoes, glassware, textile products, financial assets, and other items supplied by the British. Reflecting this reduction, the quantity of pounds demanded by Americans would decline. Simultaneously, the higher dollar price of the pound would make U.S. exports cheaper for the British. For example, an \$18,000 American automobile would cost British consumers 12,000 pounds when 1 pound trades for \$1.50, but it would cost only 10,000 pounds when 1 pound exchanges for \$1.80. If the dollar price of the pound were \$1.80, the British would supply more pounds to the foreign exchange market than Americans demand. As can be seen in Exhibit 17–2, this excess supply of pounds would cause the dollar price of the pound to decline until equilibrium is restored at the \$1.50 = 1 pound price.

At a below-equilibrium price, such as \$1.20 = 1 pound, an opposite set of forces would be present. The lower dollar price of the pound would make English goods cheaper for Americans and American goods more expensive for the British. At the \$1.20 price for a pound, the purchases of Americans from the British would exceed their sales to them, leading to an excess demand for pounds. In turn, the excess demand would cause the dollar price of the pound to rise until equilibrium was restored at \$1.50 = 1 pound.

The implications of the analysis are general. In our multicountry and multicurrency world, the demand for foreign currencies in exchange for dollars reflects the purchases by Americans of goods, services, and assets from foreigners. The supply of foreign currencies in exchange for dollars reflects the sales by Americans of goods, services, and assets to foreigners. The equilibrium exchange rate will bring the quantity of foreign exchange demanded by Americans into equality with the quantity supplied by foreigners. It will also bring the purchases by Americans from foreigners into equality with the sales by Americans to foreigners.

Changes in Exchange Rates

When exchange rates are free to fluctuate, the market value of a nation's currency will appreciate and depreciate in response to changing market conditions. Any change that alters the quantity of goods, services, or assets bought from foreigners relative to the quantity sold to foreigners will also alter the exchange rate. What types of change will alter the exchange-rate value of a currency?

Changes in Income. An increase in domestic income will encourage the nation's residents to spend a portion of their additional income on imports. When the income of a nation grows rapidly, the nation's imports tend to rise rapidly as well. As **Exhibit 17–3** illustrates, an increase in imports also increases the demand for foreign exchange (the pound in our two-country case). As the demand for pounds increases, the dollar price of the pound rises (from \$1.50 to \$1.80). This depreciation of the dollar reduces the incentive of Americans to import British goods and services, while increasing the

American consumer purchases an auto from a Japanese manufacturer.

American vacationer buys a ticket on British Airways.

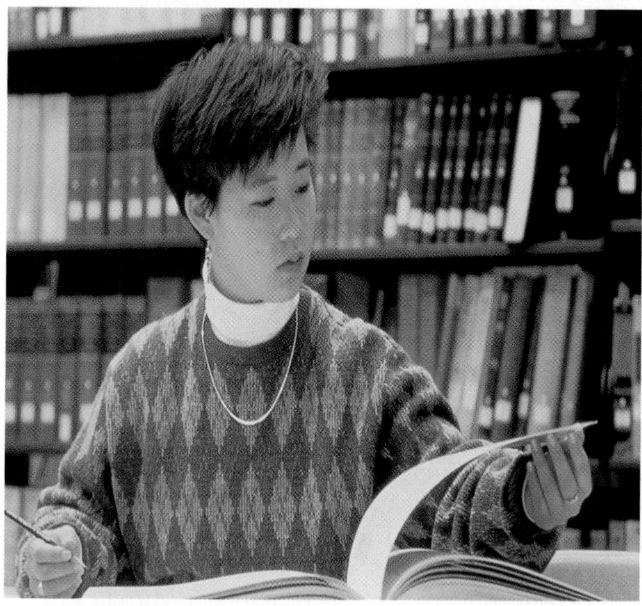
Foreign student pays tuition to Harvard..

Foreign investor purchases a bond from a U.S. corporation.

How will each of these transactions influence the demand for and supply of foreign currencies in exchange for the dollar?

EXHIBIT 17–3

GROWTH OF INCOME AND GROWTH OF IMPORTS

Other things constant, if incomes grow in the United States, U.S. imports will grow. The increase in the imports will increase the demand for pounds, causing the dollar price of the pound to rise (from $1.50 to $1.80).

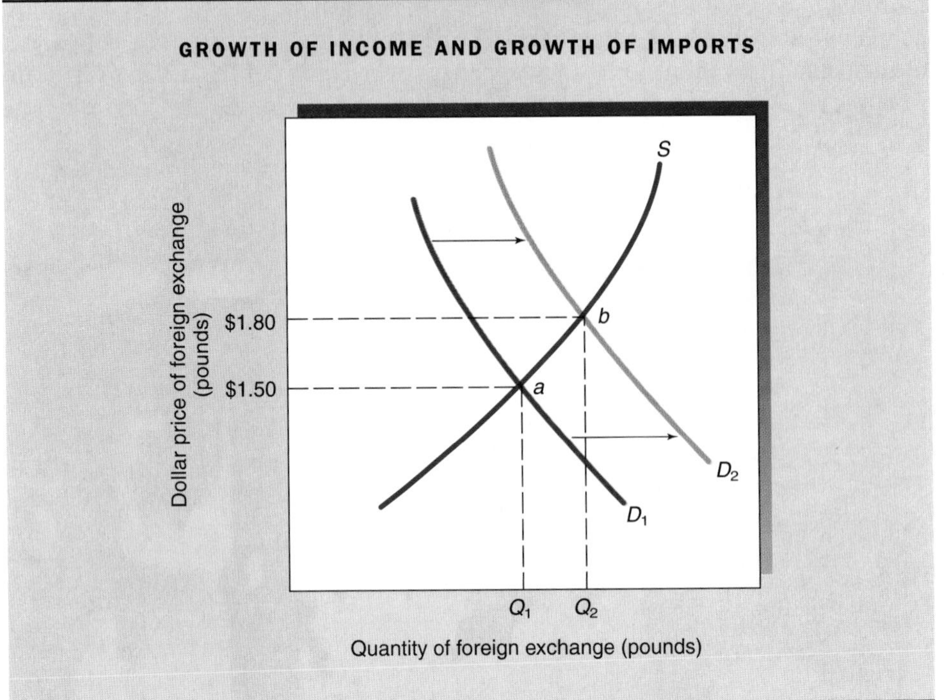

incentive of the British to purchase U.S. exports. These two forces will restore equilibrium in the foreign exchange market at a new, higher dollar price of the pound.

Just the opposite takes place when the income of a trading partner (Great Britain in our example) increases. Rapid growth of income abroad will lead to an increase in U.S. exports, causing the supply of foreign exchange (and demand for dollars) to increase. This will cause the dollar to appreciate—the dollar price of the pound will fall.

What will happen if both countries are growing? Other things constant, it is the relative growth rate that matters. A country that grows more rapidly than its trading partners will increase its imports relative to exports, which will cause the exchange-rate value of its currency to fall. Correspondingly, sluggish growth of income relative to one's trading partners will lead to a decline in imports relative to exports. ***Paradoxical as it may seem, sluggish growth relative to one's trading partners will tend to cause a nation's currency to appreciate.***

Differences in Rates of Inflation. Other things constant, domestic inflation will cause the value of a nation's currency to depreciate in the foreign exchange market, whereas deflation will result in appreciation. Suppose prices in the United States rise by 50 percent while our trading partners are experiencing stable prices. The domestic inflation will cause U.S. consumers to increase their demand for imported goods (and foreign currency). In turn, the inflated domestic prices will cause foreigners to reduce their purchases of U.S. goods, thereby reducing the supply of foreign currency to the exchange market. As **Exhibit 17–4** illustrates, the exchange rate will adjust to this set of circumstances. The dollar will depreciate relative to the pound.

EXHIBIT 17-4

INFLATION WITH FLEXIBLE EXCHANGE RATES

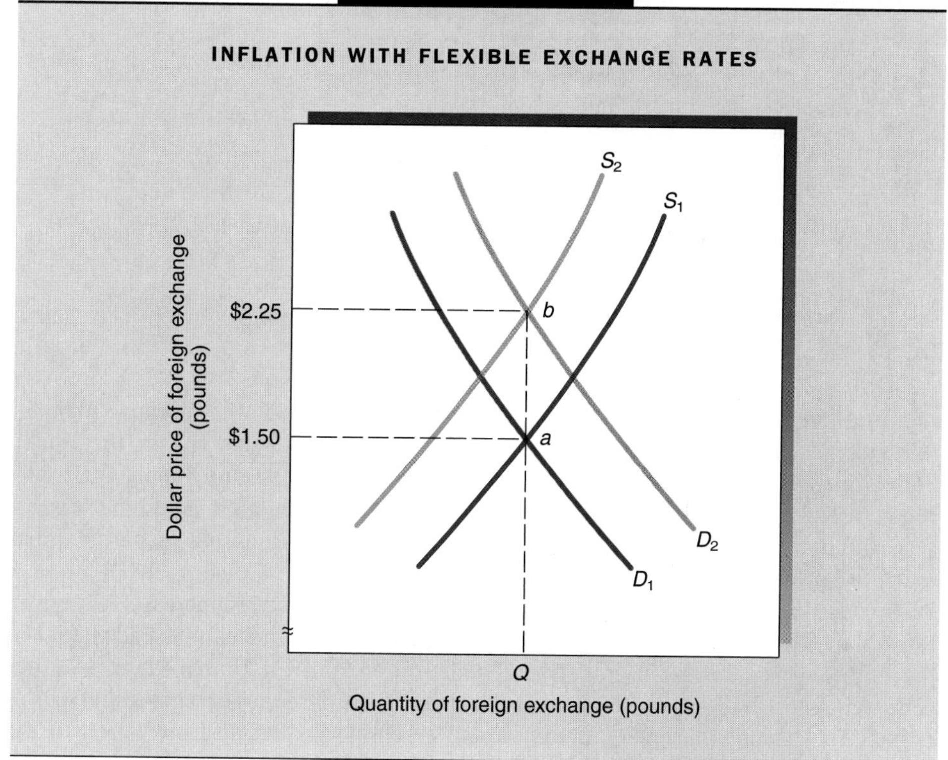

If prices were stable in Britain while the price level increased 50 percent in the United States, the U.S. demand for British products (and pounds) would increase, whereas U.S. exports to Britain would decline, causing the supply of pounds to fall. These forces would cause the dollar to depreciate relative to the pound.

Exchange-rate adjustments permit nations with even high rates of inflation to engage in trade with countries experiencing relatively stable prices.[5] A depreciation in a nation's currency in the foreign exchange market compensates for the nation's inflation rate. For example, if inflation increases the price level in the United States by 50 percent, and the value of the dollar in exchange for the pound depreciates (such that the value of the foreign currency increases 50 percent), then the prices of American goods measured in pounds are unchanged to British consumers. Thus, when the exchange-rate value of the dollar changes from \$1.50 = 1 pound to \$2.25 = 1 pound, the depreciation in the dollar restores the original prices of U.S. goods to British consumers even though the price level in the United States has increased by 50 percent.

When domestic prices are increasing more rapidly than those of one's trading partners, the value of the domestic currency will tend to depreciate in the foreign exchange market. On the other hand, if a nation's inflation rate is lower than that of its trading partners, then its currency will tend to appreciate.

Changes in Interest Rates. Financial investments will be quite sensitive to changes in real interest rates—that is, interest rates adjusted for the expected rate of inflation. International loanable funds will tend to move toward areas where the expected real rate of return (after compensation for differences in risk) is highest. ***Thus, increases in***

[5]However, high rates of inflation are likely to cause greater variability in the foreign exchange value of a currency across time periods. In turn, this increased variability of the exchange rate will generate uncertainty and reduce the volume of international trade—particularly transactions involving a time dimension. Thus, exchange-rate instability is generally harmful to the health of an economy.

THUMBNAIL SKETCH

What Factors Cause a Nation's Currency to Appreciate or Depreciate?

These Factors Will Cause a Nation's Currency to Appreciate:

1. Slow growth of income (relative to trading partners) that causes imports to lag behind exports.
2. A rate of inflation that is lower than that of one's trading partners.
3. Domestic real interest rates that are higher than real interest rates abroad.

These Factors Will Cause a Nation's Currency to Depreciate:

1. Rapid growth of income (relative to trading partners) that stimulates imports relative to exports.
2. A rate of inflation that is higher than that of one's trading partners.
3. Domestic real interest rates that are lower than real interest rates abroad.

real interest rates relative to a nation's trading partners will tend to cause that nation's currency to appreciate. For example, if real interest rates rise in the United States relative to Britain, British citizens will demand dollars (and supply their currency, pounds) in the foreign exchange market to purchase the high-yield American assets. The increase in demand for the dollar and supply of pounds will cause the dollar to appreciate relative to the British pound.

In contrast, when real interest rates in other countries increase relative to rates in the United States, short-term financial investors will move to take advantage of the higher yields abroad. As investment funds move from the United States to other countries, there will be an increase in the demand for foreign currencies and an increase in the supply of dollars in the foreign exchange market. A depreciation in the dollar relative to the currencies of the countries with the higher real interest rates will be the result. The accompanying Thumbnail Sketch summarizes the major forces that cause a nation's currency to appreciate or depreciate when exchange rates are determined by market forces.

BALANCE OF PAYMENTS

Just as countries calculate their gross domestic product (GDP) so that they have a general idea of their domestic level of production, most countries also calculate their balance of international payments in order to keep track of their transactions with other nations. The **balance of payments** summarizes the transactions of the country's citizens, businesses, and governments with foreigners. It provides information on the nation's exports, imports, earnings of domestic residents on assets located abroad, earnings on domestic assets owned by foreigners, international capital movements, and official transactions by central banks and governments.

Balance of payments
A summary of all economic transactions between a country and all other countries for a specific time period, usually a year. The balance-of-payments account reflects all payments and liabilities to foreigners (debits) and all payments and obligations received from foreigners (credits).

Balance-of-payments accounts are kept according to the principles of basic bookkeeping. Any transaction that creates a demand for foreign currency (and a supply of the domestic currency) in the foreign exchange market is recorded as a debit, or minus, item. Imports are an example of a debit item. Transactions that create a supply of foreign currency (and demand for the domestic currency) on the foreign exchange market are recorded as a credit, or plus, item. Exports are an example of a credit item. ***Because the foreign exchange market will bring quantity demanded and quantity supplied into balance, it will also bring the total debits and total credits into balance.***

Balance-of-payments transactions can be grouped into three basic categories: current account, capital account, and official reserve account. Let us take a look at each of these components.

Current-Account Transactions

All payments (and gifts) related to the purchase or sale of goods and services and income flows during the designated period are included in the **current account.** In general, there are four major types of current-account transactions: the exchange of merchandise goods, the exchange of services, income from investments, and unilateral transfers.

Current account
The record of all transactions with foreign nations that involve the exchange of merchandise goods and services, current income derived from investments, and unilateral gifts.

Merchandise Trade Transactions. The export and import of merchandise goods compose the largest portion of a nation's balance-of-payments account. When U.S. producers export their products, foreigners will supply their currency in exchange for dollars in order to pay for the U.S.-produced goods. Because U.S. exports generate a supply of foreign exchange and demand for dollars in the foreign exchange market, they are a credit (plus) item. In contrast, when Americans import goods, they will demand foreign currencies and supply dollars in the foreign exchange market. Thus, imports are a debit (minus) item.

As Exhibit 17–5 shows, the United States exported $679.3 billion of merchandise goods in 1997, compared to imports of $877.3 billion. The difference between the value of a country's merchandise exports and the value of its merchandise imports is known as the **balance of merchandise trade** (or *balance of trade*). If the value of a country's merchandise exports falls short of the value of its merchandise imports, it is said to have a balance-of-trade deficit. In contrast, the situation where a nation exports more than it imports is referred to as a trade surplus. In 1997, the United States ran a merchandise-trade deficit of $198.0 billion (line 3 of Exhibit 17–5).

Balance of merchandise trade
The difference between the value of merchandise exports and the value of merchandise imports for a nation. The balance of merchandise trade is only one component of a nation's total balance of payments. Also called simply balance of trade *or* net exports.

Other things constant, a U.S. merchandise-trade deficit implies that Americans are supplying more dollars to the exchange market in order to purchase foreign-made goods than foreigners are demanding for the purchase of American goods. If the merchandise-trade deficit were the only factor influencing the value of the dollar on the exchange market, one could anticipate a decline in the foreign exchange value of the U.S. currency. However, several other factors also affect the supply of and demand for the dollar on the exchange market.

Service Exports and Imports. The export and import of *invisible services,* as they are sometimes called, also exert an important influence on the foreign exchange market. The export of insurance, transportation, and banking services generates a supply of foreign exchange and demand for dollars just as the export of merchandise does. A Mexican business that is insured with an American company will supply pesos and demand dollars with which to pay its premiums. Similarly, when foreigners travel in the United States or transport cargo on American ships, they will supply foreign exchange and demand dollars with which to pay for these services. Thus, these service exports are credit items.

On the other hand, the import of services from foreigners generates a demand for foreign currency and supply of dollars in the exchange market. Therefore, service imports are entered into the balance-of-payments accounts as debit items. Travel abroad by U.S. citizens, the shipment of goods on foreign carriers, and the purchase of other services from foreigners are all debit items, since they create a demand for foreign exchange.

These service transactions are substantial. As Exhibit 17–5 illustrates, in 1997, U.S. service exports were $258.3 billion, compared with service imports of $170.5 billion. Thus, the United States ran an $87.8 billion surplus on its service trade transactions (line 6 of Exhibit 17–5). When we add the balance of service exports and imports to the balance of merchandise trade, we obtain the **balance on goods and services.** In 1997, the United States ran a $110.2 billion deficit (the sum of the $198.0 billion merchandise-trade deficit and the $87.8 billion service surplus) in the goods and services account.

Balance on goods and services
The exports of goods (merchandise) and services of a nation minus its imports of goods and services.

EXHIBIT 17-5

U.S. BALANCE OF PAYMENTS, 1997 (IN BILLIONS OF DOLLARS)

	Debits	Credits	Balance: Deficit (−) or Surplus (+)
Current Account			
1. U.S. merchandise exports		+679.3	
2. U.S. merchandise imports	−877.3		
3. Balance of merchandise trade (1 + 2)			−198.0
4. U.S. service exports		+258.3	
5. U.S. service imports	−170.5		
6. Balance on service trade (4 + 5)			+87.8
7. Balance on goods and services (3 + 6)			−110.2
8. U.S. investment income on U.S. assets abroad		+241.8	
9. Foreign income on foreign assets in the U.S.	−247.1		
10. Net investment income (8 + 9)			−5.3
11. Net unilateral transfers	−39.7		−39.7
12. Balance on current account (7 + 10 + 11)			**−155.2**
Capital Account			
13. Foreign investment in the U.S. (capital inflow)		+717.6	
14. U.S. investment abroad (capital outflow)	−577.2[a]		
15. Balance on capital account (13 + 14)			**+140.4**
16. Official Reserve Account Balance			+14.8
17. Total (12 + 15 + 16)			0.0

[a]*Statistical discrepancy is included in this figure.*

SOURCE: Survey of Current Business, *U.S. Department of Commerce, October 1998.*

Income from Investments. In the past, Americans have made substantial investments in stocks, bonds, and real assets in other countries. As these investments abroad generate income, dollars will flow from foreigners to Americans. The income of Americans from their investments abroad supplies foreign currency (and creates a demand for dollars) in the foreign exchange market. Thus, it enters as a credit item on the current account.

Correspondingly, foreigners hold substantial investments in the United States. As these investments earn dividends, interest, and rents, they earn income for foreigners. This income of foreigners leads to an outflow of dollars. As foreigners convert their dollar earnings to their domestic currency, the demand for foreign currency (and supply of dollars) increases in the foreign exchange market. Thus, the income of foreigners from their investments in the United States is a debit item in the balance-of-payments accounts.

As Exhibit 17–5 shows, in 1997 Americans earned $241.8 billion from investments abroad, while foreigners earned $247.1 billion from their investments in the United States. On balance, Americans earned $5.3 billion less on their investments abroad than foreigners earned on their investments in the United States. This $5.3 billion net outflow of investment income added to the deficit on current-account transactions.

Unilateral Transfers. Monetary gifts to foreigners, such as U.S. aid to a foreign government or private gifts from U.S. residents to their relatives abroad, generate a demand for foreign currencies and supply dollars in the exchange market. Thus, these gifts are debit items in the balance-of-payments accounts. Monetary gifts to Americans from foreigners are credit items. Gifts in kind are more complex. When products are given to foreigners, goods flow abroad, but there is no offsetting influx of foreign currency—that is, a demand for dollars. Balance-of-payments accountants handle such transactions as though the United States had demanded the foreign exchange and supplied the dollars with which to purchase the direct grants made to foreigners. So these items are also entered as debits. Because the U.S. government and private U.S. citizens gave $39.7 billion more to foreigners than we received from them, this net unilateral transfer was entered as a debit item on the current account in 1997.

Balance on Current Account. The difference between (1) the value of a country's current exports and earnings from investments abroad and (2) the value of its current imports and the earnings of foreigners on their domestic assets (plus net unilateral transfers to foreigners) is known as the **balance on current account.** Current-account transactions involve only current exchanges of goods and services and current income flows (and gifts). They do not involve changes in the ownership of either real or financial assets. The current-account balance provides a summary of all current-account transactions. As with the balance of trade, when the value of the current-account debit items (import-type transactions) exceeds the value of the credit items (export-type transactions), we say that the country is running a current-account deficit. Alternatively, if the credit items are greater than the debit items, the country is running a current-account surplus. In 1997, the United States ran a current-account deficit of $155.2 billion.

Balance on current account
The import-export balance of goods and services, plus net investment income earned abroad, plus net private and government transfers. If the value of the nation's export-type items exceeds (is less than) the value of the nation's import-type items plus net unilateral transfers to foreigners, a current-account surplus (deficit) is present.

CAPITAL-ACCOUNT TRANSACTIONS

In contrast with current-account transactions, **capital-account** transactions focus on changes in the ownership of real and financial assets. These transactions are composed of (1) direct investments by Americans in real assets abroad (or by foreigners in the United States) and (2) loans to and from foreigners. When foreigners make investments in the United States—for example, by purchasing stocks, bonds, or real assets from Americans—their actions will supply foreign currency and generate a demand for dollars in the foreign exchange market. Thus, these capital inflow transactions are a credit.

Capital account
The record of transactions with foreigners that involve either (1) the exchange of ownership rights to real or financial assets or (2) the extension of loans.

On the other hand, capital outflow transactions are recorded as debits. For example, if a U.S. investor purchases a shoe factory in Mexico, the Mexican seller will want to be paid in pesos. The U.S. investor will supply dollars (and demand pesos) on the foreign exchange market. Since U.S. citizens will demand foreign currency (and supply dollars) when they invest in stocks, bonds, and real assets abroad, these transactions enter into the balance-of-payments accounts as a debit. In 1997, foreign investments in the United States (capital inflow) summed to $717.6 billion, while U.S. investments abroad (capital outflow) totaled $577.2 billion.[6] Since the capital inflow exceeded the outflow, the United States ran a $140.4 billion capital-account surplus in 1997.

Official Reserve Account

Special drawing rights (SDRs)
Supplementary reserves, in the form of accounting entries, established by the International Monetary Fund (also called paper gold*). Like gold and foreign currency reserves, they can be used to make payments on international accounts.*

International Monetary Fund (IMF)
An international banking organization, with more than 180 member nations, designed to oversee the operation of the international monetary system. Although it does not control the world supply of money, it does hold currency reserves for member nations and makes currency loans to national central banks.

Governments maintain official reserve balances in the form of foreign currencies, gold, and **special drawing rights (SDRs)** with the **International Monetary Fund (IMF),** a special bank that was established in order to facilitate international transactions. Countries running a deficit on their current- and capital-account balances can draw on their reserves. Similarly, countries running a surplus can build up their reserves of foreign currencies and reserve balances with the IMF. Under the current (primarily) flexible rate system, changes in the exchange rate are generally relied on to balance the amount of goods, services, and assets purchased from foreigners and the amount sold to foreigners. Therefore, these official reserve transactions are usually quite modest relative to the total of all international transactions.

Balance of Payments Must Balance

The sum of the debit and credit items of the balance-of-payments accounts must balance. Thus, the following identity must hold:

$$\text{Current-Account Balance} + \text{Capital-Account Balance} + \text{Official Reserve Account Balance} = 0$$

However, the specific components of the accounts need not balance. For example, the debit and credit items of the current account need not be equal. Specific components may run either a surplus or a deficit. Nevertheless, since the balance of payments as a whole must balance, a deficit in one area implies a surplus in another. For example, if a nation is experiencing a current-account deficit, it must experience an offsetting surplus on the sum of its capital-account and official reserve account balances.

A current-account deficit means that, in aggregate, the citizens of a nation are buying more goods and services from foreigners than they are selling to foreigners. Under a pure flexible rate system, this excess of expenditures relative to receipts is paid for by borrowing from and selling assets to foreigners. The current system is not a pure flexible rate system; if it were, there would be no official reserve transactions. However, the official reserve transactions are generally small. In 1997, the United States ran a $155.2 billion current-account deficit and a $140.4 billion capital-account surplus. The difference between these two figures—a $14.8 billion deficit—was exactly offset by a $14.8 billion surplus in the official reserve account. Thus, the deficits and surpluses of the current-, capital-, and official reserve accounts summed to zero as is shown in Exhibit 17–5 (line 17).

Under a pure flexible rate system, official reserve transactions are zero. When this is the case, a capital-account surplus (inflow of capital) implies a current-account deficit. Similarly, a capital-account deficit (outflow of capital) implies a current-account surplus. ***With flexible exchange rates, changes in the net inflow of capital will***

[6] The statistical discrepancy is also included in the investments abroad category. This item was quite large ($99.7 billion debit) in 1997. International transactions—particularly those conducted in cash—can be difficult to monitor. As we noted when discussing the money supply, 60 percent or more of the U.S. currency supply circulates abroad. Because this "outflow" of currency is not included in balance-of-payments accounts, such movements would contribute to the statistical discrepancy. Illegal drug trade may also increase the size of this item.

influence the current-account balance. If a nation is experiencing an increase in net foreign investment, perhaps as the result of higher real interest rates, this increase in the capital-account surplus will enlarge the current-account deficit. In contrast, capital flight (outflow of capital) will move the current account toward a surplus.

MACROECONOMIC POLICY IN AN OPEN ECONOMY

During the post–Second World War period, there has been a dramatic increase in international trade and in the flow of investment capital across national boundaries. This increasing mobility of both goods and capital influences the effects of macroeconomic policy, even in a country such as the United States with a relatively small trade sector. We now live in a global economy. No country can conduct its macroeconomic policy in isolation.

Throughout this text, we have focused on the impact of macroeconomic policy within the framework of an open economy. However, we have paid little attention to the impact of macroeconomic policy on exchange rates and on the components of a nation's balance-of-payments accounts. We now turn to these issues.

MACROECONOMIC POLICY AND THE EXCHANGE RATE

Because monetary and fiscal policies exert an impact on income growth, inflation, and real interest rates, they will also influence exchange rates. These two major macropolicy tools differ with regard to their impact on the foreign exchange market. Thus, we will consider them separately.

Monetary Policy and the Exchange Rate. Suppose the United States began to follow a more expansionary monetary policy. How would this policy influence the foreign exchange market? *When the effects are not fully anticipated,* a shift to a more expansionary monetary policy will lead to more rapid economic growth, an increase in the inflation rate, and lower real interest rates.[7] As we previously discussed, each of these factors will increase the demand for foreign exchange, causing the dollar to depreciate (see prior Thumbnail Sketch). The rapid growth of income will stimulate imports. Similarly, the increase in the U.S. inflation rate (relative to our trading partners) will make U.S. goods less competitive abroad, causing a decline in exports. Simultaneously, the lower real interest rate will encourage the flow of capital abroad. ***Thus, the expected short-run effect of an unanticipated shift to a more expansionary monetary policy is a depreciation in the exchange-rate value of the dollar.***

The expected outcome of an unanticipated switch to a more restrictive monetary policy will be just the opposite. The restrictive monetary policy will retard economic growth, reduce the rate of inflation, and push real interest rates upward. Exports will grow relative to imports. Investment funds from abroad will be drawn by the high real interest rates in the United States. Foreigners will demand more dollars with

[7]As we previously noted when considering monetary policy, the impact of a policy change is dependent on whether the effects of the change are anticipated or unanticipated. Neither growth nor the real interest rate will change if people fully anticipate the effects of the change in monetary policy on the price level. In this chapter, we assume for simplicity that the price-level effects accompanying a shift in monetary policy are not fully anticipated. Clearly, this is more likely to be true in the short run than in the long run.

which to purchase goods, services, and real assets in the United States. The increase in the supply of foreign currencies and strong demand for the dollar in the foreign exchange market will cause the dollar to appreciate.

Fiscal Policy and the Exchange Rate. Fiscal policy tends to generate conflicting influences on the foreign exchange market. Suppose the United States unexpectedly shifts toward a more restrictive fiscal policy, planning a budget surplus or at least a smaller deficit. Just as with restrictive monetary policy, the restrictive fiscal policy will tend to cause a reduction in aggregate demand, an economic slowdown, and a decline in the rate of inflation. These factors will discourage imports and stimulate exports, placing upward pressure on the exchange-rate value of the dollar. However, restrictive fiscal policy will also mean less government borrowing, which will reduce real interest rates in the United States. The lower real interest rates will cause financial capital to flow from the United States. This will increase the supply of dollars in the foreign exchange market, and thereby place downward pressure on the exchange-rate value of the U.S. dollar.

Which of these two effects is likely to dominate? When answering this question, one must consider the mobility of capital relative to trade flows. ***Financial capital is highly mobile. Investors can and do quickly shift their funds from one country to another in response to changes in interest rates. In contrast, importers and exporters often enter into long-term contracts when buying and selling goods. Thus, they are likely to respond more slowly to changing market conditions. Consequently, to the extent that a more restrictive fiscal policy places downward pressure on interest rates, the outflow of capital is likely to dominate in the short run.*** At least a temporary depreciation in the nation's currency is the most likely outcome.

The analysis of expansionary fiscal policy is symmetrical. To the extent that larger budget deficits stimulate aggregate demand and domestic inflation, they will encourage imports, which will place downward pressure on the exchange-rate value of a nation's currency. However, the increased borrowing to finance larger budget deficits will push real interest rates up and draw foreign investment to the United States, causing the dollar to appreciate. In the short run, the latter outcome is more likely.

Macroeconomic Policy and the Current Account

How does macroeconomic policy affect a nation's balance on the current account? It is important to remember that the current- and capital-account balances must sum to zero under a pure flexible rate system. Thus, any deficit on the current (capital) account must be exactly offset by a capital (current) account surplus of equal size. Because unanticipated shifts in macroeconomic policy influence both the demand for imports and real interest rates, clearly they will exert an impact on both current-account and capital-account balances.

Monetary Policy and Current Account. Suppose that the Federal Reserve suddenly increases the growth rate of the money supply. How will this shift to a more expansionary monetary policy influence the U.S. balance on the current account? As we just indicated, the more rapid money growth will stimulate income, place upward pressure on the inflation rate, and reduce real interest rates. Think how this combination of factors will affect the current and capital accounts. The growth of income and higher domestic prices will stimulate imports, retard exports, and thus cause the current account to shift toward a larger deficit (or smaller surplus). At the same time, the lower domestic interest rates will encourage investors, both domestic and foreign, to shift funds from

THUMBNAIL SKETCH

How Will Monetary and Fiscal Policy Affect the Exchange-Rate and Balance-of-Payments Components?

A. The Impact of Unanticipated Shift in Monetary Policy:

	Expansionary Monetary Policy	Restrictive Monetary Policy
Exchange rate[a]	Depreciates.	Appreciates.
Real interest rates	Decline.	Increase.
Flow of capital	Capital outflow.	Capital inflow.
Current account	Shifts toward a surplus.	Shifts toward a deficit.

B. The Impact of Unanticipated Shift in Fiscal Policy:

	Expansionary Fiscal Policy	Restrictive Fiscal Policy
Exchange rate[a]	Uncertain, but the interest rate effect is likely to cause appreciation.	Uncertain, but the interest rate effect is likely to cause depreciation.
Real interest rates	Increase.	Decline.
Flow of capital	Capital inflow.	Capital outflow.
Current account	Shifts toward a deficit.	Shifts toward a surplus.

[a]Value of domestic currency

the United States to other countries where they can earn a higher rate of return. Predictably, this outflow of capital will cause a capital-account deficit and depreciation in the foreign exchange value of the dollar. In turn, the dollar depreciation will encourage exports, discourage imports, and act as a partial offset to the direct effects of the more rapid income growth. Because capital is far more mobile than goods in international markets, the outflow of capital effect will generally dominate in the short run. For a time, therefore, the shift to a more expansionary monetary policy will tend to cause an outflow of capital that will shift the capital account toward a deficit (or smaller surplus) and the current account toward a surplus (or smaller deficit).

Now consider the impact of an unanticipated shift to a more restrictive monetary policy on a nation's current-account balance. The restrictive policy will tend to slow growth and inflation, which will reduce the demand for imports. However, it will also increase real interest rates, leading to an inflow of capital and appreciation in the nation's currency. In the short run, the inflow of capital will generally dominate. Thus, the expected result of the more restrictive monetary policy is higher interest rates, an inflow of capital, a shift toward a capital-account surplus (or smaller deficit), and a shift toward a current-account deficit in the short run.

Fiscal Policy and Current Account. What impact will large budget deficits have on a nation's current account? Expansionary fiscal policy will tend to stimulate aggregate demand and push domestic interest rates upward (the *crowding-out effect*). The increase in aggregate demand will encourage the purchase of imports, and thereby shift the current account toward a deficit (or smaller surplus). Simultaneously, the higher real interest rates will both attract investment by foreigners and help keep domestic capital at home. Predictably, there will be a net capital inflow, which will shift the capital account toward a surplus.

When fiscal policy is expansionary, both the increase in imports due to the demand stimulus and the increase in the net capital inflow as the result of the higher interest rates will shift the current account toward a deficit and the capital account toward a surplus. In this way, large budget deficits will also tend to result in large current-account deficits.

Once again, the analysis is symmetrical. A shift to a more restrictive fiscal policy—for example, a reduction in the size of a budget deficit—will retard demand and reduce interest rates. As the result of the decline in aggregate demand, imports will tend to fall, shifting a nation's current account toward a surplus (or smaller deficit). Simultaneously, the low interest rates will lead to a net capital outflow, which will shift the capital account toward a deficit. Thus, restrictive fiscal policy will tend to cause a current-account surplus and a capital-account deficit. The accompanying Thumbnail Sketch summarizes the expected impacts of unanticipated shifts in monetary and fiscal policy.

MACROECONOMIC POLICY, EXCHANGE RATES, CAPITAL FLOWS, AND CURRENT-ACCOUNT DEFICITS

We are now in a position to consider the empirical evidence with regard to the impact of recent macroeconomic policy on the flow of capital and the foreign exchange value of the dollar. **Exhibit 17–6** provides data on the exchange rate, current-account balance, and net foreign investment (capital-account balance) during the last 25 years. This graphic illustrates several important points. First, the impact of the shift toward a more restrictive monetary policy and more expansionary fiscal policy during the first half of the 1980s is clearly visible. Responding to the double-digit inflation rates of 1979–1980, the Federal Reserve reduced the rate of money growth and pushed real interest rates upward in the early 1980s. The U.S. inflation rate plunged from the double-digit levels of 1979–1980 to 3.2 percent in 1983. At the same time, fiscal policy was expansionary. Increases in defense expenditures coupled with a reduction in tax rates led to a substantial increase in the federal budget deficit during the early 1980s.

Our analysis indicates that this policy combination—a more restrictive monetary policy coupled with expansionary fiscal policy—will cause higher real interest rates, an inflow of capital, currency appreciation, and a current-account deficit (see the prior Thumbnail Sketch). This is precisely what happened. In the early 1980s, real interest rates rose to historic highs. In turn, the higher interest rates led to a sharp increase in net foreign investment in the United States (frame c of Exhibit 17–6). This inflow of capital increased the demand for the dollar, causing it to appreciate sharply during 1981–1985 (frame a). The inflow of capital and appreciation of the dollar led to a dramatic increase in the current-account deficit (frame b). The annual current account of the United States shifted from a small surplus in 1981 to a deficit of more than 3 percent of GDP in the mid-1980s. These outcomes—an inflow of capital, appreciation of the dollar, and expansion in the size of the current-account deficit—are precisely what our model predicts.

APPLICATIONS IN ECONOMICS

The J-Curve Effect

As a market adjusts to a change in price, time often plays an important role. There is reason to believe that this will be true in the foreign exchange market. The impact of a currency depreciation on a current-account deficit can be broken down into a *price effect* and a *quantity effect.* A 10 percent depreciation in the dollar means that import prices increase by 10 percent in terms of dollars. Of course, this increase in the dollar price of imports will discourage purchases. However, the 10 percent depreciation also means that, *for a given quantity sold,* foreigners will earn 10 percent more dollars. Therefore, unless Americans reduce the *quantity* of their imports by more than 10 percent, their *expenditures* on imports will increase in response to a depreciation in the dollar. Similarly, the depreciation will make U.S. exports 10 percent cheaper to foreigners. Unless foreigners increase their *quantity* purchased by more than 10 percent, their demand for dollars in the exchange market will *decrease* as the result of the depreciation.

Since American and foreign-produced goods are excellent substitutes for one another, there is good reason to expect that both the U.S. demand for imports and foreign demand for U.S. exports will be highly elastic in the long run.[1] However, this may not be true in the short run. When the dollar depreciates, it will take time for American consumers to substitute away from the more expensive imports and for foreign consumers to adjust their consumption, purchasing more of the now cheaper American exports. Therefore, initially, the increase in the quantity of exports may be less than the 10 percent reduction in price. If this is the case, for a time the depreciation will actually cause the current-account deficit to worsen—the dollar expenditures on imports will rise while the dollar sales of exports will decline. With time, this situation will reverse as the U.S. demand for imports and foreign demand for U.S. exports become more elastic. Eventually, the quantity effects will dominate, and a depreciation will reduce the current-account deficit.

Economists refer to this time path of adjustment as the **J-curve effect.** A nation's current-account deficit will initially widen (slide down the hook of the "J") before it shrinks (moves up the stem of the "J") as the result of a currency depreciation. This occurs because the short-run domestic demand for imports and foreign demand for exports are inelastic. Thus, the depreciation initially increases import expenditures relative to export sales. However, in the long run, the demand for both imports and exports is elastic. Therefore, the depreciation of a nation's currency will eventually shrink the nation's current-account deficit.[2]

The J-curve effect explains why there is sometimes a substantial time lag—perhaps two or three years—between the depreciation of a nation's currency and a reduction in the current-account deficit. This was the case for the sharp reduction in the exchange-rate value of the dollar in 1985. It was nearly three years later before this depreciation began to reduce the size of the current-account deficit. (See frames b and c of Exhibit 17–6.)

[1]When demand is elastic, the quantity purchased is highly responsive to a change in price. Therefore, a change in price will cause total expenditures to change in the opposite direction. Correspondingly, *inelastic* means that the quantity purchased will be relatively unresponsive to a change in price. When this is the case, an increase in price will cause total expenditures to change in the same direction.

[2]See Jeffrey A. Rosensweig and Paul D. Koch, "The U.S. Dollar and the 'Delayed J-Curve,'" Federal Reserve Bank of Atlanta, *Economic Review,* July–August 1988, pp. 2–15, for an interesting article on the J-curve effect as it applies to the trade imbalances of the United States during the 1980s.

J-curve effect
The tendency of a nation's current-account deficit to widen initially before it shrinks in response to an exchange-rate depreciation. This tendency results because the short-run demand for both imports and exports is often inelastic, even though the long-run demand is almost always elastic.

Second, as real interest rates adjusted and the capital inflow slowed, the dollar depreciated sharply during 1986–1988. This dollar depreciation stimulated exports and discouraged imports, causing the current-account deficit to shrink during 1988 and 1989. As real GDP fell during the 1990 recession, the current account moved in balance. (Remember, slow growth of income will reduce imports relative to exports.)

Third, the strong expansion of the 1990s once again stimulated imports relative to exports, shifting the current account toward a deficit and the capital account toward a surplus. During 1997–1998, financial instability in both Latin America and Asia caused many investors to look for a safe haven. Dollar investments in U.S. stocks and bonds fit this bill. Thus, net foreign investment in the United States increased, pushing the exchange-rate value of the dollar upward. Predictably, these factors—an inflow of capital and appreciation of the dollar—resulted in a continuation of the sizable current-account deficits in the late 1990s.

EXHIBIT 17-6

THE EXCHANGE RATE, CURRENT-ACCOUNT BALANCE, AND NET FOREIGN INVESTMENT

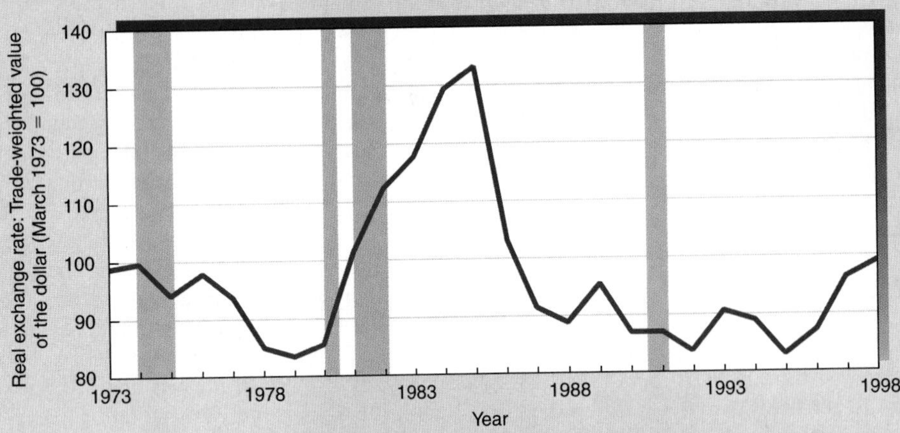

(a) Exchange-rate value of the dollar (compared with ten currencies)

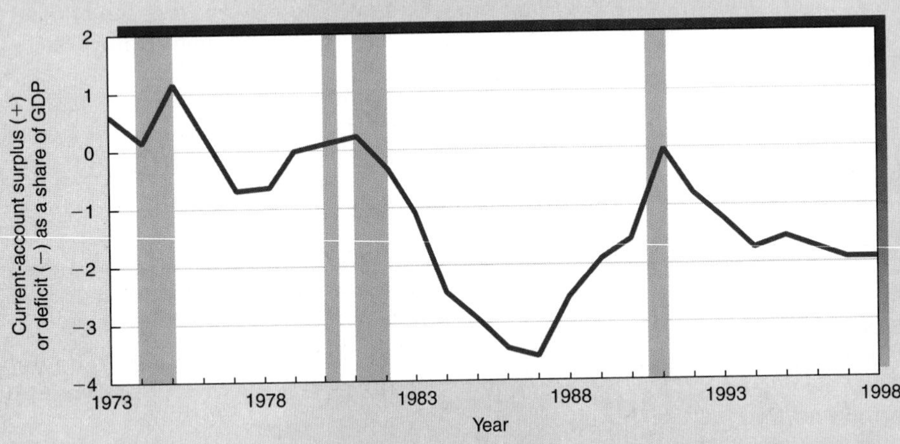

(b) Current-account balance as a share of GDP

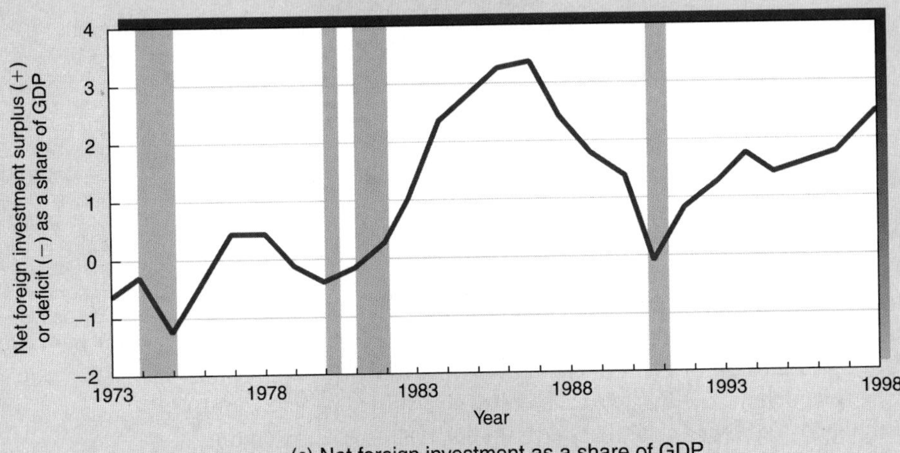

(c) Net foreign investment as a share of GDP

Note: Data are given in billions of dollars.

SOURCE: Economic Report of the President, *1999, Tables B-1, B-24, B-103, and B-110.*

Here we illustrate the relationship between the exchange rate, the current-account deficit, and net foreign investment (capital inflow). The shaded areas represent recessions.

As we have stressed throughout, the flow of capital and the current-account balance are closely related. Exhibit 17–6 clearly illustrates this point. A small capital inflow during 1977–1978 was associated with a current-account deficit of approximately the same size. When there was a small outflow of capital during 1979–1980, the current account moved to a surplus. The surge in the inflow of capital during 1982–1986 was accompanied by an equally large increase in the current-account deficit. As the capital inflow slowed during the late 1980s, the current-account deficit shrank. Later, as the inflow of capital resumed during the expansion of the 1990s, the current-account deficit widened once again. Clearly, the sizes of these two variables—net foreign investment and the current-account deficit—are closely linked.

HOW DO CURRENT-ACCOUNT DEFICITS AFFECT AN ECONOMY?

There is a tendency to think that current-account and trade surpluses are good and deficits bad. This is certainly understandable. The term *deficit* generally suggests something bad—things like excessive spending relative to income or an overdraft at the bank. In the balance-of-payments area, however, this is not always true.

What precisely is a current-account deficit? The current account measures mainly trade in goods and services. The other two current-account categories—net income from investments abroad and unilateral transfers—are generally small. Because trade in goods and services dominates current-account transactions, trade deficits and current-account deficits are closely related. Countries with large trade deficits almost always run substantial current-account deficits. Both of these deficits generally reflect that the country is importing more goods and services than it is exporting. In contrast, trade (and current-account) surpluses imply that sales of goods and services to foreigners (exports) exceed purchases from them (imports).

It is not obvious that a trade surplus is preferable to a deficit. After all, a nation that is running a trade deficit is getting more goods and services from others than it is supplying to them. What is so bad about that? Similarly, a trade surplus implies that a nation is supplying more goods and services for foreigners to consume than it is receiving from them. Is this something that people will want to continue to do?

A nation's trade deficit or surplus is an aggregation of the voluntary choices of businesses and individuals. In contrast with a budget deficit of an individual, business, or government, there is no legal entity that is responsible for the trade deficit. As Herbert Stein, a former chairman of the president's Council of Economic Advisers, once put it: "The trade deficit does not belong to any individual or institution. It is a pure-statistical aggregate, like the number of eggs laid in the U.S. or the number of bald-headed men living here."[8]

How long can a nation continue to run a current-account deficit? Perhaps surprising to some, the answer is a long time. A current-account deficit is not like business losses or an excess of household spending relative to income—conditions that eventually force decision makers to change their ways. The United States ran a current-account (trade) deficit almost every year from 1800 to 1875. On the other hand, it consistently ran current-account surpluses from 1946 to 1976. The trade accounts of other countries have followed similar lengthy periods of both deficits and surpluses.

Current-account deficits and the flow of capital. Under a pure flexible rate system, a current-account deficit implies a capital-account surplus. But it is equally true

[8]Herbert Stein, "Leave the Trade Deficit Alone," *Wall Street Journal,* March 11, 1987.

to say that a capital account surplus—that is, an inflow of foreign capital—implies a current-account deficit. In a global economy where capital moves rather freely across borders, countries with the most attractive investment environments will experience an inflow of capital. If the investments of foreigners in a country exceed those of the domestic investors abroad, foreigners will have to fill this gap. Under a flexible rate system, foreigners pay for their excess of capital purchases relative to capital sales with an excess of exports relative to imports. Thus, countries that attract a net inflow of foreign capital also tend to run current-account deficits. (see frames b and c of Exhibit 17–6.)

Are current-account deficits and an inflow of foreign capital bad? The prudent answer is: it depends on why the capital inflow is occurring and how it is used. Low-income countries often find it difficult to finance even attractive investment opportunities from their current domestic saving. When this is the case, investment funds from abroad can help them increase both their rate of capital formation and economic growth. As long as the inflow of capital is channeled into profitable investment, it enhances the growth and prosperity of a nation. Examples of this abound. Prior to 1985, Singapore ran large current-account deficits financed with an inflow of capital. Propelled by a high investment rate, it has achieved rapid growth for more than two decades and is now running a large current-account surplus. During the 1970s, South Korea ran large current-account deficits and capital-account surpluses. Like Singapore, Korea used the inflow of capital to achieve high rates of both capital formation and growth. Both economic theory and real-world experiences indicate that an inflow of capital can—if directed into profitable investments—play a positive role in the development of an economy.

Correspondingly, a current-account surplus is not always indicative of strength. For example, a country would run a current-account surplus and capital-account deficit if its profitable domestic investment alternatives were insufficient to absorb its current savings. Since domestic investors would be drawn to the more attractive investment opportunities abroad, such countries would experience an outflow of capital. In recent years, Japan has been in this position.

The current-account deficit of the United States. As part b of Exhibit 17–6 illustrates, the United States has persistently run sizable current-account deficits since 1982. The large budget deficits throughout much of this period may well have increased real interest rates and thereby contributed to both the inflow of foreign capital and the current-account deficits. However, if this were the case, the inflow of funds from abroad would have moderated both the upward pressure on interest rates and the reduction in domestic investment. When considering the significance of the current-account deficit, one should remember that the United States has a system of secure property rights, a stable monetary and political environment, and a rapidly growing labor force (compared with Europe and Japan). This makes it an attractive country in which to invest. On the other hand, the saving rate of the United States is low compared to our major trading partners. To a large degree, the U.S. current-account deficit reflects this combination of factors—an attractive domestic investment environment and a low saving rate.

INTERNATIONAL FINANCE AND EXCHANGE-RATE REGIMES

There are three major types of exchange-rate regimes: (1) flexible rates, (2) fixed rate, unified currency, and (3) pegged exchange rates. We have already explained how a flexible rate system works. We will now consider the operation of the other two.

Fixed Rate, Unified Currency System

Obviously, the 50 states of the United States have a unified currency, the dollar. In Panama, both the U.S. dollar and the Panamian balboa (available only in coins) are fully interchangeable at a one-to-one rate and equally acceptable as a means of payment. For all practical purposes, Panama has adopted the dollar as its currency. Almost two decades ago, Hong Kong linked its currency with the U.S. dollar. In 1991, Argentina did the same. Both Hong Kong and Argentina have **currency boards** that have the power to create currency only in exchange for a specific quantity of U.S. dollars (one peso = $1 in Argentina and 7.8 HK dollars = $1 in Hong Kong). Thus, the United States, Panama, Hong Kong, and Argentina have a unified currency regime.

Currency board
An entity that (a) issues a currency with a fixed designated value relative to a widely accepted currency (for example, the U.S. dollar), (b) promises to continue to redeem the issued currency at the fixed rate, and (c) maintains bonds and other liquid assets denominated in the other currency that provide 100 percent backing for all currency issued.

Beginning in 1999, 11 countries of the European Union (EU)—Belgium, Germany, Spain, France, Ireland, Italy, Luxembourg, Netherlands, Austria, Portugal, and Finland—adopted a common currency, the euro. Although the currencies of these countries will continue to circulate until 2002, each of their values is now linked to the euro at a fixed rate. Thus, these countries now have a unified currency system. In turn, the value of the euro relative to other currencies, such as the dollar and yen, is determined by market forces (flexible exchange rates).

The distinguishing characteristic of a fixed rate, unified currency regime is the presence of only one central bank with the power to expand and contract the supply of money. For the dollar, that central bank is the Federal Reserve System; for the euro, it is the European Central Bank. Those linking their currency at a fixed rate to the dollar or the euro are no longer in a position to conduct monetary policy. For example, the former central banks of the countries now using the euro no longer have the power to create money. In essence, they are now branches of the European Central Bank, much like the regional and district Federal Reserve banks are branches of the Fed.

The adoption of a currency board provides a method of unifying one currency with another that has greater credibility in international financial markets. This attribute is particularly attractive for countries like Argentina with a long history of monetary expansion and hyperinflation. ***A currency board does two things. First, it issues domestic currency at a fixed rate in exchange for a designated foreign currency.***

The symbol for the euro looks like the Greek letter epsilon, but with two center horizontal lines. This was chosen because of Greece's historical significance in European history, as well as the letter e being the first letter of the word "Europe." The two center lines are intended to represent stability. How will the euro influence future financial arrangements?

Second, the foreign currency is then invested in bonds denominated in that currency. This means that the money issued by the currency board is backed 100 percent by the foreign currency. Therefore, the holders of the money issued by the currency board know that it will always have sufficient funds to exchange the domestic currency for the foreign one at the fixed rate.

If domestic citizens are buying more (imports) from foreigners than they are selling to them (exports), the amount of the domestic currency exchanged for the foreign one will increase. This will cause the domestic money supply to fall, which will place downward pressure on the price level (rate of inflation). In turn, the lower level of prices will encourage exports relative to imports, and thereby automatically keep the value of the two currencies in line. Countries that adopt the currency board approach are no longer in a position to conduct monetary policy. Instead, they essentially accept the monetary policy of the nation to which their currency is tied. They also accept the exchange-rate fluctuations of that currency relative to other currencies outside of the unified zone.

A pure gold standard system, where each country sets the value of its currency in terms of gold and fully backs its domestic money supply with gold, is also a fixed rate, unified system. In this case, the world supply of gold (rather than a central bank) determines the total supply of money. If a country were importing more than it was exporting, its supply of gold would fall, which would reduce the domestic supply of money. This would place downward pressure on the domestic price level and bring the payments to and receipts from foreigners back into balance. Things would change in the opposite direction if a country were exporting more than it was importing. International financial arrangements approximated those of a gold standard during the period between the American Civil War and the establishment of the Federal Reserve System in 1913.

Fixed exchange rate
An exchange rate that is set at a determined amount by government policy.

Between 1944 and 1971, most of the world operated under a system of **fixed exchange rates,** where each nation fixed the price of its currency relative to others. In essence, this was a quasi-unified system. It was unified in the sense that the value of one currency was fixed relative to others over lengthy time periods. But it was not a fully unified system because the countries continued to exercise control over monetary policy. Nations maintained reserves with the International Monetary Fund, which could be drawn on when payments to foreigners exceeded receipts from them. This provided each with some leeway in its conduct of monetary policy. However, countries running persistent payment deficits would eventually deplete their reserves. This constrained the country's monetary independence and provided its policy makers with an incentive to keep monetary policy approximately in line with that of its trading partners. Under this fixed exchange-rate regime, nations confronting balance-of-payments problems often imposed tariffs, quotas, and other trade barriers in an effort to keep their payments and receipts in balance. Various restrictions on the convertibility of currencies were also common. These problems eventually led to the demise of the system.

Pegged Exchange Rates

Pegged exchange-rate system
A commitment to use monetary and fiscal policy to maintain the exchange-rate value of the domestic currency at a fixed rate or within a narrow band relative to another currency (or bundle of currencies).

A **pegged exchange-rate system** is one where a country commits itself to the maintenance of a specific exchange rate (or exchange-rate range) relative to another, stronger currency (such as the U.S. dollar) or a bundle of currencies. In contrast with the currency board approach, however, countries adopting the pegged exchange rate continue to conduct monetary policy. Thus, an excess of payments (imports) relative to receipts (exports) does not force the country to reduce its domestic money supply.

In order for a pegged rate system to be effective, a country must follow a monetary policy consistent with the fixed rate. Maintenance of the pegged rate requires the country to give up monetary independence. A nation can either (1) follow an independent monetary policy and allow its exchange rate to fluctuate or (2) tie its monetary policy to the maintenance of the fixed exchange rate. It cannot, however, maintain the convertibility of its currency at the fixed exchange rate while following a monetary policy more expansionary than that of the country to which the domestic currency is tied. Attempts to do so will lead to a financial crisis—a situation where falling foreign currency reserves eventually force the country to forgo the pegged exchange rate.

This is precisely what happened in Mexico. During 1989–1994, Mexico sought to peg the value of the peso to the U.S. dollar. At the same time, Mexico expanded its domestic money supply much more rapidly than the United States. This led to a higher rate of inflation in Mexico than in the United States. Responding to the different inflation rates, more and more people shifted away from the Mexican peso and toward the dollar. By December 1994, Mexico's foreign exchange reserves were virtually depleted. As a result, it could no longer maintain the fixed exchange rate with the dollar. Mexico devalued its currency, triggering a crisis that affected several other countries following similar policies.

More recently, much the same thing happened in Brazil and several Asian countries (Thailand, South Korea, Indonesia, and Malaysia). As in Mexico, these countries sought to maintain fixed exchange rates (or rates within a narrow band), while following monetary and fiscal policies that were inconsistent with the fixed rate. As their reserves declined, they were forced to abandon their exchange-rate pegs. This was extremely disruptive to these economies. Imports suddenly became much more expensive and therefore less affordable. Businesses (including banks) that had borrowed money in dollars (or some other foreign currency) were unable to repay their loans as the result of the sharp decline in the exchange-rate value of the domestic currency. These economies experienced sharp economic declines during 1997–1998.

The Future

Currently, international financial arrangements are in a state of flux. The recent failures of pegged rate systems have created a vacuum. Many countries are reluctant either to (a) give up their monetary policy independence as the currency board approach requires or (b) adopt a purely flexible exchange rate. Both economic theory and real-world experience indicate that either of these two approaches will work reasonably well. On the other hand, the pegged exchange approach is something like a time bomb. Pushed by political considerations, monetary policy makers in most countries are unable to follow a course consistent with the maintenance of pegged rates.

As the relative size of international exchange continues to grow, so too will the demand for currency of stable value. During the past decade, there has been a dramatic increase in the number of countries where citizens are free to use and maintain bank accounts in any currency they choose, including those issued by other governments. In most areas of the world, the U.S. dollar is the preferred foreign currency. As a result, more than half the currency issued by the Federal Reserve circulates in other countries.[9] The legalization of foreign currencies is an important structural change. The availability of competitive currencies reduces the incentive of the domestic monetary authorities to inflate. If they do, more and more people will shift to the dollar and

[9]If this currency did not circulate outside of the United States, it would be necessary for the U.S. government to have a larger quantity of interest-bearing debt outstanding. When foreigners hold dollars, in essence they are extending an interest-free loan to the U.S. government. Thus, the circulation of dollars abroad is advantageous to the United States.

other, more stable currencies. In essence, the use of a foreign currency provides citizens with an alternative to the uncertainties accompanying an unstable domestic monetary regime.

The shape of financial and exchange-rate regimes is likely to change substantially in the years immediately ahead. Much of Europe has already moved toward a unified currency. As the euro gains credibility, the four EU members (Denmark, Greece, Sweden, and the United Kingdom) that have not yet adopted the euro are likely to do so. So too are several Eastern European countries, either through a currency board arrangement or by directly joining the monetary union. It would not be surprising to see a similar trend in North and South America. Brazil, Mexico, and several other countries in the Americas may well seek currency stability through some form of linkage with the dollar. A substantial share of international trade is also conducted in Japanese yen. In the future, the dollar, euro, and yen—perhaps along with two or three other currencies—may well emerge as the dominant currencies used throughout the world for domestic as well as international trade. These developments make this an exciting time to follow international finance.

KEY POINTS

➤ Because countries generally use different currencies, international trade usually involves the conversion of one currency to another. The currencies of different countries are bought and sold in the foreign exchange market. The exchange rate is the price of one national currency in terms of another.

➤ The dollar demand for foreign exchange arises from the purchase (import) of goods, services, and assets by Americans from foreigners. The supply of foreign currency in exchange for dollars arises from the sale (export) of goods, services, and assets by Americans to foreigners. The equilibrium exchange rate will bring these two forces into balance.

➤ With flexible exchange rates, the following will cause a nation's currency to appreciate: (1) rapid growth of income abroad (and/or slow domestic growth), (2) low inflation (relative to trading partners), and (3) rising domestic real interest rates (and/or falling rates abroad). The reverse of these conditions will cause a nation's currency to depreciate.

➤ The balance-of-payments accounts provide a summary of transactions with foreigners. Transactions like imports that generate a demand for foreign currencies (and supply of the domestic currency) in the foreign exchange market are recorded as debit items. Transactions like exports that create a supply of foreign currencies (and demand for the domestic currency) are recorded as credit items.

➤ The foreign exchange market will bring the quantity demanded of foreign exchange into balance with the quantity supplied. This will also bring the total debits and total credits of the balance-of-payments accounts into balance.

➤ There are three major balance-of-payments components: (1) current account, (2) capital account, and (3) official reserve account. The balances of these three components must sum to zero, but the individual components of the accounts need not be in balance. Therefore, a deficit in one area implies an offsetting surplus in other areas. Under a pure flexible rate system, there will not be any official reserve account transactions. Under these circumstances, a current-account deficit implies a capital-account surplus (and vice versa).

➤ An unanticipated shift to a more restrictive monetary policy will raise the real interest rate, reduce the rate of inflation, and, at least temporarily, reduce aggregate demand and the growth of income. These factors will all cause the nation's currency to appreciate. In turn, the currency appreciation along with the inflow of capital will result in a current-account deficit. In contrast, the effects of a more expansionary monetary policy will be just the opposite: lower interest rates, an outflow of capital, currency depreciation, and a shift toward a current-account surplus.

➤ An unanticipated shift to a more expansionary fiscal policy will tend to increase real interest rates, lead to an inflow of capital, and cause the nation's current account to shift toward a deficit. The effects of a shift to a more restrictive fiscal policy will be just the opposite: lower interest rates, an outflow of capital, and movement toward a current-account surplus.

➤ Under a flexible exchange-rate system, an inflow of capital implies a current-account deficit. Correspondingly, an outflow of capital implies a current-account surplus. Whether a country runs a current-account deficit or surplus is largely dependent upon the attractiveness of domestic investment opportunities relative to the nation's saving rate.

➤ There are three major types of exchange-rate regimes: (1) flexible rates, (2) fixed rate, unified currency, and (3) pegged exchange rates. Eleven nations of the European Union have recently adopted a unified currency system. Countries can also use a currency board to unify their currency with another. The currencies of Hong Kong, Argentina, and Panama are unified with the U.S. dollar. In order to be effective, pegged rate systems require that a nation follow a monetary policy consistent with the maintenance of the pegged rate. Political pressure often makes this difficult to do.

CRITICAL ANALYSIS QUESTIONS

1. If the dollar depreciates relative to the Japanese yen, how will this affect your ability to purchase a Honda Accord? How will this change influence the quantity of Hondas purchased by Americans? How will it affect the dollar expenditures of Americans on Hondas?

2. How do flexible exchange rates bring about balance in the exchange-rate market? Do they lead to a balance between merchandise exports and imports? Explain.

3. "If a trade deficit means that we are getting more items from abroad than we are sending to foreigners, why is it considered a bad thing?" Answer this question.

*4. The accompanying chart indicates an actual newspaper quotation of the exchange rate of various currencies. On February 2, did the dollar appreciate or depreciate against the British pound? How did it fare against the French franc?

	U.S. Dollar Equivalent	
	February 1	February 2
British pound	1.755	1.746
French franc	0.1565	0.1575

*5. Suppose the exchange rate between the United States and Mexico freely fluctuates in the open market. Indicate which of the following would cause the dollar to appreciate (or depreciate) relative to the peso.

a. An increase in the quantity of drilling equipment purchased in the United States by Pemex, the Mexican oil company, as a result of a Mexican oil discovery
b. An increase in the U.S. purchase of crude oil from Mexico as a result of the development of Mexican oil fields
c. Higher real interest rates in Mexico, inducing U.S. citizens to move their financial investments from U.S. to Mexican banks
d. Lower real interest rates in the United States, inducing Mexican investors to borrow dollars and then exchange them for pesos
e. Inflation in the United States and stable prices in Mexico
f. An increase in the inflation rate from 2 percent to 10 percent in both the United States and Mexico
g. An economic boom in Mexico, inducing Mexicans to buy more U.S.-made automobiles, trucks, electric appliances, and television sets
h. Attractive investment opportunities, inducing U.S. investors to buy stock in Mexican firms

6. Explain why a current-account balance and a capital-account balance must sum to zero under a pure flexible rate system.

7. "A nation cannot continue to run a deficit on its current account. A healthy, growing economy will not persistently expand its indebtedness to foreigners. Eventually, the trade deficits will lead to national bankruptcy." Evaluate this view.

8. In recent years, a substantial share of the domestic capital formation in the United States has been financed by foreign investors. Is this inflow of capital from abroad indicative that the U.S. economy is in poor health? How might the United States go about reducing its current-account deficit?

*9. Suppose that the United States were running a current-account deficit. How would each of the following changes influence the size of the current-account deficit?

a. A recession in the United States
b. A decline in the attractiveness of investment opportunities in the United States
c. An improvement in investment opportunities abroad

10. Several politicians have suggested that the federal government should run a sizable budget surplus during the next decade in order to "save social security." If the

federal government does run a large surplus, what is the expected impact on interest rates, the inflow of capital, the current-account deficit, and the foreign exchange value of the dollar? Explain the reasoning underlying your answer.

*11. If foreigners have confidence in the U.S. economy and therefore move to expand their investments in the United States, how will the U.S. current-account balance be affected? How will the exchange-rate value of the dollar be affected?

12. Is a trade surplus indicative of a strong, healthy economy? Why or why not?

13. What is the J-curve effect? According to the J-curve effect, how will a depreciation in a nation's currency affect its current-account balance?

*14. "Changes in exchange rates will automatically direct a country to a current-account balance under a flexible exchange-rate system." Is this statement true or false?

*15. In recent years, many American political figures have been highly critical of the fact that U.S. imports from Japan have consistently exceeded U.S. exports to Japan.

a. Under a flexible exchange-rate system, is there any reason to expect that the imports from a given country will tend to equal the exports to that country?

b. Can you think of any reason why the United States might persistently run a trade deficit with a country such as Japan?

c. If Japan purchased substantially more American goods, would this significantly reduce the current-account deficit the United States has been running? Why or why not?

*Asterisk denotes questions for which answers are given in Appendix B.

PART 5

Applications and Special Topics in Economics

Economics has a lot to say about current issues and real world events. Why are unemployment rates substantially higher in Europe than in the United States? Why were the rates of both inflation and unemployment so high during the 1970s? Why does the current social security system face problems and what might be done to minimize them? Do labor unions increase the wages of workers? Is the world in danger of running out of natural resources? How can we best protect the environment? This section will focus on these topics and several other current issues.

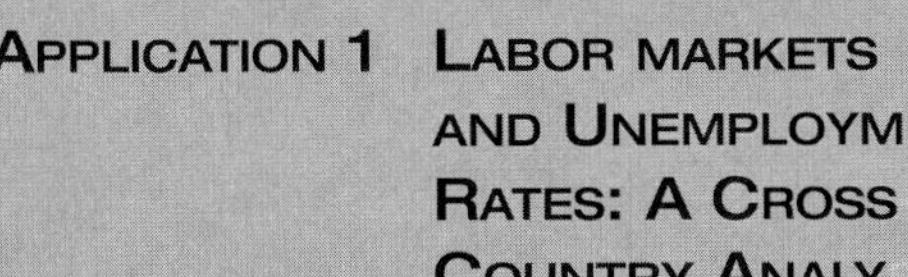

Application 1 Labor Markets and Unemployment Rates: A Cross Country Analysis

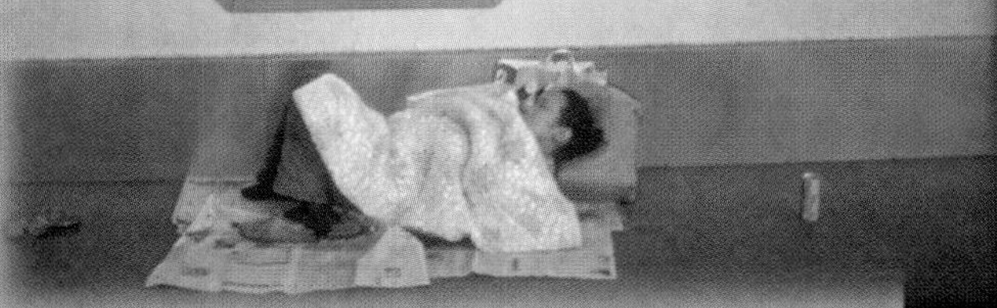

Application 2
Social Security: The Nature of the Problem and the Alternatives for Dealing with It

Application 3
The Stock Market: What Does It Do and How Has It Performed?

Application 4 How Does Government Regulation Affect Your Life?

Application 5 Income Inequality Transfers, and the Role of Government

Application 6 Do Labor Unions Increase the Wages of Workers?

Application 7 Natural Resources and the Future

Application 8 Economics and the Environment

Economics helps us better understand the real world.

APPLICATION 1

If work does not pay, people will be reluctant to work.
OECD Jobs Strategy Report[1]

Labor Markets and Unemployment Rates: A Cross-Country Analysis

APPLICATION FOCUS

- Why are unemployment rates substantially higher in Europe than in the United States?
- How do the structure of labor markets and level of unemployment benefits influence the rate of unemployment?
- How have the United Kingdom and New Zealand altered the structure of their labor markets?

[1]OECD, *OECD Jobs Strategy: Making Work Pay* (Paris: OECD, 1997), p. 7.

As we push toward the millennium, concern about persistently high rates of unemployment is widespread in Europe, Canada, and Australia. Unemployment in these three areas has remained at double-digit levels throughout most of the 1990s. At the same time, however, the unemployment rate in the United States has declined to its lowest level in nearly three decades. The U.S. rate is approximately one-half the rate of the European Union (EU). Although the Japanese unemployment rate has been rising in the 1990s, it is still substantially lower than that of the EU. Why is the unemployment rate so much higher in Europe than in the United States and Japan? Why do the Canadian and Australian unemployment rates look much like those of Europe? Does the structure of labor markets make any difference? This application will address these issues.

CROSS-COUNTRY VARIATIONS IN UNEMPLOYMENT RATES

Exhibit A1–1 shows the standardized unemployment rates during 1986–1990 and 1991–1998 for the five most populous European countries, plus Australia, Canada, Japan, and the United States.[2] These countries are all members of the Organization for Economic Cooperation and Development (OECD). They are perhaps the nine most important market economies in the world. During 1991–1998, the unemployment rate averaged 10.6 percent in Italy, 11.6 percent in France, and a whopping 20.9 percent in Spain. For the European Union as a whole, the average unemployment rate during 1991–1998 was 10.4 percent, compared to 5.9 percent for the United States and 3 percent for Japan. During the last 2 years, Germany—like France, Italy, and Spain—has also experienced double-digit rates of unemployment.

These high unemployment rates are not the result of recession. The nine economies of Exhibit A1–1 expanded in the 1990s and the inflation rate of each has been low and stable—neither rising nor falling. Under these circumstances, unemployment will move toward the natural rate, the lowest sustainable unemployment rate consistent with the economy's institutional structure. Thus, there is reason to believe that the high rates of unemployment are a long-term rather than temporary phenomenon.

Employment growth in Europe has also lagged well behind that of the United States and Japan. Total employment for the 15 European Union countries in 1997 was only 2.3 percent higher than the figure for 1980. Employment actually declined in Italy during the 1980–1997 period. The total growth of employment in Germany, France,

[2]This section borrows freely from Edward Bierhanzl and James Gwartney, "Regulation, Unions, and Labor Markets," *Regulation* (summer 1998): 40–53.

EXHIBIT A1-1

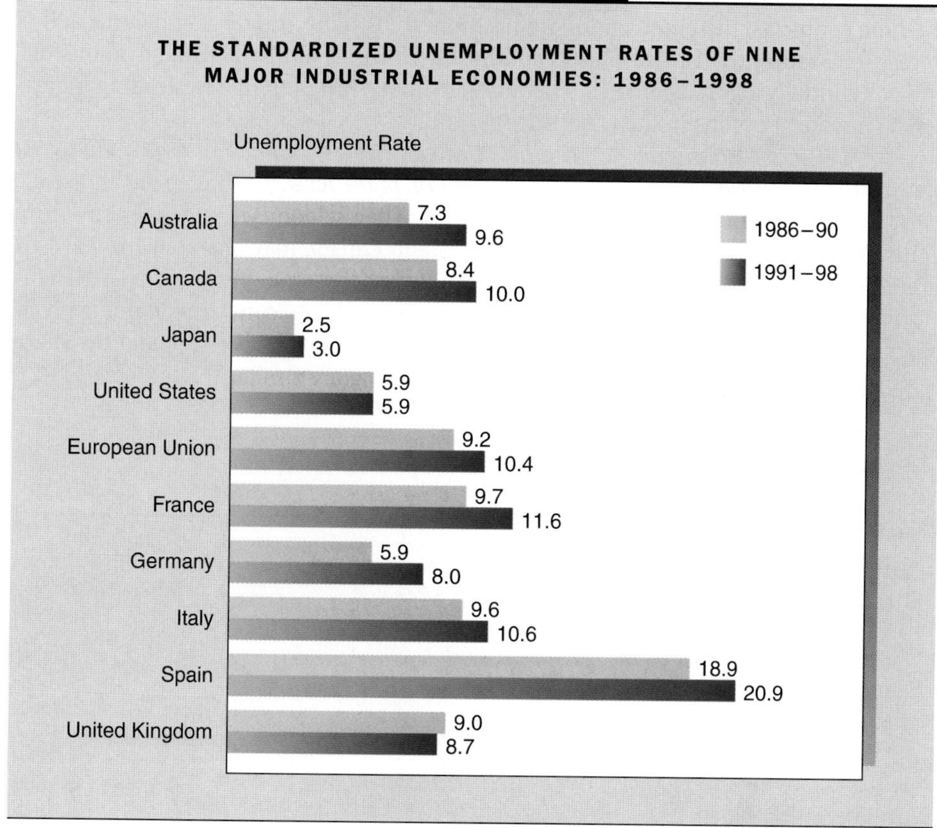

Since the mid-1980s, the unemployment rates of Australia, Canada, and the major European economies have been persistently higher than the rates for the United States and Japan.

SOURCE: OECD, *OECD Economic Outlook* (December 1998).

the United Kingdom, and Spain was 5 percent or less during this same period. By way of comparison, employment grew by 18.5 percent in Japan and by 29.5 percent in the United States.

THE STRUCTURE OF LABOR MARKETS

Labor market structural characteristics and policies differ substantially among countries. Compared to the United States and Japan, the labor markets of Europe, Australia, and Canada are characterized by (1) higher rates of unionization, (2) greater regulation, and (3) more generous unemployment assistance.[3] Let us look at the cross-country data and consider how each of these factors will influence the rate of unemployment.

[3]For additional information on this topic, see Charles Bean, "European Unemployment: A Survey," *Journal of Economic Literature,* 1995, no. 2:573–619; Sveinbjorn Blondal and Mark Pearson,"Unemployment and Other Nonemployment Benefits," *Oxford Review of Economic Policy,* 1995, no. 1:136–169; OECD, *Implementing the OECD Jobs Strategy: Member Countries' Experience* (Paris: OECD, 1997); OECD, *Making Work Pay: Taxation, Benefits, Employment and Unemployment* (Paris: OECD, 1997); and Horst Siebert, "Labor Market Rigidities: At the Root of Unemployment in Europe," *Journal of Economic Perspectives,* 1997, no. 3:37–54.

Centralized Wage-Setting

Exhibit A1–2 indicates both the percentage of the nonfarm labor force that is unionized and the share of employees whose wages are set by collective bargaining. Among the nine countries, the unionization rate is highest for Italy, Australia, and Canada; it is lowest for France, the United States, and Spain. However, the structure of unions differs substantially across countries. Therefore, membership is often a misleading indicator of the role of unions in the wage-setting process.

Collective bargaining in the United States, Canada, and Japan is decentralized—it takes place at the company or plant level. Unions in Japan are almost exclusively of the "company union" variety. They seldom set wages for an entire industry. Although unions in the United States and Canada may operate across an entire industry, the bargaining process is nearly always between a union and a single employer, or, in some cases, a single plant of the employer. These contracts do not apply to other firms. Under these circumstances, the union density (membership) and the share of workers whose wages are set by collective bargaining are similar (see Exhibit A1–2).

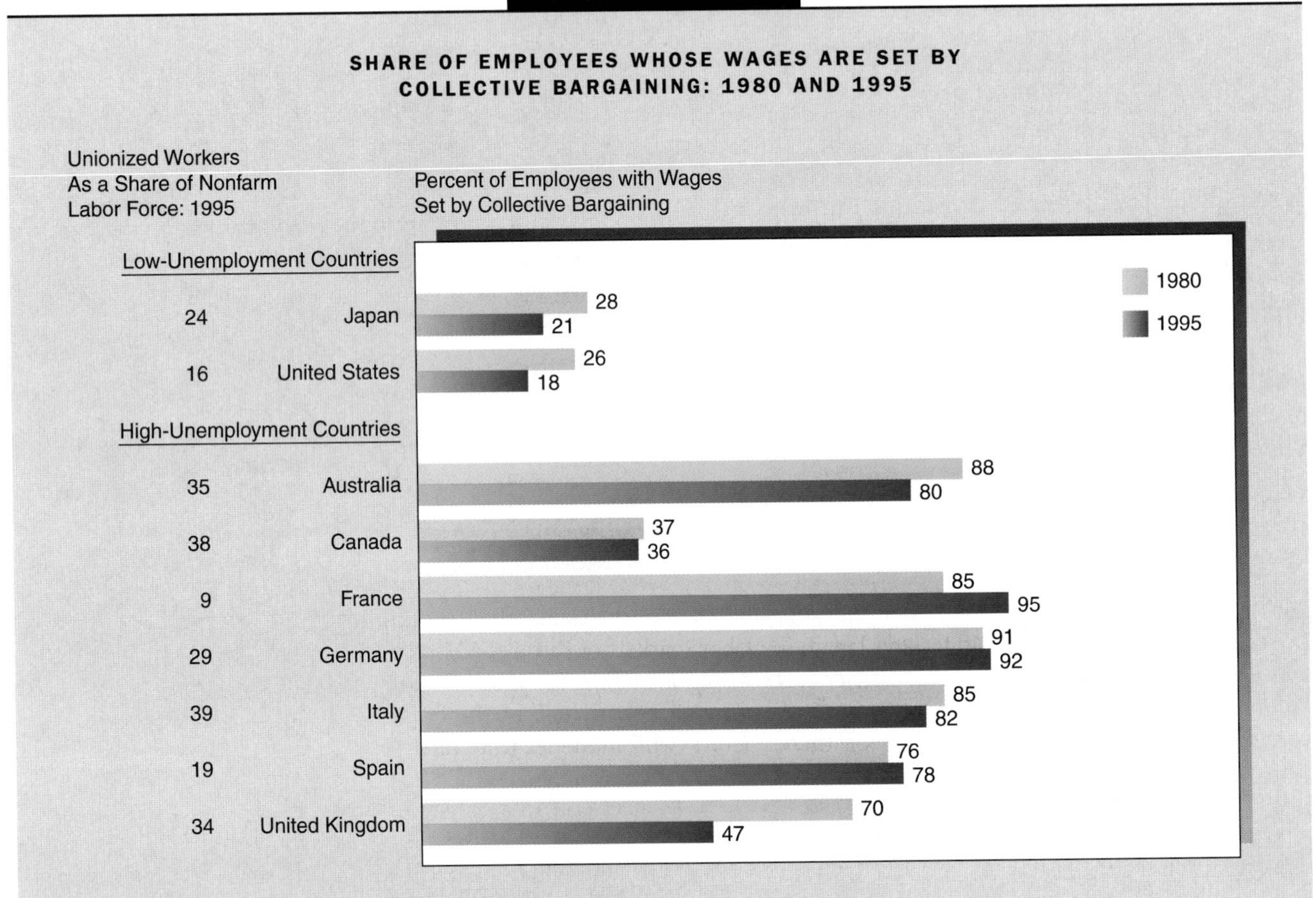

Centralized collective bargaining agreements that set wages for all workers in an industry and/or occupation are far more common in Australia and the major European economies than in the United States, Canada, and Japan.

SOURCES: OECD, Employment Outlook *(July 1994), Table 5.7; OECD,* Employment Outlook *(July 1997), Table 3.3; and OECD,* Country Surveys *(various issues).*

In contrast, the wage-setting process is highly centralized throughout most of Europe as well as in Australia. Negotiations between a union (or federation of unions) and an association of employers set the wages for all or most all workers in various industries, occupations, and/or regions. Statutory legislation extends these agreements to both nonunion employees and nonassociation employers who neither participated in the bargaining process nor agreed to the wage contracts. Sometimes political officials are also actively involved in the wage-setting process.

Therefore, as Exhibit A1–2 shows, the share of employees whose wages are set by collective bargaining in Australia and the populous countries of Europe (except for the United Kingdom in recent years) is far greater than union membership. For example, while union members were only 9 percent of the French labor force in 1995, collective bargaining set the wages for 95 percent of the employees. In Spain, Australia, Italy, and Germany, the pattern was the same. In all of these countries, highly centralized "agreements" set the wages of most workers—both union and nonunion—within various industry and occupational categories. This explains why the proportion of employees whose wages are set by collective bargaining is so much higher than union workers as a share of the workforce.

Does it make any difference whether wages are set at the firm level or for an entire industry, occupation, or region? Economic theory indicates that it does. When union members (and unionized firms) compete with nonunion workers and firms, market forces continue to play an important role. If the unionized workers push wages significantly above the competitive level, it will be more difficult for their employers to compete effectively with nonunion rivals. Thus, higher wages for union members would lead to employment reductions in the unionized sector. This will temper the bargaining process.

In contrast, the discipline of market forces is eroded when the wages for all workers and firms in an industry, an occupation, and a region are set centrally. A union that can set the wages of all firms in an industry will have considerable monopoly power. As wages are pushed up, the costs of both union and nonunion employers will rise. There will be less opportunity for nonunion firms to expand and hire workers willing to work at a lower wage. Of course, market forces will not be totally absent. Higher wages will encourage the substitution of capital for labor and make it more difficult for domestic firms to compete in international markets. Some firms will move production operations to other countries, where the services of workers of similar skill are available at a lower cost. The predictable result will be high rates of unemployment (and slow rates of employment growth) like that experienced by European countries during the last two decades.

Centralized wage-setting will have fewer adverse effects in small countries with labor forces that are relatively homogeneous in skills and education. In large countries with regional differences in cost-of-living and greater diversity among labor force participants, centrally determined wage rates will predictably lead to a substantial excess supply of workers in some areas and excess demand in others. In fact, unions and employers in high-wage regions can use the centralized wage-setting process to foist higher costs on rival firms and workers in regions where wages, reflecting educational and skill levels, would normally be lower. By pushing wages up in those regions, lower-wage and lower-skill workers are priced out of the market and rendered less competitive. The incentive for capital to move toward the low-wage regions is thus reduced.

Northern and southern Italy illustrate the significance of this strategy. Workers in southern Italy generally have fewer skills and less education than their counterparts in the North. With centralized labor contracts, however, wages in the various job categories are the same in both regions. As a result, workers in the South are less competitive and the incentive for capital to move toward that region is substantially

In Europe and Australia, union contracts often set the wages for all workers—both union and nonunion—in industry and occupational categories. The wages of more than three out of four employees are set by unions in Europe, compared to one in five in the United States.

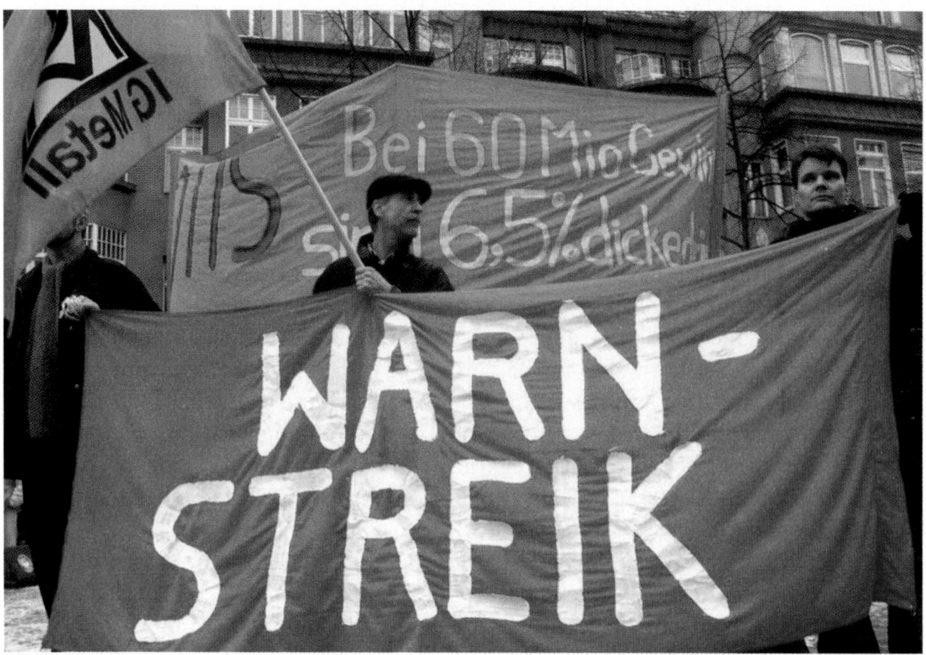

reduced. Obviously, the northern workers and their union representatives find this arrangement highly attractive. In the South, however, the results are disastrous. In recent years, unemployment rates in southern Italy have ranged between 20 percent and 30 percent—three or four times the rates of the North. Centralized wage-setting has also reduced the competitiveness of low-skill workers in several regions of Spain. As in Italy, the policy has led to both a high overall rate of unemployment and substantial regional disparity.

Regulation of Dismissal and Mandated Severance Pay

Severance pay
Pay by an employer to an employee upon the termination of employment with the firm.

European labor markets are also characterized by laws mandating various periods of prior notification and/or months of **severance pay** for the dismissal of a worker. **Exhibit** A1–3 presents data on the restrictiveness of dismissal regulations in various countries. The graph indicates the number of months of severance pay plus one-half the months of prior notification required for a no-fault dismissal of an employee. Since these mandates generally vary with seniority of the employee, the figures are the average for two workers, one with 4 years and another with 20 years of seniority.

The sum of the months of severance pay and prior notification required for a dismissal are relatively short in the United States, Japan, and Canada.[4] In contrast, they are quite lengthy in Italy and Spain. For example, Italian employers are required to give a dismissed worker with 4 years of seniority 1.1 months of notification and 3.5 months of severance pay. If the worker has 20 years of seniority, prior notification of 2.2 months and severance pay of 18 months are required. In

[4]Although there is no general notification requirement in the United States, employers with 100 or more full-time employees are required to give 60-day notice to employees dismissed as the result of a plant closing or mass layoff.

EXHIBIT A1-3

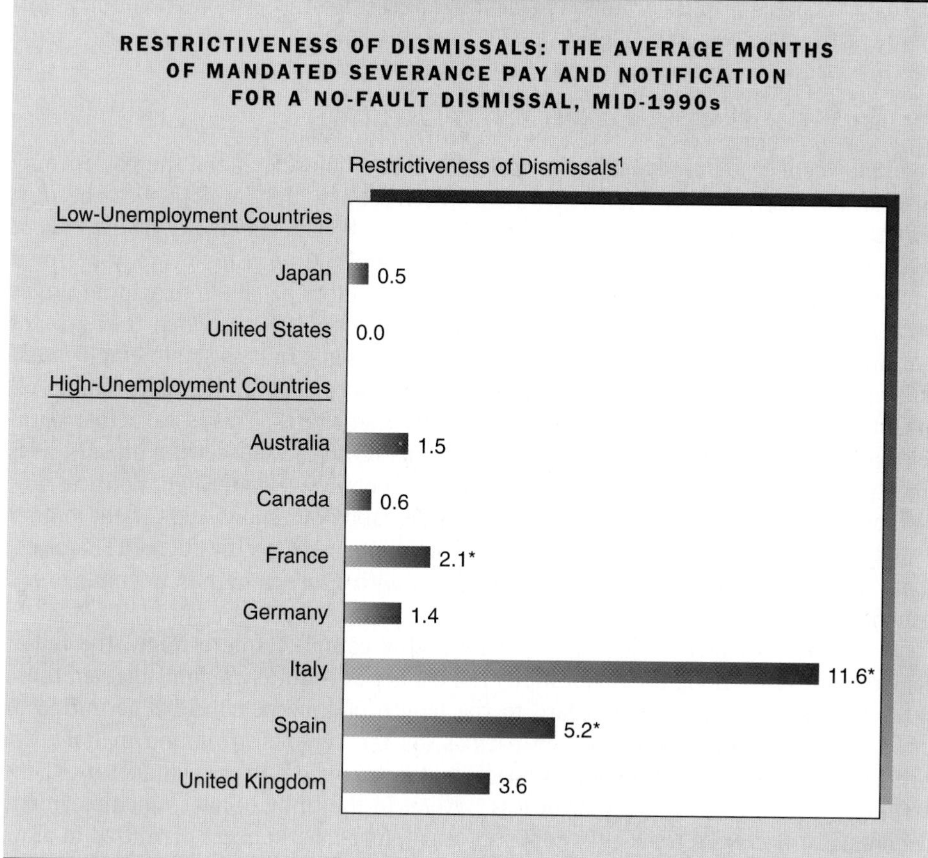

In Europe and Australia, government regulations generally require employers to give dismissed employees substantial prior notification and pay them severance pay for lengthy periods of time. These dismissal regulations are particularly restrictive in Italy and Spain.

[1]The average months of mandated severance pay plus ½ of the average months of mandated notification for the no-fault dismissal of a worker (average for workers with 4 years and 20 years of employment).
*Indicates that collective dismissals required approval from political authorities.
SOURCES: OECD, OECD Jobs Study: Evidence and Explanations *(1994), Part II, Table 6.5; and OECD,* Country Surveys *(various issues).*

addition, several European countries require political approval for mass layoffs. Employers in Italy, Spain, and France must convince various political officials that a business necessity is present before they are permitted to reduce their workforce by a sizable amount.

Proponents argue that regulations mandating notification and severance pay will help protect workers against arbitrary dismissal and provide them with greater job security. However, regulations that make it more costly to dismiss workers also make it more costly to hire them. When dismissal costs are high, employers will be reluctant to add workers during periods of strong demand because it will be costly to dismiss them if future conditions are less favorable. Thus, firms will often find that it is cheaper to expand output—particularly if the expansion is expected to be temporary—by using more capital, contracting out, or hiring part-time workers not covered by the dismissal regulations.

Furthermore, restrictive dismissal policies reduce the competition between workers with jobs and those seeking employment. They make it more expensive for employers to substitute current job seekers for established workers. In essence, the restrictions will make it extremely difficult for new entrants to find jobs and acquire labor-force experience. Thus, one of the expected side effects is high unemployment among youthful workers seeking employment. The data are consistent with this view. The unemployment rates of countries with the most restrictive dismissal policies are extremely high in the age category (15 to 24 years) where new labor-force entrants are most likely. The unemployment rate among 15- to 24-year-olds in 1996 was 42 percent in Spain, 34 percent in Italy, and 27 percent in Greece, another European country with highly restrictive dismissal policies.

Impact of Unemployment Benefits

Unemployment benefits reduce the opportunity cost of job search and thereby encourage more lengthy "spells" of unemployment. When set at a high level, they can become an attractive source of income in comparison to work. The generosity of the benefit levels may also influence unemployment in more subtle ways. Employers in seasonal and other industries offering erratic employment will often be able to pay lower wages because the benefits provide employees with income supplements when they are not working. In essence, the benefits subsidize businesses offering unstable employment and encourage the expansion of such employment.[5] More generous benefits tend to reduce the political repercussions of high unemployment rates. This is particularly important when the government is an active participant in the wage-setting process, as is the case throughout much of Europe. When the benefit levels are high, political officials will have less reason to resist the wage demands of unions even if the higher wages mean fewer jobs and higher rates of unemployment in the future. Therefore, there are good reasons to expect that countries with more generous unemployment benefits will experience higher unemployment.

Replacement rate
The share of previous earnings replaced by unemployment benefits.

Unemployment benefit systems are highly complex. Interestingly, the initial **replacement rate** among the major industrial countries is quite similar. However, there is considerable variation with regard to the length of time persons are permitted to draw benefits. The shortest duration periods for the benefits are found in Italy, the United States, the United Kingdom, Canada, and Japan, where the benefits for most unemployed workers expire in a year or less.[6] (*Note:* In the United States, unemployment benefits expire after 26 weeks.) In contrast, unemployed workers are permitted to draw benefits for two years or more in Spain, France, Germany, and Australia.

The replacement rate often varies with previous level of earnings, family size and situation, previous length of employment, and duration of unemployment. The OECD has calculated the replacement rate of member countries for recipients at two different income levels, three family situations, and three time periods of unemployment. The average replacement rates for these 18 different categories provide a reasonably good "index of generosity" for the unemployment system of each country.[7]

As Exhibit A1–4 shows, the unemployment benefits are generally more attractive (and less restrictive with regard to eligibility) in Europe, Australia, and Canada

---

[5]In several countries, including the United States, employers with more erratic employment patterns are required to pay a higher payroll tax for unemployment insurance. However, the higher tax is generally insufficient to cover the additional benefits paid to the workers laid off or dismissed by these firms.

[6]Italy uses mandated severance pay (see Exhibit A1–3) as a substitute for unemployment compensation. Until recently, only a token unemployment compensation system was present in Italy.

[7]The OECD figures cover the replacement rate for the first year of unemployment, years 2 and 3, and years 4 and 5. Because the benefits will expire after 6 months or 1 year in many countries, this average replacement rate for most countries is substantially lower than the initial replacement rate. For example, unemployment benefits initially replace 60 percent of earnings in the United States. However, since the benefits can only be drawn for 6 months, the average replacement rate over the 5-year time period is much lower than the initial figure.

EXHIBIT A1-4

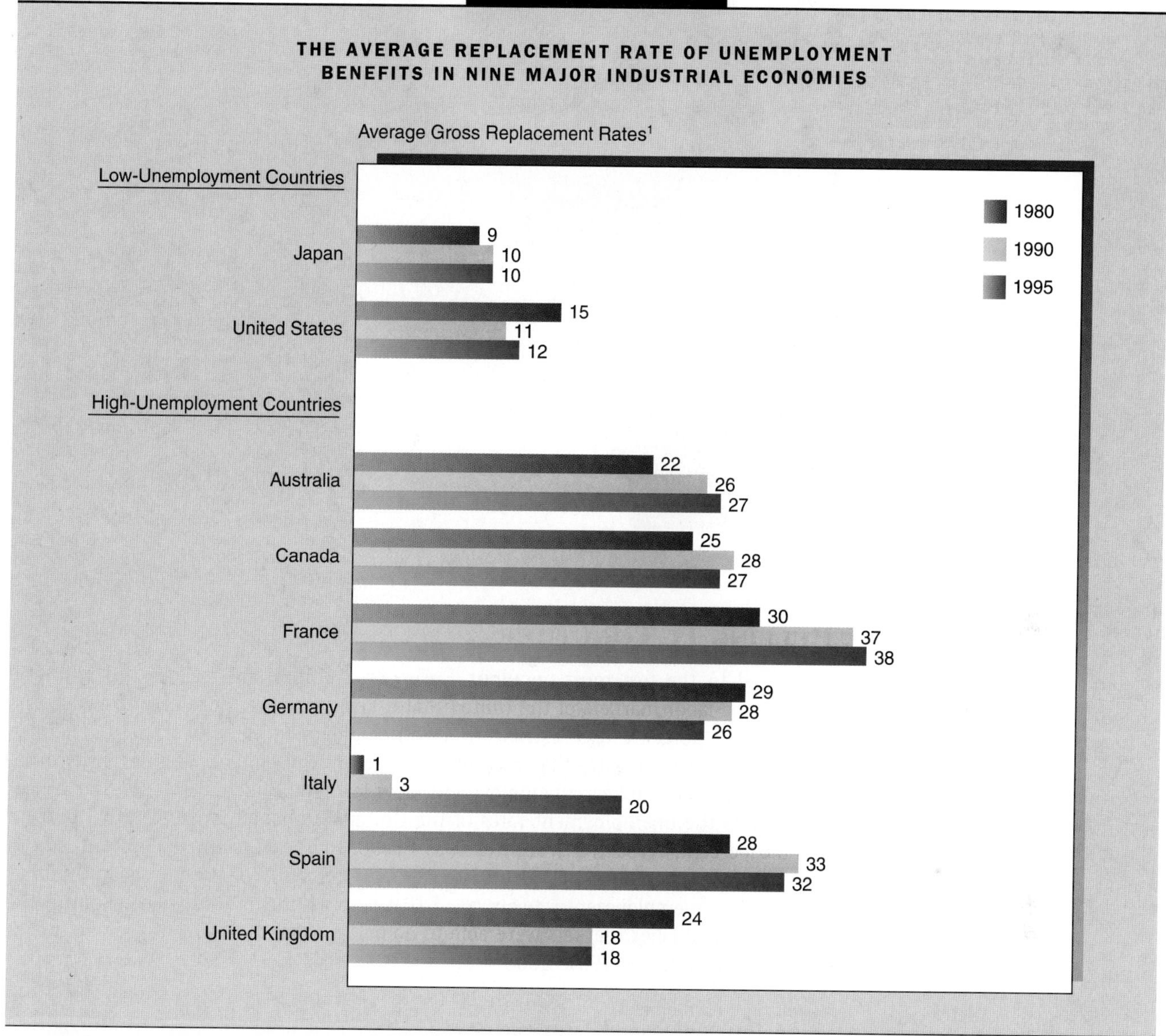

Compared to Japan and the United States, unemployment benefits in Australia, Canada, and Europe replace a larger proportion of an unemployed worker's lost earnings. How will this influence the natural rate of unemployment?

[1]*Average for two earnings levels (2/3 average and average earnings), three family situations (single, married with dependent spouse, and married with working spouse), and three duration periods (1 year, 1 to 3 years, and 3 to 5 years).*

SOURCES: OECD, OECD Jobs Strategy: Making Work Pay *(1997), Figure 2; and OECD,* Implementing the OECD Jobs Strategy: Member Countries' Experience, *Table 5.*

than in the United States and Japan. The average replacement rates of the United States and Japan generally range from one-half to one-third the replacement rates of the European countries, Australia, and Canada. Predictably, the higher unemployment benefit levels of these latter countries will encourage more lengthy periods of job search and thereby push the unemployment rate up.

Business is brisk in this German unemployment office. Compared to the United States and Japan, unemployment benefits are more generous in Europe and Australia. Higher unemployment benefits reduce the opportunity cost of job search and thereby tend to lengthen spells of unemployment. This pushes unemployment rates upward.

Pulling It Together

Compared to the five most populous European countries, as well as Australia and Canada, the labor markets of the United States and Japan are more decentralized, dismissal regulations are less restrictive, and unemployment benefits are less generous. Economic theory indicates that each of these factors will enhance the flexibility of labor markets and help keep unemployment rates low. The evidence is supportive of this view. While the unemployment rates of the United States and Japan were 5.9 percent and 3.0 percent, respectively, during 1991–1998, the average unemployment rate of the seven more interventionist countries was 11.3 percent. For the European Union as a whole, the unemployment rate averaged 10.4 percent during this period. None of the more regulated labor markets were able to do better than an 8 percent average rate of unemployment during 1991–1998.

LABOR MARKET REFORMS IN THE UNITED KINGDOM AND NEW ZEALAND

If a country moved toward a more liberal labor market, would it make any difference? The recent experience of the United Kingdom and New Zealand sheds light on this issue. These two countries have recently adopted significant reforms designed to protect the rights of workers and make their labor markets more competitive.

In the United Kingdom, the reforms focused on promotion of democratic decision making and the protection of workers' rights. The Employment Act of 1980 required secret ballot approval prior to the establishment of a closed shop. Later, legislation was adopted (1) requiring worker approval every 5 years for the continuation of a closed shop and (2) making strike action to establish a closed shop unlawful. Nonunion members were also granted legal protection against dismissal and discriminatory actions as the result of their nonunion status. Union members were given the right to join the union of their choice and granted protection against unions seeking to discipline them for failure to support a strike. These changes both weakened the monopoly power of unions and led to a more decentralized wage-setting process. Union membership in the United Kingdom fell from 50 percent of the workforce in 1980 to 34 percent in 1995. More important, centralized bargaining became less commonplace. The share of employees having their wages set by collective bargaining contracts fell from 70 percent in 1980 to 47 percent in 1995. The labor market reforms were supplemented with less-generous unemployment benefits. As Exhibit A1–4 indicates, the average replacement rate in the United Kingdom fell from 24 percent in 1980 to 18 percent in 1990 and 1995.

In New Zealand, the Employment Contracts Act of 1991 restructured the labor market even more rapidly than the English reforms. This act allowed all employees to "choose whether or not to associate with other employees for advancing the employees' collective employment interests." Employees were granted the right to negotiate labor contracts, with or without the assistance of an agent. Most significantly, while rights to strike and lockout were explicitly recognized, these weapons were permitted only at the expiration of labor contracts and then only after employee approval was obtained at the *enterprise* level. This effectively changed the wage-setting process in New Zealand from a centralized to a decentralized system. As in the United Kingdom, union membership fell and the share of employees having their wages set by union contracts declined from 67 percent in 1990 to 31 percent in 1995.

How have the labor markets of these two countries reacted to economic liberalization? In the United Kingdom, the economy expanded rapidly throughout most of the 1980s and the unemployment rate declined. Following the recession in the early 1990s, the economy rebounded nicely and by 1998, the rate of unemployment in the United Kingdom had fallen to 6.3 percent, the lowest rate achieved since the 1970s. In New Zealand, the results have been similar. New Zealand's rate of unemployment fell from 10.3 percent in 1992 to 6.4 percent during 1996–1998. The unemployment rates of both countries are now significantly lower than the rates of similarly situated countries that have followed more interventionist policies. The UK unemployment rate stands in stark contrast to the double-digit rates of the other populous European countries. New Zealand's unemployment rate is well below that of Australia, a country that continues to rely on centralized wage-setting processes.

LABOR MARKETS IN THE UNITED STATES AND CANADA

Comparisons between the United States and Canadian labor markets are quite revealing. Although the Canadian labor market is less regulated and more decentralized than those of the major European economies, it is clearly less liberal than that of the United States. Compared to the United States, the share of employees with wages set by collective bargaining is greater, dismissal regulations are more restrictive, and unemployment benefits are more generous in Canada. Furthermore, the Canadian labor market has been drifting toward the European model. Union membership has been increasing as a share of the labor force in Canada, while it has been declining in the United States. During the last decade, Canada has enacted legislation making it more difficult for employers to dismiss workers and reduce the size of their workforce. According to the OECD, the average replacement rate of Canada's unemployment benefit system has risen from 20 percent in 1970 to 25 percent in 1980 and 28 percent in 1990.

These factors show up in the unemployment statistics. During the 1960s and 1970s, the Canadian average unemployment rate was virtually the same as that of the

United States. This is no longer true. During the 1980s, the Canadian average rate of unemployment was about 2 percent greater than the rate of the United States, and in the 1990s the gap has widened to 4 percent (see Exhibit A1–1).

KEY POINTS

➤ During the last decade, the major European economies, Australia, and Canada have persistently experienced double-digit unemployment rates. In recent years, the unemployment rate of the European Union has been about twice that of the United States.

➤ When used in large and diverse labor markets, a centralized wage-setting process will push wage rates above market levels in various regions and skill categories. This will tend to cause higher rates of unemployment. Similarly, regulations that make it more costly to dismiss workers will also make employers more reluctant to hire employees. This will lead to sluggish employment growth and high rates of unemployment, particularly for youthful workers seeking to enter the workforce. High unemployment benefits will reduce the opportunity cost of job search, and thereby cause more lengthy spells of unemployment.

➤ Compared to the United States and Japan, the labor markets of Europe, Australia, and Canada are characterized by centralized wage-setting processes, more restrictive dismissal regulations, and high unemployment benefit replacement rates. There is reason to believe that these policies have contributed to the high unemployment rates of these economies.

➤ Recent reforms in the United Kingdom and New Zealand have increased the competitiveness of labor markets. The rates of unemployment in both countries have declined and are now significantly lower than the rates of similarly situated countries that have followed more restrictive labor market practices.

CRITICAL ANALYSIS QUESTIONS

*1. Compared to the situation where a union is able to organize only a portion of the firms in an industry, how does the ability to set wages for an entire industry influence the power of a labor union? What does this suggest about the relative strength of unions in Europe versus those in the United States and Japan?

2. Explain why unemployment compensation is an indirect subsidy to employers with a less stable workforce. Is it a good idea to subsidize this type of unemployment? Why or why not?

3. Suppose that legislation was passed requiring all employers in the United States to pay dismissed workers one week of severance pay for every year they were employed by the firm. What impact would this have on (a) the dismissal rate of employees, (b) the productivity of employees, and (c) the unemployment rate of youthful workers? Discuss.

4. Do you think that the United States should move toward the European labor market model characterized by more extensive collective bargaining, greater government regulation, and more generous unemployment benefits? Why or why not?

---

*Asterisk denotes questions for which answers are given in Appendix B.

APPLICATION 2

The federal government's handling of [social security] pension monies is very different from that of private pension plans.

Mark Weinberger[1]

Social Security: The Nature of the Problem and the Alternatives for Dealing with It

APPLICATION FOCUS

- Why is social security headed for problems?
- Will the Social Security Trust Fund lighten the tax burden of future generations?
- How does the social security system impact young workers and women?
- What are the alternatives to the current system?

[1]Mark Weinberger, *Social Security: Facing the Facts* (Washington, D.C.: Cato Institute, 1996), p. 2.

The social security program in the United States is officially known as Old Age and Survivors Insurance (OASI). It offers protection against the loss of income that usually accompanies old age or the death of a breadwinner. In spite of its official title, social security is not based on principles of insurance. Private insurance and pension programs invest the current payments of customers in buildings, farms, or other real assets. Alternatively, they buy stocks and bonds that finance the development of real assets. These real assets generate income that allows the pension fund (or insurance company) to fulfill its future obligations to its customers.

Social security does not follow this saving-and-investment model. Instead, most of the funds flowing into the system are paid out to current retirees and survivors in the program. In essence, the social security system is an intergenerational income-transfer program. Most of the taxes collected from the present generation of workers are paid out to current beneficiaries.

The social security retirement program is financed by a payroll tax of 6.2 percent levied on both the employee and the employer. (Additional payroll taxes finance

EXHIBIT A2-1

WORKERS PER SOCIAL SECURITY BENEFICIARY

1950

1998

2025

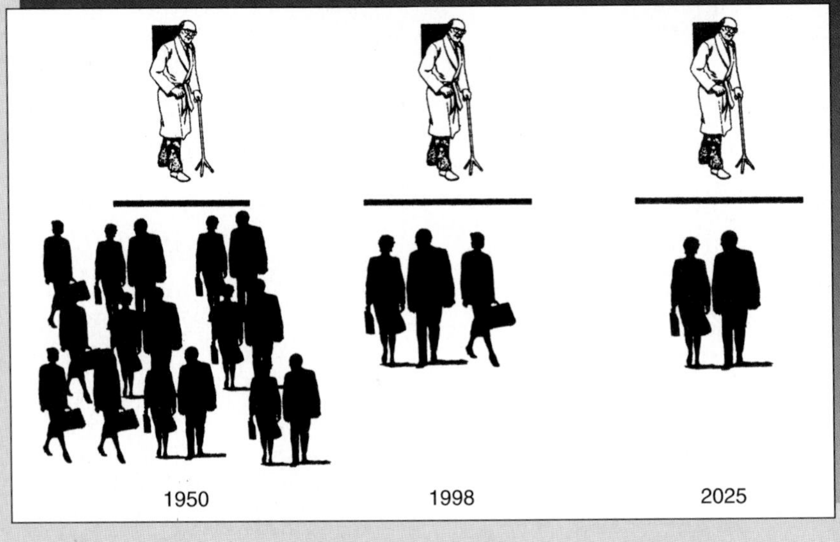

In 1950, there were 16 workers per social security beneficiary. By 1998, the figure had fallen to only 3.1. By 2025, there will be only 2 workers per retiree. As the worker/beneficiary ratio falls under a pay-as-you-go system, either taxes must be increased or benefits reduced (or both).

SOURCE: 1995 Annual Report of the Board of Trustees of the Federal Old Age and Survivors Insurance and Disability Insurance Trust Funds *(Washington, D.C.: Government Printing Office, 1995), p. 122.*

Medicare and disability programs, which are sometimes considered part of the social security program.) Therefore, the total tax for the social security retirement program is equal to 12.4 percent of employee earnings. In 1998, the tax applied to all employee earnings up to $65,400. Thus, employees earning $65,400 or more paid $8,110 (counting both employee and employer payments) in social security taxes to finance the OASI retirement program that year.

When the program began in 1935, the nation had lots of workers and few eligible retirees. As **Exhibit A2–1** illustrates, there were 16 workers for every social security beneficiary as recently as 1950. That ratio has declined sharply through the years. As a result, higher and higher taxes per worker have been required just to maintain a constant level of benefits. In 1998, there were 3.1 workers per retiree. By 2025, there will be only two workers per social security beneficiary.

Today's retirees typically receive real benefits of three or four times the amount they paid into the system, equivalent to a rate of return of more than 20 percent—far better than they could have done had they invested the funds privately. In contrast, studies indicate the workers now paying for these large benefits will not do nearly as well. For example, those now at age 35 can expect to earn a real rate of return of about 2 percent on their social security tax dollars, substantially less than what they could earn from personal investments. For two-earner couples just entering the labor force, the expected return from social security taxes is negative. ***Thus, social security has been a good deal for current and past retirees. It is not, however, a very good deal for younger workers. Workers now entering the labor force would be better off if they could invest their social security tax dollars privately.***

WHY IS SOCIAL SECURITY HEADED FOR PROBLEMS?

During the 15 years following the Second World War, the birthrate in the United States was very high. The baby boomers are now in their prime working years and their large numbers are an important factor explaining why the revenues from the social security tax currently exceed the expenditures. However, when these baby boomers move into the retirement phase of their life, the situation is going to change dramatically.

As we previously noted, the number of workers per social security retiree will fall from the current 3.1 level to only 2.0 in 2025. As **Exhibit A2–2** shows, there are now approximately 25 million persons age 70 and over in the United States. By 2030, the number of septuagenarians will soar to 47.8 million. This increase will be particularly sharp beginning around 2010. The medical expenditures of persons 70 years and over are considerably higher than those of persons a few years younger. Thus, these demographic changes will place strong pressure on the Medicare program as well as the social security retirement system.

Exhibit A2–3 shows how these demographic factors will influence the expenditures and tax revenues of the current pay-as-you-go social security retirement system. The current surplus of revenues from the payroll tax relative to retirement benefits will dissipate around 2014. The deficits will grow larger and larger as the number of beneficiaries relative to workers continues to grow throughout the 2020s and 2030s.

Between 2000 and 2030, the number of persons age 70 years and over will almost double. The medical expenses of persons in this age group are particularly high. Thus, this will place strong pressure on both the social security and Medicare programs.

SOURCES: Bipartisan Commission on Entitlement and Tax Reform, Final Report to the President *(Washington, D.C.: Government Printing Office, 1995), p. 13; and* 1995 Annual Report of the Board of Trustees of the Federal Old Age and Survivors Insurance and Disability Insurance Trust Funds, *p. 21.*

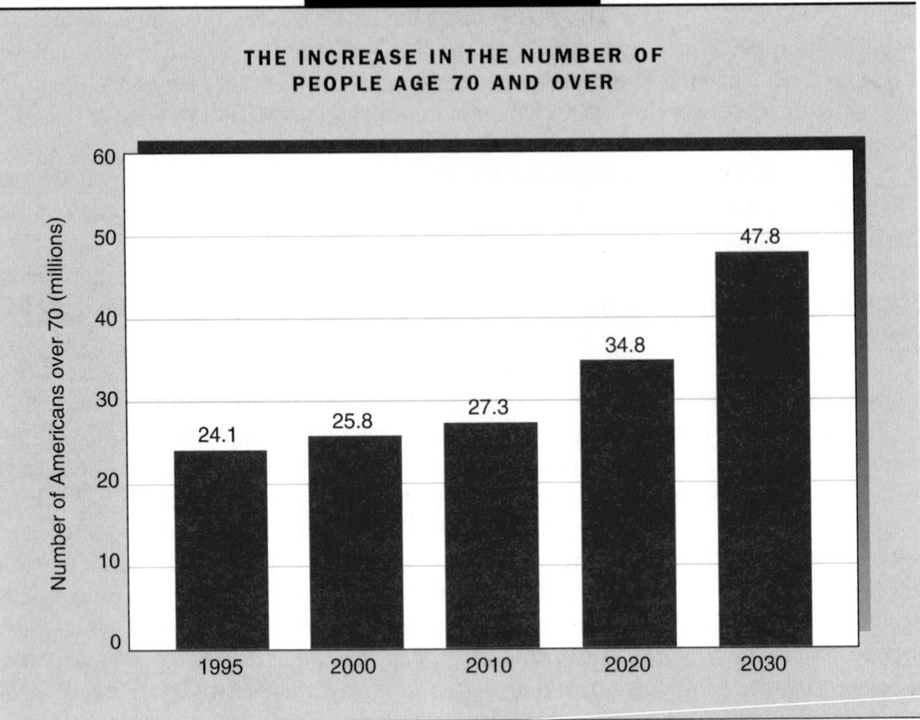

Given current payroll taxes and retirement benefit levels, the system will run larger and larger deficits during the 2014–2030 period.

SOURCE: Bipartisan Commission on Entitlement and Tax Reform, Final Report to the President *(Washington, D.C.: Government Printing Office, 1995), p. 22.*

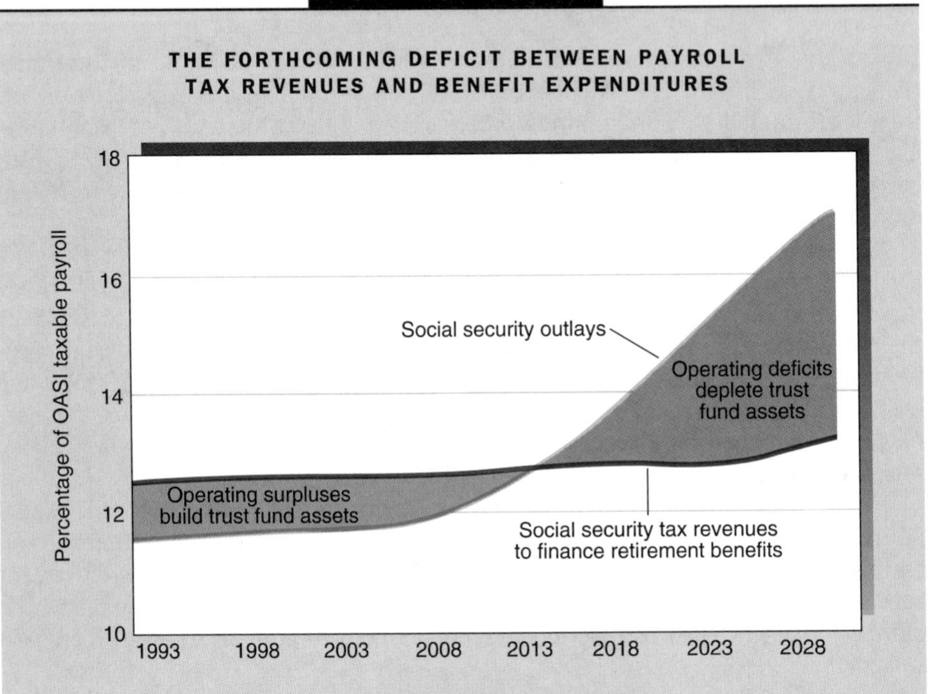

WILL THE TRUST FUND LIGHTEN THE FUTURE TAX BURDEN?

Since the mid-1980s, the revenues derived from the payroll tax have exceeded the benefits paid to current retirees. Currently, only about 80 percent of the revenues are required for the payments to current beneficiaries. Thus, the system is running a substantial surplus—about $100 billion per year. A sizable surplus is expected in the decade ahead. Under current law, the surplus is channeled into the Social Security Trust Fund (SSTF). The trust funds are used to purchase U.S. Treasury bonds.

The original idea was to build up the SSTF while the baby boomers were in the workforce and then draw on these funds later to help pay for the baby boomers' retirement benefits. If other elements of the federal budget were in balance, the social security surplus would reduce real interest rates and increase private sector investment. In turn, the higher rate of capital formation would promote economic growth and thereby make it easier to provide the benefits to the baby boomers during their retirement years. However, throughout the 1980s and most of the 1990s, the federal government ran large deficits. In essence, the surplus of the social security retirement system was used to finance current government operations. During the next decade, the social security retirement system will run a sizable surplus, expanding the size of the trust fund. Somewhere around 2014, however, the surplus will dissipate as the baby boomers begin to retire. After 2014, large deficits are projected "as far as the eye can see."

Will enlarging the trust fund make it easier to deal with the retirement of the baby boomers? Some are surprised to learn that there is little reason to believe that it will. Unlike the bonds, stocks, and physical assets held by a private insurance company, the SSTF bonds will not generate a stream of future income for the federal government. Neither are they a "pot of money" set aside for the payment of future benefits. Instead the trust fund bonds are an IOU from one government agency—the Treasury—to another—the Social Security Administration. The assets of the trust funds are a liability of the Treasury. ***Thus, no matter how many bonds are in the trust fund, their net asset value to the federal government is zero!***

THE REAL SOCIAL SECURITY PROBLEM

The real crisis faced by the pay-as-you-go system will arise around 2014 when the revenues from the payroll tax will begin to fall short of the benefits promised to retirees. As **Exhibit A2–4** illustrates, there only four ways to deal with this situation: (1) reduce benefits, (2) raise taxes and/or cut other government expenditures in order to inject additional funds into the system, (3) borrow from the general public, or (4) reform the system in a manner that will increase the rate of return earned by (or for) workers and future retirees. The presence of SSTF bonds will not change these alternatives. Of course, the SSTF bonds represent funds borrowed by the Treasury from the social security system. This makes the claim on these funds by future social security recipients more legitimate.

However, the presence of the bonds will not make it any easier to deal with future social security deficits. Remember, the federal government is both the payee and recipient of the interest and principal represented by the SSTF bonds. In order to redeem the bonds and thereby provide the social security system with funds to cover future deficits, the federal government will have to raise taxes, cut other expenditures, or borrow from the public. These options will not change with the depletion of the trust fund, an event expected to occur around 2032.

EXHIBIT A2-4

DEALING WITH THE GRAYING OF AMERICA

As the number of retirees increases relative to the number of workers, there are only four ways to deal with this situation:

THE OPTIONS

1. **Reduce benefits** (lower monthly benefits or increase retirement age).
2. **Raise taxes** and/or cut government expenditures in other areas in order to provide additional funds for the program.
3. **Borrow from the general public** (this implies higher future taxes).
4. **Reform the system** so workers can earn a higher rate of return.

The problem is not depletion of the trust funds. Instead it is the burden of soaring social security deficits on the economy beginning in about 15 years. It will not be easy to cover these deficits. If benefits are reduced, current beneficiaries and persons near retirement will—quite correctly—feel that a commitment made to them has been broken. At the same time, it will be difficult to cover the gap with tax increases and expenditure cuts. As the baby boomers retire, approximately a 50 percent increase in the payroll tax or a 30 percent increase in the personal income tax will be needed to cover the social security deficits. Tax increases of this magnitude are likely to retard economic growth, which will further aggravate the problem. Neither will it be easy to cut other expenditures. Defense spending has already been sliced substantially and the growth of the elderly population is sure to place upward pressure on Medicare spending, another major federal program. Finally, a major increase in borrowing will place upward pressure on interest rates, slowing both capital formation and economic growth. In addition, borrowing means higher future taxes just to cover the interest cost. Thus, it merely delays the problem.

REFORM ALTERNATIVES

There is increasing awareness that a pay-as-you-go system is ill-suited for the demographics of the future. In the past, when each generation was larger than its successor, it was possible to keep the taxes imposed on current workers low while still providing substantial benefits to retirees. However, the era of successively larger generations is over. This makes pay-as-you-go less attractive.

Previously, political considerations essentially ruled out major structural reform. Given the severity of the problem and unattractiveness of other alternatives, reform may now be more feasible. What type of reform would minimize the most harmful side effects accompanying the retirement of the baby boomers and subsequent generations? Several ideas have been put forth. We will consider two of the most widely discussed proposals.

Government Investment in the Stock Market

In 1999, President Clinton presented a social security plan that called for the investment of a portion of the SSTF in the stock market. Historically, the real rate of return on stocks has been about 7 percent, compared to 2 percent for government bonds. If the government could earn 7 percent rather than 2 percent on these funds, this would help make the system solvent for a longer period of time. The president's plan would cover the social security deficit for about 6 years.

The plan is not entirely new. States have invested employee retirement funds in the stock and bond markets for many years. With a few exceptions, it has worked out reasonably well. The rate of return earned by most state plans has exceeded the return on government bonds. However, the state employee retirement funds are small compared to the SSTF. Fed Chairman Alan Greenspan and others have expressed concern about the plan's impact on financial markets. In the past, the federal government has stayed out of the stock market. Many believe that this is one reason why U.S. financial markets have worked so well. If the federal government had sizable holdings, several temptations would arise. For example, would the government try to offset a downturn in the stock market with a stock buying spree? As government investment funds fell due to a shrinkage in the size of the SSTF, might this not trigger a collapse in stock prices? Might the government use the investment funds to favor some firms (perhaps those whose officers provided large political contributions) and penalize other, less politically favored firms?

The record of government-directed funds in other countries has been poor. Funds managed by the governments of Malaysia and Singapore earned 6.2 percent and 3.2 percent, respectively, during 1980–1997. Most other governments have done worse. Since 1980, funds invested by the governments of Ecuador, Egypt, Venezuela, and Peru have all earned negative returns for their citizens.[2]

Use of Payroll Taxes to Fund Personal Retirement Accounts

For those concerned about potential abuse accompanying government investment, it would be preferable to channel a portion of the payroll tax into personal retirement accounts managed by individuals. There are various ways such plans might work, but one possibility would be to allow individuals to fund their own retirement by channeling a portion of their payroll tax into a personal retirement saving account. As these retirement accounts grow, individuals could be allowed to allocate more and more of their payroll tax into them in exchange for the receipt of lower social security benefits. Rather than the government managing these funds, individuals would be permitted to choose among various stock and bond mutual funds.

In essence, this plan recognizes that social security is both a redistributional program and a mandated savings plan. For a time, people would have to continue funding the redistributional part of the program. But those willing to set aside funds for their own retirement could in effect "buy out" of the mandated saving portion of the system. Because individuals would have a property right to the funds channeled into their personal retirement accounts, the adverse incentive effects accompanying taxation would be largely avoided.

---

[2]See Peter J. Ferrara and Michael Tanner, *A New Deal for Social Security* (Washington, D.C.: Cato Institute, 1998), for evidence on this point.

Basically, there is only one way that we can simultaneously protect and improve the retirement benefits of the baby boomers and subsequent generations without increasing the tax burden on working Americans: Encourage more savings, investment, and ownership of capital by future retirees. Allowing workers to begin channeling some of their payroll tax into retirement accounts in exchange for lower social security benefits would be a step in that direction.

Some of the elderly may want to accumulate wealth by working a few extra years. Current tax treatment discourages this alternative. The working elderly are still liable for the payroll tax even though their payments add nothing to their benefit levels. If social security retirees earn more than $15,500, they confront the payroll tax, a 15 percent initial income tax liability, and a 50 cent reduction in their social security benefits for every additional dollar they earn. This combination hits them with nearly a 60 percent marginal tax rate—higher than the rate imposed on millionaires. Removal of roadblocks like this would also help future retirees provide for a better retirement.

Making Private Social Security an Option: The Experience of Chile and Other Countries

In recent years, several countries have adopted privatized social security plans. In 1993, Peru privatized its social security system. A year later, Argentina and Colombia did likewise. Still more recently, Mexico, Bolivia, and El Salvador have adopted privatized social retirement systems. The reforms in each of these countries were patterned after the system of Chile. Chile's pioneering plan was first adopted in 1980. The basics of the Chilean plan are (1) a defined contribution system and (2) privately owned and managed investment accounts. Let us consider this plan in more detail.

Workers in Chile were given an option: They could continue with the government social security program or contribute a minimum of 10 percent of their wages (up to 20 percent if they wanted earlier retirement or greater retirement benefits) into an approved private investment fund. These funds would contract to deliver retirement and insurance benefits in place of the social security program. In 1995, there were 21 alternative private "Pension Fund Administration" (AFP) companies competing for the retirement contributions of Chileans. Each AFP is a management firm with investment and operating policies regulated by the government. Each is a separate legal entity from the portfolio of stocks and bonds it manages. It receives a management fee, but has no claim on the portfolio that it manages. So if an AFP were to go bankrupt—although none has since the plan began—the holdings would remain to finance the future benefits to workers.

Ninety percent of all workers chose to leave the government system even though they had paid into it for years. They were issued "recognition bonds" that reflected the value of their previous contributions. The government pledged to buy back these bonds, with interest, from each worker upon retirement. Workers may either spend this supplemental money in retirement or use it to purchase annuities that pay a fixed amount until death.

Employers paid more than half of the payroll tax under the old Chilean system, but the current system requires no contribution from them. Instead, they were required in 1981 to provide an 18 percent raise to workers. From the raise, workers paid their own contributions.

While the Chilean plan forces employees to save, it also provides them with a property right to the funds in their retirement account. From the viewpoint of individual workers, the contributions represent earnings and an investment backed by private assets. Thus, the adverse incentive effects are minimal—substantially less than those accompanying pay-as-you-go tax plans. Furthermore, the retirement funds are clearly an asset paid for by individual workers, rather than a political favor granted by politicians. This enhances the economic and political freedom of workers. As part owners of the private economy, workers have an incentive to oppose inefficient regulations or excessive taxes placed on "business" that would hurt the economy and reduce their retirement funding. This change has helped to depoliticize the economy, as well as the pension system.

The Chilean plan has worked well for both the participants and the economy. During the first 17 years of the plan, the average rate of return earned by the contributions has been 12 percent. The contributions into the plan have led to higher rates of both saving and investment. In the 1990s, Chile's saving rate has averaged 26 percent of GDP, up from 20 percent prior to the adoption of the plan. In turn, the additional saving has stimulated capital formation and helped to strengthen the economy. Since 1985, Chile's per-capita GDP has grown at an annual rate of 5 percent. It is now one the fastest-growing economies in the world.

The Latin American countries that have moved toward private systems are much less developed than the United States. Among the high-income industrial economies, the United Kingdom has made the most dramatic moves toward privatization. Since 1986, the United Kingdom has permitted employees and self-employed workers to channel 4.6 percentage points of their payroll tax into private retirement accounts. In exchange for their participation in the private plans, employees accept a lower level of government retirement benefits. The private option has been quite popular. Approximately 73 percent of British workers now have a private plan.

Exhibit A2–5 provides information on the real rate of return earned by various private plans around the world. All of these plans have performed reasonably

EXHIBIT A2–5

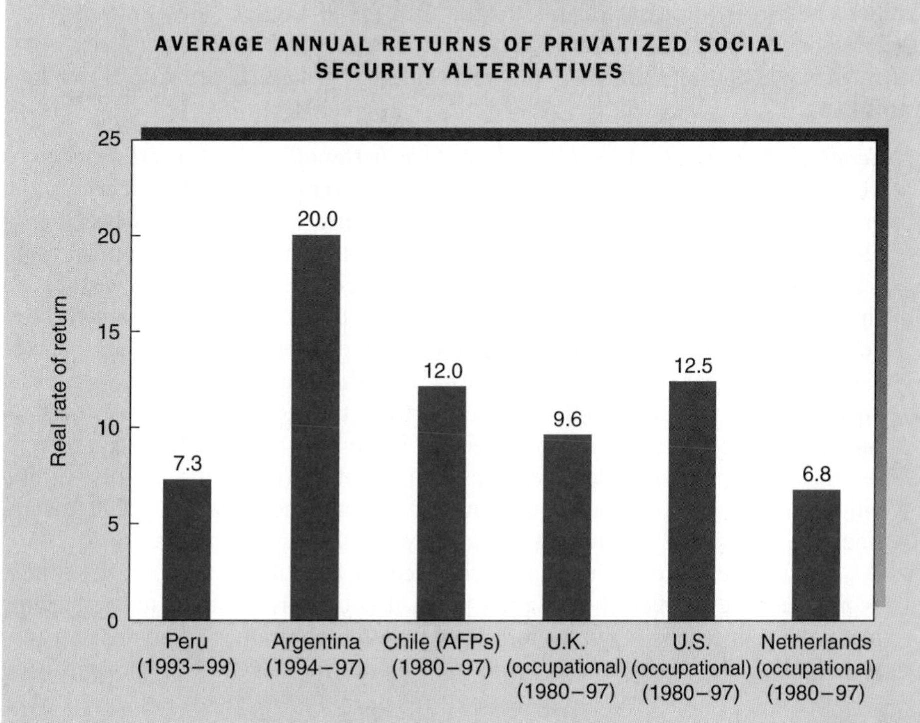

Several countries have either privatized their social security systems or provided private alternatives. The rate of return on the private alternatives is shown here. In the United States, prior to 1983, county, municipal, and state government employees were permitted to opt out of the traditional social security system. The investment rate of return of these alternative plans has been much higher than the rate earned by the social security trust fund.

SOURCE: Peter J. Ferrara and Michael Tanner, A New Deal for Social Security *(Washington, D.C.: Cato Institute, 1998), p. 150.*

well—several have earned double-digit real returns for their beneficiaries. These returns certainly compare favorably with the less than 2 percent real returns that future retirees in the United States can expect.

It is also interesting to note the experience of one group that is not part of the current social security system. Prior to 1983, county, municipal, and state government employees were permitted to opt out of the traditional social security system. More than one million state and local government employees are still participating in these retirement plans. The rate of return on the funds invested in these plans averaged 12.5 percent during 1980–1997, far higher than the returns earned by the Social Security Trust Fund.

Critics argue that private plans are more risky and that some investors will make bad decisions, leading to a higher poverty rate among the elderly. To a degree, these charges have some validity. There is certainly no assurance that individual investors will not make some bad choices. However, mutual funds provide a mechanism whereby even small, novice investors can hold a diverse portfolio of stocks and bonds while still keeping administrative costs low. Furthermore, the historical evidence indicates that when held over a lengthy time period, a diverse holding of stocks is a low-risk investment. Still, it can be expected to yield much higher returns than government bonds. (See the following application with regard to these points.) Given these factors, consideration of private investment options is likely to be an integral part of the social security debate in the years immediately ahead.

SOCIAL SECURITY AND FAIRNESS ISSUES

Social security reform is being seriously considered for several reasons. The most important is the future financial difficulties that are sure to plague the system as the number of retirees increases relative to the number of workers. But there are also other reasons to consider reform. The system exerts a discriminatory impact—one that most would consider unfair—on several different groups. Let's take a closer look at this issue.

1. ***Generations born after World War II would be better off without social security.*** As we mentioned earlier, social security has been a very good deal for current and previous retirees. Most earned a higher rate of return than would have been possible from private investments. But this will not be true for the baby-boom and subsequent generations. If tax payments into social security are viewed as an "investment" and the promised benefits a return, under current law, persons born between 1945 and 1964 will earn a rate of return of about 1.8 percent on their social security taxes. This is less than half of what they could earn on inflation-proof Treasury bonds and approximately one-fourth of the stock market's historical return (7 percent). To put this in perspective, if the baby boomers had been permitted to invest their social security taxes into private investment accounts earning only 5 percent, each of them would have, on average, more than $200,000 in additional wealth beyond the amount provided by social security benefits.[3]

   Furthermore, their future social security benefits are risky. As the system begins running a deficit in just a few years, it is conceivable their future benefits might be reduced. Is it fair to force people into a retirement plan that does so poorly? After paying high taxes while working, is the dependency accompanying

[3]These figures are from the Federal Reserve Bank of Cleveland, *Economic Trends* (March 1999): 12–13.

THE WIZARD OF ID

social security fair? People are giving more thought to questions like these as reform becomes a viable possibility.

2. *Social security discriminates against middle-income recipients.* The social security payroll tax does not apply beyond the $65,400 annual income threshold. Thus, the average payroll tax rates of persons with incomes above the cutoff are lower than for those with incomes below the cutoff. On the benefit side, the formula favors those with low incomes. In contrast, middle-income recipients pay high taxes, while receiving very little in additional benefits. Social security retirement benefits are linked to each worker's lifetime base earnings—the worker's average annual earnings for his or her 35 highest-earning years. (*Note:* The income figures are adjusted for inflation.) However, as base earnings rise, the increase in retirement benefits is far less than proportional.[4] In fact, increases in average annual earnings beyond approximately $32,000 lead to only a 15 percent increase in benefit levels. Thus, middle earners in this $32,000 to $65,000 range get virtually nothing for the additional payroll taxes they paid during their working years.[5]
3. *Social security discriminates against married women in the workforce.* This is not the intent, but nonetheless, it is the result. The problem arises because individuals are permitted to draw benefits based on either their own earnings or 50 percent of their spouse's earnings. But they cannot draw both. In the case of many working married women, the benefits based on the earnings of their spouses are approximately equal to, or in some cases greater than, benefits based on their own earnings. Thus, these married women derive virtually nothing from the payroll taxes paid during their working years.
4. *Political dependency results from the system.* The current social security system makes every group of retirees dependent on politics and politicians. Even though individuals pay throughout their working years, the current system does not give

[4]The annual retirement benefits are equal to: 90 percent of the first $5,244 of base earnings; 32 percent of base earnings between $5,244 and $31,620, and 15 percent of base earnings above $31,620. Therefore, as base earnings rise, benefits fall *as a percentage of average earnings* (and payroll taxes paid) during one's lifetime. For example, the retirement benefits of persons with base annual earnings of $10,000 sum to 62 percent of their average working-year earnings. In contrast, the retirement benefits of those with base earnings of $60,000 are only 29 percent of their average preretirement earnings. These figures are based on the 1996 formula.

[5]Compared to the poor, middle- and high-income recipients tend to live longer and therefore draw retirement benefits over a more lengthy time period. This will partially offset their lower annual benefit levels per dollar of social security taxes paid during working years.

them a clearly defined property right to future benefits. For many, this too is a fairness question. Why should Americans, high- and low-wage alike, have to beg, demand, or lobby politicians to get benefits that they were forced to pay for earlier? That is especially frustrating for those who believe that they could have purchased greater benefits more cheaply through mutual funds or other private investmentS.

Historically, social security has been viewed as almost a sacred program. Nonetheless, it now confronts several problems. The lives of today's students will be strongly affected by how these problems are dealt with in the years immediately ahead.

KEY POINTS

➤ Social security does not follow the saving-and-investment model. Most of the funds flowing into the system are paid out to current retirees and survivors under the program.

➤ While the current tax revenues exceed the payments to retirees, this will change dramatically as the baby boomers begin to move into the retirement phase of life. Beginning around 2014, the system's current surplus will shift to a deficit, which will persist for several decades.

➤ The current surplus of the social security system is used to purchase U.S. Treasury bonds. Because the federal government is both the payee and recipient of these bonds, their net asset value to the federal government is zero. They will not reduce the level of future taxes needed to cover the social security deficit when the baby boomers begin to retire.

➤ The major problem resulting from the current system is the fact that huge increases in taxes (or reductions in spending) will be required to cover the future deficits. Large tax increases would be likely to cause a slowdown in the rate of economic growth.

➤ Several potential reforms, including government investment in the stock market and moving toward privatization through personal retirement accounts, are currently under consideration. Reforms are also being considered for reasons of fairness.

CRITICAL ANALYSIS QUESTIONS

1. Is the social security system based on the same principles as private insurance? Why or why not?

*2. Why does the social security system face a crisis? Will the surplus that is currently being built up in the Social Security Trust Fund help to avert higher future taxes and/or benefit reductions when the baby boomers retire? Why or why not?

3. Do you think workers should be permitted to invest all or part of their social security contribution in private investment funds? What are the advantages and disadvantages of a private option system? If given the opportunity, would you choose the private option or stay with the current system? Why?

4. The social security payroll tax is split equally between the employee and the employer. Would it make any difference if the entire tax was imposed on employees? Would employees be helped if all the tax was imposed on employers? (*Hint:* You may want to consult Chapter 4, pages 107–109.)

5. In early 1999, President Clinton proposed that the government should invest part of the Social Security Trust Fund in the stock market. Do you think this is a good idea? Why or why not?

---

*Asterisk denotes questions for which answers are given in Appendix B.

APPLICATION 3

In investing money, the amount of interest you want should depend on whether you want to eat well or sleep well.

J. Kenfield Morley[1]

The Stock Market: What Does It Do and How Has It Performed?

APPLICATION FOCUS

- What is the economic function of the stock market?
- How are stock prices related to the interest rate?
- Why has the stock market risen so much since 1982?
- Is the stock market too high? Is it a bubble that will burst?
- How will the retirement of the baby-boomers' generation affect stock prices?

[1]As quoted in Burton G. Malkiel, *A Random Walk Down Wall Street* (New York: Norton Company, 1990), p. 287.

The market for corporate shares is called the stock market. The extremely rapid rise of stock prices in recent years has often been front page news. On the whole, investors in American stocks have done exceedingly well and this has been true over a long period. Since 1802, the returns of stock holdings have averaged 7 percent, corrected for inflation. That means that, on average, stock investments have doubled in value every 10 years.

In the 1980s and 1990s, the returns have been even higher. The Standard and Poor's 500 Index indicates the performance of the broad stock market. This index factors in the value of dividends as if they were reinvested in the market. Thus, it provides a measure of the rate of return received by investors in the form of both dividends and changes in share prices. As **Exhibit A3-1** illustrates, the S&P 500 stocks generated a 15 percent average annual rate of return during 1983–1998. Even after adjustment for inflation, the returns averaged 11.7 percent during this period.

EXHIBIT A3-1

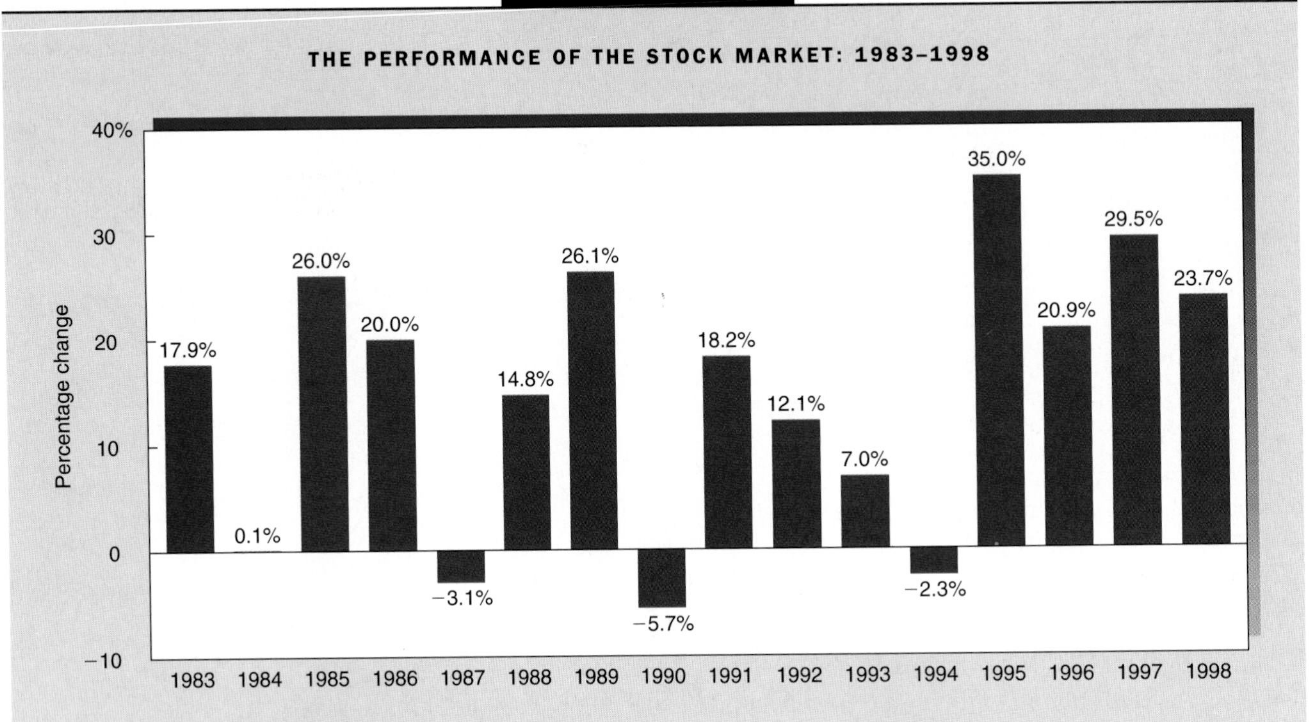

During the last 16 years, the broad S&P 500 stock index indicates that stock investors earned a 15 percent average annual rate of return. Double-digit returns were earned during 11 of the 16 years, while the returns were negative during only 3 of the years.

SOURCE: Standard and Poor's.

The prices of individual stocks can rise and fall spectacularly. Those who buy and sell stocks, especially when they try to outguess market changes, can gain or lose huge sums of money in a very short time. Is the stock market simply a giant casino? Or does it perform functions that are critical for the growth of an economy? Why has the market performed so well during the last 16 years? Will this trend continue or can we expect a downturn or even a stock market crash in the near future? How do changes in factors like the interest rate and the number of people currently in certain age categories affect the demand for stocks? This application addresses these questions and related issues.

THE ECONOMIC FUNCTIONS OF THE STOCK MARKET

The stock market performs several important functions in a modern economy. That is true even though a few active traders in the market treat it much like a casino. Those who constantly buy and sell, trying to predict the movement of each stock price and to outguess others in the market, are gambling. Most will probably lose over time, because buying and selling is itself costly. Traders looking for quick profits face a difficult task. They must frequently be right about price changes, just to break even over time. Yet it is very difficult to outguess the others in the market.

Most participants in the stock market have little special expertise. Only a few are willing to take the time to obtain detailed information on a large number of firms. Nonetheless, the stock market provides them with a means through which they can share in the profits (and the risks) of large businesses. Investment fund managers and other advisors offer, for a fee, to manage their investments. Savers have found the stock market to be an excellent place to invest their savings in order to build wealth over time. At the same time, firms seeking funds have found new stock issues to be an excellent method to identify others willing to share the risks and the opportunities that accompany their business activities. Investors and firms seeking investment capital can gain from the exchange of savings for ownership shares. For the economy as a whole, the stock market channels investment funds into profitable activities. It rewards the choice and recognition of successful business strategies. It also disciplines business decision makers who use resources in a wasteful or destructive manner. Let us look at each of these stock market functions more closely.

HOW THE STOCK MARKET WORKS FOR SAVERS AND INVESTORS

A large and rapidly growing number of savers invest as a long-term strategy. For them the stock market has been an excellent place to build wealth. Today it is possible for investors to buy shares of ownership in a wide variety of firms and hold them over long periods of time. Such a strategy can substantially reduce risk, although the stock market has no guaranteed returns.

One source of risk for a stock market investor is the fact that individual stocks can rise and fall unpredictably. Investing in any one firm is risky. But investors can reduce their risk of losses by holding a diverse **portfolio,** or collections of stocks, with small amounts of many stocks. The increases in some stock prices tend to balance out the decreases in others. That way, swings in the value of any one stock do not matter so much. The fees of stockbrokers have fallen over time. For example, trades that might have cost hundreds of dollars 15 years ago can now be made for as little as $8. An investor can economically purchase a very small ownership share in any listed firm.

Portfolio
All the stocks, bonds, or other securities held by an individual or corporation for investment purposes.

Holding shares in 20 firms from independent industries will reduce the variability of the investor's returns by about 70 percent. ***Holding shares of many firms in unconnected industries helps to reduce portfolio risk.***

Equity mutual fund
A corporation that pools the funds of investors, including small investors, and uses them to purchase a bundle of stocks.

One way an individual investor can easily purchase an interest in many firms at one time is to purchase stock in an **equity mutual fund,** a corporation that buys and holds shares of stock in many firms. A popular form of fund in recent years has been the index fund, which holds a portfolio mirroring one or another of the many stock indexes, such as the S&P 500 Index or the Dow Jones Industrials. These mutual funds do very little trading and as a result have low operating costs. They have had better yields than most of the more actively managed mutual funds—those trading more often in search of greater gains. Mutual funds with diverse holdings offer relatively low risks. As **Exhibit A3-2** shows, the combined holdings of equity mutual funds summed to approximately $3 trillion in 1998. That was about 20 percent of all publicly traded U.S. stocks. Moreover, stock ownership through these mutual funds has been growing rapidly in recent years.

A second source of risk facing investors is the fact that nearly all stocks in the market may rise or fall together, when expectations about the entire economy change. Such change can be sudden. For example, on October 19, 1987, the stocks listed in the Dow Jones Industrial Average lost more than 22 percent of their value in just one trading day. But as **Exhibit A3-3** shows, holding stocks for a longer period reduces the risk of large losses. For example, stocks in the S&P Index held for one year beginning in any month between 1950 and 1996 lost 38.9 percent in the worst case. A gain of 61 percent was the best case. But the index stocks held over any 10 years brought a small positive return of 0.5 percent in the worst case. In the best case 10-year period, the return was

EXHIBIT A3-2

The amount of money that people put into U.S. equity mutual funds, in order to hold shares in the ownership of stocks, rose dramatically in the 1990s. Purchasing shares in a mutual fund is a simple way for an individual to buy and hold an interest in a large variety of stocks with one purchase.

SOURCE: Investor Company Institute <www.ici.org>.

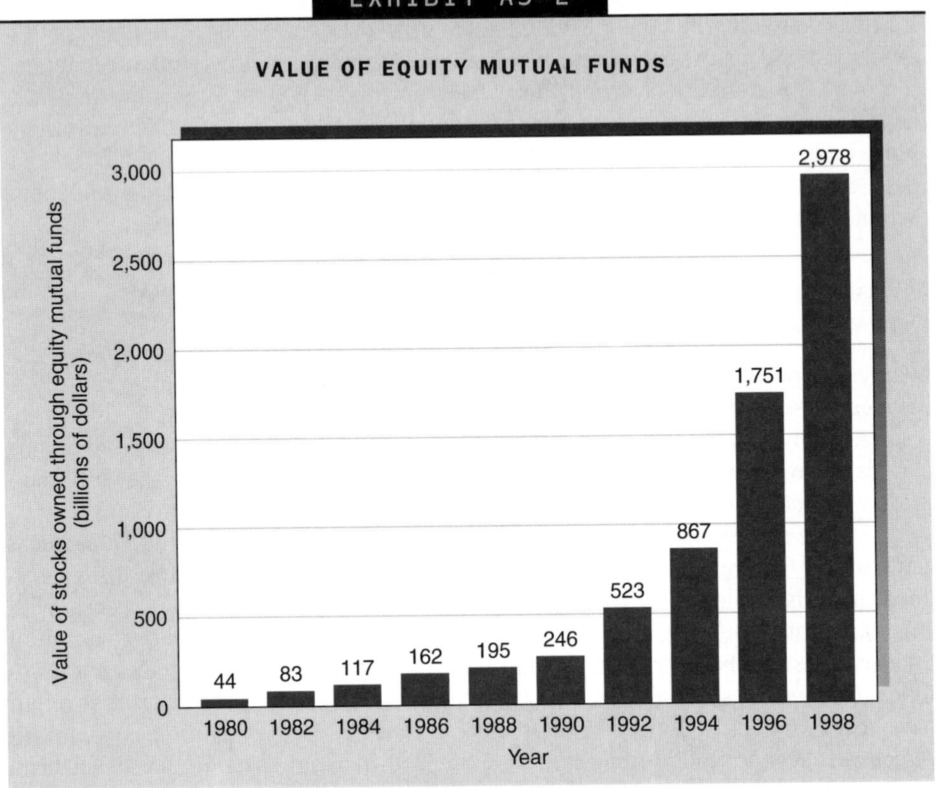

EXHIBIT A3-3

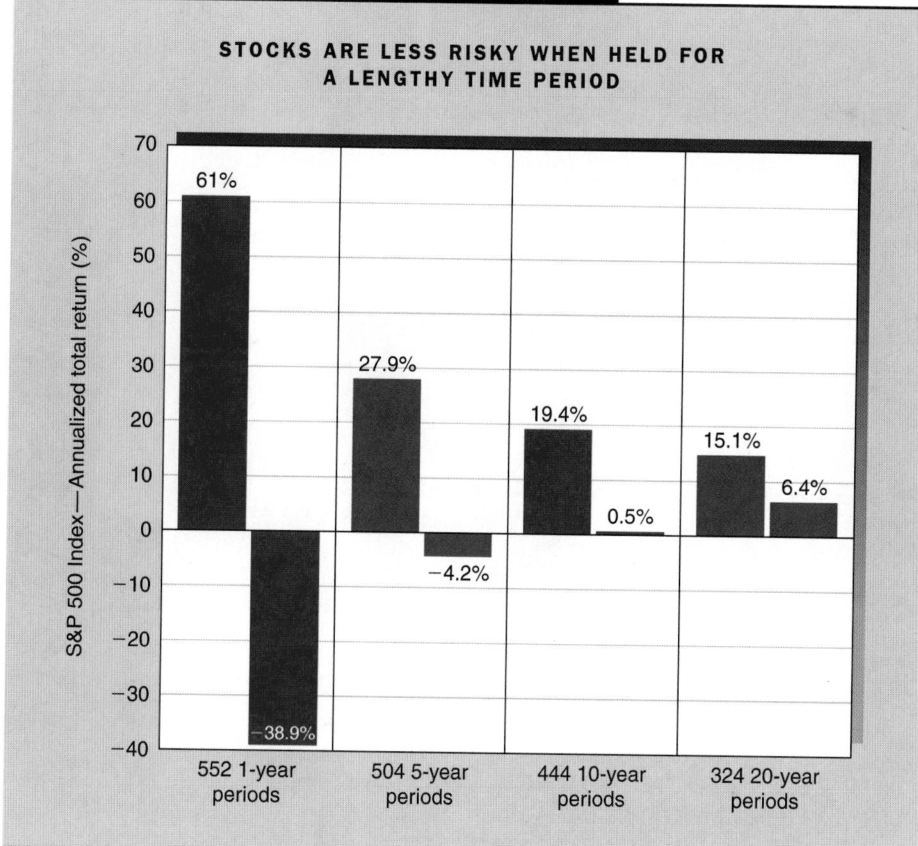

This graphic highlights the best and the worst annualized performance for each holding period from 1950 to 1996. It shows that there is less risk of a low or negative return when a portfolio of stocks (S&P 500) is held for a longer period of time.

SOURCE: Ibbotson Associates and Merrill Lynch, published in the Merrill Lynch newsletter, Insights and Strategies *3, no. 4 (1998): 1. The analysis uses "rolling time periods." The first rolling 1-year period, for example, begins on January 1, 1950, and ends on December 31, 1950. The second 1-year period begins on February 1, 1950, and ends on January 31, 1951. Similarly, the rolling 5-year periods run from January 1950 through December 1954, February 1950 through January 1955, and so on.*

19.4 percent. Over any 20-year period, 6.4 percent was the worst return, while 15.1 percent was the best. Clearly, holding a portfolio of stocks for a longer period greatly reduces the risk of very low or negative returns to the investor, although it similarly reduces the chance of very large returns.

Two decades ago, the high historical rate of return on stocks was thought to reflect their greater risk relative to bonds and other investments like savings accounts. Stocks are risky when held for a relatively short time or when only small numbers of stocks are held in one's portfolio. ***However, when a diverse set of stocks is held over a lengthy time period, historically stocks have yielded a high rate of return and the variation of that return has been relatively small. The development of stock mutual funds makes it possible for even small investors to hold a diverse portfolio, add to it regularly, and still keep transaction costs low.***

The development of equity mutual funds has both reduced the risk of stock investments and attracted large amounts of funds into the market, helping to push prices upward. Currently, many Americans are reaching retirement with substantially more wealth than they expected just a few years ago. In early 1999, U.S. households owned $11 trillion in stocks, up from $7.2 trillion at the end of 1996. More than four in every ten households now own stock, either directly or through an equity mutual fund. The wealth of these households has increased substantially as their stock holdings have risen in value.

Are stocks riskier than bonds? If held for only a short time—1 to 3 years, for example—stocks are more risky. However, when held over lengthy periods like 20 or 30 years, historically the rate of return on stocks has been both higher and less variable than that of bonds. What does this imply with regard to where persons saving for their retirement while in their 20s and 30s should place their funds?

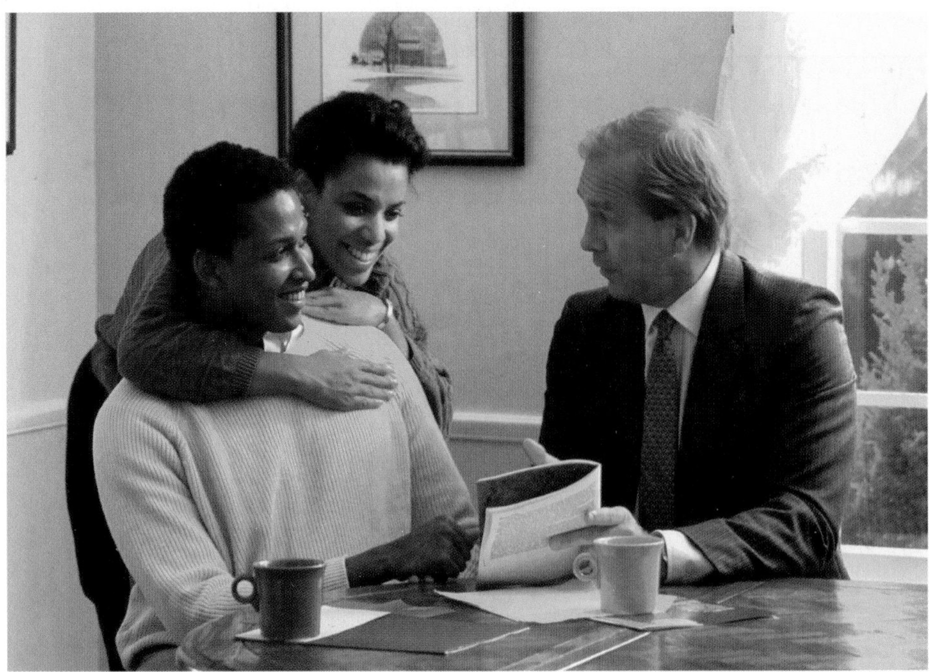

How the Stock Market Works for Corporations

To raise money to develop new products or expand output, a corporation has several options. It can use retained earnings (profits earned but not paid out to stockholders), it can borrow money, or it can sell stock. In borrowing, it promises to repay to the lender a specific amount, including principal and interest. But when it sells stock, it is selling a share of ownership in the firm. The buyer of the stock is purchasing a fractional share in the firm's future net revenues.

Primary market
Market where financial institutions aid in the sale of new securities.

Secondary Market
Market where financial institutions aid in the buying and selling of existing securities.

Newly issued stocks are sold through specialized firms to the public. A firm that issues new stock sells it in the ***primary market.*** When news reports tell us about how stock prices are changing, they are referring to ***secondary markets,*** where previously issued stocks are traded. Secondary markets make it easy to buy and sell listed stock. That is important to the primary market. The initial buyers want to know that their stocks will be easy to sell later. Entry is more attractive when exit will be easy. That helps the corporation that issues new stock to sell it for a higher price.

A stock exchange is a secondary market. It is a place where stockbrokers come to arrange trades for buyers and sellers. The largest and best known stock market is the New York Stock Exchange, where more than 2,500 stocks are traded. There are other such markets in the United States, as well as in London, Tokyo, and other trading centers around the world.

The expectation of future dividends paid from profits and gain derived from increases in share prices are the major reasons why people buy the stock of a corporation. Periodically, the firm's board of directors determines when the firm will provide dividend payments to its shareholders. A firm that earns greater profits can provide more dividend income to owners of its stock over time.

However, sometimes a firm will not pay out its profits as dividends. Instead it retains those earnings to invest in the firm. If its investments are good, they will increase the firm's future profits. The prospect of greater future profits raises the value of the stock. A good investment is simply one that increases stock value by more than the amount of the forgone dividend. In general, stockholders are happy either with profits now or with a rising stock price. Microsoft, for example, has made many stockholders rich even though it has never paid a dividend. It has used its large profits to invest even more in hiring people and increasing its ability to produce larger profits in the future. In fact, stocks in many new firms, especially those investing in high technology, rise in value before they ever earn a profit. The stock price increase is strictly due to expected future profits.

Either dividend payments or rising stock values will increase the stockholder's wealth. Of course, if the firm does not invest wisely, then future earnings will decline, as will the price of the stock. The value of a firm's stock rises (falls) when investors come to expect future profits to rise (fall). ***Thus when investors believe that a new investment by a corporation is wise—that it will increase future earnings—the stock price will rise. When a new management decision seems unwise to investors, many will sell, driving the stock price down.***

It pays for a stockholder, and especially a large stockholder such as a fund manager, to be alert to whether the firm's decisions are good ones. Those who spot a corporation's problems early can sell part or all of their stock in that firm before others notice and lower the price by selling their own stock. Those who first notice decisions that will be profitable can gain by increasing their holdings of the stock. Stockholder alertness benefits the corporation, too. The firm's board of directors can utilize the price changes resulting from investor vigilance to reward good management decisions. They often do so by tying the compensation of the top corporate officers to stock performance. How? Rather than paying these officers entirely in the form of salaries, boards of directors can integrate **stock options** into the compensation package of top executives. When good decisions drive the stock price up, the executives' options will have substantial value. On the other hand, if bad decisions cause the stock price to fall, then the options will have little or no value.

Stock options
The option to buy a specified number of shares of the firm's stock at a designated price. The designated price is generally set so that the options will be quite valuable if the firm's shares increase in price, but of little value if their price falls. Thus, when used to compensate top managers, stock options provide a strong incentive to follow policies that will increase the value of the firm.

Of course, luck can enter also, as when demand rises or falls in the firm's product market. Some boards of directors make the option price dependent on the firm's performance relative to competing firms. If the firm does well compared to others in the same market, then the reward grows. Because a firm's directors also are normally stockholders, the stock market automatically disciplines them, too. Their own rewards are larger when they choose successful corporate managers and effectively motivate them.

How the Stock Market Works for the Economy

We have seen how the stock market benefits stockholders and helps discipline corporate decision makers to be more efficient. As it does so, it is providing both information and the incentives needed to build prosperity. The secondary market in a corporation's shares constantly sends signals to the listed corporation's board of directors and managers. Changing stock prices reward good decisions and penalize bad ones. This provides executives and managers with an incentive to follow policies that increase the firm's value. In order to achieve this objective, the firm must generate an income stream that is worth more than the cost of its assets. Put another way, it must undertake productive projects.

STOCK PRICES AND THE INTEREST RATE

Underlying today's price of a firm's stock is the present value of the firm's expected future net earnings, or profit. What those future profits are worth to an investor today depends on three things: (1) the expected size of future net earnings, (2) when these earnings will be achieved, and (3) how much the investor discounts the future income. The last depends on the interest rate. As we noted in an earlier chapter, the present-value procedure can be used to determine the current value of any future income (or cost) stream. If D represents dividends (and gains from a higher stock price) earned in various years in the future (indicated by the subscripts) and i represents the discount or interest rate, the present value of the future income stream[2] is

$$PV = \frac{D_1}{(1+i)} + \frac{D_2}{(1+i)^2} + \cdots + \frac{D_n}{(1+i)^n}$$

A higher interest rate reduces the present value of future returns from holding shares of a stock. And that is true even if the size of future returns is not affected by changes in the interest rate. Stock analysts often stress that lower interest rates are good for the stock market. This should not be surprising because the lower rates of interest will increase the value of future income (and capital gains). For example, when the interest rate is 12.5 percent, the discounted value of $100 of future income to be received each year in perpetuity is $800 ($100 divided by 0.125). But when the interest rate is 5 percent, the discounted value of this same income stream is $2,000 ($100 divided by 0.05). Other things constant, lower interest rates will increase stock values.

THE STOCK MARKET SINCE 1982: WHAT CAUSED THE DRAMATIC RISE?

In March 1982, the daily closings of the Dow Jones Industrials averaged 812. Seventeen years later, on March 29, 1999, the Dow closed at 10,006. Other stock indexes showed similar increases. What factors explain this 12-fold increase in the value of stocks? Because stock prices depend on the changing expectations of millions of investors, no one can say exactly what caused the strong increase. However, most observers believe the following four factors played an important role.

- **Interest rates and inflation fell.** The interest rate on 10-year Treasury bonds stood at 13.00 percent in 1982. By March 1999, the 10-year bond rate had fallen to 5.15 percent. The lower structure of interest rates in the late 1990s compared to the early 1980s reflected a rather dramatic change in the inflationary environment. In the 2 years prior to 1982, prices had risen 10.7 percent annually; but in the 2 years prior to March 1999, prices rose only 2.5 percent annually.

  As we just noted, lower interest rates will tend to increase the discounted value of future income derived from stock ownership. In addition, there are two other reasons why lower rates of inflation and interest will tend to boost stock values. First, a lower rate of inflation will reduce the tax burden accompanying capital gains. The United States taxes nominal capital gains. Therefore, if stock prices rise with the general price level, investors will have to pay taxes on the inflation-

[2]For a specific annual income stream in perpetuity, the present value is equal simply to R/i, where R is the annual revenue stream and I is the interest rate. For example, if the interest rate is 5 percent, the PV of a $100 annual income stream in perpetuity is equal to $100/0.05, or $2,000.

ary as well as the real increases in stock values. Stability in the general level of prices, however, will eliminate the tax on the phantom inflationary gains. Second, low and stable rates of inflation reduce the uncertainty of investment and other long-term contracts. This will help both the economy and the stock markets.

- **Corporate earnings were higher.** Profits were four times larger in the 2 years prior to 1999 than in the 2 years prior to 1982. The 1990s were especially profitable. Per-share operating profits of the Dow Industrials grew 19 percent per year between 1991 and 1997. There were several reasons for this growth of profits. First, shareholders, especially pension fund and other fund managers with large stock holdings, had begun to insist that firms seek greater earnings. More corporations became willing to sell unprofitable divisions, to merge and grow, or to downsize and lay off managers and workers. Those and other painful measures were taken as shareholders insisted on and got greater productivity and profits.

  Second, boards of directors themselves, representing shareholders, more often insisted that their fellow directors hold a significant share of their wealth in the corporation's stock. They also increased the proportion of top managers' compensation paid in the form of stock options rather than salary. These measures tied the managers' rewards more closely to those of stockholders.

  Third, stockholders encouraged firms to take advantage of technological advances that allowed greater productivity. For example, new computerized systems gave managers updated information that helped firms adjust more quickly and operate more efficiently with smaller inventories. This reduced capital requirements and meant that when buyer demands changed, outdated inventories were smaller. Computers also reduced waste by allowing better fuel and industrial process management. Quicker response times and less waste increased productivity and profits.

  Fourth, greater productivity increased the firms' ability to compete internationally. The firms represented in the Dow Jones Industrial Average made 35 percent of their sales abroad in 1988. By 1999 they raised that figure to 40 percent. As lower transportation costs and reduced trade barriers expanded world trade, U.S. firms were well positioned to expand their market share.

- **The improving U.S. economy drew investment funds from abroad.** Lower tax rates, persistently low rates of inflation, and the general strength of the U.S. economy have attracted substantial investment funds from abroad during the last 15 years. In turn, this inflow of funds into the U.S. stock market has helped push stock prices higher. As **Exhibit A3-4** shows, foreign holdings of U.S. stocks amounted to $76 billion in 1982. By 1998, the figure had risen to $1.1 trillion. U.S. corporations represented a growing share of the world's stock value. The U.S. stock market rose to 53 percent of world market value in 1999, up from 29 percent in 1988.

- **Mutual funds expanded their holdings dramatically.** Stock mutual funds make it possible for even small investors to maintain a diverse portfolio of stocks. These funds have become increasingly attractive, particularly to long-term investors planning for their retirement. The recent growth of these funds has also been propelled by the movement of the baby-boom generation into the prime-earning and high-saving years of life. As the baby boomers and others have channelled record amounts into retirement plans, the pool of funds invested in stock mutual funds has grown to record levels (see Exhibit A3-2). In 1996 and 1997, stock funds gained $15 billion to 20 billion *per month.* While the flow of funds into stock mutuals slowed in 1998, it still amounted to between $10 billion and $12 billion per month. This strong demand for stocks purchased through mutual funds has boosted stock prices.

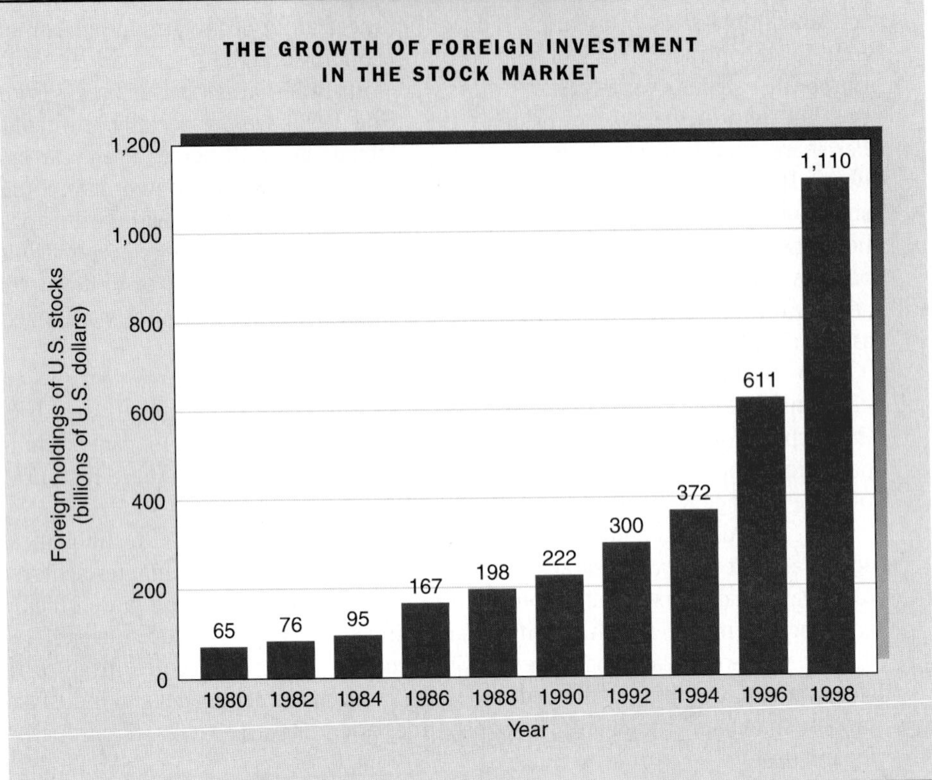

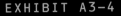

In 1982, foreign holdings of U.S. stocks amounted to $76 billion. By 1998, they had risen to more than $1 trillion. This strong demand by foreigners helped to raise U.S. stock prices to record levels.

SOURCE: Department of Commerce, Bureau of Economic Analysis.

IS THE STOCK MARKET TOO HIGH— IS IT A BUBBLE THAT WILL BURST?

The economic factors listed above helped to fuel the strong rise in stock indexes since 1982. Will they continue to push many stock prices higher? Or will these factors weaken and lead to a long-lasting collapse in stock prices? Since expectations about future earnings and stock prices drive current stock prices, no one can answer these questions with certainty. In fact, as we write, there are prominent stock market experts on both sides of this issue. Some are forecasting a continued increase in stock prices, while others predict a major correction if not impending doom.

What insights can be derived from the factors that drove stock prices up? How are these factors likely to change in the future?

Inflation and Interest Rates. Most analysts expect the rate of inflation to continue at low levels, with perhaps a slight decline. This would help keep interest rates low. Thus, the danger of a stock market collapse due to higher inflation and rising interest rates would appear to be small. On the other hand, future stock prices are unlikely to receive much of an additional boost from lower interest rates and less inflation.

Corporate Earnings. Will future corporate profits be higher in general? This is a key question. Experts differ in their forecasts, and no one can be sure of their answers. Technological advances continue and may even accelerate in the future. Stockholders continue to reward firms that are willing to try new systems and new approaches. One

EXHIBIT A3-5

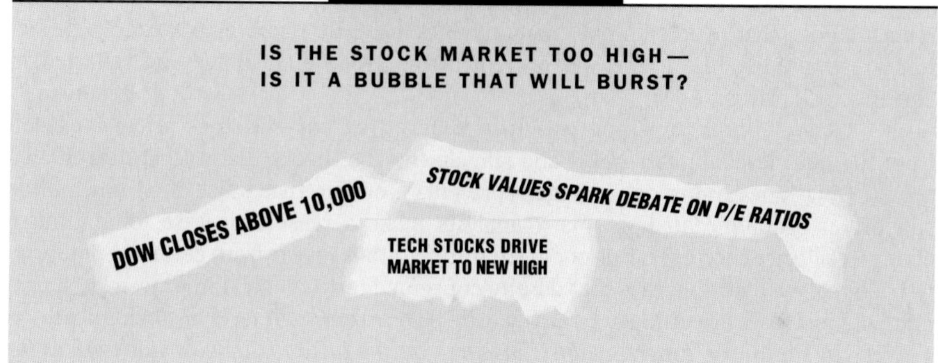

IS THE STOCK MARKET TOO HIGH—
IS IT A BUBBLE THAT WILL BURST?
DOW CLOSES ABOVE 10,000
STOCK VALUES SPARK DEBATE ON P/E RATIOS
TECH STOCKS DRIVE
MARKET TO NEW HIGH

Lower interest rates, higher corporate profits, increased inflow of foreign capital, and a huge flow of savings into stock mutual funds helped push the U.S. stock market to record highs again and again throughout 1993–1999.

indication of this is the fact that technology stocks continue to do well in the stock market, even when their current and past earnings are unimpressive. There is certainly the possibility that productivity and corporate earnings will continue to rise. Optimism about continuing increases seems plausible, but future stock price gains from this source are certainly not guaranteed.

Stock Investments from Abroad. The inflow of foreign funds into the U.S. stock market depends not only on conditions in the investment market here, but also on the situation in other nations. Continuing prosperity abroad means greater demand for stocks. But if prosperity abroad occurs, will foreign stock markets also offer better investment conditions? Greater unification of markets in Europe is occurring. Will this lead to larger or smaller European investments in the United States? If Asian markets improve strongly, will that divert demand from the U.S. stock market? Or will demand in all markets be stimulated by the rising prosperity? No one really knows whether foreigners will continue to pour money into the U.S. stock market.

Mutual Fund Investments. American workers now have much more faith in the stock market. Will they continue to pour large quantities of savings into the stock market? It seems quite possible that this can continue for some years, but once again, the future is uncertain. Continued enthusiasm may bring more new stock market investors. After all, fewer than half of all Americans currently own stock. But enthusiasm for putting savings into stocks could decline. Also, members of the baby-boom generation will begin to move into the retirement phase of life in the near future. As they do, will they sell their stock investments to finance retirement? Or will they continue to work at least part-time? Working would help delay the sale of their stocks, keeping demand stronger. Will they try to consume most of what they have saved? That would speed the selling of their stocks and tend to reduce stock prices. Most current retirees, though, try to keep much of their wealth intact. That helps insure them against poverty in an old age of uncertain length. It also allows them to pass along large portfolios to their children. If the baby boomers follow this path, then their children will be more wealthy and may demand even more stocks.

Concluding Thoughts

No one knows for sure where the U.S. stock market will go in the future. Most economists adhere to the **random walk theory** of the stock market. According to this theory, current stock prices already reflect the best known information about the future state

Random walk theory
The theory that current stock prices already reflect known information about the future. Therefore, the future movement of stock prices will be determined by surprise occurrences. This will cause them to change in a random fashion.

of corporate earnings, the health of the economy, and other factors that influence stock prices. Therefore, the future direction of stock prices will be driven by surprise occurrences, things that people do not currently anticipate. By their very nature, these factors are unpredictable. If they were predictable, they would already be reflected in current stock prices.

There is no compelling reason to believe that current stock prices must fall from the high levels of early 1999 and stay down. The theory that a level near 10,000 for the Dow Jones Industrial Average represents a bubble that must burst has limited support in economic analysis. Many analysts make a reasonable case for optimism about stock price increases. But of course this result also is far from certain. Some analysts do make a plausible case that despite continued technological improvements, productivity increases are unlikely to justify even the current high level of stock prices.

In summary, expert analysts disagree on the future course of stock prices for one fundamental reason: No one can predict the future course of savers and investors. But there are some lessons from history. Stocks have been a good long-term investment in the past. This is unlikely to change. Thus, persons investing for the long term are likely to do well if they have a substantial portion of their funds invested in a diverse bundle of stocks.

KEY POINTS

➤ The stock market has allowed many Americans without special business skills and without making specific business decisions to participate in the risks and opportunities of corporate America. Many have prospered as a result. Real returns for the past two centuries have been 7 percent per year.

➤ Buying and selling individual stocks without specialized knowledge, for a quick profit, is very risky. But holding a diverse portfolio of unrelated stocks and holding them for long periods of time greatly reduces the risk of investing in the stock market.

➤ Vigilant investors and investment fund managers, as they buy and sell stocks for their own portfolios, generate price changes that help to allocate capital efficiently and to discipline corporate decision makers in ways that benefit consumers and stockholders in general.

➤ The U.S. stock market's dramatic rise in value since 1982 has resulted from lower inflation and interest rates, rising corporate earnings, increased purchases by foreign investors, and increased stock purchases through mutual funds.

➤ Stock prices reached levels in early 1999 that were very high by historic standards. Economic analysis suggests that optimists who think stock price levels will rise significantly in the near future can make a plausible case. But pessimists can do the same for their view. In fact, investor expectations about an uncertain future determine current prices, and no one can forecast future stock prices with precision or certainty.

CRITICAL ANALYSIS QUESTIONS

*1. A friend just inherited $50,000. She informs you of her investment plans and asks for your advice. "I want to put it into the stock market and use it for my retirement in 30 years. What do you think is the best plan that will provide high returns at a relatively low risk?" What answer would you give? Explain.

2. What risks are faced by those who put a large part of their savings into the stock market? What can they do to reduce that risk while keeping their money in the market?

*3. Microsoft stock rose from less than $10 in 1995 to nearly $100 in early 1999. Microsoft has made sizable profits, but never paid a dividend. Why were people willing to pay such a high price knowing that they might not get dividends for many years?

4. In the late 1980s and through the 1990s, as U.S. stocks became more expensive, foreign investors bought more and more of them. Explain why.

*5. The stocks of some corporations that have never made a profit or paid a dividend, especially those in high-technology industries, have risen in price. What causes investors to be willing to buy these stocks?

6. New firms without proven track records are more risky than mature firms. Why are investors still willing to bid up their prices?

7. If an investment advisor gives you some hot new stock tip, is it likely to be a "sure thing"? Why or why not?

---

*Asterisk denotes questions for which answers are given in Appendix B.

APPLICATION 4

Sometimes things are not what they seem. And sometimes the illusion is more satisfying than the reality.

William R. Allen[1]

How Does Government Regulation Affect Your Life?

APPLICATION FOCUS

- How does regulation influence our lives?
- How does the regulation of health and safety differ from traditional economic regulation?
- What does public choice analysis suggest about the motivation for regulatory activities and differences between their stated objectives and actual effects?
- Who bears the cost of regulation? How do regulatory costs compare to their benefits?

[1]William R. Allen, *The Midnight Economist: Little Essays on Big Truths* (Sun Lakes, AZ: Thomas Horton and Daughters, 1997), p. 133.

As we saw in Chapter 5, markets often are not perfectly efficient. When property rights do not hold resource users, polluters, or consumers fully accountable, ideal efficiency will not result. Regulation might improve efficiency in such cases. Government regulation might also improve economic efficiency in a market that is not fully competitive. However, the actual outcomes of regulation often differ from and sometimes conflict with stated objectives. The regulatory process is complex and people may adjust to it in unforeseen ways. Further, efficiency is not the only reason why people seek to influence the regulatory process. Government regulatory restrictions on market activity can also be used by some to gain at the expense of others. For example, producers might find regulations useful to raise the costs of rival firms, or even to keep them out of the market altogether. In those cases, regulatory restrictions may reduce economic efficiency. In this application we will take a closer look at how regulation affects our lives.

REGULATION OF BUSINESS

Regulatory activity in the United States has expanded substantially in the past three decades. Federal regulatory spending and staffing levels increased rapidly in the 1970s, dropped in the early 1980s, then resumed their expansion through at least 1998. Federal spending for economic regulation in 1970 (in constant 1992 dollars) was $4.6 billion. By fiscal year 1999, it had risen to more than $15 billion. Compliance costs are much larger. For example, while the budgeted federal expenditures to make and implement environmental regulations were $6 billion in 1996, the private and public expenditures required to meet the objectives of those regulations were estimated at more than $120 billion.

TRADITIONAL ECONOMIC REGULATION

Regulation of business activity is not a new development. In 1887, Congress established the Interstate Commerce Commission (ICC), providing it with the authority to regulate both prices and levels of service in the railroad industry. In 1935, the trucking industry was also brought under the ICC's regulatory jurisdiction. State regulatory commissions began to oversee local delivery of electricity, natural gas, and telephone services as early as 1907. Federal commissions were formed during the 1930s to regulate interstate telephone service, broadcasting, airlines, natural gas pipelines, and other industries. These activities focus on **economic regulation** and usually control the product price or the structure of a particular industry rather than specifying the production processes used by business firms.

Economic regulation
Regulation of product price or industrial structure, usually imposed on a specific industry. By and large, the production processes used by the regulated firms are unaffected by this type of regulation.

Sometimes economic regulation was thought to be necessary for the protection of consumers in markets characterized by large-scale production and natural monopoly. In other instances, it was designed to preserve "orderly competition" in industries with high fixed costs and low variable costs. Railroad transport is an example of the latter. Regardless of their original purpose, regulations that fix prices and restrict entry stifle the competitive process. With time, such regulation often ends up protecting inefficient producers and limiting the options of consumers. Later, we will see some examples of this. During the late 1970s, high costs generated widespread dissatisfaction with economic regulations in several industries. Major steps toward deregulation in the ground and air transportation industries resulted. Consumers benefited substantially, and regulatory reform continues in other markets.

Recent Health and Safety Regulation of Business

Along with movement toward less economic regulation, there has been a sharp increase in **health and safety regulation.** In the late 1960s and early 1970s, people had great faith in the ability of government to improve the quality of life. The economy was prospering, and people turned their attention more toward policies to reduce health hazards and preserve environmental quality. For a wealthier nation, reducing air and water pollution and other externalities became more feasible and more desirable. Added regulation to protect individuals against risks from occupational hazards, as well as risks from newly developed drugs and other consumer products, was also demanded by various activist groups.

Health and safety regulation
Legislation designed to improve the health, safety, and environmental conditions available to workers and/or consumers. The legislation usually mandates production procedures, minimum standards, and/or product characteristics to be met by producers and employers.

Reflecting these forces, the new health and safety regulation has expanded rapidly. The expenditures, employment, and powers of such agencies as the Occupational Safety and Health Administration (OSHA), Consumer Product Safety Commission (CPSC), Food and Drug Administration (FDA), and Environmental Protection Agency (EPA) have grown rapidly. Their regulatory authority cuts across industries and involves them more in the actual operation of individual firms. In contrast with economic regulation, the health and safety mandates frequently specify in detail the engineering processes to be followed by the regulated firms and industries.

THE POLITICAL ECONOMY OF REGULATION

Regulation involves a complex set of forces, political as well as economic. Public choice analysis provides us with some insight regarding political support of regulation and how we would expect the regulatory process to work. Four factors are particularly important.

1. ***The demand for regulation often stems from special interest effects and redistribution considerations rather than from the pursuit of economic efficiency.*** The wealth of an individual (or business firm) can be increased if that person or firm becomes more efficient or expands production. Regulation introduces another possibility. Sellers can gain from regulatory policies that either reduce competition in their market or increase the costs of rival firms. Buyers can gain, at least in the short run, if a legal requirement forcing producers to supply goods below cost is passed. Regulation opens up an additional avenue whereby those most able to bend the political process to their advantage can increase their wealth.

   Public choice analysis (see Chapter 6) indicates that special-interest groups, such as well-organized, concentrated groups of buyers or sellers, can be expected to exert a disproportionate influence on the political process. Furthermore, the regulators themselves often compose a politically powerful interest group. Regulatory bureaucrats are key figures in the process. Their cooperation is important to

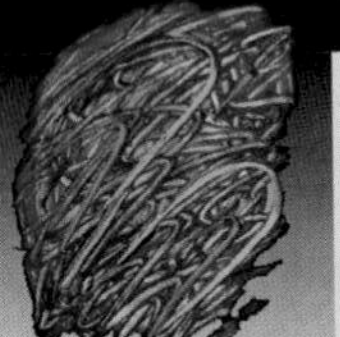

APPLICATIONS IN ECONOMICS

Taxis and Regulatory Entry Restraints

Occupational and business licensing by state and local governments often restricts entry and reduces competition. The taxicab business illustrates this point, as well as some interesting developments that may affect the future competitiveness of markets. Most cities impose regulations limiting entry into the taxi business. Some impose an absolute ban on the entry of new firms; others restrict the availability of operating licenses. For example, New York City's infamous medallion system restricts the number of taxi licenses to 12,200. These licenses are tradable. In the mid-1990s they sold for $175,000, a figure high enough to discourage many aspiring entrepreneurs, particularly those with limited capital. Taxicabs are also heavily regulated and entry severely limited in other cities, including Los Angeles, Chicago, Miami, Houston, and San Francisco. Of course, the primary effect of such regulations is less competition and higher fare prices.

Despite the presence of only three taxicab companies, the Colorado Public Utilities Commission (PUC) denied numerous requests and prohibited the entry of new firms into the Denver taxicab market for almost 50 years. Potential new entrants requesting a license were required to prove that (a) the existing service was inadequate and (b) the firms currently in the market were unable to handle the volume of traffic. Every time a potential rival sought a license, the three existing companies argued they were quite capable of handling the current demand and the PUC denied the request. In effect, the regulations imposed a three-firm oligopoly on the Denver taxicab market.

Leroy Jones, Ani Ebong, and Girma Molalegne requested a license to start Quick Pick Cabs in 1993. When their request was denied by the PUC, the entrepreneurs, along with the Institute for Justice, a public interest legal firm located in Washington, D.C., filed a suit challenging the regulations. The plaintiffs argued that the regulations limiting entry were arbitrary, excessive, and in conflict with the privileges or immunities clause of the U.S. Constitution. Thus, they asserted that their right to pursue a business and earn a living was being violated. The case attracted the attention of CBS News, *The Wall Street Journal,* and other national media. Eventually, the regulatory commission backed down and the law was changed, permitting entry except in cases where the existing firms could prove that a new rival would cause their business to fail. Obviously, this shifted the burden of proof and made it much more difficult for the existing firms to restrain entry. Subsequently, Jones, Ebong, and Molalegne started Freedom Cabs, which became Denver's first new taxicab company since 1947. By 1996, the company had grown into a thriving business with approximately 100 employees (see accompanying picture).

The Denver case is having an impact in other areas. Both Indianapolis and Cincinnati revised their regulations,

Girma Molalegne, Leroy Jones, and Ani Ebong (left to right) challenged regulations limiting entry into the taxicab market and eventually started Denver's first new cab company in almost 50 years.

(continued)

liberalizing entry into the taxi business. The Institute for Justice is assisting plaintiffs seeking to challenge restraints limiting economic freedom in other areas and occupations. In 1999, it was litigating the case of JoAnne Cornwell, a provider of African hairstyling services, who faces restrictive regulations imposed by the state of California. The state prohibits her from opening a salon or teaching her craft because she is not a licensed cosmetologist. Securing a California cosmetology license requires 1,600 hours of training, none of which actually teaches skills relevant to her specialty. Like regulations in other trades, these requirements help existing suppliers to keep out would-be competitors. It will be interesting to follow the effectiveness of these and other challenges to regulatory activities that limit entry and restrain competition.

those who are regulated. These factors suggest that there will be demand for economic regulation even if it contributes to economic inefficiency.

2. ***With the passage of time, regulatory agencies will often adopt the views of the business interests they are supposed to regulate.*** Once again, the special interest effect indicates why this is an expected result, even if the regulation initially was designed to police the actions of a business group. The personal payoff derived by *individual* consumers (and taxpayers) from a change in regulatory actions is likely to be small. Often they are lulled into thinking that because a regulatory agency exists, the "public interest" is served. In contrast, firms (and employees) in regulated industries are vitally interested in the structure and composition of regulatory commissions and agencies. Favorable actions by these regulatory bodies could result in larger profits, higher-paying jobs, and insulation from the uncertainties of competition. Thus, firms and employee groups, recognizing their potential gain, will invest both economic and political resources to influence the actions of regulatory agencies. In return for their organized support, political officials will have a strong incentive to favor their position when setting policy and making appointments to regulatory agencies.
3. ***Regulation is inflexible and slow to react to dynamic change.*** Changing market conditions often make regulatory procedures obsolete. For example, the introduction of trucking vastly changed the competitiveness of the ground transportation industry (previously dominated by railroad interests). Nevertheless, the regulation of price, entry, and routes continued for years after competitive forces had eliminated the monopoly power of firms in this industry. Similarly, city building codes that may have been appropriate when adopted have become obsolete and now retard the introduction of new, more efficient materials and procedures. In many cities regulatory procedures have prevented builders from introducing such cost-saving materials as plastic pipes, preconstructed septic tanks, and prefabricated housing units. Other local restraints are also common. Some are used primarily to stifle competition. (See the accompanying boxed feature on regulation of taxi markets.)
4. ***When approval has to be obtained from regulators, it will be difficult to introduce new products, including those that might potentially save lives.*** The activities and management of a regulatory agency, the Food and Drug Administration, for example, will come under severe scrutiny if they inadvertently permit a dangerous product on the market. The victims of such a product are specific persons and the product's harm can often be seen. In contrast, regulators face few problems if they keep a highly beneficial product—including one that would save lives—off the market. Who will know that a specific drug or other product—one that most have never heard about because the tests are still being run—*might* have saved an individual's life? Thus, the cost to the regulatory agency of the former error is much

greater than that of the latter. As a result, regulatory agencies will predictably apply tests that are too restrictive from the viewpoint of economic efficiency and consumer welfare.

THE COSTS OF REGULATION

Regulators produce benefits by ordering producers to emit less pollution, make workplaces accessible to handicapped workers, and reduce noise levels in the workplace, for example. Of course, as they do so, costs are incurred. The major cost of health and safety regulation is felt in the form of higher production costs and thus higher prices. And, of course, the process of regulation itself is costly: Employment and operating costs of regulatory agencies must be met, which means higher taxes. These costs can be substantial. According to EPA estimates, when contractors were hired in 1988 to clean up Superfund hazardous waste sites, the indirect costs—costs of such things as formulating and enforcing the rules—amounted to more than $328 for every hour spent by a worker involved in the cleanup. These figures were in addition to all payments to the firms and their employees actually planning and undertaking the work at each site.[2]

The primary cost of health and safety regulation, however, comes in the form of higher operating costs of firms striving to meet the new standards. In effect, these higher costs are like a tax. As Exhibit A4-1 illustrates, the higher cost shifts the supply curve to the left for a good affected by the regulation. Higher prices and a decline in the output of the good result. Who pays the cost? As with any tax, the burden is shared by buyers and sellers according to the elasticity of supply and demand. When consumers have more options to the taxed good, so that their demand is more elastic, they will pay

Regulation that requires businesses to adopt more costly production techniques is similar to a tax. If the regulation increases per-unit costs by t, the supply curve shifts upward by that amount. Higher prices and a smaller output result.

EXHIBIT A4-1

THE REGULATION "TAX"

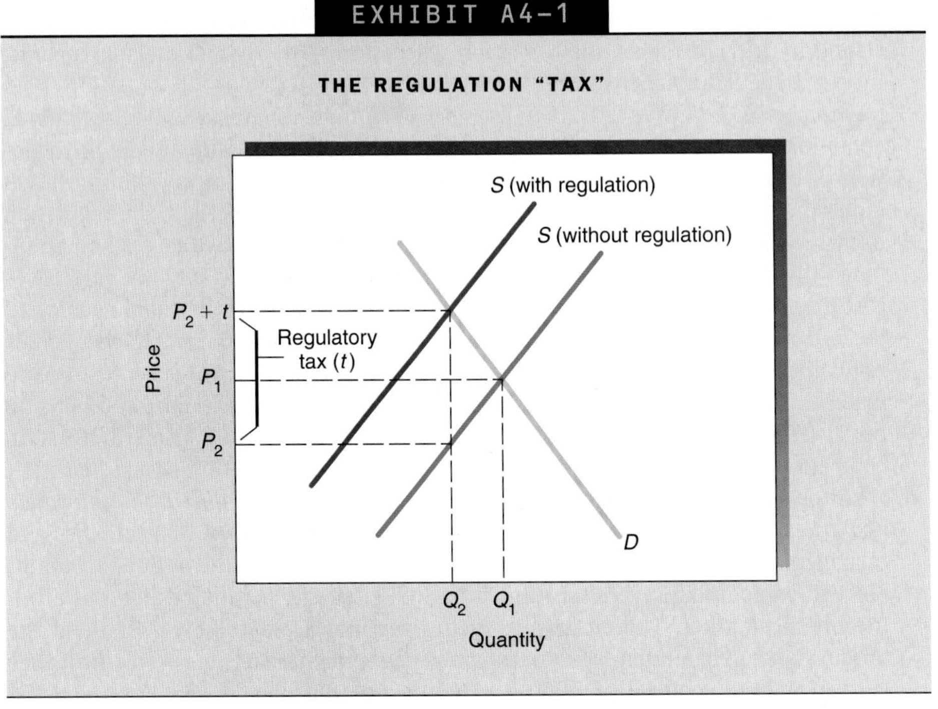

[2]These figures are from an EPA statement in the *Federal Register* 57, no. 152 (August 6, 1992). Measured in 1999 dollars, the indirect cost per hour of work would be $463.

a smaller portion of the tax. In Exhibit A4–1, the new price ($P_2 + t$) will be closer to P_1 when demand is more elastic. On the other hand, sellers will pay a smaller portion when the supply curve is more elastic, indicating that resource suppliers in the industry have reasonably attractive options in other industries. The burden imposed on sellers occurs in the form of reduced profits for investors and lower wages (and employment) for workers in the industry. In the short run, resources employed in the industry may have few alternative uses. Therefore, the short-run supply is likely to be inelastic. In the long run, of course, capital and labor are quite mobile among users, resulting in a supply curve that is more elastic.

Sometimes the opportunity cost of health and safety regulation is exceedingly difficult to calculate. For example, the FDA often bans the sale of a new drug until years of tests costing millions of dollars are completed. Two important opportunity costs of this regulation, if the drug finally proves (or would have proven) to be safe, are (1) some drugs that have a limited profit potential are never developed because of the expensive tests and delays, and (2) people who could have been helped by a drug —had it been approved—have to forgo it for several years. Deaths often result from these delays.

An important characteristic of most activities covered by health and safety regulations is a lack of information about their effects. This is not a coincidence. In most cases, the lack of information contributes directly to the demand for the regulation. For example, if consumers or their physicians knew exactly what the effects of a particular drug would be, there would be little need for the FDA to regulate its availability. Many people, though, are unaware of the precise effects of drugs, air pollution, or workplace hazards. Even when the information is available to experts, consumers may never receive it because of the cost of communicating information, particularly highly technical information. A case can be made, therefore, that we should let the experts decide which drugs, how much air pollution, and what forms of workplace safety should be sought.

Ironically, choosing regulation to protect citizens who do not understand the danger introduces a related problem: When regulators make the decisions, most of the incentive for individuals to learn about comparative risks is removed. And it is these individuals who vote and who can apply political pressure on regulators.

When the FDA announces the approval of a new, life-saving drug after several years of testing, the public can be better assured of its safety and effectiveness. However, this assurance involves costs. This extensive and time-consuming approval process means both higher drug prices and additional pain, suffering, and even loss of life for those who might have been helped by a more rapid approval of the drug.

APPLICATIONS IN ECONOMICS

Alar on Apples—Give Consumers a Choice?

In the 1980s, growers of certain apple varieties sprayed the chemical Alar on their apples to reduce apple spoilage in the orchard and to improve the color and the shelf life of the apples. But some scientists were concerned that the traces of Alar left on the apples might increase slightly the risk of cancer for children eating them. Scientists also recognized that if forbidding the use of Alar led to higher prices and even a small reduction in apple consumption, then some protection against cancer would be lost as a result of the dietary changes of consumers.

The problem of whether to ban the use of such chemicals as Alar is more general across many fruits and many chemicals. Buyers can choose either organic fruits, advertised to be grown without such chemicals, or the standard supermarket fruits. In order to choose more wisely for themselves and their families, they have an incentive to read consumer magazines and news articles, comparing opinions on both sides of the issue as more is learned by scientists. But once regulators step in to make such a decision for consumers, personal choice is restricted, and the personal incentive to learn more about the legally forbidden option virtually disappears.

In the case of Alar, citizens alarmed by the publicity campaign of an activist organization caused the EPA to consider banning the chemical, and it was removed from the market. Most citizens, who could no longer buy products treated with Alar, were unaware that the EPA's Scientific Advisory Panel did not believe that it was dangerous and therefore had repeatedly refused to recommend a ban on its use. Dr. Richard Adamson, director of the Division of Cancer Biology at the National Cancer Institute, stated that "the risk posed by Alar was no greater than eating a peanut butter sandwich."[1] This episode illustrates one of the major problems with regulation: The regulators are often more responsive to organized political pressure than to science.

[1]The quote is from Elizabeth Whelan, "The Carcinogen or Toxin of the Week Phenomenon: The Facts Behind the Scares," in *The State of Humanity,* ed. Julian L. Simon (Cambridge: Blackwell Publishers, 1995), p. 596.

The same lack of information that generates much of the demand for health and safety regulation also makes it difficult to evaluate the effectiveness of each regulatory activity. Current health and safety regulations in the United States produce high costs as well as large benefits, but these costs and benefits of regulations can only be crudely estimated. When Robert Hahn and John Hird estimated the sum of the costs and benefits from health and safety regulations, they could not even state with confidence whether the benefits exceeded the costs. They concluded that the annual costs of these regulations in the late 1980s may have exceeded the benefits by as much as $65 billion, or that alternatively, benefits may have exceeded costs by as much as $104 billion. They suggest that the benefits of health and safety regulation are probably larger than the costs, but only by a small amount.[3]

Case Study: The Costs and Benefits of Fuel Conservation Regulation[4]

Fear of global warming—which some scientists think could be caused by rising levels of carbon dioxide in the air—has led to louder calls for more fuel-efficient cars, since cars that burn less fuel emit less carbon dioxide. Legislation that would require automakers to boost substantially their average mileage per gallon (mpg) of gasoline is once again before Congress. Would such mandatory fuel economy reduce fuel usage

[3]Data are from Robert W. Hahn and John A. Hird, "The Costs and Benefits of Regulation: Review and Synthesis," *Yale Journal on Regulation* 8 (winter 1991): 233–278.

[4]This case study was written by Jane S. Shaw, Senior Associate at the Political Economy Research Center, Bozeman, Montana.

significantly? And, if so, at what cost? Responding to sharp worldwide increases in petroleum prices, Congress began mandating fuel-economy standards in 1975. The experience with this legislation provides insights with regard to both the expected impact of tighter standards and possible unintended consequences that often accompany regulation.

When the Corporate Average Fuel Economy (CAFE) standards were initially instituted, supporters argued that the standards would conserve energy and make the United States less dependent on foreign oil. However, if Congress had simply allowed gasoline prices to rise, the higher prices would have encouraged people to adjust their habits in ways best suited to their personal circumstances. Some consumers would have simply driven less; others would have saved on gasoline by buying smaller cars or having more tune-ups. Some people living far from their workplaces might have bought larger cars and carpooled; others might have moved to places where they would have a shorter commute.

Indeed, well before the CAFE standards had an impact, people began to respond to higher gasoline prices by purchasing fuel-efficient cars. According to the 1986 *Economic Report of the President,* average fuel economy in the United States increased by 43 percent between 1973 and 1979, as consumers responded to higher fuel prices. By the time the fuel-efficiency standards influenced the design of cars, which probably occurred with the 1986 model year, much fuel economy had already been achieved and gasoline prices were going down.

By that time, some consumers wanted larger cars, but the CAFE standards forced automakers to offer smaller cars. Although they could make some reductions in fuel usage by such steps as redesigning transmissions or fuel-injection systems, car companies had to reduce vehicle weight to meet the standards. Robert W. Crandall of the Brookings Institution and John Graham of the Harvard School of Public Health estimate that model year 1989 cars were on average 500 pounds lighter than they would have been without the CAFE standards.[5]

A serious problem with lighter cars is that they are less safe than larger cars. Crandall and Graham estimated that 2,200 to 3,900 lives would be lost over a 10-year period as a result of the application of the CAFE standards to the cars of the 1989 model year. A similar number of lives would likely be lost with each succeeding model year. These findings led Jerry Ralph Curry, administrator of the National Highway Traffic Safety Administration, to oppose tighter standards in 1991. Commenting on the impact of the CAFE standards in a *Washington Post* article, Curry stated, "The bottom line is drastically smaller cars and more injuries and deaths."

There have been other unintended consequences of CAFE standards. To sell enough small cars to raise the fuel-economy average, domestic automakers reduced small-car prices and raised prices for large cars. Buying decisions were distorted, and consumers paid more on balance for their cars. Because Congress required the car companies to calculate average fuel economy separately for their domestic-manufactured cars and their imports, companies could not use their smaller, more fuel-efficient imports to bring down their domestic fleets' average. This encouraged small-car production in the United States, even though it might have been cheaper to produce overseas. At the same time, Ford moved some of its large-car production out of the country in order to meet more easily the overall standards.

Predictably, the CAFE regulations led to a major lobbying effort, moving additional creative skills and energy away from productive activity. General Motors and Ford have lobbied to keep the government from tightening the standards. In contrast,

[5]Robert W. Crandall and John D. Graham, "The Effect of Fuel Economy Standards on Automobile Safety," *Journal of Law and Economics* 32, no. 1 (April 1989): 97–118.

the Chrysler Corporation, specializing in small cars, sought to keep the standards tight as a means of increasing the costs of its two major rivals.

Did the CAFE standards effectively reduce fuel use? According to the Federal Highway Administration, even though fuel usage per vehicle has fallen since 1969, total fuel consumption has been rising since 1982. With new, large cars more expensive as a result of the standards, some people probably kept their old cars longer, increasing gas consumption (and pollution). At the same time, the lower prices of small cars probably increased the total number of cars purchased. More cars on the road meant greater fuel consumption because the marginal cost of driving in a small car was lower than would otherwise have been the case, and because smaller car sizes lead people to share fewer rides. Robert A. Leone of Boston University estimates that a 2 or 3 cent tax on gasoline beginning in 1984 would have saved as much fuel as the CAFE standards, and at a substantially lower cost to society.

The experience with CAFE highlights both the inflexibility of regulation and the unforeseen side effects that often accompany it. It is not easy to mandate a specific outcome without triggering adverse consequences. As a result, regulation is generally less effective than it might first appear.

FUTURE DIRECTIONS FOR REGULATORY POLICY

Most people concede that regulation, both economic and social, is like a two-edged sword. Regulations can be beneficial, but they tend to be costly and can also be counterproductive. Some regulations are far more costly than others, even when their major goals are similar. **Exhibit A4-2** demonstrates this point. Several hundred regulations that save lives, in several agencies, were analyzed by a group of well-known risk researchers who estimated their cost per year of life saved. Some of these cost estimates for various agencies are presented here. The researchers estimated that the median cost of Federal Aviation Administration (FAA) regulations *per life year* saved was $23,000. In contrast, that of the Environmental Protection Agency was $7,600,000, or 330 times that of the FAA. Clearly, if some resources had been shifted from EPA regulatory activities to those of the FAA, more lives could have been saved for the same cost.

The cost also varied widely among the rules within each agency. The researchers suggest that if the least costly methods to save lives were chosen, the same

EXHIBIT A4-2

REGULATIONS AND DIFFERENCES IN THE COST OF SAVING LIVES

Agency	Median Cost per Life Year Saved
Federal Aviation Administration	$23,000
Consumer Product Safety Commission	$68,000
National Highway Transportation Safety Administration	$78,000
Occupational Safety and Health Administration	$88,000
Environmental Protection Agency	$7,600,000

SOURCE: T. O. Tengs et al., "Five Hundred Life-Saving Interventions and Their Cost-Effectiveness," Risk Analysis *15 (1995): 369–390.*

expenditures could save tens of thousands of additional lives per year, or alternatively, the same number of lives could be saved while expenditures could be reduced by tens of billions of dollars per year.

How can the regulations that generate large gains relative to cost be separated from those that generate few, if any, net benefits? Large gains could be realized if we could retain and expand the former, while modifying or eliminating the latter. However, it is not easy to reduce the size of an agency. Predictably, the agency's leadership will lobby for larger budgets and greater authority to achieve program goals. While there is strong support for the continuation and expansion of social regulatory activities, the voices favoring regulatory reform, and even deregulation, are growing louder. Improved empirical evidence on the effectiveness of specific regulatory policies will continue to emerge and, in some cases, will alter the direction of regulatory activities.

KEY POINTS

➤ Traditional economic regulation has generally sought to fix prices and/or influence entry into specific industries. During the 1970s, widespread dissatisfaction with economic regulation led to significant deregulation in the trucking and airline industries. This deregulation resulted in new entry, intense competition, and discount prices.

➤ Regulation involves a complex set of economic and political forces. Public choice analysis provides some insight regarding how the regulatory process can be expected to work. The following four points are particularly important:

a. The demand for regulation often stems from special-interest and redistribution considerations.
b. With the passage of time, regulatory agencies are likely to adopt the views of the interest groups they are supposed to regulate.
c. Regulation is inflexible; it will be slow to adjust to changing conditions.
d. Approval of a dangerous product will cause more problems for a regulatory agency than a failure to approve a highly beneficial product. As a result, agencies approving new products (for example, medical drugs) will generally apply tests that are too restrictive from the viewpoint of consumer welfare.

➤ While economic regulation has been relaxed in recent years, health and safety regulation has expanded rapidly. Health and safety regulation seeks to provide a cleaner, safer, healthier environment for workers and consumers. Pursuit of this objective is costly, bringing about higher product prices and higher taxes, as well as unintended safety problems. Since the costs, and particularly the benefits, are often difficult to measure and evaluate, the efficiency of social regulatory programs is both controversial and the subject of much current research.

CRITICAL ANALYSIS QUESTIONS

*1. Legislation mandating stronger side and door panels to protect drivers and passengers against side collisions presumably makes cars both safer and more expensive. The same could be said for air bags. Are laws like these necessary for auto safety? Do they save lives and make auto travel safer? Why or why not?

2. "Without legal safety requirements, products such as lawn mowers would be unsafe." Evaluate this statement.

*3. Will health and safety legislation mandating workplace and product safety standards reduce the profitability of the regulated firms? Who bears the cost and who gains the benefits of such legislation?

4. In large cities, taxi fares are often set above the market equilibrium rate. Sometimes the number of licenses is limited in order to maintain the above-market price. In other cases, licenses are automatically granted to anyone wanting to operate a taxi. When taxi fares are set above market equilibrium, compare and contrast resource allocation under the restricted license system (assume the licenses are tradable) and the free-entry system. In which case will it be easier for customers to get a taxi? In which case will the amount of capital required to enter the taxi business be greater?

5. "Regulations on the introduction of new drugs should be strengthened. Fewer people would die if more research were required prior to the introduction of new drugs. Only an economist could possibly disagree. Sure, it would cost more, but saving even one life would be worth more than whatever it costs." Evaluate this statement.

*6. "People cannot be expected to make good decisions on their own regarding auto safety. Only experts know enough to make such decisions." Evaluate this statement.

7. "Safety regulation is not an economic question. Where lives and health are at stake, economics has no place." Evaluate this statement.

*8. "If we force increased safety measures in the workplace by regulation, business may bear the cost in the short run, but capital will receive the market rate of return in the long run." Evaluate this statement, and explain your reasoning.

---

*Asterisk denotes questions for which answers are given in Appendix B.

APPLICATION 5

A society that puts equality — in the sense of equality of outcome — ahead of freedom will end up with neither equality nor freedom.

Milton and Rose Friedman[1]

Income Inequality, Transfers, and the Role of Government

APPLICATION FOCUS

- Why haven't antipoverty transfer programs been more effective?
- Do the recent welfare reforms represent a fundamental change? How will they affect the poor?
- Why do transfers generally increase the income of the intended beneficiaries by less than the amount of the transfer?
- Should the government take further action to reduce inequality?

[1]Milton and Rose Friedman, *Free to Choose* (New York: Avon Books with permission of Harcourt Brace Jovanovich, 1980), p. 139.

Perhaps surprising to some, governmental assistance programs for lower-income individuals were virtually nonexistent prior to World War II. Less-fortunate families often counted on private charity and the help of friends, family, and neighbors. Except for social security, transfer programs remained exceedingly small throughout the 1950s. Nonetheless, economic growth was persistently pushing the poverty rate to lower levels. It was against this background that the Johnson administration declared "war on poverty." There was considerable optimism that the war could be won rather easily.

THE WAR ON POVERTY: THE DREAM AND THE REALITY

President Johnson told the American people that poverty could be virtually eliminated if they were willing to spend 2 percent more of GDP on programs to assist the poor.[2] They were, and expenditures on transfer programs increased substantially. New programs targeted toward the poor—for example, food stamps, school lunches, and Medicaid—were adopted. Spending on both social security and Aid for Dependent Children was expanded, and the Medicare program, covering health-care expenditures for the elderly, was enacted. As the result of these and related programs, the role of government in the allocation of income was altered drastically.

As **Exhibit A5–1** (frame a) illustrates, transfer payments rose from 7.4 percent of personal income in 1965 to 14.4 percent in 1975. By the mid-1990s, more than 16 percent of the personal income of Americans was derived from income transfers. At the same time, government expenditures on health-care programs—primarily Medicare and Medicaid—rose sharply, reaching 6.7 percent of GDP in 1997, up from 1.5 percent in 1965. In total, expenditures on income transfers and health care rose from 7 percent of GDP in 1960 to 15 percent in 1980 and 20 percent in 1997.[3]

Furthermore, both the size of the economy and per-capita GDP rose substantially during the 1965–1997 period. As Exhibit A5–1 (frame b) shows, real income per person (measured in constant 1992 dollars) rose from $14,825 in 1965 to $27,138 in 1997. Put another way, even after adjustment for inflation, income per person in the United States nearly doubled between 1965 and 1997.

Given the growth of both transfer payments and per-capita income, what happened to the poverty rate? Perhaps surprisingly, the answer is, not much. The official

---

[2]The *Economic Report of the President: 1964* (p. 77) stated,

> Conquest of poverty is well within our power. . . . The majority of the nation could simply tax themselves enough to provide the necessary income supplements to their less fortunate citizens. The burden—one-fifth of the annual defense budget, less than 2 percent of GNP—would certainly not be intolerable.

For those interested in the spirit of that era, the 1964 Report would be an excellent document to review.

[3]These two items—income transfers and health care—now account for two-thirds of federal government expenditures.

EXHIBIT A5-1

INCOME TRANSFERS, THE GROWTH OF INCOME, AND THE POVERTY RATE

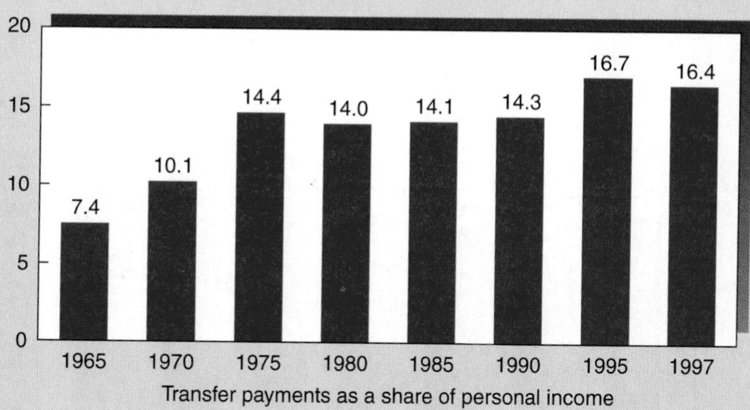

(a) Income transfers doubled *as a share of personal income* between 1965 and 1975, and they have remained at a high level.

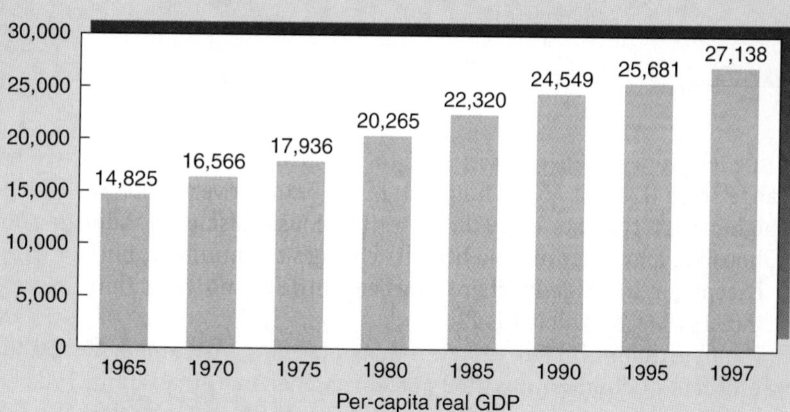

(b) Real income per person nearly doubled between 1965 and 1997.

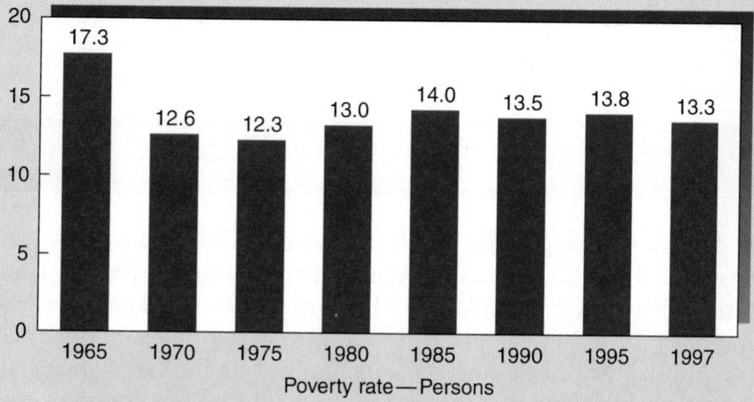

(c) Nonetheless, there has been little change in the poverty rate during the last three decades.

SOURCES: Economic Report of the President: 1998; *and U.S. Department of Commerce,* Poverty in the United States: 1997.

EXHIBIT A5–2

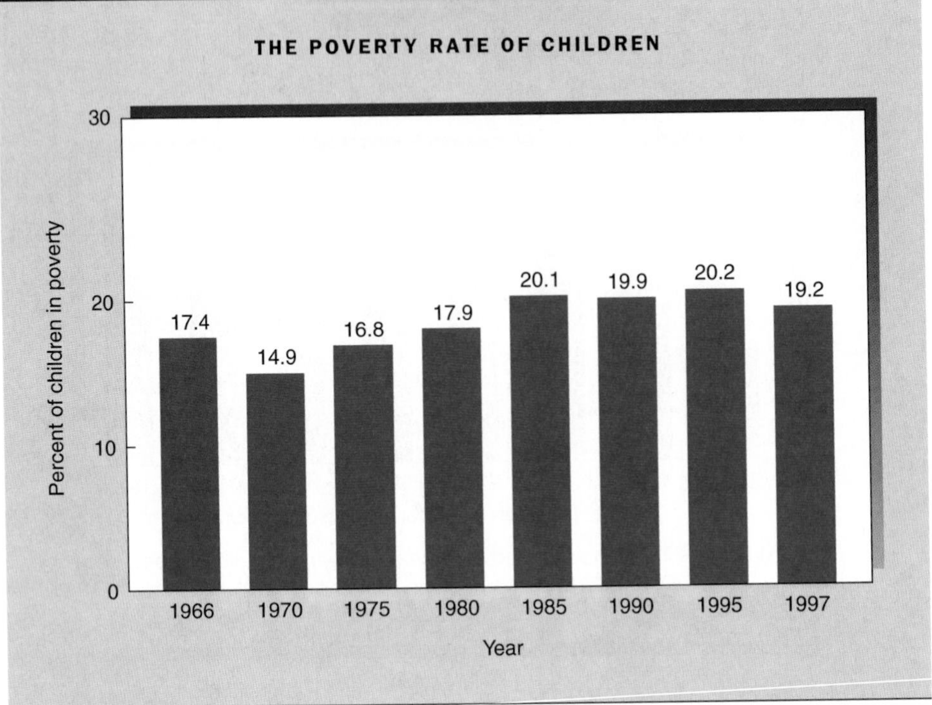

The poverty rate of children in 1997 was 19.2 percent, up from 14.9 percent in 1970.

SOURCE: Statistical Abstract of the United States *(various years).*

poverty rate fell from 17.3 percent in 1965 to 12.6 percent in 1970, but there has been little change since (Exhibit A5–1, frame c). In 1997, the poverty rate was 13.3 percent, a little higher than the rate in 1970. As we previously discussed, adjusting for food, medical, housing, and other in-kind benefits changes the numbers, but not the general pattern. Except for the elderly, there has been little or no reduction in the rate of poverty since 1970 (see Exhibit 15–8).

The figures for children are even more alarming. As **Exhibit A5–2** shows, the 1997 poverty rate of children was 19.2 percent, higher than the rate in 1966 and well above the 14.9 percent rate of 1970. After adjustment for the valuation of food, housing, medical, and other noncash benefits, the poverty rate of children was 13.3 percent in 1997. This indicates that, even when the value of in-kind benefits is counted as income, approximately one out of every seven children in America was living in poverty in 1997.

WHY WERE THE ANTIPOVERTY TRANSFERS INEFFECTIVE?

For two decades following World War II, the poverty rate steadily fell as per-capita income moved upward. Initially, as the War on Poverty expanded in the late 1960s, the poverty rate fell a little more rapidly. But this soon reversed and little progress has been registered since 1970. Now, almost three decades later, the poverty rate is virtually unchanged. Why did the results differ so dramatically from the expectations of the 1960s? Several factors contributed to the ineffectiveness of the welfare-transfer system.

1. ***The collapse of the two-parent family has substantially increased the poverty rate in recent decades.*** In 1997, the poverty rate of female-headed, single-parent

families with children was almost six times higher than the rate for two-parent families (41.0 percent compared to 7.1 percent). Children born to a single mother are thus seven times more likely to be poor than those born into a two-parent family.[4] High rates of teen pregnancy have also contributed to this problem as 55 percent of all unmarried teenage mothers find themselves on welfare within 1 year of the birth of their first child, and 77 percent are on welfare within 5 years.

Some argue that the welfare entitlement system encourages these problems by providing incentives to remain single and have more children. Having more children generally means higher levels of welfare benefits, while getting married generally lowers the level of benefits received. The evidence on this topic is mixed.[5] This issue aside, however, there is no doubt that the rising incidence of divorce, single-parent families, and births to unmarried mothers has pushed the poverty rate upward in recent decades.

2. ***The high implicit marginal tax rates that accompany the transfer system make it very difficult for low-income families to increase their earnings and thereby escape poverty.*** If a poor family earns more, its transfer benefits are reduced. Thus, additional earnings do not increase the family's spendable income by very much. Exhibit A5–3 uses the actual data for a single mother in Pennsylvania to illustrate this point. If the mother does not work, the family qualifies for $7,548 of benefits in the form of cash transfers, food stamps, housing, and medical benefits. If the mother were to take a part-time job earning $2,000 per year, she would see her benefits fall by $625, so her disposable income would rise by only $1,375 up to $8,923. In effect, she has lost $625 of her $2,000, making her implicit marginal tax rate 31.2 percent. Alternatively, she is able to keep 68.8 percent of her earnings in

EXHIBIT A5–3

EARNINGS AND DISPOSABLE INCOME FOR A SINGLE MOTHER WITH TWO CHILDREN IN PENNSYLVANIA

Annual Earnings from Work	Disposable Income (Earnings – Taxes + Transfers)	Implicit Marginal Tax Rate	Average Tax Rate on Earnings	Share of Earnings Individual Gets to Keep
$ 0	$ 7,548	—	—	—
2,000	8,923	31.2	31.2	68.8
4,000	9,290	81.7	57.4	42.6
5,000	9,473	81.7	61.5	38.5
6,000	9,657	81.6	64.8	35.2
7,000	9,840	81.7	67.3	32.7
8,000	9,956	88.4	69.9	30.1
9,000	10,523	43.3	66.9	33.1
10,000	10,937	58.6	66.1	33.9
15,000	12,606	66.6	66.3	33.7

SOURCE: Congressional Research Service, as published in the 1994 Green Book, p. 335.

[4]Of all single mothers, 77 percent are working, and the poverty rate among those who work full-time year-round is only 8 percent.

[5]See Robert Moffitt, "Incentive Effects of the U.S. Welfare System," *Journal of Economic Literature* 30, no. 1 (March 1992).

the form of disposable income. If her earnings were to increase from $2,000 to $4,000, disposable income (after taxes and transfers) would increase by only $367 (from $8,923 to $9,290). In this income range, the family faces an implicit marginal tax rate of 81.7 percent! Bear in mind that this rate is more than twice as high as the top marginal income tax rate imposed upon the very rich (39.6 percent).

The high marginal tax rates persist up the income scale. In fact, if the family earned $15,000 rather than zero, its disposable income would increase by only $5,058 (from $7,548 to $12,606) after the additional taxes (primarily the payroll tax) and the reduction in transfers are taken into account. This additional $5,058 might not even be enough to pay for the added expenses of child care and transportation, making this outcome less valuable to the family than simply not working at all. On average, the family confronts an implicit tax rate of 66 percent. If the mother got a full-time job at $7.50 per hour and worked all year to earn $15,000, she would get to keep only one-third of additional earnings. Given this incentive structure, even able-bodied adults in welfare families—particularly those headed by a single parent—have often found it unattractive to work.

3. ***When the poor opt out of the labor force because of the high implicit marginal tax rates, declining skills further limit their ability to escape poverty.*** Failure to participate in the labor force exerts a secondary effect: One's skills and work habits deteriorate. Individuals who do not use their skills for extended periods of time will find it difficult to compete with otherwise similar individuals with continuous labor-force participation. The long-term consequence of an incentive structure that discourages work is highly destructive. With the passage of time, welfare recipients—even those with substantial potential—become less and less able to support themselves.

WELFARE REFORM: CAN WE HELP THE POOR WITHOUT GENERATING ADVERSE SIDE EFFECTS?

Dissatisfaction with the current system has created pressure for reform. Beginning in the late 1980s, the federal government gave several states exemptions that allowed them to experiment with alternative approaches. Building on these efforts, a major welfare reform bill was passed in 1996. We now turn to a consideration of the central elements of that legislation.

Work Requirement. The 1996 welfare reform legislation requires most heads of families drawing benefits to begin work within 2 years. Failure to do so will lead to loss of benefits. For example, able-bodied adults with no dependents must work at least 20 hours per week in order to remain eligible for food stamps for more than 3 months (during any 3-year period).

Work requirements also apply to mothers with small children. When the welfare system was initiated, most mothers stayed home with the children, particularly if they were preschoolers. This is no longer true. More than half of the mothers with small children are now in the labor force. Thus, proponents of a strict work requirement questioned: "How can we ask families with working mothers to pay taxes to support welfare benefits without also requiring the recipients to work?"

A work requirement greatly reduces some of the worst side effects of the current system. Staying home and drawing welfare benefits is no longer an alternative to work. A work requirement also increases the incentive of recipients to search for marginally more attractive jobs and move up the job ladder. If you have to work in order to receive the benefits, you might as well work at the most attractive job you can obtain. Thus, the tendency for basic workplace skills to deteriorate from nonuse is reduced.

Time Limit for Welfare Recipients. The 1996 legislation also places a 5-year lifetime limit on the length of time a recipient can draw benefits. Persons may have more than one spell on welfare, but over their lifetime, they are limited to 5 years. States are permitted to waive this requirement for 20 percent of their recipients. During the past several decades, welfare benefits were an entitlement. In effect, they were an option to the earning of income through work. The 1996 legislation is a move away from the "entitlement" approach. It reflects the view that welfare transfers are short-term assistance designed to bridge the gap while recipients get their lives turned around.

Holding Fathers More Accountable. In recent years, several states have made a more intense effort to hold fathers, including those never married to their children's mothers, more responsible for the support of their children. Historically, fathers often escaped child support payments by moving to another state. The federal government now helps track down delinquent fathers in other states and uses other legal channels to obtain court-mandated child support payments. Some would like to see more done in this area. A special tax (for example, a 5 percent payroll tax) could be levied on fathers of children receiving welfare benefits. Alternatively, they could be required to work for free at public service jobs. Proponents of this view argue that just as we impose taxes on polluters who impose costs on society, we should do the same to irresponsible fathers who foist the cost of their actions onto society.

Evidence on the Impact of Recent Welfare Reforms

After increasing for years, welfare caseloads have been falling as the welfare system has undergone substantial change. Nationwide, the number of persons on welfare fell from 14.1 million in 1993 to 8.9 million in 1998—a 37 percent reduction. During the initial year following the 1996 legislation, welfare caseloads fell by about 2 million. Although some of this reduction can be attributed to a strong economy, state-level evidence indicates that the welfare reform accounts for a substantial portion of the reduction.

Because the reform allows states some leeway concerning how to reduce caseloads, the programs and the success of the reforms vary widely across states. Forty-two states have lowered the implicit marginal tax rates on their cash assistance programs, allowing recipients to be able to keep more of their welfare payments after they begin working. Nineteen states have adopted even stricter time limits on welfare than the 5-year limit specified in the federal reform. In addition, most states have put heavy emphasis on work requirements and welfare-to-work policies. The impact of these reforms has been substantial in some states, such as Wyoming, Wisconsin, Oregon, Colorado, and Mississippi, where caseload reductions have been in excess of 50 percent. Wisconsin's welfare reforms that began in the late 1980s have been particularly successful. Between 1987 and 1997, Wisconsin reduced its welfare caseload by more than 50 percent, and the vast majority of those moved off welfare have been moved into jobs.

Under current legislation, states get a fixed amount of federal funds regardless of their caseload level. Thus, states that are able to reduce their caseloads have extra funds available for other projects. (The reforms, however, prevented states from reducing their welfare spending by more than 25 percent, and actual decreases are averaging about 22 percent.) In contrast with the earlier situation where larger caseload levels meant more federal money, the current structure provides states with an incentive to move people from welfare to work. By the end of 1997, about half of the states were spending 80 percent or less of their spending level prior to the reforms.

What has happened to the people who moved off the welfare rolls? Nationwide, early results indicate that at least half of the former welfare recipients are now employed. In some states, such as Tennessee, the rates of movement into jobs have been as high as 64 percent. In some instances, the authorities discovered that individuals already had jobs secretly and therefore they simply stopped applying for welfare when the rules were tightened. The recent reforms have removed some of the most perverse incentive effects of the prior welfare system. While it is too early to draw definitive conclusions, there are reasons to believe that, compared to the prior situation, the revised system will work better for both the beneficiaries and taxpayers.

THE LIMITATIONS OF INCOME TRANSFERS

Before leaving the topic of transfers, one final point should be stressed. Market adjustments and competition for the transfers will erode much of the long-run gain of the intended beneficiaries. In a world of scarce resources, government must establish a criterion for the receipt of the transfers. If it did not do so, the transfers would outrun the government budget. Governments typically require transfer recipients to (a) own something (for example, land with an acreage allotment), (b) do something (for example, fill out complicated forms, pass an exam, or make political contributions), or (c) be something (for example, unemployed or poor). Once the qualification criterion is established, people will incur costs seeking to meet it until the marginal costs of qualifying increase to the level of the marginal benefits of the transfer. Therefore, the beneficiary's *net* gain will nearly always be substantially less than the cost of supplying the transfers.

Consider the following scenario. Suppose the federal government decided to give away $50 bills between 9 A.M. and 5 P.M. to all persons willing to wait in line at a teller window outside the U.S. Treasury building. No doubt, a line would form. How would people decide whether to take the steps required to obtain the subsidy? They would consider the value of the time spent waiting in line compared to the $50 transfer. A person whose time was worth $5 per hour would be willing to spend up to 10 hours waiting in line. Others whose time was worth even less, say, $3 per hour, would be willing to wait even longer. Two things are clear: (1) Long lines will emerge as people compete for the transfer and (2) the net gain of most obtaining the $50 bills will be substantially less than $50.

This simple example illustrates why the net gain of the beneficiaries is much less than the expenditures on the transfers. Qualifying for the transfer involves a cost. In the case of transfers to the poor, the cost is in the form of things like limitations on earnings; high implicit tax rates; dropping out of the labor force; skill depreciation; and reductions in charitable efforts by families, individuals, churches, and civic organizations. Thus, the net increase in income of the poor is much less than the dollars transferred.

When people must own an asset in order to receive an income transfer, that asset's value will rise until it reflects the full value of the subsidy. Regardless of whether an activity is subsidized, competition will tend to equalize the rate of return across investments of similar risk. As a result, the value of a farm subsidy will increase the value of land (or growing permits) required for the receipt of the subsidy until the rate of return in subsidized farming is equal to the rate of return in other activities. Consider another example. Several cities indirectly subsidize their local taxi industry by

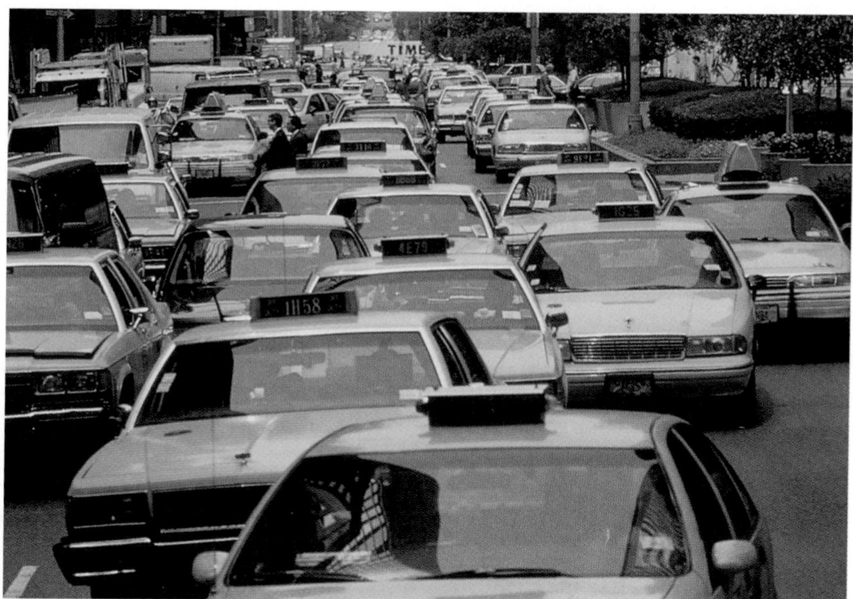

New York City and several other cities issue only a limited number of medallions required for the operation of a taxi. The licenses restrict entry and keep taxi fares high. However, the gains from this indirect subsidy are incorporated into the market value of the medallions. In the mid-1990s, taxi medallions in New York City were selling for approximately $175,000.

restricting entry into this market. With time, however, the value of this subsidy gets built into the price of licenses required for the operation of a taxi. In effect, new entrants into both subsidized farming and taxi operations pay for the subsidies in the form of higher prices for assets required for receipt of those subsidies. The long-run profitability in these and other subsidized industries is no higher than it would be if there were no subsidies. Paradoxical as it may appear, it is not easy to bestow favors upon a class of recipients in a manner that will *permanently* improve their well-being.[6]

INCOME INEQUALITY AND THE ROLE OF GOVERNMENT

The failures of antipoverty programs have not only led to welfare reform, they have also generated demands for regulatory policies designed to combat income inequality. Should the government attempt to reduce income inequality? Let us consider pro and con views of this question.

THE CASE FOR GOVERNMENT ACTION TO REDUCE INCOME INEQUALITY

The proponents of government action argue that the recent increase in economic inequality is unhealthy, unnecessary, and dangerous to the social stability of the nation. They generally believe that several factors have contributed to the increase in inequality. The list of culprits usually includes increased globalization of the economy,

[6]If transfer programs fail to provide significant long-term benefits to recipients beyond the windfall gains at the time the programs are instituted or unexpectedly expanded, what accounts for their continued political popularity? Gordon Tullock's work on the transitional gains trap provides the answer. Elimination of the programs would be costly for recipients who have adjusted to or "bought into" the programs. Even though the programs do little to improve their welfare, the current beneficiaries would be harmed by their elimination or unexpected reduction. See Gordon Tullock, "The Transitional Gains Trap," *Bell Journal of Economics* 6 (autumn 1975).

immigration, the reduction in the clout of labor unions, a decline in the real value of the minimum wage, and technological change. Thus, the agenda of those seeking to reduce inequality includes several, if not all, of the following proposals.

1. ***Erect trade barriers to protect American industries and prevent American firms from moving abroad.*** American workers cannot compete with workers in India, China, and other less-developed countries making a dollar per hour or less. Trade with such countries will merely drive our wages down to their levels. Neither can we stand idly by and allow American firms to move their plants to low-wage countries. Legislation should be adopted making it more difficult for firms to move abroad and restricting the import of goods from low-wage countries.
2. ***Restrict immigration.*** The entry of low-skill workers from less-developed countries like Mexico reduces employment opportunities and drives down the wages of Americans, particularly those with few skills. To keep this from happening, we need more restrictive immigration laws and stricter enforcement of existing laws prohibiting the employment of illegal immigrants.
3. ***Promote unions.*** Historically, unions have reduced the inequality of wages and salaries within firms. This compression of wage differentials helps to reduce the general level of income inequality. In recent decades, union membership has declined as a share of the labor force. This trend needs to be reversed. Legislation making it easier for unions to organize and more difficult for firms to resist unionization should be adopted.
4. ***Increase the minimum wage.*** An increase in the minimum wage would boost the earnings of those at the bottom of the income distribution and thereby reduce income inequality. Studies indicate that the demand for labor, including low-skill labor, is highly inelastic. Therefore, the reduction in employment accompanying the wage increase would be small.

The Case against Government Action

In response, the opponents of government action to reduce income inequality generally raise the following three points:

1. ***The underlying forces are beyond the reach of government.*** Consider the impact of technology. Even if it is true that new technologies have reduced the demand for blue-collar production workers relative to those with computer, math, and communication skills, does anyone really believe that government could devise a sensible plan that would slow the rate of technological change or make it more advantageous to those with few skills? Do we really want to freeze technology and live in a time capsule? Improvements in technology help us get more out of resources and generate a larger output that helps both the rich and the poor. Any attempt to slow this process would be a big mistake.
2. ***The proposed solutions will retard economic growth and reduce income levels across the board.*** Trade restrictions, a higher minimum wage, and labor union monopolies all distort competitive markets and promote the inefficient use of resources. Let us consider each of them. Trade restraints will not only reduce our imports, they will also reduce exports. When foreigners sell less to us (because of import restrictions), they will acquire fewer of the dollars needed to buy from us. Thus, our exports will also fall. There will not be any increase in employment—jobs "saved" by the import restrictions will be offset with jobs lost in export industries. The primary result will be greater use of our resources to produce things that

we do poorly as reflected by our inability to compete in international markets. A higher minimum wage will simply make it more difficult for inexperienced, low-skilled workers to get a start up the job ladder. Similarly, legislation promoting unions will generally reduce the job opportunities available to the least skilled and to new labor-force entrants.

3. ***The pattern of economic outcomes is not nearly so important as the process that generates the outcomes.*** The distribution of income reflects the choices and mutually advantageous exchanges between responsible adults. In a market economy, people who earn exceedingly high incomes do so because they supply goods, services, and resources that others value highly. Invariably, their actions improve the welfare of others. After all, Bill Gates did not steal nor inherit his wealth—he has received it from other individuals who happily, and voluntarily, handed over their hard-earned income to purchase his software. If individuals earn their money through voluntary exchange with others, what is unfair about this? If the process is fair, why should government try to alter the outcome? Isn't punishing the most productive members of society through high taxes to give to the least productive members an *unfair* process? It is more important to guarantee a fair and equal process (for example, equal opportunities) than to worry about the resulting outcome as measured by the distribution of income.

KEY POINTS

➤ Despite heavily increased spending on income transfers, the poverty rate in the 1990s is not much different than it was in the 1960s. Several factors contributed to the failure of the welfare system. They include high implicit marginal tax rates that discouraged work effort, depreciation in job skills that occurred when welfare recipients opted out of the labor force, and the collapse of the two-parent family.

➤ The 1996 welfare reform legislation established work requirements for most able-bodied welfare recipients, placed a 5-year lifetime limit on the receipt of welfare, and provided states with more leeway to experiment with alternative approaches. There has been a substantial reduction in the number of welfare recipients during the last few years. Evidence suggests that at least half of those who have gone off welfare now have jobs.

➤ The government must establish a qualification criterion for transfers in order to limit spending on these programs. Potential recipients will incur costs seeking to meet the criterion. Thus, the net gain of the recipient will generally be less than the expenditures on the transfer programs. It is not easy to bestow favors upon a class of recipients in a manner that will substantially and permanently improve their well-being.

➤ In an effort to reduce income inequality, some argue that the United States should increase trade barriers, place tighter restrictions on immigration, strengthen labor unions, and increase the minimum wage. In response, opponents argue that the underlying causes of the recent increases in income inequality (such as a changing family structure and technological improvements) are generally beyond the reach of government. Furthermore, they believe that the proposed "solutions" would do more harm than good.

CRITICAL ANALYSIS QUESTIONS

1. Can you think of alternatives (other than those mentioned) that would reduce income inequality? What impact would they have on economic efficiency?

2. The outcome of a state lottery game is certainly a very unequal distribution of the prize income. Some players are made very rich, while others lose their money. However, all play voluntarily. Using this example, discuss whether the fairness of the process or the fairness of the outcome is more important, and how they differ.

3. Which reforms to the welfare system do you think will be most effective at reducing the poverty rate? Why?

Can you think of additional reforms that would be effective in this area? Explain.

4. If two unmarried teenagers have a child, who should be responsible for the child's support? Is it fair to expect the taxpayer to shoulder these costs?

*5. Why is the implicit marginal tax rate confronted by low-income welfare recipients so high? How will the work requirements of the 1996 welfare reform legislation affect this marginal tax rate?

6. Suppose that one family has $100,000 while another has only $20,000. Is this outcome fair? What is your initial reaction? Compare and contrast your views of the fairness of this outcome under the following processes that might have generated this outcome.

a. The family with the higher income has both husband and wife working, while the other family has chosen for the wife to remain home with the children rather than work in the labor force.

b. The family with the higher income is headed by a person who completed a college degree, while the other family is headed by someone who dropped out of high school.

c. The family with the higher income just stole $50,000 of their income from the poorer family.

d. The family with the lower income just stole their entire $20,000 from the richer family.

e. The income of the family with the higher income is derived from farm subsidies from the government.

f. The family with the higher income received it as an inheritance from their parents who just died.

---

*Asterisk denotes questions for which answers are given in Appendix B.

APPLICATION 6

Analysts who have attributed national economic problems ranging from unemployment to wage inflation to low productivity to unions will have to find a new culprit to blame: unless there is a remarkable renaissance in unionism, critics won't have unions to kick around any more.

Richard B. Freeman[1]

Do Labor Unions Increase the Wages of Workers?

APPLICATION FOCUS

- How much of the U.S. workforce is unionized?
- Can unions increase the wages of their members? What makes a union strong? What factors limit the power of a union?
- Can unions increase the wages of all workers?

[1]Richard B. Freeman, "Contraction and Expansion: The Divergence of Private Sector and Public Sector Unionism in the United States," *Journal of Economic Perspectives* 2 (spring 1988), p. 86.

A labor union is an organization of employees, usually working either in the same occupation or same industry, who have consented to joint bargaining with employers concerning wages, working conditions, grievance procedures, and other elements of employment. The primary objective of a labor union is to improve the welfare of its members. Unions have historically been controversial. Some see them as a necessary shield protecting workers from employer greed. Others charge that unions are monopolies seeking to provide their members with benefits at the expense of other workers, consumers, and economic efficiency. Still others argue that the economic influence of unions—both for good and for bad—is vastly overrated. This application will consider the impact of unions on the wages of their members and those of other workers.

Labor union
A collective organization of employees who bargain as a unit with employers.

UNION MEMBERSHIP AS SHARE OF WORKFORCE

Historically, the proportion of the U.S. labor force belonging to a labor union has fluctuated substantially. In 1910, approximately 10 percent of nonfarm employees belonged to a union. As **Exhibit A6–1** shows, this figure rose to 18 percent in 1920. In the aftermath of the First World War, union membership declined, falling to 12 percent of nonfarm workers by 1929. Pushed along by favorable legislation adopted during the Great Depression, union membership rose from 13.5 percent of nonfarm employees in 1935 to 30.4 percent in 1945. By 1954, one-third of nonfarm workers in the United States were unionized.

Since the mid-1950s, however, union membership has waned. As Exhibit A6–1 illustrates, it declined slowly as a share of the workforce during 1955–1970, and then more rapidly during the last two decades. By 1998, union members comprised only 13.9 percent of nonfarm employees, down from 24 percent in 1979 (and 32 percent in 1954).

Several factors have contributed to this decline. First, much of the recent employment growth has been in sectors where unions have been traditionally weak. Such sectors include relatively small firms (fewer than 100 employees) in service and high-tech industries. Small firms are costly for unions to organize and thus tend to be nonunion. Also, in recent decades, employment has grown rapidly in the less-organized Sunbelt, while stagnating in the more heavily unionized Northeast and upper Middle West. This regional growth pattern has retarded the growth of union membership. Second, competition has eroded union strength in several important industries. Foreign producers have increased their market share in steel, mining, automobiles, and other heavy-manufacturing industries. Employment has thus been shrinking in these areas of traditional union strength. Deregulation in transportation and communication industries has further reduced the effectiveness of unions. As these industries have become more competitive, unionized firms have faced increased competition from nonunion producers. Finally, union membership has declined in part because workers have reduced their demand for unions over time. Consistent with a falling desire for

EXHIBIT A6–1

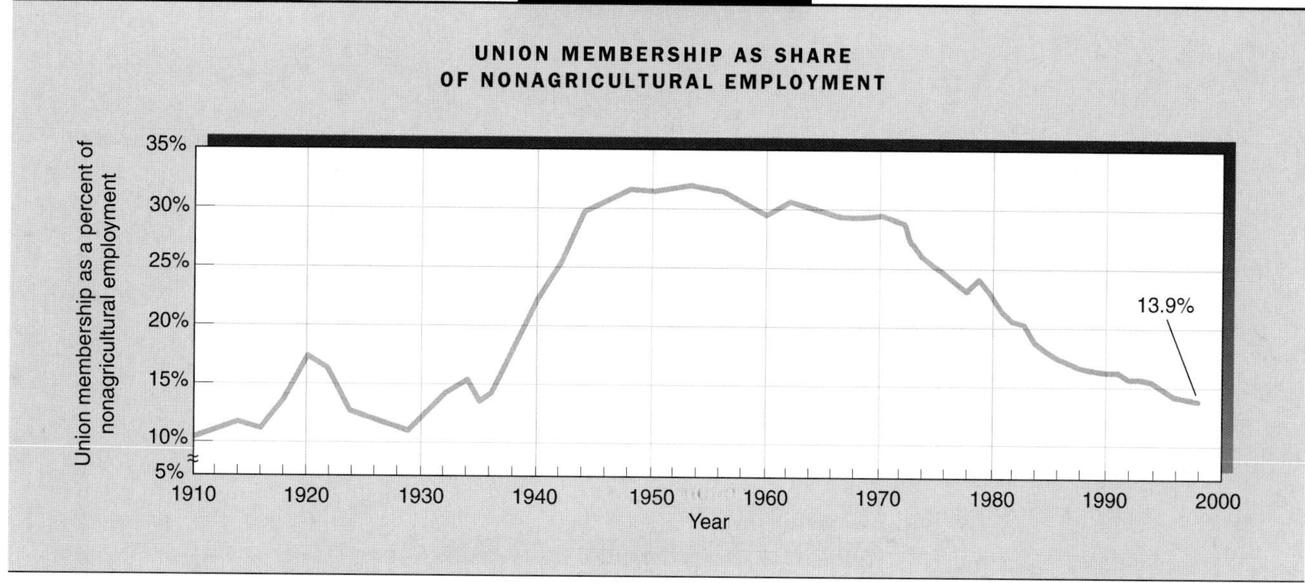

Between 1910 and 1935, union membership fluctuated between 12 percent and 18 percent of nonagricultural employment. During the 1935–1945 period, union membership increased sharply to approximately one-third of the nonfarm workforce. Since the mid-1950s, union membership has declined as a percent of nonfarm employment, and the decline has been particularly sharp since 1979.

SOURCE: Leo Troy and Neil Sheflin, Union Source Book: Membership, Structure, Finance, Directory *(West Orange, N.J.: Industrial Relations and Information Services, 1985); and Barry T. Hirsch and David A. Macpherson,* Union Membership and Earnings Data Book *(Washington, D.C.: Bureau of National Affairs, 1999). The post-1973 data are for all wage and salary workers.*

union representation, opinion surveys reveal that workers believe that unions are less effective in improving their lot now than in the past.[2]

To some extent, several of these trends reflect the impact of unions on the wages of their members. Business investment and employment will tend to move toward geographic areas, industries, and classes of firms where wages are lower *relative to productivity.* Therefore, when unions increase the wages of their members *relative to nonunion workers of similar productivity,* they also retard the growth of employment in unionized sectors.

As **Exhibit A6–2** shows, there is substantial variation in the incidence of union membership across gender, racial, and occupational groups. Men are more likely than women to belong to a union. In 1997, 16.3 percent of employed men were union members compared to only 11.6 percent of employed women. The incidence of unionization among blacks (17.9 percent) was higher than for whites (13.6 percent) and Hispanics (11.8 percent). There is substantial variation in unionization according to occupation. Less than 10 percent of the workers in technical, sales, clerical, and service occupations were unionized in 1997. In contrast, more than 20 percent of the workers in craft, operative, and laborer occupations belonged to a union.

[2]Henry S. Farber and Alan B. Krueger, "Union Membership in the United States: The Decline Continues," in *Employee Representation: Alternatives and Future Directions,* ed. Morris Kleiner and Bruce Kaufman (Madison, WI: Industrial Relations Research Association, 1993).

EXHIBIT A6–2

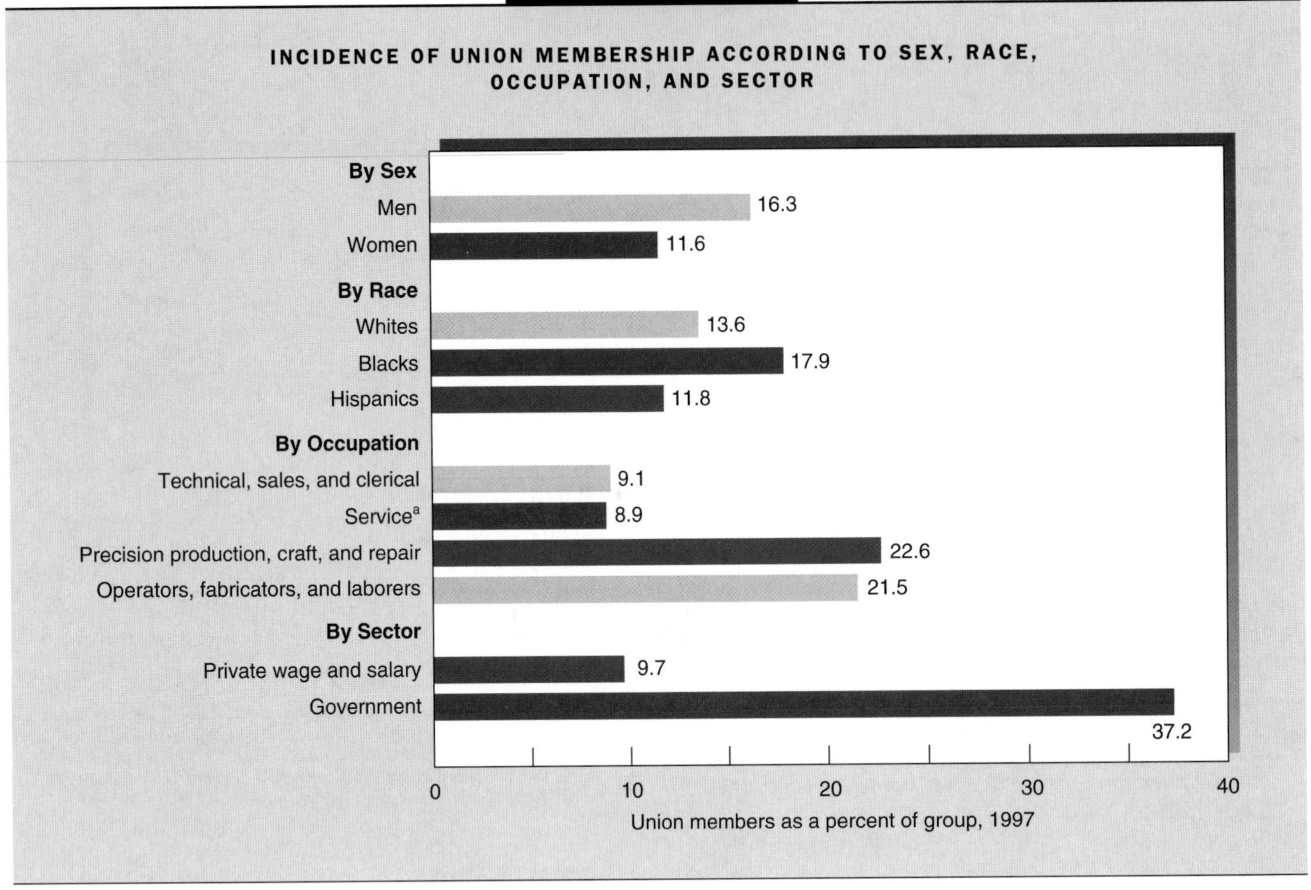

The incidence of unionism is higher among (a) men than women and (b) blacks than whites and Hispanics. Technical, sales, clerical, and service workers are far less likely to be unionized than are craft, operator, and repair workers. As a share of the workforce, unionization among government employees is nearly four times that of private sector workers.

[a]*Excluding protective service workers.*

SOURCE: Barry T. Hirsch and David A. Macpherson, Union Membership and Earnings Data Book *(Washington, D.C.: Bureau of National Affairs, 1998).*

The biggest difference in unionization is found when comparing the private and public sectors. While only 9.7 percent of the private wage and salary workers are unionized, 37.2 percent of the government employees belong to a union. And while the share of the private workforce belonging to a union has been shrinking, unionization has been increasing in the public sector. In fact, the proportion of government employees belonging to a union has more than tripled since 1960.

There is also substantial variation in the rate of unionization among states. **Exhibit A6–3** indicates the share of wage and salary employees that are unionized for the ten states with the lowest and highest unionization rates. Southern states comprise most of the group of ten with the lowest incidence of union membership. Less than 6 percent of the employees are unionized in South Carolina, North Carolina, Mississippi, and Arkansas. Heading the list of states with the highest rate of unionization are New York, Hawaii, Michigan, New Jersey, and Washington. The rate of unionization tends to be high in the industrial states of the Northeast and upper Midwest. All the ten states with the lowest incidence of unionization have **right-to-work laws,** legislation that

Right-to-work laws
Laws that prohibit the union shop—the requirement that employees must join a union as a condition of employment. Each state has the option to adopt (or reject) right-to-work legislation.

EXHIBIT A6-3

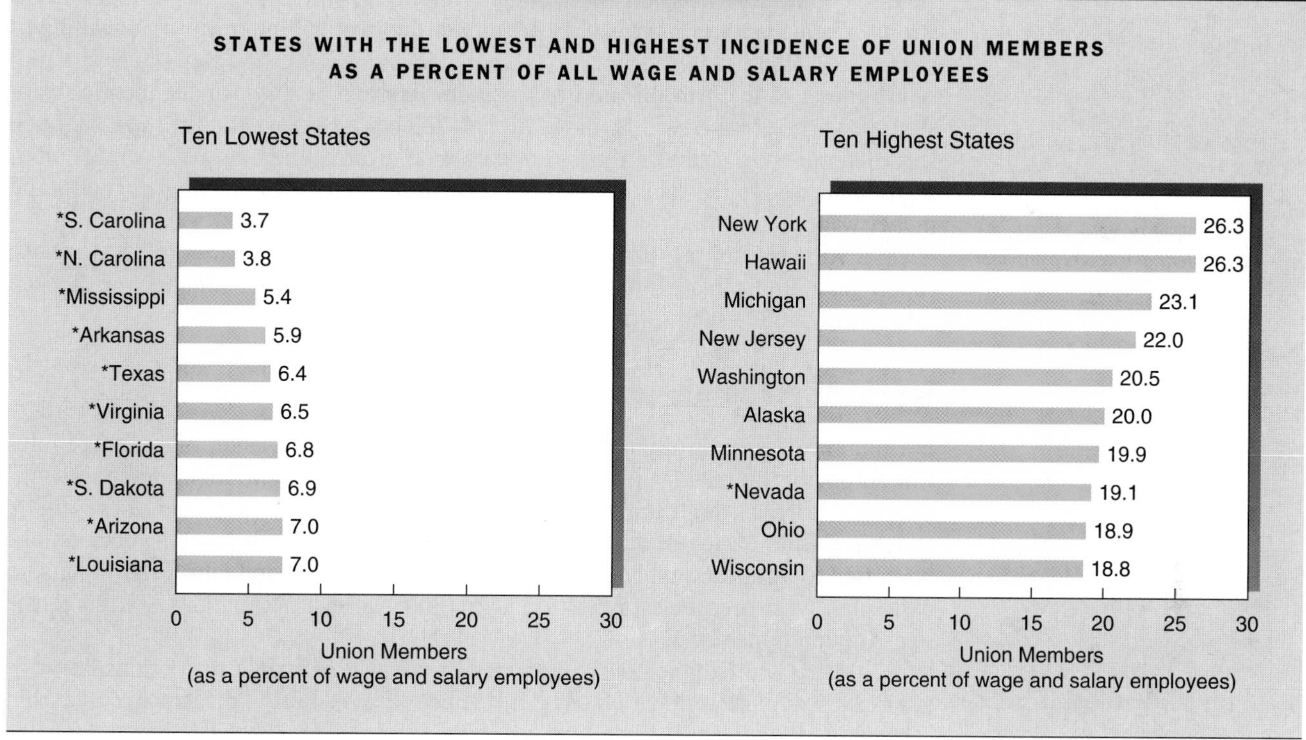

**Indicates state has a right-to-work law.*

SOURCE: Barry T. Hirsch and David A. Macpherson, Union Membership and Earnings Data Book *(Washington, D.C.: Bureau of National Affairs, 1998), Table A.*

prohibits collective bargaining agreements requiring a worker to join a union as a condition of employment. In contrast, only one (Nevada) of the ten states with the highest rate of union membership has right-to-work legislation.[3]

HOW CAN UNIONS INFLUENCE WAGES?

The union–management bargaining process often gives the impression that wages are established primarily by the talents of those sitting at the bargaining table. It might appear that market forces play a relatively minor role. However, as both union and management are well aware, market forces provide the setting in which the bargaining is conducted. They often tip the balance of power one way or the other.

High wages increase the firm's costs. When union employers face stiff competition from nonunion producers or foreign competitors, they will be less able to pass along higher wage costs to their customers. Competition in the product market thus

[3]In 1947, Congress passed the Taft-Hartley Act; Section 14-B allows states to adopt right-to-work laws. Currently, 21 states—mostly in the Sunbelt—have such legislation.

limits the bargaining power of a union. Changing market conditions also influence the balance of power between union and management. When the demand for a product is strong, the demand for labor will be high, and the firm will be much more willing to consent to a significant wage increase. When demand is weak, however, the product inventory level of the firm (or industry) is more likely to be high. Under these circumstances, wage increases will be more difficult to obtain because the firm will be much less vulnerable to a **strike** on the part of the union. (*Note:* When we speak of wage rates, we are referring to the total compensation package, including both fringe benefits and money wages.)

Strike
An action of unionized employees in which they (1) discontinue working for the employer and (2) take steps to prevent other potential workers from offering their services to the employer.

A union can use three basic strategies to increase the wages of its members: supply restrictions, bargaining power, and increased demand for union labor. We will examine each of these in turn.

SUPPLY RESTRICTIONS

If a union can successfully reduce the supply of competitive labor, higher wage rates will automatically result. Licensing requirements, long apprenticeship programs, immigration barriers, high initiation fees, refusal to admit new members to the union, and prohibition of nonunion workers from holding jobs are all practices that unions have used to limit the supply of labor to various occupations and jobs. Craft unions, in particular, have been able to restrict supply into various occupations and boost the wages of union members.

Part a of **Exhibit A6–4** illustrates the impact of supply restrictions on wage rates. Successful exclusionary tactics will reduce supply, shifting the supply curve from

The impact of higher wages obtained by restricting supply is very similar to that obtained through bargaining power. As illustrated by part a, when union policies reduce the supply of one type of labor, higher wages result. Similarly, when bargaining power is used in order to obtain higher wages (part b), employment declines and an excess supply of labor results.

EXHIBIT A6–4

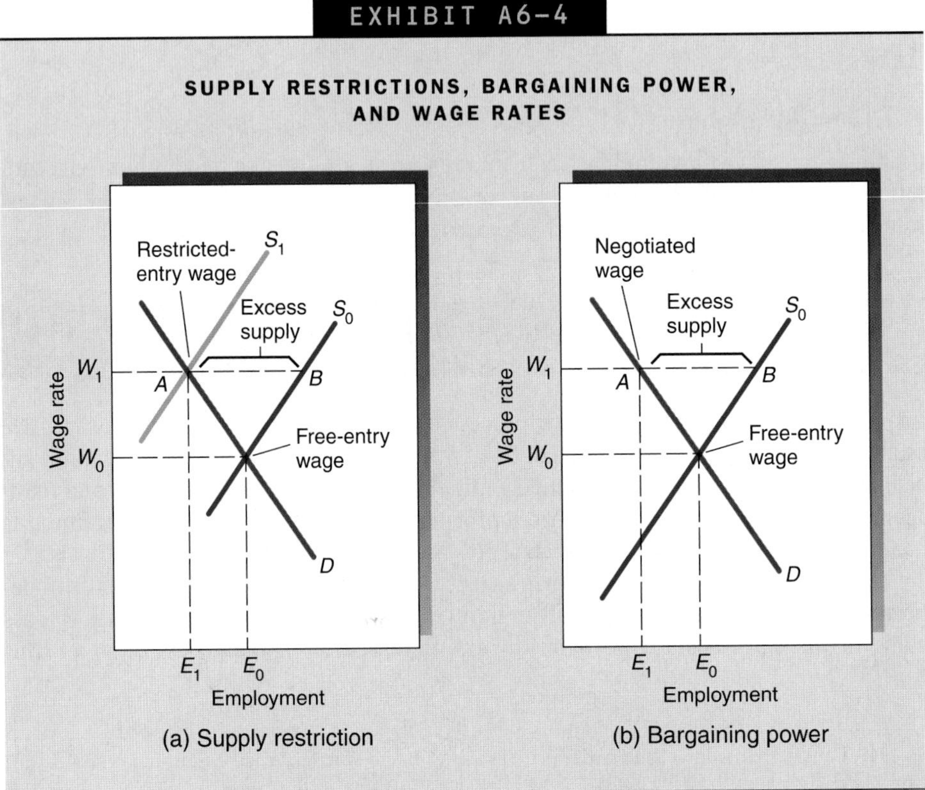

S_0 to S_1. Facing the supply curve S_1, employers will consent to the wage rate W_1. Compared to a free-entry market equilibrium, the wage rate has increased from W_0 to W_1, but employment has declined from E_0 to E_1. At the higher wage rate, W_1, an excess supply of labor, *AB*, will result. The restrictive practices will prevent this excess supply from undercutting the above-equilibrium wage rate. Because of the exclusionary practices, the union will be able to obtain higher wages for E_1 employees. Other employees who would be willing to accept work even at wage rate W_0 will now be forced into other areas of employment.

Bargaining Power

Must unions restrict entry? Why can they not simply use their bargaining power, enhanced by the strike threat, as a vehicle for raising wages? If they have enough economic power, this will be possible. A strike by even a small percentage of vital employees can sometimes halt the flow of production. For example, a work stoppage by airline pilots can force major airlines to cancel their flights. Because the pilots perform an essential function, an airline cannot operate without their services, even though they constitute only 10 percent of all airline employees.

If the union is able to obtain an above-free-entry wage rate, the impact on employment will be similar to a reduction in supply. As part b of Exhibit A6–4 illustrates, employers will hire fewer workers at the higher wage rate obtained through bargaining power. Employment will decline below the free-entry level (from E_0 to E_1) as a result of the rise in wages. An excess supply of labor, *AB*, will exist, at least temporarily. More employees will seek the high-wage union jobs than employers will choose to hire. Nonwage methods of rationing jobs will become more important.

Increased Demand

Unions may attempt to increase the demand for union labor by appealing to consumers to buy only union-produced goods. Union-sponsored promotional campaigns instructing consumers to "look for the union label" or "buy American" are generally designed to increase the demand for union-made products.

Most people, however, are primarily interested in getting the most for their consumer dollar. Thus, the demand for union labor is usually determined primarily by factors outside the union's direct control, such as the availability of substitute inputs and the demand for the product. Unions, though, can sometimes use their political power to increase the demand for their services. They may be able to induce legislators to pass laws that reduce competition from nonunion and/or foreign workers. In some areas, required inspections on construction projects will only be undertaken if the electrical or plumbing services have been performed by "licensed" (mostly union) craft workers. Unions are often supportive of import restrictions designed to increase the demand for products that they produce. During 1998–1999, the steel workers (and steel producers) sought to restrict imports of steel to the U.S. market at prices they deemed to be unfair. Garment workers have used their political muscle to raise tariffs and reduce import quotas for clothing goods produced abroad. Practices that increase the demand for goods and services produced by union labor will increase product prices as well as the wages of unionized workers. Thus, it is not surprising that both management and labor of unionized firms often join together to support various restrictions designed to reduce the competitiveness of goods produced by nonunion employees and foreigners.

WHAT GIVES A UNION STRENGTH?

Not all unions are able to raise the wages of their workers. What are the factors that make a union strong? ***Simply stated, if a union is to be strong, the demand for its labor must be inelastic. This will enable the union to obtain large wage increases while suffering only modest reductions in employment.*** In contrast, when the demand for union labor is elastic, a substantial rise in wages will mean a large loss in jobs.

There are four major determinants of the demand elasticity for a factor of production: (1) the availability of substitutes, (2) the elasticity of product demand, (3) the share of the input as a proportion of total cost, and (4) the supply elasticity of substitute inputs.[4] We now turn to the importance of each of these conditions as a determinant of union strength.

AVAILABILITY OF GOOD SUBSTITUTE INPUTS

When it is difficult to substitute other inputs for unionized labor in the production of a good, the union is strengthened. The demand for union labor is then more inelastic, and reductions in employment tend to be small if the union is able to use its bargaining power and the threat of a strike to push wages up. In contrast, when there are good substitutes for union labor, employers will turn to the substitutes and cut back on their use of union labor as it becomes more expensive. Under these circumstances, higher union wages will price the union workers out of the market and lead to a sharp reduction in their employment.

Some employers may be able to automate various production operations—in effect, substituting machines for union workers if their wages increase. When machines are a good substitute for union labor, the demand for union labor will be elastic, which will reduce the union's ability to push wages above the market level.

The best substitute for union labor is generally nonunion labor. Thus, the power of unions to gain more for their members will be directly related to their ability to insulate themselves from competition with nonunion labor. When employers are in a position to substitute nonunion labor for unionized workers, the market power of the union will be substantially reduced.

Within a given plant, a union will negotiate the wages and employment conditions for all workers, both union and nonunion. However, as union wages rise, it may be economical for unionized firms to contract with nonunion firms to handle specific operations or to supply various components used in production. Thus, contracting out often permits employers to indirectly substitute nonunion for union workers. In addition, many large firms in automobile, textile, and other manufacturing industries operate both union and nonunion plants. They may be able to substitute nonunion for union labor by shifting more and more of their production to their nonunion plants, including those located overseas or in right-to-work states where unions are generally weaker.

ELASTICITY OF DEMAND FOR PRODUCTS OF UNIONIZED FIRMS

Wages are a component of costs. An increase in the wages of union members will almost surely lead to higher prices for goods produced with union labor. Unless the demand for the good produced by union labor is inelastic, the output and employment of

[4]Alfred Marshall, *Principles of Economics,* 8th ed. (New York: Macmillan, 1920).

unionized firms will decline if the union pushes up wages (and costs). If a union is going to have a significant impact on wages (without undermining employment opportunities), its workers must produce a good for which the demand is inelastic.

Our analysis implies that a union will be unable to significantly increase wages above the free market rate when producing a good that competes with similar (or identical) goods produced by nonunion labor or foreign producers. The demand for the good produced by union labor will almost surely be highly elastic when the same product is available from nonunion and foreign producers. Thus, if higher union wages push up costs, the market share of unionized firms will shrink and their employment will fall substantially.

Both past history and recent events are consistent with this view. In the 1920s, the United Mine Workers obtained big wage gains in unionized coal fields. The union, however, was unable to halt the growth of nonunion mining, particularly in the strip mines of the West. The unionized mines soon lost the major share of their market to nonunionized fields, leading to a sharp reduction in the employment of unionized miners.

More recently, the strength of the Teamsters' union was substantially eroded when deregulation subjected the unionized segment of the trucking industry to much more intense competition from nonunion firms in the early 1980s. With deregulation, nonunion firms with lower labor costs entered the industry. Given their labor-cost advantage, many of the new entrants cut prices and were able to gain a larger market share. In contrast, the output and employment of unionized trucking firms declined. More than 100,000 Teamsters lost their jobs. Given the sharp reduction in the employment of their members, the Teamsters eventually agreed to wage concessions and a reduction in their fringe-benefit package.[5]

Deregulation of the trucking industry opened the market to nonunion trucking firms. This led to a sharp reduction in the employment of unionized (Teamsters) truck drivers in the early 1980s. Can you explain why?

[5]A study on the deregulation of the trucking industry found that the wage premium of unionized truckers fell by approximately 30 percent in the regulated sector of the industry. More drivers were employed, but the percentage of drivers who were union members fell from 60 percent prior to deregulation to 25 percent currently. See Barry T. Hirsch and David A. Macpherson, "Earnings and Employment in Trucking: Deregulating a Naturally Competitive Industry," in *Regulatory Reform and Labor Markets,* ed. James Peoples (Dordrecht, Netherlands: Kluwer Publishers, 1997).

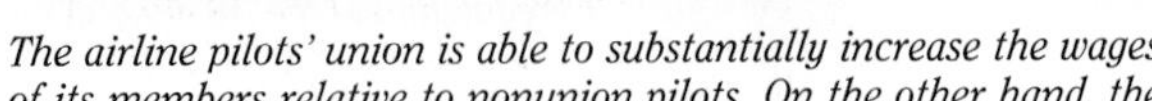

The airline pilots' union is able to substantially increase the wages of its members relative to nonunion pilots. On the other hand, the wages of union and nonunion grocery clerks are about the same. Why is the pilots' union strong and the clerks' union weak?

Union Labor as a Share of Cost of Production

If the unionized labor input comprises only a small share of total production cost, demand for that labor typically will be relatively inelastic. For example, since the wages of plumbers and airline pilots compose only a small share of the total cost of production in the housing and air travel industries, respectively, a doubling or even tripling of their wages would result in only a 1 percent or 2 percent increase in the cost of housing or air travel. A large increase in the price of such inputs would have little impact on product price, output, and employment. This factor has sometimes been called "the importance of being unimportant," because it is important to the strength of the union.

Supply Elasticity of Substitute Inputs

We have just explained that if wage rates in the unionized sector are pushed upward, firms will look for substitute inputs, and the demand for these substitutes will increase. If the supply of these substitutes (such as nonunion labor) is inelastic, however, their price will rise sharply in response to an increase in demand. The higher price will reduce the attractiveness of the substitutes. An inelastic supply of substitutes will thus strengthen the union by making the demand for union labor more inelastic.

WAGES OF UNION AND NONUNION EMPLOYEES

The precise impact of unions on the wages of their members is not easy to determine. In order to isolate the union effect, differences in other factors must be eliminated. Comparisons must be made between union and nonunion workers who have similar productivity (skills) and who are working on similar jobs.

Numerous studies have examined the effect of unions on wages. The pioneering work in this area was a 1963 study by H. Gregg Lewis of the University of Chicago.[6] Lewis estimated that, on average, union workers during the 1950s received wages between 10 percent and 15 percent higher than those of nonunion workers *with similar productivity characteristics.* The findings of other researchers using data from the 1950s and 1960s are generally consistent with the early work of Lewis.[7]

In a 1986 work, Lewis reviewed the evidence from nearly 200 studies on this topic and used more recent data to develop estimates of the union wage premium for the 1960s and 1970s.[8] **Exhibit A6–5** summarizes Lewis's findings and provides similar estimates for more recent periods. Research in this area indicates that the union–nonunion wage differential widened during the 1970s.[9] Lewis estimates that

EXHIBIT A6–5

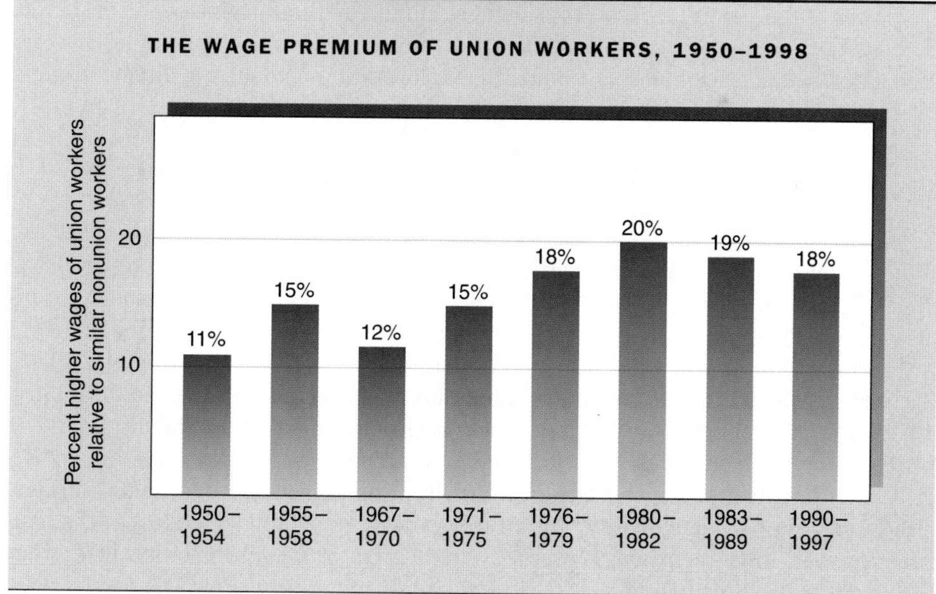

Most studies indicate that the wages of union workers have been between 18 percent and 20 percent higher than those of similar nonunion workers during the last two decades. This union–nonunion wage differential is slightly higher than during the 1950s and 1960s.

SOURCES: H. Gregg Lewis, Unionism and Relative Wages in the United States: An Empirical Inquiry *(Chicago: University of Chicago Press, 1963), p. 222; and H. Gregg Lewis,* Union Relative Wage Effects: A Survey *(Chicago: University of Chicago Press, 1986), p. 9. The 1983–1989 and 1990–1997 figures are from Barry T. Hirsch and David A. Macpherson,* Union Membership and Earnings Data Book *(Washington, D.C.: The Bureau of National Affairs, 1998).*

---

[6]H. Gregg Lewis, *Unionism and Relative Wages in the United States* (Chicago: University of Chicago Press, 1963).

[7]See Albert Rees, *The Economics of Trade Unions* (Chicago: University of Chicago Press, 1967); and Michael J. Boskin, "Unions and Relative Wages," *American Economic Review* 62 (June 1972): 466–472.

[8]H. Gregg Lewis, *Union Relative Wage Effects: A Survey* (Chicago: University of Chicago Press, 1986).

[9]See Richard B. Freeman and James L. Medoff, *What Do Unions Do?* (New York: Basic Books, 1984); Barry T. Hirsch and John T. Addison, *The Economic Analysis of Unions: New Approaches and Evidence* (Boston: Allen and Unwin, 1986); and Alison L. Booth, *The Economics of the Trade Union* (Cambridge, England: Cambridge University Press, 1995), for evidence on this point.

union workers received an 18 percent premium compared with similar nonunion workers during the 1976–1979 period, up from a 12 percent premium during 1967–1970. Labor economists Barry Hirsch and David Macpherson of Florida State University have used data from the annual *Current Population Survey* to estimate the adjusted union–nonunion wage differential during the 1980s and 1990s.[10] Their work indicates that, on average, union workers earned 18 percent to 19 percent more than *similar* nonunion employees during the past decade.[11] ***Like other research in this area, this suggests that the average union–nonunion wage differential has been between 15 percent and 20 percent during the last 25 years.***

Our theory indicates that some unions will be much stronger than others—that is, better able to achieve higher wages for their members. In some occupations, the size of the union–nonunion differential will be well above the average, while in other occupations, unions will exert little impact on wages.

Lewis estimated that strong unions, such as those of the electricians, plumbers, tool and die makers, metal craft workers, truckers (prior to the moves toward deregulation), and commercial airline pilots, were able to raise the wages of their members substantially more than the average for all unions. Other economists have found that the earnings of unionized merchant seamen, postal workers, and rail, auto, and steel workers exceed the wages of similarly skilled nonunion workers by 25 percent or more.

Unionization appears to have had the least impact on the earnings of cotton-textile, footwear, furniture, hosiery, clothing, and retail sales workers. In these areas, the power of the union has been considerably limited by the existence of a substantial number of nonunion firms. The demands of union workers in these industries are moderated by the fear of placing unionized employers at a competitive disadvantage in relation to the nonunion employers of the industry.

Unions, Profitability, and Employment in the Unionized Sector

If unions increase the wages of unionized firms above the competitive market level, the costs of those firms will rise unless (as seems unlikely) there is a corresponding increase in productivity. In the short run, the higher costs will reduce the profitability of the unionized firm. Recent research indicates that this was true during the 1970s. Barry Hirsch found that as the union–nonunion wage premium increased during the 1970s, the profitability of unionized firms lagged behind the profitability of other firms.[12]

If unions are able to transfer profits from unionized firms to union workers, clearly this is a two-edged sword. For a time, workers enjoy higher wages. In the long run, however, investment will move away from areas of low profitability. Like other

---

[10]Barry T. Hirsch and David A. Macpherson, *Union Membership and Earnings Data Book* (Washington, D.C.: The Bureau of National Affairs, 1998).

[11]The studies referred to in the text compared the wages of similarly productive union and nonunion workers at a point in time. Another approach would be to compare the change in the wages of the same worker in cases where the worker moves from a union to a nonunion job and vice versa. Research using this approach has generally placed the union wage premium at 10 percent or less, somewhat smaller than the estimates derived from cross-section studies. For evidence provided by studies using this methodology, see George Jakubson, "Estimation and Testing of the Union Wage Effect Using Panel Data," *Review of Economic Studies* 58 (October 1991): 971–991; and Richard B. Freeman, "Longitudinal Analysis and Trade Union Effects," *Journal of Labor Economics* 2 (January 1984): 1–26.

[12]Barry Hirsch, *Labor Unions and the Economic Performance of Firms* (Kalamazoo, Mich.: Upjohn Institute for Employment Research, 1991).

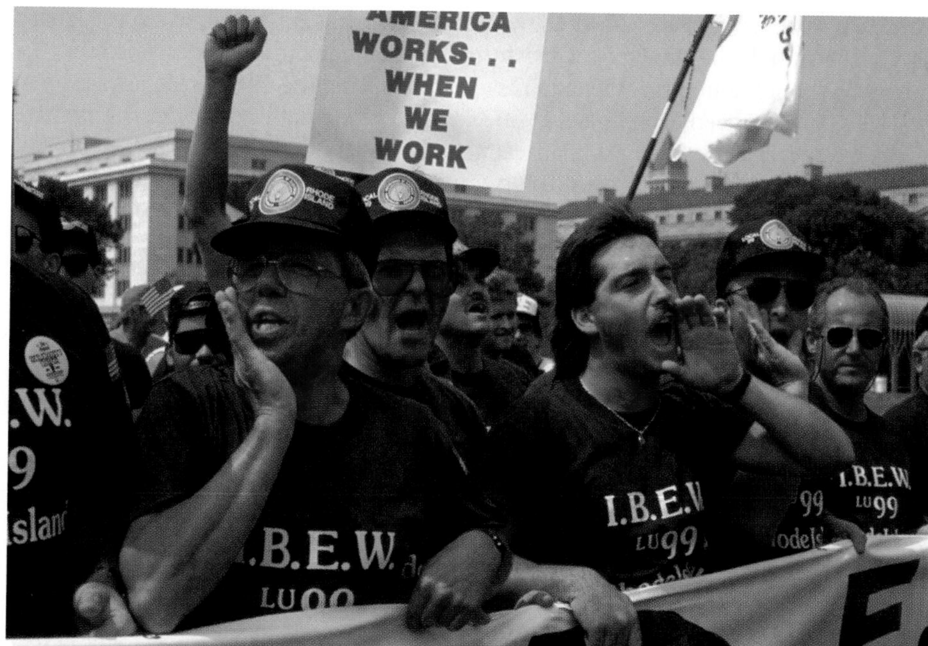

On average, unions are able to boost the wages of unionized workers by 18 to 20 percent relative to nonunion workers of similar productivity. However, there is no evidence that they are able to increase the wages of all workers or the share of income going to labor relative to capital.

mobile resources, capital may be exploited in the short run, but this will not be the case in the long run. Therefore, to the extent that the profits of unionized firms are lower, investment expenditures on fixed structures, research, and development will flow into the nonunion sector and away from unionized firms. As a result, the growth of both productivity and employment will tend to lag in the unionized sector. Investment, production, and employment will all shift away from unionized operations and toward nonunion firms. The larger the wage premium of unionized firms, the greater the incentive will be to shift production toward nonunion operations. The findings of Linneman, Wachter, and Carter are highly supportive of this view.[13] They found that industries with the largest union wage premiums were precisely the industries with the largest declines in the employment of unionized workers.

IMPACT OF UNIONS ON WAGES OF ALL WORKERS

Although unions have increased the average wages of their members, there is no reason to believe that they have increased the average overall compensation of workers—both union and nonunion. At first glance, this may seem paradoxical. However, the economic way of thinking enhances our understanding of this issue. As unions push wages up in the unionized sector, employers in this sector will hire fewer workers. Unable to find jobs in the high-wage union sector, some workers will shift to the nonunion sector. This increase in labor supply will depress the wages of nonunion workers. Thus, higher wages for union members do not necessarily mean higher wages for all workers.

[13]Peter D. Linneman, Michael L. Wachter, and William Carter, "Evaluating the Evidence on Union Employment and Wages," *Industrial and Labor Relations Review* 44 (October 1990). Linneman, Wachter, and Carter estimate that increases in the union wage premium were responsible for up to 64 percent of the decline in the union share of employment during the last two decades.

If labor unions increased the wages of all workers, we would expect labor's share of income to be directly related to union membership. This has not been the case. Even though union membership rose sharply during the 1940s, reached a peak in the 1950s, and has been declining ever since, there was virtually no change in the share of income received by labor (human capital) during this entire period. Similarly, if unions were the primary source of high wages, the real wages of workers would be higher in highly unionized countries, such as Australia, France, and the United Kingdom, than they are in the United States. But this is not what we observe.

The real source of high wages is high productivity, not labor unions. Increases in the general level of wages are dependent upon increases in productivity per hour. Income is simply the flip side of output (productivity). Of course, improvements in (1) technology, (2) the machines and tools available to workers (physical capital), (3) worker skills (human capital), and (4) the efficiency of economic organization provide the essential ingredients for higher levels of productivity. ***Higher real wages can be achieved only if the production of goods and services is expanded. Although unions can increase the wages of union workers, they cannot increase the wages of all workers unless their activities increase the total productivity of labor.***

KEY POINTS

➤ Union membership as a share of nonfarm employees has fluctuated substantially during the last 90 years. During the 1910–1935 period, union workers composed between 12 percent and 18 percent of nonfarm employees. Unionization increased rapidly during the 1935–1945 period, soaring to one-third of the workforce in the mid-1950s. Since then, union membership has waned, falling to only 13.9 percent of employees in 1998.

➤ A union can use three basic methods to increase the wages of its members: (a) restrict the supply of competitive inputs, including nonunion workers; (b) apply bargaining power enforced by a strike or threat of one; and (c) increase the demand for the labor service of union members.

➤ If a union is going to increase the wages of its members without experiencing a significant reduction in employment, the demand for union labor must be inelastic. The strength of a union is enhanced if (a) there is an absence of good substitutes for the services of union employees, (b) the demand for the product produced by the union labor is highly inelastic, (c) the union labor input is a small share of the total cost of production, and/or (d) the supply of available substitutes is highly inelastic. An absence of these conditions weakens the power of the union.

➤ Studies suggest that the wage premium of union members relative to similar nonunion workers increased during the 1970s. Since the late 1970s, the union–nonunion wage differential has been in the 18 percent to 20 percent range.

➤ Even though unions have increased the average wage of their members, there is no indication that they have either increased the average wage of all workers or increased the share of national income going to labor (human capital rather than physical capital).

➤ The real wages of workers are a reflection of their productivity rather than the share of the workforce that is unionized.

CRITICAL ANALYSIS QUESTIONS

1. Assume that the primary objective of a union is to raise wages.
   a. Discuss the conditions that will help the union achieve this objective.
   b. Why might a union be unable to meet its goal?

*2. Suppose that Florida migrant workers are effectively unionized. What will be the impact of the unionization on (a) the price of Florida oranges, (b) the profits of Florida fruit growers in the short run and in the long run, (c) the mechanization of the fruit-picking industry, and (d) the employment of migrant farmworkers?

3. The Retail Clerks Union has organized approximately one-third of the department stores in a large metro-

politan area. Do you think the union will be able to significantly increase the wages of its members? Explain.

4. "Unions cannot repeal the law of demand; they cannot have both high wages and high employment. The more successful they are at raising wages above competitive levels, the smaller the number of unionized employees."
   a. Evaluate this view.
   b. Does the success of unions at enlarging their wage premium tend to undermine their growth? Why or why not?

5. Evaluate the following statements.
   a. "An increase in the price of steel will be passed along to consumers in the form of higher prices for automobiles, homes, appliances, and other products made with steel." Do you agree or disagree?
   b. "An increase in the price of craft-union labor will be passed along to consumers in the form of higher prices of homes, repair and installation services, appliances, and other products that require craft-union labor." Do you agree or disagree?
   c. Are the interests of labor unions in conflict primarily with the interests of union employers? Explain.

6. What are the major forces that influence the ability of a union to increase the wages of the employees it represents? Why are some unions better able than others to attain higher wages for members? Explain.

*7. "If a union is unable to organize all the major firms in an industry, it is unlikely to exert a major impact on the wages of union members." Indicate why you either agree or disagree.

8. Suppose that the United Automobile Workers (UAW) substantially increases wages in the auto industry. What impact will the higher wages in the auto industry have on the following?
   a. wages of nonunion workers outside the automobile industry
   b. price of automobiles made by the UAW
   c. demand for foreign-produced automobiles
   d. profitability of U.S. automobile manufacturers

9. "Unions provide workers with protection against the greed of employers." Evaluate this statement. Be sure to consider the following questions:
   a. With whom do union workers compete?
   b. When union workers restrict entry into a market, whom are they trying to keep out?

*10. "Unions provide the only protection available to working men and women. Without unions, employers would be able to pay workers whatever they wanted." True or false?

*11. A survey of firms in your local labor market reveals that the average hourly wage rate of unionized production workers is $1.50 higher than the average wage rate of nonunion production workers. Does this indicate that unionization increases the wage rates of workers in your area by $1.50? Why or why not?

*12. Even though the wage scale of union members is substantially greater than the minimum wage, unions have generally been at the forefront of those lobbying for higher minimum rates. Why do you think unions fight so hard for a higher minimum wage?

---

*Asterisk denotes questions for which answers are given in Appendix B.

APPLICATION 7

"The End of the Lumber Supply"
Headline, *New York Times*, December 31, 1900

"Are We Running Out of Everything?"
Headline, *Newsweek*, November 19, 1973

Natural Resources and the Future

APPLICATION FOCUS

- What does the economic way of thinking have to say about resource markets?
- How do private ownership and competitive markets affect the availability and conservation of resources?
- How do regulations that weaken property rights influence conservation?
- Are we in danger of running out of vital natural resources?

The headlines above were reprinted in a 1987 book, *The Doomsday Myth: 10,000 Years of Economic Crises,* by economists Charles Maurice and Charles Smithson. As the book's title indicates, natural resource shortages, or worry about such crises, have occurred repeatedly for many centuries. And the worries continue. The cover story for *Parade* magazine on August 23, 1998, was "When Will We Run Out of Water?" Yet the crises have not kept living standards from rising, especially in the last two hundred years. What does the future hold? Will there be enough minerals, water, and other natural resources for future generations? What does economics have to say about using natural resources wisely? This application will focus on these questions and related topics.

NATURAL RESOURCE MARKETS

As we have previously stressed, the price of a good or service influences the production, quantity used, and availability of substitutes. A higher price for one good makes others more attractive as substitutes. If, for example, there is an increase in the price of movie tickets, then a host of substitutes, such as cable television subscriptions, books, and live concerts, become more attractive options for entertainment. The number of people attending movies will decline as the result of the price increase. Similar forces are at work on the supply side, since investors and workers have options as well. For example, if the price of television sets increases, those manufacturers will be able to bid more capital and labor away from other uses and will supply more TV sets at the higher price.

Are the demand and supply of natural resources shaped by similar influences? For something so basic as water, for example, are good substitutes readily available? Water is used for drinking, cleaning, irrigating crops, and for industrial processes and other purposes as well. In each use, we can substitute reduced activity (to use less with no other changes), more care (to spill less, for example), different methods of conducting the activity (perhaps drip irrigation rather than sprinklers), or equipment to recycle the water we use. **Exhibit A7–1** illustrates how several industries adjusted their water use during the California drought of the late 1980s. Firms in that area had already seen water costs rise, and many conservation measures had already been taken. During the drought they came to anticipate further cost increases as well as possible supply interruptions. Their response was to install recycling facilities and to alter their production processes in order to conserve more water. Thus, these industrial users sharply reduced their use of water per unit of output between 1985 and 1989. Other studies have shown that agricultural users and households respond to price increases in a similar manner.

When economists examine markets for water, petroleum products, access to wilderness recreation, and other natural resources, they find that the sensitivity of decision makers to price and cost is similar to that found for other goods and services. Substitutes, it seems, are everywhere. For example, when the price of gasoline rises, users find many ways to use less of it: smaller cars, less-distant vacation destinations, fewer shopping trips, and the use of public transportation or carpooling, to name just a

EXHIBIT A7-1

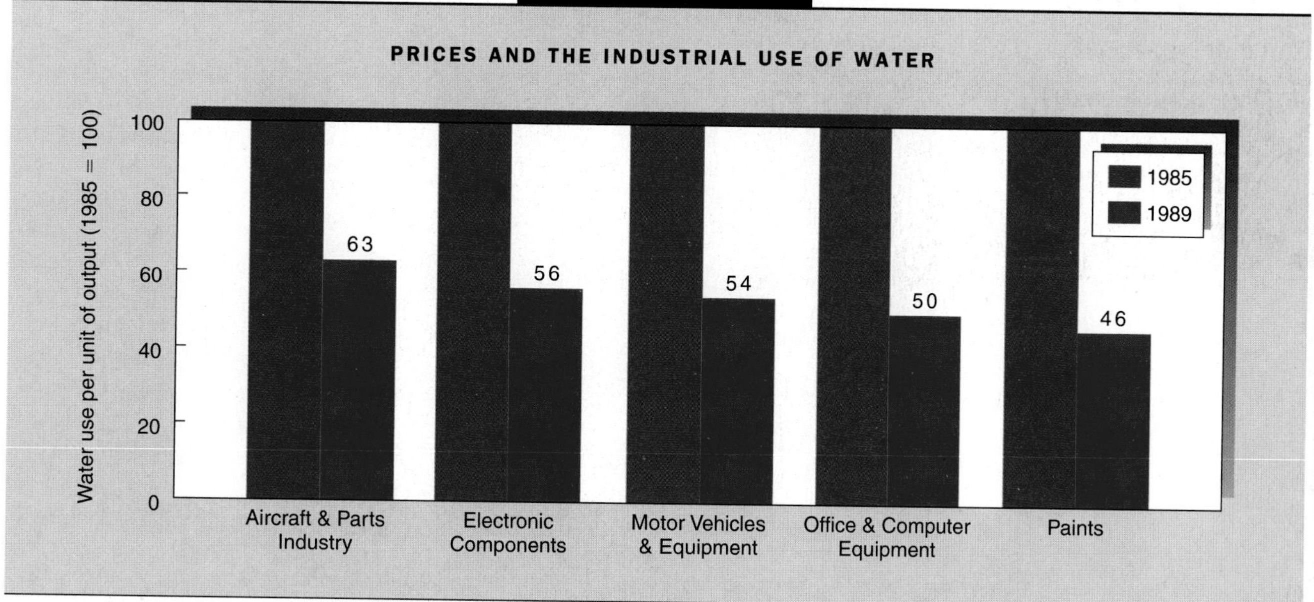

As water prices and the uncertainties of future availability increased during the 1986–1989 drought in California, industrial users cut back on their usage. As illustrated here, the amount of water used per unit of output declined by almost 50 percent in several key industries. When the use of water is expensive, people find ways to use less of it. How much water is needed to generate a gallon of paint? That depends very much on how costly water is. The "need" can be reduced if there is a good reason (such as a price increase) to do so.

SOURCE: Cost of Industrial Water Shortages, *California Urban Water Agencies, 1991; Executive Summary, Table 1-1.*

few. ***Users always seem to find ways to achieve their goals while using less of a resource that has risen in price. Like other goods and services, the amount demanded of a natural resource is negatively related to its price.***

The resource market price influences suppliers in the usual way. In the case of minerals from the earth, higher prices will induce suppliers to search for and recover more deposits of the resource. For example, when oil prices increase, wildcatters will search new territories, drillers will dig deeper, and water flooding and other techniques will be used to recover more oil from existing wells. ***Thus, the quantity supplied of oil—or any other resource—is positively related to its price.*** Similarly, as incomes grow and the demand for access to fly fishing, attractive wooded homesites, and hiking trails in relatively undisturbed natural areas increases, owners of such land will work to preserve those characteristics that make the land more valuable. When lands are owned or controlled by government, political pressures will tend to move in the same directions as market pressures, although the decision-making process is different.

As in other markets, the responsiveness of producers and users will vary with time. The longer a sharp rise or fall in price persists, the stronger the response will be to the price change. The adjustment process will require time. Users will need time to alter their equipment, for example, in order to conserve on the use of a more expensive resource. Similarly, suppliers will need time to employ more capital and labor in order to expand their output of a resource that has increased in price. Product innovation and technological change are among the additional factors that have greater impact over time, both on quantities demanded and on those supplied, in response to a price change.

When water is scarce and costly, additional capital equipment can be used to provide drip irrigation, which delivers carefully measured amounts of water to exactly the places where plants can best use it. This can greatly reduce the water input needed per acre. Capital equipment and careful planning are being substituted for water.

Economists have used statistical methods to analyze both the impact of price changes and the role of time in energy markets. **Exhibit A7–2** summarizes the findings of several studies on the price elasticities of demand for three major energy sources. For residential electricity, the estimated price elasticity of demand is 0.2 in the short run. This implies that a 10 percent rise in price would lead to a 2 percent short-run reduction in quantity demanded. The short run here means one year. When buyers have up to 10 years to respond, the long-run elasticity indicates that the same 10 percent price rise would cause a larger decline—a 7 percent reduction in residential use of electricity, if other factors remain the same.

The price elasticities of demand for natural gas and gasoline follow a similar pattern. In the short run, a change in price will lead to only a small change in amount demanded. With additional time, however, consumers will be able to adjust more fully to a price increase and come up with more and better ways to reduce consumption. Thus, the demand for both natural gas and gasoline will also be substantially more elastic in the long run than in the short run.

EXHIBIT A7–2

PRICE RESPONSIVENESS OF ENERGY FORMS: ESTIMATED PRICE ELASTICITIES OF DEMAND

	Estimated Elasticity[a]	
Fuel	Short Run	Long Run
Residential electricity	0.2	0.7
Residential natural gas	0.1	0.5
Gasoline	0.2	0.7

[a]When income and other factors such as other fuel prices are held constant, the elasticities indicate the ratio of percent change in quantity to the percent change in price causing the quantity change. Each elasticity is actually a negative number, since price and quantity demanded move in opposite directions.

SOURCE: Douglas R. Bohi, Analyzing Demand Behavior *(Baltimore: Johns Hopkins University Press, 1981), p. 159.*

Both economic theory and statistical studies indicate that resource markets are quite similar to those for other products. Higher resource prices will increase the incentive of consumers to conserve on their use of a resource and to find substitutes for it. The higher price will also bring forth additional production (supply). Lower prices will have the opposite effects, reducing the quantity supplied of the resource and increasing the quantity demanded.

PROPERTY RIGHTS AND RESOURCE CONSERVATION

When people have open access to forests, pasture land, or fishing grounds, they tend to overuse them. Providing land titles to farmers in Thailand has helped reduce damage to forests. The assignment of property titles to slum dwellers in Bandung, Indonesia, has tripled household investment in sanitation facilities. Providing security of tenure to hill farmers in Kenya has reduced soil erosion. Formalizing community rights to land in Burkina Faso is sharply improving land management. And allocating transferable rights to fishery resources has checked the tendency to overfish in New Zealand.

World Bank[1]

As the above passage indicates, the presence or absence of property rights exerts a powerful influence on the practice of conservation. Energy use in the former Soviet Union and the Eastern European nations illustrates this point. During the period when these areas were controlled by socialist governments, private property rights were absent. Most types of entrepreneurship and market exchange were prohibited by law. Production instead was centrally planned. Land and other resources were owned by the state, rather than by individuals. How did this system affect resource use and conservation?

One index of resource conservation is energy use per unit of output. In modern economies, energy constitutes more than half of all the resources utilized. Mikhail Bernstam compared the energy use in the 12 largest industrialized market economies with its use in the Eastern European socialist countries (plus socialist North Korea). The market-based industrial economies, where resources were privately owned and allocated through markets, used only 37 percent as much energy per $1,000 of output as the socialist nations in 1986. The figure had fallen from 44 percent in 1980. The same sort of comparison applies to the use of steel. Socialist economies used more than three times as much steel per unit of output as market economies.[2] The data gathered by Bernstam show that resource use per unit of output was far greater for socialist economies than for market-oriented economies.

The former Soviet bloc countries were certainly capable of using advanced technologies to conserve on their use of resources. However, without a market process where producers and consumers individually choose among competing options and individually pay for what they use, there was little incentive to do so. Why do property rights matter? Four functions of property rights are especially important from the viewpoint of resource conservation and the quality of the environment.

[1]The quoted passage is from *World Development Report,* 1992 (New York: World Bank), p. 12.

[2]The facts in this paragraph are from Mikhail Bernstam, *The Wealth of Nations and the Environment* (London: Institute of Economic Affairs, 1991), pp. 1–28.

1. ***Private property rights provide owners with the incentive to share (sell to others) resource access, while resource prices provide users with the incentive to conserve.*** Markets do not function well when sellers are denied the right to sell their assets—if they wish—to potential buyers in the marketplace. The right to sell forces each owner to confront the opportunity cost accompanying alternative uses of the resource, including uses that improve environmental quality and conserve resources for future use. Furthermore, when resources are privately owned, producers will have a strong incentive to reduce costs by conserving on their use of resources. In essence, private ownership encourages less resource usage per unit of value produced. Business firms pursuing profits have a strong incentive to implement new technologies that conserve on the use of resources. Thus, it should not be surprising that resource-saving changes tend to occur earlier in a market setting than under socialism. The experience of Eastern Europe and the former Soviet Union under socialism is consistent with this view.
2. ***A resource owner has a strong incentive to exercise good stewardship.*** Private ownership of property provides owners with an incentive to take good care of things. If the resource is well cared for, it will be more valuable and add more to the personal wealth of its owner. But if the owner allows the resource to deteriorate or be harmed by pollution, he or she personally bears the cost of that negligence in the form of a decline in the value of the resource. The value of the property right to the resource is, in a very real sense, a hostage to good care of that resource. That direct personal incentive is generally absent, however, under government ownership or control.
3. ***A resource owner has legal rights against anyone who would harm the resource.*** A private owner of a resource has more than just the incentive to preserve the value of that resource. Private property rights also provide the owner with legal rights against anyone (including a government agency) who invades—physically or by pollution—and harms the resource. Much environmental damage is prevented this way. The private owner of a forest or a farm will not sit idly by if someone is cutting down the trees or invading the property with hazardous pollutants. Lawsuits can be used to protect those rights. For example, owners of copper and lead smelters in the United States have been forced to compensate owners of agricultural crops and homes for damage from sulfur dioxide emissions. Once such a company has been successfully sued, the decision sets a legal precedent that effectively discourages further pollution.

   Before they closed it down, the owners of a smelter near Tacoma, Washington, had been sued in such a manner. After the court found the firm liable and forced it to pay damages, measures were taken to reduce future pollution. Moreover, the company recognized its accountability for costs (damages) imposed on others. As a result, whenever unusual weather conditions caused sulfur dioxide from its smokestacks to damage the foliage or the homes downwind, the company routinely made direct compensation payments to avoid the cost of further lawsuits.

   When resources are not privately owned, no individual will receive large personal rewards for bringing suit against polluters, even when the source of the pollution is clear. In the United States, fish in a river might be damaged by pollution, but they are not owned by anyone whose personal wealth depends on their safety. Political and bureaucratic authorities must be counted on to protect the resource. In England, by contrast, where fishing rights on a stream are privately owned, the owners guard jealously the quality of the water.
4. ***Changes in the value of a privately owned resource bring the anticipated future benefits and costs of today's resource decisions immediately to bear on the resource owner.*** Property rights provide long-term incentives for maximizing the

value of a resource, even for owners whose personal outlook is short term. If erosion on a tract of land reduces its future productivity, its value today falls, and the decline in the land's value reduces the owner's wealth. Fewer future services from a privately owned resource reduce the value of that resource now. In fact, as soon as an appraiser or potential buyers can see future problems, the value of the asset declines.

This is true even if the owner of the resource is a corporation, and the corporate officers, rather than the owner-stockholders, are in control. Corporate officers may be concerned mainly about the short term, not expecting to be present when future problems arise. They are concerned with current profits, but must be equally concerned with current changes in the value of the corporation's stock. If today's decision reduces future profits, it will reduce the price of the firm's stock today. Why? It is in the stockholders' interest to keep an "ear to the ground" (or to put their funds into portfolios managed by those who do) because correctly anticipating how the market will react can allow the discerning investor to buy before good news is fully captured in the stock price, or to sell before bad news is fully reflected in a falling stock price. The top corporate managers are hired and fired by the firm's board of directors, which is normally dominated by large shareholders. The top managers cannot afford to let short-sighted policies harm the interests of board members. Such self-interested scrutiny and the resultant decisions of investors, driven by the presence of property rights and the resulting resource ownership and liability for harm, provide a continual assessment of corporate strategies.

Property rights that are defined, defendable, and tradeable are vitally important for the smooth operation of markets. When property rights are present and protected, resource markets encourage resource availability, but they also promote resource conservation. To underscore the positive role of property rights, let us consider what happens when well-enforced property rights to resources are absent.

THE ENDANGERED SPECIES ACT: UNWANTED SECONDARY EFFECTS FROM WEAKER PROPERTY RIGHTS[3]

The intent of the Endangered Species Act (ESA), which the Congress passed in 1973, was to help save endangered species from extinction. To do that, the ESA gave to the U.S. Fish and Wildlife Service (FWS) the power to prohibit any land use by private owners (and government agencies) that might disturb the habitat of members of any animal species listed as endangered under the ESA. The majority of species that are listed are found on private lands. Farming, building, cutting trees, clearing brush, and even walking are activities that have been prohibited on private parcels of land where FWS biologists believe that such activities might harm a listed animal. Under the ESA, when the presence of listed species is known or suspected, the right to decide on land use is taken from the owner and given (without charge) to the agency to further its mission. The property rights of landowners are severely weakened.

Colonies of many listed species have benefited from this control. The affected landowners, however, have often been forced by ESA requirements to sacrifice highly productive activities. Although a public good—habitat provision for endangered

---

[3]Sources for this section are: Thomas R. Bourland and Richard L. Stroup, "Rent Payments as Incentives: Making Endangered Species Welcome on Private Land," *Journal of Forestry* 94, no. 4 (April 1996): 18–21; and Richard L. Stroup, *The Endangered Species Act: Making Innocent Species the Enemy,* PERC Policy Series, No. 3 (Bozeman, Mont.: PERC, April 1995).

species—is produced as a result of these sacrifices, the fact that no compensation is given to owners means that market signals and incentives are missing.

Consider the sacrifice—the opportunity cost—required to set aside the habitat favored by the red-cockaded woodpecker, a listed species found in southern pine forests from Virginia to Texas under current FWS regulations. The FWS requires that trees the birds use for nesting must be left standing for several decades beyond the time they would normally be harvested for wood. Many acres of forage must also be available around the nest. Ben Cone is one person affected by the woodpecker under the rules. He owns 7,200 acres in North Carolina. For decades he managed the land primarily for wildlife, clearcutting 50 acres of very old timber every 5 to 10 years, to gain revenue and to renew the forest. The red-cockaded woodpecker loves the old trees. So in 1991 when he wanted to cut and sell some timber, the FWS said that he must set aside any part of his land used by the woodpecker. The wildlife biologists he hired to analyze the situation told him that 1,560 acres could no longer be cut, and that the cost to him would be about $1.4 million. He told *The Wall Street Journal,* "I cannot afford to let those woodpeckers take over the rest of the property. I'm going to start massive clearcutting. I'm going to a 40-year rotation instead of a 75- to 80-year rotation." The younger trees do not draw woodpeckers to the land. He began the clearcuts, but the publicity from the case helped bring a willingness of the FWS to negotiate special arrangements with Cone to modify his strategy. Other landowners have been less fortunate.

The cost of protecting a species such as the red-cockaded woodpecker can be low or high, depending on how much land is set aside, which land, and the specific restrictions ordered by the FWS biologists. Greater habitat set-asides and stronger limits on land uses impose higher costs on landowners. The FWS provides no compensation for these costs. Properly placed, artificially drilled nesting holes, which would allow both habitat and logging on the same land, are a substitute for older nesting trees. These expenditures, however, would be a direct cost to the FWS. Thus, the agency often attempts to stretch its budget by setting aside more land with stricter controls, rather than protecting the species through habitat design.

Many landowners dread the possibility that the species will be found on their land, leading to an imposition of FWS land use restrictions. Some are even willing to risk severe punishment by illegally killing an animal before the FWS learns about it. This is sometimes referred to as the "shoot, shovel, and shut up" strategy. More often, the landowner adjusts land management in subtle ways to make that land unattractive to the listed species. The unwanted secondary effect of the ESA has been a serious reduction in habitat for listed and candidate species.

Prior to the ESA's weakening of property rights, landowners often were quite willing to help preserve declining wildlife. When fears of extinction for bluebirds arose, landowners allowed volunteers to place hundreds of thousands of nest boxes on their land and to monitor them. Owners who did not fear the loss of rights usually cooperated at low cost. The bluebird has recovered and as a result never had to be listed. Many similar efforts, large and small, have been successful in gaining landowner cooperation with little or no payment in return. But finding a landowner willing to help a species now listed under the current ESA is obviously difficult. Few will want to attract species that will bring FWS control of their land. In fact, some will no longer even welcome hikers who might discover a listed species on the land.

When regulation weakens property rights and allows regulators to ignore costs their actions impose on others, low-cost solutions to problems become less likely. ***Without the signals and incentives of the market mechanism, it is difficult to discover low-cost means of resource conservation. There is also less incentive for decision makers to use low-cost methods even when they are known.***

Preservation of endangered species such as the red-cockaded woodpecker can be achieved at a much lower cost if the incentive structure encourages local persons to assist with the protection.

We have seen that markets can, without any central planning, lead to efficient allocation of resources and to innovative resource conservation, as well as resource production. But we have also seen that markets cannot do their work without property rights, and that defendable property rights are not always present. On balance, have conservation and innovation been enough? Or are we running out of resources? Does it appear that our grandchildren and theirs will be hurt by our prosperity and economic growth? We turn now to that question.

RESOURCE MARKETS VERSUS RESOURCE DEPLETION

For centuries, various social commentators have argued that the world is about to run out of trees, vital minerals, or various sources of energy.[4] In sixteenth-century England, fear arose that the supply of wood would soon be exhausted as that resource was widely used as a source of energy. As the forests around urban areas receded, wood prices rose. People soon began substituting coal for charcoal, a wood derivative, in both personal and commercial uses. England's economic growth continued and the island nation still has forests.

In the middle of the nineteenth century, dire predictions arose that the United States was about to run out of whale oil, at that time the primary fuel for artificial lighting. As the demand for whale oil increased, many predicted that all the whales

[4]See Charles Maurice and Charles W. Smithson, *The Doomsday Myth: 10,000 Years of Economic Crises* (Stanford, Calif.: Hoover Institution Press, 1987).

would soon be gone and that Americans would face long nights without light. Whale-oil prices rose sharply from 23 cents per gallon in 1820 to $1.42 per gallon in 1850. Higher prices again motivated consumers and entrepreneurs to seek alternatives, including distilled vegetable oils, lard oil, and coal gas. By the early 1850s, coal oil (kerosene) had won out. And very soon thereafter, a new substitute for whale oil appeared: Petroleum replaced coal oil as the source of kerosene. As for whale oil, by 1896 its price had fallen to 40 cents per gallon, and even at that price few people used it. The whale-oil crisis had passed.

As people switched to petroleum, doomsday predictions about its exhaustion arose almost as soon as the resource was developed. In 1914 the Bureau of Mines reported that the total U.S. supply of oil was 6 million barrels, an amount less than the United States now produces every two years. In 1926 the Federal Oil Conservation Board informed people that the U.S. supply of oil would last only 7 years. A couple of decades later the secretary of the interior forecast that the United States would run out of oil in just a few more years.

Dire predictions about our natural resource future became a fad during the 1970s. The U.S. federal government established a Department of Energy. The first energy secretary proclaimed in 1979 that "we must rapidly adjust our economics to a condition of chronic stringency in traditional energy supplies." Oil prices peaked at $53 per barrel in 1981, then fell. By March 1999, oil prices had fallen to less than $11 per barrel.

Why Have Doomsday Projections Been Wrong?

There are two major reasons for their inaccuracy. First, "proved reserves" of a mineral resource are the verified quantity of the resource that producers have discovered and that they believe can be produced *at current levels of technology and prices.* But technology can change. In the Gulf of Mexico, for example, oil wells were thought to be fully exploited after about 30 percent of the oil was removed. With improved technology, we are now able to extract 80 percent or more of the oil from these same wells. Furthermore, a better understanding of geophysics and the increasing availability of very large, low-cost computing capabilities are now used to direct the drilling. This, too, has led to an increase in proved reserves.

Second, doomsday predictions have generally failed to consider the role of price changes. When a resource becomes more scarce, its price rises. This provides additional incentive for (1) resource users to cut back on their consumption, (2) suppliers to develop new methods of discovering and recovering larger quantities of the resource, and (3) both users and producers to search for and develop substitutes. To date, these forces have pushed "doomsday" farther and farther into the future.

In fact, the empirical evidence indicates that the relative scarcity of most resources is declining, and, as a result, the relative price of most resources is falling. The classic study of Harold Barnett and Chandler Morse illustrates this point.[5] Using data from 1870 to 1963, Barnett and Morse found that the real price of resources declined during that long period. Updates and extensions of this work indicate that resource prices are continuing to decline.

---

[5]Harold Barnett and Chandler Morse, *Scarcity of Growth: The Economics of Natural Resource Availability* (Baltimore: The Johns Hopkins University Press for Resources for the Future, 1963). For an update of this study, see Manuel H. Johnson, Fredrick W. Bell, and J. T. Bennett, "Natural Resource Scarcity: Empirical Evidence and Public Policy," *Journal of Environmental Economics and Management* 7 (September 1980): 258–269.

In 1980 the late Julian Simon, an economist, bet doomsday environmentalist Paul Ehrlich that the inflation-adjusted price of a bundle of any five natural resources of Ehrlich's choosing would decline during the 1980s. In fact, the prices of all five of the resources chosen by Ehrlich declined, and Simon won the highly publicized bet. A recent book edited by Simon, containing chapters written by a number of prominent economists and resource experts, provides a good deal of evidence that the availability of most resources continues to improve in the 1990s.[6]

Far from suggesting that doomsday is just around the corner, the price data paint a rather optimistic picture. Historical data on relative prices of key resources indicate that technology and the ever-increasing availability of substitutes tend to outrun our use of scarce natural resources. When price changes are allowed to reflect changing scarcities, constructive human responses to specific scarcities are a predictable occurrence. Just as they have been wrong in the past, doomsday forecasts that fail to incorporate human response to relative price changes are likely to be wrong in the future, so long as markets are allowed to function.

KEY POINTS

➤ In resource markets, as in other markets, incentives matter. Both the quantity demanded of a resource and the quantity supplied depend on the resource price. Substitutes abound and they influence the elasticity of both demand and supply. As in other markets, demand and supply in resource markets are generally more elastic in the long run than in the short run.

➤ Private resource ownership is important for resource conservation because it (a) is necessary for the wide, but controlled, access encouraged by the market process, (b) provides an incentive for resource stewardship, (c) gives owners legal standing against those who would overuse or harm the resource, and (d) gives future users a voice in today's markets through the capital value of resource assets.

➤ When property rights are poorly defined and enforced, problems arise. Because of the difficulties involved in specifying and enforcing ownership of some resources, property rights and market prices are not a panacea. As with other economic issues, government regulation may provide improvements when markets fail. But here, as elsewhere, it is important to recognize that government action is not an automatic corrective device.

➤ Neither economic analysis nor empirical evidence supports the view that the world is about to run out of key natural resources. When private property rights are present, increased scarcity of a natural resource increases the price of the resource and thereby encourages (a) conservation, (b) the use of substitutes, and (c) the development of new technologies capable of both enhancing supply and reducing reliance on a resource. Contrary to the doomsday view of resource scarcity, the real prices of most natural resources have been declining during the last century.

CRITICAL ANALYSIS QUESTIONS

*1. Does a resource that is not owned, and therefore is not priced, have a zero opportunity cost? Might it be treated as if it did? Explain.

2. Why is the price elasticity of demand for resources, such as water and natural gas, greater in the long run than in the short run? What examples of responses to price changes can you think of that are more complete after one year than after one week?

3. "The federal government should do a complete survey of mineral availability in the nation. It is inexcusable that we do not know how much oil, for example, the country can ultimately produce." Evaluate this statement.

*4. Why will more oil in total be produced from an oil well when the price of crude oil is higher?

*5. "Private ownership of a natural resource, such as a lake in the woods, is tantamount to setting aside that resource for the personal, selfish enjoyment of one owner.

[6]Julian L. Simon, *The State of Humanity* (Cambridge, Mass.: Blackwell Publishers, 1995), Part III, Natural Resources.

Society will be better off if it is recognized that such a resource was provided by nature, for all to enjoy." Evaluate this statement.

6. Will the world ever run out of any mineral resource? Why or why not?

*7. "Corporations should not be allowed to own forests. Corporate managers are just too short-sighted. Their philosophy is to make a profit now, regardless of the future consequences. For example, trees may be cut after growing 30 years to get revenue now, even though another 20 years' growth would yield a very high rate of return. The long-run health of our forests is too important to entrust them to this sort of management." Evaluate this statement.

8. "Since our national forests are owned by all the people, their resources will be conserved for the benefit of all, rather than exploited in a short-sighted way, to produce benefits only for the owners." Evaluate this statement.

---

*Asterisk denotes questions for which answers are given in Appendix B.

APPLICATION 8

In nearly every case, environmental problems stem from insecure, unenforceable, or nonexistent property rights.

Jane S. Shaw[1]

Economics and the Environment

APPLICATION FOCUS

- What does the economic way of thinking have to say about environmental decision making?
- Is economic growth harmful to the environment?
- How do private ownership and competitive markets affect environmental quality?
- Can government regulation help protect the environment? Will it always be successful in doing so?

[1]Jane S. Shaw, "Private Property Rights: Hope for the Environment," *Liberty* 2, no. 2 (November 1988): 55.

We have become increasingly sensitive to the environment, especially during the past 30 years. Will the quality of the environment be better in the future? Or will pollution increase as capital formation and technological improvements lead to greater production of goods and services? What does economics have to say about protecting the environment? What role can property rights and market exchange play in environmental matters? This application will focus on these questions and related issues.

ECONOMIC PRINCIPLES AND ENVIRONMENTAL DECISIONS

As we saw in the previous Application, markets coordinate the choices of people with regard to natural resource use. But what about environmental decisions, which often are made outside the market, and thus without the benefit of fully priced goods and services? There are relatively few markets for clean air, pure water, and endangered species. The absence of clearly defined and securely enforced property rights and the resulting lack of markets and decision-maker accountability are at the heart of pollution and other externality problems. Let us consider how the economic way of thinking enhances our understanding of environmental choices and problems.

1. ***Incentives matter.*** One economics professor demonstrated the importance of incentives in environmental decisions by walking into class with a lighted cigarette, taking a puff, then dropping the cigarette on the floor, and grinding it out with his shoe. Then he pointed out that he would never do such a thing in his own living room, where he personally would bear the cost of having to clean up the mess. In fact, he said, he probably would not do it if the building's janitor was watching and likely to voice strong disapproval of the behavior. Further, he said that he would be less likely to grind out the cigarette on a classroom floor if an ashtray were handy. The professor's actions regarding the surrounding environment thus depended on his expected costs.

   Do incentives matter in the preservation of wildlife? Consider the case of African elephants, which are valuable for their meat and ivory, among other factors. Poachers kill the wild elephants illegally and take the most valuable parts. A pair of elephant tusks can bring thousands of dollars on the world market. Local residents, who might most easily help prevent poaching, gain nothing from the presence of the elephants. To the contrary, elephants eat their crops, consume their scarce water, and even endanger their children. Many local residents would therefore prefer fewer of them. The control of poaching is consequently weak, and the herds in Central Africa have been declining—almost to the point of extinction.[2]

[2]See Randy Simmons and Urs Kreuter, "Herd Mentality: Banning Ivory Sales Is No Way to Save the Elephant," *Policy Review* (fall 1989): 46–49.

When landowners and local residents gain from the human use of wildlife such as elephants, they will try to protect the wildlife. But if the wildlife impose costs on local people without offsetting benefits, the wildlife may be endangered.

In some southern African nations, however, landowners are allowed to conduct elephant hunts and gain from tourism based on the presence of wildlife like elephants. In Zimbabwe, the residents of the villages near each herd are allowed to share the gains from the human use of elephants, whether from hunting or tourism. These partial private-ownership rights provide local residents with an incentive to help control poaching, and they have been quite effective in doing so. As a result, elephant herds thrive in southern African nations. There is no concern about elephants becoming extinct there. As the experience of the elephants illustrates, when people make decisions affecting the environment, their actions will be guided by expected benefits and opportunity costs, just as they are for other decisions.

2. ***The value of a good or service is subjective.*** Environmental values, like all others, are subjective. How valuable is a tract of unroaded wilderness land, relative to the same land with roads and campgrounds added to enhance recreation, or the same land developed for high-quality residential use? Individuals will differ dramatically in their evaluations of those alternatives. Some believe that wilderness is the highest and best use for such a tract of land. Others prefer more intensive recreational use or tastefully planned and easily accessible residential development, where people can be comfortable and also be in close contact with the beauty of nature.

   Consider the following question: Will persons living near a river be willing to vote for sewage plant improvements to help clean up a half-mile stretch of the river for better fishing and boating, even though that will add an extra $12 per month to their water bill? Again, we can expect people to differ in how much value they place on making a stretch of river a little cleaner. Some will be quite happy to pay the fee, while others will probably object.

3. ***Remember the secondary effects.*** As in other areas of human action, the secondary effects of environmental actions must be considered. For example, when citrus growers use chemical pesticides to protect their fruit against certain insects, the pesticides may impose some danger to consumers if they are not washed completely from the fruit. To avoid such danger to consumers, government agencies

control the use of many pesticides and have banned the use of certain compounds. That was the case for DDT, which was banned by the U.S. Environmental Protection Agency in 1972 because it was believed to be a source of human health risk and damage to wild birds. Unfortunately, the ban had unwanted secondary effects. In place of DDT, some other pesticides were used that were more risky to the workers who applied them in the fields.

In other nations, the secondary effects of banning DDT were even more tragic. In Sri Lanka, for example, where the mosquitoes that carry malaria had been controlled by DDT, the incidence of malaria had declined from 2.8 million cases in 1946 to only 110 cases in 1961. After the government of Sri Lanka stopped the use of DDT in the early 1960s, however, the number of malaria cases jumped back up to 2.5 million in 1968–1969. It is important that environmental decision makers, like those in other policy areas, be alert for secondary effects. This basic economic principle is just as important for environmental decision making as it is in other areas of human action.

Economic principles apply to the choices of people regarding natural resources and the environment just as they do to choices in other areas. But since markets and easily defended property rights are not always present, especially for air and water quality and other environmental services, observers often worry that as an economy grows, more resources will be used and additional waste will be imposed on the environment. Clearly, this is an extremely important concern. What can economists say about the effects of economic growth on environmental quality? We now turn to an examination of this important question.

IS ECONOMIC GROWTH HARMFUL TO THE ENVIRONMENT?

The need to choose between economic growth and environmental quality may seem obvious when economic activities affect the quality of our air or water. In the United States, the federal government has been asked to control polluters. Moreover, courts have historically protected the rights of those able to prove that they have been harmed by pollution. In these cases, polluters have been required to pay damages or clean up their emissions or both. As a result, certain economic activities are made more costly and specific economic outputs are reduced in order to maintain environmental quality. It is not surprising, then, that many people believe a choice must be made between economic growth on the one hand and environmental protection on the other. Yet data from around the world support a more optimistic view.

Many of the same forces that encourage economic growth, such as market institutions and improvements in technology, also help to reduce pressures on the environment. In addition, rising incomes foster the willingness and ability to pay for a cleaner, safer, more pleasant environment. Although environmental protection often imposes some cost on economic activities, growth can still proceed when the controls are intelligently applied. And growth itself, properly controlled to avoid environmental harm, has important beneficial effects on the environment.

Once people have enough income so that they are not struggling to put food on the table, they become more willing and able to take actions to reduce (or avoid) environmental damage and improve the quality of the environment. For example, as incomes have risen in North America, Europe, and other parts of the world, private actions to maintain nature preserves have proliferated. Individuals, firms, and nonprofit groups have established areas for the protection of plant and animal habitats.[3] Profit-seeking firms, such as Big Sky of Montana, find it profitable to buy large tracts of mountainous land, far more than they plan to develop, then sell some of the tracts with environmentally protective restrictions. By providing legal restrictions that protect the pristine surroundings of the resort, they increase the value of the property they sell.

Economic growth generally leads to environmental improvements because people with higher incomes are willing to pay more for environmental quality. Economist Donald Coursey has studied this topic extensively. He finds that in the United States and in other industrial nations, citizens' support for measures to improve environmental quality is highly sensitive to income changes.[4] In economic terms, willingness to pay for costly environmental measures is highly elastic with respect to income. Coursey estimates that in industrial nations the income elasticity of demand for environmental quality is 2.5. Thus, a 10 percent increase in income leads to a 25 percent increase in citizens' willingness to pay for environmental measures. According to Coursey, the demand for environmental quality has approximately the same income elasticity as the demand for luxury automobiles like the BMW and Mercedes-Benz.

Technological change is another factor that often improves the environment. Economic growth and technological change generally accompany each other. The same market processes that encourage growth also encourage technological advances. In the United States, advancing technology was itself cleaning the environment well before major environmental laws were passed.

In a market system, producers using advanced technology can profit by getting a given performance from a smaller amount of a costly resource. **Exhibit A8–1** illustrates this process for producers and users of soft-drink and beer cans. As they

EXHIBIT A8–1

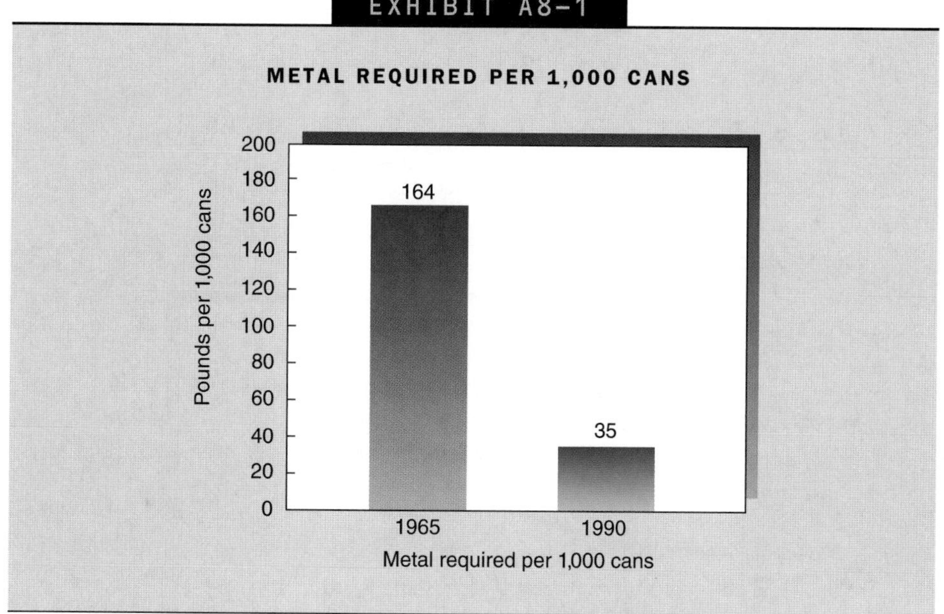

By improving their engineering techniques and switching to a thinner can made of lightweight aluminum, producers reduced their use of metal per can by almost 80 percent between 1965 and 1990.

SOURCE: Lynn Scarlett, "Make Your Environment Dirtier—Recycle," Wall Street Journal, *January 14, 1991.*

[3] Chapter 9 of *Environmental Quality* (1984), the annual report of the President's Council on Environmental Quality, describes a representative sample of these private projects, some of which date back to the nineteenth century, to benefit the environment.

[4] Donald Coursey discussed this topic in "The Demand for Environmental Quality," a paper presented in January 1993 at the annual meeting of the American Economic Association in Anaheim, California.

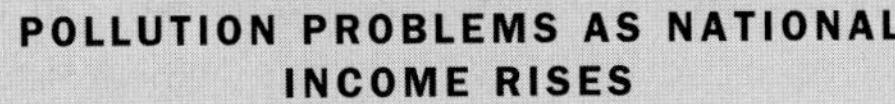
EXHIBIT A8-2

POLLUTION PROBLEMS AS NATIONAL INCOME RISES

Note: Estimates are based on cross-country regression analysis of data from the 1980s.

SOURCE: World Bank, World Development Report, *1992, p.11.*

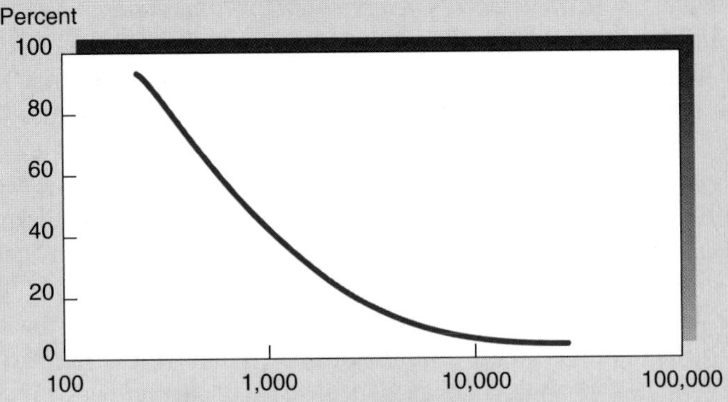

(a) Population without safe water

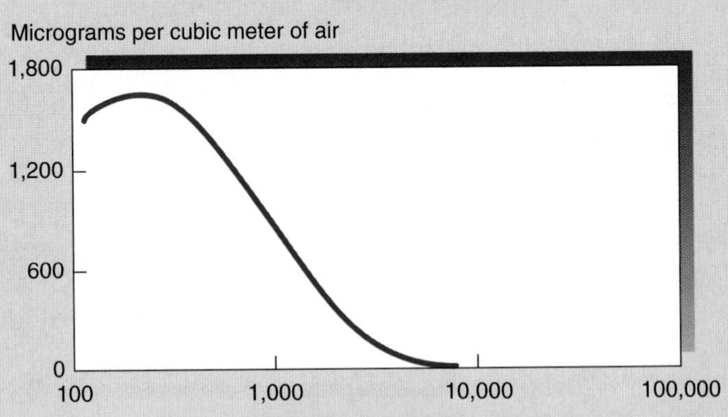

(b) Urban concentration of particulate matter

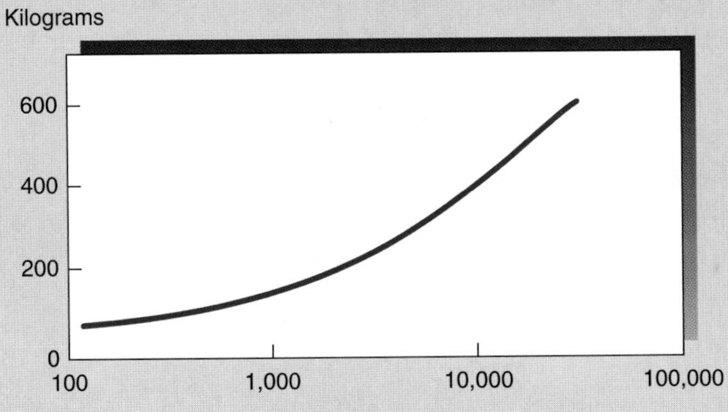

(c) Municipal waste per capita

sought greater profits, producers found ways to reduce the amount of metal used per can, and also switched to lightweight, easily recycled aluminum. As a result, less ore was dug and processed, and less energy was needed to transport both the raw materials and the filled cans, reducing pollution from the use of the cans. Because this search for lower-cost means of providing consumers with value is an ongoing process in a market economy, there is downward pressure on both resource use and waste emissions per unit of output. Of course, the increased quantity of goods and services produced is an offsetting factor. Thus, expansion in output may lead to more resource use and more pollution, depending on the amount of resource-saving technical progress that accompanies income growth.

Exhibit A8–2 illustrates the general relationship between three types of environmental problems and per-capita income. Some environmental problems are ameliorated with higher income, while others are worsened. Still others are worsened only up to a point and then improve with still higher levels of economic development. Such problems as a lack of safe drinking water (part a) are steadily reduced as income rises. As people become richer, they are more able to reduce waterborne diseases by installing sewers to handle human waste and by reducing water contamination by animals. Certain pollutants, however, such as particulates in the air (part b), tend initially to become worse as incomes increase from extremely low levels. But as income levels continue to rise, heavily used roads are paved and industrial processes become more efficient and emit smaller amounts of waste. As a result, particulate air pollution will eventually fall as per-capita income continues to increase. Once minimal income levels are achieved, economic growth generally brings cleaner air and water, along with improvements in several other aspects of environmental quality.

Unfortunately, the amount of solid waste generated normally increases steadily with economic development (part c). But proper disposal facilities can minimize the negative effects of this problem. On balance, richer seems to be environmentally better.[5] One reason lies in the fact that markets and property rights allow citizens to achieve both growth and environmental protection from identifiable polluters. Without enforceable rights to resources, both goals are more difficult to reach. We turn now to a discussion of how property rights have helped the environment in several nations around the world.

PROPERTY RIGHTS AND THE ENVIRONMENT

Income growth helps to increase the demand for environmental quality, while technological advances help to lower the cost of reducing both resource use and pollution. Yet incomes above the poverty level and an understanding of technology are not enough to protect the environment. The recent opening up of Eastern European nations and the Soviet Union exposed widespread environmental disasters. These disasters occurred despite the presence of good technical capabilities and above-average per-capita incomes in those nations.

Why did these relatively advanced nations not take better care of their environments? The answer appears to lie in the fact that property rights and market exchange were largely missing. Application 9, using the former Soviet Union and the Eastern European nations as examples, showed in some detail how property rights are

[5]The *World Development Report,* 1992 (New York: World Bank), especially Chapters 2 and 3, provides a detailed look at the connection between economic development and environmental quality.

an important factor in resource conservation. The same is true for environmental quality. More use of energy, steel, and other natural resources to produce goods and services usually means greater pollution. In addition, property rights give legal standing to those who are threatened by pollution. Owners of land and other resources in a market economy have the right to sue anyone who damages their property with pollution. Citizens have similar rights against polluters who wrongfully bombard the individuals themselves with harmful pollution. Without enforceable property rights, however, citizens must depend on government agencies to protect them. Finally, property rights promote economic prosperity and thereby spur citizen demand for greater emphasis on environmental quality.

PROPERTY RIGHTS AND THE PROTECTION OF WATER QUALITY

Could property rights help protect water quality in rivers and streams? Private ownership of fishing rights in England illustrates what happens when private ownership is present.[6] In England the adjacent landowner has title to fishing rights out to the middle of the stream. The fishing right can be rented, leased, or sold. Fishing clubs and owners of country inns are among those who have purchased those rights. Club members and guests of the inns may then have access to fishing in this area.

Some clubs are exclusive and expensive. The Houghton Club, with fewer than 25 members, owns fishing rights on 17 miles of the Test River, a fine trout fishing stream. The club's rights were estimated in 1988 to be worth more than $35 million. But fishing rights on an adjacent stretch of the same fine trout stream, a few hundred yards long, are owned by the Greyhound Inn bed and breakfast. The owner allows two guests (at about $55 each, in 1988), to fish each day. "Rough fishing" (non-trout fishing) is available from clubs organized at local pubs, for perhaps $50 per year per person. In all cases, access is strictly controlled to eliminate crowding, and the stream banks are generally kept cleared of brush and are well protected against cattle and other potential sources of pollution that might disturb the fish.

As trout fishing became more popular and the rights became more valuable over the years, fishing-rights owners became more serious about protecting their rights. In 1948, long before the first Earth Day in 1970 and 20 years before the government established authorities to control water pollution, the Anglers' Cooperative Association (ACA, later the Anglers' Conservation Association) was formed to help clubs and anglers obtain damage awards or court orders forcing intruders to cease polluting activities. The ACA won its first major case in 1951 against two chemical companies and the city of Derby for pumping untreated sewage, hot water, and tar products into the River Derwent. Through the years, it won several other cases, including a 1987 case against the Thames Water Authority for fouling the Thames River. The association has established enough court precedents that it seldom has to go to court now.

In the United States, fishing rights on most streams are owned by state governments, which might in principle sue to protect their rights just as the ACA does in England. However, without their own wealth at stake, bureaucratic decision makers seem less inclined to protect aggressively either the fish or the water quality. Instead, control of water pollution in streams is typically left up to environmental regulators. England, however, has demonstrated what seems to be a more sure and far less expen-

---

[6]This section is based on Jane S. Shaw and Richard L. Stroup, "Gone Fishin'," *Reason* 20, no. 4 (August 1988): 34–37.

sive way—private ownership of fishing rights—to protect waters that are valuable for fishing.

GOVERNMENT REGULATION AND THE ENVIRONMENT

Substantial contributions to environmental quality are made through the normal operation of property rights and a market system. However, it is sometimes difficult—if not impossible—to define, establish, and protect property rights. When pollution is local—when it exerts a significant impact on only a few people—the property rights approach can deal effectively with the problem. Most pollutants capable of doing proven and serious damage are of this sort. But this is not always the case. If the effects of an emitted substance are both serious and widespread over a large population, or if the substance has many sources, then government regulation may be more efficient.

Government regulation is an alternative method of seeking to protect and preserve the quality of the environment. Regulation, however, seldom leads to ideal outcomes, and it can be enormously expensive. The Environmental Protection Agency has estimated that environmental regulation in the United States costs about $150 billion per year. Regulation is seldom based on market signals, and so it is subject to all the problems caused by lack of information and lack of incentives that have plagued the socialist nations. It can be very wasteful.[7] Scientific uncertainty is often great in cases where regulation is demanded, and the stakes can be very high.

Consider the issue of global warming. Emissions of carbon dioxide from the efficient burning of all fuels cause no harm where they are emitted. No one's rights are being violated by the invasion of a harmful pollutant. Yet these emissions have been building up in the atmosphere. They may in the future require regulation if the buildup acts as an invisible blanket and causes the earth to warm, as some scientists claim. Such warming could change weather patterns, making hurricanes and other storms more intense, and might even result in rising sea levels around the globe. If the "worst-case scenarios" suggested by scientists were to materialize, some communities would face flooding of their lands, serious ecological disruptions, and other problems.

Some scientists and many environmental groups argue that the threat of global warming is so serious that despite high costs, the nations of the world must impose strong regulations quickly. Government limits of some sort, they point out, are the only way that carbon dioxide emissions can be controlled. Other scientists, and many policy analysts, believe that imposing strong regulation at this time would be a mistake. They point out that the science of global warming is filled with uncertainties. For example:

1. ***We do not know whether changes in the earth's cloud cover will do more to enhance the warming effects of carbon dioxide or to offset them.*** Water vapor and clouds in the atmosphere account for more than 98 percent of the total warming we now experience. Yet certain kinds of clouds reflect enough of the sun's energy that they reduce warming. So even small changes in where water resides in the atmosphere, and the form it takes, could easily overcome the impact of the buildup in carbon dioxide. All scientists agree that the atmospheric models used to predict global warming do not accurately incorporate the effects of atmospheric water vapor, although gradual improvements in the models are being made.

---

[7]For a more thorough explanation of why environmental regulation is often inefficient, and some quantitative estimates of how costly it is, see Robert Crandall, *Why Is the Cost of Environmental Regulation So High?* Policy Study No. 110 (St. Louis: Center for the Study of American Business, February 1992).

2. ***It is true that in the past, over thousands of years, added carbon dioxide has been associated with warming. But does this association mean that the carbon dioxide caused the warming?*** Studies of ice cores drilled deep into Antarctica and Greenland allow scientists to measure the levels of carbon dioxide in the atmosphere during earlier years. The evidence indicates that the warming often preceded, rather than followed, the buildup of carbon dioxide. In such cases, how could the buildup cause the warming, when the warming came first?
3. ***If warming does occur, will sea levels rise or fall?*** Warming would cause glaciers and ice caps to melt and shrink at the edges. However, warmer air carries more moisture, and the added precipitation would build up snow and ice in the still-frigid centers of the polar ice caps, increasing their thickness. Whether the net effect on the sea level would be positive or negative is unknown. Scientific experts disagree on the question.

These questions and many more are in dispute. We cannot even be sure whether the buildup and a warmer world would, on balance, be better or worse. Some people—particularly those distant from the equator—would gain from a warmer, wetter world. Also, the direct effects of added carbon dioxide are helpful to plants. Owners of greenhouses routinely purchase carbon dioxide to enrich the enclosed atmosphere and enhance plant growth. But certain diseases might also increase in a warmer world, although economist Thomas Gale Moore has shown that warmer climates are generally more healthy on balance.[8]

The cost of such policies is another consideration. One large study estimates that in the United States alone, the cost of merely stabilizing emissions at their current levels, with no net reduction, would be $95 billion in the first year, with larger costs after that. These estimated costs and the scientific uncertainties combine to make many economists unwilling to endorse strong regulations to force reductions in the emissions of carbon dioxide. As economist William Nordhaus suggested in an article about global warming, "The best investment today may be in learning about climatic change, rather than in preventing it."[9]

In sum, environmental regulation is a powerful tool, capable of providing important improvements in environmental quality, but it tends to be very costly, and its unintended consequences can be serious. The results of regulations banning DDT proved that point, as we described earlier, especially in the tragic case of Sri Lanka.

Policy makers and analysts considering environmental regulations should recognize that environmental quality is an economic good. Like food, clothing, and shelter, it is something that people are willing to pay for, though not in unlimited amounts. In addition, policy makers should recognize that the linkage between environmental quality and economic prosperity is important. Environmental regulations can exert a powerful influence, for ill as well as for good. Finally, policy makers should not forget that enforceable property rights were for many years our main form of regulating environmental pollution and allowing farsighted individuals and groups to exercise their visions of preserved natural areas. Overall, property rights continue to play a positive role in the preservation of a quality environment.

---

[8] Thomas Gale Moore, *Climate of Fear* (Washington, D.C.: Cato Institute, 1998).

[9] William Nordhaus, "Global Warming: Slowing the Greenhouse Express," in *Setting National Priorities: Policies for the Nineties,* ed. Henry J. Aaron (Washington, D.C.: The Brookings Institution, 1990), p. 207.

KEY POINTS

➤ Even though environmental decisions are often made outside a market context, the basic principles of economics still apply. Purposeful choices, influenced by prices (or their absence) and other incentives, are made without full knowledge. Values are subjective, and the secondary effects of decisions are often important.

➤ Environmental quality and economic growth tend to go together. The demand for environmental quality is positively and strongly linked to income levels.

➤ Market prices provide potential users with an incentive to conserve on their use of resources. The technological improvements spurred by market competition enhance economic growth, reduce resource waste, and enhance our ability to control pollution.

➤ When enforceable property rights cannot be put into place, government regulation is an alternative mechanism that can promote wise use of resources and the environment. However, regulatory choices are not based on information and incentives from market prices. Thus, regulation has the same potential for inefficiency and ineffectiveness faced by the socialist governments whose citizens have suffered many environmental harms.

CRITICAL ANALYSIS QUESTIONS

1. "People want clean air and clean water in their rivers, but they cannot buy them in a market. Government regulation is the only way to provide them." Evaluate this statement.

*2. Is it possible to be "too safe" when it comes to risks from chemicals, such as pesticides that might find their way into food? Why or why not? Explain.

3. Are rich people or poor people more likely to call for tighter environmental laws? Why? What does this imply about the effects of economic growth on environmental quality?

*4. "The buildup of carbon dioxide and other gases in the atmosphere threatens to warm the planet and cause enormous damage worldwide. We must immediately stop this buildup, for the sake of our grandchildren and all future generations." Why do many economists disagree with this statement? Does that indicate that these economists care less for future generations than other commentators who call for an immediate stop to the buildup? Explain.

5. Is environmental quality a good like all others? Or is it instead something that most people put before all other wants?

*6. "Unlike in a marketplace, where pollution is profitable, government control of resources and pollution can take into account the desires of all the people." What does economic thinking have to say about this statement?

7. During the last 200 years, the American buffalo has become virtually extinct. In contrast, the cattle population is now several times larger than was true 200 years ago. Why has the population of cattle grown, while that of the buffalo has fallen substantially?

*Asterisk denotes questions for which answers are given in Appendix B.

APPENDIX A

General Business and Economic Indicators

SECTION 1

GROSS DOMESTIC PRODUCT AND ITS COMPONENTS

Year	Personal Consumption Expenditures	Gross Private Domestic Investment	Government Consumption and Gross Investment	Net Exports	Gross Domestic Product (GDP)
1959	318.1	78.8	112.0	−1.7	507.2
1960	332.2	78.8	113.2	2.4	526.6
1961	342.6	77.9	120.9	3.4	544.8
1962	363.4	87.9	131.4	2.4	585.2
1963	383.0	93.4	137.7	3.3	617.4
1964	411.4	101.7	144.4	5.5	663.0
1965	444.3	118.0	153.0	3.9	719.1
1966	481.9	130.4	173.6	1.9	787.8
1967	509.5	128.0	194.6	1.4	833.6
1968	559.8	139.9	212.1	−1.3	910.6
1969	604.7	155.0	223.8	−1.2	982.2
1970	648.1	150.2	236.1	1.2	1,035.6
1971	702.5	176.0	249.9	−3.0	1,125.4
1972	770.7	205.6	268.9	−8.0	1,237.3
1973	851.6	242.9	287.6	0.6	1,382.6
1974	931.2	245.6	323.2	−3.1	1,496.9
1975	1,029.1	225.4	362.6	13.6	1,630.6
1976	1,148.8	286.6	385.9	−2.3	1,819.0
1977	1,277.1	356.6	416.9	−23.7	2,026.9
1978	1,428.8	430.8	457.9	−26.1	2,291.4
1979	1,593.5	480.9	507.1	−24.0	2,557.5
1980	1,760.4	465.9	572.8	−14.9	2,784.2
1981	1,941.3	556.2	633.4	−15.0	3,115.9
1982	2,076.8	501.1	684.8	−20.5	3,242.1
1983	2,283.4	547.1	735.7	−51.7	3,514.5
1984	2,492.3	715.6	796.6	−102.0	3,902.4
1985	2,704.8	715.1	875.0	−114.2	4,180.7
1986	2,892.7	722.5	938.5	−131.5	4,422.2
1987	3,094.5	747.2	992.8	−142.1	4,692.3
1988	3,349.7	773.9	1,032.0	−106.1	5,049.6
1989	3,594.8	829.2	1,095.1	−80.4	5,438.7
1990	3,839.3	799.7	1,176.1	−71.3	5,743.8
1991	3,975.1	736.2	1,225.9	−20.5	5,916.7
1992	4,219.8	790.4	1,263.8	−29.5	6,244.4
1993	4,459.2	876.2	1,283.4	−60.7	6,558.1
1994	4,717.0	1,007.9	1,313.0	−90.9	6,947.0
1995	4,953.9	1,043.2	1,356.4	−83.9	7,269.6
1996	5,215.7	1,131.9	1,405.2	−91.2	7,661.6
1997	5,493.7	1,256.0	1,454.6	−93.4	8,110.9
1998	5,805.6	1,368.7	1,487.5	−151.2	8,510.7

NOTE: These figures are in billions of current dollars.

SOURCES: Economic Report of the President, *1999, Table B-1; and* Survey of Current Business, *March 1999, Table 1.1.*

SECTION 1 (continued)

REAL GROSS DOMESTIC PRODUCT

Real Gross Domestic Product, 1959–1998

Year	1992 Prices (Billions of Dollars)	Annual Real Rate of Growth	Real GDP per Capita (1992 Dollars)
1959	2,210.2	7.4	12,478
1960	2,262.9	2.4	12,519
1961	2,314.3	2.3	12,595
1962	2,454.8	6.1	13,156
1963	2,559.4	4.3	13,520
1964	2,708.4	5.8	14,112
1965	2,881.1	6.4	14,825
1966	3,069.2	6.5	15,612
1967	3,147.2	2.5	15,835
1968	3,293.9	4.7	16,408
1969	3,393.6	3.0	16,739
1970	3,397.6	0.1	16,566
1971	3,510.0	3.3	16,900
1972	3,702.3	5.5	17,637
1973	3,916.3	5.8	18,479
1974	3,891.2	−0.6	18,192
1975	3,873.9	−0.4	17,936
1976	4,082.9	5.4	18,721
1977	4,273.6	4.7	19,400
1978	4,503.0	5.4	20,226
1979	4,630.6	2.8	20,571
1980	4,615.0	−0.3	20,265
1981	4,720.7	2.3	20,524
1982	4,620.3	−2.1	19,896
1983	4,803.7	4.0	20,499
1984	5,140.1	7.0	21,744
1985	5,323.5	3.6	22,320
1986	5,487.7	3.1	22,801
1987	5,649.5	2.9	23,264
1988	5,865.2	3.8	23,934
1989	6,062.0	3.4	24,504
1990	6,136.3	1.2	24,549
1991	6,079.4	−0.9	24,060
1992	6,244.4	2.7	24,447
1993	6,389.6	2.3	24,750
1994	6,610.7	3.5	25,357
1995	6,761.7	2.3	25,691
1996	6,994.8	3.4	26,338
1997	7,269.8	3.9	27,138
1998	7,552.1	3.9	28,012

SOURCES: Economic Report of the President, *1999, Table B-1; and* Survey of Current Business, *March 1999, Table 1.2.*

SECTION 2

PRICES AND INFLATION

PRICE INDEXES: 1959–1998

	GDP DEFLATOR		CONSUMER PRICE INDEX	
YEAR	INDEX (1992 = 100)	ANNUAL PERCENTAGE CHANGE	INDEX (1982–84 = 100)	PERCENTAGE CHANGE (DEC. TO DEC.)
1959	23.0	1.0	29.1	1.7
1960	23.3	1.4	29.6	1.4
1961	23.5	1.2	29.9	0.7
1962	23.8	1.3	30.2	1.3
1963	24.1	1.2	30.6	1.6
1964	24.5	1.5	31.0	1.0
1965	25.0	2.0	31.5	1.9
1966	25.7	2.8	32.4	3.5
1967	26.5	3.2	33.4	3.0
1968	27.6	4.4	34.8	4.7
1969	28.9	4.7	36.7	6.2
1970	30.5	5.3	38.8	5.6
1971	32.1	5.2	40.5	3.3
1972	33.4	4.2	41.8	3.4
1973	35.3	5.6	44.4	8.7
1974	38.5	9.0	49.3	12.3
1975	42.1	9.4	53.8	6.9
1976	44.6	5.8	56.9	4.9
1977	47.4	6.5	60.6	6.7
1978	50.9	7.3	65.2	9.0
1979	55.2	8.5	72.6	13.3
1980	60.3	9.2	82.4	12.5
1981	66.0	9.4	90.9	8.9
1982	70.2	6.3	96.5	3.8
1983	73.2	4.3	99.6	3.8
1984	75.9	3.8	103.9	3.9
1985	78.5	3.4	107.6	3.8
1986	80.6	2.6	109.6	1.1
1987	83.1	3.1	113.6	4.4
1988	86.1	3.7	118.3	4.4
1989	89.7	4.2	124.0	4.6
1990	93.6	4.3	130.7	6.1
1991	97.3	4.0	136.2	3.1
1992	100.0	2.8	140.3	2.9
1993	102.6	2.6	144.5	2.7
1994	105.1	2.4	148.2	2.7
1995	107.5	2.3	152.4	2.5
1996	109.5	1.9	156.9	3.3
1997	111.6	1.9	160.5	1.7
1998	112.7	1.0	163.0	1.6

SOURCES: Economic Report of the President, *1999, Tables B-3, B-60, and B-63; and* Survey of Current Business, *March 1999, Table 7.1.*

SECTION 3

POPULATION AND EMPLOYMENT

Population and Labor Force

Year	Civilian Noninstitutional Population Age 16+ (Millions)	Civilian Labor Force (Millions)	Civilian Labor Force Participation Rate (Percent)	Civilian Employment/ Population Ratio (Percent)
1959	115.3	68.4	59.3	56.0
1960	117.2	69.6	59.4	56.1
1961	118.8	70.5	59.3	55.4
1962	120.2	70.6	58.8	55.5
1963	122.4	71.8	58.7	55.4
1964	124.5	73.1	58.7	55.7
1965	126.5	74.5	58.9	56.2
1966	128.1	75.8	59.2	56.9
1967	129.9	77.3	59.6	57.3
1968	132.0	78.7	59.6	57.5
1969	134.3	80.7	60.1	58.0
1970	137.1	82.8	60.4	57.4
1971	140.2	84.4	60.2	56.6
1972	144.1	87.0	60.4	57.0
1973	147.1	89.4	60.8	57.8
1974	150.1	91.9	61.3	57.8
1975	153.2	93.8	61.2	56.1
1976	156.2	96.2	61.6	56.8
1977	159.0	99.0	62.3	57.9
1978	161.9	102.3	63.2	59.3
1979	164.9	105.0	63.7	59.9
1980	167.7	106.9	63.8	59.2
1981	170.1	108.7	63.9	59.0
1982	172.3	110.2	64.0	57.8
1983	174.2	111.6	64.0	57.9
1984	176.4	113.5	64.4	59.5
1985	178.2	115.5	64.8	60.1
1986	180.6	117.8	65.3	60.7
1987	182.8	119.9	65.6	61.5
1988	184.6	121.7	65.9	62.3
1989	186.4	123.9	66.5	63.0
1990	189.2	125.8	66.5	62.8
1991	190.9	126.3	66.2	61.7
1992	192.8	128.1	66.4	61.5
1993	194.8	129.2	66.3	61.7
1994	196.8	131.1	66.6	62.5
1995	198.6	132.3	66.6	62.9
1996	200.6	133.9	66.8	63.2
1997	203.1	136.3	67.1	63.8
1998	205.2	137.7	67.1	64.1

SOURCE: Economic Report of the President, *1999, Table B-35.*

SECTION 3 (continued)

POPULATION AND EMPLOYMENT

	Unemployment Rates			
Year	All Workers	Both Sexes, Age 16 to 19	Men Age 20+	Women Age 20+
1959	5.5	14.6	4.7	5.2
1960	5.5	14.7	4.7	5.1
1961	6.7	16.8	5.7	6.3
1962	5.5	14.7	4.6	5.4
1963	5.7	17.2	4.5	5.4
1964	5.2	16.2	3.9	5.2
1965	4.5	14.8	3.2	4.5
1966	3.8	12.8	2.5	3.8
1967	3.8	12.9	2.3	4.2
1968	3.6	12.7	2.2	3.8
1969	3.5	12.2	2.1	3.7
1970	4.9	15.3	3.5	4.8
1971	5.9	16.9	4.4	5.7
1972	5.6	16.2	4.0	5.4
1973	4.9	14.5	3.3	4.9
1974	5.6	16.0	3.8	5.5
1975	8.5	19.9	6.8	8.0
1976	7.7	19.0	5.9	7.4
1977	7.1	17.8	5.2	7.0
1978	6.1	16.4	4.3	6.0
1979	5.8	16.1	4.2	5.7
1980	7.1	17.8	5.9	6.4
1981	7.6	19.6	6.3	6.8
1982	9.7	23.2	8.8	8.3
1983	9.6	22.4	8.9	8.1
1984	7.5	18.9	6.6	6.8
1985	7.2	18.6	6.2	6.6
1986	7.0	18.3	6.1	6.2
1987	6.2	16.9	5.4	5.4
1988	5.5	15.3	4.8	4.9
1989	5.3	15.0	4.5	4.7
1990	5.6	15.5	5.0	4.9
1991	6.8	18.7	6.4	5.7
1992	7.5	20.1	7.1	6.3
1993	6.9	19.0	6.4	5.9
1994	6.1	17.6	5.4	5.4
1995	5.6	17.3	4.8	4.9
1996	5.4	16.7	4.6	4.8
1997	4.9	16.0	4.2	4.4
1998	4.5	14.6	3.7	4.1

SOURCE: Economic Report of the President, *1999, Tables B-35 and B-42.*

SECTION 4

MONEY SUPPLY, INTEREST RATES, AND FEDERAL FINANCES

	Money Supply Data				Interest Rate
Year	Money Supply M1 (Billions)	Annual Change in M1	Money Supply M2 (Billions)	Annual Change in M2	AAA Corporate Bonds
1959	140.0	—	297.8	—	4.38
1960	140.7	0.5	312.4	4.9	4.41
1961	145.2	3.2	335.5	7.4	4.35
1962	147.8	1.8	362.7	8.1	4.33
1963	153.3	3.7	393.2	8.4	4.26
1964	160.3	4.6	424.7	8.0	4.40
1965	167.8	4.7	459.2	8.1	4.49
1966	172.0	2.5	480.2	4.6	5.13
1967	183.3	6.6	524.8	9.3	5.51
1968	197.4	7.7	566.8	8.0	6.18
1969	203.9	3.3	587.9	3.7	7.03
1970	214.4	5.1	626.5	6.6	8.04
1971	228.3	6.5	710.3	13.4	7.39
1972	249.2	9.2	802.3	13.0	7.21
1973	262.9	5.5	855.5	6.6	7.44
1974	274.2	4.3	902.4	5.5	8.57
1975	287.4	4.8	1,017.0	12.7	8.83
1976	306.4	6.6	1,152.8	13.4	8.43
1977	331.3	8.1	1,271.5	10.3	8.02
1978	358.4	8.2	1,368.0	7.6	8.73
1979	382.9	6.8	1,475.8	7.9	9.63
1980	408.9	6.8	1,601.1	8.5	11.94
1981	436.8	6.8	1,756.2	9.7	14.17
1982	474.7	8.7	1,910.9	8.8	13.79
1983	521.2	9.8	2,127.7	11.3	12.04
1984	552.3	6.0	2,312.3	8.7	12.71
1985	619.9	12.2	2,497.7	8.0	11.37
1986	724.4	16.9	2,734.0	9.5	9.02
1987	749.7	3.5	2,832.7	3.6	9.38
1988	787.0	5.0	2,996.4	5.8	9.71
1989	794.2	0.9	3,161.0	5.5	9.26
1990	825.8	4.0	3,279.6	3.8	9.32
1991	897.3	8.7	3,379.9	3.1	8.77
1992	1,025.0	14.2	3,434.7	1.6	8.14
1993	1,129.9	10.2	3,487.5	1.5	7.22
1994	1,150.7	1.8	3,503.0	0.4	7.96
1995	1,128.7	−1.9	3,651.2	4.2	7.59
1996	1,082.8	−4.1	3,826.1	4.8	7.37
1997	1,076.0	−0.6	4,046.4	5.8	7.26
1998	1,092.3	1.5	4,412.3	9.0	6.53

SOURCE: Economic Report of the President, *1999, Tables B-69 and B-73.*

SECTION 4 (continued)

MONEY SUPPLY, INTEREST RATES, AND FEDERAL FINANCES

	Federal Budget Totals (Billions of Dollars)			National Debt	
Year	Fiscal Year Outlays	Fiscal Year Receipts	Surplus (+) or Deficit (−)	Billions of Dollars	As a Percent of GDP
1959	92.1	79.2	−12.8	287.5	58.5
1960	92.2	92.5	0.3	290.5	56.1
1961	97.7	94.4	−3.3	292.6	55.1
1962	106.8	99.7	−7.1	302.9	53.4
1963	111.3	106.6	−4.8	310.3	51.9
1964	118.5	112.6	−5.9	316.1	49.4
1965	118.2	116.8	−1.4	322.3	46.9
1966	134.5	130.8	−3.7	328.5	43.6
1967	157.5	148.8	−8.6	340.4	41.9
1968	178.1	153.0	−25.2	368.7	42.5
1969	183.6	186.9	3.2	365.8	38.6
1970	195.6	192.8	−2.8	380.9	37.8
1971	210.2	187.1	−23.0	408.2	37.9
1972	230.7	207.3	−23.4	435.9	37.0
1973	245.7	230.8	−14.9	466.3	35.7
1974	269.4	263.2	−6.1	483.9	33.6
1975	332.3	279.1	−53.2	541.9	34.9
1976	371.8	298.1	−73.7	629.0	36.3
1977	409.2	355.6	−53.7	706.4	35.8
1978	458.7	399.6	−59.2	776.6	35.1
1979	504.0	463.3	−40.7	829.5	33.2
1980	590.9	517.1	−73.8	909.1	33.4
1981	678.2	599.3	−79.0	994.8	32.6
1982	745.8	617.8	−128.0	1,137.3	35.4
1983	808.4	600.6	−207.8	1,371.7	40.1
1984	851.9	666.5	−185.4	1,564.7	41.0
1985	946.4	734.1	−212.3	1,817.5	44.3
1986	990.5	769.2	−221.2	2,120.6	48.5
1987	1,004.1	854.4	−149.8	2,346.1	50.9
1988	1,064.5	909.3	−155.2	2,601.3	52.5
1989	1,143.7	991.2	−152.5	2,868.0	53.6
1990	1,253.2	1,032.0	−221.2	3,206.6	56.4
1991	1,324.4	1,055.0	−269.4	3,598.5	61.4
1992	1,381.7	1,091.3	−290.4	4,002.1	65.1
1993	1,409.4	1,154.4	−255.0	4,351.4	67.2
1994	1,461.7	1,258.6	−203.1	4,643.7	67.8
1995	1,515.7	1,351.8	−163.9	4,921.0	68.4
1996	1,560.5	1,453.1	−107.5	5,181.9	68.6
1997	1,601.2	1,579.3	−21.9	5,369.7	67.2
1998	1,652.6	1,721.8	69.2	5,478.7	65.2

SOURCE: Economic Report of the President, *1999, Tables B-78 and B-79.*

SECTION 5

SIZE OF GOVERNMENT AS A SHARE OF GDP, 1959–1998

YEAR	FEDERAL, STATE, AND LOCAL GOVERNMENT: EXPENDITURES (% OF GDP)	REVENUES (% OF GDP)	PURCHASES OF GOODS AND SERVICES (% OF GDP)	NON-DEFENSE PURCHASES OF GOODS AND SERVICES (% OF GDP)	TRANSFER PAYMENTS TO PERSONS (% OF GDP)
1959	23.0	25.4	22.1	11.1	5.4
1960	23.1	26.4	21.5	11.1	5.6
1961	24.0	26.5	22.2	11.6	6.2
1962	24.1	26.6	22.5	11.8	5.9
1963	24.1	27.1	22.3	12.2	5.9
1964	23.7	26.1	21.8	12.5	5.7
1965	23.4	26.0	21.3	12.7	5.7
1966	24.2	26.7	22.0	12.7	5.8
1967	26.1	27.2	23.3	13.1	6.5
1968	26.8	28.7	23.3	13.2	6.9
1969	26.9	29.9	22.8	13.4	7.1
1970	28.3	28.9	22.8	14.0	8.1
1971	28.7	28.4	22.2	14.3	8.8
1972	28.5	29.5	21.7	14.2	9.0
1973	28.0	29.6	20.8	14.0	9.2
1974	29.3	30.2	21.6	14.8	10.1
1975	31.6	28.7	22.2	15.4	11.6
1976	30.6	29.5	21.2	14.8	11.4
1977	29.9	29.8	20.6	14.4	10.9
1978	28.7	29.6	20.0	14.1	10.4
1979	28.4	29.8	19.8	13.9	10.4
1980	30.2	30.0	20.6	14.3	11.4
1981	30.6	30.6	20.3	13.8	11.6
1982	32.5	30.0	21.1	14.0	12.4
1983	32.4	29.3	20.9	13.7	12.4
1984	31.1	29.3	20.4	13.2	11.5
1985	31.4	29.7	20.9	13.5	11.5
1986	31.6	29.7	21.2	13.7	11.6
1987	31.4	30.5	21.2	13.7	11.4
1988	30.7	30.0	20.4	13.4	11.3
1989	30.5	30.2	20.1	13.5	11.3
1990	31.4	30.1	20.5	14.0	11.8
1991	32.1	30.1	20.7	14.2	12.2
1992	33.1	30.0	20.2	14.2	13.6
1993	32.7	30.2	19.6	14.1	13.8
1994	31.9	30.6	18.9	13.9	13.6
1995	31.8	30.9	18.7	13.9	13.8
1996	31.3	31.5	18.3	13.8	13.8
1997	30.5	31.9	17.9	13.7	13.5
1998	29.8	32.5	17.5	13.5	13.3

SOURCES: Calculated from Economic Report of the President, *1999, Tables B-1, B-83, and B-84, and* Survey of Current Business, *March 1999, Tables 1.1 and 3.7.*

SECTION 6

BASIC ECONOMIC DATA FOR 58 COUNTRIES

	Population 1997 (Millions)	Real GNP per Capita 1997 (in 1997 Dollars)	Average Annual Growth Rate of Real GDP 1990–1997	Annual Growth Rate of Money Supply 1980–1996	Average Annual Inflation Rate 1980–1996	Gross Investment as a Share of GDP 1990–1997[1]
High-Income Countries						
Australia	19	20,170	3.7	12.0	6.0	20.8
Austria	8	21,980	1.6	6.9	3.3	23.3
Belgium	10	22,370	1.2	9.7	3.7	18.3
Canada	30	21,860	2.1	8.1	4.5	18.7
Denmark	5	22,740	2.3	8.5	4.4	19.0
Finland	5	18,980	1.1	8.7	4.9	18.1
France	59	21,860	1.3	6.1	4.7	18.9
Germany	82	21,300	2.5	6.8	2.8	22.9
Hong Kong	7	24,540	5.3	15.7	7.7	30.6
Italy	57	20,060	1.1	8.6	7.8	18.5
Japan	126	23,400	1.4	6.4	1.7	30.1
Netherlands	16	21,340	2.3	5.6	2.5	20.4
Singapore	3	29,000	8.5	12.9	2.3	34.9
Spain	39	15,720	1.6	10.2	7.6	21.9
Sweden	9	19,030	0.9	6.3	6.1	15.9
Switzerland	7	26,320	−0.1	6.6	3.2	22.5
United Kingdom	59	20,520	1.9	16.0	5.3	16.1
United States	268	28,740	2.5	6.3	4.1	16.5
Africa						
Botswana	2	8,220	5.2	17.6	11.2	27.8
Cameroon	14	1,980	0.1	3.6	7.9	—
Côte d'Ivoire	15	1,640	3.0	6.0	6.3	10.8
Ghana	18	1,790	4.3	40.4	37.8	14.0
Kenya	28	1,110	2.0	18.3	15.3	20.1
Mauritius	1	9,360	5.1	18.5	7.7	28.9
Nigeria	118	880	2.7	22.8	29.6	9.5
South Africa	38	7,490	1.5	14.9	13.1	17.1
Tanzania	31	685	2.9	27.2	29.0	22.5
Zambia	9	890	−0.5	51.9	155.0	23.6
Asia and Pacific						
Bangladesh	124	1,050	4.5	16.9	8.1	14.2
China	1227	3,570	11.9	27.0	10.1	38.5
India	961	1,650	5.9	17.0	9.4	24.3
Indonesia	200	3,450	7.5	25.1	8.8	32.8
Malaysia	21	10,920	8.7	14.8	3.6	38.5
Pakistan	137	1,590	4.4	15.5	8.5	19.2
Philippines	73	3,670	3.3	18.8	12.5	23.1
South Korea	46	13,500	7.2	18.1	6.2	36.8
Taiwan	22	13,150	6.4	15.9	4.4	22.4
Thailand	61	6,590	7.5	18.3	4.6	40.3

SECTION 6 (continued)

BASIC ECONOMIC DATA FOR 58 COUNTRIES

	Population 1997 (Millions)	Real GNP per Capita 1997 (in 1997 Dollars)	Average Annual Growth Rate of Real GDP 1990–1997	Annual Growth Rate of Money Supply 1980–1996	Average Annual Inflation Rate 1980–1996	Gross Investment as a Share of GDP 1990–1997[1]
South/Central America						
Argentina	36	9,950	4.5	207.7	194.6	17.0
Brazil	164	6,240	3.1	431.3	399.5	21.7
Chile	15	12,080	7.2	26.5	17.3	25.2
Colombia	38	6,720	4.5	29.5	23.8	19.7
Dominican Republic	8	4,540	5.0	25.9	19.1	25.0
Guatemala	11	3,840	4.1	18.1	14.2	14.9
Mexico	95	8,120	1.8	47.8	46.1	22.7
Peru	25	4,390	6.0	191.3	228.7	20.2
Venezuela	23	8,530	1.9	29.7	33.4	17.2
Middle East/Mediterranean						
Egypt	60	2,940	3.9	19.5	15.3	21.5
Greece	11	13,080	1.8	18.4	16.7	20.5
Iran	61	5,530	6.0	21.9	22.0	26.7
Israel	6	16,960	6.4	34.9	54.2	23.6
Syria	15	2,990	6.9	17.9	17.5	23.1
Turkey	64	6,430	3.6	71.8	57.4	23.8
Eastern Europe						
Bulgaria	8	3,860	−3.5	—	—	16.7
Hungary	10	7,000	−0.4	14.0	15.8	22.7
Poland	39	6,380	3.9	53.0	57.5	19.1
Romania	23	4,290	0.0	36.1	—	27.1
Russia	147	4,190	−9.0	83.4[2]	288.3[2]	26.5

[1]*When the most recent data were unavailable, investment figures from one to two years before 1990 were used to derive an eight-year average. In the case of Russia, only 1992–97 data were available.*
[2]*Derived on the basis of 1993–97 data only.*

SOURCES: World Bank, World Development Report, *1998/99; International Monetary Fund,* International Financial Statistics Yearbook, *1998;* and Statistical Yearbook of the Republic of China, *1998.*

APPENDIX B

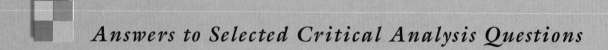

Answers to Selected Critical Analysis Questions

CHAPTER 1 The Economic Approach

2. Production of scarce goods always involves a cost; there are no free lunches. When the government provides goods without charge to consumers, other citizens (taxpayers) will bear the cost of their provision. Thus, provision by the government affects how the costs will be covered, not whether they are incurred.
4. For most taxpayers, the change will reduce the after-tax cost of raising children. Other things constant, one would predict an increase in the birth rate.
5. False. Intentions do not change the impact of the policy. If the policy runs counter to sound economics, it will lead to a counterproductive outcome even if that was not the intention of the policy. Bad policies are often advocated by people with good intentions.
7. Raising the price of new cars by requiring safety devices, which customers would not have purchased if given the choice, slows the rate of sales for new cars. Thus the older, less safe cars are driven longer, partially offsetting the safety advantage provided by the newer, safer cars. Also, drivers act a bit differently—they may take more risks—when they believe the safety devices will provide protection should they have an unexpected accident. In fact, economist Gordon Tullock says that the greatest safety device of all might be a dagger built into the center of the steering wheel, pointed directly at the driver's chest!
8. Money has nothing to do with whether an individual is economizing. Any time a person chooses, in an attempt to achieve a goal, he or she is economizing.
9. Positive economics can help one better understand the likely effects of alternative policies. This will help one choose alternatives that are less likely to lead to disappointing results.
10. Association is not causation. It is likely that a large lead, near the end of the game, caused the third team to play more, rather than the third team causing the lead.

CHAPTER 2 Some Tools of the Economist

2. This is an opportunity cost question. Even though the productivity of painters has changed only slightly, rising productivity in other areas has led to higher wages in other occupations, thereby increasing the opportunity cost of being a house painter. Since people would not supply house painting services unless they were able to meet their opportunity costs, higher wages are necessary to attract house painters from competitive (alternative) lines of work.
4. The statement reflects the "exchange is a zero sum game" view. This view is false. No private business can force customers to buy. Neither can a customer force a business to sell. Unless both buyer and seller believe the exchange is in their interest, they will not enter into the exchange. Mutual gain provides the foundation for voluntary exchange.
8. Yes. This question highlights the incentive of individuals to conserve for the future when they have private ownership rights. The market value of the land will increase in anticipation of the future harvest, as the trees grow and the expected day of harvest moves closer. Thus, with transferable private property, the tree farmer will be able to capture the value added by his planting and holding the trees for a few years, even if the actual harvest does not take place until well after his death.
9. In general, it sanctions all forms of competition except for the use of violence (or the threat of violence), theft, or fraud.
11. If the food from land, now and in the future, is worth more than the housing services from the same land, then developers will not be able to bid the land away

from farmers. However, comparative advantage determines the efficient use of a resource; thus, even the best farmland, if situated in the right location, may be far more valuable for buildings. Other, poorer land can always be made more productive by the use of different (and more costly) farming techniques, irrigation, fertilizer, and so on. Physical characteristics alone do not determine the value or the most valuable use of a resource, including land.

12. Those who get tickets at the lower price gain, while those who are prevented from offering a higher price to ticket holders may not get a ticket even though both the buyer and some ticket holders would have gained from the exchange at the higher price. Ticket holders may simply break the law, or may sell at the regulated price only to buyers willing to provide them with other favors. Price controls, if they are effective, always reduce the gains from trade.

CHAPTER 3 Supply, Demand, and the Market Process

1. Choices a and b would increase the demand for beef; c and d would affect primarily the supply of beef, rather than the demand; e leads to a change in quantity demanded, not a change in demand.
4. a. Reductions in the supply of feed grains and hay led to sharply higher prices. b. The higher feed grain and hay prices increased the cost of maintaining a cattle herd and thereby caused many producers to sell (an increase in current supply), depressing cattle prices in 1998. c. The reduction in the size of cattle herds led to a smaller future supply and higher cattle prices in 1989.
8. True. "Somebody" must decide who will be the business winners and losers. Neither markets nor the political process leaves the determination of winners and losers to chance. Under market organization, business winners and losers are determined by the decentralized choices of millions of consumers who use their dollar votes to reward firms that provide preferred goods at a low cost and penalize others who fail to do so. Under political decision making, the winners and losers are determined by political officials who use taxes, subsidies, regulations, and mandates to favor some businesses and penalize others.
10. a. Profitable production increases the value of resources owned by people and leads to mutual gain for resource suppliers, consumers, and entrepreneurs. b. Losses reduce the value of resources, which reduces the well-being of at least some people. There is no conflict.
12. In the absence of trade restrictions, modest price increases in France will attract wheat from other regions, minimizing the effects in the drought region and resulting in slightly higher prices worldwide.
15. a. Demand would increase, rising vertically by $3 per meal—the added per-meal cost previously paid separately. b. Both price and quantity will rise in response to the rise in demand.

CHAPTER 4 Supply and Demand: Applications and Extensions

4. Agreement of both buyer and seller is required for an exchange. Price ceilings push prices below equilibrium and thereby reduce the quantity sellers are willing to offer. Price floors push prices above equilibrium and thereby reduce the quantity consumers wish to buy. Both decrease the actual quantity traded in the market.
6. a. Decreases; b. Increases; c. Decreases; d. Increases.

11. The deadweight loss is the loss of the potential gains of buyers and sellers emanating from trades that are squeezed out by the tax. It is an excess burden because even though the exchanges that are squeezed out by the tax impose a cost on buyers and sellers, they do not generate tax revenue (since the trades do not take place).
14. The employment level of low-skill workers with large families would decline. Some would attempt to conceal the presence of their large family in order to get a job.

CHAPTER 5 The Economic Role of Government

1. When payment is not demanded for services, potential customers have a strong incentive to attempt a "free ride." However, when the number of nonpaying customers becomes such that the sales revenues of sellers are diminished (and in some cases eliminated), the sellers' incentive to supply the good is thereby reduced (or eliminated).
4. The anti-missile system is a public good for the residents of Washington, D.C. Strictly speaking, none of the other items is a public good since each could be provided to some consumers (paying customers, for example) without being provided to others.

CHAPTER 6 The Economics of Collective Decision Making

2. Corporate officers, while they surely care about the next few months and the profits during that time, care also about the value of the firm and its stock price. If the stock price rises sufficiently in the next few months—as it will if investors believe that current investments in future-oriented projects (planting new trees, for example) are sound—then the officers will find their jobs secure even if current profits do not look good. Rights to the profits from those (future) trees are saleable now in the form of the corporation's stock. There is no such mechanism to make the distant fruits of today's investments available to the political entrepreneurs who might otherwise fight for the future-oriented project. Only if the project appeals to today's voters, and they are willing to pay today for tomorrow's benefits, will the program be a political success. In any case, the wealth of the political entrepreneur is not directly enhanced by his or her successful fight for the project.
5. The invisible hand principle is present only when the self-interest of individuals is consistent with the general welfare. Both the special interest effect and the shortsightedness effect indicate that this will not always be the case, even when political choices are made democratically.
6. True. Since each individual computer customer both decides the issue (what computer, if any, will be purchased) and bears the consequences of a mistaken choice, each has a strong incentive to acquire information needed to make a wise choice. In contrast, each voter recognizes that one vote, even if mistaken, will not decide the congressional election. Thus, each has little incentive to search for information to make a better choice.
8. It is difficult for the voter to know what a candidate will do once elected, and the rationally ignorant voter is usually unwilling to spend the time and effort required to understand issues because the probability that any single vote will decide the issue is exceedingly small. Special interest voters, on the other hand, will know which candidate has promised them the most on their issue. Also, the candi-

date who is both competent and prepared to ignore special interests will have a hard time getting these facts to voters without financial support from special interest groups. Each voter has an incentive to be a "free rider" on the "good government" issue. Controlling government on behalf of society as a whole is a public good, requiring much private activity. Like other public goods, it tends to be underproduced.

10. No. The government is merely an alternative form of organization. Government organization does not permit us to escape either scarcity or competition. It merely affects the nature of the competition. Political competition (voting, lobbying, political contributions, taxes, and politically determined budgets) replaces market competition. Neither is there any reason to believe that government organization modifies the importance of personal self-interest.
11. When the welfare of a special interest group conflicts with that of a widely dispersed, unorganized majority, the legislative political process can reasonably be expected to work to the benefit of the special interest.

CHAPTER 7 Demand and Consumer Choice

1. Revenue will rise (fall) if students who enroll pay more (less) extra revenue than is lost due to lower enrollment. Revenue will remain the same if those who enroll pay just enough more to offset the loss from reduced enrollment. A price elasticity of 1.2 implies that raising tuition rates would reduce tuition revenue.
3. a. 0.21; 1.2. b. Substitutes; higher fuel oil prices lead to an increase in demand (and consumption) for insulation.
6. Water is usually cheaper than oil because its marginal utility at current consumption levels is less than that of oil. Since water is so abundant relative to oil, the benefit derived from an additional quart of water is less than the benefit from an additional quart of oil, even though the total utility from all units of water is far greater than the total utility from all units of oil. However, the price of a product will reflect marginal utility, not total utility.
7. Both income and time constrain our ability to consume. Since, in a wealthier society, time becomes more binding and income less binding, time-saving actions will be more common in a wealthier society. As we engage in time-saving actions (fast food, automatic appliances, air travel, and so on) in order to shift the time restraint outward, our lives become more hectic.
10. All three statements are true.
11. a. No. Even for things we like, we will experience diminishing returns. Eventually, the cost of additional units of pizza will exceed their benefits. b. Perfection in any activity is generally not worth the cost. For example, reading every page of this text three, four, or five times may improve your grade, but it may not be worth it. One function of a text is to structure the material (highlighted points, layout of graphs, and so on) so that the reader will be able to learn quickly (at a lower cost).
12. Carole.
13. False. Since the demand for agricultural products is generally inelastic, farm incomes may well increase. But the total utility of farm output reflects not only the sales revenues but also the consumer surplus. For the units produced, the utility is unchanged as the loss of consumer surplus by consumers is exactly offset by higher payments to farmers. However, both the payments to farmers and consumer surplus are lost for those units not produced. Therefore, the decline in production will reduce the total utility of farm output and the nation will be worse off as a result.

14. Deceit and dishonesty will be encouraged by methods of organization that increase the returns to such behavior. The returns to deceitful and dishonest claims will be inversely related to the ease with which they can be countered by rivals. Other things constant, the presence of rivals will tend to reduce deceitful behavior. Is a politician more or less likely to tell the truth when he or she regularly confronts rivals? Is a news medium more or less likely to be balanced and trustworthy when it faces rivals in the news business? Is a court witness more or less likely to tell the truth when there are other witnesses and cross-examination can be expected? Is a firm selling automobiles, cough drops, or hamburgers more or less likely to be honest when it faces competitors? Answers to such questions are obvious.

CHAPTER 8 Costs and the Supply of Goods

1. The economic profit of a firm is its total revenues minus the opportunity cost of all resources used in the production process. Accounting profit often excludes the opportunity cost of certain resources—particularly the equity capital of the firm and any labor services provided by an owner-manager. Zero economic profit means that the resources owned by the firm are earning their opportunity cost—that is, the rate of return is as high as the highest valued alternative forgone. Thus, the firm would not gain by pursuing other lines of business.
2. a. Sunk costs are irrelevant. b. There is an opportunity cost of one's house. c. Sunk costs should not affect one's current decision. d. There is an opportunity cost of public education even if it is provided free to the consumer.
7. At low output, the firm's plant (a fixed cost) is underutilized, implying a high average cost. As output rises toward the designed output level, average cost falls, but then rises as the designed or optimal output for that size plant is surpassed and the plant is fully utilized.
11. Because owners receive profits, clearly profit maximization is in their interest. Managers, if they are not owners, have no property right to profit and therefore no direct interest in profit maximization. Since a solid record of profitability tends to increase the market value (salary) of corporate managers, they do have an indirect incentive to pursue profits. However, corporate managers may also be interested in gaining power, having nice offices, hiring friends, expanding sales, and other activities, which may conflict with profitability. Thus, the potential for conflict between the interests of owners and managers is present.
12. a. The interest payments; b. The interest income forgone. The tax structure encourages debt rather than equity financing since the firm's tax liability is inversely related to its debt/equity ratio.
13. True. If it could produce the output at a lower cost, its profit would be greater.
15. Check list: Did your marginal cost curve cross the *ATC* and *AVC* curves at their low points? Does the vertical distance between the *ATC* and *AVC* curves get smaller and smaller as output increases? If not, redraw the three curves correctly. See Exhibit 20-6b.
18. $2,500; the $2,000 decline in market value during the year plus $500 of potential interest on funds that could be obtained if the machine were sold new. Costs associated with the decline in the value of the machine last year are sunk costs.
19. Because they believe they will be able to restructure the firm and provide better management so that the firm will have positive net earnings in the future. If the firm is purchased at a low enough price, this will allow the new owners to cover the opportunity cost of their investment and still earn an economic profit. Alterna-

tively, they may expect to sell off the firm's assets, receiving more net revenue than the cost of purchasing the firm.

CHAPTER 9 Price Takers and the Competitive Process

1. In a highly competitive industry such as agriculture, lower resource prices might improve the rate of profit in the short run, but in the long run, competition will drive prices down until economic profit is eliminated. Thus, lower resource prices will do little to improve the long-run profitability in such industries.
2. New firms will enter the industry and the existing firms will expand output; market supply will expand, causing the market price to fall until economic profit is eliminated.
5. a. Increase; b. Increase; c. Increase. Firms will earn economic profit; d. Rise (compared with its initial level) for an increasing cost industry, but return to initial price for a constant cost industry; e. Increase even more than it did in the short run; f. Economic profit will return to zero.
6. a. Decline; b. Increase; c. Decline; d. Decline.
11. a. The reduction in supply led to higher prices. b. Since demand is inelastic, the total revenue from sales increased. c. Overall, the profitability of farming increased, although some of the producers that were hardest hit by the drought experienced losses because of their sharp reduction in output.
13. b. Six or seven tons; $250 profit; c. seven or eight tons; $600 profit; d. five or six tons; $50 loss. Since the firm can cover its variable cost, it should stay in business if it believes that the low ($450) price is temporary.

CHAPTER 10 Price-Searcher Markets with Low Entry Barriers

3. The amount of variety is determined by the willingness of consumers to pay for variety relative to the cost of providing it. If consumers value variety highly and the added costs of producing different styles, designs, and sizes is low, there will be a lot of variety. Alternatively, if consumers desire similar products or if variation can be produced only at a high cost, little variety will be present. Apparently, consumers place a substantial value (relative to cost) on variety in napkins, but not in toothpicks.
4. The tax would increase the price of lower-quality (and lower-priced) automobiles by a larger percentage than higher-quality automobiles. Consumers would substitute away from the lower-quality autos since their relative price has increased. This substitution would increase the average quality of automobiles sold. Since the funds from the tax are rebated back to citizens through the lottery, one would expect this substitution effect to dominate any possible income effect.
7. No. A firm that maximizes *total* revenue would expand output as long as *marginal* revenue is positive. When marginal costs are positive, the revenue-maximizing price would be lower (and the output greater) than the price that would maximize the firm's profits.
9. Building the new resort is more risky (and less attractive) because if the market analysis is incorrect, and demand is insufficient, it probably will be difficult to find other uses for the newly built resort. If the airline proves unprofitable, however, the capital (airplanes) should be extremely mobile. However, the resort would have one offsetting advantage: If demand were stronger than expected, and profits larger, it would take competitors longer to enter the market (build a new resort), and they would be more reluctant to make the more permanent investment.

11. In a competitive setting, only the big firms will survive if economies of scale are important. When economies of scale are unimportant, small firms will be able to compete effectively.
15. a. Total revenue: $0; $8,000; $14,000; $18,000; $20,000; $20,000; Total cost: $0; $5,000; $10,000; $15,000; $20,000; $25,000; Economic profit: $0; $3,000; $4,000; $3,000; $0; −$5,000 (loss)
    b. Marginal revenue: $8,000; $6,000; $4,000; $2,000; $0; Marginal cost: $5,000; $5,000; $5,000; $5,000; $5,000
    c. Profit maximizing price: $7,000
    d. Rod will sell 2 boats at the profit-maximizing price of $7,000.
    e. Rod's economic profits will be $4,000 per week.
    f. Yes, boats 1 and 2 are the only boats for which marginal revenue is higher than marginal cost.
    g. Because of the existence of economic profit, more boat dealers will open up in the area. This will result in more competition and lower prices. The entry will continue until boat dealers' economic profits fall to zero.
    h. When demand is elastic, lowering price increases total revenue; thus Rod's demand is elastic between the prices of $9,000 and $5,000. When demand is unitary elastic, lowering price leaves revenues unchanged; thus Rod's demand is unitary elastic between the prices of $5,000 and $4,000. One could also assume that Rod's demand would eventually become inelastic below a price of $4,000 because the elasticity of demand keeps falling as one moves down along a demand curve. When this happens, Rod's total revenues will begin to fall as he continues to lower price. For example, at a price of $3,000, Rod may sell 6 boats per week, resulting in only $18,000 in revenues, which is less than the revenues Rod receives at a price of $4,000.

CHAPTER 11 Price-Searcher Markets with High Entry Barriers

1. Profits cannot exist in the long run without barriers to entry because without them new entrants seeking the profits would increase supply, drive down price, and eliminate the profits. But as the chapter shows, barriers to entry are no guarantee of profits. Sufficient demand is also a necessary condition.
3. No; No; No.
8. Product variation provides each firm in the oligopoly a chance to "cheat" by raising the quality of its products in order to entice customers away from rivals. This raises cost and helps to defeat the purpose, for the oligopolistic group, of controlling price. But if collusion has raised price much above marginal cost, there will be a powerful incentive for each firm to compete in a hidden way to get more customers.
11. Reductions in the cost of transportation generally increase competition because they force firms to compete with distant rivals and permit consumers to choose among a wider range of suppliers. As a result, the U.S. economy today is generally more competitive, in the rivalry sense, than it was 100 years ago.
12. The stock price, when the uncle bought the stock, no doubt reflected the well-known profits of Mammoth. The previous owners of the stock surely would not have sold it at a low price that failed to reflect the future dividends. In the language of the text, the uncle was not an "early bird." It is unlikely that he will profit, in the economic sense, from the purchase.
13. a. $15, profit = $110,000; b. $10.

CHAPTER 12 The Supply of and Demand for Productive Resources

3. a. Five; b. $350; c. Four. The firm will operate in the short run but it will go out of business in the long run unless the market prices rise.
4. Yes. General increases in the productivity of the labor force will cause a general increase in wages. The higher general wage rates will increase the opportunity cost of barbering and cause the supply of barbers to decline. The reduction in the supply of barbers will place upward pressure on the wages of barbers, even if technological change and worker productivity have changed little in barbering.
8. No. The dressmaker needs to employ more capital and less labor because the marginal dollar expenditures on the former are currently increasing output by a larger amount than the latter.
10. Other things constant, a lengthy training requirement to perform in an occupation reduces supply and places upward pressure on the earnings level. However, resource prices, including those for labor services, are determined by both demand and supply. When demand is weak, earnings will be low, even though a considerable amount of education may be necessary to perform in the occupation. For example, the earnings of people with degrees in English literature and world history are generally low, even though most people in these fields have a great deal of education.
12. b. 4; c. Employment would decline to 3.

CHAPTER 13 Earnings, Productivity, and the Job Market

2. U.S. workers are more productive. By investing in human capital, the laborers are somewhat responsible, but the superior tools and physical capital that are available to U.S. workers also contribute to their higher wages.
6. Although this statement, often made by politicians, sounds true, in fact, it is false. Output of goods and services valued by consumers, not jobs, is the key to economic progress and a high standard of living. Real income cannot be high unless real output is high. If job creation was the key to economic progress, it would be easy to create millions of jobs. For example, we could prohibit the use of farm machinery. Such a prohibition would create millions of jobs in agriculture. However, it would also reduce output and our standard of living.
8. The opportunity cost of leisure (nonwork) for higher-wage workers is greater than for lower-wage workers.
10. False. Several additional factors, including differences in preferences (which would influence time worked, the trade-off between money wage and working conditions, and evaluation of alternative jobs), differences in jobs, and imperfect labor mobility, would result in variations in earnings.
12. a, b, e, and f will generally increase hourly earnings; c and d will generally reduce hourly earnings.
13. a. They increase the cost of employment. Yes. b. Sure, if the higher wages are sufficient to compensate for the absence of the fringe benefits. c. No. Employees pay for them in the form of lower money wages than could be earned on comparable jobs that do not provide the fringe benefits.
15. Hourly wages will be highest in B because the higher wages will be necessary to compensate workers in B for the uncertainty and loss of income during layoffs. Annual earnings will be higher in A in order to compensate workers in A for the additional hours they will work during the year.

16. Not necessarily. Compared with married men, single men tend to be younger, have fewer dependents, be more likely to drop out of the labor force, and be less likely to receive earnings-enhancing assistance from another person. All these factors will reduce their earnings relative to married men.

CHAPTER 14 Investment, the Capital Market, and the Wealth of Nations

1. All the changes would increase interest rates in the United States.
4. No. The average outstanding balance during the year is only about half of $1,000. Therefore, the $200 interest charge translates to almost a 40 percent annual rate of interest.
6. Hints: Which has been considered to be more risky—purchasing a bond or a stock? How does risk influence the expected rate of return?
8. 6 percent.
10. a. Mike; b. Yes, people who save a lot are able to get a higher interest rate on their savings as the result of people with a high rate of time preference; c. Yes, people who want to borrow money will be able to do so at a lower rate when there are more people (like Alicia) who want to save a lot.
11. Helped. This question is a lot like prior questions involving Alicia and Mike. Potential gains from trade are present. If obstacles do not restrain trade, the low-income countries will be able to attract savings (from countries with a high saving rate) at a lower interest rate than would exist in the absence of trade. Similarly, people in the high-income countries will be able to earn a higher return than would otherwise be possible. Each can gain because of the existence of the other.
12. a. Approximately $1.277 million; b. Yes; c. The lottery earnings are less liquid. Since there is not a well-organized market transforming lottery earnings into present income, the transaction costs of finding a "buyer" (at a price equal to the present value of the earnings) for the lottery earnings "rights" may be higher than for the bond, if one wants to sell in the future.
14. No. The present value of the $500 annual additions to earnings during the next ten years is less than the cost of the schooling.

CHAPTER 15 Income Inequality and Poverty

2. Differences in family size, age of potential workers, nonmoney "income," taxes, and cost-of-living among areas reduce the effectiveness of annual money income as a measure of economic status. In general, high-income families are larger, are more likely to be headed by a prime-age worker, have less nonmoney income (including leisure), pay more taxes, and reside in higher-cost-of-living areas (particularly large cities). Thus, money income comparison between high- and low-income groups often overstates the economic status of the former relative to the latter.
4. If there were no intergenerational mobility, the diagonal numbers would all be 100 percent. If there were complete equality of opportunity and outcomes, the numbers in each column and row would be 20 percent.
6. No. The increase in marginal tax rates will reduce the incentive of the poor to earn income. Therefore, their income will rise by $1,000 minus the reduction in

their personal earnings due to the disincentive effects of the higher marginal tax rates.
7. 67 percent.

CHAPTER 16 Gaining from International Trade

1. Availability of goods and services, not jobs, is the source of economic prosperity. When a good can be purchased cheaper abroad than it can be produced at home, a nation can expand the quantity of goods and services available for consumption by specializing in the production of those goods for which it is a low-cost producer and trading them for the cheap (relative to domestic costs) foreign goods. Trade restrictions limiting the ability of Americans to purchase low-cost goods from foreigners stifle this process and thereby reduce the living standard of Americans.
3. Statements a and b are not in conflict. Since trade restrictions are typically a special interest issue, political entrepreneurs can often gain by supporting them even when they promote economic inefficiency.
5. True. The primary effect of trade restrictions is an increase in domestic scarcity. This has distributional consequences, but it is clear that as a whole, a nation will be harmed by the increased domestic scarcity accompanying the trade restraints.
6. The quota reduces the supply of sugar to the domestic market and drives up the domestic price of sugar. Domestic producers benefit from the higher prices at the expense of domestic consumers (see Exhibit 17-9). Studies indicate that the quota expanded the gross income of the 11,000 domestic sugar farmers by approximately $130,000 per farm in the mid-1980s, at the expense (in the form of higher prices of sugar and sugar products) of approximately $6 per year to the average domestic consumer. Since the program channels resources away from products for which the United States has a comparative advantage, it reduces the productive capacity of the United States. Both the special interest nature of the issue and rent-seeking theory explain the political attractiveness of the program.
8. a. No. Americans would be poorer if we used more of our resources to produce things for which we are a high opportunity-cost producer and less of our resources to produce things for which we are a low opportunity-cost producer. Employment might either increase or decrease, but the key point is that it is the value of goods produced, not employment, that generates income and provides for the wealth of a nation. The answer to b is the same as a.
9. In thinking about this issue, consider the following points. Suppose the Japanese were willing to give products such as automobiles, electronic goods, and clothing to us free of charge. Would we be worse off if we accepted the gifts? Should we try to keep the free goods out? What is the source of real income—jobs or goods and services? If the gifts make us better off, doesn't it follow that partial gifts would also make us better off?
12. While trade reduces employment in import-competing industries, it expands employment in export industries. On balance, there is no reason to believe that trade either promotes or destroys jobs. The major effect of trade is to permit individuals, states, regions, and nations to generate a larger output by specializing in the things they do well and trading for those things that they would produce only at a high cost. A higher real income is the result.
15. True. If country A imposes a tariff, other countries will sell less to A and therefore acquire less purchasing power in terms of A's currency. Thus, they will have to reduce their purchases of A's export goods.

CHAPTER 17 International Finance and the Foreign Exchange Market

4. On February 2, the dollar appreciated against the pound and depreciated against the franc.
5. Answers a and g would cause the dollar to appreciate; b, c, d, e, and h would cause the dollar to depreciate; f would leave the exchange rate unchanged.
9. Each of the changes would reduce the size of the current account deficit.
11. The current account balance will move toward a larger deficit (or smaller surplus) and the dollar will appreciate.
14. False. Flexible exchange rates bring the sum of the current and capital accounts into balance, but they do not necessarily lead to balance for either component.
15. a. No. The exchange rate will bring the sum of the current and capital accounts into balance, but it will not bring about either an overall merchandise trade balance or a trade balance with a specific country.
    b. Compared to the United States, Japan has a high savings rate. High-income countries with high savings rates tend to invest substantially abroad. In order to pay for these investments, Japan must run a current account surplus. Its trading partners—particularly those with a low saving rate like the United States—will do the opposite. In addition, Japan is a major importer of natural resources and raw materials, two product areas where the United States does not generally have a comparative advantage. Because the United States is generally not a low-cost producer of the primary products imported by the Japanese, the United States tends to export less goods and services to Japan than it imports.
    c. Americans will not want to hold the additional yen. They can be expected to use them to purchase additional foreign-produced goods, including goods supplied by the Japanese. Clearly, the trade deficit with Japan is only a part of the total current account deficit.

APPLICATION 1 Labor Markets and Unemployment Rates: A Cross-Country Analysis

1. The ability to organize only a portion of the firms in an industry leaves the organized firms in competition with the unorganized firms. When organized firms pay higher wages, they find it harder to compete with nonunion firms due to higher costs. This restricts the ability of the union to raise wages in the organized firms. Because competition from nonunion firms is less prevalent in Europe than in the United States, European unions are better able to increase the wages of union members than their counterparts in the United States.

APPLICATION 2 Social Security: The Nature of the Problem and the Alternatives for Dealing with It

2. The pay-as-you-go social security system will face a crisis sometime around 2014 when the inflow of tax revenue will be insufficient to cover the promised benefits. While the Social Security Trust Fund has bonds, they are merely an IOU from the Treasury to the Social Security Administration. In order to redeem these bonds and provide additional funds to finance social security benefits, the federal government will have to raise taxes (or pay the interest on additional Treasury

bonds it sells), or cut other expenditures, or both. Thus, the presence of the SSTF bonds does not do much to alleviate the crisis.

APPLICATION 3 The Stock Market: What Does It Do and How Has It Performed?

1. History shows that in the U.S. stock market, a relatively low risk with fairly high returns can be gained by holding a diverse portfolio of stocks in unrelated industries, for a period of 20 years or more. Mutual funds are an option that allows a person to purchase a diverse portfolio while keeping commission costs low.
3. High profits now and the expectation of higher profits in the future have driven up the price of the stock, despite the lack of dividend payment in the first years of the firm. Investors are equally happy with high dividends or the equivalent in rising stock value due to the firm's retaining of its profits for further investment.
5. Investors are buying such a stock for its rising value (price), which reflects expected future earnings and dividends.

APPLICATION 4 How Does Government Regulation Affect Your Life?

1. Making cars more safe is good, but if the cost has previously kept consumers from demanding the safety measures, it is possible that they are not worth the cost to many consumers. Some very expensive cars, such as Mercedes-Benz, had airbags when there was no requirement, but Volkswagen did not. Should only the more costly cars be sold? If so, then some people, probably the less affluent, will drive older, even less safe cars. This is not a clearcut issue.
3. Profitability may be adversely affected in the short run, but in the long run, prices will rise enough for the firms to cover their opportunity cost of production. Consumers bear the cost of such legislation and get the associated benefits, large or small.
6. Experts often do know far more about the technical options than do consumers, although consumers can and do read the advice of experts. Suppliers of safer products also make it a point to advertise data and expert opinion indicating their products are indeed safer. Nevertheless, experts usually do understand the technologies better. On the other hand, experts cannot know about how products will be used. A consumer may prefer to pay for a high degree of safety for the family car, which will carry the whole family at high speeds over long distances, while preferring a much cheaper, less-reliable car for running errands near home. Such choices are hard to allow if all vehicles are strictly regulated for safety. Decision-maker knowledge (and incentives) is, in some cases, better with consumer choice than with thorough and strict regulation.
8. The statement is essentially true. In the short run, capital may be invested in an industry such that it cannot easily be moved elsewhere. If customer demand is elastic, the industry may bear a large part of the cost burden in the short run. In the long run, however, capital is mobile. Factories don't have to be replaced, for example. If costs in the industry are high, relative to the revenues, then capital will migrate over time to other industries, and supply in the regulated industry will fall until the price buyers will pay is again high enough to provide the market rate of return to capital.

APPLICATION 5 Income Inequality, Transfers, and the Role of Government

5. Low-income welfare recipients often receive benefits from many income-tested government programs at one time. When their income increases, the benefits from each of the programs are generally reduced. Therefore, earning another $1,000 might reduce benefits by several hundred dollars. Thus, the implicit marginal tax rate is often exceedingly high. The 1996 reform law required work for able-bodied recipients, so that staying home and drawing the full benefit amount is no longer an option for most welfare recipients. For most, there is a maximum of 5 years' eligibility for welfare involving the federal government. At that point, the benefits are not available and there is no implicit tax rate.

APPLICATION 6 Do Labor Unions Increase the Wages of Workers?

2. If the union is able to raise the wages of the farmworkers: (a) The cost of Florida oranges will rise, causing supply to decline and price to rise in the long run; (b) profits of the Florida orange growers will decline in the short run, but in the long run they will return to the normal rate; (c) mechanization will be encouraged; and (d) the employment of fruit pickers will decline—particularly in the long run.
7. If only part of an industry is unionized, the costs of nonunion firms in the industry will be lower than the costs of unionized firms, if the unionized firms have higher wage rates. If the union wages are much higher than nonunion wages, then the unionized firms will be unable to compete successfully.
10. False. Competition constrains both employers and employees. Employers must compete with other employers for labor services. In order to gain the labor services of an employee, an employer must offer a compensation package superior to what the employee can get elsewhere. If the employer does not offer a superior package, the employee will work for a rival employer or choose self-employment. Similarly, employees must compete with other employees. Therefore, their ability to demand whatever wage they would like is also restrained. Thus, competition prevents both the payment of low (below-market) wages by employers and the imposition of high (above-market) wages by employees.
11. Not necessarily. Adjustment must be made for differences in (a) the productivity characteristics of the union and nonunion workers, and (b) the types of jobs they occupy (for example, work environment, job security, likelihood of layoff, and so on). Adjustment for these factors may either increase or reduce the $1.50 differential.
12. Remember, union members compete with other workers, including less-skilled workers. An increase in the minimum wage makes unskilled, low-wage workers more expensive. A higher minimum wage increases the demand for high-skill employees who are good substitutes for the low-skill workers. Union members are overrepresented among the high-skill group helped by an increase in the minimum wage. Therefore, while union leaders will generally pitch their support for a higher minimum wage in terms of a desire that all workers be paid a "decent wage," the impact of the legislation on union members suggests that self-interest rather than altruism underlies their support for the legislation.

APPLICATION 7 Natural Resources and the Future

1. Merely because a resource is unowned and unpriced, it does not follow that its opportunity cost is zero. Use of an unowned, unpriced resource might involve a high opportunity cost. Yet if there is no owner to protect it, or to allocate it to its highest-valued use, then it might indeed be treated as if it had no opportunity cost. This illustrates why private ownership of resources is important for their efficient allocation.
4. Wells are abandoned by producers when the cost of extracting and delivering additional oil exceeds its value. When the value of crude oil rises, additional oil can be produced since water flooding, steam, and chemical measures—all of which are costly—can be paid for by the higher prices gained from the extra oil.
5. Issues for thought: Are resources supplied by nature scarce? If so, what process should be used to ration them among the competing demanders? If a resource is owned by the government rather than privately, how will this affect the incentive to care for, maintain, and conserve it for the future? Do you think that government-owned property like the national forests and parks are better cared for than, for example, Disney World?
7. If an investment, such as leaving the trees to grow another 20 years, yields a higher return than other investments, then the stock price will fall if the trees are cut too soon, or will go higher if a new, more profitable investment path (leaving the trees to grow) is announced. Either way, the stock price immediately rewards good long-term decisions and penalizes bad, shortsighted ones.

APPLICATION 8 Economics and the Environment

2. Actions taken to reduce one risk can increase others. For example, banning the pesticide DDT raised risks from replacement pesticides in the United States and from malaria in Sri Lanka. It is important to consider the secondary effects of any risk-avoidance activity.
4. The cost of stopping the buildup of carbon dioxide would be very large, if it can be done. When the risk is somewhat speculative, even though it could turn out to be quite real, we must consider the reduction in wealth and prosperity that would be caused by reducing the buildup. Lower wealth and incomes would reduce our ability to reduce other risks. Then too, a warmer world would have many benefits as well as costs. We all want future generations to be better off. Whether reducing the buildup of carbon dioxide would make them better or worse off is the question.
6. Potential polluters must take into account any harm that pollution does to others, if pollution victims can enforce their property rights in court. But if enforcement of those rights is impossible because, for example, the true value of the harm or the source of the harm cannot be found, then regulation might help. However, a government regulator will have the same need for knowledge in seeking to improve the situation. Both markets and government organizations encourage resource owners and potential owners to consider their impacts on others, but neither system is perfect.

Absolute advantage A situation in which a nation, as the result of its previous experience and/or natural endowments, can produce more of a good (with the same amount of resources) than another nation.

Accounting profits The sales revenues minus the expenses of a firm over a designated time period, usually one year. Accounting profits typically make allowances for changes in the firm's inventories and depreciation of its assets. No allowance is made, however, for the opportunity cost of the equity capital of the firm's owners, or other implicit costs.

Allocative efficiency The allocation of resources to the production of goods and services most desired by consumers, at the lowest possible cost.

Appreciation An increase in the value of a domestic currency relative to foreign currencies. An appreciation increases the purchasing power of the domestic currency over foreign goods.

Asymmetric-information problem A problem arising when either buyers or sellers have important information about the product that is not possessed by the other side in potential transactions.

Automation A production technique that reduces the amount of labor required to produce a good or service. It is beneficial to adopt the new labor-saving technology if it reduces the cost of production.

Average fixed cost Total fixed cost divided by the number of units produced. It always declines as output increases.

Average product The total product (output) divided by the number of units of the variable input required to produce that output level.

Average tax rate (ATR) Tax liability divided by taxable Income. It is the percentage of income paid in taxes.

Average total cost Total cost divided by the number of units produced. It is sometimes called per unit cost.

Average variable cost The total variable cost divided by the number of units produced.

Balance of merchandise trade The difference between the value of merchandise exports and the value of merchandise imports for a nation. The balance of merchandise trade is only one component of a nation's total balance of payments. Also called simply balance of trade or net exports.

Balance of payments A summary of all economic transactions between a country and all other countries for a specific time period, usually a year. The balance-of-payments account reflects all payments and liabilities to foreigners (debits) and all payments and obligations received from foreigners (credits).

Balance on current account The import-export balance of goods and services, plus net investment income earned abroad, plus net private and government transfers. If the value of the nation's export-type items exceeds (is less than) the value of the nation's import-type items plus net unilateral transfers to foreigners, a current-account surplus (deficit) is present.

Balance on goods and services The exports of goods (merchandise) and services of a nation minus its imports of good and services.

Barriers to entry Obstacles that limit the freedom of potential rivals to enter and compete in an industry or market.

Black market A market that operates outside the legal system, either by selling illegal goods or by selling goods at illegal prices or terms.

Budget constraint The constraint that separates the bundles of goods that the consumer can purchase from those that cannot be purchased, given a limited income and the prices of the products.

Capital Resources that enhance our ability to produce output in the future.

Capital account The record of transactions with foreigners that involve either (1) the exchange of ownership rights to real or financial assets or (2) extension of loans.

Capital formation The production of buildings, machinery, tools, and other equipment that will enhance the ability of future economic participants to produce. The term can also be applied to efforts to upgrade the knowledge and skill of workers and thereby increase their ability to produce in the future.

Capitalism An economic system based on private ownership of productive resources and allocation of goods according to the signals provided by market prices.

Cartel An organization of sellers designed to coordinate supply decisions so that the joint profits of the members will be maximized. A cartel will seek to create a monopoly in the market.

Ceteris paribus A Latin term meaning "other things constant," used when the effect of one change is being described, recognizing that if other things changed, they also could affect the result. Economists often describe the effects of one change, knowing that in the real world, other things might change and have their effects, too.

Choice The act of selecting among alternatives.

Collective decision making The method of organization that relies on public-sector decision making (voting, political bargaining, lobbying, and so on) to resolve basic issues.

Collusion Agreement among firms to avoid various competitive practices, particularly price reductions. It may involve either formal agreements or merely tacit recognition that competitive practices will be self-defeating in the long run. Tacit collusion is difficult to detect. In the United States, antitrust laws prohibit collusion and conspiracies to restrain trade.

Comparative advantage The ability to produce a good at a lower opportunity cost than others can produce it. Relative costs determine comparative advantage.

Compensating wage differentials Wage differences that compensate workers for risk, unpleasant working conditions, and other undesirable non-pecuniary aspects of a job.

Competition as a dynamic process A term that denotes rivalry or competition between or among parties (for example, producers or input suppliers), each of which seeks to deliver a better deal to buyers when quality, price, and product information are all considered. Competition implies a lack of collusion among sellers.

Competitive price searcher market A market where the firms have a downward-sloping demand curve, and entry into and exit from the market are relatively easy.

Complements Products that are usually consumed jointly (for example, peanut butter and jelly). They are related such that a decrease in the price of one will cause an increase in demand for the other.

Constant-cost industry An industry for which factor prices and costs of production remain constant as market output is expanded. Thus, the long-run market supply curve is horizontal.

Constant returns to scale Unit costs that are constant as the scale of the firm is altered. Neither economies nor diseconomies of scale are present.

Consumer surplus The difference between the maximum price consumers are willing to pay and the price they actually pay. It is the net gain derived by the buyers of the good.

Consumption-opportunity constraint The constraint that separates consumption bundles that are attainable from those that are unattainable. In a money-income economy, this is usually a budget constraint.

Contestable market A market in which the costs of entry and exit are low, so a firm risks little by entering. Efficient production and zero economic profits should prevail in a contestable market. A market can be contestable even if capital requirements are high.

Corporation A business firm owned by shareholders who possess ownership rights to the firm's profits, but whose liability is limited to the amount of their investment in the firm.

Currency board An entity that (a) issues a currency with a fixed designated value relative to a widely accepted currency (for example, the U.S. dollar) (b) promises to continue to redeem the issued currency at the fixed rate, and (c) maintains bonds and other liquid assets denominated in the other currency that provide 100 percent backing for all currency issued.

Current account The record of all transactions with foreign nations that involve the exchange of merchandise goods and services, current income derived from investments, and unilateral gifts.

Deadweight loss A loss of gains from trade resulting from the imposition of a tax. It imposes a burden of taxation over and above the burden associated with the transfer of revenues to the government.

Decreasing-cost industry An industry for which costs of production decline as the industry expands. The market supply is therefore inversely related to price. Such industries are atypical.

Depreciation A reduction in the value of a domestic currency relative to foreign currencies. A depreciation reduces the purchasing power of the domestic currency for foreign goods.

Derived demand The demand for a resource; it stems from the demand for the final good the resource helps to produce.

Differential products Products distinguished from similar products by such characteristics as quality, design, location, and method of promotion.

Discounting The procedure used to calculate the present value of future income, which is inversely related to both the interest rate and the amount of time that passes before the funds are received.

Division of labor A method that breaks down the production of a commodity into a series of specific tasks, each performed by a different worker.

Dumping The sale of a good by a foreign supplier in another country at a price below that charged by the supplier in its home market.

Economic efficiency Economizing behavior. When applied to a community, it implies that (1) an activity should be undertaken if the sum of the benefits to the individuals exceeds the sum of their costs and (2) no activity should be undertaken if the costs borne by the individuals exceed the benefits.

Economic good A good that is scarce. The desire for economic goods exceeds the amount that is freely available from nature.

Economic profit The difference between the firm's total revenues and total costs.

Economic regulation Regulation of product price or industry structure, usually imposed on a specific industry. By and large, the production processes used by the regulated firms are unaffected by this type of regulation.

Economic Theory A set of definitions, postulates, and principles assembled in a manner that makes clear the "cause-and-effect" relationship of economic data.

Economies of scale Reductions in the firm's per-unit costs that are associated with the use of large plants to produce a large volume of output.

Economizing behavior Choosing with the objective of gaining a specific benefit at the least possible cost. A corollary of economizing behavior implies that, when choosing among items of equal cost, individuals will choose the option that yields the greatest benefit.

Employment discrimination Unequal treatment of persons on the basis of their race, sex, or religion restricting their employment and earning opportunities compared to others of similar productivity. Employment discrimination may stem from the prejudices of employers, customers, fellow employees, or all three.

Entrepreneur A profit-seeking decision maker who decides which projects to undertake and how they should be undertaken. A successful entrepreneur's actions will increase the value or resources.

Equilibrium A state of balance between conflicting forces, such as supply and demand.

Equity mutual fund A corporation that pools the funds of investors, including small investors, and uses them to purchase a bundle of stocks.

Excess burden of taxation Another term for deadweight loss. It reflects losses that occur when beneficial activities are forgone because they are taxed.

Exchange rate The domestic price of one unit of foreign currency. For example, if it takes $1.50 to purchase one English pound, the dollar-pound exchange rate is 1.50.

Exit The ability to withdraw from an economic relationship with another person or organization.

Explicit costs Payments by a firm to purchase the services of productive resources.

Externalities The side effects or spillover effects, of an action that influence the well-being of nonconsenting parties. The nonconsenting parties may be either helped (by external benefits) or harmed (by external costs).

Fallacy of composition Erroneous view that what is true for the individual (or the part) will also be true for the group (or the whole).

Fixed exchange rate An exchange rate that is set at a determined amount by government policy.

Flexible exchange rates Exchange rates that are determined by the market forces of supply and demand. They are sometimes called floating exchange rates.

Foreign exchange market The market in which the currencies of different countries are bought and sold.

Free rider One who receives the benefit of a good without contributing to its costs. Public goods and commodities that generate external benefits offer people the opportunity to become free riders.

Fringe benefits Benefits other than normal money wages that are supplied to employees in exchange for their labor services. Higher fringe benefits come at the expense of lower money wages.

Game theory Analyzes the strategic choices made by competitors in a conflict situation, such as decisions made by members of an oligopoly.

General Agreement on Tariffs and Trade (GATT) An organization formed following the Second World War designed to set the rules for the conduct of international trade and reduce barriers to trade among nations.

Going out of business The sale of a firm's assets and its permanent exit from the market. By going out of business, a firm is able to avoid fixed costs, which would continue during a shutdown.

Health and safety regulation Legislation designed to improve the health, safety, and environmental conditions available to workers and/or consumers. The legislation usually mandates production procedures, minimum standards, and/or product characteristics to be met by producers and employers.

Human resources The abilities, skills, and health of human beings that can contribute to the production of both current and future output. Investment in training and education can increase the supply of human resources.

Implicit costs The opportunity costs associated with a firm's use of resources that it owns. These costs do not involve a direct money payment. Examples include wage income and interests forgone by the owner of a firm who also provides labor services and equity capital to the firm.

Implicit marginal tax rate The amount of additional (marginal) earnings that must be paid explicitly in taxes or implicitly in the form of a reduction in income supplements. Since the marginal tax rate establishes the fraction of an additional dollar earned that an individual is permitted to keep, it is an important determinant of the incentive to work.

Import quota A specific limit or maximum quantity (or value) of a good permitted to be imported into a country during a given period.

Income effect That part of an increase (decrease) in amount consumed that is the result of the consumer's real income (the consumption possibilities available to the consumer) being expanded (contracted) by a reduction (rise) in the price of a good.

Income elasticity The percentage change in the quantity of a product demanded divided by the percentage change in consumer income causing the change in quantity demanded. It measures the responsiveness of the demand for a good to a change in income.

Income mobility movement of individuals and families either up or down income-distribution ranking when comparisons are made at two different points in time. When substantial income mobility is present, one's current position will be a very good indicator as to what one's position will be a few years in the future.

Increasing-cost industry An industry for which costs of production rise as output is expended. Thus, even in the long run, higher market prices will be required to induce the firms to expand the total output in such industries. The long-run market supply curve in such industries, will slope upward to the right.

Indifference curve A curve, convex from below, that separates the consumption bundles that are more preferred by an individual from those that are less preferred. The points on the curve represent combinations of goods that are equally preferred by the individual.

Inferior good A good that has a negative income elasticity, so that, as consumer income rises, the demand for that good falls.

Inflationary premium A component of the money interest rate that reflect compensation to the lender for the expected decrease, due to inflation, in the purchasing power of the principal and interest during the course of the loan. It is determined by the expected rate of future inflation.

Innovation The successful introduction and adoption of a new product or process. The economic application of inventions and marketing techniques.

International Monetary Fund (IMF) An international banking organization, with more than 180 member nations, designed to over see the operation of the international monetary system. Although it does not control the world supply of money, it does hold currency reserves for member nationals and makes currency loans to national central banks.

Invention The creation of a new product or process, often facilitated by the knowledge of engineering and scientific relationships.

Investment The purchase, construction, or development of capital resources, including both nonhuman capital and human capital. Investments increase the supply of capital.

Investment in human capital Expenditures on training, education, skill development, and health designed to increase human capital and the productivity of an individual.

Invisible hand principle The tendency of market prices to direct individuals pursuing their own interests into productive activities that also promote the economic well-being of the society.

J-curve effect The tendency of a nation's current-account deficit to widen initially before it shrinks to an exchange-rate depreciation. This tendency results because the short-run demand for both imports and exports is often inelastic, even though the long-run demand is almost always elastic.

Labor union A collective organization of employees who bargain as a unit with employers.

Laffer curve A curve illustrating the relationship between the tax rate and tax revenue. Tax revenue will be low for both very high and very low tax rates. Thus, when tax rates are quite high, a reduction in the tax rate can increase tax revenue.

Law of comparative advantage A principle that states that individuals, firms, regions, or nations can gain by specializing in the production of goods that they produce cheaply (that is, at a low opportunity cost) and exchanging those goods for other desired goods for which they are a high-opportunity-cost producer.

Law of demand A principle that states there is an inverse relationship between the price of a good and the amount of it buyers are willing to purchase. As the price of a product increases, other things constant, consumers will purchase less of the product.

Law of diminishing marginal ability The basic economic principle that, as the consumption of a commodity increases, the marginal utility derived from consuming more of the commodities (per unit of time) will eventually decline.

Law of diminishing returns The postulate that, as more and more units of a variable resource are combined with a fixed amount of other resources, employment of additional units of the variable resource will eventually increase output only at a decreasing rate. Once diminishing returns are reached, it will take successively larger amounts of the variable factor to expand output by one unit.

Law of supply A principle that states there is a direct relationship between the price of a good and the amount of it offered for sale. As the price of a product increases, other things constant, producers will increase the amount of the product supplied to the market.

Licensing A requirement that one obtain permission from the government in order to perform certain business activities or work in various occupations.

Loanable funds market A general term used to describe the broad market that coordinates the borrowing and lending decisions of business firms and households. Commercial banks, savings and loan associations, the stock and bond markets, and insurance companies are important financial institutions in this market.

Logrolling The exchange between politicians of political support on one issue for political support on another issue.

Long run (in production) A time period long enough to allow the firm to vary all factors of production.

Long run A time period of sufficient length to enable decision makers to adjust fully to a market change.

Loss Deficit of sales revenue relative to the opportunity cost of production. Losses are a penalty imposed on those who misuse resources in lower-valued uses as judged by buyers in the market.

Macroeconomics The branch of economics that focuses on how human behavior affects outcomes in highly aggregated markets, such as the markets for labor or consumer products.

Mandated benefits Fringe benefits that the government forces employers to include in their total compensation packed paid to employees.

Marginal Term used to describe the effects of a change in the current situation. For example, the marginal cost is the cost of producing an additional unit of a product, given the producer's current facility and production rate.

Marginal benefit The maximum price a consumer would be willing to pay for an additional unit. It is the dollar value of the consumer's marginal utility from the additional unit, and thus falls as consumption increases.

Marginal cost The change in total cost required to produce an additional unit of output.

Marginal product (MP) The change in total output that results from the employment of one additional unit of a resource—one workday of skilled labor, for example. Mathematically, it is the ratio of the change in total product to the change in the quantity of the variable input.

Marginal rate of substitution The change in the consumption level of one good that is just sufficient to offset a unit change in the consumption of another good without causing a shift to another indifference curve. At any point on an indifference curve, it will be equal to the slope of the curve at that point.

Marginal revenue (MR) The change in a firm's total revenue that results from the production and sale of one additional unit of output.

Marginal revenue product (MRP) The change in the total revenue of a firm that results from the employment of one additional unit of a resource. The marginal revenue product of an input is equal to its marginal product multiplied by the marginal revenue of the good or service produced.

Marginal tax rate (MTR) Additional tax liability divided by additional taxable income. It is the percentage of an extra dollar of income that must be paid in taxes. It is the marginal tax rate that is relevant in personal decision making.

Marginal utility The additional utility received from the consumption of an additional unit of a good.

Market An abstract concept that encompasses the trading arrangements of buyers and sellers that underlie the forces of supply and demand.

Market organization A method of organization that allows unregulated prices and the decentralized decisions of private property owners to resolve the basic economic problems of consumption, production, and distribution.

Market power The ability of a firm that is not a pure monopolist to earn unusually large profits, indicating that is has some mono-poly power. Because the firm has few (or weak) competitors, it has a degree of freedom from the discipline of vigorous competitions.

Means-tested income transfers Transfers that are limited to persons or families with an income below a certain cutoff point. Eligibility is this dependent on low-income status.

Microeconomics The branch of economics that focuses on how human behavior affects the conduct of affairs within narrowly defined units, such as individual households or business firms.

Middleman A person who buys and sells, or who arranges trades. A middleman reduces transaction costs.

Minimum wage Legislation requiring that workers be paid at least the state minimum hourly rate of pay.

Money rate of interest The rate of interest in monetary terms that borrowers pay for borrowed funds. During periods when borrowers and lenders expect inflation, the money rule of interest exceeds the real rate of interest.

Monopolistic competition Term often used by economists to describe markets characterized by a large number of sellers that supply differentiated products to a market with low barriers to entry. Essentially, it is an alternative term for competitive price-searcher markets.

Monopoly A market structure characterized by (1) a single seller of a well-defined product for which there are no good substitutes and (2) high barriers to the entry of any other firms into the market for that product.

Natural monopoly A market situation in which the average costs of production continually decline with increased output. Therefore, average costs of production will be lowest when a single, large firm produces the entire output demanded.

Nonhuman resources The durable, nonhuman inputs that can be used to produce both current and future output. Machines, buildings, land, and raw materials are examples. Investment can increase the supply of nonhuman resources. Economists often use the term physical capital when referring to nonhuman resources.

Nonpecuniary job characteristics Working conditions, prestige, variety, location, employee freedom and responsibilities, and other nonwage characteristics of a job that influence how employees evaluate the job.

Normal good A good that has positive income elasticity, so that, as consumer income rises, demand for that good rises also.

Normative economics Judgments about "what ought to be" in economic matters. Normative economic views cannot be proved false, because they are based on value judgments.

North American Free Trade Agreement (NAFTA) A comprehensive trade agreement between the United States, Mexico, and Canada that went into effect in 1994. Tariff barriers will continue to be phased out under the agreement until 2004.

Oligopoly A market situation in which a small number of sellers compose the entire industry. It is a competition among the few.

Opportunity cost The highest valued alternative that must be sacrificed as a result of choosing among alternatives.

Opportunity cost of equity capital The implicit rate of return that must be earned by investors to induce them to continue to supply financial capital to the firm.

Opportunity cost of production The total economic cost of producing a good or service. The cost component includes the opportunity cost of all resources, including those owned by the firm. The opportunity cost is equal to the value of the production of other goods sacrificed as the result producing the good.

Partnership A business firm owned by two or more individuals who possess ownership rights to the firm's profits and are personally liable for the debts of the firm.

Pegged exchange-rate system A commitment to use monetary and fiscal policy to maintain the exchange-rate value of the domestic currency at a fixed rate or within a narrow band relative to another currency (or bundle of currencies).

Percent value (PV) The current worth of future income after it is discounted to reflect the fact that revenues now.

Pork-barrel legislation A package of spending projects benefiting local areas at federal expense. The projects typically have costs that exceed benefits, but are intensely desired by the residents of the district getting the benefits without having to pay much of the costs.

Positive economics The scientific study of "what is" among economic relationships.

Positive rate of time preference The desire of consumers for goods now rather than in the future.

Poverty threshold income level The level of money income below which a family is considered to be poor. It differs according to family characteristics (for example, number of family members) and is adjusted when consumer prices change.

Price ceiling A legally established maximum price that sellers may charge for a good or resource.

Price controls Government-mandated prices they may be either greater or less than the market equilibrium price.

Price discrimination A practice whereby a seller charges different consumers different prices for the same product or service.

Price elasticity of demand The percent change in the quantity of a product demanded divided by the percent change in the price causing the change in quantity. Price elasticity of demand indicates the degree of consumer response to variation in price.

Price elasticity of supply The percentage change in quantity supplied, divided by the percentage change in the price causing the change in quantity supplied.

Price floor A legally established minimum price that buyers must pay for a good or resource.

Price searchers Firms that face a downward sloping demand curve for their product. The amount that the firm is able to sell is inversely related to the price that it charges.

Price takers Sellers who must take the market price in order to sell their product. Because each price taker's output is small relative to the total market, price takers can sell all their output at the market price, but they are unable to sell any of their output at a price higher than the market price.

Principal-agent problem The incentive problem arising when the purchaser of services (the principal) lacks full information about the circumstances faced by the seller (the agent) and thus cannot know how well the agent performs the purchased services. The agent may to some extent work toward objectives other than those sought by the principal paying for the service.

Private property rights Property rights that are exclusively held by an owner, or group of owners, and that can be transferred to others at the owner's discretion.

Producer surplus The difference between the minimum supply price and the actual sales price. It measures the net gains to producers and resource suppliers from market trade. It is not the same as profit.

Production possibilities curve A curve that outlines all possible combinations of total output that could be produced, assuming (1) the utilization of a fixed amount of production resources, (2) full and efficient use of those resources, and (3) a specific state of technical knowledge. The slope of the curve indicates the rate at which one product can be traded off to produce more of the other.

Profit An excess of sales revenue relative to the opportunity cost of production. The cost component includes the opportunity cost of all resources, including those owned by the firm. Therefore, profit accrues only when the value of the good produced is greater than the value of other goods that could have been produced with those same resources.

Progressive tax A tax in which the average tax rate rises with income. Persons with higher incomes will pay a higher percentage of their income in taxes.

Property rights The right to use, control, and obtain the benefits from a good or service.

Proprietorship A business firm owned by an individual who possesses the ownership right to the firm's profits and is personally liable for the firm's debts.

Public choice analysis The study of decision making as it affects the formation and operation of collective organizations, such as governments. In general, the principles and methodology of economics are applied to political science topics.

Public goods Jointly consumed goods that are not diminished when one person enjoys their consumption. When consumed by one person, they are also made available to others. National defense, flood control dams, and scientific theories are all public goods.

Purely competitive markets Markets characterized by a large number of small firms producing an identical product in an industry (market area) that permits complete freedom of entry and exit. Also called price-taker markets.

Random walk theory The theory that current stock prices already reflect known information about the future. Therefore, the future movement of stock prices will be determined by surprise occurrences. This will cause them to change in a random fashion.

Rational ignorance effect Voter ignorance resulting from the fact that people perceive their individual votes as unlikely to be decisive. Therefore, they rationally have little incentive to seek the information needed to cast an informed vote.

Rationing An allocation of a limited supply of a good or resource to users who would like to have more of it. Various criteria, including charging a price, can be utilized to allocate the limited supply. When price performs the rationing function, the good or resource is allocated to those willing to give up the most "other things" in order to obtain ownership rights.

Real rate of interest The money rate of interest minus the expected rate of inflation. The real rate of interest indicates the interest premium, in terms of real goods and services, that one must pay for earlier availability.

Regressive tax A tax in which the average tax rate falls with income. Persons with higher incomes will pay a lower percentage of their income in taxes.

Rent seeking Actions by individuals and interest groups designed to restructure public policy in a manner that will either directly or indirectly redistribute more income to themselves.

Repeat-purchase item An item purchased often by the same buyer.

Replacement rate The share of previous earnings replaced by unemployment benefits.

Residual claimants Individuals who personally receive the excess, if any, of revenues over costs. Residual claimants gain if the firm's costs are reduced or revenues increased.

Resource An input used to produce economic goods. Land, labor, skills, natural resources, and capital are examples. Our history is a record of our struggle to transform available, but limited, resources into things that we would like to have—economic goods.

Resource markets Markets in which business firms demand factors of production (for example, labor, capital, and natural resources) from household suppliers. The resources are then used to produce goods and services. These markets are sometimes called factor markets or input markets.

Resource mobility The ease with which factors of production are able to move among alternative uses. Resources than can easily be transferred to a different use or location are said to be highly mobile. Resources with few alternative uses are immobile.

Right-to-work laws Laws that prohibit the union shop—the requirement that employees must join a union as a condition of employment. Each state has the option to adopt (or reject) right-to-work legislation.

Samaritan's dilemma General assistance to those with low incomes reduces the opportunity cost of choices that lead to poverty. Thus, there is a conflict between providing income transfers to the poor and discouragement of behavior that increases the incidence of poverty.

Saving Current income that is not spent on consumption goods. Saving is a "flow" concept.

Scarcity Fundamental concept of economics that indicates that a good is less freely available than consumers would like.

Scientific thinking Development of a theory from basic postulates and the testing of the implications of that theory as to their consistency with events in the real world. Good theories are consistent with and help explain real-world events. Theories that are inconsistent with the real world are invalid and must be rejected.

Secondary effects Economic consequences of an economic change that are not immediately identifiable but are felt only with the passage of time.

Severance pay Pay by an employer to an employee upon the termination of employment with the firm.

Shirking Working at less than a normal rate of productivity, thus reducing output. Shirking is more likely when workers are not monitored, so that the cost of lower output falls on others than themselves.

Shortage A condition in which the amount of a good offering for sale by producers is less than the amount demanded by buyers at the existing price. An increase in price would eliminate the shortage.

Short run A time period of insufficient length to permit decision makers to adjust fully to a change in market conditions. For example, in the short run, producers will have time to increase output by using more labor and raw materials, but they will not have time to expand the size of their plants or to install additional heavy equipment.

Shortsightedness effect Misallocation of resources that results because public-sector action is biased (1) in favor or proposals yielding clearly defined current benefits in exchange for difficult-to-identify future costs and (2) against proposals with clearly identified current costs but yielding less concrete and less obvious future benefits.

Shutdown A temporary halt in the operation of a business firm. Because the firm anticipates returning to the market in the future, it does not sell its assets and go out of business. The firm's variable cost is eliminated by the shutdown, but its fixed costs continue.

Socialism A system of economic organization in which (1) the ownership and control of the basic means of production rest with the state, and (2) resource allocation is determined by centralized planning rather than market forces.

Special drawing rights (SDRs) Supplementary reserves, in the form of accounting entries, established by the International Monetary Fund (also called paper gold). Like gold and foreign currency reserves, they can be used to make payments on international accounts.

Special interest issue An issue that generates substantial individual benefits to a small minority while imposing a small individual cost on many other voters. In total, the net cost to the majority might either exceed or fall short of the net benefits to the special-interest group.

Stock options The option to buy a specified number of shares of the firm's stock at a designated price. The designated price is generally set so that the options will be quite valuable if the firm's shares increase in price, but of little value if their price falls. Thus, when used to compensate top managers, stock options provide a strong incentive to follow policies that will increase the value of the firm.

Strike An action of unionized employees in which they (1) discontinue working for the employer and (2) take steps to prevent other potential workers from offering their services to the employer.

Substitutes Products that serve similar purposes. They are related such that an increase in the price of one will cause an increase in demand for the other (for example, hamburgers and tacos, butter and margarine, Chevrolets and Fords).

Substitution effect That part of an increase (decrease) in amount consumed that is the result of a good being cheaper (more expensive) in relation to other goods because of a reduction (increase) in price.

Sunk costs Costs that have already been incurred as a result of past decisions. They are sometimes referred to as historical costs.

Surplus A condition in which the amount of a good offered for sale by producers is greater than the amount that buyers will purchase at the existing price. A decline in price would eliminate the surplus.

Tariff A tax levied on goods imported into a country.

Tax base The level or quantity of the economic activity that is taxed (e.g., gallons of gasoline). Because they make the activity less attractive, higher tax rates reduce the level of the tax base.

Tax incidence The manner in which the burden of a tax is distributed among economic units (consumers, producers, employees, and so on). The actual tax burden does not always fall on those who are statutorily assigned to pay the tax.

Tax rate The per-unit amount of the tax or the percentage rate at which the economic activity is taxes.

Team production A process of production wherein employees work together under the supervision of the owner or the owner's representative.

Technology The technological knowledge available at any given time. The level of technology establishes the relationship between inputs and the maximum output they can generate.

Total cost The costs, both explicit and implicit, of all the resources used by the firm. Total cost includes an imputed normal rate of return for the firm's equity capital.

Total fixed cost The sum of the costs that do not vary with output. They will be incurred as long a s firm continues in business and the assets have alternative uses.

Total product The total output of a good that is associated with alternative utilization rates of a variable input.

Total variable cost The sum of those costs that rise as output increases. Examples of variable costs are wages paid to workers and payments for raw materials.

Tournament pay A form of compensation where the top performer (or performers) receives much higher rewards than other competitors, even if the others perform at only a slightly lower level.

Transaction costs The time, effort, and other resources needed to search out, negotiate and consummate an exchange.

Utility The benefit or satisfaction expected from a choice or course of action.

Value of marginal product (VMP) The marginal product of a resource multiplied by the selling price of the product it helps to produce. For a price taker firm, marginal revenue product (MRP) will be equal to the value marginal product (VMP).

Voice The ability to communicate complaints, desires and suggestions to decision makers who may be private buyers, sellers, or decision makers in government.

Voluntary export restraint (VER) An agreement by foreign firms to limit their own exports.

World Trade Organization (WTO) The new name given to GATT in 1994; it is currently responsible for monitoring and enforcing the multilateral trade agreements among the 133 member countries.

CREDITS

LITERARY CREDITS

Exhibit A2-5 From A NEW DEAL FOR SOCIAL SECURITY by Peter J. Ferrar and Michael Tanner, 1998, p. 150. Reprinted by permission of The Cato Institute.

PHOTO CREDITS

P. 1 Left	© Bill Bachmann/The Image Works
P. 1 Top right	© Jeff Greenberg/The Image Works
P. 1 Bottom right	© Steven Rubin/The Image Works
P. 2 Left	© Robert Brenner/PhotoEdit
P. 2 Center	© Jonathan Nourok/PhotoEdit
P. 2 Right	© L. Rorke/The Image Works
P. 3 Left	© Karim Shamsi-Basha/ The Image Works
P. 3 Center	© Gary A. Conner/PhotoEdit
P. 3 Right	© Bob Daemmrich/ The Image Works
P. 4	© Tony Freeman/PhotoEdit
P. 11	Library of Congress
P. 13	© Myrleen Ferguson/PhotoEdit
P. 35	Photo courtesy of the Hoover Institution
P. 33	© Phil Sears
P. 39 Left	© David Young-Wolff/PhotoEdit
P. 39 Right	© Leo Snider/The Image Works
P. 46 Left	© Jeff Greenberg/PhotoEdit
P. 46 Top right	© James Nubile/The Image Works
P. 46 Bottom right	© Wesley Bocxe/The Image Works
P. 53 Top left	© Steven Rubin/The Image Works
P. 53 Top right	© David Young-Wolff/PhotoEdit
P. 53 Bottom left	© Paul Conklin/PhotoEdit
P. 53 Bottom right	© Steven Rubin/The Image Works
P. 54 Top	© Bob Daemmrich/The Image Works
P. 54 Bottom left	© John Neubauer/PhotoEdit
P. 54 Bottom right	© David Young-Wolff/PhotoEdit
P. 56	© PhotoDisc
P. 69	Stock Montage
P. 77	© PhotoDisc
P. 100	© John Griffin/The Image Works
P. 104	© Richard Hutchings/PhotoEdit
P. 124	© Corbis/Bettman
P. 129	© David Young-Wolff/PhotoEdit
P. 137 Left	© Bob Daemmrich/The Image Works
P. 137 Right	© Bob Daemmrich/The Image Works
P. 140	© Bill Aron/PhotoEdit
P. 141	© Tony Freeman/PhotoEdit
P. 145	Photo courtesy of George Mason University
P. 146 Left	© Tom Prettyman/PhotoEdit
P. 146 Center	© Bob Daemmrich/The Image Works
P. 146 Right	© Bob Daemmrich/The Image Works
P. 163 Top left	© Jim Harrison/Stock, Boston
P. 163 Top center	© Bill Aron/PhotoEdit
P. 163 Top right	© John Eastcott/The Image Works
P. 163 Bottom left	© John Elk, III/Stock, Boston
P. 163 Bottom center	© Bill Bachmann/The Image Works
P. 163 Bottom right	© Sven Martson/The Image Works
P. 164 Top	© Peter Menzel/Stock, Boston
P. 164 Bottom	© Richard Pasley/Stock, Boston
P. 165 Top	© Henry Horenstein/Stock, Boston
P. 165 Bottom	© Stephen Frisch/Stock, Boston
P. 166 Top	© Jeff Greenberg/The Image Works
P. 166 Bottom	© Tony Freeman/PhotoEdit
P. 167	© Joseph Nettis/Stock, Boston
P. 168	© Esbin Anderson/The Image Works
P. 174	© Mark Richards/PhotoEdit
P. 207	© Bill Bachmann/The Image Works
P. 219	© M. Greenlar/The Image Works
P. 233 Left	© A. Ramey/PhotoEdit
P. 233 Right	© John Eastcott/Stock, Boston
P. 241	© Russell Sobel
P. 244	© John Coletti/Stock, Boston
P. 247	© John Claude LeJeune/ Stock, Boston
P. 251	© Bill Aron/PhotoEdit
P. 252	Committee on Social Thought
P. 259 Top left	© Liaison Agency, Inc.
P. 259 Bottom left	© Michael Newman/PhotoEdit
P. 259 Right	© 1999 Don Couch Photography
P. 264	© Daniel Sheehan/Gamma Liaison
P. 265	© Michael Turk, Surplus Trading
P. 269 Left	© Rob Crandall/Stock, Boston
P. 269 Right	© Michele Burgess/Stock, Boston
P. 273	© Wojnarowicz/The Image Works
P. 275	© Najlah Feanny/Stock, Boston
P. 283	© Najlah Feanny/Stock, Boston
P. 292	© UPI/Bettman
P. 314	Photo by Guity Nashat, courtesy of Gary Becker
P. 323 Left	© Susan Van Etten/PhotoEdit
P. 323 Right	© David Young-Wolff/PhotoEdit
P. 327 Left	© Michael Newman/PhotoEdit
P. 327 Right	© Richard Lord/The Image Works
P. 344	© Russell Einhorn/Gamma Liaison
P. 353	© Richard Shock/ Liaison International
P. 355 Left	© Cindy Charles/PhotoEdit
P. 355 Right	© John Neubauer/PhotoEdit
P. 358 Top	© Tony Freeman/PhotoEdit
P. 358 Bottom	© Myrleen Ferguson/PhotoEdit
P. 359	© Stacy Pick/Stock, Boston
P. 369 Left	© Bill Aron/PhotoEdit
P. 369 Right	© Gary Matoso/Contact Press Images/PNI
P. 377	© Townsend P. Dickinson/ The Image Works
P. 381	Photo courtesy of Harvard University News Office
P. 398	© Paul Conklin/PhotoEdit

P. 404	© M. Antman/The Image Works
P. 409 Top left	© Tony Freeman/PhotoEdit
P. 409 Top right	© Jeff Greenberg/PhotoEdit
P. 409 Bottom	© Charles Gupton/Stock, Boston
P. 410 Top	© A. Ramey/PhotoEdit
P. 410 Bottom	© J. Nordell/The Image Works
P. 411 Top	© Paul Conklin/PhotoEdit
P. 411 Bottom	© Mark Richards/PhotoEdit
P. 412 Top	© David Young-Wolff/PhotoEdit
P. 412 Center	© Spencer Grant/PhotoEdit
P. 412 Bottom	© Jeff Greenberg/PhotoEdit
P. 413	© Tony Freeman/PhotoEdit
P. 423	© Lisa Quinones/Black Star
P. 433	© Mark Richards/PhotoEdit
P. 437	© Spencer Grant/PhotoEdit
P. 449 Top Left	© Michelle Bridwell/PhotoEdit
P. 449 Top Right	© John Neubauer/PhotoEdit
P. 449 Bottom Left	© Richard Pasley/Stock, Boston
P. 449 Bottom Right	© 1999 Don Couch Photography
P. 465	© Christian Vioujard/Liaison Agency
P. 471 Left	© Bruno Barbey/Magnum/PNI
P. 471 Right	© Steven Rubin/The Image Works
P. 472 Top	© Gary Conner/PhotoEdit
P. 472 Bottom	© J. Pickerell/The Image Works
P. 473 Left	© Tony Freeman/PhotoEdit
P. 473 Right	© Gary Conner/PhotoEdit
P. 480	© AP Photo/Hans Edinger
P. 484	© AP Photo/Hans Edinger
P. 504	© Joseph Giannetti/Stock, Boston/PNI
P. 514	Institute for Justice
P. 517	© Markel/Liaison Agency
P. 531	© Robert Brenner/PhotoEdit
P. 543	© Brian Haimer/PhotoEdit
P. 544 Left	© Lien Nibauer/Liaison International
P. 544 Right	© Frank Siteman/PhotoEdit
P. 547	© Jim West/Impact Visuals/PNI
P. 554	© Peter Menzel/Stock, Boston
P. 559	© AP Photo/Glen Mills
P. 565	© 1998 Russell & Diana Couch

CARTOON CREDITS

P. 10	SHOE reprinted by permission of Tribune Media Services.
P. 12	FAMILY CIRCUS reprinted by special permission of King Features Syndicate.
P. 15	HI AND LOIS reprinted by special permission of King Features Syndicate.
P. 37	From The *Wall Street Journal.* Reprinted by permission of Cartoon Features Syndicate.
P. 107	© John Trever, *Albuquerque Journal.* Reprinted by permission.
P. 131	© Dana Fradon, *The New Yorker* Collection, 1991, from cartoonbank.com. All Rights Reserved.
P. 156	FAMILY CIRCUS reprinted by special permission of King Features Syndicate.
P. 223	Reprinted by permission of Tribune Media Services.
P. 299	© Lee Lorenz, *The New Yorker* Collection from cartoonbank.com. All Rights Reserved
P. 315	DICK WRIGHT reprinted by permission of United Feature Syndicate.
P. 497	WIZARD OF ID reprinted by permission of Johnny Hart and Creators Syndicate, Inc.

	Population and Labor Force				Money Supply (M2)	
Year	Civilian Noninstitutional Population Age 16+ (Millions)	Civilian Labor Force Participation Rate (Percent)	Rate of Unemployment (Percent)	Civilian Employment/ Population Ratio (Percent)	Money Supply M2 (Billions)	Annual Change In M2
1959	115.3	59.3	5.5	56.0	297.8	-
1960	117.2	59.4	5.5	56.1	312.4	4.9
1961	118.8	59.3	6.7	55.4	335.5	7.4
1962	120.2	58.8	5.5	55.5	362.7	8.1
1963	122.4	58.7	5.7	55.4	393.2	8.4
1964	124.5	58.7	5.2	55.7	424.7	8.0
1965	126.5	58.9	4.5	56.2	459.2	8.1
1966	128.1	59.2	3.8	56.9	480.2	4.6
1967	129.9	59.6	3.8	57.3	524.8	9.3
1968	132.0	59.6	3.6	57.5	566.8	8.0
1969	134.3	60.1	3.5	58.0	587.9	3.7
1970	137.1	60.4	4.9	57.4	626.5	6.6
1971	140.2	60.2	5.9	56.6	710.3	13.4
1972	144.1	60.4	5.6	57.0	802.3	13.0
1973	147.1	60.8	4.9	57.8	855.5	6.6
1974	150.1	61.3	5.6	57.8	902.4	5.5
1975	153.2	61.2	8.5	56.1	1,017.0	12.7
1976	156.2	61.6	7.7	56.8	1,152.8	13.4
1977	159.0	62.3	7.1	57.9	1,271.5	10.3
1978	161.9	63.2	6.1	59.3	1,368.0	7.6
1979	164.9	63.7	5.8	59.9	1,475.8	7.9
1980	167.7	63.8	7.1	59.2	1,601.1	8.5
1981	170.1	63.9	7.6	59.0	1,756.2	9.7
1982	172.3	64.0	9.7	57.8	1,910.9	8.8
1983	174.2	64.0	9.6	57.9	2,127.7	11.3
1984	176.4	64.4	7.5	59.5	2,312.3	8.7
1985	178.2	64.8	7.2	60.1	2,497.7	8.0
1986	180.6	65.3	7.0	60.7	2,734.0	9.5
1987	182.8	65.6	6.2	61.5	2,832.7	3.6
1988	184.6	65.9	5.5	62.3	2,996.4	5.8
1989	186.4	66.5	5.3	63.0	3,161.0	5.5
1990	189.2	66.5	5.6	62.8	3,279.6	3.8
1991	190.9	66.2	6.8	61.7	3,379.9	3.1
1992	192.8	66.4	7.5	61.5	3,434.7	1.6
1993	194.8	66.3	6.9	61.7	3,487.5	1.5
1994	196.8	66.6	6.1	62.5	3,503.0	0.4
1995	198.6	66.6	5.6	62.9	3,651.2	4.2
1996	200.6	66.8	5.4	63.2	3,826.1	4.8
1997	203.1	67.1	4.9	63.8	4,046.4	5.8
1998	205.2	67.1	4.5	64.1	4,412.3	9.0

Source: *Economic Report of the President,* 1999.